DATE DUE

			PRINTED IN U.S.A.

Poetry Criticism

Guide to Gale Literary Criticism Series

For criticism on	Consult these Gale series
Authors now living or who died after December 31, 1959	*CONTEMPORARY LITERARY CRITICISM (CLC)*
Authors who died between 1900 and 1959	*TWENTIETH-CENTURY LITERARY CRITICISM (TCLC)*
Authors who died between 1800 and 1899	*NINETEENTH-CENTURY LITERATURE CRITICISM (NCLC)*
Authors who died between 1400 and 1799	*LITERATURE CRITICISM FROM 1400 TO 1800 (LC)* *SHAKESPEAREAN CRITICISM (SC)*
Authors who died before 1400	*CLASSICAL AND MEDIEVAL LITERATURE CRITICISM (CMLC)*
Authors of books for children and young adults	*CHILDREN'S LITERATURE REVIEW (CLR)*
Dramatists	*DRAMA CRITICISM (DC)*
Poets	*POETRY CRITICISM (PC)*
Short story writers	*SHORT STORY CRITICISM (SSC)*
Black writers of the past two hundred years	*BLACK LITERATURE CRITICISM (BLC)*
Hispanic writers of the late nineteenth and twentieth centuries	*HISPANIC LITERATURE CRITICISM (HLC)*
Native North American writers and orators of the eighteenth, nineteenth, and twentieth centuries	*NATIVE NORTH AMERICAN LITERATURE (NNAL)*
Major authors from the Renaissance to the present	*WORLD LITERATURE CRITICISM, 1500 TO THE PRESENT (WLC)*

ISSN 1052-4851

Poetry Criticism

Excerpts from Criticism of the Works of the Most Significant and Widely Studied Poets of World Literature

VOLUME 19

Carol T. Gaffke
Editor

GALE

DETROIT · NEW YORK · TORONTO · LONDON

STAFF

Carol T. Gaffke, *Editor*

Kathy D. Darrow, Debra A. Wells, *Assistant Editors*

Susan Trosky, *Permissions Manager*

Margaret Chamberlain, Maria Franklin, and Kimberly F. Smilay, *Permissions Specialists*
Sarah Chesney, Edna Hedblad, Michele Lonoconus, and Shalice Shah, *Permissions Associates*
Stephen Cusack, Kelly Quin, Andrea Rigby, and Jessica Ulrich, *Permissions Assistants*

Victoria B. Cariappa, *Research Manager*

Michele P. LaMeau, *Research Specialist*
Julie C. Daniel, Tamara C. Nott, Tracie A. Richardson,
Norma Sawaya, Cheryl L. Warnock,
Research Associates

Mary Beth Trimper, *Production Director*
Deborah Milliken, *Production Assistant*

C. J. Jonik, *Desktop Publisher*
Randy Bassett, *Image Database Supervisor*
Michael Ansari, Robert Duncan, *Scanner Operator*
Pamela Reed, *Photography Coordinator*

Library of Congress Catalog Card Number 91-118494
ISBN 0-7876-1546-3
ISSN 1052-4851

Printed in the United States of America

10 9 8 7 6 5 4 3 2 1

Contents

Preface vii

Acknowledgments xi

Preface

A Comprehensive Information Source on World Poetry

*P*oetry Criticism (PC) provides substantial critical excerpts and biographical information on poets throughout the world who are most frequently studied in high school and undergraduate college courses. Each *PC* entry is supplemented by biographical and bibliographical material to help guide the user to a fuller understanding of the genre and its creators. Although major poets and literary movements are covered in such Gale Literary Criticism Series as *Contemporary Literary Criticism (CLC), Twentieth-Century Literary Criticism (TCLC), Nineteenth-Century Literature Criticism (NCLC), Literature Criticism from 1400 to 1800 (LC),* and *Classical and Medieval Literature Criticism (CMLC), PC* offers more focused attention on poetry than is possible in the broader, survey-oriented entries on writers in these Gale series. Students, teachers, librarians, and researchers will find that the generous excerpts and supplementary material provided by *PC* supply them with the vital information needed to write a term paper on poetic technique, to examine a poet's most prominent themes, or to lead a poetry discussion group.

Coverage

In order to reflect the influence of tradition as well as innovation, poets of various nationalities, eras, and movements are represented in every volume of *PC*. Each author entry presents a historical survey of the critical response to that author's work; the length of an entry reflects the amount of critical attention that the author has received from critics writing in English and from foreign critics in translation. Since many poets have inspired a prodigious amount of critical explication, *PC* is necessarily selective, and the editors have chosen the most significant published criticism to aid readers and students in their research. In order to provide these important critical pieces, the editors will sometimes reprint essays that have appeared in previous volumes of Gale's Literary Criticism Series. Such duplication, however, never exceeds fifteen percent of a *PC* volume.

Organization

Each *PC* author entry consists of the following components:

- **Author Heading:** the name under which the author wrote appears at the beginning of the entry, followed by birth and death dates. If the author wrote consistently under a pseudonym, the pseudonym will be listed in the author heading and his or her legal name given in parentheses in the lines immediately preceding the Introduction. Uncertainty as to birth or death dates is indicated by question marks.

- **Introduction:** a biographical and critical essay introduces readers to the author and the critical discussions surrounding his or her work.

- **Author Portrait:** a photograph or illustration of the author is included when available.

- **Principal Works:** the author's most important works are identified in a list ordered chronologically by first publication dates. The first section comprises poetry collections and book-length poems. The second section gives information on other major works by the author. For foreign authors, original foreign-language publication information is provided, as well as the best and most complete English-language editions of their works.

- **Criticism:** critical excerpts chronologically arranged in each author entry provide perspective on changes in critical evaluation over the years. All individual titles of poems and poetry collections by the author featured in the entry are printed in boldface type to enable a reader to ascertain without difficulty the works under discussion. For purposes of easy identification, the critic's name and the publication date of the essay are given at the beginning of each piece of criticism. Unsigned criticism is preceded by the title of the journal in which it originally appeared. Publication information (such as publisher names and book prices) and parenthetical numerical references (such as footnotes or page and line references to specific editions of a work) have been deleted at the editor's discretion to enable smoother reading of the text.

- **Explanatory Notes:** introductory comments preface each critical excerpt, providing several types of useful information, including: the reputation of a critic, the importance of a work of criticism, and the specific type of criticism (biographical, psychoanalytic, historical, etc.).

- **Author Commentary:** insightful comments from the authors themselves and excerpts from author interviews are included when available.

- **Bibliographical Citations:** information preceding each piece of criticism guides the interested reader to the original essay or book.

- **Further Reading:** bibliographic references accompanied by descriptive notes at the end of each entry suggest additional materials for study of the author. Boxed material following the Further Reading provides references to other biographical and critical series published by Gale.

Other Features

- **Cumulative Author Index:** comprises all authors who have appeared in Gale's Literary Criticism Series, along with cross-references to such Gale biographical series as *Contemporary Authors* and *Dictionary of Literary Biography*. This cumulated index enables the user to locate an author within the various series.

- **Cumulative Nationality Index:** includes all authors featured in *PC,* arranged alphabetically under their respective nationalities.

- **Cumulative Title Index:** lists in alphabetical order all individual poems, book-length poems, and collection titles contained in the *PC* series. Titles of poetry collections and separately published poems are printed in italics, while titles of individual poems are printed in roman type with quotation marks. Each title is followed by the author's name and the volume and page number corresponding to the location of commentary on specific works. English-language translations of original foreign-language titles are cross-referenced to the foreign titles so that all references to discussion of a work are combined in one listing.

Citing *Poetry Criticism*

When writing papers, students who quote directly from any volume in the Literary Criticism Series may use the following general formats to footnote reprinted criticism. The first example pertains to material drawn from periodicals, the second to material reprinted from books:

[1]David Daiches, "W. H. Auden: The Search for a Public," *Poetry* LIV (June 1939), 148-56; excerpted and reprinted in *Poetry Criticism*, Vol. 1, ed. Robyn V. Young (Detroit: Gale Research, 1990), pp. 7-9.

[2]Pamela J. Annas, *A Disturbance in Mirrors: The Poetry of Sylvia Plath* (Greenwood Press, 1988); excerpted and reprinted in *Poetry Criticism*, Vol. 1, ed. Robyn V. Young (Detroit: Gale Research, 1990), pp. 410-14.

Comments Are Welcome

Readers who wish to suggest authors to appear in future volumes, or who have other suggestions, are cordially invited to contact the editors.

Acknowledgments

The editors wish to thank the copyright holders of the excerpted criticism included in this volume and the permissions managers of many book and magazine publishing companies for assisting us in securing reproduction rights. We are also grateful to the staffs of the Detroit Public Library, the Library of Congress, the University of Detroit Mercy Library, Wayne State University Purdy/Kresge Library Complex, and the University of Michigan Libraries for making their resources available to us. Following is a list of the copyright holders who have granted us permission to reproduce material in this volume of *PC*. Every effort has been made to trace copyright, but if omissions have been made, please let us know.

COPYRIGHTED EXCERPTS IN *PC*, VOLUME 19, WERE REPRODUCED FROM THE FOLLOWING PERIODICALS:

American Journal of Philology, v. 106, Summer, 1985. Copyright (c) 1985 by Johns Hopkins University Press. All rights reserved. Reproduced with permission.—*The American Poetry Review,* v. 9, July-August, 1980 for a review of "Poems of Stanley Kunitz: 1928-1978" by Gregory Orr. Copyright (c) 1980 by World Poetry, Inc. Reproduced by permission of the author.—*Arethusa,* v. 4, Fall, 1971. (c) 1971 by Arethusa. Reproduced by permission of Johns Hopkins University Press.—*The Atlantic Monthly,* v. 277, June, 1996 for "A Visionary Poet at Ninety" by David Barber. Copyright 1996 by The Atlantic Monthly Company, Boston, MA. Reproduced by permission of the author.—*The Christian Science Monitor,* August 6, 1987. (c) 1987 The Christian Science Publishing Society. All rights reserved. Reproduced by permission from The Christian Science Monitor.—*The Classical Journal,* v. 72, February-March, 1977. Reproduced by permission.—*Classical Philology,* v. 84, October, 1984. (c) 1984 by The University of Chicago. Reproduced by permission.—*Contemporary Literature,* v. 15, Winter, 1974. (c) 1974 by the Regents of the University of Wisconsin. Reproduced by permission of The University of Wisconsin Press.—*The Criterion,* v. X, July, 1931. Reprodued by permission of Faber & Faber Ltd.—*The Critical Quarterly,* v. 7, Summer, 1965 for "Fiction and Game in `The Canterbury Tales' by G. D. Josipovici. Reproduced by permission of the author.—*The Critical Review,* n. 10, 1967. Reproduced by permission.—*English Language Notes,* v, XXXI, March, 1994. (c) copyrighted 1994, Regents of the University of Colorado. Reproduced by permission.—*English Studies,* v. 72, 1991. (c) 1991 by Swets & Zeitlinger B. V. Reproduced by permission.—*Greece & Rome,* v. 8, May, 1939. Reproduced by permission of Oxford University Press.—*The Gettysburg Review,* v. 5, Spring, 1992. Reproduced by permission.—*The Hudson Review,* v. 33, Spring, 1980. Copyright (c) 1980 by The Hudson Review, Inc. Reproduced by permission.—*Iowa Review,* v. 6, Winter, 1975 for "In and About the Maximus Peoms," by Sherman Paul; v. 11, Fall, 1980 for "An Image of Man...' Working Notes on Charles Olson's Concept of Person," by Robert Creeley; v. 11, Fall, 1980 for "Charles Olson and the Postmodern Advance," by George F. Butterick. Copyright (c) 1975, 1980 by The University of Iowa. All reproduced by permission of the authors.—*Ironwood,* v. 24, Fall, 1984. Copyright (c) 1984 by Ironwood Press. Reproduced by permission.—*The Literary Half-Yearly,* v. XVIII, January, 1977. (c) 1977 The Literary Half-Yearly. Reproduced by permission.—*Modern Poetry Studies,* v. 6, Spring, 1975. Copyright 1975, by Media Study, Inc. Reproduced by permission.—*The Nation,* v. 213, September 20, 1971. Copyright 1971 The Nation magazine/The Nation Company, Inc. Reproduced by permission.—*The New Republic,* v. 203, July 2, 1990; v. 211, September 19 & 26, 1994. (c) 1990, 1994 The New Republic, Inc. Both reproduced by permission of The New Republic.—*New York Magazine,* v. 17, October 15, 1984 for "The Prime of Amy Clampitt." Copyright (c) 1997 K-III Magazine Corporation. All rights reserved. Reproduced by permission of the author.—*The New York Times Book Review,* March, 1944. Copyright 1944, renewed 1972 by The New York Times Company. Reproduced by permission.—*PMLA,* v. LXXXIII, May, 1978. Copyright (c) 1978 by the Modern Language Association of America. Reproduced by permission of the Modern Language Association of America.—*Poetics Today,* v. 5, 1984. (c) The Porter Institute for Poetics and Semiotics. Reproduced with permission.—*Poetry,* v. 93, December, 1958 for "The Thirty Years' War" by David Wagoner; v. 143, December, 1983 for a review of "The Kingfisher" by J. D. McClatchy; v. 147, December, 1985 for a review of "What the Light Was Like" by Sandra M. Gilbert; v. 165, December, 1994 for a review of "A Silence Opens" by Robert B. Shaw. (c) 1958, renewed 1986, 1983, 1985, 1994 by the Modern Poetry Association. All reproduced by permission of the Editor of Poetry and the authors.—*Proceedings of the British Academy,* v. XII, 1926; v. XVI, 1930. Copyright The British Academy 1926, 1930. Both reproduced by permission.—*The Review of English Studies,* v. IV, October, 1953 for "Milton's Hero," by Frank Kermode. Reproduced by permission of Oxford University Press and the author; v. 40, November, 1989. Reproduced

COPYRIGHTED EXCERPTS IN *PC,* VOLUME 19, WERE REPRODUCED FROM THE FOLLOWING BOOKS:

PHOTOGRAPHS AND ILLUSTRATIONS APPEARING IN *PC,* VOLUME 19, WERE RECEIVED FROM THE FOLLOWING SOURCES:

Geoffrey Chaucer
1340?-1400

English poet, prose writer, and translator.

INTRODUCTION

Widely regarded as the "father of English poetry," Geoffrey Chaucer is the foremost representative of Middle English literature. His *Canterbury Tales* is one of the most highly esteemed works in the English language, and its "General Prologue" has been acclaimed by critics as "the most perfect poem in the English language." Notable among his other works are the *Book of the Duchess, Parlement of Foules, House of Fame, Troilus and Criseyde,* and *Legend of Good Women.* Familiar with French, English, Italian, and Latin literature, Chaucer was able to meld characteristics of each in a unique body of work that affirmed the ascent of English as a literary language. Chaucer's works, which reflect his consummate mastery of various literary genres, styles, and techniques, as well as his erudition, wit, and insight, are regarded as classics of European literature.

Biographical Information

Born into a family of London-based vintners sometime in the early 1340s, Chaucer had a long and distinguished career as a civil servant, serving three successive kings—Edward III, Richard II, and Henry IV. As a member of court, he traveled to Spain in 1366 on what would be the first of a series of diplomatic missions to the continent over the next decade. In 1368 the death of Blanche, the first wife of John of Gaunt—Edward III's fourth son and the poet's courtly patron—occasioned Chaucer's composition of the *Book of the Duchess,* which was in circulation by the time he went to France in 1370. He traveled to Italy in 1372 and 1373, visiting Genoa and Florence, and upon his return to England was appointed a customs official for the Port of London, a post he would hold until 1386. Chaucer's career as a civil servant frequently took him to continental Europe over the course of the next decade, but by 1385 he was living in Kent, where he was appointed a justice of the peace. The following year he became a member of Parliament. The next few years were difficult ones for Chaucer. Linked to the royal family, he suffered as the aristocracy began to seize power in England. His fortunes rose again, however, with the return of John of Gaunt from the continent and Richard II's regained control of the government from the upstart barons. Chaucer was appointed a clerk of the king's works, but was removed from this office in 1391. The next few years were dismal for him. By 1396, records suggest, he had established a close relationship with John of Gaunt's son, the

Earl of Derby, who as King Henry IV later confirmed Chaucer's grants from Richard II and added an additional annuity in 1399. In December of that year, Chaucer leased a house in the garden of Westminster Abbey, where he lived for the remainder of his life. When Geoffrey Chaucer died on 25 October 1400, he was accorded the honor of burial in the Abbey (then traditionally reserved for royalty) and his tomb became the nucleus of what is now known as Poets' Corner.

Major Works

Inspired in large part by French court poetry, Chaucer's first major work, the *Book of the Duchess,* was written to soothe the grief of John of Gaunt after his wife's death in 1368. At the opening of the poem the narrator succumbs to sleep as he reads the story of Seyes and Alcyone. In a dream he meets a mourning Black Knight. The narrator then inquires about the Knight's anguish, and the Knight, as he relates his stornion of the work holds that Chaucer surpasses his French models in the *Book of the Duchess* by transforming the insincere courtly language and sentimental romance imagery of dying for love into a poignant reality. *House of Fame* and *Parlement of Foules* are thought to comment upon efforts to arrange a suitable marriage for the young Richard II. A dream-vision, *House of Fame* appears to be an examination of the function of poets, the nature of poetry, and the unreliability of fame. *Parlement of Foules* also takes the form of a dream-vision, and betrays the influence of Italian Renaissance literature. The work is generally seen as an allegorical disputation on love.

Troilus and Criseyde, an adaptation of Boccaccio's *Il Filostrato* (c. 1338) was long considered by some critics to be Chaucer's finest poetic achievement. A tale of thwarted love set against the backdrop of the Trojan War, the work is thought to possess a symmetry, decorum, and metaphorical quality lacking in Boccaccio's story. Likewise, Chaucer's adaptation adds depth and changes the depiction of the main characters. His Criseyde is more refined, elegant and sympathetically portrayed than her capricious predecessor; she is not degraded after deciding to accept the political betrothal to the Greek warrior Diomede rather than marry Troilus. Troilus himself is reduced to an impotent passivity, although he formulates many of the primary concerns of the story. Critics note these as tensions between erotic and intellectual spheres, interpreting the poem in one of three general ways: as a psychological novel, the first in English; as the epitome of courtly love romances; or, as a religious and philosophical allegory. The last of Chaucer's dream-vision poems, *Legend of Good Women* relates the traditional stories of such faithful women as Dido, Cleopatra, and Lucrece. Considered somewhat dull and perfunctory by some, the unfinished *Legend* is valued by critics largely for its structure as a collection of interconnected stories that prefigures the form of Chaucer's masterpiece, the *Canterbury Tales.*

Begun sometime around 1386, the *Canterbury Tales* features a series of stories told by a group of travelers on a pilgrimage to the shrine of Thomas à Becket in Canterbury, and is said to reflect the diversity of fourteenth-century English life. The pilgrims depict the full range of medieval society, and the tales they relate span the literary spectrum of the period. The *Canterbury Tales* begins with a "General Prologue," introducing the pilgrims with short, vivid sketches—beginning with a knight and his entourage, followed by several ecclesiastics and representatives of the lower classes. The stories told are generally indicative of class and personality, with certain exceptions, often for ironic effect as scholars note. The social variety of the pilgrims is highlighted by the diversity of the tales and their themes: courtly romance, racy *fabliau,* allegory, sermon, beast fable, saint's life, and, at times, a mixture of these genres. In part due to the intricacy and proposed length of the work, critics believe that Chaucer's final plan for his *Canterbury Tales* was never realized; he either died before be could place the sections he envisioned in the proper sequence or stopped work on it all together. Nevertheless, the work contains what many readers feel is a realistic depiction of Chaucer's world that points to the vast and diverse knowledge of the poet and conjures the complexity of the fourteenth-century European mind.

Critical Reception

Chaucer's genius was recognized in his own time and his works have since attracted a vast body of criticism. Praised by French and English contemporaries alike for his technical skill, he was revered as a master poet and lauded for his contributions to the English language. The outstanding English poet before Shakespeare, Geoffrey Chaucer brought Middle English to its full efflorescence. The originality of his language and style, the vivacity of his humor, the civility of his poetic demeanor, and the depth of his knowledge are continually cited as reasons for the permanence of his works. His poems continue to draw the interest of readers and critics centuries after his death and remain among the most acclaimed works throughout the English-speaking world.

PRINCIPAL WORKS

Poetry

Book of the Duchess c. 1368-1369
Anelida and Arcite c. 1373-1374
Canterbury Tales c. 1375-1400
House of Fame c. 1378-1381
Parlement of Foules c. 1378-1381
Troilus and Criseyde c. 1382-1386
Legend of Good Women c. 1386
Chaucer's Poetry: An Anthology for the Modern Reader [edited by E. Talbot Donaldson] 1975

Other Major Works

Roman de la Rose [translator; *The Romance of the Rose*] (poetry) c. 1360
Boecius de consolacione [translator; *Consolation of Philosophy*] (prose) c. 1380
Treatise on the Astrolabe (prose) c. 1391
Equatorie of the Planetis (prose) c. 1391
The Complete Poetry and Prose of Geoffrey Chaucer [edited by John H. Fisher; revised edition, 1989] (poetry and prose) 1977
A Variorum Edition of the Works of Geoffrey Chaucer [edited by Paul G. Ruggiers] (poetry and prose) 1979
The Riverside Chaucer [edited by Larry D. Benson] (poetry and prose) 1987

CRITICISM

William Blake   (essay date 1809)

SOURCE: "A Descriptive Catalogue," in *Blake: Complete Writings,* edited by Geoffrey Keynes, Oxford University Press, 1966, pp. 563-85.

[Blake is perhaps the most esteemed English poet and artist of the Romantic period. In the following excerpt from his 1809 "Descriptive Catalogue" of his paintings and drawings, he describes Chaucer's Canterbury pilgrims as examples of "universal human life."]

The characters of Chaucer's Pilgrims are the characters which compose all ages and nations: as one age falls, another rises, different to mortal sight, but to immortals only the same; for we see the same characters repeated again and again, in animals, vegetables, minerals, and in men; nothing new occurs in identical existence; Accident ever varies, Substance can never suffer change nor decay.

Of Chaucer's characters, as described in his *Canterbury Tales*, some of the names or titles are altered by time, but the characters themselves for ever remain unaltered, and consequently they are the physiognomies or lineaments of universal human life, beyond which Nature never steps. Names alter, things never alter. I have known multitudes of those who would have been monks in the age of monkery, who in this deistical age are deists. As Newton numbered the stars, and as Linneus numbered the plants, so Chaucer numbered the classes of men.

The Knight and Squire with the Squire's Yeoman lead the procession, as Chaucer has also placed them first in his prologue. The Knight is a true Hero, a good, great, and wise man; his whole length portrait on horseback, as written by Chaucer, cannot be surpassed. He has spent his life in the field; has ever been a conqueror, and is that species of character which in every age stands as the guardian of man against the oppressor. His son is like him with the germ of perhaps greater perfection still, as he blends literature and the arts with his warlike studies. Their dress and their horses are of the first rate, without ostentation, and with all the true grandeur that unaffected simplicity when in high rank always displays. The Squire's Yeoman is also a great character, a man perfectly knowing in his s hand he bare a mighty bow.

Chaucer describes here a mighty man; one who is war is the worthy attendant on noble heroes.

The Prioress follows these with her female chaplain:

> Another Nonne also with her had she,
> That was her Chaplaine, and Priests three.

This Lady is described also as of the first rank, rich and honoured. She has certain peculiarities and little delicate affectations, not unbecoming in her, being accompanied with what is truly grand and really polite; her person and face Chaucer has described with minuteness; it is very elegant, and was the beauty of our ancestors, till after Elizabeth's time, when voluptuousness and folly began to be accounted beautiful.

Her companion and her three priests were no doubt all perfectly delineated in those parts of Chaucer's work which are now lost; we ought to suppose them suitable attendants on rank and fashion.

The Monk follows these with the Friar. The Painter has also grouped with these the Pardoner and the Sompnour and the Manciple, and has here also introduced one of the rich citizens of London: Characters likely to ride in company, all being above the common rank in life or attendants on those who were so.

For the Monk is described by Chaucer, as a man of the first rank in society, noble, rich, and expensively attended; he is a leader of the age, with certain humorous accompaniments in his character, that do not degrade, but render him an object of dignified mirth, but also with other accompaniments not so respectable.

The Friar is a character also of a mixed kind:

> A friar there was, a wanton and a merry.

but in his office he is said to be a "full solemn man": eloquent, amorous, witty, and satyrical; young, handsome, and rich; he is a complete rogue, with constitutional gaiety enough to make him a master of all the pleasures of the world.

> His neck was white as the flour de lis,
> Thereto strong he was as a champioun.

It is necessary here to speak of Chaucer's own character, that I may set certain mistaken critics right in their conception of the humour and fun that occurs on the journey. Chaucer is himself the great poetical observer of men, who in every age is born to record and eternize its acts. This he does as a master, as a father, and superior, who looks down on their little follies from the Emperor to the Miller; sometimes with severity, oftener with joke and sport.

Accordingly Chaucer has made his Monk a great tragedian, one who studied poetical art. So much so, that the generous Knight is, in the compassionate dictates of his soul, compelled to cry out:

> "Ho," quoth the Knyght,— "good Sir, no more
>   of this;
> "That ye have said is right ynough I wis;
> "And mokell more, for little heaviness
> "Is right enough for much folk, as I guesse.
> "I say, for me, it is a great disease,
> "Whereas men have been in wealth and ease,
> "To heare of their sudden fall, alas,
> "And the contrary is joy and solas"

The Monk's definition of tragedy in the proem to his tale is worth repeating:

> "Tragedie is to tell a certain story,
> "As old books us maken memory,
> "Of hem that stood in great prosperity,
> "And be fallen out of high degree,
> "Into miserie, and ended wretchedly."

Though a man of luxury, pride and pleasure, he is a master of art and learning, though affecting to despise it. Those who can think that the proud Huntsman and Noble House-keeper, Chaucer's Monk, is intended for a buffoon or burlesque character, know little of Chaucer.

For the Host who follows this group, and holds the center of the cavalcade, is a first rate character, and his jokes are no trifles; they are always, though uttered with audacity, and equally free with the Lord and the Peasant, they are always substantially and weightily expressive of knowledge and experience; Henry Baillie, the keeper of the greatest Inn of the greatest City; for such was the Tabarde Inn in Southwark, near London: our Host was also a leader of the age.

By way of illustration, I instance Shakespeare's Witches in Macbeth. Those who dress them for the stage, consider them as wretched old women, and not as Shakespeare intended, the Goddesses of Destiny; this shews how Chaucer has been misunderstood in his sublime work. Shakespeare's Fairies also are the rulers of the vegetable world, and so are Chaucer's; let them be so considered, and then the poet will be understood, and not else.

But I have omitted to speak of a very prominent character, the Pardoner, the Age's Knave, who always commands and domineers over the high and low vulgar. This man is sent in every age for a rod and scourge, and for a blight, for a trial of men, to divide the classes of men; he is in the most holy sanctuary, and he is suffered by Providence for wise ends, and has also his great use, and his grand leading destiny.

His companion, the Sompnour, is also a Devil of the first magnitude, grand, terrific, rich and honoured in the rank of which he holds the destiny. The uses to Society are perhaps equal of the Devil and of the Angel, their sublimity, who can dispute.

> In daunger had he at his own gise,
> The young girls of his diocese,
> And he knew well their counsel, &c,

The principal figure in the next groupe is the Good Parson; an Apostle, a real Messenger of Heaven, sent in every age for its light and its warmth. This man is beloved and venerated by all, and neglected by all: He serves all, and is served by none; he is, according to Christ's definition, the greatest of his age. Yet he is a Poor Parson of a town. Read Chaucer's description of the Good Parson, and bow the head and the knee to him, who, in every age, sends us such a burning and a shining light. Search, O ye rich and powerful, for these men and obey their counsel, then shall the golden age return: But alas! you will not easily distinguish him from the Friar or the Pardoner; they, also, are "full solemn men," and their counsel you will continue to follow.

I have placed by his side the Sergeant at Lawe, who appears delighted to ride in his company, and between him and his brother, the Plowman; as I wish men of Law would always ride with them, and take their counsel, especially in all difficult points. Chaucer's Lawyer is a

character of great venerableness, a Judge, and a real master of the jurisprudence of his age.

The Doctor of Physic is in this groupe, and the Franklin, the voluptuous country gentleman, contrasted with the Physician, and on his other hand, with two Citizens of London. Chaucer's characters live age after age. Every age is a Canterbury Pilgrimage; we all pass on, each sustaining one or other of these characters; nor can a child be born, who is not one of these characters of Chaucer. The Doctor of Physic is described as the first of his profession; perfect, learned, completely Master and Doctor in his art. Thus the reader will observe, that Chaucer makes every one of his characters perfect in his kind; every one is an Antique Statue; the image of a class, and not of an imperfect individual.

This groupe also would furnish substantial matter, on which volumes might be written. The Franklin is one who keeps open table, who is the genius of eating and drinking, the Bacchus; as the Doctore Esculapius, the Host is the Silenus, the Squire is the Apollo, the Miller is the Hercules, &c. Chaucer's characters are a description of the eternal Principles that exist in all ages. The Franklin is voluptuousness itself, most nobly pourtrayed:

> It snewed in his house of meat and drink.

The Plowman is simplicity itself, with wisdom and strength for its stamina. Chaucer has divided the ancient character of Hercules between his Miller and his Plowman. Benevolence is the plowman's great characteristic; he is thin with excessive labour, and not with old age, as some have supposed:

> He would thresh, and thereto dike and delve
> For Christe's sake, for every poore wight,
> Withouten hire, if it lay in his might.

Visions of these eternal principles or characters of human life appear to poets, in all ages; the Grecian gods were the ancient Cherubim of Phoenicia; but the Greeks, and since them the Moderns, have neglected to subdue the gods of Priam. These gods are visions of the eternal attributes, or divine names, which, when erected into gods, become destructive to humanity. They ought to be the servants, and not the masters of man, or of society. They ought to be made to sacrifice to Man, and not man compelled to sacrifice to them; for when separated from man or humanity, who is Jesus the Saviour, the vine of eternity, they are thieves and rebels, they are destroyers.

The Plowman of Chaucer is Hercules in his supreme eternal state, divested of his spectrous shadow; which is the Miller, a terrible fellow, such as exists in all times and places for the trial of men, to astonish every neighbourhood with brutal strength and courage, to get rich and powerful to curb the pride of Man.

The Reeve and the Manciple are two characters of the most consummate worldly wisdom. The Shipman, or Sailor, is a similar genius of Ulyssean art; but with the highest courage superadded.

The Citizens and their Cook are each leaders of a class. Chaucer has been somehow made to number four citizens, which would make his whole company, himself included, thirty-one. But he says there was but nine and twenty in his company:

Full nine and twenty in a company.

The Webbe, or Weaver, and the Tapiser, or Tapestry Weaver, appear to me to be the same person; but this is only an opinion, for full nine and twenty may signify one more or less. But I dare say that Chaucer wrote "A Webbe Dyer," that is, a Cloth Dyer:

A Webbe Dyer, and a Tapiser.

The Merchant cannot be one of the Three Citizens, as his dress is different, and his character is more marked, whereas Chaucer says of his rich citizens:

All were yclothed in o liverie.

The characters of Women Chaucer has divided into two classes, the Lady Prioress and the Wife of Bath. Are not these leaders of the ages of men? The lady prioress, in some ages, predominates; and in some the wife of Bath, in whose character Chaucer has been equally minute and exact, because she is also a scourge and a blight. I shall say no more of her, nor expose what Chaucer has left hidden; let the young reader study what he has said of her: it is useful as a scarecrow. There are of such characters born too many for the peace of the world.

I come at length to the Clerk of Oxenford. This character varies from that of Chaucer, as the contemplative philosopher varies from the poetical genius. There are always these two classes of learned sages, the poetical and the philosophical. The painter has put them side by side, as if the youthful clerk had put himself under the tuition of the mature poet. Let the Philosopher always be the servant and scholar of inspiration and all will be happy.

Ralph Waldo Emerson (lecture date 1835)

SOURCE: "English Literature," in *The Early Lectures of Ralph Waldo Emerson: 1833-1836, Vol. I*, edited by Stephen E. Whicher and Robert E. Spiller, Harvard University Press, 1959, pp. 205-88.

[*Emerson, an influential literary figure and philosopher during the nineteenth century, founded the American Transcendental movement. In the following excerpt from a lecture delivered in 1835, he places Chaucer in the English literary tradition, praising him for his delightful and authentic literary portraits.*]

Geoffrey Chaucer in the unanimous opinion of scholars is the earliest classical English writer. He first gave vogue to many Provençal words by using them in his elegant and popular poems, and by far the greater part of his vocabulary is with little alteration in use at this day. He introduced several metres which from his time have been popular forms of poetic composition until ours. Moreover he either is the author or the translator of many images and fables and thoughts which have been the common property of poets ever since; and more or less exist in the common speech of men so that the reader of Chaucer finds little in his page that is wholly new. He is struck everywhere with likeness to familiar verses or tales; for, he is in the armoury of English literature. 'Tis as if he were carried back into the generation before the last, and should see the likeness of all his friends in their grand-fathers. . . .

The poems of Chaucer have great merits of their own. They are the compositions of a man of the world who has much knowledge both of books and of men. They exhibit strong sense, humor, pathos, and a dear love of nature. He is a man of strong and kindly genius possessing all his faculties in that balance and symmetry neither too little nor too much which constitute an individual a sort of Universal Man and fit him to take up into himself without egotism all the wit and character of his age and to stand for his age before posterity. He possesses many of the highest gifts of genius and those too whose value is most intelligible to all men. The milk of human kindness flows always in his veins. The hilarity of good sense joined with the best health and temper never forsakes him. He possesses that clear insight into life which ever and anon perceives under the play of the thousand interests and follies and caprices of man the adamantine framework of Nature on which all the decoration and activity of life is hung.

He possesses the most authentic property of genius, that of sympathy with his subjects so that he describes every object with a delight in the thing itself. It has been observed that it does not argue genius that a man can write well on himself, or on topics connected with his personal relations. It is the capital deduction from Lord Byron that his poems have but one subject: himself. It is the burden of society, that very few men have sufficient strength of mind to speak of any truth or sentiment and hardly even of facts and persons clean of any reference to themselves and their personal history. But the wise man and much more the true Poet quits himself and throws his spirit into whatever he contemplates and enjoys the making it speak that it would say. This power belonged to Chaucer.

With these endowments he writes though often playfully yet always as a sincere man who has an earnest meaning to express and nowise (at least in those poems on which his fame is founded) as an idle and irresponsible rhymer. He acknowledges in *House of Fame* that he prefers "sentence," that is, sense, to skill of numbers. He would make

the rime agreeable
Tho some verse fail in a syllable
And though I do no diligence
To show crafte but sentence.

But he felt and maintained the dignity of the laurel and restored it in England to its honor.

No one can read Chaucer in his grave compositions without being struck with his consciousness of his poetic duties. He never writes with timidity. He speaks like one who knows the law, and has a right to be heard. He is a philanthropist, a moralist, a reformer. He lashes the vices of the clergy. He wrote a poem of stern counsel to King Richard. He exposes the foibles and tricks of all pretenders in science [and] the professions, and his prophetic wisdom is found on the side of good sense and humanity.

I do not feel that I have closed the enumeration of the gifts of Chaucer until it is added as a cause of his permanent fame in spite of the obsoleteness of his style (now 500 years old) that his virtues and genius are singularly agreeable to the English mind; that in him they find their prominent tastes and prejudices. He has the English sincerity and homeliness and humor, and his *Canterbury Tales* are invaluable as a picture of the domestic manners of the fourteenth century. Shakespeare and Milton are not more intrinsically national poets than is Chaucer. He has therefore contributed not a little to deepen and fix in the character of his countrymen those habits and sentiments which inspired his early song.

The humor with which the English race is so deeply tinged, which constitutes the genius of so many of their writers, as, of the author of Hudibras, Smollett, Fielding, Swift, and Sterne, and which the English maintain to be inseparable from genius, effervesces in every page of Chaucer. The prologue to the *Canterbury Tales* is full of it. A pleasing specimen of it is the alarm in the farmyard in the **"Fable of the Cock and the Fox."**

[A historical feature in the English race is] the respect for women, for want of which trait the ancient Greeks and Romans as well as the Oriental nations in all ages have never attained the highest point of Civilization. A severe morality is essential to high civilization and to the moral education of man it needs that the relation between the sexes should be established on a purely virtuous footing. It is the consequence of the unnatural condition of woman in the East that even life to a woman is reckoned a calamity. "When a daughter is born," says the Chinese *Sheking*, "she creeps on the ground: she is clothed with a wrapper: she plays with a tile: she is incapable of evil or of good." Our venerable English bard fully shared this generous attribute of his nation. I suppose nothing will mr than his thorough acquaintance with the female character. He does indeed know its weakness and its vice and has not shunned to show them. I am sorry for it. Well he had observed all those traits that in rarely endowed women command a veneration scarcely to be distinguished from worship. The whole mystery of humility, of love, of purity, and of faith, in woman, and how they make a woman unearthly and divine, he well knew, and has painted better than any other in Griselda and Blanche. The story of Griselda in the *Canterbury Tales*, is, I suppose the most pathetic poem in the language. And the *Book of the Duchess*, though the introduction be long and tedious, seems to me a beautiful portraiture of true love. All the sentiment is manly, honorable, and tender. I admire the description of Blanche who knew so well how to live

That dulness was of her adrad
She n'as too sober nor too glad
In all thinges more measure
Had never I trowe creature:

George Lyman Kittredge   (essay date 1915)

SOURCE: "Troilus," in *Chaucer and His Poetry,* Harvard University Press, 1915, pp. 108-21.

[*Kittredge is renowned as the editor of the* Complete Works of Shakespeare *(with Irving Ribner) and for his collections of English and Scottish ballads as well as for his studies of Chaucer, including* Observations on the Language of Chaucer's Troilus *and* Chaucer and His Poetry *from which the following excerpt is taken. In this passage, Kittredge summarizes the situation and action of* Troilus and Criseyde *and argues that it is a superlative love tragedy.*]

Chaucer is known to everybody as the prince of storytellers, as incomparably the greatest of our narrative poets. Indeed, if we disregard the epic, which stands in a class by itself, I do not see why we should hesitate to call him the greatest of all narrative poets whatsoever, making no reservation of era or of language. His fame began in his own lifetime, and was not confined, even then, to the limits of his native country. It has constantly increased, both in area and in brilliancy, and was never so widespread or so splendid as at the present day. Besides, he is a popular poet, and this popularity—more significant than mere reputation—has grown steadily with the gradual extension of the reading habit to all sorts and conditions of men.

To most readers, however, Chaucer means only the *Canterbury Tales*; and even so, it is with but half-a-dozen of the pilgrims that they are intimately acquainted. This is manifest destiny, which it would be ridiculous to deplore: "What wol nat be, mot nede be left." Nor should we lament what Sir Thomas Browne calls "the iniquity of oblivion"; for oblivion has treated Chaucer generously. She has exempted enough of the poet's achievement to bring him popularity, which the conditions of his own time could neither afford nor promise, and she has spared besides, for such of us as care to read it, that masterpiece of psychological fiction

In which ye may the double sorwes here,
Of Troylus, in loving of Criseyde,
And how that she forsook him er she deyde.

The *Troilus* is not merely, as William Rossetti styles it, the most beautiful long narrative poem in the English language: it is the first novel, in the modern sense, that ever was written in the world, and one of the best. Authorship is a strange art: it is nearest akin to magic, which deals with the incalculable. Chaucer sat down to compose a romance, as many a poet had done before him. The subject was to be love; the ethical and social system was to be that of chivalry; the source was the matter of Troy; the material was Italian and French and Latin. His readers were to be the knights and ladies of the court, to whom the fame of the hero as a lover and a warrior was already familiar. Psychology it was to contain, or what passed for psychology in the mediæval love-poets, the analysis of emotion in terms of Chrétien de Troyes and the *Roman de la Rose*. Yet the work was not, in Chaucer's intention, to be a romance precisely. He conceived it as what scholars then called a "tragedy,"—though with a somewhat peculiar modification of the standard term. Tragedies described the malice of Fortune when she casts down men of high estate and brings them to a miserable end. This was to be a tragedy of love, and the fall of the hero was to be from happy union with his lady to the woe and ruin of her unfaithfulness. And so Chaucer took his pen in hand, and drew his quire of paper to him, and wrote a prologue.

The magician has marked out his circle, and pronounced his spells, and summoned his spirits. He knows their names, and the formulas that will evoke them, and the task that he shall require them to perform. And lo! they come, and there are strange demons among them, and when the vision is finished and the enchanter lays down his wand, he finds on his desk—a romance, to be sure, which his pen has written; a tragedy, in the sense in which he knew the word; a love-tragedy, with a background of the matter of Troy, and thousands of lines from Boccaccio, with bits of Benoit and Guido delle Colonne, and a sonnet of Petrarch's, and a section out of Boethius, and a closing prayer to the Christian God. Everything is as he had planned it. But, when he reads it over, he finds that he has produced a new thing. Nothing like it was ever in the world before.

The *Troilus* is a long poem, extending to more than eight thousand verses, but the plot is so simple that it may be set forth in a dozen sentences.

Troilus, Priam's son, and second in valor to Hector only, is a scoffer at love and lovers. On a high holiday, as he strolls idly about the temple of Pallas, heart-free and glorying in his freedom, his eye falls upon Cressida, daughter of Calchas. Her father has fled to the Greeks, to escape the doom of Troy; but Cressida remains in the city. She is a widow, young, rich, and of surpassing beauty. Troilus falls madly in love, but fears to reveal his passion. Pandarus, Cressida's uncle and Troilus' friend, coaxes the secret from him, and helps him with all his might. Cressida yields, after long wooing, and the lovers see naught but happiness before them.

One day, however, during an exchange of prisoners, Calchas persuades the Greeks to offer Antenor for Cressida, whom he fears to leave in the city of destruction. To resist is impossible. The lovers are parted; but Cressida promises to return in ten days, feeling sure that she can cajole her aged father. Her woman's wiles are fruitless: she must remain in the Grecian camp, where Diomede pays court to her assiduously. He wins her at length, though not without her bitter grief at the thought of her unfaithfulness. Troilus is slain by Achilles.

This is the barest outline, but it suffices to show the simplicity of the story. The interest lies in the details, which are told with much particularity, and in the characterization, which is complex and subtle in a high degree. Readers who look for rapid movement and quick succession of incident, are puzzled and thwarted by the deliberation, the leisureliness, of the *Troilus*. The conversations are too long for them; they find the soliloquies languid; the analysis of sentiment and emotion and passion fails to keep their minds awake. But the *Troilus* is not a tale for a spare hour: it is an elaborate psychological novel, instinct with humor, and pathos, and passion, and human nature. Condensation would spoil it. Once yield to its charm, and you wish that it might go on forever.

Fate dominates in the *Troilus*. The suspense consists not in waiting for the unexpected, but in looking forward with a kind of terror for the moment of predicted doom. The catastrophe is announced a are to hear of "the double sorrow of Troilus in loving Cressida, and how she forsook him at the last." Neither Troilus nor Cressida suspects what is to come; but we know all about it from the beginning. There is no escape for anybody. We are looking on at a tragedy that we are powerless to check or to avert.

> [*Troilus and Criseyde*] . . . is an elaborate
> **psychological novel, instinct with humor,
> and pathos, and passion and human
> nature.**
>
> —*George Lyman Kittredge*

Chaucer himself conveys the impression of telling the tale under a kind of duress. Not, of course, that there is any literal compulsion. It is rather that he is entangled, somehow, in the subject, and that, since he has begun, he is in duty bound to finish his task.

> Sin I have begonne,
> Myn auctor shal I folwen, if I conne.

There is no weariness, as in some of the tales in the *Legend of Good Women*. His interest in the matter is intense, and it never falters. But he feels the burden of the ruin that is to come. At times he even seems to struggle against the fate which has allotted him so sad a duty. He would change the tale if he could, but he must tell the truth, though it is almost more than he can bear. He would actually impugn the evidence if that were possible:—

> For how Criseyde Troilus forsook—
> Or, at the leest, how that she was unkynde—
> Moot hennesforth be mater of my book,
> As writen folk thurgh which it is in minde.
> Allas that they shulde evere cause fynde
> To speke hire harm! and if they on hire lye,
> Ywis hemself sholde han the vilenye.

So mightily is he stirred by Cressida's grief that he would extenuate her guilt, or even excuse it altogether, for sheer pity. She has been punished enough; and, after all, she was only a weak woman, "tendre-herted, slyding of corage."

> Ne me ne list this sely womman chyde
> Ferther than the story wol devyse.
> Hir name, allas! is publisshed so wyde,
> That for hir gilt it oughte y-now suffyse.
> And if I mighte excuse hir any wyse,—
> For she so sory was for hir untrouthe,—
> I-wis, *I wolde excuse hir yet for routhe.*

This extraordinary outburst works powerfully upon our feelings. The case is hopeless. There is no excuse but destiny, and destiny, though irresistible, cannot be pleaded even in extenuation. Such is the law, and Chaucer bows to its everlasting antinomy, which, like Œdipus before him, he does not pretend to reconcile.

Everywhere in the poem we find this idea of a compelling destiny. It was Troilus' fate to love; he rode by Cressida's palace on "his happy day,"—

> For which men say, may nought disturbed be
> That shal betyden of necessite.

"Swich is love," so Cressida moralizes, "and eek myn aventure" [II. 742]. The oak topples over when it receives "the falling stroke." Troilus apostrophizes the Parcæ, who settled his life for him before he was born:—

> "O fatal sustren, which, er any clooth
> Me shapen was, my destine me sponne!"

"Pleasure comes and goes in love," says Pandarus, "as the chances fall in the dice." It was Fortune that cast Troilus down, "and on her wheel she set up Diomede," but Fortune is only the "executrix of weirds," and the influences of the stars govern us mortals as the herdsman drives his cattle:—

> But O Fortune, executrice of wierdes,
> O influences of thise hevenes hye!
> Soth is that, under God, ye ben our hierdes,
> Though to us bestes been the causes wrye."

Most significant of all is the long meditation of Troilus on foreknowledge and freedom of the will in the Fourth Book. This is from Boethius, and Chaucer has been as much blamed for inserting it as Shakspere for making Hector quote Aristotle. Doubtless the passage is inartistic and maladjusted; but it is certainly not, as some have called it, a digression. On the contrary, it is, in substance, as pertinent and opportune as any of Hamlet's soliloquies. The situation is well-imagined. Cressida is to be sent to the Grecian camp. Parliament has so decided, and resistance would be vain. Troilus, in despair, seeks the solitude of a temple, and prays to almighty and omniscient Jove either to help him or to let him die. Destiny, he feels, has overtaken him, for there seems to be no likelihood that Cressida, if once she joins her father, will ever

return to Troy. What can he do but pray? Perhaps Jove will work a miracle to save him. And as he meditates, in perplexity and distress, his mind travels the weary maze of fate and free will, and finds no issue, unless in the god's omnipotence.

All this, no doubt, is un-Trojan; but that is a futile objection. We have already accepted Troilus as a mediæval knight and a mediæval lover, and we cannot take umbrage at his praying like a man of the middle ages, or arguing with himself in the mediæval manner. In details, to be sure, the passage is open to criticism, and it is undoubtedly too long; but in substance it is dramatically appropriate, and it is highly significant as a piece of exposition. For Troilus finds no comfort in his meditation. Whatever clerks may say, the upshot of the matter is that "all that comth, comth by necessitee." Whatever is foreknown, must come to pass, and cannot be avoided.

> "And thus the bifalling
> Of things that ben wist biforn the tyde,
> They mowe nat been eschewed on no syde."

The fate which darkens the loves of Troilus and Cressida is strangely intensified (in ourapprehension of it) by the impending doom of Troy. This is no mere rhetorical analogue—no trick of symbolism. Their drama is an integral part of the great Trojan tragedy. They are caught in the wheels of that resistless mechanism which the gods have set in motion for the ruin of the Trojan race. This is a vital, determining fact in their history, as Chaucer understands it, and he leaves us in no doubt as to its intense significance. Calchas, we are told at the outset, deserted Priam because Apollo had revealed the doom of Troy:—

> For wel wiste he, by sort, that Troye sholde,
> Destroyed ben, ye, wolde whose nolde.

And again and again we are reminded, as the tale proceeds, of the inevitable outcome of the ten years' war. Troilus is smitten with love when he sees Cressida in the temple. It is the great festival of Palladion, a relic, Chaucer calls it, in Christian phrase, in which the Trojans put their trust above everything. They were celebrating "Palladion's feast," for they would not intermit their devout observances, although the Greeks had shut them in, "and their cite biseged al aboute." When Pandarus finds his friend plunged in a lover's grief, despairing of ever winning the least favor from the lady he has seen in the temple, the gibe that he casts at him, "—for the nonce, To anger him and arouse him from his stupor—is an accusation of cowardice:—'Fear, perhaps, has prompted you to pray and repent, as at the approach of death.'"

> "God save hem that biseged our toun;
> And so can leye our iolitee in presse,
> And bringe our lusty folk to hevinesse!"

When Pandarus first reveals to Cressida the secret of Troilus' love, he approaches the subject carefully, so as not to startle her. "I could tell you something," he cries, "that would make you lay aside your mourning." "Now, uncle dear," she answers, "tell it us, for love of God! Is the siege over, then? I am frightened to death of these Greeks."

"As ever thryve I," quod this Pandarus,
"Yet coude I telle a thing to do yow pleye!"
"Now, uncle dere," quod she, "telle it us
For Goddes love! Is than thassege aweye?
I am of Grekes so ferd that I deye!"

Cressida felt the first thrill in her heart when she saw Troilus riding through the street on his return from battle—his helm hewn to pieces, his shield pierced with Grecian arrows and cut and broken with the blows of swords and maces,—and the people were all shouting in triumph as he passed.

Always and everywhere we are oppressed by the coming doom of the city. This it is that prompts Calchas to beg the Greeks to give up their prisoner Antenor in exchange for Cressida. They need not hesitate, he argues; one Trojan captive more or less is nothing to them,—the whole city will soon be theirs. The time is near at hand.

"That fyr and flaumbe on al the toun shal sprede,
And thus shal Troye turne in asshen dede."

And, when Hector opposes the exchange, the Trojan people, in a riotous parliament, shout out their unanimous vote in its favor, and carry the day. Hector was right, though he did not know it for he was acting, not from policy or superior foresight, but from an honorable scruple: Cressida was not a prisoner, he contended; and Trojans did not use to sell women. And the people were fatally wrong. The "cloud of error" hid their best interests from their discernment; for it was the treason of Antenor that brought about the final catastrophe. It is, then, the impendent doom of Troy that parts the lovers; and from this time forward, there is no separating their fate from the fate of the town.

When Cressida joins Calchas in the Grecian camp, she means to return in a few days. She has no doubt whatever that she can trick her father, and she has won Troilus over to her scheme. But she soon discovers that she has matched her woman's wit, not against her dotard father merely, but against the doom of Troy. No pretexts avail, not because Calchas suspects her plot, but because he knows that the city is destined to destruction. Nor does she dare to steal away by night, lest she fall into the hands of the savage soldiery. And finally, when Diomede wooes her, and gets a hearing, though little favor at first, his most powerful argument is the certain and speedy fate of Troy. He does not know that Cressida loves Troilus,—she tells him that she is heart-whole, but for her memory of her dead husband,—yet he cannot believe that so fair a lady has left no lover behind her, and he has seen her ever in sorrow. "Do not," he urges her, "spill a quarter of a tear for any Trojan; for, truly, it is not worth while. The folk of Troy are all in prison, as you may see for yourself, and not one of them shall come out alive for all the gold betwixen sun and sea!"

Thus, from first to last, the loves of Troilus and Cressida are bound up with the inexorable doom that hangs over the city. The fate of Troy is their fate. Their story begins in the temple of the Palladium; it is Calchas' foreknowledge and the people's infatuation that tear them asunder; it is the peril of the town that thwarts woman's wit, until Diomede subdues the inconstant heart. The tragedy of character grows out of the tragedy of situation.

J. M. Manly (lecture date 1926)

SOURCE: "Chaucer and the Rhetoricians," in *Proceedings of the British Academy,* Oxford University Press, 1926, pp. 95-113.

[*Manly was an esteemed professor of Medieval English known for his valuable contribution to Chaucer studies through his lectures and his eight-volume collection. The* Text of the Canterbury Tales, Studied on the Basis of All Known Manuscripts. *In the following excerpt from his published lectures, Manly describes the rhetorical styles of Chaucer's* Canterbury Tales, Book of the Duchess, Parlement of Foules, *and other poems. He traces Chaucer's style to the lessons given in medieval rhetorical texts, suggesting that Chaucer was following set conventions in his poetry, which he later imaginatively expanded.*]

. . . In investigating the sources of Chaucer's notions of literature and his conceptions of style, scholars have hitherto discussed only the writings of other authors which may have served as models for imitation. The possibility of his acquaintance with formal rhetorical theory and the precepts of rhetoricians has not been considered, not-withstanding the hint that might have been derived from the allusion to Gaufred de Vinsauf and the other passages on rhetoric scattered through his works. Even *a priori* there would seem to be a high probability that Chaucer was familiar with the rhetorical theories of his time, that he had studied the text-books and carefully weighed the doctrines. Whatever modern scholars may have said of the errors in his references and the shallowness of his classical learning—and there are few of his critics whose errors are less numerous than his—he was a man of scholarly tastes and of considerable erudition. His works bear witness to no small reading in astronomy and astrology, in alchemy, in medicine, and in philosophy and theology, as well as in the classical authors current in his day. The ancient tradition that he was educated, in part at any rate, in the law school of the Inner Temple has recently been shown to be possible, if not highly probable. The education given by the inns of court seems to have been remarkably liberal. What more likely than that the formal study of rhetoric not only was included in his academic curriculum, as one of the Seven Arts, but also occupied much of his thought and reflection in maturer years?

What, then, was medieval rhetoric? Who were its principal authorities in Chaucer's time? And what use did Chaucer make of methods and doctrines unmistakably due to the rhetoricians?

To the first two questions satisfactory answers can be readily given. Professor Edmond Faral has recently printed the chief rhetorical texts of the thirteenth and fourteenth centuries, with illuminating biographical and bibliographical notes and excellent summaries of the doctrines. To answer the third question fully would require a volume, but a provisional view of the matter can be obtained from a rapid survey of Chaucer's best-known work.

Fortunately for our inquiry, the Middle Ages knew only one rhetorical system and drew its precepts from few and well-known sources. Moreover, there was little development of the doctrines or variety in the mode of presentation. The principal sources of the doctrines were three: the two books of Cicero entitled *De Inventione,* the four books entitled *De Rhetorica, ad Herennium,* and the Epistle of Horace to Piso. Treatises based upon these were not uncommon in the earlier Middle Ages, but after the beginning of the thirteenth century the practical spirit of the time tended in the universities to substitute instruction in letter writing and the *artes dictaminis* for the more theoretical and supposedly less useful study of general rhetorical principles. It is perhaps for this reason that the treatises of Matthieu de Vendôme and Gaufred de Vinsauf, written early in the thirteenth century, retained their vogue in the time of Chaucer. These treatises are the *Ars Versificatoria* of Matthieu, and the *Documentum de Arte Versificandi* and the *Nova Poetria* of Gaufred. The first two are prose treatises, carefully defining and discussing all processes and terms and illustrating them by examples, in part drawn from earlier writers, such as Virgil, Horace, Ovid, Statius, and Sidonius, and in part composed by the rhetorician himself, either to show his skill or to pay off a grudge. For example, Matthieu is tireless in the composition of verses attacking the red-haired rival whom he calls Rufus; Gaufred, illustrating the beauties of *circumlocutio,* says it is of special value when we wish to praise or [defame] a person . . . .

The doctrine taught by these two authorities, the common medieval doctrine, falls logically and naturally into three main divisions or heads: (1) arrangement or organization; (2) amplification and abbreviation; (3) style and its ornaments.

Of arrangement they had little to say, and that little was purely formal and of small value. They treated mainly of methods of beginning and ending, distinguishing certain forms as natural and others as artificial. Artificial beginnings consisted either of those which plunge *in medias res* or set forth a final situation before narrating the events that led up to and produced it, or of those in which a *sententia* (that is, a generalization or a proverb) is elaborated as an introduction, or an *exemplum* (that is, a similar case) is briefly handled for the same purpose. It will be readily recognized that all these varieties of beginnings are in familiar use at the present day; and, curiously enough, in recent years writers for the popular magazines have shown a special fondness for beginning with an elaborately developed *sententia.*

We have not time to-day for a detailed examination of Chaucer's methods of beginning, but this is hardly necessary. The moment one undertakes a survey of his poetry in the light of rhetorical theory, one is struck by the elaborate artifice of its beginnings and the closeness of their agreement with rhetorical formulae. This artificiality has long been recognized but has been mistakenly ascribed to the influence of the poems upon which he drew for his materials. His French sources, however, are hardly responsible for these elaborate beginnings; they furnish only the raw materials which Chaucer puts together in accordance with the instructions of his masters in rhetoric. The apparent simplicity with which the **Boke of the Duchesse** begins disappears under examination: the reader is led through several long and tortuous corridors—totalling one-third of the poem—before he arrives at the real subject, which in turn is developed with amazing artificiality. The long failure of the mourning knight to make clear the nature of his loss may be regarded as an expanded form of the rhetorical figure called *occupatio.*

The **Parlement of Foules** admirably illustrates the method of beginning with a *sententia:*

> The lyf so short, the craft so long to lerne.

This is expanded into two seven-line stanzas. Then comes, not the narrative itself, but a preliminary narrative, interspersed with various rhetorical devices, including generalizations, an apostrophe, and an outline of Cicero's *Somnium Scipionis,* in all 119 lines, before the story proper begins.

This method is even more elaborately developed in the **Hous of Fame**. In fact the poet is within twenty lines of the end of Book I before he begins to tell his story. There are sixty-five lines on dreams, sixty-five more of invocation, and more than 350 telling in outline the entirely unnecessary story of Dido and Aeneas.

Even when the narrative begins in a natural manner, as in **Anelida and Arcite**, the poem is given an artificial character by prefixing an invocation or by some other rhetorical device. The beginning of the **Legend of Goode Women** combines the methods of *sententia* and *exemplum*: our belief in the joys and pains of heaven and hell, says the poet, is based, not upon experience, but upon the acceptance of the sayings of 'these olde wise'; in like manner we must accept the testimony of books—those treasuries of wisdom—about the existence of good women, though we have never known them. A few of the separate legends begin inartificially, but it was not until late in his career that Chaucer developed the method of beginning used with such masterly skill in the tales of Miller, Reeve, Summoner, and Pardoner.

Methods of ending are treated by the rhetoricians even more summarily than beginnings, the preferred forms being the employment of a proverb or general idea, an *exemplum,* or a brief summary. Chaucer is fond of some sort of explicit application of his stories. In the **"Reeve's Tale"** this takes the form of a proverb:

And therfore this proverbe is seyd ful sooth
Him thar nat wene wel that yvele dooth:
"A gylour shal hymself bigyled be."

And the **"Manciple's Tale"** ends in a stream of proverbs and proverbial sayings. But the more common form of application is a generalization or an exclamatory comment. Very common also is the ending summarizing the situation at the end of the tale. On the other hand, notwithstanding Chaucer's fondness for *exempla*, the *exemplum*-ending is very rare; perhaps the only instance, and that a doubtful one, is in the **"Friar's Tale"**:

Herketh this word, beth war, as in this cas:
"The leoun sit in his awayt alway
To sle the innocent, if that he may"

Peculiar to Chaucer are the references to other writers for further information—as in several of the legends—and the triple *demande d'amours* with which the **"Franklin's Tale"** ends.

The technical means of passing from the beginning to the body of the work—*prosecutio,* as it is called—are treated with much formality by Gaufred, though he remarks with great good sense that the prime requisite is to get on with the subject: *In ipsa continuatione, primum est continuare.*

In Chaucer, after a rhetorical beginning, the transition to the narrative itself is usually clearly and formally indicated; so, for example, in *Troilus and Criseyde*:

For now wol I gon streight to my matere.

The amount of attention devoted by the rhetoricians to the second main division, that of amplification, is to the modern reader surprising, but it results quite naturally from the purely mechanical character of the art of rhetoric as conceived by them. To them the problems of composition were not problems of the creative imagination but problems of 'fine writing'—*l'art de bien dire.* They had no conception of psychological processes or laws. The questions they raised were not questions of methods by which the writer might most perfectly develop his conception or of the means by which he might convey it to his audience. The elaborate system of technical devices was discussed only with reference to the form and structure of each device, never with reference to its emotional or aesthetic effects. As the rhetoricians conceived the matter, if a writer had something new to say, rhetoric was unnecessary; the novelty of the material relieved him of any concern for its form. But alas! this situation seldom arose. Practically everything had already been said. All the tales had been told, all the songs had been sung, all the thoughts of the mind and feelings of the heart had been expressed. The modern writer, they held, could only tell a thrice-told tale, only echo familiar sentiments. His whole task was one of finding means and methods of making the old seem new. He might therefore well begin his task of composition by choosing some familiar but attractive text—some tale, or poem, or oration, or treatise— or by making a patchwork of pieces selected from many sources. His problem would be that of renewing the expression and especially of making it more beautiful— *ornatior* is the common term.

Let no one scoff at this method as incapable of producing interesting and attractive writing. It has been practised very commonly by writers in all lands and epochs. It is recommended and taught in a widely used series of French text-books. It is the method recently revealed as pursued by that most charming of stylists, Anatole France, and is perhaps the only method by which he or Laurence Sterne could have produced such effects as they achieved.

Medieval rhetoricians assume that the writer, having chosen his subject, will find his material either too great or too small for his purpose. His problem will almost necessarily be one of amplification or abbreviation. The methods of amplifying and abbreviating are derived from the technique of style. They are therefore dealt with in their proper places when style and its ornaments are under discussion, but for the sake of clearness they are also expounded elaborately with special reference to their uses and values as means of amplification and abbreviation.

The principal means of amplification are six—some writers say eight:

Description, though perhaps not the most important, may be named first, as receiving fullest attention from both Matthieu de Vendôme and Gaufred de Vinsauf. Elaborate patterns and formulas are given for describing persons, places, things, and seasons. If the description applies to externals, the features to be described are enumerated and the order in which they are to be taken up is strictly specified; if it concerns a character, the characteristics to be mentioned are listed, and those appropriate to each sex, age, social status, employment, temperament, and career are set forth in detail. Specimens are given to illustrate the doctrines. These descriptions are not, like those in Chaucer's later work, determined by the requirements of the situation in which they occur. Their use is purely conventional, for the purpose of amplifying the material, and their construction is purely mechanical. They are merely opportunities for the writer to display his rhetorical training. It is very enlightening to compare Chaucer's later descriptions—such, for example, as those of Alysoun and Absalon in the **"Miller's Tale"**—with the early ones; for example, with that of the Duchess Blanche, which, with the exception of one or two possibly realistic touches, is nothing more than a free paraphrase of lines 563-597 of the *Nova Poetria,* composed by Gaufred de Vinsauf as a model for the description of a beautiful woman. The features described in the two passages are the same, they are taken up in the same order, and the same praise is given to each. The resemblance is still further heightened by the fact that, like Chaucer, Gaufred declines to guess at the beauties hidden by the robe—a trait hitherto regarded as characteristically Chaucerian.

There seems little doubt, indeed, that Chaucer's character sketches, widely as they later depart fromthe models offered by the rhetoricians, had their origins in them. An

American scholar has recently attempted to show that Chaucer derived them from the treatises on Vices and Virtues, with their descriptions of character types. The possibility of an influence from this source I will neither deny nor discuss, but the specimen sketches given by the rhetoricians seem entirely sufficient to account for Chaucer's interest in this type of description.

The next most important device was digression, of which two subdivisions were recognized: first, digression to another part of the same subject, anticipating a scene or an event which in regular course would come later; second, digression to another subject. Digression may obviously be made in many ways and may include many special rhetorical devices. Prominent among the special forms are the development of a *sententia* and the introduction of *exempla,* illustrating the matter in hand. These two devices are of the utmost importance for Chaucer in particular and for the Middle Ages in general. The temper of the Middle Ages being distinctly practical and its literary valuations being determined, not by the criteria of art, but by those of edification, *sententiae,* proverbs, and *exempla* were used with an ardour now difficult to appreciate. The use of *exempla* was strongly inculcated by the rhetoricians. Matthieu de Vendôme urges the writer to provide an abundance of *exempla.* . . .

But the precepts of the rhetoricians on this point had already been heeded by other writers, and in Chaucer's poems it is difficult to separate the direct influence of rhetorical theory from that of the practice of Guillaume de Machaut, whose first use of *exempla* was in his *Dit de l'Alerion* and whose later use of them gave them a vogue attested by the imitation of all hid by this astonishing fad as was any of the French imitators of Machaut. They are familiar from the series of twenty-one consecutive instances in the **"Franklin's Tale"** and the humorous accumulation of them in the controversy between the Cock and the Hen.

Third in importance among the devices of amplification may be placed apostrophe, with its rhetorical colours *exclamatio, conduplicatio, subiectio,* and *dubitatic.* It would be difficult to exaggerate the importance of apostrophe in medieval literature. Addresses to persons living or dead, present or absent, to personified abstractions, and even to inanimate objects are to be found in almost every composition with any pretensions to style from the eleventh century onward; and a special form, the *Complainte,* developed into one of the most widely cultivated types of literature. Chaucer's use of apostrophe is so frequent that no examples need be cited. Almost every tale contains from one to a dozen examples of it. Among the colours, his favourites seem to be those known as *exclamatio*—simply a passionate outcry addressed to some person or thing present or absent—and *dubitatio,* that is, a feigned hesitation what to say, a rhetorical questioning as to which of two or more expressions is appropriate to the idea and situation. Like Wordsworth's—

> O Cuckoo, shall I call thee Bird
> Or but a wandering Voice?

Fourth in order may come *prosopopeia* or *effictio,* the device which represents as speaking persons absent or dead, animals, abstractions, or inanimate objects. Widely used for purposes of amplification, this figure often furnished forth the whole of a piece of literature. Examples are numerous. A charming one contemporary with Chaucer is the *débat* in which Froissart represents his dog and horse as discussing their master and the journeys which he compels them to make with him. Chaucer uses it briefly many times, and elaborately in the principal scene of the **Parlement of Foules**.

Less important than the foregoing are the devices of *periphrasis* or *circumlocutio,* and its closely related *expolitio. Circumlocutio* was highly regarded as one of the best means, both of amplifying discourse and of raising commonplace or low ideas to a high stylistic level. It is too familiar to require discussion, but Master Gaufred seems not to have distinguished clearly between a statement expanded for the mere sake of amplification and one which expresses some important detail or phase of an idea. For example, he calls the opening lines of Virgil's *Aeneid circumlocutio* and declares, 'This is nothing else than to say, I will describe Aeneas.' And, after quoting from Boethius three lines of the metre beginning,

> O qui perpetua mundum ratione gubernas,

adds,

> *Quod nihil aliud est quam, 'O Deus.'*

These remarks and the similar ones by Matthieu de Vendôme will doubtless recall Chaucer's sly comment in the **"Franklin's Tale"** on his own rhetorical description of the end of the day:

> Til that the brighte sonne lost his hewe,
> For thorizonte hath reft the sonne his lyght,—
> This is as much to seye as it was nyght.

The colour *expolitio* includes the repetition of the same idea in different words (one form of *interpretatio*) and also the elaboration of an idea by adding the reasons or authorities, pronouncing a generalization with or without reasons, discussing the contrary, introducing a similitude or an *exemplum,* and drawing a conclusion. Although these two figures are of minor importance, they nevertheless play a considerable part in the writings of Chaucer, as of most other medieval authors.

Other devices for amplification existed, but I will spare you even the enumeration of them.

Abbreviation is joined by the rhetoricians with amplification, but is obviously of much less practical interest. The medieval writer is, as a rule, not so much concerned to abbreviate as to amplify. Master Gaufred, however, instructs his readers that in treating a well-worn subject the best means of creating an appearance of novelty is to survey the whole subject and then run quickly over the parts that predecessors have dwelt upon and dwell upon parts they have neglected. The principal means of abbreviation recommended are certain of the figures of words: asyndeton, reduction of predication, and the like. Chaucer's favourite methods are two:

(1) The use of absolute constructions—perhaps the most striking and beautiful example of this is the opening line of the second book of the *Troilus*:

Out of these blake wawes for to saile,
O wind, o wind, the weder ginneth clere!

the second line furnishing an instance of the figure called *epizeusis*.

(2) The figure called *occupatio,* that is, the refusal to describe or narrate—a figure used with special frequency in **"The Squire's Tale,"** as for example:

But for to telle yow al hir beaute
It lyth nat in my tonge, nyn my konnyng

and

I wol not tellen of hir straunge sewes

or

I wol nat taryen yow, for it is pryme

or

Who koude tellen yow the forme of daunces
So unkouthe, and so fresshe countenaunces?

. . . . .

No man but Launcelot, and he is deed.

Into the vast and tangled jungle of the medieval treatment of Style and its Ornaments we cannot venture now. Its extent may be inferred from the fact that, notwithstanding the inclusion of very long specimens of apostrophe, prosopopeia, and description (328 lines in all) the portion of the *Nova Poetria* devoted to the important subjects of 'Art in General', 'Organization', and 'Amplification and Abbreviation' occupies only 674 lines, whereas that devoted to the 'Ornaments of Style' occupies 1125. The tangle is suggested by the fact that there are recognized, defined, and discussed thirty-five colours, or figures of words, twenty figures of thought, and ten varieties of tropes, with nine more sub-varieties. These figures fall into two very distinct classes: first, those in which human emotion and aesthetic feeling have always found utterance—metaphor, simile, exclamation, rhetorical question, and the like; and second, a vast mass of highly artificial and ingenious patterns of word and thought, such as using the same word at the end of a line as at the beginning, heaped-up rhymes, and alliteration.

Like other writers in all ages, Chaucer makes extensive use of the first class of figures; of the artificial patterns he

makes only a limited use, and that solely in highly rhetorical passages, like the **"Monk's Tale,"** certain parts of the *Boke of the Duchesse*, and in the apostrophes, exclamations, and *sententiae* of other serious compositions. The humorous tales, for which the rhetoricians forbidthe use of *colores,* are entirely free from special rhetorical devices, with the single and striking exception of the **"Nun's Priest's Tale,"** a mock-heroic composition so full of rhetoric and so amusingly parodying the style of the **"Monk's Tale,"** which immediately preceded it, as to invite the suggestion that the 'high style' and its parody were purposely juxtaposed. Is it possible that Chaucer's desire to carry out this amusing contrast explains the otherwise puzzling change of the Monk from the spectacular huntsman and hard rider of the **"Prologue"** to the bookish pedant of the hundred lamentable tragedies who greets our astonished ears when he is called upon for a tale?

As no one ever pays any attention to statistics and percentages, they rest the mind. This may therefore be a fitting time to introduce a few. If we list the *Canterbury Tales* according to the percentages of the larger rhetorical devices which they contain, they form an interesting descending series, ranging from nearly 100 per cent. to 0. Highest, as might be expected, stands the **"Monk's Tale,"** with nearly 100 per cent. of rhetoric. Next comes the **"Manciple's Tale"** with 61 per cent.; then the tales of the **"Nun's Priest"** and the **"Wife of Bath"** with 50 per cent. The tales of the **"Pardoner"** and the **"Knight"** have 40 and 35 per cent. respectively; while those of the **"Man of Law,"** the **"Doctor,"** the **"Prioress,"** the **"Franklin,"** the **"Second Nun,"** and the **"Merchant"** fall between 30 and 20 per cent. The half-told tale of the **"Squire"** stands alone with 16 per cent., and slightly below it come the tales of the **"Clerk"** and the **"Canon's Yeoman,"** with 10 per cent. Quite in a class by themselves stand the tales of the **"Reeve"** and the **"Shipman,"** with about 5 per cent. of rhetoric, and those of the **"Miller,"** the **"Friar,"** and the **"Summoner,"** in which the rhetorical devices do not occupy more than 1 per cent. of the text.

Although some of these percentages are just what we should expect from the character of the tales and their probable dates, some are rather surprising. It is natural enough that the **"Monk's Tale"** should head the list, for it is professedly a collection of tragedies. But that some of Chaucer's freest and most delightful work should contain twice as much rhetoric as some of his least inspired compositions is a puzzle that demands investigation.

Let us begin by examining one of the least known and least interesting of the tales, that of the **"Manciple."** It is in fact so insignificant and so little read that I cannot even assume that all of you recall the plot. 'When Phebus lived here on earth, we are told, he had a fair young wife, whom he loved dearly, and a white Crow, whom he had taught to speak. But the wife was unfaithful and took a lover. This was observed by the Crow, who upon Phebus's return home told him. Phebus in sorrow and anger slew his wife, and then, repenting of his deed and disbelieving the charge brought against her, plucked the white feathers from the bird and doomed all crows to be black.'

We may note in the first place that the tale is not particularly appropriate to the Manciple or indeed to any other of the pilgrims, and that no effort is made to adapt it to him. It consists of 258 lines, of which 41 are devoted to describing Phebus, his wife, and the crow, and 50 to telling the incidents of the story. The remaining 167 lines—61 per cent. of the tale—are patches of rhetoric. Even this high percentage is perhaps too low, for the 25 lines of description devoted to Phebus are so conventional, so much in accordance with rhetorical formulas, that they might fairly be added to our estimate of the percentage of rhetoric. No effort was made by the author to conceive any of his characters as living beings or to visualize the action of the tale. The action, to be sure, seems in itself unpromising as the basis of a masterpiece of the story-teller's art, but so, if we consider them closely, are the basic narratives of the **"Nun's Priest's Tale"** and the tales of the **"Miller,"** the **"Reeve,"** and the **"Friar."** If Chaucer had been as well inspired when he wrote this tale as when he wrote his masterpieces, Phebus might have been as real to us as the Oxford Carpenter or the Miller of Trumpington, his wife as brilliant a bit of colour as the Carpenter's wife, and the Crow as interesting a bird as Chaunticleer or Pertelote. But he developed the tale, not imaginatively, but rhetorically. Instead of attempting to realize his characters psychologically and conceive their actions and words as elements of a dramatic situation, he padded the tale with rhetoric. Thus he thrust into it and around it 32 lines of *sententiae*, 36 of *exempla*, 18 of *exclamatio*, 14 of *sermocinatio*, 3 of technical transition, 17 of *demonstratio*, and 63 of *applicatio*—all external and mechanical additions, clever enough as mere writing, but entirely devoid of life. If the tale had been written as a school exercise, to illustrate the manner in which rhetorical padding could be introduced into a narrative framework, the process of composition could not have been more mechanical or the results more distressing.

Chaucer's greatness arose from his growing recognition that for him at least the right way to amplify a story was not to expand it by rhetorical devices, but to conceive it in terms of the life which he had observed so closely. . . .

—*J. M. Manly*

But Chaucer was endowed with the temperament, not of the rhetorician, but of the artist; and in some way he arrived at the memorable discovery that the task of the artist is not to pad his tales with rhetoric, but to conceive all the events and characters in the forms and activities of life. For this he was well prepared by native endowment and by a habit of close observation which developed early and which redeems even his earliest poems from entire banality. Owing to the loss of so much of his prentice work and the uncertain chronology of what has been preserved, we cannot trace in detail the displacement of the

older rhetorical by the new psychological methods. But certain lines in the *Hous of Fame* indicate that when he was writing that poem he at least had formed an idea of the new methods, even though he may long have continued in some respects under the dominance of the old. The lines in question are in the proems of the second and third books:

> O thought that wroot al that I mette,
> And in the tresorie it shette
> Of my brayn, now shal men se
> If any vertu in thee be;

and more specifically:

> And if, Divyne Vertu, thou
> Wilt helpe me to shewe now
> That in myn hede y-marked is.

These passages, although the first is translated from Dante, seem to me to express Chaucer's growing conviction that narration and description, instead of being mere exercises in clever phrasing, depend upon the use of the visualizing imagination.

But in spite of this recognition of the true method, and in spite of his ability later in the **"Nun's Priest's Tale"** to parody the whole apparatus of medieval rhetoric, Chaucer did not free himself at once—and perhaps never entirely—of the idea that writing which pretended to seriousness and elevated thought was improved by the presence of apostrophes and *sententiae* and *exempla,* as he had been taught by the rhetoricians. Nor could it be expected that he should. The whole weight of the medieval conception of literature was against him—the conception, I mean, that literature, like history, is of value only in so far as it can be profitably applied to the conduct of human life, a conception which not only remained in full vigour through the Middle Ages and the period we are accustomed to call the Renaissance, but even now lies at the basis of much critical theory.

Chaucer's greatness arose from his growing recognition that for him at least the right way to amplify a story was not to expand it by rhetorical devices, but to conceive it in terms of the life which he had observed so closely, to imagine how each of the characters thought and felt, and to report how in this imaginative vision they looked and acted. And if he felt obliged, as apparently he still did, in writings of serious and lofty tone, to supply *sententiae,* proverbs, *exempla,* and other fruits of erudition, he came more and more to make only a dramatic use of these rhetorical elements, that is, to put them into the mouths of his *dramatis personae* and to use only such as might fittingly be uttered by them.

It is this dramatic use of rhetorical devices which we must learn to recognize in the later and more artistic poems, and which must be taken into account in our examination of the percentages of rhetoric in the separate tales of the Canterbury pilgrimage. The mere fact that the percentage in two such masterpieces of narrative art as the tales of the **"Nun's Priest"** and the **"Wife of Bath"** is nearly twice as great as in the less successful tales of the **"Man of Law"** and the **"Doctor"** would be very misleading, if taken without further investigation. But the difference in manner of introduction and use appears immediately and is of fundamental significance. In the tales of the **"Doctor"** and the **"Man of Law"** the rhetoric is prevailingly, indeed almost exclusively, used by the narrator; that is, it is not incorporated and used dramatically but stands apart from the tale. There is even a difference between the **"Doctor's Tale"** and that of the **"Man of Law"** in manner of handling. In the **"Man of Law's Tale"** the narrative is, for the most part, broken into comparatively brief sections and the rhetoric of the narrator is freely interspersed in the forms of *apostrophe*, *exclamatio*, *collatio*, *sententiae*, and *exempla*, with various digressions on astrology. In the **"Doctor's Tale,"** on the other hand, the narrative comes in a solid block of 172 lines, preceded by 109 lines, all but 39 of which are purely rhetorical utterances of the narrator, and followed by 10 lines of rhetorical application. But both stories are, as artistic compositions, pretty crude and show no fusion of rhetorical elements. In the tales of the **"Nun's Priest"** and the **"Wife of Bath"** the situation is very different. In the **"Nun's Priest's Tale,"** although the rhetoric is scattered through the narrative as in the **"Man of Law's Tale,"** it is not the external comment of the narrator but the vitally dramatized utterance of speakers whose actions, and attitudes, and sentiments we accept as belonging to a world of poetic reality. In the **"Wife of Bath's Tale"** there are two main masses of rhetorical devices: one of them is the famous oration on 'gentilesse', poverty, and age uttered by the Fairy Wife to her humbled husband, the other is the long *exemplum* on woman's inability to keep a secret, uttered by the garrulous Wife of Bath herself. But in the latter instance no less than in the former the rhetoric is dramatic, is conformed to the character, and is motivated.

The tales of the **"Prioress"** and the **"Second Nun"** differ very slightly in percentage of rhetorical devices or in the placing of them. If we could isolate the tales—disconnect them from their narrators and the circumstances of their telling—we should probably agree that they show the same style of workmanship and may belong to the same period, a comparatively early one. But the difference between them in effect is very great. Why is this? Apart from the mere difference in appeal of the material of the two stories, is it not because in the one tale Chaucer has failed to visualize or to make his readers see the principal characters—Cecilia, Valerian, and Pope Urban remain to him and to us mere names—whereas both he and we have a vivid and charming picture of the little choir boy as he goes singing to his death? Is it not also because through some freak of chance the Second Nun herself is a mere name in the **"Prologue"** and is not mentioned at all in the pilgrimage, whereas both by the portrait in the **"Prologue"** and by the little episode of conversation with the Host the Prioress is endowed with lasting beauty and sympathetic appeal? Chaucer himself seems to have felt this. When the Prioress's tale is ended he tells us of its profound effect upon the whole party including himself; after the other tale he says, drily,

> When toold was al the lif of Seint Cecile
> Er we had ridden fully fyve mile,

we were overtaken by two men.

The tales of the **"Franklin"** and the **"Merchant"** differ only slightly in percentage of rhetorical devices from those of the **"Prioress"** and the **"Second Nun,"** but in the placing and handling of these devices, as well as in other respects, they seem to belong to a much later period of Chaucer's workmanship. The *dramatis personae* are vividly conceived and the action is clearly visualized. Both tales show, however, the persistence of the rhetorical habit and training. In the **"Merchant's Tale"** most of the rhetoric is introduced dramatically as forming the speeches of January and his advisers, but there is a long undramatic passage—inappropriate either to the Merchant or to the clerical narrator for whom the tale appears to have been originally composed. In the **"Franklin's Tale"** a fine story finely told is nearly spoiled by one hundred lines of rhetorical *exempla*. The fact that they are put into the mouth of Dorigen in her complaint against Fortune indicates that Chaucer was trying to motivate them dramatically. But what reader, modern or medieval, would not have been more powerfully and sympathetically affected if Chaucer, with the psychological insight displayed in *Troilus and Criseyde*, had caused his distressed and desperate heroine to express the real feelings appropriate to her character and situation?

It may be noted that the tales showing a low percentage of formal rhetorical devices are, with a single exception, humorous tales and all are tales which on other grounds are regarded as of late date. The exception is the **"Clerk's Tale,"** a pretty close translation from Petrarch. The small amount of rhetoric added by Chaucer in making this translation from Petrarch is in curious contrast to the large amount added in translating the **"Man of Law's Tale"** from Trivet. Can it be that his rivalry with Gower in the latter case was responsible for the rhetoric?

The absence of rhetorical devices from the humorous tales may be due in part to the specific declaration of the rhetoricians that rhetorical ornament of all sorts should be strictly excluded from such tales. But surely Chaucer's growing power of artistry, his vast observation of life, and his newly devised method of imaginative reconstruction of the scenes; characters, and events of his stories gave him such a wealth of significant detail that there was no need and no space for the older methods of amplification. *Sententiae* are reduced to single lines, mostly proverbs; *exempla* to passing allusions; apostrophes and exclamations to the briefest of utterances. For it is not only in the humorous tales that his advanced method isner's Tale" of the three roysterers who sought Death, is as vividly imagined as the tales of the Miller and the Reeve, and the long passages of rhetoric, placed between the opening twenty lines, which so ʌonderfully create background and atmosphere, and the narrative itself, are thoroughly explained and justified by their function as part of the Pardoner's sermon.

The survey we have made of Chaucer's work, hasty as it has necessarily been, has, I think, shown that he began his career, not merely as a disciple and imitator of a thoroughly artificial school of writing, but as a conscious exploiter of the formal rhetoric taught by the professional rhetoricians, and that it was only gradually and as the result of much thought and experiment that he replaced the conventional methods of rhetorical elaboration by those processes of imaginative construction which give his best work so high a rank in English literature. To treat his poems as if they all belonged to the same stage of artistic development and represented the same ideals of art is to repeat the error so long perpetrated by students of Shakespeare.

John Livingston Lowes (lecture date 1930)

SOURCE: "The Art of Geoffrey Chaucer," in *Proceedings of the British Academy,* Oxford University Press, 1930, pp. 297-326.

[*Lowes is noted for his essays and lectures on poetry and is the author of* Geoffrey Chaucer and the Development of His Genius. *In the following excerpt from one of his published lectures, Lowes provides cultural, biographical, and literary sources for Chaucer's works.*]

My subject, as I have announced it, is a theme for a volume, but titles can seldom be brief and specific at once. I mean to limit myself to an attempt to answer—and that but in part—a single question: What, aside from genius, *made* the poet of the greater *Canterbury Tales*? How, in a word, did he master a technique at its height so consummate that if often seems not to be art at all, but the effortless play of nature? And by what various roads did he travel in passing from his earlier to his later themes? That twofold evolution, of technique and subject matter, is singularly rich in human as well as literary interest, and it is worth the effort to reconstruct, as far as possible, its processes.

One of the glories of English poetry has been the interpenetration in it of personal experience—call it for brevity life, if you will—and of books. Through the one, poetry acquires its stamp of individuality; through the other it is dipped in the quickening stream of tradition which has flowed through the work of all the poets from Homer and pre-Homeric days until now. The continuity of poetry, through its participation in that deep and perpetually broadening current, is a fact perhaps more important than the newness of the channels through which from time to time it flows. The greatest poetry is, indeed, steeped in the poet's own experience and coloured by the life of his times. But it also participates in a succession almost apostolic, in which there is an authentic if incorporeal laying on of hands:

> Go, litel book . . .
>   . . . no making thou n'envye,
> But subgit be to alle poesye;

> And kis the steppes, wher-as thou seest pace
> Virgile, Ovyde, Omer, Lucan, and Stace.

That is from the close of a masterpiece which is at once sheer Chaucer and an embodiment of the tradition of the elders from Homer through the Middle Ages to a contemporary fellow poet, Boccaccio; and I suspect that no one in the long and splendid line of English poets more strikingly exemplifies than Geoffrey Chaucer the characteristic interplay, in great verse, of life and books. For he was, on the one hand, a widely experienced, busy, and versatile man of affairs, and he was also one of the most omnivorous readers in that company of glorious literary cormorants who have enriched English letters. Had he been either without the other—had there been lacking either the immediate and manifold contacts with life, or the zest of a *helluo librorum*—he would doubtless still have been a poet. But in that case not one of the poems by which he is known could even remotely have been what it is. Let me, then, rehearse as necessary background, even at the risk of seeming for the moment to abandon poetry, a few of the familiar facts.

No other English poet, in the first place, has approached Chaucer in the breadth and variety of his immediate, personal experience of life. For no other English poet—to pack a lifetime into a list—was a page in a royal household and for years Yeoman or Esquire at Court; was captured while in military service, and then ransomed by the King; was sent to Flanders, France, and Italy on half a dozen delicate and important diplomatic missions, involving royal marriages, commercial treaties, and treaties of peace; was Controller of the Customs and Subsidy of wools, hides, and wool-fells, and also Controller of Petty Customs, in the port of London; was Justice of the Peace, and member of Parliament; Clerk of the King's Works, with exacting duties and wide powers, at Westminster Palace, the Tower of London, the Castle of Berkhampstead, and at seven of the royal manors, with their gardens, millponds, and fences; Surveyor, again with large authority, of walls, ditches, gutters, sewers, bridges, causeways, et cetera, along the Thames between Greenwich and Woolwich; Clerk of the Works at Windsor; Sub-Forester, and later Forester, in control of the great royal forest domain of Petherton in Somerset; and in the intervals holder of important wardships, and associated in the management of great estates. And finally, not to omit the element of adventure, it may be doubted if there was ever another English poet who was twice robbed by highwaymen within three days. I have crammed into a catalogue, for the sake of their cumulative impact, the facts which everybody knows, but which we habitually contemplate piecemeal. And the active search still going on in the Records Office is bringing to light from time to time new items which further diversify the list. Had Chaucer never written a line of poetry, he would still have been known to his contemporaries as a trusted and capable public servant and a many-sided man of affairs.

What that rich experience meant for his art is for us the essential thing. But what it might have meant to it and by the grace of Heaven did not, it is neither irrelevant nor uninstructive to observe. Chaucer's French contemporary, Eustache Deschamps, who sent him a famous poetical epistle and who will meet us later, also led an active and a semipublic life, and into his twelve hundred *balades,* his one hundred and seventy-one *rondeaux,* his eighteen *virelais,* his fifteen *lais,* which nobody ever reads any more except as documents, he poured on occasion the minute and personal details of his variegated career— dates and places meticulously noted; incidents of his campaigns in Flanders; the racy interchange of bilingual amenities with two Englishmen as he and Othon de Graunson (Chaucer's 'flour of hem that make in Fraunce') one day rode through Calais; the fleas at the inn that night; his personal ailments; his distaste for tripe and truffles. Now Chaucer had at his fingers' ends more such themes for verse than ever Deschamps dreamed. Read sometime, for its equally sinister possibilities, the inventory in the *Life Records* which Chaucer turned in when he resigned the Clerkship of the Works—pages on pages of rakes, ladles, crowbars, hurdles for scaffolds—one remembers how 'joly Absalon', the parish clerk, played Herod 'on a scaffold hye'—, andirons innumerable, a broken cable ('frangitur et devastatur'), images made in the likeness of kings, '100 round stones called engynstones', bottles, buckets, and (from the Tower of London of all places) a frying-pan. And there were also the sewers and the gutters and the ditches. What use Deschamps would have made of such opportunities does not admit of contemplation. But only once that I can recall in the whole wide range of his poetry does Chaucer give even a hint of his participation in affairs. It was in another and a different fashion that his extraordinarily varied experience played into the hands of his art. And if in what follows I may seem for a time to have wholly forgotten that art, I can only ask you to believe that I have not.

What that experience gave to Chaucer was, of course, first of all an opportunity almost unrivalled for wide and intimate knowledge of almost every sort of actor in the human comedy. We are apt to forget in thinking of him the remarkable range of his acquaintance with men and women in virtually every station, rank, and occupation of the diversified society in which he lived. He was a member of the household, first of a prince of the blood and then of a king, and through his marriage belonged to the circle of John of Gaunt and Henry of Derby. He counted among his acquaintances and friends great nobles and knights who had travelled far, and fought in all quarters of the known world. On his missions abroad he was associated with men of wide experience and influence in State affairs; met in France and Flanders statesmen versed in diplomacy; and matched his wits in Italy with Bernabò Visconti— 'God of delyt, and scourge of Lumbardye', as he called him when the message reached him of his sudden end. The very first record that we have of him contains a reference to a visit of Prince Lionel and the Countess of Ulster, on whom he was then in attendance, to the Benedictine Nunnery of St. Leonards, at the Prioress's Stratford atte Bowe, and from then to the close of his life he had intimate knowledge in a score of ways—through members of his own family, connexions by marriage, and the infinite ramifications of the Church's influence upon affairs—

of ecclesiastics of every feather. With men of law he came, through various exigencies, into close relations, and there is reason to think that he may himself have been a member of Lincoln's Inn. He had business dealings for years with merchants and shipmen, and through his Clerkships of the Works and his Surveyorships, with masons and carpenters and hedgers and ditchers and unskilled labour of every sort. And how closely his relations with the tradesmen and the craftsmen of the guilds were bound up with his own political career, Professor Kuhl years ago made clear. Now and then one gets a glimpse of that rare and precious thing a concrete incident, as when one sees him (in that record which Miss Rickert turned up a year or so ago) going down from the Customs to Dartmouth about a Genoese tarit, the 'Saint Mary and Saint George'—its master one Johannes deNigris of Genoa—which had been driven ashore on the coast of Brittany, and which John Hawley, then Mayor of Dartmouth, was charged with robbing. And one of Hawley's ships was called the 'Maudelayne', and Chaucer had the trick of turning official business to good poetic account. There are still vast uncharted regions of the Public Records to explore, but Professor Manly's recent studies of them have given as never before—whether or not we grant this or that tentative conclusion—flesh and blood and sometimes local habitation to the sergeants of law, the merchants, franklins and shipmen, the millers and weavers, the archdeacons, canons, summoners, friars, pardoners, prioresses and nuns, whom Chaucer first knew for his day and then bequeathed to eternity.

But this wide range of his experience carries with it another consequence. We need constantly to remind ourselves of the degree to which in Chaucer's day communication had to be by word of mouth. And so the people whom he knew were also channels through which came to him news of his world—news not only of that 'little world' which to Shakespeare's John of Gaunt was England; not only, either, of that 'queasy world' (in Margaret Paston's vivid phrase) across the Channel; but also of that now looming, menacing, always mysterious world beyond, which was the Orient. And few men have ever been more strategically placed for its reception. That news of England or Wales or even Ireland should so reach him is too obvious to dwell on, fascinating as is the use he makes of it. How, for example, did he get to know of that 'Colle tregetour'— Colin the magician—whom he saw in his dream in the *House of Fame*?

> Ther saugh I Colle tregetour
> Upon a table of sicamour
> Pleye an uncouthe thing to telle;
> I saugh him carien a wind-melle
> Under a walsh-note shelle.

But Colle was actually no piquant figure in a dream. He was, as we now know, thanks to Professor Royster, a contemporary Englishman, and he later exhibited his tricks, 'par voie de nigromancie', at Orleans, precisely as the Clerk of Orleans in the **"Franklin's Tale"** produced his illusions, 'Swiche as thise subtile tregetoures playe'. And Chaucer's apposite choice of Orleans as the school of his own magician is not without interest. How, too (to draw on the *House of Fame* again), did he get to know of Bret Glascurion and of Celtic wicker houses? Did that Welsh vintner of London tell him—Lewis Johan, who was at least a friend of Chaucer once removed; or did Sir Lewis Clifford or Sir John Clanvowe, both close friends of his, and both of whom held offices in Wales? Who can say! Chaucer's London was his own vast House of Rumour, only on a smaller scale.

But men, among them scores whom Chaucer knew, were constantly going out of England and coming back to it—going out for reasons of war, or trade, or chivalry, or religion, and coming back along the trade routes and the pilgrim roads and from their military exploits, with stories, and tidings, and even manuscripts, as well as with stuffs, or spices, or cockle-shells, or battered arms. And such knights as the stately figure of the Prologue were among the great intermediaries between Chaucer's England and the rest of the world. Europe was being menaced from three directions at once. We sometimes forget that Tamerlane's life just overlapped Chaucer's at each end, and that it was in the year in which Chaucer was appointed Justice of the Peace that the Great Turk boasted that he would make his horse eat oats on the high altar of St. Peter's. And Chaucer's Knight had fought in Europe, Asia, and Africa against the Moors, the Turks, the Tartars and the heathen of the North—in Turkey, Spain, Prussia, Lithuania (then a Tartar outpost) and Russia, and also with 'that valorous champion of impossible conquests', Pierre de Lusignan, King of Cyprus, at the taking of Alexandria, and at Lyeys and Satalye. And the knight was a composite portrait of men whom Chaucer personally knew. Of the witnesses (to give a single instance) who testified with Chaucer in the Scrope-Grosvenor case, Nicholas Sambraham, Esquire, had seen Sir Stephen Scrope at the taking of Alexandria, and in Hungary, Prussia, and Constantinople, and had seen Sir Henry Scrope in Spain, and, as he says, 'beyond the great sea in many places and in many chivalrous exploits.' Sir Richard Waldegrave had seen Sir William Scrope with the King of Cyprus at Satalye in Turkey; and Sir Henry de Ferrers and John de Rither, Esquire, had seen Sir Geoffrey Scrope in Prussia and Lithuania. And these half-dozen names we know through the accident of a dispute about the bearing of certain arms. There are more, but these are enough to show that the campaigns of Chaucer's Knight were the campaigns of Chaucer's acquaintances and friends. And they, like the Knight, had been associated with fellow knights of all the other nations which, with England, were making common cause against a common foe. And such stories as circulated about those Tables of Honour, like that at the head of which the Knight had often sat 'aboven alle naciouns in Pruce,' and tales of that gallant and meteoric figure, the King of Cyprus, whose death Chaucer bewailed 'in maner of Tragedie,' and of tournaments at Tramissene and sea-fights off the coasts of Africa and Asia Minor—such stories a score of Chaucer's friends could tell. For warfare was a more leisured business then than now—witness the Barbary expedition, of which Chaucer's friends Sir Lewis Clifford and Sir John Clanvowe were members, during which warlike expedition the gay and amorous *Cent Balades*

were composed. And finally—to come closer home—it was to a meeting in France, during a pause in the Hundred Years' War, between this same friend Sir Lewis Clifford and Eustache Deschamps, that there came to Chaucer the manuscript which suggested his best-known passage outside the *Canterbury Tales*; as it was through a later meeting between the same two men, during the negotiations for a truce, that Chaucer received another manuscript which gave him rich material for the most famous portrait in the Tales themselves.

Chivalry, too, played its curious part. Don Quixote, Professor Ker once observed with chapter and verse, would have been perfectly at home with the Knights and Squires of Chaucer's day, and would not have been thought extravagant in either principles or practice. And with that dictum no student of the period will disagree. And so young Squires who, like Machaut's and Chaucer's, bore them well in arms 'in hope to stonden in [hir] lady grace', were still being sent by their ladies to win further grace, 'in-to Walakye, To Pruyse and in-to Tartarye, To Alisaundre, ne in-to Turkye', and finally charged, for the crowning exploit, to 'Go hoodles to the drye see, And come hoom by the Carrenar'. And that last injunction is a singularly apposite case in point. For we now know, as Sir Aurel Stein's latest maps and photographs at last unmistakably show, that an actual Kara-nor, or Black Lake, lies a short stone's throw from Marco Polo's highway, in the heart of Central Asia, beyond the dry, salt-incrusted bed of an ancient inland sea. And through some merchant or other this bit of flotsam and jetsam had probably drifted back along the silk routes, perhaps through Lyeys, where the Knight had fought, along with who can tell what tales of Tartary, such as that which the Squire himself was to rehearse.

For merchants, with pilgrims and shipmen, were also recognized bearers of news, and as such Chaucer, on whose own testimony I am drawing, knew them well. 'Ye ben fadres of tydinges Andtales,' exclaims the Man of Law in his apostrophe to merchants; 'Tydings of sondry regnes' he goes on, and of 'the wondres that they mighte seen or here.' And it was a merchant, he declares, who years ago told him the very tale he tells—a story which begins in Syria and wanders by way of the Pillars of Hercules to England, and back by the strait to Italy. For England, like all of Europe, was full of tales—tales which through centuries had travelled by mysterious routes from Arabia and Hindostan and Burma and Tibet and Turkey and Siberia—narratives ageless and timeless, with no abiding place; rubbed smooth in their endless passings, like pebbles rounded by the waves, or Chinese carvings polished by uncounted generations, of hands. Nor was it only merchants along the trade routes who were their vehicles. Chaucer's House of Rumour 'Was ful of shipmen and pilgrymes, With scrippes bret-ful of lesinges, Entremedled with tydinges.' And pilgrims like that notable wayfarer the Wife of Bath, who had thrice been at Jerusalem, and 'had passed many a straunge streem,' were visiting 'ferne halwes, couthe in sondry londes,' and coming back, like the merchants, with multifarious information, false and true. It was along the pilgrim roads, as we now well know, that the stories of Charlemagne and Roland and the twelve peers of France passed over the Alps into Italy. And pilgrims told their tales, and Chaucer was a marvellous listener. His Dartmouth shipman, too, whose own harbour was one of the English ports for ships from the Orient, knew 'alle the havenes, as they were, From Gootlond to the cape of Finistere, And every cryke in Britayne and in Spayne.' And Gothland, with the other havens at which he and his fellows touched, was connected through the Hanseatic trade with Novgorod, and Novgorod, like the ports in Asia Minor where Chaucer's friends had fought, had been for hundreds of years a terminus of those ancient Eastern trade-routes along which had travelled, with the merchants and the shipmen, tales like those which underlie the *fabliaux* and a dozen of the stories which the Canterbury pilgrims tell. And Chaucer sat at the receipt of custom in the port of London, 'at the quay called Wool-wharf in the Tower Ward.' And the man who, between nightfall and bedtime, had spoken with every one of the nine and twenty pilgrims at the Tabard Inn was not the man to refrain from incidental conversation with the mariners whose lawful occasions brought them to his quay.

How this or that particular tale or bit of information came to Chaucer, it is far from my present purpose to inquire. He was at the centre of a rich and varied and shifting world, and in ways without number, of which these are bare suggestions, his personal and official experience lent material to his art. And there were also books.

The range of Chaucer's reading is as extraordinary as the scope of his activities. He read in three languages besides English—French, Latin, and Italian. French he probably both knew and spoke from his childhood. Latin with little doubt he learned at school. It has hitherto been assumed that he picked up Italian in Italy, during his first visit in 1372-3. It is possible, though not yet proven, that he may have known it earlier. But in either case, the bulk of his known reading, until the great Italians swam into his ken, was French, with a good deal of Latin besides. And French he never abandoned, and Latin he read copiously to the end. The French and Italian works which he knew may best for our purpose be considered later. His wide and diversified reading of Latin, however, is both typical of his varied interests and important for its contributions, and I shall rapidly summarize it here.

Of the classics he knew in the original Ovid, especially the *Metamorphoses* (his 'owne book', as he called it), and the *Heroides*. Virgil he knew, but apparently only the *Aeneid;* the *Thebaid* of Statius; Claudian; and either in Latin or French or both, the *Pharsalia*. Cicero's *Somnium Scipionis* he read in a copy of the commentary of Macrobius which he or somebody else had thumbed to pieces—'myn olde book to-torn,' as he refers to it. Horace he quotes half a dozen times, but I doubt whether he knew either Horace or Juvenal at first hand. Dante, or John of Salisbury, or the *florilegia* may well have been intermediaries. But for Virgil, Statius, and Lucan, and also for Ovid, he had two strings to his bow. For the Middle Ages seized upon the Latin epics and made them over into their own likeness as romances. . . .

His reading in the science of his day is in some respects, I am inclined to think, the most remarkable of all. His singularly broad yet minute knowledge of medieval medicine, in which he anticipated Burton, I have elsewhere had occasion to discuss. But far more than his acquaintance with 'the lovers maladye of Hereos' is in point. Fourteenth-century medicine, like its twentieth-century descendant, was half psychology, and in its emphasis on dreams as a means of diagnosis anticipated Freud. And Madame Pertelote's diagnosis, by means of his dream, of Chauntecleer's malady, as well as her inimitable discourse on dreams as symptoms, is scientifically accurate. So is her *materia medica*. The herbs which she prescribes—'Pekke hem up right as they growe, and ete hem in'—are the medically proper herbs. And the quintessential touch is her inclusion in Chauntecleer's dietary of 'wormes' for 'a day or two.' For worms—you may read a learned and matter-of-fact chapter on *Vermes terrenae* in the *Medica Materia* of Dioscorides—were among the recognized correctives. It is easy enough to slip into one's narrative as evidence of erudition an excerpt from some learned document. But such casual exactness, imbued with delicious humour to boot, is not something which one gets up over night. In alchemy—witness the **"Canon's Yeoman's Tale"**—Chaucer was no less deeply grounded than in medicine. He had read enough in the alchemical treatises of Arnoldus de Villanova, for example, his 'Arnold of the Newe Toun,' to refer to one of Arnold's treatises a highly picturesque and abstruse dictum which he quotes, when he had actually read it in another. As for physics, one of the very best pieces of exposition, as exposition, which I know in English is the erudite Eagle's discourse in the House of Fame on the transmission of sound, and that again is founded on accepted authority. So is Chaucer's astrology, and in astronomy proper he could point with just pride to that Treatise on the Astrolabe which he wrote, with its charming Preface, for his 'litel son Lowis', using freely a Latin translation of the Arabian astronomer Messahala. These are the barest shreds and patches only. The scope and thoroughness of Chaucer's scientific reading would still be remarkable, had he read nothing else.

There, then, are the raw materials of his art—men and their doings, and books—God's plenty of each, in all conscience. And since he began with books (with which, to be sure, he never ended) it is much to the point to consider how he read. Did he have the books on our list, for example, in his own possession, and therefore ready at hand for pleasure or need? Without question a large, perhaps a very large proportion of them were his own. He declared, fairly late in his life—or rather, the God of Love asserted for him—that he had in his chest 'sixty bokes, olde and newe,' and there is no reason to doubt the statement. But that number may easily have represented three or four times sixty 'books,' in the sense in which we use the word. For book, as Chaucer employs the term, must be thought of in the light of medieval manuscripts, and a single manuscript was often a small library in itself. The 'boke' which Chaucer was reading when he fell asleep over the tale of Ceyx and Alcyone was an *omnium gatherum* of verse, and lives of queens and kings, and 'many othere thinges smale.' The 'book' (and again the word is the same) which the Wife of Bath's fifth husband revelled in contained, she declared, *Valerius ad Rufinum*, Theophrastus, Jerome against Jovinian, Tertullian, the mysterious Crisippus, Trotula, the Epistles of Eloise, the Parables of Solomon, and the *Ars Amatoria*—'And alle thise were bounden in o volume'. And one need only recall, among extant examples, the Auchinleck MS., with its more than forty separate pieces, or, for that matter, Harley 7333 among the manuscripts of the *Canterbury Tales*. Chaucer's library was a rich one for his day, and like his own clerk of Oxford who had 'at his beddes heed' his 'Twenty bokes, clad in blak or reed', and like that clerk of another kidney, 'hende Nicholas,' who likewise kept in his lodgings 'his Almageste, and bokes grete and smale . . . On shelves couched at his beddes heed', one may be fairly sure that Chaucer's sixty books were not far from his hand.

But is there any way of knowing, aside from these more or less material considerations, how he actually read? There are two subjects, and two only, on which Chaucer vouchsafes us personal information about himself—his love of books, and his imperviousness, real or assumed, to love. On those two topics he is, in William Wordsworth's phrase but with a difference, 'right voluble.' And two passages are especially in point. In one, that preternaturally intelligent bird, the Eagle of the *House of Fame*, gently chides him for his habits. He knows nothing now, says the Eagle, of what is going on about him; even 'of thy verray neyghebores That dwellen almost at thy dores, Thou herest neither that ne this.' And then follows, under cover of the Eagle's irresponsible loquacity, the most precious autobiographical touch that Chaucer left:

> For whan thy labour doon al is,
> And hast y-maad thy rekeninges,
> In stede of reste and newe thinges,
> Thou gost hoom to thy hous anoon;
> And, also domb as any stoon,
> Thou sittest at another boke,
> Til fully daswed is thy loke,
> And livest thus as an hermyte,
> Although thyn abstinence is lyte.

That picture—the account books of the customs exchanged after hours for vastly different books (the Eagle's 'another' is pregnant), and Chaucer reading on, oblivious of all else, until his eyes dazzle in his head—that picture tells more than pages, not merely of the intimate relation in which his books stood to his business, but also of the absorbed intentness with which he read. And there is another passage which illuminates yet another quality of his reading. 'Not yore agon,' he writes in the *Parlement of Foules*,

> . . . hit happed me for to beholde
> Upon a boke, was write with lettres olde;
> And ther-upon, *a certeyn thing to lerne*,
> The longe day *ful faste I radde and yerne*.

I do not know which is the more characteristic of Chaucer— the fact that he was reading with the definite purpose of learning a certain thing, or the fact that he was reading

fast and eagerly. The two belong together. You cannot divide his invincible zest from his incorrigibly inquiring spirit—that 'besy gost' of his, as he called it once, 'that thrusteth alwey newe.' And because he brought both to his books, his reading became a live and plastic thing for his art to seize on.

He was gifted, finally, with another quality of mind which is peculiarly bound up with his art. He possessed, in a word, like Virgil and Milton and Coleridge, a powerfully associative memory, which played, as he read, over the multitude of impressions from previous reading, with which his mind was stored. And the zest with which he read gave freshness to his recollections, and one can sometimes almost see the hovering associations precipitate themselves as he reads. A single phrase in Boccaccio (and I am speaking by the book) calls up the lines of a famous passage in Dante in which the same phrase occurs, and the result is a *tertium quid* of his own, enriched from the spoils of both. He finds in Boccaccio's *Filostrato*, as he works it over into his own Troilus, the lovely Virgilian simile of the lily cut by the plough and withering. But Dante, in a canto of the *Inferno,* the opening lines of which Chaucer elsewhere quotes, has a simile of falling, withering leaves. And again, through a common element, Boccaccio's lines recall the lines of Dante, and the falling leaves replace the fading lily in Chaucer's simile. And Boccaccio and Dante in turn had each in like fashion recalled his simile from Virgil. It would be easy to rehearse such instances by the score—instances, too, in which with his reminiscences of books are interwoven his recollections of experience. For that continuity of poetry of which I spoke consists in the perpetual enrichment, through just such incremental transformations, of the present through the past. And one of the happiest gifts of the gods to English poetry, at the strategic moment of its history, was that prehensile, amalgamating memory of Chaucer's which had for its playground the prodigious array of promiscuous writings which a moment ago I ruthlessly catalogued.

What now of art in its larger relations? For everything that I have so far said has been said with that definitely in view. It is perilous, in the first place, to divide Chaucer's poetic biography mechanically into periods. There was nothing cataclysmic about his development. He was not a new creature, as Professor Kittredge once observed, when he came back to London from his first visit to Italy, nor does the poet of the *Canterbury Tales* startle us by a 'leap of buds into ripe flowers.' Rather—if I too may yield to an association—'Morn into noon did pass, noon into eve.' Transitions there were, of course, but they were gradual. French poetry yielded first place to Italian, and both to an absorption in human life, in which books and men were fused as in a crucible. But even after his momentous discovery of Boccaccio and Dante, the influence of French poetry went on, though its character changed— changed (to put it briefly) from the mood of Guillaume de Lorris and Machaut to the mood of Jean de Meun and Deschamps and the *fabliaux*. And *pari passu*, as his powers developed, there came a significant shift of values, and his reading of books played a lesser and his reading of life a larger role in his art. But throughout his career, that art kept curiously even pace with his active life. It was dominantly French while he was in personal attendance on a court where French was still the more familiar language. His so-called Italian period, which was never Italian in the sense in which the earlier period had been French, coincided roughly with those activities—his missions and the customs—which brought him into various relations with Italy, Italians, and Italian letters. And when his broadening affairs afforded wider opportunities for observation, his art, keeping all that it had won from France and Italy, became at once English and universal.

Everybody knows that Chaucer began as a follower of the contemporary French school of poetry, and that the most powerful influence upon that school was the thirteenth-century *Roman de la Rose*. But the *Roman de la Rose* was influential in two entirely different ways. Guillaume de Lorris, who began it, was a dreamer of dreams and a poet of exquisite grace and charm. Jean de Meun, who continued it and multiplied its length by five, was a caustic and disillusioned satirist, trenchant, arrogant, and absolute master of a mordant pen. If Pope had taken it into his head to complete the *Faerie Queene,* or if Swift had been seized by the fancy of carrying on the *Vicar of Wakefield* in the mood of Gulliver's fierce misanthropy, we might have had an adequate parallel. And the fourteenth-century French poets, as a consequence of this strange duplex authorship, fall roughly into two schools—the sons of Guillaume de Lorris and the sons of Jean de Meun. But common to them all, and giving the framework to half their verse, was the allegorical love vision.

The contemporary Frenchmen whose influence on Chaucer was farthest reaching were three: Guillaume de Machaut, an elder contemporary; Jean Froissart, his coeval; and Eustache Deschamps, who was younger. . . .

For he found in his French models, and especially in Machaut, the framework of the vision, as that had come down, with growing elaboration on the way, from Guillaume de Lorris. And he used the machinery of the vision in the **Book of the Duchess**, the **House of Fame**, the **Parliament of Fowls**, and in the first version of the Prologue to the **Legend of Good Women**. It was the most popular and, in Machaut's expert hands, the most sophisticated device of his day, and Chaucer was then writing for a sophisticated audience. But the visions were allegorical love visions, and as such they were thick sown with artifices at which Chaucer balked. And the more thoroughly one is steeped in Chaucer, so that one sees in a measure with his eyes, the more readily one understands the impossibility of his acquiescence in the then current artificialities of the *genre*. The framework of the vision, to be sure, offered freedom in both choice and disposition of subject matter. But it was precisely in the character of the French subject matter, to judge from the cold shoulder which Chaucer turned to it, that one source of his disrelish lay. For it was obviously as barren of interest to Geoffrey Chaucer as interminable subtilizings about love—especially when nothing comes of them—have been and are to any normally constituted Anglo-Saxon. Moreover, the

visions are thickly peopled with personified abstractions. Esperance, Attemprance, Mesure, Douce Pensée, Plaisance, Desirs, Franchise, Pité, Loyauté, Espoirs, Raison, Suffisance, Patience, Paour—those are the denizens of less than half of Machaut's *Remede de Fortune*. Like Criseyde listening under trying circumstances to the 'wommanisshe thinges' of her feminine callers, Chaucer must have 'felte almost [his] herte dye For wo, and wery of that companye.' Nor was it subject matter alone which he found ⸱lien. The phraseology, too, was remote alike from his tastes and his aptitudes. There is nothing I know which rivals in its tireless facility of recurrence the later vocabulary of courtly love. If one read long enough, one is obsessed by the uncanny feeling that the phraseology walks alone, without need of the poet's intervention, and carries the poet with it of its own momentum. Specific meaning disappears. Machaut's Peronne, in that amazing Goethe-and-Bettina correspondence, the *Voir-Dit,* is 'en douceur douce com coulombelle, En loyauté loyal com turturelle.' But the same columbine phrases slip from his pen, when, in *Prise d'Alexandrie,* he describes the Emperor Charles I of Luxembourg. He too, like Peronne, is 'humbles et piteus Plus que turtre ne colombele.' In that ineffably affected jargon discriminations vanish. 'Thought and affliction, passion, hell itself, [are turned] to favour and to prettiness.' And that was not Chaucer's way.

What he found, then, in the French vision poems, was a *frame*—a frame which possessed admirable potentialities, but which for him, to all intents and purposes, was empty. And Chaucer, who in his way was not unlike Nature herself, abhorred a vacuum. He proceeded, accordingly, to fill the frame, and incidentally to set one of the great traditions of English poetry. And into the vision framework, instead of consecrated phrases, wire-drawn subtleties, *ragionamente d'amore,* and the more fantastic elements of the courtly code, he poured the stores of that reading and observation on which we have dwelt so long. 'For out of olde feldes'—and this was his discovery, as 'the longe day ful faste [he] radde and yerne'—

> For out of olde feldes, as man seith,
> Cometh al this newe corn fro yeer to yere;
> And out of olde bokes, in good feith,
> Cometh al this newe science that men lere.

And into the old bottles Chaucer poured with lavish hand a new and heady wine.

What happened may best be seen by a glance at his first three vision poems. His earliest essay, the **Book of the Duchess,** was made before he went to Italy, when his reading was almost wholly French, and when Machaut in particular was at his finger tips. It is a vision poem, with all the paraphernalia of the *genre,* and it is also an elegy— an elegy on the death of the Duchess Blanche, the first wife of his patron, John of Gaunt. But into the conventional frame he fits, with tact and feeling, and with conspicuous skill in adapting them to his ends, materials drawn from what was then his reading—to wit, in this instance, from no less than eight of Machaut's poems and one (at least) of Froissart's. Save for scattered reminiscences of the Bible, the *Roman de la Rose,* Boethius, and Benoit, there is little else. His instinct from the beginning was to enrich, and those were the stores which he then possessed. But his borrowings are interwoven with such art that for more than five hundred years nobody suspected that the poem was not all of a piece. And even when his appropriations are most unmistakable, they are still miraculously Chaucer and not Machaut. The little whelp that came creeping up, as if it knew him, to the Dreamer, and 'Hild doun his heed and joyned his eres, And leyde al smothe doun his heres'—that bewitching English puppy is Chaucer's metamorphosis of a fantastic lion, which Carpaccio would have revelled in, native to the bizarre landscape of the *Dit dou Lyon* of Machaut. And into his version of Machaut's catalogue of those remote regions to which the courtly lovers were dispatched to win their spurs, Chaucer has slipped that precious bit of hearsay about the Dry Sea and the Carrenar. The Book of the Duchess is not a masterpiece, but it is significant far beyond its intrinsic merit. For in it for the first time, with the still limited resources at his command, Chaucer loaded every rift with ore. And now the ore grew steadily richer.

For Chaucer went to Italy, and learned to read Boccaccio and Dante, and all the while that knowledge of books and men on which we have dwelt was broadening and deepening. The French influence waned as that of Italy waxed, but the shift of emphasis was gradual, and the vision poems still went on. And into the three that followed the Book of the Duchess poured those steadily growing stores. He begins the *House of Fame*—to follow what seems to me to be the true succession—a little dully, with a long résumé of the *Aeneid,* and an interlude from the *Metamorphoses.* And both the *Roman d'Eneas* and the *Ovide moralisé* were summoned, I feel certain, to his aid. Then all at once, into a desert recalled from Lucan sweeps an eagle which owed its sunlike brightness to the *Paradiso,* and the poem becomes vivid with new life. And the significant thing is not so much that the amazing eagle, throughout the flight through the air, shows himself equally at home in Ovid, and Boethius, and Theodulus, and Macrobius, and Dante's *Convito,* and can even recognize Chaucer's unspoken thoughts of Martianus Capella and Alanus, as that he is a new and unique creation—as much a person as his creator, and utterly unthinkable in any vision which Machaut and his fellows ever dreamed. And only the keenest observer of men, endowed with the rarest humour, could have conceived the inimitable conversation which goes on, as the little earth recedes to a speck and the signs of the zodiac are left behind; and the poet of the *Canterbury Tales* is already present in that immortal dialogue. Then, into the third book, ushered in, like the second, by an invocation drawn from Dante, pours a phantasmagoria which Rabelais might have envied, and which defies all summary—reminiscences of books treading on the heels of recollections of experience, in bewildering profusion. Within the compass of thirty-five lines—to take a relatively simple passage only—Chaucer's memory, as the verse flows on without a ripple, has flashed to Boethius, and the *Roman de la Rose,* and a line from the *Metamorphoses,* and some account or other which he had read in the romances of those whirling houses which were a pecu-

liarly captivating item in the romantic stock-in-trade, and Celtic wicker houses which he had either seen himself or heard of from his friends, and the noise of 'engynstones' remembered from his own campaign in France. Sketched as I am sketching it, the poem is a thing of shreds and patches. It is not so on the page. But I am putting asunder what Chaucer joined together, in order to give the barest inkling of the thronging recollections which, in his vision poems, his art curbed and concealed.

And now, in the *Parlement of Foules*, France slips gradually into the background and Italy assumes the major role. The cadre of the vision is still retained, but the familiar French couplet is discarded, and rime royal takes its place. In the last two books of the *House of Fame* Chaucer's crowding recollections are swept along as by a torrent; in the close-packed introductory sections of the *Parlement* there is a new serenity, and a sense of beauty which has been quickened and deepened alike. For the influence of Dante and Boccaccio upon Chaucer is to be sought not merely or even chiefly in his borrowings and imitations, but rather through the impregnation of his art with qualities which his earlier French masters never knew. And in the first half of the *Parlement* Chaucer's memory is busy with the Divine Comedy, and both his memory and his eyes with the *Teseide.* The Proem opens with a rendering, in a master's hand, of the first axiom of Hippocrates—

> The lyf so short, the craft so long to lerne,
> Th'assay so hard, so sharp the conquering.

It was a favourite with those elder medical authorities whom Chaucer read, and I suspect it came to him from them. Then, passing to the book which he had just been reading 'faste and yerne' all day long, he gives (I am sure for his own delight) a summary—compact and lucid and urbane—of the *Somnium Scipionis.* And night falls in the words with which Dante describes the first fall of evening in the *Inferno.* Then Chaucer's unrest before he sleeps recalls Boethius, and the thought of dreams brings back to mind the famous lines of Claudian, and because (as Chaucer shrewdly suggests) he has just been reading the dream of Scipio, Scipio himself becomes his guide. And the Proem ends with a flash of memory back to Jean de Meun.

F. N. Robinson (essay date 1933)

SOURCE: "The Legend of Good Women," in *The Works of Geoffrey Chaucer,* Houghton Mifflin Company, 1957, pp. 480-82.

[*F. N. Robinson is the editor of the widely used* The Works of Geoffrey Chaucer *noted for its extensive textual notes and introductions to Chaucer's works. In the following essay originally published in 1933, Robinson discusses the* Legend of Good Women *in relation to its sources and other works by Chaucer.*]

Next to the description of April "with his shoures sote" at the beginning of the *Canterbury Tales*, probably the most familiar and best loved lines of Chaucer are those in the Prologue to the *Legend of Good Women* which tell of his adoration of the daisy. Both passages are notable examples of the freshness and simplicity—the "vernal spirit which soothes and refreshes"—long ago praised by [James Russell] Lowell as characteristic of Chaucer. The quality is truly Chaucerian, and by no means restricted to descriptions of outward nature. But the secret of it is hard to discover. It is partly, without doubt, the effect of the language,—not of the "quaintness" falsely ascribed to Chaucer's speech by those to whom it is simply unfamiliar, but of a real simplicity of structure in early English, found also in Old French and comparable to that which distinguishes Homeric Greek from the later Attic. In part, too, the freshness of Chaucer's poetry is a reflection of his age, of a certain youthful directness in its relation to life. And in great measure it is an expression of his own mind and temperament. In any case it is not to be set down to naïve simplicity on the part of the poet or his contemporaries. Nor in the two poems which have been mentioned is the effect in question due to the avoidance of literary material or, it must be granted, to the direct observation of nature. The passage in the **"General Prologue"** follows an established convention, in which, to be sure, it surpasses all its models; and the panegyric on the daisy is almost a cento of quotations or imitations of contemporary poetry, French and perhaps Italian. Indeed the whole **"Prologue"** to the *Legend* is steeped in literary associations. The truth of its description and sentiment is not for that reason to be denied or disparaged. But the reader cannot understand the **"Prologue"** aright without knowing something of the conventions which underlie it and the fund of poetry on which it has drawn for its enrichment.

Like the *Book of the Duchess*, the *House of Fame*, and the *Parliament of Fowls*, the *Legend of Good Women* is a love-vision. But before the relation of the actual dream, the scene is set by an account of the poet's worship of the daisy on the first of May. In that passage, besides the simple delight in nature which has endeared it to generations of readers, must be recognized the skilful use of literary and social conventions. The relative merits of the flower and the leaf were a subject of poetic debate in Chaucer's time, as they were in the next century, when the poem entitled the Flower and the Leaf was composed. The ladies and gentlemen of the court—so the **"Prologue"** to the *Legend* indicates—divided themselves into two orders, devoted one to the Leaf and the other to the Flower. Similarly there is evidence, in both French and English poetry, of the existence of a cult of the marguerite. Both these courtly fashions are reflected in the **"Prologue."** In the controversy of Flower against Leaf Chaucer refuses to take sides. But he proclaims his utter devotion to the daisy, and his celebration of this queen of flowers contains many lines and phrases paralleled in Deschamps, Machaut, and Froissart, and some perhaps from Boccaccio. To complete theglorification of the daisy he invents a happy metamorphosis, worthy of the old mythologies, and represents the flower as a transformation of the queen Alceste, the leader of his "good women," who appears in his vision as an attendant of the god of Love.

According to the central fiction of the **"Prologue,"** Chaucer is condemned by the god of Love for having written heresies against his law—in particular, for having defamed women by composing the *Troilus* and translating the *Roman de la Rose*. As a penalty for his misconduct he is commanded to write a legendary of Cupid's saints—that is, of women who were good according to the standard of the religion of Love. The *Legend* thus falls at once into the ancient category of palinodes, known in literary history from the time of Stesichorus, who first wrote an ode against Helen of Troy, and then composed his Palinodia in her praise. Perhaps the most familiar Latin example of the type is Horace's "O matre pulchra filia pulchrior," and among classical writings known to Chaucer Ovid's *Ars Amatoria*, Book III, and his *Remedia Amoris* form a kind of double palinode. In mediæval French literature the fashion was revived. Jean le Fèvre, who translated the strongly antifeminist *Lamentationes Matheoli*, composed his *Leesce* as a *contrepeise,* and Nicholas de Bozon atoned for his *Char d'Orgeuil* by his counterplea *De la Bonté des Femmes*. Machaut's *Jugement dou Roy de Navarre* was not only a palinode, but may also have furnished an actual suggestion for Chaucer's *Legend*. Again in the fifteenth century, in English, the *Dialogue with a Friend* by Hoccleve, Chaucer's disciple, still continues the convention. In writing such a recantation, then, Chaucer was following a familiar custom. And perhaps the occasion of his palinode was not wholly fictitious. Just as Ovid's *Remedia Amoris* is held to have been his apology to the gossiping critics of the *Amores*, so, it has been not unreasonably suggested, Chaucer's defense of good women may have been called forth by actual condemnation of his *Troilus*.

The form of the work imposed upon Chaucer as a penance is that of a legendary, or collection of lives of saints. The good women whose tragic stories he relates are heroines of classical antiquity who suffered or died out of devotion to their lovers. They are represented as saints or martyrs on Cupid's calendar. So the *Legend* may be regarded, in the words of a recent critic, as "a cross between the Heroides of Ovid and the Legenda Aurea." In an age which produced a lover's manual of sins—the Confessio Amantis, the Ten Commandments of love, matins and lauds of love sung by the birds, paternosters and credos of love, and masses of Venus, the *Legend* affords another striking example of the adaptation of Christian ideas and institutions to the affairs of love.

Such are the varied origins and antecedents of the *Legend of Good Women*. In spite of Chaucer's uncommon skill in combining diverse elements in a simple and artistic design, he was not altogether successful in achieving unity or consistency in the **"Prologue."** He doubtless realized this himself, and for that reason gave the poem a careful revision. Even in what appears to be the later version, preserved in a single manuscript, the inconsistencies are not wholly removed, though the structure is improved and made more logical. Some of the most delightful poetry is sacrificed in the revision, so that many critics prefer the earlier version. And in fact the charm of the **"Prologue"** lies not so much in the orderly development of the argument as in the pleasant description and the happy expression of poetic feeling and fancy.

The legends themselves, regarded as narratives, are much inferior to the stories of Chaucer's latest period. They lack the variety, brilliancy, and dramatic reality of the *Troilus* or the best of the *Canterbury Tales*. Yet if compared with any contemporary narrative poems except Chaucer's own, they would be reckoned among the masterpieces of the age. They were very likely written, at least in part, earlier than the **"Prologue,"** and represent an important stage in Chaucer's literary development. Composed largely under the influence of Virgil and Ovid, they show a definite advance in narrative structure over the poems of the so-called French period of Chaucer's youth; and though they have not the interest of his more independent works, yet if read attentively and compared with their sources they reveal great care in translation and no small degree of artistry. From his painstaking study and imitation of Ovid Chaucer profited in the niceties of observation and expression.

The monotonous theme of the legend—the praise of faithful women—and its conventional treatment make the stories tiresome to the modern reader; and Chaucer himself appears to have lost interest in them, though he may never have deliberately abandoned them. The introduction to the **"Man of Law's Tale"** implies that while occupied with the *Canterbury Tales* he still had in mind the composition of more lives of good women, and he appears to have revised the **"Prologue"** as late as 1394. But he did not actually bring the series to completion, and we may well suppose that it was simply superseded in his interest by the *Canterbury Tales*. Indeed critics have questioned whether Chaucer could ever have felt real enthusiasm for the *Legend*; whether it was ever anything more than a concession to contemporary taste, or perhaps to a royal command. One scholar has gone so far as to suggest that Chaucer composed the work from the outset with satirical purpose—writing, so to speak, with his tongue in his cheek. Some of the good women, this writer reminds us, were anything but good, being guilty of murder and other crimes. Chaucer selected them and praised them, he argues, precisely for the purpose of making his ostensible defense of women ridiculous, and so of perpetrating a huge joke upon critics and patrons. This attempt to find unrecognized humor in the *Legend*, and so to rescue it from the charge of dullness, even if it seemed needful, is ill-advised. For there can be no doubt that in the mind of Chaucer and his contemporaries the heroines he celebrates were good in the only sense that counted for the purpose in hand—they were faithful followers of the god of Love. The rubric "Explicit Legenda Cleopataras Martiris" has a humor for us that it would hardly have had for the readers at the court of Richard II.

Attempts have been made to date the two versions of the **"Prologue"** on the evidence of historical allegory. But there is so much doubt about the assumed applications that the arguments are unconvincing. Recent theories on the subject are mentioned in the Explanatory Notes.

Apart from the real interest of its substance, the *Legend of Good Women* is an important landmark in versification. Chaucer, always an experimenter in meter, here employed—for the first time in English, so far as is known—the decasyllabic couplet, the principal verse-form of the *Canterbury Tales* and the "heroic couplet" of a long line of English poets.

W. H. Clawson   (essay date 1951)

SOURCE: "The Framework of the *Canterbury Tales*," in *University of Toronto Quarterly*, Vol. XX, No. 2, January, 1951, pp. 137-54.

[*In the following excerpt, Clawson explains the functions of the framing narrative within the* "General Prologue" *and throughout the* Canterbury Tales *as a linking device.*]

[The] idea of a pilgrimage as the occasion for the telling of a sequence of stories was one of the happiest devices of Chaucer's *Canterbury Tales*. [Quotations are from the *Complete Works* edited by F. N. Robinson (1933).] The religious motive of a pilgrimage made possible the coming together on a friendly footing of representatives of many social classes; and the relative safety and cheapness of such a form of travel, especially to so famous and long-established a shrine as Canterbury, promoted a holiday spirit which encouraged music and story-telling and led to the free exchange of opinions and confidences. Thus through his adoption of the pilgrimage device Chaucer was enabled to make of his **"General Prologue"** an unsurpassed social document and of his framing narrative a true human comedy.

The **"General Prologue"** presents a social group of thirty persons, larger and more diversified than the ten gentlefolk of the *Decameron* [by Boccaccio], smaller and more manageable than Sercambi's indefinitely large company [in his collection of stories, the *Novelle*, composed in 1374]. Chaucer's group of pilgrims is not schematically representative of English society but covers well enough the main social elements. The nobility and the lowest class of labourers are excluded as unlikely to travel in the fashion of this group; but the knights, the learned professions, the landed gentry, the medieval manor (through its miller and reeve), and the free agricultural labourers are all represented. The rising middle classes are well exhibited by the London merchant, preoccupied with foreign commerce, the five tradesmen with aldermanic ambitions, Harry Bailey, solid citizen and innkeeper of Southwark, and by the London cook and manciple. From the provinces come the expert cloth-weaver, Alison of Bath, and the daring sea-captain of Dartmouth. The portraits of the clergy (nearly one-third of the company) are significant for the tolerance with which Chaucer points out the foibles of the monastic orders in describing the Monk and Prioress; his greater severity in satirizing the worldliness of the Friar; and his open attack on the corrupt Summoner and the fraudulent Pardoner. His ideal portraits of the Clerk of Oxford and the Parish Priest, along with his equally favourable descriptions of the Knight and the Ploughman, perhaps reflect his own admiration at a time of changing standards of the basic ideals of earlier medieval society, as they had found expression in its fundamental classes—the men of prayer, the men of war, and the men of labour.

Each of the pilgrims . . . is revealed in such sharp and clear detail that we feel personally acquainted with him or her as an individual, and at the same time we recognize him as representative, not only of a social class, but of a type of character which may be recognized in any country and in any age.

—W.H. Clawson

An even more distinctive feature of the **"General Prologue"** is its method of characterization. Each of the pilgrims who is described is revealed in such sharp and clear detail that we feel personally acquainted with him or her as an individual, and at the same time we recognize him as representative, not only of a social class, but of a type of character which may be recognized in any country and in any age. Nothing like this series of portraits had ever appeared in literature. It is the main reason for the perennial appeal of the General Prologue. Any analysis of these portraits must be inadequate to account for their extraordinary charm. They range from sixty-two lines (the Friar) to nine lines (the Cook), and the average is thirty lines. Within this space, not a word is wasted: details of physical appearance, dress and equipment, social rank, and character evoke the whole man or woman by powerful suggestive strokes:

A sheef of pecok arwes, bright and kene,
Under his belt he bar ful thriftily,
(Wel koude he dresse his takel yemanly:
His arwes drouped noght with fetheres lowe)
And in his hand he baar a myghty bowe.
A not heed hadde he, with a broun visage.
Of wodecraft wel koude he al the usage.

His nosethirles blake were and wyde.
A swerd and bokeler bar he by his syde.
His mouth as greet was as a greet forneys.
He was a janglere and a goliardeys,
And that was moost of synne and harlotries.
Wel koude he stelen corn and tollen thries.

No small part of the realism of these portraits is their informality, their lack of regular order. We find now a detail of dress or equipment: "His bootes souple, his hors in greet estaat"; now an habitual significant action: "And evere he rood the hyndreste of oure route"; now a significant speech: "He wolde the see were kept for any thyng Bitwixe Middelburgh and Orewelle"; now a sharply drawn physical detail: "His nekke whit was as the flour-de-lys";

now a brief statement of character: "And al was conscience and tendre herte." Yet such apparently haphazard details were certainly deliberately planned to produce that effect of spontaneity that creates a sense of intimate acquaintance with each pilgrim. Manly has established the point that Chaucer drew some of the characters from real persons of his acquaintance; he has put forth a convincing argument in the case of the Host, the Prioress, the Sergeant of the Law, the Franklin, the Reeve, and the Shipman, and has established a probability for the Knight, the Miller, the Summoner, the Friar, the Pardoner, and the Wife of Bath. He carefully guarded himself from asserting that these characters were mere photographs of individuals, but he opposed the idea that they were artificial compilations, intended to present a schematized picture of medieval society. "From the experiences and observations of his life, his imagination derived the materials for its creative processes" [J. M. Manly, *Some New Light on Chaucer*, 1926].

Chaucer's characterization of the pilgrims is carried still further in the continually moving narrative of the links between the tales. The devices by which Chaucer maintains the freshness, variety, and liveliness of this background are natural and entertaining; and most important of all is the role of the Host. He dominates almost every episode along the road to Canterbury. His dignity, his independence, his experience as an innkeeper, his geniality, his tact admirably qualify him for the leadership of a personally conducted tour; and the way in which he meets the various minor and major crises of the journey gives continuous dramatic interest to the links. His sense of social values prompts him to arrange that the Knight shall tell the first tale and to call on the Monk to follow; but when the Miller insists on being heard instead, the Host yields the point to avoid a disturbance because he sees that the man is drunk. Yet ordinarily he maintains a firm ress of time, and stops any pilgrim who wanders from the point. He adapts his tone to the person he addresses, is respectful to the Knight and Man of Law, courtly to the Prioress, encouraging to the shy and aloof Clerk, bluff with the Cook. In order to keep the company entertained he jests good-humouredly with the Monk and the Priest, and he ridicules Chaucer in order to dissipate the sober mood created by the Prioress's Tale. Alert to prevent quarrels, he checks the bickering of the Friar and Summoner and reconciles the Manciple and Cook; and when he becomes involved in an angry exchange of abuse with the Pardoner he readily yields to the Knight's intervention as a peacemaker.

The Host does not let the company forget that he is the judge of the tales:

And wel I woot the substance is in me,
If any thyng shal wel reported be.

His comments on the tales keep the general scheme in mind, and further reveal his personality. His literary tastes are conservative. He cannot understand the delicate and whimsical irony of Chaucer's parody of the romances in **"Sir Thopas"**: "Now swich a rym the devel I biteche!";

and he demands the substitution of a tale, "in which ther be som murthe or som doctryne." The **"Man of Law's Tale,"** which included both entertainment and instruction, had suited him exactly: "This was a thrifty tale for the nones!" And he is well pleased with the moral allegory of Chaucer's **"Melibeus"**—partly, however, because the peace-loving Dame Prudence offered such a pleasing contrast to his own formidable wife, Goodelief. The Host prefers humorous to tragic stories. The **"Shipman's"** and the **"Nun's Priest's Tales"** are highly commended; but he strongly supports the Knight's interruption of the Monk's tragedies, agreeing with his preference for stories with a happy ending. Indeed he is so distressed by the Physician's story of Virginia that nothing can restore him but a drink or a ribald tale.

Another dramatic element of the framing narrative is the constant introduction of quarrels and disputes. These are sometimes motivated by occupational jealousy as in the case of the Miller and the Reeve, who are often brought into conflict through their duties in connection with the medieval manor, and of the Cook and the Manciple, who are rival caterers. The Friar and Summoner are also natural rivals, in that both are expert in winning money from the laity in various unscrupulous ways. The chief item of dispute that runs through several stages of the journey is the age-old war of the sexes, which perhaps begins with the Host's allusion to his wife's love of domination, is lightly touched on in the **"Nun's Priest's Tale"** of Pertelote and Chauntecleer, and rises to the importance of a discussion or debate in the Wife of Bath's frank statement of her heretical opinions on matrimony and the different replies that these call forth from the Clerk, the Merchant, and the Franklin.

Still another dramatic artifice employed in the links and prologues is what might be called the confession. Based perhaps on a literary convention which appears in the *Roman de la Rose* and in the Elizabethan soliloquy, the device is here made natural through the confidential mood inspired by the pilgrimage. The Franklin as well as the Host reveal their domestic troubles on one or two occasions; but the outstanding examples of this form of self-revelation are the **"Wife of Bath's Prologue,"** the **"Pardoner's Prologue,"** and the **"Canon's Yeoman's Prologue,"** with the first part of his tale. In each case a strongly individualized personality intimately reveals his or her principles and practice, however contrary to accepted morality; each then enforces these statements of experience by the authority of a tale by way of exemplum; and each evokes a dramatic response from other pilgrims. The Wife of Bath's account of how she won the mastery of her five husbands, with its accompanying tale of woman's sovereignty, precipitates the different kinds of irony displayed by the Clerk and the Merchant. The Pardoner's cynical confession of avarice, lechery, and gluttony, contrasted with his eloquent sermon against these sins, ends in a scene variously interpreted by the critics but accepted by all as tensely dramatic. In the **"Canon's Yeoman's Prologue"** and the preliminary part of his tale, this semi-learned confederate of a shabby alchemist, who has joined the pilgrims in the hope of getting some money to realize

his dream of achieving the transmutation of elements, finally sees that his sales talk will never convince the Host or the other pilgrims. He then breaks down and frankly describes in copious detail the constant failure of their experiments and the hopelessness of attaining their end. His tale itself is not about his own master, who seems to have been a deluded enthusiast, but about another alchemist who swindled an unsuspecting priest; at the end, he declares that the secret of alchemy will never be revealed except by the will of God.

To show that the personalities so clearly brought before us in the Prologue and the links are further revealed in the tales would take us beyond the limitations of our subject. It must suffice to note that only two of the tales are definitely known to have been written before the work was undertaken; that all the tales are sufficiently appropriate to their tellers; and that a good many of them—such, for example, as the Miller's and Reeve's, the Prioress's, the Wife of Bath's, the Friar's, the Summoner's, and the Pardoner's—were certainly written with the purpose of more fully illustrating these characters. It may be added that Chaucer's tales even more than Boccaccio's afford illustrations of every important genre in medieval literature, including not only fabliau and romance but also saint's legend, sermon, and medieval tragedy. (Saint's legend and sermon appear in Boccaccio satirically, not seriously.)

Charles A. Owen, Jr. (essay date 1953)

SOURCE: "The Crucial Passages in Five of the *Canterbury Tales*: A Study in Irony and Symbol," in *The Journal of English and Germanic Philology*, Vol. LII, No. 3, July, 1953, pp. 294-311.

[*Owen is renowned for the textual criticism in his works,* Discussions of the Canterbury Tales, Manuscripts of the Canterbury Tales *and* Pilgrimage and Storytelling in the Canterbury Tales. *In the following essay, Owen analyzes symbolic passages in the "Franklin's Tale," the "Merchant's Tale," the "Wife of Bath's Tale," the "Pardoner's Tale," and the "Nun's Priest's Tale" to show how they foreshadow and unify their plots.*]

Chaucer's Art in the *Canterbury Tales* projects a complex world. To the dramatic pose of simplicity already adopted by Chaucer in many of his narrative poems is added the complication of a group of observed narrators. The intrinsic value of each of the tales is not its final one. Behind the artificial world created in the tale are the conscious purposes of the narrator and the self-revelation, involuntary and often unconscious, involved in all artistic effort. The simplest of the plots in the *Canterbury Tales* is that of the frame. It makes the same demand of each character involved, that he ride in the company of the others to Canterbury and back and participate in the creative activity of the tale-telling. Each character projects his tale, the limited vision it embodies, and his limiting personality into the world of the pilgrimage. The plot is simple but dynamic. For each vision has the potentiality of bringing into new focus those that preceded and of influencing those that will follow. The possibilities are soon unlimited. They lead to a richness that defies final analysis but finds its most concentrated expression in passages that at once embody and expose the limited vision of created character and creating narrator. These passages foreshadow in the unwitting speech or opinion of a character the outcome of the plot and help to create symbolic values that give the narrative an added and unifying dimension. They are in a sense symbolic of the whole work: in the contrast between what *is* and what men see—of themselves and of others—lies Chaucer's deepest vein of comedy.

> . . . [I]n the contrast between what *is* and what men see—of themselves and of others—lies Chaucer's deepest vein of comedy.
>
> —*Charles A. Owen, Jr.*

Passages that foreshadow the outcome in the unwitting speech of a character are fairly numerous in the *Canterbury Tales*, but I have found only five that perform also a symbolic and unifying function. These five passages occur in five of the most important tales. It will be the purpose of this paper to analyze the five passages and to explore the multiple meanings, both within the tales and in the world of the pilgrimage, which they epitomize.

I

One of the clearest of the symbolic passages is the speech in the **"Franklin's Tale,"** where Dorigen softens her refusal to Aurelius and at the same time expresses her love for her husband:

> But after that in pley thus seyde she:
> "Aurelie," quod she, "by heighe God above,
> Yet wolde I graunte you to been youre love,
> Syn I yow se so pitously complayne,
> Looke what day that endelong Britayne
> Ye remoeve alle the rokkes, stoon by stoon,
> That they ne lette ship ne boot to goon.
> I seye, whan ye han maad the coost so clene
> Of rokkes that there nys no stoon ysene,
> Thanne wol I love yow best of any man,
> Have heer my trouthe, in al that evere I kan."

This speech of Dorigen provides the final element necessary to the plot. The happy marriage, the temporary absence of Arveragus, the enduring love of Aurelius, have all been presented. The wife's rash promise is the catalytic element that sets the others to reacting.

But because of the view we have had of Dorigen's grief, in which the rocks played so menacing a part, the rash

promise is at the same time an expression of Dorigen's love for her husband. Her mention of the rocks tells us even more certainly than her refusal that she is entirely devoted to her husband. This speech introduces for the first time in the tale the contrast, extremely important later, between the appearance of things and the reality. On the surface the speech is an agreement under certain conditions to commit adultery. Beneath the surface it is an expression of conjugal loyalty.

In fact Dorigen has endeavored without realizing it to transform the symbolic meaning of the rocks. Up to this point they have represented to her the menace of natural forces to her husband's life. Hereafter their permanence is a guarantee of her enduring love for her husband. The rocks occur to her not only because her husband's life is in danger from them but because their immutability is like her love. She has seen beyond the menacing appearance of the rocks and has invoked the symbolic value of their endurance at the same time that she has finally accepted their reality.

The changed significance of the rocks is emphasized in several ways by Chaucer. Before her rash promise Dorigen questions on grounds of reason the purpose of the rocks in God's world and prays

> "But wolde God that alle thise rokkes blake
> Were sonken into helle for his sake!
> Thise rokkes sleen myn herte for the feere."

After her promise to Aurelius it is his turn to pray for the removal of the rocks. Instead of Eterne God, he addresses Apollo, and asks him to persuade his sister Lucina to cause a two-year flood tide high enough to cover the rocks with five fathoms, or, if this is not feasible,

> "Prey hire to synken every rok adoun
> Into hir owene dirke regioun
> Under the ground, ther Pluto dwelleth inne,
> Or nevere mo shal I my lady wynne."

The parallelism of the prayers emphasizes the transformation of the symbol. The removal of the rocks is now the menace to the marriage. In both the prayers the desire to see the rocks removed is a sign of weakness, of unwillingness to accept the real world. Dorigen transcends her weakness when she accepts the permanence of the rocks. Aurelius transcends his weakness when he recognizes the quality of Dorigen's and Arveragus's love as superior to his own passion.

The rocks play an important part in the contrast between appearance and reality. There is never any question of doing away with the rocks: Aurelius's brother doesn't expect to achieve that when he proposes the trip to Orleans, nor can the magician do more than make them *seem* to vanish.

> But thurgh his magik, for a wyke or tweye,
> It semed that alle the rokkes were aweye.

Aurelius responds at first to the appearance of things.

he knew that ther was noon obstacle,
    That voyded were thise rokkes everychon.

But gradually he finds that the obstacles are still there. He himself makes no demand of Dorigen but merely reminds her of her promise. And when he hears of Arveragus's "gentillesse" and sees Dorigen's distress, he gallantly releases her. The real obstacles, like the rocks, only seem to have vanished. They are the honor, the decency, the gentility of all the people involved, and the true love of Dorigen and Arveragus for one another.

Dorigen's rash promise also functions in the tale in a way not intended by the Franklin. In addition to its other meanings it is an expression of "gentillesse" in its superficial sense. Dorigen tempers her absolute refusal in a way that makes it sound courteous, though in her heart she knows of the removal of the rocks,

"It is agayns the proces of nature."

Even while accepting the natural order, she is shirking a part of her duty in the moral. That the rocks play so great a part in the thought and fate of this soft-hearted woman is a further irony. When faced at the end with the disappearance of the rocks and the necessity of keeping her promise, she will propose to herself suicide but allow her purpose to disintegrate as she calls to mind the sad fate of women who firmly carried out such a purpose. Arveragus alone displays a firmness to which the rocks have relevance. His temporary absence makes possible the rash promise and his decision at the crisis forces Aurelius to see the "obstacles" that have only seemed to vanish. The superficial gentility of Dorigen's promise foreshadows and contrasts with the gentility of the ending, and the tale becomes a criticism of some aspects of gentility, more subtle than the Host's in the prologue to the tale, and more justified.

The Franklin presents in his tale an ideal of marriage and of "gentillesse," and manages at the same time to compliment the Knight, the Squire, and the Clerk. But his story is, without his realizing it, a critique of "gentillesse," for it is Dorigen's courteous softening of her refusal that makes the exhibition of gentility at the end necessary. The rocks which suggest the enduring value of gentility also suggest the distinctions which the Franklin in his easy acceptance of the good things of life fails to make.

II

The crucial passage in the **"Merchant's Tale"** comes in the middle of the epithalamion and sends echoes and reverberations through the two consultations and the marriage to a crowning climax in the garden scene at the end. The Merchant is showing us January's reasons for wanting to marry:

Mariage is a ful greet sacrement.
He which that hath no wyf, I holde him shent;
He lyveth helplees and al desolat,—
I speke of folk in seculer estaat.

And herke why, I sey nat this for noght,
That womman is for mannes helpe ywroght.
The hye God, whan he hadde Adam maked,
And saugh him al allone, bely-naked,
God of his grete goodnesse seyde than,
"Lat us now make an helpe unto this man
Lyk to hymself"; and thanne he made him Eve.
Heere may ye se, and heerby may ye preve,
That wyf is mannes helpe, and his confort,
His paradys terrestre, and his disport.
So buxom and so vertuous is she
They moste nedes lyve in unitee.
O flessh they been, and o flessh, as I gesse
Hath but oon herte, in wele and in distresse.

The concept of marriage as an earthly paradise has come to January late but with the blinding light of revelation: it has taken complete possession of his mind. The cautious habits and the short-sighted shrewdness of old age will be called on to support rather than examine this new vision. As in his judicious exclusion of the clergy and his appeal to example, he will use the forms of wisdom but not its substance. Marriage will carry all before it because it promises to combine the self-indulgence he has practised all his life with two things that old age makes vital to him for the first time— help for his physical weakness and the salvation of his soul. His lust for pleasure and his desire for salvation combine in the first consultation scene to blind him to the danger inherent in taking a young wife. The only danger he can foresee by the time he has chosen the girl and called his friends together the second time is so much felicity in marriage as to ruin his chance of a blissful after-life.

Besides epitomizing the precise and willful blindness of his attitude toward marriage, the passage foreshadows many of the details of his fate. The helpfulness that he anticipates in a wife will serve May as excuse for being in Damian's arms in the pear tree, and it will take the form before his very eyes of a nakedness similar to Adam's, her smock upon her breast. But as he sees in Adam's story a proof of marital bliss, so he will see in the pear tree only what his wife wants him to, an example of her care for his welfare. The "unitee" and "o flessh" receive an ironical fulfillment in the blind old man's constant clutch on his buxom and perforce virtuous May, and an additional twist in the line from his invitation to the garden,

"No spot of thee ne knew I al my lyf,"

where the irony of the contrast between his ugly passion and the romantic imagery and sacred associations of the Song of Songs (which is Solomon's!) matches the irony of his being as unconscious of the physical spot he is even then touching as he will later be of the moral spot— adultery—when he is looking at it with miraculously unblinded eyes.

The controlling images in the poem, however, are the linked ones of the garden, the blindness, and the tree. They are linked for the first time in this passage. "Heere may ye se," says the Merchant for January. But you can see in the story of Adam and Eve that a wife is man's earthly paradise, only if you are blind to the tree of the knowledge of good and evil and the forbidden fruit. As January is blind in the Garden of Eden, so is he blind in the paradise of his wife's arms:

> "A man may do no synne with his wyf,
> Ne hurte hymselven with his owene knyf."

Adam and Eve and the first sin link up in these fatuous lines with Damian,

> Which carf biforn the knyght ful many a day

and the sin soon to be committed in January's private paradise. The garden that January builds is the consummation of his folly and the symbol of his marriage. Its beauty is May, and the stone wall with which it is "enclosed al aboute" is the jealous precautions of the blind January as well as the inescapable unpleasantness of his lovemaking. There is no stone of tyranny in May's nature, and in fact we find her pliancy which January expected to be like warm wax taking a ready impression from Damian's wooing. The silver key to the garden which is January's alone is his privilege as husband, but from the warm wax of May's nature a suitable replica is provided for Damian—his privilege as lover. The blindness is the physical counterpart of the ignorance of marriage and of women that January has shown all along. It prevents him to the end from seeing the tree in the garden and the knowledge of evil which it represents. And the regaining of his sight wipes out even the alertness to danger which accompanied the blindness.

The tree plays a further and more striking part in the tale. January fails to see it in the Garden of Eden, but brings it in as an image of his own virility in the first consultation with his friends:

> "Though I be hoor, I fare as dooth a tree
> That blosmeth er that fruyt ywoxen bee
> And blosmy tree nys neither drye ne deed.
> I feele me nowhere hoor but on myn heed;
> Myn herte and alle my lymes been as grene
> As laurer thurgh the yeer is for to sene."

The image bears fruit in the final part of the story. In January's private paradise, his arms around the trunk of the pear tree, he serves his wife as stepping stone to the forbidden fruit of adultery. At the same time he becomes the symbol of his folly, cuckolded in the branches which spring from his head as horns.

The imagery of growth has structural significance. The story is essentially the growth of an idea to complete fulfillment. Starting in the mind of January, a germ with all that develops already implicit, it attains in each part of the story a new mode of actualization—first verbal expression in general terms; then the fixing of the dream to a specific woman; then the literal fulfillment. At each stage January's blindness to his own folly achieves some new fatuity linked to the imagery in which he first clothed his "vision." But the story does not stop with a single

literal fulfillment. Through Proserpina's vow it suggests repetition through the ages. And it creates in the literal world the symbolic fulfillment of the idea. The garden and the blindness, in January's mind from the beginning, are now fully materialized. No miracle can make him see the tree as horns growing from his head, nor make him see the adultery committed before his very eyes.

The Merchant has taken care to tell us that this tale is not autobiographical:

> "of myn owene soore,
> For soory herte, I telle may namoore."

Moved by the ironical moral of the **"Clerk's Tale,"** he will join the discussion opened by the Wyf of Bath and present directly a male view of marriage. The Wife and her theories are clearly in his mind for he commits the anachronism of having Justinus refer to her in the tale. His real intentions in telling the story are clear from two passages. In the prologue he says,

> "We wedded men lyven in sorwe and care. . . .
>
> As for the moore part, I say nat alle."

And in the tale itself, speaking of Argus,

> Yet was he blent, and, God woot, so been mo,
> That wenen wisly that it be nat so.
> Passe over is an ese, I sey namoore.

For the Merchant January is the type of that *rara avis*—the happily married man: Not all married men are miserable; some are blind.

The Merchant participates in the blindness of his creature January in not realizing the extent to which he is talking of his own sore in the tale. His imperceptiveness extends even to thinking that he can disguise the vulgarity of his tale in circumlocution. The circumlocutions in fact call attention to the vulgarity, just as January's blissful ignorance contrasts with but does not conceal the Merchant's disillusionment. The creator of January is evidently a converted idealist, and the bitterness of his cynicism is the measure of his former folly. He can be so penetrating in exposing January's reasons for marriage because he is really looking at his own from beyond the gulf of two shattering months of marital experience. The cynical egoist looks at the delusions of an idealistic egoist and cannot see that his bitterness betrays him.

III

The **"Wife of Bath's Tale"** is ostensibly a two-part exposition of the Wife's thesis that marriages are happy only when the woman is the master. The crucial passage occurs when the "olde wyf" at the juncture of the two parts reiterates in stronger terms her demand that the knight marry her:

> "Nay thanne," quod she, "I shrewe us bothe two!
> For thogh that I be foul, and oold, and poore,

I nolde for al the metal, ne for oore,
That under erthe is grave, or lith above,
But if thy wyf I were, and eek thy love."

The old woman's demand is not only the conclusion of the quest plot, the price the knight pays for his life, but it is also the point of departure for the husband's dilemma. The woman must first secure her man before she can offer him her alternatives. The Wife of Bath's story passes with this speech from its public to its private demonstration of the thesis. The world-wide scene of the quest dwindles to the marriage-bed of the dilemma. We pass from generally accepted theory to the practice of one woman in achieving first sovereignty then happiness in her marriage.

But the husband's dilemma and the Wife of Bath's thesis are merely the surface of the story. The old woman has already demanded that the knight marry her. In her reiteration she reveals her real desire. She wants not just a husband but a husband's love. The phrase "and eek thy love" brought here into conjunction with the woman's ugliness, age, and poverty suggests that the real dilemma in the second part of the story is the wife's rather than the husband's; it foreshadows the necessity for miracle at the end and reveals for the story a second and more valid theme, operating on the instinctive level beneath the Wife's and her heroine's theories—the quest for love.

On this level the tale as a whole progresses from rape to marriage to love with each of the three crises of the story presenting a common pattern. In each there is a problem, a theoretical solution, and a modification of theory in practice. At the beginning of the story the knight's crime of rape is to be punished by death until the ladies intervene and send him off in quest of crucial information about women. The second problem, what women most desire, is solved theoretically by the answer the knight gives the court. But it is clear from the "olde wyf's" demand that in practice one woman wants not sovereignty over husband and lover, but merely a husband and his love. The final problem is the obtaining of the husband's love, theoretically solved when he leaves the choice in his dilemma and thus the sovereignty to his wife. Actually the wife attains the knight's love by magically slipping between the horns of the dilemma and giving him exactly what he wants. The happy married life that results differs markedly from the blueprint of the Wife's thesis:

And she obeyed hym in every thyng
That myghte doon hym plesance or likyng.

The Wife of Bath had good reason to tell the story she did. It provided what she considered a good demonstration of her theory. It gave her an opportunity of discussing a number of the questions close to her heart such as the true meaning of "gentillesse," and of parodying Arthurian romance with its unrealistic notions of life and love. It had the further appeal of an imaginative wish-fulfillment, for it presented an old woman who gained a young husband and magically changed herself into everything he could desire in a wife. As a story of the quest for love it was the artistic counterpart of her life.

In its continuing contrast between theory and practice the tale repeats the unconscious revelation of the Wife's prologue. For her theory of marriage and her own practise have been worlds apart. In her first three marriages she did maintain her sovereignty, but the marriages were not happy. No doubt the Wife enjoyed the cowed submission she so cleverly exacted from her old dotards. But she is forced to admit,

And yet in bacon hadde I nevere delit.

The fourth husband with his paramour aroused her jealousy and, to her satisfaction, became jealous in his turn. The Wife of Bath took refuge in travel, and the marriage was little more than nominal. Only with the fifth, her clerk of Oxenford, did she find happiness. Jankyn she cannot name without a blessing. But in the fifth marriage the relationship of the first three was simply reversed. This time she was twice his age and forced to sign over her property before the ceremony. Like the old woman in her tale she had to win his love. At the same time, she would have us believe, she won the upper hand in the marriage. That the triumph, like that of the heroine in her tale, is nominal her own words confess:

After that day we hadden never debaat.
God helpe me so, I was to him as kynde
As any wyf from Denmark unto Ynde,
And also trewe, and so was he to me.

We have further proof of the clerk's influence over her in the stress she puts on authorities in her discussions, on the clear memory she has for the stories in the book she made him burn, and in the strange distortion she makes of the Midas story in her tale. Jankyn left his mark on more than her "ribbes," more than her hearing.

The Wife of Bath enjoyed theory on one level and life on another. Her enjoyment of both was intense and convincing, so much so that most critics and readers have appreciated her gusto without noticing the contrast between her theory and practice in both prologue and tale.

IV

In the **"Pardoner's Tale"** the crucial passage occurs at the point where the revelers find the pile of gold under the tree:

No lenger thanne after Deeth they soughte.

On the primary level of the revelers' limited vision the wealth has driven all thought of their search for Death from their minds. They now think of the pleasures the gold will buy them and plan how to get it home safely. At the same time the statement foreshadows their end. They no longer seek Death because they have found him.

The single line marks a fundamental division in the tale. On the one hand is the drunken search for Death, marked by an unwonted and a deluded altruism. They are sworn brothers. They will slay Death. Drink has given them a mission, stature, pride, contempt for others. The gold has both a sobering and a deflating effect. It brings them back to the real world from their illusions of brotherhood and of slaying Death. Yet their drunken intentions were closer to the final outcome than their sober planning and counterplanning to secure the treasure. The gold has brought them back to their narrow world. It both focuses and limits their vision. These two sections of the tale, as we shall see later, have a symbolic value for the Pardoner.

But first we must explore the complex set of meanings in the tale as a whole. What happens to the gold in the story happens to the story itself. Its value is determined by the human motives focused upon it. In itself it may be an effective warning against cupidity, showing how greed turns gold into death. But as a part of the sermon habitually delivered by the Pardoner to the "lewed peple" it is at the same time the instrument of the Pardoner's greed. And as a part of the confession made to the other pilgrims it is the expression of the Pardoner's vanity. The pilgrimage gives him the opportunity to display to an intelligent audience the full measure of his cleverness and cynicism. He hopes so to dazzle and shock them that they will fail to see the motive that drives him to the compensation of hypocrisy and greed.

The Pardoner's physical disability has isolated him from some of the normal satisfactions in life. In revenge he has rejected the professed morality of other people and uses it aginst them to attain the power and comfort that wealth brings. His income is thus a symbol of his victory over physical inadequacy and of his superiority over the normal and stupid louts who are his victims. But the victory is not one that he can fully reveal in his daily life. Here, before the pilgrims, stimulated by the intelligence of his audience and with neither the necessity nor the possibility of assuming his customary role, he can for once reveal the extent of his success, impress his companions with the amount of his income, and shock them with the cynicism that makes it all possible. He seeks at the same time to conceal the emptiness and isolation of his life by reference to the comforts and gaieties he enjoys:

> "I wol have moneie, wolle, chese, and whete. . . .
> Nay, I wolf the vyne,
> And have a joly wenche in every toun."

The task he has set himself in his confession is as wild and deluded as the drunken revelers' quest in the first part of the tale. Like the quest it has a wider range than his customary hypocrisy and is nearer the ultimate truth. But hypocrisy is his normal and sober world, and like the revelers' vision in the second part of the tale it is narrow and limited. The presumption of the pilgrim and the hypocrisy of the "noble ecclesiaste" both end in isolation. The Pardoner has also found death without recognizing it. His life is an exemplum of the futility of cynicism. And in the world of the pilgrimage, where we see the Pardoner but he cannot see himself, the crucial passage again functions.

V

The crucial passage in the **"Nun's Priest's Tale"** is not so obviously a foreshadowing of the plot as in the other instances. It comes at the juncture between the discussion of dreams and the action of the near-fatal third of May. Chauntecleer is speaking:

> "Now let us speke of myrthe, and stynte al this.
> Madame Pertelote, so have I blis,
> Of o thyng God hath sent me large grace;
> For whan I se the beautee of youre face,
> Ye been so scarlet reed aboute youre yen,
> It maketh al my drede for to dyen;
> For al so siker as *In principio*,
> *Mulier est hominis confusio*—
> Madame, the sentence of this Latyn is,
> 'Womman is mannes joye and al his blis.'
> For whan I feele a-nyght your softe syde,
> Al be it that I may nat on yow ryde,
> For that oure perche is maad so narwe, allas!
> I am so ful of joye and of solas,
> That I diffye bothe sweven and dreem."

Here the ultimate victim employs the same technique in his deception of his wife as is later to be used by the fox on him—deceitful flattery. Behind the fair words of his translation, designed to smooth the ruffled feathers of Pertelote, whose laxatives have just been scorned, lurks the malicious dig of the Latin. The cock will later be "hoist with his own petard,"

> As man that koude his traysoun nat espie
> So was he ravysshed with his flaterie

Furthermore the cock is delighted with the sound of his own voice. In the long discourse on dreams, of which this is the conclusion, he has displayed the smug assurance of the born raconteur. And it is a moot point here whether his wife's beauty or his own cleverly barbed praise of it most attracts him. The cock is indeed ready to believe that other people admire his voice.

This speech of Chauntecleer brings out the pedantry implicit from the beginning in his actions. He alone can witness and appreciate the victory he has won over his wife. The victory is a pedant's triumph and contrasts strikingly with the one the fox later wins over him, which calls forth a universal clamor.

The cock's vast learning has furthermore contributed to the easy fatalism he has fallen into as a result of his learned rebuttal on dreams. The original dream was clearly a warning dream. The beast in it, which with all his learning the cock can describe but cannot recognize as his natural enemy the fox,

> "wolde han maad areest
> Upon my body, and wolde han had me deed"

But in the examples which he uses to refute his wife's skepticism people either fail to heed the warning or they have no chance of evading the fate foretold in their dreams. The cock in effect wins the argument and forgets the dream that occasioned it. His pedantry has led him into a smug fatalism that contemplates his own coming "adversitee" as merely the concluding proof of the truth of dreams. No effort is called for—only the pursuit of what the soon-to-be-shipwrecked victim in one of the dreams called "my thynges" and the assumption of the courageous pose which Pertelote recommended and which his prowess makes ridiculous.

The cock, warned by dream and instinct against the fox and prepared by his own deft use of flattery against the technique the fox is to use, unwittingly gives himself a further warning, which he is either not learned enough or too pedantic to apply. Just as truly as the words of St. John's Gospel, woman is man's confusion, he tells his wife in Latin. But the words from the Gospel are *In principio,* in the beginning; and in the beginning Eve was Adam's confusion. So far is he from heeding the warning that the passage which contains it is full of the uxorious passion usually attributed to Adam. The cock's appreciation of his wife's charms diverts him from further thought of his own danger. Here in effect is another Adam, succumbing to the attractions of his wife when he should be using his reason. The Adam-and-Eve parallel, thus suggested for the cock-and-hen story, contributes to the mock heroics.

The passage is rich in other contributions to the mock heroic effect. It unites the language of exalted human passion with details of hen anatomy and barnyard architecture. The exalted language and the deflating details give the passage a quality that is typical of the whole poem. The courtly behavior and refined pretensions of Chauntecleer are constantly betrayed by the ludicrous activities and ignoble motives contingent upon chicken nature. The suggestion is clear: Objectively viewed, human pride and vanity are similarly betrayed. Only the simple life with frank acceptance of the necessities and limitations of the human lot, as exemplified by the widow and her menage, can have real dignity.

The contrast between Chauntecleer and his owner has a dramatic value in the Canterbury Tales. The Host in calling on the Prioress a little earlier addressed her in terms of the most exaggerated respect. Her Priest, however, he addresses with peremptory intimacy, making game of his poverty. When we remember the Prioress's pains

> to countrefete cheere
> Of court, and to been estatlich of manere,
> And to ben holden digne of reverence,

we can glimpse a guarded purpose. The sexes of the characters in the tale are reversed, as is also the ownership, but the essential relationship between poverty and wealth, between simplicity and pretension is there. The drama is carried a step further when the Priest falls into overt criticism of women. This he does at the expense of the complexity of his tale. The advice of his wife is, as we have seen, a minor detail in the cock's decision. But it is a

theme that the Priest attacks with evident relish. He brings himself up sharp with the thought of whom he might be offending, then returns to the attack indirectly by referring his listeners to the "auctors," and finally tries to ascribe the whole thing to the cock:

> "Thise ben the cokkes wordes, and nat myne;
> I kan noon harm of no womman divyne."

The inner conflict of the misogynist employed by a woman has come for a moment to the surface; then it is pushed back behind the artifice of the story, where it has been operating secretly all along. The Host's reaction to the story has thus a double irony. Not only has he failed to see the point, but he imagines the Priest, if he were only a layman, a prodigious treader of hens!

The pedantry, ridiculed in the portrait of Chauntecleer, is also attacked by the Nun's Priest in his criticism of the rhetoricians. The satire is most highly comic when Friday and Master Gaufred are brought in at the climax of the story, and Venus is reproached for not protecting her devotee on her day, when it was her influence that was partly responsible for Chauntecleer's plight. It is possible, however, to ridicule a thing and be guilty of it on occasion oneself. This trap the Nun's Priest falls into at least once when he gets himself involved in a discussion of free will and God's fore-knowledge—as a result of elaborating too far on a mock heroic color, VII 3230-50. Like Chauntecleer he is for a moment hoist with his own petard. And in struggling to get back to his tale, he suddenly finds himself involved in the criticism of women. Pedantry which leads to a criticism of women recalls the crucial passage and the cock's gibe, "*In principio,/Mulier est hominis confusio.*" The Priest in fact makes the same charge:

> Wommanes conseil broghte us first to wo,
> And made Adam fro Paradys to go,
> Ther as he was ful myrie and wel at ese.

Whatever the cause for the Priest's misogyny (it may well be a combination of intellectual contempt and involuntary attraction), there is no mistaking the animus with which he follows his hero's lead in attributing man's ills to woman. This blanket condemnation of women is a very different thing from his implied criticism of the Prioress's pretensions. In his better moments he knows, as his portrait of Chauntecleer indicates, the real significance of Adam and Eve for mankind. *Hominis confusio* is man's own frailty. That the Priest lashes out at women as his stupid cock had done measures the strength of his feelings. In a sense these *are* the cock's words, and the Priest's recognition of their unworthiness enables him to recover his composure and his story.

On the primary level then the **"Nun's Priest's Tale"** is a brilliant and complex exposure of vanity, self-esteem, and self-indulgence through the mock heroic treatment of a beast fable. On the secondary level, the Nun's Priest joins the discussions of the Pilgrims on poverty (Man of Law and Wife of Bath), women's advice (Merchant), rhetoric

(Host and Squire), and marriage. He is also presenting in the contrast between the widow and Chauntecleer a veiled comment on his position vis-à-vis the Prioress. Finally, on the level of involuntary revelation, he falls into the pedantry that he is ridiculing and uncovers for a moment in his confusion the feelings of a misogynist dependent on a woman. In this moment there is revealed a second conflict, the conflict between the artist, building with the materials of his art a world where his feelings achieve symbolic and universal expression, and the man, expressing his feelings directly.

CONCLUSION

The symbols which Chaucer employed are unobtrusive; they fit in their contexts of sentimental romance or crude realism without "shake or bind." Nothing in the tale forces them to the symbolic level. Yet the consistency with which the rocks are developed in the **"Franklin's Tale"** gives the obvious charm of the story a focused integrity which can be felt even when not clearly analyzed. The linked images of garden, tree, and blindness of the **"Merchant's Tale"** add to the bitter unity of tone an underlying unity of action: the seed of January's folly grows from the fertile soil of his figurative blindness into the successive realizations of word, fixed purpose, and deed, until it attains full maturity in the garden, the blindness, and the tree-born fruit of adultery, with the head that conceived realistically behorned.

The focus and additional dimension which symbol and image provide in the tales are also attained by the contrast or ambiguity of the narrative elements involved. The intentional pattern of the **"Wife of Bath's Tale"** and the zest with which she tells it lose none of their literal value when we see the ambiguity of the elements she uses to prove her thesis. The nature of love and marriage resists the warping efforts of her dogged feminism and provides the counterpoint of a contrasting and more valid pattern. The quest for love which dominated her life dominates her tale. The greed in which the Pardoner has taken refuge creates the skillful weapon of his tale. With one edge he cynically dupes peasants; with the other he seeks to shock the pilgrims into a recognition of his importance. For the deluded vanity of the second purpose as well as the hypocrisy of the first, the two parts of his tale present analogies; at the very center the symbol of gold as unrecognized death reveals the futile emptiness of both efforts. The concealed purpose of the Nun's Priest finds urbane expression in the contrast between the simple dignity of the people and the ostentation of the chickens in his tale. But a momentary lapse into the pedantry he is mocking in Chauntecleer confuses him and he breaks through the artifice of beast fable to direct expression of his purpose. The artistic expression, where *hominis confusio* is man's own foolish presumption, forms an ironic background for the priest's lapse into an indiscriminate and direct anti-feminism.

Chaucer, unlike the Nun's Priest, never expresses his intention directly. Present himself on the pilgrimage and in the occasional asides to the audience, he pictures himself as the simple reporter of experience, not responsible because unable to judge the questions of morals and propriety raised by the tales. Only in his own experience as narrator does the mask become penetrable, and then imaginary audience, who acquiesce in the Host's misunderstanding and crude estimate of **"Sir Thopas"** and get for their reward the prosy and long-winded idealism of the **"Melibeus."** There is implied in the episode, as in the Man of Law's wrong-headed praise while cudgeling his brains for a tale, a comment on the popular taste and on Chaucer's relation to his real audience. Chaucer did not expect to be understood fully by all his readers. Certain of his effects depend on a knowledge which few of them could have. Others, like the crucial passages that have just been analyzed, are the subtle elaborations by the artist of a design already present. They suggest a personal standard and private satisfaction in his art.

But the simplicity adopted as a mask in the tales is not entirely ironical. It is a token for the deeper simplicity that receives impressions freely and refuses to interpose the eager evaluations, artistic and moral, that prevent full recognition. This deeper simplicity reflects faithfully the paradoxes of personality, the contradictions of experience. It becomes through its forbearance a rare and delicate instrument for evaluation and judgment, and presents a total vision not to be fully appreciated from the mental and spiritual posture of the Host, nor from that of the *homme moyen du moyen âge* [average Medieval man] whom Chaucer could not only entertain but also see beyond.

E. Talbot Donaldson   (essay date 1954)

SOURCE: "Chaucer The Pilgrim," in *PMLA*, Vol. LXIX, No. 4, September, 1954, pp. 928-36.

[*Donaldson is a scholar of Medieval and Old English Literature known for his translation of* Beowulf *for modern readers and his book,* Speaking of Chaucer. *In the following excerpt, Donaldson analyzes the persona of the fictional Chaucer, the narrator of the* Canterbury Tales, *and discusses the differences and similarities between this fictional protagonist and the poem's actual author.*]

Verisimilitude in a work of fiction is not without its attendant dangers, the chief of which is that the responses it stimulates in the reader may be those appropriate not so much to an imaginative production as to an historical one or to a piece of reporting. History and reporting are, of course, honorable in themselves, but if we react to a poet as though he were an historian or a reporter, we do him somewhat less than justice. I am under the impression that many readers, too much influenced by Chaucer's brilliant verisimilitude, tend to regard his famous pilgrimage to Canterbury as significant not because it is a great fiction, but because it seems to be a remarkable record of a fourteenth-century pilgrimage. A remarkable record it may be, but if we treat it too narrowly as such there are going to be certain casualties among the elements that make up the fiction. Perhaps first among these elements is the fictional reporter, Chaucer the pilgrim, and the role he plays in the Prologue to the *Canterbury Tales* and in the links between them. I think it time that he was rescued from the comparatively dull record of history and put back into his poem. He is not really Chaucer the poet— nor, for that matter, is either the poet, or the poem's protagonist, that Geoffrey Chaucer frequently mentioned in contemporary historical records as a distinguished civil servant, but never as a poet. The fact that these are three separate entities does not, naturally, exclude the probability—or rather the certainty—that they bore a close resemblance to one another, and that, indeed, they frequently got together in the same body. But that does not excuse us from keeping them distinct from one another, difficult as their close resemblance makes our task.

The natural tendency to confuse one thing with its like is perhaps best represented by a school of Chaucerian criticism, now outmoded, that pictured a single Chaucer under the guise of a wide-eyed, jolly, rolypoly little man who, on fine Spring mornings, used to get up early, while the dew was still on the grass, and go look at daisies. A charming portrait, this, so charming, indeed, that it was sometimes able to maintain itself to the exclusion of any Chaucerian other side. It has every reason to be charming, since it was lifted almost *in toto* from the version Chaucer gives of himself in the Prologue to the *Legend of Good Women*, though I imagine it owes some of its popularity to a rough analogy with Wordsworth—a sort of *Legend of Good Poets*. It was this version of Chaucer that Kittredge, in a page of great importance to Chaucer criticism, demolished with his assertion that "a naïf Collector of Customs would be a paradoxical monster." He might well have added that a naïve creator of old January would be even more monstrous.

Kittredge's pronouncement cleared the air, and most of us now accept the proposition that Chaucer was sophisticated as readily as we do the proposition that the whale is a mammal. But unhappily, now that we've got rid of the naïve fiction, it is easy to fall into the opposite sort of mistake. This is to envision, in the *Canterbury Tales*, a highly urbane, literal-historical Chaucer setting out from Southwark on a specific day of a specific year (we even argue somewhat acrimoniously about dates and routes), in company with a group of persons who existed in real life and whom Chaucer, his reporter's eye peeled for every idiosyncrasy, determined to get down on paper—down, that is, to the last wart—so that books might be written identifying them. Whenever this accurate reporter says something especially fatuous—which is not infrequently—it is either ascribed to an opinion peculiar to the Middle Ages (sometimes very peculiar), or else Chaucer's tongue is said to be in his cheek.

Now a Chaucer with tongue-in-cheek is a vast improvement over a simple-minded Chaucer when one is trying to define the whole man, but it must lead to a loss of critical perception, and in particular to a confused notion of Chaucerian irony, to see in the **"Prologue"** a reporter who is acutely aware of the significance of what he sees but who sometimes, for ironic emphasis, interprets the evidence presented by his observation in a fashion directly contrary to what we expect. The proposition ought to be expressed in reverse: the reporter is, usually, acutely unaware of the significance of what he sees, no matter how sharply he sees it. He is, to be sure, permitted his lucid intervals, but in general he is the victim of the poet's pervasive—not merely sporadic—irony. And as such he is also the chief agent by which the poet achieves his wonderfully complex, ironic, comic, serious vision of a world which is but a devious and confused, infinitely various pilgrimage to a certain shrine. It is, as I hope to make clear, a good deal more than merely fitting that our guide on such a pilgrimage should be a man of such naïveté as the Chaucer who tells the tale of **"Sir Thopas."** Let us accompany him a little distance.

It is often remarked that Chaucer really liked the Prioress very much, even though he satirized her gently—very gently. But this is an understatement: Chaucer the pilgrim may not be said merely to have liked the Prioress very much—he thought she was utterly charming. In the first twenty-odd lines of her portrait [quotations are from *The Works of Geoffrey Chaucer,* edited by F. N. Robinson; texts and line numbers will be noted in parentheses] he employs, among other superlatives, the adverb *ful* seven times. Middle English uses *ful* where we use *very,* and if one translates the beginning of the portrait into a kind of basic English (which is what, in a way, it really is), one gets something like this: "There was also a Nun, a Prioress, who was very sincere and modest in the way she smiled; her biggest oath was only 'By saint Loy'; and she was called Madame Eglantine. She sang the divine service very well, intoning it in her nose very prettily, and she spoke French very nicely and elegantly"—and so on, down to the last gasp of sentimental appreciation. Indeed, the Prioress may be said to have transformed the rhetoric into something not unlike that of a very bright kindergarten child's descriptive theme. In his reaction to the Prioress Chaucer the pilgrim resembles another—if less—simple-hearted enthusiast: the Host, whose summons to her to tell a tale must be one of the politest speeches in the language. Not "My lady prioresse, a tale now!" but, "as curteisly as it had been a mayde,"

> My lady Prioresse, by youre leve,
> So that I wiste I sholde yow nat greve,
> I wolde demen that ye tellen sholde
> A tale next, if so were that ye wolde.
> Now wol ye vouche sauf, my lady deere?

Where the Prioress reduced Chaucer to superlatives, she reduces the Host to subjunctives.

There is no need here to go deeply into the Prioress. Eileen Power's illustrations from contemporary episcopal records show with what extraordinary economy the portrait has been packed with abuses typical of fourteenth-century nuns. The abuses, to be sure, are mostly petty, but it is clear enough that the Prioress, while a perfect lady, is anything but a perfect nun; and attempts to whitewash her, of which there have been many, can only proceed from an innocence of heart equal to Chaucer the pilgrim's and undoubtedly directly influenced by it. For he, of course, is quite swept away by her irrelevant *sensibilité*, and as a result misses much of the point of what he sees. No doubt he feels that he has come a long way, socially speaking, since his encounter with the Black Knight in the forest, and he knows, or thinks he knows, a little more of what it's all about: in this case it seems to be mostly about good manners, kindness to animals, and female charm. Thus it has been argued that Chaucer's appreciation for the Prioress as a sort of heroine of courtly romance *manquée* actually reflects the sophistication of the living Chaucer, an urbane man who cared little whether amiable nuns were good nuns. But it seems a curious form of sophistication that permits itself to babble superlatives; and indeed, if this is sophistication, it is the kind generally seen in the least experienced people—one that reflects a wide-eyed wonder at the glamor of the great world. It is just what one might expect of a bourgeois exposed to the splendors of high society, whose values, such as they are, he eagerly accepts. And that is precisely what Chaucer the pilgrim is, and what he does.

If the Prioress's appeal to him is through elegant femininity, the Monk's is through imposing virility. Of this formidable and important prelate the pilgrim does not say, with Placebo,

> I woot wel that my lord kan moore than I:
> What that he seith, I holde it ferme and stable,

but he acts Placebo's part to perfection. He is as impressed with the Monk as the Monk is, and accepts him on his own terms and at face value, never sensing that those terms imply complete condemnation of Monk *qua* Monk. The Host is also impressed by the Monk's virility, but having no sense of Placebonian propriety (he is himself a most virile man) he makes indecent jokes about it. This, naturally, offends the pilgrim's sense of decorum: there is a note of deferential commiseration in his comment, "This worthy Monk took al in pacience." Inevitably when the Monk establishes hunting as the highest activity of which religious man is capable, "I seyde his opinion was good." As one of the pilgrim's spiritual heirs was later to say, Very like a whale; but not, of course, like a fish out of water.

Wholehearted approval for the values that important persons subscribe to is seen again in the portrait of the Friar. This amounts to a prolonged gratulation for the efficiency the deplorable Hubert shows in undermining the fabric of the Church by turning St. Francis' ideal inside out:

> Ful swetely herde he confessioun,
> And plesaunt was his absolucioun.
>
> For unto swich a worthy man as he
> Acorded nat, as by his facultee,
> To have with sike lazars aqueyntaunce.

It is sometimes said that Chaucer did not like the Friar. Whether Chaucer the man would have liked such a Friar

is, for our present purposes, irrelevant. But if the pilgrim does not unequivocally express his liking for him, it is only because in his humility he does not feel that, with important people, his own likes and dislikes are material: such importance is its own reward, and can gain no lustre from Geoffrey, who, when the Friar is attacked by the Summoner, is ready to show him the same sympathy he shows the Monk.

Once he has finished describing the really important people on the pilgrimage the pilgrim's tone changes, for he can now concern himself with the bourgeoisie, members of his own class for whom he does not have to show such profound respect. Indeed, he can even afford to be a little patronizing at times, and to have his little joke at the expense of the too-busy lawyer. But such indirect assertions of his own superiority do not prevent him from giving substance to the old cynicism that the only motive recognized by the middle class is the profit motive, for his interest and admiration for the bourgeois pilgrims is centered mainly in their material prosperity and their ability to increase it. He starts, properly enough, with the out-and-out money-grubber, the Merchant, and after turning aside for that *lusus naturae,* the non-profit-motivated Clerk, proceeds to the Lawyer, who, despite the pilgrim's little joke, is the best and best-paid ever; the Franklin, twenty-one admiring lines on appetite, so expensively catered to; the Gildsmen, cheered up the social ladder, "For catel hadde they ynogh and rente"; and the Physician, again the best and richest. In this series the portrait of the Clerk is generally held to be an ideal one, containing no irony; but while it is ideal, it seems to reflect the pilgrim's sense of values in his joke about the Clerk's failure to make money: is not this still typical of the half-patronizing, half-admiring *un*understanding that practical men of business display towards academics? But in any case the portrait is a fine companion-piece for those in which material prosperity is the main interest both of the characters described and of the describer.

Of course, this is not the sole interest of so gregarious—if shy—a person as Chaucer the pilgrim. Many of the characters have the additional advantage of being good companions, a faculty that receives a high valuation in the **"Prologue."** To be good company might, indeed, atone for certain serious defects of character. Thus the Shipman, whose callous cruelty is duly noted, seems fairly well redeemed in the assertion, "And certeinly he was a good felawe." At this point an uneasy sensation that even tongue-in-cheek irony will not compensate for the lengths to which Chaucer is going in his approbation of this sinister seafarer sometimes causes editors to note that *a good felawe* means "a rascal." But I can find no evidence that it ever meant a rascal. Of course, all tritely approbative expressions enter easily into ironic connotation, but the phrase *means* a good companion, which is just what Chaucer means. And if, as he says of the Shipman, "Of nyce conscience took he no keep," Chaucer the pilgrim was doing the same with respect to him.

Nothing that has been said has been meant to imply that the pilgrim was unable to recognize, and deplore, a rascal when he saw one. He could, provided the rascality was situated in a member of the lower classes and provided it was, in any case, somewhat wider than a barn door: Miller, Manciple, Reeve, Summoner, and Pardoner are all acknowledged to be rascals. But rascality generally has, after all, the laudable object of making money, which gives it a kind of validity, if not dignity. These portraits, while in them the pilgrim, prioress-like conscious of the finer aspects of life, does deplore such matters as the Miller's indelicacy of language, contain a note of ungrudging admiration for efficient thievery. It is perhaps fortunate for the pilgrim's reputation as a judge of men that he sees through the Pardoner, since it is the Pardoner's particular tragedy that, except in Church, every one can see through him at a glance; but in Church he remains to the pilgrim "a noble ecclesiaste." The equally repellent Summoner, a practicing bawd, is partially redeemed by his also being a good fellow, "a gentil harlot and a kynde," and by the fact that for a moderate bribe he will neglect to summon: the pilgrim apparently subscribes to the popular definition of the best policeman as the one who acts the least policely.

Therefore Chaucer is tolerant, and has his little joke about the Summoner's small Latin—a very small joke, though one of the most amusing aspects of the pilgrim's character is the pleasure he takes in his own jokes, however small. But the Summoner goes too far when he cynically suggests that purse is the Archdeacon's hell, causing Chaucer to respond with a fine show of righteous respect for the instruments of spiritual punishment. The only trouble is that his enthusiastic defense of them carries *him* too far, so that after having warned us that excommunication will indeed damn our souls—

> But wel I woot he lyed right in dede:
> Of cursyng oghte ech gilty man him drede,
> For curs wol slee right as assoillyng savith—

he goes on to remind us that it will also cause considerable inconvenience to our bodies: "And also war hym of a *Significavit.*" Since a *Significavit* is the writ accomplishing the imprisonment of the excommunicate, the line provides perhaps the neatest—and most misunderstood—Chaucerian anticlimax in the **"Prologue."**

I have avoided mentioning, hitherto, the pilgrim's reactions to the really good people on the journey—the Knight, the Parson, the Plowman. One might reasonably ask how his uncertain sense of values may be reconciled with the enthusiasm he shows for their rigorous integrity. The question could, of course, be shrugged off with a remark on the irrelevance to art of exact consistency, even to art distinguished by its verisimilitude. But I am not sure that there is any basic inconsistency. It is the nature of the pilgrim to admire all kinds of superlatives, and the fact that he often admires superlatives devoid of—or opposed to—genuine virtue does not inhibit his equal admiration for virtue incarnate. He is not, after all, a bad man; he is, to place him in his literary tradition, merely an average man, or mankind: *homo,* not very *sapiens* to be sure, but with the very best intentions, making his pilgrimage

through the world in search of what is good, and showing himself, too frequently, able to recognize the good only when it is spectacularly so. Spenser's Una glows with a kind of spontaneous incandescence, so that the Red Cross Knight, mankind in search of holiness, knows her as good; but he thinks that Duessa is good, too. Virtue concretely embodied in Una or the Parson presents no problems to the well-intentioned observer, but in a world consisting mostly of imperfections, accurate evaluations are difficult for a pilgrim who, like mankind, is naïve. The pilgrim's ready appreciation for the virtuous characters is perhaps the greatest tribute that could be paid to their virtue, and their spiritual simplicity is, I think, enhanced by the intellectual simplicity of the reporter.

The pilgrim belongs, of course, to a very old—and very new—tradition of the fallible first person singular. His most exact modern counterpart is perhaps Lemuel Gulliver who, in his search for the good, failed dismally to perceive the difference between the pursuit of reason and the pursuit of reasonable horses: one may be sure that the pilgrim would have whinnied with the best of them. In his own century he is related to Long Will of *Piers Plowman,* a more explicit seeker after the good, but just as unswerving in his inability correctly to evaluate what he sees. Another kinsman is the protagonist of the *Pearl,* mankind whose heart is set on a transitory good that has been lost—who, for very natural reasons, confuses earthly with spiritual values. Not entirely unrelated is the protagonist of Gower's *Confessio Amantis,* an old man seeking for an impossible earthly love that seems to him the only good. And in more subtle fashion there is the teller of Chaucer's story of ***Troilus and Cressida***, who, while not a true protagonist, performs some of the same functions. For this unloved "servant of the servants of love" falls in love with Cressida so persuasively that almost every male reader of the poem imitates him, so that we all share the heartbreak of Troilus and sometimes, in the intensity of our heartbreak, fail to learn what Troilus did. Finally, of course, there is Dante of the *Divine Comedy,* the most exalted member of the family and perhaps the immediate original of these other first-person pilgrims.

Artistically the device of the *persona* has many functions, so integrated with one another that to try to sort them out produces both oversimplification and distortion. The most obvious, with which this paper has been dealing—distortedly, is to present a vision of the social world imposed on one of the moral world. Despite their verisimilitude most, if not all, of the characters described in the Prologue are taken directly from stock and recur again and again in medieval literature. Langland in his own Prologue and elsewhere depicts many of them: the hunting monk, the avaricious friar, the thieving miller, the hypocritical pardoner, the unjust stewards, even, in little, the all-too-human nun. But while Langland uses the device of the *persona* with considerable skill in the conduct of his allegory, he uses it hardly at all in portraying the inhabitants of the social world: these are described directly, with the poet's own voice. It was left to Chaucer to turn the ancient stock satirical characters into real people assembled for a pilgrimage, and to have them described, with all their traditional faults upon them, by another pilgrim who records faithfully each fault without, for the most part, recognizing that it is a fault and frequently felicitating its possessor for possessing it. One result—though not the only result—is a moral realism much more significant than the literary realism which is a part of it and for which it is sometimes mistaken; this moral realism discloses a world in which humanity is prevented by its own myopia, the myopia of the describer, from seeing what the dazzlingly attractive externals of life really represent. In most of the analogues mentioned above the fallible first person receives, at the end of the book, the education he has needed: the pilgrim arrives somewhere. Chaucer never completed the *Canterbury Tales*, but in the Prologue to the **"Parson's Tale"** he seems to have been doing, rather hastily, what his contemporaries had done: when, with the sun nine-and-twenty degrees from the horizon, the twenty-nine pilgrims come to a certain—unnamed—*thropes ende*, then the pilgrimage seems no longer to have Canterbury as its destination, but rather, I suspect, the Celestial City of which the Parson speaks.

If one insists that Chaucer was not a moralist but a comic writer (a distinction without a difference), then the device of the *persona* may be taken primarily as serving comedy. It has been said earlier that the several Chaucers must have inhabited one body, and in that sense the fictional first person is no fiction at all. In an oral tradition of literature the first person probably always shared the personality of his creator: thus Dante of the *Divine Comedy* was physically Dante the Florentine; the John Gower of the *Confessio* was also Chaucer's friend John Gower; and Long Will was, I am sure, some one named William Langland, who was both long and wilful. And it is equally certain that Chaucer the pilgrim, "a popet in an arm t'enbrace," was in every physical respect Chaucer the man, whom one can imagine reading his work to a courtly audience, as in the portrait appearing in one of the MSS. of *Troilus*. One can imagine also the delight of the audience which heard the Prologue read in this way, and which was aware of the similarities and dissimilarities between Chaucer, the man before them, and Chaucer the pilgrim, both of whom they could see with simultaneous vision. The Chaucer they knew was physically, one gathers, a little ludicrous; a bourgeois, but one who was known as a practical and successful man of the court; possessed perhaps of a certain diffidence of manner, reserved, deferential to the socially imposing persons with whom he was associated; a bit absent-minded, but affable and, one supposes, very good company—a good fellow; sagacious and highly perceptive. This Chaucer was telling them of another who, lacking some of his chief qualities, nevertheless possessed many of his characteristics, though in a different state of balance, and each one probably distorted just enough to become laughable without becoming unrecognizable: deference into a kind of snobbishness, affability into an over-readiness to please, practicality into Babbittry, perception into inspection, absence of mind into dimness of wit; a Chaucer acting in some respects just as Chaucer himself might have acted but unlike his creator the kind of man, withal, who could mistake a group of stock satirical types for living persons endowed with all

sorts of superlative qualities. The constant interplay of these two Chaucers must have produced an exquisite and most ingratiating humor—as, to be sure, it still does. This comedy reaches its superb climax when Chaucer the pilgrim, resembling in so many ways Chaucer the poet, can answer the Host's demand for a story only with a rhyme he "lerned longe agoon"— **"Sir Thopas,"** which bears the same complex relation to the kind of romance it satirizes and to Chaucer's own poetry as Chaucer the pilgrim does to the pilgrims he describes and to Chaucer the poet.

E. Talbot Donaldson   (essay date 1958)

SOURCE: "Troilus and Criseide," in *Chaucer's Poetry: An Anthology for the Modern Reader,* Scott, Foresman and Company, 1975, pp. 1129-44.

[*In the following excerpt from an essay originally published in 1958. Donaldson presents the theme of* Troilus and Criseyde *as a paradoxical statement in which Chaucer asserts both the importance and the transitory nature of human values.*]

Chaucer's longest single poem is his greatest artistic achievement and one of the greatest in English literature. It possesses to the highest degree that quality, which characterizes most great poetry, of being always open to reinterpretation, of yielding different meanings to different generations and kinds of readers, who, no matter how they may disagree with one another on even its most important points, nevertheless agree in sharing the profoundly moving experience the poem offers them. Its highly elusive quality, which not only permits but encourages a multiplicity of interpretations, is in no way the result of incompetence on the part of the poet, but something carefully sought after as the best way of expressing a complex vision.

Chaucer is believed to have completed the work about 1385 or 1386, with some fifteen years of productivity remaining to him. Only extraordinary resourcefulness could bring it about that, having accomplished in *Troilus* what might well seem the principal work of his life, he was able to turn to other themes and other attitudes with undiminished energy and enthusiasm for experimentation. Readers occasionally wonder why romantic love—which is both a theme and an attitude—plays so little part in the *Canterbury Tales* that employed the last years of his life: the explanation lies in *Troilus*. Chaucer was apparently aware that he could not surpass his own treatment of this subject. And magnificent as the Canterbury collection is, both in the large conception and in the individual tales, *Troilus'* grandeur remains unsurpassed.

The source of the poem is one of Boccaccio's youthful works, the *Filostrato* (the Love-Stricken, according to Boccaccio's false etymology), a passionate narrative of 5700 lines in stanzaic Italian verse, completed before 1350, probably about 1340. Boccaccio's poem, in the original

Italian and in a French translation, furnished Chaucer the essential plot, most of the narrative details—though Chaucer made a number of important additions—and even with a number of lines readily adapted to translation into English. Yet the qualities of the two poems are entirely different, and Chaucer's is, artistically speaking, by far the more original. In the clear, brilliant light of the Italian work everything seems fully realized, fully understood. One reads with interest, admiration, and excitement: the mind's eye is filled. Yet there is little in the poem that does not meet the eye, and the reader does not tend to re-create what he has seen after he no longer sees it. By contrast, Chaucer's poem is mist-enshrouded: the sun does, indeed, break through at times, but things are difficult to see steadily for more than a short period, reappear in changed shape, become illusory, vanish; as the poem progresses one finds oneself groping more and more in a world where forms are indistinct but have infinite suggestiveness; the mind creates and re-creates; and at the end one has not so much beheld an experience objectively as lived it in the emotions.

As in so many of Chaucer's poems, the guise of the narrator is important to an interpretation of the work. At the outset this seems to be the familiar one of the unloved servant of the God of Love, the man whose inexperience renders him singularly ill-fitted to write a romance, but who will nevertheless perform the pious act of translating—of all things!—an unhappy love story. As in the *Parliament of Fowls*, the value of love within the poem is heightened by the narrator's exclusion from it, his yearning toward it. But this lyrical function of the narrator is in *Troilus* less important than his dual, paradoxical function as a historian whose knowledge of the story is wholly book-derived and as an invisible yet omnipresent participant in the action. It is as a historian that he first presents himself—a rather fussy, nervous scholar who has got hold of some old books, particularly one by Lollius, that tell the story of the Trojan lovers. This he means to translate, although he complains that his sources fail to give as much information as they ought. Nevertheless, they present the essentials: the sorrow Troilus suffered before he won Criseide, and how she forsook him in the end (Bk. I). Starting out with such inadequate and unpromising data, the historian proceeds to recreate the story as if he himself were living it without knowing its outcome. His second guise, that of the participant, unlike the guise of the historian, is largely implicit, a matter of the emotional intensity and lack of objectivity with which he approaches the characters. As the poem proceeds, the tension between the two attitudes, the historian dealing with incontrovertible fact, the participant speaking from equally incontrovertible emotional experience, increases until it becomes almost unendurable. By the beginning of Book IV the narrator's love for Criseide has become such that when he finds himself forced to face the issue of her perfidy he comes close to denying the truth of his old books. *For how Criseide Troilus forsook*, he begins, forthrightly enough; but reluctance to credit the bare statement causes him to soften it:

> Or at the leeste, how that she was unkinde,
> Moot hennesforth been matere of my book,

As writen folk thurgh which it is in minde:
Allas that they sholde evere cause finde
To speke hire harm—and if they on hire lie,
Ywis, hemself sholde han the vilainye.

It is a strange historian who becomes so emotionally involved with the personages of his history that he is willing to impugn the reliability of the sources upon which his whole knowledge of those personages presumably depends.

These two divergent attitudes of the narrator come to form an image of the philosophical speculation that permeates much of the poem: is it possible in this world to maintain a single firm idea of the reality of any given human situation or character? This speculation may be best illustrated in its bearing on Criseide, upon whom so much of the emotional force of the poem centers. History records the literal fact that Criseide proved, in the end, unworthy of the love Troilus bore her. This is the flattest, most basic, and least assailable of realities. (At the time Chaucer was writing, Criseide's character may not yet have suffered the deterioration that, by Shakespeare's time, made her a kind of literary model of the unfaithful woman; nevertheless Chaucer's method of handling her is essentially what it would have been if the process had already taken place.) Despite our knowledge of the ending, the narrator's loving presentation of Criseide in the course of the poem makes us feel the powerful attraction that brought about Troilus' love; and we are even persuaded that she was worthy of it. Indeed, *Troilus* gains something of the poignancy of the elegy by the very fact that we are aware of Criseide's eventual perfidy at the same time the narrator is depicting the profound spell she casts—just as we know that Blanche, in the *Book of the Duchess*, is dead even while the Black Knight describes the charm of her vitality. History tends to pronounce judgment on the final perfidy of Criseide as effectively nullifying her positive worth as a human being; but the historical point of view does not exhaust the reality of Criseide as the heroine of the poem.

It is true that at the end of the poem we are left with two widely different versions of Criseide's reality, versions made mutually exclusive by the conventions of romance. These conventions make it impossible for a heroine worthy of love to prove faithless; and ultimately we must, of course, bow to the fact of her faithlessness. We must remember, however, that it was Chaucer's aim to make the reader suffer vicariously the experience of Troilus. The poet therefore creates in the person of Criseide one of the most alluring of heroines; and more, he persuades us that her downfall does not so much falsify our first judgment of her as compel us to see the tragic nature of reality, in which the best so often becomes the worst.

Criseide's most emphatically displayed characteristic is amiability—that is, lovability: she has almost all the qualities that men might hope to encounter in their first loves. This is perhaps the same as saying that she is above all feminine, suggesting for a young man like Troilus the compelling mystery and challenge of her sex. She is lovely in appearance, demure yet self-possessed, capable of both gaiety and gravity, glamorous in the truest sense of the word. Although she says nothing really witty, she responds to Pandarus' wit in such a way as to seem witty; her constant awareness of implications beneath the surface of the situation suggests, if it does not prove, intelligence. With her uncle and with Troilus she has the curiously endearing charm that arises from her consciousness, humorously and wryly expressed, of her own complicity in the events that befall her. The grace and tenderness with which she finally yields to Troilus (Bk. III) are almost magically appealing.

[Chaucer] creates in the person of Criseide one of the most alluring of heroines; and . . . he persuades us that her downfall does not so much falsify our first judgment of her as compel us to see the tragic nature of reality, in which the best so often becomes the worst.

—*E. Talbot Donaldson*

But Chaucer did something more than present Criseide as the completely agreeable heroine; he also suggested in her a really complex human being, filled with all sorts of latent qualities which are much more than mere enhancements of her magnetism. Chaucer's presentation, indeed, is so full as to invite his readers to find in Criseide the seeds of her eventual falseness; but Criseide's potentialities as a human being, so brilliantly sketched as partly to justify calling *Troilus* a psychological novel, elude us in the end. Several excellent critics have purported to find in this or that one of her qualities the definitive clue to her betrayal, but others continue to feel that the mainsprings of her action lie hidden. It seems to follow that if the poet were trying to make her motivation psychologically clear, he failed badly. It is, however, certain that this was not his purpose. Instead, he meant to present in Criseide a broad range of the undefined but recognizable potentialities inherent in human nature.

Our longest and seemingly most penetrating view into Criseide's character is afforded by Book II, when we are shown her reactions to the news her uncle brings her about Troilus' love. These reactions are filled with apparent clues to her basic character, but when analyzed they lead to the ambiguous conclusions. Criseide is much concerned with Troilus' high estate as a prince of Troy, and this concern might be interpreted as indicative of opportunism; conversely, because her already precarious situation in the city might make it dangerous to refuse him, her concern might be interpreted as fearfulness. If the fact of her concern, regardless of what it springs from, is taken as an indication of an overcalculating nature, then the impression is counterbalanced by her involuntary moment of intoxication when she sees Troilus, in all his martial glory, riding homeward from battle. This incident in turn might suggest an oversensual nature; but the circumspection with which, a little later, she considers the whole affair might

well reinforce an impression of her frigidity. Again, her inability to make up her mind might be taken to prove her indecisiveness and ineffectuality; on the other hand, since the problems she is facing are entirely realistic, it might be used to prove her native practicality.

The narrator is of singularly little assistance to the reader who is trying to solve the enigma. On every crucial psychological issue both he and his old books are silent. We do not know, though we may suspect, what Criseide thought when Pandarus told her Troilus was out of town the day she came to dine. We never know to what extent she was influenced by her uncle's specious, often self-contradictory, arguments. And the narrator's explanations are even worse than his silences. For instance, just after Criseide experiences the moment of intoxication mentioned above, the narrator pauses to consider the hypothetical objection of some envious person that she was falling in love too fast (Bk. II). With a fine show of indignation he protests that she did not fall in love immediately: she merely began to incline toward Troilus, who had to win her with long service. The effect of this kind of explanation—of which there are a number in the poem—is complex, not to say chaotic. The reader, who may never have thought that Criseide is proceeding too fast, is suddenly encouraged to think she is by the narrator's gratuitous denial. The reader is made, as it were, an involuntary critic of the action instead of a mere spectator. Moreover, he is made to judge Criseide according to a norm that the narrator's tone assumes to be well known but that is in fact undefined and totally unknown, namely, the decorous rate of speed with which a woman should fall in love. Finally, having cleared Criseide of a charge which only he has made, the narrator asserts, in the very next stanza, that it was not her fault but Troilus' destiny that she should fall in love with him so soon. Analyzed by the intellect alone, the passage seems to suggest that Criseide did fall in love too quickly. Yet it precedes the far longer one in which she considers the whole matter so carefully that some critics have accused her of proceeding too deliberately!

The fact is that we do not read poetry with the intellect alone, and that when poetry makes two contradictory statements they do not cancel each other out. Both remain as part of the essential poetic truth, which is not the same thing at all as logic. There is surely no abstract, logical, ideal course of action for a woman falling in love, but we can recognize the process as being truly represented by Criseide. Some parts of her nature are driving her forward with a speed that is utterly terrifying to the rest of her nature, and a bewildering variety of motives assert themselves in turn. But however we analyze these, in the long run we can say with assurance only that they are human. Any one of them, given a development which the poem resolutely refuses to permit, might become the reason for her eventual betrayal: mere timidity, mere opportunism, mere sensuality, mere inefficiency—even mere femininity. As it stands, however, we are emotionally no more prepared for the denouement than Troilus, though we have had one important advantage over him: we have been permitted to see, and have been disturbed by, suggestions of depths in Criseide that her lover could not have seen.

Our confidence in her is less serene, particularly as a result of the narrator's reassurances. It may be that her very elusiveness makes us nervous. If so, that is as it should be, since the only possible resolution of the two realities mentioned earlier lies in the unpredictability, the instability, of even the most lovely of mortal women.

Just as in later literature Criseide was to become the type of a faithless woman, so her charming, witty, intelligent uncle Pandarus was, by a worse fate, to become the type of a pimp. In a long conversation in Book III Pandarus and Troilus discuss, among other things, the implications of Pandarus' helping Troilus win Criseide. The conclusion they come to is less than satisfactory: Pandarus' help is not the act of a procurer because he receives no reward for it. Thereafter the matter is not one of the overt issues of the poem, though in his last speech to Troilus Pandarus reverts to it almost as if he foresaw the deterioration of his name Pandar to pander. And while not overt, the issue once raised can never be wholly banished from the mind. Parallel to the question the poem raises about Criseide, "Is her reality that of a worthy lover or that of an unfaithful wench?" is the question it raises about Pandarus' assistance of Troilus: "Is this the action of a loyal friend or of a mere pimp?"

History—in this case later literary history—has answered the question to the detriment of Pandarus, but the answer this poem gives is less absolute. The reader is assured by everyone—by Troilus, by Pandarus himself, by the narrator—that what Pandarus does is done wholly because of his devotion to Troilus, and surely the moralist must admit that human action is qualified by the motives of the agent. Yet, just as was the case with Criseide, when we watch his character in action we seem to glimpse potentials—undefined, to be sure—that are not of a piece with the notion of a friend acting with entire altruism. In general he seems, like his niece, a person of great charm: gay, cheerful, witty, mocking and self-mocking, friendly, helpful, practical, intelligent, sympathetic, loyal—one could hardly wish for a better companion or friend. But despite these qualities, one's confidence in him does not remain altogether secure. Perhaps his pleasure in arranging this affair is too great. The brilliant comedy he performs at the lovers' bedside—a touch of the **"Miller's Tale"**—is perhaps suggestive of some vital flaw in his nature (and the narrator does nothing to improve the situation by failing to send Pandarus off to his own chamber). Even the delightful scene of Pandarus' visit to Criseide's bedside after Troilus has departed is not without a hint of prurience. In the long run, it maybe said of the complexity of Pandarus, as of the complexity of Criseide, that it displays such a rich array of human qualities that we are at a loss in analyzing his ultimate motives and character.

Pandarus bears a relation to the problem of reality—and hence to the philosophical speculation that is carried on in the poem—in another way. He is what would generally be called today a thoroughgoing realist. Paradoxically, this seems to mean that he has no respect for reality at all. For him, things are whatever one makes them. To accomplish a given action, all one has to do is manipulate the situation so as to produce the proper pressures on the actors. It does not matter in the least if these pressures are in reality non-existent; it only matters that the actors should think them real. In putting his philosophy to work, Pandarus becomes the master-spinner of illusions. A persecutor from whom Criseide needs protection is conjured up out of thin air. A dinner party is manipulated with excruciating attention to detail so that Criseide may be introduced to Troilus under the most respectable of circumstances. When Criseide must be induced to receive Troilus in her bedchamber, a rival lover named Horaste, whom Criseide had never smiled upon and Troilus had never felt jealous of, emerges full-blown from Pandarus' fertile mind to produce the necessary pressure. And if Pandarus cannot actually produce rain, his foreknowledge that rain will come serves the magician's purpose of insuring that his dinner guest will stay the night. The love affair itself seems to result largely from the illusions Pandarus creates for the paralyzed Troilus and the passive Criseide. One would not be surprised if he were to dictate Troilus' first letter to Criseide and then to dictate her response, so close does he come to being the author of a living fiction.

Upon the significance of all this illusion-spinning the poem makes no overt comment. It even fails to distinguish clearly between real and illusory pressures exerted on Criseide: for instance, we do not know whether Pandarus' account of his discovering Troilus' love-sicknesses is in the realm of fact or merely a charming invention with which to please Criseide. But in the poem's totality the implications of Pandarus' illusions cannot be avoided, because we know that in the end Criseide's love of Troilus will prove to be a kind of illusion. Moreover, the dominant role the illusions play in the love affair, whether commented on or not, forces them on our consciousness, and once more we experience a sense of insecurity. This is embodied in the poem by the interchange between the lovers when their love is consummated; both of them, especially Troilus, express uncertainty whether such bliss can in fact be true.

Pandarus continues a realist and a would-be manipulator of realities until the end, when reality defeats him. His first reaction on hearing that Criseide must leave the city is that the love affair is finished. He tries to persuade Troilus to give her up, to forget about her, and when that practical approach fails, as it is doomed to, he tries another equally practical one, equally doomed to fail: forcefully to prevent her going. When Troilus replies, with his usual integrity, that he cannot constrain Criseide against her will, Pandarus observes that if Criseide consents to leave Troy, Troilus must consider her false. With this speech—which, incidentally, is the most strikingly revealing of several of Pandarus' reflections on Criseide in the last two books—his effective role in the poem is completed. From then on all he can do is act as go-between. His efforts to rearrange reality in order to preserve the love affair are paltry and futile. After Criseide's departure from Troy we see him upholding Troilus' hopes even when he himself recognizes their futility, and while in the earlier books Pandarus' attempts to uphold illusion did not seem offensive, now they seem the work of a half-hearted trickster. It is almost as if the reality he had tortured were having its revenge on him by redefining his actions as those of a mere procurer: for Criseide, after all, becomes little better than a whore. In the end Pandarus—and Pandarus alone—accepts history's version of Criseide: by saying, in his pathetic last speech, that he hates her, he makes clear that for him any other value she may have seemed to possess has been canceled out. He submits to the ultimate reality as Troilus, who can never "unlove" Criseide, refuses to do; yet one has felt that Pandarus' love for his niece was, in its way, as great as Troilus'.

Troilus, the hero of the poem and the most important of its personages, may seem in some respects less interesting than Pandarus or Criseide. If, however, he lacks their human variety, his *trouthe,* his integrity, makes him in the long run a more fully realized person. This integrity, the quality that he will not surrender even to keep Criseide with him, is the one human value the poem leaves entirely unquestioned: it is because of it that Troilus is granted his ultimate vision. It places him, of course, in sharp contrast with Criseide and her *untrouthe,* and since one of the meanings of *trouthe* is reality, he emerges as more real than she. The sad fact that integrity does him no practical good does not in any way impair its value; indeed, its value seems enhanced by its preventing him, at least on one occasion, from attaining an apparent good. If he had been a different person—a Diomede, for instance—he might well have used force to stop Criseide's exchange. This is what Pandarus advises and what both narrator and reader momentarily find themselves hoping for. But Troilus is acutely aware of both the public and the private implications of such an act. Criseide's exchange had been legally determined by the parliament and duly ratified by King Priam, and to prevent it forcefully would be to substitute anarchy for law: the Trojan war had itself been caused by Paris' rape of Queen Helen, and to seize Criseide would be once again to risk precipitating endless violent countermeasures. Furthermore, according to the medieval conventions of courtly love, the lover was the servant of his mistress—as the word *mistress* still suggests—and for the servant to overrule the mistress was unthinkable. As it frequently does, the courtly convention here merely articulates a real factor in the relationship of civilized men and women. A lover cannot impose his will upon his love, for unless she remains at all times possessed of free will, love itself becomes meaningless and the love affair vitiated. Similarly, to seize her would be inevitably to disclose their love affair and ruin her good name, which, according to the courtly code, he was sworn to protect. In view of these matters, for Troilus to "ravish" Criseide would be for him to violate his own nature, which, as Criseide perceives, is one of moral virtue, grounded upon truth.

But if Troilus is the only unequivocally worthwhile person in the poem, why, one must ask, is he its principal sufferer? Troilus ascribes his misery to the operation of Fortune, or malevolent fate. A heavy atmosphere of fatality does, indeed, hang over the poem, so that even if the reader had not been told the outcome of the love affair he might feel it inevitable that Troilus should in the end fall, like Troy. Yet with one exception all the specific incidents, although the narrator may invoke for them the causality of the

stars, seem equally attributable to the action of one of the three actors in the love tragedy. The exception is the intervention of Criseide's forgotten father Calchas, an intervention that comes from his sure foreknowledge of the city's doom and that is beyond the control of Pandarus or the lovers. Elsewhere causality is ambiguous. For instance, the narrator ascribes to astrological influences entirely remote from Criseide's control the rain which prevented Criseide's leaving her uncle's house. On the other hand, we are aware that the rain had been foreseen by Pandarus, so that what may be deemed fate in its relation to Criseide is at the same time mere machination on the part of Pandarus. Nor are we sure enough of Criseide's state of mind in accepting her uncle's invitation—the narrator has been marvelously ambiguous about that too—clearly to exonerate her from an acquiescence in a foreseen fate so prompt as to make fate's role negligible. But here as elsewhere the impression of fatal influence is not canceled out by the impression of human responsibility: both impressions remain and even unite into a single impression poetically truer than either by itself. Similarly, Troilus' failure to prevent Criseide from leaving Troy, while it is the result of his own free will, might still be ascribed to fate, for in order to have stopped her Troilus would have had to be someone other than Troilus, and this he could not be.

In a more universal and more tragic sense, the impossibility of a human being's becoming anything but what he is is one of the principal points—perhaps the principal point—that the poem makes, and it is toward this point that the poem has been steadily moving. The form, as has been said above, is that of a history, the end of which is known, being lived by personages who do not know their end, and presented at times as if neither narrator nor reader knows it. Preoccupied constantly during the presentation with the charm and delight of humanity as represented by Criseide and Pandarus, we can little more believe that things will turn out as they do than can Troilus. The fact that they turn out as they do almost seems, at times, a violation of our idea of reality; within the poem we are now and again apt to ascribe the ending to a malevolent fate which, in order to bring about what it foresees, contorts and constrains events and persons from their natural course. This is the ultimate conclusion of which Troilus is capable in his lifetime. His long soliloquy in Book IV on predestination and free will comes in its tortured circularity to nothing more than a statement that what God has foreseen must be—that free will does not exist. This soliloquy, of course, precedes any suspicion on his part of Criseide's infidelity, so that he is not forced to consider the problem of her free will operating evilly. When suspicions have once occurred, he is no longer able to think even as clearly as he does here, but vacillates pathetically between the two conflicting realities, Criseide's apparently true love and Criseide's faithlessness. His still relatively happy ignorance stops him in his soliloquy from going to the extreme of accusing his god of devising a plot that does not fit its characters; but this is an accusation that occasional readers have, with some reason, made against Chaucer the poet, just as Chaucer the narrator comes close to making it against his old books.

But to the profoundly medieval, profoundly Christian Chaucer there could be no other plot because there could be no other characters. According to some medieval thinkers, the whole duty of the historian was to find in recorded history the image of instability: it is in this sense that the **"Monk's Tale"** presents history, bad as the tale is. The premise underlying such a definition of history is that natural, fallen man is unstable. Chaucer, while surely not bound to any arbitrary point of view, presents in *Troilus and Criseide* a pattern of human instability. Criseide is its chief exponent in terms of human character; Pandarus in terms of human action. Troilus comes, because of his *trouthe,* as near to stability as man may come; but within a world where mutation is the law—and in a world in which the stability of a Christian God does not exist—it does him no good. Given Boethius or Christian doctrine, Troilus might have progressed beyond the point he does in his soliloquy on foreordination. As it is, he concludes where Boethius began in his *Consolation of Philosophy,* before Philosophy had persuaded him that he must not commit himself wholly and exclusively to this unstable world. Troilus' *trouthe* is, as has been said above, a real value; but within the terms set by the poem, it must remain only a moral value, imitating one aspect of God, who is *Trouthe,* but hopelessly limited in other respects. Despite its alternate meaning, reality, it cannot help Troilus perceive ultimate reality, which only God can perceive; conversely, it cannot defend him against illusion—the illusion of Criseide's stability, of the enduring power of human love. It cannot, in short, enable him to see that of all the conflicting realities the poem presents none is in the end real, since compared to the reality of God no earthly substance has reality.

The poem comes to its tragic conclusion by no such bald statement as the above. We have seen how in the ambiguity of the characterization of Criseide and Pandarus there has been, since the beginning, the potential of instability. One might say that in their very elusiveness, their unknowability, resides equally the image of unreality. And we have since the beginning been fully aware of where the story is leading, though our willingness to forget is the product of Chaucer's art. As the poem approaches its climax—or anticlimax—the poet so manipulates us that while we continue our intense involvement with the characters, we begin to see them increasingly in the light of historical generalization. Halfway through the fifth book this manipulation appears most brilliantly. It is the ninth night after Criseide's departure, and we are taken to the Greek camp to see how she is faring with her plots to return to Troy, as she had promised, on the tenth day. Her pathetic soliloquy, so futile, so devoid of resource, so spiritless, leaves us infinitely saddened. The narrator, seemingly in hot pursuit of his story, turns quickly to Diomede, and for a moment we enter that blunt, aggressive, unillusioned mind. Diomede's interior monologue completed, the narrator, as if suddenly recalling his own failure to characterize Diomede earlier, gives us a one stanza pen-portrait of him. And then, by a curious afterthought, he gives a three-stanza description of Criseide and a two-stanza description of Troilus. The quality of these is, contextually, strange in the extreme: they are impersonal, trivial, oversimplified—as if a historian had collected all the information there was about several persons of no special significance and were listing it, not because of its inherent interest, but because the historian's duty is to assemble and preserve any sort of scraps turned up during his research. And indeed these scraps are in a very real sense the oldest historical material relating to the story of Troilus and Criseide, the sparse material from which the full-grown story eventually sprang. Chaucer's source for the portraits is not Boccaccio, but rather a sixth-century narrative of the fall of Troy ascribed to Dares the Phrygian. This book pads out its paltry fiction with brief descriptions of important people concerned with the Trojan war, among them Diomede, Troilus, and Criseide, described just as Chaucer describes them in Book V but still some centuries removed from the relationship later writers were to give them. When, nearing the end of his poem, Chaucer saw that it was time to turn from the guise of the passionately committed participant to the guise of the objective, remote, detached historian, he did so with a vengeance. Perhaps nowhere else in the poem are the two conflicting versions of reality more boldly juxtaposed. Certainly nowhere else is the shock so great as when the historian, having listed a miscellany of Criseide's attributes, some trivial but all agreeable enough, brings the portrait to the muted conclusion:

> Tendre-herted, sliding of corage—
> But trewely I can nat telle hir age.

Sliding of corage: the simple unemphatic statement of Criseide's instability of heart is not even the climax of the portrait. From the point of view of the realistic historian, human nature is capable only of anticlimax.

The sudden re-emergence of the detached historian at this point in Book V provides a kind of foretaste of the dominant mood in which the poem concludes; but the narrator's other guise continues to reappear whenever Criseide is mentioned. Indeed, Chaucer's manipulation of the two guises, and through them of the reader, is nowhere more adroit than in his handling of Criseide's betrayal. Time and again while the narrative inexorably demonstrates the progress of her infidelity the narrator leaps to her defense, and by the very inadequacy of the defense reinforces the reader's condemnation of her. The most striking instance of this technique occurs after Diomede has visited Criseide on the eleventh day, when she has already broken her promise to Troilus. The interview she has with Diomede is not described; instead the narrator rapidly summarizes all the later history of her amorous dealings with the Greek. And then, having given to the whole history of her treachery the emotional impact of a single action committed in a day or two, he indignantly asserts that while his books are silent on this subject, all this successful wooing by Diomede must have taken a long time! As if this were not enough, he carries us back to Troy to show us Troilus, standing on the walls, still scanning the outlying roads for his beloved. Months of action have rushed by in the Greek camp, but in Troy it is still only the tenth day, the day Criseide is to return.

Thus the poem moves with mounting emotional force to its conclusion. The actual ending of the poem—generally though incorrectly called its epilogue—gathers up with extraordinary effectiveness the many moods and many attitudes which have alternated in the course of the narrative. There is both low and high comedy—and perhaps high truth, too—in the poet's prayer to "every lady bright of hue," that she not blame him for Criseide's faithlessness, and in his baldly illogical claim that he has told the story "not only" that men should beware of women but "mostly" that women should beware of men. There is comedy also in the poet's self-conscious fear that he has failed to make himself clear, that readers will mis-scan his lines and miss his meaning. The works of the great poets of the past with which he fears his "little book" (of more than eight thousand lines) might be compared make him nervous. His successive echoes of the first line of the *Aeneid* and of the first line of the *Iliad* suggest that he is afraid he ought to have written not a love poem but a martial epic—if only he were up to it. In any case, may God give him power to write a comedy.

These outbursts of nervousness—which are perhaps a kind of mocking image of man's inability to make sense of the materials his own history provides him—intrude upon the story before it is actually finished, and almost by an afterthought the poet returns to it in order to tell the end of Troilus. Inevitably enough, history does not permit Troilus to kill Diomede or to be killed by him: even that meager satisfaction is denied to our sense of the way things ought to be. Instead, Troilus is killed by Achilles. Only when he has been thus freed from his earthly misery is he rewarded for his earthly fidelity: he is admitted into heaven, a heaven that is physically pagan but theologically Christian. (It is not the first time in medieval literature that *trouthe* allows a non-Christian to enter into a Christian heaven, for according to both Langland and Dante the same quality had raised to heaven the Emperor Trajan.) From his remote sphere Troilus is granted that vision of the world he lately left which enables him to see in full perspective the pettiness and fragility to which he had committed his being: his *trouthe,* finally receiving its philosophic extension, is made whole. But Troilus' is not the ultimate vision in the poem. His could come only after his death, but to the Christian reader the vision is possible at all times during his life. In the last lines of the poem Chaucer gathers up all the flickering emotions, the flickering loves with which he has been dealing and unites them into the great harmony of the only true and perfect love. All the conflicting realities and illusions of the old story are subsumed under the one supreme reality.

Thus the conclusion asserts most solemnly the principle—toward which the poem has been steadily moving—that man's nature and his works are and must be unstable and unreal. Some readers are apt to feel, however, that the poet's final statement cancels all the human values which his own loving treatment has made real; that he is, in effect, saying either that he ought not to have written the poem or that the reader ought not to have read it. This feeling is natural enough in view of Chaucer's entirely specific condemnation of all things mortal except man's ability to love God. But it must be borne in mind that the ending is a part of the poem, and no matter how sincere a statement it is on the part of the poet, the ending combines with all the other parts of the poem to produce the poem's own ultimate meaning. As has been said before, nothing a poet writes is ever canceled out by anything else he writes, and both the haunting loveliness of the story of Troilus and Criseide and the necessity of rejecting it remain valid for the reader. And also, one may suppose, for Chaucer. For the lines in which he condemns the world—

> . . . and thinketh al nis but a faire,
> This world that passeth soone as flowres faire—

poignantly enhance the very thing that he is repudiating. It is in the quality of these lines, taken as an epitome of the quality of the whole poem, that the ultimate meaning of *Troilus* lies. The simultaneous awareness of the real validity of human values—and hence our need to commit ourselves to them—and of their inevitable transitoriness—and hence our need to remain uncommitted—represents a complex, mature, truly tragic vision of mankind. The prayer of the poem's last stanza suggests the poet's faith that his vision is also subsumed under the vision of the Author of all things.

G. D. Josipovici   (essay date 1965)

SOURCE: "Fiction and Game in *The Canterbury Tales,*" in *The Critical Quarterly,* Vol. 7, No. 2, Summer, 1965, pp. 185-97.

[*In the following excerpt, Josipovici explains the function of the game motif as a method of resolving immoral aspects of the "Miller's Tale" and "The Pardoner's Prologue and Tale," and as a method of ironic self-revelation that reveals the folly of the pilgrims.*]

Wherever we turn in *The Canterbury Tales* [quotations are taken from *The Poetical Works of Chaucer,* ed. by F. N. Robinson (1933)] we are faced with a conflict between the moral and the immoral, the edifying and the unedifying, the religious and the secular. This conflict is first suggested by the narrator in the **"General Prologue"**; it provides the theme of a number of the headlinks; it forms the substance of the Pardoner's Prologue and Epilogue, and dominates the Parson's Prologue; and the work concludes with the Retractation, which appears to reflect Chaucer's final stand on this central issue. Yet *The Canterbury Tales,* unlike so many medieval works, including *Troilus and Criseyde,* does not find itself irremediably split in an attempted allegiance atone and the same time to the religious and to the secular. Although the conflict between the two stands at the centre of the poem it does not imply any submission by Chaucer to the conventions of his age at the expense of his artistic design. On the contrary, Chaucer uses this conflict to conduct a bold and original strategy whose aim is to free his poem from moral jurisdiction and ensure its autonomy as a fictional construct.

The first enunciation of the conflict occurs towards the close of the **"General Prologue."** The narrator has just finished telling of the dress, appearance, and number of the pilgrims, and explained why they were all assembled at the Tabard. Before going on with his story he pauses and addresses the reader:

> But first I pray yow, of youre curteisye,
> That ye n'arette it nat my vileynye,
> Thogh that I pleynly speke in this mateere,
> To telle yow hir wordes and hir cheere,
> Ne thogh I speke hir wordes proprely.
> For this ye knowen al so wel as I,
> Whoso shal telle a tale after a man,
> He moot reherce as ny as evere he kan
> Everich a word, if it be in his charge,
> Al speke he never so rudeliche and large,
> Or ellis he moot telle .
> He may nat spare, although he were his brother;
> He moot as wel seye o word as another.
> Crist spak hymself ful brode in hooly writ,
> And wel ye woot no vileynye is it.
> Eek Plato seith, whoso that kan hym rede,
> The wordes moote be cosyn to the dede.

On the face of it Chaucer is here merely protecting himself against possible charges of immorality. He is, he says, a mere reporter of stories and events. He writes down what he sees and hears, and he would be failing in his duty as impartial recorder were he to pass over in silence those tales that might cause offence: neither the manner nor the matter of the tales are to be imputed to him. The narrator appeals to a higher authority, truth, fidelity to fact, to exonerate him from charges of bawdiness. But beneath this concern lest he be accused of indecency lies another, and graver, concern: to free his poem from the bondage to reality and ensure its status as fiction. Paradoxically this can only be done by having the narrator insist on his purely reportorial status. The explanation of this paradox lies in the frequently noted fact that the pilgrim narrator of *The Canterbury Tales* is not to be identified with Chaucer, but is the poet's ironic creation. . . .

It is not only in the **"General Prologue"** that the pilgrim narrator affirms his purely reportorial status. He repeats his assertion in the Prologue to the **"Miller's Tale,"** where his passive role is emphasized by making the drunken miller insist on telling his bawdy tale despite the vigorous efforts of the Host and the Reeve to stop him. It seems that he is determined to tell his story whether the pilgrims like it or not, and the narrator warns his readers that those who are squeamish should move on to less offensive tales. And he concludes:

> The Millere is a cherl, ye knowe wel this;
> So was the Reve eek and othere mo,
> And harlotrie they tolden bothe two.
> Avyseth yow, and put me out of blame;
> And eek men shal nat maken ernest of game.

In other words, if the reader should choose to read the ensuing tale he should not be offended even if it does turn out to be bawdy because none of it is meant to be taken seriously, it is all part of a game. Chaucer is once more assuring us that this is a fiction and not to be confused with reality. Unlike the pilgrims, who must listen to the Miller whether they like it or not, the reader is free to skip the tale if he chooses; but even if he doesn't, to take offence at such a tale is to make the same sort of error as is made by those listeners who send money for the relief of the heroine of a radio serial. It is to forget that *The Canterbury Tales* is not a veridical report but a game played by Chaucer with his readers.

Chaucer is able to introduce the notion of game at this point because here his game with the reader coincides with another game, played within his poem by the pilgrims. It is the pilgrim narrator as well as the poet who insists that the words of the Miller are only a "game." The kind of relationship which Chaucer has established between himself, his poem, and the reader, is mirrored in the relationship established *within the poem* between the pilgrim storytellers, their material, and their audience.

It is the Host who first suggests that the pilgrims play a game to relieve the boredom of the journey to Canterbury, and it is he who lays down the rules for this game when the company assents to his suggestion. Each person is to tell two tales on the way to the shrine and two on the way back; the teller of the best tale is to be given dinner by all the other pilgrims; and anyone who fails to abide by the decisions of Harry Bailly is to pay a forfeit. The pilgrims agree to these rules, and, with the drawing of the shortest "cut" by the Knight on the following morning, the game is on. The ensuing tales, then, are not simply stories told to pass away the time on the road to Canterbury; they are part of a game, with rules of its own, which all the pilgrims have e of *The Canterbury Tales* stands a game, mirroring that other game, which poet and reader have agreed to play. Both games take place within a context of real life, but, because they are games, the participants are answerable to none of the laws which govern real life, but only to those rules which they have agreed upon beforehand.

The Host, who has set himself up as arbiter, has, it soon transpires, very clear ideas as to what it is he requires from a story. His words to the Clerk form perhaps the best summary of his attitude:

> Telle us som myrie tale, by youre fey!
> For what man that is entred in a pley,
> He nedes moot unto the pley assente.
> But precheth nat, as freres doon in Lente,
> To make us for oure olde synnes wepe,
> Ne that thy tale make us nat to slepe.

The primary requirement is that the story must not be boring. The Host is willing to listen to a tale in the high style or the low style, in prose or verse, a saint's life or a fabliau. But if he considers the tale boring then he has no hesitation in cutting it short and asking for something better. The ultimate crime of the story-teller is to send his audience to sleep, for to do so is to destroy the very *raison d'être* of the story: you cannot very well tell a tale without listeners, as he points out to the Monk.

It is partly for this reason too that the Host warns pilgrim after pilgrim not to preach. A sermon for the Host represents the acme of boredom. But there is another reason for his dislike of preaching, which is related to the desire that a story should hold the listener's interest, but which must not be confused with it. What the Host particularly dislikes about preaching is that the preacher has designs on his listeners. Although Harry Bailly never loses a chance to attack or ridicule preachers, he has nothing against them as such. His attitude is that they have no place in his game. The whole point of a game, after all, is that it is freely joined, that the only laws are the rules that have been agreed upon beforehand. Hence propaganda of any sort, however exalted the motive, has no place in a game.

The Parson is obviously the chief offender in this respect. In the **"General Prologue"** we see him as an ideal figure who, with the Knight, the Plowman and the Clerk is contrasted to all the other pilgrims by the fact that with him the word does indeed stick close to the deed: "first he wroughte, and afterwards he taughte." In all the other ecclesiastics—and most of the laymen—the gap between the word and the deed, the habit and the person, is more or less large, and one of the functions of the irony in the **"General Prologue"** is to reveal the degree of deviation. In the Prologue we are given an idealized description of the Parson, and we have to accept it since we are not allowed to see him in action. But later, on two separate occasions before he tells his own tale we do so see him, and in both he is involved in a quarrel with the Host.

In the Epilogue to the **"Man of Law's Tale"** Harry Bailly turns to him and asks him for a tale, "by Goddes dignitee." The Parson's only answer is to reprove him for swearing; whereupon he turns to the other pilgrims in mock surprise, and warns them that they "schal han a predicacioun," that "this Lollere heer wil prechen us somwhat." But at once the Shipman leaps in:

> "Nay by my fader soule, that schal he nat!"
> Seyde the Shipman; "heer schal he nat preche;
> He schal no gospel glosen here ne teche."

This time the Parson subsides into silence, but the next time he and Harry Bailly clash it is he who wins the victory. For some unknown reason Chaucer changed his mind about the number of tales he was going to tell, and in the Parson's Prologue it transpires that all the tales have been told except for that of the Parson. The Host thus turns to him:

> "Sire preest," quod he, "artow a vicary?
> Or arte a person? sey sooth, by thy fey!
> Be what thou be, ne breke thou nat oure pley;
> For every man, save thou, hath toold his tale . . .
> Telle us a fable anon, for cokkes bones!"

But once again the Parson reprehends him. He will take part in the "pley," but only on his own terms:

> "Thou getest fable noon ytoold for me;
> For Paul, that writeth unto Thymothee,
> Repreveth hem that weyven soothfastnesse,
> And tellen fables and swich wrecchednesse . . .
> For which I seye, if that yow list to heere
> Moralitee and vertuous mateere,
> And thanne that ye wol yeve me audience,
> I wol ful fayn, at Cristes reverence,
> Do you plesaunce leefful, as I kan."

The figure who emerges from these two scenes is not that of the ideal ecclesiastic of the **"General Prologue,"** but a type as common as the Friar and the Summoner: a medieval Puritan rigidly opposed to any form of swearing and to all but overtly moral tales on the grounds that they are lies and hence conducive to sin. And as we must weigh the words of the Friar and the Summoner against their deeds, so it would be incorrect to see Chaucer everywhere behind the Parson. Medieval scholars have for a long time now been stressing that it would be wrong to see the **"Parson's Tale"** as deliberately boring in the way that the **"Monk's"** is meant to be, and they have insisted that there is no irony in the apparent discrepancy between the Host's admonition to "be fructuous, and that in litel space," and the length and dryness of the ensuing sermon. Sermons in the middle ages were one of the only forms of entertainment, they remind us, and men were quite used to even longer ones than the Parson's. At the same time they have been pointing out that it was traditional in the middle ages to end a collection of tales with a particularly moral one, as Boccaccio does in the *Decameron,* for instance. Such warnings are certainly necessary, for there is nothing easier than to foist one's own sympathies on an ironic writer. But they tend, I believe, to do less than justice to Chaucer's artistry, and to blur the larger patterns of the poem.

In his *Essay on the "Vita Nuova"* C. S. Singleton has convincingly argued that only Dante, in the whole of the middle ages, was able to reconcile, artistically, human and divine love. Even ***Troilus and Criseyde***, so poised a work in almost every respect, ultimately fails to reconcile the two, and, however one may justify the moral with which it ends, is a lesser work for the failure. The problem, of course, is not simply one of reconciling the love of woman and the love of God. It is equally the problem of reconciling the work of art with the Cot rest in the creations of this world, but must use them to come to God. As such, the problem is less epistemological than artistic. Dante's solution was to make of Beatrice an analogy for Christ. Beatrice is not an allegory of Christ, as Renaissance interpreters believed. Only *through* her, as Singleton and Charles Williams have shown, can Dante come to God. The method of analogy was never Chaucer's, but in the ***Canterbury Tales*** he hit upon a solution that left him as much artistic freedom as Dante had enjoyed, but of a kind new to the middle ages. He stressed the fact that his poem was a fiction. What this means is that every episode, every statement in the poem is enveloped in a web of irony which cannot be broken by reference to laws or rules in operation outside the fictional construct. So that if, from one point of view we assent to the rightness of the Parson's telling the last tale of all, and accept as the necessary prelude to salvation a sermon on penitence, from another the ironic device of the fictional narrator permits us to question the validity of the Parson's methods, and frees us from taking at its face value the retractation which follows. The Parson's sermon becomes an element of the poem, to be listened to as morality by the pilgrims, but read as fiction by the reader. For if the game devised by the Host breaks down at the close of the journey, the game played by Chaucer with his readers holds to the end.

What the Host objects to in the Parson is his tendency to destroy the game by substituting his own rules for those agreed to by the pilgrims. But Harry Bailly is not so disinterested himself as he would have one believe. To begin with there is the question of the prize dinner. Whoever wins, part of the spoils will go to the keeper of the Tabard who has undertaken to prepare the meal. But there is another, less material advantage which accrues to the organiser of the game: his role as docent allows him to indulge his love of mockery and sarcasm and his need toder cover of the rules. Thus he can insult the Cook and the Monk to their faces, while avoiding their censure by immediately reminding them to

> . . . be nat wroth for game;
> A man may seye ful sooth in game and pley.

The Parson refuses to play the game. He confuses fiction with falsehood, and stands firm in his determination to preach a sermon rather than tell a tale. The Host plays the game, but he is even more at fault than the Parson for he plays it for his own ends. So long as it is he who is making the jokes he is only too eager to invoke the game as an excuse; but as soon as the joke turns on himself he forgets all about the game and its rules in his blind anger at the joker. As the Pardoner concludes his tale the Host finds that for the first time the joke is on him, and he does not like it.

"The Pardoner's Prologue and Tale" stands at the centre of *The Canterbury Tales*. It reveals the final turn of the ironic screw. Other tales had been told with another end in view than the winning of the prize dinner. The Miller had told a tale about a carpenter who aimed higher than was natural and so fell lower, and the Reeve had replied in similar vein with a story about a miller. The pilgrims could sit back and laugh at the knaves who fool others only to be fooled in their turn through lack of self-knowledge, and the reader could laugh with them. But the Pardoner has designs upon the whole company of pilgrims, and so, implicitly, upon ourselves, the readers.

What the Pardoner does is to tell the company that he is going to fool them, and then to go ahead and do it. As the pilgrims drink in the conclusion of the tale of the three rioters and submit to the inevitable moral:

> Now, goode men, God foryeve yow youre trespas,
> And ware yow fro the synne of avarice!
> Myn hooly pardoun may yow alle warice,

> So that ye offre nobles or sterlynges,
> Or elles silver broches, spoones, rynges.

they automatically reach into their pockets, only to be brought up sharp by the sudden realisation that the Pardoner is only going through his old routine, which he had explained at length in his Prologue. The reaction of the Host is violent in the extreme:

> But, by the croys which that Seint Eleyne fond,
> I wolde I hadde thy coillons in myn hond
> In stide of relikes or of seintuarie.

The Pardoner grows speechless with indignation at this, and a fight seems to be about to break out when the Knight interposes, reminding Harry Bailly of what he had himself so often said to cover up his own insults, that all this is nothing but a game:

> Namoore of this, for it is right ynough!
> Sire Pardoner, be glad and myrie of cheere;
> And ye, sire Hoost, that been to me so deere,
> I prey yow that ye kisse the Pardoner.
> And Pardoner, I prey thee, drawe thee neer,
> And, as we diden, lat us laughe and pleye.

It would be a mistake to imagine that the Host is angry because the Pardoner has asked him for money. What arouses his indignation is that the Pardoner has fooled him. The Pardoner is not out to make money off the pilgrims, otherwise he would never have revealed to them so candidly his methods of doing so in his Prologue. What he is out for is to prove the power of his words, and in order to succeed he has to make the pilgrims see that he has been able to fool them despite their previous knowledge of his methods. In that moment between the conclusion of his tale and the outraged cry of the Host, the moment when the power of his rhetoric wears off enough to be recognised as such, he has won his victory. And as the power he is allowed to exercise over others under cover of the game seemed more important to the Host than the money he might make over the prize dinner, so we may be sure that the Pardoner would not have foregone his mental triumph for all the relics in the world.

But what in fact has the Pardoner done that was so obnoxious? After all, he has only played the game to its limits. His tale is the very reverse of that of the Parson, since it accepts itself as merely a tale. Although on the one level it is aimed at making a fool of everybody, on another level it is not aimed against anyone—except those who refuse to recognise it as a fiction, a tale told as part of a game. . . .

"The Pardoner's Prologue and Tale" stands at the centre of *The Canterbury Tales* because it is a paradigm of the whole poem. All the tales, and the poem as a whole, can be seen as an effort to bring to the consciousness of the reader the fact that it is easier to lay down rules for others than to abide by them oneself, easier to invoke the game when it is oneself who is making the jokes than when one is the victim of a joke. This is the theme of the tales of the Miller, the Reeve, the Merchant, and the Nun's Priest. But it is also the theme of the debate between the Miller and the Reeve, the Friar and the Summoner. The Miller is as blind to the mote in his own eye as is John the Carpenter, the gull of his tale. But the Reeve, who points this out to him, and goes on to tell a tale of a gulled miller, is equally blind. All the pilgrims and the characters in their tales are quite capable of seeing the folly of others, but none is capable of seeing that he too is tainted. And the regression from John the Carpenter to the Miller to the Reeve can end only with one person: the reader. After he has laughed with the Miller at John, and with Chaucer and the Reeve at the Miller, and with Chaucer at the Reeve, the reader suddenly finds, as the Host found at the close of the Pardoner's tale, that the joke is on himself. And at this point there us only one way of escape: to acknowledge one's folly and learn from the game. The Pardoner's ironic self-revelation is a mirror of Chaucer's insistence that his poem is not truth but fiction.

Norman Knox   (essay date 1965)

SOURCE: "The Satiric Pattern of *The Canterbury Tales,*" in *Six Satirists,* edited by Beekman W. Cottrell *et al.,* Carnegie Institute of Technology, 1965, pp. 17-34.

[*Knox has written a study of irony in literature from 1500 to 1755. In the following essay, Knox analyzes the forms of irony in the* Canterbury Tales.]

Suppose we put to ourselves this question: To what extent, precisely, are the *Canterbury Tales* a work of satire? From one point of view we might answer the question very easily, simply by running through the *Tales* collecting an exhibit of disengaged passages and episodes which strike us as obviously satiric. But suppose we put the question this way: To what extent are the *Canterbury Tales* as a whole a work of satire? We now face difficulties, at least two of them, which we did not have as long as we considered the *Tales* only a collection of bits and pieces.

The first difficulty is that in fact the *Tales* are a collection of bits and pieces. What we have are nine fragments of a structure which Chaucer drew up plans for but which, whether because of weariness, boredom, or death, he never finished. We are not sure how these particular pieces were meant to fit in, nor how Chaucer might have changed their shape as he worried them into place. On the other hand, everyone knows what his overall plan was. Now when a writer, after trotting out thirty characters in a row, informs us that we are about to hear 120 short stories, it is not unreasonable to suppose that the thirty narrators are merely glue to hold the stories together, that telling the stories themselves is what he really wants to do. Again, even in the light of Chaucer's overall plan, we seem to be dealing with fragments. If in this sense we are dealing with a collection of fragments, then the question we started out from is idle, for such a collection is not very susceptible to being talked about as a whole. Fortunately for our enterprise, it is now generally agreed that Chaucer's plan

was more ambitious than we might at first glance suppose. Refusing to content himself with a perfunctory framework, he apparently hoped so to With this critical backing, then, we may go ahead on the assumption that it is not entirely idle to talk about the nature of the *Canterbury Tales* as a whole, even though our conception of that whole must always remain hypothetical.

Our second difficulty becomes clear when we review the variety of the fragments we do have. They range from earthy, uproarious farce through sophisticated burlesque, religious and romantic idealism, to superb melodrama. No tales in the collection are more uproariously funny than the fabliaux. Four of them find the thread of their plots in the clever tricks by which a young bachelor manages to seduce another man's wife. Ordinarily we might take this somewhat seriously, but in Chaucer's tales the characters themselves are not deeply involved emotionally in the event—though of course they are involved in less profound ways; equally important, the plot of each tale becomes such a magnificently intricate machine for discomfiting certain of the characters that we lose our sense of reality in watching it work itself out.

An instructive contrast with the fabliaux is the **"Franklin's Tale."** Here too a handsome young fellow wants to seduce another man's wife. But the young fellow is a squire, the husband a knight, and his wife a noble lady. Adultery is important to these people, not because their emotions are deeply involved, but because their ideals of behavior are. Consequently, even though the squire calls in a magician to remove all the rocks from the coast of Brittany, he cannot bring himself, his prize in his grasp, to act less nobly than he should. The event does not occur and all the characters leave the stage feeling very noble indeed. We are now clearly into the realm of ideals: knights and squires, great ladies and beautiful damsels, magnificent tournaments and undying, unrequited love. On the whole, Chaucer asks us to take the tales which deal with these matters with some seriousness, but in the unfinished **"Sir Topaz,"** he gives us an amusing burlesque of their preposterous aspects.

Chaucer adopts a more consistently serious tone in the tales which celebrate Christian faith and related virtues. The plot pattern of these tales is a simple and familiar one: in each, a heroine—all the protagonists are women except one, who is a small boy—a heroine of saint-like perfection undergoes a terrible trial of her faith or virtue. These do not desert her and her cause emerges triumphant, either because of her own actions or because of the miraculous intervention of Heaven. No doubt for us these tales seem in many ways bigoted, violent, naive. But they also express the passionate faith and the intense morality—at least on the theoretical level—so often to be found in the Middle Ages. In the **"Parson's Tale"** and the **"Tale of Melibee"** Chaucer gives us a more reasonable and discriminating expression of these characteristics—and a duller one. Neither is really a story at all. There is a good deal of hard-headed worldly wisdom in the **Melibee,** and several of the other Canterbury tales are of the sort often used to illustrate and teach such wisdom. For instance, both the **"Manciple's"** and the **"Nun's Priest's"** tales are at bottom fables, like Aesop's fables, the characters animals whose small adventures point a moral.

These are the **Canterbury Tales**, and the difficulty is clear enough. When we put the label *satire* under *Gulliver's Travels* we are allowed to go our ways in peace, for *Gulliver's Travels* is one of the things everyone means when he talks about satire. But when, after looking at the miscellany I have sketched above, we put the question whether this is satire, we come face to face not only with the problem of defining the nature of the **Canterbury Tales** as a whole, insofar as we can, but also withthe problem of defining the farthest outskirts of meaning in our term. I would be happier if we could skirt the maze of definition in this corner of the critical garden, but we cannot. Unless we establish a few elementary distinctions we will not reach any conclusion at all. "Satire," Northrop Frye asserts in his broadly based *Anatomy of Criticism,* as useful a book for matters of this sort as we will find, "satire is militant irony: its moral norms are relatively clear, and it assumes standards against which the grotesque and absurd are measured. Sheer invective or name-calling . . . is satire in which there is relatively little irony: on the other hand, whenever a reader is not sure what the author's attitude is or what his own is supposed to be, we have irony with relatively little satire." Frye has gone directly to the center of the maze, for if it is difficult to define *satire,* a reader of current literary criticism may be pardoned for feeling that it is impossible to define *irony*. But let us try. Perhaps, if we keep matters as basic and as simple as possible, we can find the distinctions we need.

One distinction sometimes made by the better college textbooks—and not made often enough by professional critics—is that between irony of language and irony of situation. If I happen to see a truck driver, his face distorted with brute fury, swearing and gesturing at a traffic officer, and if I turn to a companion and say, "There's pretty fellow," I am using irony of language: the meaning of the words I use does not fit the object we both see in front of us. Suppose, then, that as the officer, ready to give as good as he got, walks over to the truck driver, there arrives on the scene a little old lady thrusting up a massive poster: "Have You Made Your Peace With God?" It may strike me that the little old lady and the two men, though they are all situated on the same streetcorner, are not really operating in the same world, and if it does so strike me, I am aware of irony in the situation.

The above distinction may seem an unimpressive one, but no other is as fundamental, whether we think in terms of the history of literary criticism or of the theory of literary structure. Irony of language arises out of the interaction between two of the levels of any literary structure: the verbal level and the level that is often called the *world* created in our imaginations. Irony of situation, on the other hand, arises out of the interaction between two elements at the *world* level, and it need not depend any more on the verbal level than does any other element in the imagined world. Again, when we turn to the history of literary terms, we find that before the late eighteenth century, the word *irony* was virtually always used to mean irony of language. Irony of situation, as a meaning available in the word *irony* itself, seems to be the invention of the last two centuries.

If this distinction is fundamental, it ought to lead us to some useful observations, and I think it does. Let us examine three.

(1) If we have a solid historical understanding of a literary text, solid in relation to the author, the language, and the cultural milieu, we can say with some certainty whether and where that text exhibits irony of language. We know what the author means by the words he uses, and the world to which these words correspond or do not correspond, complex as it may be, is in front of us. Of course there are borderline cases, but they are borderline because our historical understanding of the text is not fine enough. On the other hand, we cannot say with the same kind of certainty whether a given text "contains" irony of situation. The reason is simply that here a good deal depends on the reader's "philosophy of life," to use a handy phrase. Every teacher has, at one time or another, been obliged to *tell* his students that there is an ironic conflict in the world of a Hardy poem, a conflict which Hardy "put into" the poem, and teachers of the metaphysical poets are nowadays obliged to warn students that Donne probablydid not "put into" his poems all the ironic conflicts which critics of a few years ago were determined to see there. But suppose a "world picture" or an author's personal "world view" does not control us? Then everything depends on the point of view—the reader's point of view. For the extreme Platonist who thinks the world ought to be one clear, unbroken light, everything except a blank mirror is riddled with irony. This explains why it is so easy for graduate students and other industrious critics to turn out paper after paper on "Irony in———."

The above observation may also help us to a convenient name for the irony of situation. *Verbal irony* is an accurate and widely accepted name for many of the ironies of language; I intend to use it to cover all of them. When we want to talk about the irony of situation, however, we are confronted with a number of terms that are either too narrow or too broad: *Socratic irony, Sophoclean irony, dramatic irony, irony of fate, cosmic irony, philosophic irony*, and worst of all, the word *irony* without a modifier—a popular usage which confuses the whole issue. Since the term *Philosophic irony* has had some currency, since it has narrowed the meaning in the direction we want to go, and since the irony of situation does in fact depend on the philosophic angle from which a situation is viewed, I intend to adopt that term to cover all the ironies except verbal ones.

(2) In his analysis of the ironic *mode,* to return to Northrop Frye for a moment, he points out that the writer who specializes in this mode generally presents his ironic world without comment. That is, he employs philosophic irony but not verbal irony. In the broad historical categories Frye works in, this is probably true enough, but we should not go on to suppose that there is a necessary antagonism between verbal and philosophic irony. They may coexist

in all sorts of ways, and it is perhaps worth saying that only some of these ways have been usefully explored, in, for instance, studies of dramatic and Socratic irony.

(3) Finally, to make the last of our three observations, we can say that verbal irony is always used at least partly for the purposes of satire or, much less frequently, of compliment; philosophic irony, on the other hand, may be used for the purposes of satire or it may not. And this brings us, at last, back to Chaucer.

What I wish to do, now that some of the ground has been cleared, is to examine certain aspects of irony in the *Canterbury Tales*, aspects which will exhibit several of the basic kinds of verbal and philosophic irony both in Chaucer and in general, and having done this, I will return to our initial question. Let us begin with the **"Pardoner's Tale."**

It is the time of the plague when thousands are dying. Three young men, drunk and riotous, hear the hand-bell clink as a coffin is borne past the tavern on the way to church. "Whose corpse is in that coffin passing by?" one of the men calls to the serving lad. "He was a friend of yours," is the answer; "a privy thief, they call him Death . . . speared him through the heart. . . ." The youths are infuriated. Inquiring where Death lives, they set out in a rush to kill him. On their way they meet an old man, one of the most ambiguous and haunting figures in English literature. He is not eager to give directions, but when they insist he points to a grove of trees where, he says, Death is waiting. For us the warning is clear, of course, but the drunken youths cannot grasp it. What they find under the tree is a great pile of gold. Visions of endless wealth and pleasure fill their minds; death is forgotten. One runs eagerly into town to fetch bread and wine while the other two stay to guard the gold—and to plot the death of their absent friend. Knowing this, we follow the third youth into an apothecary's shop. "Sell me some poison," he says, "I have a lot of rats I want to kill . . . I'll get even . . . with vermin that destroy a man by night." We think at once of his two comrades waiting, weapons in hand, under the tree, but he, of course, is all unconscious of the sinister meaning in his excuse. When he returns to his comrades, his wine bottles filled with poison, they murder him. "Now for a drink. Sit down and let's be merry," one of the murderers says. And Chaucer has him add, "For later on there'll be the corpse to bury." And he drinks the poisoned wine.

What we have here in the **"Pardoner's Tale"** is the pattern of ironies sometimes called Sophoclean, sometimes dramatic, sometimes a combination of dramatic irony and the irony of fate. But let us analyze the pattern in our own terms. The dominant irony is philosophic, and so plain I don't suppose anyone would doubt that Chaucer put it in. The chief characters set out to find happiness, first by seeking the death of Death, then by pursuing the glorious life a pile of gold is reputed to bring. All their efforts lead only to the grave. Some readers, possibly, feel "the mockery which our ultimate achievement casts on rosy expectations," to quote Robert K. Root, but I do not myself think that the weight of the irony falls in quite this direction.

The wages of sin is death: events turn out ironically because the supernal powers are moral powers and the aspirations of the three youths are sinful. If satire is militant irony in which the moral norms are clear, then the **"Pardoner's Tale"** is, surely, to some extent satiric. It becomes more certainly so if one feels, as I do, that the young men's inability to grasp life by the right handle makes them seem rather stupid, even in places grotesque, a feeling that may come from the way Chaucer mixes realism and allegory in this particular story.

At the verbal level of this tale there are several ironies like "For later on there'll be the corpse to bury." When the Old Man advises the three youths that they will find Death under a tree, his statement conflicts with the actual fact, for they find gold there, and in its second meaning it conflicts with the view of the situation taken by the youths: they cannot see death in the gold. It is perfectly true, of course, that in this second sense the statement accurately reflects the ultimate turn of events and that we as the audience should suspect this, but we are not, after all, part of the *world* of the tale, and if the three youths, who are part of that world, could see the truth in the statement, it would immediately cease to be ironic. From the point of view of dramatic effect, however, an important function of these verbal ironies is to bring into focus for the audience the whole dramatic shock of the ironic situation, which for a startled moment we see in all clarity. We may even find a parallel to the duplicity of the events in the duplicity of the language.

Verbal ironies of this sort have also their independent effect, aside from underlining the philosophic irony, and here, as elsewhere, it is satiric, for no character can survive the unrecognized passage of a meaning over his head without incurring some loss. The reader inevitably convicts him of general stupidity, moral stupidity, a wrong view of life, a wrong view of himself, or whatever. In the **"Pardoner's Tale,"** the three roisterers seem to be convicted not only of moral obtuseness but of a certain stupid, though superficially shrewd, vulgarity, and at times there is even an element of grotesque comedy in the tone, though that is on the whole not, we would agree, comic. In this tale, then, verbal and philosophic irony are working together to reach the same satiric ends. And we can probably say that although the philosophic irony could exist alone, it is not easy to see how the verbal irony could; its philosophic basis in this case is essential.

We might now pursue the sort of analysis we have just made through a number of the Canterbury tales, and perhaps it would be a profitable thing to do. No doubt we would find considerable variety, as I suggested in my review of the tales at the beginning of this essay, variety in the importance of the part, if any, which satiric ironies play, variety in the tone they are given, and even variety in the norms the stories appeal to. But if I may take this variety for granted, I would like to turn now not to further analysis of individual tales but to our image of the *Canterbury Tales* as a whole, an image in which the tales are parts of a larger pattern. From this point of view, I suspect, the exact nature of the various tales will not be so important as the fact that they are various, and we will also see more directly some kind of answer to our initial question.

We recall that some thirty people are making the pilgrimage. Obviously there is opportunity for all sorts of tension and excitement in a group like this. At the beginning things go quietly. It is a bright April morning and the pilgrims have ambled as far as St. Thomas's watering-place. For the first story our Host turns to the Knight, who recounts a tale of chivalry and romantic love. All the pilgrims, especially the gentlefolk, agree it is a noble story. "Come on, Sir Monk," says the Host, now it is your turn. But by this time the Miller is very drunk, "straddled on his horse, half-on, half-off, and in no mood for manners." He is determined to tell a very funny story about an old carpenter and his wife. At this the Reeve, who is himself a carpenter and not young, looks up to shout, "Give over with your drunken harlotry." But nothing will stop the Miller, who tells his riotous tale to the amusement of nearly everyone. The Reeve, however, is still angry. I'll pay you back for that story, he says, and proceeds to tell a fabliau about how a miller's eye was bleared. This so amuses the Cook, who claws his back for joy, that he asks leave to tell a little joke that occurred in his city, and we get still a third fabliau. So the first fragment ends.

The second begins with a tale of Christian virtue and fortitude told, perhaps surprisingly, by the Man-of-Law, who does not strike us as an especially devout person. Thinking to preserve the decorous tone, our Host, with his habitual harmless profanity, asks the Parson for a tale, whereupon the Parson reproves him for swearing. "Ho! . . . I smell a Lollard in the wind," exclaims the Host, at which the Shipman starts. There will be no heretical preaching while he is around, he exclaims. "My jolly body has a tale to tell!" And he swings into a fabliau. He is followed by the Prioress, who as a virgin dedicated to the Church quite appropriately tells a story celebrating the miracle of the Virgin. Soberness descends upon the crowd. Hoping to shake them up again the Host turns to Chaucer, poking fun at Chaucer's plump, well-padded figure and his elvish silence. Without anger Chaucer begins the **"Tale of Sir Topaz."** Suddenly the Host breaks in: "No more of this for God's dear dignity!" he exclaims; "My ears are aching from your frowsty story!" Chaucer is mildly offended, but acquiesces and now tells the prose Tale of Melibee. In this Dame Prudence, a remarkably wise woman and wife, argues that husbands should trust their wives and follow their advice. Much struck by Dame Prudence, the Host describes for his fellow pilgrims his own battling shrew of a wife. In fact the question whether husband or wife should rule the roost seems a sore one for a number of pilgrims, for when his turn comes the Nun's Priest, who works under the thumb of a woman, goes out of his way to illustrate how misleading women's advice really is. The Wife of Bath determinedly reasserts wives' prerogatives, and in passing takes a dig at all clerks like the Priest. Each in his turn—the Clerk, the Merchant, the Squire and the Franklin—all, directly or indirectly through the tales they tell, have something to say on this interesting subject. And so the procession moves on amidst quar-

rels and sudden friendships, jokes, and unexpected revelations. Itis the unpredictable, confusing, characteristic human chaos, and as we move along with it we gradually become aware of a unity in the *Canterbury Tales*.

In modern English—or American—life probably nothing except an air-raid shelter would gather into one group, a group with a common purpose, such a diverse collection of individuals as were the Canterbury pilgrims. But medieval religion was accepted as solid fact by everyone, the Miller and the Reeve as well as the Prioress and the Parson. In observing its rites everyone felt himself a member of one community. Chaucer does not in fact represent everyone among his pilgrims, but so diverse are the social types he does represent that he gives us the impression almost of a complete society joined in pilgrimage. As we watch it move along the road across southern England, there grows up in us the sense of a longer pilgrimage moving toward another goal, a goal of which Canterbury is the local symbol.

But I have said nothing of another element which also brings unity and something more to the unfinished *Tales*. I am thinking of the role played by their narrator, the pilgrim Chaucer. We have been talking as though the *Canterbury Tales* were a play the author of which never appears, but in fact when the poem begins the first character we meet is Chaucer himself. As W. W. Lawrence says, he takes us into his confidence at once, as though we were "dear and intimate friend[s], from whom he will keep no secrets and whom he will never willingly deceive————." It all happened, Chaucer begins, exactly as I will tell you, for I was there:

> . . . one day
> In Southwark, at *The Tabard,* as I lay
> Ready to go on pilgrimage and start
> For Canterbury, most devout at heart,
> At night there came into that hostelry
> Some nine and twenty in a company
> Of sundry folk happening then to fall
> In fellowship, and they were pilgrims all
> That towards Canterbury meant to ride.
> **("General Prologue,"** *The Canterbury Tales,*
> translated by Nevill Coghill)

So obviously candid and unpremeditated are his words, so almost naive, that we trust him at once. Here is a fellow who will indeed tell us what happened; he has not the self-consciousness to distort and color things.

"While I have time and space," he goes on, let me describe the other pilgrims. He begins with the Knight, his son the Squire, and their servant the Yeoman, and clearly he admires them all. "A most distinguished man . . . a true, perfect knight," he says, and his son was just what a fine young squire should be, handsome, brave and strong, courteous, "a lad of fire." All the facts he gives us confirm his judgment. Here, indeed, were admirable people. As he turns now to the Prioress, her too he finds admirable. She never, he points out, swore any oath worse than "By St. Loy," who, we know, had been a remarkably diplomatic, courteous, and handsome saint. She spoke extremely dainty French, in the manner of the English school at Stratford, and her manners were exquisite. She was always "straining to counterfeit a courtly kind of grace." Especially appealing was her tender-heartedness; if she saw a mouse in a trap or a dog beaten she would burst into tears. And finally, he says, she wore a bright golden brooch on which was engraved, "Love conquers all." For the first time we hesitate, somehow, to concur with the judgment of our honest guide. His prioress sounds very charming, yes, but there is a note of affectation about her, and we pause for a moment over the question whether a prioress, who devotes her life to religion and the education of young girls, ought to swear at all, even by so nice a saint as St. Loy. We are bothered too by her straining after courtly graces when she has in a sense rejected the worldly court. Should she not weep for the sorrows of men, rather than for those of small mice and mistreated puppies?—But we are being overcritical. We are breaking this gracious woman on the wheel of large ethical and social standards she had not the slightest intention of offending against. Still, a hint of doubt remains as we turn to the Monk.

Here, certainly, there can be no doubt. Our guide is all enthusiasm. "A manly man," he says of the Monk, "fit to be an Abbot," fit really to be exhibited as the paragon of monks: plump, bright-eyed, full of the zest of life. He loved good food and hunting, owned a fine horse and greyhounds swift as birds. His monk's garb was the finest to be had, trimmed with the most expensive fur in the country, the hood fastened with a gold pin in the shape of a lover's knot. As for studying old books, working the land, turning his back upon worldly temptations and riches, as St. Benedict and St. Augustine require of monks, he rejected them all as old-fashioned notions. "And," our honest Chaucer relates,

> I said I agreed with his opinion;
> What! Study until reason lost dominion
> Poring on books in cloisters? Must he toil
> As Austin bade and till the very soil?
> Was he to leave the world upon the shelf?
> Let Austin have his labor to himself.

Is this our admirable Chaucer speaking? Surely he is not taken in by such arrogant hypocrisy. Even as practical, hard-headed men of the world we expect the proprieties to be observed. A man of God should at least pretend a little. This fellow openly flouts the very doctrines he is expected to live by. And here is Chaucer praising him, even going him one step better! Honest as our guide seems to be, we begin to suspect him of gullibility, and the further we read the stronger our suspicion becomes. Apparently he accepts everything. He accords the same praise, the same objectivity, to the most flagrant cheats and liars among the pilgrims as he does to the most upright and conscientious of them. In fact, the worse they are the more enthusiastic he becomes.

He does have, however, one redeeming trait. As you will understand, he says, "I'm short of wit," and we are happy to see that he recognizes this handicap. When later in the pilgrimage the lawyer speaks slightingly of Chaucer's poetry, Chaucer himself very sensibly keeps quiet, and when the Host pokes fun at his plumpness and shyness, he replies:

> "Host, . . . I hope you are not one
> To take it in bad part if I'm a dunce;
> I know only a rhyme which, for the nonce,
> I learnt."

And he recites the hilariously bad **"Rime of Sir Topaz,"** so bad that the Host stops him in exasperation. Well, we think, it is awful stuff if you take it seriously, but at the same time it very cleverly exaggerates and thereby reveals what is wrong with the worst metrical romances. Perhaps the Host is a little obtuse not to see this. But Chaucer seems totally unaware that he has beguiled the Host into betraying himself.

This, then, is our pilgrim Chaucer. Virginia Woolf catches his character exactly. As his simple, friendly, ingenuous narrative proceeds, suddenly, she says, "out from behind peeps the face of Chaucer, grinning, malicious, in league with all foxes, donkeys, and hens . . . witty, intellectual, French, at the same time based upon a broad bottom of English humor." The game he plays is as old as Socrates and the *eiron* of Greek comedy. "What a very stupid fellow I am," these mockers tell us, "but my friend here is most admirable, most admirable indeed. You can see that for yourself." And as they turn the searchlight of their praise on this character or that, every wart, wrinkle, and blemish is exposed by the merciless glare, and woe unto those who are not, indeed, praiseworthy.

Let us stand back, now, from this character and this scene, and see what in general we have. We have, first, two groups of verbal ironies: Chaucer's comments and verbal performances which misrepresent himself; his comments which misrepresent the other pilgrims. Few of these are doubtful. Nothing we know of Chaucer allows us to accept him as "short of wit," and nothing we know of fourteenth century norms allows us to accept the Monk as genuinely "fit to be an abbot." Both groups of ironies function satirically in two ways. They both force us to take a hard look at the actual nature of the object: at Chaucer's delightful sophistication, at the Monk's hard-boiled worldliness; and they both hold up to ridicule the characters over whose heads the ironies pass unrecognized; Harry Bailey is caught flat-footed by Sir Topaz, and the Monk by Chaucer's praise. The norms applied throughout are definite and positive, the norms of Geoffrey Chaucer's sensitive intelligence, both moral and artistic: the Monk is wrong, and Harry Bailey is wrong.

The verbal ironies have also an effect similar to that we observed in the **"Pardoner's Tale."** Quite early in the **"Prologue,"** I would say, we become aware of the part we must play in Chaucer's game—when he agrees so heartily with the Monk, to be exact. Now that we know our author is capable of sly irony, we read on looking for other ironies, and so often do we find them that by the time we end the **"Prologue,"** our suspicions are aroused by every incongruity, we are hounds sniffing after the slightest scent of a quarry. Thus Chaucer, by lighting a fire under our critical faculties, illuminates the whole world of the *Canterbury Tales*. After the Prologue, he himself, as author or as pilgrim, seldom appears, but we are never quite able to lose ourselves in the fictional world he creates. Having alerted us, he is now able to disappear into this world, offering it to us without open comment and with apparent fidelity to the characters and limitations of his people, but we, if ever we are tempted to accept these people uncritically, on their own terms, are brought up sharp by a malicious little smile on Chaucer's good-natured face.

It is tempting to see Chaucer as a writer in Northrop Frye's ironic mode, a writer who in fact does present his world without comment. But such a view is mistaken. I have pointed out some of the verbal ironies through which Chaucer judges his world, and although it is true that he more often than not seems to disappear, that he presents his characters with apparent fidelity to their natures, if we recall the burlesque exaggeration of Sir Topaz, of the **"Nun's Priest's Tale,"** of the Wife of Bath, we realize that very often he does not in fact disappear, does not present his people with strict fidelity to their natures, but simply finds a subtler form of verbal irony to serve as vehicle for his satiric judgments. And even when he genuinely withdraws, it takes a while, as I have suggested, for the critical faculties of his audience to run down.

Let us examine now what we have in the way of philosophic ironies. We notice first that there are a number which are of a familiar and obviously satiric nature, analogous, perhaps, to the kind we found in the **"Pardoner's Tale."** An instance we can be certain of is the Pardoner himself: he preaches magnificently against the very vice he himself is most passionately found of. The ironic conflict here makes a satiric comment on the Pardoner's public image, very much as the ironic conflict between aspiration and accomplishment in the Pardoner's Tale makes a satiric comment on a wrong view of the moral universe. We can be certain Chaucer put this irony in, both because it is so obvious and because the Pardoner himself points it out. But what of the Prioress? Devout and tender-hearted, she takes sadistic pleasure in the torture of the Jews. We may appeal to historical prejudices, but one wonders whether Chaucer was really limited to these, and the question remains open.

It becomes even more puzzling if we take another step backward in order to see some of the larger relationships in the *Tales*. Consider the relationship between the teller of the tale and the tale he tells. When, for example, the Wife of Bath asserts the eternal right of women to dominate their husbands, it is the Clerk who answers her. His story celebrates the duty of absolute obedience in wives. Do we smile when we recall that the Clerk is a cloistered scholar, lean, sober, studious, and unmarried? Or consider the relationship between two tales which Chaucer places cheek by jowl. For instance, the Monk, fat and arrogant, entertains the company with seventeen tragedies, each

relating the sad fate of a great and prosperous man brought low by ill-fortune. He is followed by the Nun's Priest, silent, poor, and thin, a man who never has been and never will be prosperous, but who nevertheless tells a delightfully humorous fable in pointed contrast to the Monk's lugubrious tragedies. To point the contrast further, he decorates his comic little tale of a fox and a chicken with all the tragic paraphernalia the Monk has just used. Or consider certain of the relationships of a character to himself. The Pardoner, as we have said, is a complete religious hypocrite, fattening his purse by preaching against the very sin he is himself the most guilty of—avarice. And he is unrepentant; in fact, he is proud of his cleverness and moral hardness. But when he tells his dark tale of riot and death, it is not the other pilgrims who are impressed, it is he, and for a moment, quite unintentionally, he seems to reveal beneath his hard, braggadocio surface the fear and self-hatred which he hides chiefly from himself.

Finally, I want to suggest a set of relationships which is so complex that it is better experienced than explained, but I shall try. We know, as did Chaucer's readers in his own time, that he was an artist of wide reputation, and when we read the *Canterbury Tales* we know that this wise and practiced artist is telling us a story. In that story we make the acquaintance of another Chaucer, the pilgrim Chaucer, who is both like and unlike the first Chaucer we know, and he too is telling us the story. In his story are some thirty other pilgrims, and they, each in their turn, also tell the story. And in each of their stories are characters who, at their own level, have their own reality. The *Canterbury Tales* are in this aspect very like a set of Chinese boxes. As we read along we are quite often aware of only one box, as when we watch the pageantry of the Knight's Tale. Sometimes we are aware of two boxes at once, as when we think of the relationship between the Clerk's Tale and the Clerk who is telling it, or of the relationship between the real Chaucer and Chaucer the innocent pilgrim. But every once in a while Chaucer rattles three or four boxes at once, and the resultant ironies pretty much defy description. In his book on Chaucer G. K. Chesterton, alone among the critics I am familiar with, has made an attempt to describe one important effect of these interrelationships.

> The Poet is the Maker; he is the creator of a cosmos; and Chaucer is the creator of the whole world of his creatures. He made the pilgrimage; he made the pilgrims. He made all the tales that are told by the pilgrims. . . . Then in due course, as the poet is also a pilgrim among other pilgrims, he is asked for his contribution. He is at first struck dumb with embarrassment; and then suddenly starts a gabble of the worst doggerel in the book. . . . [He] can only defend himself by saying sadly that this is the only poem he knows. . . . The point is in the admirable irony of the whole conception of the dumb or doggerel rhymer who is nevertheless the author of all the other rhymes; nay, even the author of their authors. . . . But the irony is wider and even deeper than that. . . . Chaucer has made a world of his own shadows, and, when he is on a certain plane, finds himself equally shadowy. It has in it all the

mystery of the relation of the maker with things made. There falls on it from after even some dark ray of the irony of God, who was mocked when He entered His own world, and killed when He came among His creatures. . . .

That is laughter in the grand style. . . . It is the presence of such things, behind the seeming simplicity . . . which constitutes . . . the greatness of Chaucer.

The question that naturally arises in our minds as we read Chesterton's remarks and consider the sort of ironic juxtapositions I sketched above, the first question that has to be answered, is whether all this irony is really there. Are we writing our own *Canterbury Tales*? We may answer the question by saying that for the reader who feels these philosophic ironies strongly, they are there. Right you are if you think you are. And if it is not taken in a naive way, this is a sensible answer. But it does not get rid of one historical question. If Chaucer ever re-read all the manuscripts at once, did he see that he had put these ironies in? Did he feel them as an essential element in the work he envisioned? We may well wonder. After all, what we read are fragments, fragments which probably create accidental impressions that would not be created if our responses were controlled by a complete work of art. And does not any long, comprehensive, various work inevitably generate the sort of ironies we are dealing with here? If we read half a dozen fragments of *Tom Jones* or the *Decameron*, could we are not take off on a flight of fancy like Chesterton's?

Granting that these considerations should make us cautious, I am nevertheless inclined to think that Chaucer fully intended the ironic world some readers feel. He was, after all, an ironic fellow. We are certain of many of his verbal ironies, and they are not the narrow, virulent irony of dogmatic controversy but the irony of a fine discrimination and an unfailing sense of proportion. Moreover, the world view that was second nature to a man of Chaucer's age made an ironic vision of human life quite as available as does our own. Indeed, if we divest ourselves of the provincial superiority of modernism, we will see that the medieval view perhaps led more naturally than ours does to such a vision. We will remember Dante gazing down from Saturn: "With my sight I turned back through all and every of the seven spheres, and saw this globe such that I smiled at its sorry semblance"; and we will remember Troilus gazing down from the eighth sphere at "this little spot of earth . . . thiswretched world," and laughing.

An awareness of this medieval vision helps us to accept the presence of broad philosophic ironies in the *Canterbury Tales*. It also helps us to see the exact nature of those ironies and thus to answer the question from which we started: To what extent, precisely, are the *Canterbury Tales* as a whole a work of satire? A comparison with *Point Counter Point*, to choose a modern novel which is in many ways similar to the *Tales* (even in the Chinese boxes of creator and creation), will be useful here. That novel is notoriously full of philosophic irony. When we examine the lives of Lucy, Walter,

Illidge, the Tantamounts, old Bidlake, Webley, Quarles Junior and Senior, we find that in every case the event of the character's hopes and aspirations is only ironic defeat. When we move from the world of one character to the world of another, we find that from the point of view of A, B is wrong, from the point of view of B, C is wrong, and so on around the circle. Everything is cancelled out by something else and in the end we can only turn up empty hands.

It is tempting to read the *Canterbury Tales* in this way. The Clerk and the Wife of Bath, the fabliaux and the **"Franklin's Tale,"** Chaucer the Creator and Chaucer the gabbling storyteller, all seem to balance each other off. Yet no sooner do we make such a statement than we realize how wrong it is, for everything in the *Canterbury Tales* is not really cancelled out by something else. We recall the firmness of Chaucer's verbal irony, we realize that the Wife and the fabliaux cancel out the Clerk and the **"Franklin's Tale"** only on this little spot of earth, and we hear Troilus laughing in the eighth sphere. Chaucer does not leave us with empty hands; as Virginia Woolf remarks, "we absorb morality at every pore." No doubt, in the practical chaos of our pilgrimage through this world, it does seem that every human vision is partial and all human life pointlessly ironic, but from the eighth sphere we may laugh and turn our faces upward.

If, then, satire is "militant irony," if "its moral norms are relatively clear, and it assumes standards against which the grotesque and absurd are measured," the *Canterbury Tales* as a whole, a comprehensive pattern which governs all the individual tales, romantic, tragic, farcical, melodramatic, do indeed seem to be satiric. But if Chaucer had finished his work, had taken his commuly back to the Tabard for a grand feast celebrating the end of their successful journey, would not the *Tales*, like Dante's great poem, be a comedy? The answer to this question is probably yes—and irrelevant. We do not have the finished work, and because we do not, the pattern of what we do have is that of satire. Not, I hasten to add, satire of the gloomy sort that *Gulliver* and the *Dunciad* end with. Though at bottom Chaucer's view of humanity was probably not widely different from Swift's, he seems to have been the most cheerful and serene of men. The native cast of his mind led him, as it led Dryden, to understand and to appreciate many sides to many questions. But his awareness of the grain of truth or of humanity in conflicting points of view did not make him depressed and neurotic, as it makes so many of our modern ironists. He accepted this state of affairs, this confusion and contradiction, as the inevitable condition of human life; like Sophocles, he knew that "all the generations of mortal man add up to nothing." But in the *Canterbury Tales* he chose to face the human condition not with sorrow or anger but with serene laughter from the eighth sphere.

Ian Robinson   (essay date 1967)

SOURCE: "Chaucer's Religious Tales," in *The Critical Review*, No. 10, 1967, pp. 18-32.

[*Robinson is the noted author of* Chaucer and the English Tradition *and* Chaucer's Prosody: A Study of the Middle English Verse Tradition. *In the following essay, Robinson discusses the religious motifs used in the "Prioress's Tale," the "Clerk's Tale," and the "Man of Law's Tale."*]

Of the devotional and moral *Canterbury Tales*—a surprisingly large proportion of the whole work—the potentially interesting ones are the Prioress's, the Man of Law's and the Clerk's; and about these three there is a deep-seatedly mistaken critical tradition, namely that they are all pretty much the same sort of thing. Mr R. O. Payne is one of the most interesting modern writers on Chaucer, and when he follows the tradition it is time to protest on behalf of the **"Clerk's Tale."** Mr Payne writes of these three tales, when calling them all saints' legends,

> In only one of these is the protagonist literally a saint, but in form and effect, as well as in the characters of the protagonists, they are so much alike that the distinction is doctrinal rather than literary. (*The Key of Remembrance.*)

The statement is very representative of what many people think of the three tales. It is also common to be exasperated by both the "litel clergeoun" of the **"Prioress's Tale"** and Constance and Patient Griselda. All three are felt to be representatives of a rather sickly-sweet goodness, a goodness simply of its time and place, with nothing to say to *our* world. The three tales also appear to share a sentimentality, particularly about mothers and infants, which may make the reader want afterwards to rinse his mind in something like the **"Miller's Tale."**

A variation on the common view is to find Chaucer's emotion effective but to see it as the enemy of any real religious depth or artistic control. The influential statement of this view of the **"Clerk's Tale"** is Mrs Elizabeth Salter's *Chaucer, the Knight's Tale and the Clerk's Tale* (*Studies in English Literature,* 1962)—a work which uses an unpromising opportunity to treat these poems with due seriousness. Nevertheless, it seems to me that the three tales are quite different, that the various reactions I have been describing are fully appropriate to none of them, and that the **"Clerk's Tale,"** at any rate, is one of Chaucer's most arresting and daring performances. And I hope that I may be able to show this by arguing against Mrs Salter's central proposition that "the more vividly [Griselda] emerges as a sentient being, the less will be her power to move and instruct as a pure religious symbol." Perhaps if we can see a connection between the symbol and the vividly pathetic character we can simultaneously vindicate the tale's religious feeling and rescue it from sentimentality.

A feeling that the **"Clerk's Tale"** is not to be dismissed comes out of our two best critics in an oddly tentative way. Mr John Spiers is here at his most tantalizing, making some very leading remarks which he doesn't follow up—the most interesting of all in fact coming in his section on the **"Man of Law's Tale":**

There is the same quality of tenderness for Griselda and her child in the **"Clerk's Tale."** The natural human feeling has acquired a peculiar sanctity and grace which we should hesitate to find sentimental. (*Chaucer the Maker.*)

But he leaves it there. Mr Muscatine records this impression:

> [The **"Clerk's Tale"**] requires rereading; and with successive readings one's indifference turns to tolerance, then to admiration. (*Chaucer and the French Tradition.*)

But he too, beyond a few hints that I shall try to use later, doesn't explore very far how the tale works to create that admiration. And Mr Sledd, in another widely-read essay (reprinted in *Chaucer, Modern Essays in Criticism,* ed. Wagenknecht) makes interesting suggestions about the necessity of connecting the moral and the action of the **"Clerk's Tale"** and of defending it against the more extreme charges of sentimentality. But instead of following his ideas through, he lapses into the very odd notion that the tale is "a fairly straight-forward, middling kind of yarn"—which doesn't get us far either.

I

The **"Prioress's Tale"** is the easiest of the three to grasp, though the critics have not generally found it so. The tale is occasionally found detached from the other *Canterbury Tales* and bound up in pious collections, so it must have been acceptable to some people in the fifteenth century as an ordinary Miracle of the Virgin, presumably to be read aloud for the edification of pious audiences. On the other hand it has occasionally been seen by later critics as a satire on the form. F. N. Robinson comments in his edition that the latter view is "certainly wrong." But how do we know? And if he is right, are we forced into the former view?

The **"Prioress's Tale"** fits easily into one useful account of what Chaucer is doing in *The Canterbury Tales*. He tells us so much about what mattered to people in the fourteenth century by showing ways of life in action, being judged by their action and interaction, and he does this by taking over the heterogeneous literary traditions he found and relating them to one another. The **"Prioress's Tale"** is the clearest example of the process. So it would be a mistake to ask whether Chaucer is *pro* or *anti* the Prioress's kind of piety. He is evidently in a way superior to it, able to view if from a height.

Much of what the Prioress says, both in her **"Prologue"** and in her **"Tale,"** has a genuinely touching beauty and even, sometimes, has more strength than one might expect. Her **"Prologue"** links her own tender feelings with a much more powerful-seeming God than she seems to worship in the **"General Prologue."** And, recalling some of her tenderness in the **"Tale"** itself, I find it hard to sympathize with those moderns who *only* sneer at her.

The swetnesse hath his herte perced so
Of Cristes mooder that, to hire to preye
He kan nat stynte of syngyng by the weye.

That does express to me a touchingly delicate religious sentiment, and there is quite a lot like it in the tale.

But the tale is not to be taken at its face value as a Miracle of the Virgin. The religious feeling,though sometimes so beautiful, is seen to be both damagingly limited and in some ways perverse. The limitation comes out, for example, in the Prioress's use of her favourite word *litel*. The school is *litel* (though it contains "children an heep"); the hero is a "litel clergeoun, seven yeers of age," and the *litel* son (of a widow, of course). Even his grammar is a little one:

This litel child, his litel boke lernyng . . .

and when he is finally dead,

in a tombe of marbul stones cleere
Enclosen they his litel body sweete.

There is a similar force of limited emotion behind the Prioress's use of *innocent*—and those who argue that because *innocent* is a technical term in theology the Prioress is not using it sentimentally ignore the way the poem works. The Prioress is tenderly sentimental about the martyr in much the same way as she is about her dogs in the **"General Prologue."**

We can enjoy this tenderness, but to do so will establish the devotion, also, as *litel*. Perhaps "charming" is the word for it. What is not so charming is the Prioress's attitude to the Jews. There the sentimentality becomes, in its wilful thoughtlessness, actually wicked; the tenderness is seen to be connected, by way of unintelligence, with something the opposite of tender. Her view of the Jews is, as you might expect, a naive and simple one:

Ther was in Asye, in a greet citee,
Amonges Cristene folk, a Jewerye,
Sustened by a lord of that contree
For foule usure and lucre of vileynye,
Hateful to Crist and to his compaignye—

which is a simple example of the usual mediæval Christian party line on the Jews. For the Prioress, whose *conscience* has nothing to do with intelligence, it is simply natural and right that the Jews (all of them?) should commit a murder out of mere hatred of Christianity. At the end of the tale there is a surprising concatenation of piety and tenderness about the martyr with rancorous and savage injustice to the Jews—both equally part of the Prioress's religion:

This child with pitous lamentacioun
Up taken was, syngynge his song alway,
And with honour of greet processioun
They carrien hym unto the nexte abbay.
His mooder swownynge by the beere lay;
Unnethe myghte the peple that was theere
This newe Rachel brynge fro his beere.

With torment and with shameful deeth echon
This provost dooth thise Jewes for to sterve
That of this mordre wiste, and that anon.
He nolde no swiche cursednesse observe.
"Yvele shal have that yvele wol deserve";
Therfore with wilde hors he dide hem drawe,
And after that he heng hem by the lawe.

Not only the murderers, but everyone who knew of the murder, are killed; you could hardly call it execution, since death precedes trial. First the Jews are tortured to death then the trial takes place and the corpses are hanged.

Any apology for the Prioress would be sure to bring out the unreality of her religion, its discontinuity with any real world. It might be said that her hatred of the Jews cannot be equated with modern anti-semitism: as a provincial Englishwoman she had probably never seen a Jew in her life; the pogroms were well over in England by Chaucer's day, the Jews having been allowed to leave (after several requests, and taking with them only portable property) in 1290. But if this hatred is not inspired by real Jews it becomes as unreal and limited as the love for the martyr. And if the unreality of this anti-semitism means that the Prioress is not a dangerous character, the charm of her religion is hardly rescued. That religion is a kind of private luxury which could sustain nobody in adversity and could tell nobody anything about God.

II

The **"Man of Law's Tale"** and the **"Clerk's Tale"** are more difficult because in them Chaucer is committing himself further. Neither has the perfection of the **"Prioress's Tale,"** but they show it to be a minor perfection. (Cf. Lawrence's remark, "Give me a little splendour and I'll leave perfection to the small fry.") We see the Prioress's religion in its charm and depravity, but I know of no reason for supposing that it mattered much more to Chaucer than it does to us. In the **"Man of Law's Tale"** he commits himself *not* to place the piety in such a detached and central way. In fact the great weakness of the tale is that in it Chaucer seems to be stifling his critical intelligence—which, however, occasionally breaks out with disastrous results. What is he trying to do in the **"Man of Law's Tale"**?

He seems to me to be trying to create the aura of magical significance that can sometimes be found at that end of the range of Saints' Lives which continues without a break into folk-tales. Shakespeare could bring ghosts and witches into his plays: where could Chaucer go for anything comparable? Perhaps *folk-ballads* is the most obvious answer; but Chaucer, as a courtly poet, was cut off from the folk poems as effectively as Alexander Pope. If he is trying for the sense of the numinous there is a good reason why he should not be trying to "place" it. It is one thing to put the Prioress's religion in perspective, another to do the same thing for a ghost: a criticized ghost would disappear. Only Shakespeare can laugh at a ghost without destroying it. The equivalent of ghosts in the **"Man of Law's Tale"** is the feeling of miraculous sanctity. And the best bits of the tale are those where Chaucer for a moment brings it off:

> That oon of hem was blynd and myghte nat see,
> But it were with thilke eyen of his mynde
> With whiche men seen, after that they ben blynde . . .

and so on. But such places are only a small fraction of a long tale, and in the rest Chaucer seems to be filling out his flagging inspiration with whatever comes to hand. The tale gives him a chance to indulge in the kind of touching sentiment found in the **"Prioress's Tale,"** and here too it is beautiful enough. Little children and their mothers were certainly a chance for Chaucer's emotionality—though, to use the most obvious comparison, it is a pity that Chaucer's feeling is so facile compared with Dante's in the Ugolino of Pisa episode (*Inferno*, xxxiii, used in Chaucer's **"Monk's Tale"**).

But Chaucer often seems to be trying to get at the right feelings without doing any work for them. So he has to strain to keep it up. Several different sets of celestial machinery are switched in; as well as God there is Fortune, Satan and several of the astrological deities, all used to inflate the feeling of significance. The astrology here seems (very unlike the gods in the **"Knight's Tale"**) to be there only to impress the reader, and it may misfire by provoking him to answer the rhetorical questions *wrong*:

> Imprudent Emperour of Rome, allas!
> Was ther no philosophre in al thy toun?
> Is no tyme bet than oother in swich cas?
>   [NO! Or at any rate the stars won't tell you
>   which time is best.]
> Of viage is ther noon eleccioun,
> Namely to folk of heigh condicioun?
> Noght whan a roote is of a burthe yknowe?
>   [Certainly not. Roots of births have nothing to do
>   with it.]

One may be similarly tempted into rude answers to the series of rhetorical questions during Constance's first marooning:

> Who kepte hire fro drenchyng in the see?
> Who kepte Jonas in the fisshes mawe
> Til he was spouted up at Nynyvee? . . .

Who indeed?

Another sign of strain is the very frequent resort to apostrophe. Nobody can do anything wrong, whether it be Satan or the Sultaness or one of the careless messengers, without receiving a solemn denunciation in high style ("O messager, fulfild of dronkenesse!" &c.).

The result of this straining for effect is that the tale fails to make its moral point and, in a way, takes its revenge on the morality. When we come to such lines as these we are plainly meant to receive a strong moral, embodied by the tale:

> But natheless she taketh in good entente
> The wyl of Crist, and knelynge on the stronde,
> She seyde, "Lord, ay welcome be thy sonde!"

—which is one sign that Chaucer needs the story to be more than a convenient cloak for the moral. The same lines in the **"Clerk's Tale"** might have been more convincing. Similarly, the first villainess of the piece has to be the Sultaness; but she seems to me a relatively heroic figure, defending the things she believes in against the weak caprice of her son.

The final sign that Chaucer can't keep up the mysterious holiness is the occasional lapse into the manner of the Wife of Bath, which produces in this context something very like a snigger:

> Housbondes been alle goode, and han been yoore;
> That knowen wyves; I dar sey yow na moore. . . .
>
> They goon to bedde, as it was skile and right;
> For though that wyves be ful hooly thynges,
> They moste take in pacience at nyght
> Swiche manere necessaries as been plesynges
> To folk that han ywedded hem with rynges,
> And leye a lite hir hoolynesse aside,
> As for the tyme,—it may no bet bitide.

The use of such a key term as *pacience* in such a way must carry over to, and attack, its use in other contexts; the atmosphere is destroyed; the tale cannot bear the intrusion of Chaucer's other, better styles.

The result is that the **"Man of Law's Tale"** is Chaucer's nearest approach to Lydgate. It seems to come not from anyone's soul—the Man of Law's or Chaucer's—but from a rather mechanical exercise in the rhetorical art of religious tale-telling. But what of the **"Clerk's Tale"**?

III

Even before facing the central problem of the **"Clerk's Tale"** we can see that it is much better written than the **"Man of Law's Tale."** Take, to begin with, the very different openings of the two poems. In the **"Man of Law's Tale"** the poet's emphases are in all the wrong places and attention quickly wanders. The verse-form isn't doing anything in particular except to announce that the poem is to be taken solemnly whether or not it deserves to be.

> In Surrye whilom dwelte a compaignye
> Of chapmen riche, and therto sadde and trewe . . .

These rich merchants are of no importance in the tale but they are introduced with an emphasis suitable to the tale's hero. The tale's heroine, however, slips in almost unawares in a subordinate clause:

> Sojourned han thise merchantz in that toun
> A certain tyme, as fil to hire plesance.
> And so bifel that th' excellent renoun

Of the Emperoures doghter, dame Custance,
Reported was, with euery circumstance,
Unto to thise Surryen marchantz in swich wise,
Fro day to day, as I shal yow devyse.

This is second-rate verse. The enjambement is careless,
as if this were the first way the poet thought of putting
things, but which turned out not to be the best. Chaucer's
padding lines and half-lines often serve to highlight an
intense statement by their side, but there is no good reason
why the sense of this stanza should stop, as it does, a line
and a half before the end. Contrast the **"Clerk's Tale"**:

Ther is, right at the west style of Ytaille,
Doun at the roote of Vesulus the colde,
A lusty playn, habundant of vitaille,
Where many a tour and toun thou mayst biholde,
That founded were in tyme of fadres olde,
And many another delitable sighte,
And Saluces this noble contree highte.

A markys whilom lord was of that lond,
As were his worthy eldres hym bifore;
And obeisant, ay redy to his hond,
Were alle his liges, bothe lasse and moore.
Thus in delit he lyveth, and hath doon yoore,
Biloved and drad, thurgh fauour of Fortune,
Bothe of his lordes and of his commune.

The first stanza does not introduce any of the tale's major
figures but it does establish very carefully the tone as
well as the scene. The deliberation and quiet definiteness
establish right from the start a tone that is later seen to be
specifically the Clerk's, and which is maintained throughout the poem. (Muscatine writes very well of the Clerk's
style in *Chaucer and the French Tradition*.) In this passage Chaucer manages to focus attention on the more
important words in a way that makes the passage, though
slower and more formal, as careful as anything in the
Wife of Bath. In fact the verse has a considerable density
of meaning despite what Muscatine calls the "frugality"
of the style. When Walter is introduced in the second
stanza it is in this already established tone, and with a
care and emphasis fitting his importance in the tale. In
parallel with "Saluces" he is named in the last line of the
third stanza. (Griselda is introduced in a very similar way
at the beginning of Part II.) And the regularity of the
metre here is very far from removing the verse from the
life of the spoken language. The rhetorical balances between and within the lines help the metre in its task of
measuring the delivery peech. The rhetorical groupings
of the last-quoted couplet convey by their repetition and
variation of phrase-pattern something weightier than one
might expect from the unaided metre.

The first two parts of the tale, before Griselda's trials
begin, may be found attractive by many readerswho can't
stand the rest. There is nothing thin about the tale's frugality; the control and economy of style and content are
apparent, but there is no deprivation in the poor life of
Janicula and Griselda, which reminds one of the opening
scene of the **"Nun's Priest's Tale,"** seen with less partic-

ularity. We are not told the name of Griselda's sheep, but
she does live in a world from which sheep are not excluded.
And the description of Griselda, though it concentrates on
her morality, is far from suggesting that she is unattractive or sexless:

But for to speke of vertuous beautee,
Thanne was she oon the faireste under sonne;
For povreliche yfostred up was she,
No likerous lust was thurgh hire herte yronne.
Wel ofter of the welle than of the tonne
She drank, and for she wolde vertu plese,
She knew well labour, but noon ydel ese.

But though this mayde tendre were of age,
Yet in the brest of hire virginitee
Ther was enclosed rype and sad corage . . .

But here we are still on the edge of the tale's problems.
The main one is, of course, how to see Griseld as a moral
heroine. In a most obvious way she is exactly the opposite, and in several places the Clerk has to disclaim any
intention of making her a model for wives. A wife who
allows the children to be carried off apparently to a violent
death is a wicked woman. So the Clerk says,

This storie is seyd, nat for that wyves sholde
Folwen Grisilde as in humylitee,
For it were inportable, though they wolde—

"this story is told not to make wives imitate Griselda in
humility, for that would be *intolerable*—even if they wanted
to." But it is equally clear that in another sense Griselda
is a moral example. The Clerk continues:

But for that every wight, in his degree,
Sholde be constant in adversitee
As was Grisilde; therefore Petrak writeth
This storie, which with heigh style he enditeth.

For, sith a womman was so pacient
Unto a mortal man, wel moore us oghte
Receyven al in gree that God us sent . . .

But how can that follow if Griselda ought not to have
been so patient to a mortal man? Griselda can only be a
moral example if at certain crucial moments we can discount or forget her wickedness. How could that be?

Professor Muscatine writes, "The whole ordonnance of the
poem invites, constrains a symbolic reading" (*Chaucer and
the French Tradition*), but does not take his own hint. Let
us try to (Why should the form of the **"Clerk's Tale"** present
difficulties to a generation at home with *Measure for Measure*?) The first part of the tale could hardly announce more
plainly that we are not reading a novel, that the characters—
if that is the right word—are not to be shown naturalis-
tically any more than the actions, but are there for the sake
of their further significance. (Though there are naturalistic
touches, which have their place in the tale, as I shall argue.)
It is rather obvious that in the **"Clerk's Tale"** we are somewhere between fable, parable and allegory.

Let us see what will happen if we opt for the last term. Consider, out of context, some of the things Griselda says to Walter, and let us try to forget for the moment the situations in which these speeches occur:

> Wondrynge upon this word, quakynge for drede,
> She seyde, "Lord, undigne and unworthy
> Am I to thilke honour that ye me beede,
> But as ye wole youreself, right so wol I.
> And heere I swere that nevere willyngly,
> In werk ne thought, I nyl yow disobeye,
> For to be deed, though me were looth to deye. . . ."

> She seyde, "Lord, al lyth in youre plesaunce.
> My child and I, with hertely obeisaunce,
> Been youres al, and ye mowe save or spille
> Youre owene thyng; werketh after youre wille.

> "Ther may no thyng, God so my soule save,
> Liken to yow that may displese me;
> Ne I desire no thyng for to have,
> Ne drede for to leese, save oonly yee.
> This wyl is in myn herte, and ay shal be;
> No lengthe of tyme or deeth may this deface,
> Ne chaunge my corage to another place. . . ."

> "I have," quod she, "seyd thus, and evere shal:
> I wol no thyng, ne nyl no thyng certayn,
> But as yow list. Nought greveth me at al,
> Though that my doghter and my sone be slayn,—
> At youre comandement, this is to sayn.
> I have noght had no part of children tweyne
> But first siknesse, and after, wo and peyne.

> "Ye been oure Lord, dooth with youre owene
>   thynge
> Right as yow list; axeth no reed at me.
> For as I lefte at hoom al my clothyng,
> Whan I first cam to yow, right so," quod she,
> "Lefte I my wyl and al my libertee,
> And took youre clothyng; wherfore I yow preye,
> Dooth youre plesaunce, I wol youre lust obeye.

> "And certes, if I hadde prescience
> Youre wyl to knowe, er ye youre lust me tolde,
> I wolde it doon withouten necligence;
> But now I woot youre lust, and what ye wolde,
> Al youre plesance ferme and stable I holde;
> For wiste I that my deeth wolde do yow ese,
> Right gladly wolde I dyen, yow to plese.
> "Deth may noght make no comparisoun
> Unto youre love. . . ."

Out of context these all seem quite clearly to be addresses by the Christian soul to God. Would they have been out of place in Rolle or Julian of Norwich? And considered as devotional verse these passages are perhaps more convincing than anything in Rolle in the restraint and dignity that accompany their deeply felt submission to the divine will. It cannot be merely accident that Griselda's words fit another situation so exactly.

There are plenty of hints in the tale that Griselda is either the Christian soul or the Church in its union with Christ, and that Walter is God. Look how Janicula phrases his reply to Walter:

> "Lord," quod he, "my willynge
> Is as ye wole, ne ayeynes youre likynge
> I wol no thyng, ye be my lord so deere;
>   Right as yow lust, governeth this mateere."

At Griselda's first meeting with Walter,

> doun up on hir knes she gan to falle,
> And with sad contenance kneleth stille,
> Til she had herd what was the lordes wille—

not, you note, *this* lord's will. In answer to his question, "Where is youre fader, O Grisildis?" she

> with reverence, in humble cheere,
> Answerde, "Lord, he is al redy heere."

And much later in the tale Griselda exclaims

> "O goode God! how gentil and how kynde
> e semed . . ."

where it would make good grammatical sense to take *Ye* as God.

But in another way Walter is very obviously not God, and the Clerk has to say or imply this repeatedly to avoid imputing pointless cruelty to God. Can the tale only make its point if we take the religious passages out of context? If so it is a failure, of course. Yet there has to be some separation of the meaning from the figure that expresses it if the Clerk is not to be blasphemous. Is that an admission of the tale's failure?

The function of the context, the tale, must be to give the patience of the Christian soul a particular life that even as the finest general statement it must lack. Some connection between the literal and figurative meanings is therefore necessary; but I have argued that some disconnection is also necessary. Here the delicacy of the Clerk's task is clear: Chaucer has to detach the religious passages from the context in every way but one, leaving only the thread of *pacience* to connect them with the tale; but with that thread he has to draw across from the tale the emotional poignancy that is not found in the doctrine on its own.

The tale, then, depends on the generation of emotion and its bearing across to the partly detached doctrine. I have shown the detachment by quoting key passages out of context. There remains the question of the tale's pathos and its connection with the doctrine.

Some people cannot stand the emotions of the **"Clerk's Tale"** (and other people cannot bear them). I find especially that young women can rarely forgive or forget that Griselda fails to stand up to her husband. I can't always take this in the necessary way myself, but sometimes I manage to; of moral comment on Griselda is an unnecessary refusal to suspend disbelief, a refusal to let the tale be itself. Here of course we have to follow the Clerk along another tightrope: if he makes the situations too real Griselda, as a real woman, will disgust us; if too unreal there will not be the involvement that enriches the doctrine. Certainly we need some flexibility and delicacy of response to move between the tale's different levels; but to do so it is only necessary to follow the directions of the tale itself, which is one of the most delicately controlled of all Chaucer's works. The model of what is to happen is given in the episode of Walter's proposal. There, surely, we can respond warmly and without qualms to Griselda's realization that she is the chosen one; and we can do that without any knowledge of Walter's personality. The feeling is then channelled by Griselda's words into the other context, the religious one. Why should this be so difficult?

And generally speaking, the pathetic scenes throughout the tale are overwhelmingly successful in their creation of poignant emotion. If we are taking the tale properly we can respond with strong compassion and pity. Why not? He would be hard-hearted indeed who refused to share Griselda's joy or grief merely because the tale is not a novel. If it *were*, it wouldn't be so moving. Griselda has something in common with the characters of folk or fairy tale: a naturalistic Cinderella would bore children. We need to avoid the cynicism or the demand for naturalism that can destroy the tale.

When the children are so callously removed by the Fell Sergeant, some critics find Griselda's calm unemotional, a sign of coldness. The very opposite seems to me to be the case: Griselda is more poignant here, when she must allow herself no murmur, than she is at the end of the tale, when she can show the ordinary signs of her feeling by fainting. These are the places where Chaucer seems to have profited by his reading of the Ugolino of Pisa episode. In the **"Clerk's Tale"** we have the best of the tender mother and child situations that so appealed to Chaucer; it is the best in itself and also because here, at last, Chaucer is doing something with it more important than placing it or wallowing in it.

> And thus she seyde in hire benigne voys,
> "Farweel my child! I shal thee nevere see.
> But sith I thee have marked the with the croys
> Of thilke Fader—blessed moote he be!—
> That for us deyde upon a croys of tree,
> Thy soule, litel child, I hym bitake,
> For this nyght shaltow dyen for my sake."

We bear across the emotion of these situations to the doctrine.

The "human touches" (if the phrase is still possible) make their point too. For all the frugality of the tale, it need not altogether cut itself off from the ordinary world, as the **"Man of Law's Tale"** has to. The Clerk scores mild but precise debating points against the Wife, joking about marriage as slavery, and hitting the right nail squarely on

the head when he calls her doctrine that of a sect. Before Griselda can fall on her knees before the Lord she has to put down her water-pot. The ladies who are to array the bride do not like to handle her old clothes, the suggestion being not that they are dirty but that they are unfashionable. The multitude welcoming Walter's second wife is as fickle as any in Shakespeare, and remark that the new wife is more beautiful and younger than Griselda. And Griselda's faint is such a real one that the children have to be torn from her hard grip. All these things help to provide a background for the action.

But even if you concede all this, is it not still true that the Clerk's example is a bad one? Isn't it a dangerously chosen example because, with that plot, thoughts about Griselda's unsatisfactoriness must intrude? Wouldn't another example have shown *pacience* better and without leading to these objections?

The tale is not about consequences. It is not a tragedy embodying its moral in the fable so that the moral is not extractable and can only be stated by a performance of the tragedy. The Clerk needs a tale for his moral, but not in that way. His tale would have made its point equally well, I suspect, without the happy ending. The Clerk, being a very orthodox Christian, has to show that all things work together for good to them that love God; but would the quality of Griselda's patience have been impaired if the tale had ended with her retirement to obscurity, and Walter's second marriage? The value of Griselda's response to adversity is not that it is finally rewarded, but in itself, heroic patience in a particular situation.

> [God] suffreth us, as for our excercise,
> With sharpe scourges of adversitee
> Ful ofte to be bete in sondry wise . . .

And the point of the "exercise" is in the submission itself. Or, as Muscatine puts it,

> Walter's lack of motivation is an advantage in presenting this theme. This is *pure* chastening, *pure* correction. Griselda's trial is a trial because there is no reason for it. (*Chaucer and the French Tradition*)

The Clerk is not trying to convert us to Christianity; he is not telling a tale to show the *advantages* of patience. Rather, the tale is a genuine philosopher's example; it makes a doctrine clearer. The Clerk is saying that Christian patience, submission to God's will, is *as if* a wife should behave like Griselda, even without hope that the husband is really kind. And as a philosopher's extreme example the tale shows what God may require of a Christian soul, and suggests the kind of sense a Christian soul might make of the demand. The marriage agreement is not what a husband has any right to require of a wife, but the suggestion that it is what God may require of us can give the reader the kind of shock about the inevitable conditions of human life that is one mark of the powers of a great poet. The tale, that is, makes its point in a way that can challenge us as well as that scholarly fiction the fourteenth-century audience.

It puts the case that, whatever the consequences, Griselda's patience is best for her. (Would it have been better for her to revile Walter and return home bitterly to Janicula? The Tale's final realistic touch is the revelation that that is exactly what Janicula expects.) Would it be better for the Christian to renounce God if he feels that God has renounced him? By holding on to her sense that her marriage has existed—her one insistence to Walter is that she *has been* his true wife—Griselda in a way preserves the sense the marriage has made. Perhaps she could have responded similarly if Walter had died.

By putting Christian patience so starkly and so poignantly, the Clerk challenges us to see it and make up our minds about it.

But if the reader feels something monstrous in Griselda's patience, too—something demanding rebellion against such a God—perhaps that is implied as well, at least as a possible response to the Clerk's challenge. We might reject the doctrine, having seen it clearly for the first time. I confess that the "Clerk's Tale" is for me the chanciest of Chaucer's great things. Sometimes I hate Griselda's patience. But at other times I admire it as a heroic human possibility. In either case I am clear—as nowhere else in mediæval literature—about what this religion is and what it demands. *That,* I think, is the triumph of the tale.

Even so, the "Clerk's Tale" is such an extreme that if it alone had survived of Chaucer's works we should probably have thought of Chaucer as a brilliantly fanatical contemporary of Langland. The tale needs the Wife's "Prologue" as an opposite extreme to balance it, and it needs the famous Envoy with which Chaucer breaks the Clerk's spell and brings us back to a more ordinary world.

Paul Beekman Taylor   (essay date 1991)

SOURCE: "The Uncourteous Knights of *The Canterbury Tales*," in *English Studies*, Vol. 72, No. 3, 1991, pp. 209-18.

[*Taylor is the author of* Chaucer's Chain of Love. *In the following essay, he examines Chaucer's portrayal of flawed knighthood by analyzing the "Franklin's Tale," the "Physician's Tale," the "Wife of Bath's Tale," and the "Merchant's Tale."*]

Although the pilgrim-knight whom hazard honours as the first teller of tales is portrayed by Chaucer in great detail as a warrior who serves both secular and religious causes, the Knight's own tale tells of knights in the service of ideals of courtesy. Indeed, the eight tales which feature knights concern love rather than war, and this emphasis reflects the predominant literary tastes of Chaucer's day, if not the general recognition of the declining value of the knight on horseback in military operations. [From the time of the First Crusade, when Norman and Frankish knights struck terror into the Saracens as invincible fighting machines, until the Battle of Crécy in 1346 when the knight

proved himself obsolete in battle, knighthood was, first and foremost, a military ideal in service of the Church. It is by martial standards of the day that recent studies measure Chaucer's Knight, for example Terry Jones, *Chaucer's Knight* (London, 1980) and, in rebuttal, John H. Pratt, 'Was Chaucer's Knight Really a Mercenary?' *Chaucer Review*, 1987. By Chaucer's day the knight was idealized for his courtesy, for his figurative rather than real protection of the Faith.] There are surprisingly few knights in *The Canterbury Tales*, considering how freely the title is attributed in *The Legend of Good Women* and *Troilus and Criseyde*. Besides Theseus, Palamon and Arcite in "The Knight's Tale," there is the false accuser of Constance in "The Man of Law's Tale," the rapist of "The Wife of Bath's Tale," the Franklin's Arveragus, the Merchant's Januarie, the Physician's Virginius, Chaucer's own Thopas and the Second Nun's knights of Christ in her hagiographical account of Cecilie. Of these, only the first three take part in wars, though it is Theseus's mediation in the love contest between the two unruly knights that is the topic of the Knight's story. The last knights—Cecilie's husband and his brother—embody ideals of spiritual service that match Theseus's secular service. Between these poles, however, are six tales which display knights who fail, more or less, the ideals of courtesy attached to their title. The peril in which these knights place both image and person of women suggests that Chaucer is framing a timely argument against a knighthood whose ideals are belied by its exemplars, whose understood service to love is performed in disservice to women.

From its inception in the Carolingian epoch, knighthood was associated with a common defence of Church and womanhood, the latter as image of the former. Chaucer's Parson explains that 'certes, the swerd that men yeven first to a knyght, whan that he is newe dubbed, signifieth that he sholde defend hooly chirche' [Quotations are from *The Riverside Chaucer*, 3rd ed.]. The text of that ceremony requires the knight to protect *ecclesiarum, viduarum et orphanorum* ('Church, widows and orphans') as well as to fight the heathen. Langland's Holy Church tells Piers that knights are to defend its truth and punish its transgressors [in *Piers Plowman*], while the French poetic tradition of Crétien and his followers call upon the knight to display strength, courage, fair bearing, loyalty, generosity, courtesy, leadership and dedication to just causes. This list accords closely with the virtues of knighthood recommended in Palamon by his rival Arcite to Emily:

> 'To speken of a servent properly,
> With alle circumstances trewely—
> That is to seyen, trouthe, honour, knyghthede,
> Wysdom, humblesse, estaat, and heigh kyndrede,
> Fredom, and al that longeth to that art.'

There is no need to multiply such lists of knightly virtue. They appear throughout the prose and poetic corpus of medieval western Europe. The protection of women is typologically bound to the defence of Holy Church because the exegetes had identified women as reflections of the Virgin Mary and, hence, figures of Church. *Virgo Maria est ecclesia*, says Hildibert. As the Church mediates between God and man, women mediate between husband and children in the popular model of the family. [David Herlihy, 'The Making of the Medieval Family,' *Journal of Family History*, 1983. Herlihy notes that the ancient Germanic tradition of according a higher *wergild* value to women during their child-bearing years pertains to the bourgeois medieval English notion of the marketable value of family members.]. The love between husband and wife which produces offspring, in fulfillment of God's command to wax and multiply, is *honesta copulatio*, and the child-bearing bed an image of the church altar. These are but commonplace truisms, but they need to be rehearsed in order to show why knights are, ideally, the mediating bond between spiritual and worldly love. They are figures of Christ and of that universal governing force Theseus identifies as the *faire cheyne of love*. A knight is, therefore, a servant of love, whether fighting the heathen or protecting oppressed damsels.

With the establishment of the ideal arrive its counter-figures. An early anonymous Latin poem, probably from the twelfth century, exposes clerks and knights who serve venereal instead of charitable love. . . .

As protectors of the ideals of love, knights would be expected to be ideal lovers themselves, exercising *moderatio* in choice and performance of love. Knights should love as Pandarus counsels Troilus, 'in a worthy place' (*Troilus*). The social history of Chaucer's Europe reveals, however, a common interpretation of this hierarchal harmony to mean that while one should *love* another of the same social worth, one can *lust* lower. Alison, of **"The Miller's Tale,"** is

> . . . a prymerole, a piggesnye,
> For any lord to leggen in his bedde,
> Or yet for any good yeman to wedde.

The point seems innocuous in context, but it is likely that Chaucer's audience would know that women like Alison were married off for economic reasons in which they, themselves, had no say. If Malyn in **"The Reeve's Tale"** addresses a courtly aubade to the clerk who rapes her, it is because this lover will be, most likely, the highest of social rank she will have amorous dealing with in her squalid environment. Violent amorous pursuits were not infrequent in Chaucer's day. Groups of young knights perpetrated gang rapes in southeast France which were considered by the ruling class as "acceptable amusement for the young men who felt frustrated by their inability to marry before they were sufficiently established" [Mary Wade Labarge, *Women in Medieval Life*, 1986.]. Lower class women were fair game and those who were viewed askance as fairies were prime targets [Duby, *The Knight*. He remarks: 'When they imagined themselves winning, by violent and dangerous means, these enticing, elusive, dominating fays, they must have felt they were conquering their anxieties and returning to the warm bosom of their earliest infancy.' Psychoanalytic speculation aside, women who were considered to possess 'magical' powers were more often attacked with impunity than others.]. Rapine love seems to Jean de Meung the rule rather than the

exception. Chaucer's Parson, in his lugubrious exposition of the sin of lechery, establishes a hierarchy of deleterious love in association with the senses, or wits. Eyes, ears, and so forth, incite lust, where reason should mediate spiritual love.

It is this deficiency of the senses that quickens the lust which characterizes Chaucer's knights. Palamon and Arcite desire Emily from first sight, though the former compares her to a goddess, while the latter is attracted to her as a *creature*. Theseus, after mediating the griefs of the Theban women, converts the disorderly pursuit of the two knights for Emily into a structured contest whose reward is marriage. When that plan goes awry by the untimely and unexpected death of Arcite, Theseus calls Emily and Palamon together for a marriage which will serve the political alliances of the state. As a philosophical justification for the union, Theseus makes his renowned 'Great Mover' speech in which he celebrates the fair chain of love and the holy bond of matrimony which reflects it in the secular world. In keeping with the historical context and the typological structure of the tale, Theseus attributes the bond of love, the Divine Logos, if you will, to Jupiter. In the mythographic tradition, ironically, it is Jupiter who ushers in the age of lechery:

> . . . Jupiter the likerous,
> That first was fader of delicacye,
> Come in this world.
>
> ('The Former Age')

At any rate, Theseus protects Emily's interests by turning her pursuers' squabble into an honourable quest for marriage. In doing so, however, as Emily herself reveals in her futile prayer to Diana to preserve her virginity, the woman's own desires are not taken into consideration. Theseus uses his sister-in-law as a peace-web.

"The Franklin's Tale" is a parodic reflection of the Knight's story in contemporary and domestic setting. Like the Knight's tale of Theseus, the Franklin's story of Arveragus and Dorigen ends happily, in re-established order; but, where in the Knight's story Theseus ties a political knot by means of a marriage, the Franklin's plot is achieved by a succession of untyings. Arveragus releases his wife from her marriage vows, Aurelius releases her from her rash promise, and the clerk of Orleans releases Aurelius from his debt. Where Theseus resets in place, over and over again, an order he compares to the created order of the universe, Arveragus, Dorigen and Aurelius proceed in their comic triangle of love by unthreading fabrics of order. The tale begins with Arveragus surrendering his 'natural' superiority over his wife to her will in all marital matters except his public posture, on the grounds that:

> Love wol nat been constreyned by maistrye,
> Whan maistrie comth, the God of Love anon
> Beteth his wynges, and farewel, he is gon!
> Love is a thyng as an spirit free.

By this comic image the Franklin trivializes the philosophic concept of love and reduces it to a sprite in fear of a cage. Such a notion is only a symptom of the tale's confusion of love and knighthood. Arveragus leaves his wife unprotected as he goes off to enhance his chivalric honour. Dorigen, alone and fearful, looks at the black rocks of Brittany as threats to her love and calls upon God to view his own works. The address parodies Theseus's exposition of universal design, but where Theseus the man celebrates the harmony of order in nature apparent to the intellectual eye, Dorigen the woman laments the 'foul confusion' of nature before her eyes. It is no surprise that a mind which reads nature so poorly should read Aurelius's offer of service as an invitation to adultery. Her offer of her body to him, should he remove the rocks, is a false promise, quite different from Theseus's promise of Emily's hand to the winner in the lists. It is not necessary to spin out here the comic complications which follow. It is sufficient to recall that Arveragus, once he hears of Dorigen's contract, releases her from their vital marital bond to send her off to honour a frivolously contracted bond of adultery, though he takes the precaution, curiously, of protecting her this time with a maid and squire. Where Theseus had exposed a universe ordered by a perceptible providential design, Arveragus, Dorigen and Aurelius are finally restored to order by a series of gratuitous and contingent repudiations of bonds. When Arveragus orders Dorigen to keep her word to Aurelius, he exercises his will in a fashion comparable to Theseus's marrying of Emily, but where Theseus is fulfilling a noble service of love, Arveragus is pandering to the basest service of love.

"The Physician's Tale" also treats the issue of knightly protection of love. Virginius is, as Theseus and Arveragus, a noble knight. Under his guard is a daughter Virginia whose perfection of nature is detailed in a passage which occupies more than a third of the entire tale. Her body and its controlling virtues reflect Theseus's view of the cosmos. All is moderate and self-sustained. She is an image of unfallen nature, an example of governance. When the magistrate Apius schemes to possess her, Virginius, instead of permitting his daughter to exercise her virtues of self-governance to protect herself or to convert the lust of her suitor to honourable affection, decides to kill her, apparently for no better reason than to defend his and her public honor. [In the *Roman de la Rose* version of the story, Apius resorts to his fraud only after direct confrontation with Virginia fails.] Her pleas to mercy are ignored, and she finally yields herself to her father's will, ironically, in God's name. The operations of will untempered by mercy and uninstructed by reason—that is, at least, an understanding of man's just participation in God's creation—contrast with Theseus's ordering according to the merciful interests of women and with Arveragus's misguided but well-intentioned reconciliation of his wife with her pledge of body. All three tales feature knights who exercise their will to subject women to a personal view of order and value in the universe. Theseus's mastery of Emily may strike the modern reader as lacking a sense of equality between the sexes, but is, in its context, a benign operation. Arveragus's fault is a failure of protection and a subjection of an essential bond to a deleterious one, but the gratuitous generosity of man finally turns to

comedy the materials of tragedy. Virginius wastes life and destroys the nature which reflects universal order. He kills what he cannot master. All three knights are married, in the prime of life, and enjoy public worth.

The knightly concern in **"The Man Law's Tale," "The Wife of Bath's Tale"** and **"The Merchant's Tale"** shifts from protection of woman to ways of loving them. These are tales of amorous pursuit, assaults on the bodies of women. Thwarted in his advances to Constance, the Man of Law's knight kills Hermengyld and accuses Constance of the crime. Unlike Virginius's killing of his daughter, there are no mitigating circumstances here, and the fact that God's hand materializes to strike the knight dead implies that the knight's crime of perjury implicates the bond of Divine Love. Comparable in culpability is the rapist-knight of the Wife's tale. Berefting a maid of her virginity, the Parson reminds the pilgrims, is casting her out of the 'hyeste degree that is in this present lif, and bireveth hire thilke fruyt that the book clepeth the hundred fruyt.' His crime, then, is tantamount to murder, but all the more odious being motivated by pride of lust. Echoing distantly the deference of judgement to woman's mercy, penance is set by Guenevere. The punishment fits the crime, since the knight is condemned to discover and express publicly what women most desire privately. The answer is mastery, or sovereignty over men, a sort of turning the tables on the knight who had exercised sexual sovereignty over the maid. It is a fairy woman's counsel that gives the knight the saving reply, and this is a turning of the tables of protection by knights, for it is *she* who saves *his* life. Her price is a promise of marriage, but the fact that she is old, ugly and poor complicates the issue. His marriage would not be a bond to a worthy object; nor would it be a bond for the lawful reason to beget children for the common profit. In effect, the old hag, shape-shifting from old to young, appropriates the role of a knight in amorous pursuit. She imposes her body upon him, against his will. She counsels him in such a way as to persuade him to render his sovereignty to her. When she offers him, finally, a decisive choice between having her fair and fickle or foul and true, he returns the choice to her. His will has been chastised if not his reason, and she rewards his will by promising both youth and fidelity. As we might expect of a woman playing the role of a sexual predator knight, the reward has already been promised for her own sake, for even before she reveals the choice, she reveals its profit:

> 'But nathlees, syn I knowe youre delit,
> I shall fulfille youre worldly appetit.'

Now, while it may be argued that, like Theseus, she is acting as a mediator to convert a savage sexual pursuit to an ordered marriage, it appears that she is mediating between *his* will and *her own* lust. She is engaging the knight in an amorous combat, duelling with words rather than with the blunted weapons of the *mêlée* in which Palamon and Arcite participate. What she has done, effectively, is to convert his will to her own sexual profit. She rapes with words.

Januarie, the knight of **"The Merchant's Tale,"** has much in common with the Wife's knight as well as with the hag. He marries a young woman in order to serve his personal delight rather than to serve the common profit in the engendering of children. To give Januarie credit where it is due, he does mention children as a motive for marriage, as well as the bonds of marriage as a protection against the sin of fornication, but it would seem that both arguments are mounted in order to justify the purchase of a servant to his lust. After all, he 'buys' May by 'scrit and bond.' Januarie presents himself as a grotesque parody of the 'First Mover' Theseus posits as the maker of the chain of love. First of all, he spends considerable time entertaining images of the young girls he has seen, or not seen, in the marketplace. The Merchant identifies Januarie's entertainment as 'heigh fantasye and curious bisynesse,' [For 'fantasy' the *Oxford English Dictionary* has 'the faculty of delusive images, deluded images produced by such a faculty' (see *Troilus* V), 'a liking directed by caprice' Wife's prologue (III), and 'an amorous fancy' **"Monk's Tale"** (VII). Januarie's 'fantasy' is related, of course, to a sexual drive inappropriate to his age.] and I suspect that these terms direct us to the neo-platonic figure of the God who contains in his mind an image of what does not yet exist. This figure is known throughout the Middle Ages, from Chalcidius and Boethius through Bernard Silvester and William of Conches, as the *Opifex* and the *artifex*. The latter term designates the Divine Architect who reifies his eternal plan by the Word of love, or *Logos*. It is a stock figure in Chaucer's works. Pandarus recognizes in himself an architect of deceitful love in *Troilus* (III). So Januarie conceives of himself in his love-making, exclaiming to May in the nuptial bed:

' . . . Allas! I moot trespace
To yow, my spouse, and yow greetly offende
Ere tyme come that I wil doun descende.
But nathelees, considereth this,' quod he,
'Ther nys no werkman, whatsoevere he be,
That may bothe werke wel and hastily.'

The Biblical echoes need no glossing here, but Januarie's amatory dalliance is ironic in this context. God *does* work Creation in no time at all, and his shaping of the world is no trespass, while Januarie's rapine reach is one of a series of amatory gestures which trangress May's body without creating life. The descent of the Holy Spirit to impregnate the Virgin Mary is not quite the same thing as Januarie's stumble down the stairs after his sexual visit. After a while, however, May learns the Hag's lesson on mastery and works to convert Januarie's desire to her use. She hints at a pregnancy both to flatter her husband and to justify her inordinate hunger for the pears in the tree where her lover awaits. When his eyes are opened to the adulterous liaison, her words blind him to the truth by convincing him of what he would like to believe. This is not unlike the Hag's knight who is convinced of a reward by words rather than by acts.

What aligns **"The Merchant's Tale's"** denouement with the ending of **"The Wife of Bath's Tale"** is the manner in which crimes of knights are redressed by women who succeed, one way or another, in submitting the body of their knights to their own will. May uses Januarie's back for her ascent into the tree to enjoy the kind of love that Januarie himself is well-acquainted with. The Hag's knight becomes the means by which the hag recovers her youth and sexual vitality, in thought if not in deed. [Yielding to an ugly lover's expressed wish is a common disenchantment device in medieval folk-tale and romance.] It is the word, the secular reflection of the creative *logos,* that chastizes and purges the excessive lust of rapine knights.

The tales of Sir Thopas and Saint Cecilia present two extreme views of otherworldly love, the former as fantasy pursuit and the latter as spiritual pursuit. Both tales concern the quest for an idea rather than for a person. Chaucer's tale of Sir Thopas is a comic travesty of amorous idealism. In outward array as well as accomplishment, Thopas is a knight *par excellence:* he sings, dances, wrestles and hunts. He falls in love to the thrustel's song (VII), and once his outward ear is incited to an amorous quest, his inward eye sights, in a dream, an elf-queen as his *lemman,* a term for a loverfound most typically in Chaucer's day in lyric references to Christ. If Januarie's *heigh fantasye* paraded images of women he had seen at one time or another, Thopas's amorous imagination pictures what, as far as we know, does not even exist. Pursuit of an invisible love is, of course, pursuit of the Virgin Mary and a quest for spiritual love. The identification of Chaucer's Fairy Queen with the Virgin Mary is made by Edmund Spenser in the first book of his *Fairie Queene,* and it is likely that Chaucer's immediate audience understood the implicit allusion. Thopas makes the identification himself, paratactically, when he wakes from his dream and exclaims: 'O seynte Marie, benedicite!' (VII). Since Thopas's love is never joined to an image outside of his own fantasy, it is autistic. It is puerile, and like Januarie's love for May, it is sterile. The expense of energy during his quest for the elf-queen procures him nothing but words. It is fitting that his quest be blocked by a giant Olifaunt, whose name, according to Boethius, signals 'gretnesse or weighte of body' countering the 'stablenesse and the swift cours of the hevene.' [This is Chaucer's translation of *The Consolation,* Book III. In the context of Thopas's ridiculous quest it is perhaps worth mentioning that for Chaucer's pronunciation, *quene* 'whore' and *queene* 'queen' would be virtually homophonous.] Thopas's vapid and fruitless pursuit in a doggerel style of its teller, which matches the hero's gallop, is a carnival mirror of knightly love chases. It is a caricature of misdirected gestures of love.

As if to direct the imagination towards a spiritual love manifest in nature, the Second Nun tells a tale in which angles are seen, flowers of martyrdom smelled and eternal truths heard from the mouth of Pope Urban. If Thopas is engaged in a labyrinthine pursuit attended by multitudinous trivial details of speech and gesture, the Second Nun's Cecile points a narrow and direct path toward a truth that is evident to man's senses. More significant, perhaps, is the fact that Valerian and Tiburce *earn* their knighthood, for Cecile rewards their faith with the title 'Cristes owene knyghtes leeve and deere' (VIII). The career of these two is a chastising example to earlier tales of knights. For example, whereas Theseus's secular design is based on the authority of Jupiter, Cecile makes knights of her husband and his brother in order to arm them against a command to sacrifice to Jupiter. Theseus mediates a disordered pursuit in order to conform it to his political design, while Cecile preaches a withdrawal from worldly pursuits in favour of a spiritual design. While Theseus argues that Jupiter's cosmic order is apparent to the eye (intellectual or physical), Cecile explains a manifestation of spirit in nature which binds this world with the next. Like the Wife's hag and the Merchant's May, Cecile converts husbands to her will, but her motives are not private and personal, but public and universal. There is no question of begetting children in marriage for her, because in her austere and radical view of this world's service to the next, there is profit only in renouncing physical things for spiritual good. Val awarded knighthood for renouncing everything that marks the mundane knights of earlier tales. They disdain their own nature as well as social honour. Their title of 'knight' is a distant ideal, a service to one sense of love alone.

Chaucer's knights in *The Canterbury Tales*, apart from the rarified models presented by the Second Nun, are uniform in submitting women to their will. They abuse both image and body of women to an extent that feminists would be justified in labelling 'sexual imperialism.' The threat against body is prevalent. Virginius kills his daughter, a maiden is raped by a knight, Arveragus threatens to kill Dorigen if she makes her contract with Aurelius public, and then orders her to surrender her body. May submits to the perverse sexual appetite of Januarie, Hermengyld is murdered and Constance falsely accused by the Man of Law's knight, and even Theseus cannot escape the charge that he neverdefers to Emily's opinion in the question of her marriage. Thopas is an extreme case, for whatever image of elf-queen he holds in his mind, it is wholly his; that is, Thopas's woman is a product of a male fantasy, and fully subject to its delights. If tnere is a singular flaw that can be pointed to as the cause of flawed service of love, it is man's deficiency of sense, or wits. Chaucer's knights, with the exception of the well-instructed knights of Cecile, misread nature. Theseus posits a perfectly ordered creation to justify his mundane ambitions, but dislocates nature violently when he dislodges the denizens of the forest from their habitat, and when he changes the use of the earth by bringing sunlight to where it never was before. In effect, he destroys the very design he celebrates. Virginius kills his daughter, failing to protect her, but also failing to recognize in her virtues a power to protect herself. Arveragus renders up his will to a wife whose senses and reason, if we judge her address to God before the black rocks as evidence, are manifestly insufficient. The Wife's knight cannot contain his lust, Januarie's lust is excessive for his age, and Thopas does not even care to distinguish, if he could, dream images from real persons.

Chaucer's knights reflect three errors in their service of love. The first is subjection of woman's bodies to male wills for the sake of public order and honour. Theseus, Arveragus and Virginius are more or less culpable of this fault. The second error is the rapine pursuit of woman's bodies for pride of lust, and the knights of the Man of Law, the Wife of Bath and the Merchant are so guilty. The third error is fantasy pursuit, the quest of an ideal in the absence of a person. So Palamon loves until he is brought into Emily's company, and so Thopas pursues an image of his own fancy. Chaucer plays in his art with shifting distances between ideals and practices, and it would seem that his careful selection of knights in the tales serves his exposition of flawed knighthood.

Carol Falvo Heffernan (essay date 1995)

SOURCE: "*The Book of the Duchess:* Chaucer and the Medieval Physicians," in *The Melancholy Muse: Chaucer, Shakespeare and Early Medicine,* Duquesne University Press, 1995, pp. 38-65.

[*In the following excerpt, Heffernan analyzes the narrator of the* Book of the Duchess *in terms of medieval concepts of depression.*]

Comparing Chaucer's understanding of mental states, as it appears in *The Book of the Duchess*, with those ideas recorded in medical texts makes even more evident the human values in the poem to which generations of readers have responded. Examining Chaucer thus is not an unliterary approach. Even Robert Jordan [in *Chaucer's Poetics and the Modern Reader*], examining the poem to uncover the general principles that preside over its status as literary discourse, gets dangerously close to meaning (for a critical theorist) when he points to the fact that 1,000 lines of this 1,300-line poem are elegiac. It has been called "the most historically contextualized of Chaucer's early narrative poems" [Edwards, Robert R. *The Dream of Chaucer: Representation and Reflection in the Early Narratives.* Further references to this text will be given in parentheses]. Chaucer himself makes the poem part of the history of his time by tying it to the death of John of Gaunt's wife, Blanche; he has Queen Alceste, in *The Legend of Good Women*, refer to the poem as "the Deeth of Blaunche the Duchesse." As this historical reference dictates the gravity of the poem's opening, so its other historical components sharpen and season its tone. Medical knowledge is one of those components.

The varying ways in which Chaucer's *Book of the Duchess* portrays and addresses melancholy deserve a more comprehensive examination, particularly in terms of what medical texts reveal. Descriptions of three diseases are almost always found in close proximity to one another in early medical treatises: melancholy, *heroes* and mania. Distinguishing between them is complicated by the fact that these diseases had a number of symptoms in common. It is not surprising, therefore, to find that Stanley Jackson begins his study, *Melancholia and Depression,* with these words:

> In the terms *melancholia* and *depression* and their cognates, we have well over two millennia of the Western world's ways of referring to a goodly number

of different dejected states. At any particular time during these many centuries the term that was in common use might have denoted a disease, a troublesome condition of sufficient severity and duration to be conceived of as a clinical entity; or it might have referred to one of a cluster of symptoms that were thought to constitute a disease.

But as a point from which to begin, it is probably safe to generalize by saying that medieval physicians meant by *depression* or *melancholia* a disease in which sadness and fear were dominant emotions and the imagination disordered, by *mania* a disease in which the prime emotion was anger with some disturbance of the imagination and, to a lesser degree, reason, and by *hereos*—a disease that always ended in mania—a type of melancholia characterized by an obsessive preoccupation with a beloved person. . . .

In their efforts to identify the disease the narrator of *The Book of the Duchess* has suffered for eight long years, several modern scholars have already attempted a more complete evaluation of the evidence. John Hill pointed out that "One of the most prominent symptoms of love melancholy, fixation on the object of desire is missing" [Hill, John M. *The Book of the Duchess*, Melancholy, and that Eight-Year Sickness." *Chaucer Review*, 1974] Judith Neaman concluded that the narrator suffers from ordinary melancholy, the main consequence of which is an inability to write [Neaman, Judith. "Brain Physiology and Poetics in *The Book of the Duchess*." *Res Publica Litterarum*, 1980] and, in a recent note, I argued that the narrator of Chaucer's poem is an example of a neglected variety of melancholy known in the medical literature as *melancholia canina* [in "That Dog Again: *Melancholia Canina* and Chaucer's *Book of the Duchess*." *Modern Philology*, 1986]. In broader terms, John B. Friedman, in a 1969 *Chaucer Review* article, described the narrator of the poem as spiritually distressed ["The Dreamer, the Whele, and Consolation in *The Book of the Duchess*," *Chaucer Review*, 1969]. In discussing Chaucer's concern with poetic subjectivity, Robert Edwards, in his recent book on the dream visions, has made a telling observation, "We might take this [the account of the narrator's mental state] as the originary gesture of his narrative for he explicitly identifies the narrator's interior world as 'our first mater' and 'my first matere." That is, the primary subject of Chaucer's poem is the anguished inward life of the narrator, to which the outward dream bears witness.

I think on reconsidering the evidence—the poem itself and the medical treatises—that the pathological condition described in *The Book of the Duchess*, both in its symptomatology and treatment, cannot be identified as a clearcut case of lovesickness as set forth in discussions by classical and medieval physicians. Furthermore, making clear distinctions between *amor hereos*, melancholy and mania is difficult because early descriptions of these diseases—particularly their treatments—tend to overlap. The difficulty is worth coping with, however; exploring Chaucer's poetic descriptions of melancholy and the medical discussions of the disease by classical and medieval physicians reveals the kind of striking similarities that imply close interrelationships between medieval poetry and medieval medicine. In studying the resemblances between Chaucer's poetry and medieval medical thinking on melancholy, more light can be shed on the poet's keen psychological perceptiveness, as well as on the breadth of knowledge that fed his poetic imagination. Early physicians may have diagnosed and written about mental disorders, but Chaucer's poetry contributed much to popularizing their thinking.

Part of the task of this chapter will be to examine the way sleeping, reading and talking are used by classical and medieval physicians to treat the symptoms of mental diseases and the extent to which Chaucer's suffering narrator-dreamer employs these same three "cures."

SLEEPLESSNESS

The Book of the Duchess begins with a portrait of a narrator rendered sleepless by a great sorrow; whether it be "unfulfilled desire" [Robertson, Jr., D. W. and Bernard F. Huppé. *Fruyt and Chaf: Studies in Chaucer's Allegories*, 1963] or "a general, unfathomable state of *melancholia*" (Hill) is not immediately clear.

> I have gret wonder, be this lyght,
> How that I lyve, for day ne nyght
> I may nat slepe wel nygh noght;
> I have so many an ydel thought,
> Purely for defaute of slep.
>
> (*Duchess*)

The passage, [F. N.] Robinson points out in the Explanatory Notes to his edition, resembles both the opening of Froissart's *Paradys d'Amours* and several passages in Machaut's *Dit de la Fonteinne Amoureuse*. He adds that the situation described was one which "according to medieval theory or general human experience would have led to dreams." The problem of whether Chaucer or other medieval poets had direct knowledge of scientific treatises or were drawing on observable human experiences is one we will put aside for now and return to later in the chapter. Suffice to say, at this juncture, the comment is correct; a dream does occur, but not until the theme of sleep is worked through. The narrator goes on at length with a discourse about his condition in which the word "sleep" frequently appears, as, for example, in this brief excerpt:

> And wel ye woot, agaynes kynde
> Hyt were to lyven in thys wyse,
> For nature wolde nat suffyse
> To noon erthly creature
> Nat longe tyme to endure
> Withoute slep and be in sorwe.

Something is dangerously wrong; life cannot be maintained for long without sleep. In an effort to conquer his sleeplessness, the narrator turns to reading the eleventh book of Ovid's *Metamorphoses,* the story of Ceyx and Alcyone, married lovers separated by death. Suspending for now discussion of what the narrator may have gained by his emotional involvement with the grieving wife of

Ovid's tale, we see immediately that the discovery of the god of sleep is crucial for him. Chaucer handles the section on the intervention of the god with a light, comic touch that throws the tragic circumstances into high relief. To answer Alcyone's prayer for information about her husband's fate, Juno sends a messenger in quest of a revelatory dream from the Cave of Sleep. The messenger can hardly rouse the god, in a passage Chaucer modulates comically without allowing the tone to become jarring:

> This messager com fleynge faste
> And cried, "O, ho! awake anoon!"
> Hit was for noght; there herde hym non.
> "Awake!" quod he, "whoo ys lyth there?"
> And blew his horn ryght in here eere,
> And cried "Awaketh!" wonder hye.

The poem continues the elaboration of the theme of sleep in the following section, in which the narrator, much struck by his reading of the account of "the goddes of slepyng," prays to the newly discovered Morpheus who brought sleep to Queen Alcyone:

> Me thoghte wonder yf hit were so,
> For I had never herd speke, or tho
> Of noo goddes that koude make
> Men to slepe, ne for to wake,
> For I ne knew never god but oon.
> And in my game I sayde anoon
> (And yet me lyst ryght evel to pleye).

If only Morpheus will let him "slepe a lyte," the narrator will offer the comic sacrifice of a featherbed "Of down of pure dowves white" and a black and gold sleeping chamber. No sooner is the promise made than he promptly falls asleep and becomes a dreamer who has "so ynly swete a sweven" that no one, not even Joseph or Macrobius, could interpret his dream.

In early medical treatises, the inability to sleep is a serious symptom, and it follows naturally enough that inducing sleep is curative. One of the first medical writers to discuss mental diseases and, in particular, melancholy and mania, was Soranus of Ephesus, who studied medicine at Alexandria and practiced at Rome during the reigns of Trajan and Hadrian. According to his editor and translator, I. E. Drabkin, "Soranus' works, in common with Hippocratic and Galenic writings, were among those most widely excerpted and translated" (Aurelianus, *On Acute Diseases*). His foremost translatorwas the African, Caelius Aurelianus, who probably lived in the fifth century. His major contribution to communicating Greek medicine to the Middle Ages is his translation of two important works by Soranus, the *Acute Diseases* (three books) and the *Chronic Diseases* (five books). Charles Talbot, the eminent authority on medieval medicine in England, has called this translation by Caelius Aurelianus "the main link in the transmission of ancient medical thought to the Middle Ages" ["Medicine." In *Science in the Middle Ages*, 1978]. The fate of this lengthy and popular work was to undergo changes and abridgements: the portion on acute diseases appeared alone early, with the name "Aurelius" as author; the second half on chronic diseases was circulated in

the seventh century under the name "Aesculapius." These two abridgements spawned many other smaller compilations, some of which were practical, others more theoretical (Talbot). The two treatises examine both melancholy and mania; the latter is described as "a major disease; it is chronic and consists of attacks alternating with periods of remission; it involves a state of stricture."

The question of sleep is taken up only in the section of the book that considers mania. Aurelianus cites "continual sleeplessness" as one of the "observable causes" of mania. Among its symptoms he lists "light and short sleep," "tossing in sleep," as well as "sleep marked by great fear and turmoil." He observes that "in most cases of mania, at the time of an actual attack, the eyes become bloodshot and intent. There is also continual wakefulness." Here it is a symptom or effect, not a cause. The prescribed cures were physical as well as chemical. First he writes that "If the patient is wakeful, prescribe passive exercise, first in a hammock and then in a sedan chair. The rapid dripping of water may be employed to induce sleep, for under the influence of its sound patients often fall asleep." Dripping water appears within the context of sleep in both the ***Book of the Duchess*** and the Ceyx and Alcyone myth of Ovid's *Metamorphoses:*

> ther were a fewe welles
> Came rennynge fro the clyves adoun,
> that made a dedly slepynge soun,
> And ronnen doun ryght by a cave
> That was under a rokke ygrave
> Amydde the valey, wonder depe.
> There these goddes lay and slepe,
> Morpheus and Eclympasteyr,
> That was the god of slepes heyr,
> That slep and dide noon other werk.
>
> *(**Duchess**)*

> But from the bottom of the cave there flows the stream of Lethe, whose waves, gently murmuring over the gravelly bed, invite to slumber. Before the cavern's entrance abundant poppies bloom, and countless herbs, from whose juices dewy night distils sleep and spreads its influence over the darkened lands.
>
> *(Metamorphoses)*

Ovid's passage includes not just Lethe's drowsy streams but other allusions as well to gentle murmuring waves, blooming poppies and numerous night-distilling herbs, all of which make it a comprehensive poetic treatment of Morpheus. At a later point in his discussion of mania and ways of enabling the patient to sleep, Caelius Aurelianus observes that some physicians take a psychopharmacological approach and "try to produce a deep sleep with certain drugs, fomenting the patient with poppy and causing stupor and drowsiness rather than natural sleep." Of the latter approach he is obviously critical, as he adds, "in so doing, they constrict the very parts which require relaxing measures."

READING

Another frequently discussed cure for melancholy is reading; the narrator's insomnia, it will be recalled, was the cause of his turning to Ovid's tale. In *Chaucerian Fiction,* the chapter entitled *"The Book of the Duchess:* The Kindly Imagination," Robert Burlin observes that the poem "differs from the later dream-visions in that we find the dreamer literally 'using' a work of fiction. The story of Seys and Alcyone, directly or indirectly taken from Ovid's *Metamorphoses,* serves therapeutically to divert the narrator from an insomnia induced by an imprecisely defined melancholy." The narrator, unable to sleep, turns to an old romance because he thinks "it beter play/Then play either at ches or tables" (*Duchess*). Now the narrator can view someone else's sorrow—Alcyone's—made beautiful and distant by art, which allows him to sublimate and, perhaps, transcend his own sorrow. Such fables as the narrator turns to were intended by their creators to be reflected upon by those in need of counsel:

And in this bok were written fables
That clerkes had in olde tyme,
And other poetes, put in rime
To rede and for to be in minde,
While men loved the lawe of kinde.

We cannot evade sorrow, but we can assert our human nature through reflection. As Chaucer retells Ovid's tale, he enlarges on the sufferings of Queen Alcyone, separated from her husband, so that the narrator may concentrate on a loss other than, but similar to, his own:

Such sorowe this lady to her tok
That trewly I, that made this book,
Had such pittee and such rowthe
To rede hir sorowe that, by my trowthe,
I ferde the worse al the morwe
Aftir to thenken on hir sorwe.

Ovid's tale deepens the narrator's understanding of his own sorrow. The tale of Alcyone's grief, her husband Ceyx's message in her dream—"I nam but ded"—and her death, precipitated by the blunt, stunning news, offers a lesson about *the lawe of kinde*: sorrow must come to an end. The husband's message is clear on this point, "farewel, swete, my worldes blysse!/I praye God youre sorwe lysse." While the narrator empathizes with Alcyone's story, he does not come to terms with the fact of her sudden death. Chaucer, in fact, abruptly cuts off the story, omitting Ovid's reunion of the lovers after death as birds, and lets the narrator drop off to sleep without the Roman poet's happy ending.

The narrator's dream is itself a kind of fable, for, indeed, when he awakens he thinks to himself,

"Thys ys so queynt a sweven
That I wol, be process of tyme,
Fonde to put this sweven in ryme
As I kan best."

That is, he will make of his dream something like Ovid's tale of Ceyx and Alcyone. When the dreamer encounters the sorrowing black knight in the dream, he finds him beyond the consolations offered by life—he is not interested in the hunt—or by art:

Nought al the remedyes of Ovyde,
Ne Orpheus, god of melodye,
Ne Dedalus with his playes slye.

The black knight, whose name suggests a melancholic condition, is like the dreamer; his sorrowing heart "gan faste faynte" and "his spirites wexen ded". Here, as in Froissart's *Paradys,* imitated at the beginning of *The Book of the Duchess*, the connection between the loss of a loved one and lovesickness is explicit. Moreover, also like the dreamer, he wonders "how hys lyf myght laste", for "he had wel nygh lost hys mynde." For both the grieving dreamer and the black knight, "a tale" becomes the path to gaining "more knowynge of hys [the knight's] thought." In reality, of course, the conversation of the two within the dream framework *is* literature. The black knight's account of his courtship of the lady White memorializes his feelings about her and is a kind of romance. His account of her appearance, even if accurate, is conventional to romance literature, specifically Machaut's *Remede de Fortune* and the *Jugement dou Roy de Behaingne:*

And goode faire White she het;
That was my lady name ryght.
She was bothe fair and bryght;
She hadde not hir name wrong.
Ryght faire shuldres and body long
She had, and armes, every lyth
Fattyssh, flesshy, not gret therwith;
Ryght white handes, and nayles rede,
Rounde brestes; and of good brede
Hyr hippes were; a streight flat bak.

Not only is White's beauty like something out of a story-book, but so is her virtue. She is likened to the fabulous bird of legend, "The soleyn fenix of Arabye" and, for her "debonairte," to "Hester in the Bible." Much of *The Book of the Duchess* grows out of the dreamer-turned-poet recording the black knight's description of his lost lady. His memory of her is already a fiction, caught in the images of his suffering mind. In the end, without any solution, religious or philosophical, to the problem of mortality, the black knight is able to say plainly, "she ys ded!" As Burlin so aptly summarizes, "in purely human terms: the perceptive powers of the imagination in intimate cooperation with memory bring about a release from the paralysis of sorrow." Interestingly, the imagination, over time an important element of the cure, is also an aspect of the disease, since, in love melancholy, it is the imagination that is affected, trapped by the image of the beloved so that the sufferer abandons all other bodily needs, including food and sleep. One could argue that the reading of Chaucer's narrator-dreamer strongly colors the contents of the dream, so that the preoccupations of the waking life are carried on in sleep. While the dream at first offers Ovidian coincidence of detail, it also gradually shows the way to escape.

The therapeutic effect of literature, especially in treating mental disease, was recognized by the ancients, and they continued to praise it up until Chaucer's day and beyond. Glending Olson observes of this poem, "however original and humorous Chaucer may be in describing his [the narrator's] means of falling asleep, it is worth noting that his invention in the **Book of the Duchess** seems predicated on a psychology of reading and sleeping that is explained in the *Tacuinum*," a Latin manual on hygiene translated from the Arabic in the thirteenth century. Olson's quote from this work, however, indicates that it is no more than an item from a table on sleep: "*Confabulator*: a teller of stories should have good discernment in knowing the kind of fictions in which the soul takes delight." The idea of the therapeutic good of pleasurable reading is explicit enough, but, as we shall see, many other more learned and elaborated statements on "literatherapy" were abroad in Chaucer's day in the medical literature (and some of these embody ideas that still hold weight today).

Among the many early physicians who give space to the importance of literary diversion is Paul of Aegina who, in discussing lovesick persons, comments that these are frequently "wasted" by physicians who misdiagnose their ailment and prescribe "quietude"; whereas, "wiser ones" who are more skilled at diagnosis advise, among other treatments, "spectacles and amusing stories" (*The Seven Book*). Such entertainment is likewise prescribed for melancholy by Avicenna in his *Canon of Medicine* and by Bartholomaeus Anglicus in *De Proprietatibus Rerum,* and for both melancholy and *amor hereos* by Valescus de Taranta in the *Philonium* (fol. 11r and 13r). Clearly the idea that the pleasures of literary diversion gave melancholics relief had currency in Chaucer's day; it would have had to be a virtual commonplace to have sifted down into a manual on health such as the *Tacuinum*. But the appearance of the idea in Avicenna and Bartholomaeus Anglicus has added significance in terms of the interplay of poetry and science during the Middle Ages, because Chaucer could easily have encountered their works.

Avicenna was readily available, and we know Chaucer was acquainted with his work, for in the **"Pardoner's Tale"** he mentions the distinctive chapter and fen divisions of the *Canon*'s structure when he discusses the symptoms of poisoning:

> But certes, I suppose that Avycen
> Wroot nevere in no canon, ne in no fen,
> Mo wonder signes of empoisonyng
> Than hadde thise wrecches two, er hir endyng.

J. A. W. Bennett, who considers Chaucer's learning unmatched by any other late medieval English poet, even though he never took a university degree, is persuaded that his interest in and proximity to Oxford and the rich holdings of the Merton College Library may have contributed to his achievements. As a lifelong servant of kings, Chaucer would have attended court at the palace of Woodstock, regularly used by Edward and Richard, which was eight miles to the north of Oxford and only accessible from London (where Chaucer lived) by passing through Oxford (Bennett). The first appearance of Chaucer's name, in fact, occurs in the Woodstock household accounts for 1357. The poet associates his pilgrim clerk with Oxford, names two men with close ties to Oxford in his writing,

"philosophical" Strode and Bishop Bradwardine, gives his tale of student life an Oxford setting, and credits his physician pilgrim with a knowledge of medical works so vast that he could not have owned them all. Bennett comments, "I can find no record of any collection containing them except Merton College." If Chaucer himself spent time at Oxford, and if he went to the Merton College Library, one of the works he could have read there was Avicenna's *Canon*. The *Canon* contains a long section on signs of melancholy care, followed by a section on its cure. While emphasizing somatic cures such as bathing, drinking wine and being rubbed with aromatic oils, Avicenna also includes "listening to songs" in the context of such pastimes as hunting and sensual delights. Equally accessible was Bartholomaeus Anglicus's *De Proprietatibus Rerum,* translated into Middle English by John of Trevisa in the fourteenth century. This encyclopedia also advises literary entertainment for the relief of those who are cast down— "þe remedye of þise is þat þe sike man be ileide in a ly3t place and þat þere be iangelinge and grete spekinge and disputesoun," "by swete voys and song[es] and armonye, accord, and musik, sike men and mad and frenetek come ofte to hire witt a3ee and hele of body"—albeit of a distinctly oral, lyric nature.

But by far the most detailed discussion of the therapeutic value of literary entertainment appears in Caelius Aurelianus's *Chronic Diseases,* as he considers cures for mania:

> . . . have the patient read aloud even from texts that are marred by false statements. In this way he will exercise his mind more thoroughly. And for the same reason he should also be kept busy answering questions. This will enable us both to detect malingering and to obtain the information we require. Then let him relax, giving him reading that is easy to understand; injury due to overexertion will thus be avoided. For if these mental exercises overtax the patient's strength, they are no less harmful than passive exercise carried to excess.

> And so after the reading let him see a stage performance. A mime is suitable if the patient's madness has manifested itself in dejection; on the other hand, a composition depicting sadness or tragic terror is suitable in cases of madness which involve playful childishness. For the particular characteristic of a case of mental disturbance must be corrected by emphasizing the opposite quality, so that the mental condition, too, may attain the balanced state of health. And as the treatment proceeds, have the patient deliver discourses or speeches as far as his ability and strength permit. And in this case the speeches should all be arranged in the same way, the introduction to be delivered with a gentle voice, the narrative portions and proof more loudly and intensely, and the conclusion, again, in asubdued and kindly manner. This is in accordance with the precepts of those who have written on vocal exercise (Greek *anaphonesis*). An audience should be present, consisting of persons familiar to the patient, by according the speech favorable attention and praise, they will help relax the speaker's mind.

A related cure in **The Book of the Duchess** is the process of "talking it out"—the backbone of current day psychotherapies—as exemplifed by the conversation between the black knight and the dreamer.

Talking

Years ago, at a time when some critics accused the dreamer of stupidity and lack of tact, Joseph E. Grennen [in "*Hert-Huntyng* in the *Book of the Duchess*." *Modern Language Quarterly*, 1964] stated flatly, "The dreamer does clearly see himself in the role of physician" and cited the supporting lines:

> But certes, sire, yif that yee
> Wolde ought discure me youre woo,
> I wolde, as wys God helpe me soo,
> Amend hyt, yif I kan or may.
> Ye mowe preve hyt by assay;
> For, by my trouthe, to make yow hool
> I wol do al my power hool.
> And telleth me of youre sorwes smerte;
> Paraunter hyt may ese youre herte,
> That semeth ful sek under your syde.

Penelope Doob [in *Nebuchadnezzar's Children: Conventions of Madness in Middle English Literature*] cites this passage as well and observes that the minor but very fine fifteenth century poet, Thomas Hoccleve, uses the same technique in the *Regement of Princes* (ca. 1412), wherein the poet depicts himself as a melancholic wandering in a state of distraction who has the good fortune to be found by a benevolent beggar (Doob). This man insists on getting Hoccleve to talk with him and tell "the verray cause of þin hyd maladye." Hoccleve is generally thought to be describing his own madness, and Doob credits him with "considerable scientific and medical knowledge." It is likely that Hoccleve is drawing on his personal experience combined with medical learning; there is also a strong probability that he is consciously reworking Chaucer's dialogue. Like the narrator in *The Book of the Duchess*, Hoccleve's beggar uses talk as a diversion from grief. Actually, as noted earlier, Chaucer's dreamer wants to establish contact with the bereaved knight even before the above-cited passage:

> Anoon ryght I gan fynde a tale
> To hym, to loke wher I myght ought
> Have more knowynge of hys thought.

Far from stupid or clumsy, the dreamer's desire to intervene flows from his sense of the enormity of the black knight's grief,

> Hit was gret wonder that Nature
> Myght suffre any creature
> To have such sorwe, and be nat ded,

gathered from tactful eavesdropping while the knight sange his "complaynte":

> "I have sorwe so gret won
> That joye gete I never non,
> Now that I see my lady bryght,
> Which I have loved with al my myght,
> Is fro me ded and ys agoon."

The second half of the poem essentially relates the conversational give-and-take between the dreamer and bereaved knight, whereby the latter is enabled to express his sorrow directly to himself and another person. When, for instance, the black knight avoids the truth by losing it in the indirection of the figure of the chess game, the dreamer's conscious pose of obtuseness—"But ther is no man alyve her / Wolde for a fers make this woo!"—gently prods the knight in the direction of unburdening his heart. As the dreamer well knows, the sorrow springs from the loss of a human being, and his remark opens the floodgates of memory. The bereaved knight spends some 300 lines detailing the beauty and virtues of his "lady dere." After that space of recollection, the dreamer poses the unavoidable question, "Sir . . . where is she now?" which, briefly avoided, leads finally to the open confession, "she ys ded!" This frees the knight to return home to his castle and presumably to reenter the world of active living. The "hert-huntyng" is done, heart's ease has been achieved, and the dreamer awakens thereafter with the book about "the goddes of slepyng" in his hand. By that point two mourners have been restored: the black knight of the dream is ready to resume the work of governance and the dreamer feels nearly ready to put the strange dream into "ryme / As I kan best." It seems reasonable to view the second half of *The Book of the Duchess* as mostly detailing the progress of, as Robertson and Huppé so aptly put it, "the poet's discovery of his mourning self through facing its simulacrum." This is a rather sophisticated development of one of the more frequent pieces of advice offered by early medical writers: that melancholics ought to get out and speak with friends. . . .

On the basis of this examination of *The Book of the Duchess*, and in light of earlier scholarly discoveries about the interchange between medieval physicians and medieval poets, it appears that Geoffrey Chaucer knew well the medieval thinking and practices of his time, though it is impossible to ascertain how much of the medical writing he knew firsthand. But what, finally, can be said about the narrator's eight-year sickness? Is it *amor hereos?* melancholy? mania? Hill, as mentioned in opening this chapter, astutely observes that "One of the most prominent symptoms of love melancholy, fixation on the object of desire, is missing." Chaucer's narrator emphasizes, rather, that "al is ylyche good to me—/ . . . for I have felynge in nothing," (*Duchess*), and that he is always dazed and dizzy. Hill's diagnosis of the disease is "head melancholy," a term borrowed from Robert Burton's *Anatomy*, which leaves the narrator "in danger of dying from default of sleep caused by his sorrowful *ymagynacioun*" (Hill). It may be that there is only dazed numbness without fixation on the object of desire because White *is* dead: the ideal woman has become inaccessible forever. My own earlier comments on the poem in terms of *melancholia canina* would not, however, rule out *amor hereos;* indeed, that category of melancholy may embrace *hereos*. The tenth century physicians Rhazes and Haly Abbas are responsible for a loose association of *melancholia canina* with *amor hereos* that could lend support to the view that frustrated love is, indeed, the cause of the narrator's eight-year sickness. In Rhazes's *Continens*, for instance, he links the two categories of melancholy in a chapter heading: "Concerning Coturub." But again, as the present examination shows, symptoms as well as treatments for lovesickness, melancholy and mania tend to overlap. The narrator's initial complaint of insomnia is a serious symptom shared by each of the three diseases. His recourse to reading Ovid is a sensible diversion that, again, is prescribed by early physicians for all three mental diseases. Moreover, the dialogue between the narrator and black knight, a benefit to both participants, is also in accord with treatments recommended for each of these diseases.

In the final analysis, a definitive diagnosis is not only hard to make but unnecessary, as lovesickness, melancholy and mania are not only perceived but treated in many of the same ways. Implicit in Chaucer's description of Arcite's mental condition in the **"Knight's Tale"** is the poet's understanding of the interrelationship of the three mental conditions—*amor hereos,* mania and melancholy. He says of Arcite's psychological state that it was

> Nat oonly lik the loveris maladye
> Of Hereos, but rather lyk manye,
> Engendred of humour malencolik
> Biforn, in his celle fantastik

It appears that Lowes began the scholarly journey from a very fruitful place.

Chaucer's passage on Arcite's mental state expresses a psychological subtlety that suggests his comprehension of the extremes of human behavior went beyond merely being in touch with medical commonplaces of his day. It is, nonetheless, difficult to know just how much direct knowledge Chaucer had of the writings of that rather comprehensive list of medical authorities cited in the portrait of his physician pilgrim. In *Chaucer's Physician,* Huling Ussery discusses John of Arderne as a reasonable model for the physician, in preference to John of Gaddesden, who died too early (1349) to be a reasonable candidate. Chaucer probably had heard that "Peter de Barulo *alias* Master Peter de Salernia, physician" was arrested in 1387 and may have been acquainted with one of his treatises. For all we know, this possibly unscrupulous man was a model for the physician pilgrim. But such evidence does not make it possible to prove that Chaucer read the writing of medieval medical authorities; we are simply assured that it was not *im*possible. Rossell Hope Robbins, an indefatigable tracker of manuscripts, in his essay, "The Physician's Authorities," points out that in the fourteenth century, ten of Chaucer's authorities were among the 230 medical works in St. Augustine's Abbey at Canterbury; nine appear among 208 medical books in the fifteenth century catalogs of Christ Church, Canterbury; and all except two, Gaddesden and Rufus, are also found in the library of Dover Priory. Thus it was possible for Chaucer to consult medical treatises firsthand. Of course, the availability of texts only makes their reading possible, no more; I have never read *The Magic Mountain* though a copy is on a bookshelf in the living room. Yet over an over again, one senses behind Chaucer's verse not just the intuition of poetic insight but actual scientific learning. When, for instance, right before the dreamer offers his help to the Black Knight, Chaucer conveys the man's danger, expressing poetically his unnatural state of cold joylessness and nature's mechanism for correcting it, the poet does so in a way clearly informed by a knowledge of contemporary physiology. One hardly needs the evidence of parallel medical texts to feel convinced of a meeting of poetic vision and scientific knowledge in this passage:

> Hys sorwful hert gan faste faynte,
> And his spirites wexen dede;
> The blood was fled for pure drede
> Doun to hys herte to make hym warm—
> For wel hyt feled the herte had harm—
> To wite eke why hit was adrad
> By kynde, and for to make hyt glad.

The ability of poets and physicians to see in parallel ways accounts for the ease with which they move in and out of one another's territory—not merely human nature, there for mutual viewing, but their works *about* that nature.

A. J. Minnis   (essay date 1995)

SOURCE: *"The Book of the Duchess,"* in *Oxford Guides to Chaucer: The Shorter Poems,* edited by A. J. Minnis *et al.,* Clarendon Press, 1995, pp. 73-90.

[*Minnis is a scholar of Medieval Literature and the author of many notable works including* Chaucer and the Pagan Antiquity *and* Chaucer's Boece and the Medieval Tradition of Boethius. *In the following excerpt, Minnis uses historical information and analyses of verse form, rhetoric, and style to praise Chaucer's* The Book of the Duchess.]

Blanche of Lancaster died on 12 September 1368, perhaps of the plague. Two major monuments were constructed to preserve her memory. One was a poem by Geoffrey Chaucer, this being (as far as we know) his first substantial composition; he was probably in his mid-twenties at the time of Blanche's death. The other was the work of her husband, John of Gaunt, the third surviving son of King Edward III. In 1374 he commissioned from master mason Henry Yevele a splendid alabaster tomb, surmounted by sculptures of the duchess and himself. Perpetual masses were to be said for her soul at an adjoining altar, and a memorial service held on 12 September of each year. Gaunt's will contained the directive, 'My body to be buried . . . beside my most dear late wife Blanche, who is there interred.' And that was done. However, the tomb of Gaunt and Blanche, which was located in the north arcade of the choir of old St Paul's cathedral church in London, perished in the Great Fire. Chaucer's poem has survived. Is it a record, however idealized, of a genuine love-affair, or an elaborate piece of prince-pleasing which plays fast and loose with the facts, assuming that the poet knew them? Many critics have felt obliged to speculate on the nature of the royal relationship, since on it hangs—or at least they have made to hang—their views on the negotiations between artifice and life, conventional discourses and emotional integrity, which are made by the *Book of the Duchess*.

It has been argued that Gaunt's first marriage was dictated by political expediency every bit as much as his second, to Constance of Castile. Worse still, in some medieval accounts he appears as an inveterate womanizer: having fathered an illegitimate daughter before he met Blanche, during the time of his marriage to Constance he took Katherine Swynford as his mistress (they were to marry in 1396). Indeed, it has even been suggested (though hard evidence is lacking) that this affair began while he was married to Blanche. Katherine had been one of Blanche's ladies-in-waiting and the governess of her daughters. Chaucer could hardly have been unaware of such events, if it is true that his wife Philippa was the sister of Gaunt's long-time mistress.

One would give much to know what the poet had in mind as he wrote the *Book of the Duchess* and as he looked back on it in later years. But that knowledge will, of course, never be forthcoming, and in the absence of such intimate biographical detail we may isolate the appropriate critical issues by means of a modern meditation on a medieval tomb—not Blanche's lost tomb, to be sure, but one belonging to the Howard family, once earls and countesses of Arundel, which may be seen in Winchester Cathedral. Philip Larkin's poem "An Arundel Tomb" raises questions concerning the artistic imitation (or is it illusion?) of feeling and the needs of the audience which confronts such an image, questions which lead us into vital regions of the aesthetics of Chaucer's poem.

> Side by side, their faces blurred,
> The earl and countess lie in stone,
> their proper habits vaguely shown
> As jointed armour, stiffened pleat

What these people really felt for each other has also become 'blurred,' as the poem will make abundantly clear. In what sense do they 'lie in stone'? The earl's left-hand gauntlet is empty, and

> One sees, with a sharp tender shock,
> His hand withdrawn, holding her hand.

But this serves to perplex as well as please. Is this a true or false image of historical reality? 'They would not think to lie so long', the repetition of 'lie' underlining the double meaning of the word: the sculptures lie together there as part of the tomb, and yet they may be perpetuating an untruth. (The fact that the hand-clasp is the result of later 'restoration' of the tomb serves to reinforce Larkin's point!) The next line, 'Such faithfulness in effigy,' is similarly ambiguous. That particular effigy could be an accurate representation of genuine fidelity; yet, taken in its entirety, the phrase also suggests something grimly static and cold, the life-affirming quality of fidelity in love being impossible to preserve artificially.

The role of the artist, the sculptor responsible for this fabrication, is then considered. Maybe the holding of hands

was simply a grace-note ('A sculptor's sweet commissioned grace') which he added on his own initiative (though of course he had been paid to display his skill), in the hope that its rarity would aid the memory of the beholders. If so, it would seem that time has reversed such priorities. Now tourists stare uncomprehendingly at the Latin names 'around the base,' not being able to understand this dead language. What seems to be familiar, what they fancy they recognize, is that hand-clasp; here is something which transcends temporal and linguistic differences. 'Only an attitude remains'—the configuration of the sculptures, existing irrespective of, and maybe even despite, what the original attitudes of the medieval lord and lady may have been. It seems to affirm that human love is durable. Certainly, that is what (the poem's assumed) 'we' *want* to believe; what is seen on the tomb appears

>   to prove
> Our almost-instinct almost true:
> What will survive of us is love.

But the poem will not allow 'us' to luxuriate in such a sentiment, tempting though that may be. It persists in asking, *does* love survive, in general, and is this what has happened in the case of the Howards, whose identities are lost in the past?

Time is not passive; it has not merely permitted the effigy to travel unhindered in its 'supine stationary voyage' down to the present. Rather, it is a power which effects transformation.

> Time has transfigured them into
> Untruth. The stone fidelity
> They hardly meant has come to be
> Their final blazon

In this case it may have exercised a heightening, and hence a distorting, effect on something which owes more to art than to life, more to fiction than to truth. The medieval aristocrats may not have lived up to their image; 'hardly meant' evinces at once possible misunderstanding and firm affirmation—the hard stone declares its own meaning. The 'attitude' of love has thus been created by art; art has the power, as it were, to 'make' love. But are we dealing, then, with a lie? In terms of historical truth, maybe—though we shall never know. But the desire of human beings to believe in the survival of love in itself constitutes a major truth. Hence one can justifiably speak of an 'almost-instinct' as being 'almost true.' The agnostic modern, seeking to avoid sentimentality and dubious of the existence of a destiny which shapes our ends, is not prepared to go any farther than that. Yet this almost-truth is, in Larkin's terms, a fact of the first magnitude.

Due to the carefully wrought ambiguity of this poem, neither element of the balance is allowed to dominate. It cannot be said that this has always been the case in modern interpretation of Chaucer's 'lie' in verse, the *fabula* of the *Book of the Duchess*. Some have been convinced that time, with the help of Chaucer's artistic 'grace' (whether specifically 'commissioned' or not) has transfigured Gaunt and Blanche into untruth. The possibility that John of Gaunt had committed adultery with Katherine in Blanche's lifetime has occasionally been raised, with Gaunt's wish to be buried beside his first duchess being taken as indicative of his thankfulness for her acquiescent forbearance. Then there is the question, did Gaunt do enough on Blanche's death? One may contrast, for example, Richard II's order, on the death of his queen in 1394, that the royal manor at Sheen be destroyed; he had once enjoyed happiness with her there. (As Clerk of the Works, Chaucer had overseen alterations to that royal residence.) But, even by the standards of the age, this was an extravagant expression of grief; it can hardly be taken as a norm against which to measure Gaunt's behaviour and find it wanting.

Others have perceived an even more elaborate web of intrigue, which included Chaucer's own wife and the poet himself. For instance, it has been suggested that Gaunt may have had an affair with Philippa, the issue of which was Thomas Chaucer. Such a claim, however, rests on an extraordinarily partial interpretation of such evidence as does exist and a determination to make gaps in the historical record into significant silences. Moreover, it is quite unnecessary: such links as we know Chaucer to have had with Gaunt certainly did not require him to have been in the position of a 'contented cuckold' (as B. J. Whiting puts it) who merited some compensation, and 'in later years the fact that the duke truly loved Chaucer's sister-in-law may be reason enough why he granted financial favors' to her kin, to quote Donald Howard [in *Chaucer and the Medieval World*].

But let us concentrate on the relationship between Gaunt and Blanche. It has often been declared or implied that love is the most important thing that has survived of them. Sydney Armitage-Smith, in his 1904 biography of John of Gaunt, saw Blanche's death as marking the end of the best years of Gaunt's life. 'Of the sincerity of the Duke's grief there need be no question'; his 'gratitude to the memory of his first wife never failed.' Monkish attacks on Gaunt's subsequent affair with Katherine are trivialized as 'merely the venom of the cloister,' and there is special pleading with reference to the 'standard of English society in the fourteenth century,' which is supposed to have been 'not exacting' in matters of personal morality. Gaunt's conduct, Armitage-Smith believes, was 'if no better . . . certainly no worse' than that of others. Writing over eighty years later, Howard follows in Armitage-Smith's footsteps by seeing Gaunt's life with Blanche as marking the end of his golden age: 'Her death . . . wrought a change in his character. He was to be thereafter a man possessed by ambitions.' Concerning the quality of Gaunt's first love, while noting that 'Medieval knights of royal lineage are often depicted as unfeeling military leaders whose relationships with women were exploitative and wanting in sentiment,' Howard prefers to throw his own weight behind the belief that 'they could love their wives with towering and noble emotion,' and unhesitatingly takes the commemorative masses and services which Gaunt ordered, along with his declared desire to be buried beside Blanche, as firm evidence that he 'loved her deeply.' A similar dichotomy pervades Derek Brewer's approach. Evincing a robust willingness to accept medieval *realpolitik* and mores, he refuses to be surprised by Gaunt's prompt remarriage: 'Private sentiment could not weigh against public policy; and there was anyway a hardboiled acceptance of death in the fourteenth century.' However, these general facts of late medieval life certainly do not, in Brewer's opinion, rule out the possibility that profound 'private sentiment' could have existed in this case: 'Lancaster's genuine love for Blanche and his grief at her death are not to be questioned' [*Chaucer and His World*]. Chaucer's poem, he continues, is 'not so much an idealized account of life as the ideal truth to which life was so fortunate to approximate.'

George Kane, *pace* Chaucer's poem, is determined to portray Gaunt with warts and all, and to remind us that they were clearly visible before, as well as after, his time with Blanche. 'There was nothing [in the *Book of the Duchess*] about the daughter Gaunt fathered before he married Blanche'; nor could one know from it that 'Gaunt's marriage to Blanche had in fact been arranged by his father to consolidate the kingship' [*Chaucer*]. Yet, later, Kane declares that although this was an arranged marriage, 'It turned into a love match.' 'Lovely Blanche . . . never lost her place in his heart,' as is manifest by his wish to be buried beside her. However, Chaucer's latest biographer, Derek Pearsall, has challenged such reasoning. 'It was usual to be buried next to one's first wife,' he claims, 'especially when she was the foundation of one's fortune.' And the phrase 'my most dear late wife,' apparently so appropriate as applied to Blanche, is also applied to Constance of Castile (who died in 1394). Anyway, declares Pearsall, here we are dealing with 'the routine commonplaces of inky clerks' [*Life of Chaucer*].

How, then, can one possibly sum up Gaunt's behaviour in love? 'A spectacular man to whom the rules might not seem to apply' is Kane's verdict. Thus, Gaunt's best side is presented to the beholder: here is one who was not numbered in the roll of common men. And this is, of course, precisely what the *Book of the Duchess* shows and says, inasmuch as its Man in Black is an idealized figure of Gaunt. In the final analysis, we cannot claim familiarity with Gaunt. Similarly, there is considerable distance between the observer and the observed in the *Book of the Duchess*, the poet persona and the Gaunt-surrogate being divided by rank and experience. These matters will be discussed below. Suffice it to say here that Chaucer's portraits of Gaunt and Blanche, though idealized representations, are no effigies upon which the narrator can project his meditations—which is what is happening in the Larkin poem. For in the *Book of the Duchess* it is the black knight who is dominant, who imposes his meditations on a beholder, the narrator, a subordinate who can listen and learn even if he cannot fully understand. He, the marvelling reporter, invites his audience to share in his admiration. And in Chaucer's poem, art, far from turning feelings into stone, serves to conserve them—but here too the pleat has stiffened, inasmuch as they are presented in forms which owe much to the ritualizing processes of literary decorums and conventions. Whether or not this is a 'lie' or an approximation to ideal truth (to echo Brewer's phrase) is impossible to tell. History allows either opinion, and gainsays neither. . . .

Chaucer's use of the octosyllabic couplet . . . encourages the feeling that we are in the presence a young poet who is heavily influenced by French fashion. This was the verse-form used in the *Roman de la Rose*. Chaucer seems to have translated this extraordinarily influential poem into English, at least one fragment of which may have survived. It was also the measure of several of the direct sources of the **Book of the Duchess**, most notably Guillaume de Machaut's *Remede de Fortune* and *Dit de la Fonteinne Amoureuse* (c. 1360), and the *Ovide moralisé*, which was written between 1316 and 1328 by an anonymous Franciscan.

Some lines have one syllable more and others one syllable less. This cannot be put down to inexperience, however, since this variation is found also in the later **House of Fame**. Moreover, sometimes a trochee functions as the first, second, or indeed the third foot in place of the iambus. And on occasion Chaucer allows an extra syllable before the caesura and a short foot after it. All this indicates Chaucer's preference for a looser verse-form—by contrast with Gower, who in his *Confessio Amantis* creates octosyllabic couplets of exceptional regularity with apparent ease. The current consensus is that Chaucer cannot be judged strictly by French metrical standards, given that he seems to have been influenced by the freer English tradition of four-beat lines. Certainly there is no justification for thoroughgoing editorial attempts to 'restore' smooth octosyllabics.

Further, there is, perhaps, a general tendency to regard the octosyllabic couplet as a highly reductive measure, cramping and homogenizing in its limited scope. This should be resisted. An effective antidote is offered by the work of a contemporary master of the form, Tony Harrison. To take but two examples, his controversial poem on the Gulf War, "A Cold Coming," and his film poem "The Gaze of the Gorgon" prove beyond any shadow of a doubt that octosyllabics can accommodate both savage satire and subtle sensitivies, and are eminently capable of ranging from hope to horror, from the sublime to the ridiculous, from the tender to the obscene, even within a few lines. All the more reason to give Chaucer the benefit of the doubt.

At two points in the **Book of the Duchess** a more complicated rhyme scheme is used. This is in the case of the 'enclosed lyrics,' the Man in Black's initial 'compleynte' about his lost 'lady bryght' and the very first 'song' which, according to his reminiscences, he wrote in expression of his feelings for her. The latter rhymes *aabbaa*. The former has a more elaborate scheme, *aabbaccdccd,* which seems to be imperfect. All the manuscripts agree here, but normally one would expect a second couplet rhyming on *a*, though as a genre the complaint can take many forms. In William Thynne's 1532 edition of Chaucer the line 'Now have I tolde the, sothe to say' appears after the indubitably authentic line 1180, but Thynne may simply have made it up.

By including lyrics in this way and highlighting them as discrete units within the narrative (we are told when a recital is about to begin, and some comment is made to

mark its completion), Chaucer was following in the footsteps of the Old French poets. The fiction of overhearing and recording a superior's lyric was almost certainly indebted to Machaut's *Fonteinne Amoureuse,* in which the patron's accomplished complaint is transcribed admiringly by the narrator. But the 'intercalated lyric' is a common feature of the *dit amoreux* genre. To take one of the most influential *dits* of them all as an example, in Machaut's *Remede de Fortune* the narrator composes a lay about his feelings for his lady and a complaint about Fortune. (At the end of the latter Machaut presents the I-persona as debating and struggling alone ('per moy debatus'). That particular phrase calls to mind Chaucer's statement that the Man in Black's complaint is 'to hymselve,' and later, in **Troilus and Criseyde**, Troilus will be described as 'disputyng with hymself' in the 'matere' of fate and fortune.) Subsequently Hope sings a *chant royal* and a *baladele* to comfort and cheer the lover. Duly revitalized, he composes a *ballade* to his lady, and prays to Love. The climax comes when he actually performs a *chanson baladee* before her, after which she consents to be called his beloved; overjoyed, he sings a *rondelet* as he takes his leave. It could be said that here poetic production is being put in place of amatory experience, an effect which is even more obvious in Machaut's *Voir Dit* (c. 1364), wherein the lover-narrator and the beloved, Toute-Belle, exchange poems and verse letters, and when their relationship blossoms, each writes a lyric by way of celebration. Jean Froissart's *Prison Amoureuse* (c. 1360), which is fundamentally a sequence of lyrics and letters, is an obvious attempt to surpass the *Voir Dit;* similarly, Froissart's *Paradys d'Amours* (c. 1362-9) includes examples of the *rondel, rondelet, lay, virelay,* and *ballade,* which the characters sing with pleasure and much self-congratulation. Nominally these lyric performances record and reflect the psychological history of the narrator and/or some authority figure, but above all else they are an ostentatious display of technical virtuosity, the narrative functioning as a show-case.

Chaucer is rather more interested in having the intercalated lyric fulfil a definite narrative function. Thus, it is the Man in Black's complaint that first tells us that his beloved is dead; thereby the scene is set for the lengthy conversation which follows. And the composition of his very first song in honour of the lady White is also presented as an event of real significance in the furtherance of the story. Knowledge of the bereaved lover's past emotions helps us to understand his present ones. The fact that there are only two lyrics, rather than a formidable arsenal, makes them all the more effective in these terms; they function symmetrically as a neatly contrasting pair. The point which I want to emphasize, however, is that these lyrics keep the action moving rather than hold it up; to some extent this is due, of course, to the fact that they are a lot shorter than most of the effusions in the French *dits,* but different literary priorities are the major determining factor. When John Lydgate came to produce his own version of Chaucer's poem, the *Complaynt of a Loveres Lyfe* (written during the period 1398-1412), he returned to the French manner of doing things which we have just described, the result being a poem which comprises a sequence of quite static set pieces. The actual complaint of 'a man / In black and white, colour pale and wan' occupies some 356 lines within a poem of 681 lines, thus constituting over half its total length. Lydgate's eavesdropping narrator does not actually converse with the grieving knight, but carefully records what he said—to entertain the audience!

> A pene I toke and gan me fast[e] spede
> The woful pleynt[e] of this man to write,
> Worde by worde as he dyd endyte:
> Lyke as I herde and coud him tho reporte
> I haue here set, youre hertis to dysporte.

And he utters a twenty-five-line prayer to 'lady Venus' on the knight's behalf. The poem ends with two envoys, of eight lines each, the first to 'Princes' and 'womanhede' in general and the second to his 'luyves quene' in particular. Here direct human contact is avoided, Lydgate being more interested in the aureate encrustation of disembodied emotions than the creation of selfhoods or with their interaction. The contrasts with the **Book of the Duchess** are striking.

Chaucer's interest in the intercalated lyric was by no means confined to the **Book of the Duchess**. **Anelida and Arcite** contains an elaborate 'compleynt,' and a 'roundel' in praise of St Valentine's Day appears near the end of the **Parliament of Fowls**. In the F Prologue to the **Legend of Good Women** a 'balade' beginning 'Hyd, Absolon, thy gilte tresses clere' is recited ('seyn') by the I-persona, while in the G Prologue it is sung by the group of ladies which accompanies the God of Love; these performances have an ornamental function in the main. Moreover, in **Troilus and Criseyde** there is a *Canticus Troili* at i. 400-20 (on the contrary emotions characteristic of love) and another at v. 638-44 (on the torment caused by Criseyde's absence). In the second book Antigone sings 'cleere' a 'Troian song,' which encourages Criseyde to sympathetic to Troilus, while the final book includes two verse letters, one from Troilus to Criseyde, the other, Criseyde's reply. More unusually, in the third book Boethian philosophy is recast in the form of yet another *Canticus Troili*, sung by the overjoyed prince in celebration of the consummation of his love. As Ardis Butterfield has argued so well, this may be regarded as a development of the French practice of lyric enclosure, less surprising given the manifest debt of some of the *dits amoreux,* particularly the *Remede de Fortune,* to the *Consolatio philosophiae*. Clearly, Old French verseforms and intercalating techniques exercised an influence on Chaucer which lasted well into his so-called Italian period.

Moving on now to discuss the poem's style, with special reference to its rhetoric, it may be said that Chaucer took a calculated risk in introducing idiomatic dialogue, which is generally awkward to handle in verse. Lines 1042 ff. work very well, the tricky exchange at 1045-7 being handled with especial skill. Then again, a wonderfully comic effect is achieved at lines 184-6, when Juno's messenger wakes up Morpheus ('Who clepeth ther?' / 'Hyt am I'). But lines 1309-10 pose problems even for some of the poem's greatest admirers.

> 'She ys ded!' 'Nay!' 'Yis, be my trouthe!'
> 'Is that youre los? Be God, hyt ys routhe!'

For a climax to a long apotheosis of love and the lady, is not this rather disappointing? Of course, it could be said that here at last the poem's displacing and ritualizing decorums have been left behind, as the plain fact of death is confronted in plain speech. But there is a hint of something else, something which feels uncomfortably like bathos. The chime of the rhyme diminishes the emotional force of the exchange, making it sound inappropriately pat and curt. A similar effect occurs at the end of the 'poem within the poem', the story of Ceyx and Alcyone, when the traumatized queen is dismissed rather brusquely:

> . . . 'Alas!' quod she for sorwe,
> And deyede within the thridde morwe.

Here, however, the effect can be justified as part and parcel of the 'game' which the narrator may be playing with the ancient text. Alternatively, Chaucer could have been striving to construct a blunt statement of the facts of death, a theory which can claim support from the emphasis on earthly transience that is characteristic of the entire passage which culminates with this couplet.

The prevailing impression given by the poem, however, is of an enthusiastic and highly ambitious writer who is in love with rhetoric. This may be illustrated with reference to Chaucer's long *descriptio* of 'faire White', which occupies lines 817-1041, with a brief continuation at lines 1052-87, making a grand total of some 261 lines of verse. Chaucer took the account of a beautiful lady (who, incidentally, proves unfaithful) as seen through the eyes of her lover from Machaut's *Jugement dou Roy de Behaingne* (composed before 1342), and embellished it further, developing its theme with devices of *amplificatio* (amplification, enlargement) and enriching its language with the ornaments of style. Both descriptions follow a set pattern, as recommended by the medieval arts of poetry and followed with extraordinary consistency by generations of medieval poets writing in the several European vernaculars as well as in Latin. Medieval gentlemen certainly preferred blondes, and ladies with golden hair, thin brown eyebrows, slender waists, swelling bellies (suggesting child-bearing potential), and of lily and rose complexion are ubiquitous in literature and painting.

The rhetoricians had listed the personal attributes which should be included in a description, including name, nature, style of life, fortune, quality, diligence, and the like. Chaucer is particularly interested in the lady's name, whereas in the *Behaingne* Machaut was not:

> And goode faire White she het;
> That was my lady name ryght.
> She was bothe fair and bryght;
> She hadde not hir name wrong.

By the interpretation of a person's name something good or bad about them may be intimated, declares Matthew of Vendôme in his *Ars versificatoria* (written before 1175).

For example, Maximus lives up to his great name in nobility and soul (Ovid, *Epistulae ex Ponto*), whereas Caesar 'takes his name from his achievement' (a reference to one of Matthew's own examples of *descriptio*). Similarly, 'faire White' is white by name and white and bright by nature. Moreover, she is determined to live up to her good name: 'She loved so wel hir owne name.' The *artes poetriae* advocate an emphasis on a person's rank, and that certainly is being placed here: the lady White knows who she is, and the poem makes sure that we know it too. Her beauty functions to confirm her high birth and impeccable breeding.

Chaucer takes Machaut's statement that the lady's hair 'was like strands of gold, neither too blond nor too brown,' and builds it up into a *circumlocutio* or roundabout statement, which ends with an affirmation of his conclusion:

> For every heer on hir hed,
> Soth to seyne, hyt was not red,
> Ne nouther yelowe ne broun hyt nas;
> Me thoughte most lyk gold hyt was.

In his *Documentum de modo et arte dictandi et versificandi* Geoffrey of Vinsauf—the 'Gaufred, deere maister soverayn' referred to in the **"Nun's Priest's Tale"**—says of this device, 'instead of speaking of a thing directly, we move about [it] in a circle.' And certainly that is what is happening here.

Exclamatio, exclamation which expresses vehemently some emotion, occurs at lines 895-7 and 919-20 (cf. 1075, etc.). Chaucer employs *repetitio,* repetition of a word or phrase at the beginning of several lines, at 827-9 ('Of . . . '), 869-70 ('Hyt . . .'), 906-7 and 911-12 ('And . . .'), 927-8 ('Ne . . . '), 988-9 ('And . . . '), 1025-6 ('To . . . '), 1038-40, ('My/Myn . . .'), etc. Then there is *interrogatio,* where a question is asked for rhetorical effect and not as a request for information. The comparison of White to the phoenix in order to emphasize her uniqueness is of course an *exemplum* (cf. 1052-87, where a formidable arsenal of *exempla* may be found, White being likened to Penelope and Lucrece). The older poet was to exploit the funny side of the ponderous use of *exempla* in ***Troilus and Criseyde***. There Troilus, having been warned against excessive weeping like Niobe (who turned into stone when grieving), tells Pandarus that he has had enough:

> 'What knowe I of the queene Nyobe?
> Lat be thyne olde ensaumples, I the preye'.

But that is some time away in the future, and of course the context is very different. To be sure, the Man in Black is hardly impressed with the role model of Socrates as recommended by the dreamer, but he is too polite to protest much, even when his companion provides him with five further *exempla* for good measure. Later, he himself demonstrates a fatal attraction to the device.

There are, however, aspects of Machaut's account in the *Behaingne* which Chaucer abbreviates rather than amplifies. The descriptions of the lady's 'forehead, eyebrows,

nose, mouth, teeth, chin, haunches, thighs, legs, feet, flesh' and the statement of her age are all omitted, as Derek Brewer succinctly puts it. This was probably due to decorum: Chaucer could not be too familiar in textualizing the wife of the powerful Gaunt, a woman who had been one of the most eminent heiresses throughout England. Indeed, some of the specimen descriptions provided in the *artes poetriae* include rather salacious passages, as when Matthew of Vendôme, having described a woman's ivory teeth, milky forehead, snowy neck, star-like eyes, rosy lips, narrow waist, and 'luscious little belly,' moves on to consider her 'sweet home of Venus': 'The sweetness of savour that lies hid in the realm of Venus / The judging touch can fortell.' This voyeurism (fairly standard in Matthew) sees the female body very much in terms of its sexual attractions to the male. Machaut's lover was more circumspect: 'Of the rest, which I did not see, I can assure you . . . that it was in perfect accord with Nature, pleasing in shape and contour. This remaining part, which I wish to speak no more of here, must be held without comparison to be sweeter and more beautiful than any other.' Chaucer took discretion even further—

> I knew in hir noon other lak
> That al hir lymmes nere pure sewynge
> In as fer as I had knowynge.
>   *perfectly proportioned*

—even though he is putting these words in the mouth of the man who, within the narrative, subsequently wins her. The Man in Black is, of course, speaking of White as she was when he first knew her, rather than from the point of view of a husband married to her for nine years (the length of time that Gaunt was married to Blanche).

Not that Chaucer is averse to elaborating on the traditional physical attributes: he moves away from Machaut in adding plumpness to the arms and red fingernails to the customarily white hands and in noting her straight flat back and long body. Moreover, he describes her speech, as goodly, friendly, soft, and reasonable; here he was following another poem of Machaut's, the *Remede de Fortune*. Matthew of Vendôme recommends the inclusion of this attribute, for someone's character can be established through reference to a 'cultivated manner of speaking', as when Ovid says that grace was not absent in the 'eloquent speech' of Ulysses (*Metamorphoses*). Of course, some aspects of Machaut's description simply did not apply to Blanche, as, for example, her age. The Machaut lady, the subject of so much male praise and the cause of so much sorrow on account of her infidelity, is fourteen and a half years old. Heroines in medieval literature can be, by today's standards, surprisingly young, probably a reflection of the medieval belief that women matured and died earlier than men. For instance, Emilia in Boccaccio's *Teseida* (the primary source of the **"Knight's Tale"**) is only 15 when she marries Palemone. By contrast, Chaucer makes no comment about how old his Emelye was, and professes ignorance of the age of Criseyde (***Troilus and Criseyde***). He also avoids mentioning White's age. Blanche was 27 when she died, and thus past her prime (as envisioned in Chaucer's day), and so it may have been delicacy which prompted him to avoid that matter. Against this, it may be noted that Froissart described her as having died 'fair and young'—but then, he was vague about her age, remarking that she was 'about twenty-two years old,' which is a considerable underestimate. Returning to Blanche as textualized by Chaucer, there is another possible reason for his silence. She was slightly (at the most one year) younger than Gaunt, and so the specification of her age might have made her greater maturity seem implausible, even allowing for the belief that women were thought to mature earlier. But of course, it would be quite naïve to talk as if White *is* Blanche or the Man in Black *is* Gaunt, for we are dealing with fictions which maintain some distance from their real-life equivalents, in a manner which owes much to the practice of the *dits amoreux.*

Moreover, certain aspects of White which Chaucer wished to describe simply had no precedent in the *Behaingne*. Her moral qualities are emphasized, qualities markedly absent in the case of the lady in Machaut's poem, who left her adoring knight for another man. Once again, Chaucer follows the precepts and the practice of the rhetoricians. Matthew of Vendôme includes in his series of model *descriptiones* an account of the virtuous woman, here identified as Marcia, wife of Cato. This paragon is said to reject 'feminine deceits,' display understanding, and radiate trustworthiness. 'The honesty of her speech portends / The value of her virtue'; she 'lacks guile,' the 'goodwill of her gaze' not being 'a craving for Venus' sport . . . Marcia is strong in mind.' Similarly, White is friendly but not forward; no prude (she enjoys dancing and modest 'pleye') but certainly no flirt. Her glance is direct, quite lacking in coquettishness and sexual allure, as is her behaviour in general. Her intelligence is disposed to all goodness, and she is incapable of wronging anyone. In her dealings with men she is honest and straightforward, giving no encouragement where none is meant and not being the type to set a suitor elaborate tests of love, sending him off to foreign lands to win 'worshyp' before he can enter her presence again. However, she is not to be won easily; the black knight has to 'serve' her for a year before she takes him into her 'governance,' thereby making a man of this rather callow youth. Marcia, Matthew of Vendôme concludes, is a fit wife for the wise Cato. White, Chaucer's poem implies, was the perfect match for the Man in Black.

Geoffrey of Vinsauf, in his *Poetria nova* (composed between 1200 and 1213), recommends that *descriptio* be delightful as well as large, 'handsome as well as big.' In order that the mind should be 'fully refreshed,' he continues, 'her conventional nature should not be too trite'; 'more unusual usages' should therefore be sought. In similar vein, Matthew of Vendôme declares that a writer is at fault when he employs 'a superfluous flourish of words and ornamented speech and grasps at clouds and vacuities.' In the *Book of the Duchess* Chaucer's verse sometimes comes perilously close to doing just that. It must be said, of course, that medieval vernacular poetry is generally designed for oral performance, or at least circumscribed by strategies which had developed to enhance oral delivery. Here is literature composed above all else to be *heard,* when read aloud to a company or indeed to oneself (whether the words were declaimed or mouthed), 'silent reading' being a rarity. Hence the rhetorical nature of so much medieval literature. We are dealing with 'performance texts' *par excellence,* works which require room to create their effects, long periods to build up their descriptions, since the writer cannot rely on his public reading and rereading a passage until all its significance is grasped (this being the usual means in which poetry is experienced in an age of print rather than script).

After all due allowance is made for these factors, however, it may be said that Chaucer has not as yet learned that big may not be beautiful and that more can mean less. On the other hand, certain passages in the *Book of the Duchess* have an exquisite charm which is scarcely rivalled by anything he was to write later: the lightsome dream-chamber, the lush landscape through which the mysterious dog leads the dreamer, White dancing 'so comlily' and laughing with her friends, the black knight's description of how he and she lived as one, and so forth. And as a whole the poem has retained its power to move.

FURTHER READING

Bibliography

Allan, Mark and Fisher, John H. *The Essential Chaucer: An Annotated Bibliography of Major Modern Studies.* London: Mansell Publishing Limited, 1987, 243 p.

   A descriptive guide to twentieth-century Chaucer studies cross referenced by Chaucer's titles, subjects of his works, and topics of studies.

Hahn, Thomas, edited by. *The Chaucer Bibliographies.* Toronto: University of Toronto Press, 1983-.

   The definitive bibliography of Chaucer studies, anticipated to be sixteen volumes; to date volumes on *Anelida and Arcite,* the translations, scientific works and apocrypha, and on the "General Prologue" to the *Canterbury Tales* and the "Knight's Tale" have been completed. Noted for its thorough annotations of each entry making it an excellent reference source.

Hammond, Eleanor Prescott. *Chaucer: A Bibliographical Manual.* Reprint. New York: Peter Smith, 1933, 579 p.

   Bibliography of works by Chaucer and of historical biographies and criticism on Chaucer written from the fifteenth through the nineteenth centuries. This is the standard guide for reference to works up to 1900 and contains excellent introductory material for a beginning study of Chaucer's background.

Leyerle, John and Quick, Anne. *Chaucer: A Bibliographic Introduction.* Toronto: University of Toronto Press, 1986, 321 p.

   A descriptive bibliography of twentieth-century criticism arranged in sections by Chaucer's titles and cultural topics.

Morris, Lynn King. *Chaucer Source and Analogue Criticism: A Cross-Referenced Guide*. New York: Garland Publishing, 1985, 584 p.

> Cross-lists criticism of Chaucer by authors, titles, subjects, and genres.

Biography

Brewer, Derek S. *Chaucer and His World*. New York: Dodd, Mead and Company, 1978, 224 p.

> Presents Chaucer as an influential cultural and literary figure of fourteenth-century England; provides a portrait of his early life and civic career; and explores the psychology of his poetry.

Bronson, Bertrand H. *In Search of Chaucer*. Toronto: University of Toronto Press, 1960, 117 p.

> A study of Chaucer's works as a key to discovering his personality.

Crow, Martin M. and Olson, Clair C., eds. *Chaucer Life-Records*. Oxford: Clarendon Press, 1966, 755 p.

> Provides the 493 records of Chaucer's life in their original form and language with editorial explanations.

Gardner, John [Champlin]. *The Life and Times of Chaucer*. New York: Alfred A. Knopf, 1977, 347 p.

> Narrative biography that reconstructs Chaucer's personal and literary life from interpretations of his poetry and fourteenth-century history.

Howard, Donald R. *Chaucer: His Life, His Works, His World*. New York: E. P. Dutton, 1987, 636 p.

> A comprehensive study that uses cultural and political history and Chaucer's works to construct a thorough and readable portrait of his life.

Hulbert, James Root. *Chaucer's Official Life*. New York: Phaeton Press, 1970, 96 p.

> Uses historical records to describe Chaucer's political life.

Wagenknecht, Edward. *The Personality of Chaucer*. Norman: University of Oklahoma Press, 1968, 168 p.

> Describes Chaucer's personality based on his poetic sentiments.

Criticism

Arathoon, Leigh A., ed. *Chaucer and the Craft of Fiction*. Rochester, MI: Solaris Press, 1986, 430 p.

> Collection of fourteen examinations of Chaucer's narrative art.

Astell, Ann W. *Chaucer and the Universe of Learning*. Ithaca, NY.: Cornell University Press, 1996, 254 p.

> Argues that the Ellesmere tale-order was not editorial but was Chaucer's design and that it creates an astrological sequence and a philosophical survey in its arrangement.

Barney, Stephen A., ed. *Chaucer's Troilus: Essays in Criticism*. Hamden, CT: Archon Books, 1980, 323 p.

> Reprints seminal essays on *Troilus and Criseyde* along with three original pieces.

Baum, Paull F. *Chaucer's Verse*. Durham, NC: Duke University Press, 1961, 145 p.

> Describes the meter, rhyme patterns, and stanzaic forms of Chaucer's poetry.

Beichner, Paul E. "Chaucer's Pardoner as Entertainer." *Medieval Studies* XXV (1963): 160-72.

> Maintains that the Pardoner's intent is to entertain, not to raise funds from the other pilgrims, as some critics have claimed.

Bennett, H. S. *Chaucer and the Fifteenth Century*. Oxford: Clarendon Press, 1947, 326 p.

> Presents an overview of Chaucer's time and literary accomplishments.

Bennett, J. A. *The Parlement of Foules: An Interpretation*. Oxford: Clarendon Press, 1957, 217 p.

> Offers an examination of the poem's sources and literary traditions.

Benson, C. David. *Chaucer's Drama of Style: Poetic Variety and Contrast in the 'Canterbury Tales.'* Chapel Hill: University of North Carolina Press, 1986, 183 p.

> Analyzes the dramatic and Christian elements of the tales; focuses special attention on the fabliaux, the religious tales, the Pardoner's tales, and the character of Chaucer, the pilgrim.

Boitani, Piero and Mann, Jill, eds. *The Cambridge Chaucer Companion*. Cambridge: Cambridge University Press, 1986, 262 p.

> Collection of fifteen essays for the "student approaching Chaucer for the first time," covering the major works and providing some historical context.

—— and Torti, Ann, eds. *Poetics: Theory and Practice in Medieval English Literature*. Cambridge: D. S. Brewer, 1991, 207 p.

> Contains nine essays on Chaucer by notable Chaucerian scholars such as A. J. Minnis, Charles Owen, Jr., Paul Taylor, and Helen Cooper.

Bowden, Muriel. *A Reader's Guide to Geoffrey Chaucer*. New York: Farrar, Straus and Giroux, 1964, 212 p.

> Introduction to Chaucer backgrounds and straightforward analyses of Chaucer's major works intended to help the beginning reader develop an understanding and appreciation; includes a useful glossary of selected Chaucer vocabulary.

Brewer, Derek S., ed. *Chaucer and Chaucerians: Critical Studies in Middle English Literature*. Montgomery: University of Alabama Press, 1966, 278 p.

> Collection of nine essays by prominent Chaucer scholars.

——. *Chaucer: The Poet as Storyteller*. New York: Macmillan, 1984, 150 p.

Includes Brewer's new and previously published essays that explore how Chaucer's poetry operates within fourteenth-century narrative traditions.

Cooper, Helen. *Oxford Guides to Chaucer: The Canterbury Tales*. Oxford: Clarendon Press, 1989, 437 p.

Provides a summary of criticism about the *Canterbury Tales* in easily accessible sections.

Dinshaw, Carolyn. *Chaucer's Sexual Poetics*. Madison: University of Wisconsin Press, 1989, 310 p.

Feminist analysis of Chaucer's poetry that finds Chaucer noteworthy for "the thoroughness, flexibility and variety" of his female characters.

Donaldson, E. Talbot. *Speaking of Chaucer*. New York: W. W. Norton and Company, 1970, 178 p.

A collection of essays, some previously published and classic, by an outstanding critic and Chaucer scholar.

Eliason, Norman E. *The Language of Chaucer's Poetry: An Appraisal of the Verse, Style and Structure*. Copenhagen: Rosenkilde and Bagger, 1972, 250 p.

A general analysis intended to add to the novice reader's appreciation of Chaucer's poetry.

Faulkner, Dewey R., ed. *Twentieth Century Interpretations of the Pardoner's Tale: A Collection of Critical Essays*. Englewood Cliffs, NJ: Prentice-Hall, 1973, 123 p.

Collection of new and reprinted essays concerning the major critical views of the "Pardoner's Tale."

Fisher, John H. *The Importance of Chaucer*. Carbondale: Southern Illinois University Press, 1992, 198 p.

Explores Chaucer's significance to English language and literature.

Frank, Robert Worth, Jr. "Structure and Meaning in the *Parlement of Foules*." *PMLA* 71, No. 3 (June 1956): 530-39.

Argues that the *Parlement of Foules* reflects courtly love conventions in unconventional ways.

Gardner, John [Champlin]. *The Poetry of Chaucer*. Carbondale: Southern Illinois University Press, 1977, 408 p.

A thematic and historical analysis of Chaucer's major works.

Jordan, Robert M. *Chaucer's Poetics and the Modern Reader*. Berkeley: University of California Press, 1987, 182 p.

Discusses the rhetorical poetics of Chaucer's major works.

Kirby, Thomas A. *Chaucer's Troilus: A Study in Courtly Love*. Gloucester, MA: Peter Smith, 1958, 337 p.

Analyzes *Troilus and Criseyde* as a work that uses the classical conventions of courtly love.

Klassen, Norman. *Chaucer on Love, Knowledge, and Sight*. Cambridge: D. S. Brewer, 1995, 225 p.

Volume XXI of the Chaucer Studies series, this work provides a scholarly study of Chaucer's love poetry and its relationship to metaphysical visual motifs and fourteenth-century natural philosophy.

Knight, Stephen. *Rymyng Craftily: Meaning in Chaucer's Poetry*. Sydney: Angus and Robertson, 1973, 247 p.

Reveals the connections between the aesthetics of Chaucer's poetry and its meaning in *Troilus and Criseyde, Parlement of Foules* and selections from the *Canterbury Tales*.

Lewis, C. S. "Chaucer." In *The Allegory of Love: A Study in Medieval Tradition*, pp. 157-97. London: Oxford University Press, 1953.

Shows how Chaucer's works utilize allegorical modes and the traditions of courtly love.

Lowes, John Livingston. *Geoffrey Chaucer and the Development of His Genius*. Boston: Houghton Mifflin Co., 1934, 246 p.

Collection of six lectures that give an overview of cultural and literary influences upon Chaucer and analyses of his major works.

Malone, Kemp. *Chapters on Chaucer*. Baltimore, MD: Johns Hopkins Press, 1951, 240 p.

Discussions of Chaucer's major poems intended as a guide for the beginning student of Chaucer.

Manly, J. M. *Some New Light on Chaucer: Lectures Delivered at the Lowell Institute*. New York: Henry Holt and Company, 1926, 305 p.

Identifies the pilgrims of the *Canterbury Tales* with real people to varying degrees of certainty and includes shorter chapters on Chaucer's background and artistic style.

McAlpine, Monica E. *The Genre of Troilus and Criseyde*. Ithaca, NY: Cornell University Press, 1978, 252 p.

Examines the *Troilus* as a tragedy in the Boethian sense, in which tragedy is a thematic device used to reveal rich depictions of human reality rather than an organizational device that shapes the representation of human experience.

McDonald, Charles O. "An Interpretation of Chaucer's *Parlement of Foules*." *Speculum* XXX, No. 3 (July 1955): 444-57.

Suggests that the work is a survey of various kinds of love and that it is unified by the figure of Nature.

Miller, Robert P., ed. *Chaucer: Sources and Backgrounds*. New York: Oxford University Press, 1977, 507 p.

Reprints excerpts from Chaucer's sources in modern translation and provides related background material arranged by subject.

Muscatine, Charles. *Chaucer and the French Tradition: A Study in Style and Meaning*. Berkeley: University of California Press, 1957, 282 p.

Examines traditions of French poetry as they apply to Chaucer.

Myles, Robert. *Chaucerian Realism*. Cambridge: D. S. Brewer, 1994, 153 p.

Volume XX of the Chaucer Studies series, this work provides an intricate study using semiotics and linguistics to present Chaucer's work as psychologically realistic; two chapters pertain specifically to the "Friar's Tale."

Quiller-Couch, Sir Arthur T. *The Age of Chaucer*. London: J. M. Dent and Sons, 1926, 158 p.

A description of fourteenth-century life as it relates to Chaucer's works.

Richardson, Cynthia C. "The Function of the Host in the *Canterbury Tales*." *Texas Studies in Literature and Language* XII, No. 1 (Spring 1970): 325-44.

Suggests that, for Chaucer, Harry Bailly represents the superficial and uncritical audience.

Robertson, D. W., Jr. *A Preface to Chaucer: Studies in Medieval Perspectives*. Princeton, NJ: Princeton University Press, 1962, 519 p.

Contends that all medieval poetry, including Chaucer's, was intended to be interpreted allegorically.

Robinson, Ian. *Chaucer and the English Tradition*. Cambridge: Cambridge University Press, 1972, 296 p.

Assesses Chaucer's native English qualities and compares his work with that of his contemporaries to show how he "created" the forms of English literature.

Rowland, Beryl, ed. *Companion to Chaucer Studies*. London: Oxford University Press, 1968, 409 p.

Invaluable collection of critical articles concerning many aspects of Chaucerian scholarship. Each essay contains its own bibliography.

Ruggiers, Paul G. *The Art of the Canterbury Tales*. Madison: University of Wisconsin Press, 1965, 265 p.

Examines the structure of the *Canterbury Tales* and finds Chaucer's view of humanity to be comprehensive and sympathetic.

Taylor, Paul Beekman. *Chaucer's Chain of Love*. London: Associated University Press, 1996, 215 p.

A philological study of *The Legend of Good Women, Parliament of Fowls, Troilus and Criseyde,* the "Knight's Tale" and other selections intended to show that Chaucer's works express a spiritual love of God and life.

Wasserman, Julian N. and Blanch, Robert J., eds. *Chaucer in the Eighties*. Syracuse, NY: Syracuse University Press, 1986, 258 p.

Collection of sixteen modern interpretations of Chaucer's poetry.

Woo, Constance, and Matthews, William. "The Spiritual Purpose of the *Canterbury Tales*." *Comitatus*, No. 1 (December 1970): 85-109.

Presents evidence for considering the poem as primarily spiritual in intent and purpose.

Woolf, Virginia. "The Pastons and Chaucer." In *The Common Reader,* pp. 13-38. New York: Harcourt, Brace and Co., 1925.

Stresses that Chaucer should be read as a whole, not in select pieces taken out of context, to fully appreciate his art.

Amy Clampitt
1920-1994

American poet.

INTRODUCTION

Clampitt emerged on the literary scene in 1983 with the
publication of *The Kingfisher*. Surprisingly, this first
collection earned her a reputation as one of America's
foremost poets. Her poems resonate with rich and varied
language, and are filled with detailed images from classical literature. In her subsequent collections, *What the Light
Was Like* (1985), *Archaic Figure* (1987), *Westward* (1990),
and *A Silence Opens* 1994), Clampitt built on her reputation for virtuoso use of language, metaphors, and meticulous detail. Her intellectual language and construction
have led to comparisons with Marianne Moore and Gerard Manley Hopkins. Those same qualities are also the
most oft-cited flaws in Clampitt's poetry: at times her
heavy language and ornamentation seem to overwhelm
the subject.

Biographical Information

Clampitt was born and raised in Iowa, living on the farm
owned by her Quaker parents. As a child she was often
left alone to amuse herself, and spent much of her time
reading. Clampitt's grandfather, a farmer who loved
books, set an early example for her, having written a
memoir of his life on the prairie. By the age of nine,
Clampitt herself was writing Shakespearian sonnets, but
initially wanted to write fiction, believing that being a
novelist was more acceptable to her peers than being a
poet. Clampitt attended Grinnell College in her native
Iowa where she received a B.A. with honors in English in
1941. She earned a graduate fellowship to Columbia
University and moved to New York City after leaving
Grinnell. Clampitt soon discovered that graduate work
was not to her liking, and she left Columbia and took a
job with Oxford University Press where she remained until
1951. After a five-month European vacation, Clampitt
returned to New York in 1952 and worked as a reference
librarian for the National Audubon Society and subsequently as a free-lance editor. Her time spent in Europe
would later provide a rich source of material for her poetry,
and inspired much of the collection *Archaic Figure*. She
resumed writing poetry in the early 1960s, inspired in
part by the social turmoil and issues of the time. The
1960s gave her, she said, the courage to write poetry, but
it wasn't until the mid 1970s that a collection (*Multitudes,
Multitudes*, 1974) was published. With the publication of
The Kingfisher came overnight acclaim and recognition
for the then 63 year-old poet; more importantly, Clampitt

was able to make her living as a poet, giving readings,
teaching, and holding grants such as the Guggenheim Fellowship. Clampitt continued to write prolifically, producing new poems and collections at a remarkable rate
until her death from cancer in 1994.

Major Works

Clampitt's first collection *Multitudes, Multitudes* (1974)
offered little indication of the bright future that lay ahead.
The style felt somewhat forced and heavy-handed, yet
some critics argue that the collection is not without merit.
Many of the themes that were to occupy her later work
were present in the fledgling collection, including mythology, war, and ancient Greece. Clampitt became known
to the reading public through poems published in the *New
Yorker*, the *Atlantic Monthly*, and other periodicals, and
was championed by Stanley Moss, the *New Yorker*'s long-
time poetry editor. Many of her previously published
poems were collected in *The Kingfisher* (1983), Clampitt's
first commercially-published collection, which shocked
and dazzled the literary community by its assured and
distinctive voice. Noted critics, including Helen Vendler

and Frederick Turner, expressed amazement at the depth and complexity of Clampitt's verse. Hailed as a watershed in modern American poetry and called "the most brilliant debut in recent American literary history" by Edmund White, *The Kingfisher* instantly accorded Clampitt a high place in American literary circles and assured her future as a poet. She was immediately compared with Marianne Moore, Elizabeth Bishop, Gerard Manley Hopkins and many other famous poets.

Her next collection—*What the Light Was Like* (1985)—sometimes suffers by comparison, but some critics note an increased Keats-like rhetoric, and, indeed, its centerpiece was the tribute "Voyages: A Homage to John Keats." In all of her works, critics observe that she maintains an enthusiastic interest in structure, rhythm, meter, and texture laced with classical allusions, references to science and literature, and a wealth of details. Her work dealing with her childhood is considered among her best, and her treatment of the beauty of farm life interspersed with the pain of adulthood is evidence of her thoughtfulness and subtle understanding. *Archaic Figure* (1987) earned both enthusiastic praise and criticism: praise for her frequently brilliant use of rhythm and poetic phrasing, and criticism of her overly literary style In *Westward* (1990) Clampitt made extensive use of landscape as a vehicle to deal with unsatisfactory relations, sexual identify and loneliness. The collection was highly praised by critics. Clampitt's last work, *A Silence Opens* (1994) is filled with "curious, almost random-seeming detail [collected] with magpie thoroughness." Critics note her fascination with the shifting perceptions of history which in this collection she described as, "the shadowy, predatory tent show / we know as history." In the collection, Clampitt sought to give voice to those persons marginalized by the record of the past, as in the poem "Matoaka" about the Native American known to history as Pocahontas.

Critical Reception

Clampitt's poetry has met almost universal acclaim for its complex use of language and allusion. Marked by a resonant voice, allusive wit and texture, her work draws on the experiences of poets who came before her, especially Gerard Manley Hopkins and Marianne Moore. Critics agree that Clampitt's love of details and powers of observation are her key strengths, and they work to the best advantage in her land- and sea-scape poems. Clampitt's poetry is nothing if not intellectual, and the life of the mind and ideas are central to her poems. It has been remarked that a reader would do well to have a dictionary or two on hand while reading Clampitt. The vocabulary and literary allusions that enrich her verse has also been criticized as being too academic, too forced, and over the head of most modern readers. Still, the depth of meaning is undeniable and to simplify her language or structure would be to strip her poetry of its uniqueness and its force. What most distinguishes Clampitt's poetry is her ability to weave together the myriad of ideas (nothing was beyond her notice) with the life of the mind and the spirit into a whole which reflected the curiosity of an agile mind.

PRINCIPAL WORKS

Poetry

Multitudes, Multitudes 1974*
The Kingfisher 1983
A Homage to John Keats 1984
What the Light Was Like 1985
Archaic Figure 1987
Westward 1990
A Silence Opens 1994

* Self-Published Collection

CRITICISM

J. D. McClatchy (review date 1983)

SOURCE: "Short Reviews," in *Poetry,* Vol. 143, No. 3, December, 1983, pp. 163-67.

[*In this brief review of* The Kingfisher, *McClatchy comments on Clampitt's similarities to Marianne Moore, especially in their use of language, their exuberance, and their moralism.*]

"It is a privilege to see so / much confusion," said Marianne Moore. By "confusion" she meant the world's own welter, its facts, artifacts, curios, and contradiction. And by "privilege" she meant their moral ordering. Amy Clampitt is a poet in the mold of Moore. For several years now I have been excitedly following Clampitt's poems as they appeared in magazines. As Leigh Hunt said of Congreve, they were "full as an egg of some kind of wit or sense in almost every sentence." Some of the poems—**"Times Square Water Music," "Exmoor," "Good Friday,"** and **"Marginal Employment"** come back to mind—even sounded like Moore. But it was not that studied resemblance that attracted me so much as a deeper affinity: the curiosity and exuberance both poets share, their canny moralism, a disposition to view the world through the spectacles of language, their love of (in Clampitt's phrase) "the ramifying / happenstance, the mirroring / marryings of all likeness."

Now that the poems have been brought together in a book, their achievement seems all the more remarkable—and somewhat different from what it had seemed before. Clampitt is a virtuoso, and she has two of a virtuoso's faults, both easily blinked at. Her cadenzas are sometimes too heavily ornamented, so that her skill overwhelms her subject, and her program is too long. Yet, asked which adjective, which poem I would strike, I am hard pressed. My caution is based on an impression, not on strictures, and may pass when I am more used to Clampitt's voice. It is luxuriant, frisky, and "escapes / our mere totting-up," but it is not a voice to catch up the more delicate traceries of piquant embellishment, or to propound the sweep and mischief of original ideas. Her effects are bold, often nervy, and buoyed both by tradition and by the community of solitaries. A close observer of the natural world and of its "perishing residue / of pure sensation," she knows enough too to ask "What is real except / what's fabricated?" Her descriptions, then, are both; a sea-surface, for instance, is most itself when seen as something else: "this windsilver / rumpling as of oatfields, / a suede of meadow, / a nub, a nap, a mane of lustre / lithe as the slide / of muscle in its / sheath of skin."

Clampitt has a genius for places, and her book has many landscapes in it: Maine, her native Iowa, Mexico, Greece, Italy—the local color of each place freshly seen through anecdote and detail. All of these advantages together would make her an admirable poet, but she is more seriously ambitious, and her arrangement of poems in *The Kingfisher* leaves me with a sense of her as a more brooding poet than I had previously expected. Just to recall some of the strongest poems in the book—**"A Procession at Candlemas," "The Kingfisher," "Beethoven, Opus 111," "The Quarry,"** and **"Imago"**—is to realize her imagination is deeply historical. All her angles—topographical, political, memorial—are manifestations of her concern for how men have lived with themselves in time. The six poems of the book's final section confirm this, and in a harrowing way. Never journalistic, never strident or self-righteous ("The purest art has slept with turpitude, / we all pay taxes."), they explore the causes and the cost of human suffering. One, **"The Dahlia Garden,"** is especially disturbing. It tells the story of Norman Morrison, a young Quaker activist who immolated himself in front of the Pentagon in 1965. It is a story that might have been rendered with the sentimentality of current political poetry. Instead, Clampitt makes it strange and urgent. Minds—those of bureaucrats and of martyrs—fill up with darkness: "overland, the inching caravans / the blacked-out troop trains / convoys through ruined villages / along the Mekong // merging / with the hydrocarbon-dark, headlight-inflamed Potomac // the little lights the candles / flickering on Christmas eve / the one light left burning / in a front hallway kerosene- / lit windows in the pitch dark / of back-country roads." That darkness is a terrible energy. In one version it is oil:

    . . . hydrocarbon unearthed
    and peeled away, process by process,
    in stages not unlike the stages
    of revelation, to a gaseous plume
    that burns like a bush . . .

In another, fanaticism:

    Hermaphrodite of pity and violence, the chambered
    pistil and the sword-bearing archangel,
    scapegoat and self-appointed avenger, contend,
    embrace, are one. He strikes the match.

The poet works to unite "system with system into one terrible mandala." The result is a very powerful poem, the product of a large, confident, humane imagination.

Patricia Morrisroe (essay date 1984)

SOURCE: "The Prime of Amy Clampitt," in *New York*, Vol. 17, No. 41, October 15, 1984, pp. 44-8.

[*In this essay, Morrisroe credits Clampitt's poetry with the power to turn the everyday into the magical through its powerful, evocative language.*]

"It's all very strange," says Amy Clampitt in her small, bird-like voice. "For years, nobody wanted to read my poems. I'd submit them to magazines and get them back without a word of encouragement. Now there's all this commotion, and it's nice. But sometimes I wonder what all the fuss is about."

In just two years, the "fuss" has turned Clampitt, a former Audubon Society librarian, into one of the major voices in American poetry. Her first book, *The Kingfisher,* published in 1983, was immediately hailed for its technical mastery and rich, allusive language. *The New York Review of Books* praised Clampitt's "distinguished mind"; *The New York Times Book Review* recognized her "dazzling" vocabulary; and *The Nation* called *The Kingfisher* "one of the most brilliant debuts in recent American literary history."

It was also one of the *latest* debuts. Clampitt is in her early sixties, and her first poem wasn't published until 1978. At an age when most poets have done the bulk of their work, Clampitt is just beginning her public career. "A few years ago, nobody knew who she was," says poet and critic J. D. McClatchy. "And now you can't pick up *The New Yorker* without reading an Amy Clampitt poem. The situation is extremely uncommon. Unknown poets rarely burst upon the scene as though they'd sprung full-blown from the brow of Jove."

And they rarely have the confidence to produce work that ignores current trends. Unlike the pared-down language that characterized much of American verse in the seventies, Clampitt's work returns to what critics call the "hard tasks."

"She didn't follow the latest fads or slavishly imitate what was popular," says McClatchy. "She was interested in structure, rhythm, meter, texture, and not in writing down whatever popped into her head."

"Much of the poetry published in the sixties and seventies was very spontaneous and spare," says Helen Vendler, critic and professor of English at Boston University. "There was a kind of trance-like looseness of construction, as though the poet had taped his own telephone conversation."

In contrast, Clampitt's work is laced with classical allusions and references to science, literature, and Freud. "Clampitt isn't afraid to let you know she's traveled and read books," says McClatchy. "And she presumes you've done the same. It's poetry for grown-ups."

It's also more restrained than the "confessional" poems of such contemporary writers as Sylvia Plath and Anne Sexton.

Before they died, each had recorded her private life in vivid detail, including divorces, love affairs, and in the case of Plath, her repeated suicide attempts. Many of the confessional poets had undergone psychoanalysis, and their writing reflected a struggle with identity and self-esteem.

Although Clampitt doesn't avoid painful subjects, her power comes more from language than from personal experience. "Amy doesn't bleed all over the page," says Howard Moss, poetry editor of *The New Yorker*. "There is the feeling that something exists beyond herself."

Although Clampitt's language is sometimes criticized as "overly decorated" or, as one person put it, "like Arnold Schwarzenegger flexing his muscles," she also has an extremely delicate touch. Exotic words ripple down the page, and even if the reader doesn't always understand them, they don't stop the musical flow of the poem. Winds arrive with "lariats and tambourines of rain," gales "stand up on point in twirling fouettés of debris," and the fog is described as "floss of mercury, deshabillé of spun aluminum, furred with a velouté of looking-glass."

The intensity of her response to nature can turn the mundane into the magical without turning the magical into a prettified cliché. On the lookout for beach glass, she sees "amber of Budweiser, chrysoprase / of Almadén and Gallo, lapis / by way of (no getting around it, / I'm afraid) Phillips' Milk of Magnesia, with now and then a rare / translucent turquoise or blurred amethyst / of no known origin."

But she is not merely a "nature poet"; nor is her descriptive talent limited to transforming Budweiser into amber. Clampitt is concerned with what it takes to survive in the natural world—her poems reverberate with this—and the mood of *The Kingfisher* deepens as it moves beyond the impressionistic seascapes to darker scenes depicting the deaths of her parents, and tragic love affairs. As she writes in **"A Procession at Candlemas,"** "sooner or later every trek becomes a funeral procession," and *The Kingfisher* is no different. It begins, with **"The Cove,"** on a note of warmth and innocence, "inside the snug house," where "cross-stitch domesticates the guest room," and ends, with **"The Burning Child,"** in the "killing chambers," where people, "herded from the cattle cars," have been stripped of "clothes, of names, of chattels."

In all these poems, Clampitt's voice is at once that of a frail creature buffeted by natural forces and that of a scientist trying to analyze and transcend those forces. It is certainly not an imitation of a phone conversation, nor an excruciating investigation of her own psyche. It is beautiful, sad, uplifting, and, above all, remarkably mature. As the painter Delacroix said, to be 20 and a poet is to be 20; to be 40 and a poet is to be a poet.

"I really don't know what to say," Clampitt says when approached about a magazine profile. Sitting at Confetti Cafe on Madison Avenue, she looks tired and pale, as though the prospect of being a major poet was already sapping her strength. Reed-thin, she speaks in a soft voice

that can barely be heard above the noise in the restaurant. As the room fills up with noisy people, many of them women carrying Bergdorf shopping bags, Clampitt, whose hair is neatly tucked into a beret, seems out of place, like Wedgwood china in a high-school cafeteria.

"I never wanted to be a celebrity," she says. "I don't want to reach millions of people. I'd much rather have 30 or 40 readers than be famous and appear on *Good Morning America*."

Clampitt, who was born "with an overdose of aesthetic leanings," grew up on a 125-acre farm in Iowa. The oldest of five children, she loved the outdoors, and many of her poems re-create the sense of wonder that a child brings to the natural world. Her earliest memories are of the violets that grew like a "cellarhole of pure astonishment" in the undergrowth of a woodlot.

While Clampitt remembers the bluebells and the "waterfall of bridlewreath below the porch," she has darker memories too. In Clampitt's mind, the school bus was a torture chamber in which she was ruthlessly picked on by other children. "You never recover from that kind of teasing," she says. "Kids have an unerring instinct to find people who are vulnerable. And I was sensitive. But perhaps that's not such a bad thing. To paraphrase Henry James, I think all poets should aspire to be someone on whom nothing is lost."

What wasn't lost on Clampitt was the sense of cultural isolation she felt growing up in midwestern farm country. "There was the feeling that anything interesting came from somewhere else," she says. "We weren't near the ocean, and we weren't near New York. The sources of things seemed very far away."

This sense of isolation was heightened by Clampitt's belief, as she writes in **"Black Buttercups,"** that the "gray world of adulthood" didn't hold much promise. Her mother was preoccupied with domestic chores and with raising five children. "She was a good example of the housewife kept in the shade," Clampitt says. "She was my father's wife. It was only after he died that she became her own person. It's distressing to contemplate. Perhaps that's the reason I never married."

Though Clampitt doesn't consider herself a feminist poet, she doesn't shy away from themes that highlight a mother's "mumbling lot." In **"Meridian,"** she writes about waking on the front porch on a warm summer day and watching the early morning turn to "apathy at the meridian, the noon / of absolute boredom: flies / crooning black lullabies in the kitchen, / milk-soured crocks, cream separator / still unwashed: what is there to life / but chores and more chores, dishwater, / fatigue, unwanted children."

Clampitt describes her father, who was raised a Quaker, as "a man of enormous feelings that were mostly repressed." Intelligent and college-educated, he turned down a job as a high-school principal to become a farmer. It was a decision Clampitt never understood. Yet he also devoted much of his time to anti-war activity and attended vigils in Washington. Though he didn't play piano himself, he bought one so his family could play.

"There was something about my childhood that was idyllic," she says. "But I was always aware that my parents were unhappy. So I grew up with all these layers and interminglings. There was the natural world that was frightening and beautiful, and the adult world that was frightening and painful."

For Clampitt, poetry provided a seductive escape. She started writing at around eight but claims it was "really stupid stuff." In high school, she composed a few sonnets that "weren't bad," although she never seriously thought about poetry as a career. "Who wanted to be a *poetess*?" she says.

Later, at Grinnell College, she majored in English and "fell in love" with Gerard Manley Hopkins, the nineteenth-century British poet and Jesuit priest. Like Clampitt, Hopkins used his mystical insights into nature to raise certain fundamental questions about the human condition. "I was attracted to his intensity," she says. "He was somebody who wrote about vivid sensations." But she didn't write much poetry in college. In those days, she had two goals: to live near the ocean and to get a job in publishing. The first was realized when she received a graduate fellowship to Columbia University. Before the year was out, she stopped attending classes. She thought Columbia was a "mill for getting advanced degrees," and even worse, she hated the setting. "The wind off the Hudson never stopped blowing," she says. "It just howled and howled."

She reached her second goal when she got a job as a secretary at Oxford University Press, where she won a trip to England by entering an essay contest. "Growing up in the Midwest, I didn't get a sense of history," she says. "England changed my perspective on life." Two years later, she returned to Europe. By then, she had quit her job at the publishing company and used her savings to travel.

When she returned to New York, she decided to write a novel. It was rejected by several publishers, and today Clampitt admits, "It wasn't very good." Her money was running out, so she found a job with the Audubon Society as a reference librarian. She spent her lunch hours bird-watching in Central Park and wrote occasional book reviews for *Audubon* magazine. One book in particular captured her imagination. It was a biography of Charles Darwin, whose theory of evolution would become a recurrent theme in her poetry.

Though she stayed at the Audubon Society for seven years, it was not a happy period. She liked learning about biology but didn't like being a librarian. She wrote novels but couldn't get published. And most of all, she hated the fifties. "I felt like a misfit," she says. "Everybody was married, and I didn't want that. But I didn't want to move up in the business world, either. So I didn't have a husband *or* a career. Ultimately, I became a recluse because

I didn't have a niche. I'm not saying I'm to be pitied. It's just that I was an anomaly.

"For a long time, I didn't have anything to do with men," she says. "I didn't see any future in a relationship, and frankly, I was scared of the idea. I'd had enough troubles already." Some of those troubles involved a relationship detailed in **"The Kingfisher."** Clampitt describes the poem as "a novel trying to work itself into a piece of cloisonné." She met a man in England "in a year the nightingales were said to be so loud they drowned out slumber." They continued the relationship in New York "among the Bronx Zoo's exiled jungle fowl" and the thrushes of Wall Street. But the affair ended, and Clampitt was left with the memory of "a kingfisher's burnished plunge" as it took her "down on down, the uninhabitable sorrow."

During her time at the Audubon Society, Clampitt did not write poetry. "I was paralyzed," she says. "I didn't have any confidence in myself, and you need a lot to be a writer. Of course, the confidence could stem from the sheer rage of being a misfit, but for me it had to be found in a quieter way."

The first small step out of this creative black hole came when Clampitt quit her job and returned to Iowa to help her parents with a family problem. She worked in a contractor's office and wrote another novel, which was also never published. But that didn't matter to Clampitt. "What was really important was that I was finally able to explain myself to my parents," she says. "After years of unspoken disappointments, we finally seemed to understand one another. My parents' friends thought I was 'interesting,' and this made my parents feel better about me. They stopped thinking I was a weirdo because I wasn't married. For the first time in my life, I felt free."

Back in New York, Clampitt was further liberated by the cultural changes of the sixties. "If the fifties had gone on forever, I would have never been a poet," she says. "But suddenly it was okay to be unconventional." She became a freelance editor, earning a reputation for her ability to fix up difficult manuscripts. Clampitt also became involved in the peace movement, and from 1967 until 1970 she directed most of her energy into protest. "I guess I inherited a good bit of that from my father," she says. In 1971, Clampitt took part in the "daily death toll," in which protesters sprawled in front of the White House gates to symbolize the number of Vietnamese killed that day. "We all wore Vietnamese hats and had to designate our occupations on banners. I chose 'poet.' It was the first time I really thought of myself that way."

Clampitt was now writing poetry in earnest, but she couldn't get published.

Finally, in 1978, her work was brought to the attention of Howard Moss, who has been poetry editor of *The New Yorker* since the early fifties. "I fell in love with it immediately," he says. "We were all waiting for someone like Amy to come along, someone who didn't pretend that life was simple. Right away, I knew that she was the real thing."

When Clampitt received a check for her first poem published in *The New Yorker*, she immediately sent her mother flowers. At the time, Clampitt was in her late fifties, and it was the first significant money she had ever earned as a writer.

Since then, Clampitt's work has appeared in *The Atlantic*, *The Nation*, *The New Republic*, and numerous poetry magazines. In 1982, she won a Guggenheim Fellowship. A year later, *The Kingfisher* was published as part of the highly regarded Knopf Poetry Series. The book is currently in its fifth printing, having sold close to 7,500 copies. Considering that popular volumes of poetry rarely sell more than 1,000, this makes *The Kingfisher* a bestseller. Though she cannot live off of her book royalties, she is a paid writer in residence at the College of William and Mary in Virginia and gets fees for her poetry readings. For the first time in her life, Clampitt is earning her living solely as a writer.

"Whenever I used to get upset about my life," Clampitt explains, "my friends used to tell me, 'Amy, don't worry, your time hasn't come.'"

"Now I guess it has," she says. And Clampitt is taking full advantage of it, writing at a furious pace that astonishes editors and friends. "She's like a mesmerist who puts her hands over the wand and suddenly thousands of words float onto the page," says Alice Quinn, Clampitt's editor at Knopf.

Some months after *The Kingfisher* was published, she handed Quinn a second volume of poetry, which will be published next spring. *What the Light Was Like* contains 40 poems, most of which were written between 1981 and 1982. "I just hope she doesn't burn herself out," says an acquaintance. "She seems to be working *awfully* hard."

But Clampitt has a simple answer. "I have to make up for lost time," she explains. "Younger poets have several decades to produce their life's work. I don't."

So she writes her poetry on buses and trains and just about everywhere, including the small Greenwich Village apartment that she has rented for over 30 years. Now that she has a little more money and a lot more freedom, she is constantly on the move. In the past two years, she has traveled to England and Greece and has crisscrossed the United States. Clampitt doesn't fly unless it's absolutely necessary, so she usually takes a bus. "Humans weren't meant to be up in the air," she says. Clampitt likes to travel in order to indulge what she calls her bohemian instincts, but there is also a deeper reason. "There's something about being in motion that stimulates the creative process," she says. "It shakes you loose from the usual way of seeing." Certain smells and sights associated with various cities frequently trigger Proustian remembrances. "The event could have happened years ago," she says, "and suddenly it comes flooding back—strange sounds, the color of the light in Venice. I get a picture in my mind. But now it's more exciting than it was the first time around."

Clampitt's ideas frequently stem from sensations, but she builds on her initial response, adding layer upon layer until the end product is both sensual and intellectually complex. In **"Beethoven, Opus 111,"** Clampitt writes of a concert given by a pianist in New York City. The music brings back memories of her father, who gave his children music lessons "to demonstrate that one, though he may grunt and sweat at work, is not a clod." She draws a parallel between the farmer "hacking at sourdock, at the strangleroots of thistles" and the deaf composer with his ear trumpet, pounding at the keys of his piano, "rehearsing the unhearable." Initially, it is an odd comparison.

By the end of the poem, however, the farmer and the composer have become one, not only in their frustration but in their ability to rise above it. As Beethoven's Opus 111 ends in a life-affirming swell, Clampitt's father, who has been suffering from cancer for months, dies peacefully. "Dying, / for my father, came to be like that / finally— in its messages the levitation / of serenity, as though the spirit might / aspire, in its last act / to walk on air."

This is dense, complex stuff, and it's not surprising that Clampitt often spends months composing a poem. When she isn't travelling, she likes to write in front of a window, preferably one with a view. "All I really need is a tree," she says. Clampitt writes on the backs of discarded legal announcements because she likes the texture of the vellum sheets. Besides, she adds, "it's much less intimidating to write on a small piece of paper."

After she has completed a first draft, she reads it aloud to "her best friend," a lawyer who has been her close companion for the past fifteen years. "He has a very good ear," she says, "and he'll tell me if something doesn't sound quite right." When it doesn't—and this happens frequently—Clampitt returns to work. A typical poem requires at least twenty revisions.

Clampitt has little patience for the concept of the "tortured poet." "I know there are people like that," she says, citing the example of Dylan Thomas staggering from tavern to tavern. "But I don't think you have to suffer in order to write. Intensity doesn't always have to be centered on unhappiness. I realized at some point that if I was going to be a poet then I'd have to be a professional and treat it like a business. I couldn't sit around and wait for the muse to strike. I had to accept that writing is hard work, and that it will *always* be hard work."

These days, it's the work that keeps her going, and not the literary acclaim. She avoids parties and doesn't hobnob with editors and critics. In fact, Clampitt says she is afraid of literary people. "They make me feel uncomfortable," she says. "They use too many critical terms, and I don't know what they're talking about."

Most of her new friends are younger poets who also shun the limelight. "In this business," says Nicholas Christopher, author of *On Tour With Rita*, "there are two types of people: the poets and the politicians. Amy is a true poet. When I first met her, in 1982, she was studying the *Iliad* in ancient Greek at Hunter College. I asked her why she was doing it, and she told me she just wanted to hear the rhythm of the words. Amy is different from a lot of poets. She doesn't live for grants and academic positions. She isn't looking to be a star."

Poet Mary Jo Salter agrees. "Amy rarely mentions her success," she says. "She's much more interested in talking about a rare flower she spotted, or a stray cat she befriended. She is totally *of* this world, and yet at times completely *above* it." Or to quote from the title of the second section of *The Kingfisher*, she is both "airborne" and "earthbound."

It is an Indian-summer morning. Clampitt is wearing a cotton print dress, and a scarf is tied around her head. Although her hair is gray and deep circles ring her eyes, she looks amazingly young and vibrant. As she talks, she gazes at the geraniums in a nearby window box. "Pretty," she says, although the leaves are wilted and the pink blossoms are turning brown.

Soon she is leaving on another trip. As usual, she is vague about when she will return. When asked if this is a happy period, she shrugs her shoulders as if happiness weren't really the issue.

"When I received my honorary degree at Grinnell College," she says, "I had three minutes to give a little speech. In that short time, I wanted to say something important. The words really had to count. I talked about our society and how we are fast becoming a country of analgesics and soporifics. We watch television so much that we are conditioned to believe whatever nonsense comes out of that box. We look for the quick and easy answer, always the happy ending.

"As a poet, I'm trying to sort out values," she says. "To discriminate between the authentic and the phony—to preserve what's worth preserving."

Like Beethoven at the keyboard and the farmer in the field, Clampitt, in her late middle years, is composing a message of serenity, "as though the spirit might aspire, in its last act, to walk on air."

Sandra M. Gilbert (review date 1985)

SOURCE: "Six Reviews," in *Poetry*, Vol. 147, No. 3, December, 1985, pp. 156-58.

[*In this review of* What the Light Was Like, *Gilbert criticizes Clampitt's obvious and, in her opinion, tedious use of literary references and excessively poetic phrasing.*]

Especially on the East Coast, Amy Clampitt has been widely hailed as the latest wonder woman of contemporary poetry. Perhaps most notably, Helen Vendler enthusiastically commended this writer's first volume, *The Kingfisher*, for the variety, the complexity, and, indeed,

the difficulty of its vocabulary, but more recently—and more extravagantly—Mona Van Duyn (on the cover of *What the Light Was Like*) has characterized Clampitt as the offspring of a fantasy marriage between Marianne Moore and Gerard Manley Hopkins. The phenomenon represented by this suddenly made and meteorically ascending reputation is an interesting one, suggesting that some readers are almost desperately nostalgic for the good old pre-"Beat," pre-"Deep Image," pre-"Confessional" days when poems were well wrought urns, poets' personalities were (as T. S. Eliot had recommended) decorously "extinguished," and teachers of verse were priestly interpreters who fostered "appreciation" by urging students to "explicate" tough allusions, hard words, and intricate stanza patterns.

For Amy Clampitt's work wears both learning and linguistic craftsmanship like academic insignia—fancy hoods and stripes on a doctoral gown, certifying aesthetic achievement by openly affiliating individual talent to the increasingly imperilled high cultural tradition for which so many intellectuals lately find themselves yearning. Through overt or covert allusions to texts by Homer, Sappho, Virgil, Petrarch, George Eliot, John Keats, William Butler Yeats, William Carlos Williams, Robert Frost, Wallace Stevens—and to many another monument of unaging intellect—Clampitt demonstrates that Western Civ. still lives and sophomore survey courses can pay off for reader and writer alike. Similarly, through her affinity for sonnets and sestinas, complex stanza patterns and elegant half-rhymes, she proves that verse-writing might actually be a teachable (and traditional) skill whose rules transcend the vagaries and mysteries of "breath units," "organic" forms, and "concrete" compositions.

That Clampitt's special interests tend to assuage a number of specialized anxieties does not, of course, mean that this poet lacks talent. Besides its skillful, sometimes even brilliant exploitation of old-fashioned resources of rhyme and meter whose time for revival has at last arrived, the verse in *What the Light Was Like* is often marked by the inventive urbanity one associates with Marianne Moore and Elizabeth Bishop in their more relaxed moments. In **"Gooseberry Fool,"** for instance, she observes that

> . . . gooseberry virtues
> take some getting
> used to, much as does trepang,
> tripe à la mode de Caen,
> or having turned thirteen.
> The acerbity of all things green
> and adolescent lingers in
> it . . .

while in **"Low Tide at Schoodic"** she notes how "a warbler . . . all nerves turned to / alarums, dapper in a yellow domino, / a noose of dark about his throat, / appends his anxious signature" to the granite sea-edge, "the planar windowpanes of tidepools." When she writes directly about childhood memories, moreover, Clampitt often achieves real dramatic power. Though the elegiac **"Black Buttercups,"** for instance, is (to my mind) marred by some of the characteristics that have become this writer's "hallmarks"—classical allusion (a pond that is "the Acheron / of dreadful disappointed Eros"), unabashedly "poetic" phrasing ("lucent chalices")—it vividly elegizes the lost house of childhood "where even now / the child who wept to leave still sits / weeping at the thought of exile."

Nevertheless, much of the work in *What the Light Was Like* is for the most part too tediously—and easily—literary. Yes, if you took Poetry 101 at any decent university you'll guess the references: "An ordinary evening in Wisconsin," "Something there is that doesn't / love a Third Avenue tenement," and "Much having traveled in the funkier realms of Ac- / ademe" are only a few of the more obvious ones. But if you didn't get an A in the course and can't find the others for yourself, the author is only too willing to help you out with footnotes which, unlike Marianne Moore's arcane and cryptic citations, explain the obvious with self-congratulatory fervor. About a clever sestina entitled **"The Reedbeds of the Hackensack,"** for example, Clampitt pontificates that "Allusions to and / or borrowings from the poems of William Carlos Williams, Dante, Milton, Keats, and Shakespeare will be noted in this poem, which may be regarded as a last-ditch [note the pun] effort to associate the landscape familiarly known as the Jersey Meadows with the tradition of elegiac poetry," while a witty occasional poem called **"A Cure at Porlock"** comes *tout ensemble* with a *Norton-Anthology*-style footnote to Coleridge's famously interrupted opium dream.

Most depressingly—and vapidly—"literary," however, is the sequence entitled *Voyages: A Homage to John Keats*, which functions as a kind of centerpiece for this volume and which is, appropriately enough, dedicated to the Clampitt enthusiast and Keats scholar Helen Vendler. Alas, this Hollywood version of a great and greatly moving life ought more properly to have been labelled *The John Keats Story* or maybe just *Keats!* (though the latter would probably be the right title for the musical comedy avatar). To give the unwary Keats lover an idea of what I mean: when the young poet decides to write "The Eve of St. Agnes," Clampitt recounts his feelings thus:

> He must have whistled at the notion that struck
> him now. And then blushed. Or vice versa. A
> girl going to bed on St. Agnes' Eve—that very
> night, or near it—without supper, so as to
> dream of the man she was to marry. Imagine
> her. Imagine. . . . He blushed now at the
> audacity. But the thing had taken hold:
> St. Agnes' Eve. A girl going to bed. . . .

And when the pained artist suddenly and poignantly gains confidence, Clampitt describes the experience as follows:

> "I think
> I shall be among the English
> poets after my death." There,
> he'd said it.

There are some wonderful moments in *What the Light Was Like* but it would be better for Amy Clampitt if, at least for a while, she tucked her notes from Poetry 101 away in a trunk. There, I've said it.

J. D. McClatchy (essay date 1989)

SOURCE: "Amy Clampitt: The Mirroring Marryings," in *White paper on Contemporary American Poetry,* Columbia University Press, 1989, pp. 311-28.

[*In the excerpt below, McClatchy explores Clampitt's poetic voice, especially her use of literary allusions and the themes of death and completion.*]

When Amy Clampitt's *The Kingfisher* was published in 1983, reactions were as extravagant as the texture of the poems themselves. Those reactions came in two waves. The praise prompted a success; the success prompted attacks. About *The Kingfisher* and the books she has written since, opinions have been sharply divided: enthusiasts applaud their unfashionably rich rhetoric, their allusiveness and virtuosity, while detractors dismiss them as overstuffed and regressive. Because the two sides have been so insistent, their conflicting claims signal perhaps the most unusual debut in recent literary history. But because this is an old debate about American poetry, its resumption in this case was not a surprise. The oddly surprising factor was the poet's age. She was born in 1920, and even in a country with many famously belated debuts (by Whitman, Frost, Stevens), hers at sixty-three seemed remarkable. The further surprise is that *The Kingfisher* was not her first book.

She too had her long foreground. *Multitudes, Multitudes*, a full-length collection of twenty-six poems, was privately published in 1973. In retrospect, it may seem like a lost original, but actually it reads like a feebler, paler version of the book she published a decade later. All the poems in *Multitudes, Multitudes* are carefully dated at the bottom, and many go back to the mid- and late-sixties. Even then her style was recognizably her own. The syntactical sprawl, the glut of adjectives, the periphrasis and flurry of appositional phrases, the layering of references—all of these seem in place from the start. The same echoes of Hopkins, Stevens, and Keats that one hears in later books sound more faintly in this book too. One difference is the several character studies here, in the manner of Jarrell or early Lowell. They reflect Clampitt's still earlier efforts to write novels. In later books the impulse is reserved for personal poems of an affectionately comic note (like **"Rain at Bellagio"**), but this is also the ground from which her historical pastiches grew. In fact, the titles of many poems here might come from later books: **"The Eve of All Souls," "The Skylarks of Mykonos," "Hera of Samos," "The Christmas Cactus."** Her religious temperament, which seeks both to accommodate the world and transcend it, is even more strongly evident in these early poems, and focused here by the subject that has consistently animated her work: death. Because of this obsession—the fact and the idea of death—she is an obliquely "political" poet. If she deploys Greek mythology here, she also visits Attica prison. Her literary cast of mind never blinds her to Vietnam, or South Africa, or welfare hearings. But politics is only a trope for her larger sense that "nothing in the world is safely kept." Those ways in which laws, cultures, historical circumstance, injustice, or art, or love may shape and control us—these fascinate Clampitt from the beginning. Her concentration on details—odd bits of life or language—is finally her way to keep these huge forces in check. But by momentarily avoiding them, she allows them to rush into her poems with greater impact. This balance of restraint and engulfment gives all her work its peculiar strength.

Whatever *Multitudes, Multitudes* may have predicted, *The Kingfisher* announced a poet of lavish gifts. But they were unwanted gifts—or unwanted by those readers used to the workshop whimsy, the surreal bleats, and drab earnest verse that have been the stock-in-trade of younger American poets for two decades. It is true that there is a risky nostalgia in Clampitt's style, and in her partisans' reaction to it. "If a poet gets a large audience very quickly," T. S. Eliot once wrote, "that is a rather suspicious circumstance: for it leads us to fear that he is not really doing anything new, that he is only giving people what they are already used to, and therefore what they have already had from the poets of the previous generation." Some critics who disliked *The Kingfisher* took her for the New Formalism's extremist. But she is not, strictly speaking, an overly "formal" poet. She occasionally works in prescribed forms, though with less success than in more amiably free-form runs of rhythmical verse. It's her *rhetoric* the critics were actually scorning or admiring. And her rhetoric does recall, say, the stately grace of Richard Wilbur's poems of the 1950s. To some, her style marked a return to the sedate sort of poetry (the tag "academic" is usually attached to the complaint) dominant before Black Mountain and the Beats. But as I've said, this skirmish is a continuing one, and a useless one. The rhetorical range of American poetry has historically been a wide one, and nourished by its extremes. It is middlebrow writing—correct and empty—that has been the true enemy of both sides, and Clampitt has always written as if she had absorbed W. H. Auden's advice: "Be subtle, various, ornamental, clever, / And do not listen to those critics ever / Whose crude provincial gullets crave in books / Plain cooking made still plainer by plain cooks."

One gets the sense from Clampitt's poems of both attention paid and amplitude given; or as she puts in it one poem, of her being at once "earthbound" and "fired-up." Admittedly, what some find exuberantly literary, others find merely bookish; what seems complex and heightened to some will strike others as clotted or gassy; one reader's figured meaning is another's decoration. What is clear is that she has studied and learned a great deal—from the landscape and lifeblood of literature, as well as from the encyclopedia of the eye's observations. Clampitt is a virtuoso, and she has two of a virtuoso's faults, both easily blinked at. Her cadenzas are sometimes too heavily ornamented, so that her skill overwhelms her subject; and her program is too long. Her style is luxuriant, frisky, and "escapes / our mere totting-up." Stanzas, for this poet, are

"little rooms / for turmoil to grow lucid in," and indeed her poems are each a series of refocusings: close-up and dissolve. Her effects are bold, often nervy, and buoyed both by tradition and by the community of solitaries. Wallace Stevens, in his "Adagia," said that "things seen are things as seen." A close observer of the natural world and of its "perishing residue / of pure sensation," Clampitt knows enough too to ask "What is real except / what's fabricated?" Her descriptions, then, are both; a sea-surface, for instance, is most itself when seen as something else: "this windsilver / rumpling as of oatfields, / a suede of shadow, / a nub, a nap, a mane of lustre / lithe as the slide / of muscle in its / sheath of skin."

The right word for Clampitt's style, of course, is *baroque*. That is to say, her poems are both intricate and full, their extensions defined by outsized syntactical gestures, by images and diction that introduce harmonic dissonances. This doesn't preclude a quiet dignity, but that is not the first note in her lyre. As in a baroque painting, the "action" of her poems is in the middle ground. The busy foreground pushes at a reader; her lines are crowded, overbright, and their extraneous detail sometimes makes them difficult to parse at first sight. The background of her poems, though, is softer, darker: traditional themes that structure and sustain the dramatic shape and force of her verse. It could be said she is a poet of light, light that separates and joins objects. One thinks of the atmospheric effects in her outdoor settings, or the firelit interiors of her nineteenth-century studies. And it is light, the fall and play of it, that figures so strongly in baroque art. Similarly, both the foreground and background of her poems are heavily allusive. Clampitt, like any baroque artist, pillages the art of the past. She looks at the world through language, so that what she sees is charged by the transforming power of metaphor. But—and this disturbs many readers—she looks at the world through art as well. It seems ridiculous to me that this art-about-art is so often deplored as etiolated and derivative in poetry; few object to it in, say, painting or music, perhaps because there it is recognized as a quintessential Romantic concern. Art models life, sets ideal or ironic standards, and so is a moral presence in poems—certainly in Clampitt's. It is her method to order, clarify, and illuminate experience. Art is to the poet what ideas are to the philosopher.

"It is a privilege to see so / much confusion," said Marianne Moore. By "confusion" she meant the world's own welter, its facts, artifacts, curios, and contradictions. And by "privilege" she meant their moral ordering. Clampitt is a poet in the mold of Moore. Some of the poems in *The Kingfisher* even sound like Moore—**"Times Square Water Music," "Good Friday," "Marginal Employment,"** and the appropriately named **"Exmoor."** But it is not that studied resemblance that attracts me so much as a deeper affinity: the curiosity and exuberance both poets share, their shrewd moralism, a disposition to view things through the spectacles of language, their love of (in Clampitt's phrase) "the ramifying / happenstance, the mirroring / marryings of all likeness." To have, for instance, Moore's "A Grave" in mind while reading Clampitt's **"Beach Glass"** is helpful. The same setting and point of view, the same indeterminate "you" addressed, the same thematic concerns—the sea as a "collector" and a grave, the ocean in which (here is Moore's conclusion) "dropped things are bound to sink—/ in which if they turn and twist, it is neither with volition nor consciousness." Of course the details are different. As she walks along her beach, Clampitt's eye is quicker than Moore's, more capacious, less sententious. What Moore notices are gorgeous or dire anomalies, timeless and detached in their moment of having been noticed. By contrast, Clampitt's details—"last night's / beer cans, spilt oil, the coughed-up / residue of plastic"—tend always to implicate some human drama behind them. This adds depth to a poem without narrative detours. And in her more deliberate way, she moves from the smaller particular to the grander generalization. The bits of beach glass she comes upon—the amber of Budweiser, chrysoprase of Gallo, lapis of Milk of Magnesia—are charming for their sea-changes. But she goes on to make her point about the stuff of human making. The myth of the engulfed cathedral is as much a part of these lines as is the religion of commercialism; and all of it is reduced to the Nothing that is everything is this poet's mind. It is poem that turns back in on itself, on its "looking":

> The process
> goes on forever: they come from sand,
> they go back to gravel,
> along with the treasuries
> of Murano, the buttressed
> astonishments of Chartres,
> which even now are readying
> for being turned over and over as gravely
> and gradually as an intellect
> engaged in the hazardous
> redefinition of structures
> no one has yet looked at.

The word that literally sticks out in that final stanza—"gravely"—is her nod to Moore's poem; and her sense of intellectual "redefinition" is both a tribute paid and a sly statement of her own terms.

When the English edition of *The Kingfisher* appeared in 1984, Faber had changed her into a different, and lesser poet for the British audience. It makes a certain sense to have deleted very local poems about life in New York City; they may not travel well. But also gone were some of the best poems in the book—its entire last section, in fact, some long and difficult poems that show more powerfully than many others how historical her imagination is. Part of that history is personal. Earlier poems that have set her parents to rest—**"Beethoven, Opus 111"** and **"A Procession at Candlemas"**—are part of her ambivalent project in this book to come to terms with her own past. The several poems about her Iowa childhood present a very mixed image, and some crucial motifs. In most of them, a real or imaged "habitat of magic" (a phrase from **"The Quarry"**) that is safe, enclosed, aloof from the immensities of the Midwest plains which are most often described in terms of water: "only waves / of chlorophyll in motion, the darkened jetsam / of bur oaks, a serpentine

of woodlot." The child-poet's eye looks for lines, for "fine manners." But it was barbed wire or nodes of evergreen and maple that "gave the prairie grid / what little personality it had." While the tantrums of big weather blow over here, the child is drawn elsewhere:

> Deep in it, under
> appletrees like figures in a ritual, violets
> are thick, a blue cellarhole
> of pure astonishment.
> It is
> the earliest memory. Before it,
> I/you, whatever that conundrum may yet
> prove to be, amounts to nothing.

"Astonishment" is a key word in Clampitt's vocabulary, and may account for her heaping of terms, as a way to understand and praise what stuns her. Or, it being her "earliest memory," an attempt to retrieve a primal image (the mother's breast, someone would suggest), or to compensate for a speechless wonder. But what fascinates me about this moment in **"The Woodlot"** is that the word "astonishment" comes from the same root that gives us "tornado," so that beneath the surface of the poem, beneath that apparent sharp contrast, her fear and her refuge from that fear are the same emotion. This is a peculiar but entirely characteristic maneuver on Clampitt's part.

"Imago" is the fullest version of these contrasts and mirrorings in *The Kingfisher*. It is a poem about growing up, and about growing away. The poem's term for this is "unfathomable evolvings." Her choice of adjective is apt, because the metaphor of the sea—and the sensation of *flux*—is everywhere, as an image for the vast waterless plains of Iowa, and for her unconscious yearnings ("A thirst for something definite so dense / it feels like drowning"). The portrait of the child here begins by juxtaposing two sorts of stories she is given: the tall tales of the western migration, and the fairy tales she reads on her own: Indians and merfolk. An image from the first—an infant daughter's headstone, "so small it might be playing house"—leads into the fabled palace the young girl is reading about in her farmhouse parlor. The severe and formless Iowa of Grant Wood and of provincial expectations is contrasted in the child's imagination with the "hard and handsome," dark and mysterious world of European culture:

> the abysm of history,
> a slough to be pulled out of
> any way you could. Antiquity, the backward
> suction of the dark, amounted to a knothole
> you plugged with straw, old rags, pages
> ripped from last year's Sears Roebuck catalog,
> anything, to ward off the blizzard.

A knothole through which forbidden pleasures might leak into the staid Iowa farmhouse is, of course, also the child's peephole, and similar to the cellarhole in **"The Woodlot"**—her access to astonishment. It is "the Italy / of urns and cypresses" that lures her, as it had Keats; a world theatrical and even lurid. At this point in the poem the knothole looks back at her from

a pair of masks whose look, at even
this remove, could drill through bone:
the tragic howl, the comic rictus,
eyeholes that stare out of the crypt
of what no grownup is ever heard to speak of.

But the last stanza, the longest in the poem, abruptly changes the tone of the poem. We are back home, on prayer meeting night. Here Clampitt plays with two meanings of "born-again." There are the worshipful revivalists surrounding her. And then there is herself, as if reborn through the eyehole into a new knowledge. Rather than speak autobiographically, she introduces a luna moth, after its metamorphosis from caterpillar "the emblem / of the born-again." The earlier knotholes next become the eyeholes on the luna moth's wing—the imago, both moth and totemic image of the unconscious—that predictably draws the child away to the East and to Art, as in the fairy tale the child had been reading about "the merfolk who revert to foam, / eyeing at a distance the lit pavilions / that seduced her, their tailed child, / into the palaces of metamorphosis." That she is drawn *underwater* is Clampitt's way of mingling the terms and fortunes of her two opposed states.

She can also move these terms beyond the personal. All her angles—topographical, political, memorial—are manifestations of her concern for how men have lived with themselves in time. The six poems of *The Kingfisher*'s final section confirm this, and in a harrowing way. Never journalistic, never strident or self-righteous ("The purest art has slept with turpitude, / we all pay taxes"), they explore the causes and the cost of human suffering. One, **"The Dahlia Gardens,"** is especially disturbing. It tells the story of Norman Morrison, a young Quaker activist who immolated himself in front of the Pentagon in 1965—another kind of terrible, emblematic moth in this book. It is a story that might have been rendered with the sentimentality of much political poetry. Instead, Clampitt makes it strange and urgent. Minds—those of bureaucrats and of martyrs—fill up with darkness:

> overland, the inching caravans
> the blacked-out troop trains
> convoys through ruined villages
> along the Mekong
>
> merging
>
> with the hydrocarbon-dark, headlight-inflamed
>   Potomac
>
> the little lights the candles
> flickering on Christmas eve
> the one light left burning
> in a front hallway kerosene-
> lit windows in the pitch dark
> of back-country roads.

That darkness is a terrible energy. In one version it is oil:

> . . . hydrocarbon unearthed
> and peeled away, process by process,

in stages not unlike the stages
of revelation, to a gaseous plume
that burns like a bush. . . .

In another, fanaticism:

> Hermaphrodite of pity and violence, the chambered
> pistil and the sword-bearing archangel,
> scapegoat and self-appointed avenger, contend,
> embrace, are one. He strikes the match.

The poet works to unite "system with system into one terrible mandala."

Metaphor is the figure of speech that embodies change, and even violence, and it is change and process, borders and shorelines, in-between states, "the unrest whose home—*our / home*—is motion," that are central to *What the Light Was Like* (1985). The poems in this book are grouped into five sections that move from **"The Shore"** to **"The Hinterland"** to **"The Metropolis,"** and back again. What changes is not just the locale, but the register and the vantage, and the way turmoils are contained. We start in a cottage on the Maine coast, then move to (and because it is the scene of her past, revisit) an Iowa farmhouse on the inland sea, then to an apartment on Manhattan island. Each is a marginal existence, a fugitive vision. The book opens with **"A Baroque Sunburst,"** ends at nightfall, and in between flicker images of light and dark. Those images, along with a crosshatching of allusions and themes, and its bracing structure, make this the most unified and resolute of all her books.

A familiar narrative device for this poet—one she shares with Elizabeth Bishop, A. R. Ammons, and others—is the ramble, during which unconsidered trifles are snatched up as symbols. Her favorites are her plucky city adventures and her walks in Maine, along its bogs and tidal flats, a shoreline that stands between solid familiarity and oceanic flux. The opening of **"Low Tide at Schoodic"** can stand in for her method in all these poems, whereby abstractions and images are allegorically loaded onto the plain object of mediation. The move here from surf to still tidepool, the movement of both the water and the walker, is brilliantly told in terms of palace revolution:

> Force, just here, rolls up
> pomaded into vast blue curls
> fit for the Sun King, then crumples
> to a stuff of ruffs and kerchiefs
> over ruined doorposts, the rubble
> of an overthrow no one remembers
> except through cooled
> extrapolation—tunnels
> underneath the granite,
> the simmering moat, the darkened sill
> we walk on now,
> prowling the planar windowpanes of tidepools
> for glimpses of kelp's ribboned whips,
> the dead man's fingers.

This book also includes versions of *The Kingfisher*'s more ambitious poems. Poems here about the death of

Clampitt's brother echo earlier poems about her parents; the title poem, about the death at sea of a Maine fisherman and how "the iridescence / of his last perception, charring, gave way to unreversed, / irrevocable dark," is a muted echo of the more anguished and searching poem **"The Dahlia Gardens."** But other poems here—**"Black Buttercups"** and **"A Curfew"** particularly—have a more urgent, personal, and thereby affecting note to them. The title poem reminds us "that what you love most is the same as what you're / most afraid of—God, / in a word." As before, it is love that draws Clampitt to the world's "wallowing and glitter," and it is fear that pulls her back from a vision of that world as a manifestation of dark, unknowable will.

The book's literal and figurative centerpiece is **"Voyages,"** a sequence of eight poems subtitled **"A Homage to John Keats,"** in part a costume drama drawn from Keats' letters and poems and from biographies of the poet, and in part a displaced study of these same themes of love and fear. It is nearly impossible not to draw an appealing portrait of Keats. Even so, Clampitt's pastiche is strikingly successful, circling as it does Keats' "own recurring dream of being warm," of the "fine weather, health, Books, a contented Mind" that animated and eluded his short life. **"Voyages"** is also an extraordinary act of literary self-definition. The ways she identifies her own writing with Keats'—with his lush impetuosity, his taste for grandeur, his regard for the literature of the past as "a Refuge and a Passion"—are illuminating.

But with good reason she concentrates more on Keats' life than on his work, and previous poems in the book forge stronger links between the two poets. We think of Clampitt's dead younger brother (to whose memory her book is dedicated) when she speaks of Keats' beloved Tom. We think of her own early prairie life when Keats contemplates his brother George's emigration to the wilds of America. The loss of both brothers to the cold immensities is several times contrasted with the warm, feminine indoors which nurtures the poet in "that imaginary place, that stanza / where nothing at all had happened," and prompts him, in turn, to open the casement window on the real: "The cold outside was real. / Dying was real . . ."

But it is not only the "continual allegory" of Keats' life that Clampitt is appropriating for herself as a way to make her turmoil lucid. She is interested, her footnote says, in "the powerful way in which literature can become a link with times and places, and with minds, otherwise remote." To that end, having joined herself to Keats, she enjoins a subsequent line of poets—Walt Whitman, Hart Crane, Wallace Stevens, and Osip Mandelstam—in which she means to take her place. All of them are poets of immensities: Whitman and Crane, of the sea; Stevens, of the auroras; and Mandelstam, of the cold. All of them countered their fears with trust in a redemptive art, their sense of engulfment with the imagination's posthumous whispers out of time. Clampitt's daring here is, in Pound's phrase, to have gathered from the air a live tradition, her voice one with theirs:

How clannish
the whole hand-to-hand, cliffhanging trade,

the gradual letdown, the hempen slither,
precarious basketload of sea drift
gathered at Margate or at Barnegat:
along Paumanok's liquid rim, the dirges,
nostalgia for the foam: *the bottom of
the sea is cruel.* The chaff, the scum
of the impalpable confined in stanzas,

a shut-in's hunger for the bodiless
enkindlings of the aurora—all that
traffic in the perilous. That summer,
orphaned of sublimity, he'd settled for
the way an oatfield's stalks and blades
checquered his writing tablet with their
quivering. But after, back in Hampstead,

the samphire-gatherer's mimic god-deliverer
still bled metonymy: an ordinary field of
barley turned to alien corn's inland sea-
surfaces, and onto every prairie rolling,
sans the samphire trade's frail craft, un-
basketed, undid the casement of the homesick,
stared once more, and called an image home.

"Life," remarked Wallace Stevens, "is not people and scene but thought and feeling." **"Voyages"** is both. It is a poem whose livelihood trades in character sketch and minutely observed setting, but whose life is what it thinks of them and how it invokes and quickens our feeling about them.

Clampitt herself has said that her third book, *Archaic Figure* (1987), "differs from *The Kingfisher* and *What the Light Was Like* rather more than either of those books differed from the other." But because her talent has unfolded rather than developed, I prefer to view the book as the third panel of a triptych. Many poems in all three books could go in any of the collections. The entire last section of *Archaic Figure* is largely leftovers. But the earlier parts of this book complete the large-scale self-portrait and historical inquiry that the triptych undertakes. The autobiographical intimacies of *The Kingfisher* dramatize a sequence of private initiations into womanhood, and the literary homages in *What the Light Was Like* are a process of affiliation. Those two movements, simultaneously away from and into the self, are here combined into the poet's studies of *women artists*—George Eliot, Margaret Fuller, Dorothy Wordsworth. None led an untroubled life, none is what we would call a triumphant artist. They are apt choices, then, for what Clampitt says the book's central concern is: "the experience of women, as individuals and as a part of human history." For this poet, that experience has been a very mixed one.

Two figures dominate the book. One, its figurehead on the dust jacket, is a headless female statue from a votive group in the Heraeum of Samos (now in East Berlin), by the sculptor Geneleos from about 560 B.C. The delicate figure, with her tresses and gathered, pleated chiton, is called *Orinthe,* or "Little Bird." The opening, the titular or dedicatory poem of the book, **"Archaic Figure,"** broods on this figure—the austere, elusive virgin beyond time—"that saw—or so to us it seems—/ with unexampled clarity to the black core / of what we are, of everything we were to be, / have since become." The other and opposing figure is Medusa. She might also be considered, in the long run, a headless figure, but we most often think of her *as a head*—in this instance, one that completes the headless statute of Orinthe. The Medusa could be thought of as the female counterpart of the Minotaur: monstrous because the most "human" part of the person is bestial, murderous, irrational. Clampitt's monster is, typically, more pathetic. She stands as an emblem of the body itself, or of the fallen body, subjected to time and brute force:

> The tentacles, the brazen phiz whose glare
> stands every fibril of the mind on end—
> lust looked at backwards at it were,
> an antique scare tactic, either self-protection
> or a libel on the sex whose periodic
> blossom hangs in ungathered garland
> from the horned clockwork of the moon:
> as cause or consequence, or both, hysteric
> symptoms no doubt figure here. She'd been
> a beauty till Poseidon, in a flagrant
> trespass, closed with her on Athena's temple floor.

She is a sympathetic but still forbidding figure throughout the book, as in later poems she is associated first with Athena, and later with the slightly grotesque George Eliot. She may as well be the presiding force in the long poem **"An Anatomy of Migraine"**—the modern pathological manifestation of the old myth? It is not just horrific pain, the very pain of existence itself, that she represents, though she is the constant reminder in this book that "we are animals, mire-born, / mud-cumbered, chilled and full of fear." In the poem **"Hippocrene"** she is said to be the "harbinger of going under, / of death by water." The indirect reference is to Virginia Woolf; to those headaches and depressions that signaled the onset of her fatal madness. The motif of drowning goes back to her earliest poems, and if we make the appropriate connections, it is possible to see Orinthe and Medusa as embodiments of the two principles—restraint and engulfment—that have fascinated Clampitt's imagination in all four books.

I want to take these connections one step further. **"The Nereids of Seriphos"** in *Archaic Figure* makes an explicit link between the Greek landscape that Clampitt is drawn to and the Midwest plains of her childhood. They are both, let us call them, elemental landscapes, and they are joined by others in her books, notably by the Maine coastline. There is a blessed indifference, a cruel sanctity to these places, and they may continually be contrasted with the doomed happiness and plenitude of both the nineteenth-century households she re-imagines and the Manhattan apartment and blocks where she dwells. The latter world is an interior one, cozy but crossed with upheaval and destruction: one she identifies herself with. The other is outdoors, vast, an image of eternity: one she has fled but revisits. Both are part of what she calls "this

/ botched cumbersome, much-mended, / not unsatisfactory thing" that is existence itself. The mixed state, the middle ground: it is here Clampitt's poems mark their boundaries, replenishing themselves to soothe an old uneasiness, pushing against and beyond the scramble of natural facts and human history toward the calm of ideas about life. And those ideas, in their turn, are lit by the light of her style—a light "that's always shifting—from / a nimbus gone beserk / to a single gorget, a cathedral train of blinking, or / the fogbound shroud / that can turn anywhere into a nowhere."

Blake Morrison (review date 1990)

SOURCE: "The Cross-Country Poet," in *The New Republic*, Vol. 203, No. 1, July 2, 1990, pp. 29-32.

[*In his review of* Westward, *Morrison attributes Clampitt's appeal to English readers to her attention to detail, her willingness to include the Old World and its history, and her search for emotional roots.*]

Amy Clampitt's new book opens with a bold piece of imaginative transportation, **"John Donne in California,"** setting down a poet who alluded to America but never visited it among the giant redwoods and "New World lizards" of the West:

> Is the Pacific Sea my home? Or is
> Jerusalem? pondered John Donne,
> who never stood among these strenuous,
> huge, wind-curried hills, their green
> gobleted just now with native poppies'
> opulent red-gold . . .

Donne is far from being the only figure, or indeed the only literary figure, to be uprooted in the course of Clampitt's collection. The central theme of the book, as dominant in the last poem as in the first, is of men and women driving westward—pioneers, settlers, immigrants, dreamers, poets. But Donne is the right person for Clampitt to start with, for the poem of his that she cites and expects us to turn to (though uncharacteristically she gives no source in the endnotes) is a "Hymne to God my God, in my sicknesse," in which Donne imagines his prostrate body as a map (and his doctors as cartographers) and celebrates a heavenly union of East and West. "Is the Pacifique Sea my home? Or are/The Eastern riches? Is Jerusalem?" asks Donne (and Clampitt after him), implying an answer he had already reached in one of his sermons: "In a flat Map, there goes no more, to make West East, though they be distant in an extremity, but to paste that flat Map upon a round body, and then West and East are all one."

Nearly four centuries after Donne, the idea of West and East being united, "all one," remains as frail a conceit as it has always been, but in the euphoria of the present moment, with the bad old empires on their sickbeds all around the globe, it is proper that Clampitt, if ever so obliquely, should catch something of that utopian dream. She is not a political poet, but nor is she so unworldly as she sometimes sounds, and her collection, susceptible to historical changes, offers its own special version of late twentieth-century glasnost. It is no coincidence that **"The Prairie,"** which closes her collection, should offer us another fusion of East and West, comparing the experiences of Anton Chekhov in the Russian steppes with those of her own grandfather in the American prairies.

So *Westward*, despite its title, is as much about the East as the West, the Atlantic as the Pacific, Europe as North America. Clampitt calls the opening section of it "Crossings," and it is a word she has earned the right to use, for she is a great poet of crossings over, mediation, cultural exchange. In Europe, or at any rate in Britain, we are very conscious of this: Clampitt, it seems, is the first American poet since Robert Lowell to explore the continuities between her country and ours.

Until Clampitt's arrival, it had become a critical commonplace to assert that American poetry and British poetry were no longer on speaking terms. Since that brief, glorious moment in the late 1950s when the British and American poetic traditions took a parallel course, with the marriage of Ted Hughes and Sylvia Plath an initially beneficent but finally tragic symbol of the union, the two traditions have been all but severed. Indeed, the suspicion had begun to arise that they have always been implacably opposed, and that separatists like Poe, Whitman, and Williams, for whom being in the American grain meant kicking against the old colonialist British heritage, had it right.

Part of Clampitt's attraction (to us at least) is that she offers a more hopeful version of the relationship between Old World and New. She finds it, for example, in the image of her grandfather, a late nineteenth-century pioneer, whom she describes composing a sonnet in the middle of the prairies. "We have listened too long to the courtly muses," wrote Emerson, and sought instead American "self-trust." Clampitt's grandfather, terrified of the infinite spaces, lacking self-trust and clinging to the reassurances of the Mayflower legacy, cannot oblige him:

> There crowd my mind (he wrote) vague fancies
> of Aeolian harpings, twined with weird oaks'
> murmurings . . .

Aeolian harpings in Dakota: it is an image that admits dislocation, opposition, even a faint sense of the ridiculous. But for Clampitt's grandfather, a prey to terrible anxieties and crying "Lost, Lost," those Aeolian harpings are a way of finding himself, or at least of comforting a troubled mind. So Clampitt does not judge it reprehensible that the Old World should continue to penetrate the New. She goes on to ask whether it still does so a century later:

> Can the courtly muses
> of Europe, those bedizened crones, survive
> the manholes, the vaunt and skitter of Manhattan, or
> consort with the dug-in, the hunkering guardians
> of the Dakotas?

The answer, for her, is that they can and they do. *Westward*, like her three earlier books, is forever turning up connections and continuities: between the European skylark and the North American meadowlark; between a New England violet and a field pansy in Holland; between Scottish heather and blueberries in Maine; between the history of Virginia and the mockingbirds and warblers who move through the state's colonial habitats unheedingly, "ignorant of royal grants, crests / charters, sea power, mercantile / expansion, the imperative to / find an opening, explore, exploit . . ."

For Old World readers, touchy these days about seeming marginal, it is reassuring to find themselves reinstated on the map in this way. The welcome the British gave to *The Kingfisher*, Clampitt's first book, must have had a lot to do with such feelings of gratitude, though perhaps we didn't recognize it at the time: at last an American poet who made us feel we mattered; at last an American poet we could appreciate without having to feel defensive about our own achievements; at last, after futile endeavors to get a grip on Ashbery and Ammons, an American poet we could understand. This may be simply another way of saying that Clampitt is an Anglophile, and it is true that, though the guiding spirits of *The Kingfisher* were Elizabeth Bishop and Marianne Moore, the book also displayed a rich appreciation of such components of English life as damp bed sheets, Peak Frean biscuits, hassocks, toasting forks, sheepdogs, windowboxes, and rain.

That same Anglophilia has since manifested itself in more literary appreciations—of Coleridge, the Wordsworths, Hopkins, George Eliot, Virginia Woolf, and above all of Keats, to whom Clampitt dedicated one of the sequences in her second book, *What the Light Was Like*. In *Archaic Figure*, her last collection, Clampitt's imagination moved outward and backward to Greece, leading her into a reclamation of female deities and toward her most feminist collection to date. But even here, a reverence for English figures like Dorothy Wordsworth and George Eliot were central to the pattern. And in the new book it is impossible to read beyond the first page without feeling that the British (or the Irish) are at the back of it—whether Hopkins, whose compounding technique is imitated in Clampitt's image of "lofted strong-arm / redwoods' fogfondled silhouette," or Seamus Heaney, whom one glimpses in "the frail wick of metaphor I've brought to see by."

Yet Anglophilia will not quite serve as an explanation for why it is that Clampitt should have been taken up so enthusiastically on our side of the Atlantic as on her own. One might as easily explain her appeal in terms of what, for the British reader, is its exotica: in birds, beasts, and flowers (porcupines, turtles, sundews, the sea mouse, the beach pea, the grosbeak) familiar to us only from books. It is true that such natural phenomena must look exotic to readers in New York, too, but they are hardly likely to feel the vertiginous thrill that British readers do on reading a Clampitt poem about, for example, a whippoorwill. A whippoorwill! My Columbia Encyclopedia, referring me to "Goatsucker," gives me a fuller description than Clampitt can offer, but she has the better explanation of why it is that rare birds like the whippoorwill should exert such fascination:

> The webbiness,
> the gregariousness of the many are what
> we can't abide.
> We single out for notice
>
> above all what's disjunct, the way birds are,
> with their unhooked-up, cheekily anarchic
> dartings and flashings, their uncalled-for color . . .

A taste for the exotic is not one that Clampitt would necessarily like to see attributed to her, though, and not only because it might raise questions about her centrality. In **"Nothing Stays Put,"** she wonders whether the exotic can really be said to exist in a world where distance has collapsed, where nowhere is more than a plane-hop away, and where supermarket shelves blaze with the "largesse" of the tropics. Clampitt, who grew up a Puritan and can still sound like one, recoils from this unmerited glut ("we are not entitled"), much as an earlier poem of hers recoiled from central heating.

But this isn't so much a recoil from the contemporary world as a desire to suggest that "the strange and wonderful" can be indigenous, too. She is drawn to, and likes to draw our attention to, the neglected, the remote, the out of the way; and there is nowhere like one's own doorstep for finding them. This holds for people as well. The human beings Clampitt likes to celebrate, women mostly, are also neglected and out of the way, and often come associated with a particular piece of indigenous yet exotic fauna: one with a "potted hedge of rubber trees," another with *Rosa rugosa,* a third with the "ubiquitous, unaspiring" beach pea.

The sympathy that Clampitt brings to her descriptions of people and plants does indeed make us feel that they are "strange and wonderful," but this is not because she likes to wow us with their oddities. On the contrary, she has a humdrum care to represent them accurately. Even the whippoorwill sounds pretty familiar by the time Clampitt has finished with it:

> Night after night, it was very nearly enough,
> they said, to drive you crazy: a whippoorwill
> in the woods repeating itself like the stuck groove
> of an LP with a defect, and no way possible
> of turning the thing off.
>
> And night after night, they said, in the insomniac
> small hours the whipsawing voice of obsession
> would have come in closer, the way a sick
> thing does when it's done for— . . .

An evocation like this might serve better than the Columbia Encyclopedia in helping you to recognize the whippoorwill's call. Such an ability in a poet should never be underestimated, and Clampitt has it in abundance. Bishop, who had it too, said of Moore that "if she speaks of a chair you can practically sit on these poets how a fin-

icky notation—of flowers, plants, herbs, birds, animals—can not only displace the need for handbooks and field guides, but create a poetry of its own. Nothing is beneath notice, nothing—not even grasses—too humble to delineate:

> the oats grow tall,
> their pendent helmetfuls
> of mica-drift, examined stem
> by stem, disclose
>
> alloys so various, enamelings
> of a vermeil so
> craftless, I all but despair of
> ever reining in a
>
> metaphor for . . .

But rein in her metaphors she does, of course: the "liquid millennium" of the dawn chorus, the "charred and single coal" of an oriole, the "yearning seedling choir" of canary droppings in a cage. The rush of physical impressions can threaten to overwhelm not only the reader but the poet, too, who describes herself a couple of times as "fazed," and who in her most intense moments comes across as the sort of woman you might meet at dusk on the shoreline with an armful of shells, driftwood and fishing net—wide-eyed, pantheistic, half-cracked. But she is prepared to risk a reputation for genteel craziness so long as that also allows her a place in posterity as (to adapt Hardy) a woman who used to notice such things.

The contradictions of such a persona—the poet whose genius for noticing is also held to be an eccentricity, whose careful attention to the look of things is held to be, socially, a carelessness—are ones she writes well about in **"The Field Pansy,"** which uncovers a connection between three different kinds of flowers, and speaks of

> this gushing insouciance that appears at the same
>   time capable
> of an all but infinite particularity: sedulous, patient,
>   though
> in the end (so far as anyone can see) without
>   consequence.
> What is consequence? What difference do the
>   minutiae
> of that seeming inconsequence that's called beauty
>
> add up to? . . .

Phrased as a question though this is, it offers an implicit defense of Clampitt's art, which will put up with being called "inconsequential" so long as it has the consequence of capturing and creating beauty.

It is a difficult double-act to perform—insouciance on the one hand, sedulousness on the other—and Clampitt does not always bring it off. At times her thoroughness becomes a self-defeating pedanticism, as if she has thought out and read up on her subject to the point where there is nothing left to discover in the act of writing the poem, and where a scholarly paper (or indeed one of her ample source notes) might serve equally well. At this point her poetry can sound academic, prone to an Eng. Lit. piety (all *hommages* to the giants) and to a fussy, ornate, affected vocabulary—"the zenith's frescoed-by-/Tiepolo cerulean."

But if at its worst her poetry smells of the lamp, at its best it works like a flashlight, purposeful in its glare but always likely to chance on bright objects in the dark. Her casual-seeming line breaks help this effect of spontaneity: resistant to rhymes and end stops, it is a verse that stays alert to lucky breaks, sudden insights, the brief epiphanies of a life lived on the move. Her poetry is full of lists, accumulating and itemizing in verbless sentences the riches of things read or observed ("spring mud and summer dust,/ burdocks, beatings, piety," "Collectives. Tractor lugs. / Names: brunizem and chernozem; culm / rhizome and stolon"). More usually, though out of the same restlessly notating spirit, she prefers long sentences. **"Iola, Kansas,"** for example, is one long sentence running over eight stanzas and bringing us the Midwest as seen from a Greyhound:

> we're in Kansas now, we've turned off the freeway,
> we're meandering, as again night falls, among
>   farmsteads,
> the little towns with the name of a girl on the
>   watertower,
> the bandstand in the park at the center, the churches
>
> alight from within, perpendicular banalities of glass
> candy-streaked purple-green-yellow (who is this
>   Jesus?),
> the strangeness of all there is, whatever it is,
>   growing
> stranger, we've come to a rest stop, the name of the
>   girl
>
> on the watertower is Iola: no video, no vending
>   machines,
> but Wonder Bread sandwiches, a pie: "It's
>   boysenberry,
> I just baked it today," the woman behind the
>   counter
> believably says, the innards a purply glue . . .

Whether this stands up, grammatically, as a sentence is doubtful (". . . growing stranger, we've come to a rest stop" surely requires stronger punctuation than a comma), but there can be no doubt that it is the *mode juste*, the commas and the colons acting like rest stops on a long journey, the full stop delayed for the end.

The long sentence, often broken up by one or several sets of parentheses, has become an increasing feature of Clampitt's work and has never seemed more appropriate than in *Westward*. It expresses the rootlessness and the restlessness that is her subject here, the feeling of drawn-out journeys and great movements and migrations, of destinations finally arrived at but even then perhaps only provisionally, and certainly only after several detours so elaborate that the direction in which we are moving looks

to have been forgotten. The most spectacular example of this comes in the title poem itself, which is an account of a journey Clampitt took to Iona, in the Western Isles of Scotland, home of St. Columba and Christianity.

Beginning in London, among the "reverse" migrants of a spent commonwealth, those from the fringe returning to the old imperial heart, Clampitt heads northward and westward, her journey becoming a symbol for all the "embarkations, landings, dooms, conquests" of people in search of God, or of the promised land. It takes two interminable sentences toward the end before Clampitt brings us to "the brim of an illumination" about

> a zeal ignited somewhere to the east,
> concealed in hovels, quarreled over,
>
> portaged westward: a basket weave, a
> fishing net, a weir to catch, to salvage
> some tenet, some common intimation for
>
> all flesh, to hold on somehow till
> the last millennium: as though the routes,
> the ribbonings and redoublings, the
>
> attenuations, spent supply lines, frayed-
> out gradual of the retreat from empire, all
> its castaways, might still bear witness.

This is Clampitt's most high-flown and religious version of what the westward impulse means. As the title poem, it acquires a certain definitiveness. But other meanings multiply throughout the course of the book. **"Westward"** is the search for gold, money, jobs, opportunity, a home; it is a flight from the fear of infinite spaces; it is the urge to civilize, colonize, tame, subdue, settle; it is an existential quest, the search for a freedom to "throw one's life away" as one chooses:

> This being what all the rush
> of westward-the-course-of-empire
>   finally comes down to:
>
> to be free, as Isabel Archer pig-
> headedly put it, to meet one's fate,
> to take one's chances, try on
> disguises . . .

Above all, "westward" is Clampitt's own search for roots, the return she makes from points east to the "evangel-haunted prairie hinterland" of her upbringing, a "farmhouse childhood, kerosene-lit, tatting and mahogany-genteel," which she left as an "intemperate" teenager to head for the "glittering shambles / of enthrallments and futilities" that goes by the name of Manhattan. As that image shows, Clampitt now shrinks from the vacuity of urban "monoculture": the color and generosity of what she finds in nature are a reproach to the gray human alternative in Manhattan, "every pittance under lock and key / a party to the general malfeasance." But this is not to say that there was anything especially wholesome about her ancestor-settlers, "far from hot baths," who, social outcasts of a kind, fled to discover new worlds but soon enough were imposing a "neat and fearful grid of settlement" that would enable them in turn to find someone else more vagrant "to look down on." Clampitt, in other words, is not sentimental about her roots.

Hovering over her book is a play on the word "settled": conscious (from reading his privately printed pamphlet) of her grandfather's unsettled mind, she tries to settle something in her own mind. Is not settlement primarily an attempt to ward off spiritual unsettlement? Is it not therefore doomed to failure, however often roots are put down and civilization spreads? And isn't man's natural state, however much he may seek to be at rest some-where, to be mobile? Some such suggestion underlies **"The Prairie"** and allows its ending, which might otherwise be a sad record of Clampitt's failed homecoming, to have an air of exhilaration about it:

> No one
>
> I know or ever heard of lives there now.
> On Summit, from some long-obliterated
> snapshot, I thought I recognized the house
>
> a great-aunt lived in once: the number
> not quite right, the tenant an old
> deaf Mexican who did not understand.

Not being able to return to where you came from leaves you freer to be what you are: that would seem to be the almost joyous consolation Clampitt takes from her frustrated journey. It is the same exultant note that one hears at the end of **"Iola, Kansas"**:

> and through some duct in the rock I feel my heart
>   go out,
> out here in the middle of nowhere (the scheme is a
>   mess)
> to the waste, to the not knowing who or why, and
>   am happy.

It is this surrender that makes Clampitt a more truly modern poet than her occasional snappishness at contemporary urban culture would lead you to think. In the brightness and the diversity and the "unhooked-up" independence of the bird world she finds a model ("free as a bird") to live by; and in the migrations of her ancestors she confirms her own migrating spirit, which, unlike theirs, will never seek to find *the* place to settle. *Westward* is not her most accessible book, but it is her most self-aware one. Failing to come home at the end of it, she can now be said to have truly arrived.

Helen Vendler   (review date 1991)

SOURCE: "Imagination Pressing Back," in *The New Yorker,* Vol. LXVII, No. 16, June 10, 1991, pp. 103-11.

[*In this review of* Westward, *Vendler examines Clampitt's use of landscape as a means "to resolve questions of*

sexual identity, of unsatisfactory family relations, of the expectations of society. . . ."]

For Amy Clampitt, landscape is the refuge to which, for its serenity, its visual variety, its biological laws, she turns in order to resolve questions of sexual identity, of unsatisfactory family relations, of the expectations of society, of the history of Iowa (whence she fled, in her twenties, to Greenwich Village). Reading, of course, was one resource of this bookish child, but nothing in her reading—not even Andersen or the Greek myths—ever gave her the pure wordless solace of the earth's changing sights and sounds.

Landscape was for Clampitt the first aesthetic realm, and in a central poem, **"The Field Pansy,"** from her new collection, *Westward* she tells the story of all aesthetic people dismayed to discover that the beauty that so assuages and reassures them does absolutely nothing for someone else:

> Life was hard in the hinterland, where spring
>   arrived
> with a gush of violets, sky-blue out of the ground
>   of the woodlot,
> but where a woman was praised by others of her
>   sex for being
> Practical, and by men not at all, other than in a
>   slow reddening
> about the neck, a callowly surreptious wolf-whistle:
>   where the mode
>
> was stoic, and embarrassment stood in the way of
>   affect:
> a mother having been alarmingly seen in tears, once
>   only
> we brought her a fistful of johnny-jump-ups from
>   the garden,
> "because you were crying"—and saw we'd done the
>   wrong thing.

The second stanza here is the final one of the poem, and, though all the others have five lines, it has only four, because the mother's rebuffing response shocks the child (and the later poet) into silence, represented by an aborted line of stifled feeling.

What, then, is the use of beauty, if it can heal oneself but not others? "What difference do the minutiae / of that seeming inconsequence that's called beauty / add up to?" It seems to Clampitt that some beauty-diffusing impulse in the universe itself is in question, an impulse that strews the earth with all the evolutionary varieties of pansy enumerated in the poem:

> . . . a gathering, a proliferation
>
> on a scale that, for all its unobtrusiveness, seems to
>   be
> worldwide, of what I don't know how to read
>   except as an
> urge to give pleasure . . .

I know I'm leaving something out
when I write of this omnipresence of something like
    eagerness,

this gushing insouciance that appears at the same
    time capable
of an all but infinite particularity.

Clampitt admires Hopkinsian inscape without seeking (as
Hopkins often did) the best sunset, the most striking cloud-
scape, the most boisterous weather. Her poetry crosses
Hopkinsian "gush" ("He gushes, but he means it," a
schoolmate of Hopkins said) with a Wordsworthian appreciation of the common and the unobtrusive: the field
pansy is a cousin of the "violet by a mossy stone, / Half
hidden from the eye."

In her Maine poems Clampitt notices the recrudescent
mosses and sundews, everyday plants, as a stay against
decay, and admires, in **"High Noon,"** an elderly woman
who is still bestowing, however faded herself, unfaded
flowers on the young. The poem ends by reflecting on a
photograph of the elderly woman in her youth:

> When the sun
> leaves the zenith (if it ever does) of that
> monochrome, it will utter its frivolous last
>   gasp in a smother of roses.

"Frivolous," perhaps, to those who do not understand a
death accompanied by roses rather than by prayers, but a
sentiment not unknown to Ronsard, watering a rose tree
on a young girl's grave, "*Afin que vif et mort ton corps
ne soit que roses.*"

Violets and roses are the luxuriant, bright side of Clampitt's
imagination, pressing back against the inhumanity of the
social order. (Clampitt's father was a Quaker, and her
first book included a poem in memory of a self-immolated
Quaker martyr protesting the war in Vietnam.) In **"Westward,"** the symbol of social disorder is not war but the
modern city. Clampitt's indictment of New York includes
herself among the (relatively helpless) authors of "the
general malfeasance." Here is the Dantesque description
of "half-stupefied Manhattan" from the sinister opening
of the long poem **"The Prairie"**:

> The wind whines in the elevator shaft. The
>   houseless
> squinny at us, mumbling. We walk attuned
> to the colubrine rustle of a proletariat
>
> that owes nobody anything, through a Manhattan
> otherwise (George Eliot's phrase) well wadded
> in stupidity—a warren of unruth, a propped
>
> vacuity: our every pittance under lock and key
> a party to the general malfeasance. Saurian,
> steam-wreathed rancors crowd the manholes,
> as though somebody grappled with the city's
> entrails: Laocoön, doomsayer, by a god
> or gods undone.

From that beginning in New York City, her own milieu,
Clampitt traces, in a long and complicated arc, the parallel stories of her grandfather and Anton Chekhov, born in
the same year. Chekhov wrote that the steppe cried out
for a bard; Clampitt feels—in spite of her early escape to
New York—the obligation to commemorate the prairie
past that formed her sense of life. The flight of the poet
from the "settled life" of the Midwest community takes
place late in the poem, almost anonymously, in a reprise
of the opening:

> Dreams of escape: out of the settled life's
> fencerow patrols, into their licensed overthrow:
>
> excess, androgyny, the left wing; anonymity-
> celebrity: escape achieved that's no escape,
> the waiting misstep, the glassy fjord-leap.
>
> Living anxious. The wind a suicidal howling
> in the elevator shaft. The manholes' stinking,
> steaming entrails. Dreams, now and again,
>
> lopsided fantasies of going back, weak-kneed,
> through the underbrush, and getting even.

Such brief selections from a lengthy poem give only a
glimpse of Clampitt's rhythmic adroitness as she mimics
the jump-starts and cowerings of the mind. In the end, she
pursues the family line back to a house, dimly remembered from a snapshot, of a great-aunt in Pasadena: "The
number / not quite right, the tenant an old / deaf Mexican
who did not understand." The evanescence of personal
history is palpable as the poem closes with the descendant
of the homesteader unable to communicate with the Hispanic immigrant. This is a place where the American landscape—ever-changing under the soles of its westward-
moving population—cannot give solace. Its failure to
provide aesthetic reassurance is coupled with its failure to
provide an enduring home for anyone.

Like landscape, femaleness has for Clampitt its disappointments; whatever the ultimate rewards to the contemporary woman artist, she and her avatars—Dorothy Wordsworth, Emily Dickinson—were unsuccessful girls, judged
by the common standards of their societies. In **"My Cousin
Muriel,"** a cousin of the speaker is dying in California,
and old memories arise while death, unspeakable, "stirs
like a stone":

> The air of rural Protestant New England
>
>   . . . infused the hinterland
> my cousin Muriel and I both hailed from:
> a farmhouse childhood, kerosene-lit,
> tatting-and-mahogany genteel. "You
> were the smart one," she'd later say. . . .
>
> [She played] the whole trajectory of
> being female, while I played the dullard,
> presaged. She bloomed, knew how to flirt,
> acquired admirers. I didn't.

Clampitt has faced the question of being female before, mercilessly, in her elegy for her mother, **"Procession at Candlemas"**; here she confronts, in the frightening and frightened poem **"A Hedge of Rubber Trees,"** what she herself might have become, uprooted in New York—a sodden recluse. She recounts her temporary alliance with a displaced eccentric:

> Unclassifiable castoffs, misfits, marginal cases:
> when you're one yourself, or close to it, there's
> a reassurance in proving you haven't quite gone
> under by taking up with somebody odder than you
> are.

Finally, the acquaintance with the elder eccentric founders. The poet does not excuse her own part in the separation:

> The West Village was changing. I was changing.
> The last
> time I asked her to dinner, she didn't show.
> Hours—
> or was it days?—later, she phoned to explain: she
> hadn't
> been able to find my block; a patrolman had steered
> her home.
> I spent my evenings canvassing for Gene McCarthy.
> Passing,
> I'd see her shades drawn, no light behind the
> rubber trees.
> She wasn't out, she didn't own a TV. She was in
> there,
> getting gently blotto. What came next, I wasn't
> brave
> enough to want to know.

Earlier, the recluse had dreamed that her own face in the mirror was "covered over . . . with gray veils." The lethal effacement of the spinster by society, partly because of her inability or refusal to compromise, partly because of the revulsion felt by the sexual for the asexual, is a theme not much treated in poetry. It is there in Clampitt, but unsentimentally; the recluse speaks of her cohort of roaches, "ruefully, as of an affliction that / might once, long ago, have been prevented." Landscape and "beauty" and "art," and even church (where the speaker and the recluse met), are powerless to cope with the disintegrative force of the city.

If, then, Clampitt's imagination at its most stringent cannot rest in landscape (whatever its exaltations), or in solidarity with women, or in institutional remedies, or in art, where will it find an anchor? The title poem of **"Westward,"** in partial answer, takes Clampitt to the island of Iona, off the western coast of Scotland. She goes there partly because Keats went there, partly because Lycidas drowned in the Irish Sea, partly because St. Columba "made his pious landfall" there, partly because it is "the raw edge of Europe." On Iona, "the prospect / is to the west." At the same time, "the retrospect / is once again toward the interior." Facing both ways, back to Europe and forward to the New World, Clampitt imagines the dogged wanderings of what one can only call the Western

religious imagination, guarding something that will be of use and solace to everyone (as art is not, as sexual identity is not, as even the beauty of the earth is not). Clampitt does not know where to locate the current home of the religious impulse, but she recalls its past, the trail of "the mind's / resistance to the omnipresence of what / moves but has no, cannot say its name." Naming and the religious impulse are for Clampitt (if I understand her correctly) the same. Carrying the Word has led, in the West, to all the "embarkations, landings, dooms, conquests, / missionary journeys, memorials" of human endeavor. **"Westward"** ends with a brilliantly entropic summary of those Christian journeyings from the Holy Land to Europe and on to the New World:

> Columba
> in the skin-covered wicker of that coracle,
>
> lofting these stonily decrepit preaching
> posts above the heathen purple; in their
> chiseled gnarls, dimmed by the weatherings
>
> of a millennium and more, the braided syntax
> of a zeal ignited somewhere to the east,
> concealed in hovels, quarreled over,
>
> portaged westward: a basket weave, a
> fishing net, a weir to catch, to salvage
> some tenet, some common intimation for
>
> all flesh, to hold on somehow till
> the last millennium: as though the routes,
> the ribbonings and redoublings, the
>
> attenuations, spent supply lines, frayed-
> out gradual of the retreat from empire, all
> its castaways, might still bear witness.

This Protestant witnessing to the Word is an old theme in American literature, but its belatedness (to use Harold Bloom's word) in **"Westward"** suggests that its frailty belies its reassurances. Nonetheless, Clampitt insists that the saving Word has to be one available to all, not solely to readers of literature or people of one nationality.

Clampitt's formality in her prophetic moments, such as this one, means that her religious moments are estranged somewhat from the lines that speak of roaches and "getting gently blotto" and also from her botanizing lines. She is unwilling to give up on landscape or on the day-to-day (the deathbed journeys, the waits in clinics, the bus rides). Yet, above nature and above the quotidian, her imagination stubbornly aspires to something she cannot locate socially or institutionally, or even aesthetically. This "bearing witness" can be compromised or attenuated by circumstance, but it nonetheless stands all alone, "hugely politic" (Shakespeare's phrase). Clampitt, while recognizing the same tyrannies and historical corruptions in the pursuit of the absolute which so dismay Bidart, preserves a sense of the undamaged conscience reborn among human beings. It is for her a bulwark against the ultimate insufficiency of beauty and history alike. And though the power of her faith in that inner light is unmistakable, she does not always convince this reader of the reliability of a universal Word, reinvented by every culture.

Amy Clampitt   (essay date 1993)

SOURCE: "Lasting the Night," in *Where We Stand: Women Poets on Literary Tradition,* W.W. Norton & Company, 1993, pp. 28-30.

[*In this essay, Clampitt recalls her initial lack of self-assurance and reflects upon the development of her poetic voice.*]

By the time I graduated from high school I had discovered the poems of Edna St. Vincent Millay, then very much in fashion. The spring of 1937 is a long time ago, and it may be that I only imagine what I seem to recall—namely, aspiring to what the first of her Figs from Thistles called "burning at both ends." Oh yes, I was going to be a Writer, but that was no more than ancillary. To put it another way, it meant getting out—out of the rural scene where my own psychic halts and festinations, my lunges toward self-definition, were all egregiously out of sync.

Looking back, I'm not sure how much gender had to do with this quasi-paralysis. My parents had been similarly lacking in assurance; but I have a sense that it was my father, as head of the household, on whom the burden of anxiety chiefly fell. *His* father had left a poignant record, whose importance to me can scarcely be exaggerated, of anxiety amounting almost to terror. It may be that my mother and my grandmothers suffered no less; but if so, they set down no such record. For my mother there was the recourse of tears, which made everybody feel guilty, whereas for the men in my family, whatever feeling was openly expressed took the form of anger. Setting things down could make a difference, as I seem to have known from an early age; but the legacy of self-doubt remained.

Why were we all so unsure of ourselves, so fearful of exposure, so open to ridicule, to throttling worry about what other people might think or say? It wasn't simply money, though we were pinched for it. As I would learn much later, such anxieties had been known to Virginia Woolf; and it was she, through the language of *The Waves,* who seemed to be speaking to and for an isolation so precarious that I, as a college sophomore, hadn't dared suppose it could be the plight of anyone else. Her being a novelist, so called, rather than a poet, had perhaps something to do with the kind of writer I now intended to be.

Back in high school, I'd written a number of sonnets—Shakespeare, not Millay, being the real exemplar, so far as I remember. But in those days (however improbable it might seem, given the ever-dwindling margin of concern with what is wistfully called "the examined life" as a matter of public discourse), the notion of becoming a poet was more fraught with ridicule than now. The sources of this paradox are for cultural historians to mull over. One

effect of the sixties was a general blurring of the old stereotypes, that of the poet among them. I seem to remember, from Ernie Kovacs' long-gone gallery of losers, one Percy something—was it Silvertonsils? He was, at any rate, unmistakably, effeminately, The Poet. Nowadays, live poets from time to time make an appearance on television—marginally but without (so far as I know) being lampooned. Men once sneered at Culture because they felt in some way threatened by it, in much the same way (I believe) that they felt threatened by women. The way men feel threatened by women has changed; as for the feminine aspect associated with Higher Things, the sneer would seem to have been replaced by indifference. In my own reluctance to assume the label of poet(ess), gender must thus have been a factor, but one so pervasive that I hardly knew how to think about it.

Others did, certainly: the most vivid member of the campus literary elite (who would go on to write prose, not verse) addressed herself, in a poem I still remember, to Milton's "He for God only, she for God in him"—though in a tone more adoring of a particular male than bitter concerning the female condition.

Having geared myself toward prose, I never considered taking a course in verse writing. One had been offered, taught by a woman who never, if I remember correctly, got past the rank of assistant professor. (The department included two other women; all three were single, and their position on campus and beyond was, accordingly, the more anomalous.) After college, I was not to attempt anything in verse for something like fifteen years. As for that alluring First Fig, I can only say that lasting the night, and still more the feat of getting through the day, had given me pause. During those years, sporadically, I tried my hand at fiction. The reluctant and gradual conclusion that I must after all be, if anything, a poet, coincided more or less with the upheavals of the sixties. The exhilaration of those upheavals was liberating for me, bringing me as near as I've ever come to the equivalent of "burning at both ends." The anxiety that had kept me throttled now lift of possibility. I am simplifying, I suppose; but as though for the first time, I felt free to be a poet. It was even, in the lingo of the moment, a neat thing to be.

I was reading Sylvia Plath in those days, and at the same time I was aware of scathings from the blast furnace of radical feminism. My response to both was initially one of resistance: a poem entitled **"After Reading Sylvia Plath"** began, if I remember right, by saying, "No, no, I do not want it," and one called **"Models"** ended with an appalled repudiation of what I had heard at one high-pitched gathering, where women were "afraid of not agreeing, it will mean they are not brave." If I did pick up, perhaps, a bit of swagger, a change of manner, from what was being resisted, it was little more that that. Emily Dickinson had not yet spoken to me, nor had Marianne Moore; the few anthologized pieces I knew would remain impenetrable for a while longer. The day would come when, awakened to the inclusiveness and particularity of Marianne Moore's work, I would discover in it a new way of proceeding. Even then, the poets whose longtime influence chiefly obtained were Keats and Hopkins, Milton and Donne. No wonder, then, that an offering to the editors of *Aphra* came back with the complaint, "We don't hear *your* voice." From other periodicals, years of silence—broken finally, as it happens, by an editor who happened to be male.

Do I feel left out? From the perspective of one who has been helped more by men than by women, the question has a ring of almost comic irrelevance—the one reasonable answer being, Of course, who doesn't? My own case (as one critic, a woman, a bit crossly called it) may itself be irrelevant, a mere anomaly. Or is it perhaps that to be anomalous is finally inseparable from what makes a poet, of either sex?

Phoebe Pettingell   (review date 1994)

SOURCE: "Poetry in Review," in *The Yale Review,* Vol. 82, No. 3, July, 1994, pp. 170-73.

[*In the following review of* A Silence Opens, *Pettingell discusses the importance of history in Clampitt's poetry.*]

Can it really be only eleven years ago that readers of poetry discovered Amy Clampitt? Back then, in 1983, even sympathetic critics were taken aback by the rich density of her rhetoric. Nobody had expected a revival of almost nineteenth-century lushness of language and imagery—especially in an era where an almost anorectic plain style still retained popularity. Reviews tackled her anomalies by tracing her diverse influences: John Donne and John Keats, Gerard Manley Hopkins and Marianne Moore. Sometimes these explanations verged on the patronizing, yet few could deny that this sixty-three-year-old knew quite well what she was about, and, furthermore, had already captured an appreciative audience. Today she has become a measure of comparison: newcomer poets who write lengthy, lyrical musings about chains of associations with spiritual overtones and who employ recondite vocabulary are said to sound like Clampitt. Her voice is so distinctive, such a feature of the current scene, that we would probably recognize an unsigned poem of hers if we encountered it on the moon.

Her most recent volume is *A Silence Opens*. As did its four predecessors, it continues to chart complex topographies of associations and ideas. In the past, a few of these winding trails led to dead ends or lost themselves in the undergrowth. The best examples certainly ranged over considerable territory as well, yet proved absorbing pilgrimages leading to some epiphany. Now her quests are pursued with a sterner, more single-minded focus. One further notes changes in the itinerary. What she calls "strolls" or "rambles" (though usually they constitute rather bracing hikes) tend increasingly to spelunk in interior caves of the psyche.

This is not to say she has abandoned her vignettes of loved places. Clampitt knows how to bring a still life into motion with tropes both homely and startling. She memorably evokes "the humped, half-subterranean / potato barns, the tubers / like grown stones" on Long Island, which she calls by Whitman's favorite appellation, "Paumanok"; an Iowa "bobbed, hairpinned / and pompadoured with farmsteads" (**"Homeland"**); Maine seacoasts blurred by "Fog all day, skim / milk to gruel / and back" (**"At Easterly"**); New York vistas which yield glimpses "through early-morning mists" of Asian women moving surreptitiously "with raised / poles harvesting the dun produce / of a stand of ginkgo trees" in Cental Park (**"Manhattan: Grace Church"**). Though she has been a resident of New York for years, this poet makes her evocations of this city *unheimlich,* frequently sinister. Its breakdown is symbolized by the corrosion of "Hart Crane's great cabled lyre" spanning the East River, or, further out in the harbor, "the decades-sodden / pilings, bile and verdigris" shoring up the Statue of Liberty (**"The Staten Island Ferry"**). These rusting landmarks are more than simple metaphors of urban decay; they represent physical dissolutions in general, bringing the poem to the brink where "the mind gropes toward its own recessional." Not for nothing has Clampitt included her translation of the ninth canto of the *Inferno* earlier in the book. It allows us to understand that the horrors witnessed every time one steps out in "the foul thoroughfare" of New York make it, in some sense, another City of Lucifer, where, like Dante and Virgil, we may glimpse the abyss.

There are some very somber poems in *A Silence Opens*. **"Sed de Correr"** is an extended contemplation of exiled writers. The title is taken from César Vallejo, and can be roughly translated as the "thirst for running away." His own sad life suggests others, including those of Lorca, Woolf, and Kafka, as he dreams up the notion of

> metamorphosing
> escape in the form—O no, not of a bird,
> not he who so fled the open, but of an insect
> gravitating unerringly toward the dark:
> those feelers, that lustrous, chitinous
> lodging among interstices, among systems
> we've lost track of the workings of,
> and to whose advantage, outwitting
> the gathering impasse of language, the screech
> of its decibels, the mumble of its circumlocutions,
> the mutter, all over Europe, of what sooner and
>   sooner
> was bound, was about to happen.

This is one way of reminding readers why modern literature can't be "straightforward" or "easily accessible": we live in societies where "plain speaking" has become the tool of propaganda, oversimplification, disinformation. In the way Clampitt fashions her passage about the famous cockroach, one can understand how Kafka presages the linguistic alterations of poets like Paul Celan—a Holocaust survivor who wrote in a fractured syntax, omitting many words because his native tongue had been corrupted by the unspeakable uses to which it had been put under the Nazis: "the mumble of its circumlocutions," its "deathfugues."

Clampitt has long evinced a fascination with what she here calls "the shadowy, predatory tentshow / we know as history"—a dead-on metaphor, when one recollects the media furor over Columbus's demotion from National Icon to White Male European Oppressor of native peoples. "**Matoaka**" considers another paragon beloved of grade-school textbooks who is currently undergoing revision. We know this figure better as "Pocahontas," the name that the Elizabethan adventurer, Captain John Smith, gave her; we all learned that she pleaded for his life from her father, the "Indian" chief. A few years later, she married one of the founders of the Virginia Colony, an early to-bacco farmer. As a Christian convert, now baptized "Rebecca," she sailed to England, became a nine days' wonder in Jacobean London, then died while awaiting the ship that was to return her to her own continent. What ought we to make of this person now? the poem asks. More to the point, can we possibly imagine how she saw herself? (The book's title is a line derived from these queries.) Obviously, no final answer is possible since

> The stories we tell ourselves keep changing.
> Bronze-immobilized, the heathen
>   princess, demure in
>
> feathered deerskin, turns to bric-a-brac.
> As kings have also done. As words do,
> the words we used once, whatever they
>   once stood for gone.

We seem to keep on trying to rearrange shards of the past, hoping to resolve them into some pattern which will help us understand our own times. This poem is, at once, an essay on the shape-shifting our language, ideas, and ideals undergo, and a bridge that imaginatively spans the gulf between present and past so as to excavate lost lives and fossilized words. Still, the themes turn out to be modern, after all. They concern the role history has tra-ditionally assigned to women; why our culture now es-chews inspiring parables "in favor of / the hidden, dis-creditable motive" of ancestors; what provokes our deep nostalgia for certain places and people we never knew, but whose presences haunt us nonetheless. "**Matoaka**" stands as one of Clampitt's most resonant poems to date, touching on anxieties and discontents that are hallmarks of the way we live and think. Ultimately, she speaks "to the mystery / of what we are."

Robert B. Shaw (essay date 1994)

SOURCE: "High Reachers," in *Poetry,* Vol. 165, No. 3, December, 1994, pp. 158-65.

[*In the following review of* A Silence Opens, *Shaw praises Clampitt's ability to impose an order upon the multitude of small details that leads the reader to the poem's moral message.*]

Amy Clampitt's latest book [*A Silence Opens*], like her earlier ones, is at first a little intimidating in its bursts of abundance. It can seem like a cornucopia out of control. Rather than shrinking back, it is best to allow oneself to be engulfed; what seems a welter proves to have a fair amount of order after all. The plenitude in question is both in subject matter and style; geographically and philologically, the poet is well-travelled. While the mul-tiple shifts in location throughout the book may recall Elizabeth Bishop, the style is closer to that of Bishop's mentor Marianne Moore. Like Moore, Clampitt collects curious, almost random-seeming details with magpie thor-oughness, and arranges them in patterns of unexpected significance. Discursiveness can teeter on the brink of digressiveness, but both poets manage to pull firm, un-breaking threads of argument through the maze-like paths of their poems. The sentences themselves can seem maze-like: complex, even Jamesian in syntax, they overreach the bounds of tidy-looking stanzas, creating a counter-point to these with their grammatical suspensions and dragooning of prose rhythms.

In a time when philosophy and literary criticism have tended to question the capacity of language to render either personal experience or external reality, Clampitt is brac-ingly unabashed in pursuing her vocation of fitting words to the world. Her enthusiasm is obvious in the authority and verve she brings to describing the localities that count most for her. The midwest prairies of her childhood, Manhattan where she has spent much of her life, the New England coast, sites in England and the Continent, all make appearances here as in her earlier volumes. There are a few new additions to the gazetteer as well. Perhaps the most imposing poem in the book concerns Virginia in the days of the first English settlements. Entitled "**Ma-toaka**" (the actual name of the princess most of us learned in school to call Pocahontas), this could be read as a darker, more skeptical rewriting of Moore's sedately en-chanting travelogue "Virginia Britannia." Clampitt directs an unsparing light on "the shadowy predatory tentshow / we know as history" in this model of intricate construc-tion. With Matoaka's own story in the foreground—her marriage to John Rolfe and voyage to England, where she soon died—the poem brilliantly captures the moment of two cultures, of the old world and the new, confronting one another:

>   the gartered
> glitterings, the breathing
> propinquity of faces: through
>   a pomandered fog
>
> of rooms and posturings arises,
> stunningly vivid still yet
> dim with distance, a figure
>   long gone from Jamestown,
>
> an ocean's retching, heaving
> vertigo removed, and more: from
> girlhood's remembered grapevines,
>   strawberries, sun-
>
> warm mulberries, leapfrog,
> cartwheels, the sound of streams,

of names, of languages: Pamunkey,
    Chickahominy. . . .

The subduing of nature by artifice and the greed and
mendacity of colonialists (Captain John Smith and Sir
Walter Raleigh serve as representative figures) are themes
woven into the tapestry; so is the role of tobacco,

    the golden weed

King James once railed against
(correctly, it latterly appears)
as noxious, till persuaded there was
    money to be made. . . .

Throughout, the poem stresses how little can be known of
this woman whose constantly changing names—Matoaka,
Pocahontas, Rebecca Rolfe—symbolize her exploitative
displacement. "A silence opens"—the gap in the historical
record; and yet by the end of the piece Clampitt has compensated for this with her imaginative leaps of empathy:

        to stroll thus
    is to move nearer,

in imagination, to the nub,
the pulse, the ember of what she was—
no stranger, finally, to the mystery
    of what we are.

This is surely one of her richest poems. It is well accompanied by others such as **"Hispaniola," "Paumanok,"**
and **"Brought from Beyond,"** which similarly expose the
spoliation and enslavement which are the most troubling
parts of the explorers' heritage, the treasure looted for
"the gilding of basilicas":

O Marco Polo and Coronado, where do
    these things, these

fabrications, come from—the holy places,
ark and altarpiece, the aureoles,
the seraphim—and underneath it all
    the howling?

Clampitt's ability to make a moral point briefly and tellingly may be another legacy of Marianne Moore. Both
poets are adept at avoiding tedious preachiness, and both
draw their moral conclusions as if inevitably from a tissue of meticulous observations.

The poems centering on the colonial past are grouped in
the first section of the volume. Its further contents are
more personal in focus. Many of them are fine and memorable. **"Handed Down"** is a much more modest piece
about the New England coast than the splendid earlier
elegy **"What the Light Was Like"**; still, it manages to
be an effective dirge not merely for one drowned fisherman but for a vanishing way of life:

        It's the names,
    the roll call handed on and let down

in heavy seas, the visibility near zero,
the solitude total, night falling—it's the names
of the dead, kept alive, they still hold on to.

Elsewhere she lets down her own net of memory and
retrieves scenes which are elemental in their clarity. "The
wizened resins / of remembering turn into plunder" as she
recalls huddling in her family's storm cellar in **"Homeland"**:

        Such
    extravaganzas of suspense—

the brassy calm, the vapors' upthrust,
the lurid porches of foreboding
we lived among, they could be thought of

as a kind of homeland: the unease,
the dim notion of a down-to-earth
transcendence that brought us in,

that raises from the apple bin
long-dormant resonances
of an oncoming winter.

Here, as often before, she speaks as a connoisseur of what
Frost liked to call "inner weather." Such exercises of
memory yield insights of various kinds—moral, historical, psychological, or esthetic—and rise at moments to
perceptions that can only be called religious. Again in the
final poem, as in **"Matoaka,"** "a silence opens," but it is
not here the silence of unrecorded history but that of
ineffable experience, the mystic's discovery of "the infinite love of God" which exists

    past parentage or gender
    beyond sung vocables
    the slipped-between
    the so infinitesimal
    fault line
    a limitless
    interiority

This last poem is notable for its daring in pursuing such
a subject, and for its humility which does not profess to
understand more than mortal intelligence is equipped to.

Other intriguing or well-fashioned poems upon which I
haven't room to comment include **"Bayou Afternoon,"**
"A Cadenza," "Matrix," and **"The Horned Rampi-
on."** Any lapses? Well, here and there those marathon
sentences seem more straggling than artfully attenuated.
A few poems (I think of **"Seed"** in particular) are over-
loaded with literary allusion. A translation from Dante's
Inferno coexists somewhat awkwardly with its surroundings. These cavillings aside, this is a book Amy
Clampitt's readers should welcome wholeheartedly, with
appreciation of the wholeheartedness that evidently went
into the writing. For many readers her generosity of spirit
has proved—as I expect it will for many more in the
future—to be something enlightening and wholesomely
contagious.

FURTHER READING

Criticism

Berger, Charles. "Poetry Chronicle." *Raritan* No. 3 (Winter 1991): 119-33.

    Discusses Clampitt's work in context of *Westward* and calls Clampitt a formidable elegist.

Birkerts, Sven. "Amy Clampitt/Christopher Janecorkery." in *The Electric Life: Essays on Modern Poetry*, pp. 305-08. New York: Williams Morrow and Company, Inc., 1989.

    Compares *The Kingfisher* with *What the Light Was Like* and says the newer collection is strong and shows a sense of wholeness though sometimes the Baroque degenerates to Rococo.

Kirby, David. "Life's Goofy Splendors." *New York Times Book Review* (23 December 1990): 16.

    Discusses Clampitt's *Westward* collection and says there is a "ceaseless current of laughter in it reflecting an appreciation of the incongruity inherent in everything."

Logan, William. "The Habits of Their Habitats." *Parnassus: Poetry in Review* 12/13, No. 21, (1985): 463, 477-86.

    Describes what he calls Clampitt's Baroque poetry as f illed with a profusion of "gorgeous" details, and says that she has established herself as the supreme poet of place.

McClatchy, J. D. "Earthbound and Fired-Up." *The New Republic* 192, No. 16 (22 April 1985): 38-40.

    Compares Clampitt with W.H. Auden, finding both to be subtle and complex.

Ramazani, Jahan. "American Family Elegy II." in *Poetry of Mourning*, pp. 293-333. Chicago: The University of Chicago Press, 1994.

    Discusses Clampitt's mourning for her parents through poems in *The Kingfisher*.

Weisman, Karen A. "Staring Before the Actual." *Criticism*, Vol. 36, No. 1 (Winter 1994): 119-37.

    Scholarly look at "Voyages: A Homage to John Keats" in the collection *Westward* which says Clampitt's romanticism is a refraction of the complex relationship of American Modernism to British Romanticism.

Additional coverage of Clampitt's life and career is contained in the following sources published by Gale Research: *Contemporary Literary Criticism*, Vol. 32; *Contemporary Authors*, Vols. 110, 146; *Contemporary Authors New Revision Series*, Vol. 29; and *Dictionary of Literary Biography*, Vol. 105.

Nikki Giovanni
1943-

(Born Yolande Cornelia Giovanni) American poet, essayist, children's author, and editor.

INTRODUCTION

A strong yet controversial figure in American poetry, Giovanni came into prominence amid the social upheavals of the late-1960s and early-1970s. Though originally recognized mainly for its militant, revolutionary, Black-Power stance, Giovanni's poetry explores a full range of themes—from childhood and family to sexuality and romantic love—and draws images and rhythms from sources as varied as the Bible, hymns, rhythm-and-blues, jazz, popular music, and colloquial speech. Never quite becoming a manifesto, but being much more than mere reporting, Giovanni's poems are highly personal statements of rage and love, capable of tenderness, humor, and irony. Energetically individualistic—even to the point of contradiction—Giovanni's poetry attempts to transmit the voice of an active witness, a witness who not only observes but also creates—and is created by—life's changing circumstances.

Biographical Information

Born to middle-class parents in Knoxville, Tennessee, Giovanni soon moved with her family to the predominantly black community of Lincoln Heights, Ohio. In her work, Giovanni typically portrays childhood as a positive experience, reflecting the fact that, in her various reminiscences, she remembers her own childhood as "groovy," a time spent in a nurturing environment with a supporting family. Growing up, Giovanni was especially devoted to, and spent a great deal of time with, her maternal grandmother, Louvenia Terrell Watson, a proud and outspoken woman who, early in her life, moved to Tennessee from her home in Albany, Georgia, fearing a possible lynching due to anti-white views she had expressed. Though assertiveness, pride, and a deep concern for the lives of women—the intellectual and emotional heirlooms Watson passed on to Giovanni—became consistent features in her poetry, Giovanni's social and political views—typified in her reading of the radical individualist, Ayn Rand, and in her support of Barry Goldwater—were generally conservative. These views underwent massive transformation during Giovanni's studies at Fisk University where Giovanni not only accepted the radicalism she encountered in some of her classmates, but she herself became active, spearheading the effort for the reinstatement of the campus chapter of the Student Nonviolent Coordinating Committee. Though she received her bachelor's degree in history, Giovanni also participated in the literary scene at Fisk, attending a creative writing workshop taught by

novelist John Oliver Killens and editing a campus literary magazine. In 1969, after further schooling and social and political activism, Giovanni took a teaching position at Rutgers University, and, following the immense success of her first two books, began giving readings and lectures on college campuses nationwide. This allowed her to engage in conversations with key figures in African-American literature, including James Baldwin and Margaret Walker. Giovanni has received many awards, including *Mademoiselle*'s "Highest Achievement Award" and numerous honorary doctorates. Giovanni quickly came to be called "The Princess of Black Poetry." In 1969, Giovanni also gave birth to her son, Thomas, an event which—like the extensive travel Giovanni engaged in the early1970's—some critics argue had a profound effect on her poems, broadening their scope, making them less angry and more domestic. Giovanni is currently a Professor of English at Virginia Polytechnic Institute and State University.

Major Works

Released during the late-1960s and early-1970s when the quest for civil rights and Black liberation was being supplanted by the drive for revolution and Black power, Giovanni's early volumes of poetry—*Black Feeling, Black Talk* (1968), *Black Judgement* (1968), and *Re: Creation* (1970)—gained immediate recognition and notoriety for their overtly militant, revolutionary content and tone; however, these volumes also include intimate poems of joy and of sorrow, hinting at thematic and emotive possibilities which grow and develop in subsequent volumes. Life changes, especially the birth of her son, and intensified introspection brought about by work on the autobiographical essays of *Gemini* (1971), led Giovanni to *My House* (1972), a volume which highlights the existence of a private and as well as a public, political life. Written mostly as lyrical monologues from various personae, the poems of *My House* are divided into two sections: "The Rooms Inside," which focuses on personal relationships, and "The Rooms Outside," which focuses on people as they struggle in physical and emotional realms outside of the homelike and familial. *The Women and the Men* (1975) continues Giovanni's interest in relationships, but also signals an increased, conscious interest in revisiting and revising her own past, including her earlier, militant tendencies. Giovanni's work finally goes full circle, for although remembrance becomes elegy in *Cotton Candy on a Rainy Day* (1978), a volume focusing on the missed possibilities and the transitory nature of life, many of the poems in *Those Who Ride the Night Winds* (1983) manage to tap out in a new form—short paragraphs punctuated with ellipses—meditative lyrics praising those who, like Giovanni, took risks and sought change.

Critical Reception

Although it was immensely popular when it first appeared, Giovanni's poetry has long been a subject of much critical dispute. Even though early critics—very often supporters of Black liberation and/or Black power movements—generally liked Giovanni's poetry even in spite of what some saw as political naivete or narrowness, they increasingly were alienated by what was perceived to be Giovanni's gradual shift from the political to the romantic; however, critics without a direct stake in the social movements of the 60s and 70s generally praised what they perceived to be the increased scope and humanity Giovanni's poems from the mid-70s. Artistically, although critics acknowledge the fact that Giovanni has composed some strong, lyrical poems, many believe the poems suffer from not following through, from not attaining a full-enough realization. More recent criticism attempts to make way for new readings of Giovanni's work by freeing her writing from outmoded political contexts and oppressive aesthetic assumptions.

PRINCIPAL WORKS

Poetry

Black Judgement 1968
Black Feeling, Black Talk 1968

Re: Creation 1970
Black Feeling, Black Talk/ Black Judgement 1970
The Poem of Angela Yvonne Davis 1970
Spin a Soft Black Song: Poems for Children 1971
My House: Poems 1972
Ego Tripping and Other Poems for Young Readers 1973
The Women and the Men 1975
Cotton Candy on a Rainy Day 1978
Vacation Time: Poems for Children 1980
Those Who Ride the Night Winds 1983
The Selected Poems of Nikki Giovanni 1995
The Sun Is So Quiet: Poems 1996

Other Major Works

Night Comes Softly: An Anthology of Black Female Voices [editor] (sketches) 1970
Gemini: An Extended Autobiographical Statement on My First Twenty-Five Years of Being a Black Poet (essays) 1971
Truth Is on Its Way (recording) 1971
A Dialogue: James Baldwin and Nikki Giovanni [with James Baldwin] (interviews) 1973
Like a Ripple on a Pond (recording) 1973
A Poetic Equation: Conversations Between Nikki Giovanni and Margaret Walker [with Margaret Walker] (interviews) 1974
The Way I Feel (recording) 1975
Legacies: The Poetry of Nikki Giovanni (recording) 1976
The Reason I Like Chocolate (recording) 1976
Images of Blacks in American Culture: A Reference Guide to Information Sources [editor, with Jessie Carney Smith] (handbook) 1988
Sacred Cows . . . and Other Edibles (essays) 1988
Appalachian Elders: A Warm Hearth Sampler [editor, with Cathee Dennison] (sketches) 1991
Grand Mothers: A Multicultural Anthology of Poems, Reminiscences, and Short Stories About the Keepers of Our Traditions [editor] (reminiscences) 1994
Racism 101 (essays) 1994
Shimmy Shimmy Shimmy Like My Sister Kate: Looking at the Harlem Renaissance Through Poems (essays) 1996

CRITICISM

Suzanne Juhasz (essay date 1976)

SOURCE: "'A Sweet Inspiration . . . of My People': The Poetry of Gwendolyn Brooks and Nikki Giovanni," in *Naked and Fiery Forms: Modern American Poetry by Women, A New Tradition*, Harper and Row, 1976, pp. 144-75.

[*In the following excerpt, Juhasz reads Giovanni's poetry as a record of her attempts to meld her roles as a black, a woman, and a poet by defining those roles "in terms of two primary factors . . . : power and love."*]

In 1972 I heard Gwendolyn Brooks read her poetry at Bucknell University, a small, private, expensive upper-middle-class school in central Pennsylvania. The Black Student Alliance had turned out in full force (some seventy-five people) to pay tribute to this most famous of black poets, the "poet laureate of Chicago." The reading was about blackness, both in the subject matter of the poems and in the ambience of the event itself. The black students were dressed in their finest, not in the jeans they daily wore (the uniform of the white middle-class students to whose school they had been brought), proclaiming that this was their poet and their evening, that tonight we whites were the guests. It was a moving experience, but it was also a full room with poor ventilation, and in spite of myself I grew drowsy. Then Brooks read a poem that woke me abruptly, electrifying me and the rest of the audience with its urgency, its humor, and, above all, its sound. I admit to having thought: now she's really writing what before she was only talking about—and at her age! But it was not her own poem that Brooks had just read. It was her tribute as one black woman poet to another, younger one; a poet who was able to say what she said in the way she said it because Gwendolyn Brooks had lived and written; yet it was a poem that Brooks herself could never have written. It was Nikki Giovanni's **"Beautiful Black Men."** The differences between these two poets and the links that bind them are the subject of this essay on the black woman poet. Gwendolyn Brooks is the first black woman poet to achieve prominence in twentieth-century America; Nikki Giovanni is one of the most recent. Their sisters include Lucille Clifton, June Jordan, Sonia Sanchez, Mari Evans, Alice Walker, and Johari Amini.

[Giovanni] . . . comes to her art knowing that she is as female as she is black and that somehow she must, in her own life and art, express how these aspects of herself come together and define her.

—*Suzanne Juhasz*

The black woman suffers from not a double but a triple bind. Being doubly oppressed, because of race and sex, she experiences conflict between being poet and woman, poet and black, black and woman. Frequently, she must deal with the issue as one of priorities (which comes first: poet, black, woman?) and of identities (is she a poet who happens to be a black woman, a black who happens to be a woman poet, a woman who happens to be a black poet?). Is it possible to be a black woman poet?. . . .

"Nikki, / isn't this counterrevolutionary . . . ?"

Nikki Giovanni is one of those "young Africans"; one of those young black poets who come to their craft with that political consciousness regarding the source and purpose of their writing that Don Lee has articulated. She writes: [in *Gemini*]

Poetry is the culture of a people. We are poets even when we don't write poems; just look at our life, our rhythms, our tenderness, our signifying, our sermons and our songs. I could just as easily say we are all musicians. We are all preachers because we are One. And whatever the term we still are the same in other survival/life tools. The new Black Poets, so called, are in line with this tradition. We rap a tale out, we tell it like we see it; someone jumps up maybe to challenge, to agree. We are still on the corner—no matter where we are—and the corner is in fact the fire, a gathering of the clan after the hunt. I don't think we younger poets are doing anything significantly different from what we as a people have always done. The new Black poetry is in fact just a manifestation of our collective historical needs.

She also comes to her art knowing that she is as female as she is black and that somehow she must, in her own life and art, express how these aspects of herself come together and define her. She has always defined herself as a black woman, seeing Women's Liberation as a white woman's movement; seeing black women as different from both white women and black men: "But white women and Black men are both niggers and both respond as such. He runs to the white man to explain his 'rights' and she runs to us. And I think that's where they are both coming from. . . . We Black women are the single group in the West intact." But her ideas about the black woman's role in the movement have changed over the past several years, I think, moving from a more traditional view (black womanhood comes second to black revolution) to one that is stronger and more individualistic. In *Gemini* she writes: "I don't really think it's bad to be used by someone you love. As Verta Mae pointed out, 'What does it mean to walk five paces behind him?' If he needs to know he's leading, then do it—or stop saying he isn't leading." Yet even at that time, her pride in black women undercuts such a position.

Because it's clear that no one can outrun us. We Black women have obviously underestimated our strength. I used to think, why don't they just run ahead of us? But obviously we are moving pretty fast. The main thing we have to deal with is, What makes a woman? Once we decide that, everything else will fall into place. As perhaps everything has. Black men have to decide what makes a man.

Two years later, in *A Dialogue,* she argues passionately with James Baldwin: "Black men say, in order for me to be a man, you walk ten paces behind me. Which means nothing. I can walk ten paces behind a dog. It means nothing to me, but if that's what the black man needs, I'll never get far enough behind him for him to be a man. I'll never walk that slowly." Baldwin tries to maintain that black men need black women to give them their manhood *because* the white world takes it away from them. "They've got you; they've got you by the throat and by the balls. And of course it comes out directed to the person closest to you." He says that the woman's role in this civilization is to understand, "to understand the man's point of view," "to understand that although I may love you, in this world

I can't come with nothing." He needs to be her *provider,* because only with her can he act like a real man. But Giovanni refuses to allow the man to define her and her role any more. "I've seen so many people get so hung up on such crappy, superficial kinds of things that, for lack of being able to bring a steak in the house, they won't come. I can get my own damn steak." She redefines him: "If the man functions as a man he is not necessarily a provider of all that stuff"; "I'm looking for beauty in the eyes of those I love or want to love, you know? I'm already deprived of almost everything that we find in the world. Must I also be deprived of you?"

> . . . black men—to me, as a woman, which is all I can say—have to say, Okay, I can't go that route; it doesn't work. And it's so illogical to continue to fight that, to continue to try to be little white men. Which is what you're still trying to be. We have our dashikis and your hair is growing, but you're still trying to be little white men. It doesn't work. . . . I demand that you be the man and still not pay the rent. Try it that way.

As a woman, as a black, as a black woman, Giovanni defines herself in terms of two primary factors, which she sees as related: power and love.

> I was trained intellectually and spiritually to respect myself and the people who respected me. I was emotionally trained to love those who love me. If such a thing can be, I was trained to be in power—that is, to learn and act upon necessary emotions which will grant me more control over my life. Sometimes it's a painful thing to make decisions based on our training, but if we are properly trained we do. I consider this a good. My life is not all it will be. There is a real possibility that I can be the first person in my family to be free. That would make me happy. I'm twenty-five years old. A revolutionary poet. I love.

In the relatively brief (I am discussing a five-year period, 1968 to 1972) evolution of her poetry, she develops these attitudes in formal and thematic terms, maturing as a black woman poet.

"Where's your power Black people"

Power and love are what are at issue in Nikki Giovanni's poetry and life. In her earlier poems (1968-1970), these issues are for the most part separate. She writes of personal love in poems of private life; of black power and a public love in political poems. She won her fame with the latter.

> Nigger
> Can you kill
> Can you kill
> Can a nigger kill
> Can a nigger kill a honkie
> Can a nigger kill the Man
> Can you kill nigger
> Huh? nigger can you
> kill
>
> ("**The True Import of the Present Dialogue,**
> **Black vs. Negro**" [in *Black feeling* . . .])

In poems such as the above, Giovanni speaks for her people in their own language of the social issues that concern them. Her role is that of spokeswoman for others with whom she is kin except for the fact that she possesses the gift of poetry: "i wanted to be / a sweet inspiration in my dreams / of my people . . ." ("**The Wonder Woman**" [in *My House*]). The quotation is from a later poem in which she is questioning that very role. But as she gains her fame, the concept of poet as "manifesting our collective historical needs" is very much present.

In defining poetry as "the culture of a people," Giovanni, in the statement from *Gemini* quoted earlier, uses "musician" and "preacher" as synonyms for "poet." All speak for the culture; all *speak,* with the emphasis on the sound they make. Making poems from black English is more than using idioms and grammatical idiosyncrasies; the very form of black English, and certainly its power, is derived from its tradition and preeminent usage as an oral language. So in Giovanni's poems both theme and structure rely on sound patterns for significance.

> i wanta say just gotta say something
> bout those beautiful beautiful beautiful outasight
> black men
> with they afros
> walking down the street
> is the same ol danger
> but a brand new pleasure

In the opening stanza of "**Beautiful Black Men (with compliments and apologies to all not mentioned by name),**" [in *Black feeling* . . .] the idiom ("outasight") is present, so is the special syntax ("they afros"), but more centrally are the rhythms of speech employed to organize the poetic statement. The statement is political, because the poem, like many of hers from this period, is meant to praise blackness: in praising, to foster, to incite. For the proper pride in and achievement of blackness is revolutionary. The poem is not a treatise, however; it is an emotionally charged utterance that, as it develops, creates through its own form the excitement about which it is speaking. In the first stanza, the repetitions, the emphases that the pause at line breaks creates, the accelerations within lines because of lack of pauses, all achieve the tenor of the speaking voice. As the poem progresses, the excitement that the speaker feels as she describes her subject is communicated by her voice on the page:

> sitting on stoops, in bars, going to offices
> running numbers, watching for their whores
> preaching in churches, driving their hogs
> walking their dogs, winking at me
> in their fire red, lime green, burnt orange
> royal blue tight tight pants that hug
> what i like to hug

The beautiful men are catalogued in action, they then turn and focus on the speaker herself (all of them "winking at me"), and finally they merge into an essence of color, clothing, and sexuality. The verbal process consistently builds image upon image as it accelerates pitch.

jerry butler, wilson pickett, the impressions
temptations, mighty mighty sly
don't have to do anything but walk
on stage
and i scream and stamp and shout

Giovanni becomes quite literally a spokeswoman: she
speaks out for black women, appreciating their men now
embodied in the musicians who present publicly the image
of the black man as a powerful and beautiful star. She
raises her voice in praise, screaming, shouting her response.

see new breed men in breed alls
dashiki suits with shirts that match
the lining that complements the ties
that smile at the sandals
where dirty toes peek at me
and i scream and stamp and shout
for more beautiful beautiful beautiful
black men with outasight afros

A sense of humor is never lacking in Giovanni's poetry—
serious purpose does not negate the ability to laugh! Here
she mocks with affection the black male's love of splendor
as it accompanies his dislike of cleanliness. What comes
through in her tone is love as well as clear-sightedness,
both qualities giving her the right to appreciate "beautiful,
beautiful, beautiful black men." From wanting to say,
having to say, something about beautiful black men, the
poem moves, gathering speed and intensity as it goes, to
a scream, a stamp and a shout that impel the person reading
to likewise shout, likewise praise—to *feel* as the speaker
feels.

Such a feeling is not separate from the one called for in
poems like **"Poem (No Name No. 2)"**:

Bitter Black Bitterness
Black Bitter Bitterness
Bitterness Black Brothers
Bitter Black Get
Blacker Get Bitter
Get Black Bitterness
          NOW
          (*Black feeling, Black talk/Black judgement*)

—or in **"Of Liberation"**:

BLACK STEP ONE:
Get the feeling out (this may be painful—endure)
BLACK STEP TWO:
Outline and implement the program
All honkies and some negros will have to die
This is unfortunate but necessary
          (*Black feeling, Black talk/Black judgement*)

For the sound and the feeling go together to create the
needed power:

Honkies always talking 'bout
Black Folks
Walking down the streets

Talking to themselves
(they say we're high—
or crazy)

But recent events have shown
we know who we're talking
to
          (**"A Short Essay of Affirmation Explaining Why
          [with Apologies to the Federal Bureau of
          Investigation],"** *Black feeling, Black talk/Black
          judgement*)

In these early poems, Giovanni is concerned about the
political, public implications of her own life, as well; of
the fact of her womanhood:

it's a sex object if you're pretty
and no love
or love and no sex if you're fat
get back fat black woman be a mother
grandmother strong thing but not a woman
gameswoman romantic love needer
man seeker dick eater sweat getter
fuck needing love seeking woman
          (**"Woman Poem,"** *Black feeling, Black talk/Black
          judgement*)

Using techniques similar to those with which she calls for
black power, she can evoke the powerlessness of women.
In **"All I Gotta Do"** [in *Re:Creation*] phrases that repeat,
that halt at line breaks and recur in changing but always
inconclusive combinations create Giovanni's frustration
at the gap between her individual needs and the means (or
lack of them) allotted her by society for fulfilling them.
"All i gotta do," "sit and wait," "cause i'm a woman,"
"it'll find me"—wanting it, needing it, getting it, having
it—these are the formulaic phrases. Their arrangement
makes the poem.

all i gotta do
is sit and wait
sit and wait
and its gonna find
me
all i gotta do
is sit and wait
if i can learn
how

In stanza 1, the formulaic phrases are used to set out
society's rules. The rules do not seemso difficult, the
opening phrase attests—"all i gotta do," that's all. Yet a
change is rung (through parallel structures) between the
hoped-for results (if the game is properly played) that it
will "find me" and an inherent difficulty in playing properly:
"if i can learn / how." The single word "if," because its
setting is so spare, controlled, simple, carries enormous
weight: weighing by its problematic stance the *unnatural*
societal rules against the natural woman.

what i need to do
is sit and wait

cause i'm a woman
sit and wait
what i gotta do
is sit and wait
cause i'm a woman
it'll find me

In the second stanza, the phrase "sit and wait" occurs three times, a drumbeat behind "need to do," "gotta do," with their causal relation to the central fact supporting the whole enterprise: "cause i'm a woman." Everything follows from that irrevocable fact—especially the end result, "it'll find me": passivity is absolutely necessary for success.

you get yours
and i'll get mine
if i learn
to sit and wait
i want mine
and i'm gonna get it
cause i gotta get it
cause i need to get it
if i learn how

"Sit and wait" continues into the third stanza to remind us of the rules. Another person has been introduced into the poem, someone who does get "his." The urgency of the speaker's own desire for getting is now underlined: "want," "gonna," "gotta," "need to"; and it comes smack up against the terms for carrying desires through: "cause," "cause"—"if."

thought about calling
for it on the phone
asked for a delivery
but they didn't have it
thought about going
to the store to get it
walked to the corner
but they didn't have it

Giovanni's irrepressible humor, the ability to see the comic element present in any life-and-death situation, bubbles to the surface in the fourth stanza, providing, as humor often does, both momentary relief and incisive insight. Calling on the phone, asking for a delivery, walking down to the corner store—acts such as these lead to frustration only. Stores aren't where "it" is found, and, more importantly, one is not supposed to *ask*.

called your name
in my sleep
sitting and waiting
thought you would awake me
called your name
lying in my bed
but you didn't have it
offered to go get it
but you didn't have it
so i'm sitting

The "you" referred to previously (as having gotten his) now reappears—very obviously a he. "Called your name"

becomes a repeated action in the fifth stanza, seemingly a less active kind of initiative-taking than going to the corner store. But it, too, proves unsuccessful, because it is too overt: if asked for it, he doesn't "have it." In such a situation, one should never then offer "to go get it"! "Sitting and waiting," as it repeats and repeats, becomes more and more a plaintive *accusation*.

all i know
is sitting and waiting
waiting and sitting
cause i'm a woman
all i know
is sitting and waiting
cause i gotta wait
wait for it to find
me

The final stanza is formed by the now-familiar formulaic phrases alone—combined, repeated, repeated, combined—and it is this form that creates the poem's concluding sadness, bitterness, and resignation. "Sitting and waiting" is twice repeated and once reversed, "waiting and sitting." Each phrase is allowed a line to itself, so that the importance of the act is tied to its ceaselessness.

The poem began with the line "all i gotta do." This stanza reorganizes these key words, presenting an opening phrase, "all i know" (the lesson, through the act of the poem, has been thoroughly learned), throwing "gotta" into the seventh line and changing "do" into "wait," thus firmly equating action with nonaction: "cause i gotta wait." The sense of unwavering causation, a train of rules and results whereby society is created (implicit throughout the poem is the double meaning of the word "gotta," linking rule and reward—to have to, to achieve), is finally underlined by the balancing of "cause i'm a woman" with "cause i gotta wait": woman equals waiting. The poem's speaker has learned her lesson: the word "if" no longer appears. What she waits for, "it," has never been defined. It need not be, for the poem has demonstrated that whatever she might want (with whatever degree of intensity) must find her. In the opening stanza, this idea was expressed with an optimism ("its gonna find / me") that was, however, almost immediately undercut by "if i can learn / how." In the last stanza, the uncertainty is expressed with total resignation: "wait for it to find / me." "It" may or may not come, but there is *nothing* the speaker can do about it. Exactly the opposite is required: the less she does do, the more possible becomes the awaited reward; the workings of society are totally out of her hands. The "me" of the poem's last line is alone and alien.

That "me," that lonely woman, is responsible for many private love poems. She seems to have little to do with the spokeswoman who is the black (political) poet. She writes poems like **"Rain"** from *Re: Creation*.

rain is
god's sperm falling
in the receptive
woman how else

to spend
a rainy day
other than with you
seeking sun and stars
and heavenly bodies
how else to spend
a rainy day
other than with you

These love poems are private and describe the woman enacting rather than criticizing the socially prescribed female role. They speak for Giovanni only and are not meant to incite anybody to any kind of revolution. Such a private/public dichotomy in her work may be neat, but it contains too great a degree of ambivalence for a woman poet like Giovanni to feel comfortable with it or to maintain it for long. How can the woman who sees herself as a sweet inspiration of her people and the woman who has been trained not only to sit and wait but also to need and to value interpersonal, private relationships be the same poet? In **"Adulthood"** (*Black feeling, Black talk/ Black judgement*), she writes about going to college and learning that "just because everything i was was unreal / i could be real"—not from "withdrawal / into emotional crosshairs or colored bourgeois / intellectual pretensions," "But from involvement with things approaching reality / i could possibly have a life." What about not merely black reality, but her own reality? And what is the relation between them? Especially as through her poetry she becomes a genuine public personality, she needs to ask these questions. And what about the revolution?

"dreams of being a natural / woman"

A poet may be musician, preacher, articulator of a culture, but she or he is also a dreamer. In a series of poems about herself as dreamer, Giovanni explores the conflicting and confusing relations between her roles as poet, woman, and black.

In **"Dreams"** (*Black feeling, Black talk/Black judgement*), she describes her younger years—"before i learned / black people aren't / supposed to dream." She wanted, she says, to be a musician, a singer, a Raelet or maybe Marjorie Hendricks, grinding up against the mike screaming "baaaaaby nightandday." But then she "became more sensible":

and decided i would
settle down
and just become
a sweet inspiration

(The significance of the black singer—the musician as articulating the culture—appears throughout her work, as in **"Revolutionary Music"** [in *Black feeling* . . .]: "you've just got to dig sly / and the family stone / damn the words / you gonna be dancing to the music" . . . "we be digging all / our revolutionary music consciously or un / cause sam cooke said 'a change is gonna come.'")

A few years later, in **"The Wonder Woman"** (*My House*), she must deal with the fact of having become that sweet inspiration. "Dreams have a way / of tossing and turning themselves / around," she observes; also that "the times / make requirements that we dream / real dreams." She may have once dreamed of becoming a sweet inspiration of her people:

. . . but the times
require that i give
myself willingly and become
a wonder woman.

The wonder woman is a totally public personage who cannot—must not—integrate her personal needs and experiences into that role if they do not coincide. Giovanni makes this clear in poems about female stars, like Aretha Franklin, and in poems about herself, such as **"Categories"** (*My House*).

sometimes you hear a question like "what is
your responsibility as an unwed mother"
and some other times you stand sweating profusely
   before
going on stage and somebody says "but you are
   used
      to it"
or maybe you look into a face you've never seen
or never noticed and you know
the ugly awful loneliness of being
locked into a mind and body that belong
to a *name* or *non-name*—not that it matters
cause *you* feel and *it* felt but you have
a planetrainbussubway—it doesn't matter—
   something
to catch to take your arms away from someone
you might have thought about
putting them around if you didn't
have all that shit to take you safely away

"Categories" goes on to question even black/white divisions (political and public), if they can—and they do—at times violate personal reality, describing in its second stanza an old white woman "who maybe you'd really care about" except that, being a young black woman, one's "job" is to "kill maim or seriously / make her question / the validity of her existence."

The poem ends by questioning the fact and function of categories themselves (". . . if this seems / like somewhat of a tentative poem it's probably / because i just realized that / i'm bored with categories"), but, in doing so, it is raising the more profound matter of the relations between society and self. The earlier **"Poem for Aretha,"** 1970 (*Re: Creation*), begins with a clear sense of the separation between public and private selves:

cause nobody deals with Aretha—a mother with
   four
      children—having to hit the road
they always say "after she comes
home" . . .

Again Giovanni explains the significance of the musician/ artist to society: "she is undoubtedly the one person who puts everyone on / notice," but about Aretha she also says, "she's more important than her music—if they must be / separated." (It is significant that the form of both these poems is closer to thought than speech. No answers here, only questions, problems.)

One means of bridging the gap between public and private is suggested in **"Revolutionary Dreams,"** 1970 (*Re: Creation*).

> i used to dream militant
> dreams of taking
> over america to show
> these white folks how it should be
> done
> i used to dream radical dreams
> of blowing everyone away with my perceptive
>　　powers
> of correct analysis
> i even used to think i'd be the one
> to stop the riot and negotiate the peace
> then i awoke and dug
> that if i dreamed natural
> dreams of being a natural
> woman doing what a woman
> does when she's natural
> i would have a revolution

"Militant" and "radical" are poised against "natural" here, as they were in **"Categories."** But this poem makes the connection to gender: the "natural dreams," of a "natural woman" who doeswhat a woman does "when she's natural." The result of this juxtaposition is "true revolution." Somehow the black woman must be true to herself as she *is* to be both a poet and a revolutionary, for the nature of the revolution itself is in question. Revolutions are not only in the streets, where niggers must be asked if they can kill. Revolutions do not occur only in male terms, as Giovanni had begun to understand, humorously, in **"Seduction"** (*Black feeling, Black talk/Black judgement*), in which the male keeps talking politics ("The Black . . ."; "The way I see we ought to . . .; "And what about the situation . . ."; "the revolution . . .") while she is resting his hand on her stomach, licking his arm, unbuckling his pants, taking his shorts off. The poem is, however, set in some hypothetical future: "one day." It concludes with that future:

> then you'll notice
> your state of undress
> and knowing you you'll just say
> "Nikki,
> isn't this counterrevolutionary . . . ?"

The implicit reply is no, but it is not until her 1972 volume, *My House*, that Giovanni can make this answer with self-confidence. In the poems of *Black feeling, Black talk/ Black judgement* and of *Re: Creation,* the doubts are present, and possibilities for solution occur and disappear. However, *My House* as a book, not only the individual poems in it, makes a new statement about the revolution, about the very nature of political poetry, when the poet is a black woman.

Earlier, in **"My Poem"** (*Black feeling, Black talk/Black judgement),* she had written:

> the revolution
> is in the streets
> and if i stay on
> the 5th floor
> it will go on
> and if i never do
> anything
> it will go on

Perhaps, but it will not be the same revolution, she has realized; and she has also come to understand that it will take place, as well, on the fifth floor.

In "On the Issue of Roles," Toni Cade, editor of one of the first collections of essays about being black and female, *The Black Woman,* makes a comment that seems to me to be a valuable gloss to the statement of Giovanni's *My House.*

> If your house ain't in order, you ain't in order. It is so much easier to be out there than right here. The revolution ain't out there. Yet. But it is here. Should be. And arguing that instant-coffee-
>
> ten-minutes-to-midnight alibi to justify hasty-headed dealings with your mate is shit. Ain't no such animal as an instant gorilla.

Ida Lewis points [in the introduction to *My House*] with a different vocabulary to the same phenomenon: "A most interesting aspect of her [Giovanni's] work is the poet's belief in individualism at a time when the trend in the Black community is away from the individual and towards the mass." In *My House,* Giovanni is trying to be a natural woman doing what a woman does when she's natural— in doing so, dreaming natural dreams, having a revolution. She is integrating private and public; in doing so, politicizing the private, personalizing the public. This action is occurring in poetry.

My House is divided into two sections, "The Rooms Inside" and "The Rooms Outside." The inside rooms hold personal poems about grandmothers, mothers, friends, lovers—all in their own way love poems. **"Legacies,"** in which the poet describes the relationship between grandmother and granddaughter, is a very political poem.

> 　"i want chu to learn how to make rolls" said the
> 　　old
> woman proudly
> but the little girl didn't want
> to learn how because she knew
> even if she couldn't say it that
> that would mean when the old one died she would
> 　be less
> dependent on her spirit so
> she said
> 　　"i don't want to know how to make no rolls"

Black heritage is explained in personal terms. The little girl in the poem recognizes an impulse to be independent, but the speaker recognizes as well the importance of the old woman, of her love, to the grandchild in achieving her own adulthood. Although the poem ends by observing that "neither of them ever / said what they meant / and i guess nobody ever does," it is the poem itself that provides that meaning through its understanding.

Overtly political are poems like **"Categories"** or **"The Wonder Woman,"** but also political are the gentle love poems (**"The Butterfly," "When I Nap"**), and indeed all the poems that are about Giovanni as private person; for in various dialogues and dialects they all make this statement:

> . . . i'm glad
> i'm Black not only
> because it's beautiful but because it's me
> and i can be dumb and old and petty and ugly
> and jealous but i still need love
>
> **("Straight Talk")**

The poems of the rooms outside are not calls to action from the public platform; they are dreams, some funny, some apocalyptic, of old worlds and new. In each of these poems, *My House*'s equivalent to the earlier poems of black feeling and black judgment, the poet stresses the element of personal vision.

> the outline of a face on a picture isn't really
> a face or an image of a face but the idea of an
>   image
> of a dream that once was dreamed by some artist
> who never knew how much more real is a dream
>   than reality
>
> so julian bond was elected president and rap brown
>   chief
> justice of the supreme court and nixon sold himself
> on 42nd street for a package of winstons
> (with the down home taste) and our man on the
>   moon said
>   alleluia
> and we all raised our right fist in the power sign
> and the earth was thrown off course and crashed
>   into the sun
> but since we never recognize the sun
> we went right on to work in our factories
> and offices and laundry mats and record shops
> the next morning and only the children
> and a few poets knew
> that a change had come
>
> **("Nothing Makes Sense")**

This artist has begun to learn—through a process of coming to terms with herself as black woman, black poet, that art can create as well as reflect reality, as revolutions do.

It is fitting to the purpose of *My House* that its final poem, which is in "The Rooms Outside," is **"My House."**

> i only want to
> be there to kiss you
> as you want to be kissed

> when you need to be kissed
> where i want to kiss you
> cause it's my house
> and i plan to live in it

The first stanza follows Giovanni's familiar oral structure. Phrases stand against one another without the imaginative extensions of figurative language: word against word, repeating, altering, pointing. A love poem, to one particular lover. It starts in a tone reminiscent of both **"Beautiful Black Men"** and **"all i gotta do"**—the woman is there to adore her man: "i only want to / be there to kiss you"; "as you want"; "as you need." But although the gentle tone persists, an extraordinary change is rung with a firm emphasis on the personal and the possessive in the last three lines: "where i want to kiss you," "my house," "i plan." She is suiting his needs to hers as well as vice versa.

> i really need to hug you
> when i want to hug you
> as you like to hug me
> does this sound like a silly poem

In terms of one (important) action, hugging—touching—the point is clarified. The woman of **"all i gotta do"** has forgotten, or chosen to forget, the rules!

> i mean it's my house
> and i want to fry pork chops
> and bake sweet potatoes
> and call them yams
> cause i run the kitchen
> and i can stand the heat

Nonetheless, she makes it clear that she is still very much of a woman, using the traditionally female vocabulary of cooking and kitchens to underscore her message. But this woman is active, not passive: she means, wants, bakes, calls, runs. She orders experience and controls it. The element of control asserts itself not only through direct statement—"cause i run the kitchen"—but through vocabulary itself: "i mean"; "[i] call them yams" (in the latter phrase asserting blackness itself through control of language: "yams" and not "sweet potatoes"). She controls not only through need and desire but through strength, ability: "i can stand the heat."

> i spent all winter in
> carpet stores gathering
> patches so i could make
> a quilt
> does this really sound
> like a silly poem
> i mean i want to keep you
> warm

For love is not unrelated to action, strength, control. All of these qualities can be directed to that end in a significant way: "i want to keep you / warm." Gathering patches; no longer waiting for "it" to find her. And making poems about gathering patches—is that silly?

and my windows might be dirty
but it's my house
and if i can't see out sometimes
they can't see in either

The house and its elements are beginning to assume symbolic proportions, surely emphasized by the fact that the poem has been continually calling attention to its existence as a poem. The house is a world; it is reality.

english isn't a good language
to express emotion through
mostly i imagine because people
try to speak english instead
of trying to speak through it
i don't know maybe it is
a silly poem

I am making a message, both poet and poem are insisting; and now they explain how messages work. "Trying to speak through" language rather than speaking it means that word and thing are not identical: that words are not yams, and thus language frees the poet to create realities (dreams) and not just to copy them. So that somehow this not-very-silly poem is carrying out a revolution.

i'm saying it's my house
and i'll make fudge and call
it love and touch my lips
to the chocolate warmth
and smile at old men and call
it revolution cause what's real
is really real
and i still like men in tight
pants cause everybody has some
thing to give and more
important need something to take

and this is my house and you make me
happy
so this is your poem

The act of naming, of using language creatively, becomes the most powerful action of all—saying, calling. Calling fudge love, calling smiling at old men revolution is creative (rather than derivative) action that expresses more than her own powers as woman and poet. In **"Seduction"** there was a significant gap between language (rhetoric) and action, between male and female. In that fable, men and words were allied and were seen by the woman poet as impotent. The woman was allied with action (love), but she was, in the poem, mute. The man calls her action "counterrevolutionary." Now, in **"My House,"** the woman's action, love (an overt expression of the personal, private sphere), is allied to language. Giovanni brings her power bases together in this poem, her dominion over kitchens, love, and words. No longer passive in any way, she makes the food, the love, the poem, and the revolution. She brings together things and words through her own vision (dream, poem) of them, seeing that language (naming) is action, because it makes things happen. Once fudge has been named love, touching one's lips to it becomes an act of

love; smiling at old men becomes revolution "cause what's / is really real." Real = dream + experience. To make all this happen, most of all there must exist a sense of self on the part of the maker, which is why the overriding tone of the poem is the sense of an "i" who in giving need feel no impotence from the act of taking (both become aspects of the same event). Thus this is *her* house and he makes her happy, thus and only thus—"cause" abounds in this poem, too: this, her poem, can be his poem. Not silly at all.

In bringing together her private and public roles and thereby validating her sense of self as black woman poet, Giovanni is on her way towards achieving in art that for which she was trained: emotionally, to love; intellectually and spiritually, to be in power; "to learn and act upon necessary emotions which will grant me more control over my life," as she writes in *Gemini*. Through interrelating love and power, to achieve a revolution-to be free. She concludes her poem **"When I Die"** (*My House*) with these lines:

and if i ever touched a life i hope that life knows
that i know that touching was and still is and will
    always
        be the true
revolution

These words of poetry explain the way to enact a dream, one that is "a real possibility": "that I can be the first person in my family to be free . . . I'm twenty-five years old. A revolutionary poet. I love."

Wherever Nikki Giovanni's life as poet will take her, she will go there in full possession of her self. Rather than reiterating the fact of Gwendolyn Brooks in that admirable achievement, let me conclude with Giovanni's poem **"For Gwendolyn Brooks."**

brooks start with cloud condensation
allah crying
for his lost children

brooks babble
from mountain tops to settle
in collecting the earth's essence
pure spring fountain
of love knowledge
for those who find
and dare drink
of it

　　　　　　　　　　　　　　　　　　　　　(*Re: Creation*)

William J. Harris (essay date 1983)

SOURCE: "Sweet Soft Essence of Possibility: The Poetry of Nikki Giovanni," in *Black Women Writers (1950-1980): A Critical Evaluation*, Doubleday, 1984, pp. 218-28.

[*In the following essay, Harris regards Giovanni as "a good popular poet" whose work responds to the complex events of her time yet sometimes suffers from a lack of a more complete realization.*]

Even though Nikki Giovanni has a large popular audience, she has not gained the respect of the critics. Michele Wallace calls her "a kind of nationalistic Rod McKuen"; Eugene Redmond claims her poetry "lacks lyricism and imagery"; Haki Madhubuti (Don L. Lee) insists she lacks the sophistication of thought demanded of one with pretensions of a "political seer" and finally, Amiri Baraka and Saunders Redding, united on no other issue, declare in their different styles that she is simply an opportunist. These critics illustrate the problem of evaluating Nikki Giovanni dispassionately. Her limitations notwithstanding, there is a curious tendency of normally perceptive critics to undervalue her, to condescend to her rather than to criticize her.

When Michele Wallace compares Giovanni to McKuen, she is suggesting that both are popular poets. This is true enough, but still there is a crucial difference between them: McKuen is a bad popular poet; Giovanni is a good one. He is a bad popular poet because he presents conventional sentiments in a shamelessly sloppy form. His retellings of conventional stories in conventional ways, without a trace of thought or feeling, have won him a ready audience. In essence, he is the genius of the unexamined life; he is the opposite of a serious artist who is dedicated to the exploration of his life. The serious artist deals in fresh discoveries; McKuen in clichés. Giovanni, on the other hand, is a popular poet but also a serious artist because she tries to examine her life honestly.

The popular writer is usually easy to read and topical; that is, he or she writes in a language which is direct and immediate rather than arcane or esoteric, and speaks of problems and situations that are obviously relevant to the general reader's life. This is neither good nor bad but simply the nature of the genre. Most critics, poets, and teachers are uncomfortable with the popular form. Since the language is unspecialized and the experience everyday, the critic and teacher are left virtually withvery little to say, an embarrassing situation. Therefore, even the good popular poet is often ignored: one sees more essays on Wallace Stevens than on Langston Hughes. That the good popular poet is not analyzed is not the *poet's* fault; rather, current critical vocabularies and even values seem inadequate to deal with him. The good popular poet faces the complexity of life in his or her poems even though he does not embody it in their form. Langston Hughes may be one of America's greatest popular poets; he writes of celebrated subjects in a direct manner with the precision, toughness of language, and emotion which derive from the blues tradition. Conversely, McKuen's poetry derives from the tradition of pop song: at best the world of sentimentality, at worst the world of cynical lies. McKuen's carelessness of form, which can be found by randomly opening any of his books, testifies to his carelessness of thought and feeling. As Pound says: "Technique is the test of sincerity. If a thing isn't worth getting the technique to say, it is of inferior value."

Giovanni is a good popular poet: she is honest, she writes well-crafted poems, and, unlike McKuen, she pushes against the barriers of the conventional; in other words, she responds to the complexities of the contemporary world as a complex individual, not as a stock character in anybody's movie about Anyplace, U.S.A. In fact, much of Giovanni's value as a poet derives from her insistence on being herself; she refuses to go along with anybody's orthodoxy. Since she is always reacting to her multifarious environment, it is not surprising that her career has already gone through three distinct stages: first, the black militant; then the domestic lover; and now the disappointed lover. Therefore, it is clear that her move from Black militant poet to domestic woman poet is not a contradiction, as some critics maintain, but only a response to her times: the seventies and eighties call for different responses than did the sixties. Unlike Madhubuti she is not doctrinaire; she does not have a system to plug all her experiences into. She examines her time and place and comes to the conclusions she must for that time and place.

Giovanni does have weaknesses. At times she does not seem to think things through with sufficient care. Furthermore, she often does not bother to finish her poems; consequently, there are many unrealized poems in her oeuvre. Finally, not unlike a movie star, she is possibly too dependent on her public personality. In other words, she can be self-indulgent and irresponsible. Paradoxically, her shortcomings do grow out of the same soil as her strengths, that is, out of her independence of mind, her individuality, and her natural charm.

Since her first book in 1968, Nikki Giovanni has published a number of volumes of poetry, including *Black Feeling, Black Talk/ Black Judgement* (a combined edition, 1970), *Re:Creation* (1970), *My House* (1972), *The Women and the Men* (1975), and her most recent work, *Cotton Candy on a Rainy Day* (1978), and even though her attitudes have changed over the years, the books are unified by her personality. Like many poets of the period she is autobiographical and her personal stamp is on all her work. There is also a consistency of style, even though there is a change of mood: the poetry is always direct, conversational, and grounded in the rhythms of Black music and speech. Her poems are also unified in that they are written from the perspective of a Black woman. Moreover, her themes remain constant: dreams, love, Blackness, womanhood, mothers, children, fathers, family, stardom, fame, and sex. In addition to her poetry books, she has published an autobiography, *Gemini,* two extended interviews—one with Margaret Walker, one with James Baldwin—and a number of children's books.

In Giovanni's first stage she wrote several classic sixties poems expressing the extreme militancy of the period. These include **"The True Import of Present Dialogue, Black vs. Negro,"** and **"For Saundra."** In 1968 Giovanni spits out:

> Nigger
> Can you kill
> Can you kill
> Can a nigger kill
> Can a nigger kill a honkie

The poem these lines are taken from, **"The True Import of the Present Dialogue, Black vs. Negro,"** is intended to incite violence by asking for the literal death of white America. It captures the spirit of the sixties, that feeling that Armageddon, the final battle between good and evil, is imminent. It is informed by the example of Frantz Fanon, the Black revolutionary author of *The Wretched of the Earth,* whose book Eldridge Cleaver called "the Bible" of the Black liberation movement. In it, Fanon declares: "National liberation, national renaissance, the restoration of nationhood of the people, commonwealth: whatever may be the headings used or the new formulas introduced, decolonisation is always a violent phenomenon." Cleaver correctly claims that Fanon's book "legitimize[s] the revolutionary impulse to violence." No matter how romantic that moment now seems, there was then a sincere feeling that it was a time of revolution; and Giovanni, along with Madhubuti, Baraka and others, expressed these revolutionary ideas in their poems. Furthermore, Giovanni's poem **"The True Import of Present Dialogue, Black vs. Negro"** embodies more than the literal demand for the killing of whites: it also expresses a symbolic need on the part of Blacks to kill their own white values:

> Can you kill the nigger
> in you
> Can you make your nigger mind
> die

Eliot has said that poetry should not deviate too far from common speech; these Black revolutionary poets—in a sense Eliot's heirs—demonstrate that they have absorbed the subtleties of their language. For example, in the above poem Giovanni exploits the complex connotations of the term "nigger"; she uses it in this stanza to suggest the consciousness that wants to conform to white standards; consequently, to kill the "nigger" is to transform consciousness. In more general terms, the entire poem is cast in the form of a street chant: the rhythm is intended to drive the reader into the street, ready to fight. In fact, the source of much of the form utilized in the 1960s Black Arts Movement is street language and folk forms such as the chant and the dozens, a form of ritualized insult.

Giovanni's **"For Saundra"** provides the rationale for the New Black Poetry:

> i wanted to write
> a poem
> that rhymes
> but revolution doesn't lend
> itself to be-bopping
>
>   . . . . .
>
> maybe i shouldn't write
> at all
> but clean my gun

In short, Giovanni is saying that the times will not allow for poems which are not political in nature, which do not promote revolution. In the 1960s art had to subordinate itself to revolution. Ron Karenga insisted: "All art must reflect and support the Black Revolution."

Even though such revolutionary figures as Karenga and Baraka stressed collective over individual values, Giovanni remains an individual, implicitly questioning the call for revolutionary hatred in the very titles of such poems as **"Letter to a Bourgeois Friend Whom Once I Loved (and Maybe Still Do If Love Is Valid)."** She feels the tension between personal and revolutionary needs—a tension that runs throughout her work in the revolutionary period. Baraka demands: "Let there be no love poems written/until love can exist freely and cleanly." Giovanni understands that there are times of hate but also realizes that to subordinate all feeling to revolutionary hate is too abstract and inhuman.

Yet Giovanni's independence can be irresponsible. At times she seems a little too eager to gratify human desires at the expense of the revolution. She confides in **"Detroit Conference of Unity and Art"** (dedicated to former SNCC leader H. Rap Brown):

> No doubt many important
> Resolutions
> Were passed
> As we climbed Malcolm's ladder
> But the most
> Valid of them
> All was that
> Rap chose me

Even a nonrevolutionary reader would question the political commitment of the above lines. If one is going to set herself up as a serious poetprophet—and Giovanni has—one had better be concerned about the revolutionary business at a meeting, not one's love life. This is the sort of frivolousness that Giovanni's critics, such as Madhubuti and Wallace, rightfully attack. However, at other times, Giovanni's frivolousness was refreshing in those tense and serious days of revolt. **"Seduction"** delightfully points out that the revolution cannot be conducted twenty-four hours a day. The poem centers around a brother so earnestly involved in the revolution that he does not notice that the poet has stripped both of them. The poem concludes:

> then you'll notice
> your state of undress
> and knowing you you'll just say
> "Nikki,
> isn't this counterrevolutionary . . . ?"

Part of Giovanni's attractiveness stems from her realization that for sanity, there must be sex and humor, even in revolutionary times.

When the revolution failed her, Giovanni turned to love and began writing a more personal poetry, signaling the onset of the second stage of her career. The literature of the seventies was quite unlike those of the hot and hopeful sixties. Addison Gayle writes about certain important differences between the sixties and the seventies in his excellent autobiography, *Wayward Child:*

Beyond my personal despair, there was that occasioned by the disappointments of the seventies, following so close upon the successes of the sixties, the return on almost all levels, to the old feelings of hopelessness, cynicism, and apathy, which, until the era of Martin King and Malcolm X, Stokely Carmichael, and H. Rap Brown, had so immobilized a race of people.

For Giovanni, too, idealism of the sixties had been replaced by the despair of the seventies. In a poem of the seventies she asserts:

> i've always prided myself
> on being a child of the sixties
> and we are all finished
> so that makes being
> nothing

The sixties stood for endless possibility; the seventies for hopelessness and frustration. However, in *My House* she seeks an alternative to public commitment and finds one in domestic love. Giovanni is not the only Black figure to seek new alternatives in the seventies: Cleaver found God; Baraka found Marxism; Julian Bond shifted allegiances from the activist organization SNCC to the staid NAACP. Giovanni finds her answers in **"My House"**:

> i'm saying it's my house
> and i'll make fudge and call
> it love and touch my lips
> to the chocolate warmth
> and smile at old men and call
> it revolution cause what's real
> is really real
> and i still like men in tight
> pants cause everybody has some
> thing to give and more
> important need something to take
>
> and this is my house and you make me happy
> so this is your poem

Giovanni has exchanged the role of revolutionary Mother Courage, sending her Black troops into battle, for the role of domestic Black woman, making fudge for her Black man. While the poem may make the reader uncomfortable— has it set the feminist movement back fifty years?—one can sympathize with Giovanni's desire to retreat into domestic comforts in the face of a disappointing world. In **"My House"** she declares her domesticity loudly, militantly, perhaps to give herself confidence in her new role. Later she will celebrate the domestic more quietly and convincingly. In **"Winter"** from *Cotton Candy* she observes:

> Frogs burrow the mud
> snails bury themselves
> and I air my quilts
> preparing for the cold
> Dogs grow more hair
> mothers make oatmeal
> and little boys and girls
> take Father John's Medicine

> Bears store fat
> chipmunks gather nuts
> and I collect books
> For the coming winter

Here Giovanni gathers supplies to retreat from the cold world; however, it is only for a season. And unlike **"My House,"** this poem creates a snug place one would want to retire to; Giovanni has become more comfortably at home in the domestic world of **"Winter"** than in the brash **"My House."**

If she implicitly questioned "pure" revolution earlier, in the seventies she questions all ideologies that try to define or categorize her. In **"Categories"** she writes:

> and sometimes on rainy nights you see
> an old white woman who maybe you'd really
>   care about
> except that you're a young Black woman
> whose job it is to kill maim or seriously
> make her question
> the validity of her existence
>
>   . . . . .
>
>   and if this seems
> like somewhat of a tentative poem it's probably
> because i just realized that
> i'm bored with categories

This suspicion of categories persists into *Cotton Candy*:

> i am in a box
> on a tight string
> subject to pop
> without notice
>
>   . . . . .
>
> i am tired
> of being boxed
>
>   . . . . .
>
> i can't breathe

And we see in **"A Poem Off Center"** that Giovanni especially resents being boxed in as a writer:

> if you write a political poem
> you're anti-semitic
> if you write a domestic poem
> you're foolish
> if you write a happy poem
> you're unserious
> if you write a love poem
> you're maudlin
> of course the only real poem
> to write
> is the go to hell writing establishment poem
> but the readers never know who

you're talking about which brings
us back
to point one

She has amusingly illustrated the dangers of literary categories. It is not surprising that this maverick does not want to be fenced in by anybody—friend or foe. She will not go along with anybody's orthodoxy.

By the third stage of her career, love, too, has failed Giovanni. In the title poem from her latest book, *Cotton Candy on a Rainy Day* (1978), she notes:

what this decade will be
  known for
There is no doubt it is
  loneliness

and in the same poem she continues:

If loneliness were a grape
  the wine would be vintage
If it were a wood
  the furniture would be mahogany
But since it is life it is
  Cotton Candy
    on a rainy day
The sweet soft essence
  of possibility
Never quite maturing

        . . . . .

I am cotton candy on a rainy day
  the unrealized dream of an idea unborn

Cotton Candy is Giovanni's bleakest book and reflects the failure of both revolution and love in the late seventies. Possibility has become stillborn.

Cotton Candy's bleak title poem provides a good example of the problems the reader faces in trying to evaluate Giovanni. Even though the poem is not a total success, it is better than it appears on casual reading. At first the title seems totally sentimental: "cotton candy" conjures up images of sticky, sappy love—it seems to catapult us into the world of Rod McKuen. In fact, the publisher exploits this aspect of Giovanni's art by giving us a sentimental soft-pink cover featuring a drawing of a dreamy, romantic woman. It's a Rod McKuen cover. Despite the poem's sometimes vague language which suggests the conventional popular poem, **"Cotton Candy"** has serious moments which save it from the world of pop songs and greeting cards. When we look closely at the cotton candy image we see it refers to a world of failed possibility; and the language, at least for a few lines, is stately and expressive of a generation:

The sweet soft essence
  of possibility
Never quite maturing

A curious aspect of Giovanni's appeal has little to do with her language per se but with the sensibility she creates on the page. It isn't that she does not use words effectively. In fact, she does. Not only did she use Black forms effectively during the sixties; in the seventies she mastered a quieter, less ethnic, free verse mode. However, on the whole what is most striking about Giovanni's poetry is that she has created the charming persona of "Nikki Giovanni." This persona is honest, searching, complex, lusty, and, above all, individualistic and charmingly egoistical. This is a verbal achievement having less to do with the surface of language than with the creation of a character, that is, more a novelistic achievement than a lyric one.

> **. . . What is most striking about Giovanni's poetry is that she has created the charming persona of "Nikki Giovanni." This persona is honest, searching, complex, lusty, and, above all, individualistic and charmingly egoistical.**
>
> **—William J. Harris**

Giovanni's lust is comedic (see **"Seduction"**) and healthy; it permeates her vision of the world. Only a lusty woman would bring this perspective to the world of politics:

Ever notice how it's only the ugly
honkies
who hate
like hitler was an ugly dude
same with lyndon

and only a lusty woman could write these joyful lines:

i wanta say just gotta say something
bout those beautiful beautiful beautiful outasight
black men
with they afros
walking down the street
is the same ol danger
but a brand new pleasure

A source of her unabashed lustiness could be the tough, blues-woman tradition. She could be following in the footsteps of Aretha Franklin's "Dr. Feelgood." The following Giovanni poem explicitly exploits and updates the blues/soul tradition:

its wednesday night baby
and i'm all alone
wednesday night baby
and i'm all alone
        . . . . .

but i'm a modern woman baby
ain't gonna let this get me down

i'm a modern woman
ain't gonna let this get me down
gonna take my master charge
and get everything in town

This poem combines the classic blues attitude about love—
defiance in the face of loss—with references to contemporary antidotes to pain: charge cards.

The poem **"Ego Tripping,"** one of her best poems,
grounded in the vital Black vernacular, features her delightful egotism. The poem is a toast, a Black form where
the hero establishes his virtues by boasting about them.
Her wonderfully healthy egotism, which is expressed succinctly in these witty lines: "show me some one not full
of herself/and i'll show you a hungry person" abounds in
"Ego Tripping":

I was born in the congo
I walked to the fertile crescent and built
        the sphinx
I designed a pyramid so tough that a star
            that only glows every one hundred years falls
            into the center giving divine perfect light
I am bad

In a way **"Ego Tripping"** is an updating of Hughes' "The
Negro Speaks of Rivers" from a woman's perspective.
Hughes' poem is a celebration of the collective Black
experience from the primordial time to the present. Giovanni's poem creates a giant mythic Black woman who
embodies and celebrates the race across time. The poem
doesn't only claim that Giovanni is Black and proud: it
creates a magnificent Black woman whose mere gaze can
burn out a Sahara Desert and whose casual blowing of
her nose can provide oil for the entire Arab world. In a
word, she is "bad!" Since it is not Giovanni speaking
personally but collectively, it is not a personal boast but
a racial jubilee.

Giovanni is a frustrating poet. I can sympathize with her
detractors, no matter what the motives for their discontent. She clearly has talent that she refuses to discipline.
She just doesn't seem to try hard enough. In **"Habits"**
she coyly declares:

    i sit writing
    a poem
    about my habits
    which while it's not
    a great poem
    is mine

It isn't enough that the poem is hers; personality isn't
enough, isn't a substitute for fully realized poems. Even
though she has created a compelling persona on the page,
she has been too dependent on it. Her ego has backfired.
She has written a number of lively, sometimes humorous,
sometimes tragic, often perceptive poems about the contemporary world. The best poems in her three strongest
books, *Black Feeling, Black Talk/ Black Judgement, Re:
Creation*, and *Cotton Candy*, demonstrate that she can be
a very good poet. However, her work also contains dross:
too much unrealized abstraction (flabby abstraction at
that!), too much "poetic" fantasy posing as poetry and too
many moments verging on sentimentality. In the early
seventies, after severely criticizing Giovanni's shortcomings,
Haki Madhubuti said he eagerly awaited the publication
of her new book, *Re: Creation*; he hoped that in it she
would fulfill the promise of her early poetry. Even though
it turned out to be one of Giovanni's better books, I find
myself in a similar situation to Madhubuti's. I see that not
only does Giovanni have promise, she already has written
some good poems and continues to write them. Yet I am
concerned about her development. I think it is time for
her to stand back and take stock of herself, to take for
herself the time for reflection, the vacation she says Aretha
deserves for work well done. Nikki Giovanni is one of
the most talented writers to come out of the Black sixties,
and I don't want to lose her. I want her to write poems
which grow out of that charming persona, not poems which
are consumed by it. Giovanni must keep her charm and
overcome her selfindulgence. She has the talent to create
good, perhaps important, poetry, if only she has the will
to discipline her craft.

John W. Cromer on *My House*

A poem is a delicate, tremulous thing existing somewhere
between the heart and the mind. The poet Nikki Giovanni
looks upon her world with a wide open penetrating gaze.
She sees her world as an extension of herself, she sees
problems in the world as an extension of her problems,
she sees herself existing amidst tensions, heartache, and
marvelous expressions of love. But the tensions, heartaches,
and expressions of love do not overwhelm the poet. She
controls her environment—sometimes with her mind, often
with her heart.

My House is the poetic expression of a vibrant black
woman with a special way of looking at things. A strong
narrative line runs through many of the poems: a familiar
scene is presented, and the poet comments upon the people
or the events. The poems are short, the language is simple;
each poem contains a single poignant image. The people
in Nikki Giovanni's poems are insulated from one another
by carefully constructed walls of personal superiority: the
old lady in **"Conversation"** is proud of the knowledge
she assumes she has because of her advanced age; the
woman in **"And Another Thing"** maintains an uncertain
status by constantly talking.

John W. Cromer, in English Journal, *April, 1973.*

Margaret B. McDowell (essay date 1986)

SOURCE: "Groundwork for a More Comprehensive Criticism of Nikki Giovanni," in *Studies in Black American
Literature*, Vol. 2, Penkeville Publishing Company, 1986,
pp. 135-59.

[*In the following essay, McDowell argues for a more comprehensive criticism of Giovanni's work, claiming that it is generally misinterpreted and poorly assessed due to earlier criticism biased by "the critics' misperceptions, their insistence on half-truths, or their . . . political and personal convictions."*]

I.

The nature of Nikki Giovanni's poetry cannot be fully understood nor its significance in recent literary history be established unless critics provide more perceptive interpretations and assessments of her work than they have done in the first fifteen years of her career. Such informed appraisals are long overdue, and her reputation has suffered from the neglect of her work by serious critics. Those who would contribute now to more comprehensive and open-minded judgments of her work will undoubtedly wish to consider the early contradictory appraisals of her poetry to ascertain what is genuine in them as a basis for this more comprehensive undertaking. I shall summarize, accordingly, the extreme reactions which Giovanni's poetry evoked primarily during the first five years of her career (1969-1974). And I will speculate on possible explanations for these contradictory responses and mediate among the early conflicting judgments, because they significantly affect her reputation to this day.

> The written response to Giovanni's poetry shows relatively little evidence of the application of objective criteria or of clearly formulated critical postulates.
>
> —*Margaret B. McDowell*

It is my general conclusion that much of the writing on Giovanni's poetry has been predicated on the critics' misperceptions, their insistence on half-truths, or their rigid and demanding political and personal convictions. Academic literary critics have been inclined to generalize about Black poetry and have failed to recognize the relationships present between the poetry and Black speech or Black music. They have tended also to discover aesthetic excellence only in poetry of intricate symbolic or intellectual complexity. On the other hand, political reviewers of Giovanni's work have overestimated the necessary function of poetry in the furtherance of Black Cultural Nationalism and Pan-Africanism, and they have underestimated her poetry affirmation of Afro-American culture and her realistic portrayals of individual Afro-Americans and their experience. In writing of her poetry, critics have allowed personal and political attitudes not merely to affect their judgment but to dominate it. For example, they have used, in place of objective criteria, the tenet that poets should subordinate their individual creativity to the rhetorical needs of the political or racial group. They have placed excessive value on consistency in the views expressed from poem to poem and book to book as if the

persona of a poem is always the author herself and the experience depicted is autobiographical. They have demanded that the author's personal behavior be approved if her poetry is to be judged favorably. Some reviewers have sought in Giovanni's poetry an ideal for Black womanhood and been disappointed either by the assertiveness, impudence, and strength they found in the poetry or, conversely by the acknowledgment of emotional vulnerability, disillusionment, and fatigue which can also be found in it. The written response to Giovanni's poetry shows relatively little evidence of the application of objective criteria or of clearly formulated critical postulates In the total body of criticism on her, no systematic, career-long examination of her techniques, her development, or the shifts in her interests and viewpoint can be found. In the reviews, one finds ardent enthusiasm for "the Princess of Black Poetry" and also cutting and humiliating attacks on both the poet and her poetry, but only a handful of writings reflect an open-minded, sensitive, and careful reading of all her work.

The judgments one infers from the popular response to Nikki Giovanni's poetry may ultimately provide more reliable critical assessment than that gleaned from "professional" sources, because such popular judgments are often made by listeners as well as readers and depend on reactions to the immediate clarity of lines; the impact of tone rhythm, and language; and the integrity of the realism in Giovanni's depiction of Afro-Americans and their experience. The response at the popular level reflects the views of large numbers of people from a wide variety of backgrounds. However, such judgment comes, in part, from the shared enthusiasm of the crowd and the charismatic personality of the poet as well as from the poetry itself, and while the emphasis on the poetry's orality is important in criticism of Giovanni, the listener cannot fully assess the damage done to a poem by a single flawed line or by an awkward beginning, and he or she is equally likely to overlook the rich ambiguities and ironies found in the best of Giovanni's lyrics.

In the past, Giovanni claimed that the criticism of her work was irrelevant. But her attitude appears to have changed. Recently, she has implied that "harder questions" than those asked last year challenge her work this year. Her statements in recent interviews with Claudia Tate [in *Black Women Writers at Work,* 1983] and Arlene Elder [in *MELVS,* 9, No. 3, 1982] may, in themselves, provide guidance for an effective critique of an author's achievement throughout a career—particularly of an author like Giovanni, who is still experimenting with technique, growing as an artist, and broadening her vision.

A consideration of the difficulties which Giovanni experienced in the 1970s in establishing her early reputation and of her own recently expressed views on the criticism she has received to the present time might serve to indicate those aspects of her work which call for further scrutiny. Among the subjects that have never had full discussion and that demand considerable systematic and reasonable criticism are (1) an identification of her goals, (2) a definition of her techniques, (3) discrimination among her aesthetic successes and failures, (4) an analysis of the changes in her processes of invention and of revision, (5) an identification of the objects of her satire and its purposes, (6) an analysis of her use of folk materials, (7) the compilation of a history of the oral presentations of her poetry (before various kinds of audiences in stage performances, on records, and on television), (8) an examination of her status as a writer of books for children, (9) a determination of the shifts in her interests as related to the forms that she has used, (10) an exploration of the alleged inconsistencies in her work, and (11) a sensitive analysis of the flexibility, the ironies, and the ambiguities that add grace and substance to her poems—particularly those in which she develops "the women and the men" themes. Her use of Black music (jazz, blues, spirituals, folk, and popular), which enriches the patterns to be found in her poetry and her recourse to stylized elements in Black conversation are also important features of her work that contribute to the "orality" for which she is famous, and these subjects need further investigation.

Each of Giovanni's successive volumes has been marred by the inclusion of some misbegotten poems or prosaic or sentimental lines (which usually occur at the beginnings or ends of poems). These failures repeatedly have claimed disproportionate attention in reviews, blurred the focus of her critics, and delayed the acknowledgment of her developing stature. Consequently, I would view as a first priority in the building of a comprehensive criticism of Giovanni the publication of a collection of her poems, selected with exceeding care. Such a volume seems crucial to the serious assessment of her achievement from 1968 to the present and to a more general awareness of her continued promise as a mature poet. With such an ordered and trimmed presentation of her work, critics might begin to see her poetry in its proper place in the history of Afro-American poetry and in its relation to the work of other American poets of the present time. Her critics, acting largely upon personal and political beliefs and preferences, have delayed such observation of Giovanni's work from the perspective of American literary history. While a chronological presentation of the selected poems could encourage developmental studies of the poet, arguments could be made for arrangement by topic, theme, or form.

If Giovanni is eventually to receive her merited place in the history of American literature, it is time for critics to examine the marked division in the response that her work has elicited (a division that began in 1971 and that widened greatly in 1972 and 1973). In 1972 the audiences for her poetry and its readers were highly enthusiastic; academic critics ignored her; radical Black critics, having praised her a year or two earlier, attacked her, mostly on ideological and personal grounds; and newspaper and magazine reviewers wrote brief generalizations and seemed to be reading each other's reviews rather than her poems. A disinterested consideration of her work as literary art appeared impossible when those who read her work praised it extravagantly, sharply attacked it, disregarded it, or commented on it in general formulas. Nor did it seem possible later in the 1970s for writers to consider her career in its totality in order that they might ascertain her development

as a thinker and an artist as each new volume appeared and that they might appraise her achievement for what it had gradually become. On the basis of her first widely-read collection, *Black Feeling, Black Talk/Black Judgement* (1970), critics casually placed her in the context of current Afro-American poetry by classifying her with "the Black revolutionary poets" and by referring to her work as representative of "the new Black poetry of hate." Following the reactions which met *My House* (1972) and later volumes, wherein she includes few political poems, no critic has seriously confronted the whole body of her poetry and its relationship to the developments in Afro-American poetry since 1960, and to modern poetry in general.

II.

Before she gained the attention of the critics and the public with *Black Feeling, Black Talk/Black Judgement*, Giovanni had attained a modicum of distinction as a promising scholar and writer, receiving honors from universities and grants from funding agencies for the humanities. She graduated in 1967 from Fisk University (her maternal grandfather, a Latin teacher, had earlier graduated from Fisk; her parents, both social workers, had graduated from Knoxville College, also in Tennessee). At her graduation she received honors in history, a formative discipline in her life. She has continued to read history as her recreation, and it has influenced her perspective on many contemporary issues. In 1967 she won a Ford Foundation Fellowship to study at the University of Pennsylvania; in 1968, a National Foundation of the Arts grant to study at the School of Fine Arts, Columbia University; and in 1969, a grant from the Harlem Council of the Arts.

She had also by 1970 grown in political and racial perspicacity and had gone through several phases of awareness of, and commitment to, Black causes. From early childhood she knew that her gradfather had changed teaching jobs and smuggled her grandmother, Louvenia, out of Georgia to Knoxville, Tennessee, one night, after hiding her under blankets. Louvenia had, as an "uppity" pioneer member of the NAACP, offended white people with her outspoken assertion of her rights. Nikki Giovanni's moving portrayal of Louvenia in *Gemini* (1970) suggests convincingly the effect of her independent, yet emotionally vulnerable, ancestor upon her. In Cincinnati, where her parents worked in social services, Giovanni learned as a child about urban poverty, the difficulties that Blacks face in attaining equal justice, and the struggles that Blacks undergo for economic survival in a Northern industrial city. During the times she lived in Knoxville, Tennessee, she saw, through her grandmother's eyes, the relative powerlessness of Blacks in confronting the racism of the white population in a smaller Southern town. For example Giovanni in 1967 thought Louvenia had been figuratively "assassinated" by the people who so wanted "progress" in Knoxville that they re-routed a little-used road, necessitating the displacement of her grandmother and her neighbors from the houses in which they had lived most of their lives. She felt that the elderly people grieved to death in alien surroundings.

In *Gemini* Giovanni tells an anecdote about herself at age four. She threw rocks from the porch roof at enemies who chased her older sister from school. She thought her sister should not fight her own battle: she might "maim" her hands, not be able to take her music lessons, and, as a consequence, the music teacher's family might starve. The story anticipates Giovanni's willingness and energy to enter the fight at hand (as in Black Cultural Nationalist enterprises between 1967 and 1969), but it also suggests that the motivation for her militance lay in helping the Black community rather than in gaining power for herself. In college her political activism intensified. Her ambivalence about the politically moderate family heroes—Martin Luther King, Jr., and Roy Wilkins—led her to found a campus chapter of SNCC during the period of Stokely Carmichael's leadership of that organization. As a graduate student at the University of Pennsylvania and then at Columbia (and simultaneously as a teacher at Queen's College and then at Rutgers University) for about two and a half years before the birth of her son (Thomas Watson Giovanni), she supported the Black activists in the leftist and radical Black Arts, Black Theater, and Black History groups; and she spoke at conferences in Detroit, Newark, Wilmington, and New York during the time that Amiri Baraka, Larry Neal, and Ron Karenga became leaders of Black Cultural Nationalism. Although she has consistently retained her commitment to the Black Aesthetic principles that all genuine Black art explore and affirm the Afro-American experience, she has always been ambivalent and cautious about the expectation that noteworthy Black art be "useful" in promoting the struggle for social and political power—and especially about the mixing of paramilitary activity with poetry. She has never believed that self-determination for a people negated the need for individual self-determination.

By 1969 she had openly dissociated her work from the demands that prescriptive didacticism was making upon her as an artist. By that time, Baraka and his associates had gained national domination of the Black Liberation Movement through para-military means in the Committee for a Unified New Ark, had violently challenged the supremacy of parallel California groups and their leaders, and, between 1970 and 1974, had fought for the support of major coalitions in the Pan-African organizations. Giovanni retreated from such extreme political action, and, as her dialogue with James Baldwin (1973) and some later poems show, she had begun again to appreciate the effectiveness of Martin Luther King. Only occasionally in the 1970s did she write about Black revolution, and then she addressed in prose issues related to equal justice, as in the cases of Angela Davis and H. Rapp Brown.

Giovanni still sees the need for continuing the Black revolution, but she contends that the revolution started four hundred years ago in America rather than in the 1960s and that one confronts its struggles, and experiences its victories, constantly. In frequent public and printed remarks, she undoubtedly alienated certain younger Black critics in the early 1970s as she dissociated her goals for Afro-American power from the more radical politics of the Black Nationalists and the Pan-African liberation groups.

In her interview with Arlene Elder, Giovanni describes Africa as the world's richest continent and oldest civilization but indicates that she does not feel a closer relationship to it than to all of the other places on "this little earth" in which she wishes to travel everywhere freely with her son. She regards her poetry as having been little influenced by African culture, because she is Western by birth and no traditionalist. (Curiously, because she views the Near East as an extension of the African continent, she sees the influence of the Bible upon her poetry as African in origin.) The subject matter of her poems has consistently been Afro-*American*.

Giovanni's willingness to limit her political efforts to Afro-American causes has continued to bring her negative criticism, even today, partly because she so openly calls herself a Black American "chauvinist." Since the feminist movement has increasingly linked American women with those in developing nations, some feminist critics of Giovanni have also seen her focus as self-centered. The evidence that political disapproval of her exclusive focus on Afro-American needs, and not on African needs, *still* affects her literary reputation can be seen in the exclusion of her poems from the fine anthology, *Confirmation: An Anthology of African American Women,* edited by Amiri and Amina Baraka (New York: Quill, 1983). The book includes works by forty-nine practicing women poets, and since Giovanni is frequently considered to be today's most widely-read Black American woman poet, perhaps the most widely-read living Black American poet, period, her absence from this volume is startling. A terse footnote in the prefatory material states that Giovanni's contributions were rejected at press time because she traveled in South Africa in 1982.

III.

The most significant development in Giovanni's career has been her evolution from a strongly committed political consciousness prior to 1969 to a more inclusive consciousness which does not repudiate political concern and commitment, but which regards a revolutionary ethos as only one aspect of the totality of Black experience. Her earlier political associates and favorable reviewers of the late 1960s often regarded her development after 1970 with consternation, as representing a repudiation of her racial roots and of political commitment, without perhaps fully understanding the basis for her widened concerns and interests. Giovanni's shift in interest from revolutionary politics and race as a collective matter towards love and race as they affect personal development and relationships brought strong reviewer reaction. (The shift to less favorable criticism, which is apparent in the reviews of *My House,* is also evident in the late notices of *Gemini,* Giovanni's most widely reviewed book.) The problems involved in studying the relationship between this shift in her poetry and the somewhat delayed shift from favorable to less favorable criticism, as her artistry grew, are complex. And they are further complicated by the fact that, at the very time the negative reviews of her poetry markedly increased, her popularity with readers surged dramatically ahead. Witness the late sales of *Gemini* (1971) and ***Black***

Feeling/Black Talk/ Black Judgement (1970), the new sales of *My House* (1972), and the record-breaking sales of two of her early albums of recorded poetry. Her audiences around the country grew markedly in size and enthusiasm in 1972, and feature articles and cover stories on "the Princess of Black Poetry" appeared in over a dozen popular magazines in 1972 and 1973.

Studying the relationships between the positive and negative reviews and between the opinions of reviewers and popular audiences is made more difficult by an anomaly presented by Giovanni's *Black Feeling, Black Talk/Black Judgement*: two-thirds of the poems in this 1970 volume are brief, introspective lyrics which are political only in the most peripheral sense—that they mention a lover as someone the speaker met at a conference, for instance. The remaining third, poems which are strongly political and often militant, received practically all the attention of reviewers. Critics ignored almost completely the poems that foreshadow nearly all the poetry Giovanni was to write in the next thirteen years. In short, the wave of literary reviews that established Giovanni's national reputation as a poet also established her image as a radical. Yet, by the summer of 1970, when these reviews began to appear, Giovanni had been writing solely non-political, lyric poetry for a year. The label "the poet of the Black revolution" which characterized her in the popular media was alreadya misnomer in 1970, when it began to be popularly used.

The change in stance had, in fact, appeared by 1969, when Giovanni published an article criticizing the leaders of Black Cultural Nationalism. In it, she also rejected the rigidity and the prescriptiveness of the Black Aesthetic, the proponents of which insisted that committed Black writers like herself could only write about changing the Black situation in America in terms of power. She further charged that Black Arts groups had become exclusive and snobbish, and she attacked the Movement's male activists for demanding the subservience of Black women to the male leaders of the cause. In general, she concluded that she could no longer as an artist subordinate her poetry to the politics of revolution. Entitled "Black Poets, *Poseurs*, and Power," the essay appeared first in the June, 1969, issue of *Black World*. The aggressive Black leaders of the revolution must surely have read it, but apparently few of her other readers knew of the essay. Since Giovanni had no popular following prior to 1970, her 1969 essay did not become a widely discussed matter in the literary world.

At least initially, readers also seem to have paid scant attention to the philosophical conclusions that Giovanni had arrived at and had announced in her casually organized and conversational essay when it was reprinted in *Gemini*, a collection of prose pieces, in 1971. Most would have been more interested in her angrily expressed charge that the Black Cultural Nationalists "have made Black women the new Jews." Black readers of *Gemini* would have focused, too, on her reaction to the 1968 electoral campaign in Newark: the Black citizens of Newark, she contends, seemed more fearful of their "liberators" than they did

the corrupt white politicians who had oppressed them in the past. That Giovanni had, by 1971, felt *some* repercussions from the publication of her article might account for her remark, in *A Dialogue: James Baldwin and Nikki Giovanni*, that "the young Black critics are, I think just trying to hurt people, and the white critics don't understand."

Ruth Rambo McClain, reviewing Giovanni's 1970 poetry collection *Re: Creation* in the February, 1971, issue of *Black World*, is one of the first critics to recognize the change in Giovanni's subject and form. McClain regards the many lyrics in *Re: Creation* as "tight controlled, clean—too clean" and sees in Giovanni not only "a new classical lyrical Nikki, exploring her new feeling," but "an almost declawed tamed panther." *Re: Creation*, a small collection, contains a few poems on revolution, the imprisonment of Blacks, and the hatred of white oppressors (perhaps written prior to having arrived at the conclusions Giovanni presents in "Black Poets, *Poseurs*, and Power"). Most of those who reviewed her two 1970 books of poetry wanted more poems of this sort and referred to them as *sharp, vital, energetic,* or *non-sentimental*. A few more detached critics saw the rhetoric in them as somewhat posed and artificial but did not object on political grounds.

Most of the reviews and essays on Giovanni in 1971 recognized no impending change in her work. For example, A. Russell Brooks, writing on "The Motifs of Dynamic Change in Black Revolutionary Poetry" in the September, 1971, issue of *CLA Journal* (pp. 7-17), includes Giovanni in his list of nine poets "in the forefront" of revolutionary poetry, and he identifies her as "one of the first two or three most popular black poets." Placing his comments on her between those on Don L. Lee (Haki Madhubuti) and LeRoi Jones (Amiri Baraka), he refers to Lee as the most impatient, Giovanni as the most popular, and Jones as "the Dean of Black Revolutionary Artists." However, in a later review of *A Dialogue* (*CLA Journal,* December, 1973, pp. 291-294), Brooks speaks of Giovanni's "marked change in her mode of looking at the world and writing about it" as reflected not only in *My House* but "fairly well indicated" in *Re: Creation* and *Gemini*. In a 1971 article entitled "The Poetry of Three Revolutionists: Don L. Lee, Sonia Sanchez, and Nikki Giovanni" (*CLA Journal*, September, 1971), R. Roderick Palmer failed to acknowledge Giovanni's shift in vision, seeing her, among these three figures, as the *true* revolutionary: "the most polemic, the most incendiary; the poet most impatient for change, who . . . advocates open violence." Palmer, like many other readers, failed to recognize the preponderance of the lyric mode in the collections of 1970, the preponderance of poems devoted to self-analysis, love, and the exploration of personal relationships; he mistakenly remarks that she "occasionally lends herself to less explosive themes."

On February 13, 1972, June Jordan, herself a Black poet, reviewed *Gemini* in the New York *Times Book Review* in a generally favorable way. She notes that the paragraphs of Giovanni's prose slide about and loosely switch tracks" but feels that two essays are unusual for their serious, held focus and for their clarity." She singles out for special comment the 1969 article "Black Poets, *Poseurs,* and Power" and the last essay in *Gemini*, "Gemini—A Prolonged Autobiographical Statement on Why," which closes with the statement "I really like to think a Black, beautiful, loving world is possible." More directly than had McClain, Jordan remarks on what she also identifies as an impending transition in Giovanni's work—because of the attitudes she sees revealed in these two essays. She agrees with Giovanni that the growing militarism in the Black Arts Movement is deplorable and that the Black community itself is the loser when violent strategies pit Black against Black and leave the real enemies laughing at the sidelines." She observes that Giovanni, in "Black Poets, *Poseurs*, and Power," was telling the world in 1969 of a change occurring in her poetry and in herself. In speaking of the closing essay in the book, Jordan concludes: "When you compare the poetry [apparently she refers here to the revolutionary poems included in the 1970 volumes] with the ambivalence and wants expressed in this essay, it becomes clear that a transition is taking place inside the artist. . . . She is writing, 'I don't want my son to be a George or a Jonathan Jackson!'" A few months later, the publication of ***My House***, without revolutionary poems and with most of its lyrics written after 1969, proved June Jordan's careful and perceptive interpretation of Giovanni's intent to have been accurate.

Two of Giovanni's friends wrote positively of her new emphasis on personal values in 1972. Howard University Press editor Paula Giddings, who provided the preface for Giovanni's ***Cotton Candy on a Rainy Day*** (1978), in a brief review of *Gemini* in *Black World* (August 1972), contends that Giovanni's concern for individual Black self-determination places her in a long standing tradition of Black literature. Ida Lewis, Editor of *Encore*, a magazine for which Giovanni wrote a twice-monthly column beginning in 1975 (as well as many other articles), mentions in her preface to ***My House*** that Giovanni already "has been re-proached for her independent attitudes by her critics. . . . But Nikki Giovanni's greatness is not derived from fol-lowing leaders, nor has she ever accepted the burden of carrying the revolution. Her struggle is a personal search for individual values. . . . She jealously guards her right to be judged as an individual." These two sets of remarks make it evident that Giovanni had heard that attacks on her work were soon to appear in print. In the preface to ***My House***, Lewis quotes Giovanni as saying of such Black critics: "We are the *only* people who will read someone out of the race—the entire nation—because we don't agree with them."

In the same month that Jordan's review appeared, Black critic Peter Bailey published a favorable feature story in *Ebony* (February, 1972) on Giovanni's rapidly growing popular reputation, but he ominously suggested, as did Lewis, that the negative reaction from certain Black art-ists and politicians loomed just ahead for Giovanni and her poetry. Unlike Jordan, Giddings, and Lewis, however, Bailey saw her popular reputation as a partial *cause* for the accelerating attack on her work, whereas Jordan had

referred to it as a "guarantee" of the interests of her work: "Like it or not," writes Bailey, "—and some people don't like it—she has become a cultural force to be dealt with She's a much-anthologized poet and she's a lecturer who commands a vast audience. . . . There are black artists—those in what she called 'the black-power literary establishment'—who are convinced that Nikki's emergence as a 'star' will hinder her development as a *black* poet."

Since the bulk of Giovanni's Black political associates and fellow artists did not understand the basis for her widened concerns as a poet and saw only her apparent retreat from revolutionary politics, few critics who sup-ported the Black Aesthetic applauded her. Dudley Randall (editor of the Broadside Press), Ida Lewis, Paula Gid-dings, and probably June Jordan recognized the impera-tive of the artist to follow her or his own vision if one's imaginative poetry is to flourish. Most others regarded Giovanni's new position as a failure in nerve, even a betrayal. In their reviews they commented disapprovingly about her diminished political and racial commitment in turning to the lyric and away from revolutionary themes, and they judged harshly the poems that dealt with sex, love, and family relationships.

These critics seldom attacked either specific poems or specific lines; they simply opposed Giovanni's new ideo-logical orientation. Repeatedly, they stereotyped her un-favorably—as a woman crying for a lover she could not hold, as a mother abandoned with a baby—frustrated and resentful, longing for the return of her man. While she was insultingly derided for "singing the blues," she was almost as often stereotyped as a frivolous woman, joking, laughing, enjoying herself when serious issues of race and revolution needed to be addressed, and as an overly ambitious and successful woman, who had compromised to accommodate and please everyone in order to gain popularity, wealth, and applause. This second stereotype—the too-happy woman—was labeled the "ego-tripper." (**"Ego-Tripping"** is the name of one of her most popular poems which she often reads to audiences. It derives from folk origins—the tall-tale, the amusing boaster whose ex-aggeration increases throughout the story or song and has no bounds as explicit details accumulate into a semblance of invulnerable realism. *Ego-Tripping* is also the name of her 1973 book for young people.)

Those reviewers who promoted the stereotype of Giovanni's crying the blues for a lost love said that her poems were sad and lacking in energy; those promoting the ego-tripper stereotype complained that her poems were irrelevant, frivolous, trivial, and derived from European lyric tradi-tions. Giovanni's son was five when this kind of attack was most blatantly made—certainly not an infant—; in 1969 and 1970 when he *was* an infant and when her rev-olutionary poetry was occupying reviewers, no such ref-erences were made. The image of the woman sitting alone and weeping over a sacrificed future must have seemed strange to the crowds who knew of the strenuous speaking and travel schedule which she maintained in the early '70s. In addition, she was writing the poems published in

The Women and the Men in 1975, and both preparing her dialogues with Margaret Walker and with James Baldwin for publication in 1973 and 1974, respectively, and producing two books of children's poems, written for her son. During part of this time she also continued to teach at Rutgers University.

In any event, whether critics' animosity arose from their disapproval of independent motherhood, envy of Giovanni's success and popularity, or anger at her political withdrawal from the Black Cultural Nationalist activity and failure to support Pan-African groups, the bitterness of their reviews is startling. They are as extreme in their negation as were the crowds which welcomed Giovanni wherever she spoke or read her poetry extreme in their enthusiasm. Hilda-Njoki McElroy prefaces her review of *A Dialogue* in the December, 1973, issue of *Black World* by satirizing the book as "Who's Afraid of James Baldwin and Nikki Giovanni: A Comedy for White Audiences," starring N. Giovanni who, as a "super cool, funny woman[,] reveals her vulnerability." McElroy then refers to Giovanni's recent honors as "accolades and awards from the enemy."

Kalamu ya Salaam (Val Ferdinand) launched a still harsher attack upon Giovanni's integrity in an essay which purports to be a late review of *My House* and of her record album *Like a Ripple in the Pond* (*Black World,* July, 1974). This critic—who edits the *Black Collegian,* is associated with the Nkombo Press in New Orleans, and writes essays, poetry, and plays—had won the Richard Wright Prize for Criticism in 1970. He was active in the Congress of Afrikan People and the Afrikan Liberation Support Committee, and a few months later published a long report on his assessment of African Liberation Day entitled "Tell No Lies, Claim No Easy Victories" *Black World,* October, 1974). He is obviously sympathetic to Baraka's progress in the early 1970s towards dominance in the Pan-African groups as he won strength also for the CFUN (Committee for a Unified New Ark). Given Salaam's political background, it is not surprising that he disapproved of Giovanni's 1969 statement on the Black Cultural Nationalists and her refusal to participate in the African liberation groups. Nevertheless, the sense of shock which he expresses in his review rings false, because he is writing about a change that occurred in her work five years before and should have been clear to everyone two years earlier with the publication of *My House.*

In his essay Salaam centers on a quotation from Baraka which describes the Black actress Ruby Dee in a mournful pose, sitting at a window on a rainy day. (Ruby Dee had, since 1940, played roles in *Agamemnon, King Lear, Boesman and Lena,* and *A Raisin in the Sun* and taken other parts in stage plays, films, and television dramas. Like Giovanni, she had produced poetry readings against a background of jazz and gospel music.) Quoting Baraka, "Ruby Dee weeps at the window . . . lost in her life . . . sentimental bitter frustrated deprived of her fullest light. . . ." Salaam continues, "This describes *Nikki* perfectly." He then contends that Giovanni has moved from revolutionary poetry to sad lyricism in *My House* because she is la-

menting a lover who has abandoned her, and she now is, like "a whole lot of Ruby Dees, sitting . . . waiting . . . the footsteps of us brothers come back home." His supposed pity for her suddenly assumes a harsher tone: "Nikki has gone quietly crazy." Referring to her lyric about the experience of being a bridesmaid, he taunts her by saying, "A lot of the seeming insanity and nonsense that Nikki verbalizes . . . must be understood for what it is: Broken dreams. Misses. Efforts that failed. I betcha Nikki wanted to be married. . . ." This fictionalized biography completed, Salaam attacks Giovanni's poetry for its sentimentality, its romanticism, and its being influenced by European tradition ("strictly European literature regurgitated"). He scolds her for turning from the unremitting analysis of "collective oppression" in order to "sing the blues" about personal problems. She should have known that "just love" is not an appropriate theme for poetry, because love is an intensely personal experience between only two individuals and, thus, is counter-revolutionary. He concludes that Giovanni does not have the right to "do whatever . . . she feels like doing" because she is, as a Black, still "in captivity." She should see the limits of her poetry withinthe message "The revolution is, and must be, for land and self-control. And good government."

IV.

It is my contention that Giovanni's rejection of the pressure to write primarily a didactic, "useful" political poetry was not only a sign of her integrity but an inevitable sign of her development. A truly comprehensive criticism of her work must be willing to recognize both her continuing commitment to the attainment by Black people of power in America and a commitment to personal freedom for herself as a woman and an artist. Critics need not only to see the importance of politics in her life but to perceive also that a commitment to politics, pursued with ideological rigor, inevitably becomes constricting to an artist. That Giovanni still writes political poetry can be understood by attending to the anger which she expresses in each volume at the oppression of Blacks, women, and the elderly; she continually deplores also the violence which oppression spawns. She illustrates the conflict between ideological commitment, exacted by political beliefs, and the demands of the artistic sensibility which tend to find such commitment confining and stultifying. She illustrates in her own work and career the same arc that the poets of the Auden generation in England illustrated: the passing beyond a doctrinal basis for one's poetry to a work responsive to an illuminating of the whole of the individual's experience. Giovanni's case is both complicated and made clearer by her connections with the Black Liberation Movement, which has not yet won all its objectives, particularly her affinities to the work of those closely tied to Marxist-Leninist ideology and Pan-African goals.

Giovanni has been viewed by some of her politically ardent contemporaries in the liberation groups as having deserted the movement with which she was at first visibly associated. Her revolutionary poem in *Black Feeling, Black Talk/Black Judgement* made her into a heroic figure for some Blacks, and the myth of her fiery opposition to tyranny was slow to die—even though she had moved away from Black Cultural Nationalism before most of those who hailed the strenuous and dominant voice in her poems knew that she existed. A more comprehensive criticism would permit critics to consider that Giovanni may have gained rather than lost as a result of the development of a personal idiom and of a more lyrical stance in her post-1970 work. In her response to Peter Bailey's questions early in 1972 about the "reproach" from Black activists that was gathering about her and her work, Giovanni displayed again the defiance and staunch independence captured in the anecdote from *Gemini* which features the four-year-old Nikki holding the fort with stones on her porch roof, ready to fight back against detractors: "I'm not about telling people what they should do. . . . The fight in the world today is the fight to be an individual, the fight to live out your own damn ego in your own damn way. . . . If I allow you to be yourself and you allow me to be myself, then we can come together and build a strong union. . . . I'm an arrogant bitch, culturally speaking" (*Ebony,* February, 1972).

If the verbal and structural forthrightness of Giovanni's poetry in some measure accounts for the paucity of academic criticism of it, this elemental quality accounts also for her popular acclaim by thousands who come to hear her read her work.

—Margaret B. McDowell

In her poetry Giovanni has chosen to communicate with the common reader, as well as with artists and critics; consequently, she has used graphic images from everyday Afro-American life and stressed the "orality" of her usually short poems, often by assimilating into them the rhythms of Black conversation and the heritage from jazz, blues, and the spirituals—reflecting these origins both in rhythmic patterns and borrowed phrases. She has tended to focus on a single individual, situation, or idea, often with a brief narrative thread present in the poem. Her choice of such simple forms has meant that academic critics might well be less interested in her work than in that of the more complex and intellectualized poets most often associated with modernism, such as T. S. Eliot, Ezra Pound, and W. H. Auden. She avoids the allusions to classical literature and mythology, the relatively obscure symbolism, the involved syntax, the densely-packed idiom, and the elliptical diction often characteristic of such poets. If the verbal and structural forthrightness of Giovanni's poetry in some measure accounts for the paucity of academic criticism of it, this elemental quality accounts also for her popular acclaim by thousands who come to hear her read her work. Like a folksinger, she senses the close relationship of poetry with music, since her poetry, like music, depends on sound and rhythm and is incomplete without oral performance and without an audience. (At times, especially in her children's poetry, she relates her poems to a third such art, dance.)

Throughout the 1970s Giovanni read her poetry and lectured on campuses, at churches, and on radio and television. Paula Giddings reported in the preface to Giovanni's *Cotton Candy on a Rainy Day* (1978) that Giovanni appeared before as many as two hundred audiences a year during the 1970s, commanding substantial speaking fees. Today she continues to make public appearances but on a less strenuous schedule. As a poet of the people, Giovanni renews the tradition of the bard, prophet, or witness who sings or chants to inform the people, to subvert tyranny, and to bring an audience together as a community to celebrate a cause or person or a heritage, or to establish a basis for sympathy and understanding of one another's suffering or problems. For Giovanni's audience participation at a poetry reading can be as much a part of the aesthetic experience as congregational expression may be part of worship experience.

Giovanni's acceptance by the public was strong in 1970 and grew in 1971 with the publication of *Gemini*, and in 1972 and 1973 it greatly increased, in counterpoint to the negative reviews of *My House* during those years. In 1969 the *Amsterdam News*, a Black New York weekly found in 1909, listed her as one of the ten most admired Black women in America. By 1970 and 1971 journalists and television speakers generally referred to her as "the star" or "the Princess of Black Poetry." June Jordan, in reviewing *Gemini,* commented in 1972 that the book's interests were "guaranteed by Miss Giovanni's status as a leading black poet and celebrity," and she referred to Giovanni's "plentiful followers" who claimed her as "*their* poet," so directly did she speak to them (*The New York Times Book Review,* 13 February, 1972).

The popular media both reflected her burgeoning popular reputation and strengthened its further growth. Besides the many feature articles on her poetry and personality in major popular magazines, over a dozen in 1972 and 1973 alone, she frequently appeared on late-night television talk shows, and she read her poetry regularly on *Soul,* a one-hour television show of music, dance, drama, and literature for young people (sponsored by the Ford Foundation). In 1970 she established her own company, NikTom Records, Ltd., and then recorded albums on which she read her poetry against a musical background—first, gospel; and later, blues, jazz, rock, and folk. Two early albums were best-sellers, and one received the national AFTRA Award for Best Spoken Album in 1972.

Giovanni says that she speaks for no one but herself, but she actually has become, in her poems, the speaker for many diverse groups and individuals. She has revealed a sincere interest in the people from many backgrounds who come to hear her or who write to her. Though in her early work she made use of a militant rhetoric with images of violence, she deplored—even in her first major volume— the actual violence seemingly endemic to American life.

In one of her first poems, **"Love Poem: For Real,"** she mourned the fact that "the sixties have been one long funeral day." In her poetry she is ardently sympathetic to those who have died uselessly and goes on in each new volume to lament the senselessness of the results of prejudice and intolerance, the public tragedy that she makes personal tragedy in her poetry—from the Ku Klux Klan murders of civil rights workers in Philadelphia, Mississippi, through the assassinations of public leaders in the 1960s, to the murders of kidnapped children in Atlanta.

She has attracted feminists with her portrayals of the women in her family and of elderly Black women. They have noted her frequent dedications of poems to women and have been impressed by her courageous assertion that she had her baby in 1969 because she wanted a baby, could *afford* to, and didn't want a husband. The more traditional leadership of the National Council of Negro Women, moreover, has honored her with a life membership, and she has praised their inclusive program of advocacy and membership policy. Young protesters against the draft and Viet Nam involvement crowded her campus lectures, but she also encouraged high school students at assemblies (often Black students) to avoid an alignment with "hippie" groups and to follow a disciplined life—to aim higher, work harder, and demand bigger rewards. After the inmates of the Cook County Jail presented her with a plaque, she boasted that prisoners and students were her best supporters. She relished ceremonies in which mayors from Gary, Indiana, to Dallas, Texas, gave her keys to their cities. With more somber pomp and ceremony, she was in three years (1972-1975) awarded four honorary doctorates.

One example of the acclaim Giovanni received in 1972 and 1973 can be found in an event honoring her which combined the setting of the Kennedy Center for the Performing Arts, a formally attired audience of government dignitaries and other celebrities, a several-month-long publicity promotion in the *Ladies' Home Journal*, and the financial backing of Clairol (a large manufacturer of hair products) with a one-hour television extravaganza which pre-empted network programs. In 1972 Giovanni received one of seven "Highest Achievement Awards" from *Mademoiselle* as "one of the most listened to of the younger poets" (*Mademoiselle*, January, 1972). In the more highly publicized *Ladies' Home Journal* "Women of the Year" contest in 1973, she became one of the eight winners (from among eighty nominees on ballots printed in the magazine, which thirty thousand subscribers clipped, marked, signed, and mailed that month). A jury of prestigious women who made the final choices for the list included Shirley Temple Black; Margaret Truman Daniels; Eunice Kennedy Shriver; the presidents of the National Organization for Women, the General Federation of Women's Clubs, the National Council of Negro Women, Women in Communications, and two women's colleges; the dean of a medical college; a recruiter for high-level positions in the Nixonadministration; and a woman Brigadier General in the U. S. Air Force. Besides Giovanni, the list itself included such famous women as Katharine Graham, publisher of the *Washington Post*; Shirley Chisholm, recently a Presidential candidate; and actress Helen Hayes. Other nominees included Coretta King; Dorothy Day; Judge Shirley Hofstedler; sculptor Louise Nevelson; historian Barbara Tuchman; authors Joyce Carol Oates, Anne Sexton, and Pearl Buck; musicians Beverly Sills, Joan Baez, Carly Simon, and Ethel Waters; athletes Billie Jean King, Chris Evert, and Peggy Fleming; feminists Bella Abzug, Betty Friedan, Gloria Steinem, and Aileen Hernandez; former ambassador Patricia Harris; sex researcher Virginia Masters; Patricia Nixon; Julie Nixon Eisenhower; and Rose Kennedy. The awards (pendant-pins with three diamonds, specially designed for the occasion by Tiffany's) were presented by Mamie Eisenhower, news commentator Barbara Walters, and Senator Margaret Chase Smith. The ceremony, hosted by actress Rosalind Russell, was viewed by an estimated television audience of thirty million.

The nomination ballots had identified Giovanni as a "Black consciousness poet," and the award presentation statement cited her as "a symbol of Black awareness." Although it also described her somewhat patronizingly as a person "rising above her environment to seek the truth and tell it," readers of her poetry know that its "truth" derives not from her rising above her environment but from her having remained so close to it. This mass-media event offers evidence of the poet's rapid rise to celebrity and provides evidence of the widespread recognition of her and her poetry. This popular acclaim would seem to be an affirmation of her decision four years earlier to write on a wide variety of subjects and to reach as wide a number of people of differing backgrounds and personal characteristics as possible.

V.

The problems arising from Giovanni's early critical reception linger. As we move in the direction of providing a more adequate base of understanding and assessment of her work, it is fortunate that three good sources of Giovanni's own views on the criticism of poetry (particularly her own work) have appeared in the last two years: the verse preface to Giovanni's *Those Who Ride the Night Winds* (1983), the 1983 interview with Claudia Tate in *Black Women Writers at Work*, and the 1982 interview with Arlene Elder.

As I mentioned earlier, negative criticism of Giovanni—often based on personal or political bias rather than sound literary assessment—gains strength by pointing to a particularly poor poem or an unfortunate line. Giovanni's process of revision (or discarding all or part of a poem), therefore, has special relevance in her continued development. As she describes her process of revision to Claudia Tate, she essentially discards an entire poem if it appears to present several problems or a major problem. Otherwise, when she discovers a recalcitrant line or two, she "starts at the top" and rewrites the entire poem—perhaps a dozen times—rather than working on a particular line or phrase. She finds this radical rewriting necessary to insure the poem's unity: "A poem's got to be a single stroke." It is particularly important to understand this characteristic process, established over fifteen years, as one begins to criticize Giovanni's forthcoming works. According to Arlene Elder's introduction to her interview with Giovanni, the poet is about to embark on an experiment with much longer poems (1,200-1,500 lines) after a career of writing short poems. Since one cannot rewrite a long poem a dozen times upon encountering problems in a few lines, Giovanni's revision process may radically change.

One already sees changes of probable significance between Giovanni's most recent book, *Those Who Ride the Night Winds*, and her books of the 1970s. In many of the poems she is using a "lineless" form: the rhythmic effects come from measured groups of words or phrases of fairly regular length separated from each other by ellipses, but appearing otherwise to be prose paragraphs. Except for works before 1970, she has (more than other contemporary Black poets, such as Sonia Sanchez or Haki Madhubuti) avoided such unconventional typographical devices as capitalizing all the words in a line, separating a single syllable between lines (Bl-Ack), or spelling for the sake of puns (hue-man, Spear-o-Agnew, master-bate). She has probably done so, in part, because of the artificiality of these tricks—but more often because she stresses the oral nature of her poetry, and such typography has little effect on the spoken word. One wonders, then, whether she is, in her latest volume, moving away from the emphasis on the oral. She may also be seeking a bridge between the freedom of prose and the more exact structuring of poetry. In this book she also includes a number of poems about individual white people—John Lennon, John F. Kennedy, and Billie Jean King, for example. New critics of Giovanni will need to know her earlier work and the nature of its development to understand and evaluate the changes that appear to be approaching in her career.

From the Tate interview, one learns much that is significant about Giovanni's views on good criticism. She now claims that she does not care whether her critic is black or white, but the individual should understand her work, or try to do so, before writing on it. In her view critics must not permanently "brand" a work so that other critics unconsciously embrace that judgment. They should not expect consistency within an author's canon, since such an expectation denies the fact that an artist may grow and change. In reviewing a book, they should place it in the context of the rest of the author's work. They should not assume that the voice ordering the poem and the experience described in the poem are necessarily autobiographical. They should not aim to injure an author personally by referring to private matters instead of concentrating on the work apart from the author's life. They should not question a writer's integrity because they happen to disagree with the ideas expressed in the work. Giovanni's comments, though offhanded, are pithy: "There would be no point to having me go three-fourths of the way around the world if I couldn't create an inconsistency, if I hadn't *learned* anything." "You're only as good as your last book. . . . God wrote one book. The rest of us are forced to do a little better." "You can't quote the last book as if it were the first."

In her preface to *Those Who Ride the Night Winds*, Giovanni invites her readers to hurry along with her as

she flies the uncharted night winds, because she is *changing,* and because—as the Walrus said—the time has come to talk of *many* things. If she still feels distrust of critics, in this preface she suggests a willingness to listen, as in the interviews she suggests a desire to be energized as a poet by "better questions this year than last." In spite of her mixed experience with critics, she does not see herself as their victim, because she knows that she was free to choose a safer occupation than that of writer and did not do so. In the "lineless" poetry she uses in her new book—the first unconventional typography she has used since 1970—she puns on the "bookmaker" as a professional gambler and her own game of chance as a "maker of books": "Bookmaking is shooting craps . . . with the white boys . . . downtown on the stock exchange . . . is betting a dime you can win . . . And that's as it should be . . . If you wanted to be safe . . . you would have walked into the Post Office . . . or taken a graduate degree in Educational Administration . . . you pick up your pen . . . And take your chances . . ."

Giovanni's critics, who often limit themselves to reviews of her separate books, devote little attention to her development from year to year and provide little specific analysis of the significant aspects of the form and structure of her poetry. No critic has fully discussed the variety of her subjects and her techniques. Beyond this, personal bias and political needs, rather than a commitment to judgments based on sound theoretical postulates, dominate much of the criticism which does exist on her work. Those who have attacked her poetry most severely have failed to understand Giovanni's compulsion to follow her own artistic vision as well as her continued commitment to Afro-American culture. Her great popularity among readers of many ages, classes, races, and economic backgrounds is at variance with the neglect of her work by critics or their tendency to patronize her and her work. Sympathetic and sophisticated studies of her work are a prime necessity if she is to achieve the recognition due her as a literary artist. Such studies, it is hoped, would encourage her to achieve her full potential as a poet and would also attain for her the reputation that the corpus of her work calls for.

Nikki Giovanni with Claudia Tate (interview date 1983)

SOURCE: An interview in *Black Women Writers at Work*, Continuum, 1983, pp. 60-78.

[*In the following interview, Giovanni discusses her work's development, considers the effects of race and gender on writing, and provides insight into her own creative process.*]

Nikki Giovanni began her literary career as a poet in the late sixties during the so-called "Black Revolution," and much of her verse at that time encouraged social and political activism among Black Americans. Her later work also addresses contemporary issues, but the focus falls instead on human relationships rendered from the vantage point of a mother, a lover, and a women. Giovannni's language remains startling, energetic, enraged, and loving. . . .

[TATE]: *The black revolutionary fervor of the sixties seems to be gone. We no longer even hear the rhetoric. Does this suggest that the revolution is over?*

[GIOVANNI]: I bought three new windows for my mother's basement. Have you ever bought windows for your mother's basement? It's revolutionary! It really is.

I have a problem I think I should share with you. For the most part this question is boring. We're looking at a phenomenon as if it were finished. Everyone says, "Well, what happened to the revolution?" If you want to deal with states [dialectical transitions] you have to deal with Marx. But I'm not into that. From where I am, I see a continuous black revolution going on for the last four hundred years in America. There has been a continuous revolution of black people for the last two thousand years. And it's not letting up.

When you look at the decade from 1954 to 1964, you're forced to say black Americans won their objectives. We didn't like the segregated buses. We didn't like the segregated schools. We didn't like the way we were treated in stores. We didn't like the housing patterns. We didn't like the number of doctors or lawyers we had. We didn't like our lack of professionals. We won. But looking at the late seventies, there's no way you can consider the Bakke decision to be favorable. It was 5-4. It was really a bad decision. Close cases make bad law. There's no question Bakke should have come in 9-0 either way, if it's going to be definitive. Then you would have had a law. You don't have a law now.

I'm looking for a riot. I'm living in a city that kills cops like people kill flies. Cincinnati, Ohio is leading the nation in the number of policemen killed. We're number one. The black community seems to be saying, "Well, you can play Nazi, but we ain't playing Jew." And black folks have been shooting back. We're saying, "Wait a minute. Who do you think you're playing with?" Nobody's going back to 1954. No matter what the rollback is. It's not even going back to '64. No matter what "let's take the breather" is.

When people start to say "What happened to the sixties," we've got to remember, "Hey, this is the eighties and what are we going to do now?" Where are we going because it's going to continue. My generation didn't start the bus boycotts. But we decided where they should go. Now it's time again to decide on a direction. We weren't the first generation to say "This ain't right." But we were the first to know we had to fight in terms of our bodies. We recognized we were going to have to go to jail, and we were going to have to get killed. And all of that is really sad. We were going to get beaten; our houses were going to get bombed. But we went on the line. I mean bodies, a lot of bodies. I'm not the first poet, neither is

Carolyn Rogers nor Gwen Brooks, to say, "Hey, this is intolerable." Neither was Langston Hughes, nor Claude McKay. We're talking about a struggle for freedom that keeps going on and on. People are tending to approach the whole problem like, "Oh! Wow! It's all over. It's been done." This is not a movie!

Sure the militant posture has left contemporary writing. First of all it was boring. That's a very serious word for me; I use it a lot, I realize, but what do you want? You want me to rewrite "Nigger can you kill/Can you kill/ Nigger can you kill?" I wrote it. It's not just that it's written, but I wrote it. And I wasn't even the first person to write it. Nor will I be the last. But I did it *my* time. Now it's time for me to do something else.

Your earlier works, **Black Feeling, Black Talk/ Black Judgment** *and* **Re: Creation,** *seem very extroverted, militant, arrogant. The later work,* **The Women and the Men** *and* **Cotton Candy on a Rainy Day,** *seem very introverted, private, lonely, withdrawn. Does this shift in perspective, tone, and thematic focus reflect a conscious transition?*

I'll tell you what's wrong with that question. The assumption inherent in that question is that the self is not a part of the body politic. There's no separation.

I'm not a critic of my own work. It's not what I'm supposed to be about. I think literary analysis gives academics something to do. Books are generally amusement parks for readers. They will ultimately make a decision about which book to ride. But as for critics, they have to write a book as interesting as the one they're criticizing or the criticism is without validity. If they succeed, then the book they're writing about is only their subject; it is not in itself necessary. The critics could have written about anything. And after all, they've got to have something to do. It's Friday and it's raining, so they write a critique of Nikki Giovanni. It's not serious. And I'm not denigrating myself; it's just that it's no more serious than that.

Is there a black aesthetic? If so, can you define it?

It's not that I can't define the term, but I am not interested in defining it. I don't trust people who do. Melvin Tolson said you only define a culture in its decline; you never define a culture in its ascendancy. There's no question about that. You only define anything when it's on its way down. How high did it go? As long as it's traveling, you're only guessing. So too with the black aesthetic.

As the black-aesthetic criticism went, you were told that if you were a black writer or a black critic, you were told *this* is what you should do. That kind of prescription cuts off the question by defining parameters. I object to prescriptions of all kinds. In this case the prescription was a capsulized militant stance. What are we going to do with a stance? Literature is only as useful as it reflects reality. I talk about this in *Gemini*; I also say it's very difficult to gauge what we have done as a people when we have been systematically subjected to the whims of other people.

One essay in Gemini *discusses the effects of slavery on Phillis Wheatley's life and work.*

You talk to Margaret Walker about Phillis because I would like to be very clear about her. There is nothing wrong with the poems she wrote. And I dare say, from what I see of history, there was no particular reason why Phillis Wheatley didn't mean exactly what she said. There is no reason for me to reject what Phillis Wheatley had to say about her experience. And I don't. People get upset because she talks about Africa in terms of how delighted she was to discover Christianity. Well, from what little I know, she might have been damned delighted. Life for an African woman can be very difficult even today, and she was writing in the eighteenth century. We can't talk about freedom for the African woman *now*. That's a battle yet to be fought.

I just want to be clear on Phillis because I think she gets a bad rap. People haven't read her and don't know a damn thing about her and don't want to empathize with her life. I think she had a difficult life. If she could say she was delighted to be on these shores, then we have to look at that.

Critics should do one thing and that is understand the work. It doesn't make any difference whether they are white or black, they should try to understand the work. I've been so consistent on this point that I would just like to point out my consistency. (People never read what I say, and I don't know where they get what they come up with.) I can both read and appreciate literature, as I was taught to do. I can do this with Shakespeare, though I am not a great lover of Shakespeare. Therefore, it is incomprehensible to me that Robert Bone, a white critic, can't read and appreciate Nikki Giovanni, a black poet. I think I'm probably brighter and more sensitive than he is, and I'm saying Bone because he's the first white critic who comes to mind. I have not created a totally unique, incomprehensible feat. I can understand Milton and T. S. Eliot, so the critic can understand me. That's the critic's job.

We have made literature in the Western world a big bugaboo. I remember when I was in a humanities class, we read Theodore Dreiser's *Sister Carrie* because it was short enough to be put intoa six-week course. But if you're going to read Dreiser, there's only *An American Tragedy*. He *didn't* write anything else! If you're going to read Tom Wolfe, you're going to read *Look Homeward, Angel*. That's what you're going to have to do. If you're going to read Thomas Mann, you're going to read *The Magic Mountain*. But we generally don't read a writer's best work. So people end up not liking literature. And they are discouraged, absolutely discouraged from reading literature because we've given them the worst but what was most convenient. What we've been taught for the last five generations of public education is expediency. And that's what we are dealing with right now. Kids say, "If I'm going to read shit why should I read?" That's exactly what it comes down to. Why should I read the worst of some author? Because it's safer; it's sanitized, and he or she

she didn't use bad words. And all of us let this happen, because we have our jobs or whatever.

Poetry is the most mistaught subject in any school because we teach poetry by form and not by content. I remember reading Edna St. Vincent Millay—and nobody was reading Millay, you know, except me and the teacher. I really liked "I Burned My Candle at Both Ends," and I wanted to discuss the poem in class. But I was told, "We don't discuss that." It had nothing to do with the fact of how one can read Edna St. Vincent Millay and not read that poem. But we did! Another time I was reading *The Well of Loneliness* [by Radclyffe Hall] and I wanted to do a book review on it. Miss Delaney said, "My dear, we don't review books like that." What the hell! If you can't review what you want, if schools aren't interested in teaching literature on the level of serious reading, how are we going to get a critic?

I read an article called "The Great Literary Hoax" in *Atlantic* magazine. The guy says every book that comes out is treated as a literary event. Of course, they mostly aren't. If you look at the Nobel list and the Pulitzer list, you'll be lucky if you find two books worth reading. I'm serious! You're a Ph.D. and I would bet that you haven't read ten books on both lists. Nobody does. You know why? Because they're shit. These books get awards because they're safe. But they're shit. The National Book Award list isn't a whole lot better, but at least I was able to read ten or so books on that list. I can't say that for the Pulitzer Prize list. These lists don't reflect our best literature. They don't support excellence in any way, shape, or form. Mediocrity is safe.

If there were just one critic, and it doesn't matter what color, race, none of that, who looked at literature and decided he or she was going to write a book saying what was really great for whatever reason, it would never see the light of day. The critic controls nothing. He or she has to submit their book to a publisher. For example, you have to submit your book to an editor who will probably be Jewish and won't like the fact that you're black. If you were white, you would have to submit it to an editor who probably won't like the fact that you're a woman. Even if you were a white man, you would have to submit it to an editor who probably can't read. Winning is very hard. And I'm just being serious. I'm not saying give up because I'm not a give-up. Something's got to change. Sure, people say what's the point in trying. But of course, there's a point in trying. At some point those of us who are about what is called "truth" have to be as willing to fight for our reality as those who are fighting against us. I could grow up in America and think the Civil War was an awful thing, and I grew up black in Tennessee. And it might be a long time before I'd realize, hey, you motherf—ers are *crazy*! This is *me* you're talking about. I know we're talking about a lot of different things here; it's all got to be connected. Otherwise I could answer yes or no.

Writers have to fight. Nobody's going to tell you that you're going to have to change three words in your book. It doesn't come down like that. People think, "Oh, they're going to mess with my work." They're not. It never happens like that. It's just going to be that you get no response. We who are interested have to be as willing to fight as those who fight against us. "Life is not a problem," as I said in **Cotton Candy** [**on a Rainy Day**]. "It is a process," and we have to make choices. We frequently act like life is a drama, think there's a problem to be resolved with a climax. So we're always dissatisfied because there are no answers.

Is there validity to "For Colored Girls Who Have Considered Suicide When the Rainbow Is Enuf" and "Black Macho and the Myth of the Superwoman," and the subsequent criticism these works incite?

Evidently there is validity or it wouldn't fly. You're essentially asking does it have a motor? It's got to have a motor or it wouldn't fly. Otherwise it'd just sit out on the runway. I have problems with this man-woman thing because I'm stuck on a word. The word's "boring."

I can't think of anything that could interest me less. I've turned down a lot of contracts on this topic. The man-woman thing is a boring subject. It's essentially a dead end. It's going to come down to one of two things: either you're going to take off your clothes or you're not. Men and women do that. Show me a man and a woman and that's what's going to happen. You show me a man without a woman and something else will happen. Show me a woman without a man and something else will happen. But as long as there are men and women, there's no race; there's no color; there's no age. As long as they're men and women, they're going to do what men and women have been doing for the last two million years. This man-woman thing is not even a case of making a mountain out of a mole hill. We don't even have a mole hill yet! It's sort of like cotton candy. We're just spinning around.

I remember in Harlem there used to be these "Save Our Men Meetings" and I was invited to one. I try to get along with people. I'm not as difficult to get along with as people think. I went to the Save Our Men Meeting, and I said, "What are we talking about? Which men do you own? Save my car, yeah. I've got a Peugeot out there on the street, and I'd like to save it. I'd like to save my record collection because I really like it. But I don't *have* a man." I have a *relationship* with a man, and he has a *relationship* with me. Certain things are going to happen to make it either a good or a bad relationship. If it's a good relationship, everybody's happy. If it's a bad one, there's going to be a change.

I'm not inextricably tied to black men. Black women who say "I don't want anybody but a black man" are saying they're afraid because there are men other than black American men. There are men all over the world. If you can't find one, try another. You could just be out of sync. If you're fat and you're living in Paris, you're going to have a problem with men. Because French men like their women thin. Hey, try the Caribbean, where they like them fat.

I loved "For Colored Girls." First of all Ntozake is an extremely bright, sensitive, *good poet*. She writes exceptionally well. She has a lot of developing to do and that's not meant as a negative comment. I don't see how anybody could take it as a negative statement. Furthermore, I don't see how anybody can be overly sensitive about her work. It's really a case of if the shoe fits, you simply have to wear it. I mean that's all she's done. She said, *"Here I am."* Ntozake's naked on that stage. She's naked in that book. And if you don't like it, lump it. "For Colored Girls" is not a love poem. I love it. It's one of my favorite poems. But it's not a love poem.

Ntozake's naked on that stage, but not because she's writing from experience. I resent people who say writers write from experience. Writers don't write from experience, though many are hesitant to admit that they don't. I want to be very clear about this. If you wrote from experience, you'd get maybe one book, maybe three poems. Writers write from empathy. We cheapen anything written when we consider it an experience. Because if it's someone else's experience we don't have to take it seriously. We really don't. We could say, "That's what happened to Ntozake. Isn't that a shame?" No, that's not what happened to Ntozake! I don't know whether it did or it didn't. That's not the point. The point is *that's what happened; that's what still happens*. Writers write because they empathize with the general human condition.

I wrote a poem about a black man, and Don Lee wrote the most asinine thing I've ever read. His criticism was that Nikki Giovanni's problem is that she's had difficulty with a man. *Kirkus Review's* critical response to **The Women and the Men** was "Oh she's just in love." If *Kirkus* never reviews another book of mine I'll be more than happy. My life is not bound in anything that sells for $5.95. And it will never be. No matter what you're seeing, it's not me. If I'm not bigger than my books, I have a problem. I have a serious problem. I don't take my books personally because they're not personal. They reflect what I have seen, and I stand behind them because they are about reality, truth. I'm not America's greatest writer, but I'm credible.

The truth I'm trying to express is not about my life. This is not an autobiography we're talking about. *Gemini* is barely one, and it comes close. It was what I said it was, an autobiographical essay, which is very different from autobiography. Even autobiographies are not real because we only remember what we remember. And the truth has to be bigger than that, and if it isn't there's something wrong with your life. What we remember is only a ripple in a pond. It really is. And where does the last ripple go and who sees it? You never see the end of your own life. We put too much emphasis in the wrong places. And what we do to writers, particularly, is we try to get away from what is being said. We brand them. Of course, I'm back to the critics again.

The point of the writer is to remind us that nuclear energy, for example, is not just some technical, scientific thing, not that Pluto is the last planet and it's freezing, but that such things are comprehensible to the human mind.

We've got to live in the real world. If we don't like the world we're living in, change it. And if we can't change it, we change ourselves. We can do something. If in 1956 I didn't like the way the world was, it was incumbent upon me to at least join a picket line. I didn't have to join a picket line happily. I didn't have to join it with full knowledge of what this could mean to me. None of that was required of me. It was only required that I try to make a change so that ten years later I'll be able to go to Knoxville, Tennessee, and I'll be able to walk down Gay Street without having to move aside for some cracker. And in ten years we did. That was a limited goal, but I won. All I'm trying to say is, okay, if you can't win today, you can win tomorrow. That's all. My obligation is to win, but winning is transitory. What you win today, you start from ground zero on the next plateau tomorrow. That's what people don't want to deal with.

You're only as good as your last book. And that's what writers have a problem with. You say you wrote a book twelve years ago. Hey, I'm real glad, but I want to know what you are doing now. I complained about [Ralph] Ellison in *Gemini* in this regard. And I think it's a valid complaint. God wrote one book. The rest of us are forced to do a little better. You can't live forever on that one book. No matter how interesting, or how great, or how whatever, you are forced to continue, to take a chance. Maybe your next book won't be as good as your last. Who knows?

A lot of people refuse to do things because they don't want to go naked, don't want to go without guarantee. But that's what's got to happen. You go naked until you die. That's the way it goes down. If you don't want to play, you're not forced to. You can always quit. But if you're not going to quit, play. You've got to do one or the other. And it's got to be your choice. You've got to make up your own mind. I made up my mind. If you're going to play, play *all* the way. You're going to sweat, and you're going to get hit, and you're going to fall down. And you're going to be *wrong*. Probably nine times out of ten you're going to be wrong, but it's the tenth time that counts. Because when you come up right, you come up right beautifully. But after that you have to start again. We as black people, we as people, we as the human species have got to get used to the fact we're not going to be right most of the time, not even when our intentions are good. We've got to go naked and see what happens.

Do women writers record human experience in fundamentally different ways than men?

I think men and women are different. I think most of these differences have to do with what would have to be considered as conditioning. A woman writer was expected to write little love stories. She was expected to deal with emotions. Women were not really allowed to encouraged to do anything else. So women's published works went down in a certain way. If you were a woman, and you were identifiably a woman, and you sent a manuscript to a publisher, it was not going to be about Buck Rogers because women didn't write science fiction. It wasn't

Executive Suite [a popular novel published in 1977 by Cameron Hawley], not that *Executive Suite* is a great novel. But women weren't supposed to write business novels. They were supposed to write little homely, lovely novels that were quite safe, and they sold for a quarter and everybody lived happily ever after.

Do you see an evolution in Afro-American writing in terms of theme, craft, perspective?

There has never been a time since we discovered literature that we have not both petitioned white writers and recognized their basic bestiality. As black Americans living in a foreign nation we are, as the wandering Jew, both myth and reality. Black Americans have no home now or ever. We have been here too long to go any place else. I'm not saying we cannot migrate. Twenty of us or 20,000 of us can certainly go to Africa. We can go, but Africa would be a new experience, and we would also be strangers there. This is what black Americans reject. And it's probably human nature to reject the fact that we will always be strangers. But our alienation is our great strength. Our strength is that we are not comfortable any place; therefore, we're comfortable *every place*. We can go any place on earth and find a way to be comfortable.

I'm always saying to the kids—and it's a big joke—that if I were anything from outer space, I would make a point to come into a black community because that's the only place where I would *at least* be given a chance. The first response of black people would not be to shoot me, stamp me out, poison me, or somehow get rid of me. They would be curious about me. They would not do what your average cracker would do which is to wipe me out.

We who are black have to recognize our basic powerlessness, and that's a strength. It's not power; it's strength. We have nothing to protect. What was especially great during the period between '68 and '74 was the mass consciousness that there was nothing for us to protect. We said if the best you have to offer is Richard Nixon, then go to hell! That attitude blew the country's mind. The country said how can we get back to those people. The country sent a lot to us. It sent the women [women's liberation]. It sent "the man." It offered jobs. But you don't hear blacks saying "God Bless America." In fact, nobody cares if the flag goes up or down. When you hear the national anthem, you know we're going to play ball. That's all the anthem seems to be for—to open a ball game. When they finish singing it, the proper expression is "play ball."

Black American consciousness has finally assumed dominance all over the world. I'm serious about this. We're setting the tone. If we function well, we will continue to set it. There's little alternative to the black American consciousness. The alternative is essentially destruction.

We talk about what writers should be doing. Well, we've got to look beyond the block. We've got to do a lot of thinking. You asked a question a while back about my evolution as a writer. A lot has happened. I don't want anybody to think it's just me. It's all of us. It has to do with the way we conceptualize the world. We are earthlings. When Viking II took off we became earthlings. Nobody knows what an earthling is, and how an earthling relates to other earthlings. Is a whale an earthling? If it is, do we have a right to kill it? Is a baby seal an earthling? If it is, is it all right to hit it in the head? And if it's all right to hit a baby seal in the head, which it is, then it's perfectly all right to napalm the Vietnamese. It's also all right to shoot elephants because they're eating up tree bark. We don't have to draw the line. Then it's okay to shoot blacks because they want some land. And if it's not all right, then who's going to stop it?

The choice is between what we do and what they do. As blacks—and I've been consistent on this point—we are not seeking equality. We're seeking superiority. I happen to be a black American chauvinist. I think black Americans are potentially the political tone-setters of the world, though our interest in power has been very low. If black Americans were as interested in power as we are in basketball, we would dominate. There's no question about it. We can do anything we want to do. We ought to quit listening to what people are saying about us. We were talking earlier about *Black Macho*. Hey, they won't even be real. Who will remember? Hey, it's the latest chewing gum. It's Mellow Yellow, the fastest soft drink in the world. So when you look at what we've done as a people, you see we've taken our consciousness and used it for survival.

The fact that we have survived says something for humanity. We are a part of the oldest people on earth, and as black Americans we are also the latest distinct group. Black Americans are different. It's the attitude. The black American attitude is a strange thing. It can really get you. It bothers me sometimes. Everything is so "f—-ing laid-back." But that's a black attitude. Laid-back is not a country or Western attitude. Laid-back is a colored attitude; it always was. It's an attitude blacks have adopted to survive because if we couldn't take it easy, we couldn't take it at all. If we stayed hot, we'd burn up. I'm a hot person and therefore a bit apart from that attitude. I stay hot. I think things can be changed. If you were to look at my personality you'd see I'm always hot. I can't take intolerable situations. Somebody's got to go down. You or me. It "don't" matter. But my attitude, in effect, is not necessarily atypical, if you put me in the group. The group as a whole learns to take it easy. I'm not worried that the white boys are playing with DNA because I'll change them before they change me. I come from a people who learned how to run with hot people.

What makes a poet different from a John Doe who's cleaning gutters?

The fact that I write poetry and do it well makes me different. I dare say I probably wouldn't clean gutters nearly as well. Though if it came to cleaning gutters, I could do it. If I am a better poet, it's because I'm not afraid. If artists are different from ordinary people, that's because we are confident about what we are doing. That's

the difference between what I would consider to be a serious artist and those who are in it for the fun. A lot of people are always into thinking they can become famous. Kids are always asking how one becomes famous. Well, I don't know. You know if you're talking fame, you're not a serious person.

If you didn't think this book is important and that you could do it, you wouldn't be here. You think it's important. I don't have to think it's important and I'm part of it. Margaret doesn't; Gwen doesn't. Nobody has to think it's important but you. It's your book; it's not my book. What people have to realize is, the difference between those who are serious and those who are not is simply that the former take it seriously. It wouldn't matter to you if nobody else took your book seriously. If it did, you wouldn't write it. You wouldn't care if all of us wrote you back and said this is not a serious project. You'd just go out and find yourself fourteen other writers. But we didn't respond to you that way because you take it seriously. But if you had written and said what you think we should do, you wouldn't get a response from anybody. You know people write me and say, "I want to be a writer. What should I write about?" How the hell should I know what one should write about?

Nobody's going to tell me what to write about because it's about me dancing naked on that floor. And if I'm going to be cold, it's going to be because I decided to dance there. And if you don't like to dance, go home. It's that simple. So the artistic attitude is that you take your work seriously. However, we writers would all be better off if we didn't deceive ourselves so frequently by thinking everything we create is important or good. It's not. When you reread something you need to be able to say, "Gee, that wasn't so hot. I thought it was really great ten years ago." But sometimes you can say, "Hey, it's not so bad."

What about the prose?

I don't reread my prose because I'm kind of afraid. I suppose one day I will. At least I would like to think so. But I'm very much afraid to be trapped by what I've said. I don't think life is inherently coherent. I think what Emerson said about consistency being the hobgoblin of little minds is true. The more you reread your prose the more likely you're going to try to justify what you've said. I don't really object to being an asshole. I don't take it personally.

If I never contradict myself then I'm either not thinking or I'm conciliating positions and, therefore, not growing. There has to be a contradiction. There would be no point to having me go three-fourths of the way around the world if I couldn't create an inconsistency, if I hadn't learned anything. If I ever get to the moon, it would be absolutely pointless to have gone to the moon and come back with the same position.

That's been a quarrel I've had with my fellow writers of the sixties. If you didn't learn anything what was the point of going through a decade? If I'm going to be the same at thirty-eight as I was at twenty-eight, what justifies the ten years to myself? And I feel that's who I've got to justify it to—ME.

Though I don't reread my prose, I do reread my poetry. After all that's how I earn my living.

How do you polish the poems?

A poem is a way of capturing a moment. I don't do a lot of revisions because I think if you have to do that then you've got problems with the poem. Rather than polish the words, I take the time to polish the poem. If that means I start at the top a dozen times, that's what I do. A poem's got to be a single stroke, and I make it the best I can because it's going to live. I feel if only one thing of mine is to survive, it's at least got to be an accurate picture of what I saw. I want my camera and film to record what my eye and my heart saw. It's that simple. And I keep working until I have the best reflection I can get. Universality has dimension in that moment.

Do you have a particular writing method—a special place, a special time for writing?

One thing for sure I can say about me is that if my book is going to bust, it's going to bust in public. It is either going to be so bad or so good. That's true of most of my books. Nothing is ever half way with me. It's shit or it's great. That's my attitude. I think that's the only way to go. Now other people are much more cautious. They'll do the safe thing and handle it right. Jean Noble put twelve years into *Beautiful Are the Souls of My Black Sisters*. Jean's book is beautiful, and I'm glad she did. Alex put twelve years in *Roots*. I couldn't be happier he did. I'm glad for Alex; I'm glad for me because I've got galleys. But I could no more put twelve years into anything. Nothing is worth twelve years to me. I can't grow a garden. I can't see waiting that long just for some vegetables. Some people can do it; I'm not one of them. I believe in accepting the limits of my competency.

That's weakness. Yeah, I'll admit it. I just don't get a thrill out of seeing tomatoes grow. I do get a thrill seeing my poems, and I will take the time for them. But if after a year I was working on a poem, not a book but a poem, I would say something's wrong with either the poem or me. That's probably not the best way to be a writer. I wouldn't even want to consider myself an example. I'm essentially undisciplined. I do a lot of thinking, a lot of reading, but I wouldn't recommend my writing method. On the other hand I can't be like Hemingway and get up at six o'clock every morning and write for two hours. He had a wife who got up and cooked his breakfasts. I don't have time to sit there and write for two hours whether I have something to say or not. I write when it's compelling.

I'm not good at moving. I understand why Andrew Wyeth felt that if he left Brandywine he wouldn't be able to paint. It's very difficult for an artist to move. Richard Wright moved to Paris, and people said his work suffered. He didn't live long enough to re-establish his con-

nection with his new place. I think people really overlook this. I never knew Wright, but I'm sure there was a lack of connection. It was very difficult for me to move from Cincinnati to New York. And it was equally difficult for me to move from New York back to Cincinnati. I have to feel at home in order to write. No matter what kind of little shack home is; I have to be at home. I'm very territorial.

How do you regard your audience?

I have always assumed that whoever is listening to a reading of mine, whether it be from my first book [*Black Feeling, Black Talk*] to the most recent, whether a kid or a senior citizen, deserves to hear my best. I think a lot of writers make the assumption that the people in the audience are not generally very bright. So they don't give them their best because they think they won't understand it. I also think there ought to be improvement in every subsequent piece of work.

We were talking about my writing habits. If my next book isn't at least an emotional improvement over my last book, I would never submit it to a publisher. I like to think there's growth. If there's no growth, there's no reason to publish. But I think the people who read me are intelligent. That's one reason I continue to be read because I do make this assumption: if you're reading me, you've got something going for yourself. That's arrogant. Writers are arrogant.

I would really feel badly if somebody said, "Well, I read you in '69 and I'm glad to say, you haven't changed. That would *ruin my day*. That would send me into a glass of something, and I don't drink. I'd have to say who are you and what have you read because I think I've changed. I mentioned Don [Lee] earlier; he doesn't really understand my work. Michele has not read me. There's no way I can be convinced that Michele Wallace has read me. She quoted the wrong books. I have written fifteen books. You can't quote the last book as if it were the first. You can't make a critical judgment based on one book. It doesn't work. She was not only quoting out of context in terms of time, she was quoting out of context in terms of the books. "Black Macho" is bad history.

We were talking about the sixties. I think what happened to a lot of writers—as well as some other people—was they decided what they wrote in '65 was right, and they began to repeat it. If I've grown, and I have, if I share that growth, and I do, then my readers are allowed to grow. I expect growth. I expect a better question from my audience this year than last year. I really do. If I don't get it I'm prone to say, "I'm really bored with you people." I expect intelligence, and I think I have a right to expect it. I don't care if they're paying me. I expect them to be as interested in talking to me, whether they're asking a question or making a statement, as I am in talking to them. And if they're not, one of us is in the wrong place. And since I don't make those kinds of mistakes, it's simple. They can say, "You can't put that on us." I say, "Sure I can, because if I don't who will?"

I have a heavy foot. And the advantage of that is not necessarily that I speed. It's that I will go in the wrong direction fast enough to recognize it and turn around and still beat you. We're going to make mistakes. It's not what so-and-so says that defines a mistake. It's what I decide is an error: that was wrong; that was dumb; that was insensitive; that was stupid. . . . But I've got to go on and try again. That's the only thing we really have to learn.

I'd like to beat the winners. That's the only fun. I wouldn't want to be the only black poet in America. It's not even interesting. I want to be among the best. And it's going to take a lot of poets because we don't even have enough to make a comparison. I'm looking for a golden age, and I would very much like to be a part of it. But there's no race now. In twelve years I produced fifteen books. That's not bad. I would like to have a little more attention.

I'm looking for a golden age, and the only way that's going to happen is for a lot of people to have a lot of different ideas. We don't need just one idea. That's my basic quarrel with some writers, and it remains. We don't need somebody telling us what to think. We need somebody to encourage us to think what we want to think. That was the problem with the black aesthetic. That's why *Negro Digest* went out of business—because it was boring.

On this level you critics do bear responsibility. I'm going to be very clear about this. You critics really praise what you understand. The fact that you understand it is almost suspect. Because once you get the critics all saying, "Well, that's really good," then you have to know something's wrong. If the ideas and concepts of a work are all that comprehensible, then the work hasn't broken any new ground. There has to be something new. That's why Toni Morrison is so great. Alice Walker's *Third Life of Grange Copeland* is great.

That book comes down to Grange, the father, who has to decide that Brownfield is not worth living. Before he will let Brownfield destroy the future, he will kill him. Only Grange could have killed him. He created him and it was an error. That's why pencils have erasers. He said I have made a mistake, but it cannot continue. Now that was a hell of a statement Alice made. A lot of people didn't like it. They can jump on Ntozake, but Ntozake didn't kill him. Alice killed him. She said Brownfield must die. Even *he* recognized that he shouldn't live, but he didn't have the strength to kill himself. It was up to his father. In Toni's *Sula* it is the mother who says, hey, you're a junkie; you've got to go. You're my own and I'm going to take care of you. In *Song of Solomon,* which was comprehensible on most levels, you have Milkman and if anybody should have killed his mother, Milkman should have killed his. Toni made a statement about flying away that people haven't dealt with yet—Milkman's act of wanting to just fly away. We know he didn't. He couldn't have. So where was he? Where is he? That's like the end of a horror movie. Toni made a statement in *Solomon,* but since it is easier to deal with than *Sula* the statement got obscured. *Sula* disturbed the critics because in the beginning there

are two women and at the end there is Nel who remarks that "they were girls together." That's a hell of a statement because black women have never been allowed to say they were girls together in print. Critics have not gotten to Toni yet. They just don't understand Toni. That's probably one of the reasons she is very hesitant to talk to people. I don't blame her. If I wrote a book like that I wouldn't give interviews either. Because somebody is bound to ask a dumb question that shows he or she missed the point of the whole book. "Tell me, Ms. Morrison, why do you think Nel missed Sula?"

In terms of American writers, for the three novels Toni's written, let alone any to come, Toni's in. Who else is writing? Who else is doing it? There's no question. It's black women. What's happening with black women is great. Black women are flying. Ask a black woman what is she doing? She'll say, "I'm going to do what I have to do, and I'm really happy for you; I wish you no harm, but I've got to go." I think we are beginning to unleash a lot of energy because there's going to be competition, especially among black women writers. We haven't gotten to the point where black men and women compete, despite what you hear. The competition is among ourselves. What you're seeing in the media isn't important. Very few black women are writing out of respect or concern for what white people think. I don't care whether the [*New York*] *Times* reviews me or not. If it can review Michele, it doesn't need to review me. If the *Times* can review Michele, there's no way it can review Jean Noble. It had to make a choice, so it took what it understood.

If you look through **Cotton Candy** you'll hear a lot of music. 'Cause if you're in trouble, you don't whistle a happy tune and hold your head erect. You hummm. You hum a basic gospel tune. Can you imagine what a slave ship must have sounded like? Imagine what a slave ship must have sounded like to the women. All the slave-ship stories we've heard so far have been from men. All the men heard was the agony of the men. That's valid. But just imagine what a slave ship must have sounded like to a woman. The humming must have been deafening. It had to be there. The hum, the gospel, the call-and-response came over because it's here. The men didn't bring it over. I'm not knocking the men. They brought the drum for sure. But they didn't bring the hum; they didn't bring the leader-call; they didn't bring the field hollers, because they didn't know them. They were not field men. They were hunters. Hunters don't make noise. So what we're hearing in the music is the women. People have just continued to overlook the impact of the women. We women won't. We women were the ones in the fields in Africa. The music is not something we learned on these shores. We were communal even then, and as we got into bigger fields, we would call to one another. If you didn't answer back, we went to see about you. The hum, the holler, the leader-call are women things. The men didn't do them. Black men were out hunting in Africa, but in America they were in the fields with the women. They learned the women things from women. So what you're hearing in our music is nothing but the sound of a woman calling another woman.

Martha Cook   (essay date 1990)

SOURCE: "Nikki Giovanni: Place and Sense of Place in Her Poetry," in *Southern Women Writers: The New Generation,* University of Alabama Press, 1990, pp. 279-99.

[*In the following essay, Cook discusses the theme of place in Giovanni's poems, arguing that Giovanni's most important poems are not the early, militant poems, but those which are greatly concerned with place, home and family.*]

Nikki Giovanni's poetry has been most often viewed by literary critics in the tradition of militant black poetry; the first serious critical article on her work, in fact, is R. Roderick Palmer's "The Poetry of Three Revolutionists: Don L. Lee, Sonia Sanchez, and Nikki Giovanni" (*College Language Association Journal,* September 1971). More recent critics, especially Suzanne Juhasz in her *Naked and Fiery Forms: Modern American Poetry by Women, A New Tradition* (1976), have emphasized the developing feminism in Giovanni's poems. No critic has yet focused on what I see as the key to reading Giovanni, her position in the rich tradition of Southern poetry, proceeding unbroken from Richard Lewis in the eighteenth century through Poe, Henry Timrod, and Sidney Lanier, on through the Fugitives and Jean Toomer, down to James Dickey and Ishmael Reed today. By focusing specifically on the sense of place, a vital element in Southern literature, I have identified a group of poems that represents Giovanni at her best, technically and thematically.

Before looking at specific themes, subjects, images, and symbols, I should survey the significant aspects of Nikki Giovanni's life and career. She was born on 7 June 1943 in Knoxville, Tennessee, to a middle-class black couple, Jones Giovanni, a probation officer, and his wife, Yolande, a social worker. It is clearly a mark of Giovanni's respect for her mother that she sometimes gives her formal name as Yolande Cornelia Giovanni, Jr. When she was young, the family lived "in Wyoming, Ohio, which is a suburb of Cincinnati, which some say is a suburb of Lexington, Kentucky." [Unless otherwise indicated, autobiographical material is taken from *Gemini*] Later they moved to the black community of Lincoln Heights. Nikki often visited her much-beloved Watson grandparents in Knoxville and attended Austin High School there. She closely identified her grandparents with their home on Mulvaney Street; when her grandmother Louvenia was forced by urban renewal to move to Linden Avenue, Giovanni explained her own feelings of displacement: "There was no familiar smell in that house." Giovanni's Southern roots were further strengthened during her years at Fisk University in Nashville. She began college immediately after high school; though difficulties in maturing during the turbulence of the 1960s resulted in a gap in her college work, she eventually graduated with honors in history in 1967. She is remembered for her radical activities on campus, especially her role in reestablishing the Fisk chapter of the Student Nonviolent Coordinating Committee. She also studied with John Killens and edited the Fisk literary magazine.

Giovanni continued her involvement in the civil rights movement of the 1960s, primarily through her writing. Right out of college, she began publishing articles, poems, and book reviews in journals such as *Negro Digest* and *Black World.* Consistently attacking elitism in the black arts movement, she praised writers whom she viewed as presenting a realistic yet positive picture of black life, both new voices, such as Louise Meriwether, author of the 1970 novel *Daddy Was a Number Runner,* and established ones, such as Dudley Randall. During the late 1960s, she worked to organize the first Cincinnati Black Arts Festival and the New Theatre in that city, as well as a black history group in Wilmington, Delaware. She also took courses at the University of Pennsylvania School of Social Work and the Columbia University School of Fine Arts and taught at Queens College of the City University of New York and Livingston College of Rutgers University.

Randall's Broadside Press, invaluable for its support and encouragement of black poetry, brought out two small collections of Giovanni's poems, ***Black Feeling, Black Talk*** (1968), which she had first printed privately, and ***Black Judgement*** (1969), including many poems that contributed to Giovanni's early reputation as a militant poet who advocated the violent overthrow of the white power structure in America. Many readers found these poems exciting and inspiring, and the poet Don L. Lee pointed [in *Dynamits Voices I: Black Poets of the 1960s,* 1971] to "lines that suggest the writer has a real, serious commitment to her people and to the institutions that are working toward the liberation of Black people." However, he goes on, "when the Black poet chooses to serve as political seer, he must display a keen sophistication. Sometimes Nikki oversimplifies and therefore sounds rather naive politically." Giovanni offered further support for fellow black writers by founding a publishing cooperative, NikTom, Ltd. One of its significant projects is her edition of a collection of poems by black women, *Night Comes Softly: Anthology of Black Female Voices* (1970), with contributors ranging in age from seventeen to eighty-four, from unknowns to Sonia Sanchez to Gwendolyn Brooks.

In addition to her literary creations, Giovanni marked her twenty-fifth year by having a child, though she did not marry his father. She was living in New York, where she was writing poetry and serving on the editorial board of the journal *Black Dialogue.* One suspects that the humor used to describe her pregnancy and the birth of her son in the essay "Don't Have a Baby Till You Read This" masks to some degree the fears and uneasiness with which she faced life as a single parent. However, she amusingly recounts planning for a daughter's birth in New York, but giving birth prematurely to a son while visiting her parents in Ohio. Through this experience, she learns that one is always a child to one's parents; finally, she asserts herself and goes "home" to New York with her own child. Of her decision to have a child alone, she said later [in Peter Bailey's "Nikki Giovanni: 'I am Black, Female, Polite . . . ,' *Ebony,* February 1972], "'I had a baby at 25 because I *wanted* to have a baby and I could *afford* to have a baby. I did not get married because I didn't *want* to get married and I could *afford* not to get married.'" Giovanni has remained unmarried and has consistently viewed her single motherhood as a positive choice.

By 1969, Sheila Weller [in "To Be a Poet," *Mademoiselle,* December 1969] had called Giovanni "one of the most powerful figures on the new black poetry scene—both in language and appeal." Weller goes on to indicate that the woman she is interviewing is not the woman she expected from reading her poetry: "The tense anger that wires many of Nikki's poems is in direct contrast to the warm calm she generates." Giovanni said of herself at the time of the interview, "'I've changed a lot over the last few months.'" When her next volume of poetry, *Re: Creation* (1970), was published by Broadside, a reviewer for *Black World* [February 1971] was concerned that the poems were not so radical and militant as those in Giovanni's earlier volumes, describing the poet as transformed "into an almost declawed, tamed Panther with bad teeth," yet conceding, "a Panther with bad teeth is still quite deadly." Seeing her changes as positive rather than negative, as strengthening her work rather than weakening it, *Time* noted in a 1970 article on black writers ["The Undaunted Pursuit of Fury," 6 April 1970] that "already some, like Nikki Giovanni, are moving away from extreme political activism toward more compassionate and universal themes."

In 1970, the firm William Morrow issued Giovanni's first two Broadside books under the title *Black Feeling, Black Talk/ Black Judgement.* This publication, followed in 1971 by the prose volume *Gemini: An Extended Autobiographical Statement on My First Twenty-Five Years of Being a Black Poet* (Bobbs-Merrill), brought her such attention as a lengthy review by Martha Duffy in *Time* ["Hustler and Fabulist," 17 January 1972]. Duffy particularly praises the autobiographical sections of *Gemini,* emphasizing: "On the subject of her childhood, Miss Giovanni is magical. She meanders along with every appearance of artlessness, but one might as well say that Mark Twain wrote shaggy-dog stories." Of Giovanni's propagandistic writing, Duffy observes: "Hers is a committed social rage. She is capable of scalding rhetoric, but the artist in her keeps interrupting."

The year 1971 also marked the publication of Giovanni's first volume of poetry for children, *Spin a Soft Black Song*. The poems, enhanced by excellent illustrations by Charles Bible, offer realistic images of black urban life and positive images of black identity. The same year, she recorded the first of several poetry readings combined with gospel music or jazz. "Truth Is on Its Way" includes a number of poems from Giovanni's Broadside volumes, with music by the New York Community Choir under the direction of Benny Diggs. According to *Harper's Bazaar* [in Gwen Mazer's "Lifestyle: Nikki Giovanni," July 1972], Giovanni introduced the album at a free concert in a church in Harlem. Following her performance, "the audience shouted its appreciation."

Peter Bailey summed up Giovanni's public role as follows: "Nikki, the poet, has become a personality, a *star*." At that time, in 1972, Giovanni seemed to see herself in the tradition of confessional poetry, like so many twentieth-century American women poets, but with the particular

perspective of the black American: "'When I write poetry, . . . I write out of my own experiences—which also happen to be the experiences of my people. But if I had to choose between my people's experiences and mine, I'd choose mine, because that's what I know best.'" Her next volume of poems is entitled *My House* (1972). In the introduction, Ida Lewis, editor and publisher of *Encore,* for which Giovanni was serving as an editorial consultant, calls her "the Princess of Black Poetry," saying lightheartedly: "I've seen Nikki mobbed in Bloomingdale's department store by Black and white customers; I've walked with her down Fifth Avenue and watched a man who was saying 'hi' to her walk into an oncoming taxi." Yet Lewis concludes in a serious vein, emphasizing that Giovanni "writes about the central themes of our times, in which thirty million Blacks search for self-identification and self-love." The star, the princess, at the age of twenty-nine was taken seriously enough to be awarded an honorary doctorate by Wilberforce University, the oldest black institution of higher education in America. Even after the publication of her next two volumes of poetry, Alex Batman [in *Dictionary of Literary Biography,* vol. 5] considered *My House* her "finest work."

Giovanni's next album, "Like a Ripple on a Pond," again with the New York Community Choir, features selections from *My House*. The volume and the album were criticized by *Black World* [July 1974] reviewer Kalamu ya Salaam for failing to live up to the promise of Giovanni's earlier work. Salaam is particularly hard on the poems, citing their sentimentality and romanticism. He is accurate in some cases, yet he is harshly critical of the sequence of African poems that other critics have seen as one of the strongest elements of the volume. Giovanni's next volume of poetry for children, *Ego-Tripping and Other Poems for Young People* (1973), includes a selection of previously published poems illustrated by George Ford. The title poem is an especially good example of her theme of racial pride and her interest in the places associated with her African heritage.

In 1971, Giovanni had taped a program for the WNET series "Soul!"; this appearance was transcribed, edited, and published in 1973 as *A Dialogue: James Baldwin/ Nikki Giovanni*. The volume offers insight into both the works and the personal lives of these two important black writers, as does a similar volume apparently inspired by that experience, *A Poetic Equation: Conversations between Nikki Giovanni and Margaret Walker,* published by Howard University Press in 1974. The latter is perhaps the more interesting, as it gives these black women writers of succeeding generations the opportunity to react to contemporary political and literary issues.

The early 1970s were clearly a period of change and growth for Giovanni, as she was coming to terms with the legacy of civil rights activism and her own personal concerns as a woman and a mother. In 1973, a number of public figures were asked by *Mademoiselle* to describe their views of the previous decade in a so-called epitaph. Giovanni's contribution, a mock radio-drama called "Racism: The Continuing Saga of the American Dream," was obviously a difficult chore; she commented [in "The 60's: Over and Out . . . ," *Mademoiselle*, May 1973], "'I had to use a light touch. To approach the '60s any other way right now would be too painful.'" A warmer side of Giovanni is seen in her contribution to a *Mademoiselle* [December 1973] feature entitled "A Christmas Memory," where she concludes, "Christmas to me is a special link to the past and a ritual for our future."

During this period of increasing strength in the feminist movement in America, Giovanni seems to have become more aware of the personal and political significance of sex roles and of sex discrimination. "'Roles between men and women are changing. . . . We no longer need categories,'" she said in an interview [with Mazar]. "'There is no reason why my son can't cook and rock with his teddy bear as well as swim and play ball.'" Giovanni's next volume of poetry, *The Women and the Men* (1975), reflects her growing awareness of such issues but also hints at difficulties in the creative process. Three years after *My House*, she offers a volume including a number of poems from the 1970 *Re: Creation* (which did deserve wider circulation than it had received); the new poems do not generally demonstrate meaningful development in theme or technique. Yet *The Women and the Men* brought Giovanni further attention in the media, including prepublication of three poems in *Mademoiselle* (September 1975). Jay S. Paul [in *Contemporary Poets,* 1980] has called it "her richest collection of poems." The mid-seventies also produced another album, "The Way I Feel," with accompanying music by Arif Mardin and liner notes by Roberta Flack.

In addition to Giovanni's growing concern with feminist themes, in the 1970s, she further explored her heritage as a black American. In *Gemini,* she writes of her father's journey from Ohio to Knoxville College as a journey to his "spiritual roots"—his grandfather had been a slave in eastern Tennessee—and also tells the story of how her maternal grandparents were forced to leave Georgia because her grandmother refused to submit to white domination. Another essay in the volume describes her own trip to Haiti in search of "sunshine and Black people"; feeling like a foreigner, she went on to Barbados, where she gained a deeper understanding of the sense of displacement of West Indian immigrants in American society, clearly analogous to the position of blacks who were brought to this country as slaves. In 1975, she traveled to Africa, where she spoke in several countries, including Ghana, Zambia, Tanzania, and Nigeria.

Giovanni continued to receive recognition in the mid-1970s, with, for example, honorary doctorates from the University of Maryland, Princess Anne Campus, Ripon University, and Smith College. Another honor was more controversial. According to Jeanne Noble [in *Beautiful Also Are the Souls of My Black Sisters . . .* , 1978], "Nikki's winning the Ladies' Home Journal Woman of the Year Award in 1974 meant to some young revolutionaries that she was joining forces with the very people she often considered foes. But, she does not shun confrontation or even violence if whites provoke it." In fact, Giovanni had for some time been more concerned with broader themes

of identity and self-knowledge than with her earlier militancy, though she remained politically active. "While her poetry is full of Black pride," *African Woman* [May/June 1978] explains, "she transcends colour to deal with the challenge of being human."

Giovanni's next volume of poetry, *Cotton Candy on a Rainy Day* (1978), represents a definite, if not wholly positive, change. Paula Giddings's introduction emphasizes the development she sees in Giovanni and her work: "If Nikki, in her idealism, was a child of the sixties then now, in her realism, she is a woman of the seventies." She also notes, "*Cotton Candy* is the most introspective book to date, and the most plaintive." Alex Batman describes the distinctive features of this volume in a similar way: "One feels throughout that here is a child of the 1960s mourning the passing of a decadeof conflict, of violence, but most of all, of hope. Such an attitude, of course, may lend itself too readily to sentimentality and chauvinism, but Giovanni is capable of countering the problems with a kind of hard matter-of-factness about the world that has passed away from her and the world she now faces."

Giddings further says of the *Cotton Candy* volume that it represents "the private moments: of coming to terms with oneself—of living with oneself. Taken in the context of Nikki's work it completes the circle: of dealing with society, others and finally oneself." Giddings's description of Giovanni's work may reveal why her development of new themes and techniques was slow. Perhaps she had to come to terms with herself, doing so to a certain degree through her poetry, before she could truly deal with others and with society. Indeed, her poetry is in many ways a mirror of the social consciousness of the 1960s, followed by the self-centeredness of the 1970s. Yet Giddings's comments do not predict what might follow such an inwardly focused collection, what one might expect from Giovanni's poetry in the 1980s. Anna T. Robinson, in a short monograph entitled *Nikki Giovanni: From Revolution to Revelation,* [1979] believes that *Cotton Candy* is "a pivotal work in Nikki Giovanni's career. It will mandate that she be evaluated as a poet rather than a voice for a cause."

The title of the volume *Cotton Candy on a Rainy Day* is ironic; the poems are not lighthearted or optimistic, as the positive connotations of cotton candy suggest. Giovanni's next volume has an ambiguous and perhaps also ironic title, *Those Who Ride the Night Winds* (1983). Having read *Cotton Candy on a Rainy Day*, one might anticipate a journey into the further gloom night can symbolize. However, the dedication indicates that night may offer possibilities not readily apparent: "This book is dedicated to the courage and fortitude of those who ride the night winds—who are the day trippers and midnight cowboys— who in sonic solitude or the hazy hell of habit know— that for all the devils and gods—for all the illnesses and drugs to cure them—Life is a marvelous, transitory adventure—and are determined to push us into the next century, galaxy—possibility." The form of the poems shows an interesting development in technique. Most are written in long verse paragraphs with abundant ellipsis marks, a stream-of-consciousness form that is not traditionally "poetic" but produces a sense of openness and forward movement with thematic significance.

The reasons behind the changes in Giovanni's poetry between the 1978 and 1983 volumes may well lie in her decision to move back to Lincoln Heights with her son and share her parents' home after her father suffered a stroke. Although she maintained an apartment in New York City, she devoted time, energy, and money to making a place for herself in Ohio again. She has more than once spoken of the difficulties she has encountered in this situation, not to complain, but simply to explain. For example, she said in 1981 [in Stephanie J. Stokes's "My House': Nikki Giovanni," *Essence*, August 1981], "'No matter what the situation is or what the financial arrangements are, you are always their child. . . . If you're in your parents' house or they're in yours, it's still a parent-child relationship.'" When her son was born, Giovanni apparently needed to assert her independence, but she had matured enough not to feel her sense of identity threatened by her family. Though she spoke [in Claudia Tate's interview in *Black Women Writers at Work*, 1983] of the need "to feel at home in order to write," she seems to have made the adjustment rapidly, for during that period, she published her third volume for children, new poems with the title *Vacation Time* (1980).

The poems in *Those Who Ride the Night Winds* transcend such categories as black/white, male/female, reality/fantasy. "In this book," Mozella G. Mitchell [in *Dictionary of Literary Biography*, vol. 41] points out, "Giovanni has adopted a new and innovative form; and the poetry reflects her heightened self knowledge and imagination." A look down the table of contents reveals new kinds of subjects, with poems to Billie Jean King, John Lennon, and Robert F. Kennedy, as well as to Lorraine Hansberry, Martin Luther King, Jr., and Rosa Parks. Having once stated that she wrote primarily from personal or at least from racial experiences, Giovanni recently contradicted herself [in the Tate interview] in the best Emersonian sense: "I resent people who say writers write from experience. Writers don't write from experience, though many are hesitant to admit that they don't. I want to be very clear about this. If you wrote from experience, you'd get maybe one book, maybe three poems. Writers write from empathy. . . . Writers write because they empathize with the general human condition." *Those Who Ride the Night Winds* is an impressive illustration of the effectiveness of that kind of empathy and the value of change. "'Only a fool doesn't change,'" Giovanni once commented. [in M. Cordell Thompson's "Nikki Giovanni: Black Rebel with Power in Poetry," *Jet* 25 May 1972] In the preface to this volume of poems, she alludes to both Lewis Carroll and the Beatles as she announces: "I changed . . . I chart the night winds . . . glide with me . . . I am the walrus . . . the time has come . . . to speak of many things . . ." Having changed, Giovanni has reached maturity as a poet, with a volume that satisfies the reader, yet promises more complex and challenging poems in the future.

Giovanni has continued to receive recognition for her work in the 1980s in the academic world, with honorary doctor-ates from the College of Mount St. Joseph on-the-Ohio and Mount St. Mary College, and with teaching positions at Ohio State University, Mount St. Joseph, and Virginia Polytechnic Institute and State University. She also continues to reach the larger world outside the academy, as indicated by her being named to the Ohio Women's Hall of Fame and as the Outstanding Woman of Tennessee, both in 1985. She was chosen co-chairperson of the Literary Arts Festival for Homecoming '86 in Tennessee, the Duncanson Artist-in-Residence of the Taft Museum in Cincinnati in 1986, and a member of the Ohio Humanities Council in 1987.

Some of these honors and positions indicate that Nikki Giovanni has maintained close ties with the South of her birthplace, despite having lived more years away from the South than in it. What the South as a place means to her is of considerable significance in looking at the body of her poetry. Like many writers of the Southern Literary Renaissance before her, Giovanni left the South after her graduation from college. Louis D. Rubin, Jr., speaking of earlier writers such as Allen Tate and Robert Penn Warren, has pointed out: [in "Southern literature: the Historical Image," in *South: Modern Southern Literature in its Cultural Setting*, 1961] "Almost all the young Southern writers at one time or another packed their suitcases and headed for the cities of the Northeast, toward the center of modernity, toward the new. Some turned around and came back to stay; others remained." These remarks apply to succeeding generations of Southern writers, such as William Styron and Ralph Ellison, and on to Alice Walker and Nikki Giovanni, who continue to be influenced by the South and their often ambivalent feelings toward it, even though they may have felt compelled to leave.

The ambivalence of black Southerners toward the region has been in the past compared to the way Jews might feel about Germany: "They love the South . . . for its beauty, its climate, its fecundity and its better ways of life; but they hate, with a bitter corroding hatred, the color prejudice, the discrimination, the violence, the crudities, the insults and humiliations, and the racial segregation of the South, and they hate all those who keep these evils alive,". [George Schuyler, "What the Negro Thinks of the South," in *Black American Literature: Essays, Poetry, Fiction, Drama*, 1970] Though the South has changed, there has been much in Giovanni's lifetime to cause pain for the black Southerner. Still she has acknowledged the South as a symbolic home, commenting earthily: "I can deal with the South because I love it. And it's the love of someone who lived there, who was born there, who lost her cherry there and loved the land. . . ." In the opening essay of *Gemini*, Giovanni describes "going home" to speak in Knoxville, Tennessee, and looking for familiar place—Vine Street, the Gem Theatre, Mulvaney Street. "All of that is gone now," she realizes. Even so, after a tour of the city, "I was exhausted but feeling quite high from being once again in a place where no matter what I belong. And Knoxville belongs to me. I was born there in Old Knoxville General and I am buried there with Louvenia. . . . And I thought Tommy, my son, must know about this. He must know we come from somewhere. That we belong."

This theme of belonging has occurred in Giovanni's poetry since the beginning, in poems set in the South and in other places as well. The best of her poetry throughout her career has been concrete, with references to specific places, rooms, furniture, people, colors, qualities of light and dark. When she is abstract, her poetry is sometimes still successful in a political but not a critical sense. This kind of concreteness has been identified as one of the essential elements in Southern literature by Robert B. Heilman, in a seminal study entitled "The Southern Temper," where he distinguishes between what he terms "a sense of the concrete" and merely employing concrete images. The overriding importance of place in Southern literature has often been noted, for example, by Frederick J. Hoffman, whose essay "The Sense of Place" is a landmark in the criticism of modern Southern poetry and fiction. Looking closely at the body of Giovanni's poetry, one finds places large and small, houses and continents, places she has lived in or traveled to, places important in the history of black people, places from the past and in the present, metaphorical places, places of fantasy, symbolic places. To emphasize this sense of place in her work is to see it, along with the best literature of the South, not as provincial but as universal.

While Giovanni has received more attention first for her militant poems on racial themes and later for her feminist writing, the poems that will finally determine her position in the canon of American poetry are, almost without exception, ones in which place functions not only as a vehicle, but also as a theme. In her most recent work, her themes are becoming increasingly complex, reflecting her maturity as a woman and as a writer. Traditionally in Southern writing, place has been associated with themes of the past and the family; these themes are seen in Giovanni's poems of the late 1960s and the early 1970s, with the added dimension of a desire to understand the faraway places from which black slaves were brought to the American South. Her later poetry reflects a changing consciousness of her role in society as a single woman, the need to adjust her concept of home and family and of the importance of smaller places, such as houses and rooms, to fit her own life, a life that many American women and men, black and white, can identify with. In her best poems, places grow into themes that convey the universal situation of modern humanity, a sense of placelessness and a need for security.

In her first collection of poems, Giovanni expresses themes anticipated by the title *Black Feeling, Black Talk*. But already she demonstrates occasionally her gift for the original, individual image, for example, as she evokes the days and places of childhood in **"Poem (For BMC No. 2)"**:

> There were fields where once we walked
> Among the clover and crab grass and those
> Funny little things that look like cotton candy
>
> There were liquids expanding and contracting
> In which we swam with amoebas and other Afro-
>   Americans

This poem is a striking contrast to the best-known poem from this volume, **"The True Import of Present Dialogue, Black vs. Negro (For Peppe, Who Will Ultimately Judge Our Efforts),"** with its repetition of the lines "Nigger / Can you kill." Like **"Nikki-Rosa"** and **"Knoxville, Tennessee"** from her next volume, **"Poem (For BMC No. 2)"** recalls a time and place that endure in memory, even in the face of violence and hatred.

One of Giovanni's finest poems is set in this homeland of the past. **"Knoxville, Tennessee,"** written at the height of the unrest of the civil rights movement of the 1960s, develops a theme of security, of belonging, through simple yet highly effective images of nature, of family, of religion. Although it is almost imagistic, it builds to an explicit thematic statement:

> I always like summer
> best
> you can eat fresh corn
> from daddy's garden
> and okra
> and greens
> and cabbage
> and lots of
> barbecue
>
>   . . . . .
>
> and be warm
> all the time
> not only when you go to bed
> and sleep

The simple diction, the soothing alliteration, the short lines to emphasize each word, all create a feeling of love for this place and these people that transcends topical issues.

Giovanni later wrote a prose description of Christmas in Knoxville using images of winter rather than summer, yet conveying the same feeling of warmth: "Christmas in Knoxville was the smell of turnip greens and fatback, perfume blending with good Kentucky bourbon, cigars and cigarettes, bread rising on the new electric stove, the inexplicable smell of meat hanging in the smokehouse (though we owned no smokehouse), and, somehow, the sweet taste of tasteless snow." As Roger Whitlow notes, [in *Black American Literature: A Critical History,* 1973] though, this kind of warmth is "rare" in Giovanni's early work. Still, Giovanni's use of this Southern place from her past speaks to the same aspects of Southern life as poems by James Dickey or prose by Eudora Welty.

Most of the poems in *Black Judgment* are militant in subject and theme; one of the most effective is **"Adulthood (For Claudia),"** in which Giovanni catalogs the violence of the decade, the deaths of leaders from Patrice Lumumba to John F. Kennedy to Martin Luther King, Jr., and of lesser-known civil rights workers such as Viola Liuzzo. In another poem from this volume, **"For Saundra,"** Giovanni seems to explain why poems of political rhetoric dominate her first two volumes. The persona speaks of the difficulty of composing poems in revolutionary times; for example,

> So i thought
> i'll write a beautiful green tree poem
> peeked from my window
> to check the image
> noticed the schoolyard was covered
> with asphalt
> no green—no trees grow
> in manhattan

She concludes that "perhaps these are not poetic / times / at all." Although the thrust of the poem is toward the civil rights strife of the late 1960s, the reader also senses something of the alienation and displacement of a Southerner in the urban North.

Giovanni uses the South and its people to develop the specific theme of the past in **"Alabama Poem"** from her next collection, *Re: Creation*. A student at Tuskegee Institute meets an old black man and then an old black woman whose remarks indicate that knowledge must be gained through experience, must be inherited from the past. The persona speculates in conclusion: "if trees would talk / wonder what they'd tell me." Her words do not seem ironic; rather she seems to have learned a valuable lesson in her walk along this Southern country road. Though the images in this poem are sparse, the rural place and its people are seen to be of vital significance to one who seeks knowledge. The theme of the necessity of learning from the past what one needs to live in the present links this poem by Nikki Giovanni to a rich tradition in Southern writing, especially from the Fugitive poets of the 1920s to the present.

A more challenging use of the concreteness of place and the thematic significance of the past can be seen in the complex, ironic poem **"Walking Down Park,"** also from *Re:Creation*. Speculating about the history of New York City, the speaker wonders what a street such as Park Avenue looked like "before it was an avenue," "what grass was like before / they rolled it / into a ball and called / it central park." She even thinks:

> ever look south
> on a clear day and not see
> time's squares but see
> tall birch trees with sycamores
> touching hands

Questioning why men destroy their environment, she returns to days of the past, musing, "probably so we would forget / the Iroquois, Algonquin / and Mohicans who could caress / the earth." Possibly this relationship with nature, which characterized the Indians of an earlier time, can be recaptured:

> ever think what Harlem would be
> like if our herbs and roots and elephant ears
> grew sending
> a cacophony of sound to us

Here through a complex set of images Giovanni connects the situation of blacks in contemporary America with the past of the American Indian, another oppressed minority group, as well as with their African heritage. **"Walking Down Park"** thus becomes a statement of a longing for happiness, related in the mind of the speaker not only to life in the past, which allowed for a closeness to nature lost in contemporary urban life, but also to a specific place from the past—Africa.

One of the most important examples of the ways Giovanni employs places in her poetry is her use of houses, both literal and metaphorical, from the past and in the present. In **"Housecleaning,"** another poem from *Re: Creation*, the persona speaks first of her pleasure in ordinary chores essential to maintaining a house, then turns tidying up into a metaphor to describe aptly the chores necessary in human relationships as well. The growing sense of independence and identity in this poem anticipates the major themes of Giovanni's next volume, *My House*.

At this point, in the early 1970s, Giovanni is still using the lowercase "i," which R. Roderick Palmer identifies [in "The Poetry of Three Revolutionists: Don L. Lee, Sonia Sanchez, and Nikki Giovanni," *College Language Association Journal*, September 1971] as a common device in revolutionary poetry, more then the uppercase. Perhaps she intends to symbolize the concept she has often invoked, that one retains qualities of childhood, even when striving for maturity. She uses this device in a poem from *My House* set, as is **"Knoxville, Tennessee,"** in a place that now exists only in memory. In **"Mothers,"** Giovanni depicts a woman remembering her mother sitting in a kitchen at night:

> she was sitting on a chair
> the room was bathed in moonlight diffused through
> those thousands of panes landlords who rented
> to people with children were prone to put in
>   windows

Recalling a poem her mother taught her on this particular night, the persona determines to teach the same poem to her son, to establish with him the relationship she had with her mother. This relationship is re-created for the reader in the simple description of a place remembered, especially in the quality of light Giovanni uses as the central image of the poem.

In the title poem, Giovanni uses homes and houses to represent the movement toward maturity, symbolized by the movement away from the places, homes, of one's childhood toward establishing a home for oneself, or an identity as a mature person. Like Giovanni's poems about childhood, **"My House"** is characterized by images of warmth and security, emphasizing that in her house the speaker is in complete control:

> i mean it's my house
> and i want to fry pork chops
> and bake sweet potatoes
> and call them yams

cause i run the kitchen
and i can stand the heat

. . . . .

and my windows might be dirty
but it's my house
and if i can't see out sometimes
they can't see in either

As Suzanne Juhasz emphasizes, [in *Naked and fiery forms* . . . , 1976] the woman speaker "orders experience and controls it. . . . She controls not only through need and desire, but through strength, ability. . . ." In contrast to the child persona of **"Knoxville, Tennessee,"** the "i" here has discovered that she is an autonomous being who can shape at least the smaller places of her world to suit her own needs and desires; at the same time, the "i" is willing to take responsibility for her actions, to pay the price for such control.

In this context, the title poem of the volume *My House* takes on a deeper level of meaning. In fact, Erlene Stetson has identified [in the tradition to *Black Sister: Poetry by Black American Women, 1746-1980,* 1981] the house as a dominant symbol in poetry by women, especially black women, explaining: "The house represents the historic quest by black women for homes of their own—apart from the house of slavery, the common house of bondage, the house of the patriarchy. The house embodies women's search for place and belonging and for a whole and complete identity. . . . In addition, the house is a symbol for place—heaven, haven, home, the heart, women's estate, the earthly tenement, the hearth—and for region—Africa, the West Indies, America, Asia, the North, and the South." Stetson does not emphasize, as she might, that this use of place as symbol is particularly significant in the tradition of Southern literature to which Nikki Giovanni and a number of other black women poets belong.

Many of Giovanni's poems are set, as I have mentioned, in Africa. For Giovanni, as for black Southerners and other black Americans in the twentieth century, the significance of this place lies mostly in the past—a past with which each individual must come to terms. Like other Southern writers in the period since World War I, Giovanni recognizes that no one can live in the past or relive the past, yet there is no meaningful life in the present or the future without an understanding of, often involving a confrontation with, the past. In a three-poem sequence in *My House*, she creates powerful images of the displacement of a people who in their racial past were forced to leave their homeland involuntarily.

The first poem in the group, **"Africa I,"** describes a plane journey to Africa. During the flight, the speaker dreams of seeing a lion from the plane but is jarred by the statement of a companion that "there are no lions / in this part of africa." Her response is quick: "it's my dream dammit." The poem closes at the journey's end, with the following thoughts:

we landed in accra and the people
clapped and i almost cried wake up
we're home
and something in me said shout
and something else said quietly
your mother may be glad to see you
but she may also remember why
you went away

Seeing Africa as a woman, a mother, as she did in the fantasy poem **"Ego-Tripping,"** Giovanni movingly illustrates how the significance of this place relates to the past of these tourists, visitors, just as the significance of an adult's mother usually lies more in the past than in the present. In one's personal past as well as in one's racial past may exist harsh memories difficult to confront. Yet coming to terms with the past is necessary in order to grow and mature, as an individual or as a people.

"They Clapped," the third poem in this sequence, demonstrates even more explicitly that the dream of Africa and the reality, the past and the present, are not the same. The black American tourists clap because they are so happy to be landing in "the mother land"; then they see the realities of poverty and disease, as well as of their own foreignness. As they leave to return to America, they appear to have come to terms with the past in a way that frees them for their lives now and later. Giovanni uses the metaphor of possession, a subtle allusion to the horrors of slavery in the past, to convey the theme of displacement:

they brought out their cameras and bought out
   africa's drums
when they finally realized they are strangers all
   over
and love is only and always about the lover not the
   beloved
they marveled at the beauty of the people and the
   richness
of the land knowing they could never possess either

they clapped when they took off
for home despite the dead
dream they saw a free future

So the physical confrontation with this place serves to make these tourists aware of their historical past as past rather than as present or future. They have learned too that, as modern men and women, they are "strangers all over," that in a very important sense they do not belong anywhereexcept in the place they must create for themselves as individuals. Thus Giovanni reminds the reader that the visitors to Africa are returning home, to America.

Many of the best poems in Giovanni's next volume, *The Women and the Men*, such as **"Ego-Tripping"** and **"Walking Down Park,"** originally appeared in *Re: Creation*. The new African poems, including **"Africa"** and **"Swaziland,"** are less successful than the Africa sequence in *My House* because they depend more on abstract diction than concrete images to convey themes. Yet one new symbolic poem, **"Night,"** uses complex metaphorical language to contrast New York City with Africa and the Caribbean. The latter are both portrayed as places where the night is strong, natural, black:

> in africa night walks
> into day as quickly
> as a moth is extinguished
> by its desire for flame
>
> the clouds in the caribbean carry
> night like a young man
> with a proud erection dripping
> black dots across the blue sky
> the wind a mistress of the sun howls
> her displeasure at the involuntary
> fertilization

In contrast, the night in New York is seen to be unnaturally white, with humans being unable to adjust to their environment:

> but nights are white
> in new york
> the shrouds of displeasure
> mask our fear of facing
> ourselves between the lonely
> sheets

Again Giovanni contrasts the natural environment of the warm Southern country and continent with the literal and metaphorical cold of the urbanized northeastern United States, dominated by white culture. The images of masking and of death suggest that no one, black or white, can live a meaningful life in a place like New York. However, the negative images in the earlier sections of the poem—death, rape—reveal the generally grim situation for modern man or woman in Africa, in the Caribbean, anywhere.

Perhaps acknowledging the desire to succumb to loneliness, to the temptations of the solitary life, allowed Giovanni herself to move forward, to change in a way that profoundlyaffected her poetic subject matter and technique.

—Martha Cook

The volume *Cotton Candy on a Rainy Day* contains mostly poems relying on images of placelessness or homelessness rather than security, or dominated by ideas rather than strong central images. The title poem sets a fairly pessimistic tone for the volume yet hints at what may follow in Nikki Giovanni's career. Characterizing the seventies as a decade of loneliness, Giovanni uses the image of cotton candy poignantly:

> But since it is life   it is
>   Cotton Candy

> on a rainy day
> The sweet soft essence
>   of possibility
> Never quite maturing

Though she speaks of a lack of maturity, in this poem Giovanni uses an uppercase "I" to define the speaker, acknowledging perhaps unconsciously a certain kind of maturity that seems to have been missing in earlier poems such as **"My House,"** regardless of their bravado.

At any rate, the speaker is characterized as a lonely, placeless person, yet one who can write a prescription to improve her own condition:

> Everything   some say   will change
> I need a change
>   of pace   face   attitude and life
> Though I long for my loneliness
> I know I need something
> Or someone
> Or . . . . . .

Perhaps acknowledging the desire to succumb to loneliness, to the temptations of the solitary life, allowed Giovanni herself to move forward, to change in a way that profoundly affected her poetic subject matter and technique.

This sense of placelessness is perhaps seen most clearly in an urban poem different from those in Giovanni's earlier volumes. **"The New Yorkers"** focuses on the so-called bag people, "night people" who seem to "evaporate during the light of day," others who are seen during the day but appear to have nowhere to go at night. Of these placeless people, she comments:

> How odd to also see the people
> of New York City living
> in the doorways of public buildings
> as if this is an emerging nation
> though of course it is

In addition to its commentary on American society in the 1970s, the poem provides a commentary on the persona's shaky self-image, as "an old blind Black woman" says on hearing her voice, "You that Eyetalian poet ain't you? I know yo voice. I seen you on television." Yet the old woman feels the poet's hair and determines that she is truly black; symbolically, her identity is intact.

Among the innovations in *Those Who Ride the Night Winds* is a different sense of place, a sense of space, of openness, as well as a concern with "inner" rather than "outer" space, both striking contrasts with earlier uses of place in Giovanni's work. For example, in **"This Is Not for John Lennon (And This Is Not a Poem),"** the speaker implores:

> . . . Don't cry for John Lennon cry for ourselves . . .
> He was an astronaut of inner space . . . He celebrated
> happiness . . . soothed the lonely . . . braced the weary

... gave word to the deaf ... vision to the insensitive
... sang a long low note when he reached the edge of
this universe and saw the Blackness ...

This view of John Lennon leads to the conclusion that
"those who ride the night winds do learn to love the stars
... even while crying in the darkness. ..." In other
words, only those who travel far enough, metaphorically,
to confront the harshness of reality are able to transcend
it, as Lennon did.

An extreme example of this philosophy is seen in **"Flying
Underground."** Dedicated to the children of Atlanta who
died in the mass murders of the early 1980s, the poem
develops the idea that in death these innocent children
"can make the earth move ... flying underground. ..."
Giovanni thus takes the entrapment of the place "underground"—literally, the grave—and transforms it into a
sense of freedom and possibility. The reader is reminded
of the old slave's cry so often invoked by Martin Luther
King, "Free at last," a phrase Giovanni used with effective
irony in a poem on his death, published in *Black Judgement*.

The concluding poem in *Those Who Ride the Night
Winds,* **"A Song for New-Ark,"** is an appropriate end to
an impressive volume. Giovanni characterizes the city of
Newark, New Jersey, where she once lived, in predominantly negative terms, stressing, as she did in the earlier
poem **"Walking Down Park,"** the destruction of nature to
create this urban environment: "I never saw old/jersey ...
or old/ark ... Old/ark was a forest ... felled for concrete
... and asphalt ... and bridges to Manhattan. ..." After
drawing analogies between city dwellers and the rats that
plague them, the poet-persona closes:

> When I write I want to write ... in rhythm ...
> regularizing the moontides ... to the heart/beats ...
> of the twinkling stars ... sending an S.O.S. ... to
> day trippers ... urging them to turn back ... toward
> the Darkness ... to ride the night winds ... to
> tomorrow ...

She moves from the confinement of a physical, earthly
place to the openness and freedom of outer space and
places of fantasy.

In addition to this new sense of place, Giovanni displays
a new sense of herself as a poet in *Those Who Ride the
Night Winds*. In **"A Song for New-Ark"** and also in **"I
Am She,"** Giovanni seems confident of the role she has
chosen for herself, secure in her place in society. As she
says in the latter poem, "I am she ... who writes ... the
poems. ..." Again the ellipses give the sense of openness, of more to come from this poetic talent. While the
poems in this volume seem to reflect Giovanni's own
feeling that she has reached maturity as a poet, there are
still indications of the necessity of coping with the demands
of modern life. She acknowledges the presence of loneliness, not as she did through the poems in the volume
Cotton Candy on a Rainy Day, where loneliness seemed
to be a problem for which she could at the time see no

solution, but in a way that indicates the strength of her
inner resources. In the poem **"The Room with the Tapestry Rug,"** she creates a persona who confronts loneliness by seeking out "the room ... where all who lived
... knew her well. ...." The room holds memories of the
past, symbolized by a garment created by a member of
her family who was important in her childhood, used in
a literal and metaphorical way to keep out the cold.

But Giovanni moves beyond this fairly traditional symbol,
refusing to let the room be only a place of confinement
and protection from the larger world; it becomes a place
where she can also find comfort in the cool air from
outside, while luxuriating in the security of her own space:

> If it was cold ... she would wrap herself ... in the
> natted blue sweater ... knitted by a grandmother ...
> so many years ago ... If warm ... the windows were
> opened ... to allow the wind ... to partake of their
> pleasure ...

The closing paragraph of the poem indicates the resources
of the persona beyond her memories of the past: "Her
books ... her secret life ... in the room with the tapestry
rug. ...." Here she shows not only the need for but the
fact of control over the places in her own life.

In the 1970s, such poems as **"My House"** conveyed an
important theme of the development of a strengthening
identity as a single woman; in the 1980s, such poems as
"The Room with the Tapestry Rug" and **"I Am She"**
illustrate not only the strength but also the depth and
range of that identity. It is appropriate that a volume that
so strongly exhibits Giovanni's talents as a writer should
also attest to the importance of literature and art in her
life, an importance reflected as well in her continued involvement in efforts to bring people and the arts together.

These examples from Nikki Giovanni's poetry—and her
prose as well—demonstrate that, for her, place is more
than an image, more than a surface used to develop a
narrative or a theme, just as place functions in the best
poetry of the Southern tradition lying behind her work.
Further, the changing sense of place in these poems can
be seen to reveal Giovanni's developing sense of herself
as a woman and as a poet. Suzanne Juhasz, Anna T.
Robinson, and Erlene Stetson all emphasize in their recent
critical discussions the growing feminist consciousness
they find in Giovanni's work. Her use of place is broader
than simply a feminist symbol, though, just as her poetry
has developed beyond purely racial themes. The relationships of people to places and the ways people have responded to and tried to control places are important themes
for Giovanni, as are the ways places sometimes control
people. Greatest in thematic significance are the need to
belong to a place or in a place and the necessity of moving
beyond physical places to spiritual or metaphysical ones.

Looking at Giovanni's poetry in the context of Southern
literature expands rather than limits the possibilities for
interpretation and analysis. In fact, this approach reveals
that within the body of her work lies a solid core of poems

that do not rely on political or personal situations for their success. Rather, they develop universal themes, such as coming to terms with the past and with the present so that one may move into the future—again, themes that have been and continue to be of particular significance in Southern poetry. These themes mark her work as a contribution to the canon not just of Southern poetry, of black poetry, of feminist poetry, but also of contemporary American poetry. However, Giovanni's response to any generalization, any categorization, would probably echo the closing line of her poem **"Categories,"** from *My House*. Emphasizing her uniqueness as an individual, she might well proclaim, "i'm bored with categories."

Further Reading

Criticism

Fowler, Virginia C. *Nikki Giovanni*. New York: Twayne, 1992, 192 p.
> Substantial overview of Giovanni's poetry from its beginnings through *Those Who Ride the Night Winds*.

Giddings, Paula. "Nikki Giovanni: Taking a Chance on Feeling." In *Black Women Writers (1950-1980): A Critical Evaluation*, pp. 211-17. Garden City, NY: Doubleday, 1984.
> Overview of earlier work which critiques *Those Who Ride the Night Winds* as being overly-simplistic for the older Giovanni.

Giovanni, Nikki. "An Answer to Some Questions on How I Write: In Three Parts." In *Black Women Writers (1950-1980): A Critical Evaluation*, pp. 205-10. Garden City, NY: Doubleday, 1984.

Provides insight into Giovanni's creative process and habits.

Lee, Don L. "Nikki Giovanni." In *Dynamite Voices I: Black Poets of the 1960's*, pp. 68-74. Detroit: Broadside Press, 1971.
> Reviews *Black Feeling, Black Talk* and *Black Judgement*, appreciating many of the poems but finding the longer, militant poems overly-simplistic.

McLain, Ruth Rambo. Review of *Re: Creation*. *Black World* XX, No. 4 (February 1971): 62-4.
> Expresses regret over the fact that Giovanni's latest collection of poems is "too clean," the work of a "tamed Panther."

Salaam, Kalamu Ya. Review of *My House* and *Like a Ripple On a Pond*. *Black World* XXIII, No. 9 (July 1974): 64-70.
> Claims *My House* is sentimental and romantic, and views *Like a Ripple On a Pond* as a lesser version of what Giovanni already did with *Truth Is On Its Way*.

Interviews

Bonner, Carrington. "An Interview with Nikki Giovanni." *Black American Literature Forum* 18, No. 1 (Spring 1984): 29-30.
> Discussion of *Those Who Ride the Night Wind*, Giovanni's supposed trip to South Africa, and the situation of Black writing at the time.

Fowler, Virginia C., ed. *Conversations with Nikki Giovanni*. Jackson: University Press of Mississippi, 1992, 220 p.
> Collects interviews with Giovanni from throughout her career.

Additional coverage of Giovanni's life and career is contained in the following sources published by Gale Research: *Contemporary Literary Criticism*, Vols. 2, 4, 19, 64; *Black Literature Criticism*; *DISCovering Authors*; *Authors in the News*, Vol. 1; *Black Writers*, Vol. 2; *Contemporary Authors*, Vols. 29-32R; *Contemporary Authors Autobiography Series*, Vol. 6; *Contemporary Authors New Revision Series*, Vols. 18, 41; *Children's Literature Review*, Vol. 6; *Dictionary of Literary Biography*, Vols. 5, 41; *Major Twentieth-Century Writers*; and *Something About the Author*, Vol. 24.

Stanley (Jasspon) Kunitz
1905-

American poet, essayist, editor, translator, and journalist.

INTRODUCTION

One of the longest-surviving poets from the generation that came of age under the influence of T. S. Eliot and W. H. Auden, Kunitz is considered an important, if somewhat critically neglected, voice in contemporary American poetry. He exercised a subtle influence on such major poets as Theodore Roethke and Robert Lowell, and has provided encouragement to hundreds of younger poets as well. Kunitz's career is generally divided into two phases. While his early poetry collections, including *Intellectual Things* (1930) and *Passport to the War* (1944), earned him a reputation as a technically accomplished metaphysical poet, his later work, beginning with *The Testing-Tree* (1971), showed Kunitz writing a simpler, more emotional poetry that embraced the physical world. Although Kunitz has always been admired by his peers, especially since the publication of *Selected Poems, 1928-1958* (1958), which was awarded a Pulitzer Prize in 1959, the classification of his work into two, easily defined categories and his reputation as a "poet's poet" have tended to deter critical interest in his work. While Kunitz's style changed over the years, the subjects of his poems have remained constant. He is known for his sensitive exploration of such themes as the simultaneity of life and death, the search for the lost father, love, generation and decline, and the movement from the unknown to the known. Consistently praised for his skillful craftsmanship, Kunitz incorporates the rhythms of natural speech in his poetry and displays a fine ear for the musical cadence of phrases.

Biographical Information

Born in Worcester, Massachusetts, Kunitz was the third and last child of Russian-Jewish parents. His father, Solomon, a dress manufacturer, committed suicide just months before his birth, and his mother, Yetta, who took over the family business, would not allow Kunitz to mention his father's name. Kunitz received B.A. and M.A. degrees from Harvard, where he was recognized as a promising poet and awarded the coveted Lloyd McKim Garrison Medal for Poetry. In 1927, when Kunitz was denied a teaching appointment at Harvard because of the school administration's concerns about his religious ancestry, he rejected the academic life as a profession but continued writing poetry in private. He worked briefly as a reporter for the *Worcester Telegram* before beginning a long association with the W. H. Wilson Publishing Company of New York, where he served as editor of the Wilson Library

Bulletin from 1928 until 1943 and worked on eight biographical dictionaries about famous authors between 1931 and 1980. In the late 1920s, Kunitz contributed poems to a variety of magazines, including the *Dial,* the *Nation,* and the *New Republic,* and by early 1929, his first collection, *Intellectual Things,* was accepted by the largest publishing house in the country, Doubleday, Doran. While most of the reviews of *Intellectual Things* and Kunitz's second collection of poems, *Passport to the War,* were complimentary, it was not until the publication of the Pulitzer Prize-winning *Selected Poems, 1928-1958* that Kunitz began to elicit any substantial critical attention. In 1946, as a result of his friendship with Roethke, Kunitz began teaching at Bennington College in Vermont, and he continued to teach at a number of American colleges, including Yale and Columbia, until 1985. In the 1960s and 1970s Kunitz also gained recognition for his translations of the works of several Russian poets, among them Anna Akhmatova, Andrei Voznesensky, and Yevgeny Yevtushenko. In addition, he became well known as an advocate of poetry and the arts; he directed the YM-YWCA Poetry Workshop in New York, was general editor of the prestigious "Yale Series of Younger Poets," headed the poetry section at the Library of Congress, and traveled as a cultural exchange lecturer to Poland, Israel, Egypt, Ghana, Senegal, and the former Soviet Union.

Major Works

Kunitz's early poetry collections, *Intellectual Things, Passport to the War,* and *Selected Poems, 1928-1958,* earned him a reputation as an intellectual poet. Reflecting Kunitz's admiration for the English metaphysical poets John Donne and William Blake, these intricate poems, rich in metaphor and allusion, were recognized more for their craft than their substance. *The Testing-Tree,* with its conversational tone, looser forms, and shorter lines, marked a departure to a simpler, more open style. In a *Publishers Weekly* article, Kunitz commented on his two styles: "My early poems were very intricate, dense and formal. . . . They were written in conventional metrics and had a very strong beat to the line. . . . In my late poems I've learned to depend on a simplicity that seems almost nonpoetic on the surface, but has reverberations within that keep it intense and alive. . . ." Elsewhere he remarked, "Since my *Selected Poems* I have been moving toward a more open style, based on natural speech rhythms. *The Testing-Tree* embodied my search for a transparency of language and vision. Maybe age itself compels me to embrace the great simplicities, as I struggle to free myself from the knots and complications, the hang-ups, of my youth. I keep trying to improve my controls over language, so that I won't have to tell lies." The change in Kunitz's style is reflected in his treatment of his most common themes. As critics have noted, Kunitz has been more inclined to expose his feelings in his later work, particularly with regard to the suicide of his father. Such poems as "The Portrait," "Open the Gate," and "Father and Son," which concern a son's quest for his father, show Kunitz to be more willing to confront his personal trauma than in his earlier verse. Critics have also focused on Kunitz's interest in the idea of the simultaneity of life and death, which Kunitz described as "a rather terrifying thought that is at the root of much of my poetry." Kunitz's exploration of such serious themes has prompted critics to applaud his courage and to describe him as a risk taker, although they also note that his tone is more optimistic in such later collections as *Next-to-Last Things* (1985) and *Passing Through* (1996).

Critical Reception

The highly crafted nature of Kunitz's initial works stalled critical attention, and it was not until he was awarded the Pulitzer Prize that critics began to take any significant interest in his poetry. Still, academic critics have been much less receptive to Kunitz than his peers. For many years the standard critical view was that Kunitz was too imitative, lacking any recognizable style of his own. As this argument runs, in his early works Kunitz was a derivative practitioner of the modernist-metaphysical mode, and in his later works he switched to the confessional mode made popular by such poets as Lowell and John Berryman. In addition, Kunitz's poetry has not achieved the wide readership many believe it merits, largely because of his reputation as a "poet's poet," which he earned because of his technical virtuosity and his work as an ambassador of his art. Most critics have preferred the later work to the earlier, and in recent years Kunitz has been consistently praised for the power and intensity of his lyric poems, while continuing to be admired for his meticulous attention to the subtleties of sound and sense. Kunitz has also continued to be recognized by his peers as an important voice in contemporary American poetry. He was awarded a National Endowment for the Arts fellowship in 1984, the Bollingen Prize in Poetry in 1987, and, in the same year, the Walt Whitman award citation of merit, with designation as State Poet of New York.

PRINCIPAL WORKS

Poetry

Intellectual Things 1930
Passport to the War: A Selection of Poems 1944
Selected Poems, 1928-1958 1958
The Testing-Tree: Poems 1971
The Coat without a Seam: Sixty Poems, 1930-1972 1974
The Terrible Threshold: Selected Poems, 1940-1970 1974
The Lincoln Relics 1978
Poems of Stanley Kunitz: 1928-1978 1979
The Wellfleet Whale and Companion Poems 1983
Next-to-Last Things: New Poems and Essays (poetry and essays) 1985
Passing Through: The Later Poems, New and Selected 1996

Other Major Works

Living Authors: A Book of Biographies [editor, as Dilly Tante] (biography) 1931
Authors Today and Yesterday: A Companion Volume to "Living Authors" [editor, with Howard Haycraft and Wilbur C. Hadden] (biography) 1933
British Authors of the Nineteenth Century [editor, with Howard Haycraft] (biography) 1936
American Authors, 1600-1900: A Biographical Dictionary of American Literature [editor, with Howard Haycraft] (biography) 1938
Twentieth-Century Authors: A Biographical Dictionary of Modern Literature [editor, with Howard Haycraft] (biography) 1942
British Authors before 1800: A Biographical Dictionary [editor, with Howard Haycraft] (biography) 1952
European Authors, 1000-1900: A Biographical Dictionary of European Literature [editor, with Vineta Colby] (biography) 1967
Poems of Akhmatova [editor and translator, with Max Hayward] (poetry) 1973
Robert Lowell: Poet of Terribilita (lecture) 1974
Story under Full Sail [translator, from the poetry of Andrei Voznesensky] (poetry) 1974

*A Kind of Order, a Kind of Folly: Essays and Conversa-
tions* (essays and conversations) 1975
World Authors, 1970-1975 [editor, with John Wakeman]
(biography) 1980
The Essential Blake [editor] (poetry) 1987

CRITICISM

Poetry (review date 1930)

SOURCE: "Prelude to Adventure," in *Poetry*, Vol. 36,
No. 4, July, 1930, pp. 218-23.

[*In the following review of* Intellectual Things, *the critic
states that Kunitz shows promise as a poet, praises his
gift for melody but cautions him against stylization.*]

Enough of the probing seriousness and curiosity of a keen
poetic intelligence is exhibited in [*Intellectual Things*] to
warrant a considerable confidence in the talents of the
author, and in his future work. With a public career little
more than a year old, he has issued a collection marked
by unquestionable faults and insecurities, but one in which
a trait of real lyric individuality emerges.

Mr. Kunitz shares his faults with a large company of
contemporaries, and they may be traced largely to an
attempt, in many ways laudable, to develop a new lyric
fashion. In his case certain merits indicate that genuine
style will result, provided the poet is willing to cultivate
his positive assets at the cost of real labor and with the
sacrifice of those superficial devices which result from
mere vanity. These weaknesses grow from an effort at
stylization not always justified by its results. Mr. Kunitz
is fond of making a conventional idea accept new dimensions and uses within the poems. These dimensions, however, are not very successfully described since the traditional stanzaic forms and contours abound, and the uses
are never too well defined in relation to the final philosophical conclusions. For instance, in **"Promise Me"** he
performs a sort of verbal gymnastic without making his
neo-Elizabethan statement count for anything new:

> Only, when loosening clothes, you lean
> Out of your window sleepily,
> And with luxurious lidded mien
> Sniff at the bitter dark—dear she,
> Think somewhat gently of, between
> Love ended and beginning, me.

In **"Sad Song"** he very dangerously wastes his words:

> I married me a fay,
> I was a merry gnome;
> The wind stole my love away,
> In the dark the whistler came.
> I married me a fay.
> Sweet bird, sweet bird, fly home, *etc.*

Through the book these sleights of absurdity crop up.
There is too much talk about odd unnatural symbols, and
too little constructive use made of them. In **"Promenade
on Any Street"** we are taken no farther beyond the manifold imitations of Eliot than the last trite couplet:

> Beneath his gray felt hat
> Leaps thought, the acrobat.

This combination of strained attitude and gyrating syntax
is enough to wear down the patience of the reader. We
have had too many minor Prufrocks and Senlins, and too
many star-goaded Robarteses, to meet another without
diffidence.

The reader's patience, however, finds its reward in the
best poems of this collection, four or five of which are so
good that vigorous caution against the prevailing defects
is fully justified. Mr. Kunitz possesses what in a musician
would be called a melodic gift—a special ability to define
and sustain fluently the verbal and tonal pattern upon
which his poem is built. The presentation of such patterns
necessarily involves a good deal of creative courage, and
Mr. Kunitz plunges into his elaborate imagery, conceits,
and phraseology with none of the hesitation that detains
the poet stricter in matters of form and logic. In **"Very
Tree," "Twilight," "Postscript,"** and particularly in **"Poem,"**
the symbolic configuration is undoubtedly too bold, and far
too involved to hold the idea together. But **"Change," "For
the Word Is Flesh," "Deciduous Branch,"** and **"Rape of
the Leaf,"** elaborate as they are in concept, are expressed
with clarity and smooth linear directness. **"Deciduous
Branch"** shows its descriptive charm in its first stanza:

> Winter, that coils in the thickets now,
> Will glide from the fields; the swinging rain
> Be knotted with flowers; on every bough
> A bird will meditate again.

"Eagle" has admirably caught the swift thrust of its idea:

> The dwindling pole,
> Tall perpendicular in air,
> Attenuates to be a bird
> Poised on a sphere.
>
> No flag projects
> This tensile grace, this needle-word;
> Only, in rigid attitude,
> The ball, the bird.

The sonnets, though too often rhetorically expanded toward the end, are founded on such substantial lines as:

> So intricately is this world resolved
> Of substance arched on thrust of circumstance, . . .
>
> Parting, I take with me completed June,
> Remembered hoard of time in thought compact.

No sonnet quite fulfils the promise of these first phrases,
but each is well weighted and deftly pointed toward its

goal. It is when he gives rein to his creative facility that Mr. Kunitz works best, and for that reason the conventional epigrams of **"Benediction," "Promenade,"** and **"Dissect This Silence"** fail to refresh or convince the reader. The hint of MacLeish's influence in **"Night-Piece"** and **"Invasions"** may indicate one source of Mr. Kunitz's method, yet this, along with several older echoes, may hardly be mentioned against the individuality elsewhere strongly displayed.

An impressive personality is outlined in the best poems here, and it will be interesting to see how far and how substantially, during the next few years, that outline is filled in. In a half-dozen lyrics far more than the familiar two-dimensional self-portrait of the novice is presented. **"Master and Mistress," "Night-piece," "Organic Bloom," "Soul's Adventure," "Vita Nuova,"** might well have been held for a future volume where they would still bear the scrutiny demanded by the more secure and deliberate art of maturity.

Mark Schorer (review date 1944)

SOURCE: A review of *Passport to the War*, in *The New York Times Book Review*, March 26, 1944, p. 26.

[*In the following review of* Passport to the War, *Schorer comments that Kunitz's "'metaphysical' style" has become less imitative since the publication of his first volume of poetry.*]

[Stanley Kunitz] made a . . . cautious selection of influences and, from the beginning, showed himself to be a first-rate rather than a second-rate poet by integrating those influences with his own vision of experience to produce what may be called a style. Half of his present book. [*Passport to the War*] consists of selections from his first book, *Intellectual Things* published in 1930, and comparison is gratifying. For it shows clearly, in the first place, that many of his early poems were exactly as good as they were then taken to be; poems like **"Organic Bloom"** and **"In a Strange House"** have lost none of their splendor.

Comparison shows, in the second place, how the poet has developed. From the beginning he was a "metaphysical" poet in the triple sense that he was interested in the analysis of, not the mere submission to experience; that that analysis was made by means of imagery predominantly intellectual in its manipulation; and that the images were drawn from every corner of the poet's experience. But he was also "metaphysical" in the less satisfactory sense that he echoed, quite directly, certain seventeenth-century poets, particularly Donne and Marvel: like those poets and unlike the best modern poets, he depended, rather monotonously, on metaphor rather than symbol (an *indirect* "sensuous apprehension of experience.") Finally, in the earlier poems he sometimes wrote ineptly, with awkward or forced lines, and sometimes slackly and tritely:

> I wept for my youth, sweet pas-
>   sionate young thought,
> And cozy women dead that by my
>   side
> Once lay: I wept with bitter long-
>   ing, not
> Remembering how in my youth
>   I cried.

Now the "metaphysical" style has become entirely his own, and he writes with terse, fresh imagery at nearly every point:

>   I thought I heard
> A piece of laughter break upon
>   the stair
> Like glass, but when I wheeled
>   around I saw
> Disorder, in a tall magician's hat,
> Keeping his rabbit-madness
>   crouched inside,
> Sit at my desk and scramble all
>   the news.

With this consolidation of method has gone no stiffening in the ability to explore the possibilities of technique—notice his attractive experiment in false rhymes called **"Confidential Instructions."** Kunitz has now (it would seem) every instrument necessary to the poetic analysis of modern experience. Time and time again in his new poems he achieves, with precision and fullness, his aim.

David Wagoner (review date 1958)

SOURCE: "The Thirty Years' War," in *Poetry*, Vol. 93, No. 3, December, 1958, pp. 174-78.

[*In the following essay, Wagoner predicts that the publication of* Selected Poems, 1928-1958 *will bring an end to critical neglect of Kunitz's poetry.*]

One of the most depressing literary curiosities of the past three decades has been the neglect of Stanley Kunitz's poetry. His earlier books—*Intellectual Things* (1930) and *Passport to the War* (1944)—received uniformly high praise from reviewers (for the single exception, see his poem **"A Choice of Weapons,"** but serious critical attention appeared to stop there. Now, at last, the *Selected Poems 1928-1958* marks what will surely be the end of Kunitz's quiet Thirty Years' War for a place among the very best poets of our time. Let us hope that the Peace of Westphalia will be celebrated in anthologies and perhaps even on the most important prize lists.

The eighty-five poems in the book exhibit a simultaneously delightful and frightening mind. Its ways are intricate, surprising, and clear; but they occasionally lead so deep or so far forward that the reader performing Pound's "dance along the intellect" discovers himself in a country where he is his own most dangerous enemy, where he is forced to choose sides at the bottom of his own mind. This is, therefore, "difficult" poetry in the true sense: most people do not take kindly to those who make crucial disturbances.

An early poem called **"The Words of the Preacher"** reads in part:

> Taking infection from the vulgar air
> And sick with the extravagant disease
> Of life, my soul rejected the sweet snare
> Of happiness; declined
> That democratic bait, set in the world
> By fortune's old and mediocre mind.
>
> To love a changing shape with perfect faith
> Is waste of faith; to follow dying things
> With deathless hope is vain; to go from breath
> To breath, so to be fed
> And put to sleep, is cheat and shame—because
> By piecemeal living a man is doomed, I said. . . .
>
> Into the middle of my thought I crept
> And on the bosom of the angel lay,
> Lived all my life at once; and oh I wept
> My own future to be;
> Upon his death-soft burning plumage wept
> To vie with God for His eternity.

It ought to be enough to say these lines are memorable; but they seem, instead, permanent outside of any mind, like sculpture. What might have been merely heavy rhetoric or bombast from a lesser poet, is here a statement of cause, act, and effect-to-be, *bitten* into art with unmistakable finality. Poem after poem is of this sort: a model of what language taken to its end should be.

Reviewers of contemporary fiction frequently speak of cerebral and muscular (or gutsy) style, in all the gradations from afflatus to flatulence; the anatomical metaphor in these poems would vary between bone and nerve—the essentials of form and impulse. Kunitz is formal in the dramatic sense, not rigidly, not like a child clinging to a jungle-gym in a whirlwind. Maintaining his balance within a poem, among increasingly intense imagery, movement, and substance, he is able to find the shape of his thought in a manner unknown to the free-association, oh-look-what-I-just-spelled, I'll-tell-you-*my*-dream poets who appear to think, mistakenly, that even their postcards to each other are interesting.

The following poem, **"Among the Gods,"** should have been a piece of pure arrogance. It isn't.

> Within the grated dungeon of the eye
> The old gods, shaggy with gray lichen, sit
> Like fragments of the antique masonry
> Of heaven, a patient thunder in their stare,
>
> Huge blocks of language, all my quarried love,
> They justify, and not in random poems,

> But shapes of things interior to Time,
> Hewn out of chaos when the Pure was plain.
>
> Sister, my bride, who were both cloud and bird
> When Zeus came down in a shower of sexual gold,
> Listen! we make a world! I hear the sound
> Of Matter pouring through eternal forms.

When I try to imagine a poem written on this subject by nearly anyone else, I flinch. But Kunitz justifies his hubris by the extraordinary act of the poem itself: the unanswerable argument. (Yet somewhere in a Beat notebook the attempt undoubtedly lies: "I'm turned on, man, I'm on! I'm strapped to that crazy great hornblowing Gasser of a God, the mainline Screw!" *etc.* for twenty pages.)

In mood and subject, the poems range widely but perhaps not as widely as some could wish. Kunitz moves from the forceful lyric to the tour de force, but always with clenched fists. Although his ear is delicate, he seldom allows that part of his gift to predominate. This seems to me unfortunate because his obviously flexible technical skill might be put to singing simply, a task it would perform beautifully. I don't think it is presumptuous here to cavil at the missing poem because, if my guess is right, it is one of the reasons for Kunitz's neglect. His work is so charged with passionate ferocity, even when its source is ostensibly lyrical, that it becomes very nearly unbearable if taken in bulk. Put the case: (1) his attacks on the center of his own and the reader's mind are rarely feints, and again and again, the thrusts go home; (2) anthology-making is a notoriously jading profession, and few of today's scissorsmen are noted for their staying power. *Ergo* . . . well, one is tempted to see a causal relationship.

Another small complaint: the poems are neither dated nor arranged chronologically. Work covering a very long period of time is mixed into five not entirely useful thematic patterns; and because the books containing the earlier poems are long since out of print, most readers will have no way to trace the growth of the poet. The legendary cry of "New lamps for old" once led to confusion as well as magic.

But these matters lose almost all their importance in the face of the achievement the book represents: imagination functioning repeatedly at the highest pitch. There appear to be no discernible contemporary influences, but there are amazing confluences in which love, art, and death lie fused. I am tempted to quote half the book, but one example of this phenomenon will have to suffice—in a poem about the setting-out of the hero, **"The Way Down,"** which begins:

> Time swings her burning hands.
> I saw him going down
> Into those mythic lands
> Bearing his selfhood's gold,
> A last heroic speck
> Of matter in his mind
> That ecstasy could not crack
> Nor metaphysics grind.

I saw him going down
Veridical with bane
Where pastes of phosphor shine
To a cabin underground
Where his hermit father lives
Escaping pound by pound
From his breast-buckled gyves;
In his hermit father's coat,
The coat without a seam,
That the race, in its usury, bought
For the agonist to redeem,
By dying in it, one
Degree a day till the whole
Circle's run.

And by the time the reader has finished the remaining two parts of the poem, he can believe it is all happening again. Language and imagery have become uncanny, and the lines are duplicating, in themselves and by themselves, the peril and importance of that life-renewing journey. When this occurs in literature, we should be grateful, as Kunitz himself apparently is, for all of us, in the last lines of a poem that ends the book and speaks of "The spiral verb that weaves / Through the crystal of our lives." He has seen, recognized, suffered, and used

This laurel-sparking rhyme
That we repeat in time
Until the fathers rest
On the inhuman breast
That is both fire and stone,
Mother and mistress, one.

Harvey Gross (essay date 1965)

SOURCE: "The Generation of Auden," in *Sound and Form in Modern Poetry: A Study of Prosody from Thomas Hardy to Robert Lowell,* University of Michigan Press, 1965, pp. 279-82.

[*In the following excerpt, Gross focuses on meter and sound in Kunitz's poetry, praising him for his technical accomplishments.*]

. . . Kunitz' acknowledged masters are Donne, Baudelaire, and Eliot. He pays each the formal compliment of allusion or translation; in the blank-verse poem **"The Class Will Come to Order"** a celebrated line from *The Relique,*

A bracelet of bright hair about the bone

appears in witty paraphrase:

Absurd though it may seem,
Perhaps there's too much order in this world;
The poets love to haul disorder in,
Braiding their wrists with her long mistress hair,
And when the house is tossed about our ears,
The governors must set it right again.
How wise was he who banned them from his state!

A great variety of movement and tone shades the feeling in these lines. The only outstanding metrical departure is the shortened first line (trimeter rather than pentameter), but Kunitz' ear for quantity and monosyllabic harmonies is nearly unmatched among American poets. The quality of sinuous beauty which inheres in the fourth line,

Brai ding | their wrísts | with her lóng mís | tress háir

is produced by the strategically placed short *i*'s as well as by the reversed first foot and the double foot standing in the third and fourth positions.

Especially worthy of commentary are the monosyllabic lines, "the glory of our verse and language." **"The Class Will Come to Order"** ends with two delicately ambiguous lines, one of eight, the other of ten syllables:

I smiled but I did not tell them,
I did not tell them why it was I smiled.

The gentle tug between speech stress and metrical stress teases the meaning first one way, then another. Emphasizing the metrical pattern,

I smiled but *I* did not tell *them*

we get an antithesis between *I* and *them;* the poet *I,* kept his secret from *them,* the class. If we let rhetorical stress override the metrical pattern,

I smiled but I did *not tell* them

the strong *tell* enforces the act of *not* telling. The whole assertion is further modified in the last line where *not* and *them* now appear in metrically unstressed positions, and *tell* and *why* receive the emphasis:

I díd | not téll | them whý | it wás | I smíled.

Our next example, also in blank verse, comes from **"The Thief."** Again, we note an extraordinary refinement of language and feeling singing through a much varied music:

Pick-pocket, pick-thank music plucks the strings
For the rag-madonna with perdurable babe
Most dolorously hallowing the square
Where Caesar walks three steps to meet Bernini,
Whose sumptuous art runs wild
From gate to gate, pausing in tiptoe-joy
Only to light a torch of fountains, to set
His tritons dancing, or at a blest façade
To cast up from his wrist a flight of angels,
Volute on volute, wing on climbing wing.
In the middle of my life I heard the waters playing.

This long verse-paragraph winds through many syntactical delays, holding back a full stop until the tenth line. The last line, with its echo from Dante and its lengthened meter (irregular hexameter), stabilizes the rhythmic flow of the previous lines.

Kunitz is as deft in stanza and rhyme as he is in blank verse. A measured tetrameter and wire-tight irony hold in balance compassion, fury, chagrin, amusement—and a final resolution of all these:

> I thought of Judith in her tent,
> Of Helen by the crackling wall,
> Of Cressida, her bone-lust spent,
> Of Catherine on the holy wheel:
> I heard their woman-dust lament
> The golden wound that does not heal.
>
> What a wild air her small joints beat!
> I only poured the raging wine
> Until our bodies filled with light,
> Mine with hers and hers with mine,
> And we went out into the night
> Where all the constellations shine.
>
> from **"She Wept, She Railed"**

In another mood and stanza the qualities are lyric grace and Arcadian serenity; the somewhat "medieval" imagery is complemented by a stiff, archaic trimeter movement:

> The lily and the swan
> Attend her whiter pride,
> While the courtly laurel kneels
> To kiss his mantling bride.
>
> Under each cherry-bough
> She spreads her silken cloths
> At the rumor of a wind,
> To gather up her deaths,
>
> For the petals of her heart
> Are shaken in a night,
> Whose ceremonial art
> Is dying into light.
>
> from **"When the Light Falls"**

"Ceremonial art" well describes Kunitz' meticulously realized poems. . . .

Jean H. Hagstrum (essay date 1967)

SOURCE: "The Poetry of Stanley Kunitz: An Introductory Essay," in *Poets in Progress*, Northwestern University Press, 1967, pp. 38-58.

[*In the following essay, Hagstrum identifies major themes in Kunitz's poetry and traces the development of his technique, examining poems from* Intellectual Things, Passport to the War, *and* Selected Poems, 1928-1958.]

Stanley Kunitz provides his readers with the excitement, rarely encountered in modern poetry, of exploring both the guilty and the joyful recesses of the personality. Of guilt alone, we have perhaps had more than our share, and the pilgrimage from sin to salvation has become—who would have believed it a generation ago?—almost fashionable. But relatively few have moved, as Mr. Kunitz has in his thirty-year poetic career, from darkly morbid psychic interiors to a clean, well-lighted place, where personality is integrated through love and art—love that draws nourishment from the unabashedly physical and art that, though complex, rests on the honest simplifications of life.

I

Though Kunitz's literary life and manner are difficult, one of his central ideas is extremely simple. He has said, "Let life happen to you . . . Life is right," and he believes that modern neurosis in part stems from the morbid separation of art from life that characterizes our culture. The naked prose statements will impress only those who admire the dignified Johnsonian ability to state without fear of triteness the essential commonplaces of life and art. But expressed in his poetry the same idea possesses verbal vigor and imagistic shock, especially in that series of brilliant life-death antitheses whose polarities constitute the major contention of his major poetry.

In the early poetry the negative or life-denying side of the contrast receives the greater emphasis and is embodied in the important image of the skeleton and in other images that cluster about it. Kunitz imagines bones as clean, hygienic, disinfected, shapely, sharp—the

> bonecase (melted down)
> Shimmers with scaly wit—

but irrevocably and horribly dead. The death-image is composed not of decay, blood, exposed viscera, smells of disintegration, but of harsh, dry, and defined things like needles, spines, spikes, sand, stones, leafless branches, scalpels, peeled nuts, and shadows on the wall. In **"The Surgeons"** death is symbolized by skillful, professional savages who open the brain of a child, dissipate its dreams, and cut away all pity and love. These men of knife and bone are systematic, amputating men who hate tradition and passion and whose despair of the future matches their scorn of the past.

Kunitz's symbols of life, which seem to predominate in the later poems, are better if one prefers the constructive and wholesome to the bitterly angry. The old-clothes man, unlike the surgeons, does not create but mobilizes wounds. He collects the decaying coats behind the door, the scraps and rags of past experience—dead ambitions, buried love, lost innocence. But this tatterdemalion army, as ragged as Jack Falstaff's, is an invincibly human one:

> Let
> The enemies of life beware
> When these old clothes go forth to war.

In a recent poem, **"The Thief,"** in which the poet curses a *ladrone* who picked his pocket clean in a crowded Roman train, Kunitz gives his favorite antithesis an autobiographical context. The unpleasant loss evokes recollections of both historical Rome and the poet's own personal Rome, which he remembers from the lantern slides shown at school. But that Rome, he now knows, was a "pedagogic lie," and the careful reader of Kunitz sees that that Rome ("the frozen pure") has become a symbol of stony, skeletal death. But the real Rome, with its elbowing mobs, its thieves, its jogging *carrozze,* and its stones baroquely shaped by Bernini, is all motion, impure like *e*motion, flawed by mutability,

> and yet thereby
> More lovely and more graced, perhaps
> More true.

Kunitz likes the blooming, bacterial rot the surgeon cuts away to expose his dead and flinty surfaces. For the poet, the blood, the guts, the "bubbling brain, exploding life's gray tumor," and the "green-celled world" where our "blind moulds" kiss have their compensatory side: they blaze with life as well as death. Alexander Pope recoiled in horror from the crawling maggoty world which in the *Dunciad* he created to symbolize Grub Street. But Kunitz finds decay a pre-condition of existence, the very compost in which life sprouts:

> In fierce decay I'll find a stripe
> Of honey sweetening the tart
> Old brain. I shall not know again such ripe
> Beauty of the burst, dark heart.

Kunitz believes, in Gospel phrase, that "Except a corn of wheat fall to the ground and die, it abideth alone; but if it die, it bringeth forth much fruit":

> I lie awake, hearing the drip
> Upon my sill; thinking, the sun
> Has not been promised; we who strip
> Summer to seed shall be undone.
>
> Now, while the antler of the eaves
> Liquefies, drop by drop, I brood
> On a Christian thing: unless the leaves
> Perish, the tree is not renewed.

II

Kunitz has said in prose that "every poem must be loaded with a full charge of experience" and in verse,

> I, being rent
> By the fierce divisions of our time, cried death
> And death again, and my own dying meant.

We cannot, without more information than we now possess, trace the poetry back to its biographical source. But as critics we must ask that unsophisticated, essential, and difficult question: does the poetry have on it the bloom of first-hand experience?

Kunitz was born in 1905 of Russian-Jewish parents, and in his verse there is the shadowy outline of a changing response to his Jewish heritage. The following early lines seem to sound a note of revolt against the family and its traditions:

> Now I must tread the starry wrack
> And penetrate the burning sea.
> Iscariot, I may come back,
> But do not wait for me.

In **"For the Word is Flesh"** the poet apparently confesses to hearing "the fierce / Wild cry of Jesus on the holy tree" at the very moment he says to his dead father that he has

> of you no syllable to keep,
> Only the deep rock crumbling in the deep.

And the impression from the earlier poetry is confirmed by a comment on his boyhood days in one of his latest poems,

> For nothing pleased me then in my legacy.

World War II seems, from the evidence of the poetry and from that alone, to have restored the poet's ties with his personal past, for the following lines must surely be autobiographical (The man of the first lines is, I believe, Hitler, the ancestors of the third and following lines are his immigrant parents, and the second paragraph refers to the Nazis, persecuting the Jews and perhaps also invading Russia):

> When I stand in the center of that man's madness,
> Deep in his trauma, as in the crater of a wound,
> My ancestors step from my American bones.
> There's mother in a woven shawl, and that,
> No doubt, is father picking up his pack
> For the return voyage through those dreadful years
> Into the winter of the raging eye.
>
> One generation past, two days by plane away,
> My house is dispossessed, my friends dispersed,
> My teeth and pride knocked in, my people game
> For the hunters of man-skins in the warrens of
>   Europe,
> The impossible creatures of an hysteriac's dream
> Advancing with hatchets sunk into their skulls
> To rip the god out of the machine.

Two of Kunitz's best poems, **"For the Word is Flesh"** (from the 1930 volume) and **"Father and Son"** (from the 1944 volume), represent strongly diverse responses to antithetical father-images, or, if the biographical identifications I propose are wrong, antithetical responses to the same father-image, or perhaps something more complicated than either of these alternatives. (The two poems are obviously now intended to be read together since they are printed on opposite pages in the 1958 volume.) The earlier poem belongs to the period of Kunitz's impatience with his heritage—or lack of one—and his horror at the surgically produced skeletons of modern life. Among these enemies of life he has placed his father—or at least a generic father whom the speaker of the poem addresses— now a lipless skeleton:

Let sons learn from their lipless fathers how
Man enters hell without a golden bough.

It may be relevant to note that Kunitz's father died a
suicide at thirty-eight, a few weeks before his son was
born, and to quote the poet's comment, "Of my father I
know almost nothing except that he was a free-thinker
and a Mason who left behind a collection of good books."

In the later father-poem tenderness has replaced anger.
This poem, I suggest hesitantly, is addressed not to
Kunitz's father but his stepfather, Mark Dine, "of all men
I have known . . . the gentlest," who lived with the family
only six years before he died of a heart attack. The step-
son was then fourteen. In the poem from which I quote
here only the last paragraph, the spirit of Mark Dine has
been transmuted to unalloyed poetic gold:

> At the water's edge, where the smothering ferns
>   lifted
> Their arms, "Father!" I cried, "Return! You know
> The way. I'll wipe the mudstains from your clothes;
> No trace, I promise, will remain. Instruct
> Your son, whirling between two wars,
> In the Gemara of your gentleness,
> For I would be a child of those who mourn
> And brother to the foundlings of the field
> And friend of innocence and all bright eyes.
> O teach me how to work and keep me kind."
> Among the turtles and the lilies he turned to me
> The white ignorant hollow of his face.

The two father-poems also represent responses to the poet's
national and religious heritage. In the first he confesses
that he "cannot blur / The mirrored brain with fantasies of
Er," but in the second a suffering and chastened man
seeks wisdom in the Gemara of his father's gentleness.

Kunitz's love poetry has always been perceptive and
persuasive. Neither Puritanical or prurient, it never stri-
dently tempts us to eat forbidden fruit. It has sometimes
been tremblingly tender, as in **"Night-piece,"** when men
sigh good night,

> put out their bodies like a light,
> And set their brains adrift upon their blood,

and urge, "Let us be shy again like feathered things"; and
sometimes jealously amorous as in **"The Science of the
Night,"** when the lover, his manhood lying on a rumpled
field, his beloved sprawled carelessly in sleep, imagines
that she returns to people and places he has never known.

Kunitz's poetry introduces two Ladies, an Early Lady and
a Later Lady, who must correspond to his experience in
the subtle way that art always corresponds to the reality
out of which it springs. The Early Lady is imprecisely
outlined. She appears fleetingly in the surrealist landscape
of the first poems; and the experiences in which she figures
are frustrating ones, not unlike the situation in Gertrude
Stein's most beautiful story, *Melanctha,* in which one lover's love is too early and the other's is tragically too late:

For love is coming or is passing by,
And none may look upon her features plain.

How shall these tarry, how shall these meet,
When he must remember and she forget?
Her baby-heart is running down a street
Already ended, his to a place not yet.

The Later Lady has provided both lover and artist with
his deepest fulfillments. Although a person of an earlier
secret life lived apart from his own and although a person
of a wild, adventuring spirit for whom the boldest astronomical imagery may even be restrained, this Lady has
also evoked the most delicate, urbane, and courtly poetry
Kunitz has as yet written. The Lady, herself an artist,
transforms the raw music of life to measured harmony;
metaphysical of mind, she provokes and appreciates the
subtlest intellectual joke. But even the Early Lady—a Dark
Lady who spoke the serpent's word—is never really lost
to life and experience. She may, like the ooze of souls, be
too virulent to die. She may be one of the blind wounds
the old-clothes man comes to mobilize. In any event, she
has taught the poet a hard, hard lesson:

> We learn, as the thread plays out, that we belong
> Less to what flatters us than to what scars.

III

Kunitz has published three volumes of poetry, in 1930,
1944, and 1958. *Intellectual Things*, the first of these,
contained fifty poems, most of them short lyrics in the
modern metaphysical manner made fashionable by T. S.
Eliot.

The bold images and scenes remind one of Donne, but
the urbane language, the exquisitely flowing music, and
the syntactical precision recall Marvell. Donne's sense of
evil in the marrow, his moral and psychological frankness,
his imaginative originality in combining geography, mathematics, science, and statecraft with love-making and
worship—all these have their impressive counterparts in
Kunitz. But Donne serves a modern purpose; and his tight,
though outrageously literal scholastic logic, his firm sense
of intellectual outline, his essential fidelity to nature even
when his combinations disfigure its surface, Kunitz distorts
into an imagistic surrealism that provides intense experience without providing paraphrasable meaning. Man dissolves in a cooking vat of chemicals that stands alone on
a crumbling rock. A poetic speaker compares himself to
a crystal bead in a crystal ball, "So pure that only Nothing
could be less." Twilight invades a room in which glowing
lions congregate and in which the poet, also tawny, awaits
the approach of night, as the day and his heart spill their
blood to slake his lips, when suddenly the moon, tawny
like man and lion, materializes at the door. A human body
swells in corruption until in death it becomes a whale
that, like a derelict vessel, is pillaged by the curious. Lovers
eat their ecstatic hearts and kiss in "complicate analysis
of passionate destruction." The poet creeps deep into his
own self, where he lies on the burning plumage of an
angel and so lives his entire life all at once.

In thus delineating Kunitz's surrealist landscape, I have been guilty of separating image and context. In its proper place the imagery does more than shock. It attacks the modern simplifications of human nature that reduce it to one dimension and omit the vital parts. Kunitz's outrage is that of the anti-body against a destroying foreign presence. Blood, organ and sinew swell in protest, and a feverish brain tries to expel the attackers of our vital centers.

"Single Vision," which I have chosen to represent the 1930 volume, is so tightly coherent that it must be quoted in full. The action seems to be this: one of Kunitz's surgeons, a lost man, rises in a resurrection scene that recalls Donne and, in one image—though if there was conscious intent it must have been to draw a contrast—Piero della Francesca's great painting in which Christ rises with a banner in his hand. The rising man is a Kunitzian skeleton, taught to reject love and the blood and to refine away the flesh. But as he rises, persisting life rises with him and all that goes with life—the unused evil in the bones, the stain of reality on the brain, and the pride of blood unimaginably unfurled at his side. In sympathy with these life-symbols, the skeleton, now in remorse, sheds the tears of the soul and then slips into the silence of the bony and dusty grave which modern, life-disinfecting, hollow men have prepared for him:

> Before I am completely shriven
> I shall reject my inch of heaven.
>
> Cancel my eyes, and, standing, sink
> Into my deepest self; there drink
>
> Memory down. The banner of
> My blood, unfurled, will not be love,
>
> Only the pity and the pride
> Of it, pinned to my open side.
>
> When I have utterly refined
> The composition of my mind,
>
> Shaped language of my narrow till
> Its forms are instant to my will,
>
> Suffered the leaf of my heart to fall
> Under the wind, and, stripping all
>
> The tender blanket from my bone,
> Rise like a skeleton in the sun,
>
> I shall have risen to disown
> The good mortality I won.
>
> Directly risen with the stain
> Of life upon my crested brain,
>
> Which I shall shake against my ghost
> To frighten him, when I am lost.
>
> Gladly, as any poison, yield
> My halved conscience, brightly peeled;

> Infect him, since we live but once,
> With the unused evil in my bones.
>
> I'll shed the tear of souls, the true
> Sweat, Blake's intellectual dew,
>
> Before I am resigned to slip
> A dusty finger on my lip.

In 1944 Kunitz's second volume of verse, **Passport to the War**, appeared, containing fifty poems in all, twenty-six of which had not before appeared in book-form and twenty-four of which were re-published from the earlier volume. Lines like

> The silence unrolling before me as I came,
> The night nailed like an orange to my brow,

and others, recalling early De Chirico,

> Through portal and through peristyle
> Her phantom glides, whose secret mouth,
> The absence of whose flagrant smile,
> Hangs on my chimney like a wreath of cloud,

show that the earlier metaphysical-surrealist manner continues. But it is now combined with themes of contemporary political and social reality; and a new style of expression, that may suggest Robert Frost, introduces greater colloquial flexibility and greater human warmth. Anger remains, but it is a satirical anger aimed at recognizable targets: Hitler, the Nazis, the Bitch Goddess Success, military men of any nation, and a new, dangerously pervasive savagery. **"Reflections by a Mailbox," "Night Letter,"** and **"Father and Son"**—unfortunately all too long to quote in full—add new power to the old without obliterating the Kunitzian signature, which remains unmistakable throughout his entire career.

The best moments are still those that explore the individual's soul. The new social themes remain languid until they disturb the psyche. But though not notable in themselves as programs of action or ways of life, the new social reality has brought drama and scene into sharper focus even in the metaphysical moments. Consider the increased intensity of that stunning poem about evil in the dream and in the soul, **"The Fitting of the Mask,"** the inspiration for which Kunitz seems to have derived from a passage he greatly admired in Rilke's *Journal of My Other Self*. I quote the poem entire as an example of the new power of the 1944 collection:

> "Again I come to buy the image fated."
> "Your valued image, sir, and that's a pity,
> Is gone, I mean the youth, the undefeated,
> Whose falcon-heart, winged with the golden shout
> Of morning, sweeps windward from his native city,
> Crying his father's grief, his mother's doubt."
>
> "You knew I cared, and that I'd come for him;
> The traffic hindered me; you should have known."
> "Ah there, that's bad! But my poor memory's dim
> As a bell that rings the tide in; I lose track

Of things to keep and things to sell, and one
Can never be quite certain who'll come back."

"Enough! There was another face, a bright
Pathetic one I'll take, from whose wild stain
Of sympathy a man could borrow light."
"Our catalogue describes him 'Fool of Love,
Fragile and dear, tinctured with mortal pain,
Buys grain of his grain and eats the chaff there-
of.'"

"Your cataloguer has the cynic touch,
But I'll forgive him. Is our business over?"
"Be patient, sir. You would not thank me much
Or recommend my baffling merchandise
If I should offer this unblessed believer,
This torn-cheek, with the chasm in his eyes."

"Old man, I'm in a hurry to proceed,
And everyone, you know, must wear a mask
Give me a countenance to meet my need
Or malice will expose me at the dance."
"Oh sir, we'll try, but it's no easy task
To make adjustments to your circumstance;

And now, while my assistant turns the key
And in the windows now the lights go out,
For it is closing time irrevocably
Until new features sit upon the forms,
I'll sing a little ditty to the ghost
That occupies this world of empty frames.

[*Sings:*]
Good-fellow's lost among our Psychic Cases,
The Angry Man has turned a ghastly blue,
Munich exhausted all our Judas-faces.
And what are we to do, and what to do?
The Optimist was mangled in a sock,
The rats conferred and ate The Wandering Jew,
There's nothing left that's decent in our stock,
And what are we to do, and what to do?

But look!—here's something rare, macabre, a true
Invention of the time's insomniac wits.
Perhaps we ought to sell it to the zoo.
Go to the darkening glass that traps your shames
And tell me what you see."

               "O Prince of Counterfeits,
This is the Self I hunted and knifed in dreams."

Kunitz's *Selected Poems 1928-1958* contained eighty-five poems, of which one-third were new and the remaining were republished from the two earlier volumes. The latest poems make the old metaphysical boldness even bolder and intensify the already unparaphrasable imagistic intensity. At the same time, the long colloquial line of 1944 has now become a marvel of flexible strength. Suffusing these familiar effects is a golden romanticism that had earlier been only a hesitant *soupçon* of better things to come—a strain that from the beginning invoked poets of the romantic generation, notably Blake.

The title *Intellectual Things* (1930) was adapted from Blake's famous sentence, "For the tear is an intellectual thing," which Kunitz used as the epigraph of that volume. In a memorable phrase Kunitz defined the "tear of souls" (in contrast to modern, dry-as-dust, skeletal powder) as the "true sweat, Blake's intellectual dew." Some four poems in that volume, none of which Kunitz has chosen to reprint, are vaguely Blakean and romantic: **"Death in Moonlight," "Sad Song," "Thou Unbelieving Heart"** (which contains lovely lines but may not be as fully integrated as at first appears), and **"Elemental Metamorphosis"** (which contains a stronger recollection of Wordsworth's "Three Years She Grew" and "A Slumber did my Spirit Seal" than of anything in Blake). But except for certain lines these poems did not achieve the magic of the *Songs of Innocence and Experience* because they are too lush or because they remain flat and smooth and imprecise, like the romantics at their least impressive. In **"Open the Gates"** of the 1944 collection, however, Kunitz, perhaps unconsciously, has achieved an effect in the first two stanzas that is authentically Blakean—but recalling not so much the purely lyrical Blake as the verbal-visual Blake of emblems like the frontispiece to *Jerusalem* or the haunting "Death's Door":

    Within the city of the burning cloud,
    Dragging my life behind me in a sack,
    Naked I prowl, scourged by the black
    Temptation of the blood grown proud.

    Here at the monumental door,
    Carved with the curious legend of my youth,
    I brandish the great bone of my death,
    Beat once therewith and beat no more.

In the 1958 volume the Blakean strain grows into something fresh and lovely: in the poem to the delicate white mouse, **"The Waltzer in the House"**; in the emblematic allegory, **"The Way Down"**; in the exquisite **"As Flowers Are,"** a lovely poem that draws on the wars and loves of the flowers—Erasmus Darwin refined into quintessential Blake; but above all in that delicate aubade, **"When the Light Falls,"** a poem of urbane compliment which combines Ben Jonson's courtly, classical elegance and Blake's power of deep and elemental suggestion:

    When the light falls, it falls on her
    In whose rose-gilded chamber
    A music strained through mind
    Turns everything to measure.

    The light that seeks her out
    Finds answering light within,
    And the two join hands and dance
    On either side of her skin.

    The lily and the swan
    Attend her whiter pride,
    While the courtly laurel kneels
    To kiss his mantling bride.

    Under each cherry-bough
    She spreads her silken cloths

At the rumor of a wind,
To gather up her deaths,

For the petals of her heart
Are shaken in a night,
Whose ceremonial art
Is dying into light.

Kunitz's poetic virtuosity is such that it fully vindicates his own aesthetic belief that meaning in verse is "a product of the total form." But like his peers and even his betters, he is not an absolutely impeccable craftsman, and there are some fifteen separate occasions on which one reader grieved in reading the latest collection, from which the poet has excluded what he considers his earlier failures—grief usually over a word, line, or image, only rarely over an entire poem or one of its crucial sections.

Kunitz has said that "there is only one artist, the true, recurrent, undying wanderer, the eternally guilty, invincibly friendly man." It is tempting to apply that sentence to its author. The joyous love lyrics, the austere but amiable reviews of younger men's work, his comments on his teaching experiences, in which he has delighted in engaging the inquisitive spirits of even the faltering beginners—all this makes us want to say of him that he must be "an invincibly friendly man."

As poet Mr. Kunitz appears also as the "eternally guilty" man:

But why do I wake at the sound,
In the middle of the night,
Of the tread of the Masked Man
Heavy on the stairs . . . ?
Agh! I am sometimes weary
Of this everlasting search
For the drama in a nutshell,
The opera of the tragic sense,
Which I would gladly be rid of.

But Mr. Kunitz need not be embarrassed. **"Complicate"** guilt is one of his most excitingly exploited themes, absolutely without the theatricality he seems to impute to it in the lines just quoted.

What can Kunitz mean when he calls the artist the "true, recurrent, undying wanderer," and can this part of the sentence also be applied to him? I think it can, and I judge it to mean that a poem—to interpret Kunitz by Kunitz—"repeats for us man's spiritual ascent, identifying whoever shares in its beauty with those obscure thousands under the hill of time [this image Kunitz has used more than once in his poetry] who once climbed . . . and climb again the forbidding slope." That is, a true work of art is a kind of secular All Souls' Day sacrament, that brings us into communion with struggling men of all days and ways, with dead poets who have celebrated those struggles, and with the heroes of myth and legend who have memorably embodied them for the whole race. **"The Approach to Thebes"** reveals the true poetic "wandered" in the full meaning of Kunitz. Oedipus, who speaks the

lines of the poem, has encountered and overcome the Sphinx. He now approaches Thebes, about to become its king—not joyfully but in solemn sadness since a prophetic vision reveals to him the horrors that will with the years be heaped upon his head. But he comes prepared: the winning of the Sphinx has irrevocably tied him to life itself. In overcoming her, he has mastered it:

In the zero of the night, in the lipping hour,
Skin-time, knocking-time, when the heart is pearled
And the moon squanders its uranian gold,
She taunted me, who was all music's tongue,
Philosophy's and wilderness's breed,
Of shifting shape, half jungle-cat, half-dancer,
Night's woman-petaled, lion-scented rose,
To whom I gave, out of a hero's need,
The dolor of my thrust, my riddling answer,
Whose force no lesser mortal knows. Dangerous?
Yes, as nervous oracles foretold
Who could not guess the secret taste of her:
Impossible wine! I came into the world
To fill a fate; am punished by my youth
No more. What if dog-faced logic howls
Was it art or magic multiplied my joy?
Nature has reasons beyond true or false.
We played like metaphysic animals
Whose freedom made our knowledge bold
Before the tragic curtain of the day:
I can bear the dishonor now of growing old.

Blinded and old, exiled, diseased, and scorned—
The verdict's bitten on the brazen gates,
For the gods grant each of us his lot, his term.
Hail to the King of Thebes!—my self, ordained
To satisfy the impulse of the worm,
Bemummied in those famous incestuous sheets,
The bloodiest flags of nations of the curse,
To be hung from the balcony outside the room
Where I encounter my most flagrant source.
Children, grandchildren, my long posterity,
To whom I bequeath the spiders of my dust,
Believe me, whatever sordid tales you hear,
Told by physicians or mendacious scribes,
Of beardless folly, consanguineous lust,
Fomenting pestilence, rebellion, war,
I come prepared, unwanting what I see,
But tied to life. On the royal road to Thebes
I had my luck, I met a lovely monster,
And the story's this: I made the monster me.

The sensitive and trained reader of these lines cannot escape believing that the Sphinx of the legend the poet has made to correspond profoundly to the Later Lady of the love-lyrics and that therefore Oedipus must be, in ways too deep to follow, a richly autobiographical character. The poem virtually equates the mastery of the lovely monster with the mastery of life itself, and that equation measures both the difficulties and the rewards of the conquest.

Kunitz has said, "No poetry is required of any of us. Our first labor is to master our worlds." No poetry is indeed required, but it is most welcome when, like that of Stanley

Kunitz, it authentically reports the breaking and the making of a poet and his world.

Stanley Moss (review date 1971)

SOURCE: "Man with a Leaf in His Head," in *Nation*, Vol. 213, No. 8, September 20, 1971, pp. 250-51.

[*Praising the artistry and maturity of* The Testing-Tree, *Moss considers some of Kunitz's major themes, including the opposition of life and death, the search for the unknown father, religion, and nature.*]

In his *Selected Poems*, published in 1958, Stanley Kunitz gave us some dozen poems that are likely to guide people guided by poetry, as long as English is read. He has "suffered the twentieth century," confronted tragic experience, given it form—in the course of the poems, triumphed over it. Now we have thirty additional poems. I have spent a month with *The Testing-Tree* in my pocket or within reach, blessed and tortured by its artistry. The new book brings a new open style; complications have been made apparently simple. When passionless, open simplicity is the crab grass of our literature, Kunitz's poems often begin with the naked truth. The new style faces that exacting passion.

In *The Testing-Tree* Kunitz's language ruthlessly prods the wounds of his life. His primordial curse is the suicide of his father before his birth. The poems take us into the sacred woods and houses of his 66 years, illuminate the images that have haunted him. Yet nowhere in the fiber of this book is there a thread of malice, anger, hatred, envy, pique; not a sneer, not a "sidelong pickerel smile," nor does Kunitz turn the other cheek. What he has managed is to turn the "conscience kind." In a time when literature seems to edge us toward suicide, or lead us into hell, Kunitz stands with Roethke on "the terrible threshold" and says, "I dance for the joy of surviving."

Call *The Testing-Tree* an ocean, take a stand along the shore, and a wave of change or counterchange will send you sprawling. But caution be damned. It is not Kunitz's sense of personal measure that leads; it is hallucination, apparition, that draws him and the reader to a state beyond reason.

Drawn deep into the underground of selfhood, Kunitz must "find, create in the past in order to become fully alive in the present." Is there another poet so haunted by the unknown? In a letter, referring to himself as a character in *The Divine Comedy*, Dante wrote: "'. . . . he saw certain things which he who thence descends cannot relate'; and he tells the reason, saying 'that the intellect is so engulfed' in the very thing for which it longs, . . . 'that memory cannot follow.'" I believe this is the territory Kunitz has staked out for himself. Where it is God for whom Dante longed, Kunitz, by some process for which the poem itself is the verb, searches for secret reality and the meaning of the unknown father. He moves from the

known to the unknown to the unknowable—not necessarily in that order.

Kunitz's poetry keeps a watchful eye on the 20th century. Of the thirty poems in *The Testing-Tree*, twelve clearly show a mind "engaged in history," and may be read as "parables for our time." History enters a number of poems where ideally and lifelessly it might have been excluded— for example, in the gentlest of love poems for his daughter. Nothing Kunitz has ever written in any way touching on history contradicts the findings of **"Night Letter"** among the *Selected Poems*: that history, no matter how dreadful or dreary, is a history of the human heart. He is among a bare handful of poets we have who can think in poetry.

In an essay Kunitz makes this central statement: "The hard and inescapable phenomenon to be faced is that we are living and dying at once. My commitment is to report the dialogue." The Kunitz dialogue, an explosion of opposites conceiving knowledge, is the molten core of the book. Out of this fire Kunitz has pulled a wonderful variety of forms. Here is Kunitz, for example, moving as life does from the comical-ridiculous to the tragic within the course of two lines:

> That coathanger neatly whisked your
>   coat
> right off your back. Soon it will want
>   your skin.

He has said, with a salute to Gerard Manley Hopkins, that he prefers a poem steeped in the "taste of self." Often, Kunitz's self and his "I" are used in separate ways. The "I" poems usually deal with temporal material; he is the speaker and he tells of events that actually happened. The song he says he sang when his child was ill we are certain he sang; the FBI really called; the number and kind of trees he planted are as stated. Kunitz's diggings are never in the fiefdoms of American regionalism. He pursues his own living and dying.

Then there is another self, his persona. As this self, he may appear as a prophet gardener, a Pacific salmon, a Lutheran minister who plotted to assassinate Hitler, a Jew in the desert. The poet is partly observer, partly the thing observed. He must be true to himself and, at the same time, he must speak within the confine of what the imagined or actual character might say, feel and do. As this self, he deals with aging, dying, moral and spiritual survival. He reaches to become something "beyond the merely human"— he prepares to die.

In **"The King of the River,"** the major poem on aging and dying, Kunitz's dialogue appears in its purest form:

> The great clock of your life
> is slowing down,
> and the small clocks run wild.
> For this were you born.

Among the useful notes in the back of the book, one on this poem reminds us of the two-week period in the life of the Pacific salmon during which it leaves the ocean, swims up river in full strength and beauty, spawns, turns old and colorless, and dies. The phenomenon is studied by geriatric medicine because the same process in the human takes twenty to forty years. Such concentration of living and dying offers ideal raw matter. (A similar concentration occurs in the poem around the hanged anti-Nazi pastor, thanks to the time structure provided by the S.S.) Here is the opening of **"King of the River"**:

> If the water were clear enough,
> if the water were still,
> but the water is not clear,
> the water is not still,
> you would see yourself,
> slipped out of your skin,
> nosing upstream,
> slapping, thrashing,
> tumbling
> over the rocks
> till you paint them
> with your belly's blood:
> Finned Ego
> yard of muscle that coils,
> uncoils.

Who peers into the water sees not himself, or the water in himself, but a self slipped out of its skin into a conditional world of the imagination. Much of the poem is written in the conditional mood. The word "I" never appears except late in the poem when the wind speaks. It is not by chance that "Finned Ego" is capitalized. Something of the great "I Am" must dart through the reader's mind. The poem aches for the unknowable, the unattainable. Rhythm and counter-rhythm and silence add to the meaning of argument and counter-argument. The **"King of the River"** is a dialogue, the method Socratic. Each passage—I hesitate to use the word stanza—with its unique rhythms, actions and stops, is a "question," answered by the closing lines of the poem. Here are the opening lines of the four sections:

> If the water were clear enough,
> if the water were still . . .
>
> If the knowledge were given you, . . .
>
> If the power were granted you
> to break out of your cells, . . .
>
> If the heart were pure enough, . . .

In fact, the "questions" are not questions but conditional statements; truth and language coil and uncoil simultaneously. Within the syntax of the poem, self and nature join and become something more lasting, if not holy.

In the closing passage of **"King of the River"** and **"Around Pastor Bonhoeffer"** a common action occurs. The self, the actor in each poem, has come to the "threshold of the last mystery," . . ."at the brute absolute hour" the dying-living being is turned back to face his origins, "the salt

kingdom," the world. The Extermination Camp section of **"Bonhoeffer"** closes with these lines:

> Oh but he knew the Hangman!
> Only a few steps more
> And he would enter the arcanum
> where the Master
> would take him by the shoulder,
> as He does at each encounter,
> and turn him round
> to face his brothers in the world.

As I see it, the final instruction is that at death man must face his fellow men, judge them and in turn be morally and spiritually judged. There is something Talmudic about it. Basic to the Jewish concept of atonement is the position that if you wrong a man, only he can forgive you, not God. (If you wrong God, you must ask forgiveness from him.) Kunitz has given us some of the great religious poems of our century. He is so personal in his spiritual attention (I struck out devotion) that to discuss his religion seems more of an affront than a service. He sees himself as a stranger. The sense of exile, which runs through the grain of his work, is a poet's exile, but it is also a Jew's. In **"An Old Cracked Tune,"** after the street song, Kunitz puts it like this:

> My name is Solomon Levi,
> the desert is my home,
> my mother's breast was thorny,
> and father I had none.
>
> The sands whispered, "Be separate,"
> the stones taught me, "Be hard."
> I dance for the joy of surviving,
> on the edge of the road.

There is no major American poet so free of place names as Kunitz. In **"The Mound Builders,"** in apparent contradiction, he travels through various places in the South, but he stops at Macon, Ga., where he quickly digs through the mounds of seven civilizations.

In an early poem he told us:

> If I must build a church,
> Though I do not really want one,
> Let it be in the wilderness
> Out of nothing but nail-holes.

Some poets have taken nature as a teacher. Frost saw it as indifferent, Melville as malignant. Thoreau, who certainly tried harder than most to be intimate with nature, had to admit:

> I still must seek the friend
> Who does with nature blend,
> Who is the person in her mask,
> He is the man I ask . . .

As a boy Kunitz threw his stones against "the indefatigable oak, tyrant and target," in a battle for "Love, poetry and for eternal life." We know the man in the poems has planted 10,000 trees. He is at peace with nature:

> I held a fantail of squirming roots
> that kissed the palm of my dirty hand,
> as if in reply to a bird.

Kunitz, now in his mid-60s, has found his way. His self, poetry and nature are worked with as one consubstantive stuff. This accomplishment, so simply presented in **"King of the River"** and **"The Mulch,"** should occasion a national holiday. He has become a mulch, a protector locked into nature. He is "a man with a leaf in his head." The leaf is both growing and memorized.

Stanley Kunitz with Cynthia Davis (interview date 1972)

SOURCE: An interview with Stanley Kunitz, in *Contemporary Literature*, Vol. 15, No. 1, Winter, 1974, pp. 1-14.

[*In the following interview, which was conducted on March 9, 1972, at Kunitz's home in New York, Kunitz comments on a number of subjects pertinent to his work, including the relationship between poetry and myth, his poetic development, the function of intellect and passion in poetry, the poet's position in society, his influences, his aversion to being called a "confessional poet," and the themes of guilt, love, and life and death in his verse.*]

[Davis]: *Mr. Kunitz, you said once to a group of students studying your poetry that no one has the "right answers" in interpretation, and that after it's published the poem belongs as much to them as to you. Are you generally reluctant to explain your poems?*

[Kunitz]: I often don't really know what a poem means, in rational terms. There are so many currents that flow into the poem, of which the poet himself can't be totally aware. Years after you have written a poem, you come back to it and find something you didn't know was there. Sometimes, I grant, a poet can be helpful about a specific image or an obscure portion of his poem.

Do you think it's helpful to talk about the circumstances that led to your writing a poem?

If they can be recalled, they may, in some cases, prove illuminating. But, as a general rule, the poem ought to have released itself from the circumstances of its origin.

Is that related to the idea of myth—poetry as myth?

Yes, it's that, but it's also related to my feeling that the poem has to be found beyond the day, that it requires a plunge into the well of one's being, where all one's key images lie. The occasion for a poem, which may have been something quite casual, is not the true source of the poem—it has only helped to trigger the right nerves.

When I asked about myth, I was thinking of the idea that I find in the poems of "The Coat without a Seam" [*a section in* **Selected Poems, 1928-1950,** *hereafter referred to as* **SP**] *especially, the idea that myth is something constant that can be expressed in many different kinds of circumstances, but that goes beyond circumstances—even beyond the individual. So a great poem speaks to everyone because all share a common condition.*

Jung spoke of archetypal images that go beyond the individual persona and that pertain to the collective history of the race.

Is that a reason for your use of dream and hallucination in the poetry—to reach that archetypal material?

I think of dream as an actual visitation into that world, as a clue to secrets of which one is only faintly aware in ordinary consciousness.

But you wouldn't agree with the "psychic automatism" of the surrealists?

No. Because I think a poem is a combination of unconscious and conscious factors. One is trying to reach a level of transcendence; at the same time, one has to keep a grip on language, not to let it run away with itself. Automatic writing is such a bore!

Is your use of metaphysical techniques—exploiting the metaphor in extended conceits—one of the ways of exercising that conscious control over language, giving form to the raw materials of the unconscious mind?

The image leads you out of yourself into a world of relatives. The beautiful risk to take is to extend the image as far as you can go, until it turns in upon itself. The danger is in jumping off into absurdity, but that's part of the risk.

Perhaps we can consider some of these questions by talking about changes in your development. You eliminated almost half of the poems in **Intellectual Things** (*1930*) *in later volumes. Was that because they were technically unsuccessful, or because you no longer agreed with the ideas you expressed in them?*

My main feeling was that they were immature. Maybe I felt a little embarrassed reading them, so I thought it would be better to drop them, that's all.

I felt that many of the poems in that book placed much greater emphasis on the power of the intellect than later poems. I'm thinking of poems like **"Mens Creatrix,"** *in which you seem to talk about the superiority of the intellect over the emotions. I wondered if perhaps one of the reasons for elimination of such poems was that you had changed your emphasis.*

I doubt it. Certainly when I was writing the poems in **Intellectual Things,** I meant to demonstrate, if I could, not that the poem was a cerebral exercise, but the contrary, that the intellect and the passions were inseparable—which is the whole point of the Blake epigraph to the book, "The tear is an intellectual thing."

Then why the poems in which you talk about putting away passion, or subduing it by intellectual power?

It's not a question of putting it away or rising above it. Remember, I'm thinking back a good many years, so that I wouldn't swear to this—but my recollection is that my characteristic figure at this stage, in speaking of mind and heart, was of each devouring and being devoured by the other, an act of mutual ingestion. In **"Beyond Reason"** [from *Intellectual Things,* hereafter referred to as *IT*] I spoke of taming the passions "with the sections of my mind"—as though it were a sort of dog food—but then I wanted to "teach my mind to love its thoughtless crack."

One of the poems that impressed me on this theme was "Motion of wish" (**IT**).

I'll take a look at it and see whether you're right or not. . . . Yes, I think the lines you were thinking of were ". . . wish may find / Mastery only in the mind." This poem I haven't looked at in so long, but as I read it now, I see these lines as the key to understanding of the poem: ". . . mariners eat / One lotus-moment to forget / All other moments, and their eyes / Fasten on impossible surprise." And then the end: "A man may journey to the sun, / But his one true love and companion / Sleeps curled in his thoughtful womb. / Here will the lone life-traveler come / To find himself infallibly home." But you have to consider here that the mind is the eater of the passions, and the passions rest in that mind, so that what one is asserting is a sense of the unity of all experience, not a separation.

And the mind contains that sense of unity.

Yes. The mind stands for the whole experiential and existential process. I think that the confusion here is to think that when I talk of mind in this volume, that I'm talking about brain. I'm not talking about brain; I'm talking about the whole process of existence.

What about poems like "Very Tree" (**IT**), *where is seems that what you're saying is that you perceive the essence of the tree—its treeness—and discard its particulars? That the particulars are not important?*

One of my great influences was Plato, and I was very deep in Platonic lore, especially at this period of my first work. The theme is the idea of tree, treeness, as opposed to the shadow of the idea.

But you're not really suggesting that particulars of experience are unimportant?

You arrive at universals through the perception—the clear perception—of what Blake called "Minute Particulars."

These earlier poems are much more abstract than your later work, aren't they?

I suppose so. That may have been the Platonic influence, as much as anything else that I can think of.

Did you become dissatisfied with that kind of approach?

As I became more of a political being, I wanted to fasten my poems to the reality of the day. I turned away from poems that began with the grandeur of generality. I wanted to find the general through breaking the kernel of particulars.

Is this why, in **Passport to the War** *(1944), you make so many references to contemporary events? As concretions for your general themes?*

Don't you think that that is possibly simply the result of maturing a bit and having more experience of the world? At the time of writing *Intellectual Things*, I was in my early twenties and was an innocent in so many ways. I had developed intellectually more than I had emotionally or experientially.

This volume, especially the war poetry, seems very different even from your later poetry.

It was my darkest time.

Do you still have the same feelings about the conditions of the modern world and what it does to man?

I've never stopped being a dissenter. I have no use for a superior technology that breeds hatred, injustice, inequality, and war.

What do you think the poet's position should be in relationship to that kind of society?

Number one, he must not become a subscribing member of it. Since the beginning of the Industrial Revolution, the poet has been the prophetic voice of a counterculture. Poetry today speaks more directly to the young than ever before because they recognize its adversary position.

Then you think it's more difficult to be a poet now than it was before the nineteenth century?

The poet before the Industrial Revolution could identify himself with State or Church, but he certainly has not been able to do so since. That's why he is a creature apart.

You often talk about guilt in **Passport to the War**. *Sometimes it's played upon by society, but sometimes you seem to say that everyone carries a load of guilt around with him. What is this guilt caused by and directed at?*

When I speak of **"The Guilty Man"** [from *Passport to the War*, hereafter referred to as *PW*], I don't mean someone who has sinned more than anybody else. I mean the person who, simply by virtue of being mortal, is in a way condemned; he's mortal and he's fallible, and his life is inevitably a series of errors and consequences. Since he cannot really see the true path—it is not given to him to see it, except in moments of revelation—he is denied the rapture of innocence.

Like Original Sin?

Without the theological furniture.

Is this related to the existentialist idea of the fear of freedom?

I was making noises like an existentialist before I knew what it was to be one. I keep on trying to record my sense of being alive, which means in practice my sense, from moment to moment, of living and dying at once, a condition of perpetual crisis.

In particular, when I read **"The Fitting of the Mask"** (**PW**), *I thought of Sartre's "bad faith": the attempt to conceal one's own being from oneself.*

If we did not wear masks, we should be frightened of mirrors.

You say in **"Night Letter"** (**PW**) *that you "believe in love" as the salvation from this fear of one's own being and from the evils of modern society. Are you speaking primarily of love for mankind or personal love?*

Abstract love is not love at all. One expresses love in relation to another—that's the germinal node. I don't really care much for people who are always talking about love for mankind and hate their neighbors.

The treatment of the love theme is another difference I found between the first volume and later ones. In **Intellectual Things**, *the love poetry is often about relationships that fail; it isn't until the later poetry that you really celebrate fulfilling relationships.*

That's more or less to be expected. After all, the disasters of early love are legendary and part of one's education. For that reason, among others, poets in their youth tend to be melancholy. "When I was young," said Yeats, "my Muse was old; now that I am old, my Muse is young."

It wasn't, then, that you had a more pessimistic conception of the relationship?

I've always been an optimist about love. Three marriages are the proof.

I'd like to talk a little about **Selected Poems**. *Perhaps we could begin with a poem that seems central to that volume,* **"The Approach to Thebes"** *That poem ends with these lines: ". . . I met a lovely monster, / And the story's this: I made the monster me." Is this just acceptance of one's fate?*

More than that. . . . I have a theory about monsters. I remember, a few years ago, telling Mark Rothko, who was a dear friend of mine, that every genius is a monster. Mark thought about that for some time, and then, with the

typical vanity of an artist, said, "You mean I'm a monster?" I replied, "Well, I'm not talking about anybody in this room." But of course I was. The adversary artist in our time pays a price, in human terms, for his excess of ego and sensibility. He has had to sacrifice too much; he is poisoned by ambition; and he carries too big a load of griefs and shames—that's the hunch on his back. You're not likely to find him open, generous, or joyous. Rothko, incidentally, killed himself by slashing his wrists not long after our discussion. I have a poem about him, entitled **"The Artist,"** in *The Testing-Tree*.

And the burden of monsterdom is placed on mythic heroes, too?

Yes.

There's one mythic hero that you seem to consider more than others, and that's Christ. Why is the Christian myth more important in your poetry than other myths?

Because it shakes me more. It is the supreme drama of guilt and redemption. I have no religion—perhaps that is why I think so much about God.

When you speak of myth in poetry, you mean a re-creation of the human drama embodied in religious myths such as this?

Poetic myth is nourished by all the great traditions.

Then you are saying that all myths attempt to do the same thing, to tell the same story.

All myths are the same myth; all metaphors are the same metaphor. When you touch the web of creation at any point, the whole web shudders.

And poetry has the same function as myth?

Metaphorically.

You draw many parallels between the poet and the mythic hero. Do you, like so many poets, see the poet as supreme example of affirmative action, of what a man can be?

As I said a while back, he can be a monster. But ideally he is the last representative free man, in that he is beholden to nobody but himself and his own vision of truth. Almost anybody else you can think of is beholden to others: the pastor to his congregation, the politician to the public, the actor to his audience. But the poet, since he is not a commodity, is more blessed than others—he can strive toward the absolute purity of his art.

Aren't you beholden to your publisher and your readers, at least in some measure financially?

No, I don't think so. One manages to survive. If I felt for a moment that I had to write lies in order to publish, I would stop publishing. It wouldn't matter that much. I could still go on writing.

You're especially concerned with the question of what it is to be a poet in "The Coat without a Seam," and nearly all of the poems in that section are new in **Selected Poems**. *Why is it that you became more concerned with poems about poetry in that volume?*

I'm not sure that I did. Periodically one tries to redefine and reassert one's vocation—not always in obvious terms. Wallace Stevens made a career out of doing precisely that. "Poetry," he wrote, "is the subject of the poem." As you rightly perceived, I keep trying to relate poetic function with mythic or heroic destiny.

You note that relationship in other sections, too, in poems like "Green Ways."

I wonder whether you caught the logic of the various sections in the **Selected Poems**. They were meant to indicate my primary thematic concerns.

Perhaps you would talk about a couple of those sections; for example, "The Terrible Threshold."

That title—"The Terrible Threshold"—comes, of course, from one of the poems, **"Open the Gates,"** where the poet sees "The end and the beginning in each other's arms." I think of the poems in this section as visionary experiences, culminating in a moment of illumination.

In speaking to a group of students studying **"Prophecy on Lethe"** (SP), *you said that that moment was one of fleeting awareness, and that you couldn't state what that awareness was of. If you can't state what you see in that moment of epiphany. . . .*

I don't have to state it. The awareness is in the poem, not in my memory of it. Come to think of it, I don't even remember what the last lines were!

"With your strange brain blooming as it lies / Abandoned to the bipeds on the beach; / Your jelly-mouth and, crushed, your polyp eyes."

I see all those death images piled up on that shore. The key word, the transcendental word, for me is "blooming."

There's a movement there toward a sense of identity, isn't there? First an anonymous figure floating on the stream, and at the end you speak directly to the "you."

Death-in-Life. Life-in-Death. The glory of the senses. . . .

This is what I was trying to get at: I saw the poem as, at least partially, a myth of the birth of consciousness, moving from a Being-in-Itself state—unconscious and no perception—to that sense of identity that you have because you're conscious. And of course, a sharper awareness of your own sensuous perceptions. I don't know whether that would be valid or not.

Thanks—I'll buy it. It just occurs to me that there's a comparable evolution in my later poem, **"Green Ways."** I hadn't seen the affinity before.

And part of the point of "Green Ways" is that it is the duty of the conscious being to accept his consciousness, isn't it?

More than that, he must affirm his vegetable and mineral existence, as well as his animal self.

Not discarding them with consciousness, then.

Accepting them, in the fullness of the life-process.

Could you talk a little about "The Serpent's Word" section also?

Those are love poems, or deal with the love experience. The phrase is always the key to the section that it heads; here it's from the line. "Who taught me the serpent's word, but yet the word." Which takes us back to the Garden of Eden.

In "The Dark and the Fair" (SP), the source of that line, there's a Fair Lady and another Dark Lady, and the Dark Lady replaces the Fair. The Dark Lady is from the past; is she symbolic of the Fall?

She's Lilith, in the poem.

There is another poem in "The Serpent's Word" that I find more difficult than most, "As Flowers Are."

That poem records the changes in a field through the seasons. And at the same time, it offers by implication a metaphor of the aspects of love. From week to week each species of flower, each hue, struggles to gain possession of the field.

Is that the "war" of the flowers?

Yes. The yellows and whites of spring yield to the hot tones of summer, a riot of colors. The chill nights bring the lavenders in; and, with the first frost, the whole field turns bronze. It's a parable, I suppose.

I think I see it now.

It's not so difficult, if you listen to the music.

You've said that in an open society, poetry tends to become hermetic, more difficult, and very private. Do you think this is true of your own poetry?

The important question is, do I still think we live in an open society. Certainly America seems to me less open than it was. And certainly my work has undergone a sea-change. Robert Lowell wrote something to the effect that I've broken with my "passionately gnarled" earlier style and am writing in a language that "even cats and dogs can understand." Perhaps in my age I've managed to untie some of the knots of my youth. I want to say what I have to say without fuss. I want to strip everything down to essentials.

You talked about some of these ideas in **Passport to the War**, *and that volume also had a more open style than the first one.*

Poets are always wanting to change their lives and their styles. Of the two, it's easier to change the life.

In that last volume, **The Testing-Tree** *(1971), you included several of your translations of other authors. Why did you pick those particular ones?*

Obviously because I liked them as poems. And because they seemed to have an affinity with my own work. For example, I've been working on the poems of Anna Akhmatova for several years—they make up my next book. I've been so absorbed in her verse that it would be surprising if I hadn't been affected by it. Incidentally, I tend to think of a book as a composition, a joining of parts into an architectural whole, not just a throwing-together of the poems as written. A book ought to have an interior logic: these few translations seemed to me to fit into the logic of this particular book. I deliberately excluded scores of others.

Are they fairly strict translations?

Close, but not slavishly close. Translating poetry is an exercise in paradox. "Be true to me!" says the poem to its translator. And in the next breath, "Transform me, make me new!" If you follow the original, word for word, and lose the poetry—as you must, if you insist on a literal rendering—your translation is a dud. But if you find the poetry in a free act of the imagination, it's a lie. I'm reminded of the citizen in Kafka's aphorism who's fettered to two chains, one attached to earth, the other to heaven. No matter which way he heads, the opposite chain pulls him back with a jolt. That's pretty much the condition of the translator.

Do you read the originals yourself?

My knowledge of Russian is rudimentary. Though my parents came from Russia, I am not a Russian linguist or scholar. So I nearly always translate with somebody whom I can depend on for roots and connotations and allusions. Max Hayward helped me with Akhmatova, as he did before with Voznesensky.

Did you do many translations earlier?

A few . . . from French, Spanish, and Italian. I included one of my Baudelaire translations in *Selected Poems*. He was important to me.

You spoke of the "internal logic" of a volume of poetry. Does **The Testing-Tree** *have a definite logic for its sections, as* **Selected Poems** *does?*

A logic, but less definite, perhaps. I shuffled those poems all around. The first section is the overture, anticipating the main themes. Section two is dominated by poems of place; three, political; four deals with the role and character of the artist.

The title poem seems most like your earlier poems in theme.

Not in form, certainly. But that and **"King of the River"** go back to the mythic.

Were they written earlier?

No. Quite late.

Would you say, then, that your themes are the same, that you're just expressing them in a different way?

A man's preoccupations and themes aren't likely to change. What changes is the extent to which he can put the full diversity of his moods and interests and information into his poems. Formal verse is a highly selective medium. A high style wants to be fed exclusively on high sentiments. Given the kind of person I am, I came to see the need for a middle style—for a low style, even, though that may be outside my range.

I was interested in Robert Lowell's review of **The Testing-Tree** *because I thought that he was saying, among other things, that the new poetry was more like his, more like confessional poetry.*

I've always been an intensely subjective poet. There's never been any shift from that.

The sort of open description of autobiographical detail that appears in your last volume is generally considered confessional poetry.

Confession is a private matter. Most so-called confessional poetry strikes me as raw and embarrassing—bad art.

Do you think you've been influenced by any of the confessional poets? Lowell and Roethke?

In the first place, you musn't call Roethke a confessional poet.

He would have vomited at the thought. We were friends for thirty years, till his death, swapping manuscripts and criticism. My friendship with Lowell dates from the publication of my *Selected Poems* in 1958. *Intellectual Things* had brought Roethke and me together—he was still unpublished. But these are more than literary friendships. In these long and deep associations it's idle to discuss who influences whom. Friendship is a sustained act of reciprocity. We have all been touched by our interchange. Vulnerable human beings affect each other; that's all there is to it.

You wouldn't then put yourself in any group?

Now or at any stage, I can't imagine to what group I could possibly be attached. A one-to-one relationship is the limit of my herd instinct.

What earlier poets would you say influenced you greatly?

Donne and Herbert and Blake were my first major influences—Donne and Herbert stylistically, Blake prophetically. I must have learned something, too, from Wordsworth's "Prelude" and his "Intimations of Immortality." For awhile I steeped myself in Keats and Tennyson. After that, almost nobody until Hopkins overwhelmed me during my college years. And Yeats, of course, whom I consider to be the great master of the poem in English in this century. I suppose Eliot to a degree, though I opposed him, quarreling with his ideas, his criticism, and what I thought of as his poverty of sympathy. His theory of the depersonalization of poetry struck me as false and destructive. My work didn't fit into that picture of his at all. Both Roethke and I felt from the beginning that the Eliot school was our principal adversary. We fought for a more passionate art. Nevertheless I was so aware of his existence that even in a negative way I was influenced by him. So was Roethke. That Eliot rhythm had an hypnotic effect.

I'd like to go back for a moment to the question we discussed earlier, your differences from confessional poets. Your latest volume is certainly more directly autobiographical than the others. Rosenthal justifies the use of autobiographical material in confessional poetry by the poet's assumption that the literal self is important and that it becomes symbolic of the world—what happens to the self is what the modern world does to man. How does your idea of poetry differ from that?

I phrase it differently. I say that the effort is to convert one's life into legend, which isn't quite the same thing. Secrets are part of the legend. My emphasis isn't on spilling everything. It's on the act of transformation, the ritual sense, the perception of a destiny.

Is it possible to see these mythic connections even if you're not a poet?

I'm not contending that the poet is set apart from others. On the contrary, he is more like others than anybody else—that's his nature. It's what Keats meant by negative capability, the predisposition to flow into everyone and everything. A poetry of self-indulgence and self-advertisement is produced by the egotistical sublime—Keats's phrase again—and is simply ugly. God knows a poet needs ego, but it has to be consumed in the fire of the poetic action.

Then your view is almost the reverse of the confessional one; you begin with a general idea of the human condition.

The only reason you write about yourself is that this is what you know best. What else has half as much reality for you? Even so, certain details of your life can be clouded by pain, or fear, or shame, or other complications, that induce you to lie, to disguise the truth about yourself. But the truth about yourself is no more important than the truth about anybody else. And if you knew anybody else as well as you know yourself, you would write about that other.

Stanley Kunitz with Robert Boyers (interview date 1972)

SOURCE: "'Imagine Wrestling with an Angel': An Interview with Stanley Kunitz," in *Salmagundi*, No. 22/23, Spring/Summer, 1973, pp. 71-83.

[*In the following interview, which is an edited transcript of a public interview conducted at Skidmore College in April, 1972, Kunitz discusses, among other subjects, trends in contemporary poetry, the process of composing verse, the function of poetry, the work of up-and-coming poets, his influences, and the practice of labeling poets.*]

[Boyers]: *Whenever I go and visit people who are interested in poetry, there seems to be constant reference to Stanley Kunitz as the "poets' poet." Have you heard yourself described in this way? What do you think these people mean?*

[Kunitz]: When it was said of Spenser, it was meant to be a compliment. Nowadays it would depend on the inflection. I'm a bit leery of it.

I was wondering if the fact that people speak of you in these terms suggests that they have in mind another kind of poetry which is more immediately contemporary, more popular among the young on college campuses, and whether this isn't the poetry, this other poetry, that the best poets themselves consider inferior, perhaps not poetry at all?

That may be so, but it's dangerous to think of poetry as being divided into two kinds—a high art and a low art. No poet can afford to be out of touch with the commonplace. In my youth I suppose I rather willed myself on being an hermetic poet. But for years I have tried to make my work more open and accessible, without sacrificing its complex inner tissue. Film, jazz, and rock have been very much a part of my world of experience.

You read many poetry manuscripts. Can you give us some notions of what the younger poets, those who've not published volumes, are writing?

The most notable characteristic of the poetry written by the young—in their 20's or 30's—is its variety. There is no dominant strain that I can detect. So much depends on local interest—regional associations, university teachers who happen at the moment to be available to them as models. A few years ago it seemed to me that the New York School had many adherents over the country, but I think there are fewer now—it seems to have exhausted its potentiality. Certainly Robert Bly and company have a number of acolytes who follow their precepts thundered from on high—but that's only one aspect of the scene. You can find almost as many different styles as you can find poets.

In particular I was interested in one poet who was awarded the Yale Series Prize, Hugh Seidman, in many ways a remarkable poet. Now many of his poems seem to me to be haphazardly put together, and he seems to trust a good deal to what one might call the "happy accident," the chance hit, which is matched, I guess, by a great many unlucky misses. I wonder if you might speak a little bit about that kind of poetry, a poetry which includes the "happy accident."

The concept of chance is inseparable from the act of poetry. Verse that is precalculated and preordained inevitably goes dead. There has to be room for accidents in the writing of a poem. You leave yourself open to the possibility of anything happening and you hope that it will work—if it doesn't that's your hard luck.

In the volume The Contemporary Poet as Artist and Critic, *there is a symposium having to do with your poem "Father and Son," a very beautiful poem. There is some talk in the symposium about the line in the poem which reads "The night nailed like an orange to my brow." In the course of your response, you speak of the line as an example of that special kind of risk which poets must take, and which constitutes a kind of signature, a unique signature of the poet. Could you speak a little bit about the relationship between a good risk and a bad risk in poetry?*

I don't think that you can tell beforehand whether the risk is a good one or a bad one—but if you take no risks, I doubt that much will happen. I want to venture beyond what I know to be safe and correct, to grapple with a possibility that doesn't yet appear.

And would you say that in taking the risk with a line that doesn't seem readily to yield its private associations even to a reader who's armed with the elementary biographical information, you would justify that risk simply on the basis of what you felt strongly at the time the poem was being composed? That is, must one always take into account the presence of the reader who perhaps won't be able to pick up the association?

In the first place the poet hasn't invited the reader to become the judge of his poem—he enters the scene after the event. It is the reader's choice—he can either continue to work with the poem, or he can decide that it offers him nothing, and if he so chooses, that's his privilege. The poet ought not to complain if the reader decides that he doesn't like that particular poem, or that he can't understand it, and turns to another poem, or to somebody else's work. A poet who begins by saying, "I am myself and only myself," is in no position to demand, "You must read me and love me." My own preference is for a poetry that looks fairly simple on the surface, but that moves mysteriously inside its skin.

I'm very interested also in raising the whole question of composition, the process of composition, and I've come upon all sorts of preferences in poets who come at their poems in a great variety of ways. Roethke, for instance, speaks in the Letters *of carrying around a phrase in his pocket, scrawled on a piece of paper for a very long time, and then of allowing that single phrase or image to develop over perhaps several years, and then watching that phrase lead to others, and finally building an entire poem out of that one single image; or I think of Dylan Thomas establishing a whole string of end rhymes and then sort of backing into the poem, filling in the text that leads to the end rhyme. How do you compose a poem?*

I'm a night bird, so that most of my poems happen in the small hours and usually after a long struggle to clean my mind out—to get rid of the day—that's the first step. The

poem usually ripples out from something buried. Perhaps you turn over the leaves of your notebook and come across a phrase 5 years old, or 15 years old, that leaps out of the page—it's ready now to be played with. And then you begin pushing words and rhythms around. But to me it's mainly dredging, dredging down into the unconscious—trying to find associations, links with the whole life and with the secrets of the life, not with the obvious materials. And so the poem slowly builds. I say it over and over again—whatever I have of it—the lines with which I begin—it's a kind of incantation and maybe a form of self-hypnosis, who knows, but gradually the rhythm begins to take over, and then I know that nothing is going to stop the poem from happening.

Do you think it's possible for a reader of poems, like yourself for instance, to perceive, in reading the poem for the first time, whether it was written with one approach rather than another, whether a poem suggests in its very contours, its surface contours, whether it was constructed out of an image which gave birth to others, or whether it was originally an "idea poem," emerging from a particular thematic concern, a political idea, for instance? Do poems yield that kind of information, do you think?

In the kind of poem I'm talking about the stitching between thoughts and feelings is invisible. I don't really care much for "idea poems" as such. They're a form of illustration.

Who were the poetic models that you adopted and followed as a young poet? Were you, for instance, taken by T. S. Eliot, as others were who came of age in the 1920's and '30's?

I was moved by him but I resisted him—I think that's the answer there—one could not help but be moved by him because he was a poetic event. Certainly "The Wasteland" shook my world at the moment of its appearance. I can still remember the thrill of picking up my copy of *The Dial* in which it appeared. Subsequently I became a kind of adversary. His definition of poetry as an objective act, a depersonalized performance, was contrary to my own conviction that the art and the life were bound together. I sought a more passionate voice. And I scorned his politics.

Were there other models that you felt closer to in that time, in the '20's, for instance?

Contemporaries? No. The poets who meant most to me then were Yeats (the later Yeats) and Hopkins. I studied both intensively. Hardy was another of my admirations.

Did you study Thomas a good deal, later on, in the '40's and the beginning of the '50's?

Not particularly—though there are five or six of Thomas's poems that I admire. You're talking now of literary fashions—something I have no use for. In the '20's and '30's, one had to follow Eliot in order to have an audience. In the late '30's, into the '40's, one had to be Audenesque. Then Thomas was the rage. Later the Beats had their turn.

And so it goes. The easiest poet to neglect is one who resists classification.

In thinking of tastes and fashions in poetry, I've often been fascinated by a number of things the late Sir Herbert Read used to say about poetry, feeling that a sort of betrayal was involved in a poet's going back over ground that had been amply covered by other poets. Do you think that there is such a thing as regression in the life of poetry, and perhaps more to the point, what is the nature of the function of innovation in poetry? Is it necessary that great poets be radical innovators? Can you conceive of a great poet who is an aesthetic reactionary?

Pound more or less covered that ground when he set aside a category of inventors among the poets. They are not necessarily the strongest voices of an age, but they often have great influence. Pound affected his contemporaries more than, let us say, Yeats did, who was not an inventor, but I would be willing to say flatly that Yeats is the greater poet.

You would say, then, that the whole idea of regression in the life of poetry is not really a viable notion, that it is possible to go back over old ground, and to do things which are essentially similar to what earlier poets perfected?

The trouble with Read's idea is that the idea of regression, like the idea of progress, has no aesthetic relevance. The way backward and the way forward are the same. A rediscovery of the past often leads to radical innovation. We know, for example, that Picasso was inspired by African sculpture, that the art of the Renaissance is linked with the resurgence of classic myth. Poetic technique follows the same route. At the moment I can think of Hopkins, who went back to Old English for his sprung rhythm; of Pound, who turned his ear on Provencal song; of Berryman, who dug up inversion and minstrel patter for his *Dream Songs*. These are all acts of renewal, not tired replays of the style of another period—which is the last thing I am prepared to defend. Pound was, of course, right, in his criticism of "The Wasteland" manuscript, when he dissuaded Eliot from trying to compete with Pope in the matter of composing heroic couplets. As he said, Pope could do it better. In general, a poet has to rework—not imitate—the past, and the success of his reworking is dependent on the degree of his contemporary awareness. If a poet has an ear for the living speech—whose rhythmic pattern is ever so slightly modified from generation to generation—he has at least the foundation of a style, the one into which he was born. I recall that Roethke and I used to challenge each other to guess the dates of the most obscure poems we could find. Over a long period we become so expert at the game that we almost never missed by more than ten years. It was simply because the voice, the stylistic voice, of any decade is unmistakable.

Is there such a thing as a direct relation between the poet and the particular moment of his culture, conceived as a political situation? What I'm referring to is the kind of statement we've heard from Denise Levertov of late, where

the claim is made that a poet who is of his time must necessarily reflect the moment of his culture, especially when that culture is in crisis and turmoil, that to indulge a strictly personal kind of poetry at a time when one's own country is engaged in destroying thousands of people in Vietnam, for instance, is to do something that is totally irresponsible and runs counter to the whole life of poetry. Does that make any sense to you?

The war disgusts and outrages me, just as it does Denise, but I'm not inclined to tell other poets what they may or may not write. Each of us has to be trusted with his own conscience. The fanatic is the direct opposite of the poet. It's no accident that most of the poetry of confrontation is such appalling stuff. What could be more spiritually stultifying than an exclusive diet of anti-war or anti-Nixon tracts? An age in crisis needs more than ever to be made aware of the full range of human possibility.

In that respect, what do you see as the basic function of your own art? Is it essentially designed to give pleasure, is it educative, does it serve the function of rendering the general experience more complex?

Let me try to reply in an historical context. Modern poetry, in the long view, springs out of the Age of Enlightenment and the Industrial Revolution. When faith withered and the Church could no longer satisfy the universal need for otherness, poetry became the alternative medium of transcendence. The poet assumed, or reasserted—from an earlier tribal structure—an ambiguous but socially disturbing role with prophetic or shamanistic implications. One of his functions—as Blake clearly understood—was to serve as defender of the natural universe and of natural man against the greed and ambition of the spoilers and their faceless agents. Politically, I see the poet as the representative free man, the irreconcilable adversary of the Nation-State.

Is there any useful connection to be made, in a general sense, between age and creativity? Many have claimed that the creative powers wane with the advancing years, yet we all know of very wonderful poets who seemed to have their powers grow stronger with the passage of the years. For me, for instance, the major period of William Carlos Williams is his final period, though that is not the case, of course, with people like Eliot or Stevens. Is there any general relationship that's worth pointing to?

The determining factor there is the relationship between the life and the work. Yeats has a phrase, "radical innocence," that I cherish. As I interpret it, it's the capacity for perpetual self-renewal, as opposed to a condition of emotional exhaustion or world-weariness; it's waking each day to the wonder of possibility; it's being like a child—which is not to say being childish. "There lives the dearest freshness deep down things"—Hopkins' line—that's an expression of radical innocence. With Blake, it's the very essence of his art and of his prophetic function. The poets of radical innocence stay alive till the day they die—and, even then, they take that last step as an adventure. . . .

Do you especially care for the work of poets whose names are frequently linked with Lowell as part of the confessional school? Do you feel any kinship with poets like Snodgrass, or Sylvia Plath? Is this where the energy of our best poetry has been?

I must tell you that, like most poets, I hate labels. I'm not quite sure what confessional poetry is, though certain critics have seen fit to discuss me as a late convert to that school. I guess I resent that. I've always admired a fierce subjectivity; but compulsive exhibitionism—and there's plenty of that around—gobs of sticky hysteria—are an embarrassment. Perhaps I sound more censorious than I intend. One of my premises is that you can say anything as long as it is true . . . but not everything that's true is worth saying. Another is that you need not be a victim of your shame . . . but neither should you boast about it. In this context maybe Roethke showed me a way of coping with affliction. Nearly all his adult life he was a manic-depressive, subject to intermittent crack-ups of devastating violence. In the beginning he was terribly ashamed of these episodes and tried to conceal them, even from his closest friends. When he was sent away to a mental hospital, he pretended that he had gone off on vacation. The onset of his best work coincided with his discovery that he need not feel guilty about his illness; that it was a condition he could explore and use; that it was, in fact, convertible into daemonic energy, the driving power of imagination. At the same time he began to read Jung, who clarified for him the act of psychic regression, that is, of reliving one's embryonic passage through fish-shape, frog-shape, bird-shape until one is born human. That knowledge, that deep metamorphic awareness, became the source of Roethke's strength in his major poems. What they speak of is archetypal experience—which has nothing to do with being a "confessional" poet.

You've spoken of your own work in terms of the note of tragic exaltation. Can you describe what this constitutes, how you see this tonality functioning in your poems? Does it bear relation to what we get in classical tragedy, for instance?

Not much—but maybe in so far as Recognition is an element of Greek tragedy. It's easier to locate the feeling than to define it. I could offer some lines as a touchstone: "I stand on the terrible threshold, and I see / The end and the beginning in each other's arms." Or Mandelstam, at a greater distance, saying: "Only the flash of recognition brings delight." Or Pascal invoking "the eternal silence of the infinite spaces." Not everybody detects the exaltation, for it's a far more secret thing than terror or despair. Imagine wrestling with an angel, the darkest one of the tribe. You know you're doomed to lose. But that weight on your shoulder!

Do you read much besides creative or imaginative literature? Do you keep up with developments in psychoanalysis, in aesthetics, in the sciences, and so on?

I try to, except for aesthetics, which seems to me an arid subject. Astrophysics has always fascinated me. And any-

thing to do with the natural universe. Right now I'm deep in whales.

But you do feel that the most exciting things at the moment are still poetry, that the work of young and coming poets is still more exciting and alive than work done in other areas?

No doubt I'm prejudiced, but I honestly believe that the poetic imagination is capable of embracing the actualities of our time more fully than any other discipline, including the scientific. That's one explanation of my involvement with the graduate writing program at Columbia, with the Yale Series of Younger Poets, and with the Fine Arts Work Center in Provincetown, Massachusetts, where young writers and artists can find a loosely structured community, created for their benefit. Has anyone noticed how the poetic and scientific imaginations are beginning to draw together for mutual sustenance? Perhaps it's an instinctive alliance determined by our crisis of survival. You mentioned Seidman earlier, my first poetry choice at Yale. He was trained as a physicist, and is an expert on the computer. My second choice, Peter Klappert, was a student of zoology, who planned to be a veterinarian. Michael Casey, who came back from Vietnam with his collection of *Obscenities,* was another physics major, who expected to become an engineer, till the Yale award threw him off his course. Robert Hass's book isn't out yet, but its title, *Field Guide,* suggests that it isn't incompatible with the others. Love and botany are his twin preoccupations. Different kinds of intellect may be turning to poetry out of desperation, but it's a good sign, nevertheless.

You mentioned last night that you've been working on a long poem. Is there any special reason why you haven't written one before now, and could you speak a little bit about the general failure of our poets to write successful long poems, in most cases even to undertake them?

The problem of the long poem, like that of the novel, is related to our loss of faith in the validity of the narrative continuum. Joyce invented a technique for coping with a new time sense, but that required a superhuman effort, which no longer seems consistent with an anti-heroic age. The collapse of Pound's *Cantos* remains a central symptomatic event. Technically he understood the problem, as his contribution to the making of "The Wasteland" proves, but his own project was too indeterminate, and he had overreached himself in the matter of scale. As a collection of fragments, of fairly limited scope, "The Wasteland" seems better adapted for enduring the weathers of an age. I suppose the last major effort to build a solid block of marble was Hart Crane's—and "The Bridge" has its magnificence, but it is the magnificence of failure. "Mistress Bradstreet" and "Howl" arepassionate apostrophes, but their architecture is too frail for the weight of their rhetoric. Berryman's *Dream Songs* and Lowell's *Notebook*—to be called *History* in its next incarnation—don't aspire to the unity of the long poem. Essentially they're poetic sequences, like the sonnet cycles of the Elizabethans. I am half-persuaded that the modern mind is too distracted for the span of attention demanded by the long poem, and that no single theme, given the disorder of our epoch, is capable of mobilizing that attention. But I am only half-persuaded.

I also wanted to ask you about the whole question of obscurity in the poem, something that Randall Jarrell suggests in a number of places to the effect that in an age which is so apt to appropriate poets, to convert them into acrobats of a sort, it may in fact be the business of the poet to be obscure, to challenge this audience, to make readers uncomfortable, to make them work for whatever pleasures they can get from the poem. Do you feel any sympathy with that?

During the heyday of the New Criticism, there were poets who trafficked in obfuscation, providing grist for the critics who trafficked in the explication of obfuscation. A beautiful symbiotic relationship! Poets today tend to be clearer—sometimes all too clear. I strive for a transparency of surface, but I should be disappointed if my work yielded all its substance and tonality at first reading. "Never try to explain," I say somewhere. A poem is charged with a secret life. Some of its information ought to circulate continuously within its perimeters as energy. And that, as I see it, is the function of form: to contain the energy of a poem, to prevent it from leaking out.

You spoke last night at dinner of the frustrations of so many contemporary artists, and this led you to reflect on the idea of the poet as monster. Would you care to expatiate?

It's a notion that enters into several of my poems—for instance, **"The Approach to Thebes,"** and later **"The Artist,"** which grew out of my friendship with Mark Rothko. So many of my attachments are to the world of painters and sculptors. I recall a conversation with Mark one evening, in which I referred to Picasso—not without admiration—as a monster. And then I added Joyce's name, for good measure. Mark was troubled by my epithet. I tried to explain to him why, in the modern arts, the words "genius" and "monster" may be interchangeable. His face darkened. "You don't mean me, do you?" he asked. Less than a year later he was dead, by his own hand. What is it in our culture that drives so many artists and writers to suicide—or, failing that, mutilates them spiritually? At the root of the problem is the cruel discrepancy between the values of art and the values of society, which makes strangers and adversaries out of those who are most gifted and vulnerable. The artist who turns in on himself, feeds off his own psyche, aggrandizes his bruised ego is on his way to monsterdom. Ambition is the fire in his gut. No sacrifice is judged too great for his art. At a certain point he becomes a nexus of abstract sensations and powers, beyond the realm of the personal. That's when the transformation into monster occurs. I don't mean to imply that everybody is worthy of that designation—it requires a special kind of greatness . . . Sylvia Plath's, for example. If we search among the poets of an older generation for the masters who were whole, who excelled in their humanity, who fulfilled themselves in the life as well as in the work, whom can we name? Not most of "the best among us"—in Pound's words. Certainly not Pound himself, not Eliot, not Yeats, nor Frost, nor Stevens . . . the list could be extended indefinitely. I am told that Pasternak was a notable exception, and I know, closer to home, that William Carlos Williams was another. Then I have to pause. They make a shining pair. The young around us give me hope that eventually they'll have plenty of company. But the condition may well be the creation of a new society.

Robert Weisburg   (essay date 1975)

SOURCE: "Stanley Kunitz: The Stubborn Middle Way," in *Modern Poetry Studies,* Vol. 6, No. 1, pp. 49-73.

[*In the following essay, Weisburg relates Kunitz's poetry to that of his contemporaries and discusses his major themes as they emerge in* Selected Poems, 1928-1958: *disease: generation, or the past: and monstrosity.*]

"The easiest poet to neglect is one who resists classification" [quoted from "Imagine Wrestling with an Angel: An Interview with Stanley Kunitz," in *Salmagundi* (Spring Summen 1973); all subsequent quoted comments of Kunitz are also extracted from this interview]. Had he spoken of himself, Stanley Kunitz might rather have said that we neglect the poet who becomes classified too early and too narrowly. Since a brief, if sympathetic, article by Jean Hagstrum in 1958, Kunitz's impressive canon has aroused no critical interest. Instead, he has been dubiously honored, by almost universal agreement, as a strange phenomenon called the "poet's poet," and the only recent study of him, by Marjorie Perloff in the *Iowa Review,* explicitly sustains this official view. In what sense is Kunitz "the poet's poet"? The title first assumes that his verse is of minor interest in itself, but that his literary relationships as peer and mentor have merited him a grateful, if condescending, nod from the historians of contemporary poetry. More specifically, the title has generally implied fixed critical views of the nature of his verse. In his early work as represented in *Selected Poems* he is a skillful but derivative practitioner of the modernist-metaphysical mode, limited in subject, a bit abstruse in imagery, and interesting chiefly as a technician. In the late poems in *The Testing Tree* he is again the skillful derivative, this time as a late convert to the confessional mode.

We will see the real Kunitz when we look askance at our categories of classification. It seems absurd, but may be necessary, to say that his career as a sane, mature, and stable eye in the storm of modern literary lives is no reason to slight his work. The notion that his field of vision is narrow is challenged by his own remark about political poetry: "An age in crisis needs more than ever to be made aware of the full range of human possibility." We must ask whether narrowing his material may, ironically, have helped us to widen that range. And if we avoid the self-fulfilling prophecy of typing the late poems as pallid confessionals, we might see that there are magnificent autobiographical poems, like his **"King of the River,"** which "derive" from a tradition of personal poetry far older than that born in 1959 with Robert Lowell's *Life Studies*. We may come to see Kunitz as a still point in the turning world of recent poetry, a poet whose dynamic order will remind us of what subject matter may be worth a poet's excluding.

What has been seen as the safe path of the "poet's poet" has been a stubborn middle way. Kunitz has felt no need to encompass the extremes of his contemporaries when he can remain at their point of intersection. He need not journey all the way to either hell or Byzantium to dramatize the condition of the poet caught in between: to deny this is to assume an ethic and aesthetic of Faustian aspiration which he would say destroys more good poetry than it creates, because it destroys good poets. Kunitz lives among the classic paradoxes of modern literature and has learned that a sane irony produces a poetry as useful as the most audacious plumbing and soaring.

Born in 1905, Kunitz emerged as a poet in one of the dourest literary periods in America, a time of the odd convergence of such literary influences as T. S. Eliot's, and such philosophical influences as Marx's and Freud's. W. H. Auden is the mediator between these influences and a large if loose group of young American poets who came of age between the wars, and whose pre-war poetry now, in retrospect, seems so stylized in its cultivated, impersonal, and often ideological despair. In **"The Dark and the Fair,"** Kunitz recalls a literary gathering (it ideally would have included Randall Jarrell, Delmore Schwartz, Karl Shapiro, Lowell, and Theodore Roethke) and sums up its mood:

> A roaring company that festive night;
> The beast of dialectic dragged his chains,
> Prowling from chair to chair in the smoking light,
> While the snow hissed against the windowpanes.
>
> Our politics, our science, and our faith
> Were whiskey on the tongue; I being rent
> By the fierce divisions of our time, cried death
> And death again, and my own dying meant.

This recalls a whole mode of poetry most obvious in the painfully psychological, probing poems of the first Auden volume, and such Jarrell poems as "The Winter's Tale" that follow. In them the poet, having absorbed a lot of Freud and Marx (in the sense of analytic approach if not actual ideology) attempts a hawk's-eye survey of a somber pre-war world and sees nothing but life-denial. It is revealing that even here, the poet finds the source of this vision in personal depression and not in the results of comprehensive social analysis. Kunitz offers a poem quite directly in this mode in **"Night Letter"**:

> I suffer the twentieth century,
> The nerves of commerce wither in my arm;
> Violence shakes my dreams; I am so cold,
> Chilled by the persecuting wind abroad,
> The oratory of the rodent's tooth,
> The slaughter of the blue-eyed open towns,
> And principle disgraced, and art denied.
> My dear, it is too late for peace. . . .

"Night Letter" embodies attitudes of its moment in its arch, world-weary tone, its often contrived yearning for a "faith, and especially its agonizing debate with history as Satan. ("Gerontion" is the great model here.) It is certainly close to the early poems of Schwartz, to Shapiro's bitter social ironies, and even, without the acrobatics of style, to the Lowell of *Lord Weary's Castle*. It was a generation, in its self-conscious anti-Romanticism, all too ready to adopt the Romantic youthful pose of exhausted cynicism tinged with rootless religious idealism. Those most deeply involved in this mode, of course, sought release from it after the war's conclusion induced in America a sense of relief and security; the free-form and ultimately the confessional followed the impersonally cynical in our poetic history.

Kunitz's membership in this group needs qualification. Despite sharing the tone and diction, he shows little inclination toward any ideology or faith-based view of the world (as Auden ultimately does), and he only slowly, if at all, follows the path of confessional liberation of Lowell and Jarrell, for example. Yet, years later, he still clings to some of the central concerns of this group, especially the burden of the past (though for him it is *always* personal, never collectively historical) and the possibilities of healing what Eliot decried as our dissociation of sensibility in a verse that fuses an active critical intelligence and a Romantic temperament. Perhaps this makes Kunitz the truest member of this group, again, the still point at its center, a subtle guide to the development of contemporary poetry amidst the extremer tendencies of his fellows.

Selected Poems 1928-1958 is organized, the poet tells us, not by chronology, but by similarities of "argument," of theme. Two outstanding themes appear in it, and perhaps a third emerges to unite the two. The first theme unifies a great number of poems that make the agonies of love a metaphor of mortality in general. The poet pictures these agonies through complex metaphysical imagery as a wound, or, more often, a festering disease from which we may seek escape into pure vision, but to which we return as the *felix culpa* of poetry: love and life are a venereal disease. The second major theme is that of generation, of the poet's three-phase struggle with his past. First, the poet tries to escape the responsibility that the ghosts of the past place on him; then he ecstatically embraces them in a transcendent illumination; and finally, as in the first theme, rejecting a rarefied vision for the salvation he finds in the fecund ditch of life, he learns to "endure" (a central word in Kunitz) the agonies of the generative process. This does not mean to make peace with the past by transcending time, but to make peace with time itself. Ultimately, the wound and the generative process are one, and it is the poet's job to celebrate them.

It is the poems of the first theme that undoubtedly caused critics to type Kunitz as an extreme formalist, but it is important to see a substantial change within them even in *Selected Poems*. We might say that Kunitz does begin with poems that *do* all too self-consciously offer themselves as reincarnations of John Donne:

And even should I track you to your birth
Through all the cities of your mortal trial,
As in my jealous thought I try to do,
You would escape me—from the brink of earth
Take off to where the lawless auroras run,
You with your wild and metaphysic heart.
My touch is on you, who are light-years gone.
We are not souls but systems, and we move
In clouds of our unknowing. . . .

            (**"The Science of the Night"**)

Kunitz here displays the typical dilemma of his generation—and excess of sheer stylistic talent all too vulnerable to string influence—as if he were too enthusiastically filling Eliot's request for a re-association of sensibility. The burden of talent and influence produces an immensely interesting and rich lyric which yet seems to stifle the poet's true voice, as if an almost unconscious insincerity may have been the curse attached to the Eliot-Auden inheritance. At other times we may feel the poet fully to blame for conceiving himself as the restorer of the Elizabethan World Picture:

So intricately is this world resolved
Of substance arched on thrust of circumstance,
The earth's organic meaning so involved
That none may break the pattern of his dance; . . .

       (**"So Intricately Is This World Resolved"**)

The problem is that at the base of a good metaphysical yoking-conceit must be some sort of conflict between an order and a violence, and if the violence is insufficiently realized in the poem, if it seems just a tame, cultivated violence and not the genuine violence of a convincing emotional experience, the order in the conceit will seem more clever than dynamic.

But as *Selected Poems* progresses, a more sincere voice does emerge in the poems of this first theme; a more forceful, less genteel, violence of language reveals a genuine emotional core, and Kunitz seems to achieve the difficult synthesis he may well have thought Eliot was asking for. He manages to bring to his immediate experience a Renaissance sense of wit and decorum, including metrical formality, and use it to express and contain his personality, not suppress it through derivative stylization. We might even imagine him in these poems conducting a secret argument with Eliot. The poet has acknowledged himself a respectful adversary of Eliot: "His definition of poetry as an objective act, a depersonalized performance, was contrary to my own conviction that art and life were bound together. I sought a more passionate voice. And I scorned his politics." Kunitz undoubtedly is wrong in seeing a crude art-life split in Eliot, but he takes Eliot at his word in making a poetry of intelligence and emotion possible again, very close to the original Renaissance model. This is opposite to what Eliot did in his own verse, which was to transform the metaphysical mode so thoroughly into modernist-free verse as to make the metaphysical influence more a critical catalyst than a true poetic model.

The new voice emerges gradually. We see in **"No Word"** still the almost excessively thick imagery, yet the wit in this poem conceals a contemporary, common subject—the "no word" is the telephone call that does not come—and so the metaphysical style begins to connect with a true experience:

No message. May the mothering dark,
Whose benediction calms the sea,
Abater of the atrocious spark
Of love and love's anxiety,
Be kind; and may my self condone,
As surely as my judge reprieves,
This heart strung on the telephone,
Folded in death, whom no voice revives.

At the end here, the poet moves toward Eliot in weaving an object of common experience into the conceit, and the effect is startling and emotionally convincing. Recalling Eliot's distinction between the "rhetorics" of Henry James and John Milton, we might see the twists and turns of the verse approaching the vacillations of an active emotional mind, and not just self-consciously elaborating the conceit. The woman of the poem remains as remote as in **"The Science of the Night"**—but remote as a real woman might be to a man, and not, as in the previous poem, remote merely because abstract. Here she is simply distant and cold, and takes on some implied substance through the poet's own tension.

We see another advance in **"The Words of the Preacher."** The diction is no more contemporary, and in some ways the emotional experience no more precise. But the poem has an *energy* that other of Kunitz's metaphysical lyrics lack. And so it succeeds as one of Ezra Pound's early experiments in traditional forms succeeds, by investing the form with new vigor and whole, yet being, in a sense, a purely imitative poem. Equally important though, the poem begins to develop the disease conceit that will dominate the rest of the volume:

Taking infection from the vulgar air
And sick with the extravagant disease
Of life, my soul rejected the sweet snare
Of happiness; declined
That democratic bait, set in the world
By fortune's old and mediocre mind.

To love a changing shape with perfect faith
Is waste of faith; to follow dying things
With deathless hope is vain; to go from breath
To breath, so to be fed
And put to sleep, is cheat and shame—because
By piecemeal living a man is doomed, I said.

This verbal energy, or, more specifically, this invigorating sense of a speaking voice, is precisely what most imitative verse lacks. Many poems of the thirties compound the weakness by seeming uncertain of *who* is speaking at all. The potential energy in a good "homage" may be dissipated by the poet's anxiety to force sincerity, and the result is the insincerity we have seen already. Here, the poet displays a rare Pound-like sense of play with the metaphysical style. The poem deals with his serious theme, yet borrows from the early Pound the redeeming power of play in rejuvenating the old form. This sense of play is a significant movement for Kunitz, for the poems get richer as they turn from a forced Elizabethan elegance to the sharper emotional thrust that is more natural to him.

For Kunitz, the *felix culpa* is man's attachment to this "extravagant disease" (the metaphor has the metaphysical *vigor* of such Yeats metaphors as "dying animal" and "fecund ditch"), and like W. B. Yeats, he gradually lays claim to this middle ground, this scrimmage of mortality between nihilism and rarefied vision as the distinct arena of his poetry. Kunitz's best poems refuse to decorate the physical life with Elizabethan elegance, or transcend it for a permanence he finds all the more threatening. Again, the poems are strongest where the commitment to this mortal arena is most honest, where the metaphysical images heighten rather than tame the tension.

Three poems stand out in particular, and it might be well to begin with **"By Lamplight,"** which, with revealing irony, may well evoke from a sensitive but incautious reader the odd notion that a poem written decades ago is "Plathian":

> Welcome, eccentric life,
> Attracted to my star,
> Let there be festival
> Perverse and singular.
> Let any drop of poison
> Grow legs and crawl and eat:
> The malice of unreason
> A man can tolerate.
> The stumblers and the clowns
> Are wired with their will
> To live, to live, to live:
> They do not mean to kill.
> Sweet beetles, comrade moths,
> The bonfires in your head
> Are neither coals of hell
> Nor the rose in the marriage-bed.
> I heard all summer long
> (Dance, monsters, hairy forms!)
> The idiot on the leaf
> Babbling of the dust and storms,
> And in this rough heart made
> A little thin-legged song
> Out of my greening blood
> To swell the night's harangue.

The synthesis of order and violence becomes, for Kunitz, not just the *felix culpa* of diseased mortality, but the growth of poetry itself. The poem is, in origin, simply the meditation of the midnight poet on the gross insect life orbiting around his lamp. This insect life becomes for him the "hairy forms," the "festival" of perverse mortality which he not only welcomes into his brain, but makes his poetry of. The disease image is repeated at the end, almost as an image of a kind of festering mental gangrene, but the grossness of physicality is absorbed into the thoroughly healthy, unmorbid vigor of the poem. Kunitz chooses here the middle ground between "the coals of hell" and "the

rose in the marriage-bed"—his territory is absolute neither in extreme damnation nor perfected symbolic harmony. It is only after acknowledging this powerful embrace of reality that the rhymed (often slant rhymed) and well-varied iambic trimeter, which encloses the abberrant circles of the insects, should be noted for the poem's formal success.

We can begin, then to understand the common misconception of Kunitz. The violence of his theme is not over-cultivated; he is rarely a gardener poet, and as seen, in the best short poems, the violence is anything but elegant. It is simply that he lives, or once lived, in a very symbolic universe, so that we are offered little of the *explicit* private or public material of violence that we have come to expect in contemporaries. Kunitz, in fact, is a devout Romantic in his adherence to the natural world as his model for human experience, though he has successfully transformed nature from Wordsworthian harmony and sublimity to the modern disfigurement he must deal with, especially by dealing more with *man's* body than with earth's body. So it is a very conscious, controlled limitation of explicit subject matter, rather than any over-refinement, that may make the poems seem genteel to the contemporary ear: The disease of mortality in Kunitz *is* a disease; but the poet has decided that the more he documented it, the less he would make music of it.

A more striking example of this balance is **"Off Point Lotus,"** a poem which as well as any in Kunitz demonstrates the inadequacy of using the label "confessional" to measure the personal. The poem is wholly and impressively personal in the sense that a reader knowing nothing of the poet's life will still intuit that it has been written out of a private experience and that the reader will need no explicit evidence of that experience. His intuition will derive, rather, from the thoroughly uncontrived verve with which the Odysseus myth is taken up, and from the lucid connections the poem makes to others in the volume to establish itself as a stage in the construction of a coherent poetic character:

> Three years I lolled in that country of the girls,
> Thick with their wine, their loose idolatry,
> Nor saw that I was only prince of gulls,
> Nor heard the ambiguous whisper of the sea.
>
> Used . . . used! Eating their morphine leaf,
> I breathed a cloud of self-congratulations
> To pillow me, while my boat slapped on the wharf
> And a gang of spiders scribbled invitations.
>
> All right, my bully-boys, you who connived
> My fall, I thank you for your dirty part,
> I kiss you for each lie you took to wife
> And for that salt you packed around my heart.
>
> Good-bye, old things, I am forever lost!
> My crazy vessel dances to the rail,
> Sea-drunken since I left that barbarous coast,
> The stain of anger spreading on my sail.

The manipulation of tone is the great strength of this poem, and tone is just that factor which makes a self-consciously mythic or conventional poem "personal" in the Kunitz sense.

Again, referring to the earlier metaphysical lyrics, we can recall a somber archness disturbingly in excess of the experience as it is offered to us in the poems. Here, the harshness is distributed on both sides of the lotus experience: the self-irony of "lolled," in the subtle shift to a confident irony toward his seducers in the third stanza. Kunitz alludes to the disease theme in the rather painful salt image and in the blood-wine stain at the end, but the infection of carnal and liquorous ecstasy becomes his moving force and even his emblem on the sail. He does not offer these figures as precontrived conceits, as a more obvious metaphysical poet would. Rather, they are not conceits at all: they emerge from the emotional logic of the poem's imagery. Again, keeping half an eye on the triumphant **"King of the River,"** it is the subordination of a rich—and thoroughly traditional—symbolic material to an original and active mind and heart caught moving through the contours of our fundamental experiences that characterizes the best Kunitz poems. Once this symbolic material has been established as the "connecting tissue" of the volume, we can, as if with libretto in hand, sway to the diverse emotional music.

One wants to say that **"Hermetic Poem"** is so "Roethkean," until one realizes how well it epitomizes this first theme of Kunitz:

> The secret my heart keeps
> Flows into cracked cups.
>
> No saucer can contain
> This overplus of mine:
>
> It glisters to the floor,
> Lashing like lizard fire
>
> And ramps upon the walls
> Crazy with ruby ills.
>
> Who enters by my door
> Is drowned, burned, stung and starred.

The reader suffers the four fates of the poem not in any indulgent disarray of poetic effects, but in a controlled perilous journey of a sensibility through appetite, to pain, to poetry.

Much as the first theme is of a journey through pain, the second is a journey through guilt; pain and guilt are the loci of the poetry. In this theme of guilt we may see a parallel development from an agonizing awareness, to a magniloquent vision of transcendence, and finally to a middle ground that does not undermine the vision but balances it with a subtler possibility of enduring a bitter, but liberating, tension between the guilt and the vision. Thus may the development be seen in bare outline, but as with the first theme, a very close reading of the poems

reveals a complicated journey in and out of these three phases, with an emerging emphasis on the last phase toward the end of the volume and in the finest poems in *The Testing Tree*.

As the pain came from love, so the guilt comes from time, and in **"The Signal from the House,"** the poet boldly announces the theme, and immediately casts it into its central metaphor. His "father's house" is the repository of ghosts who fail him, as we shall see, in not offering him a clear spiritual heritage, in not giving him a Word to take into the future, and whom he fails in his refusal or inability to make peace with them. The poems of what we might thus call the generation theme oscillate between these two failures, but it is the latter failure that provides the drama for this first announcement:

> I said to the watcher at the gate,
> "They also kill who wait."
>
> I cried to the mourner on the stair,
> "Mother, I hate you for those tears."
>
> To mistress of the ruined hall,
> The keeper of the sacred heart,
>
> I bought the mind's indifference
> And the heavy marble of my face:
>
> For those who were too much with me
> Were secretly against me:
>
> Hostages to the old life,
> Expecting to be ransomed daily
>
> And for the same fond reason
> From the deep prison of their person,
>
> Their lantern shining in the window
> had signaled me, like a cry of conscience,
>
> Insisting that I must be broken
> Upon the wheel of the unforsaken.

Aside from being another example of a work intensely personal while in no clear way being confessional, the poem succeeds as a conscious metaphysical conceit where earlier ones failed, in that again, it energizes an old form: here what we might call the dramatic reversal structure of such a George Herbert poem as "The Collar." The reversal arises from the speaker's defiant but uncertain attitude toward the dead, exemplified by his attitude to the mourners, whom he chides for mediating between him and the father he wants to forget but cannot. He resists identifying with the mourners—who are imagined as respectful worshippers as well as the bereaved—and adopts the pose of "marble indifference."

The action significantly connects with the well-known poem **"The Thief,"** in which Kunitz ultimately rejects the marble past of Rome for the squalid and fertile modern city that stands on its ruins. In **"The Signal from the**

House," the same pose is offered only to be shown in its futility. The undertone of guilt and paranoia at the center of the poem turns suddenly at the end to a direct acknowledgement of the wheel, the medieval torture of time to which he is committed. The father-haunted-house metaphor is woven into the metaphors of the sacred chapel and of the psychological kidnapping, and all merge in the final torture which the poet presents in impressive understatement. Here, as in the next poem of the theme, we begin with an ironic Miltonic echo, which reminds us at the end, that the poet must join those "waiting," enduring the responsibilities the unburied dead foist on us.

Now it is just this stance of serving and waiting that **"Open the Gates"** contradicts, and it is important to see this as a very deliberate contradiction, as Kunitz establishes the opposite pole of the theme. **"Open the Gates"** is a poem of visionary impatience with time, a storming of the door out of the haunted house and into heaven, and though its goal is rejected by later poems, it still stands as a brilliant, terse revelation of a *possibility*. Even if modified later, this possibility by its power, still maintains a constant valence in Kunitz's mind. Without this poem as opposite pole, even **"King of the River"** might be weakened in its dramatic placement in his canon:

> Within the city of the burning cloud,
> Dragging my life behind me in a sack,
> Naked I prowl, scourged by the black
> Temptation of the blood gone proud.
>
> Here at the monumental door,
> Carved with the curious legend of my youth,
> I brandish the great bone of my death,
> Beat once therewith and beat no more.
>
> The hinges groan: a rush of forms
> Shivers my name, wrenched out of me.
> I stand on the terrible threshold, and I see
> The end and the beginning in each other's arms.

The past, personal as well as cultural, is even more clearly a guilty burden in this poem. Kunitz creates an impersonal sense of visionary possibility of unity rising out of the personal theme of **"The Signal from the House,"** which is reiterated in the sense of skulking guilt and shame at the end of the first stanza here. An earlier poem, **"Among the Gods,"** had platonically celebrated "the sound / Of matter pouring through eternal forms," as if the music of that cascade will be his true poetry. In **"Open the Gates,"** in the final metamorphosis of the concluding scene of St. Augustine's *Confessions* into a brilliant, Yeatsian sexual metaphor, the process reverses, and the forms ecstatically rush *out* of the speaker, and he stands, purged, before "the terrible threshold" through which he sees time embraced into a unity. The commitment to physicality in such poems as **"Among the Gods"** seems coldly abstract compared to the sexual excitement of the return to Platonic purity in **"Open the Gates,"** his "Byzantium." . . .

Selected Poems, Kunitz tells us, is classified into themes and arguments, and the absence of chronological structure teases us into abstracting a line of development that the arrangement of poems may obscure. As such, having discerned the two basic themes of disease and generation, we may have to add a third, not just to tie our two themes into a conclusion, but to account for a number of impressive poems which fall in between or outside these themes. Let us call it the theme of monstrosity.

Kunitz has explicitly defined for us a concept of the contemporary artist as a potential monster:

> What is it in our culture that drives so many artists and writers to suicide—or, failing that, mutilates them spiritually! At the root of the problem is the cruel discrepancy between the values of art and the values of society, which makes strangers and adversaries out of those who are most gifted and vulnerable. The artist who turns in on himself, feeds off his own psyche, aggrandizes his bruised ego, is on the way to monsterdom. Ambition is the fire in his gut. No sacrifice is judged too great for his art. At a certain point he becomes a nexus of abstract sensations and powers, beyond the realm of the personal.

He then refers to two poems in particular, **"Approach to Thebes,"** and **"The Artist,"** from *The Testing Tree*, which elaborate this notion. The Oedipus figure of the latter poem lives to tell his story, and so, though "spiritually mutilated" by his incest with his "flagrant source" (the pun suggests, in terms of the generation theme, the dangers of the beginning and the end embracing), survives as a poet to bequeath his monstrous legend to his posterity. And such would be a tolerable notion of the role of the poet, as bequeather except we see a more terrifying picture of the poet as monster in Mark Rothko's suicide in **"The Artist,"** and most especially in an amazing poem that Kunitz does not mention, **"Prophecy on Lethe."**

> Echo, the beating of the tide,
> Infringes on the blond curved shore;
> Archaic weeds from sleep's green side
> Bind skull and pelvis till the four
> Seasons of the blood are unified.
>
> Anonymous sweet carrion,
> Blind mammal floating on the stream
> Of depthless sound, completely one
> In the cinnamon-dark of no dream—
> A pod of silence, bursting when the sun
>
> Clings to the forehead, will surprise
> The gasping turtle and the leech
> With your strange brain blooming as it lies
> Abandoned to the bipeds on the beach;
> Your jelly-mouth and, crushed, your polyp eyes.

A poem like this may explain why the poet resists what he calls elsewhere "the Faustian dog that chews my penitential bones," why he resists a poetry of visionary prophecy, to which he is clearly attracted, why he sets against the great monsters of poetry such figures as William Carlos Williams and Boris Pasternak "who were whole, who excelled in their humanity, who fulfilled themselves in the life as well as in the work." It explains, in fact, the whole middle way of Kunitz's poetry, a refusal to embrace "the Truth" so violently that he will ruin himself into abstracted monsterhood—the danger being, of course, that it *is* the truth that he fears. But the poet is honest enough to acknowledge what he is willing and not willing to do, and **"Prophecy on Lethe"** suggests that he has come close enough to the terror of the truth to know what he would choose to keep clear of.

"Prophecy" makes monstrosity much more precise and suicidal than **"Approach to Thebes."** It alludes to the myth of Echo and Narcissus and makes the poet a bit of each, doomed to inwardness, reduced to two separate parts: a carrion and a voice. Like Oedipus, the implicit poet figure bequeaths a poetic legend to posterity. The bequest turns out to be his own frightening monster-self, tossed on the shore of normal reality from the sea of Truth—inward truth—that the self has descended to. It is swollen, decayed, contorted; it has seen some Medusa, and it cannot tell the story but only offer itself as a warning. Yet the warning cannot even be heard or understood, since the animal imagery or the poem pictures the poet as having passed into a wholly new species, inexplicable to "the bipeds on the beach." He has passed, in fact, all the way through poetry to silence, the visionary embrace having separated itself from the voice it left underwater. Instead of the beginning and the end in each other's arms, we get the "skull and pelvis" bound and blurred beyond human recognition and denied voice and vision. The heroic poet has been harmonized into grotesquerie. Kunitz acknowledges that not every poet can be a monster, that it "takes a special kind of greatness," such as Sylvia Plath had, and here we have the poet's refusing to join what has become the post-confessional suicidal school. We can only say that if it seems he lacks that "greatness," his poetry is ennobled nevertheless by the way he refuses to desire it.

So perhaps the truest final note of *Selected Poems* comes in the wry realism of **"Revolving Meditation,"** which tries to put poetry into a perspective of the larger question of the whole, healthy life, arguing that there may be something "beyond all this fiddle."

> Imagination makes
> Out of what stuff it can,
> An action fit
> For a more heroic stage
> Than body ever walked on.
> I have learned,
> Trying to live
> With this perjured quid of mine,
> That the truth is not in the stones,
> But in the architecture;

Kunitz is willing to risk that his poetry may suffer the consequences of his believing that mere is something worth more than poetry, though it is that risk which ironically produces many of his best poems. To those who cry for a leap into the Truth, he responds:

> But I fly towards Possibility, . . .
>
> Careless that I am bound
> To the flaming wheel of my bones,
> Preferring to hear, as I
> Am forced to hear,
> The voice of the solitary
> Who makes others less alone,
> The dialogue of lovers,
> And the conversation of two worms
> In the beam of a house,
> Their mouths filled with sawdust.

We can relate the worm-riddled house to the Broken Tower here, and see the poet making what he can of the decaying process, which is also the march of pure stain upon stain toward the sun. He wants poetry to bring him fulfillment *in* life, not beyond or beneath it.

The Testing Tree shows us some of that fulfillment in the possibilities of poetry once the struggle with "the brave god" has been relaxed, the battles for the truth over. **"The Artist,"** the poem on Rothko, provides us with a bridge to Kunitz's latest volume, since it reassures us that the poet is now beyond any interest in self-consumption:

> At last he took a knife in his hand
> and slashed an exit for himself
> between the frames of his tall scenery.
> Through the holes of his tattered universe
> the first innocence and the light
> came pouring in.

It takes a full appreciation of the early Kunitz to receive the full ironic bite of those lines. The artist here is denied even the grotesque legacy of **"Prophecy on Lethe"**; he achieves not even destruction, but pure dissolution. *The Testing Tree* is the offering of a poet who has learned—and hopefully taught—his lesson, and the appealing personal—*not* confessional—warmth of the volume is a model of what a deliberately, maturely limited aesthetic can produce.

"Illumination," which in some ways recapitulates **"Open the Gates,"** uses a light tone to make a serious new point about the possibilities of vision—in fact, to deliberately deepen the ambivalence of the value and feasibility of the visionary embrace he once tried so resolutely to assert. The poet here, with obvious irony, catalogs the ills of his life:

> the parent I denied,
> the friends I failed,
> the hearts I spoiled,
> including at least
> my own left ventricle—

Then, with even subtler irony, the illumination is promised, but not delivered. And yet the poem leaves him—and us—with the strangest feeling that perhaps the illumination was accomplished--but not as intended:

> "Dante!" I cried
> to the apparition

entering from the hall,
laureled and gaunt,
in a cone of light.
"Out of mercy you came
To be my Master
and my guide!"
To which he replied:
"I know neither the time
nor the way
nor the number on the door . . .
but this must be my room,
I was here before."
And he held up in his hand
the key,
which blinded me.

This poem subsumes all the conflicts about vision shaping the earlier poetry in a healthy irony exactly opposed to the deadly irony of his Auden-influenced work. Having moved among extremes of feeling and thought, the poet has created as the great sanity and health-inducing element of his poetry the manipulation of tone as the great limiter and negotiator among extremes. There is a lessened risk here; after all, **"The Artist"** did see a light the poet cannot allow into this poetry. But Kunitz finds ample poetic freedom in dramatizing the vicissitudes of the mind and heart tracing out their boundaries, and his subtlest and most mature manipulation of tone is also his most lucid map of the geography of the mind and heart, and finally the richest poem of his career.

"King of the River" fuses the emotional intensity of the early poems with the terse and yet conversational style of the other poems of this volume. It is his most distilled statement and most finely crafted lyric. Ironically, both Kunitz and Lowell (in "Waking Early Sunday Morning") have been moved by Yeats to write about *salmon*. Yeats, a great influence on the early poems, may be seen as an antagonist here. "Sailing to Byzantium" itself is, of course, ambivalent in its nostalgia and desire for the fish-filled sensual river of generation—or we might say simply its nostalgia *for* desire. But the thrust of Yeats's poem is to assert the primacy of monuments of unaging intellect as the right goal of the imagination. Kunitz, in effect, is reconstituting Yeats's "Dialogue of Self and Soul" and throwing it in the face of Byzantium, by actively committing himself to corruption. The bruised, battered human muscle of Kunitz's poem, "glazed with madness," is only slightly less grotesque in physical form than the polyp-eyed corpse of **"Prophecy on Lethe,"** yet it becomes a figure not of terror, but of heroic endurance and imagination. The poet embraces, not the dissolving of the beginning into the end, but his constant oscillation on the "two-way ladder / between heaven and hell." And the waving orchestration of the poem, parallel to the coiling and uncoiling of this generative human muscle, celebrates the same ambiguities of his attitude toward time and eternity. Kunitz renews Yeats's "fecund ditch" in his "orgiastic pool," and the rapid and almost grotesque birth, copulation, and aging to ward death of the salmon becomes the happiest metaphor of the poet's career. As in **"The Illumination,"** where he subsumed the dilemma over vision,

here he perfectly dramatizes the tensions of nostalgia and desire in the contours of the verse—in the "if-but-then" sequence which builds irony into the very structure of the poem:

If the power were granted you
to break out of your cells,
but the imagination fails
and the doors of the senses close
on the child within,
you would dare to be changed,
as you are changing now,
into the shape you dread
beyond the merely human.

The finest irony of all is that the visionary poet fails to see that the shape he aspires to assume, he may be assuming all his life. To be visionary for Kunitz is to want orgiastic death, which is what we are having all along if we will slow down our senses to notice. Normal experience is all the orgy toward death a poet needs, and all the monstrosity he can afford. We are going nowhere as rapidly and as grandiloquently as we need to, so to endure is to be as apocalyptic as we need be.

James Finn Cotter   (review date 1980)

SOURCE: A review of *Poems of Stanley Kunitz: 1928-1978,* in *The Hudson Review,* Vol. 33, No. 1, Spring, 1980, pp. 131-50.

[*Cotter reviews* Poems of Stanley Kunitz: 1928-1978, *briefly remarking on Kunitz's poetic development.*]

[In *The Poems of Stanley Kunitz, 1928-1978*, Kunitz] arranges his poems in reverse chronological order, but the strategem cannot hide the nature of his poetic development. His early poems launch a direct assault on the Self, using myth (**"For Proserpine"**), rhetoric (**"O Sion of my heart"**), and melancholy (**"I wept for my youth"**) as the traditional arsenal for one's siege. No wonder Kunitz decided not to begin his book with such rusty stuff; too bad it had to be included at all. Kunitz began to find his idiom in his second volume, published in 1944, with poems like **"Father and Son,"** although here too the Self-conscious rears its easy head: "At the water's edge, where the smothering ferns lifted / Their arms, 'Father!' I cried, 'Return!'" The exclamation may work, but the metaphor does not. In his 1958 *Selected Poems*, flashes of humor and humanity enliven **"The Thief," "The War Against the Trees,"** and **"Rover."** Where early Kunitz sounded like late Yeats, the poet discovered his own story and image in the autobiographical **"A Testing-Tree,"** a poem that merits a place in any anthology of modern verse. A late bloomer, Kunitz has fashioned some of his finest poems in the last decade. Ego and Self join hands in **"What of the Night?," "Quinnapoxet," "The Lincoln Relics," "The Quarrel,"** and **"The Illumination."** Here the personal voice controls poetic intensity, not the other way round. **"Route Six,"** for example, begins:

The city squats on my back.
I am heart-sore, stiff-necked,
exasperated. That's why
I slammed the door,
that's why I tell you now,
in every house of marriage
there's room for an interpreter.

He proposes that he and his wife jump into the car, with their cat, to head for Cape Cod: "We'll drive non-stop till dawn" until they see "Light glazes the eastern sky / over Buzzards Bay." The poem concludes with a simple statement: "The last stretch toward home! / Twenty summers roll by." What begins in ego ends in illumination of Self, light and a sniff of salt air summing up an instant of life more than would acres of solitary contemplation.

Gregory Orr   (review date 1980)

SOURCE: A review of *Poems of Stanley Kunitz: 1928-1978,* in *American Poetry Review,* Vol. 9, No. 4, July/August, 1980, pp. 36-41.

[*Orr explores what he identifies as Kunitz's major theme: the son's quest for the father.*]

If Stanley Kunitz is a major poet, then he must have a major theme. What is that theme? Something that for the moment I'll call "the son's quest for the father." As all authentic major themes of this century must, it represents a fusion of personal crisis with an impersonal, universal significance. For the process of fusing personal and impersonal, the phrase Kunitz uses in relation to his own work is "to convert life into legend." I would assert that there must be a certain balance between the personal and impersonal in such an endeavor. In terms of the father-quest theme, Kunitz's early work (*Selected Poems*) is weighted toward the impersonal, and it is only in *The Testing Tree* that the poems approach the unadorned personal source. With the extra-ordinary simplicity and understatement that is his genius in the later work, he tells us the most essential tale of his life and his work:

My mother never forgave my father
for killing himself,
especially at such an awkward time
and in a public park,
that spring
when I was waiting to be born . . .

("**The Portrait**")

Let us not underestimate how difficult such simplicity of statement is, nor how great a struggle Kunitz must go through before he can achieve such a straightforward telling of what he elsewhere calls "the curious legend of my youth" (**"Open the Gates"**).

Now that I've spoken of the personal source, the private source; now that I've applied such a grand label as "the son's quest for the father"—what is it that this theme might mean to a reader who does not share the personal crisis that gave rise to it? Kunitz's quest for the father is no less than a quest for the source of his being, a quest for his identity. In a world where forces conspire constantly to destroy our individual sense of identity, a poet's struggle to discover (or create) and affirm his identity is a representative human struggle. If he is triumphant in his quest to affirm his own being in a confrontation with loss and death, then our sense of self is enhanced.

People seek the biological and psychological source of their being in order to understand who they are. But in Kunitz's case, this quest for the biological and psychological source must confront at the very beginning of life the ultimate contradiction of human meaning: death, and self-willed death at that. This quest for the father is by definition—at least in terms of the physical world—doomed to utter failure. So it is removed to the level of the imagination (or legend) because the impossibility of the task does not affect the *necessity* of the quest. One must have meaning. In Kunitz's case, the quest for the meaning of his personal existence, his being, is intimately, biologically tied up with non-being. And this non-being is mysterious because it is surrounded by silence, because (on the literal level) who can say *why* someone commits suicide?

The theme of the Quest for the Father takes numerous forms in the body of Kunitz's work. We might start by saying that it is there at the beginning, in the earliest poem Kunitz includes [in *The Poems of Stanley Kunitz, 1928-1978*], **"Vita Nuova."** And it is there at the end, explicitly in the next-most-recent poem, **"What of the Night?,"** and implicitly in the most recent, **"The Knot."** One can say, in terms that Kunitz himself might employ, that the theme of the son and the father is the alpha and omega of Kunitz's poetic vision.

In his first appearance, the father is simply part of a quest that we, as readers, participate in, but whose source and motive we don't understand. The speaker in **"Vita Nuova"** announces that a certain level of personal spiritual accomplishment will be achieved when he "wears his father's face":

Now I will peel that vision from my brain
Of numbers wrangling in a common place,
And I will go, unburdened, on the quiet lane
Of my eternal kind, till shadowless
With inner light I wear my father's face.

(**"Vita Nuova"**)

Why this should be the culmination of a quest for identity we do not know, though it works well in the imagistic context. What the speaker seeks is a single self among the multiple selves (this single self to "wear the father's face"); perhaps this self is a growing outward of the "gentler self" within his external physical self (this is not necessarily clear). The other touchstone of all Kunitz's work that is present in **"Vita Nuova"** is *intensity*: the final word of the poem, its final aspiration is "intense":

My dark will make, reflecting from your stones,
The single beam of all my life intense.

Intensity will be the standard by which Kunitz measures all language and all statement in his poetry.

The title itself, from Dante's *Vita Nuova* points to the physical death of a loved one as the moment of spiritual rebirth (or birth to the spiritual) of the survivor. Dante's poem is at the source of all poems of human loss which look forward (spiritual allegory) rather than backward (elegy). . . .

Although the son's quest for the father manifests itself at crucial moments in numerous earlier poems, the theme is best explored in two individual poems where it dominates the entire dramatic situation: **"Father and Son"** and **"Open the Gates."**

"Father and Son"

Now in the suburbs and the falling light
I followed him, and now down sandy road
Whiter than bone-dust, through the sweet
Curdle of fields, where the plums
Dropped with their load of ripeness, one by one.
Mile after mile I followed, with skimming feet,
After the secret master of my blood,
Him, steeped in the odor of ponds, whose
        indomitable love
Kept me in chains. Strode years, stretched
        into bird;
Raced through the sleeping country where
        I was young,
The silence unrolling before me as I came,
The night nailed like an orange to my brow.

How shall I tell him my fable and the fears,
How bridge the chasm in a casual tone,
Saying, "The house, the stucco one you built,
We lost. Sister married and went from home,
And nothing comes back, it's strange,
        from where she goes.
I lived on a hill that had too many rooms:
Light we could make, but not enough of warmth,
And when the light failed, I climbed under the hill.
The papers are delivered every day;
I am alone and never shed a tear."

At the water's edge, where the smothering
        ferns lifted
Their arms, "Father!" I cried, "Return! You know
The way. I'll wipe the mudstains
        from your clothes;
No trace, I promise, will remain. Instruct
Your son, whirling between two wars,
In the Gemara of your gentleness,
For I would be a child to those who mourn
And brother to the foundlings of the field
And friend of innocence and all bright eyes.
O teach me how to work and keep me kind."

Among the turtles and the lilies he turned
        to me
The white ignorant hollow of his face.

It is a most direct telling of the quest: a poem of seeking and beseeching. The father is called "the secret master of my blood." This is Kunitz's primary situation: the incredible urgency of the speaker and the impossibility of what he seeks. First, the pursuit (stanza 1); then the son's account of his life, "my fable and my fears" (stanza 2). What the father made ("the house, the stucco one . . .") has been lost. A bad omen for the son (who was also "made" by the father) that is shown to be an accurate prediction two lines later with another house ("I lived on a hill . . ."). There is a failure here for the son ("light we could make, but not enough of warmth . . .")—a failure of feeling, an inadequacy of feeling. In stanza 3 the son's motive for the pursuit emerges: he believes that the father "knows the way," that he can instruct his son as fathers ordinarily do, are expected to do. The terms of aspiration that the speaker expresses (child, brother, then friend) recapitulate human growth from infancy to family link to adulthood: all that has been lost because of the absence of the father and his instructions. It is when this situation of beseeching has reached its peak of poignancy that the horrible, sudden resolution of the final two lines occurs. The father's face is "ignorant" (the knowledge cannot come from this source), "hollow" (the decay of death is real): both facts are revealed in the final physical gesture of the father's turning back at the last moment before he disappears under the surface of the pond. It is a moment of ghastly revelation, perhaps ironically heightened by the presence of "turtles" and "lilies"—both with Biblical overtones germane to the poem.

"Open the Gates"

Within the city of the burning cloud,
Dragging my life behind me in a sack,
Naked I prowl, scourged by the black
Temptation of the blood grown proud.

Here at the monumental door,
Carved with the curious legend of my youth,
I brandish the great bone of my death,
Beat once therewith and beat no more.

The hinges groan: a rush of forms
Shivers my name, wrenched out of me.
I stand on the terrible threshold, and I see
The end and the beginning in each other's arms.

Again we have that incantatory energy that animates Kunitz's best work. **"Father and Son"** is a rather straightforward telling of his tale (minus one crucial detail: the suicide) in which he expresses his personal anguish and his imaginative link of that anguish to his father's absence. **"Open the Gates"** is that 'quest' tale told at a mythic, Blakean level, with almost no personal contamination. (I say "almost": I think the meaning of the line "curious legend of my youth "is only fully revealed by the later poem, **"The Portrait"**). **"Open the Gates"** is a poem of archetypal vision and yet the whole thing is anchored by, suffused with and emanating a strange sexual energy. The final two lines represent a fusion of Apocalypse (the opening of St. John's *Revelations*: Alpha and Omega) and Freud's Primal Scene. Kuntiz somehow witnesses, even participates in his own engendering.

I've said that I believe the major theme in Kunitz's work is the quest of the foundations of one's being. Because of the "curious legend" of Kunitz's youth, when Kunitz turns to the biological source (which is also the spiritual/ metaphysical source) he confronts a mysterious absence that becomes a haunting, obsessive presence.

Sometimes this seeking leads to spiritual fathers who might also guide and instruct Kunitz. For example, Dante in **"The Illumination"** and Lincoln in **"The Lincoln Relics."**

At other times, the father's ghost or some analogue is the active seeker, and the speaker (Kunitz) is either passive or pursued. I would call this version of the story "the mysterious summons." We find an example in the early poem **"Revolving Meditation"**:

> But why do I wake at the sound,
> In the middle of the night,
> Of the tread of the Masked Man
> Heavy on the stairs,
> And from the street below
> The lamentation of the wounded glove?

Or these lines from the next-most recent poem, **"What of the Night?,"** lines that are also linked to the father:

> What wakes me now
> like the country doctor
> startled in his sleep?
> Why does my racing heart
> shuffle down the hall
> for the hundredth time
> to answer the night bell?
> Whoever summons me has need of me . . .

In yet another version of the story, Kunitz's father appears as an apparition:

> Bolt upright in my bed that night
> I saw my father flying;
> the wind was walking on my neck,
> the windowpanes were crying.
>
> ("Three Floors")

This child's vision of his father flying about in his bedroom is so similar to the apparition of Lincoln that Kunitz describes in **"The Lincoln Relics"** that it further confirms the link in Kunitz's imagination between his father and Lincoln:

> In the Great Hall of the Library,
> as in a glass aquarium,
> Abe Lincoln is swimming around,

> dressed to the nines
> in his stovepipe hat
> and swallowtail coat . . .

A third and far more mythic form that the father takes in Kunitz's work is that of a tree in the "ancestral wood." Here the father is more likely to be grand, a kind of fusion of stag, oak, and vegetation deity as in section 3 of **"The Way Down"**:

> O father in the wood,
> Mad father of us all,
> King of our antlered wills,
> Our candelabrum-pride
> That the pretender kills,
> Receive your dazzling child . . .

In the marvelous poem **"The Testing Tree,"** the father is both the tree the son confronts and a spirit whose blessing the son seeks for his ordeal:

> There I stood in the shadow,
>   at fifty measured paces,
>   of the inexhaustible oak,
> tyrant and target,
>   Jehovah of acorns,
>   watchtower of thunders,
> that locked King Philip's War
>   in its annulated core
>   under the cut of my name.
> Father wherever you are
>   I have only three throws
>   bless my good right arm.

Here we are in the imaginative territory of *The Golden Bough* with its rituals of struggle and renewal in the woods. This shows another imaginative level at which Kunitz's quest for the father can be apprehended. Related to the identification of the father with trees and vegetation deities is his association in Kunitz's imagination with ponds. The ultimate confrontation between father and son in **"Father and Son"** takes place as the father or his ghost is entering a pond. In **"Goose Pond,"** a "white-lipped boy" is born up from the pond and, as he climbs out on the bank, meets "his childhood beating back / To find what furies made him man." In the late poem **"Quinnapoxet,"** Kunitz is fishing in an abandoned reservoir when he has a vision of his father and mother approaching him. In **"The Testing Tree,"** a recurring dream has Kunitz look down a well at an albino walrus who has his father's gentle eyes. It's not necessary for us to understand why the father is associated with these different figures, situations, and natural phenomena; the important thing is to recognize that the theme of the father and the son's quest can take numerous forms.

In identifying the father's presence in various forms in various kinds of poems, I do not mean to be reductive. For one thing, Kunitz's father exists at the very start on the level of legend. Kunitz has no father in the sense that most people do, and so the word "father" which most people use concretely is for Kunitz and Kunitz's work already a symbolic reality.

"The Portrait"

My mother never forgave my father
for killing himself,
especially at such an awkward time
and in a public park,
that spring
when I was waiting to be born.
She locked his name
in her deepest cabinet
and would not let him out,
though I could hear him thumping.
When I came down from the attic
with the pastel portrait in my hand
of a long-lipped stranger
with a brave moustache
and deep brown level eyes,
she ripped it into shreds
without a single word
and slapped me hard.
In my sixty-fourth year
I can feel my cheek
still burning.

At first it might seem that we do not need to know the information contained in **"The Portrait"** in order to appreciate what Kunitz is about. And yet, we do. What is more, Kunitz needs to know this information, needs to introduce it into the body of his work. This is the pivotal poem in his whole work, the poem which makes possible the greatness of the later poems. When I say Kunitz needs to know, I mean that the poem acknowledges and integrates certain important pieces of information about his life, certain pieces until now missing from the puzzle. Without these pieces, Kunitz cannot hope to achieve his ambition of "converting life into legend." Now the essential elements of the "life" are present and a true growth can occur that is as rare and powerful as that of later Yeats.

Not only do we learn for the first time that Kunitz's father was a suicide, but also that it was before Kunitz's birth, and perhaps most significantly, that Kunitz's mother "never forgave." For almost the first time, the mother appears and her role becomes clear. As long as Kunitz confined the dynamic of his imaginative life to Father-Son, it seemed impossible to go beyond simple seeking and confronting (**"Father and Son"**). But when he introduces the mother and her role, suddenly the possible dynamics are greatly extended. Soon other figures enter the poems: Frieda, Kunitz's daughter, his wife, the woman of **"After the Last Dynasty,"** and others. All this is made directly possible by the mother's entrance.

For the first time it is not simply the father's death and mysterious absence which are seen to exert power over the whole of Kunitz's life. The mother's role in the persistence of suffering is revealed: it is *her* slap on his cheek

that still burns fifty years or more later. The persistence of trauma is central to Kunitz's work: the struggle to be healed that takes a whole lifetime of imagination. This poem reveals that it is not simply the father's absence, but also the mother's rage that combine to trap the boy/adult Kunitz. Even later in Kunitz's work, the mother's slap ("my cheek/still burning.") becomes the "gashed thumb" of the poem **"Quinnapoxet."** In **"Quinnapoxet,"** Kunitz receives a wound from a fish in the "abandoned reservoir"; this wound he shares with his father whose apparition approaches him "with his face averted / as if to hide a scald." It is the father's scald (the suicide wound) and Kunitz's hurt thumb that represent a link between father and son. Kunitz signals to his father:

I touched my forehead
with my swollen thumb
and splayed my fingers out—
in deaf-mute country
the sign for father.

Even the form of Kunitz's wound, a "swollen thumb," has to do with a male, phallic life-force, a life-force "hurt" into being, yet potent. Through this shared wound (scald and gashed thumb) Kunitz does indeed fulfill in a strange way the prophecy of inheritance of that earliest poem, **"Vita Nuova"**; he does indeed "wear his father's face" (as he also did in the "burning cheek" of **"The Portrait"**). . . .

"The Lincoln Relics" is one of the ultimate poems of Kunitz's father-son theme. Here that personal theme fuses with the less personal theme of the individual and the state. (I'd say Kunitz's three enduring themes are: father-son, love, and the individual and the state). Again the challenge is to affirm being in the face of non-being. Death, violence, and negation must be overcome by some authentic act of imagination and affirmation fused together. In section 1, Kunitz rejects the miracles associated with saints' relics and yet affirms the human spirit that Lincoln represents for him:

Cold-eyed, in Naples once,
while the congregation swooned,
I watched the liquefaction
of a vial of precious blood,
and wondered only
how the trick was done.
Saint's bones are only bones
to me, but here,
where the stage is set
without a trace of gore,
these relics on display—
watchfob and ivory pocket knife,
a handkerchief of Irish linen,
a button severed from his sleeve—
make a noble, dissolving music
out of homely fife and drum,
and that's miraculous.

The paradox that the Lincoln relics are homely and yet noble is what Kunitz chooses to affirm as "miraculous." We are in the territory of a spirit-father here: a legendary father, grand, mysterious, and martyred. I am not in any way trying to say Lincoln is merely a substitute for his father. What I mean is that Kunitz's past gives him a peculiar sensitivity to this situation of father figures who are heroic yet doomed, and who are genuinely worthy of our love. Kunitz has access to this theme because of his own "curious legend" *and* because of the way his imagination has transformed that legend. Again, Kunitz is an extraordinary human spirit in that he encounters at the start of his life a devastating negation *and* he overcomes (transforms or transfigures) that negation through a major and constantly renewed act of affirmative imagination.

Space doesn't permit me to examine this wonderful poem at length, but only to say that once again (as with so many of the later poems), there is a steady deepening of the father-son theme; it is for Kunitz an inexhaustible mine always capable of yielding new insights, new discoveries about the human spirit, if only he has the courage to dig deeper and deeper into it. As he says near the end of **"The Testing Tree"**:

> It is necessary to go
>> through dark and deeper dark
>>> and not to turn . . .

I want to make only a minor observation about the conclusion of **"The Lincoln Relics."** Kunitz's own youth and old age are themes here; the quiet imminence of his own life's end as well as the awareness that Lincoln is "slipping away from us / into his legend and his fame." From this double desolation Kunitz's imagination spontaneously generates a new affirmation of the life spirit: the final section of the poem hints briefly at the possibility of Lincoln's reincarnation in a young man glimpsed in a crowd. In this way, the poem is a further stepping toward the future, a direction that we first encountered strongly in **"Journal for my Daughter."**

"The Layers"

> I have walked through many lives,
> some of them my own,
> and I am not who I was,
> though some principle of being
> abides, from which I struggle
> not to stray.
> When I look behind,
> as I am compelled to look
> before I can gather strength
> to proceed on my journey,
> I see the milestones dwindling
> toward the horizon
> and the slow fires trailing
> from the abandoned camp-sites,
> over which scavenger angels
> wheel on heavy wings.
> Oh, I have made myself a tribe
> out of my true affections,
> and my tribe is scattered!
> How shall the heart be reconciled
> to its feast of losses?

> In a rising wind
> the manic dust of my friends,
> those who fell along the way,
> bitterly stings my face.
> Yet I turn, I turn,
> exulting somewhat,
> with my will intact to go
> wherever I need to go,
> and every stone on the road
> precious to me.
> In my darkèst night,
> when the moon was covered
> and I roamed through wreckage,
> a nimbus-clouded voice
> directed me:
> "Live in the layers,
> not on the litter."
> Though I lack the art
> to decipher it,
> no doubt the next chapter
> in my book of transformations
> is already written.
> I am not done with my changes.

At this point we are facing Kunitz's art stripped down to its essentials, and yet the poem contains everything his art is about. Here are the key situations and words all fused into one whole drama: "struggle," "being," the intensity of the spiritual allegory, "affections," affirmation out of deepest desolation, "transformation." All this and age as well. The final test of a poetry of this sort might be its ability to affirm in the face of personal death. We have moved even beyond that other great poem of age, **"King of the River,"** whose final triumph was a series of intense paradoxes:

> forever inheriting his salt kingdom,
> from which he is banished
> forever.

In **"The Layers,"** Kunitz moves past paradox into pure, strange statement: exultant, quiet, confident: "I am not done with my changes. . . ."

Kunitz's imagination has one purpose: to affirm being over nonbeing. But it is always a struggle. To read Kunitz rightly we must accept that there is a hurt, a negation, at the beginning of Kunitz's life that resonates and persists through the whole life and that affects all the important aspects of his life. This negation is not only the primary negation of death (his father's suicide and the early death of a beloved stepfather telescoped together), but the secondary negation of the mother's unwillingness or inability to "forgive."

Kunitz's primary experience is *loss* or absence. This fixes a deeply sombre color to his experience of a primary reality: *change*. If change is real, it can be a negative change (death, nonbeing: the ignorant hollow) or positive, affirmative change (metamorphosis, transformation, other "triumphs" of imagination that fuse with being and the life-force). The stakes are high. When poets in our time have struggled with nonbeing, it has often ended badly: Berryman's suicide, Sylvia Plath and Hart Crane; Roethke's and Lowell's periodic bouts of madness. These poets express that confrontation with nonbeing which is a primary human encounter; we need to hear as much about it as possible, because we share it. . . .

Metamorphosis, desire, memory, vision, love, transformation, myths of quest, dream, will, revelation—it's as though each of the later poems puts forward another profound strategy of affirmation, another new way to endorse and participate in the life force and overcome the ever-present negation. It is not "himself" that he remakes in each of the later poems, it is the human spirit that he rebuilds from its foundations. He discovers, in "gathering strengths to proceed on his journey" (**"The Layers"**), what resources the human spirit has at its disposal to affirm against the realities of negation and despair. It is not simply imagination that affirms. This ceaseless crisis of the spirit demands an affirmation of the whole being that requires great courage and dignity. Kunitz's work is deeply grounded in the tragic sense: an intense, simultaneous awareness of man's dignity and his weakness:

> In a murderous time
>   the heart breaks and breaks
>   and lives by breaking.
> It is necessary to go
>   through dark and deeper dark
>   and not to turn.

What we discover as we open ourselves more and more to Kunitz's work is that poetry can deal with the deepest issues of the individual human life. It *is* that triumphant endeavor we once hoped and believed it was. There is something of utmost human importance going on here. This is the poetry of the human spirit: matters of life and death and language; the spirit and the world fuse into one vision that affirms without falsifying.

Stanley Kunitz (essay date 1984)

SOURCE: "The Layers," in *Ironwood,* Vol. 24, Fall, 1984, pp. 71-4.

[*In the following essay, Kunitz discusses poetic imagination and explains the genesis of his poem "The Abduction."*]

A few months ago a graduate student at a Midwestern university sent me an elaborate commentary on an early poem of mine, requesting my seal of approval for his interpretation. Since I could scarcely recall the lines in question—they had been produced in my twenties—I needed first of all to reacquaint myself with them, almost as if they had been written by a stranger. Something quite disturbing happened to me. As I began to read, the apparent subject-matter crumbled away, and what I heard was a cry out of the past, evoking images of an unhappy time, the pang of a hopeless love affair, in a rush of memory

that clouded the page. When I turned to my correspondent's thesis, I found that a large portion of it was devoted to an analysis and classification of prosodic devices, fortifying his perception of the poem as an example of metaphysical wit. Such discrepancies are not isolated occurrences. The readers of a poem perceive it as a verbal structure, about which they are free to speculate; whereas the poet himself is irrevocably bound to the existential source.

Even with the advantage of inside knowledge, including specific information about the occasions and intentions of what he has written, the poet is less likely than his critics to assume that he fully understands the operations of the creative faculty. Reason certainly enters into the work of the imagination, but the work has its own reasons. In my later years I have wanted to write poems that are simple on the surface, even transparent in their diction, but without denying that much of the power of poetry has its origins in the secrecy of the life and in the evocativeness of language itself, which is anciently deep in mysteries.

One of the great resources of the poetic imagination is its capacity to mount thought on thought, event on event, image on image, time on time, a process that I term "layering." The life of the mind is largely a buried life. That is why the ideal imagination, i.e., the Shakespearean one, can be compared to Jerusalem or Rome, cities sacred and eternal, great capitals built on their ruins, mounted on successive layers of civilization.

To a poet of my age each new poem presents itself in a double aspect, as a separate entity demanding to be perfected and, conversely, as an extension of the lifework, to which it is joined by invisible psychic filaments. In this latter aspect, all the poems of a lifetime can be said to add up to a single poem . . . one that is never satisfied with itself, never finished.

Poems do not want to explain themselves, even to the mind that makes them. Those most deeply embedded in this history of the self are the most reluctant to betray their ancestry and motivations. A fairly recent poem, I recall, seemed to come to me out of nowhere—a gift, to be sure, for which one ought to be thankful, but delivered suspiciously without a postmark and wrapped in bafflement. Examining it now, I can at least initiate an effort to identify some of its sources in the multifoliate tissue of experience and memory.

"The Abduction"

> Some things I do not profess
> to understand, perhaps
> not wanting to, including
> whatever it was they did
> with you or you with them
> that timeless summer day
> when you stumbled out of the wood,
> distracted, with your white blouse torn
> and a bloodstain on your skirt.
> "Do you believe?" you asked.

Between us, through the years,
from bits, from broken clues,
we pieced enough together
to make the story real:
how you encountered on the path
a pack of sleek, grey hounds,
trailed by a dumbshow retinue
in leather shrouds; and how
you were led, through leafy ways,
into the presence of a royal stag,
flaming in his chestnut coat,
who kneeled on a swale of moss
before you; and how you were borne
aloft in triumph through the green,
stretched on his rack of budding horn,
till suddenly you found yourself alone
in a trampled clearing.

That was a long time ago,
almost another age, but even now,
when I hold you in my arms,
I wonder where you are.
Sometimes I wake to hear
the engines of the night thrumming
outside the east bay window
on the lawn spreading to the rose garden.
You lie beside me in elegant repose,
a hint of transport hovering on your lips,
indifferent to the harsh green flares
that swivel through the room,
searchlights controlled by unseen hands.
Out there is childhood country,
bleached faces peering in
with coals for eyes.
Our lives are spinning out
from world to world;
the shapes of things
are shifting in the wind.
What do we know
beyond the rapture and the dread?

Ostensibly **"The Abduction"** began for me in Province-town, Massachusetts, in the middle of a summer night when I woke and turned to gaze on the face of my sleeping wife: "You lie beside me in elegant repose, / a hint of transport hovering on your lips." In the actual writing, these were my first lines. Some thirty years before, in another place and a different life, a similar circumstance had engendered the opening of **"The Science of the Night"**:

I touch you in the night, whose gift was you,
My careless sprawler,
And I touch you cold, unstirring, star-bemused,
That have become the land of your self-strangeness.

It strikes me that in both **"The Science of the Night"** and **"The Abduction,"** the epithet for the body abandoned to its night-self is "indifferent," a word less accusatory than poignant, born of the knowledge that when we are most ourselves, as in sleep, we are most withdrawn from others, even those we love. That capacity for withdrawal may be one of the conditions of the creative life.

In this connection I am reminded of a passage in one of Henry James's late letters, whose eloquence has long haunted my ears:

The port from which I set out was, I think, that of the *essential loneliness of my life*—and it seems to me the port, in sooth, to which again finally my course directs itself. This loneliness (since I mention it!)—what is it still but the deepest thing about one? Deeper about me, at any rate, than anything else, deeper than my 'genius,' deeper than my 'discipline,' deeper than my pride, deeper above all than the deep counter-minings of art.

When I review the genesis of **"The Abduction,"** its subterranean strategies ("counter-minings," in James's phrase), I see that there are two women in the poem, maybe three, combined into a single figure. The image of the woman stumbling out of the woods came to me in a dream, just as I have recorded it, two or three months after I had put aside, in discouragement, my initial lines. Physically she resembled the "careless sprawler" of **"The Science of the Night,"** who had kept a guilty secret from me; but the scenario of her fantastic adventure clearly derived from a book I had been reading, written by a friend, about UFO abductions. One of the documents in the book is the transcript of an hypnotic session with a subject named Virginia, detailing her encounter in a glade with "a beautiful deer . . . a mystical deer." I might add that among the books of my youth that fired my imagination were Grimm's fairy tales, Ovid's *Metamorphoses,* Bulfinch's mythologies, and *Gawain and the Green Knight.* Shape-shifting remains for me a viable metaphor.

In the vaults of memory everything unforgotten is equally real. Echoes of what we have read, dreamed, or imagined co-exist in the mind with remembrances of "actual" happenings. The experience of poetry itself is part of the reality that enters into the making of a poem. I venture that there is a connection, however tenuous, between my account of "the engines of the night thrumming" and Milton's mysterious evocation, in "Lycidas," of "that two-handed engine at the door," but I doubt that anyone else would even guess at the linkage. Somewhat more palpable, I suppose, is the rhythmic allusion, at the end of my poem, to Yeats's celebrated question, "How can we know the dancer from the dance?"

"The Abduction" came to me, in all its aspects, as a poem of transformation. Once the transforming spirit had asserted itself, a host of preternatural images, not all of which I can identify, arrived in a cluster. Certainly the view through the bay window and the apparition of the green flares belong to the distant summer of 1928, at Yaddo in Saratoga Springs, when the ghost of a child, the daughter of the house, who had drowned years before in the lily pond at the foot of the rose garden, invaded my chamber in the tower, shattering the casement—or so I believed. And just as certainly the vision of the bleached faces peering in at me goes even further back to the night-terrors of my childhood in Worcester, where the wind-tossed branches of the elm scraped on the glass of the fatherless house.

Nothing that I have said is meant to suggest that a poem, any poem, is at best an inspired pastiche, reducible to the sum of its constituent elements. One has hoped against the odds that it is something more, something at once capricious, idiosyncratic, and whole; not only bits and pieces, not only parts of speech, not only artful play, but one's own signature, the occult and passionate grammar of a life.

Stanley Kunitz with Peter Stitt (interview date 1990)

SOURCE: An interview with Stanley Kunitz, in *The Gettysburg Review,* Vol. 5, No. 2, Spring, 1992, pp. 193-209.

[*In the following excerpt from his interview with Stitt, which occurred on May 3, 1990, Kunitz discusses his childhood, his education, his early aspirations to be a poet, the publication of his first book, his relationship with Theodore Roethke, and the physicality of language.*]

[Stitt]: *What sort of childhood did you have?*

[Kunitz]: As I look back on it, my main impression is of how lonely I was. Aside from school, where of course I did have a degree of companionship, it was a childhood without much company outside the household itself, largely because, for so much of that time, we were living far out at the edge of the city without any neighbors. My main refuge was the woods that lay behind the house, where I wandered every day. That is where I invented the game I write about in **"The Testing-Tree."** I would throw three rocks at the tree, and the results would determine my fate. In retrospect I realize that those three throws of the stone against the patriarchal oak reveal much of the meaning of my life, at that point and in the future. If I hit the target with only one stone, somebody would love me. If I hit it twice, I should be a poet. And if I hit it three times, I should never die. That was the game, and I think it expresses my deepest yearnings.

How old were you at that time?

I must have been in my early teens. Thirteen or fourteen.

It is interesting that you should have wished to be a poet at that age. When were you first conscious that this was your desire?

It is hard for me to define exactly. I was writing from the very beginning, from the moment I went to school. Writing was what gave me the most gratification. I was also reading omnivorously. Every week I would walk to the public library, about three and a half miles from where we lived, and I would pick out this great bundle of books. The librarian would say, "Now, Stanley, you are permitted to take only five books, no more. That's the limit." So I would wrestle with the problem of which five books out of this big bundle I should take. The regulation was that you could do this only once a week; I do not know why

there was such a limitation. But I would always be back a day or two later, wanting five more books. So eventually she consented to bend the rules and let me have those extra books. Then I would trudge all the way home and devour them. My taste was indiscriminate. I did not know what I was reading—I just grabbed anything that caught my eye.

I take it this was going on even before you were twelve.

Yes, it started early. I still have—on yellow sheets of sketch paper—a collection of short stories I wrote at the age of eleven, recounting my adventures in the far north. All of them are very detailed, very tragic and desperate. They are about survival. I am mushing through snow and ice with my team of huskies. We are lost in this terrible storm, and one by one they start dropping off, dying of the cold. Finally, there is just one left and we sort of keep each other warm. No doubt I was influenced by Jack London. . . .

Let me go back to what you were saying about your early reading and writing. Was Worcester the sort of community that would support that kind of activity on the part of a very young man?

It was hardly an ideal environment. The Worcester that I knew was largely an immigrant city. It was built on seven hills, like ancient Rome—as the town fathers liked to boast—and each hill was inhabited by a different ethnic group: Irish, Swedes, Armenians, Italians, Jews, etc. Each group was isolated from the others. In fact, you were apt to encounter animosity and even some violence if you strayed into the wrong neighborhood. I bitterly resented the all-too-visible signs of parochialism and sectarianism and vowed to make my escape at the first opportunity. Sherwood Anderson's *Winesburg, Ohio,* with its depressing picture of the frustrations of small-town existence, was a book that reinforced my determination.

In high school, I founded a literary magazine called *The Argus,* in which I published early poems and other writings. In the old WASP section of Worcester, there was a group called The Browning Society, staunch survivors of what had once been a flourishing network of chapters. I have no idea how it came about, but as a young poet and editor I was granted the privilege of joining them. The elderly ladies of the Society, in their prim hats and long dresses, drank tea and discussed the poetry of Robert Browning in reverential terms. That was my first taste of the literary life, that invitation to The Browning Society.

Let me add that despite the reservations I have expressed about the Worcester environment, I remain forever grateful for the quality and breadth of instruction I received in the local schools, particularly at Classical High, a sort of magnet school, though the term hadn't been invented yet. I still treasure the hand-inscribed copy of *Bartlett's Familiar Quotations* that the faculty presented to me at graduation. No prize since then has meant as much to me. Those teachers, I believe, were superior to almost any you would find today in the public school system. I'm not even sure you could find their equivalent in the private sector.

Was there a special teacher at Classical High School who encouraged your poetry?

One such teacher was Perry Howe, the coach of the debating and declamation teams. In those days debating and declaiming were taken very seriously—there were interschool competitions in both categories, and silver cups were given to the winning teams. I was chosen captain of teams that successfully defended Classical's championship record. These were big events, held in the main auditorium of the city, with overflow audiences of students and parents in attendance. One of our first debates was on the subject of granting suffrage to women; fortunately, we drew the right side. Perry Howe helped me to overcome my native shyness and taught me how to project my voice.

I am indebted most of all to Martin Post, whom students joked about because of his love of poetry. One day he tossed aside the textbook from which he was reading to us a set of soporific quatrains—you know, the kind of didactic verse they fed to youngsters then—and reached into his pocket, saying, "I want you to hear some real poetry." That was my introduction to Robert Herrick: "Get up! get up for shame! . . . / Get up, sweet slug-a-bed and see / the dew bespangling herb and tree." And those other unforgettable lines: "Whenas in silks my Julia goes, / Then, then, methinks, how sweetly flows / That liquefaction of her clothes." I had never heard such delightful music. Right after school I dashed to the public library on Elm Street and took home Herrick's poems. I have been smitten with them ever since.

In another session of his class, Martin Post went over to the piano, struck a sequence of bass notes, and asked us, "What color did you hear?" In the midst of the snickers, when I saw that nobody else was tempted to respond, I raised my hand. The bottom notes, I said, were black, but a bit higher in the scale they moved toward the purple. Then Mr. Post put me to the test with the high, tinkling notes at the other end of the keyboard. I told him the topmost notes sounded white or crystal, moving downward toward the yellow. He turned to me and said, "Stanley, you're going to be a poet." Years later I read about the new findings by psychologists in their study of sensory perception. At birth all our five senses are fused; their differentiation is a developmental process. So that synaesthesia, the translation of one sense into the language of another, is tantamount to a return to a state of innocence. It is one of the great metaphorical resources of the poetic imagination. What was it Emily Dickinson wrote?: "To the bugle, every color is red." I don't know where Martin Post got his information.

Tell me something more about the magazine you founded, The Argus. *How long did that go on and how much writing did you do for it?*

I must have been a sophomore when I started it. Publication continued for a good many years after my departure.

Eventually the school shut down: classical education was no longer considered to be essential. Somewhere I have a file of *The Argus* tucked away. Among my contributions, I can recall, were parodies of Poe's "Raven" and Longfellow's "Excelsior." I suppose that parody was my way of learning metrics, as effective a discipline as any I know of. Perhaps, too, I was already beginning to distance myself from the nineteenth-century worthies who dominated the literary landscape.

How did you happen to go to Harvard after high school?

This was the period in which there were heavy restrictions on the number of Jews in the colleges. Even as valedictorian of my class, I had no assurance of being admitted to the college of my choice, especially since I needed financial assistance. The principal of Classical High School, Kenneth Porter, had his heart set on my going to Amherst, but failed to persuade his alma mater to accept me. Fortunately, Harvard—which I scarcely dared dream of—came through with the grant of a handsome scholarship. This despite its notorious two per cent quota.

I recall that you were an English major at Harvard. Did you receive any encouragement there as a writer?

In my second year I took a course in composition with visiting professor Robert Gay. His requirement was the submission of a one-page typed manuscript every day, Monday to Friday, on any topic of our choice—an heroic assignment, since he read and commented on every paper. After a month or so, he wrote on one of my papers, "You are a poet—Be one!" That was an even clearer signal than Martin Post had given me, and I tried, as best I could, to apply myself accordingly. In my senior year I was awarded the Garrison Medal in Poetry. During my graduate year, 1927, I took a course in versification with Robert Hillyer, but not with any appreciable benefit, since I resisted the mechanics of his approach to prosody.

Alfred North Whitehead came to Harvard, from England, while I was still an undergraduate. I knew his work and was eager to study with him, but his only offering was in advanced mathematical theory and philosophy. When I inquired about auditing his lectures, I was told that as an English major with inadequate scientific background I did not qualify. So I went to Whitehead himself. He examined my record and asked, "Why do you want to study with me?" I replied, in the firmest tones I could command, "Because I admire your work extravagantly and because I hope to be a poet." He looked at me in some astonishment and said, "You're in."

But I ended up bearing no great love for Harvard. This is an old story now, but I don't want it forgotten. After graduating *summa cum laude,* I assumed I would be asked to stay on as a teaching assistant. When I inquired of my counselor why I had not been approached, he said that he had wondered about it himself and would discuss the matter with the head of the department, Professor John Livingston Lowes, who was famous for his book on Coleridge and his course on the Romantic poets. He came back, looking embarrassed, and delivered his message, carefully giving each syllable equal weight: "What I've been told is simply this—'Our Anglo-Saxon students would resent being taught English by a Jew.'" That really shocked me. I felt crushed and angry. At that point I abandoned all thought of an academic career. How could I foresee then that eventually I would thank heaven for having been deflected from that course? After I received my master's, I left Harvard for good. During the previous summers I had been working as a cub reporter on the *Worcester Telegram*. Now I returned to Worcester as a full-fledged member of the staff and a few months later became assistant Sunday feature editor. . . .

I take it that you were also working on your poetry at this time?

I was working on the poems that constituted my first book, writing them at night and feeling good when they began to appear in various magazines, including *Poetry, The Nation, The Dial, Commonweal,* and *The New Republic.* Early in 1929 I put my poems together and sent them in the mail to the biggest publishing house in the country then: Doubleday, Doran. Only a few weeks later I had a telephone call from an editor who identified himself as Ogden Nash; he had read my poems with pleasure and wanted to congratulate me on the acceptance of my manuscript. Would I please come in to talk things over? So that is how I got my first book published. I felt that I was fortune's child. By the time *Intellectual Things* came out, in the spring of 1930, I was abroad. . . .

How did you happen to meet Theodore Roethke?

In the late thirties, when I was living in Bucks County, Pennsylvania—this was after the breakup of my marriage with Helen Pearce—Ted drove down in his jalopy from Lafayette College, where he was teaching, and knocked at my door. He was wearing a voluminous raccoon coat, and he had my book, *Intellectual Things*—much of which he knew by heart—under his arm.

He was very large, very formidable, and he stood on the doorstep reciting lines out of my poems. Then he said, "May I come in? I'd like to talk with you." With an introduction like that, he was more than welcome. Of course, he had also brought his own poems with him in manuscript. He was working on the poems that were to constitute his first volume, which I titled for him, *Open House.* It was clear to me from the start that Ted was a force of nature, a real poet. The poems he was writing then were by no means great—they were quite formal, somewhat imitative, and restricted in range. But there were signs everywhere of his ultimate destiny.

He was the first poet I had met whose passion for poetry was like mine—who had the same rather terrifying immersion in the poetic medium and who had read everybody. Through the years we learned a lot from each other, though I, being a little older and having already published, was certainly at first in the position of being more his mentor than he was mine. Later he was to open doors

of the imagination for me, particularly during the period when he erupted into the poems of *The Lost Son.* To me those were the most important poems written by anyone in my generation. . . .

You once said, "The language of the poem must do more than convey experience, it must embody it." Does that mean for you the physicality of language?

Definitely. The poems that mean most to me are the ones to which I respond physically as well as intellectually or aesthetically. When we say that we are moved or stirred or shaken by a poem we are describing a kinaesthetic response to fields of verbal energy. In the dynamics of poetry, all the sounds are actions. It is as though some intrinsic gesture of the soul itself were being expressed through the resonances of language. In that context the marriage of sense with sound seems to me to be a deep metaphysical action.

Is this why you love the Metaphysical poets so much, and why your own work has been grouped with that of the new metaphysical poets?

I don't care much for these groupings. Through the various stages of my work, I've been put into some rather strange company. But seriously, I'm inclined to think of myself less as a metaphysical than as an existential poet. To me, the struggle of words to be born, to arrive at the level of consciousness, is like the struggle of the self to become a person. I think that what the poet is trying to do is to bring words out from the darkness of the self into the light of the world. That is like the primordial act of creation, what Coleridge meant when he spoke of the repetition in the finite mind of the infinite I AM.

As you were talking about the physicality of the language, which would seem to imply the necessity of a rich verbal texture, it occurred to me to ask if you have that same feeling about your more recent poems, those beginning with **The Testing-Tree.**

Some years ago, in commenting on my later work, I said I was trying to write poems with a surface so simple and transparent that you could look through them and see the world. I didn't mean to suggest that I had lost interest in the orchestration of the world within. Texture is more than a superficial phenomenon and is not to be confused with the maintenance of a high style. My main concern is with psychic texture, which is a deeper and more complex thing.

When you compose your poems, is there that same sense of actual physical engagement?

I have never known how to compose poems except by saying them. The problem always has been to discover a rhythm on which I can ride. When that happens, I am on my way. A poem springs to life when its energy begins to flow from one's deepest wells.

In my interview with him, James Wright quoted you as having said to him when he was a young poet: "You've got to get down into the pit of the self, the real pit, and then you have to find your own way to climb out of it. And it can't be anybody else's way. It has to be yours."

Very sound advice!

Do you write regularly, say a little bit every day?

No.

How do you know when it is time to write a new poem?

I have never been able to sit down and write a poem as an act of will. My poems seem to have wills of their own. They keep their own schedules secret, and they don't answer the phone. They usually come to me at night with a phrase or image that starts troubling my sleep, gradually hooking up with other words and images, often counter-images, searching—as I've already indicated—for a controlling rhythm. It's a slow process.

Have you ever had poems come to you ready-made, a kind of spontaneous perfect composition?

Miracles happen now and then, but not if you count on them.

I am going to name a few poems and see if you have anything to say about the story behind the poem or its genesis: "End of Summer."

That's one I happen to have written about. It dates back to the time I was living in Bucks County. I was hoeing in the corn field when I heard a clamor in the sky—it was the season for the wild Canadian geese to be flying south. Great v-shapes, constellations of them. Something in that calling of the birds disturbed me. I dropped my hoe, ran into the house, and started to write. After the geese delivered their message to me, they flew out of the poem. They told me to make an important decision, to change my life, and I did. It is a poem about migration.

How about the poem "No Word"?

That's simple. I don't believe anyone has ever asked me about it before. I was waiting for a telephone call from someone who meant a lot to me, and the call did not come. Well, it did finally come, but too late.

How about "Open the Gates"?—Jim Wright's favorite of your poems.

"Open the Gates" originated in a dream. The landscape suggests the cities of the plain, Sodom and Gomorrah, from which I am fleeing—at least that was my interpretation on waking. In the climactic action, the monumental door I knock on is the door of revelation. Many of my poems speak of a quest, the search for the transcendent, a movement from darkness into light, from the kingdom of the profane into the kingdom of the sacred. As a rule, I don't feel I'm done with a poem until it passes from one realm of experience to another.

Your interest in politics is profound, as we see in your devotion to poets who have lived under totalitarian governments. But your poems are never overtly political.

Well, almost never. I maintain that to live as a poet in this society is to make a definite political statement. The politics is inherent in the practice of the art, as well as in the life. At the same time I feel that poetry resists being used as a tool. The truth is that we are suffering from an excess of political rhetoric and a dearth of the compassionate imagination.

David Barber (review date 1996)

SOURCE: "A Visionary Poet at Ninety," in *The Atlantic Monthly,* Vol. 277, No. 6, pp. 113-16, 118-20.

[*In the following excerpt from a review of* Passing Through, *Barber marvels at Kunitz's "exemplary resilience" and "inexhaustible" curiosity.*]

Here, in a trim volume that nobody could wish shorter, [*Passing Through: The Later Poems, New and Selected*], is virtually the entire windfall of Kunitz's "later" poetry: the selected contents of *The Testing-Tree* (1971), **"The Layers"** (the constellation of new poems that led off his 1979 edition of *The Poems of Stanley Kunitz*), and *Next-to-Last Things: New Poems and Essays* (1985), along with nine poems appearing for the first time in a book. Not a lifetime's work but something more seasoned and concentrated and surpassing—work with a lifetime steeped in it. In contrast to *The Poems of Stanley Kunitz*, a more substantial compilation that showed Kunitz over a span of some fifty years moving beyond his clenched and seething early style, *Passing Through* allows readers to follow the clean arc of Kunitz's late three decades of composition in splendid isolation.

It is, above all, a book of revelations. From the beginning Kunitz's was a poetry consecrated to transfiguring moments of insight and rapture, and it is startling to discover how active that core of exaltation has remained. For Kunitz, as for no other first-rank American poet of his time who comes readily to mind, the lyric poem has been a portal into mystical apprehension, an article of faith thathe does not shrink from making explicit in the preface to *Passing Through*, "Instead of a Foreword." Conceding nothing to postmodern anxiety and exhaustion, Kunitz uses his prologue to extol the poet's vocation, as "a form of spiritual testimony," and poetry as "ultimately mythology, the telling of the stories of the soul." . . .

Even for poets nowhere near Kunitz's age, a volume of selected poems is usually, in one studied way or another, the formal unveiling of a monument, a hopeful brief for literary posterity. But no such ceremony intrudes on *Passing Through*: even in its closing pages, where the latest of these later poems appear, Kunitz doesn't once seem to be posing for a marble bust or auditioning for the anthologies. Instead one enters the presence of an indomitable elder spirit writing with alertness, tenacity, and finesse, still immersed in the life of the senses and persisting in the search for fugitive essences. Neither resigned nor becalmed, Kunitz's newest poems are by turns contemplative, confiding, mythic, and elegiac. If they have the measured and worldly tone that befits an old master, they also have the ardent and questing air of one whose capacity for artless wonder seems inexhaustible. "What makes the engine go?" Kunitz asks in **"Touch Me,"** as he kneels in his cricket-riddled garden and marvels "like a child again / . . . to hear so clear / and brave a music pour / from such a small machine." And the answering line speaks for the persistence of Kunitz's music as well: "Desire, desire, desire."

Perhaps the ultimate tribute to this book is to say that one closes it with no certainty that it's going to stand as the poet's last word. Little in these poems puts one in mind of postscripts or epitaphs, and even Kunitz's most pronounced valedictory gestures seem somehow to steal a march on the gloaming. Consider, for example, the closing lines of the book's title poem, which, its epigraph informs us, was composed on the poet's seventy-ninth birthday.

> The way I look
> at it, I'm passing through a phase:
> gradually I'm changing to a word.
> Whatever you choose to claim
> of me is always yours;
> nothing is truly mine
> except my name. I only
> borrowed this dust.

It should be noted that **"Passing Through"** is addressed to Kunitz's wife, Elise Asher; this is no last will and testament but a love poem. The whole effect is vintage Kunitz: lines unforced and seemingly spontaneous yet so ineffable that one can almost imagine them having been inscribed on papyrus. To write this calmly and collectedly, with a sanity so finely tempered that it acquires a spooky prescience, one has to have done more than simply endure. And such is clearly the story behind the exemplary resilience of grand old man Stanley Kunitz: the fullness of time hasn't just left his senses intact but has concentrated his mind wonderfully. That dust has moved mountains.

FURTHER READING

Biographies

Guston, Philip. *A Celebration for Stanley Kunitz on His 80th Birthday.* New York: Sheep Meadow Press, 1986, 159 p.
  A collection of reminiscences and testimonials by friends and other admirers of Kunitz.

Criticism

Claire, William F. Review of *A Kind of Order, a Kind of Folly,* by Stanley Kunitz. *The American Scholar* 45, No. 4 (Autumn 1976): 598.

Notes Kunitz's many varied interests, including his knowledge of the visual arts and involvement in the work of younger poets.

Davis, Cynthia A. "Stanley Kunitz and the Transubstantial Word." *The Literary Review* 24, No. 3 (Spring 1981): 413-26.
  Studies the development of Kunitz's use of language in relation to the dominant archetypal patterns in his poetry: death and rebirth, the quest, the night journey, and the lost father.

Henault, Marie. *Stanley Kunitz.* Boston: Twayne, 1980, 164 p.
  A comprehensive biography and critical assessment of Kunitz's life and works.

Lieberman, Laurence. Review of *The Testing-Tree,* by Stanley Kunitz. *The Yale Review* (Autumn 1971): 82-5.
  Praises the poetic voice of many individual poems, but finds the collection uneven as a whole.

Orr, Gregory. *Stanley Kunitz: An Introduction to the Poetry.* New York: Columbia University Press, 1985, 297 p.
  The most comprehensive study of Kunitz's poetry, dealing mainly with the theme of father and son relationships.

Perloff, Marjorie. "The Testing of Stanley Kunitz." *The Iowa Review* 3, No. 1 (Winter 1972): 93-103.
  Identifies the strengths and weaknesses of *The Testing-Tree,* focusing on the poem "Journal for My Daughter."

Ryan, Michael. "Life Between Scylla and Charybdis." *American Poetry Review* 14, No. 5 (September/October 1985): 28-30.
  Considers Kunitz a poet of polarities and praises him for setting a moral example for younger poets.

Shaw, Robert. "A Book of Changes." *The New York Times Book Review* (22 July 1979): 1, 20.
  Views Kunitz's writing as calculated risk taking that has succeeded.

Voigt, Ellen Bryant. "On Tone." *New England Review & Bread Loaf Quarterly* 12, No. 3 (Spring 1990): 249-66.
  Discusses the poem "My Sisters" as an example of the clarity of Kunitz's writing, focusing on Kunitz's use of powerful sensory images.

Interviews

Moss, Stanley. *Interviews and Encounters with Stanley Kunitz.* New York: Sheep Meadow Press, 1993, 241 p.
  A comprehensive collection of interviews with Kunitz.

Packard, William. An interview with Stanley Kunitz. *New York Quarterly,* No. 4 (Fall 1970): 9-22.
  A conversation in which Kunitz discusses his education, his early experiences as an editor, the political layerings in "Mound Builders," and the opening lines of his poems.

Additional coverage of Kunitz's life and career is contained in the following sources published by Gale Research: *Contemporary Literary Criticism*, Vols. 6, 11, 14; *Contemporary Authors*, Vols. 41-44R; *Contemporary Authors New Revision Series*, Vol. 26; *Dictionary of Literary Biography*, Vol. 48; and *Major Twentieth-Century Writers*.

John Milton
1608-1674

English poet, essayist, dramatist, and historian.

INTRODUCTION

Milton is recognized as one of the greatest writers in the English language and as a thinker of world importance. He is best known for *Paradise Lost* (1667), an epic poem recounting the Biblical story of humanity's fall from grace. This work and its sequel *Paradise Regained* (1671) are celebrated for their consummate artistry and searching consideration of God's relationship with the human race. In addition to these great works, Milton also wrote "Lycidas," "Il Penseroso" and "L'Allegro," a series of sonnets on personal and political themes, as well as a number of fine minor poems. His prose works include *Areopagitica* (1644) and *The Doctrine and Discipline of Divorce* (1643), both powerful essays in defense of individual liberty.

Biographical Information

Born in Cheapside, London in 1608, the son of a prosperous scrivener and notary, Milton was from an early age immersed in literary and intellectual activity. His father provided his son with a private tutor, retaining him even after Milton had entered St. Paul's School. Milton was a model student: he excelled in Latin, Greek, and Hebrew; wrote poetry in Latin and English; and studied the classics, modern languages, and music voraciously. (Milton acknowledged that in his youth he rarely quit his books before midnight, and he attributed his later blindness to excessive reading by lamp- and candlelight.) His studies—especially music and the classics—remained lifelong interests for Milton and colored much of his literary work. Milton entered Christ's College, Cambridge in 1625. There, his handsome face, delicate appearance, and lofty but unpretentious bearing earned him the sobriquet "the Lady of Christ's." At first unpopular, Milton eventually made a name for himself as a rhetorician and public speaker. While at Cambridge he probably wrote "L'Allegro," and "Il Penseroso," and "On the Morning of Christ's Nativity," three of his earliest great poems in English. Upon leaving the university in 1632 with an A.M. degree, Milton retired to Hammersmith for three years and later to Horton, Buckinghamshire, where he devoted himself to intense study and writing. To this period scholars ascribe the composition of some of Milton's finest non-epic poems, including "Lycidas," "Arcades," and the sonnet "How Soon Hath Time." While still in Hammersmith, he also wrote his first extended work, Comus (1637), a masque, on commission for the Bridgewater family. In May 1638, Milton embarked on an Italian journey which was to last

nearly fifteen months. The experience, which he described in *Defensio secunda pro populo anglicano* (*Second Defense of the People of England,* 1654), brought him into contact with the leading men of letters in Florence, Rome, and Naples, including Giovanni Battista Manso, Marquis of Villa, who had been an intimate of the epic poet Torquato Tasso. Scholars view the Italian tour as seminal in Milton's literary development; a new self-confidence emerged in the letters he wrote during his travels, and it was in Italy that Milton first proposed to write a great epic. Upon his return to England, Milton wrote the Italian-inspired *Epitaphium Damonis* (*Damon,* 1640) a Latin elegy on his longtime friend Charles Diodati. Critics have seen this work as Milton's first heralding of his ambition to be a great poet inthe Renaissance vein, the author of classically inspired works on elevated themes. With the coming of the English Civil War and Commonwealth, Milton's life changed utterly as his attentions shifted from private to public concerns. Abruptly he left off writing poetry for prose, pouring out pamphlets during the early 1640s in which he opposed what he considered rampant episcopal tyranny. Around this time, Milton also published *The Doctrine and Discipline of Divorce,* in which he maintained that incompatibility is a valid reason for divorce (a work presumably inspired by his own unhappy marriage to Mary Powell) and *Areopagitica,* a now-classic plea for unlicensed printing in England. Over the next few years Milton worked on other prose works, including his *History of Britain* (1670) and *De doctrina christiana* (*A Treatise of Christian Doctrine,* unpublished until 1825). The execution of Charles I in 1649 prompted *The Tenure of Kings and Magistrates,* a radical assertion of the right of a people to depose or execute a ruling tyrant, which confirmed Milton's left-wing politics. The Restoration of Charles II in 1660 left Milton disillusioned and hastened his departure from public life; he lived for a time in peril of his life, but for reasons not entirely clear he was spared harsh punishment.

The remaining fourteen years of Milton's life were spent in relatively peaceful retirement in and around London. Now completely blind—he had been since 1652—Milton increasingly devoted his time to poetry. Secretaries, assisted sometimes by Milton's two nephews and his daughter Deborah, were employed to take dictation, correct copy, and read aloud, and Milton made rapid progress on projects he had put off many years before. During the making of *Paradise Lost,* Milton spent mornings dictating passages he had composed in his head at night. *Paradise Lost* was published in 1667, followed in 1671 by *Paradise Regained. Samson Agonistes,* a metrical tragedy, appeared in the same volume as *Paradise Regained.* Milton died in November 1674, apparently of heart failure. His funeral, wrote John Toland in 1698, was attended by "All his learned and great friends in London, not without a friendly concourse of the Vulgar. . . ."

Major Works

Most of Milton's works (with the exception of the verse dramas *Comus* and *Samson Agonistes*) fall neatly into two categories, poetry and prose, and there is very little crossover of theme or purpose from one category to the other; poetry was chiefly an artistic medium for Milton, prose being reserved for exposition only. In his first poetic successes, the twin lyrics "L'Allegro" and "Il Penseroso," Milton contrasted the active and contemplative lives. The imagery, drawn from classical mythology and English folklore, is cultivated and stylized, and both works are tightly argued. Critics agree that with "Lycidas," his next major work, Milton came into his own as a poet. In editing his poems in 1645, he called this pastoral a "Monody" in which "the Author bewails a learned Friend, unfortunately drown'd . . . on the Irish Seas, 1637. And by occasion foretells the ruin of our corrupted Clergy then in their height." The purpose of the poem was twofold: to honor the late Edward King, a former schoolmate of Christ's College, and to denounce hireling, incompetent clergy—a perennial concern of Milton's. Incidentally, the poem reveals Milton's own philosophical ambitions, later undertaken in *Paradise Lost:* to justify God's ways to men. Many critics consider "Lycidas" the finest short poem in the English language.

Milton's best-known works are also his longest ones: *Paradise Lost, Paradise Regained* and *Samson Agonistes.*

Of these, *Paradise Lost* is deemed the supreme achievement by far. Milton had long planned an epic which was to be to England what Homer's works were to Greece and the Aeneid was to Rome. Originally, he contemplated an Arthurian subject for his national poem, but later adopted a Biblical subject: the Fall of Man as described in the Book of Genesis. As a classicist, Milton was powerfully aware of his antique precedents; he therefore began the poem in medias res, invoking his muse and plunging into the action with a description of Satan in Hell—actually the poem's third crisis, which chronologically follows Satan's revolt in Heaven and descent with his followers through Chaos to Hell. The remainder of the poem treats Satan's deception of Eve in Eden, her deception of Adam, their fall from perfect fellowship with god and with each other, and their banishment from Paradise. Everywhere the poem is strong in its appeal to the ear, the intellect, and the visual imagination. While the iambic pentameter is the norm, Milton played with the model, contriving syllable and stresses to complement the sense. (Commentators attribute many of Milton's superb metrical effects to his deep knowledge of music and his acutely sensitive ear.) Descriptive passages evoke images at once vague and minute, exposing in precise detail the character (but usually not the exact composition) of Heaven, Pandemonium, Chaos, and the universe. Eden is revealed as a sensuous feast. Milton's high purpose in the poem, to "justify the ways of God to men," is ever in the forefront of the action. Critics agree that this challenging objective, made all the more difficult by the complicated issue of divine foreknowledge of the Fall, is effected chiefly by imbuing Adam with a will as well as a mind of his own, enabling him to disobey God and thus mar an omnipotent Creator's perfect creation. *Paradise Regained*—more a dramatic poem than an epic—completes the action of *Paradise Lost.* Shorter and conceptually much simpler that the earlier work, it depicts Christ in the wilderness overcoming Satan the tempter. By this action, Christ proves his fitness as the Son of God, thereby preparing himself for his human, substitutionary role in the Crucifixion. Written in the tradition of dramatic tragedy, *Samson Agonistes* departs from the form and theme of *Paradise Lost* and *Paradise Regained,* but it is clear that Milton recognized affinities among the three works. Like Christ in *Paradise Regained,* Samson is terribly isolated, "Eyeless in Gaza at the mill with slaves," and undergoes a severe testing of his spiritual strength. He triumphs, gaining renewed faith in God and an improved understanding of his soul.

Critical Reception

More criticism has been devoted to Milton than to any English author save Shakespeare and perhaps Chaucer. While celebrated as a poet in his lifetime, Milton was scorned by many contemporaries for his anti-clerical and anti-moralist stances, although some noted persons, such as Andrew Marvell, rose to his defense. Soon after Milton's death, *Paradise Lost* began to draw increased attention and praise from such critics as John Dryden, who considered Milton as an epic poet comparable in stature to Homer and Virgil. With the notable exception of Samuel Johnson, who dismissed "Lycidas" as cold and mechanical and *Paradise Lost* as stylistically flawed, critics throughout the eighteenth and nineteenth centuries upheld Milton's achievement unabated, for various reasons: William Blake and Percy Bysshe Shelley considered *Paradise Lost* a precursor of Romanticism, ennobling Satan as a tragic rebel; William Wordsworth hailed Milton's libertarian ideals; Matthew Arnold viewed Milton as exemplifying English genius. In the 1920, a group of critics, led by T. S. Eliot, began to attack what they perceived as the wooden style and structure of Milton's epics; Eliot, while conceding Milton's talent, lamented his influence on later poets, who, he argued, often created torturously boring, rhetorical verse in imitation of the earlier poet. In the 1940s and 50s, Milton's puritan ideology and grand style drew fire from some of the New Critics, most notably the English academic F. R. Leavis. For Leavis, as for Robert Graves, aesthetic judgement was curiously close to a visceral, strangely personal dislike of Milton himself. Milton's star, however, was on the ascendent. Critics including Cleanth Brooks, C. S. Lewis, William Empson, and Frank Kermode sympathetically defended the poet's brilliance and integrity, drawing a fresh generation of readers to the epic splendors of Milton's poetry. While the rise of the women's movement in the 1970s provoked controversy over sexism in *Paradise Lost,* Harold Bloom made Milton's poetry central to his theory of literary influence, reinstating the poet's dominant role in English literature. It would be difficult to overestimate Milton's importance in English letters. In *Paradise Lost* he gave his country its greatest epic, surpassing, most commentators believe, even Spenser in the magnitude of his achievement in this form. And as the author of "Lycidas," "L'Allegro" and "Il Penseroso" he established himself as a master of the shorter poem. His scope was wide, his sweep broad, and his capacity for thought deep—the touchstone of intellectual achievement. For, in the words of James Russell Lowell, "If [Milton] is blind, it is with excess of light, it is a divine partiality, an overshadowing with angels' wings."

PRINCIPAL WORKS

Poetry

"Lycidas" 1638; published in *Obsequies to the Memorie of Mr. Edward King, Anno. Dom. 1638*
Epitaphium Damonis 1640
Poems of Mr. John Milton, Both English and Latin, Compos'd at Several Times 1645
Paradise Lost: A Poem Written in Ten Books 1667; also published as *Paradise Lost: A Poem in Twelve Books* [enlarged edition] 1674
Paradise Regained Poem in IV Books. To Which Is Added Samson Agonistes 1671
The Poetical Works of Mr. John Milton 1697
A Complete Collection of the Historical, Political, and Miscellaneous Works of John Milton, Both English and Latin, with Some Papers Never Before Publish'd 1698

A Common-place Book of John Milton 1876
The Sonnets of John Milton 1883
The Works of John Milton. 18 vols. 1931-1938

Other Major Works

A Maske Presented at Ludlow Castle, 1634, on Michaelmas Night, before the Right Honorable John Earle of Bridgewater, Viscount Brackly (drama) 1637
The Reason of Church-Government Urg'd against Prelaty (essay) 1642
The Doctrine and Discipline of Divorce, Restor'd to the Good of Both Sexes from the Bondage of Canon Law (essay) 1643
Areopagitica: A Speech of Mr. John Milton for the Liberty of Unlicenc'd Printing, to the Parliament of England (essay) 1644
The Tenure of Kings and Magistrates, Proving That It is Lawfull, and Hath Been Held So Through All Ages, for Any Who Have the Power, to Call to Account a Tyrant, or Wicked King (essay) 1649
Pro populo anglicano defensio, contra Claudii Anonymi (essay) 1651
Defense of the People of England, 1692
Defensio secunda pro populo anglicano (essay) 1654
The History of Britain, That Part Especially Now Call'd England, from the First Traditional Beginning, Continu'd to the Norman Conquest (history) 1670
The Works of Mr. John Milton (essays) 1697
De doctrina christiana libri duo posthumi [*A Treatise of Christian Doctrine*] (essay) 1825
Complete Prose Works of John Milton. 8 vols. (essay, history, and letters) 1953

* This work is commonly known as *Comus: A Maske.*

CRITICISM

William Hazlitt (essay date 1818)

SOURCE: "Of Shakespeare and Milton," in *Lectures on the English Poets,* Humphrey Milford and Oxford University Press, 1924, pp. 85-103.

[*In the following excerpt, Hazlitt provides an overview of Milton's religious sensibilities, his political commitments, and his literary influences from Biblical and Classical writings.*]

. . . Milton's works are a perpetual invocation to the Muses; a hymn to Fame. He had his thoughts constantly fixed on the contemplation of the Hebrew theocracy, and of a perfect commonwealth; and he seized the pen with a hand just warm from the touch of the ark of faith. His religious zeal infused its character into his imagination; so that he devotes himself with the same sense of duty to the cultivation of his genius, as he did to the exercise of virtue, or the good of his country. The spirit of the poet, the patriot, and the prophet, vied with each other in his breast. His mind appears to have held equal communion with the inspired writers, and with the bards and sages of ancient Greece and Rome;—

> Blind Thamyris, and blind Mæonides,
> And Tiresias, and Phineus, prophets old.

He had a high standard, with which he was always comparing himself, nothing short of which could satisfy his jealous ambition. He thought of nobler forms and nobler things than those he found about him. He lived apart, in the solitude of his own thoughts, carefully excluding from his mind whatever might distract its purposes or alloy its purity, or damp its zeal. "With darkness and with dangers compassed round," he had the mighty models of antiquity always present to his thoughts, and determined to raise a monument of equal height and glory. "piling up every stone of lustre from the brook," for the delight and wonder of posterity. He had girded himself up, and as it were, sanctified his genius to this service from his youth. "For after," he says, "I had from my first years, by the ceaseless diligence and care of my father, been exercised to the tongues, and some sciences as my age could suffer, by sundry masters and teachers, it was found that whether aught was imposed upon me by them, or betaken to of my own choice, the style by certain vital signs it had, was likely to live; but much latelier, in the private academies of Italy, perceiving that some trifles which I had in memory, composed at under twenty or thereabout, met with acceptance above what was looked for; I began thus far to assent both to them and divers of my friends here at home, and not less to an inward prompting which now grew daily upon me, that by labour and intense study (which I take to be my portion in this life), joined with the strong propensity of nature, I might perhaps leave something so written to after-times as they should not willingly let it die. The accomplishment of these intentions, which have lived within me ever since I could conceive myself anything worth to my country, lies not but in a power above man's to promise; but that none hath by more studious ways endeavoured, and with more unwearied spirit that none shall, that I dare almost aver of myself, as far as life and free leisure will extend. Neither do I think it shame to covenant with any knowing reader, that for some few years yet, I may go on trust with him toward the payment of what I am now indebted, as being a work not to be raised from the heat of youth or the vapours of wine; like that which flows at waste from the pen of some vulgar amourist, or the trencher fury of a rhyming parasite, nor to be obtained by the invocation of Dame Memory and her Siren daughters, but by devout prayer to that eternal spirit who can enrich with all utterance and knowledge, and sends out his Seraphim with the hallowed fire of his altar, to touch and purify the lips of whom he pleases: to this must be added industrious and select reading, steady observation, and insight into all seemly and generous arts and affairs. Although it nothing content me to have disclosed thus much beforehand; but that I trust hereby to make it manifest with what small willingness I endure to

interrupt the pursuit of no less hopes than these, and leave a calm and pleasing solitariness, fed with cheerful and confident thoughts, to embark in a troubled sea of noises and hoarse disputes, from beholding the bright countenance of truth in the quiet and still air of delightful studies."

So that of Spenser:

> The noble heart that harbours virtuous thought,
>   And is with child of glorious great intent,
> Can never rest until it forth have brought
>   The eternal brood of glory excellent.

Milton, therefore, did not write from casual impulse, but after a severe examination of his own strength, and with a resolution to leave nothing undone which it was in his power to do. He always labours, and almost always succeeds. He strives hard to say the finest things in the world, and he does say them. He adorns and dignifies his subject to the utmost: he surrounds it with every possible association of beauty or grandeur, whether moral, intellectual, or physical. He refines on his descriptions of beauty; loading sweets on sweets, till the sense aches at them; and raises his images of terror to a gigantic elevation, that "makes Ossa like a wart," In Milton, there is always an appearance of effort: in Shakespeare, scarcely any.

Milton has borrowed more than any other writer, and exhausted every source of imitation, sacred or profane; yet he is perfectly distinct from every other writer. He is a writer of centos, and yet in originality scarcely inferior to Homer. The power of his mind is stamped on every line. The fervour of his imagination melts down and renders malleable, as in a furnace, the most contradictory materials. In reading his works, we feel ourselves under the influence of a mighty intellect, that the nearer it approaches to others, becomes more distinct from them. The quantity of art in him shows the strength of his genius: the weight of his intellectual obligations would have oppressed any otherwriter. Milton's learning has the effect of intuition. He describes objects, of which he could only have read in books, with the vividness of actual observation. His imagination has the force of nature. He makes words tell as pictures.

> Him followed Rimmon, whose delightful seat
> Was fair Damascus, on the fertile banks
> Of Abbana and Pharphar, lucid streams.

The word *lucid* here gives to the idea all the sparkling effect of the most perfect landscape.

And again:

> As when a vulture on Imaus bred,
> Whose snowy ridge the roving Tartar bounds,
> Dislodging from a region scarce of prey,
> To gorge the flesh of lambs and yeanling kids
> On hills where flocks are fed, flies towards the
>   springs
> Of Ganges or Hydaspes, Indian streams;
> But in his way lights on the barren plains

Of Sericana, where Chineses drive
With sails and wind their cany waggons light.

If Milton had taken a journey for the express purpose, he could not have described this scenery and mode of life better. Such passages are like demonstrations of natural history. Instances might be multiplied without end.

We might be tempted to suppose that the vividness with which he describes visible objects, was owing to their having acquired an unusual degree of strength in his mind, after the privation of his sight; but we find the same palpableness and truth in the descriptions which occur in his early poems. In **"Lycidas"** he speaks of 'the great vision of the guarded mount,' with that preternatural weight of impression with which it would present itself suddenly to 'the pilot of some small night-foundered skiff': and the lines in the **"Penseroso,"** describing 'the wandering moon,

> Riding near her highest noon,
> Like one that had been led astray
> Through the heaven's wide pathless way,'

are as if he had gazed himself blind in looking at her. There is also the same depth of impression in his descriptions of the objects of all the different senses, whether colours, or sounds, or smells—the same absorption of his mind in whatever engaged his attention at the time. It has been indeed objected to Milton, by a common perversity of criticism, that his ideas were musical rather than picturesque, as if because they were in the highest degree musical, they must be (to keep the sage critical balance even, and to allow no one man to possess two qualities at the same time) proportionably deficient in other respects. But Milton's poetry is not cast in any such narrow, common-place mould; it is not so barren of resources. His worship of the Muse was not so simpleor confined. A sound arises "like a steam of rich distilled perfumes"; we hear the pealing organ, but the incense on the altars is also there, and the statues of the gods are ranged around! The ear indeed predominates over the eye, because it is more immediately affected, and because the language of music blends more immediately with, and forms a more natural accompaniment to, the variable and indefinite associations of ideas conveyed by words. But where the associations of the imagination are not the principal thing, the individual object is given by Milton with equal force and beauty. The strongest and best proof of this, as a characteristic power of his mind, is, that the persons of Adam and Eve, of Satan, &c. are always accompanied, in our imagination, with the grandeur of the naked figure; they convey to us the ideas of sculpture. As an instance, take the following:

> He soon
> Saw within ken a glorious Angel stand,
> The same whom John saw also in the sun:
> His back was turned, but not his brightness hid;
> Of beaming sunny rays a golden tiar
> Circled his head, nor less his locks behind
> Illustrious on his shoulders fledge with wings

> Lay waving round; on some great charge employ'd
> He seem'd, or fix'd in cogitation deep.
> Glad was the spirit impure, as now in hope
> To find who might direct his wand'ring flight
> To Paradise, the happy seat of man,
> His journey's end, and our beginning woe.
> But first he casts to change his proper shape,
> Which else might work him danger or delay:
> And now a stripling cherub he appears,
> Not of the prime, yet such as in his face
> Youth smiled celestial, and to every limb
> Suitable grace diffus'd, so well he feign'd:
> Under a coronet his flowing hair
> In curls on either cheek play'd; wings he wore
> Of many a colour'd plume sprinkled with gold,
> His habit fit for speed succinct, and held
> Before his decent steps a silver wand.

The figures introduced here have all the elegance and precision of a Greek statue; glossy and impurpled, tinged with golden light, and musical as the strings of Memnon's harp!

Again, nothing can be more magnificent than the portrait of Beelzebub:

> With Atlantean shoulders fit to bear
> The weight of mightiest monarchies:

Or the comparison of Satan, as he 'lay floating many a rood,' to 'that sea beast,'

> Leviathan, which God of all his works
> Created hugest that swim the ocean-stream!

What a force of imagination is there in this last expression! What an idea it conveys of the size of that hugest of created beings, as if it shrunk up the ocean to a stream, and took up the sea in its nostrils as a very little thing! Force of style is one of Milton's greatest excellences. Hence, perhaps, he stimulates us more in the reading, and less afterwards. The way to defend Milton against all impugners, is to take down the book and read it.

Milton's blank verse is the only blank verse in the language (except Shakespeare's) that deserves the name of verse. Dr. Johnson, who had modelled his ideas of versification on the regular sing-song of Pope, condemns the *Paradise Lost* as harsh and unequal. I shall not pretend to say that this is not sometimes the case; for where a degree of excellence beyond the mechanical rules of art is attempted, the poet must sometimes fail. But I imagine that there are more perfect examples in Milton of musical expression, or of an adaptation of the sound and movement of the verse to the meaning of the passage, than in all our other writers, whether of rhyme or blank verse, put together (with the exception already mentioned). Spenser is the most harmonious of our stanza writers, as Dryden is the most sounding and varied of our rhymists. But in neither is there anything like the same ear for music, the same power of approximating the varieties of poetical to those of musical rhythm, as there is in our great epic poet.

The sound of his lines is moulded into the expression of the sentiment, almost of the very image. They rise or fall, pause or hurry rapidly on, with exquisite art, but without the least trick or affectation, as the occasion seems to require. . . .

Dr. Johnson and Pope would have converted his vaulting Pegasus into a rocking-horse. Read any other blank verse but Milton's,—Thomson's, Young's, Cowper's, Wordsworth's,—and it will be found, from the want of the same insight into 'the hidden soul of harmony,' to be mere lumbering prose.

To proceed to a consideration of the merits of **Paradise Lost**, in the most essential point of view, I mean as to the poetry of character and passion. I shall say nothing of the fable, or of other technical objections or excellences; but I shall try to explain at once the foundation of the interest belonging to the poem. I am ready to give up the dialogues in Heaven, where, as Pope justly observes, "God the Father turns a school-divine"; nor do I consider the battle of the angels as the climax of sublimity, or the most successful effort of Milton's pen. In a word, the interest of the poem arises from the daring ambition and fierce passions of Satan, and from the account of the paradisaical happiness, and the loss of it by our first parents. Three-fourths of the work are taken up with these characters, and nearly all that relates to them is unmixed sublimity and beauty. The two first books alone are like two massy pillars of solid gold.

> **[Milton's] religious zeal infused its character into his imagination; so that he devotes himself with the same sense of duty to the cultivation of his genius, as he did to the exercise of virtue, or the good of his country.**
>
> —*William Hazlitt*

Satan is the most heroic subject that ever was chosen for a poem; and the execution is as perfect as the design is lofty. He was the first of created beings, who, for endeavouring to be equal with the highest, and to divide the empire of heaven with the Almighty, was hurled down to hell. His aim was no less than the throne of the universe; his means, myriads of angelic armies bright, the third part of the heavens, whom he lured after him with his countenance, and who durst defy the Omnipotent in arms. His ambition was the greatest, and his punishment was the greatest; but not so his despair, for his fortitude was as great as his sufferings. His strength of mind was matchless as his strength of body; the vastness of his designs did not surpass the firm, inflexible determination with which he submitted to his irreversible doom, and final loss of all good. His power of action and of suffering was equal. He was the greatest power that was ever overthrown, with the strongest will

left to resist or to endure. He was baffled, not confounded. He stood like a tower; or

> ——————————— As when Heaven's fire
> Hath scathed the forest oaks or mountain pines.

He was still surrounded with hosts of rebel angels, armed warriors, who own him as their sovereign leader, and with whose fate he sympathizes as he views them round, far as the eye can reach; though he keeps aloof from them in his own mind, and holds supreme counsel only with his own breast. An outcast from Heaven, Hell trembles beneath his feet, Sin and Death are at his heels, and mankind are his easy prey.

> All is not lost; th' unconquerable will,
> And study of revenge, immortal hate,
> And courage never to submit or yield,
> And what is else not to be overcome,

are still his. The sense of his punishment seems lost in the magnitude of it; the fierceness of tormenting flames is qualified and made innoxious by the greater fierceness of his pride; the loss of infinite happiness to himself is compensated in thought, by the power of inflicting infinite misery on others. Yet Satan is not the principle of malignity, or of the abstract love of evil—but of the abstract love of power, of pride, of self-will personified, to which last principle all other good and evil, and even his own, are subordinate. From this principle he never once flinches. His love of power and contempt for suffering are never once relaxed from the highest pitch of intensity. His thoughts burn like a hell within him; but the power of thought holds dominion in his mind over every other consideration. The consciousness of a determined purpose, of "that intellectual being, those thoughts that wander through eternity," though accompanied with endless pain, he prefers to nonentity, to "being swallowed up and lost in the wide womb of uncreated night." He expresses the sum and substance of all ambition in one line. "Fallen cherub, to be weak is miserable, doing or suffering!" After such a conflict as his, and such a defeat, to retreat in order, to rally, to make terms, to exist at all, is something; but he does more than this—he founds a new empire in hell, and from it conquers this new world, whither he bends his undaunted flight, forcing his way through nether and surrounding fires. The poet has not in all this given us a mere shadowy outline; the strength is equal to the magnitude of the conception. The Achilles of Homer is not more distinct; the Titans were not more vast; Prometheus chained to his rock was not a more terrific examples of suffering and of crime. Wherever the figure of Satan is introduced, whether he walks or flies, "rising aloft incumbent on the dusky air," it is illustrated with the most striking and appropriate images: so that we see it always before us, gigantic, irregular, portentous, uneasy, and disturbed—but dazzling in its faded splendour, the clouded ruins of a god. The deformity of Satan is only in the depravity of his will; he has no bodily deformity to excite our loathing or disgust. The horns and tail are not there, poor emblems of the unbending, unconquered spirit, of the writhing agonies within. Milton was too magnanimous and open an antagonist to support his argument by the by-tricks of a hump and cloven foot; to bring into the fair field of controversy the good old catholic prejudices of which Tasso and Dante have availed themselves, and which the mystic German critics would restore. He relied on the justice of his cause, and did not scruple to give the devil his due. Some persons may think that he has carried his liberality too far, and injured the cause he professed to espouse by making him the chief person in his poem. Considering the nature of his subject, he would be equally in danger of running into this fault, from his faith in religion, and his love of rebellion; and perhaps each of these motives had its full share in determining the choice of his subject.

Not only the figure of Satan, but his speeches in council, his soliloquies, his address to Eve, his share in the war in heaven, or in the fall of man, show the same decided superiority of character. To give only one instance, almost the first speech he makes:

> Is this the region, this the soil, the clime,
> Said then the lost archangel, this the seat
> That we must change for Heaven; this mournful
>   gloom
> For that celestial light? Be it so, since he
> Who now is sov'rain can dispose and bid
> What shall be right: farthest from him is best,
> Whom reason hath equal'd, force hath made
>   supreme
> Above his equals. Farewel happy fields,
> Where joy for ever dwells: Hail horrors, hail
> Infernal world, and thou profoundest Hell,
> Receive thy new possessor; one who brings
> A mind not to be chang'd by place or time.
> The mind is its own place, and in itself
> Can make a Heav'n of Hell, a Hell of Heav'n.
> What matter where, if I be still the same,
> And what I should be, all but less than he
> Whom thunder hath made greater? Here at least
> We shall be free; th' Almighty hath not built
> Here for his envy, will not drive us hence:
> Here we may reign secure, and in my choice
> To reign is worth ambition, though in Hell:
> Better to reign in Hell, than serve in Heaven.

The whole of the speeches and debates in Pandemonium are well worthy of the place and the occasion—with Gods for speakers, and angels and archangels for hearers. There is a decided manly tone in the arguments and sentiments, an eloquent dogmatism, as if each person spoke from thorough conviction; an excellence which Milton probably borrowed from his spirit of partisanship, or else his spirit of partisanship from the natural firmness and vigour of his mind. In this respect Milton resembles Dante (the only modern writer with whom he has anything in common), and it is remarkable that Dante, as well as Milton, was a political partisan. That approximation to the severity of impassioned prose which has been made an objection to Milton's poetry, and which is chiefly to be met with in these bitter invectives, is one of its great excellences. The author might here turn his philippics against Salmasius to

good account. The rout in Heaven is like the fall of some mighty structure, nodding to its base, "with hideous ruin and combustion down." But, perhaps, of all the passages in *Paradise Lost*, the description of the employments of the angels during the absence of Satan, some of whom "retreated in a silent valley, sing with notes angelical to many a harp their own heroic deeds and hapless fall by doom of battle," is the most perfect example of mingled pathos and sublimity. What proves the truth of this noble picture in every part, and that the frequent complaint of want of interest in it is the fault of the reader, not of the poet, is that when any interest of a practical kind takes a shape that can be at all turned into this, (and there is little doubt that Milton had some such in his eye in writing it), each party converts it to its own purposes, feels the absolute identity of these abstracted and high speculations; and that, in fact, a noted political writer of the present day has exhausted nearly the whole account of Satan in the *Paradise Lost*, by applying it to a character whom he considered as after the devil (though I do not know whether he would make even that exception) the greatest enemy of the human race. This may serve to show that Milton's Satan is not a very insipid personage.

Of Adam and Eve it has been said, that the ordinary reader can feel little interest in them, because they have none of the passions, pursuits, or even relations of human life, except that of man and wife, the least interesting of all others, if not to the parties concerned, at least to the bystanders. The preference has on this account been given to Homer, who, it is said, has left very vivid and infinitely diversified pictures of all the passions and affections, public and private, incident to human nature—the relations of son, of brother, parent, friend, citizen, and many others. Longinus preferred the *Iliad* to the *Odyssey,* on account of the greater number of battles it contains; but I can neither agree to his criticism, nor assent to the present objection. It is true, there is little action in this part of Milton's poem; but there is much repose, and more enjoyment. There are none of the everyday occurrences, contentions, disputes, wars, fightings, feuds, jealousies, trades, professions, liveries, and common handicrafts of life; "no kind of traffic; letters are not known; no use of service, of riches, poverty, contract, succession, bourne, bound of land, tilth, vineyard none; no occupation, no treason, felony, sword, pike, knife, gun, nor need of any engine." So much the better; thank Heaven, all these were yet to come. But still the die was cast, and in them our doom was sealed. In them

> The generations were prepared; the pangs,
> The internal pangs, were ready, the dread strife
> Of poor humanity's afflicted will,
> Struggling in vain with ruthless destiny.

In their first false step we trace all our future woe, with loss of Eden. But there was a short and precious interval between, like the first blush of morning before the day is overcast with tempest,the dawn of the world, the birth of nature from "the unapparent deep," with its first dews and freshness on its cheek, breathing odours. Theirs was the first delicious taste of life, and on them depended all that was to come of it. In them hung trembling all our hopes and fears. They were as yet alone in the world, in the eye of nature, wondering at their new being, full of enjoyment and enraptured with one another, with the voice of their Maker walking in the garden, and ministering angels attendant on their steps, winged messengers from heaven like rosy clouds descending in their sight. Nature played around them her virgin fancies wild; and spread for them a repast where no crude surfeit reigned. Was there nothing in this scene, which God and nature alone witnessed, to interest a modern critic? What need was there of action, where the heart was full of bliss and innocence without it! They had nothing to do but feel their own happiness, and "know to know no more." They toiled not, neither did they spin; yet Solomon in all his glory was not arrayed like one of these." All things seem to acquire fresh sweetness, and to be clothed with fresh beauty in their sight. They tasted as it were for themselves and us, of all that there ever was pure in human bliss. "In them the burthen of the mystery, the heavy and the weary weight of all this unintelligible world, is lightened." They stood awhile perfect, but they afterwards fell, and were driven out of Paradise, tasting the first fruits of bitterness as they had done of bliss. But their pangs were such as a pure spirit might feel at the sight—their tears "such as angels weep." The pathos is of that mild contemplative kind which arises from regret for the loss of unspeakable happiness, and resignation to inevitable fate. There is none of the fierceness of intemperate passion, none of the agony of mind and turbulence of action, which is the result of the habitual struggles of the will with circumstances, irritated by repeated disappointment, and constantly setting its desires most eagerly on that which there is an impossibility of attaining. This would have destroyed the beauty of the whole picture. They had received their unlooked-for happiness as a free gift from their Creator's hands, and they submitted to its loss, not without sorrow, but without impious and stubborn repining.

> In either hand the hast'ning angel caught
> Our ling'ring parents, and to th' eastern gate
> Led them direct, and down the cliff as fast
> To the subjected plain; then disappear'd.
> They looking back, all th' eastern side beheld
> Of Paradise, so late their happy seat,
> Wav'd over by that flaming brand, the gate
> With dreadful faces throng'd, and fiery arms:
> Some natural tears they dropt, but wip'd them soon
> The world was all before them, where to choose
> Their place of rest, and Providence their guide.

Samuel Taylor Coleridge (essay date 1818)

SOURCE: "Milton," in *Coleridge's Miscellaneous Criticism,* Constable & Co., 1936, pp. 157-65.

[*In the following excerpt, Coleridge praises the sublime simplicity of* Paradise Lost.]

If we divide the period from the accession of Elizabeth to the Protectorate of Cromwell into two unequal portions, the first ending with the death of James I. the other comprehending the reign of Charles and the brief glories of the Republic, we are forcibly struck with a difference in the character of the illustrious actors, by whom each period is rendered severally memorable. Or rather, the difference in the characters of the great men in each period, leads us to make this division. Eminent as the intellectual powers were that were displayed in both; yet in the number of great men, in the various sorts of excellence, and not merely in the variety but almost diversity of talents united in the same individual, the age of Charles falls short of its predecessor; and the stars of the Parliament, keen as their radiance was, in fulness and richness of lustre, yield to the constellation at the court of Elizabeth;—which can only be paralleled by Greece in her brightest moment, when the titles of the poet, the philosopher, the historian, the statesman and the general not seldom formed a garland round the same head, as in the instances of our Sidneys and Raleighs. But then, on the other hand, there was a vehemence of will, an enthusiasm of principle, a depth and an earnestness of spirit, which the charms of individual fame and personal aggrandisement could not pacify,—an aspiration after reality, permanence, and general good,—in short, a moral grandeur in the latter period, with which the the low intrigues, Machiavellic maxims, and selfish and servile ambition of the former, stand in painful contrast.

The causes of this it belongs not to the present occasion to detail at length; but a mere allusion to the quick succession of revolutions in religion, breeding a political indifference in the mass of men to religion itself, the enormous increase of the royal power in consequence of the humiliation of the nobility and the clergy—the transference of the papal authority to the crown,—the unfixed state of Elizabeth's own opinions, whose inclinations were as popish as her interests were protestant—the controversial extravagance and practical imbecility of her successor—will help to explain the former period; and the persecutions that had given a life and soul-interest to the disputes so imprudently fostered by James,—the ardour of a conscious increase of power in the commons, and the greater austerity of manners and maxims, the natural product and most formidable weapon of religious disputation, not merely in conjunction, but in closest combination, with newly awakened political and republican zeal, these perhaps account for the character of the latter aera.

In the close of the former period, and during the bloom of the latter, the poet Milton was educated and formed; and he survived the latter, and all the fond hopes and aspirations which had been its life; and so in evil days, standing as the representative of the combined excellence of both periods, he produced the *Paradise Lost* as by an after-throe of nature. "There are some persons (observes a divine, a contemporary of Milton's) of whom the grace of God takes early hold, and the good spirit inhabiting them, carries them on in an even constancy through innocence into virtue, their Christianity bearing equal date with their manhood, and reason and religion, like warp and woof, running together, make up one web of a wise and exemplary life. This (he adds) is a most happy case, wherever it happens; for, besides that there is no sweeter or more lovely thing on earth than the early buds of piety, which drew from our Saviour signal affection to the beloved disciple, it is better to have no wound than to experience the most sovereign balsam, which, if it work a cure, yet usually leaves a scar behind." Although it was and is my intention to defer the consideration of Milton's own character to the conclusion of this Lecture, yet I could not prevail on myself to approach the *Paradise Lost* without impressing on your minds the conditions under which such a work was in fact producible at all, the original genius having been assumed as the immediate agent and efficientcause; and these conditions I find in the character of the times and in his own character. The age in which the foundations of his mind were laid, was congenial to it as one golden aera of profound erudition and individual genius;—that in which the superstructure was carried up, was no less favourable to it by a sternness of discipline and a show of self-control, highly flattering to the imaginative dignity of an heir of fame, and which won Milton over from the dear-loved delights of academic groves and cathedral aisles to the anti-prelatic party. It acted on him, too, no doubt, and modified his studies by a characteristic controversial spirit, (his presentation of God is tinted with it)—a spirit not less busy indeed in political than in theological and ecclesiastical dispute, but carrying on the former almost always, more or less, in the guise of the latter. And so far as Pope's censure of our poet,—that he makes God the Father a school divine—is just, we must attribute it to the character of his age, from which the men of genius, who escaped, escaped by a worse disease, the licentious indifference of a Frenchified court.

Such was the *nidus* or soil, which constituted, in the strict sense of the word, the circumstances of Milton's mind. In his mind itself there were purity and piety absolute; an imagination to which neither the past nor the present were interesting, except as far as they called forth and enlivened the great ideal, in which and for which he lived; a keen love of truth, which, after many weary pursuits, found a harbour in a sublime listening to the still voice in his own spirit, and as keen a love of his country, which, after a disappointment still more depressive, expanded and soared into a love of man as a probationer of immortality. These were, these alone could be, the conditions under which such a work as the *Paradise Lost* could be conceived and accomplished. By a life-long study Milton had known—

> What was of use to know,
> What best to say could say, to do had done.
> His actions to his words agreed, his words
> To his large heart gave utterance due, his heart
> Contain'd of good, wise, fair, the perfect shape;

and he left the imperishable total, as a bequest to the ages coming, in the *Paradise Lost.*

Difficult as I shall find it to turn over these leaves without catching some passage, which would tempt me to stop, I propose to consider, 1st, the general plan and arrangement of the work;—2ndly, the subject with its difficulties

and advantages;—3rdly, the poet's object, the spirit in the letter, the ἐνθύμιον ἐν μύθω, the true school-divinity; and lastly, the characteristic excellencies of the poem, in what they consist, and by what means they were produced.

1. As to the plan and ordonnance of the Poem.

Compare it with the *Iliad,* many of the books of which might change places without any injury to the thread of the story. Indeed, I doubt the original existence of the *Iliad* as one poem; it seems more probable that it was put together about the time of the Pisistratidae. The *Iliad*—and, more or less, all epic poems, the subjects of which are taken from history—have no rounded conclusion; they remain, after all, but single chapters from the volume of history, although they are ornamental chapters. Consider the exquisite simplicity of the *Paradise Lost*. It and it alone really possesses a beginning, a middle, and an end; it has the totality of the poem as distinguished from the *ab ovo* birth and parentage, or straight line, of history.

2. As to the subject.

In Homer, the supposed importance of the subject, as the first effort of confederated Greece, is an after-thought of the critics; and the interest, such as it is, derived from the events themselves, as distinguished from the manner of representing them, is very languid to all but Greeks. It is a Greek poem. The superiority of the *Paradise Lost* is obvious in this respect, that the interest transcends the limits of a nation. But we do not generally dwell on this excellence of the *Paradise Lost*, because it seems attributable to Christianity itself;—yet in fact the interest is wider than Christendom, and comprehends the Jewish and Mohammedan worlds;—nay, still further, inasmuch as it represents the origin of evil, and the combat of evil and good, it contains matter of deep interest to all mankind, as forming the basis of all religion, and the true occasion of all philosophy whatsoever.

The FALL of Man is the subject; Satan is the cause; man's blissful state the immediate object of his enmity and attack; man is warned by an angel who gives him an account of all that was requisite to be known, to make the warning at once intelligible and awful; then the temptation ensues, and the Fall; then the immediate sensible consequence; then the consolation, wherein an angel presents a vision of the history of men with the ultimate triumph of the Redeemer. Nothing is touched in this vision but what is of general interest in religion; anything else would have been improper.

The inferiority of Klopstock's Messiah is inexpressible. I admit the prerogative of poetic feeling, and poetic faith; but I cannot suspend the judgment even for a moment. A poem may in one sense be a dream, but it must be a waking dream. In Milton you have a religious faith combined with the moral nature; it is an efflux; you go along with it. In Klopstock there is a wilfulness; he makes things so and so. The feigned speeches and events in the Messiah shock us like falsehoods; but nothing of that sort is felt in the *Paradise Lost*, in which no particulars, at least very few indeed, are touched which can come into collision or juxtaposition with recorded matter.

But notwithstanding the advantages in Milton's subject, there were concomitant insuperable difficulties, and Milton has exhibited marvellous skill in keeping most of them out of sight. High poetry is the translation of reality into the ideal under the predicament of succession of time only. The poet is an historian, upon condition of moral power being the only force in the universe. The very grandeur of his subject ministered a difficulty to Milton. The statement of a being of high intellect, warring against the supreme Being, seems to contradict the idea of a supreme Being. Milton precludes our feeling this, as much as possible, by keeping the peculiar attributes of divinity less in sight, making them to a certain extent allegorical only. Again, poetry implies the language of excitement; yet how to reconcile such language with God? Hence Milton confines the poetic passion in God's speeches to the language of scripture; and once only allows the *passio vera,* or *quasihumana* to appear, in the passage, where the Father contemplates his own likeness in the Son before the battle:—

> Go then, thou Mightiest, in thy Father's might,
> Ascend my chariot, guide the rapid wheels
> That shake Heaven's basis, bring forth all my war,
> My bow and thunder; my almighty arms
> Gird on, and sword upon thy puissant thigh;
> Pursue these sons of darkness, drive them out
> From all Heaven's bounds into the utter deep:
> There let them learn, as likes them, to despise
> God and Messiah his anointed king.

3. As to Milton's object:—

It was to justify the ways of God to man! The controversial spirit observable in many parts of the poem, especially in God's speeches, is immediately attributable to the great controversy of that age, the origination of evil. The Arminians considered it a mere calamity. The Calvinists took away all human will. Milton asserted the will, but declared for the enslavement of the will out of an act of the will itself. There are three powers in us, which distinguish us from the beasts that perish;—1, reason; 2, the power of viewing universal truth; and 3, the power of contracting universal truth into particulars. Religion is the will in the reason, and love in the will.

The character of Satan is pride and sensual indulgence, finding in self the sole motive of action. It is the character so often seen *in little* on the political stage. It exhibits all the restlessness, temerity, and cunning which have marked the mighty hunters of mankind from Nimrod to Napoleon. The common fascination of men is, that these great men, as they are called, must act from some great motive. Milton has carefully marked in his Satan the intense selfishness, the alcohol of egotism, which would rather reign in hell than serve in heaven. To place this lust of self in opposition to denial of self or duty, and to show what exertions it would make, and what pains endure to accomplish its end, is Milton's particular object in the character of Satan. But around this character he has thrown a singularity of daring, a grandeur of sufferance, and a ruined splendour, which constitute the very height of poetic sublimity.

Lastly, as to the execution:—

The language and versification of the *Paradise Lost* are peculiar in being so much more necessarily correspondent to each than those in any other poem or poet. The connexion of the sentences and the position of the words are exquisitely artificial; but the position is rather according to the logic of passion or universal logic, than to the logic of grammar. Milton attempted to make the English language obey the logic of passion as perfectly as the Greek and Latin. Hence the occasional harshness in the construction.

> **The connexion of the sentences and the position of the words are exquisitely artificial, but the position is rather according to the logic, than to the logic of grammar.**
>
> *—Samuel Taylor Coleridge*

Sublimity is the pre-eminent characteristic of the *Paradise Lost*. It is not an arithmetical sublime like Klopstock's, whose rule always is to treat what we might think large as contemptibly small. Klopstock mistakes bigness for greatness. There is a greatness arising from images of effort and daring, and also from those of moral endurance; in Milton both are united. The fallen angels are human passions, invested with a dramatic reality.

The apostrophe to light at the commencement of the third book is particularly beautiful as an intermediate link between Hell and Heaven; and observe, how the second and third book support the subjective character of the poem. In all modern poetry in Christendom there is an under consciousness of a sinful nature, a fleeting away of external things, the mind or subject greater than the object, the reflective character predominant. In the *Paradise Lost* the sublimest parts are the revelations of Milton's own mind, producing itself and evolving its own greatness; and this is so truly so, that when that which is merely entertaining for its objective beauty is introduced, it at first seems a discord.

In the description of Paradise itself you have Milton's sunny side as a man; here his descriptive powers are exercised to the utmost, and he draws deep upon his Italian resources. In the description of Eve, and throughout this part of the poem, the poet is predominant over the theologian. Dress is the symbol of the Fall, but the mark of intellect; and the metaphysics of dress are, the hiding what is not symbolic and displaying by discrimination what is. The love of Adam and Eve in Paradise is of the highest merit—not phantomatic, and yet removed from every thing degrading. It is the sentiment of one rational being towards another made tender by a specific difference in that which is essentially the same in both; it is a union of opposites, a giving and receiving mutually of the permanent in either, a completion of each in the other.

Milton is not a picturesque, but a musical, poet; although he has this merit that the object chosen by him for any particular foreground always remains prominent to the end, enriched, but not incumbered, by the opulence of descriptive details furnished by an exhaustless imagination. I wish the *Paradise Lost* were more carefully read and studied than I can see any ground for believing it is, especially those parts which, from the habit of always looking for a story in poetry, are scarcely read at all,—as for example, Adam's vision of future events in the 11th and 12th books. No one can rise from the perusal of this immortal poem without a deep sense of the grandeur and the purity of Milton's soul, or without feeling how susceptible of domestic enjoyments he really was, notwithstanding the discomforts which actually resulted from an apparently unhappy choice in marriage. He was, as every truly great poet has ever been, a good man; but finding it impossible to realize his own aspirations, either in religion, or politics, or society, he gave up his heart to the living spirit and light within him, and avenged himself on the world by enriching it with this record of his own transcendant ideal.

Matthew Arnold   (essay date 1879)

SOURCE: "A French Critic on Milton," in *Mixed Essays,* Smith, Elder, & Co., 1903, pp. 266-70.

[*In the following excerpt, Arnold describes Milton as the supreme English poet.*]

Milton has always the sure, strong touch of the master. His power both of diction and of rhythm is unsurpassable, and it is characterised by being always present—not depending on an access of emotion, not intermittent, but, like the grace of Raphael, working in its possessor as a constant gift of nature Milton's style, moreover, has the same propriety and soundness in presenting plain matters, as in the comparatively smooth task for a poet of presenting grand ones. His rhythm is as admirable where, as in the line

And Tiresias and Phineus, prophets old—

it is unusual, as in such lines as—

With dreadful faces throng'd and fiery arms—

where it is simplest. And what high praise this is, we may best appreciate by considering the ever-recurring failure, both in rhythm and in diction, which we find in the so-

called Miltonic blank verse of Thomson, Cowper, Wordsworth. What leagues of lumbering movement! what desperate endeavours, as in Wordsworth's

And at the 'Hoop' alighted, famous inn,

to tender a platitude endurable by making it pompous! Shakespeare himself, divine as are his gifts, has not, of the marks of the master, this one: perfect sureness of hand in his style. Alone of English poets, alone in English art, Milton has it; he is our great artist in style, our one first-rate master in the grand style. He is as truly a master in this style as the great Greeks are, or Virgil, or Dante. The number of such masters is so limited that a man acquires a world-rank in poetry and art, instead of a mere local rank, by being counted among them. But Milton's importance to us Englishmen, by virtue of this distinction of his, is incalculable. The charm of a master's unfailing touch in diction and in rhythm, no one, after all, can feel so intimately, so profoundly, as his own countrymen. Invention, plan, wit, pathos, thought, all of them are in great measure capable of being detached from the original work itself, and of being exported for admiration abroad. Diction and rhythm are not. Even when a foreigner can read the work in its own language, they are not, perhaps, easily appreciable by him. . . . We natives must naturally feel it yet more powerfully. Be it remembered, too, that English literature, full of vigour and genius as it is, is peculiarly impaired by gropings and inadequacies in form. And the same with English art. Therefore for the English artist in any line, if he is a true artist, the study of Milton may well have an indescribable attraction. It gives him lessons which nowhere else from an Englishman's work can be obtain, and feeds a sense which English work, in general, seems bent on disappointing and baffling. And this sense is yet so deep-seated in human nature,—this sense of style,—that probably not for artists alone, but for all intelligent Englishmen who read him, its gratification by Milton's poetry is a large though often not fully recognised part of his charm, and a very wholesome and fruitful one.

As a man, too, not less than as a poet, Milton has a side of unsurpassable grandeur. A master's touch is the gift of nature. Moral qualities, it is commonly thought, are in our own power. Perhaps the germs of such qualities are in their greater or less strength as much a part of our natural constitution as the sense for style. The range open to our own will and power, however, in developing and establishing them, is evidently much larger. Certain high moral dispositions Milton had from nature, and he sedulously trained and developed them until they became habits of great power.

Some moral qualities seem to be connected in a man with his power of style. Milton's power of style, for instance, has for its great character *elevation;* and Milton's elevation clearly comes, in the main, from a moral quality in him,—his pureness. 'By pureness, by kindness!' says St. Paul. These two, pureness and kindness, are, in very truth, the two signal Christian virtues, the two mighty wings of Christianity, with which it winnowed and renewed, and still winnows and renews, the world. In kindness, and in all which that word conveys or suggests, Milton does not shine. He had the temper of his Puritan party. We often hear the boast, on behalf of the Puritans, that they produced 'our great epic poet.' Alas! one might not unjustly retort that they spoiled him. However, let Milton bear his own burden; in his temper he had natural affinities with the Puritans. He has paid for it by limitations as a poet. But, on the other hand, how high, clear, and splendid is his pureness; and how intimately does its might enter into the voice of his poetry!

G. K. Chesterton (essay date 1908)

SOURCE: "The Taste for Milton," in *A Handful of Authors,* Sheed and Ward, 1953, pp. 75-7.

[*In the following excerpt, Chesterton sees Milton as a seventeenth-century individualist, standing apart from the Classical tradition on which he drew.*]

Of all poets Milton is the one whom it is the most difficult to praise with real delicacy and sincerity of definition. Of all poets Milton is the one whom it is most easy to praise with mere facile phraseology and conventional awe. There is one thing about Milton which must have been generally observed—that he is really a matured taste, a taste that grows. Shakespeare is really for all ages, for all the seven ages of man.

But Milton at his best is absolutely nothing to childhood. I do not mean that children cannot enjoy Milton; children can enjoy the Post Office directory. That is the kingdom of heaven; to enjoy things without understanding them. But I say that children cannot enjoy the Miltonism of Milton; the thing that no one but Milton can do. A boy does not appreciate that wonderful and controlled style, which, like a well-managed war-horse, even capers and caracoles rather by restraint than impetus. A boy does not feel the lift of those great lines, as of a great eagle leaving the nest,

> That with no middle flight presumes to soar
> Above the Aonian mount.

I think a great part of the trouble which the ordinary mind has in appreciating Milton (or, rather, Milton in pleasing the ordinary mind, for please remember that the popular mind is much more important than Milton) lies in the mistake of always describing him as a pure and classical writer. Really he was a highly complex and in some ways too modern writer. The perfectly classical can be understood by anybody. No charwoman would say that the tale of Ulysses coming back in rags to the woman who had been faithful to him was not a touching tale. No dog-fancier in the street would be indifferent to the death of Argus. No man in the street could ever say upon his conscience that the Venus of Milo was not a fine woman.

It is the secondary and distorted art which really and suddenly loses the sympathies of the people. The char-

woman would fail in seeing the peculiar pathos of Mr. Robert Elsmere, who wanted to be a curate and also an agnostic. The dog-fancier would be justly indifferent to the rhetoric of the numerous modern animal lovers who could not look after a dog for a day. And the man in the street will not admit that the women of Aubrey Beardsley are fine women, because they are not. The tastes of the man in the street are classical.

And if Milton were really as straightforward as Homer or the Elgin Marbles he would be, in practice, uproariously popular. The real reason that he cannot make his glory quite as broad as it is undoubtedly deep and high is that there was in him something of the modern individualist, something of the social schismatic. He had that weird and wicked ambition of the modern artist; he wanted "to think for himself". But Dante and Dickens wanted to think for other people also.

Milton stands between the very social society in which Dante lived and the very social society which Dickens always desired and occasionally experienced, with that fastidious isolation which belongs to art in our time and belonged to religion in his time. He is the seventeenth-century individualist. He is the perfect Calvinist; the man alone with his God. He is also the perfect artist; the man alone with his art. No man, perhaps, has ever had such power over his art since the arts of humanity were made. And yet there is something that makes one turn to the firesides of the *Pickwick Papers,* and even to the fires of the Purgatorio.

Douglas Bush (essay date 1939)

SOURCE: "Milton," in *The Renaissance and English Humanism,* University of Toronto Press, 1939, pp. 101-29.

[*In the following essay, Bush analyzes the influence of Christian humanism on Milton's poetry.*]

It may be more candid than diplomatic to acknowledge at the start that admirers of Milton have always been, consciously or not, on the defensive. They certainly must be nowadays, when for the first time since the seventeenth century Milton has ceased to be an active force in poetry. We may think that modern poets could still learn something from him, and if the poets thought so too we might be spared some headaches. But, so far from being an influence in contemporary work, Milton is damned as the man who crushed the fruitful metaphysical movement and kept poetry in bondage for three centuries. Mr. Eliot has even complained of Milton's obscurity. One may have, as I have, a great admiration for Mr. Eliot's writing in both verse and prose and still find a certain pleasure in visualizing the author of *The Waste Land* as he struggles with the meaning of *Paradise Lost.*

Among the various reasons for Milton's unpopularity doubtless the chief one is that in his major poems he treated on a heroic scale, and with a too confident simplicity, themes and problems which seem remote and no longer of vital concern to us. We think in purely human terms and know that

> malt does more than Milton can
> To justify God's ways to man.

Instead of Milton, who expounds a lofty faith in God and human reason, we prefer a smaller poet like Donne, whose sceptical uncertainties and staccato realism are more congenial to a generation which has lost its way. Milton is too big, too sternly strenuous, to allow us to feel at ease in his presence; he could never be taken under the maternal wing of Christopher Morley. Like Dante, Milton is not what P. G. Wodehouse would call a "matey" person. Put beside Chaucer or Shakespeare, with their crowd of human characters, with their benevolent interest, half humorous, half divine, in the stuff of common life, Milton seems cold, inhuman, an unapproachable Jehovah of poetry.

But this discourse is not supposed to be an arraignment of Milton. I am merely indicating a consciousness of these and all the other charges, old and new, and if some are damaging to Milton, some are damaging to the reader. My purpose is to outline the growth and the main principles of Milton's thought, with reference to our general theme. I say "main principles" because there are many subtleties and ramifications which must be neglected, at the risk of making his mind appear more simple than it was. I shall not, therefore, be discussing Milton's poetry as poetry, and in discussing his major ideas and attitudes I shall have to incur the guilt of repeating commonplaces both about him and about Christian humanism. There is no other way of showing that he is the last voice of an essentially medieval tradition, that, with due allowance for the lapse of five centuries, Milton stands shoulder to shoulder with that twelfth-century humanist—and defender of tyrannicide—John of Salisbury. Yet Milton appears at a moment when Christian humanism is succumbing to such internal and external enemies as have been described. In England and Europe generally, in the troubled period of Milton's lifetime, humanism has grown less religious and religion less humane. We shall try to see in him the normal fusion and the occasional friction of classical and Christian elements. We shall try to see also what a noble anachronism the old humanistic faith has become in an increasingly modern and scientific world.

Milton's ardent study began in childhood and, no less than Bacon, he took all knowledge for his province. It was partly as a young Baconian, partly as a young Platonist, that he attacked the sterile Aristotelianism of the Cambridge curriculum and pleaded for genuine and fruitful examination of man's outer and inner world. What might be called Milton's academic valedictory, on the theme that learning brings more blessings to men than ignorance, at first sight seems only a tissue of Renaissance platitudes. But it also sets forth an intensely personal faith, the boundless optimism and ambition of a young idealist of genius who feels himself standing on the threshold of a new era, who sees no obstacle in the way of man's conquest of nature and of all individual and social problems. And he aspires, with a half-concealed but proud self-confidence, to be one of the makers of that new era, to be the oracle of many nations, whose home comes to be visited as a shrine. When we follow the course of Milton's life and work, we can measure the depth of his later pessimism only by appreciating the sublime and, as we cynically say, the unrealistic optimism of his earlier years.

That is one aspect of Milton's youthful humanism. We have other aspects in his Latin poems. These too are outwardly conventional—as long as bishops and beadles were subject to mortality Milton did not lack a theme—but in the personal pieces the obscurity of a learned language encouraged the young poet to express his own moods with more spontaneous frankness than he allowed himself in his native tongue. It is springtime and Cupid is busy everywhere. The young man's pulses are stirred by the awakening life of nature and by the beauty of girls in the parks, yet they are no Corinnas or Circes, and Milton's sensuous paganism is quite innocent. Indeed, lest he give a wrong impression, he assures his friend Diodati that, like Ulysses, he clings to the magical herb moly, by which he means Christian virtue. Thus the young Renaissance artist and the young puritan live in happy harmony together and, while Milton is finding that he cannot subscribe slave by taking holy orders, he has conceived of heroic poetry as a not less but more sacred and exalted calling. No other English poet has so earnestly and so repeatedly dedicated himself to the classical office of poet-priest, and most of his important poems may be regarded, directly or indirectly, as successive spiritual stock-takings.

We may read **"L'Allegro"** and **"Il Penseroso"** simply as tone poems, two ideal moods of a bookish and high-minded young man in the country, as lovely expressions of a serene tranquillity which their militant author never again enjoyed. But these companion pieces, written probably during Milton's later days at Cambridge, we may take also as an *ave atque vale,* a half-unconscious good-bye to carefree youth and an embracing of a life of mature seriousness. Keats, surveying Milton's work as a whole, discerned in him a conflict between the pleasures and the ardours of song, a conflict which is writ large in Keats himself. In Milton's twin poems there is no conflict as yet, but we who know what is to come can foresee possible discord between two modes of art and life. In fact he had already, in his sixth elegy, contrasted the irresponsible singer of wine and gaiety with the ascetic poet of truly heroic themes. And in the sonnet on his twenty-fourth birthday, written, it would seem, after the two lyrical pieces, Milton pledges himself to a religious life:

> Yet, be it less or more, or soon or slow,
> It shall be still in strictest measure even
> To that same lot, however mean or high,
> Toward which Time leads me, and the will of
>   Heaven.
> All is, if I have grace to use it so,
> As ever in my great Task-Master's eye.

In this solemn acceptance of the divine will we are accustomed to hear the puritan note, the sense of personal responsibility to God, but these lines are also a partial echo of one of the most religious of ancient poets, Pindar.

When we look forward five or six years to the most elaborate and impassioned of Milton's earlier self-examinations, namely **"Lycidas,"** we find that the cheerful and the thoughtful ideals are no longer complementary but antagonistic. **"L'Allegro,"** we might say, raises his voice for the last time to ask:

> Alas! what boots it with uncessant care
> To tend the homely, slighted, shepherd's trade,
> And strictly meditate the thankless Muse?
> Were it not better done, as others use,
> To sport with Amaryllis in the shade,
> Or with the tangles of Neaera's hair?

But Milton has put away childish things, and **"Il Penseroso"** replies, in a sterner mood than his earlier self had felt:

> Fame is the spur that the clear spirit doth raise
> (That last infirmity of noble mind)
> To scorn delights and live laborious days. . . .

If the whole passage on the heavenly reward of the virtuous and arduous life, for all its classical ornament, suggests that Milton's Hebraic zeal is drying up his aesthetic sensibility, we may remember the letter written to Diodati in the same year as **"Lycidas."** In it Milton declares his God-given passion for beauty in all the forms and appearances of things. The words are both an aesthetic and a religious affirmation.

The conflict in Milton has more than one aspect. He felt keenly both the charms of contemplative retirement and the duties of the active life. But that conflict did not become a reality until he returned from abroad in 1639. A more immediate problem for a young poet of the Renaissance was the conflict between the sensuous and the ethical impulses in his nature. There was never, of course, any question of an actual lapse from his own high standards of personal conduct, but it was more difficult for him, with his temperament and in his age, than it had been for Spenser to reconcile the two motives in his poetry. Three years before **"Lycidas"** he had written *Comus*. The traditional masque glorified youth and love and jollity; *Comus* is a sermon on temperance. With all the sensuous passions of a young man and a poet, Milton still holds the precious moly and has not stooped to sensual gratification. Comus is allowed to plead the case for "natural" license, but his arguments—like Satan's—betray their own speciousness; he is the representative, not of true freedom, but of slavery. And the Lady, meeting him first on the level of the natural reason, rises with "sacred vehemence" to the religious defence of "sun-clad" Chastity. If her or Milton's ideal seems at moments negative, there is a far more powerful positive impulse which we can understand if we look back a little into his spiritual evolution. In a pamphlet of 1642, defending himself as usual, Milton

recalled some of his earlier reading. At first he had been captured by the smooth elegiac poets of Rome, but their fleshliness was less satisfying than their art. He had passed on to the two famous renowners of Beatrice and Laura. There grew the belief that "he who would not be frustrate of his hope to write well hereafter in laudable things, ought himself to be a true poem; that is, a composition and pattern of the best and honourablest things. . . ." From Dante and Petrarch, Milton was led to the fables and romances of knighthood, and such works proved, not the fuel of loose living, but incitements to virtue. Next came Plato, with his lofty idealism, his conception of the Eros which leads to divine knowledge and beauty. And, finally, there was St. Paul, with his ultimate claim that "the body is for the Lord, and the Lord for the body." The ideal of chasity in *Comus,* then, is not merely negative, it is a positive and all-embracing way of life. And the best evidence is found, not in the exposition of Pauline or Platonic or Spenserian moral ideas, but in that indefinable purity of tone which instantly possesses and elevates us when we begin—

> Before the starry threshold of Jove's court
> My mansion is. . . .

Milton returned from his prolonged continental travels to maintain himself as a private schoolmaster and to follow with eager interest the course of events which was soon to issue in civil war. But in such a time it was reserved only for God and angels to be lookers-on, and Milton was not God nor, except at rare moments, an angel. With mingled zeal and reluctance he plunged into pamphleteering. The heroic poem which was to win immortal fame had to be indefinitely postponed for the writing of prose tracts which are now, except for scholars, mostly dead. But we need not lament the twenty years Milton gave to prose and public affairs. He would not have been Milton if he had not been able to sacrifice his hopes to the claims of public duty. He belongs to that great tradition which stretches back through Spenser and Dante to the writers of Greece and Rome, the tradition of the poet who is an active citizen and a leader of his age. To Milton the romantic notion of the artist as an isolated or anti-social figure would have been not only reprehensible but unintelligible. Further, though he knew the magnitude of his sacrifice, since poetry was his right hand and prose his left, yet he had always desired the fame of a great leader, an oracle of nations, and his work as a publicist, if in one sense a forced betrayal of his destiny, was also an integral part of its fulfilment. It consoles him in his blindness to recall his defence of liberty, "Of which all Europe talks from side to side." Finally, the poetry itself was not altogether a loser. The noble sonnets on public men and events are close in spirit to the patriotic odes in which Horace reminded decadent Rome of the old Roman virtues. And the major poems were strengthened by their author's experience in the arena. As he says in one of his apologies for delaying his appointed task, the truly heroic poet must have, among other things, "insight into all seemly and generous arts and affairs." To echo Gibbon, the secretary to the Council was not useless to the historian of Pandemonium.

Most of us, if we have any radical instincts at all, manifest them in youth, and then our arteries harden and our heads soften. The circumstances of Milton's early life might well have made him a contented conservative, but the older he grew the more radical he became. I can barely mention the chief battle-fronts on which he served.

First in importance among his prose works stands *Areopagitica,* the most eloquent defence of individual liberty and the power of truth in the language. The tract is a vivid reminder of its author's double affiliations. In form it is a classical oration, but it grew out of a puritan controversy over the rights of religious minorities. While for the modern reader it stands alone, at the time it was unheeded by the host of other pamphleteers.

Milton's early notoriety was especially due to the treatises in which he pleaded for divorce on the ground of incompatibility. I will say just three things about these works. First, modern research has freed Milton from the odium of having begun the series during his honeymoon; we know now that he began it a year later. Secondly, his plea for easier divorce was based, not on a week-end view of marriage, but on a high conception of its sanctity, of that marriage of minds which the Bible and the law did not recognize. Thirdly, notwithstanding the common prejudice against Milton's "Turkish contempt of females," he did not ignore the right of women as well as men to release from unworthy mates. If Milton always regarded man as the superior being, so did everyone else; how many men really think otherwise now?

To proceed with the main ideas of the prose tracts, in religious faith Milton moved from trinitarianism toward Arian and other heresies—though in essentials the theology of *Paradise Lost* remained orthodox enough to darken Sunday afternoon for many generations of evangelical readers. Milton's huge treatise on Christian doctrine, which was not published till 1825, was an attempt to define his own beliefs and, apparently, to provide a fundamental creed which all Christians might accept. As for religion on its external or institutional side, he changed from Anglicanism to Presbyterianism; then, seeing that the Presbyterians did not want religious freedom but only wanted to be top dog, he became an Independent with a capital "I"; his final position was independency with a small "i." Milton himself declared: "I never knew that time in England, when men of truest religion were not counted sectaries"; and, as Sir Herbert Grierson says, "he *was* a sect."

In politics, the supporter of monarchy became the defender of the regicides, a champion of a free republic who observed Cromwell's growing power with uneasiness.

In education, Milton damned the logical studies of the universities as an asinine feast of sow-thistles and brambles, and urged a more practical and certainly a more heroically comprehensive curriculum. His letter on education is the last of the long series of humanistic treatises which had begun nearly three hundred years before, and it has all the main features of the tradition. It is aristocratic.

It aims at training the ablest young men to be useful and cultivated citizens, not scholars. In substance the programme is mainly classical, though less predominantly literary than that of most earlier humanists, for Milton recognizes the study of nature and science generally. His emphasis on religion and virtue, on the discipline of the moral judgment and the will, is no special mark of puritan zeal, for that had been the chief end of Christian humanism in all ages and all countries.

When we survey Milton's whole body of writing in prose and verse, we see that his various ideas and principles start from a passionate belief in the freedom of the will. There, of course, he breaks utterly with Calvinistic doctrine. Over a century earlier Erasmus had challenged Luther on just that ground. No humanist who had learned from the ancients the dignity of human reason could accept predestination and the depravity of man. In all problems, divorce, religion, politics, education, censorship of the press, Milton goes where reason leads him. No ordinance, he declares—in words which from a religious man at that time are rather bold—no ordinance, human or from heaven, can bind against the good of man. People have a way of associating the classics with mellow Toryism, but for Milton the classics were a trumpet and a sword. While Milton the artist learned his art chiefly from the ancient poets, to Milton the humanist and publicist Athens and Rome were the nurseries of individual and republican liberty. No wonder that Hobbes, recoiling from the chaos of the times to plead for absolutism in government, exclaims, with men like Milton in mind:

> And by reading of these Greek and Latin authors men from their childhood have gotten a habit, under a false show of liberty, of favouring tumults, and of licentious controlling the actions of their sovereigns, and again of controlling those controllers; with the effusion of so much blood as I think I may truly say there was never anything so dearly bought as these western parts have bought the learning of the Greek and Latin tongues.

At the same time we should remember the Protestant conception of "Christian liberty" which Professor Woodhouse has emphasized, that aristocratic distinction between the regenerate and the unregenerate which in Milton coalesces with the aristocratic principle of classical humanism. And, to echo Professor Woodhouse further, Milton's classical humanism sets him apart from merely religious puritans and leads him to interpret the regenerate state in humanistic, that is, in rational and ethical terms.

Dr. Tillyard remarks that if Milton had been stranded in his own paradise, he would have eaten the apple and immediately justified the act in a polemical pamphlet. We need not query a cheerful epigram, but we may notice that romantic idea which is still to be met, outside universities—namely, that Milton was of the devil's party without knowing it, that Satan was his real hero. Certainly the Satan of the first two books of *Paradise Lost* would not be the splendid figure he is if Milton himself had not been a rebel against authority, yet we are intended to see that from the very beginning Satan's heroic strength is vitiated by a fatal taint. For Satan is an example, on the grand scale, of perverted reason and perverted will, and the later books record his progressively shameful degradation. Milton never fought for the right of the individual to do as he pleases. While the traditional orthodoxy of the humanistic creed was modified by Milton's vigorous individualism, none the less he conceives of liberty as the right of man's disciplined reason to self-government, and one who loves liberty must first be wise and good. Hence the supreme importance of education, above all in the sacred and humane writings which provide ethical as well as intellectual training.

It is no accident that Milton's four long poems deal with one great theme, the human will confronted by temptation. Among the various motives inherent in, or read into, the chosen fables, perhaps the most obvious and recurrent are the sensual. Such emphasis is partly puritan and partly Miltonic. Milton's first marriage, apparently, gave a shock to his self-confidence which reverberates in the poems composed many years later. If he, a man elect, had not allowed his senses to betray his reason, he had at least shown a terrible lack of discernment. However large or small the personal factor, and in our days it is only too likely to be exaggerated, it is clear in the first place that Milton's ethical doctrine was not a copy-book abstraction but a vital reality which was proved on his pulses. In the second place, and this is what concerns us here, Milton's various treatments of the theme of temptation are as much classical as Christian. The battle is not merely between the love of God and the sinful flesh, it is between reason and unreason, "knowledge" and "ignorance." Milton uses the ethical psychology of Plato which had contributed so much to the rational framework of Spenser's moral allegory. Plato's thought, as Professor Hughes says, is built into the ethics of Milton's poems as substantially as some parts of the Bible are built into their plots. (One may sometimes wish for more gleams in Milton of that white light of Platonism which glows in Vaughan or Browne, but in the main the humanistic tradition had been unmystical.) If one may venture, in these days of psychological laboratories when moral responsibility has been shifted to defective glands, to recall again the naïve ideas of ancient thinkers, the kernel of the matter is that reason, the highest and most human of human faculties, should control the irrational passions and appetites.

Here I must quote those eloquent and familiar sentences from the central passage of *Areopagitica* which explain the ethical substance and purpose of Milton's major poems, explain indeed the whole character of his Christian humanism. It may be observed that his conception of God's plan that human virtue should prove itself by resisting evil is a favourite idea of Lactantius, and Milton quotes him in his *Commonplace Book:*

> I cannot praise a fugitive and cloistered virtue, unexercised and unbreathed, that never sallies out and sees her adversary, but slinks out of the race, where that immortal garland is to be run for, not without dust and heat. Assuredly we bring not innocence into the world, we bring impurity much rather; that which purifies us is trial, and trial is by what is contrary.

> That virtue therefore which is but a youngling in the contemplation of evil, and knows not the utmost that vice promises to her followers, and rejects it, is but a blank virtue, not a pure; her whiteness is but an excremental whiteness. Which was the reason why our sage and serious poet Spenser, whom I dare be known to think a better teacher than Scotus or Aquinas, describing true temperance under the person of Guyon, brings him in with his palmer through the cave of Mammon, and the bower of earthly bliss, that he might see and know, and yet abstain. . . .

> Many there be that complain of divine Providence for suffering Adam to transgress; foolish tongues! When God gave him reason, he gave him freedom to choose, for reason is but choosing; he had been else a mere artificial Adam, such an Adam as he is in the motions. We ourselves esteem not of that obedience, or love, or gift, which is of force: God therefore left him free, set before him a provoking object, ever almost in his eyes; herein consisted his merit, herein the right of his reward, the praise of his abstinence. Wherefore did he create passions within us, pleasures round about us, but that these rightly tempered are the very ingredients of virtue? . . .

> This justifies the high providence of God, who, though he commands us temperance, justice, continence, yet pours out before us even to a profuseness all desirable things, and gives us minds that can wander beyond all limit and satiety.

This last sentence, with its verbal anticipations of *Paradise Lost*, is a particular reminder of Milton's method of justifying the ways of God to men. He distorts the biblical fable in order to put it on a humanistic and rational basis. Adam and Eve do not simply disobey an arbitrary decree, they allow their reason, their faculty of moral choice, to be overruled by their passions and appetites. Coming to *Paradise Regained*, the uninstructed reader might naturally expect the subject to be the crucifixion and redemption, but the doctrine of vicarious atonement, though central in traditional Christianity, is distasteful to Milton; he accepts it, of course, but in a dryly legal way. For him paradise is regained when Christ, the personification of ideal human reason and will, conquers the conqueror of Adam.

But if Milton's ethical scheme is always rational, it is not always equally human and humane. In *Comus*, beautiful as the writing is, the ethical sermon, despite its Platonic and Christian radiance, has the unrealistic, inflexible assurance that goes with the exalted idealism of youth. In *Paradise Regained*, as Professor Rice has made clear, Milton is consciously trying to show Christ's human humility and constancy of faith; yet his hero is perfect and cannot sin, and the poem, as the presentation of a moral struggle and victory, is relatively unreal and cold. In *Paradise Lost*, Adam and Eve are at first artificial beings in an artificial world, but they are humanized by sin and suffering, and their author is too when he contemplates them. In dealing with the fall itself Milton turns from epic narrative to intimate drama, and the deep sympathy manifested there culminates in the marvellous close. The great cosmic and supernatural background, the epic war between God and Satan, which had been rendered with such heroic pomp and circumstance, with such sweep of imagination—all this, in Professor Stoll's words, gives place to a twilight picture of two human beings alone in the world:

> Some natural tears they dropped, but wiped them
>   soon;
> The world was all before them, where to choose
> Their place of rest, and Providence their guide:
> They hand in hand, with wandering steps and slow,
> Through Eden took their solitary way.

Milton is an unfailing master of the classical quiet ending, but here, as in Greek drama, quietness means serenity only to those who miss the mingled tragedy and hope, irony and pity, in a symbolic picture of life itself reduced to its elemental terms. And if in *Paradise Lost* the theological frame melts away, no such frame obtrudes at all in *Samson Agonistes*. This, the one great English drama on the Greek model, is the most deeply humanized treatment of Milton's perennial theme, and it remains, not the most beautiful, but the most wholly alive, the most permanently moving, of all his works. Samson is a completely human being in a completely real world, a great man who has lived greatly and sinned greatly. If he differs from his Greek counterparts, Heracles, Prometheus, and the aged Oedipus, through his faith in the God of Israel, what we feel most is the tragic drama that goes on in Samson's own soul.

There is profound pessimism in the later books of *Paradise Lost*, and it reaches its depth in *Samson,* where the hero's triumphant martyrdom scarcely mitigates the effect of Milton's arraignment of God. The sheltered idealist had grown up thinking that England was full of John Miltons who had only to be shown the right way to follow it. In *Areopagitica* his optimism runs high. When God is beginning a new and greater reformation, "what does He then but reveal Himself to His servants, and, as His manner is, first to His Englishmen?" Among the first to be informed of divine intentions would be John Milton, who craved an honourable share in the great work. Now the fields are white for harvest; there can be no lack of reapers.

> Methinks I see in my mind a noble and puissant nation rousing herself like a strong man after sleep, and shaking her invincible locks. Methinks I see her as an eagle mewing her mighty youth, and kindling her undazzled eyes at the full mid-day beam, purging and unscaling her long-abused sight at the fountain itself of heavenly radiance. . . .

Sixteen years later, when the wheels are moving rapidly to bring back Charles Stuart, Milton makes a last appeal for a free republic. But with all its detailed plans this tract is an admission of defeat. The vision of a noble and puissant nation has faded into the light of common day, and men worthy to be for ever slaves are rushing to put their heads under the yoke. The good old cause is dead, and the work of a large part of Milton's life is undone.

While he seems, outwardly, to have had a fairly cheerful old age, the stress and stimulus of composition heightened his realization of heroic past and ignoble present. He can declare himself still able to sing with voice unchanged,

> though fallen on evil days,
> On evil days though fallen, and evil tongues,
> In darkness, and with dangers compassed round,
> And solitude,

but his voice is changed, even in these very lines.

Milton had never been a democrat in the modern sense of the word. He did not believe that one man's opinion was as good as another's. But, both as humanist and as puritan, he had believed passionately in the collective wisdom, inspiration, and effectual power of the best men, whether Platonic philosopher-kings or puritan "Saints." There is little of that faith left in his later works. Samson, God's chosen hero, is now "Eyeless in Gaza at the mill with slaves." Milton tries to find a basis for hope in the scroll of future history revealed to Adam, but Adam hears no such story of national courage and triumph as Aeneas heard from Anchises:

> Truth shall retire
> Bestuck with slanderous darts, and works of Faith
> Rarely be found; so shall the world go on,
> To good malignant, to bad men benign,
> Under her own weight groaning, till the day
> Appear of respiration to the just,
> And vengeance to the wicked. . . .

Milton's hope of a new reformation, then, will be realized only at the day of judgment, when the evil world is cleansed by fire, and that is small comfort here and now. But if his old faith in men has proved vain, something can still be done by individual man; he can at least rule himself. So when Adam has learned the rational and Christian virtues, he has no need of an earthly paradise, he has a paradise within him, happier far. So Christ, man's perfect model, maintains his integrity against the allurements of the world. So Samson, resisting selfish and sensual temptations, achieves an inner regeneration which makes his outward fate of no account.

There are two special topics, both related to Milton's Christian humanism, with which we may end. When we think of his lifelong devotion to the classical authors who taught him his craft, who inspired alike his love of liberty and his love of discipline, it cannot be other than a painful shock to come upon that violent denunciation of Greek culture in *Paradise Regained*. And the shock is all the greater for the eulogy of Hellenism which precedes it:

> Athens, the eye of Greece, mother of arts
> And eloquence, native to famous wits
> Or hospitable, in her sweet recess,
> City or suburban, studious walks and shades.
> See there the olive-grove of Academe,
> Plato's retirement, where the Attic bird
> Trills her thick-warbled notes the summer long. . . .

And so on. But this beautiful evocation of Athens and her legacy to the world, written from the heart if ever anything was, is put in the mouth of Satan, and in an almost strident voice Christ answers with a repudiation of the vain philosophy, oratory, and poetry of Greece, which cannot approach the sacred truth of Hebrew writings.

It is painful indeed to watch Milton turn and rend some main roots of his being, but we must try to understand him. His harsh condemnation is relative rather than absolute; we know that his favourite authors up to the end were ancients, and this very poem owes much to them. Yet, with a strenuous and disappointed life behind him, Milton has come more and more to hold fast to ultimate things. If he, a warfaring Christian, must choose between the classical light of nature and the Hebrew light of revelation, he cannot hesitate, whatever the cost. For if our supreme task in this world is the conduct of our own lives, then Christ comes before Plato. It would be wrong to say simply that in old age the puritan has conquered the humanist. What is true is that Milton holds the traditional attitude of the Christian humanist with a more than traditional fervour inspired by the conditions of his age and by his own intense character.

The place of the Bible and the church in the humanistic tradition we have seen, and Milton himself had always put the sacred writings first, even if his own reason had sometimes strained their elasticity. So this outburst in *Paradise Regained*, uniquely elaborate and vehement though it is, contains nothing essentially new. One could trace a consistent attitude from the beginning. We have seen how his conception of love and chastity rose from Ovid to Plato and finally St. Paul. Though the classics form the staple of his educational programme, Milton expressly puts the Bible on a higher level. In apologizing, as a pamphleteer, for the postponement of that heroic poem he is going to write, he affirms its superiority to the ancient epics, not because he is a greater artist than Homer and Virgil—as artist Milton is humble enough—but because he is a Christian. His epic is not "to be obtained by the invocation of dame memory and her siren daughters; but by devout prayer to that eternal Spirit, who can enrich with all utterance and knowledge, and sends out his seraphim, with the hallowed fire of his altar, to touch and purify the lips of whom he pleases." The claim is repeated in those several invocations in *Paradise Lost* which, outwardly imitations of classical addresses to the Muse, are really prayers. And while throughout the poem he employs mythological allusions, many of them among the most beautiful things he ever wrote, so sternly does he feel that the highest truth must be kept pure that again and again he takes pains to label these myths pagan fiction. Such facts testify to the sincerity and consistency of Milton's Christian faith. They testify also to the dilemma facing a puritan bred in the tradition of Renaissance classicism.

The second and last topic involves a similar question of apparent inconsistency. Along with temperance in the moral sphere Adam learns the necessity of temperance in the pursuit of secular and scientific knowledge. This is not an incidental but an integral part of Milton's subject, and we may ask how such a position can be taken by the man who had been receptive to Baconian ideas, who had given science an exceptional place in his educational scheme, and who had written with such power in defence of free inquiry. A partial answer to this question has, I hope, already been given. We have seen that from the Middle Ages onward the Christian humanists, under the banner of Cicero, Plato, and Christ, attacked the various tribes of Aristotelians because neither logic nor natural science, however good in themselves, taught the right conduct of life. For that highest wisdom, they said, one must go first to the sacred, secondly to the classical, authors. Like all intelligent men Milton was interested in the new astronomy, but, like all Christian humanists, he feared the danger of confusing wisdom and knowledge, law for man and law for thing. In 1642, for instance, he had distinguished between "that knowledge that rests in the contemplation of natural causes and dimensions, which must needs be a lower wisdom, as the object is low," and "the only high valuable wisdom," which is the knowledge of God and the true end of man's life.

In the following decades it might well seem that the rising tide of science and scientific philosophy threatened to sweep away religious and humane values altogether, and a consciousness of that movement, along with larger and sadder experience of life, would only intensify Milton's religious and humanistic reaction. Even if individual scientists retained their Christian faith, the implications of science seemed plain. For Milton as for Christian humanists of all ages (including the Cambridge Platonists), the physical and metaphysical world is a divine order with a divine purpose, and man is a being endowed with divine reason and divine will. For the scientific philosopher, such as Hobbes, the universe is a purely mechanical system of bodies moving in time and space. God and man alike have been pushed out of the real world, for real knowledge is mathematical knowledge. God is the initial cause of motion. The human faculties, which for the humanist are all that matters, have become mere bundles of secondary qualities which cannot be measured. The human mind is a blank wall which receives physical sensations. Memory, the mother of the Muses, is decayed sensation. The will, for Milton the helm of man's ship, is only the last, the effectual, appetite. Is it any wonder the Christian humanist believes that free speculation has undermined fundamental values, that Adam is taught to check the roving mind or fancy, which lures men into philosophic mazes, and to recognize that the prime wisdom is that which illuminates the moral problems of daily life?

The inevitable and basic antithesis which Miss Nicolson has pointed out between Milton and Hobbes is the same as that between Petrarch and the Averroists—or between Arnold and Huxley. The end of all learning and eloquence, said Erasmus, is to know Christ and honour Him. Of the two definitions of education in Milton's prose tract the less familiar but not less Miltonic one is this:

> The end, then, of learning is to repair the ruins of our
> first parents by regaining to know God aright, and out

of that knowledge to love Him, to imitate Him, to be like Him, as we may the nearest, by possessing our souls of true virtue, which, being united to the heavenly grace of faith, makes up the highest perfection.

Nearly a quarter of a century later that definition is expanded, one might say, in Milton's final summing-up of the lesson of *Paradise Lost*. If in his early days he had had some Baconian dreams of the conquest of nature, now, in his age, he has no thought of an earthly paradise; Adam-to repeat that all-important line-has a paradise within him, happier far. . . .

F. R. Leavis (essay date 1947)

SOURCE: "Milton's Verse," in *Revaluation: Tradition and Development in English Poetry,* W.W. Norton & Co., 1963, pp. 42-61.

[*In the following essay. Leavis dismisses Milton's poetry as puritanical and pedantic.*]

Milton's dislodgment, in the past decade, after his two centuries of predominance, was effected with remarkably little fuss. The irresistible argument was, of course, Mr. Eliot's creative achievement; it gave his few critical asides—potent, it is true, by context—their finality, and made it unnecessary to elaborate a case. Mr. Middleton Murry also, it should be remembered, came out against Milton at much the same time. His *Problem of Style* contains an acute page or two comparing Milton with Shakespeare, and there was a review of Bridges' *Milton's Prosody* in *The Athenæum* that one would like to see reprinted along with a good deal more of Mr. Murry's weekly journalism of that time. But the case remained unelaborated, and now that Mr. Eliot has become academically respectable those who refer to it show commonly that they cannot understand it. And when a writer of Mr. Allen Tate's repute as critic, poet and intellectual leader, telling us that Milton should be "made" to "influence poetry once more," shows that he too doesn't understand, then one may overcome, perhaps, one's shyness of saying the obvious.

Mr. Tate thinks that if we don't like Milton it is because of a prejudice against myth and fable and a preference for the fragmentary: "When we read poetry we bring to it the pseudo-scientific habit of mind; we are used to joining things up in vague disconnected processes in terms that are abstract and thin, and so our sensuous enjoyment is confined to the immediate field of sensation. We are bewildered, helpless, confronted with one of those immensely remote, highly sensuous and perfectly make-believe worlds that rise above our scattered notions of process."

Not every one will find this impressive. If we are affected by the pseudo-scientific habit of mind to that degree, some would suggest, we probably cannot read poetry at all. But if we can and do read poetry, then our objection to Milton, it must be insisted, is that we dislike his verse and believe that in such verse no "highly sensuous and perfectly make-believe world" could be evoked. Even in the first two books of *Paradise Lost*, where the myth has vigorous life and one can admire the magnificent invention that Milton's verse is, we feel, after a few hundred lines, our sense of dissatisfaction growing into something stronger. In the end we find ourselves protesting—protesting against the routine gesture, the heavy fall, of the verse, flinching from the foreseen thud that comes so inevitably, and, at last, irresistibly: for reading *Paradise Lost* is a matter of resisting, of standing up against, the verse-movement, of subduing it into something tolerably like sensitiveness, and in the end our resistance is worn down; we surrender at last to the inescapable monotony of the ritual. Monotony: the variety attributed to Milton's Grand Style in the orthodox account can be discoursed on and illustrated at great length, but the stress could be left on "variety," after an honest interrogation of experience, only by the classically trained.

Here, if this were a lecture, would come illustrative reading-out—say of the famous opening to Book III. As it is, the point seems best enforcible (though it should be obvious at once to any one capable of being convinced at all) by turning to one of the exceptionally good passages—for every one will agree at any rate that there are places where the verse glows with an unusual life. One of these, it will again be agreed, is the Mulciber passage at the end of Book I:

> The hasty multitude
> Admiring enter'd, and the work some praise
> And some the Architect: his hand was known
> In Heav'n by many a Towred structure high,
> Where Scepter'd Angels held thir residence,
> And sat as Princes, whom the supreme King
> Exalted to such power, and gave to rule,
> Each in his Hierarchie, the Orders bright.
> Nor was his name unheard or unador'd
> In ancient Greece; and in Ausonian land
> Men called him Mulciber; and how he fell
> From Heav'n, they fabl'd, thrown by angry Jove
> Sheer o're the Chrystal Battlements: from Morn
> To Noon he fell, from Noon to dewy Eve,
> A Summers day; and with the setting Sun
> Dropt from the Zenith like a falling Star,
> On Lemnos th' Ægæan Ile: thus they relate,
> Erring . . .

The opening exhibits the usual heavy rhythmic pattern, the hieratic stylization, the swaying ritual movement back and forth, the steep cadences. Italics will serve to suggest how, when the reader's resistance has weakened, he is brought inevitably down with the foreseen thud in the foreseen place:

> The hasty multitude
> Ad*mir*ing enter'd, and the wórk some praise
> And *some* the Architect: his hánd was known
> In Héav'n by many a Tówred structure high,
> Where Scépter'd Angels held thir résidence,
> And *sat* as Princès . . .

But from "Nor was his name unheard" onwards the effect changes. One no longer feels oneself carried along, resigned or protesting, by an automatic ritual, responding automatically with bodily gestures—swayed head and lifted shoulders—to the commanding emphasis: the verse seems suddenly to have come to life. Yet the pattern remains the same; there are the same heavy stresses, the same rhythmic gestures and the same cadences, and if one thought a graph of the verse-movement worth drawing it would not show the difference. The change of feeling cannot at first be related to any point of form; it comes in with "ancient Greece" and "Ausonian land," and seems to be immediately due to the evocation of that serene, clear, ideally remote classical world so potent upon Milton's sensibility. But what is most important to note is that the heavy stresses, the characteristic cadences, turns and returns of the verse, have here a peculiar expressive felicity. What would elsewhere have been the routine thump of "Sheer" and "Dropt" is here, in either case, obviously functional, and the other rhythmic features of the verse are correspondingly appropriate. The stress given by the end-position to the first "fell," with the accompanying pause, in what looks like a common, limply pompous Miltonicism—

> and how he fell
> From Heav'n, they fabl'd, thrown . . .

—is here uncommonly right; the heavy "thrown" is right, and so are the following rise and fall, the slopes and curves, of the verse.

There is no need to particularize further. This much room has been given to the fairly obvious merely by way of insisting that the usual pattern of Milton's verse has here an unusual expressive function—becomes, indeed, something else. If any one should question the unusualness, the doubt would be soon settled by a little exploration. And to admit the unusualness is to admit that commonly the pattern, the stylized gesture and movement, has no particular expressive work to do, but functions by rote, of its own momentum, in the manner of a ritual.

Milton has difficult places to cross, runs the orthodox eulogy, but his style always carries him through. The sense that Milton's style is of that kind, the dissatisfied sense of a certain hollowness, would by most readers who share it be first of all referred to a characteristic not yet specified—that which evoked from Mr. Eliot the damaging word magniloquence.' To say that Milton's verse is magniloquent is to say that it is not doing as much as its impressive pomp and volume seem to be asserting; that mere orotundity is a disproportionate part of the whole effect; and that it demands more deference than it merits. It is to call attention to a lack of something in the stuff of the verse, to a certain sensuous poverty.

This poverty is best established by contrast, and tactical considerations suggest taking the example from Milton himself:

> Wherefore did Nature powre her bounties forth,
> With such a full and unwithdrawing hand,

Covering the earth with odours, fruits, and flocks,
Thronging the Seas with spawn innumerable,
But all to please, and sate the curious taste?
And set to work millions of spinning Worms,
That in their green shops weave the smooth-hair'd
     silk
To deck her Sons, and that no corner might
Be vacant of her plenty, in her own loyns
She hutch't th' all-worship ore, and precious gems
To store her children with; if all the world
Should in a pet of temperance feed on Pulse,
Drink the clear stream, and nothing wear but Freize
Th' all-giver would be unthank't, would be
     unprais'd,
Not half his riches known, and yet despis'd,
And we should serve him as a grudging master,
As a Penurious niggard of his wealth,
And live like Natures bastards, not her sons,
Who would be quite surcharged with her own
     weight,
And strangl'd with her waste fertility;
Th' earth cumber'd, and the wing'd air dark't with
     plumes,
The herds would over-multitude their Lords,
The Sea o'refraught would swell, and th' unsought
     diamonds
Would so emblaze the forhead of the Deep,
And so bestudd with Stars, that they below
Would grow inur'd to light, and com at last
To gaze upon the Sun with shameless brows.

This is very unlike anything in *Paradise Lost* (indeed, it is not very like most of *Comus*). If one could forget where one had read it, and were faced with assigning it to its author, one would not soon fix with conviction on any dramatist. And yet it is too like dramatic verse to suggest Milton. It shows, in fact, the momentary predominance in Milton of Shakespeare. It may look less mature, less developed, than the verse of *Paradise Lost*; it is, as a matter of fact, richer, subtler and more sensitive than anything in *Paradise Lost*, *Paradise Regained* or *Samson Agonistes*.

Its comparative sensuous richness, which is pervasive, lends itself fairly readily to analysis at various points; for instance:

> And set to work millions of spinning Worms,
> That in their green shops weave the smooth-hair'd
>   silk . . .

The Shakespearian life of this is to be explained largely by the swift diversity of associations that are run together. The impression of the swarming worms is telescoped with that of the ordered industry of the workshop, and a further vividness results from the contrasting "green," with its suggestion of leafy tranquillity. "Smooth-hair'd" plays off against the energy of the verse the tactual luxury of stroking human hair or the living coat of an animal. The texture of actual sounds, the run of vowels and consonants, with the variety of action and effort, rich in subtle analogical suggestion, demanded in pronouncing them, plays an essential part, though this is not to be analysed in abstraction from the meaning. The total effect is as if words as words withdrew themselves from the focus of our attention and we were directly aware of a tissue of feelings and perceptions.

No such effect is possible in the verse of *Paradise Lost*, where the use of the medium, the poet's relation to his words, is completely different. This, for instance, is from the description, in Book IV, of the Garden of Eden, which, most admirers of Milton will agree, exemplifies sensuous richness if that is to be found in *Paradise Lost*:

> And now divided into four main Streams,
> Runs divers, wandring many a famous Realme
> And Country whereof here needs no account,
> But rather to tell how, if Art could tell,
> How from that Sapphire Fount the crisped Brooks,
> Rowling on Orient Pearl and sands of Gold,
> With mazie error under pendant shades
> Ran Nectar, visiting each plant, and fed
> Flours worthy of Paradise which not nice Art
> In Beds and curious Knots, but Nature boon
> Powrd forth profuse on Hill and Dale and Plaine,
> Both where the morning Sun first warmly smote
> The open field, and where the unpierc't shade
> Imbround the noontide Bowrs: Thus was this place,
> A happy rural seat of various view:
> Groves whose rich Trees wept odorous Gumms and
>   Balme,
> Others whose fruit burnisht with Golden Rinde
> Hung amiable, Hesperian Fables true,
> If true, here onely, and of delicious taste . . .

It should be plain at once that the difference was not exaggerated. As the laboured, pedantic artifice of the diction suggests, Milton seems here to be focussing rather upon words than upon perceptions, sensations or things. "Sapphire," "Orient Pearl," "sands of Gold," "odorous Gumms and Balme," and so on, convey no doubt a vague sense of opulence, but this is not what we mean by "sensuous richness." The loose judgment that it is a verbal opulence has a plain enough meaning if we look for contrast at the "bestudd with Stars" of Comus's speech; there we feel (the alliteration is of a different kind from that of the Grand Style) the solid lumps of gold studding the "forehead of the Deep." In the description of Eden, a little before the passage quoted, we have:

> And all amid them stood the Tree of Life,
> High eminent, blooming Ambrosial Fruit
> Of vegetable Gold . . .

It would be of no use to try and argue with any one who contended that "vegetable Gold" exemplified the same kind of fusion as "green shops."

It needs no unusual sensitiveness to language to perceive that, in this Grand Style, the medium calls pervasively for a kind of attention, compels an attitude towards itself, that is incompatible with sharp, concrete realization; just as it would seem to be, in the mind of the poet, incompatible with an interest in sensuous particularity. He exhibits a feeling *for* words rather than a capacity for feel-

ing *through* words; we are often, in reading him, moved to comment that he is "external" or that he "works from the outside." The Grand Style, at its best, compels us to recognize it as an impressive stylization, but it functions very readily, and even impressively, at low tension, and its tendency is betrayed, even in a show piece like the description of Eden, by such offences as:

>   Thus was this place,
> A happy rural seat of various view:
> Groves whose rich Trees wept odorous Gumms and
>   Balme,
> Others whose fruit burnisht with Golden Rinde
> Hung amiable, Hesperian Fables true,
> If true, here onely, and of delicious taste . . .

—If the Eighteenth Century thought that poetry was something that could be applied from the outside, it found the precedent as well as the apparatus in Milton.

The extreme and consistent remoteness of Milton's medium from any English that was ever spoken is an immediately relevant consideration. It became, of course, habitual to him; but habituation could not sensitize a medium so cut off from speech—speech that belongs to the emotional and sensory texture of actual living and is in resonance with the nervous system; it could only confirm an impoverishment of sensibility. In any case, the Grand Style barred Milton from essential expressive resources of English that he had once commanded. Comus, in the passage quoted, imagining the consequences of the Lady's doctrine, says that Nature

>   would be quite surcharged with her own weight,
> And strangl'd with her waste fertility;
> Th' earth cumber'd, and the wing'd air dark't with
>   plumes,
> The herds would over-multitude their Lords,
> The Sea o'refraught would swell . . .

To cut the passage short here is to lame it, for the effect of Nature's being strangled with her waste fertility is partly conveyed by the ejaculatory piling-up of clauses, as the reader, by turning back, can verify. But one way in which the verse acts the meaning—not merely says but does— is fairly represented in the line,

> Th' earth cumber'd, and the wing'd air dark't with
>   plumes,

where the crowding of stressed words, the consonantal clusters and the clogged movement have a function that needs no analysis. This kind of action in the verse, together with the attendant effects of movement and intonation in the whole passage, would be quite impossible in the Grand Style: the tyrannical stylization forbids. But then, the mind that invented Milton's Grand Style had renounced the English language, and with that, inevitably, Milton being an Englishman, a great deal else.

"Milton wrote Latin as readily as he did English." And: "Critics sometimes forget that before the **'Nativity Ode'**

Milton wrote more Latin than English, and one may suggest that the best of the Latin is at least as good as the best of the English." At any rate, one can believe that, after a decade of Latin polemic, Latin idiom came very naturally to him, and was associated with some of his strongest, if not necessarily most interesting, habits of feeling. But however admirable his Latin may be judged to be, to latinize in English is quite another matter, and it is a testimony to the effect of the "fortifying curriculum" that the price of Milton's latinizing should have been so little recognized.

"This charm of the exceptional and the irregular in diction," writes Mr. Logan Pearsall Smith in his extremely valuable essay on English Idioms, "accounts for the fact that we can enjoy the use of idiom even in a dead language which we do not know very well; it also explains the subtlety of effect which Milton achieved by transfusing Greek or Latin constructions into his English verse." But Milton's transfusing is regular and unremitting, and involves, not pleasant occasional surprises, but a consistent rejection of English idiom, as the passage quoted from Book IV sufficiently shows. So complete, and so mechanically habitual, is Milton's departure from the English order, structure and accentuation that he often produces passages that have to be read through several times before one can see how they go, though the Miltonic mind has nothing to offer that could justify obscurity— no obscurity was intended: it is merely that Milton has forgotten the English language. There is, however, a much more important point to be made: it is that, cultivating so complete and systematic a callousness to the intrinsic nature of English, Milton forfeits all possibility of subtle or delicate life in his verse.

It should be plain, for instance, that subtlety of movement in English verse depends upon the play of the natural sense movement and intonation against the verse structure, and that "natural," here, involves a reference, more or less direct, to idiomatic speech. The development in Shakespeare can be studied as a more and more complex and subtle play of speech movement and intonation against the verse. There is growing complexity of imagery and thought too, of course, but it is not to this mainly that one would refer in analysing the difference between a characteristic passage of *Othello* and Romeo's dying lament: the difference is very largely a matter of subtle tensions within, pressures upon, the still smooth curves of the still "regular" verse of *Othello*. No such play is possible in a medium in which the life of idiom, the pressure of speech, is as completely absent as in Milton's Grand Style. That is why even in the most lively books of **Paradise Lost** the verse, brilliant as it is, has to the ear that appreciates Shakespeare a wearying deadness about it. That skill we are told of, the skill with which Milton varies the beat without losing touch with the underlying norm, slides the cæsura backwards and forwards, and so on, is certainly there. But the kind of appreciation this skill demands is that which one gives— if one is a classic—to a piece of Latin (we find writers on Milton "appreciating" his Latin verse in the same tone and spirit as they do his English).

"An appreciation of Milton is the last reward of consummated scholarship." Qualified as Mark Pattison prescribes, one may, with Raleigh, find that Milton's style is "all substance and weight," that he is almost too packed to be read aloud, and go on to acclaim the "top of his skill" in the choruses of *Samson Agonistes*. But the ear trained on Shakespeare will believe that it would lose little at the first hearing of a moderately well-declaimed passage, and that *Samson Agonistes* read aloud would be hardly tolerable, because of its desolating exposure of utter loss—loss in the poet of all feeling for his native English. The rhythmic deadness, the mechanical externality with which the movement is varied, is the more pitifully evident because of the personal urgency of the theme and the austerity: there is no magniloquence here. To arrive here, of course, took genius, and the consummation can be analytically admired. But then, there have been critics who found rhythmic subtlety in *Phœbus with Admetus* and *Love in the Valley*.

Up to this point the stress has fallen upon Milton's latinizing. To leave it there would be to suggest an inadequate view of his significance. His influence is seen in Tennyson as well as in Thomson, and to say that he groups with Tennyson and Spenser in contrast to Shakespeare and Donne is to say something more important about him than that he latinized. The force of associating him with Spenser is not that he was himself "sage and serious", and in contrasting him with Donne one is not, as seems also commonly to be thought, lamenting that he chose not to become a Metaphysical. The qualities of Donne that invite the opposition are what is shown in this:

> On a huge hill,
> Cragged, and steep, Truth stands, and hee that will
> Reach her, about must, and about must goe;
> And what the hills suddennes resists, winne so;
> Yet strive so, that before age, deaths twilight,
> Thy Soule rest, for none can worke in that night.

This is the Shakespearian use of English; one might say that it is the English use—the use, in the essential spirit of the language, of its characteristic resources. The words seem to do what they say; a very obvious example of what, in more or less subtle forms, is pervasive being given in the image of reaching that the reader has to enact when he passes from the second to the third line. But a comparison will save analysis:

> For so to interpose a little ease,
> Let our frail thoughts dally with false surmise.
> Ay me! Whilst thee the shores, and sounding Seas
> Wash far away, where ere thy bones are hurld,
> Whether beyond the stormy Hebrides,
> Where thou perhaps under the whelming tide
> Visit'st the bottom of the monstrous world;
> Or whether thou to our moist vows denied,
> Sleep'st by the fable of Bellerus old,
> Where the great vision of the guarded Mount
> Looks toward Namancos and Bayona's hold . . .

The contrast is sharp; the use of the medium, the attitude towards it in both writer and reader, is as different as possible. Though the words are doing so much less work than in Donne, they seem to value themselves more highly—they seem, comparatively, to be occupied with valuing themselves rather than with doing anything. This last clause would have to be saved for Tennyson if it were a question of distinguishing fairly between Milton and him, but, faced with the passage from Donne, Milton and Tennyson go together. Tennyson descends from Spenser by way of Milton and Keats, and it was not for nothing that Milton, to the puzzlement of some critics, named Spenser as his "original": the mention of Tennyson gives the statement (however intended) an obvious significance.

The consummate art of **"Lycidas,"** personal as it is, exhibits a use of language in the spirit of Spenser—incantatory, remote from speech. Certain feelings are expressed, but there is no pressure behind the words; what predominates in the handling of them is not the tension of something precise to be defined and fixed, but a concern for mellifluousness—for liquid sequences and a pleasing opening and closing of the vowels. This is the bent revealed in the early work; the Shakespearian passage in *Comus* is exceptional. Milton, that is, some one will observe of the comparison, is trying to do something quite other than Donne; his bent is quite different. Exactly: the point is to be clear which way it tends.

The most admired things in *Comus*—it is significant—are the songs.

> Sweet Echo, sweetest Nymph that liv'st unseen
>   Within thy airy shell
>   By slow Meander's margent green,
> And in the violet imbroider'd vale
>   Where the love-lorn Nightingale
> Nightly to thee her sad Song mourneth well . . .

Quite plainly, the intention here is not merely to flatter the singing voice and suit the air, but to produce in words effects analogous to those of music, and the exquisite achievement has been sufficiently praised. The undertaking was congenial to Milton. Already he had shown his capacity for a weightier kind of music, a more impressive and less delicate instrument:

> Blest pair of Sirens, pledges of Heav'ns joy,
> Sphear-born harmonious Sisters, Voice, and Vers,
> Wed your divine sounds, and mixt power employ
> Dead things with inbreath'd sense able to pierce,
> And . . .

We remember the Tennysonian felicity: "God-gifted organ voice." **"At a Solemn Musick,"** though coming from not long after 1630, anticipates unmistakably the "melodious noise" of *Paradise Lost*, and suggests a further account of that sustained impressiveness, that booming swell, which becomes so intolerable.

This, then, and not any incapacity to be interested in myth, is why we find Milton unexhilarating. The myth of *Paradise Lost*, indeed, suffers from deficiencies related to those of the verse. "Milton's celestial and infernal regions are

large but insufficiently furnished apartments filled by heavy conversation," remarks Mr. Eliot, and suggests that the divorce from Rome, following the earlier breach with the Teutonic past, may have something to do with this mythological thinness. But it is enough to point to the limitations in range and depth of Milton's interests, their patent inadequacy to inform a "sense of myth, of fable, of ordered wholes in experience." His strength is of the kind that we indicate when, distinguishing between intelligence and character, we lay the stress on the latter; it is a strength, that is, involving sad disabilities. He has "character," moral grandeur, moral force; but he is, for the purposes of his undertaking, disastrously single-minded and simple-minded. He reveals everywhere a dominating sense of righteousness and a complete incapacity to question or explore its significance and conditions. This defect of intelligence is a defect of imagination. He offers as ultimate for our worship mere brute assertive will, though he condemns it unwittingly by his argument and by glimpses of his own finer human standard. His volume of moral passion owes its strength too much to innocence—a guileless unawareness of the subtleties of egotism—to be an apt agent for projecting an "ordered whole of experience." It involves, too, a great poverty of interest. After the first two books, magnificent in their simple force (party politics in the Grand Style Milton can compass), *Paradise Lost*, though there are intervals of relief, becomes dull and empty: "all," as Raleigh says, "is power, vagueness and grandeur." Milton's inadequacy to myth, in fact, is so inescapable, and so much is conceded in sanctioned comment, that the routine eulogy of his "architectonic" power is plainly a matter of mere inert convention.

> **. . . A good deal of *Paradise Lost* strikes one as being almost as mechanical as bricklaying . . .**
>
> *—F. R. Leavis*

But even if the realized effect were much less remote than it actually is from the abstract design, even if the life and interest were much better distributed, the orthodox praise of Milton's architectonics would still be questionable in its implications. It would still be most commonly found to harbour the incomprehensions betrayed by the critic cited in the opening of this chapter.

> 'In his time (as in ours) there was a good deal to be said for the Spenserian school against the technical break down to which the Jacobean dramatists had ridden English verse. Webster is a great moment in English style, but the drama was falling off, and blank verse had to survive in a non-dramatic form, which required a more rigid treatment than the stage could offer it. In substance, it needed stiffer and less sensitive perceptions, a more artificial grasp of sensation, to offset the supersensitive awareness of the school of Shakespeare, a versification less imitative of the flow of sensation and more architectural. What poetry needed,

Milton was able to give. It was Arnold who, in the 1853 preface to his own poems, remarked that the sensational imagery of the Shakespearian tradition had not been without its baleful effect on poetry down to Keats: one may imitate a passage in Shakespeare without penetrating to the mind that wrote it, but to imitate Milton one must be Milton; one must have all of Milton's resources in myth behind the impulse: it is the myth, ingrained in his very being, that makes the style.'

If that is so, the style, as we have seen, condemns the myth. Behind the whole muddled passage, of course, and not far behind, is the old distinction between the "Classical style" and the "Romantic"—the "Romantic" including Shelley (and one presumes, Swinburne) along with Shakespeare. It is enough here to say that the inability to read Shakespeare (or the remoteness from the reading of him) revealed in such a passage and such a distinction throws the most damaging suspicion upon the term "architectural." The critic clearly implies that because Shakespeare exhibits "more sensitive perceptions," and offers a "versification more imitative of the flow of sensation," he is therefore indifferent to total effect and dissipates the attention by focussing, and asking us to focus, on the immediate at the expense of the whole. As a matter of fact, any one of the great tragedies is an incomparably better whole than *Paradise Lost*; so finely and subtly organized that architectural analogies seem inappropriate (a good deal of *Paradise Lost* strikes one as being almost as mechanical as bricklaying). The analysis of a Shakespeare passage showing that "supersensitive awareness" leads one into the essential structure of the whole organism: Shakespeare's marvellous faculty of intense local realization is a faculty of realizing the whole locally.

A Shakespeare play, says Professor Wilson Knight, may be considered as "an extended metaphor," and the phrase suggests with great felicity this almost inconceivably close and delicate organic wholeness. The belief that "architectural" qualities like Milton's represent a higher kind of unity goes with the kind of intellectual bent that produced Humanism—that takes satisfaction in inertly orthodox generalities, and is impressed by invocations of Order from minds that have no glimmer of intelligence about contemporary literature and could not safely risk even elementary particular appreciation.

Robert Graves (essay date 1947)

SOURCE: "The Ghost of Milton," in *The Common Asphodel: Collected Essays on Poetry, 1922-1949,* Hamish Hamilton, 1949, pp. 321-5.

[*In the following excerpt, Graves assesses Milton as "a minor poet with a remarkable ear for music, before diabolic ambition impelled him to renounce the true Muse and bloat himself up . . . into a towering rugged poet."*]

. . . With all possible deference to his admirers, Milton was not a great poet, in the sense in which Shakespeare

was great. He was a minor poet with a remarkable ear for music, before diabolic ambition impelled him to renounce the true Muse and bloat himself up, like Virgil (another minor poet with the same musical gift) into a towering, rugged major poet. There is strong evidence that he consciously composed only a part of *Paradise Lost*; the rest was communicated to him by what he regarded as a supernatural agency.

The effect of *Paradise Lost* on sensitive readers is, of course, over-powering. But is the function of poetry to overpower? To be over-powered is to accept spiritual defeat. Shakespeare never overpowers: he raises up. To put the matter in simple terms, so as not to get involved in the language of the morbid psychologist: it was not the Holy Ghost that dictated *Paradise Lost*—the poem which has caused more unhappiness, to the young especially, than any other in the language—but Satan the protagonist, demon of pride. The majesty of certain passages is superhuman, but their effect is finally depressing and therefore evil. Parts of the poem, as for example his accounts of the rebel angels' military tactics with concealed artillery, and of the architecture of Hell, are downright vulgar: vulgarity and classical vapidity are characteristic of the passages which intervene between the high flights, the communicated diabolisms.

The very familiarity of **"Lycidas"** discourages critical comment and it is usually assumed—though I disagree with this—that Dr. Johnson showed a lack of poetic feeling when he criticized the falsity of its sentiments and imagery:

> It is not to be considered as the effusion of real passion: for passion runs not after remote allusions and obscure opinions. Passion plucks no berries from the myrtle and ivy, nor calls upon Arethuse and Mincius, nor tells of rough satyrs and fauns with cloven hoof. Where there is leisure for fiction there is little grief.

Milton's effusion was certainly not spontaneous; in 1637 he had been invited to collaborate in a projected memorial anthology in honour of Edward King, his late fellow-student at King's College, Cambridge, and was apparently the last to send in his piece. It is unlikely that his grief for King was any more sincere than the admiration he had expressed for Shakespeare seven years previously when similarly invited to compose a commendatory sonnet for a new edition of the Plays (the first of his poems to be printed); and young King's appointment by Royal mandate to a vacant College Fellowship seems to have so embittered Milton, who considered that he had the first claim to it himself, as to turn him into an anti-monarchist. There is authentic emotion in **"Lycidas,"** but it springs, as in his **"Lament for Damon,"** from the realization that young intellectuals of his generation are as liable as anyone else to die suddenly; Fate's latest victim might well have been John Milton, not Edward King; which would have been a far more serious literary disaster. It also springs, but more obscurely, from the Fellowship grudge—apparently the irrelevant attack, in the second part of the poem, on Bishops who are unfaithful to their flocks, was aimed at William Chappell, his hated former College tutor, recently promoted Bishop of Ross, as being the enemy who had secured King his Fellowship. Dr. Johnson was rightly scandalized by the sudden change at this point in the poem from "the vulgar pastoral . . . in which appear the heathen deities Jove and Phoebus, Neptune and Aeolus . . ." to a satire on contemporary Church Government. He writes:

> The shepherd is now a feeder of sheep and afterwards an ecclesiastical pastor, a superintendent of a Christian flock. Such equivocations are always unskilful; but here they are indecent.

When he adds that **"Lycidas"** "has no art," this is true only in the sense that it is a poem strangled by art. Johnson sturdily resisted the musical spell which the opening lines cast on more sensitive readers:

> Yet once more, O ye Laurels, and once more
> Ye Myrtles brown, with Ivy never-sear,
> I com to pluck your Berries harsh and crude,
> And with forc'd fingers rude,
> Shatter your leaves before the mellowing year.

and did not trouble to examine carefully the principles on which they were written.

So far as I know, nobody has ever pointed out that in the extravagantly artful interlacing of alliteration throughout this passage Milton is adapting to English metrical use the device of *cynghanedd*, or recurrent consonantal sequences, used by the Welsh bards whom he mentions appreciatively early in the poem. It may well be that he learned of the device when he visited the Court of the President of Wales, for whom he had written *Comus*, in 1634.

The initial consonants of the first lines are an alliterative interlace of Y.M.L. which is interrupted by the harshness of the alliterative pairs B.B., C.C., and F.F., and which, after *Shatter*, reappears to decorate the "dying close." The interlace of C.S.D. in the next two lines is linked to the foregoing with another B.B.:

> . . . leaves before the mellowing year.
> Bitter constraint, and sad occasion dear,
> Compels me to disturb your season due . . .

Then follows a more complicated interlace: a P.H.N.L. sequence connected to the C.S.D. sequence by a bridge of D's, and followed by a watery succession of W's to close the stanza.

> For *Lycidas* is dead, dead ere his prime
> Young *Lycidas,* and hath not left his peer:
> Who would not sing for *Lycidas*? he knew
> Himself to sing, and build the lofty rhyme.
> He must not flote upon his watry bear
> Unwept, and welter to the parching wind,
> Without the meed of som melodious tear.

It was naughty of Johnson to pretend that 'the diction is harsh, the rhymes uncertain, the numbers unpleasing': the sound of the poem is magnificent; only the sense is deficient. In the opening lines *Brown*, introduced for its resonance and as an alliterative partner to *Berries*, suggests a false contrast between myrtle leaves which go brown and ivy leaves that stay green; whereas both sorts of leaf go brown in old age and fall off after younger leaves have taken their place. Laurel is sacred to Apollo, the god of poetry; ivy to Dionysus-Osiris, the god of resurrection; myrtle to Venus, goddess of love. But ivy and myrtle drop out of the poem immediately and seem to have been introduced only for the melodious sound of their names; and though it is clear from the next lines that Lycidas' death, in August before the year has mellowed, has unseasonably forced Milton's hand, he does not explain why he has to shatter the leaves of these trees while plucking the unripe berries. If he needs the berries, though of these three sorts only myrtle berries are edible, when they ripen in mid-winter, he does not have to disturb the leaves; if he needs a wreath he can cut a young shoot and shatter neither berries nor leaves. Clearly *Shatter* is used merely for its violence of sound; the presumed sense is "I have come to pluck your berries and leaves before the year has mellowed," but this is not conveyed.

And if he needs a wreath, for whom is it intended? For himself, later to converse with Apollo and have his ears encouragingly touched, or for the laureate hearse of his fellow-poet? The exigencies of his complicated metrical scheme have blurred the logic of the stanza—*parching* and *melodious* are further examples of words chosen for their sound at the expense of meaning—but his musical craftsmanship has lulled successive generations of readers into delighted acquiescence, and in Johnson's words "driven away the eye from nice examination." It is enough for them to catch the general drift: that a poet has died before his time, shattering the hopes of his friends, and that a fellowpoet, suddenly aware that he is human too, is fumbling broken-heartedly among the evergreens with a confused notion that he ought to weave someone—but whom?— a garland of some sort or other; and that he feels vaguely (but is too downhearted to work the theory out) that the Bishops are to blame for everything.

Frank Kermode **(essay date 1953)**

SOURCE: "Milton's Hero," in *Review of English Studies,* Vol. IV, No. XVI, October, 1953, pp. 317-30.

[*In the following essay, Kermode examines the depiction of Christ in* Paradise Regained, *establishing Christian heroic virtue as distinct from pagan.*]

The heroic poem, said Davenant, should "exhibit a venerable and amiable image of heroic virtue"; this virtue, he considered, had best be Christian. Cowley, choosing a Christian hero, concurred, and Milton, dealing as usual with the substance and not the shadow, made Jesus his exemplary hero. From the virtue of the angry Achilles, even from that of the dedicated Aeneas, to that of Christ, is a long step, but recent scholarship has shown how the magnanimity of the Aristotelian prescription had been Christianized, so that "the extinction of appetite by reason," could be an heroic agony, and Milton's Christ could debel Satan and appetite not by acting but by suffering. My purpose here is not so much to develop these inquiries as to show that *Paradise Regain'd* contains within itself the reasons why its hero is as he is and not otherwise, and that Milton's thought was, on this deeply important subject, always and heroically consistent.

It is essential, to begin with, that we should not hesitate to accept Milton as a hero. He clearly aspired, in a remarkably unaffected way, to heroism, and thought it necessary to his day labour, "not presuming to sing high praises of heroick men . . . unlesse he have in himselfe the experience and the practice of all which is praiseworthy." This is not merely to say that Milton was in love with the breathed and exercised virtue of Guyon; that in his life and work he honoured the virtue which heroically rejects. He had in mind a more sharply defined heroic pattern. He cast himself as well as his Christ in this heroic mould; hence a degree of resemblance between them which has dangerously and unnecessarily been called identity. We know that from early days Milton called Christ "Most perfect Heroe"; what more does he say of his own heroism?

Like Adam, Milton was formed for contemplation and valour, not for either, but for both. He thought of his long secluded nonage as the formal period of preparation for the heroic life. The "degree of merriment" which, on Dr. Johnson's orders, we are to allow ourselves at the story of his return from Italy, need not obscure the fact that the long preparation was over; the hero went forth into the world. While he was still at Horton, Milton commented elaborately upon his long holding back from the world in the letter, written in 1632 and preserved in the Trinity MS., which ends with the sonnet on his twenty-third birthday. This letter, written perhaps to no one in particular, is a careful apology for his long seclusion, an apology perhaps the more necessary in that his long stay at Horton was only just beginning. His seclusion, he says, is not the result of an affected love of learning, "whereby a man cuts him self off from all action and becomes the most helplesse, pusilanimous & unweapon'd creature in the world, the most unable & unfit to doe that which all mortals aspire to." Rather is it the desire to be properly equipped for the great action when the time comes, "not taking thought of being late, so it give advantage to be more fit, for those that were latest lost nothing when the maister of the vineyard came to give each one his hire"; thus he excuses himself from the reproach that, having reached an age to obey Christ's command that all should "labour while yet there is light," he remains inactive. His is not the crime which preceded "the terrible seasing of him that hid the talent"; for he is preparing for the day when the talent matures.

Here Milton is conscious not only of the biblical *loci*, but also of the traditional Stoic positions on the life of retirement and the life of action. Apart from an orthodox defence of learning, he has a fairly open allusion to Seneca's *De Tranquillitate Animi*, with its debate between the philosopher and the young student Serenus, whose longing for glory disturbs his studies. The dialogue concerns the nature and purpose of different kinds of retirement. That Milton was thinking of this dialogue is confirmed by the sonnet **"When I consider how my light is spent,"** written twenty years later. Its opening line is reminiscent of the sonnet **"On his being arrived at the age of twenty-three"**; it is as if Milton had refreshed his memory of the earlier poem and the letter of which it was a part. Christ commanded us to labour while there was light; but does he require our labour when there is no light? "There is," as Warton said, "a pun on the doctrine in the Gospel." But there is also a reference to the letter in which this parable was earlier quoted, and the later sonnet alludes also to the other parable, the parable of the one talent which is death to hide. Now Patience prevents the fond question "Can anything be asked of me in this hopeless plight?" by another amalgam of Seneca and Christian imagery in the sestet. This new seclusion of blindness is another retreat. What is recommended to the devotee of Virtue who is driven by Fortune from the active life? Not inertia; he is not useless. "Nunquam enim quamvis obscura virtus latet, sed mittit sua signa." His proper course is to serve still; for Milton to wait upon the Lord; for Seneca to champion the cause of Virtue. . . . And this is true no matter what gifts Fortune may have withdrawn. . . .

Thus Milton, in two poems separated by twenty years, considers the pattern of heroic retirement, and seeks authority not only in the Scriptures but also in classical antiquity. The retreat at Horton, and the retreat of his blindness are alike considered in relation to a classical heroic scheme.

> He grew up in the privacy of his own family, and till his age was quite mature and settled, which he also passed in private, was chiefly known for his attendance upon the purer worship, and for his integrity of life. He had cherished his confidence in God, he had nursed his great spirit in silence. . . . He was a soldier above all the most exercised in knowledge of himself; he had either destroyed, or reduced to his own control, all enemies within his own breast—vain hopes, fears, desires. . . . To evince his extraordinary, his little less than divine virtue, this mark will suffice; that there lived in him an energy, whether of spirit or genius, or of discipline established . . . by the rule of Christ and of sanctity.

The first two sentences could have been spoken of Christ, and the whole, with small change, of Milton himself, though the hero here celebrated is Cromwell,

> Who from his private Gardens, where
> He liv'd reserved and austere,
>   As if his highest plot
>   To plant the Bergamot,
> Could by industrious Valour Climbe
> To ruine the great work of Time,
>   And cast the Kingdome old
>   Into another Mold.

Milton offers us a Cromwell on the model of the younger Scipio, though he has Christianized the model. And a little later in the *Second Defence* he speaks of Fairfax and how he unites "exemplary sanctity of life with the highest courage." "In your present secession, like that of Scipio Africanus of old at Liternaum, you hide yourself as much as possible from the public view. It is not the enemy alone you have conquered; you have conquered ambition, and what itself conquers the most excellent of mortals, you have conquered glory." So does Milton shape the Parliamentary generals by the pattern of Christian heroic virtue. Scipio, the model of ancient heroism, the true exemplar of the nice balance of active and contemplative, who understood the causes of retreat and was never less alone than when alone; Scipio has a key position in the pattern, whether the issue of heroism be conquest or 'the better fortitude Of Patience and Heroic Martyrdom.'

Christian heroism may take either of these courses, though the latter is more Christ-like, "above Heroic." In Milton's tragedy Samson, Manoah, and the Chorus, in the course of their patient inquiry into the true significance of Samson's life, have to treat of this topic. The sham code-ridden honour of Harapha is discomfited, and the Chorus comments upon his departure; heroism is comely and reviving, but the higher heroism is the active, which quells 'the mighty of the earth' "with plain Heroic magnitude of mind And celestial vigour arm'd." But the chorus supposes, ironically, that Samson is no longer to be thought of as an active hero:

> . . . Patience is more oft the exercise
> Of Saints, the trial of thir fortitude,
> Making them each his own Deliverer,
> And Victor over all
> That tyrannie or fortune can inflict . . .
>   Sight bereav'd
> May chance to number thee with those
> Whom Patience finally must crown.

But Samson is precisely the hero who debels the tyrant by plain heroic magnitude, having with Job-like patience endured suffering. The lesson of Samson becomes clear: God seems to desert his heroes, but does not. Virtue, the staple of heroism, is never allowed to die, but always rises from the ashes of suffering and acting heroes. This is the new acquist of true experience, that virtue is "vigorous most When most unactive deem'd." To the end Milton was preoccupied with the hero as the Christian *electus,* with the reconciliation of Christian and classical schemes of heroism, and the problem of why God apparently deserts his champion and allows him to be maimed and humiliated. *Samson Agonistes* is particularly concerned with the last of these issues, which is raised insistently by the accounts of the Old Testament heroes and also by Milton's own life. The Passion of Christ presents it in its most acute and terrible form. This accounts for that likeness which has been so often held against the poet.

To make his Christ unchallengeably exemplary Milton shaped *Paradise Regain'd* to contain a hero who complete and transcends the heroic data, not merely exemplary in his patience and heroic martyrdom, but gaining exemplary rewards, which transcend the rewards of pagan heroism—sensual satisfactions, glory, power, even secular knowledge.

The action of *Paradise Regain'd* concerns the primary heroic crisis, the emergence of the hero from seclusion. He is tempted; this is what Milton calls a "good temptation . . . whereby God tempts even the righteous for the purpose of exercising or manifesting their faith and patience, as in the case of Abraham and Job." This ordeal is necessary to the Redeemer. "For that he himself hath suffered being tempted, he is able to succour them that are tempted." It is also necessary to Christ as Hero; he must be refined for a greater conquest, he must "lay down the rudiments of his great warfare" before the battle with Sin and Death.

Having established the situation of crisis, the poem looks back to the youth of Christ. It had been spent in learning. Like Cato, like Cromwell, Christ had been

> Serious to learn and know, and thence to do,
> What might be publick good.

"Therefore, above my years The Law of God I read," says Christ, perhaps, as Dunster suggests, with an allusion to the *Aeneid*—ante annos animumque gerens curamque virilem. He aspired to heroic acts, to rid Israel of the Roman yoke "till truth were freed"; the comely and reviving acts of the chosen hero of God. He is intended to carry out, in his own way, the prophecy of Anchises, "to teach the erring soul . . . the stubborn only to subdue." His mother has cautioned him against haste:

> High are thy thoughts
> O Son, but nourish them and let them soar
> To what highth sacred vertue and true worth
> Can raise them, though above example high.

And so "The time prefixt I waited", living "private, unactive, calm, contemplative" and addicted . . . To contemplation and profound dispute." Now, at the moment of emergence, he finds "all his great work to come before him set." The faithful cannot understand his departure into the wilderness, nor can his mother; he himself has a serene confidence in, but no rational understanding of, this vocation. But he knows, as they do not (though his mother hints at it) that his moment has come, as it came to Aeneas and Cato, to Cromwell and Milton.

So he goes forth, not like the pagan heroes to honour, but to "trouble." He goes not to act but to suffer, not to receive but to reject; to achieve "by Humiliation and strong Sufferance," and by his weakness to "o'ercome Satanic strength." He must resist the permitted strength of Satan as Job did; this is a different heroism from that of any pagan. The contrast between these heroisms is a leading theme of the poem, which resounds with the names of heroes who augment or illuminate by contrast the total and exemplary heroism of Christ.

The name of Scipio dominates the allusions to pagan heroism, and he is often present when not named. When Christ is led into loneliness,

> But with such thoughts . . .
> Lodg'd in his brest, as well might recommend
> Such Solitude before choicest Society

Milton is referring us to the delicious solitude of Cicero's Scipio; so too when Christ is "Sole but with holiest meditations fed." As Scipio and Alexander rejected women, Belial need not expect Christ to fall to them. In the Third Book Satan flatters Christ; he is wise, he is capable of glory; but how shall he achieve it, sunk in his affection for the private life? Glory is "the flame of most erected spirits"; in failing to seek it, Christ lags behind some more timely happy spirits who had gone in quest of it— Alexander, Pompey, Machabeus, Scipio . . . But the answer is firm: Satan is himself the type of those insatiable for glory; and

> If young *African* for fame
> His wasted Country freed from *Punic* rage,
> The deed becomes unprais'd, the man at least . . .

In fact Scipio had explicitly rejected this devil's idea of glory, and was free from the vulgar error which makes honour dependent upon reputation and the verdict of the mob. In no detail does Christ fall short of the model of ancient heroes.

In another place Christ compares himself with the heroes of the past—with "Quintus, Fabricius, Curius, Regulus"; those who accomplished great things in poverty, or by self-sacrifice. To rule oneself is better than to be a king, and, as Regulus showed, "to lay down Far more magnanimous, then to assume." This group of heroes is named, together with the Old Testament group—Jephtha, David, and Gideon, *Heros rege major*—in Christ's reply to the temptation of wealth, which is carried on entirely in these terms.

> And what in me seems wanting, but that I
> May also in this poverty as soon
> Accomplish what they did, perhaps and more?

The virtues of these heroes are included in Christ. There are others, chiefly Job and Socrates, Christ's heathen type, "for truths sake suffering death unjust." Socrates had achieved what might be achieved by the light of nature; he was the hardest of the pagans to reject, but he did not know the truth as Christ and his successors knew it; and the new way of knowing it is the key to the heroism of humiliation. It was not available to Socrates and Scipio, and so no pagan equivalent of the true heroism will do, not even that which despises honour and gain, and drinks the cup of humiliation.

Satan professes his inability to understand how Christ proposes to be a hero. "What dost thou in this World?" he asks. The answer, we know, is suffer and reject. Satan's bewilderment, though feigned, is not uncongenial to us, however, for in dismissing the old hero Milton has dismissed the old rewards of heroism; and one consequence of the relative neglect of the poem is that the exact nature of the new rewards proposed for the new hero escapes the modern reader. Milton for excellent reasons describes them very obliquely; they are suggested by the very rewards they displace; they supersede the old rewards exactly as the new hero supersedes the old. I propose to examine this process of supersession as it occurs at four places in the poem: the banquet, the debate upon honour, the rejection of Rome, and the rejection of Athens.

There has been some debate as to why Milton, having recorded in the First Book the temptation of the stone, proceeds to an account of Satan's illusory banquet; a device which appears to repeat the initial appeal to Christ's hunger. The reason is that the first temptation is canonical, the second a quasi-allegorical development of it which is essential to the structure of the poem. Milton follows the hint in St. Matthew, who alone speaks of the angels ministering to Jesus after the temptations. This ministration, it is natural to assume, was partly of food; and Milton balances this celestial banquet with a banquet of sense, which Jesus rejects so that he may attain to the higher angelicbanquet. There is a suggestion of this scheme in Giles Fletcher's *Christs Victorie on Earth*. In both poems Satan offers Christ a banquet of sense. We are perhaps most familiar with this expression from Chapman's poem, which describes a systematic assault on the senses of the erotic Ovid; each sense in turn is elaborately described. Ultimately the banquet of sense is the antitype of the celestial banquet of the *Symposium* as Ficino explained it. The theme occurs with rich suggestiveness in *Timon of Athens*—the banquet having satisfied all the senses save sight, Cupid brings in a masque for its benefit:

> The five best senses
> Acknowledge thee their patron. . . . Th'ear,
> Taste, touch, smell, pleas'd from thy table rise;
> They only now come but to feast thine eyes.

This banquet is associated with Timon's self-deception on the issues of honour, friendship, nature, and so forth. The obscurer banquet in *The Tempest* concerns the depravity of Antonio and his friends. Milton uses a banquet to enforce the sensual arguments of Comus in his Masque. Now, in ***Paradise Regain'd***, Satan appeals to the sight with the beautiful youths and nymphs, to the smell with "the wine That fragrant smell diffus'd"; to the ear— "Harmonious Airs were heard Of chiming strings, or charming pipes"; and then he completes the tale with taste and touch:

> No interdict
> Defends the touching of these viands pure,
> Thir taste no knowledge works, at least of evil. . . .

The sensual impact proceeds from the highest, "the eye itself, That most pure spirit of sense," to the lowest, touch and taste.

The adverbs describing the tone of Christ's responses to the temptations of Satan are always significant. At this point he replies "temperately." Temperance is not so appropriate to his continued fast as to his rejection of sensuality as it is summed up in the banquet. Christ says that he may have at will a celestial banquet,

And call swift flights of Angels ministrant
Array'd in Glory on my cup to attend.

At the end of the poem he has his proper reward:

A table of Celestial Food, Divine,
Ambrosial, Fruits fetcht from the tree of life,
And from the fount of life Ambrosial drink.

In place of the sensual banquet, the material gratifications of the conqueror, he has a celestial banquet, a banquet of love and of heavenly glory.

I have already, in speaking of Scipio's function in the poem, alluded to Christ's rejection of honour, and I need not dwell long upon it here. Christ, like Milton, distinguishes between honour which depends on opinion—*insipientium opinio*—and honour more absolute, of which Cicero spoke as "amplitudinem animi et quasi quandam exaggerationem quam altissimam animi" which enables a man in conquering himself to conquer all things. This distinction is as old as Plato, and its most familiar exposition in English is the debate on honour between Hector and his brothers in *Troilus and Cressida*; Hector holds that true honour

Holds his estimate and dignity
As well wherein 'tis precious of itself
As in the prizer.

This is the most explicit statement of one of Shakespeare's most insistent themes. Milton develops the idea in a predictable way; the honour which resides in reputation is the honour of the old hero, and it is subject to envious and calumniating time. With it go all temporal distinctions and rewards. But the Christian equivalent of honour is not appraised by the common breath, and certainly does not derive its life from that source. The truth and the rewards of honour are determined "by perfet witnes of all judging *Jove*." No Christian can be in doubt about the distinction.

Fame, I confess, I find more eagerly pursued by the heathen than by the Christians of these times. The immortality (as they thought) of their name was to them, as the immortality of the soul to us: a strong reason to persuade to worthiness. Their knowledge halted in the latter; so they rested in the first; which often made them sacrifice their lives to that which they esteemed above their lives, their fame. Christians know a thing beyond it: and that knowledge causes them to give but a secondary respect to fame; there being no reason why we should neglect that whereon all our future happiness depends, for that which is nothing but a name and empty air. Virtue were a kind of misery, if fame alone were all the garland that did crown her. Glory alone were a reward incompetent for the toils of industrious man. This follows him but on earth; in heaven is laid up a more noble, more essential recompense.

So the poet of **"Lycidas"** dismisses his fears; so, in the Horton letter and sonnet, he justifies his calling. So, to

Satan's reproaches concerning his tardiness in the pursuit of fame, Jesus "calmly" replies:

For what is glory but the blaze of fame,
The peoples praise, if always praise unmixt?
And what the people but a herd confus'd,
A miscellaneous rabble, who extol
Things vulgar, & well weigh'd, scarce worth the
  praise? . . .
This is true glory and renown, when God
Looking on the Earth, with approbation marks
The just man, and divulges him through Heaven
To all his Angels, who with true applause
Recount his praises; thus he did to *Job*. . . .

In exchange for the glory which resides in the opinion of the rabble, the Christian hero receives that which is measured by the knowledge of God. Christ's conquest "unarm'd" is celebrated at the end of the poem by a choir of angels, singing "Heavenly Anthems of his victory."

In the Third Book Satan offers Jesus the military power of Parthia. Jesus is "unmov'd" in his rejection. The "cumbersome Luggage of war" is "argument Of human weakness rather then of strength." But immediately, at the opening of the Fourth Book, Satan returns to the argument of earthly power. Milton takes extraordinary measures to emphasize the desperation of Satan's case, for his return to the attack is signalled by three powerful formal similes which are all the more impressive in that the poem is so stripped of "ornament." The Tempter embarks on his great eulogy of Rome,

Whose wide domain
In ample Territory, wealth and power,
Civility of Manners, Arts, and Arms,
And long Renown thou justly may'st prefer
Before the *Parthian*.

To this temptation Jesus also replies "unmov'd." Rome is degenerate and base, though "once just"; it conquered well, but governs ill; his own kingdom, when it comes, "shall be like a tree Spreading and overshadowing all the Earth, Or as a stone that shall to pieces dash All Monarchies besides throughout the world."

It has recently been observed that Satan's eulogy of Rome is cast in the form of an *encomium urbis*. The prototype is the prophecy of Anchises in *Aeneid*, vi, but Milton may here be borrowing more directly from Claudian. On the Roman valuation, Rome was *urbs aeterna*, and the culmination of the Roman *imperium* was the great climax of history. When Satan showed Christ the vision of Rome he was offering him the sum of pre-Christian civilization; wealth, glory, military power. Now Christ has truly been shown "The kingdoms of the world in all their glory." But his kingdom is not of this world. Just as the sensual banquet and the earthly glory have their heavenly counterparts, so the *civitas terrena* is replaced by the *civitas Dei*. Christ could no more be in doubt about the true nature of the earthly city than was the Red Cross Knight when he had seen the true Jerusalem;

For this great Citie that does far surpas,
And this bright Angels towre quite dims that towre
  of glas.

St. Augustine tolerated the Roman *imperium,* but expected it to give way to the heavenly justice. The Romans had never made good their boast, *parcere subiectis,* and their imperfect justice would be superseded by the *civitas Dei.* Milton repeats the charge against Rome; and the hero, in rejecting the earthly city makes certain of the heavenly, to which he alludes in the language of Daniel's prophecy of the stone and the tree. Since Rome stands for temporal power and glory, and, under Tiberius, for brutality and vicious sensuality, this is an inclusive temptation, and the unmoved rejection of it is the refusal of all the rewards possible to un-Christian heroism of the active sort. Dunster, who is usually acute, remarks that it provokes the crisis of recognition, the impudent requirement that Christ should "fall down, And worship" which provokes the retort, "plain thou nowappear'st That Evil one."

There remains one more temptation before the explicit challenge of the supernatural battle over Jerusalem. It seems the cruellest and most difficult of all; the sweetness of the tempter's suggestions, the uncompromising austerity of Christ's reply, are more than anything else responsible for the coldness with which this poem has always been received.

Satan, arguing somewhat too easily, contends that since Christ is not active he must be contemplative. He therefore tempts him with the learning of Greece

  let extend thy mind o're all the world
In knowledge. . . .
All knowledge is not couch't in *Moses* Law . . .
The *Gentiles* also know, and write, and teach
To admiration, led by Natures light.

There follows the glorious encomium of Athens; most modern readers know very well that they are here if nowhere else of the devil's party. But Christ makes a "sage" reply. It disturbs us that Milton, who in the past had resoundingly acknowledged his love of Greek learning and philosophy, should write this calm rejection; but its consistency is undeniable. The light of nature is superseded by "Light from above, from the fountain of light"—it is characteristic of the situation that this line should itself be redolent of Platonism. The heroes of pagan contemplation are systematically rejected: Socrates because of the avowed and inevitable uncertainty of his knowledge, Plato, who "to fabling fell"—an objection to Plato which is, ultimately, Platonic—Sceptics, Epicureans, Stoics—these because they failed to understand the impossibility of virtue without grace. The lack of divine knowledge renders all Greek learning supererogatory.

          many books
  . . . are wearisom; who reads
Incessantly, and to his reading brings not
A spirit and judgment equal or superior,
(And what he brings, what needs he elsewhere

  seek)
Uncertain and unsettl'd still remains,
Deep verst in books and shallow in himself. . . .

It has been observed that the force of Christ's reply is not independent of classical allusion; in fact it seems to me to owe something to Seneca's Epistle lxxxviii, which treats of intemperate learning and the tenuous relationship of learning to virtue. There is a conventional element in the rejection of useless learning which was heard in English long before Milton; but Milton specializes in the Puritan manner, identifying useful learning with the Law, and dismissing, like St. Augustine who is throughout this passage not far from his mind, the dissensions of the gentile philosophers in favour of the concord of the canonical scriptures. The hero willingly forgoes Athens for Sinai, and Parnassus for Sion. The rejection of Greek poetry in favour of 'Sion's songs, to all true tasts excelling' echoes previous attempts in English to establish the supremacy of Hebrew poetry, and Milton himself had always given a notional credence to the doctrine. Here, as elsewhere, he applies the full weight of his humanism to the antihumanist cause. He himself was a hero, but not the exemplar of heroism.

Pagan learning, then, is to Christian learning as Socrates is to Christ; as Scipio is to Christ; as the earthly honour to the heavenly and the earthly city to the heavenly; as nature to grace. Milton's devotion to his theme is responsible for the cold, unrhetorical diction of the poem, from which he has banished "swelling Epithetes" and much that might recall the pagan epic. But he does not make such sacrifices "unmov'd"; and there is in this section of the poem a profound and moving turbulence.

The last temptation translates the conflict to the plane of violent action. Christ will not throw himself down from the pinnacle; it is Satan-Antaeus who must fall, with such consolation as he can derive from his at last certain knowledge of the nature of his antagonist. At this point the supernatural powers of Christ are asserted, at first simply in his standing inactive. Immediately he receives his supernatural rewards, heavenly glory, and the banquet of celestial love; the angels also affirm his divine nature, "light of light Conceiving," and his coming reign.

        Heir of both worlds,
    Queller of Satan, on thy glorious work
    Now enter, and begin to save mankind.

The whole poem, then, is concerned to establish the character of Christian heroic virtue as distinct from pagan, and to establish the heavenly nature of the rewards which supersede the earthly recompense of the old heroes.

This is certainly in accordance with the doctrines of Tasso in his *Discorso della Virtù Heroica, et della Charità.* There we learn that heroic virtue includes all the other virtues in a nobler recension, but that pagan heroism and charity are only shadows of the Christian type; even Scipio's saving his father's life is only "ombra e figura della Christiana Charità, la quale nel nascimento di Christo cominciò, &

in Christo hebbe la sua perfettione . . .." Heroic Virtue
and Charity resemble each other in many ways, and both
seek a reward of glory. But Charity is the greater; and it
is Charity that inspires the Christian hero.

> niun Heroe espose cosi lietamente la vita per la patria,
> come l'huom caritativo l'espone per Christo; e i Curtii,
> e i Decii, e i Marcelli, e gli altri famosi Romani,
> Barbari, e Greci, non possono in alcu[n]o modo a i
> Martiri di Christo, o a' Machabei esser' agguagliati.

This is, as M. Y. Hughes suggested, the background of
the poem; but *Paradise Regain'd* is self-supporting, and
thus far more complicated structurally than is usually
supposed. Milton had a terrible appetite for essentials. He
took no ready-made theodicy for *Paradise Lost*, no pre-
fabricated hero for *Paradise Regain'd*. We learn, and we
find the lesson hard, why Christ is the exemplary hero by
watching him in the act of confuting or transcending all
the known modes of heroism. We are taught the rewards
of Christian heroism by a demonstration based on the
superseded rewards of the old heroes. We are shown the
difficult victory of a love superior to that expounded by
Plato and his equal Xenophon. The "first and chiefest
office" of this love is to die. When the struggle was
over,Christ, like Socrates after his victory for love, "home
to his Mothers house private return'd." The "heir of both
worlds" had shown how the Christian hero must deserve
his reward. "Blessed is the man that endureth temptation;
for when he is tried he shall receive the crown of life."

M. H. Abrams (essay date 1961)

SOURCE: "Five Types of Lycidas," in *Milton's Lycidas:
The Tradition and the Poem,* University of Missouri Press,
1983, pp. 216-35.

[*In the following essay, Abrams surveys interpretations of
"Lycidas."*]

Most modern critics base their theories on the proposition
that a poem is an object in itself. And all critics endorse
enthusiastically at least one statement by Matthew Arnold,
that the function of criticism is "to see the object as in
itself it really is." The undertaking is surely valid, and
laudable; the results, however, are disconcerting. For in
this age of unexampled critical activity, as one poetic
object after another is analyzed under rigidly controlled
conditions, the object proves to be highly unstable, and
disintegrates. In the pages of the critics we increasingly
find, under a single title, not one poem but a variety of
poems.

Milton's **"Lycidas"** is a convenient case in point, because
it is short enough to be easily manageable, has been ex-
plicated many times, and is almost universally esteemed.
If not every reader goes all the way with Mark Pattison's
judgment that it is "the high-water mark of English Poesy,"
still critics agree about its excellence as closely as they
ever do in evaluating a lyric poem. My point is that, on

the evidence of their own commentaries, critics agree about
the excellence of quite different poems. They present us
not with one **"Lycidas"** but with discriminable types of
"Lycidas"—five types, I have announced in my title. I
feel confident that with a little more perseverance I could
have distinguished at least seven, to equal William Empson's types of ambiguity. But in these matters distinctions, as Mr. Empson's procedure demonstrates, can be
rather arbitrary. And even five types of **"Lycidas"** are
enough to confront the literary theorist with an embarrassing problem: Is a poem one or many? And if it is one,
how are we to decide which one?

For the first type, take **"Lycidas"** as it was commonly
described in the period between the first volume of Mas-
son's monumental *Life of Milton* (1859) and the critical
age ushered in by T. S. Eliot and I. A. Richards a generation ago. This traditional reading (in which I was educated)
was conveniently epitomized by J. H. Hanford in his
Milton Handbook. Individual discussions varied in emphasis and detail; but when in that lost paradise of critical
innocence readers looked at **"Lycidas,"** they agreed that
they saw an elegiac poem about Edward King, a contemporary of Milton's at Christ's College, who had been
drowned when his ship suddenly foundered in the Irish
Sea. To depersonalize his grief and elevate its occasion,
Milton chose to follow the elaborate conventions of the
pastoral elegy, as these had evolved over the 1800 years
between the Sicilian Theocritus and the English Spenser;
he ended the poem with a traditional consolation at the
thought of Lycidas resurrected in heaven, and found in
this thought the strength to carry on his own concerns. In
two passages, many commentators agreed—they often
called them digressions—Milton uttered his personal concerns in a thin fictional disguise. In one of these Milton
expressed his own fear that "th' abhorred shears" might
cut him off before he could achieve the poetic fame to
which he had dedicated his life. In the other Milton,
through St. Peter, voiced a grim warning to the corrupt
English clergy of his time.

Writing in 1926, on the extreme verge of the New Criticism, Professor Hanford was so imprudent as to close his
discussion with the statement that **"Lycidas"** bears its
meaning plainly enough on its face." It contains, to be
sure, a minor verbal crux or two, such as the nature of the
"two-handed engine at the door"; but, he roundly asserted,
"there has been little room for disagreement regarding its
larger features."

Only four years later E. M. W. Tillyard published in his
Milton an analysis of **"Lycidas"** which in its opening
tucket sounded the new note in criticism: Most criticism
of **"Lycidas"** is off the mark, because it fails to distinguish between the nominal and the real subject, what the
poem professes to be about and what it is about. It assumes that Edward King is the real whereas he is but the
nominal subject. Fundamentally **"Lycidas"** concerns—

But before we hear what **"Lycidas"** is really about, we
ought to attend to Tillyard's distinction between "nominal"
and "real" poetic meaning. For this modern polysemism,

which splits all poems—or at least the most noteworthy poems—into two or more levels of meaning, one overt and nominal (which other readers have detected) and the other covert but essential (whose discovery has usually been reserved for the critic making the distinction) is extraordinarily widespread, and we shall find it repeatedly applied to **"Lycidas."** The lamination of poetic significance is variously named. Tillyard elsewhere distinguishes between conscious and unconscious, and direct and oblique meanings. Other critics make a parallel distinction between manifest and latent, ostensible and actual, literal and symbolic, or particular and archetypal significance. And at the risk of giving away a trade secret, it must be confessed that most of the time, when we critics come out with a startling new interpretation of a well-known work, it is through the application of this very useful interpretative stratagem.

The procedure is indispensable in analyzing works for which there is convincing evidence that they were written in the mode of allegory or symbolism. But it is worth noting that the distinction was developed by Greek commentators, interested in establishing Homer's reputation as a doctor of universal wisdom, who dismissed Homer's scandalous stories about the gods as only the veil for an esoteric and edifying undermeaning. The same strategy was adapted by Philo to bring the Old Testament into harmony with Greek philosophy, and by the Church Fathers to prove that the Old Testament prefigured the New Testament, and by medieval and Renaissance moralists in order to disclose, behind Ovid's pagan and ostensibly licentious fables, austere ethical precepts and anticipations of the Christian mysteries. From the vantage of our altered cultural prepossessions, it appears that the distinction between nominal and real meaning has not infrequently been used as a handy gadget to replace what an author has said with what a commentator would prefer him to have said.

We are braced now for Tillyard's disclosure of the real subject of **"Lycidas."** Fundamentally **"Lycidas"** concerns Milton himself; King is but the excuse for one of Milton's most personal poems." The main argument for this interpretation is that **"Lycidas"** is generally admitted to be a great poem, but "if it is great, it must contain deep feeling of some sort"; since this feeling is obviously not about King, it must be about Milton himself. Milton, Tillyard maintains, expresses his own situation and feelings and attitudes, not only in the obviously allegorical passages about driving afield and piping with Lycidas, or in the passages on fame and the corrupt clergy which had been called personal by earlier critics, but from beginning to end of the poem. How radical Tillyard's formula is for translating objective references to subjective equivalents is indicated by his analysis of the poem's climactic passage:

> The fourth section purports to describe the resurrection of Lycidas and his entry into heaven. More truly it solves the whole poem by describing the resurrection into a new kind of life of Milton's hopes, should they be ruined by premature death or by the moral collapse of his country. . . . Above all the fourth section describes the renunciation of earthly fame, the abnegation

of self by the great egotist, and the spiritual purgation of gaining one's life after losing it.

Only such an interpretation, Tillyard claims, will reveal the integrity of the poem, by making it possible "to see in **'Lycidas'** a unity of purpose which cannot be seen in it if the death of King is taken as the real subject." Furthermore, the value of the poem really resides in the ordered and harmonized mental impulses for which the objective references are merely a projected correlative: "What makes **'Lycidas'** one of the greatest poems in English is that it expresses with success a state of mind whose high value can hardly be limited to a particular religious creed."

From this interpretation and these grounds of value John Crowe Ransom (to speak in understatement) disagrees. His premise is that "anonymity . . . is a condition of poetry." Milton very properly undertook to keep himself and his private concerns out of his memorial verses, and to do so assumed the identity of a Greek shepherd, the "uncouth swain" of the last stanza, who serves as a dramatis persona, a "qualified spokesman" for the public performance of a ritual elegy. As for the problem with which Tillyard confronted us—if the passion is not for King, for whom can it be except Milton himself?—Ransom solves it by dissolving it. There is no passion in the poem, and so no problem. "For Lycidas [Milton] mourns with a very technical piety." The pastoral conventions are part of the poetic "make-believe," and the whole poem, whatever more it may be, is "an exercise in pure linguistic technique, or metrics; it was also an exercise in the technique of what our critics of fiction refer to as 'point of view.'"

This is the poem, at any rate, that Milton set out to write and almost succeeded in writing. But his youth and character interfered and forced into the writing three defiant gestures of "rebellion against the formalism of his art." One of these is the liberty he took with his stanzas, which are almost anarchically irregular and include ten lines which do not rhyme at all. Another is St. Peter's speech; in Ransom's comment on this passage, we hear a voice out of the past—the Cavalier critic gracefully but firmly putting the stiff-necked and surly Puritan in his place: it expresses, he says, "a Milton who is angry, violent, and perhaps a little bit vulgar . . . Peter sounds like another Puritan zealot, and less than apostolic." The third instance of Milton's self-assertion is his "breach in the logic of composition"; that is, he shifts from the first-person monologue with which the poem opens to dialogues with Phoebus and others, then abruptly to the third person in the last stanza, where the uncouth swain is presented in "a pure narrative conclusion in the past [tense]." It follows that Ransom's concluding evaluation turns Tillyard's precisely inside-out. The sustained self-expression, on which Tillyard had grounded both the unity and excellence of the elegy, according to Ransom breaks out only sporadically, and then so as to violate the integrity and flaw the perfection of the poem. "So **'Lycidas,'** for the most part a work of great art, is sometimes artful and tricky. We are disturbingly conscious of a man behind the artist."

One might, of course, demur that given Ransom's own criteria, two of the items he decries as arrogant gestures of Milton's originality are exactly those in which he closely follows established conventions. The scholarly annotators— at whom, as he passes, Ransom turns to smile—tell us that the models for Milton's stanzas, the elaborate *canzone* employed by several Italian lyrists of the sixteenth century, were not only variable in structure, but also included unrhymed lines for the sake of that seeming ease and freedom which is the aim of an art that hides art. As for St. Peter's diatribe, Milton inherited the right to introduce rough satire against the clergy into a pastoral from a widespread convention established by Petrarch, who was hardly vulgar, nor a Puritan, nor even a Protestant. In Ransom's third exhibit, one element—Milton's putting the elegy into a narrative context in the conclusion, without a matching narrative introduction—is not, apparently, traditional. But it is at any rate odd to make Milton out to assert his own egoism in the passage which specifically assigns the elegy to another person than himself; a person, moreover, who is the entirely conventional rural singer of a pastoral elegy.

But this begins to seem captious, and does not represent the measure of my admiration for the charm and deftness of Mr. Ransom's essay, which thrusts home some important and timely truths about the dramatic construction of 'Lycidas' by the artful device of overstatement. It is, one might hazard, a virtuoso exercise in critical point of view.

Let the commentary by Cleanth Brooks and John Hardy, in their edition of Milton's **Poems** of 1645, represent 'Lycidas,' type four. At first glance it might seem that to these explicators the poem is not really about King, nor about Milton, but mainly about water. They turn to the first mention of water in lines 12-14 and discover at once the paradox that the "tear" which is the "meed" paid to Lycidas by the elegiac singer is of the same substance, salt water, as the "wat'ry bier," the sea on which the body welters. As the poem develops, they say, "the 'melodious tear' promises to overwhelm the 'sounding Seas.'" For the tear is the elegy itself, which derives its inspiration from the "sacred well" of the muses, and flows on through a profusion of fountains, rivers, and streams, in richly ambiguous interrelations of harmonies, contrasts, and ironies, until, by the agency of "resurrection images," all of which "have to do with a circumvention of the sea," we are transferred to a transcendent pastoral realm where Lycidas walks "other streams along" and the saints wipe the tears forever from his eyes.

The base of the critical operation here is the assumption that "the 'poetry' resides in the total structure of meanings." The primary component in this structure is "imagery," of which the component parts are so organically related, through mutual reflection and implication, that it does not matter where you start: any part will lead you to the center and the whole. The key to both the form and value of "Lycidas," then, which Tillyard had found in the ordering of mental impulses, and Ransom in the all-but-successful maintenance of impersonal elegiac conventions, Brooks and Hardy locate in the evolution and integration

of the imagery: "Lycidas" is a good poem not because it is appropriately and simply pastoral and elegiac—with . . . all the standard equipment-but because of its unique formal wholeness, because of the rich 'integrity' of even such a single figure as that in the lines 'He must not flote upon his wat'ry bear / Un-wept. . . .'"

It turns out, however, that these images are only provisionally the elements of the poem, since in Milton they are used as vehicles for a more basic component, "certain dominant, recurrent symbolic motives." The fact, hitherto mainly overlooked, is that "Milton is a symbolist poet to a considerable extent." Accordingly we must again, as in Tillyard's essay, penetrate the ostensible meaning to discover the real meaning of "Lycidas," though a real meaning which in this case is an abstract concept. "What," they ask, "is the real subject" of "Lycidas"?

> If Milton is not deeply concerned with King as a person, he is deeply concerned, and as a young poet personally involved, with a theme—which is that of the place and meaning of poetry in a world which seems at many points inimical to it.

Specifically, the early part of the poem presents the despairing theme that nature is neutral, emptied of the old pastoral deities ("to say nymphs are ineffectual is tantamount to denying their existence"); and this concept is transcended only by the movement from philosophic naturalism to Christian supernaturalism, in the pastoral imagery of the conclusion in heaven.

Perhaps other readers share my disquiet at this discovery. Leaving aside the validity of assuming that "Lycidas" is essentially a symbolist poem of which the real subject is a theme, there remains the difficulty that the theme seems to be startlingly anachronistic. Milton, we are told, writing in 1637, and echoing a complaint about the nymphs which is as old as Theocritus' first Idyll, presents us with the world-view involving "an emptied nature, a nature which allows us to personify it only in the sense that its sounds seem mournful. . . . The music of nature . . . has also been stilled." But wasn't it Tennyson who said this, in an elegy published in 1850?

> And all the phantom, Nature, stands—
>   With all the music in her tone,
>   A hollow echo of my own,—
> A hollow form with empty hands.

As for the concept imputed to Milton, with respect to the place of poetry in an inimical world, that "Nature is neutral: it is not positively malignant, but neither is it beneficent"—isn't this exactly the thesis laid down in 1926 by I. A. Richards in a very influential little book, *Science and Poetry*? In our own age, Mr. Richards said,

> the central dominant change may be described as the *Neutralization of Nature,* the tranference from the Magical View of the world to the scientific. . . . There is some evidence that Poetry . . . arose with this Magical View. It is a possibility to be seriously considered that Poetry may pass away with it.

At any rate, it is by a notable sleight of explication that Brooks and Hardy convert to the real meaning that Nature does not sympathize with the poet's sorrow and "has no apparent respect for the memory of Lycidas" the very passage in which Milton explicitly states the contrary: that nature, which had responded joyously to Lycidas' soft lays when he was alive, now mourns his death:

> Thee Shepherd, thee the Woods, and desert Caves,
> With wilde Thyme and the gadding Vine o'regrown,
> And all their echoes mourn.

We go on to the fifth type of **"Lycidas,"** the archetypal version, which entered the critical ken after the vogue of the writings in comparative anthropology of James G. Frazer and in analytical psychology of C. G. Jung. This mode of criticism, like the last, begins by isolating images or patterns of imagery; now, however, the focus is on images which reflect the agents and events of myth or folklore. The favorite legends are those which (according to some folklorists) concern beings who were once nature deities—the dead and risen gods of Syria, Egypt, and Greece associated with the dying or reaping of the crops in the fall and their revival in the spring.

Richard P. Adams, investigating "The Archetypal Pattern of Death and Rebirth in **"Lycidas,"** discovers that the poem is throughout "a remarkably tight amalgam of death-and-rebirth imagery." These images begin with the initial reference to the evergreen plants, the laurel, myrtle, and ivy, and continue through the allusions to the hyacinth, the rose, and the violet, which had their mythical genesis in the blood of a mortal or deity. The many water-images are here interpreted as fertility symbols; the allusion to the death of Orpheus is said to bring in a myth whose similarities to "the deaths of Adonis, Attis, Osiris, and other fertility demigods have been pointed out by modern scholars"; while the poet's speculation that the body of Lycidas perhaps visits "the bottom of the monstrous world" parallels the descent into water and the dragon fight "which is often a feature of death-and-rebirth cycles."

Adams is content with a fairly traditional interpretation of the subject of **"Lycidas"**: Milton's concern was not with Edward King, but "with the life, death, and resurrection of the dedicated poet, and specifically with his own situation at the time." Northrop Frye, however, in his essay on "Literature as Context: Milton's **"Lycidas,"** contends that the "structural principle" of the poem, the formal cause which "assimilates all details in the realizing of its unity," is "the Adonis myth," and that "Lycidas is, poetically speaking, a god or spirit of nature, who eventually becomes a saint in heaven." The archetypal reading here provides us with a new principle of unity, a new distinction between ostensible and implicit meaning, and a new version of what the poem is really rather than nominally about. In an earlier essay, Frye put the matter bluntly: "Poetry demands, as Milton saw it, that the elements of his theme should be assimilated to their archetypes. . . . Hence the poem will not be about King, but about his archetype, Adonis, the dying and rising god, called Lycidas in Milton's poem."

It will not do to say, as one is tempted to say, that these five versions of **"Lycidas"** really give us the same poem, in diversely selected aspects and details. The versions differ not in selection or emphasis, but in essentials. Each strikes for the heart of the poem; each claims to have discovered the key element, or structural principle, which has controlled the choice, order, and interrelations of the parts, and which establishes for the reader the meaning, unity, and value of the whole. Nor will it help put Humpty Dumpty together again to carry out the proposal we sometimes hear, to combine all these critical modes into a single criticism which has the virtues of each and the deficiency ofnone. To provide a coherent reading, a critical procedure must itself be coherent; it cannot be divided against itself in its first principles. A syncretic criticism is invertebrate, and will yield not an integral poem, but a ragout.

When there is such radical and many-sided disagreement about the real but nonliteral and esoteric meaning of the poem, the best hope of remedy, I think, lies in going back to Milton's text and reading it with a dogged literalness, except when there is clear evidence that some part of it is to be read allegorically or symbolically. This is what I propose, very briefly, to attempt. In a way, this puts me in a favorable position. A drawback in writing as a new critic is that it would be embarrassing to come out with an old reading; while I can plead that I have deliberately set out to labor the obvious, and can take comfort from the number of earlier critiques with which I find myself in agreement.

Looked at in this way, **"Lycidas"** turns out to be in some sense—although in some cases a very loose sense—about Edward King, about Milton, about water, about the problem of being a poet in an inimical world; and it is undoubtedly about at least one God (Christ) who died to be reborn. But it is about none of these in the central way that it is about certain other things that, to the literal-minded reader, constitute the essential poem Milton chose to write.

First, it is about—in the sense that it presents as the poetic datum, Milton's elected fiction—a nameless shepherd, sitting from morn to evening in a rural setting and hymning the death of a fellow poet-pastor, who is not Edward King but, specifically, Lycidas. The reason all our interpreters except Ransom treat the stated elegist rather casually, if at all, is that they tend to take as premise that a poem is an object made of words, or "a structure of meanings." So indeed it is. But as a starting point for criticism, it would be more inclusive and suggestive to say that a poem is made of *speech,* because the term "speech" entails a particular speaker. In **"Lycidas"** the speaker is an unnamed rustic singer whose speech refers to a state of affairs, describes the appearance and quotes the statements of other speakers, including Phoebus, Camus, and St. Peter, expresses his own thoughts and changing mood, and conveys, by immediate implication, something of his own character. The poem is therefore clearly a dramatic lyric, with a setting, an occasion, a chief character, and several subordinate characters (who may, however, be regarded as representing the speaker's own thoughts, objectified for dramatic purposes as standard personae of the pastoral ritual).

Tillyard is surely right, as against Ransom (and earlier, Dr. Johnson), in finding deep feeling in the poem, but he confronts us with the spurious alternative that the feeling must be either about King or about Milton himself. The feeling is occasioned by the death of Lycidas and the thoughts plausibly evoked by that event; and it is experienced and expressed not by Milton, but by a singer Milton is at considerable pains to identify as someone other than himself. Precisely what Milton himself thought and felt during the many hours—probably days—in which he labored over **"Lycidas,"** despite Tillyard's assurance, is beyond all but the most tenuous conjecture; although it is safe to say that, among other things, he was thinking how he might put together the best possible pastoral elegy. But we know precisely what the uncouth swain thought and felt, because the expression of his thoughts and feelings constitutes the poem, from the bold opening, "Yet once more, O ye Laurels . . . ," up to, but not including, the closing eight lines, when the author takes over as omniscient narrator: "*Thus* sang the uncouth Swain. . . ."

Readers of the poem at its first appearance knew that it was one of thirteen *Obsequies to the Memorie of Mr. Edward King,* and undoubtedly some also knew that the J.M. who signed the last obsequy was John Milton, whose circumstances and relations to King bore some resemblance to those presented in the poem. Such knowledge, however, does not displace but adds a particular historical reference to the two chief persons of the literal poem. **"Lycidas"** is not simply "about" King; it is a public ceremonial on the occasion of King's death, and the decorum of such a performance requires that the individual be not only lamented but also honored. And how could King be honored more greatly than to be made an instance of the type of poet-priest, identified by the traditional name "Lycidas," and to be lamented by a typical pastoral singer—in Ransom's phrase, a "qualified spokesman" for the public performance of a ritual elegy—whose single voice is resonant with echoes of poets through the ages mourning other poets untimely cut off? My insistence here may seem to be much ado about trivia, and, provided we are ready to fill out the details when pertinent, it can be a harmless critical shorthand to say that it is Milton who sings a lament for Edward King. But entirely to disregard these elementary circumstances may be the beginning of critical arrogance, which can end in our substituting our own poem for the one Milton chose to write.

The pastoral singer sets out, then, both to lament and to celebrate Lycidas. But consideration of this particular death raises in his mind a general question about the pointless contingencies of life, with its constant threat that fate may slit the thin-spun thread of any dedicated mortal prior to fulfillment and so render profitless his self-denial. This doubt, it should be noted, is not an ulterior "theme" beneath the ostensible surface of the poem. It is, explicitly, a topic in the thought of the lyric speaker, a stage in his soliloquy, which the speaker's continued meditation, guided by the comments of other imagined characters, goes on to

resolve. This turn away from Lycidas to the circumstance of those who have survived him is not insincere, nor does it constitute a digression or an indecorously personal intrusion. It is entirely natural and appropriate; just as (to borrow a parallel from J. M. French) it is altogether fitting and proper for Lincoln, in the course of the *Gettysburg Address,* to turn from "these honored dead" to concern for "us the living." After all, the doubts and fears of the lyric speaker concern the insecurity of his own life only in so far as he, like Lycidas, is a member of the genus Poet, and concern the class of poets only in so far as they share the universal human condition.

While initially, then, we may say that the presented subject of **"Lycidas"** is a pastoral singer memorializing the death of a dedicated shepherd poet-and-priest, we must go on to say that—in a second and important sense of "subject" as the dynamic center, or controlling principle, of a poem—its subject is a question about the seeming profitlessness of the dedicated life and the seeming deficiency of divine justice raised by that shocking death in the mind of the lyric speaker. That the rise, evolution, and resolution of the troubled thought of the elegist is the key to the structure of **"Lycidas,"** Milton made as emphatic as he could. He forced it on our attention by the startling device of ending the elegy, in a passage set off as a stanza in ottava rima, not with Lycidas, but with the elegist himself as, reassured, he faces his own destiny with confidence. But there is no occasion for Lycidas to feel slighted by this dereliction, for has he not been left in heaven, entertained and comforted by a chorus of saints, and given an office equivalent to St. Michael's, as guardian of the western shore?

If this, in barest outline, is the subject and the structural principle of the poem, what are we to make of the thematic imagery which, in the alternative interpretation by Brooks and Hardy, motivate andcontrol its development?

"Lycidas" indeed, as these critics point out, incorporates many water and sheep-and-shepherd images; it also has song-and-singer images, flower images, stellar images, wide-ranging geographical images, even a surprising number of eye, ear, and mouth images. The usual strategy of the imagist critic is to pull out a selection of such items and to set them up in an order which is largely independent of who utters them, on what occasion, and for what dramatic purpose. Freed from the controls imposed by their specific verbal and dramatic contexts, the selected images readily send out shoots and tendrils of significance, which can be twined into a symbolic pattern—and if the critic is sensitive, learned, and adroit, often a very interesting pattern. The danger is, that the pattern may be largely an artifact of the implicit scheme governing the critical analysis.

From our elected point of view, the images in **"Lycidas"** constitute elements in the speech—some of it literal and some figurative, allegoric, or symbolic—which serve primarily to express the perceptions, thoughts, and feelings of the lyric speaker. These images constitute for the reader a sensuous texture, and they set up among themselves, as

Brooks and Hardy point out, various ambiguities, contrasts, and harmonies. But in **"Lycidas,"** the procession of images is less determining than determined. If they steer the meditation of the speaker, it is only in so far as they cooperate in doing so with more authoritative principles: with the inherited formulas of the elegiac ritual, and with these formulas as they in turn (in Milton's inventive use of pastoral conventions) are subtly subordinated to the evolving meditation of the lyric speaker himself. In effect, then, the imagery does not displace, but corroborates the process of feelingful thought in the mind of a specified character. This, it seems to me, is the way Milton wrote "Lycidas"; there is no valid evidence, in or out of the poem, that he constructed it—as T. S. Eliot might have done—out of a set of ownerless symbols which he endowed with an implicit dynamism and set to acting out a thematic plot.

For the mythic and archetypal interpretation of **"Lycidas,"** as it happens, there is a more plausible basis in Milton's ideas and characteristic procedures. As a Christian humanist of the Renaissance, Milton was eager to save the phenomena of classical culture, and thus shared with the modern archetypist an interest in synthesizing the ancient and modern, the primitive and civilized, pagan fable and Christian dogma, into an all-encompassing whole. And Milton knew, from divers ancient and Renaissance mythographers, about the parallel to the death and resurrection of Christ in ancient fables and fertility cults—about what in *Paradise Lost* he called the "reviv'd Adonis," and the "annual wound" of Thammuz, identified with Adonis by the Syrian damsels who lamented his fate "in amorous ditties all a Summer's day." But these facts are not adequate to validate a reading of **"Lycidas"** as a poem which is really about Adonis, or any other pagan fertility god. In **"Lycidas"** Milton makes no allusion whatever to Adonis, and he refers to Orpheus only to voice despair that even the Muse his mother was helpless to prevent his hideous death. In his references to these fables in *Paradise Lost*, Milton specifies that the story of the Garden of revived Adonis is "feign'd," lists Thammuz-Adonis among the "Devils [adored] for Deities," and describes the mother of Orpheus as "an empty dream." For though a humanist, Milton is a Christian humanist, to whom revelation is not one more echo of archetypal myths but the archetype itself, the one Truth, which had been either corrupted or distortedly foreshadowed, "prefigured," in various pagan deities and fables. There is a world of difference between Milton's assumption that there is only one religion and Blake's archetypal assertion that "All Religions are One."

By conflating Christian and non-Christian story into equivalent variations on a single rebirth pattern, the tendency of an archetypal reading is to cancel dramatic structure by flattening the poem out, or even—in the extreme but common view that we get closer to the archetype as we move back along the scale toward the vegetational cycle itself—by turning the poem inside out. For if we regard the rebirth theme as having been revealed in the opening passage on the unwithering laurel, myrtle, and ivy, and as merely reiterated in later passages on Orpheus, on water,

on sanguine flowers, and in the allusion to Christ and the risen Lycidas, then the denouement of the poem lies in its exordium and its movement is not a progress but an eddy.

The movement of **"Lycidas,"** on the contrary, is patently from despair through a series of insights to triumphant joy. We can put it this way: read literally, the elegy proper opens with the statement "Lycidas is dead, dead ere his prime"; it concludes with the flatly opposing statement "Lycidas your sorrow is *not* dead." Everything that intervenes has been planned to constitute a plausible sequence of thoughts and insights that will finally convert a logical contradiction into a lyric reversal by the anagnorisis, the discovery, that for a worthy Christian poet-priest a seeming defeat by death is actually an immortal triumph.

Milton achieves this reversal by a gradual shift from the natural, pastoral, and pagan viewpoint to the viewpoint of Christian revelation and its promise of another world, the Kingdom of Heaven. He carefully marks for us the stages of this ascent by what, to contemporary readers, was the conspicuous device of grading the levels of his style. For as Milton said in the treatise *Of Education*, issued seven years after **"Lycidas,"** decorum (including "the fitted stile of lofty, mean, or lowly" to the height of the matter) "is the grand master peece to observe." The problem of stylistic decorum had been particularly debated in connection with the pastoral, which had troubled Renaissance theorists by the duplicity of its stylistic requirements, since it typically dealt with high matters under the lowly guise of a conversation between two uncouth swains. Milton's comment on the fitted style probably was an echo of Puttenham's statement that "decencie," or "decorum"—the just proportioning of the "high, meane, and base stile"—is "the chiefe praise of any writer"; and Puttenham had also pointed out that, though the normal level of pastoral was the "base and humble stile," the form was often used "under the vaile of homely persons and in rude speeches to insinuate and glaunce at greater matters."

Accordingly Milton's singer opens the poem with a style higher than the pastoral norm: "Begin, and somewhat loudly sweep the string" is what he bids the muses, echoing the *"Sicelides Musae, paulo maiora canamus"* with which Virgil had elevated the pitch of his Fourth, or "Messianic," Eclogue. (Puttenham had remarked concerning this pastoral that, because of its lofty subject, "Virgill used a somewhat swelling stile" and that under the circumstances, "this was decent.") The initial level of **"Lycidas"** suffices for the early pastoral and pagan sections on sympathizing nature, the nymphs, and the death of Orpheus. But this last reference evokes the despairing thought: what boots the ascetic life for those who, like Lycidas, stake everything on a treacherous future? The immediate comfort is vouchsafed the singer in a thought in which the highest pagan ethics comes closest to the Christian: the distinction between mere earthly reputation and the meed of true fame awarded by a divine and infallible judge. The concept is only tangentially Christian, however, for the deities named in this passage, Phoebus and Jove, are pagan ones. Nevertheless "that strain," the singer observes, "was of a higher mood," and he therefore readdresses himself to Arethuse and Mincius, waters associated with the classical pastoralists, as a transition back to the initial key: "But now my *Oat* proceeds. . . ."

The next modulation comes when St. Peter raises by implication the even more searching question why a faithful shepherd is taken early, while the corrupt ones prosper. He himself gives the obscurely terrifying answer: the two-handed engine stands ready to smite at the door; infallible justice dispenses punishment as well as rewards. This time the "dread voice" has been not merely of "a higher mood," but of an entirely different ontological and stylistic order, for it has "shrunk" the pastoral stream and frightened away the "Sicilian Muse" altogether. It is not only that the voice has been raised in the harsh rhetoric of anger, but that it belongs to a pastor, and expresses a matter, alien to the world of pagan pastoral. A Christian subject is here for the first time explicit. The appearance and speech of Peter, although brought in, as Milton said in his subtitle, "by occasion," is far from a digression. It turns out, indeed, to be nothing less than the climax and turning point of the lyric meditation, for without it the resolution, inadequately grounded, would seem to have been contrived through Christ as a patent *Deus ex machina*. The speech of Peter has in fact closely paraphrased Christ's own pastoral parable (John 9:39-41; 10:1-18), addressed to the Pharisees, in which He too had denounced those who remain blind to the truth, who climb into the sheepfold, and who abandon their sheep to the marauding wolf, and had then identified Himself as the Good Shepherd who lays down His life for His sheep—but only, He adds, "that I might take it again." Once Christ, the shepherd who died to be born again, is paralleled to the dead shepherd Lycidas, though by allusion only, the resolution of the elegy is assured—especially since Peter, the Pilot of the Galilean Lake, is the very Apostle who had been taught by Christ, through faith and force of example, to walk on the water in which he would otherwise have drowned (Matthew 14:25-31). The elegiac singer, however, is momentarily occupied with the specific references rather than the Scriptural overtones of Peter's comment, with the result that the resolution, so skillfully planted in his evolving thought, is delayed until he has tried to interpose a little case by strewing imaginary flowers on Lycidas' imagined hearse. But this evasion only brings home the horror of the actual condition of the lost and weltering corpse. By extraordinary dramatic management, it is at this point of profoundest depression that the thought of Lycidas' body sinking to "the bottom of the monstrous world" releases the full implication of St. Peter's speech, and we make the leap from nature to revelation, in the great lyric peripety:

> Weep no more, woful Shepherds weep no more,
> For *Lycidas* your sorrow is not dead,
> Sunk though he be beneath the watry floor . . .
> So *Lycidas,* sunk low, but mounted high,
> Through the dear might of him that walk'd the
> 　　waves. . . .

This consolation is total, where the two earlier ones were partial. For one thing, we now move from the strict judg-

ment of merit and demerit to the God who rewards us beyond the requirements of justice by the free gift of a life eternal. Also, the elegist has had the earlier promises of reward and retribution by hearsay from Apollo and Peter, but now, in a passage thronged with echoes from the Book of Revelation and soaring, accordingly, into an assured sublimity of style, he has his own imaginative revelation, so that he, like St. John in that Book, might say: "And I saw a new heaven and a new earth." His vision is of Lycidas having lost his life to find a better life in a felicity without tears; in which even that last infirmity of noble mind, the desire for fame, has been purged "in the blest Kingdoms meek of joy and love," the earthly inclination to Amaryllis and Neaera has been sublimated into the "unexpressive nuptial Song" of the marriage of the Lamb, and the pastoral properties of grove, stream, and song serve only to shadow forth a Kingdom outside of space and beyond the vicissitude of the seasons. But the meditation of the lyric singer, as I have said, is ultimately concerned with the dead as they affect the living; so, by way of the Genius of the shore, we redescend to the stylistic level of plain utterance and conclude with the solitary piper at evening, facing with restored confidence the contingencies of a world in which the set and rise of the material sun are only the emblematic promise of another life.

We are all aware by now of a considerable irony: I undertook to resolve the five types of **"Lycidas"** into one, and instead have added a sixth. But of course, that is all a critic can do. A critique does not give us the poem, but only a description of the poem. Whatever the ontological status of **"Lycidas"** as an object-in-itself, there are many possible descriptions of **"Lycidas"**—as many, in fact, as there are diverse critical premises and procedures which can be applied to the text.

In the bewildering proliferation of assumptions and procedures that characterizes the present age, we need a safeguard against confusion, and a safeguard as well against the sceptical temptation to throw all criticism overboard as a waste of time. I would suggest that we regard any critique of a poem as a persuasive description; that is, as an attempt, under the guise of statements of fact, to persuade the reader to look at a poem in a particular way. Thus when a critic says, with assurance, "A poem means *X*," consider him to say: "Try reading it as though it meant *X*." When he says, **"Lycidas"** is really about Milton himself," quietly translate: "I recommend that you entertain the hypothesis that **"Lycidas"** is about Milton, and see how it applies." From this point of view, the best interpretation of **"Lycidas"**—we can say, if we like to use that philosophical idiom, the reading which approximates most closely to *Lycidas* as an object-in-itself— is the one among the interpretations at present available which provides the best fit to all the parts of the poem in their actual order, emphases, and emotional effects, and which is in addition consistent with itself and with what we know of Milton's literary and intellectual inheritance and his characteristic poetic procedures.

The persuasive description of **"Lycidas"** which I have sketched must be judged by the degree to which it satisfies these criteria of correspondence and coherence. To be sure it has a serious handicap, when measured against the startling discoveries in recent years of what **"Lycidas"** is really about. It is singularly unexciting to be told at this date that **"Lycidas"** is really what it seems—a dramatic presentation of a traditional pastoral singer uttering a ritual lament and raising in its course questions about untimely death and God's providence which are resolved by the recognition that God's Kingdom is not of this world. But surely this is the great commonplace in terms of which Milton, as a thoroughly Christian poet, inevitably thought. We cannot expect his innovations, on this crucial issue, to be doctrinal; the novelty (and it is entirely sufficient to make this an immense feat of lyric invention) consists in the way that the pastoral conventions and Christian concepts are newly realized, reconciled, and dramatized in the minute particulars of this unique and splendid poem.

I would not be understood to claim that the alternative readings of **"Lycidas"** I have described are illegitimate, or their discoveries unrewarding. They freshen our sense of old and familiar poems, and they force readers into novel points of vantage that yield interesting insights, of which some hold good for other critical viewpoints as well. I am as susceptible as most readers to the charm of suddenly being brought to see a solidly dramatic lyric flattened into an ornate texture of thematic images, or to the thrill of the archetypal revelation whereby, as Jane Harrison described it, behind the "bright splendors" of "great things in literature" one sees moving "darker and older shapes." But in our fascination with the ultra-violet and infra-red discoveries made possible by modern speculative instruments, we must take care not to overlook the middle of the poetic spectrum. The necessary, though not sufficient condition for a competent reader of poetry remains what it has always been—a keen eye for the obvious.

Stanley Fish   (essay date 1975)

SOURCE: "What It's Like to Read 'L'Allegro' and 'Il Penseroso,'" *Milton Studies,* Vol. VII, 1975, pp. 77-98.

[*In the following essay, Fish offers a performative reading of "L'Allegro" and "Il Penseroso."*]

I have only one point to make and everything else follows from it: **"L'Allegro"** is easier to read than **"Il Penseroso."** This I assume is hardly news, but if one were a subscriber to the *Times Literary Supplement* in 1934, the matter might seem to be shrouded in considerable doubt, for on October 18 of that year J. P. Curgenven initiated a remarkable correspondence by asking and answering the question, "Who comes to the window in **"L'Allegro,"** line 46?" Curgenven is disturbed by those who construe "come" as dependent on "hear," which thus, he says, "gives the crude rendering: 'to hear the lark . . . to come, in spite of sorrow, and at my window bid good morrow!'" "Surely," he exclaims, "'come' is dependent on 'admit' and parallel to 'live' and 'hear,' and thus it is **"L'Allegro"**

who comes to his own window and bids good morrow". Curgenven attributes the alternative mistaken reading to two causes: "the expectation of finding inaccuracies in Milton's descriptions of natural phenomena" and the presence in earlier poetry of "some striking references to birds singing their good morrows" and among these, some larks. He duly cites these references, admitting in passing that Milton had no doubt read the poems in question. It is only the first of many curiosities in this exchange that Curgenven spends so much time marshaling evidence in support of the position he opposes.

One week later (October 25) the question is taken up again by T. Sturge Moore, who finds Curgenven's reading "unnatural." "Yet," he goes on, "I agree . . . that to make the lark come is absurd." Moore, it seems, has another candidate. "Surely [a word that appears often in this correspondence, but with a diminishing force], it is *Mirth* [who] is begged to come to the window. The poet has asked to be admitted of her crew . . . and runs on to enumerate advantages he hopes to gain . . . breaking off he resumes his petition: *Then,* as lark and sun rise, is the moment for the Goddess to come and bid him good morrow." A third week (November 1) finds Professor Grierson joining the fray to argue for the one reading that both Moore and Curgenven dismiss out of hand. It *is* the lark who comes, not in nature, but in the mind of the speaker who might well think, in spiteof the natural error, that he was being wakened by the bird. A poet, Grierson reminds us, "is not a scientist, . . . he tells truth in his own way." On November 8, B. A. Wright becomes the first of several fence straddlers. He agrees with Curgenven that the syntax and the pronunciation of lines 39-48 are "perfectly clear" (a statement belied by the existence of his letter) and that the poet is himself the subject of the infinitive "come" as he is of the infinitives "live" and "hear." Noting, however, that Mr. Moore understands Mirth to be the subject of "come," Wright admits that this makes good sense and is grammatically typical of Milton. "Either of these interpretations," he concludes, "seems to me possible," although he "cannot with Professor Grierson imagine Milton imagining the lark first 'at his watch towre in the skies' and then still singing at his own bedroom window." (Notice that this assumes what is by no means certain, that it is the lark, not "dull night," who is "startled.") Grierson for his part continues to defend the lark (on November 15) but concedes that "if we are to judge by strict grammar then the most defensible meaning is that it is the cheerful man who comes to the window". "If I am in error," he continues, "I should prefer to take 'Then to come' as a boldly elliptical construction which leaves it quite indefinite who it is that comes." This retreat of course is more strategical than sincere, but it points toward the only conclusion the exchange will finally allow.

In the weeks that follow, old positions are restated and new ones put forward. Tillyard appears (November 15) to support Wright and the cheerful man by alluding, as he often did, to the *First Prolusion.* Joan Sargeaunt offers to remind us "of Bishop Copleston's sly dig at the literal seriousness of critics," presumably (although I am not sure) *she* intends some sly dig at the length and heat of the present correspondence and agrees with Grierson when he declares, "It is vain to argue these questions." Wright, however, will have none of that. It is a matter, he insists, of "Milton's poetic honour. Professor Grierson would seem to imply that any reader is entitled to his own interpretation of the lines," but no one, Wright thunders, is entitled to an interpretation which "makes Milton talk nonsense." Grierson's reading of the lines, he continues, is possible only "when they are isolated from their context." Grierson rather wearily replies "I am afraid Mr. Wright is growing indignant with me which is a sign I should stop." He goes on long enough, however, to insist that "there remain some difficulties" (an understatement, I think) and to declare that where there is doubt, "surely [that word again] one may allow some freedom of interpretation." And indeed the limits of freedom had already been extended by B. R. Rowbottom, who on November 22 had proposed still another interpretation. "Neither 'Mirth' nor 'The Lark' nor 'The Cheerful Man' is 'then' to come and bid good-morrow at the window through the Sweet-Briar, or the Vine, or the twisted Eglantine, in spite of sorrow, but the 'Dawn' . . . while the Cock scatters the rear of darkness thin.'

The controversy ends on November 29 with a letter from W. A. Jones, The County School, Cardiganshire, who reports that his classes of school children "invariably and without noticing any difficulty understand the lines." Whether or not the editors took this as a comment on the entire affair is a matter of conjecture, but at any rate they append a footnote to Jones' letter: "We cannot continue this correspondence."

The point, of course, is that this correspondence could have been continued indefinitely, but even in its abbreviated form, it allows us to make some observations.

1. The proponent of each reading makes concessions, usually by acknowledging that there *is* evidence for the readings he opposes.

2. Each critic is able to point to details which do in fact support his position.

3. But in order fully to support his respective position every one of the critics is moved to make *sense* of the lines by supplying connections more firm and delimiting than the connections available in the text.

4. This making of sense always involves an attempt to arrange the images and events of the passage into a sequence of logical action.

Thus V. B. Halpert, a latecomer to the controversy in 1963, argues for the lark on the basis of the temporal adverb "then," which, she says, signals a break from the simple infinitive construction of "to live" and "to hear" and therefore indicates the beginning of a new action with a new agent—the lark, who "after startling the dull night will then leave its watch tower and come to the poet's window." "In other words," Halpert concludes, "the word *then* signifies a sequence of events." Perhaps so, but it is

a sequence which Edith Riggs, who is also committed to making the lines "make perfect sense," finds "unhappy" and "dangerously close to *non*-sense." She proposes a new sequence, one that puts "night" rather than the lark in the watchtower: "The lark, the first of day's forces, startles the enemy from his watch tower in the sky . . . Night is routed and forced to flee." Whether or not the routed night also stops at the poet's window to bid him good-morrow, Miss Riggs does not say (although nothing I can think of would debar her from saying it); she simply concludes on a note of triumph I find impossible to share: "The new reading thus rids the poem of a jarring image and replaces it by one . . . more meaningful within the total context of the passage."

What are we to make of all this? I find myself at least partly in Grierson's camp, and finally in the camp of Jones' children; for if the entire exchange proves anything, it is that Milton does not wish to bind us to any one of these interpretations. I do not mean (as Grierson seems to) that he left us free to choose whatever interpretation we might prefer, but that he left us free *not* to choose, or more simply, that he left us free. As Brooks and Hardy observe, the reader of these lines "is hurried through a series of infinitives . . . the last of which is completely ambiguous in its subject." I would only add that the ambiguity is *so* complete that unless someone asks us to, we do not worry about it, and we do not worry about it (or even notice it) because while no subject is specified for "come," any number of subjects—lark, poet, Mirth, Dawn, Night—are available. What is *not* available is the connecting word or sustained syntactical unit which would pressure us to decide between them, and in the absence of that pressure, we are not obliged to decide. Nor are we obliged to decide between the different (and plausible) sequences which choosing any one of these subjects would generate:

1. If it is the lark who comes to the window, he does so while the cock "with lively din" scatters the rear of darkness thin, and the two birds thus perform complementary actions.

2. If it is the dawn that comes to the window, she does so while the cock with lively din scatters the rear of darkness thin and is thus faithful to our understanding of the relationship between cock's crowing and dawn.

3. If it is the poet (L'Allegro) who comes to the window, he does so in response to lark, cock, and dawn; that is, while they are performing their related functions.

4. And if it is Mirth who comes to the window, the action allies her with lark, cock, and dawn in the awakening of L'Allegro.

All of these readings hang on the word "while" in line 49, but since "while" is less time-specific than other temporal adverbs, it does not firmly call for any one of these and, more to the point, it functions equally well, that is, equally *loosely,* in all of them. Rather than insisting on a clear temporal relationship among the events it connects, "while" acts as a fulcrum around which those events swirl, supplying just enough of a sense of order to allow us to continue, but not so much that we feel compelled to arrange the components of the passage into an intelligible sequence. In short, "while" neither directs nor requires choice; instead, it *frees* us from choice and allows us—and I mean this literally—to be careless. This is also the effect of the two "ors" in the preceding couplet: "Through the Sweet-Briar or the Vine, / Or the twisted Eglantine." The "ors" divide alternative images, each of which registers only for a split second before it is supplanted by the next. We are neither committed to any one of them, nor required to combine them into a single coherent picture. The effect of the couplet extends both backward—softening the outline of the window and of *who*ever or *what*ever has come to it—and forward—removing the pressure of specificity from the weakly transitional "while."

I intend the phrase "weakly transitional" precisely, for it exactly captures the balance Milton achieves by deploying his connectives. If there were no transitions, the freedom of the poem's experience would become a burden, since a reader would first notice it and then worry about it; and if the transitions were firmly directing, a reader would be obliged to follow the directions they gave. Milton has it both ways, just as he does with a syntax that is not so much ambiguous as it is loose. Twentieth-century criticism has taught us to value ambiguities because they are meaningful, but these ambiguities, if they can be called that, protect us from meaning by protecting us from working. They are there, not to be noticed, but to assure that whatever track a reader happens to come in on, he will have no trouble keeping to it; no choice that he makes (of lark, poet, Goddess, etc.) will conflict with a word or a phrase he meets later. Anything fits with anything else, so that it is never necessary to go back and retrace one's effortless steps.

Rosemond Tuve has written that the pleasures enumerated in **"L'Allegro"** all have "the flat absence of any relation to responsibility which we sometimes call innocence." What I am suggesting is that the experience of *reading* the poem is itself such a pleasure, involving just that absence; for at no point are we held responsible for an action or an image beyond the moment of its fleeting appearance in a line or a couplet. Moreover it is a *flat* absence in the sense that we are not even aware of having been relieved of it. That is why Cleanth Brooks is not quite right when he declares that the unreproved pleasures of **"L'Allegro"** "can be had for the asking"; they can be had *without* the asking.

The result is an experience very much like that described by William Strode in "Against Melancholy," a poem that has been suggested by J. B. Leishman as a possible source for **"L'Allegro"**:

> Free wandring thoughts not ty'de to muse
> Which thinke on all things, nothing choose,
> Which ere we see them come are gone.

"Take no care," Strode enjoins in line 18, but Milton goes him one better by *giving* no care, by not asking that we

put things together, or supply connections, or make inferences, or do anything at all. Rather than compelling attention, the verse operates to diffuse attention, either by blurring the focus of its descriptions—the Sweet-Briar *or* the Vine *or* the twisted Eglantine—or by breaking off a description if its focus threatens to become too sharp, or by providing so many possible and plausible sequences that it finally insists on none. As a result we move from linguistic event to linguistic event with almost no hostages from our previous experience and therefore with no obligation to relate what we are reading to what we have read.

Critics have always been aware of the curious discreteness that characterizes **"L'Allegro,"** both as an object and as an experience, but in general they have responded either by downgrading the poem, so capable, as D. C. Allen observes, of "desultory rearrangement," or by attempting to rescue it from the charge of disunity and fragmentation. In 1958 Robert Graves went so far as to suggest that in the course of composing **"L'Allegro"** Milton misplaced sixteen lines, probably over the weekend. The lines beginning "Oft listening" and ending with every shepherd telling his tale under the hawthorn in the dale originally followed the account of the Lubber fiend as "Crop full out of the door he flings, / Ere the first cock his matins rings." By restoring the original order, Graves asserts, we make the poem very much less of a "muddle" (that is, we make *sense* of it). Otherwise, he points out, we are left with this improbable sequence of events:

> While distractedly bidding good-morrow, at the window, to Mirth, with one ear cocked for the hounds and horn . . . [he] sometimes, we are told, "*goes walking, not unseen, by hedgerow elms, on Hillocks green.*" Either Milton had forgotten that he was still supposedly standing naked at the open window—(the Jacobeans always slept raw)—or the subject of "walking" is the cock, who escapes from the barnyard, deserts his dames, ceases to strut, and anxiously aware of the distant hunt, trudges far afield among ploughmen and shepherds in the dale. But why should Milton give twenty lines to the adventures of the neighbor's wandering cock? And why, "*walking not unseen*"? Not unseen by whom?

Graves is not unaware of the impression he is making. "Please do not think I am joking," he implores, and at least one critic has taken him seriously. Herbert F. West, Jr., admits that such an accident of misplacement is "possible" and that Graves' emendation "does little apparent danger to the text" and even seems to "smooth over some difficult spots." And so it does. The poet now looks out of his window to say, quite naturally, "Straight mine eye hath caught new pleasures," and it is the Lubber fiend who walks not unseen on hillocks green where he is espied, one assumes, by plowman, milkmaid, mower, and shepherd. The sequence ends as he listens to each shepherd tell his tale under the hawthorn in the dale, making for a perfect transition to the next section, which begins with line 115: "Thus done the Tales, to bed they creep." Yet Graves' emendation should, I think, be rejected and rejected precisely *because* of its advantages; for by providing continuity to the plot line of the poem, it gives us something to keep track of, and therefore it gives us *care*.

It is Milton's wish, however, to liberate us from care, and the nonsequiturs that bother Graves are meant to prevent us from searching after the kind of sense he wants to make. "Not unseen by whom?" he asks, and he might well have asked, why *not* unseen, a formula which neither relates the figure of the walker to other figures nor declares categorically the absence of such a relation, leaving the matter not so much ambiguous as unexamined. Or he might have asked (perhaps did ask) what precisely is the "it" that in line 77 "sees"? This question would only lead to another, for the pronoun subject is no more indeterminate than the object of "its" seeing—the beauty who is the cynosure of neighboring eyes. Is she there or is she not? "Perhaps," answers Milton in line 79, relieving us of any responsibility to her or even to her existence. This in turn removes the specificity from the adverbial of place which introduces the following line: "Hard by, a Cottage chimney smokes." Hard by what? Graves might well ask. In this context or noncontext the phrase has no pointing function at all. It merely gets us unburdened into the next line and into the next *discrete* scene, where with Corydon and Thyrsis we rest in "secure delight," that is, in delight *se cura,* delight without, or free from, care.

It is the promise of "secure delight," of course, that is at the heart of the pastoral vision, although it is the literary strength of the pastoral always to default on that promise by failing to exclude from its landscape the concerns of the real world. Milton, however, chooses to sacrifice that strength in order to secure the peculiar flatness of effect that makes reading **"L'Allegro"** so effortless. The details of this landscape are without resonance; they refer to nothing beyond themselves and they ask from us no response beyond the *minimal* and literary response of recognition. This lack of resonance is attributable in part to the swift succession of images, no one of which claims our attention for more than a couplet. Each couplet is self-enclosed by ringing monosyllabic rhymes, and the enclosures remain discrete. Continuity is provided by patterns of alliteration and assonance (mountains-meadows), which carry us along but do not move us to acts of association or reflection. The "new pleasures" which the eyes of both speaker and reader catch are new in the sense of novel, *continually* new, following one another but not firmly related to one another. From lawns to mountains to meadows and then to towers, the sequence is so arranged as to discourage us from extrapolating from it a composite scene, the details of which would then be interpretable. Neither time's winged chariot nor anything else is at the back of these shepherds, and the verse in no way compels us to translate them into figures for the young poet or the weary courtier or the faithful feeder of a Christian flock. In other words, we know and understand the quality of their untroubled (careless) joy because it is precisely reflected in the absence of any pressure on us to make more of their landscape than its surfaces present. (This introduces the interesting possibility that while **"L'Allegro"** is the easier of the two poems to read, it was the more difficult to write. In **"Il Penseroso"** Milton can exploit the traditions his verse invades; in **"L'Allegro"** he must simultaneously introduce them and denude them of their implications, employing a diction and vocabulary rich in complex associations without the slightest gesture in the direction of that complexity. In **"L'Allegro"** it is not so much what the images do, but what they do not do. The poem is a triumph of absence.)

There is then here, as elsewhere, a one-to-one correspondence between the pleasures celebrated in the poem and the pleasure of reading it, and this correspondence inheres in the careless freedom with which *any* activity, including the activity of reading, can be enjoyed. The tournaments of lines 119-24 belong in **"L'Allegro"** because the knights and barons bold who take part in them hazard nothing, not life or death or even honor. Their high triumphs are triumphs of style and involve a fidelity to forms which have no meaning beyond the moment of their execution. Like us they areengaged in an activity from which the consequences (hostages to time) have been carefully removed.

The activities of **"L'Allegro"** are consistently like this, without consequences as they are without antecedents. Only once is a consequence even threatened, when the Lydian airs are said to "pierce" the meeting soul— "Lap me in soft *Lydian* Airs, / Married to immortal verse, / Such as the meeting soul may pierce"; but the first two words of the following line, "In notes," blunt the potential thrust of "pierce" exactly as the lances and swords of the knights and barons bold are blunted and rendered harmless. It has been suggested that Milton's conception of Lydian music is taken from Cassiodorus, who attributes to it the power to restore us with relaxation and delight, "being invented against excessive cares and worries." Whether or not this is Milton's source, it is surely a description of the effect his music, *his* invention, has on us. We are delighted because we are relaxed, and we are relaxed because the cares to which other poems bind us—the care of attending to implications, the care of carrying into one line or couplet the syntax and sense of previous lines and couplets, the care of arranging and ordering the details of a poetic landscape, the care of rendering judgments and drawing conclusions, the care, in sum, of sustained (and consecutive) thought—these are here not present. The figure of Orpheus as he appears in lines 145-50 is thus a perfect surrogate for the reader; the music he hears calls him to nothing, as we have been called to nothing by the verse. He is enwrapped in its harmonies, resting on "heapt Elysian flow'rs" as we rest, unexercised, on the heaped (not arranged) flowers of the poem's images and scenes, insulated from the resonances and complications which might be activated in another context (the context, in fact, of **"Il Penseroso"**). This music *merely* meets the ear and the ear it meets has no answering responsibility (of which there is the "flat absence") beyond the passive responsibility of involuntary delight. When Graves discovered that **"L'Allegro"** was "rather a muddle," it was after many years of reading the poem. I had however, he explains, never before "read it carefully." The point that I have been making is that no one asked him to, and that his period of *mis*reading began when he decided to accord the poem the kind of careful attention from which it was Milton's gift to set us free.

If I am right about **"L'Allegro,"** the other critics who have written on it are necessarily wrong; for to a man they have sought to interpret the poem, while it is my contention that interpretation is precisely what it does not invite, because its parts are arranged in such a way as to exert no interpretive pressures. Of course it would be easy to turn this argument into a criticism by saying that what I have demonstrated here is that **"L'Allegro"** lacks unity. This would certainly be true if unity were defined (narrowly) as the coherence of formal elements, but it is the absence of that coherence which is responsible for the unity I have been describing, a unity not of form, but of experience. That is to say, what unifies **"L'Allegro"** is the consistency of the demands it makes, or rather declines to make, on the reader, who is thus permitted the freedom from care ("secure delight") which is the poem's subject. It is this freedom which is banished when **"Il Penseroso"** opens by declaring "Hence vain deluding joys." "Vain" here is to be taken as fruitless or without purpose, and it refers not to an abstraction, but to a mode of experiencing, a mode in which the brain is quite literally "idle" because it is "possessed" by a succession of "gaudy shapes" and fancies "which ere we see them come are gone." This is of course the experiential mode of **"L'Allegro,"** and it should not surprise us to find that the experience of reading **"Il Penseroso"** is quite different.

Like **"L'Allegro,"** **"Il Penseroso"** offers alternative genealogies in its opening lines; but where in the first poem these are indifferently presented, in the second, one is specifically preferred to theother; and the fact of the preference is rooted in a judgment we are required to understand and in a distinction (or series of distinctions) we are pressured to make. That pressure is felt as soon as we hear, "Hail divinest Melancholy, / Whose Saintly visage is too bright / To hit the sense of human sight." These lines turn on a paradox, and it is in the nature of a paradox that a reader who recognizes it is already responding to the question it poses. What kind of light is so bright that it dazzles and, in effect, darkens the sense of human sight? An answer to this question is readily available in the Christian-neo-Platonic opposition between the light of ordinary day and the "Celestial light" which "shines inward" revealing "things invisible to mortal sight." There is no more familiar commonplace in Renaissance thought, but even so, in order to recall it, a reader must reach for it; that is, he must *do* something, engage in an activity, and it is an activity in which he is asked to continue as the passage unfolds:

> And therefore to our weaker view,
> O'erlaid with black staid Wisdom's hue.
> Black, but such as in esteem,
> Prince *Memnon's* sister might beseem,
> Or that Starr'd *Ethiop* Queen that strove
> To set her beauties praise above
> The Sea Nymphs, and their powers offended.
> Yet thou art higher far descended.

The single word "therefore" in line 15 can stand for everything that distinguishes the companion poems. It is a word that could never appear in **"L'Allegro"** because it oper-

ates to *enjoin* the responsibility (to backward and forward contexts) from which that poem sets us free. The lines that follow "therefore" add to the responsibility, for in the course of reading them we are asked to do several things at once. First we must suspend one line of argument and attend to another, but that argument in turn unfolds in stages, so that we are continually revising our understanding of what we have just read; and, moreover, the effect of our revised understanding extends in every instance backward to the Goddess Melancholy, whose precise characterization remains the goal of our consecutive attention. Obviously, that attention is not only consecutive, but strenuous. A phrase like "Black, but" asks us simultaneously to recall the pejorative associations of black and to prepare ourselves for a more positive view of the color; but no sooner has that view been established than it too is challenged, first by the imputation to Cassiopeia of impiety and then (more directly) by the qualificatory "Yet" of line 22. In this context (the context not of the verse, but of our *experience* of the verse), there are at least three possible readings of that line: (1) the obvious literal reading: "Your lineage is more impressive than that of Memnon's sister or Cassiopeia." (2) The secondary literal reading: "You come to us from a loftier height than does Memnon's sister or Cassiopeia, that is, from the stars." (3) What we might call the moral reading: "You are higher precisely because you have descended, because you have been willing to accommodate yourself to our 'weaker view' by being black and low rather than bright and high ('starry')."

In **"L'Allegro,"** the availability of alternative readings operates to minimize our responsibility to any one of them and therefore to any consecutive argument; here it is precisely because we have been following a consecutive argument that the alternative readings become available. In neither poem are we required to choose between the readings; but whereas in one the absence of choice is a function of the absence of interpretive pressure, in the other that pressure is so great that we are asked to choose every reading, because each of them goes with one of the interpretive strains we have been led to pursue and distinguish.

Here then is a way of answering the questions that have so often been put to these two poems. Do they share patterns of imagery, or is the presence in them of light and shadow consistently and meaningfully opposed? Are they to be read as the hyperbolic rhetoric of their invocations suggests, or are those invocations directed at the excess of the complementary means they present? Is there mirth in **"Il Penseroso"**'s melancholy and melancholy in **"L'Allegro"**'s mirth? So long as these (and other) questions have been asked in the context of an examination of the text, there has been no hope of answering them, for as the history of the criticism shows, the observable evidence will support any number of answers. But if we turn our attention from the text to the experience it gives, an unambiguous and verifiable answer is immediately forthcoming. Every point of contact is a point of contrast, not in the poems (where the details could be made to point in either direction), but in the nature of the activities they require of their readers. The activities required of us by **"Il Penseroso"** are consistently strenuous. Rather than permitting us to move from one discrete unit to another, the verse of the second poem continually insists that we carry into the present context whatever insights we have won from previous contexts, which are in turn altered or expanded retroactively. As a result our attention is not diffused but concentrated, and the distinction made in the opening lines—between an idle brain captive to a succession of unrelated images and a mind that is "fixed"—is precisely realized in the reading experiences of the two poems.

A fixed mind is one that keeps steadily before it an idea or a project to which it relates whatever new particulars come into its ken. Here the idea is the Goddess Melancholy and the project is the understanding of the way of life she presents. It is of course our project, and because it is ours, it gives interpretive direction to our movement through the poem, providing us with ready-made contexts—it is *we* who have made them—into which the details of the verse are immediately drawn. Thus when the Goddess Melancholy materializes in the form of the "pensive Nun," the lines describing her habit and gait are resonant with significance because we bring the significances with us. The Nun's "robe of darkest grain" is capable of any number of interpretations, but the reader who has negotiated the preceding lines will immediately identify its color as the dark hue of staid Wisdom and distinguish it from the boasting blackness of Cassiopeia. Forgetting oneself to marble and gazing downward with an unseeing stare is at the very least ambiguous behavior, but it is disambiguated when the same reader recalls that the dimming of natural vision and the stilling of bodily motion are preliminary to the descrying of a light that is too bright to hit the sense of human sight. As a figure in the landscape, the Nun displays less and less energy, but at the same time she is being energized from within by the meanings *we* attach to her dress and actions, until at line 45 she stands (frozen) before us as an embodiment of all the mythological and philosophical associations to which we have been called by the verse.

In a way I am simply giving body to an observation made by D. C. Allen. In **"L'Allegro,"** Allen points out, "there is an abrupt division between the invitation and the main body of the poem," while in **"Il Penseroso,"** the transition is "more fluid and skillful." For Allen, however, abruptness and fluidity are properties of formal structures, and his distinction is a value judgment (presumably if the transitions of **"L'Allegro"** were more fluid, it would be a better poem). But in my terms, abruptness and fluidity are properties of experiences, and the distinction is not between a skillful and an unskillful arrangement, but between the different experiences provided by arrangements that are indifferently skillful. The components of either poem offer ample possibilities for making connections (that is, for fluidity), but it is only while reading **"Il Penseroso"** that we are pressured to make them. The source of that pressure is the verse, and it is exerted both silently and explicitly: silently when we are asked to manage units of sense and syntax larger than the couplet,

and explicitly when we are directed in line 49 to add ("And add to these retired Leisure"). What we are to add are Melancholy's companions, Peace, Quiet, Spare Fast, the Muses, retired Leisure, and first and chiefest (although last to be called) the Cherub Contemplation. Were this list in **"L'Allegro,"** we would receive its items discretely ("Straight mine eye hath caught new pleasures"); but here we are asked to relate them both to each other and to the master abstraction of which they are all manifestations. Moreover, the point of relation is not something they share on the surface—on its face the list is quite heterogeneous—but something that is available only when we extrapolate from the surface to an underlying pattern of significance. The content of that pattern is a two-stage sequence—withdrawal from the busy companies of men followed by an ascent to the realm of pure and heavenly forms—and this of course is precisely the sequence that has just been acted out by the pensive Nun, who is herself a realization of the paradoxes exploited in the opening lines. "The poetic components of **'Il Penseroso,'**" declares Allen, "seem to glide out of each other by brilliant acts of association." The point I have been making is that these acts are ours, and we perform them with a self-consciousness that is continually returning us to the first link in the associative chain, which in every case is found to be isomorphic with the last. The Cherub Contemplation is the first and chiefest even though he brings up the rear, because the values he declares explicitly, that is by name, were present in the first and in every other of their incarnations.

We see then that the pattern of experience in **"Il Penseroso"** is as consistent as the quite different pattern in **"L'Allegro."** It is a pattern of continually exerted pressure, and it moves us to a set of sustained and related activities: generalizing, abstracting, reflecting, recalling, synthesizing. Not only are these activities sustained, but they have a single object, the precise elucidation of the nature of melancholy; and this continues to be true when the focus of the poem shifts to the speaker, for in his wanderings he repeatedly acts out the sequence that joins the other figures we have encountered. Three times he retires from the light of day into an enclosure: first in some "removed place" where light is taught to counterfeit a gloom, later in twilight groves that have been sought specifically to escape the Sun's flaring beams, and finally in the "Cloister's pale" where the light streaming through the windows is deemed religious *because* it is "dim." Three times as day's garish eye is shut out and earthly sounds are stilled, Il Penseroso becomes physically inactive, sitting in some high and lonely tower, or asleep by a hallowed brook, or standing motionless as the pealing organ blows to the full-voiced choir below. And three times, as his body forgets itself to marble, his spirit soars, in the company of Plato (as together they explore "what vast Regions hold / The immortal mind that hath forsook / Her mansion in this fleshly nook," under the aegis of "some strange mysterious dream," and in response to the ecstasy-making sounds of the "Service high and Anthems clear":

> With antic Pillars massy proof
> And storied windows richly dight,
> Casting a dim religious light.

There let the pealing Organ blow,
To the full voic'd choir below,
In Service high and Anthems clear,
As may with sweetness, through mine ear,
Dissolve me into ecstasies,
And bring all Heav'n before mine eyes.

In this penultimate scene we are once again returned to the master images whose exfoliation has been the stimulus to our interpretive efforts. The worshiper in the "Cloister's pale" assumes exactly the position assumed earlier by the pensive Nun, and like her he is the very embodiment of Peace, Quiet, Spare Fast, the Muses, retired Leisure, and the Cherub Contemplation. Even the pattern of word play is the pattern we experienced in the opening lines, and we are moved by it to make the same distinctions we made then. The basic distinction is between two kinds of perception, the physical and the spiritual. They share a vocabulary, but that vocabulary is so placed that we cannot help but be aware of its two fields of reference. In line 160 the ruling adjective is "dim," but line 163 ends with a strong stress on the adjective "clear." The same apparent clash exists between the adverb "below" in line 162, which refers to the spatial positioning of the organ and the choir, and the adjective "high" in line 163. The clash in both cases is only apparent, because as we come upon them we understand "high" and "clear" to refer not to spatial and sensible, but to spiritual categories; but since that understanding follows immediately upon a sequence in which spatial and sensible categories *are* operative, it signals a transference from outer to inner space. That transference is completed by the pointed juxtaposition in lines 164 and 166 of "through mine ear" and "before mine eyes." No word in the poem is more emphasized than "eyes"; it marks the end of a line, of a couplet, and of a section; and as we read it we know, with the full weight of everything we have learned, that it cannot be read literally, and that this is the eye of the mind which now opens, as it has opened so many times before, to a light that is too bright to hit the sense of human sight. Milton, the *Variorum Commentary* observes at this point, "is here summing up the whole process of self-education described in the poem"; but whatever has been described in the poem (and that has long been a matter of dispute), the process and the education have taken place in the reader.

Let me say, lest there be any misunderstanding, that I am not here offering an interpretation of **"Il Penseroso,"** but arguing that interpretation is the activity to which the poem moves us, and that it is this which distinguishes it from **"Il Allegro."** In another sense, however, the poems are not to be distinguished; for in both there is a congruence of experience with thematic materials. The bards in **"Il Penseroso"** sing of "Trophies hung" and therefore of tournaments in which something more than the applause of ladies is at stake. In place of a domesticated goblin who performs kitchen chores in return for a "cream bowl," the voice of **"Il Penseroso"** speaks to us of Daemons "Whose power hath a *true* consent / With Planet or with Element"; and it is precisely this "power" that Orpheus displays when he bests Pluto in a line whose stresses

communicate and create a sense of urgency that is wholly alien to **"L'Allegro"**: "And made Hell grant what Love did seek."

The singing of Orpheus, like everything else in **"Il Penseroso,"** has both purpose and consequence; and purpose and consequence are also what characterize our efforts as readers. There is here as in **"L'Allegro"** a one-to-one correspondence between the activities *in* the poem and the activity of reading it, and these activities merge in a single line: "Where more is meant than meets the ear." More is indeed meant by **"Il Penseroso"** than meets the ear, and the responsibility for that meaning rests with the ear that is met, an ear that is asked not only to take in a succession of sounds, but to relate them to each other and to a complex of significances in which they are implicated. It is just this kind of sustained mental effort, the effort of synthesizing, generalizing, and abstracting, to which the pensive man pledges himself in the poem's closing lines:

Where I may sit and rightly spell
Of every star that Heav'n doth shew,
And every Herb that sips the dew;
Till old experience do attain,
To something like Prophetic strain.

To spell is to decipher, to puzzle out, to consider, to think; to engage in just those actions the poem requires of its readers. Here then is another point of contact between the two poems that is finally a point of contrast. In both, the speaker and reader are united by the kind of acts they do or do not perform. In **"Il Penseroso,"** as Bridget Lyons has observed, we are continually aware of a consciousness through which the phenomena of experience are being filtered. In other words, we are continually aware of the presence in the poem of a mind, and our awareness takes the form of matching exertions. **"L'Allegro,"** on the other hand, is striking for the absence of mind; there is, it would seem, no one at home. The first-person pronoun only occurs once before the final couplet, and it is followed immediately by the lines that were the occasion of the *TLS* correspondence. They are in turn so variously interpretable that any sense of a continuous and controlling presence is progressively weakened; nor is it reinforced when the speaker appears again in line 69 as a disembodied eye: "Straight mine eye hath caught new pleasures." Even this synecdochical identity is blurred when it is absorbed into a speculation about "neighboring eyes" (the progression is from "I" to "eye" to "eyes") which may or may not be there. The same imprecision of reference and sequence that removes the pressure of consecutive thought also prevents us from finding in the poem a consecutive thinker; and in the absence of a consciousness whose continuing and active presence would give the poem unity, we are that much less inclined to unify it. If no one is at home, then we can be on holiday too.

In both poems, then, the speaker and the reader are to be identified, and this identification suggests a new answer to an old question: who or what are **"L'Allegro"** and **"Il Penseroso"**? **"L'Allegro"** and **"Il Penseroso"** are the reader; that is, they stand for modes of being which the reader realizes in his response to the poems bearing their names. The formal and thematic features of each poem are intimately related to its meaning, not because they reflect it, but because they *produce* it, by moving the reader to a characteristic activity. In short, the poems *mean* the experience they give; and because they so mean, the conditionals with which they end are false:

> These delights if thou canst give,
> Mirth with thee I mean to live.
>
> These pleasures *Melancholy* give,
> And I with thee will choose to live.

These conditionals are false because the conditions they specify have already been met. The delights and pleasures of Mirth and Melancholy are even now ours, for in the very act of reading we have been theirs.

In conclusion, I would like to turn away from the poems to consider the larger implications of my analysis. More specifically, I would like to pose a question. What is it that a procedure focusing on the reader's experience can do? First of all it can deal with **"L'Allegro,"** which has, for the most part, been unavailable to other critical vocabularies. This is not to say that the experience of **"L'Allegro"** has been unavailable, but that the readers who have had that experience have been compelled by their theoretical assumptions either to allegorize it or to devalue it. In fact it is difficult to see how a formalist criticism, committed as it is to "care" both as a criterion for composition and as a condition of serious reading, could accept my description of **"L'Allegro."** For the formalist, reading poetry is equivalent to noticing and *sharing in* the craft and labor that produced it. A poem that asked for no such answering attention would therefore be suspect; and indeed when this paper was first read at a public meeting, a member of the audience rose to ask, with some indignation, why I was attacking **"L'Allegro."** Presumably it was inconceivable to him that an account of the poem that did not tie up, but multiplied loose ends could be praise. In this connection, the recently published *Variorum Commentary* is instructive. Time and again the editors note the presence in the poem of interpretive puzzles, and time and again the sifting of evidence leads to an indeterminate conclusion. The question, who comes to the window at line 46, is debated for a full four pages which end with the recording of a difference of opinion between the two editors. A discussion of alternative versions of line 104 breaks off with the admission that in either version the syntax is "somewhat obscure" and suggests a "degree of carelessness." (Carelessness indeed!) Even the simple phrase "tells his tale" in "every Shepherd tells his tale" has had, we are told, "alternative explanations," but after a survey of those explanations, we read that "all that is certain is that the shepherds were sitting"; anything else, "the reader must decide for himself."

The point of course is that he need not, and that these and other "obscurities" exist precisely so that he will not feel pressured to make the sense the editors seek. These same editors are continually turning up evidence for the reading

offered in this paper (when for example they gloss "wanton" as "uncontrolled by plan or purpose" and "giddy" as "incapable of steady attention"), but they are unable to see the evidence for what it is because they are committed to a single criterion of formal unity (which is at base a criterion of cognitive clarity). As it turns out, however, that is exactly the wrong criterion to apply to a poem like **"L'Allegro"** which grows out of what Thomas Rosenmeyer has recently called the "disconnective decorum" of the Theocritan pastoral. As Rosenmeyer describes it, this decorum is tied to "a perception of a world that is not continuous, but a series of discrete units, each to be savored for its own sake." A poem displaying this decorum will be "best analyzed as a loose combination of independent elements," since "the poet provides few if any clues . . . for consolidation." The poem, Rosenmeyer continues, does not have a plot, so that it is protected "against the profundities and syntheses which . . . plot . . . is always on the verge of triggering." "Consequently," he concludes, "the artlessness of the poem is not there for a reason, but exists of itself, which also means that it is harder to explain." An analysis in terms of the reading experience has, I submit, been able to explain it, because it is not tied to an evaluative bias which both directs and crowns its procedures.

This success (if you will agree that it is one) is finally attributable to a larger capability I would claim for experiential analysis: it provides a firm basis for the resolving of critical controversies. As I have argued elsewhere, formalist procedures are unable to settle anything, because in the absence of constraints the observable regularities in a text can be made to point in any number of directions. But if the focus of analysis is the reader's experience, a description of that experience will at the same time be an interpretation of its materials. Rather than two operations (description and interpretation) whose relationship is problematical, there is only one, and consequently many of the directions in which values might have been irresponsibly assigned are automatically eliminated.

As a final example, consider the question most often asked of **"L'Allegro"** and **"Il Penseroso."** Is the mode of being presented in one poem to be preferred to the mode of being presented in the other? As it is usually posed, this is a spatial question: that is, it is to be answered by examining the two poems as objects and toting up the attitudes or judgments they contain. Not surprisingly, this procedure has led only to disagreement and dispute. If, however, we turn the spatial question into a temporal one, an unambiguous answer is immediately forthcoming because preference or choice is no longer an issue. The pressure for choice is the creation of the assumptions of the critics who make it. The experience of the poems, however, exerts no such pressure, because in the order of their reading the faculties of judgment and discrimination come into play only in **"Il Penseroso."** Were that order reversed, the reflective self-consciousness encouraged by **"Il Penseroso"** would also encourage a critical attitude toward the flatness of implication characteristic of **"L'Allegro,"** and we would be unable to read that poem with the innocence (absence of responsibility) which is both its subject and its gift. The present order, the order Milton gave us, allows the pleasure of reading **"L'Allegro"** to be an unreproved pleasure free, and only then does it introduce us to another pleasure (by giving us another experience) which does not so much reprove the first as remove it from memory. Allen ends his fine essay on the poems by speaking of "a ceaseless passing from one chamber of experience to the next." It is that passing, rather than any after-the-fact judgment one could make on it, that I have tried to describe.

Harold Bloom (essay date 1975)

SOURCE: "Milton and His Precursors," in *A Map of Misreading,* Oxford University Press, 1975, pp. 125-43.

[*In the following essay, Bloom identifies the literary antecedents of* Paradise Lost.]

No poet compares to Milton in his intensity of self-consciousness as an artist and in his ability to overcome all negative consequences of such concern. Milton's highly deliberate and knowingly ambitious program necessarily involved him in direct competition with Homer, Virgil, Lucretius, Ovid, Dante and Tasso, among other major precursors. More anxiously, it brought him very close to Spenser, whose actual influence on *Paradise Lost* is deeper, subtler and more extensive than scholarship so far has recognized. Most anxiously, the ultimate ambitions of *Paradise Lost* gave Milton the problem of expanding Scripture without distorting the Word of God.

A reader, thinking of Milton's style, is very likely to recognize that style's most distinctive characteristic as being the density of its allusiveness. Perhaps only Gray compares to Milton in this regard, and Gray is only a footnote, though an important and valuable one, to the Miltonic splendor. Milton's allusiveness has a distinct design, which is to enhance both the quality and the extent of his inventiveness. His handling of allusion is his highly individual and original defense against poetic tradition, his revisionary stance in writing what is in effect a tertiary epic, following after Homer in primary epic and Virgil, Ovid, and Dante in secondary epic. Most vitally, Miltonic allusion is the crucial revisionary ratio by which *Paradise Lost* distances itself from its most dangerous precursor, *The Faerie Queene,* for Spenser had achieved a national romance, of epic greatness, in the vernacular, and in the service of moral and theological beliefs not far from Milton's own.

The map of misprision move[s] between the poles of *illusio*—irony as a figure of speech, or the reaction-formation I have termed *clinamen*—and allusion, particularly as the scheme of transumption or metaleptic reversal that I have named *apophrades* and analogized to the defenses of introjection and projection. As the common root of their names indicates, *illusio* and allusion are curiously related, both being a kind of mockery, rather in the sense

intended by the title of Geoffrey Hill's poem on Campanella, that "Men are a mockery of Angels." The history of "allusion" as an English word goes from an initial meaning of "illusion" on to an early Renaissance use as meaning a pun, or word-play in general. But by the time of Bacon it meant any symbolic likening, whether in allegory, parable or metaphor, as when in *The Advancement of Learning* poetry is divided into "Narrative, representative, and allusive." A fourth meaning, which is still the correct modern one, follows rapidly by the very early seventeenth century, and involves any implied, indirect or hidden reference. The fifth meaning, still incorrect but bound to establish itself, now equates allusion with direct, overt reference. Since the root meaning is "to play with, mock, jest at," allusion is uneasily allied to words like "ludicrous" and "elusion," as we will remember later.

Thomas McFarland, formidably defending Coleridge against endlessly repetitive charges of plagiarism, has suggested that "plagiarism" ought to be added as a seventh revisionary ratio. Allusion is a comprehensive enough ratio to contain "plagiarism" also under the heading of *apophrades,* which the Lurianic Kabbalists called *gilgul* . . . Allusion as covert reference became in Milton's control the most powerful and successful figuration that any strong poet has ever employed against his strong precursors.

Milton, who would not sunder spirit from matter, would not let himself be a receiver, object to a subject's influencings. His stance against dualism and influence alike is related to his exaltation of unfallen *pleasure,* his appeal not so much to his reader's senses as to his reader's yearning for the expanded senses of Eden. Precisely here is the center of Milton's own influence upon the Romantics, and here also is why he surpassed them in greatness, since what he could do for himself was the cause of their becoming unable to do the same for themselves. His achievement became at once their starting point, their inspiration, yet also their goad, their torment.

Yet he too had his starting point: Spenser. Spenser was "the soothest shepherd that e'er piped on plains," "sage and serious." "Milton has acknowledged to me, that Spenser was his original," Dryden testified, but the paternity required no acknowledgment. A darker acknowledgment can be read in Milton's astonishing mistake about Spenser in *Areopagitica,* written more than twenty years before *Paradise Lost* was completed:

> . . . It was from out the rind of one apple tasted, that the knowledge of good and evil, as two twins cleaving together, leaped forth into the world. And perhaps this is that doom which Adam fell into of knowing good and evil, that is to say of knowing good by evil. As therefore the state of man is, what wisdom can there be to choose, what continence to forbear, without the knowledge of evil? He that can apprehend and consider vice with all her baits and seeming pleasures, and yet abstain, and yet distinguish, and yet prefer that which is truly better, he is the true warfaring Christian. I cannot praise a fugitive and cloistered virtue, unexercised and unbreathed, that never sallies out and sees her adversary, but slinks out of the race, where that

immortal garland is to be run for, not without dust and heat. Assuredly we bring not innocence into the world, we bring impurity much rather; that which purifies us is trial, and trial is by what is contrary. That virtue therefore which is but a youngling in the contemplation of evil, and knows not the utmost that vice promises to her followers, and rejects it, is but a blank virtue, not a pure; her whiteness is but an excremental whiteness; which was the reason why our sage and serious poet Spenser, whom I dare be known to think a better teacher than Scotus or Aquinas, describing true temperance under the person of Guyon, brings him in with his palmer through the cave of Mammon, and the bower of earthly bliss, that he might see and know, and yet abstain. . . .

Spenser's cave of Mammon is Milton's Hell; far more than the descents to the underworld of Homer and Virgil, more even than Dante's vision, the prefigurement of Books I and II of *Paradise Lost* reverberates in Book II of *The Faerie Queene*. Against Acrasia's bower, Guyon enjoys the moral guidance of his unfaltering Palmer, but necessarily in Mammon's cave Guyon has to be wholly on his own, even as Adam and Eve must withstand temptation in the absence of the affable Raphael. Guyon stands, though at some cost; Adam and Eve fall, but both the endurance and the failure are independent. Milton's is no ordinary error, no mere lapse in memory, but is itself a powerful misinterpretation of Spenser, and a strong defense against him. For Guyon is not so much Adam's precursor as he is Milton's own, the giant model imitated by the Abdiel of *Paradise Lost*. Milton re-writes Spenser so as to *increase the distance* between his poetic father and himself. St. Augustine identified memory with the father, and we may surmise that a lapse in a memory as preternatural as Milton's is a movement against the father.

Milton's full relation to Spenser is too complex and hidden for any rapid description or analysis to suffice, even for my limited purposes in this [essay]. Here I will venture that Milton's transumptive stance in regard to all his precursors, including Spenser, is founded on Spenser's resourceful and bewildering (even Joycean) way of subsuming his precursors, particularly Virgil, through his labyrinthine syncretism. Spenserian allusiveness has been described by Angus Fletcher as collage: "Collage is parody drawing attention to the *materials* of art and life." Fletcher follows Harry Berger's description of the technique of *conspicuous allusion* in Spenser: "the depiction of stock literary motifs, characters, and genres in a manner which emphasizes their conventionality, displaying at once their debt to and their existence in a conventional climate—Classical, medieval, romance, etc.—which is archaic when seen from Spenser's retrospective viewpoint." This allusive collage or conspicuousness is readily assimilated to Spenser's peculiarly metamorphic elegiacism, which becomes the particular legacy of Spenser to all his poetic descendants, from Drayton and Milton down to Yeats and Stevens. For Spenser began that internalization of quest-romance that is or became what we call Romanticism. It is the Colin Clout of Spenser's Book VI who is the father of Milton's "Il Penseroso," and from Milton's visionary stem the later Spenserian transforma-

tions of Wordsworth's Solitary, and all of the Solitary's children in the wanderers of Keats, Shelley, Browning, Tennyson and Yeats until the parodistic climax in Stevens' comedian Crispin. Fletcher, in his study of Spenser, *The Prophetic Moment,* charts this genealogy of introspection, stressing the intervention of Shakespeare between Spenser and Milton, since from Shakespeare Milton learned to contain the Spenserian elegiacism or "prophetic strain" within what Fletcher calls "transcendental forms." In his study of *Comus* as such a form, *The Transcendental Masque,* Fletcher emphasizes the "enclosed vastness" in which Milton, like Shakespeare, allows reverberations of the Spenserian resonance, a poetic diction richly dependent on allusive echoings of precursors. *Comus* abounds in *apophrades,* the return of many poets dead and gone, with Spenser and Shakespeare especially prominent among them. Following Berger and Fletcher, I would call the allusiveness of *Comus* still "conspicuous" and so still Spenserian, still part of the principle of echo. But, with *Paradise Lost*, Miltonic allusion is transformed into a mode of transumption, and poetic tradition is radically altered in consequence.

Fletcher, the most daemonic and inventive of modern allegorists, is again the right guide into the mysteries of *transumptive allusion,* through one of the brilliant footnotes in his early book, *Allegory: The Theory of a Symbolic Mode.* Studying what he calls "difficult ornament" and the transition to modern allegory, Fletcher meditates on Johnson's ambivalence towards Milton's style. In his *Life of Milton,* Johnson observes that "the heat of Milton's mind might be said to sublimate his learning." Hazlitt, a less ambivalent admirer of Milton, asserted that Milton's learning had the effect of intuition. Johnson, though so much more grudging, actually renders the greater homage, for Johnson's own immense hunger of imagination was overmatched by Milton's, as he recognized:

> Whatever be his subject, he never fails to fill the imagination. But his images and descriptions of the scenes or operations of Nature do not seem to be always copied from original form, nor to have the freshness, raciness, and energy of immediate observation. He saw Nature, as Dryden expresses it, *through the spectacles of books;* and on most occasions calls learning to his assistance. . . .

> But he does not confine himself within the limits of rigorous comparison: his great excellence is amplitude, and he expands the adventitious image beyond the dimensions which the occasion required. Thus, comparing the shield of Satan to the orb of the Moon, he crowds the imagination with the discovery of the telescope, and all the wonders which the telescope discovers.

This Johnsonian emphasis upon allusion in Milton inspires Fletcher to compare Miltonic allusion to the trope of transumption or metalepsis, Puttenham's "far-fetcher":

> Johnson stresses allusion in Milton: "the spectacles of books" are a means of sublimity, since at every point the reader is led from one scene to an allusive second

scene, to a third, and so on. Johnson's Milton has, we might say, a "transumptive" style. . . .

Here is the passage that moved Johnson's observation, *Paradise Lost*, Book I, 283-313. Beelzebub has urged Satan to address his fallen legions, who still lie "astounded and amazed" on the lake of fire:

> He scarce had ceas't when the superior Fiend
> Was moving toward the shore; his ponderous shield
> Ethereal temper, massy, large and round,
> Behind him cast; the broad circumference
> Hung on his shoulders like the Moon, whose Orb
> Through Optic Glass the *Tuscan* Artist views
> At Ev'ning from the top of *Fesole,*
> Or in *Valdarno,* to descry new Lands,
> Rivers or Mountains in her spotty Globe.
> His Spear, to equal which the tallest Pine
> Hewn on *Norwegian* hills, to be the Mast
> Of some great Ammiral, were but a wand,
> He walkt with to support uneasy steps
> Over the burning Marl, not like those steps
> On Heaven's Azure, and the torrid Clime
> Smote on him sore besides, vaulted with Fire;
> Nathless he so endur'd, till on the Beach
> Of that inflamed Sea, he stood and call'd
> His Legions, Angel Forms, who lay intrans't
> Thick as Autumnal Leaves that strow the Brooks
> In *Vallembrosa,* where th' *Etrurian* shades
> High overarch't imbow'r; or scatter'd sedge
> Afloat, when with fierce Winds *Orion* arm'd
> Hath vext the Red-Sea Coast, whose waves
>   o'erthrew
> *Busiris* and his *Memphian* Chivalry,
> While with perfidious hatred they pursu'd
> The Sojourners of *Goshen,* who beheld
> From the safe shore thir floating Carcasses
> And broken Chariot Wheels, so thick bestrown
> Abject and lost lay these, covering the Flood,
> Under amazement of thir hideous change.

The transumption of the precursors here is managed by the juxtaposition between the far-fetching of Homer, Virgil, Ovid, Dante, Tasso, Spenser, the Bible and the single near-contemporary reference to Galileo, "the Tuscan artist," and his telescope. Milton's aim is to make his own belatedness into an earliness, and his tradition's priority over him into a lateness. The critical question to be asked of this passage is: why is Johnson's "adventitious image," Galileo and the telescope, present at all? Johnson, despite his judgment that the image is extrinsic, implies the right answer: because the expansion of this apparently extrinsic image crowds the reader's imagination, by giving Milton the true priority of *interpretation,* the powerful reading that insists upon its own uniqueness and its own accuracy. Troping upon his forerunners' tropes, Milton compels us to read as he reads, and to accept his stance and vision as our origin, his time as true time. His allusiveness introjects the past, and projects the future, but at the paradoxical cost of the present, which is not voided but is yielded up to an experiential darkness, as we will see, to a mingling of wonder (discovery) and woe (the

fallen Church's imprisonment of the discoverer). As Frank Kermode remarks, *Paradise Lost* is a wholly contemporary poem, yet surely its sense of the present is necessarily more of loss than of delight.

Milton's giant simile comparing Satan's shield to the moon alludes to the shield of Achilles in the *Iliad,* XIX, 373-80:

> . . . and caught up the great shield, huge and heavy
>   next, and from it
> the light glimmered far, as from the moon.
> And as when from across water a light shines to
>   mariners from a blazing
> fire, when the fire is burning high in the mountains
>   in a desolate
> standing, as the mariners are carried unwilling by
>   storm winds over the
> fish-swarming sea, far away from their loved ones;
> so the light from the fair elaborate shield of
>   Achilleus shot into the high
> air.
>
> (Lattimore version)

Milton is glancing also at the shield of Radigund in *The Faerie Queene,* V, v, 3:

> And on her shoulder hung her shield, bedeckt
> Upon the bosse with stones, that shined wide,
> As the faire Moone in her most full aspect,
> That to the Moone it mote be like in each respect.

Radigund, Princess of the Amazons, is dominated by pride and anger, like Achilles. Satan, excelling both in his bad eminence, is seen accurately through the optic glass of the British artist's transumptive vision, even as Galileo sees what no one before him has seen on the moon's surface. Galileo, when visited by Milton (as he tells us in *Areopagitica*), was working while under house arrest by the Inquisition, a condition not wholly unlike Milton's own in the early days of the Restoration. Homer and Spenser emphasize the moonlike brightness and shining of the shields of Achilles and Radigund; Milton emphasizes size, shape, weight as the common feature of Satan's shield and the moon, for Milton's post-Galilean moon is more of a world and less of a light. Milton and Galileo are *late,* yet they see more, and more significantly, than Homer and Spenser, who were *early.* Milton gives his readers the light, yet also the true dimensions and features of reality, even though Milton, like the Tuscan artist, must work on while compassed around by experiential darkness, in a world of woe.

Milton will not stop with his true vision of Satan's shield, but transumes his precursors also in regard to Satan's spear, and to the fallen-leaves aspect of the Satanic host. Satan's spear evokes passages of Homer, Virgil, Ovid, Tasso and Spenser, allusions transumed by the contemporary reference to a flagship ("ammiral") with its mast made of Norwegian fir. The central allusion is probably to Ovid's vision of the Golden Age (Golding's version, I, 109-16):

> The loftie Pyntree was not hewen from mountaines
>   where it stood,

In seeking straunge and forren landes to rove upon
   the flood.
Men knew none other countries yet, than where
   themselves did keepe:
There was no towne enclosed yet, with walles and
   ditches deepe.
No horne nor trumpet was in use, no sword nor
   helmet worne.
The worlde was suche, that souldiers helpe might
   easly be forborne.
The fertile earth as yet was free, untoucht of spade
   or plough,
And yet it yeelded of it selfe of every things
   inough.

Ovid's emblem of the passage from Golden Age to Iron
Age is reduced to "but a wand," for Satan will more truly
cause the fall from Golden to Iron. As earlier Satan subsumed Achilles and Radigund, now he contains and met-
aleptically reverses the Polyphemus of Homer and of
Virgil, the Tancredi and Argantes of Tasso, and the proud
giant Orgoglio of Spenser:

   a club, or staff, lay there along the fold—
   an olive tree, felled green and left to season
   for Kyklops' hand. And it was like a mast
   a lugger of twenty oars, broad in the beam—
   a deep-sea-going craft—might carry:
   so long, so big around, it seemed.
          (*Odyssey,* IX, 322-27, Fitzgerald version)

   . . . we saw
   upon a peak the shepherd Polyphemus;
   he lugged his mammoth hulk among the flocks,
   searching along familiar shores—an awful
   misshapen monster, huge, his eyelight lost.
   His steps are steadied by the lopped-off pine
   he grips. . . .
          (*Aeneid,* III, 660-66; Mandelbaum version)

These sons of Mavors bore, instead of spears,
   Two knotty masts, which none but they could
lift;
Each foaming steed so fast his master bears,
   That never beast, bird, shaft, flew half so swift:
Such was their fury, as when Boreas tears
   The shatter'd crags from Taurus' northern clift:
Upon their helms their lances long they brake,
And up to heav'n flew splinters, sparks, and smoke.
          (*Jerusalem Delivered,* VI, 40, Fairfax version)

So growen great through arrogant delight
   Of th'high descent, whereof he was yborne,
      And through presumption of his matchlesse
   might,
      All other powers and knighthood he did
   scorne.
      Such now he marcheth to this man forlorne,
      And left to losse: his stalking steps are stayde
   Upon a snaggy Oke, which he had torne
   Out of his mothers bowelles, and it made
His mortall mace, wherewith his foemen he

dismayde.

          (*Faerie Queene,* I, vii, x)

The Wild Men, Polyphemus the Cyclops and the crudely
proud Orgoglio, as well as the Catholic and Circassian
champions, Tancredi and Argantes, all become late and
lesser versions of Milton's earlier and greater Satan. The
tree and the mast become interchangeable with the club,
and all three become emblematic of the brutality of Satan
as the Antichrist, the fallen son of God who walks in the
darkness of his vainglory and perverts nature to the ends
of war-by-sea and war-by-land, Job's Leviathan and Be-
hemoth. Milton's present age is again an experiential
darkness—of naval warfare—but his backward glance to
Satanic origins reveals the full truth of which Homer,
Virgil, Tasso give only incomplete reflections. Whether
the transumption truly overcomes Spenser's Orgoglio is
more dubious, for he remains nearly as Satanic as Milton's
Satan, except that Satan is more complex and poignant,
being a son of heaven and not, like the gross Orgoglio, a
child of earth.

The third transumption of the passage, the fiction of the
leaves, is surely the subtlest, and the one most worthy of
Milton's greatness. He tropes here on the tropes of Isaiah,
Homer, Virgil and Dante, and with the Orion allusion on
Job and Virgil. The series is capped by the references to
Exodus and Ovid, with the equation of Busiris and Satan.
This movement from fallen leaves to starry influence over
storms to the overwhelming of a tyrannous host is itself
a kind of transumption, as Milton moves from metonymy
to metonymy before accomplishing a final reduction.

Satan's fallen hosts, poignantly still called "angel forms,"
most directly allude to a prophetic outcry of Isaiah 34:4:

   And all the host of heaven shall be dissolved, and the
   heavens shall be rolled together as a scroll; and all
   their host shall fall down, as the leaf falleth off from
   the vine, and as a falling fig from the fig tree.

Milton is too wary to mark this for transumption; his
trope works upon a series of Homer, Virgil, Dante:

   . . . why ask of my generation?
   As is the generation of leaves, so is that of
      humanity.
   The wind scatters the leaves on the ground, but the
      fine timber
   burgeons with leaves again in the season of spring
      returning.
   So one generation of men will grow while another
      dies. . . .
          (*Iliad,* VI, 145-50, Lattimore version)

   thick as the leaves that with the early frost
   of autumn drop and fall within the forest,
   or as the birds that flock along the beaches,
   in flight from frenzied seas when the chill season
   drives them across the waves to lands of sun.
   They stand; each pleads to be the first to cross
   the stream; their hands reach out in longing for

the farther shore. But Charon, sullen boatman,
now takes these souls, now those; the rest he
  leaves;
thrusting them back, he keeps them from the beach.
      (*Aeneid*, VI, 310-19; Mandelbaum version)

. . . But those forlorn and naked souls changed color,
their teeth chattering, as soon as they heard the cruel
words. They cursed God, their parents, the human race,
the place, the time, the seed of their begetting and of
their birth. Then, weeping loudly, all drew to the evil
shore that awaits every man who fears not God. The
demon Charon, his eyes like glowing coals, beckons
to them and collects them all, beating with his oar
whoever lingers.

As the leaves fall away in autumn, one after another,
till the bough sees all its spoils upon the ground, so
there the evil seed of Adam: one by one they cast
themselves from that shore at signals, like a bird at its
call. Thus they go over the dark water, and before
they have landed on the other shore, on this side a
new throng gathers.

      (*Inferno*, III, 100-120, Singleton version)

Homer accepts grim process; Virgil accepts yet plangently
laments, with his unforgettable vision of those who stretch
forth their hands out of love for the farther shore. Dante,
lovingly close to Virgil, is more terrible, since his leaves
fall even as the evil seed of Adam falls. Milton remembers standing, younger and then able to see, in the woods
at Vallombrosa, watching the autumn leaves strew the
brooks. His characteristic metonymy of shades for woods
allusively puns on Virgil's and Dante's images of the
shades gathering for Charon, and by a metalepsis carries
across Dante and Virgil to their tragic Homeric origin.
Once again, the precursors are projected into belatedness,
as Milton introjects the prophetic source of Isaiah. Leaves
fall from trees, generations of men die, because once one-
third of the heavenly host came falling down. Milton's present
time again is experiential loss; he watches no more autumns,
but the optic glass of his art sees fully what his precursors
saw only darkly, or in the vegetable glass of nature.

By a transition to the "scattered sedge" of the Red Sea,
Milton calls up Virgil again, compounding two passages
on Orion:

Our prows were pointed there when suddenly,
rising upon the surge, stormy Orion
drove us against blind shoals. . . .
      (*Aeneid*, I, 534-36; Mandelbaum version)

. . . he marks Arcturus,
the twin Bears and the rainy Hyades,
Orion armed with gold; and seeing all
together in the tranquil heavens, loudly
he signals. . . .
      (*Aeneid*, III, 517-21; Mandelbaum version)

Alastair Fowler notes the contrast to the parallel Biblical
allusions:

He is wise in heart, and mighty in strength: who hath
hardened himself against him, and hath prospered?

. . . Which alone spreadeth out the heavens, and
treadeth upon the waves of the sea.

Which maketh Arcturus, Orion, and Pleiades, and the
chambers of the south.

      (Job 9:4, 8-9)

Seek him that maketh the seven stars and Orion, and
turneth the shadow of death into the morning, and
maketh the day dark with night: that calleth for the
waters of the sea, and poureth them out upon the face
of the earth: The LORD is his name. . . .

      (Amos 5:8)

In Virgil, Orion rising marks the seasonal onset of storms.
In the Bible, Orion and all the stars are put into place as
a mere sign-system, demoted from their pagan status as
powers. Milton says "hath vexed" to indicate that the sign-
system continues in his own day, but he says "o'erthrew"
to show that the Satanic stars and the hosts of Busiris the
Pharaoh fell once for all, Pharaoh being a type of Satan.
Virgil, still caught in a vision that held Orion as a potency,
is himself again transumed into a sign of error.

I have worked through this passage's allusions in some
detail so as to provide one full instance of a transumptive
scheme in *Paradise Lost*. Johnson's insight is validated,
for the "adventitious image" of the optic glass is shown
to be not extrinsic at all, but rather to be the device that
"crowds the imagination," compressing or hastening much
transumption into a little space. By arranging his precursors in series, Milton figuratively reverses his obligation
to them, for his stationing crowds them between the visionary truth of his poem (carefully aligned with Biblical
truth) and his darkened present (which he shares with
Galileo). Transumption murders time, for by troping on a
trope, you enforce a state of rhetoricity or word-conscious-
ness, and you negate fallen history. Milton does what
Bacon hoped to do; Milton and Galileo become ancients,
and Homer, Virgil, Ovid, Dante, Tasso, Spenser become
belated moderns. The cost is a loss in the immediacy of
the living moment. Milton's meaning is remarkably freed
of the burden of anteriority, but only because Milton himself is already one with the future, which he introjects.

It would occupy too many pages to demonstrate another
of Milton's transumptive schemes in its largest and therefore most powerful dimensions, but I will outline one,
summarizing rather than quoting the text and citing rather
than giving the allusions. My motive is not only to show
that the "optic glass" passage is hardly unique in its arrangement, but to analyze more thoroughly Milton's self-
awareness of both his war against influence and his use of
rhetoricity as a defense. Of many possibilities, Book I,
lines 670-798, seems to me the best, for this concluding
movement of the epic's initial book has as its hidden
subject both the anxiety of influence and an anxiety of
morality about the secondariness of any poetic creation,
even Milton's own. The passage describes the sudden

building, out of the deep, of Pandaemonium, the palace of Satan, and ends with the infernal peers sitting there in council.

This sequence works to transume the crucial precursors again—Homer, Virgil, Ovid and Spenser—but there are triumphant allusions here to Lucretius and Shakespeare also (as Fowler notes). In some sense, the extraordinary and reverberating power of the Pandaemonium masque (as John Hollander terms it, likening it to transformation scenes in court masques) depends on its being a continuous and unified allusion to the very idea of poetic tradition, and to the moral problematic of that idea. Metalepsis or transumption can be described as an extended trope with a missing or weakened middle, and for Milton literary tradition is such a trope. The illusionistic sets and complex machinery of the masque transformation scene are emblematic, in the Pandaemonium sequence, of the self-deceptions and morally misleading machinery of epic and tragic convention.

Cunningly, Milton starts the sequence with a transumption to the fallen near-present, evoking the royal army in the Civil War as precise analogue to the Satanic army. Mammon leads on the advance party, in an opening allusion to Spenser's Cave of Mammon canto, since both Mammons direct gold-mining operations. With the next major allusion, to the same passage in Ovid's *Metamorphoses* I that was evoked in the Galileo sequence, Milton probes the morality of art:

> Let none admire
> That riches grow in Hell; that soil may best
> Deserve the precious bane. And here let those
> Who boast in mortal things, and wond'ring tell
> Of *Babel*, and the works of *Memphian* Kings,
> Learn how thir greatest Monuments of Fame,
> And Strength and Art are easily outdone
> By Spirits reprobate, and in an hour
> What in an age they with incessant toil
> And hands innumerable scarce perform.

Milton presumably would not have termed the *Iliad* or the *Aeneid* "precious bane," yet the force of his condemnation extends to them, and his anxiety necessarily touches his own poem as well. Pandaemonium rises in baroque splendor, with a backward allusion to Ovid's Palace of the Sun, also designed by Mulciber (*Metamorphoses* II, 1-4), and with a near-contemporary allusion to St. Peter's at Rome and, according to Fowler, to Bernini's colonnade in the piazza of St. Peter's. Mulciber, archetype not only of Bernini but more darkly of all artists, including epic poets, becomes the center of the sequence:

> Men call'd him *Mulciber;* and how he fell
> From Heav'n, they fabl'd, thrown by angry *Jove*
> Sheer o'er the Crystal Battlements: from Morn
> To Noon he fell, from Noon to dewy Eve,
> A Summer's day; and with the setting Sun
> Dropt from the Zenith like a falling Star,
> On *Lemnos* th' *Ægæan* Isle: thus they relate,
> Erring; for he with this rebellious rout

> Fell long before; nor aught avail'd him now
> To have built in Heav'n high Towrs; nor did he
>   scape
> By all his Engines, but was headlong sent
> With is industrious crew to build in hell.

The devastating "Erring" of line 747 is a smack at Homer by way of the *errat* of Lucretius (*De rerum natura,* I, 393, as Fowler notes). The contrast with Homer's passage illuminates the transumptive function of Milton's allusiveness, for Homer's Hephaistos (whose Latin name was Vulcan or Mulciber) gently fables his own downfall:

> . . . It is too hard to fight against the Olympian.
> There was a time once before now I was minded to
>   help you, and he caught
> me by the foot and threw me from the magic
>   threshold,
> and all day long I dropped helpless, and about
>   sunset
> I landed in Lemnos. . . .
>   (*Iliad,* I, 589-93, Lattimore version)

Milton first mocks Homer by over-accentuating the idyllic nature of this fall, and then reverses Homer completely. In the dark present, Mulciber's work is still done when the bad eminence of baroque glory is turned to the purposes of a fallen Church. So, at line 756, Pandaemonium is called "the high capital" of Satan, alluding to two lines of Virgil (*Aeneid,* VI, 836 and VIII, 348), but the allusion is qualified by the complex simile of the bees that continues throughout lines 768-75, and which relies on further allusions to *Iliad,* II, 87-90 and *Aeneid,* 430-36, where Achaian and Carthaginian heroes respectively are compared to bees. One of the most remarkable of Milton's transumptive returns to present time is then accomplished by an allusion to Shakespeare's *Midsummer Night's Dream,* II, i, 28ff. A "belated peasant" beholds the "Faery Elves" even as we, Milton's readers, see the giant demons shrink in size. Yet *our* belatedness is again redressed by metaleptic reversal, with an allusion to *Aeneid,* VI, 451-54, where Aeneas recognizes Dido's "dim shape among the shadows (just as one who either sees or thinks he sees . . . the moon rising)." So the belated peasant "sees, or dreams he sees" the elves, but like Milton we *know* we see the fallen angels metamorphosed from giants into pygmies. The Pandaemonium sequence ends with the great conclave of "a thousand demi-gods on golden seats," in clear parody of ecclesiastical assemblies re-convened after the Restoration. As with the opening reference to the advance-party of the royal army, the present is seen as fallen on evil days, but it provides vantage for Milton's enduring vision.

So prevalent throughout the poem is this scheme of allusion that any possibility of inadvertence can be ruled out. Milton's design is wholly definite, and its effect is to reverse literary tradition, at the expense of the presentness of the present. The precursors return in Milton, but only at his will, and they return to be corrected. Perhaps only Shakespeare can be judged Milton's rival in allusive triumph over tradition, yet Shakespeare had no Spenser to subsume, but only a Marlowe, and Shakespeare is less clearly in overt competition with Aeschylus, Sophocles, Euripides than Milton is with Homer, Virgil, Ovid, Dante, Tasso.

Hobbes, in his *Answer to Davenant's Preface* (1650), had subordinated wit to judgment, and so implied also that rhetoric was subordinate to dialectic:

> From knowing much, proceedeth the admirable variety and novelty of metaphors and similitudes, which are not possibly to be lighted on in the compass of a narrow knowledge. And the want whereof compelleth a writer to expressions that are either defaced by time or sullied with vulgar or long use. For the phrases of poesy, as the airs of music, with often hearing become insipid; the reader having no more sense of their force, than our flesh is sensible of the bones that sustain it. As the sense we have of bodies, consisteth in change and variety of impression, so also does the sense of language in the variety and changeable use of words. I mean not in the affectation of words newly brought home from travel, but in new (and withal, significant) translation to our purposes, of those that be already received, and in far fetched (but withal, apt, instructive, and comely) similitudes. . . .

Had Milton deliberately accepted this as challenge, he could have done no more both to fulfill and to refute Hobbes than *Paradise Lost* already does. What Davenant and Cowley could not manage was a complete translation to their own purposes of received rhetoric; but Milton raised such translation to sublimity. In doing so, he also raised rhetoric over dialectic, *contra* Hobbes, for his far-fetchedness (Puttenham's term for transumption) gave similitudes the status and function of complex arguments. Milton's wit, his control of rhetoric, was again the exercise of the mind through all her powers, and not a lower faculty subordinate to judgment. Had Hobbes written his *Answer* twenty years later, and after reading *Paradise Lost*, he might have been less confident of the authority of philosophy over poetry.

Sandra M. Gilbert (essay date 1978)

SOURCE: "Patriarchal Poetry and Women Readers: Reflections on Milton's Bogey," *Publications of the Modern Language Association,* Vol. LXXXXIII, No. 3, May, 1978, pp. 368-81.

[*In the following essay, Gilbert studies the influence of* Paradise Lost *on female writers.*]

To resurrect "the dead poet who was Shakespeare's sister," Virginia Woolf declares in *A Room of One's Own,* literate women must "look past Milton's bogey, for no human being should shut out the view." The perfunctory reference to Milton is curiously enigmatic, for the allusion has had no significant prior development, and Woolf, in the midst of her peroration, does not stop to explain it. Yet the context in which she places this apparently mysterious

bogey is highly suggestive. Shutting out the view, Milton's bogey cuts women off from the spaciousness of possibility, the predominantly male landscapes of fulfillment Woolf has been describing throughout *A Room.* Worse, locking women into "the common sitting room" that denies them individuality, it is a murderous phantom that, if it didn't actually kill "Judith Shakespeare," has helped to keep her dead for hundreds of years, over and over again separating her creative spirit from "the body which she has so often laid down."

Nevertheless, the mystery of Woolf's phrase persists. For who (or what) *is* Milton's bogey? Not only is the phrase enigmatic, it is ambiguous. It may refer to Milton himself, the real patriarchal specter or—to use Harold Bloom's critical terminology—"Covering Cherub" who blocks the view for women poets. It may refer to Adam, who is Milton's (and God's) favored creature, and therefore also a Covering Cherub of sorts. Or it may refer to another fictitious specter, one more bogey created by Milton: his inferior and Satanically inspired Eve, who has also intimidated women and blocked their view of possibilities both real and literary. That Woolf does not definitely indicate which of these meanings she intended suggests that the ambiguity of her phrase may have been deliberate. Certainly other Woolfian allusions to Milton reinforce the idea that for her, as for most other women writers, both he and the creatures of his imagination constitute the misogynistic essence of what Gertrude Stein called "patriarchal poetry. . . ."

Literary women, readers and writers alike, have long been "confused" and intimidated by the patriarchal etiology that defines a solitary Father God as the only creator of all things. For what if such a fiercely masculine cosmic Author is the sole legitimate model for all earthly authors? Milton's myth of origins, summarizing a long misogynistic tradition, clearly implied this question to the many women writers who directly or indirectly recorded anxieties about patriarchal poetry. A minimal list of such figures would include Margaret Cavendish, Anne Finch, Mary Shelley, Charlotte and Emily Brontë, Emily Dickinson, Elizabeth Barrett Browning, George Eliot, Christina Rossetti, H.D., and Sylvia Plath, as well as Stein, Nin, and Woolf herself. In addition, in an effort to come to terms with the institutionalized and often elaborately metaphorical misogyny Milton's epic expresses, many of these women devised their own revisionary myths and metaphors.

Mary Shelley's *Frankenstein,* for instance, is at least in part a despairingly acquiescent "misreading" of *Paradise Lost,* with Eve-Sin apparently exorcised from the story but really translated into the monster that Milton hints she is. Emily Brontë's *Wuthering Heights,* by contrast, is a radically corrective "misreading" of Milton, a kind of Blakean Bible of Hell, with the fall from heaven to hell transformed into a fall from a realm that conventional theology would associate with "hell" (the Heights) to a place that parodies "heaven" (the Grange). Similarly, Elizabeth Barrett Browning's "A Drama of Exile," Charlotte Brontë's *Shirley,* and Christina Rossetti's "Goblin

Market" all include or imply revisionary critiques of *Paradise Lost*, while George Eliot's *Middlemarch* uses Dorothea's worship of that "affable archangel" Casaubon specifically to comment upon the disastrous relationship between Milton and his daughters. And in her undaughterly rebellion against that "Papa above" whom she also called "a God of Flint" and "Burglar! Banker—Father," Emily Dickinson, as Albert Gelpi has perceptively noted, was "passionately Byronic," and therefore, as we shall see, subtly anti-Miltonic. For all these women, in other words, the question of Milton's misogyny was not in any sense an academic one. On the contrary, since it was only through patriarchal poetry that they learned "their origin and their history"—learned, that is, to define themselves as misogynistic theology defined them—most of these writers read Milton with painful absorption.

Considering all this, Woolf's 1918 diary entry on *Paradise Lost*, an apparently causal summary of reactions to a belated study of that poem, may well represent all female anxieties about "Milton's bogey," and is thus worth quoting in its entirety.

> Though I am not the only person in Sussex who reads Milton, I mean to write down my impressions of *Paradise Lost* while I am about it. Impressions fairly well describes the sort of thing left in my mind. I have left many riddles unread. I have slipped on too easily to taste the full flavour. However I see, and agree to some extent in believing, that this full flavour is the reward of highest scholarship. I am struck by the extreme difference between this poem and any other. It lies, I think, in the sublime aloofness and impersonality of the emotion. I have never read Cowper on the sofa, but I can imagine that the sofa is a degraded substitute for *Paradise Lost*. The substance of Milton is all made of wonderful, beautiful, and masterly descriptions of angels' bodies, battles, flights, dwelling places. He deals in horror and immensity and squalor and sublimity but never in the passions of the human heart. Has any great poem ever let in so little light upon one's own joys and sorrows? I get no help in judging life; I scarcely feel that Milton lived or knew men and women; except for the peevish personalities about marriage and the woman's duties. He was the first of the masculinists, but his disparagement rises from his own ill luck and seems even a spiteful last word in his domestic quarrels. But how smooth, strong and elaborate it all is! What poetry! I can conceive that even Shakespeare after this would seem a little troubled, personal, hot and imperfect. I can conceive that this is the essence, of which almost all other poetry is the dilution. The inexpressible fineness of the style, in which shade after shade is perceptible, would alone keep one gazing into it, long after the surface business in progress has been despatched. Deep down one catches still further combinations, rejections, felicities and masteries. Moreover, though there is nothing like Lady Macbeth's terror or Hamlet's cry, no pity or sympathy or intuition, the figures are majestic; in them is summed up much of what men thought of our place in the universe, of our duty to God, our religion.

Interestingly, even the diffident first sentence of this paragraph expresses an uncharacteristic humility, even nervousness, in the presence of Milton's "sublime aloofness and impersonality." By 1918 Woolf was herself an experienced, widely published literary critic, as well as the author of one accomplished novel, with another in progress. In the preceding pages she has confidently set down judgments of Christina Rossetti ("She has the natural singing power"), Byron ("He has at least the male virtues"), Sophocles' *Electra* ("It's not so fearfully difficult after all"), and a number of other serious literary subjects. Yet Milton, and Milton alone, leaves her feeling puzzled, excluded, inferior, and even a little guilty. Like Greek or metaphysics, those other bastions of intellectual masculinity, Milton is for Woolf a sort of inordinately complex algebraic equation, an insoluble problem that she feels obliged—but unable—to solve ("I have left many riddles unread"). At the same time, his magnum opus seems to have little or nothing to do with her own, distinctively female perception of things ("Has any great poem ever let in so little light upon one's own joys and sorrows?"). Her admiration, moreover, is cast in peculiarly vague, even abstract language ("how smooth, strong and elaborate it all is"). And her feeling that Milton's verse (not the dramas of her beloved, androgynous Shakespeare) must be "the essence, of which almost all other poetry is the dilution" perhaps explains her dutiful conclusion, with its strained insistence that in the depths of Milton's verse "is summed up much of what men thought of our place in the universe, of our duty to God, our religion." Our? Surely Woolf is speaking here "as a woman," to borrow one of her own favorite phrases, and surely her conscious or unconscious statement is clear: Milton's bogey, whatever else it may be, is ultimately his cosmology, his vision of "what *men* thought" and his powerful rendering of the culture myth that Woolf, like most other literary women, sensed at the heart of Western literary patriarchy.

The story that Milton, "the first of the masculinists," most notably tells to women is of course the story of woman's secondness, her otherness, and how that otherness leads inexorably to her demonic anger, her sin, her fall, and her exclusion from that garden of the gods which is also, for her, the garden of poetry. In an extraordinarily important and yet also extraordinarily distinctive way, therefore, Milton is for women what Harold Bloom (who might here be paraphrasing Woolf) calls "the great Inhibitor, the Sphinx who strangles even strong imaginations in their cradles." In a line even more appropriate to women, Bloom adds that "the motto to English poetry since Milton was stated by Keats: 'life to him would be death to me'". And interestingly, Woolf herself echoes just this line in speaking of her father years after his death. Had Sir Leslie Stephen lived into his nineties, she remarks, "His life would have entirely ended mine. What would have happened? No writing, no books;—inconceivable." For whatever Milton is to the male imagination, to the female imagination Milton and the inhibiting Father—the Patriarch of patriarchs—are one.

For Woolf, indeed, even Milton's manuscripts are dramatically associated with male hegemony and female subordination. One of the key confrontations in *A Room* occurs when she decides to consult the manuscript of

"Lycidas" in the "Oxbridge" library and is forbidden entrance by an agitated male librarian

> like a guardian angel barring the way with a flutter of black gown instead of white wings, a deprecating, silvery, kindly gentleman, who regretted in a low voice as he waved me back that ladies are only admitted to the library if accompanied by a Fellow of the College or furnished with a letter of introduction.

Locked away from female contamination at the heart of "Oxbridge's" paradigmatically patriarchal library—in the very heaven of libraries, so to speak—there is a Word of power, and the Word is Milton's.

Although *A Room* merely hints at the cryptic but crucial power of the Miltonic text and its misogynistic context, Woolf clearly defined Milton as a frightening "Inhibitor" in the fictional (rather than critical) uses she made or did not make of Milton throughout her literary career. Both *Orlando* and *Between the Acts,* for instance, her two most ambitious and feminist revisions of history, appear quite deliberately to exclude Milton from their radically transformed chronicles of literary events. Hermaphroditic Orlando meets Shakespeare, the enigmatic androgyne, and effeminate Alexander Pope—but John Milton simply does not exist for him-her, just as he doesn't exist for Miss La Trobe, the revisionary historian of *Between the Acts.* As Bloom notes, one way in which a poet evades anxiety is to deny even the existence of the precursor poet who causes anxiety.

When, however, Woolf does allude to Milton in her fiction, as she does in her first novel, *The Voyage Out,* her reference grants him his pernicious power in its entirety. Indeed, the motto of the heroine, Rachel Vinrace, might well be Keats's "Life to him would be death to me," for twenty-four-year-old Rachel, dying of some unnamed disease mysteriously related to her sexual initiation by Terence Hewet, seems to drown in waves of Miltonic verse. ". . . Terence was reading Milton aloud, because he said the words of Milton had substance and shape, so that it was not necessary to understand what he was saying. . . . [But] the words, in spite of what Terence had said, seemed to be laden with meaning, and perhaps it was for this reason that it was painful to listen to them." Milton's invocation to "Sabrina Fair," the goddess "under the glassy, cool, translucent wave," seeks the salvation of a maiden who has been turned to stone, but these words from *Comus* have a very different effect on Rachel. Heralding illness, they draw her toward a "deep pool of sticky water," murky with images derived from Woolf's own episodes of madness, and ultimately they plunge her into the darkness "at the bottom of the sea". Would death to Milton, one wonders, have been life for Rachel?

Charlotte Brontë would certainly have thought so. Because Woolf was such a sophisticated literary critic, she may have been at once the most conscious and the most anxious heiress of the Miltonic culture myth. But among earlier women writers it was Charlotte Brontë who seemed most aware of Milton's threatening qualities, particularly

of the extent to which his influence upon women's fate might be seen as—to borrow a pun from Bloom—an unhealthy *influenza*. In *Shirley* she specifically attacked the patriarchal Miltonic cosmology, within whose baleful context she saw both her female protagonists sickening, orphaned and starved by a male-dominated society. "Milton was great; but was he good?" asks Shirley Keeldar, the novel's eponymous heroine.

> [He] tried to see the first woman, but . . . he saw her not. . . . It was his cook that he saw; or it was Mrs. Gill, as I have seen her, making custards, in the heat of summer, in the cool dairy, with rosetrees and nasturtiums about the latticed window, preparing a cold collation for the reactors,—preserves, and "dulcet creams"—puzzled "What choice to choose for delicacy best. . . ."

Shirley's allusion is to the passage in Book V of *Paradise Lost* in which housewifely Eve, "on hospitable thoughts intent," serves Adam and his angelic guest an Edenic cold collation of fruits and nuts, berries and "dulcet creams." With its descriptions of mouth-watering seraphic banquets and its almost Victorian depiction of primordial domestic bliss, this scene is especially vulnerable to the sort of parodic wit Brontë has Shirley turn against it. But the alternative that Brontë and Shirley propose to Milton's Eve-as-little-woman is more serious and implies an even severer criticism of *Paradise Lost*'s visionary misogyny. The first woman, Shirley hypothesizes, was not an Eve, "half doll, half angel," and always potential fiend. Rather, she was a Titan, and a distinctively Promethean one at that:

> ". . . from her sprang Saturn, Hyperion, Oceanus; she bore Prometheus. . . . The first woman's breast that heaved with life on this world yielded the daring which could contend with Omnipotence: the strength which could bear a thousand years of bondage,—the vitality which could feed that vulture death through uncounted ages,—the unexhausted life and uncorrupted excellence, sisters to immortality, which . . . could conceive and bring forth a Messiah . . . I saw—I now see—a woman-Titan. . . . she reclines her bosom on the ridge of Stilbro' Moor; her mighty hands are joined beneath it. So kneeling, face to face she speaks with God. That Eve is Jehovah's daughter, as Adam was his son."

Like Woolf's concept of "Milton's bogey," this apparently bold vision of a titanic Eve is interestingly (and perhaps necessarily) ambiguous. It is possible, for instance, to read the passage as a comparatively conventional evocation of maternal Nature giving birth to *male* greatness. Because she "bore Prometheus," the first woman's breast nursed daring, strength, vitality. At the same time, however, the syntax here suggests that "the daring which could contend with Omnipotence" and "the strength which could bear a thousand years of bondage" belonged—like the qualities they parallel, "the unexhausted life and uncorrupted excellence . . . which . . . could . . . bring forth a Messiah"—to the first woman herself. Not only did Shirley's Eve bring forth a Prometheus, then, she was herself a Prometheus, contending with Omnipotence and defying bondage. Thus, where Milton's Eve is apparently submissive, except for one moment of disastrous rebellion in which she listens to the wrong voice, Shirley's is strong, assertive, vital. Where Milton's Eve is domestic, Shirley's is daring. Where Milton's Eve is from the first curiously hollow, as if somehow created corrupt, "in outwardshow / Elaborate, of inward less exact," Shirley's is filled with "unexhausted life and uncorrupted excellence." Where Milton's Eve is a sort of divine afterthought, an almost superfluous and mostly material being created from Adam's "supernumerary" rib, Shirley's is spiritual, primary, "heavenborn." Finally, and perhaps most significantly, where Milton's Eve is usually excluded from God's sight and, at crucial moments in the history of Eden, drugged and silenced by divinely ordained sleep, Shirley's speaks "face to face" with God. We may even speculate that, supplanted by a servile and destructive specter, Shirley's Eve is the first avatar of that dead poet whom Woolf, in her revision of this myth, called Judith Shakespeare and who was herself condemned to death by Milton's bogey.

Besides having interesting descendants, however, Shirley's titanic woman has interesting ancestors. For instance, if she is herself a sort of Prometheus as well as Prometheus' mother, she is in a sense closer to Milton's Satan than to his Eve. Certainly "the daring which could contend with Omnipotence" and "the strength which could bear a thousand years of bondage" are qualities that recall not only the firm resolve of Shelley's Prometheus (or Byron's or Goethe's or Aeschylus') but "the unconquerable will" Milton's fiend opposes to the "tyranny of Heav'n." In addition, the gigantic size of Milton's fallen angel ("in bulk as huge / As whom the Fables name of monstrous size, / Titanian, or *Earthborn*') is repeated in the enormity of Shirley's Eve. She "reclines her bosom on the ridge of Stillbro' Moor" just as Satan lies "stretched out huge in length" in Book I of *Paradise Lost* and just as Blake's fallen Albion (another neo-Miltonic figure) appears with his right foot "on Dover cliffs, his heel / On Canterburys ruins; his right hand [covering] lofty Wales / His left Scotland." But of course Milton's Satan is himself the ancestor of all the Promethean heroes conceived by the Romantic poets who influenced Brontë. And as if to acknowledge that fact, she has Shirley remark that under her Titan-woman's breast "I see her zone, purple like that horizon: through its blush shines the star of evening"— Lucifer, the "son of the morning" and the evening star, who is Satan in his unfallen state.

Milton's Satan transformed into a Promethean Eve may at first sound like a rather unlikely literary development. But even the briefest reflection of *Paradise Lost* should remind us that, despite Eve's apparent passivity and domesticity, Milton himself seems deliberately to have sketched so many parallels between her and Satan that it is hard at times for the unwary reader to distinguish the sinfulness of one from that of the other. As Stanley Fish has pointed out, for instance, Eve's temptation speech to Adam in Book IX is "a tissue of Satanic echoes," with its central argument, "Look on me. / Do not believe," an exact duplicate of the antireligious empiricism embedded in Satan's earlier temptation speech to her. Moreover, where Adam

falls out of uxorious "fondness," out of a self-sacrificing love for Eve, which, at least to the modern reader, seems quite noble, Milton's Eve falls for exactly the same reason that Satan does: because she wants to be "as Gods" and because, like him, she is secretly dissatisfied with her place, secretly preoccupied with questions of "equality." After *his* fall, Satan makes a pseudolibertarian speech to his fellow angels in which he asks, "Who can in reason then or right assume / Monarchy over such as live by right / His equals, if in power and splendor less, / In freedom equal?" After *her* fall, Eve considers the possibility of keeping the fruit to herself "so to add what wants / In Female Sex, the more to draw [Adam's] Love, / And render me more equal."

Again, just as Milton's Satan—despite his pretensions to equality with the divine—dwindles from anangel into a dreadful (though subtle) serpent, so Eve is gradually reduced from an angelic being to a monstrous and serpentine creature, listening sadly as Adam thunders, "Out of my sight, thou Serpent, that name best / Befits thee with him leagu'd, thyself as false / And hateful; nothing wants, but that thy shape, / Like his, and colour Serpentine may show / Thy inward fraud." The enmity God sets between the woman and the serpent is thus the discord necessary to divide those who are not opposed or mutually hostile but too much alike, too much attracted to each other. In addition, just as Satan feeds Eve with the forbidden fruit, so Eve—who is consistently associated with fruit, not only as Edenic chef but also as the womb, the bearer of fruit— feeds the fruit to Adam. And finally, just as Satan's was a fall into generation, its first consequence being the appearance of the material world of Sin and Death, so Eve's (and not Adam's) fall completes the human entry into generation, since its consequence is the pain of birth, death's necessary opposite and mirror image. And just as Satan is humbled and enslaved by his desire for the bitter fruit, so Eve is humbled by becoming a slave not only to Adam the individual man but to Adam the archetypal man, a slave not only to her husband but, as de Beauvoir notes, to the species. By contrast, Adam's fall is fortunate, among other reasons because, from the woman's point of view, his punishment seems almost like a reward, as he himself suggests when he remarks that "On mee the Curse aslope / Glanc'd on the ground, with labour I must earn / My bread; what harm? Idleness had been worse . . ."

We must remember, however, that Eve's relationship to Satan, as Milton delineates it, is even richer, deeper, and more complex than these few points suggest. Her bond with the fiend is strengthened not only by the striking similarities between them but also by her resemblance to Sin, who is, as it were, his female avatar and, indeed, the only other female who graces (or, rather, disgraces) *Paradise Lost*. Brontë's Shirley, whose titanic Eve is reminiscent of the Promethean aspects of Milton's devil, does not appear to have noticed this relationship, even in her bitter attack upon Milton's little woman. But we can be sure that Brontë herself, like many other female readers, did—if only unconsciously—perceive the likeness. For not only is Sin female, like Eve, she is serpentine, as Satan is and as Adam tells Eve *she* is. Her body, "woman to the waist, and fair, / But [ending] foul in many a scaly fold / Voluminous and vast, a serpent arm'd / With mortal sting," seems to exaggerate and parody female anatomy just as the monstrous bodies of Spenser's Error and Duessa do. In addition, with her fairness ironically set against foulness, Sin parodies Adam's fearful sense of the tension between Eve's "outward show / Elaborate" and her "inward less exact." Moreover, just as Eve is a secondary and contingent creation, made from Adam's rib, so Sin, Satan's "Daughter," burst from the fallen angel's brain like a grotesque subversion of the Greco-Roman story of wise Minerva's birth from the head of Jove. In a patriarchal Christian context the pagan goddess Wisdom may, Milton suggests, become the loathsome demoness Sin, for the intelligence of heaven is made up exclusively of "Spirits Masculine," and the woman, like her dark double, Sin, is a "fair defect / Of Nature."

If Eve's punishment, moreover, is her condemnation to the anguish of maternity, Sin is the only model of maternity other than the "wide womb of Chaos" with which *Paradise Lost* presents her, and as a model Milton's monster provides a hideous warning of what it means to be a "slave to the species." Birthing innumerable Hell Hounds in a dreadful cycle, Sin is endlessly devoured by her children, who continually emerge from and return to her womb, where they bark and howl unseen. Their bestial sounds remind us that to bear young is to be, not spiritual, but animal, a *thing* of flesh, an incomprehensible and uncomprehending body, while their ceaseless suckling presages the exhaustion that leads to death, companion of birth. And Death is indeed their sibling as well as the father who has raped (and thus fused with) his mother, Sin, in order to bring this pain into being, just as "he" will meld with Eve when in eating the apple she ends up "eating Death."

Of course, Sin's pride and her vulnerability to Satan's seductive wiles make her Eve's double too. It is at Satan's behest, after all, that Sin disobeys God's commandments and opens the gates of hell to let the first cause of evil loose in the world, and this act of hers is clearly analogous to Eve's disobedient eating of the apple, with its similar consequences. Like both Eve and Satan, moreover, Sin wants to be "as Gods," to reign in a "new world of light and bliss." And surely it is not insignificant that her moving but blasphemous pledge of allegiance to Satan ("Thou art my Father, thou my Author, thou / My being gav'st me: whom should I obey / But thee, whom follow?") foreshadows Eve's most poignant speech to Adam ("but now lead on;/ . . . with thee to go, / Is to stay here; without thee here to stay, / Is to go hence unwilling; thou to mee / Art all things under Heav'n . . .," as if in some part of himself Milton meant not to instruct the reader by contrasting two modes of obedience but to undercut even Eve's "goodness" in advance. Perhaps it is for this reason that, in the grim shade of Sin's Medusa-like snakiness, Eve's beauty, too, begins (to an experienced reader of *Paradise Lost*) to seem suspect: her golden tresses waving in wanton, wandering ringlets suggest at least a sinister potential, and it hardly helps matters that so keen a critic as Hazlitt thought her nakedness made her luscious as a piece of fruit.

Despite Milton's well-known misogyny, however, and the highly developed philosophical tradition in which it can be placed, all these connections, parallels, and doublings among Satan, Eve, and Sin are shadowy messages, embedded in the text of *Paradise Lost*, rather than carefully illuminated overt statements. Still, for sensitive female readers brought up in the bosom of a "masculinist," patristic, neo-Manichean church, the latent as well as the manifest content of such a powerful work as *Paradise Lost* was (and is) bruisingly real. To such women the unholy trinity of Satan, Sin, and Eve, diabolically mimicking the holy trinity of God, Christ, and Adam, must have seemed even in the eighteenth and nineteenth centuries to illustrate that historical dispossession and degradation of the female principle which was to be imaginatively analyzed in the twentieth century by Robert Graves, among others. "The new God," Graves wrote in *The White Goddess,* speaking of the rise of the Judaic-Pythagorean tradition whose culture myth Milton recounts,

> claimed to be dominant as Alpha and Omega, the Beginning and the End, pure Holiness, pure Good, pure Logic, able to exist without the aid of woman; but it was natural to identify him with one of the original rivals of the Theme of the [*White Goddess*] and to ally the woman and the other rival permanently against him. The outcome was philosophical dualism with all the tragi-comic woes attendant on spiritual dichotomy. If the True God, the God of the Logos, was pure thought, pure good, whence came evil and error? Two separate creations had to be assumed: the true spiritual Creation and the false material Creation. In terms of the heavenly bodies, Sun and Saturn were now jointly opposed to Moon, Mars, Mercury, Jupiter and Venus. The five heavenly bodies in opposition made a strong partnership, with a woman at the beginning and a woman at the end. Jupiter and the Moon Goddess paired together as the rulers of the material World, the lovers Mars and Venus paired together as the lustful Flesh, and between the pairs stood Mercury who was the Devil, the Cosmocrator or author of the false creation. It was these five who composed the Pythagorean *hyle,* or grove, of the five material senses; and spiritually minded men, coming to regard them as sources of error, tried to rise superior to them by pure meditation. This policy was carried to extreme lengths by the God-fearing Essenes, who formed their monkish communities within compounds topped by acacia hedges, from which all women were excluded; lived ascetically, cultivated a morbid disgust for their own natural functions and turned their eyes away from World, Flesh and Devil.

Milton, who offers at least lip service to the institution of matrimony, is never so intensely misogynistic as the fanatically celibate Essenes. But a similar misogyny, though more disguised, obviously contributes to Adam's espousal of Right Reason as a means of transcending the worldly falsehoods propounded by Eve and Satan (and by his vision of the "bevy of fair women" whose wiles betrayed the "sons of God"). And that the Right Reason of *Paradise Lost* did have such implications was powerfully understood by William Blake, whose fallen Urizenic Milton must reunite with his female Emanation in order to cast off his fetters and achieve imaginative wholeness. Perhaps even more important for our purposes here, in the visionary epic *Milton,* Blake reveals a sure grasp of the psychohistorical effects he thought Milton's misguided "chastity" had not only upon Milton, but upon women themselves. While Milton-as-noble-bard, for instance, ponders "the intricate mazes of Providence," Blake has his "six-fold Emanation" howl and wail, "Scatter'd thro' the deep / In torment." Made up of his three wives and three daughters, this archetypal abandoned woman knows very well that Milton's antifeminism has deadly implications for her own character as well as for her fate. "Is this our Feminine Portion," Blake has her demand despairingly. "Are we Contraries O Milton, Thou & I / O Immortal! how were we led to War the Wars of Death[?]." And, as if to describe the moral deformity such misogyny fosters in women, she explains that "Altho' our Human Power can sustain the severe contentions . . . our Sexual cannot: but flies into the [hell of] the Ulro. / Hence arose all our terrors in Eternity!"

Still, although he was troubled by Milton's misogyny and was radically opposed to the Cartesian dualism that Milton's vaguely Manichean cosmology anticipated, Blake did portray the author of *Paradise Lost* as the hero—the redeemer even—of the poem that bears his name. Beyond or behind Milton's bogey, the later poet saw, there was a more charismatic and congenial figure, a figure that Shirley and her author, like most other female readers, must also have perceived, judging by the ambiguous responses to Milton recorded by so many women. For though the epic voice of *Paradise Lost* often sounds censorious and "masculinist" as it recounts and comments upon Western patriarchy's central culture myth, the epic's creator often seems to display such dramatic affinities with rebels against the censorship of heaven that Romantic readers might well conclude with Blake that Milton wrote of God "in fetters" and was "of the Devils party without knowing it." And so Blake, blazing a path for Shirley and for Shelley, for Byron and for Mary Shelley, and for all the Brontës, presented what was to become his famous interpretation of Satan as the real, burningly visionary god—the Los—of *Paradise Lost*, with "God" as the rigid and death-dealing Urizenic demon. His extraordinarily significant misreading clarifies not only the lineage of, say, Shelley's Prometheus but also the ancestry of Shirley's titanic Eve. For if Eve is in so many negative ways like Satan the serpentine tempter, why should she not also be akin to Satan the Romantic outlaw, the character whom T. S. Eliot considered "Milton's curly-haired Byronic hero"?

That Satan is throughout much of *Paradise Lost* a handsome devil and therefore a paradigm for the Byronic hero at his most attractive is, of course, a point frequently made by critics of all persuasions, including those less hostile than Eliot was to both Byron and Milton. Indeed, Satan's Prometheanism, the indomitable will and courage he bequeathed to characters like Shirley's Eve, almost seems to have been created to illustrate some of the crucial features of Romanticism in general. Refusing, like Shelley's Prometheus, to submit to the "tyranny of Heaven," and stalking "apart in joyless revery" like Byron's Childe Harold, Milton's Satan is as alienated from celestial society as any of the early nineteenth-century poets *maudit* who made him their emblem. Accursed and self-cursing, paradoxical and mystical ("Which way I fly is hell; myself am Hell . . . Evil be thou my Good," he experiences the guilty double consciousness, the sense of a stupendous self capable of nameless and perhaps criminal enormities, that Byron redefined in *Manfred* and *Cain* as marks of superiority. To the extent, moreover, that the tyranny of heaven is associated with Right Reason, Satan is Romantically antirational in his exploration of the secret depths of himself and of the cosmos. He is antirational, too—and Romantic—in his indecorous yielding to excesses of passion, his Byronic "gesture fierce" and "mad demeanor." At the same time, his aristocratic egalitarianism, manifested in his war against the heavenly system of primogeniture that has unjustly elevated God's "Son" above even the highest angels, suggests a Byronic (and Shelleyan and Godwinian) concern with liberty and justice for all. Thunder-scarred and world-weary, this black-browed devil would not, one feels, have been out of place at Missolonghi.

Significantly, Eve is the only character in *Paradise Lost* for whom a rebellion against the hierarchical status quo is as necessary as it is for Satan. Though in one sense oppressed, or at least manipulated, by God, Adam is after all to his own realm what God is to his: absolute master and guardian of the patriarchal rights of primogeniture. Eve's docile speech in Book IV emphasizes this: "My Author and Disposer, what thou bidd'st / Unargu'd I obey; so God ordains, / God is thy Law, thou mine: to know no more / Is woman's happiest knowledge and her praise." But the dream she has shortly after speaking these words to Adam seems to reveal her true feelings about the matter in its fantasy of a Satanic flight of escape from the garden and its oppressions: "Up to the clouds / . . . I flew and underneath beheld / The Earth outstretcht immense, a prospect wide / And various . . .," a redefined prospect of happy knowledge not unlike the one Woolf imagines women viewing from their opened windows. And interestingly, brief as is the passage describing Eve's flight, it foreshadowed fantasies that would recur frequently and compellingly in the writings of both women and Romantic poets. Byron's Cain, for instance, disenchanted by what his author called the "politics of paradise," flies through space with his seductive Lucifer like a masculine version of Milton's Eve, and though Shirley's Eve is earthbound—almost earthlike—innumerable other "Eves" of female origin have flown, fallen, surfaced, or feared to fly, as if to acknowledge in a backhanded sort of way the power of the dream Milton let Satan grant to Eve. But whether female dreams of flying escapes are derived from Miltonic or Romantic ideas, or from some collective female unconscious, is a difficult question to answer. For the connections among Satan, Romanticism, and concealed or incipient feminism are intricate and far-reaching indeed.

Certainly, if both Satan and Eve are in some sense alienated, rebellious, and therefore Byronic figures, the same is true for women writers as a class—for Shirley's creator as well as for Shirley, for Virginia Woolf as well as for "Judith Shakespeare." Dispossessed by her older brothers (the "Sons of God"), educated to submission, enjoined to silence, the woman writer—in fantasy if not in reality—must often have "stalked apart in joyless revery," like Byron's heroes, like Satan, like Prometheus. Feeling keenly the discrepancy between the angel she was supposed to be and the angry demon she knew she often was, she must have experienced the same paradoxical double consciousness of guilt and greatness that afflicts both Satan and, say, Manfred. Composing herself to saintly stillness, brooding narcissistically like Eve over her own image and like Satan over her own power, she may even have feared occasionally that like Satan—or Lara, or Manfred—she would betray her secret fury by "gestures fierce" or a "mad demeanor." Asleep in the bower of domesticity, she would be unable to silence the Romantic-Satanic whisper—"Why sleepst thou Eve?"—with its invitation to join the visionary world of those who fly by night.

Significantly, Eve is the only character in *Paradise Lost* for whom a rebellion against the status quo is as necessary as it is for Satan.

—Sandra M. Gilbert

Again, though Milton goes to great lengths to associate visionary prophetic powers with Adam, God, Christ, and the angels, that visionary night world of poetry and imagination, insofar as it is a *demonic* world, is more often subtly associated in *Paradise Lost* with Eve, Satan, and femaleness than with any of the "good" characters except the epic speaker himself. Blake, of course, saw this quite clearly. It is the main reason for the Satan-God role reversal he postulates. But his friend Mary Wollstonecraft and her Romantic female descendants must have seen it too, just as Byron and Shelley did. For though Adam is magically shown, as in a crystal ball, what the future holds, Satan and Eve are the real dreamers of *Paradise Lost*, possessed in the Romantic sense by seductive reflections and uncontrollable imaginings of alternative lives to the point where, like Manfred or Christabel or the Keats of "The Fall of Hyperion," they are so scorched by visionary longings they become fevers of themselves, to echo Moneta's words to Keats. But even Satan's and Eve's suffering sense of the hellish discrepancy between their aspiration and their position is a model of esthetic nobility to the Romantic poet and the Romantically inspired feminist. Contemplating the "lovely pair" of Adam and Eve in their cozily unfallen state, Mary Wollstonecraft confesses that she feels "an emotion similar to what we feel when children are playing or animals sporting," and on such occasions "I have, with conscious dignity, or Satanic pride, turned to hell for sublimer subjects." Her deliberate, ironic confusion of "conscious dignity" and "Satanic pride," together with her Romantic reverence for the sublime, prefigures Shelley's Titan as clearly as Shirley's titanic woman. The imagining of more "sublime" alternative lives, moreover, as Blake and Wollstonecraft also saw, reinforces

the revolutionary fervor that Satan the visionary poet, like Satan the aristocratic Byronic rebel, defined for women and Romantics alike.

That the Romantic esthetic has often been linked with visionary politics is, of course, almost a truism. From the apocalyptic revolutions of Blake and Shelley to those of Yeats and D. H. Lawrence, moreover, revisions of the Miltonic culture myth have been associated with such repudiations of the conservative, hierarchical "politics of paradise." "In terrible majesty," Blake's Satanic Milton thunders, "Obey thou the words of the Inspired Man. / All that can be annihilated must be annihilated / That the children of Jerusalem may be saved from slavery." Like him, Byron's Lucifer offers autonomy and knowledge—the prerequisites of freedom—to Cain, while Shelley's Prometheus, overthrowing the tyranny of heaven, ushers in "Life, Joy, Empire, and Victory" for all of humanity. Even D. H. Lawrence's Satanic snake, emerging one hundred years later from the hellishly burningbowels of the earth, seems to be "one of the lords / of life," an exiled king "now due to be crowned again," signaling a reborn society. For in the revolutionary cosmologies of all these Romantic poets, both Satan and his other self, Lucifer ("son of the morning"), were emblematic of that liberated dawn in which it *would* be bliss to be alive.

It is not surprising, then, that women, identifying at their most rebellious with Satan, at their least with rebellious Eve, and almost all the time with the Romantic poets, should have been similarly obsessed with the apocalyptic social transformations a revision of Milton might bring about. Mary Wollstonecraft, whose *A Vindication of the Rights of Women* often reads like an outraged commentary on *Paradise Lost*, combined a Blakean enthusiasm for the French Revolution—at least in its early days—with her "pre-Romantic" reverence for the Satanic Sublime and her feminist anger at Milton's misogyny. But complicated as it was, that complex of interrelated feelings was not hers alone. For not only have feminism and Romantic radicalism been consciously associated in the minds of many women writers, Byronically (and Satanically) rebellious visionary politics have often been used by women as metaphorical disguises for sexual politics. Thus Brontë, in addition to creating an anti-Miltonic Eve in *Shirley,* uses the revolutionary anger of the frame-breaking workers with whom the novel is crucially concerned as an image for the fury of its dispossessed heroines. Similarly, as Ellen Moers has perceptively noted, Englishwomen's factory novels (like Gaskell's *Mary Barton*) and American women's antislavery novels (like Stowe's *Uncle Tom's Cabin*) submerged or disguised "private, brooding, female resentment" in ostensibly disinterested examinations of larger public issues. More recently, even Virginia Woolf's angrily feminist *Three Guineas* purports to have begun not primarily as a consideration of the woman question but as an almost Shelleyan dream of transforming the world—abolishing war, tyranny, ignorance, and so on—through the formation of a female "Society of Outsiders."

But of course such a society would be curiously Satanic, since in the politics of paradise the Prince of Darkness was literally the first Outsider. And even if Woolf herself did not see far enough past Milton's bogey to recognize this, a number of other women, both feminists and anti-feminists, did. In late nineteenth-century America a well-known journal of Romantically radical politics and feminism was called *Lucifer the Light-Bearer,* for instance, and in Victorian England Mrs. Rigby wrote of Charlotte Brontë's Byronic and feminist *Jane Eyre* that "the tone of mind and thought which has overthrown authority and violated every code human and divine abroad, and fostered Chartism and rebellion at home"—in other words, a Byronic, Promethean, Satanic, and Jacobin tone of mind—"is the same which has also written *Jane Eyre.*"

Paradoxically, however, Brontë herself may have been less conscious of the extraordinary complex of visionary and revisionary impulses that went into *Jane Eyre* than Mrs. Rigby was, at least in part because, like many other women, she found her own anger and its intellectual consequences almost too painful to confront. Commenting on the so-called "condition of women" question, she told Mrs. Gaskell that there are "evils—deep-rooted in the foundation of the social system—which no efforts of ours can touch; of which we cannot complain: of which it is advisable not too often to think." Still, despite her refusal to "complain," Brontë's unwillingness to think of social inequities was more likely a function of her anxiety about her own rebelliously Satanic impulses than a sign of blind resignation to what Yeats called "the injustice of the skies."

The relationship between women writers and Milton's curly-haired Byronic hero is, however, even more complicated than I have so far suggested. And in the intricate tangle of this relationship resides still another reason for the refusal of writers like Brontë consciously to confront their obsessive interest in the impulses incarnated in the villain of *Paradise Lost.* For not only is Milton's Satan in certain crucial ways very much *like* women, he is also, much more obviously, enormously attractive to women. Indeed, as Eliot's phrase suggests—and as Byron's own life indicates—he is in most ways the incarnation of worldly male sexuality: fierce, powerful, experienced, simultaneously brutal and seductive, devil enough to overwhelm the body and yet enough a fallen angel to charm the soul. As such, however, in his relations with women he is a sort of Nietzchean *Übermensch,* giving orders and expecting homage to his "natural"—that is, masculine—superiority, as if he were God's shadow self, the id of heaven, Satanically reduplicating the politics of paradise wherever he goes. And yet, wherever he goes, women follow him, even when they refuse to follow the God whose domination he parodies. As Sylvia Plath so famously noted, "Every woman adores a Fascist, / The boot in the face, the brute / Brute heart of a brute like you." Speaking of "Daddy," Plath was of course speaking also of Satan, "a man in black with a Mein Kampf look." And the masochistic phenomenon she described helps explain the unspeakable, even unthinkable sense of sin that also caused women like Woolf and Brontë to avert their eyes from their own Satanic impulses. For if Eve is Sin's as well as Satan's double, then Satan is to Eve what he is to Sin—both a lover and a daddy.

That the Romantic fascination with incest derived in part from Milton's portrayal of the Sin-Satan relationship may be true but is in a sense beside the point here. That both women and Romantic poets must have found at least an analogue for their relationship to each other in Satan's incestuous affair with Sin is, however, very much to the point. Admiring, even adoring Satan's Byronic rebelliousness, his scorn of conventional virtues, his raging energy, the woman writer may have secretly fantasized that she *was* Satan—or Cain, or Manfred, or Prometheus. But at the same time her feelings of female powerlessness manifested themselves in her conviction that the closest she could really get to being Satan was to be his creature, his tool, the witchlike daughter-mistress who sits on his right hand. Leslie Marchand tells a revealing little story of Mary Shelley's stepsister, Claire Clairmont, that brilliantly illuminates this movement from self-assertive identification to masochistic self-denial. Begging Byron to criticize her half-finished novel, rebellious Claire (who was later to follow the poet to Geneva and bear his daughter Allegra) is said to have explained that he *must* read the manuscript because "the creator ought not to destroy his creature."

Despite Brontë's vision of a Promethean Eve, *Shirley* betrays a similar sense of the difficulty of direct identification with the assertive Satanic principle and the need for women to accept their own instrumentality, for her first ecstatic description of an active, indomitable Eve is followed by a more chastened story. In this second parable, the "first woman" passively wanders alone in an alienating landscape, wondering whether she is "thus to burn out and perish, her living light doing no good, never seen, never needed" even though "the flame of her intelligence burn[s] so vivid" and "something within her stir[s] disquieted. . . ." Instead of coming from that Promethean fire within her, however, as the first Eve's salvation implicitly did, this Eva's redemption comes through a Byronic-Satanic god of the night, called "Genius," who claims her, a "lost atom of life," as his bride. "I take from thy vision, darkness. . . . I, with my presence, fill vacancy," he declares, explaining that "Unhumbled, I can take what is mine. Did I not give from the altar the very flame which lit Eva's being?" Superficially, this allegorical narrative may be seen as a woman's attempt to imagine a malemuse with whom she can interact in a way that will parallel the male poet's congress with his female muse. But the incestuous Byronic love story in which Brontë embodies her allegorical message is more significant here than the message itself.

It suggests to begin with that, like Claire Clairmont, Brontë may have seen herself as at best a creation of male "Genius"—whether artwork or daughter is left deliberately vague—and therefore a being ultimately lacking in autonomy. Finding her ideas astonishingly close to those of an admired male (Byron, Satan, "Genius") and accustomed to assuming that male thought is the source of all female thinking, just as Adam's rib is the source of Eve's body, she supposes that he has, as it were, invented her. Her autonomy is further denied even by the incestuous coupling that appears to link her to her creator and to make them equals. For, as Helene Moglen notes, the devouring ego of the Satanic-Byronic hero found the fantasy (or reality) of incest the best strategy for metaphorically annihilating the otherness—the autonomy—of the female. "In his union with [his half-sister] Augusta Leigh," Moglen points out, "Byron was in fact striving to achieve union with himself," just as Manfred expresses his solipsistic self-absorption by indulging his forbidden passion for his sister, Astarte. Similarly, the enormity of Satan's ego is manifested in the sexual cycle of his solipsistic production and reproduction of himself, first as Sin and later as Death. Like Byron, he seems to be "attempting to become purely self-dependent by possessing his past in his present, affirming a more complete identity by enveloping and containing his other, complementary self." But, as Moglen goes on to remark, "to incorporate 'the other' is also after all to negate it. No space remains for the female. She can either allow herself to be devoured or she can retreat into isolation."

It is not insignificant, then, that the fruit of Satan's solipsistic union with Sin is Death, just as death is the fruit of Manfred's love for Astarte and ultimately, I would argue, of all the incestuous neo-Satanic couplings envisioned by women writers from Mary Shelley to Sylvia Plath. To the extent that the desire to violate the incest taboo is a desire to be self-sufficient—self-begetting—it is a divinely interdicted wish to be "as Gods," like the desire for the forbidden fruit of the tree of knowledge, whose taste also meant death. For the woman writer, moreover, even the reflection that the Byronic hero is as much a creature of her mind—an incarnation of her "private, brooding, female resentments"—as she is an invention of his offers little solace. For if in loving her he loves himself, in loving him she loves herself, and is therefore similarly condemned to the death of the soul that punishes solipsism.

But of course such a death of the soul is implied in any case by Satan's conception of his unholy creatures: Sin, Death, and Eve. As a figure of the heavenly interloper who plays the part of false "cosmocrator" in the dualistic patriarchal cosmology that Milton inherited from Christian tradition, Satan is in fact a sort of artist of death, the paradigmatic master of all those perverse esthetic techniques that pleasure the body rather than the soul and serve the world rather than God. From the golden palace he erects at Pandemonium to his angelic impersonations in the garden and the devilish machines he engineers as part of his war against God, he practices false, fleshly, death-devoted arts (though a few of them are very much the kinds of arts a Romantic sensualist like Keats sometimes admired). As if following Milton even here, Byron makes the Satanic Manfred similarly the master of false, diabolical arts. And defining herself as the "creature" of one or the other of these irreligious artists, the woman writer would be confirmed not only in her sense that she was part of the "effeminate slackness" of the "false creation" but also in her fear that she was herself a false creator, one of the seductive "bevy of fair women" for whom the arts of language, like those of dance and music, are techniques "Bred only . . . to the taste / Of lustful appetance," sinister parodies of the language of the angels and the music of the spheres. In the shadow of such a

fear, even her housewifely arts would begin, like Eve's cookery—her choosing of delicacies "so contriv'd as not to mix / Tastes"—to seem suspect, while the poetry she conceived might well appear to be a monster birth, like Satan's horrible child Death. Fallen like Anne Finch into domesticity, into the "dull mannage of a servile house" as well as into the slavery of generation, she would not even have the satisfaction Manfred has of dying nobly. Rather, dwindling by degrees into an infertile drone, she might well conclude that this image of Satan and Eve as the false artists of creation was finally the most demeaning and discouraging avatar of Milton's bogey.

What would have made her perception of this last bogey even more galling, of course, would have been the magisterial calm with which Milton, as the epic speaker of *Paradise Lost*, continually calls attention to his own art, for the express purpose, so it seems, of defining himself throughout the poem as a type of the true artist, the virtuous poet who, rather than merely delighting (like Eve and Satan), delights while instructing. A prophet or priestly bard and therefore a guardian of the sacred mysteries of patriarchy, he serenely proposes to justify the ways of God to men, calls upon subservient female muses for the assistance that is his due (and in real life upon slavish daughters for the same sort of assistance), and at the same time wars upon women with a barrage of angry words, just as God wars upon Satan. Indeed, as a figure of the true artist, God's emissary and defender on earth, Milton himself, as he appears in *Paradise Lost*, might well have seemed to female readers to be as much akin to God as they themselves were to Satan, Eve, or Sin.

Like God, for instance, Milton-as-epic-speaker creates heaven and earth (or their verbal equivalents) out of a bewildering chaos of history, legend, and philosophy. Like God, he has mental powers that penetrate to the furthest corners of the cosmos he has created, to the depths of hell and the heights of heaven, soaring with "no middle flight" toward ontological subjects "unattempted yet in Prose or Rhyme." Like God, too, he knows the consequence of every action and event, his comments upon them indicating an almost divine consciousness of the simultaneity of past, present, and future. Like God, he punishes Satan, rebukes Adam and Eve, moves angels from one battle station to another, and grants all mankind glimpses of apocalyptic futurity, when a "greater Man" shall arrive to restore paradisal bliss. And like God—like the Redeemer, like the Creator, like the Holy Ghost—he is male. Indeed, as a male poet justifying the ways of a male deity to male readers, he rigorously excludes all females from the heaven of his poem, except insofar as he can beget new ideas upon their chaotic fecundity, like the Holy Spirit "brooding on the vast Abyss" and making it pregnant.

Even the blindness to which this epic speaker occasionally refers makes him appear godlike rather than handicapped. Cutting him off from "the cheerful ways" of ordinary mortals and reducing Satan's and Eve's domain of material nature to "a universal blanc," it elevates him above trivial fleshly concerns and causes "Celestial light" to "shine inward" upon him so that, like Tiresias, Homer, and God, he may see the mysteries of the spiritual world and "tell / Of things invisible to mortal sight." And finally, even the syntax in which he speaks of these "things invisible" seems somehow godlike. Certainly the imposition of a Latinate sentence structure on English suggests both supreme confidence and supreme power. *Paradise Lost* is the "most remarkable Production of the world," Keats dryly decided in one of his more anti-Miltonic moments, because of the way its author forceda "northern dialect" to accommodate itself "to greek and latin inversions and intonations." But not only are Greek and Latin the quintessential languages of masculine scholarship (as Virginia Woolf, for instance, never tired of noting), they are also the languages of the Church, of patristic and patriarchal ritual and theology. Imposed upon English, moreover, their periodic sentences, perhaps more than any other stylistic device in *Paradise Lost*, flaunt the poet's divine foreknowledge. When Milton begins a sentence "Him the Almighty," the reader knows perfectly well that only the poet and God know how the sentence—like the verse, the book, and the epic of humanity itself—will come out in the end.

That the Romantics perceived, admired, and occasionally identified with Milton's bardlike godliness while at the same time identifying with Satan's Promethean energy and fortitude is one of the more understandable paradoxes of literary history. Though they might sometimes have been irreligious and radically visionary with Satan, poets like Wordsworth and Shelley were after all fundamentally "masculinist" with Milton, even if they revered Mary Wollstonecraft (as Shelley did) or praised Anne Finch (as Wordsworth did). In this respect, their metaphors for the poet and "his" art are as revealing as Milton's. Both Wordsworth and Shelley, for instance, conceive of the poet as a sort of divine ruler, an "unacknowledged legislator" in Shelley's famous phrase and "an upholder and preserver" in Wordsworth's more conservative words. As such a ruler, a sort of inspired patriarch, he is, like Milton, the guardian and hierophant of sacred mysteries, inalterably opposed to the "idleness and unmanly despair" of the false, effeminate creation. More, he is a virile trumpet that calls mankind to battle, a fiercely phallic sword that consumes its scabbard, and—most Miltonic of all—a godlike "influence which is moved not, but moves," modeled upon Aristotle's Unmoved Mover.

No wonder then that, as Joseph Wittreich puts it, the author of *Paradise Lost* was "the quintessence of everything the Romantics most admired . . . the Knower moved by truth alone, the Doer . . . causing divine deeds to issue forth from divine ideas, the Sayer who translates the divine idea into poetry. . . . Thus to know Milton was to know the answers to the indistinguishable questions—What is a poet? What is poetry?" Virginia Woolf, living in a world where the dead female poet who was "Judith Shakespeare" had laid aside her body so many times, made the same point in different words: "This is the essence, of which almost all other poetry is the dilution." Such an assertion might seem jubilant if made by a man. But the protean shadow of Milton's bogey seems to darken the page as Woolf writes.

Michael Wilding (essay date 1987)

SOURCE: "Milton's Early Radicalism," in *Dragons Teeth: Literature in the English Revolution*, Oxford University Press, 1987, pp. 7-27.

[*Wilding argues that Milton's democratic radicalism was present in his early work as well as his later writings.*]

How radical was the young Milton? Can we find evidence of a political commitment in the poetry associated with his Cambridge years? Is there anything in the early work that looks forward to the revolutionary?

Milton's *Poems* of 1645 has generally been seen as an unpolitical or apolitical volume, as embodying Milton's youthful poems of the age before the revolution. For those who find the image of Milton the revolutionary politically embarrassing, it is still possible to preserve Milton in the pantheon of great literary, figures, by focusing on this allegedly prepolitical gathering of the "minor poems." The "New Critical" reading of the 1645 volume offered in the commentary by Cleanth Brooks and John E. Hardy, presented a poet shorn of the political. The New Critical, depoliticizing approach to Milton was never as critically exciting as the application of the approach to the metaphysical poets. Milton never became a central figure in new critical practice, despite the earlier essay on **"L'Allegro"** and **"Il Penseroso"** in Brooks's *The Well Wrought Urn* But the negative aspects of the approach, the removal of the socio-political context, had their effect and the Brooks and Hardy readings achieved a pervasive influence.

Louis Martz developed the approach in his elegant essay, "The Rising Poet, 1645."

> Here is the picture of a youthful poet, free from adult cares, sometimes wandering alone, amusing himself, sometimes making music for his friends or acquaintances, sometimes writing in his native vein, sometimes evoking a strain from idealized antiquity— but with a light and dancing posture that we do not usually associate with John Milton: *et humum vix tetigit pede*. It is clear, from many indications, that Milton has designed his book with great care to create this impression.

> The entire volume strives to create a tribute to a youthful era now past—not only the poet's own youth, but a state of mind, a point of view, ways of writing, ways of living, an old culture and outlook now shattered by the pressures of maturity and by the actions of political man.

But whereas Brooks and Hardy had essentially ignored the political, Martz presents a political motive behind the nonpolitical impression. He argues that the volume is contrived to present an unpolitical impression, a commitment to "the transcendent values of art" rather than "the political situation."

Meanwhile, the facing title page prepares us for a volume that will contain songs of unlabored elegance, in the recent courtly style: "The Songs were set in Music by Mr. Henry Lawes Gentleman of the Kings Chappel, and one of His Maiesties Private Musick"— a notice quite in line with Moseley's preface, which associates Milton's volume with the poems of Waller that Moseley had published a year before. Waller, as everyone knew, had been exiled for his plot against Parliament on the King's behalf; nevertheless Moseley insists on saying: "that incouragement I have already received from the most ingenious men in their clear and courtious entertainment of Mr. Waller's late choice Peeces, hath once more made me adventure into the World, presenting it with these ever-green, and not to be blasted Laurels." This bland ignoring, or bold confronting, of the political situation, with its emphasis upon the transcendent values of art, is maintained by reprinting here from the 1637 edition, Henry Lawes's eloquent dedication of Milton's *Mask* to a young nobleman with strong Royalist associations; by the Latin poems in memory of the bishops of Winchester and Ely; by the complimentary writings prefixed to the Latin poems, showing the high regard that Milton had won in Catholic Italy; by Milton's admiration for Manso, the fine old Catholicpatron of Tasso; and by other aspects of the volume, notably the sonnet beginning: "Captain or Colonel, or Knight in Arms, / Whose chance on these defenceless dores may sease." This is not a poem of presumptuous naïveté but of mature awareness, in which the poet, as Brooks and Hardy say, with a "wry humor . . . contemplates a little ruefully but still with a fine inner confidence, the place of the poet in a jostling world of men at arms."

Immediately certain separations need to be made in Martz's account between Milton's activities and those of his publisher. Martz stresses the Waller connection. Milton may not have known of Moseley's intention, may not have agreed with it, may have gone along with it as many an author has gone along with a publisher's promotional strategy that he or she was not in agreement with. Milton may have tacitly accepted the image Moseley was creating. At the same time, the head-notes to the poems themselves and the arrangement of the volume allow a radical theme to be perceived in the volume. Both Moseley as publisher and Milton as writer would have been aware of the advantages of appealing both to Protestant radicals and to royalist aesthetes: a larger audience than appealing to only one sectarian group. Moseley may have endured Milton's radicalism as Milton may have endured Moseley's conservatism. The permutations are multiple. My point is to stress the multifaceted nature of the 1645 volume. Thomas Corns has argued that the 1645 *Poems* show Milton engaged in "a further attempt to dissociate himself from the archetypal sectary," an image with which his polemical writings had identified him. "It contains a number of poems which in no way square with his ideological position by 1645, but which serve to restate his social status and aspirations." And Corns concludes

> Milton's volume of poetry indicates clearly enough in its maturer items the Puritanism of the poet. Milton draws attention to it. **"Lycidas"** is introduced as foretelling "the ruine of our corrupted Clergy then in

their height" . . . The abiding impression, however, of any browser selecting this volume in Moseley's bookshop early in 1646 must surely have been of the eminent respectability of its author. Over and over again the volume declares his wealth, his establishment connexions, his contact with European culture, and his scholarship.

Dr Corns is surely right in pointing to the contradictions within the 1645 volume between Milton's gestures at respectability and his gestures at radicalism. In part the contradictions may have been tactical, in part they may have expressed contradictions within Milton's own political thinking. But in exploring these contradictions it is necessary that both the conservative and the radical impulses should be explored. And though the apolitical, conservative, and respectable reference of the 1645 volume has been established, the radical impetus has been comparatively little examined. Christopher Hill has stressed that

> Although at the age of seventeen Milton wrote conventional Latin elegies on two bishops, the Vice-Chancellor and the university bedel, he never composed poems to royalty. Edward King, his junior contemporary, between 1631 and 1637 contributed to six collections of Latin verse celebrating royal births, marriages, etc.

But apart from such important negative, contextual evidence, what signs of radicalism can be read in the poems themselves?

When **"Lycidas"** was reprinted as the culminating item in the English poems in the 1645 volume, it was prefaced by an introductory five lines not present on its first appearance in the memorial volume for Edward King:

> In this monody the author bewails a learned friend, unfortunately drowned in his passage from Chester on the Irish Seas, 1637. And by occasion foretells the ruin of our corrupted clergy then in their height.

The first sentence exists in the Trinity manuscript. But the reference to "our corrupted clergy" appears only in the 1645 volume. It is a sentence that draws attention to the radical attack from the Pilot of the Galilean lake:

> How well could I have spared for thee, young swain,
> Enow of such as for their bellies' sake,
> Creep and intrude, and climb into the fold?

If the reader of 1638 missed decoding the pastoral, the reader of 1645 could not avoid the denunciation, could not avoid seeing the poet as placed unambiguously with the forces of reform. And the poet's gifts of political prophecy are likewise made unavoidable:

> But that two-handed engine at the door,
> Stands ready to smite once, and smite no more.

The attack and the promise of doom were written when the clergy were "then in their height." It is not a convenient piece of hindsight, but a committed exercise of radical foresight. As Haller remarked in *The Rise of Puritanism,*

> The blazing distinction of its author's genius and character has made it difficult for later generations to understand clearly how intimately and completely he was related to his own time. Milton's poem, with its extraordinary denunciation of the prelatical church, has become one of the most admired poems in literature. Yet, it was an expression of the same spirit which had been long making itself heard in the Puritan pulpit and which was at the moment clamoring in the reckless pamphlets of Prynne and Lilburne.

The 1645 superscription draws attention to the apocalyptic political note in **"Lycidas."** But the careful reader in 1638 as well as in 1645 would have detected a threatening gesture to established order in the poem's opening phrase, "Yet once more . . . ." Brooks and Hardy remark that "Evidently this is not the first time he has come forward with an immature performance, and this is the usual gloss. But, as a number of commentators "have remarked, there is a heavy resonance to "Yet once more," for all its seeming innocuousness. The allusion is to the Epistle to the Hebrews 12: 25-7:

> See that ye refuse not him that speaketh. For if they escaped not who refused him that spake on earth, much more shall not we escape, if we turn away from him that speaketh from heaven: whose voice then shook the earth: but now he hath promised, saying, Yet once more I shake not the earth only, but also heaven. And this word, Yet once more, signifieth the removing of those things that are shaken, as of things that are made, that those things which cannot be shaken may remain.

Both the King James and the Geneva Bibles make cross-reference to Haggai 2: 6-7:

> For thus saith the Lord of hosts; Yet once, it is a little while, and I will shake the heavens, and the earth, and the sea, and the dry land; And I will shake all nations, and the desire of all nations shall come: and I will fill this house with glory, saith the Lord of hosts.

The opening phrase, then, establishes the note of doom, of the judgement of the Lord, of the Second Coming. The earth and the heavens will be shaken, and those things that do not stand firm will be removed. And the conclusion of the poem, with Lycidas entertained by

> all the saints above,
> In solemn troops, and sweet societies
> That sing, and singing in their glory move,
> And wipe the tears for ever from his eyes

makes an allusion to Revelation 7: 17, "wipe away all tears from their eyes." The references are inescapably apocalyptic. The political pressures about to erupt in the revolution are sensed by the poet-prophet. Doom is spelled out for the corrupt clergy. And the vision of renewal, of the New Jerusalem, is caught in the final line:

Tomorrow to fresh woods, and pastures new.

The two indisputable points of emphasis in any collection of poems are the opening and closing positions. If we would argue that Milton deliberately used the concluding position to make a radical political assertion with **"Lycidas,"** then it is likely that he would make similar use of the opening position. And we notice there is a brief, situating gloss attached to the title of the first poem of the 1645 volume: **'On the Morning of CHRISTS / Nativity. Compos'd 1629.'** Typographically "Compos'd 1629" is presented as part of the title. It does not have the explicit political proclamation of the head-note to **"Lycidas,"** but it clearly makes some proclamation; why else is it there?

The frequent assumption that Milton was somehow apologizing for early work, distancing himself from juvenilia by attaching dates in this volume has never seemed to me persuasive. Milton does not seem the sort of writer to be apologetic. There were a few poems from the Cambridge years not included in the 1645 volume; if he did not feel the poems were adequate to stand alone, then why not leave them with the uncollected? Rather than see the attached date as an apology, we might better see it as a political hint. The date worked into the **"Lycidas"** head-note, 1637, serves to establish that the poem denounced the clergy at the time of their height and foretold their ruin. The date 1629 puts **"On the Morning of Christ's Nativity"** way back in the pre-revolutionary days. And in those days the poet is shown as looking forward to better times to come. We are offered a glimpse of the apocalypse, delayed but promised.

> For if such holy song
> Enwrap our fancy long,
>   Time will run back, and fetch the age of gold,
> And speckled vanity
> Will sicken soon and die,
>   And lep'rous sin will melt from earthly mould
> And hell itself will pass away,
> And leave her dolorous mansions to the peering
>   day.

The process has begun. And even though "The babe lies yet in smiling infancy," Milton looks forward to the Crucifixion, and from the Crucifixion forward again to the Second Coming:

> When at the world's last session,
> The dreadful judge in middle air shall spread his
>   throne.

XVIII

> And then at last our bliss
> Full and perfect is,
>   But now begins; for from this happy day
> The old dragon under ground
> In straiter limits bound,
>   Not half so far casts his usurped sway . . .

Commentators have remarked how Milton moves from his ostensible theme of the nativity to a vision of apocalypse. What I would stress here are the political uses of apocalypse. Although millenarian beliefs were not confined to the radicals, their expression increasingly implied a revolutionary component. At the time the poem was composed, millenarian speculations were suppressed. Joseph Mede's *Key to Revelation* had appeared in Latin two years earlier, but no English translation appeared until 1643 when a committee of the House of Commons ordered one. Hill points out that "no vernacular translation of the seminal works on Revelation and Daniel by Brightman, Mede, Pareus or Alsted was published in England until after the meeting of the Long Parliament."

"On the Morning of Christ's Nativity," then, introduces a vernacular glimpse of apocalypse at a historical moment when such visions were suppressed because of their radical Utopian political implications. The poet reminds us of the date. And it is reissued as the opening proclamation to a collection of poems at an historical moment when apocalyptic pronouncements were part of the vanguard of revolutionary ideology. Between composing and publishing the poem Milton had written that powerful apocalyptic vision concluding *Of Reformation Touching Church-Discipline in England* (1641), looking forward to:

> that day when thou the Eternall and shortly-expected King shalt open the Clouds to *judge the* severall Kingdomes of the World, and distributing *Nationall Honours* and *Rewards* to Religious and just *Commonwealths,* shalt put an end to all Earthly *Tyrannies,* proclaiming thy universal and milde *Monarchy* through Heaven and Earth.

It is a vision that reminds us that apocalyptic imagery was not a "purely literary" matter, nota matter of pure aesthetics. In the context of the 1640s, a vision of apocalypse was a revolutionary vision. And in 1645 the parade of defeated pagan gods invited a reading that allowed an analogy with the parade of defeated bishops, clergy, and courtiers—Strafford, Laud, and the rest of that crew.

> The oracles are dumb,
> No voice or hideous hum
>   Runs through the arched roof in words deceiving.
> Apollo from his shrine
> Can no more divine,
>   With hollow shriek the steep of Delphos leaving.
> No nightly trance, or breathed spell,
> Inspires the pale-eyed priest from the prophetic cell.

That 'arched roof' invites a Gothic image. Here we can see the English unpurged church as much as any remote Hellenic ritual, the priest and the cell allowing a ready impression of Roman Catholic leanings.

XXI

> In consecrated earth,
> And on the holy hearth,
>   The lars, and lemures moan with midnight plaint,
> In urns, and altars round,
> A drear and dying sound
>   Affrights the flamens at their service quaint . . .

We are accustomed to the critical procedure that glosses "all-judging Jove" in **"Lycidas"** as the Christian God. Classical references can be decoded for a contemporary, Christian meaning. It is no remote or illegitimate reading that would see in "consecrated earth" "altars," and "service quaint" a reference to established Anglican ceremonial, the resented altar rather than the table, the quaint idolatrous rituals. As Milton was to write in *Of Reformation:*

> the Table of Communion now become a Table of separation stands like an exalted platforme upon the brow of the quire, fortifi'd with bulwark, and barricado, to keep off the profane touch of the Laicks, whilst the obscene and surfeted Priest scruples not to paw, and mammock the sacramentall bread, as familiarly as his Tavern Bisket.

> Peor, and Baalim,
> Forsake their temples dim . . .

English churches are readily referred to as temples particularly if the fetishism of church buildings is being denounced. "O Spirit, that dost prefer / Before all temples the upright heart and pure" Milton was to write in *Paradise Lost*

> And mooned Ashtaroth,
> Heaven's queen and mother both,
>   Now sits not girt with tapers' holy shine . . .

Once the pursuit of correspondence is begun, it is hard not to read this as a dismissal of the Roman Catholic cult of Mary.

> In vain with timbrelled anthems dark
> The sable-stoled sorcerers bear his worshipped ark.

What are these but black surpliced clergy promenading to church music—music so denounced by radical Puritans who held it was the work of Antichrist, introduced by the Pope in 666 AD. And to see this whole "damned crew" "troop to the infernal jail" had an undoubted prophetic touch when the twelve bishops did indeed troop off to jail in the Tower in 1641/2.

This is a contextual reading. The events of the early 1640s draw out a reading that was only prophetically implicit in the Cambridge of 1629. But the arrangement of the 1645 volume encourages the emergence of this reading, not only with the opening poem balancing the explicitly radical attack on the clergy of the concluding poem, but with the two psalms immediately following **"On the Morning of Christ's Nativity."** Again they are prefaced with a temporal headnote. "This and the following Psalm were done by the Author at fifteen years old." There is no need to read in this any apology for immaturity. Psalm 136 has endured more widely than any of Milton's verses through its incorporation and happy popular acceptance in the English hymn book. If any implication of immaturity remains, it is in the context of truth spoken out of the mouths of babes and sucklings, of powerful, irrefutable, prophetic, Christian utterance from the young poet.

Our babe to show his Godhead true,
Can in his swaddling bands control the damned
  crew.

Not a blasphemous assumption of Godhead; but none the
less a clear indication of prophetic possession in youth,
the year preceding his matriculation at Cambridge. For
what is the subject of these two psalms? We tend too
readily to pass them by, see them as part of that psalm-
versifying of Protestant tradition, and disregard their quite
specific content.

When the blest seed of Terah's faithful son,
After long toil their liberty had won
                              (Psalm 114, 1-2)

In bloody battle he brought down
Kings of prowess and renown.
                              (Psalm 136, 62-3)

In 1634 Milton turned to Psalm 114 again, translating it
into Greek hexameters and sending a copy to Alexander
Gill. With the victories of the Parliamentary army of 1645,
these versions take on a prophetic significance.

To bring out the full political implications of the young
Milton's prophetic vision, we need to look at that recurrent image of the Cambridge poems, the music of the
spheres. As Arthur Barker remarked, "The force with
which this idea struck Milton's imagination is indicated
by the fact that from the '[**Nativity**] **Ode**' to '**Lycidas**'
he was almost incapable of writing on a serious subject
without introducing the music." In the context of the
image of the music of the spheres, the prophetic note
takes on an unavoidable millenarian political edge. The
lost music can be regained; there can be a new golden
age.

XIII

Ring out, ye crystal spheres,
Once bless our human ears.

And the poet begs the music to ring out for a quite specific social purpose:

XIV

For if such holy song
Enwrap our fancy long
  Time will run back, and fetch the age of gold.

The age of gold is glossed in political terms, not only in
moral terms. "Lep'rous sin will melt from earthly mould,"
but also

XV

Yea Truth, and Justice then
Will down return to men,
  Orb'd in a rainbow; and like glories wearing
Mercy will sit between . . .

Truth, Justice, and Mercy have their undeniable reference
to earthly administrations as well as to any larger spiritual
context. As J. B. Broadbent remarked, "The second descent, of Mercy, Truth and Justice, has only the abstract
effect of a reference to eschatology, because Milton is
thinking of political rather than spiritual qualities". And
the conclusion of **"At a Solemn Music"** suggests the
achievement of that music on earth prior to the transcending
of the material realm:

O may we soon again renew that song,
And keep in tune with Heav'n, till God ere long
To his celestial consort us unite,
To live with him, and sing in endless morn of light.

It might be argued that truth, justice, and mercy are easy
abstractions. Is there any social specificity in Milton's
vision that would entitle us to see a more fleshed-out
incipient radicalism? The description of "the Heav'n-born-
child / All meanly wrapp'd in the rude manger" **"On the
Nativity,"**30-1) certainly allows a sympathy for the poor.

Nature in awe to him
Had doff'd her gaudy trim,
  With her great master so to sympathize.

Milton was later to use the circumstances of Christ's
humble birth to make a radical point. "For notwithstanding the gaudy superstition of som devoted still ignorantly
to temples, we may be well assur'd that he who disdaind
not to be laid in a manger, disdains not to be preachd in
a barn" (*Considerations touching the likeliest means to
remove hirelings out of the church,* 1659). And the vision
of the shepherds "Sat simply chatting in a rustic row"
again asserts a lowly simplicity. It serves to contrast
Christ's heavenly majesty with the humility of his descent to earth, but it serves too to elevate the humble
and to devalue the earthly proud; the first shall be last and
the last shall be first. Hugh Richmond has remarked on the
aesthetic consequences of this note of humility, this rejection of an élitist standpoint.

The theme of a saviour "All meanly wrapt in the rude
manger" encourages in Milton a quaint particularity
more characteristic of the humble craftsman than the
sophisticated academic . . . the virtues admired in **"On
the Nativity"** derive from this modest recognition of
the Christian rhythm: its acceptance of the humble,
quaint, discontinuous nature of experience, which gave
the art of anonymous medieval craftsmen a vivid
particularity denied to the arid theorizing of the
pretentious Schoolmen. Few but scholars and specialists
now regularly read even an Aquinas, while millions
still delight in the statuary and paintings of the forgotten
artisans who were his contemporaries.

Although, as Milton wrote in the vacation exercise of
1628, "my hand has never grown horny with driving the
plough . . . I was never a farm hand at seven or laid
myself down full length in the midday sun," he did not
fail to remind himself in *The Reason of Church-government Urg'd against Prelaty* (1641) that "ease and leasure
was given thee for thy retired thoughts out of the sweat

of other men." Against the often-presented image of the élitist Milton, we need to reassert his stress on Christ's humble birth, on the simplicity of the shepherds, on the simple manual labour of Adam and Eve, contrasted with the tyrannical pomp of Satan's authoritarian regime in *Paradise Lost*.

So far we have stressed the threatening aspect of the apocalyptic note, the warnings of doom on the ungodly. But the vision of the Second Coming was a vision of universal peace. And so in **"On the Morning of Christ's Nativity"**

III

But he her fears to cease,
Sent down the meek-eyed Peace,
  She crowned with olive green, came softly sliding

Down through the turning sphere
His ready harbinger,
  With turtle wing the amorous clouds dividing,

And waving wide her myrtle wand,
She strikes a universal peace through sea and land.

IV

No war, or battle's sound
Was heard the world around . . .

Rosemond Tuve has stressed the theme of peace in the poem:

Encouraged to do so by Milton's own unifying use of great ancient images towards one thematic end, we could make shift to indicate the theme of this nativity hymn in two symbolic words: *our peace*. Only, however, if they are understood to carry all those wide and deep meanings he has gathered in, touching the redemption of all nature from guilty error, reconciliation and restored participation in the divine harmony, and final union with the divine light; traditional in poetry and liturgy of the season, these were to Milton most familiarly accepted and most natural in the form given them in the New Testament epistles.

But in noting "all those wide and deep meanings" gathered around peace, Miss Tuve ignores the political. Yet a vision of peace is of course a political vision. It cuts across those vested power-interests that need and create and maintain war. The political context is presented clearly enough by Milton; the implements of warfare—the products of organized political societies—are stressed:

The idle spear and shield were high up hung,
The hooked chariot stood
Unstained with hostile blood,
  The trumpet spake not to the armed throng . . .

It is organized warfare that is alluded to; not just spear and shield but the chariot, product of a technological state; not something that can be dismissed as a small brawl, but "the armed throng." And the political organization behind the warfare now brought to a halt is spelled out as monarchy:

And kings sat still with awful eye,
As if they surely knew their sovran Lord was by.

They sit there still before the wand of peace. Their reactions are not shown; the blankness of their portrayal is indication enough that Milton could not spell out what had happened to them, a lack of comment that indicates the inexpressible anti-monarchical feeling. In times of press censorship and severe repression, it is the negative evidence that we need to turn to. When monarchy appears again in the poem it is in connection with the Satanic reaction to the beginning of the new age:

          for from this happy day
The old dragon under ground
In straiter limits bound,
  Not half so far casts his usurped sway,
And wroth to see his kingdom fail,
Swinges the scaly horror of his folded tail.

It is a kingdom; and the phrase "usurped sway" evokes the idea of other usurping kings; the Norman Yoke, that imposition of tyranny on the English people by the usurping power of William the Conqueror, one of the most powerful radical images of the revolutionary and pre-revolutionary period.

To find political radicalism in the non-prophetic early poems as well as in the prophetic ones would strengthen our case. **"L'Allegro"** seems an initially unlikely locus for the political: but the force with which the political has been denied here suggests a significant repression.

Come, and trip it as you go
On the light fantastic toe,
And in thy right hand lead with thee,
The mountain nymph, sweet Liberty;
And if I give thee honour due,
Mirth, admit me of thy crew
To live with her, and live with thee,
In unreproved pleasures free . . .

It is hard to see how "sweet Liberty" could be construed as anything other than liberty. It is not luxury or licence or anything pejorative. It is a positive value that has an unavoidable political meaning. Switzerland, that Protestant mountainous stronghold of religious freedom, may be implied. Yet Cleanth Brooks in his influential essay in *The Well Wrought Urn* dismisses this natural reading:

If, under the influence of Milton's later political career, we tend to give Liberty any political significance, we find her in **"L'Allegro"** in very strange company, consorting with

Jest and youthful Jollity
Quips and Cranks, and wanton Wiles
Nods, and Becks, and Wreathed smiles . . .

Sport that wrincled Care derides
And Laughter holding both his sides.

But the passage Brooks quotes precedes the introduction of "Liberty"; jest, jollity, quips, and cranks are presented as the qualities or companions of Mirth. Liberty is a more serious quality that Milton distinguishes from Mirth. Brooks offers no argument for his rejection of the political reading of liberty here. He implies that a knowledge of Milton's later career pollutes the reading, but liberty would have meant liberty whatever Milton's later career. And the introduction of Dr Johnson does not clinch Brooks's case. "Dr Johnson, always on the alert to ruffle up at the presence of Milton's somewhat aggressively republican goddess, does not betray any irritation at the presence of Liberty here." That Dr Johnson made no political interpretation here does not preclude such an interpretation. Brooks went on to make another distortion that has proved remarkably influential in later readings:

> The first scene is a dawn scene—sunrise and people going to work: the ploughman, the milkmaid, the mower, and the shepherd. But though we see people going to work, we never see them *at* their work.

But when we turn to that first scene, Brooks's case simply falls down:

> While the ploughman near at hand,
> Whistles o'er the furrowed land,
> And the milkmaid singeth blithe,
> And the mower whets his scythe,
> And every shepherd tells his tale
> Under the hawthorn in the dale.

Stanley Fish has pointed to the pervasive ambiguity of syntax and image and reference in **"L'Allegro"** and "Il Penseroso." What Brooks did was to accentuate one aspect of the ambiguous and repress the other. The phrases in the poem that can be read as indicating people going to work can as readily be interpreted as accounts of their being engaged in work. The ploughman who "whistles o'er the furrowed land" may be whistling across a ploughed field on his way to work; or the whistles may express the song of his labour and the speed with which he is ploughing. The milkmaid who "singeth blithe" may as readily be singing while she works as not. The shepherd who "tells his tale" can be telling a tale while keeping an eye on the sheep; or he may be counting them, telling his sheep, keeping tally. The clinching case is the mower who "whets his scythe." Cleanth Brooks writes as if the sharpening of the scythe was not work, but some relaxed occupation of the mower's leisure time. But the scythe has to be constantly resharpened, and the whetting is part of the rhythm and activity of mowing as much as the strokes cutting the grass.

The work presented is joyous. In **"L'Allegro"** labour is delight. It is a vision like William Morris's haymaking in *News from Nowhere*; fulfilling, enjoyable. Yet the exhausting quality of the labour is not repressed: this is not a false or purely decorative pastoral. To read of

Mountains on whose barren breast
The labouring clouds do often rest

is to be reminded of the hardship of physical rural labour, of the need for rest, of the harshness of the places of rest available to the labourer. When we are shown the cottage "hard by" the towers and battlements, the "hard" picks up the "barren breast" of the mountains on which the "labouring clouds . . . rest" to remind us of the hard life of the cottager; its implications spread into the cottage life, not the castle or crenellated manor-house. And it is not easy to see how labour can be evacuated from the picture of the cottagers

> Hard by, a cottage chimney smokes,
> From betwixt two aged oaks,
> Where Corydon and Thyrsis met,
> Are at their savoury dinner set
> Of herbs, and other country messes,
> Which the neat-handed Phillis dresses;
> And then in haste her bower she leaves,
> With Thestylis to bind the sheaves;
> Or if the earlier season lead
> To the tanned haycock in the mead . . .

Brooks comments "we do not accompany them to the haycock, nor do we feel the sun which tans it." But the demands of labour cannot that easily be denied. The emphatic present tense stresses the present activity of dressing the dinner and rushing off to work; the "haste" with which Phillis leaves the bower to bind the sheaves emphatically stresses a hurried meal, hurried because of the pressing demand of labour; and the alternative "or if the earlier season lead" similarly stresses that whatever season there is pressing work. There is always some demand.

As a result of his case, Brooks has to distort the poem further by treating unambiguous images of labour as somehow exceptions. He writes:

> Nobody sweats in the world of **"L'Allegro"**—except the goblin:

> Tells how the drudging Goblin swet,
> To ern his Cream-bowle duly set,
> When in one night, ere glimps of morn,
> His shadowy Flale hath thresh'd the Corn . . .

(Perhaps it is overingenious to suggest that in this scene—the only depiction of strenuous activity in the poem—Milton has "cooled" it off by making the flail "shadowy," by presenting it as part of a night scene, and by making the labourer, not a flesh-and-blood man, but a goblin. And yet the scene has been carefully patterned: it is balanced by the passage in **"Il Penseroso,"** where the spectator having taken refuge from the sun listens

> While the Bee with Honied thie,
> . . . at her flowry work doth sing . . .

Goblins and bees are the only creatures presented "at work" in the two poems.)

But rather than excepting goblins and bees, we might more profitably see them as thematic reinforcements of the image of labour. All nature labours: human male and female—ploughman and milkmaid; the labouring clouds; the insect world, the bee, type and reminder of human social labour here as in Marvell's "The Garden"; and the supernatural world. Labour is not something separate from life, either here, or in Adam and Eve's gardening labour in Eden, or in the description of God as "my great task-master" in **"Sonnet 7."**

The significance of Brooks's denial of the presence of labouring activity in **"L'Allegro"** is brought into political focus by some comments of Raymond Williams in *The Country and the City*:

> The whole result of the fall from paradise was that instead of picking easily from an all-providing nature, man had to earn his bread in the sweat of his brow; that he incurred, as a common fate, the curse of labour. What is really happening, in Jonson's and Carew's celebrations of a rural order, is an extraction of just this curse, by the power of art: a magical recreation of what can be seen as a natural bounty and then a willing charity: both serving to ratify and bless the country landowner, or, by a characteristic reification, his house. Yet this magical extraction of the curse of labour is in fact achieved by a simple extraction of the existence of the labourers. The actual men and women who rear the animals and drive them to the house and kill them and prepare them for meat; who trap the pheasants and partridges and catch the fish; who plant and manure and prune and harvest the fruit trees; these are not present; their work is all done for them by a natural order. When they do at last appear, it is merely as the "rout of rural folke" or, more simply, as "much poore" . . .

It is this extraction of the existence of the rural labourers in the representative rural poetry of the early seventeenth century that Milton confronts and resists. Brooks attempts to subsume **"L'Allegro"** to this dominant, quasi-pastoral, patrician, land-owning vision. And his attempt to do so when detected reveals the politics of Milton's vision more clearly. The labourers are present; indeed, the labourers are introduced before the landowners, gentry, and aristocrats are encountered in the poem. The labour of the rural workers is recognized, given a dignity and an aesthetic beauty in commemoration, and its hardships acknowledged. The human basis for Milton's stand against the forces of oppression—bishops, monarchs, all the figures of power and authority that he confronted—lies here in a recognition and sympathy for the labouring class.

And "labour and intent study" are the destined lot of the prophetic poet. Inspiration works dialectically with the medium; the medium needs to have a store of knowledge and a developed wisdom, across which inspiration can play. Describing the first steps in his decision to become a writer, Milton recalled in *The Reason of Church-Government Urg'd Against Prelaty* that, encouraged by the response his early poems had received from members of the private Academies of Italy,

> I began thus farre to assent both to them and divers of my friends here at home, and not lesse to an inward prompting which now grew daily upon me, that by labour and intent study (which I take to be my portion in this life) joyn'd with the strong propensity of nature, I might perhaps leave something so written to aftertimes, as they should not willingly let it die.

Labour and intent study and inward prompting—the Protestant drive. And prophetic millenarianism has a long tradition of radical, revolutionary associations. The surprise would be if Milton's prophetic apocalyptic note were unpolitical. The repression of apocalyptic commentary under Laud was from a recognition of its revolutionary potential. In that time of brutal censorship, the political had to be expressed covertly, in literary code. By 1645 the political situation had changed and the code could be openly translated. From that perspective we can rediscover the radicalism of Milton's earlier years.

On Milton's sociability:

One can imagine the blind poet visiting a coffee house to hear the *Gazette* read aloud and listen to the news from across the city. As his health worsened, perhaps he believed or hoped that coffee's medicinal properties could relieve his gout as its advertisements promised. Milton would clearly have appreciated the coffee houses' temperance: they did not serve alcohol during the Commonwealth, and many remained 'temperance establishments' at the Restoration. Whereas Parker envisions Milton 'dwelling apart, holding high converse with the best minds of the past', Milton's contemporaries portray a more outgoing man who enjoyed conversing with real people—the *'chief Scene'* and 'main end' of visiting a coffee house. Milton's daughter Deborah described him as 'Delightful Company, the life of the Conversation'; Aubrey concurs that Milton was 'Extreme pleasant in his conversation', and Toland, too, notes that 'He was affable in Conversation'.

*"'Where Men of Differing Judgements Croud':
Milton and the Culture of the Coffee Houses," in*
Seventeenth Century, *Vol. 9, No. 1, Spring 1994.*

Catherine Gimelli Martin (essay date 1993)

SOURCE: "Demystifying Disguises: Adam, Eve, and the Subject of Desire," in *Renaissance Discourses of Desire*, University of Missouri Press, 1993, pp. 237-58.

[Martin explores the role of desire in Milton's depictions of Paradise.]

One of the chief innovations in Milton's conception of paradise is his frank acceptance of desire as an essential and inalienable attribute of the human condition. Free of "dishonest shame," Adam and Eve need neither the "mere shows of seeming pure" nor any of the other "troublesome disguises which wee wear." Yet not merely the "Hypocrites austere" the poet condemns for "defaming as impure what God declares / Pure," but many modern readers also question the innocence of this portrayal of uninhibited "connubial Love." What *seems* to be "free to all"—desire—may not *be* free and, in fact, has been interpreted as something less than pure and more than patriarchal, as the mystified voice of patriarchy itself.

In fact, though Adam demanded, and God seemed to grant, a consort fit "to participate / All rational delight," our first view of the human pair suggests that they are unequal, "as thir sex not equal seem'd." However, since this observation is conveyed not only through the potentially misleading verb of "seeming," but actually through the eyes of Satan himself, many of the poem's more sympathetic readers have been inclined to reject these "appearances" as deceptive. Yet unfortunately for this line of defense, all else that Satan observes about our "Grand Parents" turns out to be accurate not only from his own but from the narrator's point of view. If we are to dispute the inequality he attributes to Eve, then we must doubt both that she and Adam are "Lords of all," since they only *seem* so, and also suppose that Satan's gaze is no more correct in observing how they are *formed* than how they seem. Furthermore, although both male and female merely *seem* worthy of the image of their maker, it is their "seeming" to reflect this image that allows them to be "plac't" in "true filial freedom," while their purported inequality is reinforced by the description of Eve being *"form'd"* for "softness" and "sweet attractive grace," Adam "for contemplation . . . and valor." Finally, since Satan's observations prove especially reliable whenever his success is at stake, and since his observations here are not only useful to his plans but mixed with an unfeigned if ambivalent sense of admiration, it seems most plausible to assume that not merely his torment but his gaze is sharpened as he spies upon the pair, seeing

> Two of far nobler shape erect and tall,
> Godlike erect, with native Honor clad
> In naked Majesty seem'd Lords of all,
> And worthy seem'd, for in thir looks Divine
> The image of thir glorious Maker shone,
> Truth, Wisdom, Sanctitude severe and pure,
> Severe, but in true filial freedom plac't;
> Whence true autority in men; though both
> Not equal, as thir sex not equal seem'd;
> For contemplation hee and valor form'd,
> For softness shee and sweet attractive Grace,
> He for God only, shee for God in him.

Whatever the conflicting connotations of the verbs in this passage, their ultimate effect is to confirm the ironically appropriate inconsistency of Satan's gaze, a gaze not fundamentally different from our own. Sharing some of his dis-ease but also his awe, we are thus led into a paradisal paradox without any "seeming" resolution.

At the heart of this paradox lie the unresolved questions of whether Eve's weaker attributes can be reconciled with her full reflection of God's image, and whether her belat-

edness also implies a secondariness in dignity and power. The centrality of these issues is further stressed by the fact that the observation of her inherent "softness" is immediately followed and seemingly summarized by the most decisive statement of the difference between the two, their sequential and apparently subordinationist creation, "He for God only, Shee for God in Him." If this difference is taken literally, what, if anything, can remain of their "true filial freedom"; does it not thereby become an empty technicality, or even a covert form of domination that, as Christine Froula concludes, not only "transsexualizes" Eve's autonomous desire, but also serves as a means of "silencing and voiding . . . female creativity"? However, like the defense of Edenic desire that would dismiss Satan's "seeming" point of view entirely, an unproblematic acceptance of this point of view—which requires dismissing Eve entirely—raises as many problems as it resolves. Like a large number of the solutions proposed both by Milton's detractors and his defenders, Froula's account omits many of the epic's actual ambiguities by drawing upon inherited assumptions about the "orthodoxly" Puritan, patriarchal poet and, consequently, about the uniform, didactic purpose supposedly informing what is actually an unconventional, evolutionary epic. Yet just as surely as Milton's Eden contrasts with the conventionally static Paradise, his portrayal of the "yet sinless" Adam and Eve resists the conventional treatment by emphasizing the constant alteration, development, and reciprocity of capacities that belong at once to general human subjects and to specific male and female prototypes.

Thus any atemporal reading of this "allegory of desire" tends to ignore how the poem exploits traditional, even courtly models of male and female subjectivity only to subvert them, just as it exploits Edenic gates and boundaries primarily to subordinate *them* to individual choice. As Adam's "sudden apprehension" reveals in the aftermath of Eve's "tainted" dream, even Satan's most forceful incursions into Eden can easily be undone by the willing subject: "Evil into the mind of God or Man / May come and go, so unapprov'd, and leave / No spot or blame behind." Similarly, God's provisions for "advent'rous Eve" are not only ambiguous but also ultimately impermanent. Although she is initially depicted as the vine to Adam's elm, she later proves more of a quester, at least in the physical, heroic sense, than he is, while he takes on the guiding and corrective functions that Spenser would assign a feminine "conscience" or soul like Una's. In this way not only are both sexes "transsexualized," but the substitutions and transferences of this process are never stabilized into a new hierarchy. A dialectic of assertion and subversion is finally the *most* characteristic element of the landscape and life of this paradise; and in spite of the intimate connections between the former and the latter, no permanent alteration in matter or spirit ever occurs that is not subject to the reversal implicit in the free act of the desiring subject. Hence, lacking Eve's permission, Satan proves no Archimago; he can impose on her only the most transitory and ultimately unreal loss, a mere inquietude. Correspondingly, since all Edenic boundaries exist primarily to mark the threshold of choice, not of purity or contamination, its gender roles like its other "barriers" characteristically remain "virtue proof" *because*—not *in spite of*—the potentially "errant" suggestions that surround them.

For these as well as a number of related reasons, the paradisal paradox can only be untangled by emphasizing that although the epic portrayal of gender (as of all physical appearances) grants each a power and a dignity of their own, the poem's characteristic mode of emblematic outline and qualification, statement and revision, ultimately depicts Eve's subjection to Adam's authority as more apparent than real. "Impli'd" but not coerced, even the most fundamental precept of her submission—that it be "requir'd with gentle sway"—remains open to her own as well as to Adam's interpretation. In fact, the multiple meanings of "requir'd" underscore the ambiguity of Milton's interpretation of biblical headship (1 Cor. 11:3-10; Eph. 5:23) in ways that make the verbal qualifications surrounding this "sway" far more meaningful than those surrounding "seeming." To *require* can mean either to request *or* to exact, but since the "yet sinless" Eve is not always "submiss," the former, not the latter sense predominates. Similarly, her emblematic role as Adam's vine fails to limit her to a largely passive or decorative function; while she may (and does) choose simply to complement his "masculine" sturdiness, she equally may and does choose to surpass and enthrall this "elm." Yet these like the poem's other vicissitudes are no more "tainted" than Eve's dream. While many critics have condemned this along with other aspects of her supposedly coy or flirtatious femininity, the variety of her moods, like the various walks and "seasons" of Eden, and like the "sweet reluctant amorous delay" with which she responds to Adam, supply an ambiguity necessary not only to the representation of her own freedom, but to that which she shares with all God's creation. The conditionality of her response and its complex potential for acceptance, withdrawal, or both, is the source and warrant of its independence as well as of its "attractive grace." Significantly, then, while J. Hillis Miller objects to Eve's admixture of "coy submission" and "modest pride," qualities that for him suggest a "wantonness" too experienced for innocence, he cannot help noting that it effectively places "her above Adam or outside his control and identifies her with Milton's independent power of poetry. Eve's curly tendrils imply independence as well as subjection."

Yet if these observations cast considerable doubt upon Froula's charge that "Eve is not a self, a subject at all; she is rather a substanceless image, a mere 'shadow' without object until the voice unites her to Adam," in some respects the human pair *does* appear to be separate and not equal in a way that clearly implies Eve's inferiority. Although both receive "true autority" in reflecting their maker's "Truth, Wisdom, Sanctitude severe and pure," Adam seems the more exact copy, as the contemplation of "His fair large Front and Eye" declare. As noted above, Eve's gifts seem considerably less: softness, sweetness, attractiveness and Grace, even if the latter is taken to include spiritual as well as physical gifts. If this in turn implies a relay system of sexual authority and desire whereby Adam is made for God and Eve for God-in-him, the "part-ness" of

his partner can in fact be taken as literally as Froula does. Must Eve interpret her creator only through Adam, or even worship him only through him—a seemingly idolatrous possibility? Furthermore, if she independently understands the will of the "presence Divine" directly, why does she so often need Adam's guidance, even in interpreting her own dream? In order accurately to define the nature of Eve's "subjection" to the God-in-him and the nature of a difference posed as a series of continuities-within-difference—as Eve's loose tendrils, for instance, at once repeat and modify the "manly clusters" of Adam's hair—we must then turn to the archetypal descriptions of awakening life to which Froula also turns: Eve's creation narrative in book 4, and Adam's parallel narrative in book 8. Only here and in what follows can we discover the cumulative effect of comparing Adam to Eve as contemplation to Grace, as clusters to tendrils, truth to quest, and finally, as vision to revision—comparisons that on at least three occasions relate them not only to each other, but to Raphael and finally to the whole heavenly order.

Although Eve relates the story of her awakening consciousness first, this fact need not, as several feminist critics remind us, grant it any kind of priority. First and last, like "Great / Or Bright infers not Excellence," as Raphael is at some pains to teach Adam. And while Adam finally understands what Eve earlier had "suddenly apprehended," that "to know / That which before us lies in daily life, / Is the prime Wisdom," Raphael's implicit approval of her reliance on experience over abstraction, like his mild disapproval of Adam's more abstract "roving," fails wholly to elevate her form of apprehension over his. As book 9 will make abundantly clear, not only do both modes have their dangers, but each is tied to clear-cut sexual differences that Raphael's ritual hailing of the pair reinforces. Playing upon his name, Raphael greets Adam as more than clay, as a creature fit to invite "Spirits of Heaven." Eve is on the other hand hailed as a type of Mary, "Mother of Mankind, whose fruitful Womb / Shall fill the World." The implication here is that Adam is intrinsically closer to the Spirits of Heaven, and Eve to her nursery, for whose "tendance" she leaves the discourse on astronomy. Hence once again the apparent mutuality of gender roles appears to dissolve into what Froula terms the "ontological hierarchy" of *Paradise Lost*.

However, this hierarchy is again modified or "corrected" by Raphael's narration of Satan's fall. The moral of this story is that "filial freedom" is opposed to the rigid "Orders and Degrees" that Satan upholds in the spurious name of "liberty" and depends instead upon an acceptance of difference. Since Adam's role in regard to Eve is far less priestly or exalted than that which Satan envied in the Son, both humans uttering prayers "unanimous," we must then question if their difference can also be a form of freedom, if not of equality as we have come to know it. This problem is magnified by the tremendous evolution in recent concepts of equality. As Joseph Wittreich points out in *Feminist Milton*, earlier female readers were likely to interpret gender differences as "evidence of distinction, not inequality"; early feminists, too, generally supported a concept of male and female mutuality in which "ideally their different qualities blend." For modern feminists after Freud, however, difference signifies domination. Thus for Froula, the whole point of the temporal priority of Eve's birth narration is to subsume it in Adam's; to inculcate the idea that "Eve can only 'read' the world in oneway, by making herself the mirror of the patriarchal authority of Adam." The mothering waters of the lake to which Eve is intuitively drawn, like her own reflected image, are thus canceled by the "invisible voice" that leads her to Adam, the voice at once of God/Adam/Milton and Patriarchy.

Yet as suggested above, this interpretation fails to account for the full scope of the mirroring process that connects Adam to Eve as vitally as Eve to her lake. In this process a recognition of difference *precedes* one of continuity, which in both narratives is represented as a gradual series of differentiations and corrections. The uniformity of this process is underscored by the fact that Eve's awakening response is *not* in fact to her own reflection, but like Adam's, to the questions surrounding her existence: "what I was, when thither brought, and how." Her next response is to a "murmuring sound / Of waters" that brings her to "a liquid Plain . . . Pure as th' expanse of Heav'n." Already aware of the existence of the Heavens, which symbolize the mental orientation of both human genders, her fascination with their replication both beneath and above her then causes her to seek an answering existence. While unlike Adam she finds this in the form of her own reflection, which Narcissus-like responds with "looks / Of sympathy and love," Eve is an unfallen *anti*-Narcissus who, as she later acknowledges, is merely "unexperienc't." Unlike the conceited creature who prefers self-absorption to another's love, but like the child of Lacan's mirror stage, initially incapable of separating self (the form recumbent on the green bank) from Other (reflection, watery womb, or Mother), and *like* Adam, she needs an external stimulus, God's voice, to help her make this distinction and hail her into the symbolic order. In this respect Eve provides an archetypal model of awakening consciousness fully as much as Adam does; her "hailing" into the symbolic order, like his, initiates her dis- and re-union with a creature like herself ("whose image thou art,") but *without* any confusion or shadow-barrier between them.

Entering the landscape of names/language/difference, Eve thus gains a new title and position, "Mother of human Race." This title, along with the acceptance and the renunciation it implies, exalts more than it limits her, since it allies her with the Son. Like him, she becomes an example of the interdependence of growth and sacrifice: both are able to reflect the Father's creative design only by renouncing self-love, yet both are appropriately rewarded by achieving the potential to produce "Multitudes like thyself," not merely like the Father or Adam. Hence, just as the Son's descent "to assume / Man's Nature" neither lessens nor degrades his own but grants him even greater equality with God, "equally enjoying / God-like fruition," so Eve can enjoy "God-like fruition" only by quitting her virgin, self-mirroring independence. In return she, too, gains restoration and exaltation within an expanded mirroring process, the potential for limitless reflexivity in the space of Edenic marriage, an exchange of desire that is alone fecund.

Hence the poet's striking revision, in fact reversal, of the Narcissus myth also illuminates his use of pagan images to describe Eve in another controversial passage, when Adam on Eve

> Smil'd with superior Love, as *Jupiter*
> On *Juno* smiles, when he impregns the Clouds
> That shed *May* Flowers; and press'd her Matron lip
> With kisses pure . . .

This, too, suggests that love, like life itself, can be created only by the alternation of similarity with difference—as when God "conglob'd / Like things to like, the rest to several place / Disparted." Extending the metaphor, Adam and Eve may be understood as a primally innocent Jove and Juno "disparted" from all negative connotation, representatives of the masculine and feminine principles of sunbeam and cloud, male seed and female mist mingling in a flowerlike, gentle form of "sway." The sun shines down on the cloud for purposes of propagation inseparable from sexual delight, but inseparable also from the mysterious, asexual process of equality-within-difference imaged by Father and Son. Yet here we must once again address our recurrent problem; if Eve is represented as Son/Juno/cloud, the necessary principle of reception and nurture, then perhaps, as Mary Nyquist proposes, her desire is after all secondary: her-story actually a his-story of learning the "value of submitting desire to the paternal law." Continuing to weigh these stories, then, as to whether they blend into a kind of ur-story, we must next turn to Adam's reminiscences to Raphael in book 8 to see what actual limitations are imposed on Eve's desires by their different births.

Adam's first sensation, unlike Eve's, is tactile. While it is natural enough for him first to feel the sunlight on his skin, given that he awakes in sunlight, Eve in shade, this difference again suggests that Adam is to Eve as strong "male" light of the Sun to shaded "female" light of the Moon. However, the passage primarily serves to emphasize that Adam's natural affiliation, like Eve's, is with the heavens; the sun causes him to look upward much as the reflection of the heavenly expanse led her to gaze downward. In both cases a sensation of touch or sound motivates their sight, and causes them to assume the "Godlike erect" inclination they share with the angels. This is the essence not of Adam's but of *their* kind, which "upright with Front Serene" displays a "Sanctity of Reason" made "to correspond with Heav'n." Like the Son worshiping equally "with heart and voice and eyes," the love they render the Father like that they give each other is the exclusive prerogative of neither. Yet as the contrast between their awakening in shade or sunlight and then gazing either upward or downward also suggests, the organs of "voice and eyes" are experienced differently by male and female. Eve is led upon her awakening from sounds to sights, and thence back again to the invisible voice. Adam, on the other hand, is led from tactile sensations to gaze at the "ample Sky," and finally to see a "shape Divine" in his dream. So marked is his preference for the organ of sight that he even represents the "liquid Lapse of murmuring Streams" as what he *saw*.

Yet with an alternation characteristic of the poem, Adam's next impulse reasserts his analogy to Eve. Seeking a creature with an answering face, he searches among all

> Creatures that liv'd, and mov'd, and walk'd, or
>   flew,
> Birds on the branches warbling: all things smil'd,
> With fragrance and with joy my heart o'erflow'd.
> Myself I then perus'd, and Limb by Limb
> Survey'd. . . . .
> But who I was, or where, or from what cause,
> Knew not;

First stopping to survey himself, Adam's attempt to find an answering reflection of life does not then focus, as does Eve's, on his own image, although his motive seems the same: to find a living being who will return his gaze and fill his void. Moreover, his attempts like Eve's are at once enabling and impairing; although he immediately perceives his difference from the creatures who smile back at him, and thus passes more spontaneously from the Imaginary to the Symbolic stage, his difficulty in locating the Law's source—the Father himself—is actually greater than hers. Attempting to answer the questions that also trouble Eve, "who I was, or where, or from what cause," he appeals to the Sun and Earth: "ye that live and move, fair Creatures, tell / Tell, if ye saw, how came I thus, how here?" Eve's affinity both with the sounds of creation and her own body is, taken as a whole, inadequate; but Adam's sense of difference and alienation is, if anything, more so. The *natural* response of neither is sufficient to identify themselves *or* their creator; without direct revelation from God to Eve through his voice, to Adam through his vision, both would become idolaters either of Mother Goddess or Father Sun.

Thus, these narratives show Adam and Eve erring in related but inverse directions. Adam attempts to "read" nature sheerly through tactile and visual stimuli and through analytic comparisons that allow him more rapidly to develop his symbolic consciousness. He questions his existence through rational contemplation, which allows him to conclude that his being is "Not of myself; by some great Maker then, / In Goodness and power preeminent." Eve is also led to make comparisons but relies more on auditory sensations and on analogies rather than differences between inner and outer, higher and lower forms: her interest in the lake is prompted by the fact that it seems both a "liquid plain" and "another Sky." Yet if Adam is led by his sight, both physical and rational, into a more immediate entrance into the rational-symbolic order, Eve is equally adept in intuiting that her existence is alternately material and spiritual, just as the watery elements of earth and sky are alternately watery plain and fluid heavenly expanse. Neither Adam *nor* Eve is able to perceive the Deity unaided; God must intercept *both* Adam's confused search ("thus I call'd, and stray'd I knew

not whither,") and Eve's pining with "vain desire." Adam is more dramatically depicted as seeking and conversing with his Maker, but only in a dream, and dream and voice are generally regarded as equivalent modes of prophetic knowledge. In any case, these modes reverse in books 9 and 10, where God speaks to Eve in a dream, to Adam through the prophetic voice of Michael.

Since analogy as well as difference is stressed in these scenes, it is not surprising that the first decree of the "shape Divine" is strictly parallel, if gender specific. The Father names Eve "Mother of human Race" and Adam the "First Man, of Men innumerable ordain'd / First Father." Following this, it is true, Adam is explicitly instructed in the uses and prohibitions of his garden, initiating a dialogue between Adam and his creator not later granted Eve. We must assume, however, that Adam instructs Eve in their joint authority over Eden, since Eve unequivocally considers the garden her responsibility, and since God declares both "authors to themselves in all." Most significantly, neither Adam nor Eve knows God by any name more explicit than "Whom thou sought'st I am," an obvious variant of the Mosaic "I am that I am." Adam's question concerning intimate address, "O by what Name, . . . how may I / Adore thee," is never answered; Adam and Eve are to know the "author" through whom they become authors of mankind only through verbs of being and through spontaneous dialogue, listening, response, and vision. The Puritan poet carefully resists any suggestion of Adam's priestly functions in regard either to divine worship or to the prohibitions this authority could sanction. Nor is God's fatherly instruction of Eve actually less than of Adam, even if it occurs offstage. As Adam describes his first sight of her to Raphael,

> On she came,
> Led by her Heav'nly Maker, though unseen,
> And guided by his voice, nor uninform'd
> Of nuptial Sanctity and marriage Rites:
> Grace was in her steps, Heav'n in her Eye,
> In every gesture dignity and love.

With "Heav'n in her Eye" Adam must acknowledge Eve his sister as well as spouse, "one Flesh, one Heart, one Soul." The name he gives her, "Woman," is not her name in the personal but only in the generic sense; Adam has wit enough to recognize his own species. Eve's name is no more "Woman" than Adam's is "Man"; titles are hardly names. It is only by a considerable distortion of the text, then, that Froula claims that God "soothes Adam's fears of female power . . . by bestowing upon Adam 'Dominion' over the fruits of this creation through authorizing him to name the animals *and* Eve." Far from subtracting from her female power, Eve's auditory response to the symbolic order forms a necessary complement to Adam's visual mode.

Yet even if we can assert that Adam lacks the complete authority over Eve that Froula claims he has, and if, by now, it is clear that their difference is one of degree and not of kind, a final charge of the feminist critique of the hierarchy of Edenic desire remains to be addressed. Eve's more guided transition from the Imaginary to the Symbolic stage, her greater reliance on the intuitive, responsive ear as opposed to Adam's rational, active eye, appear in fact to suggest that Milton, like Freud, traces a "progress in spirituality" that places the female sex on a lower evolutionary rung. And this objection could in fact be supported, had not the Christian poet set a much higher value than Freud upon the primacy of the Imaginary, which for him performs an intuitive, wholistic communion with the body of a universe he insists is divine, and had not Eve's greater access to this communion actually granted her a source of authority fully equivalent—and hence potentially even superior—to Adam's. In this respect Froula, too, must accord Eve abilities that are more than merely complementary; she remarks that while "Adam's need to possess Eve is usually understood as complemented by her need for his guidance, [yet] . . . Milton's text suggests a more subtle and more compelling source for this need: Adam's sense of inadequacy in face of what he sees as Eve's perfection."

However, Froula sees Adam's "alienation from his body" and even from God not as parallel to the sense of inadequacy Eve also feels, but as the direct cause of his subjugation of her. This view is challenged by the fact that Eve's ability to arrange thoughts and words, not merely domestic delights, clearly surpasses Adam's in a way that he finds both sustaining and inspiring. In highly cadenced and evocative blank verse, she turns her love for him into what James Turner calls an "aria," eighteen lines that have "the grace and recapitulative pattern of an Elizabethan sonnet." The author and not merely the singer of the piece, her voice is as authentic as her verse original; she creates a form that claims Adam as the demystified object of her own desire. Not Adam's "coy mistress" forever eluding him on the banks of an Edenic Umber, *she* is the sonneteer praising him because "With thee conversing I forget all time." Inverting Marvell's clever carpe diem to his lady, this lady seizes the day and the object of a desire to which she is also subject. Hierarchy is undermined by role reversal, which, as Turner notes, blurs "the usual division of faculties into 'male' and 'female'; . . . [Milton's] Eve is more logocentric and intelligent than the conventional treatment, and his Adam, even in his prime, more emotionally susceptible."

Yet the implications of Eve's invention are broader still. She concludes her aria with a question suggested by the theme of her composition; tracing the course of an Edenic day, its "seasons and thir change," she wonders what the purpose of the most mysterious of these changes, the procession of "glittering Star-light," might mean: "But wherefore all night long shine these, for whom / This glorious sight, when sleep hath shut all eyes?" Adam is immediately aware both of the skill of her song and the importance of this question; addressing her as "Daughter of God and Man, accomplisht *Eve*," his reply supplies "manly" balance to her poetic skill as he offers a "hymn" to God's providence. Yet neither here nor elsewhere does his authority silence Eve; it only complements hers. Further, his conjecture that the stars "shine not in vain" is in turn supplanted by a higher authority, and what this authority

reveals combines as it elevates the male and female responses to creation. Before informing them of the several possible arrangements of the universe and even hinting at the possibility of life on other planets, Raphael cautions that although experiential knowledge may at times exceed abstract, all forms of knowledge, in fact all life, are ultimately relative. Each should "Solicit not thy thoughts with matters hid," but instead invest their energies in affairs closer to hand—not because of any divine prohibition or even because of the threat now posed by Satan, but because human understanding like the human body itself will be refined by obedience, so that in "tract of time" the human couple may become "Ethereal, as wee." At this point they would enjoy not only the intuitive understanding of the angels, but also their fully unencumbered sexual freedom, which can "either Sex assume, or both." Yet Raphael also acknowledges that their present state is not lacking sufficient perfection that they might then actually prefer to continue their earthly existence; no simple value can be attached to the process of "rising" in and for itself.

However, Raphael's final, private discourse with Adam also offers the most problematic representation of the poem's hierarchy of desire. Although seeming to agree with Adam in his opinion of Eve as "resembling less / His Image who made both, and less expressing / The character of that Dominion giv'n / Oe'r other Creatures," he adds that Adam's ambivalence as to whether Eve corresponds to this, or to his other view of her "As one intended first, not after made / Occasionally," lies in his own perceptions, not in Nature. Yet Raphael never precisely reveals what "Nature" dictates concerning Eve's role; he simply warns against "attributing overmuch to *things* less excellent" (emphasis supplied). Since these "things" refer neither to Eve nor to her accomplishments per se but only to her "fair outside," Raphael suggests that Adam can best appreciate and guide her by weighing her merits against his. Even this vaguely patriarchal advice must, however, in turn be weighed against its broader context, one in which the entire discussion between Adam and Raphael mirrors those previously initiated between Adam and Eve. As the prelude to Eve's sonnet included a didactic statement of obedience, a summation of the Pauline doctrine of headship—"what thou bidd'st / Unargu'd I obey; so God ordains, / God is thy law, thou mine"—so Adam now mimics Eve's procedure in conversing with Raphael. A statement of submission is followed by a tribute to Raphael's sensory powers—a tribute that similarly bestows the powers of the subject on their object. Just as Eve had deferred to Adam by attributing her rich sensory experience of Eden, her "nursery," to his presence, by her example Adam now demonstrates his humility (which is also his authority) by granting Eve his first-born prerogatives of Wisdom, Authority, and Reason. The result of this exchange is simultaneously to exalt masculine and feminine dignity; Eve is its synthesis for him as he had been it for her. She now becomes a vision of masculine virtue in feminine form: "Greatness of mind and nobleness thir seat / Build in her loveliest."

Still, like Raphael, the reader cannot immediately evaluate the full meaning of this transference, let alone how patriarchal, antipatriarchal, or even uxorious its assumptions may be, until it is tested against the background of Edenic gender relations as a whole. Here for the third time we have observed Adam and Eve performing a similar interchange, Eve responding, Adam recapitulating and interpreting her more spontaneous activity. She first questioned the purposes and motions of the stars, a query that Adam elaborates and poses to Raphael, while a little earlier she had narrated her experience of creation to Adam, a story that so delights him that he then adopts it as a means of entertaining the angel. On the third occasion Eve set another pattern by first acknowledging the principle of marital headship, then giving Adam a verse account of the experiential value, greater than all of Eden, she found in his company; she made her gifts, her perceptual and poetic skill, a supreme tribute to him. Later Adam gives Raphael a similar acknowledgment of his "official" superiority, then adds an experiential account of the supreme value of his conversation, a "process of speech" that figuratively synthesizes and transcends "masculine" and "feminine" gender traits. His compliment in fact paraphrases the very words that Eve had used to express her love for him. He tells Raphael,

> For while I sit with thee, I seem in Heav'n
> And sweeter thy discourse is to my ear
> Than Fruits of Palm-tree pleasantest to thirst
> And hunger both.

While Adam recognizes Raphael's differing "Grace Divine" as superior just as clearly as he sees that Eve's difference from himself can imply some relative superiority or inferiority between them, at the same time he can do no better than follow her example. While for Eve "Nor grateful Ev'ning mild, nor silent Night / With this her solemn Bird, nor walk by Moon, / Or glittering Star-light mild, without thee is sweet," now for Adam no fruits of Eden can supply the sweetness of Raphael's words. Significantly, their theoretical affinities here reverse, since Adam is more domestic and Eve more astronomical in her metaphors.

Whatever this reversal may mean in the abstract, the concrete result is the same. As in the Father's relation to the Son, submission merits exaltation and, more importantly, reciprocity. Orders exist to be broken and transformed: as in the "one first matter" Raphael describes, energy and light flow both upward and downward. Anything more rigid or circumscribed would disturb the harmonious intercourse of the universe, as Raphael in response acknowledges:

> Nor are thy lips ungraceful, Sire of men,
> Nor tongue ineloquent; for God on thee
> Abundantly his gifts hath also pour'd
> Inward and outward both, his image fair:
>
> . . . . .
>
> Nor less think wee in Heav'n of thee on Earth
> Than of our fellow servant, and inquire
> Gladly into the ways of God with Man:

> For God we see hath honor'd thee, and set
> On Man his Equal Love.

In this exchange, the discourse of "rational delight" is made the simultaneous prop and leveler of hierarchies; Adam can scarcely be as superior to Eve as Raphael is to himself, and yet his graceful deference merits acknowledgment of angel and man as "fellow servants" enjoying God's "Equal Love." In contrast, duplicitous self-promotion leads Satan, like Adam and Eve after their fall, to bestiality. Nor is their postlapsarian descent depicted as the effect of a divine curse upon those who exceed hierarchical boundaries, but merely as the natural and immediate outcome of Adam's failure correctly to apply Raphael's advice. Instead of skillfully weighing Eve's gifts with his, which would include balancing her more accurate interpretation of Raphael's instruction against his equally accurate intuition about Satan's most likely strategy, Adam is distracted by a temporary loss of face that he fails to see has little or nothing to do either with his true authority or with Eve's true love for him. Atypically yet fatally, his regard for her sense of responsibility toward her garden, her determination, and her well-reasoned (if over-confident) acceptance of trial as a concomitant of Edenic life makes him lose his ability to direct and guide the admirable qualities that, unmodified, like both their garden and his own desire, "tend to wild." Yet if his error perhaps increases Eve's all-too-human liability to err, it cannot be said to produce her fall unless all we have seen of her, including God's pronouncement that *both* were created "sufficient to have stood," is rendered meaningless. Rather, Adam's failed conversation with Eve, his temporary but not-yet-tragic loss of appreciation for their radical relativity, becomes truly tragic only when Eve, like Adam overvaluing her momentary victory, chooses to forsake successful conversation not merely with Adam but with herself and her God. Indulging in a "process of speech" that is actually a process of rationalization, she begins to dream of synthesizing and supplanting Adam's gift for abstract understanding with her own for intuitive thinking and experimentation. Inevitably, this self-centered desire for rising leads her to overvalue the fallacious "evidence" of the wily serpent/Satan. Then and only then does she develop a sinful appetite for what is neither properly hers nor Adam's, the seemingly effortless but ultimately illusory ascent that throughout the poem is shown to be the essence of all descent.

Yet finally, the eternally authentic and not exclusively Edenic power of innocent desire is confirmed both because and in spite of loss of Eden. Self-knowledge and recognition of difference, the basis of both growth and exchange, are reestablished as the proper and in fact only channels of true union and communion between spiritual beings. And while both before and after the Fall this union is only temporary, this is because it must first be temporal, the result of free and rational choice in time, the mark of "Grace Divine." It is not God alone who raises his creatures "deifi'd" by his communion to "what highth thou wilt," but Adam can merit and Raphael bestow this same equality. By precisely the same means, the human genders may alternately exalt one another, so that ideally each is fit both to initiate and "to participate / all rational delight". Further, their capacity to do so directly follows from the fact that Eve is *not* the body to Adam's head nor the senses to his intelligence; as experience, beauty, hearing, Eve is analogous not merely to Christ, but to the poet himself. Milton can conceive her function in this way because he conceives poetry, like reason, as the necessary but not sufficient condition of Grace. Its sufficient condition depends neither exclusively upon Adam's more visual and analytic understanding nor upon Eve's auditory and intuitive imagination, but upon a process of "weighing" and blending both. This process of harmonizing her gifts with his is what Raphael recommends to Adam after showing him how dialectically to sift through his motives, and what allows Eve to initiate their recuperation after the Fall. Then, significantly, Eve again spontaneously intuits the necessity of weighing and accepting responsibility, while Adam's self-righteous sense of the betrayal of his "higher" functions (as well as his emotional confusion) leads him into a momentary loss of all hope and even all remembrance of Raphael's subtle lessons.

Thus the question of "whence true autority in men," in Milton's universe one among many variants of the question of "whence true autonomy," can be accurately resolved only by at once refining and broadening our understanding of the universal basis of "Union or Communion," that semimysterious conversation in which difference, including the ultimate difference between God and his creation, is resolved in an act of complementarity inseparable from simultaneous Other and self-reflection. Autonomy hence becomes a metonymy of male and female gifts and desires that, in perfect balance, generates the synecdoche of divine intercourse and human marriage alike. Raphael counsels Adam (and his heirs) not to upset the balance of this exchange, which by resting upon an unstable and thus freely adaptable form of reflexivity, can achieve a liberating potential that is neither moderate nor conservative but extreme. Because in this system hierarchy is dependent upon temporal interpretation and initiative, not upon innate "natural dispositions," the inner harmony of its balance is at once subject to radical alternation and role reversal and to radical joy, the true analog of the heavenly union revealed/concealed behind Raphael's rosy blush, "Love's proper hue." Yet behind even this disguise are demystified glimpses—of an original sexual union precedent to original sin, of the unencumbered embraces of the angels, "Union of Pure with Pure/Desiring," and of the mutual glorification of the Father and Son, whose balanced energies produce the spontaneous desire to exalt and multiply the Other, the *universal* desire that "to fulfill is all . . . Bliss."

FURTHER READING

Biography

Muir, Kenneth. *John Milton.* London: Longmans, Green, 1955, 196 p.
    Defends Milton against the attacks of modern critics.

Wilson, A. N. *The Life of John Milton.* Oxford: Oxford University Press, 1983, 278 p.
    Offers a detailed literary biography, with excellent historical context.

Criticism

Bowra, C. M. "Milton and the Destiny of Man." In *From Virgil to Milton,* pp. 194-247. New York: St. Martin's Press, 1967.
    Discusses epic form in *Paradise Lost.*

Broadbent, John (ed). *John Milton: Introductions.* Cambridge: Cambridge University Press, 1973, 344 pp.
    Offers a variety of essays on Milton and seventeenth century culture.

Corthell, Ronald J. "Milton and the Possibilities of Theory." In *Reconsidering the Renaissance,* edited by Mario A. Di Cesare, pp. 489-99. Binghamton: Medieval and Renaissance Texts and Studies, 1992.
    Comments on recent theoretical approaches to Milton.

Daiches, David. "Some Aspects of Milton's Pastoral Imagery." In *More Literary Essays,* Edinburgh, London: Oliver & Boyd, 1968, pp. 96-114.
    Examines the influence of Greek and Latin bucolic poetry on Milton's work.

Empson, William. *Milton's God.* London: Chatto and Windus, 1961, 343 p.
    Analyzes the theology of *Paradise Lost.*

Friedman, Donald. "Harmony and the Poet's Voice in Some of Milton's Early Poems." *Modern Language Quarterly,* Vol. XXX (1969): 523-34.
    Discusses Milton's creation of his poetic persona in poems before *Paradise Lost.*

Frye, Northrop. "Literature as Context: Milton's 'Lycidas.'" In *Comparative Literature,* pp. 44-55. Chapel Hill, NC: University of North Carolina Press, 1959.
    Uncovers the mythic framework of "Lycidas."

Kermode, Frank. *The Living Milton.* New York: Barnes & Noble, 1968, 179 p.
    Collects influential examples of Milton criticism.

Knight, G. Wilson. "The Frozen Labyrinth: An Essay on Milton." In *The Burning Oracle: Studies in the Poetry of Action,* pp. 59-113. London: Oxford University Press, 1939.
    Finds Milton's poetry to be chillingly forbidding.

Lewalski, Barbara K. "Milton on Women—Yet Once More." *Milton Studies,* Vol. VI (1974): 3-19.
    Discusses the limitations of feminist criticism of *Paradise Lost.*

McCarthy, William. "The Continuity of Milton's Sonnets." *Publications of the Modern Language Association,* Vol.

LXXVII, No. 2 (January 1977), pp. 96-109.
  Finds patterns in Milton's sonnets related to his career as a poet.

Patrick, J. Max and Roger H. Sundell (eds.) *Milton and the Art of Sacred Song*. Madison, WI: University of Wisconsin Press, 1979, 154 p.
  Includes essays on Christian language and thought in Milton's poetry.

Samuel, Irene. "The Development of Milton's Poetics." *Publications of the Modern Language Association,* Vol. LXXXXII, No. 2 (March 1977): 231-40.
  Comments on Milton's attitudes to the art of poetry.

Shawcross, John. *Milton: The Critical Heritage*. New York: Barnes & Noble, 1970, 276 p.
  Collects 18th and 19th century critical responses to Milton's poetry.

Steadman, John M. *Milton's Biblical and Classical Imagery*. Pittsburgh, PA: Duquesne University Press, 1984, 258 p.
  Identifies classical and scriptural motifs in Milton's poetry.

Tillyard, E.M. *Studies in Milton*. London: Chatto & Windus, 1960, 176 p.
  Presents essays on subjects ranging from *Paradise Lost* to Milton's humor.

Untermeyer, Louis. "Blind Visionary: John Milton." In *Lives of the Poets,* pp. 170-92. New York: Simon and Schuster, 1959.
  Traces biographical influences on Milton's poetry.

Wilding, Michael. *Dragon's Teeth: Literature in the English Revolution*. Oxford: Clarendon Press, 1987, 286 p.
  Includes several new historicist essays on Milton's poetry and politics.

Additional coverage of Milton's life and career is contained in the following sources published by Gale Research: *Literature Criticism*, Vol. 9; *DISCovering Authors*; *World Literature Criticism, 1500 to the Present*; *Concise Dictionary of British Literary Biography 1660-1789*; and *Dictionary of Literary Biography*, Vols. 131, 151.

Charles Olson
1910-1970

(Full name Charles John Olson) American poet and essayist.

INTRODUCTION

Olson was a major figure in the Black Mountain school of Post-modernist American poetry. Beginning his career as a poet in middle age, he developed considerable influence as a lecturer at Black Mountain College in North Carolina, as well as through his poems and essays on literary theory. Deeply influenced by Ezra Pound and William Carlos Williams, he attempted to carry on their innovations while discovering his own radically new means of expression. Seeking to break from conventional poetics, he tried to make his work spontaneous, reflecting the rhythms of ordinary conversation. He rejected the traditional European-influenced system of symbols, images, and classical allusions in poetry, preferring to express a world view that was multicultural yet specifically rooted in the American of his time.

Biographical Information

While growing up in Massachusetts, Olson spent his summers in the fishing village of Gloucester, which would later become the focus of what critics regard as his most important work, the three-volume epic cycle known as *The Maximus Poems*. An outstanding student, he received his bachelor's and master's degrees from Wesleyan University. By 1939, Olson had completed all requirements for a doctorate at Harvard except for his dissertation, but chose to accept a Guggenheim Fellowship to write a book on Herman Melville, which was eventually published as *Call Me Ishmael* (1947). After working in the Office of War Information during World War II, he built what seemed to be a promising career with the Democratic National Committee, but abandoned politics in his mid-thirties in order to concentrate on literature. In 1948 he assumed a temporary teaching post at Black Mountain College, and returned in 1951 to serve as a lecturer and as the school's rector. There he became the charismatic leader of what became known as the Black Mountain Poets, a group that included Robert Creeley, Joel Oppenheimer, and Robert Duncan. When Black Mountain College closed in 1956, Olson returned to Gloucester, where, living among fishermen in very modest circumstances, he devoted himself to writing *The Maximus Poems*.

Major Works

Olson's literary output was prolific, divided between poetry and prose works that expounded his theories about writing.

His essay "Projective Verse," first published in 1950, became a manifesto for the Post-modernist poetry movement in America. In his lectures and essays Olson argued that poetic language must be spontaneous, expressing what is actually seen and felt, rather than obeying conventional rules of logic and order. In his major poetic works "The Kingfishers" and *The Maximus Poems,* as well as the shorter poems contained in the collections *Y & X* (1948), *In Cold Hell*, *In Thicket* (1953), and *The Distances* (1960), Olson demonstrates ideas advocated in his essays on poetics, particularly the rejection of tradition-bound, Eurocentric ways of thinking and a striving towards less artificial, more direct methods of writing and experiencing life. The *Maximus* cycle is his most ambitious work, intended to follow in the tradition of major twentieth century verse epics such as Pound's *Cantos,* Williams' *Paterson,* and Hart Crane's *The Bridge*. The subject of the poem is Gloucester, both its historic past and present condition, from the point of view of Maximus, a character representing the poet himself. Among the themes treated in the *Maximus* cycle are the values and heroism of the working people of Gloucester, and how what might have been an idyllic community has been violated by modern American consumer culture.

Critical Reception

During his lifetime, Olson inspired admiration within his circle of colleagues and students. He also attracted controversy with his radical challenges to traditional and Modernist literary conventions. Because his seemingly cryptic, often ungrammatical manner of writing can be difficult to read, contemporary reviewers expressed frustration with and skepticism about his methods. As Postmodernism became an established literary movement, critics focused on exploring Olson's characteristic themes and style, often comparing his theoretical writings with his own verse.

PRINCIPAL WORKS

Poetry

Y&X 1948
In Cold Hell, In Thicket 1953
O'Ryan 2.4.6.8.10 1959
The Distances 1960
The Maximus Poems 1960
O'Ryan 1,2,3,4,5,6,7,8,9,10 1965
Selected Writings (poetry and prose) 1965
'West' 1966
The Maximus Poems, IV, V, VI 1968
Archaeologist of Morning 1970
The Maximus Poems, Volume Three 1975
The Collected Peoms of Charles Olson 1987
A Nation of Nothing but Poetry: Supplementary Poems 1989

Other Major Works

Call Me Ishmael: A Study of Melville (criticism) 1947
Mayan Letters (essays) 1953
Projective Verse (essay) 1959
A Bibliography on America for Ed Dorn (prose) 1964
Human Universe and Other Essays (essays) 1965
Proprioception (essays) 1965
Letters for Origin 1950-1956 (essays) 1969
The Special View of History (essays) 1970
Additional Prose: A Bibliography on America, Proprioception, and Other Notes and Essays (essays and prose) 1974
Muthologos: The Collected Lectures and Interviews (interviews and lectures) 1978
Charles Olson and Robert Creeley: The Complete Correspondence (letters) 1980

CRITICISM

Times Literary Supplement (review date 1970)

SOURCE: "Anti-Poetic Fisher of Men," in *Times Literary Supplement,* No. 3585, November 13, 1970, p. 1315.

[In the following review, the critic offers a negative assessment of The Maximus Poems.*]*

Whoever dislikes the poetry of Charles Olson should take note of the abundant testimony of his admirers. Not all of them can be dismissed as friends, pupils, and debtors. Young men who have never met him privately celebrate the magical effect of his public performances. Young women stammer out eulogies of his inspiring example. Yet the story lingers in one's mind of the professorial friend whom Olson saw cupping a hand to an ear while the poet was reading his work in a Harvard auditorium, and whom Olson asked to leave because his attentive presence made a proper delivery of the verses impossible.

Sympathetic attention is not what **The Maximus Poems** call for. The patient reader may suppress a fatigued sense of déjà vu as he glimpses Crane's *The Bridge* (or Waldo Frank's introduction to it) in some elements of **Maximus**, and Williams's *Paterson* in others. But his impression of the author as a devalued Pound must remain; for the doctrine and mannerisms of the *Cantos* pervade Olson's collection.

Suppose one forcibly ignores one's experience of the real thing and determines to treat the **Maximus** sequence as an independent design: what pleasures will reveal themselves? Readers who have no acquaintance with deep sea fishing and no knowledge of American colonial history may be entertained by the snatches of John Smith's prose or the anecdotes of disasters at sea. Connoisseurs of grammar may relish Olson's habit of omitting relative pronouns and the prepositions of time or place. Rhetoricians may study his addiction to aposiopesis. Puzzle-solvers will be happiest of all, tracing "mettle" on page 131 to Corinthian bronze on page 123, or connecting the "nasturtium" on page 93 with the "nose-twist" on page 36.

The unhappy few who listen for lines that engrave themselves on the tables of memory, for rhythmic subtlety or the undeniably right choice of words, for grace of sound or felicity of perception, for a fresh, true insight into the human condition—in other words, for significant art—will feel generally thwarted. Mr. Olson is too busy with his lofty programmes of metrics and sociology to sink to mere pleasurable art; he is too busy recommending craftsmanship to exemplify it. Finally, one comes to suspect that in his own person Olson exerted a magnetic force that he failed to infuse into his writing.

It is no accident that one of the most coherent poems in the collection is about the devices by which a false poet establishes a real reputation ("**Letter 5**"). Here the unfortunate Ferrini, editor of a little magazine called *Four Winds,* comes under a cannonade for using his publication to promote his own career:

> what sticks out in this issue is verse
> from at least four other editors
> of literary magazines.

Hatred of those who have received unmerited recognition is a driving impulse behind Olson's work. The poet identifies himself with unappreciated artisans, forgotten colonists, unsung fishermen. The virtues he admires are modest heroism, craftsmanship for its own sake. Whether he embodies them remains a question.

Olson chose "Maximus" for his pseudonym partly because he was tall but more because he wished to suggest an imaginative energy that gives men their greatest spiritual stature, the energy everyone has access to but few men tap. On those few, says Olson, depends the health of the *polis,* or true community; and when the leaders of the people end their attachment to a craft or to a primary industry (such as fishing), when they abandon themselves to blind money-making, absentee ownership, advertising, then the true community crumbles. The poet, the fisherman, represent types of *local* vocations rooted in specific places, strengthening the *polis.* Even in nature the bird building its nest shows the same kind of radical, constructive art.

Maximus addresses himself to his own city (Gloucester, Mass., a fishing port), which he hopes to save from the corruption he says has ruined most of America. He wishes to open the doors of perception in his fellow townspeople:

> that all start up
> to the eye and soul
> as though it had never
> happened before

The argument is as familiar as it is pathetic and self-contradictory; for if the way of life the poet recommends ever did exist, and if it were as satisfying as he claims, no people would abandon it. Contrariwise, if artless men are to be converted to such a faith, Olson's kind of poem is hardly the best instrument for the task. If the poet does not falsify the fisherman's work, he does sentimentalize the fisherman.

The free forms of the poems seldom add depth to the doctrine; for, in accordance with his literary programme, Olson leaps in mid-line from the poet's surroundings while writing to the memories his impressions provoke, or from minute autobiography to extracts from historical documents, or from economic theory to invective against America. Most of his language is deliberately flat, slangy, anti-poetic. But the surface of toughness dissolves in the few lyric passages, which could not be softer or more conventional—especially those dealing with springtime. It is an easy step from the moralization of landscapes to the denunciation of their spoilers. Olson follows a well-worn path when he calls for the destruction of those he would also like to save, and he says (addressing a bulldozer):

> clean the earth
> of sentimental
> drifty dirty
> lazy man

Is the poet excluded from this category?

Robert von Hallberg (essay date 1974)

SOURCE: "Olson's Relation to Pound and Williams," in *Contemporary Literature,* Vol. 15, No. 1, Winter, 1974, pp. 15-48.

[*In the following essay, von Hallberg discusses the defining influence of Ezra Pound and William Carlos Williams on Olson's poetry.*]

Charles Olson's name comes up often in discussions of the influence of Pound and Williams on younger poets, and rightly so. Shortly before Olson's death, Gerard Malanga asked him whether he could have written *The Maximus Poems* without having known Pound's and Williams' work. Olson answered: "That's like asking me how I could have written without having read." But there has been so little notice taken of the matters that divided Olson, Pound, and Williams that at least one Poundian has glibly dismissed Olson's poetics as almost wholly derivative and surely inferior to Pound's work. Anyone interested in understanding the course of American poetry over the last sixty or seventy years and the directions open to it in the future is likely to be frustrated by this myopic blurring of distinctions. In truth, the story of Olson's relationship to Pound and Williams is a detailed and complex one that casts light on all three poets and especially on their long poems.

They can all be understood as post- or antisymbolists, and Olson was most explicit about this issue: "It doesn't take much thought over Bill's proposition—'Not in ideas but in things'—to be sure that any of us intend an image as a 'thing,' never, so far as we know, such a non-animal as symbol" [*Human Universe and Other Essays,* 1967]. It is this allegiance, and more specifically Williams' poem "This Is Just to Say," that are behind **"Letter 9"**:

> I, dazzled
>
> as one is, until one discovers
> there is no other issue than
> the moment of
>
>   the pleasure of
>   this plum,
> these things
> which don't carry their end any further than
> their reality in
> themselves

Allegiance to Williams' dictate here means absolute opposition to Eliot, whom Olson recognized to be in the symbolist tradition. He ends an early poem, **"ABC's,"** with a cryptic reference to this conflict:

> Words, form
> but the extension of
> content
>
> Style, est verbum
>
> The word
> is image, and the reverend reverse is

Eliot
Pound
is verse

As long as words simply extend content into form, they can be said to be images; the word and its referent are so closely tied that the one is a transparent image of the other. But the symbolist program—the "reverend reverse"—takes the word itself, its sound and connotations, to be image enough, never mind its referent. The difference between these two approaches is not a matter of "mere" technique; it reflects a conflict between two notions of the function of art. The symbolists aspire to an order of reality beyond and above the mundane experiences of common, actual people, beyond what Mallarmé calls "ici-bas." The function of this nonmimetic art is to express the yearning to transcend. Olson, though, had no desire to write off the mundane and the actual: ". . . no / *Transcendence*—the ideal / in the occurrence without any raising / of the issue" [*Archeologist of Morning*, 1970]. For him the importance and integrity of art rested on the accuracy of its representation, its mimesis: "Image / can be exact to fact, or / how is this art twin to what is, / what was, / what goes on?". The symbolists, Olson thought, by projecting their subjectivity onto objects, impose a hierarchical order on experience. In **"La Torre"** this order is a tower that must be brought down to the level of the beach, where a new spatial order will form:

> To begin again. Lightning
> is an axe, transfer
> of force subject to object is
> order: destroy!
>
>> To destroy
>> is start again, is a factor of
>> sun, fire is
>> when the sun is out, dowsed. . . .
>
> Let the tower fall!
> Where space is born
> man has a beach to ground on

Olson began his career as *chef d'école* in 1950 with the publication of his manifesto "Projective Verse." The essay begins with the distinction between the projective and the nonprojective—between friends and foes—Pound and Williams on one side and, all too predictably, Milton and Wordsworth on the other. He was deliberately constructing a bridge to span the more than forty years since Pound and Williams began their careers, to extend a line of continuity from Pound and Williams to the younger poets beginning their work in the late forties and early fifties—a task that now looks complete. Few modern poets begin their careers so at ease with the immediately preceding generation of poets: continuity is so alien to what is thought of as "modern" that Olson referred to himself as a post-modern.

But even in the conclusion to this essay some haziness lurks about the precise lessons to be learned from Pound's work:

For I would hazard the guess that, if projective verse is practiced long enough, is driven ahead hard enough along the course I think it dictates, verse again can carry much larger material than it has carried in our language since the Elizabethans. But it can't be jumped. We are only at its beginnings, and if I think that the *Cantos* make more "dramatic" sense than do the plays of Mr. Eliot, it is not because I think they have solved the problem but because the methodology of the verse in them points a way by which, one day, the problem of larger content and of larger forms may be solved [*Selected Writings*, 1966].

All that is clear is that very early in his literary career Olson intended to write a long poem of large scope, and that Pound's life's work stood as a model of how one might proceed with this kind of project. In March of the following year Olson wrote to Robert Creeley in more detail about Pound's methodology:

why I still beat up against this biz of, getting rid of nomination, so that historical material is free for forms now, is

Ez's epic solves problem by his ego: his single emotion breaks all down to his equals or inferiors (so far as I can see only two, possibly, are admitted, by him, to be his betters—Confucius, & Dante. Which assumption, that there are intelligent men whom he can outtalk, is beautiful because it destroys historical time, and

thus creates the methodology of the Cantos, viz, a space-field where, by inversion, though the material is all time material, he has driven through it so sharply by the beak of his ego, that, he has turned time into what we must now have, space & its live air.

Pound's methodology obliterates chronology. Selected individuals and events of the *Cantos* exist simultaneously in an eternal present. In a letter to Cid Corman of about the same time Olson shows some sense of the dangers of Pound's method; he refers to the exceptional "drive of EP—who never for a moment let his hand slip off the Johnson rod to his own loco. HIS energy as the thing to be put to USE by ANYTHING of the past—never let the PAST for its own sake ('human positionalism') slide him off . . .". Pound may steer a steady course, but for his successors, like Olson, the dangers remain real. On the one hand, Olson might fall into an excessive subjectivism ("let his hand slip off the Johnson rod to his own loco"), because Pound's triumph over time occurs in Pound's own mind. Or he might lapse into antiquarianism, which resurrects the past because of its presumed inherent value ("let the PAST for its own sake . . . slide him off"), not because of its use in the present. In fact, Olson did feel that Pound moved perilously close to antiquarianism, when he used the past as a stick to beat the shabby and unruly present; after a visit with Pound in Saint Elizabeth's Olson wrote: "In Pound's case, however, I feel he has not cleared his course of the dangers: I think of the presence in his work of the worship for past accomplishments and a kind of blindness to the underground vigor of a present." But this criticism was less a dismissal of Pound than an indication of the direction Olson saw open to his own work.

Pound's ability to break free of the restrictions of chronology signified to Olson a level of consciousness different from and more archaic than that of Pound's contemporaries; this is what Olson called "the major thing, the mytho-culture measure of him." Olson did not mean that Pound is a Blakean or Yeatsian maker of myths; Pound is more the realist than either Blake or Yeats: "Now clearly Ezra Pound is no parabolist, no Christian, and no mythist! So what can he teach us? He can reinforce the secular at the base of myth. For Ezra is one of the real forerunners, the documentarians. The 'world' is very much a creature to his delight, a Dioce." In 1970 *The Special View of History* was published posthumously. In this slim volume, which grew out of a seminar given by Olson at Black Mountain College in 1955 or 1956, he sums up the significance of the last 2,500 years in a way that glosses his reference to Pound's "mytho-culture measure":

> But you will see what happened the moment the mythological was displaced by the rational (date, sometime around 440 B.C. Socrates) but datable back from that date to some point inside and after Heraclitus (contemporary of Buddha and Confucius and Pythagoras—the latter the real ignored and crucial figure now to be restored.):

> because the will and culture was always ready to put out the light (any one of us has the danger to sleep), if you do what the rational does—to seek one explanation—or to put it more evenly, undo the paradox (the rational mind hates the familiar, and has to make it ordinary by explaining it, in order not to experience it), you can easily see why the West has been halved, and each of the persons in it for nigh unto two and a half millenia.

Pound's mythological vision apprehends the familiar directly, free of that rationality that cannot live with a paradox. Pound's is the whole vision, 2,500 years old, not weakened by the "halving" of subject and object. But that is not to say Pound is an anachronism; for Olson he is something of a prophet:

> Except as none of us will ever be satisfied, we are quite making it, except for that I am persuaded that at this point of the 20th century it might be possible for man to cease to be estranged, as Heraclitus said he was in 500 B.C., from that with which he is most familiar. At least I take Heraclitus' dictum as the epigraph of this book. For all this I know increased my impression that man lost something just about 500 B.C. and only got it back just about 1905 A.D.

Too frequently in Olson's prose pivotal terms and phrases remain abstract and barely defined. Sometimes the poetry actually helps one to understand the prose. One is so used to consulting tomes like Yeats's *A Vision* for clues to his most opaque poems that it may seem peculiar and preposterous when a poet's poetry glosses his expository prose. Yet should it? Olson's tendency to clarify in his poetry terms and ideas which are fuzzy in his prose may indicate that he simply had better control of the language of his

poetry than that of prose, which ought to be no surprise at all. Heraclitus' sentence—"Man is estranged from that with which he is most familiar"—is a case in point. The first half of **"Maximus, to himself,"** one of the few lyric passages of the sequence, puts some flesh on Heraclitus' statement:

> I have had to learn the simplest things
> last. Which made for difficulties.
> Even at sea I was slow, to get the hand out, or to
>   cross
> a wet deck.
>   The sea was not, finally, my trade.
> But even my trade, at it, I stood estranged
> from that which was most familiar. Was delayed,
> and not content with the man's argument
> that such postponement
> is now the nature of
> obedience,
>
>   that we are all late
>   in a slow time,
>   that we grow up many
>   And the single
>   is not easily
>   known
>
> It could be, though the sharpness (the *achiote*)
> I note in others,
> makes more sense
> than my own distances. The agilities
>
>   they show daily
>   who do the world's
>   businesses
>   And who do nature's
>   as I have no sense
>   I have done either.

The poem explains how it feels to be estranged from the familiar, and how for a poet this means being alienated from his community, his society. Olson as a poet-critic makes "dialogues" and discusses "ancient texts," but he lives in a community of people who fish, people who work with "the known," the world of real things. In their world he is slow, slow to learn, slow even—perhaps I should say especially—to move his body from place to place. Even as a writer he was slow to get started, thirty-five years old before his first poems were published. The contemporary angst of dispersion and fragmentation ("we grow up many") took its toll on him before he focused his energies on the single activity that would give his life its integrity. He was distanced from the physical world around him and distanced from the community in which he lived. Dulled, slow, even clumsy, Olson long felt out of touch with the physical world most familiar to him.

Pound's mythological vision is the antidote to that estrangement. History began, Olson thought, with the fall from the mythological vision: "(I should think, if one stopped long enough, one could expose a fallacy here which has dominated all living—literally—since the 5th Century BC, when, for the first time, that unhappy consciousness of 'history'—and which consciousness begets 'culture' (art as taste, inherited forms, Mr Eliot—indeed, Mister Pound as he preaches the 'grrrate bookes') came into existence" [*A Bibliography on America For Ed Dorn*, 1964]. The mythological vision skips over history, over 2,500 years of it, to recover and reinstate a dialectical unity: "You see, I cannot stress enough how WILL has been now so long a misplaced force—will, and Beauty. For they go together, and are either disparate twins which produce death and culture, or they are what mythologically they once were, Venus and Adonis, love and desire" [*Special View of History*]. It is the will that engages man with the real world and transforms desire into action. The emphasis on action quite properly conjures up shades of the ideal active man, the hero; for Olson envisions a man who is of more than human proportions: "I have this dream, that just as we cannot now see & say the size of these early HUMAN KINGS, we cannot, by the very lost token of their science, see what size man can be once more capable of, once the turn of the flow of his energies that I speak of as the WILL TO COHERE is admitted, and its energy taken up" [*Human Universe and Other Essays*]. And Pound is the poet of will, *directio voluntatis*: "Ep's poems are—after the early Guido's—one long extrapolation, canzone, on WILL: how, to get it, up" [*Letters for Origin*, 1970].

Because Olson never singled out one particular canto as an illustration of Pound's mythological vision, it is difficult to point with authority at such an example. But Canto 17 seems to be the sort of poem Olson had in mind. The achievement of that canto is that the barriers between the actual scene before Pound's eyes, Venice at dawn, and his vision of Dionysus, and his recollection of the political history and cultural development of Venice, and even the geochemical formation of marble from trees and algae and limestone, all these barriers dissolve in a single sustained vision. But the limitation of Pound's vision is no less real: the actual, the historical, the geochemical, and the mythological come together in Pound's mind. In Olson's judgment Pound's ego assumes too much responsibility; it brings to coherence the elements of experience Olson wanted to cohere, but it does so through the vision of one man, through a vision which lacks a firm enough anchor in the contemporary objective reality outside of Pound's mind. What it comes down to is that Pound's vision is too much his own; his idiosyncratic interpretations of history and socioeconomic problems, for instance, are finally not shareable. Olson admired and clearly learned from the Pound whose focus was societal and historical, though he had nothing but contempt for Pound's judgment in these matters: "Wrong as he is, to my mind, in his conclusions on authority, and obscured, as fascists canbe, by a mania to save the Constitution, no one can deny the seriousness with which he has examined civic responsibility." Olson felt that Pound's "conclusions may be wrong. But the process is a thing to protect." In 1951 Olson wrote to Creeley about how the idiosyncrasies of both Pound and Edward Dahlberg leave them on the peripheries of society too vulnerable to an easy dismissal: "what burns me, is, they never speak, in their slash at the State or the Economy, basically, for anyone but themselves. And thus, it is Bo-

hemianism." In reaction against this aspect of Pound's method Olson was wise to turn to Williams, though he did so in a hesitant way. In the same letter to Creeley Olson said of *Paterson* and the *Cantos*:

> each of the above jobs are HALVES, that is, I take it (1) that the EGO AS BEAK is bent and busted but (2) whatever it is that we can call its replacement (Bill very much a little of it) HAS, SO FAR, not been able to bring any time so abreast of us that we are in this present air, going straight out, of ourselves, into it. . . . Perhaps, as I sd before, I am only arguing with myself, that is, I am trying to see how to throw the materials I am interested in so that they take, with all impact of a correct methodology AND WITH THE ALTERNATIVE TO THE EGO-POSITION.

Olson took very seriously his sense of Williams' failures. But the redeeming quality of *Paterson* for him was that it encompasses so much that is not Williams, so much of Paterson, New Jersey: "the primary contrast, for our purposes, is BILL: his Pat is exact opposite of Ez's, that is, Bill HAS an emotional system which is capable of extensions & comprehensions the ego-system (the Old Deal, Ez as Cento Man, here dates) is not." Yet Olson thought that Williams' work is ultimately undone by an inability to properly handle time; Pound's accomplishment is exactly Williams' failure: "by making his substance historical of one city (the Joyce deal), Bill completely licks himself, lets time roll him under as Ez does not, and thus, so far as what is the more important, methodology, contributes nothing, in fact, delays, deters, and hampers, by not having busted through the very problem which Ez has so brilliantly faced, & beat."

Olson saw two really different problems in *Paterson* which led him to make so severe a judgment of Williams. The first is that Williams simply never went back far enough into history, at least never after writing *In the American Grain* (1925). Although *In the American Grain* traces the origins of America into the tenth century, nearly all the historical elements of *Paterson* date from the eighteenth and nineteenth centuries. In *The Bibliography on America for Ed Dorn* Olson explains just how far back in time one must go: "And if I say it don't end short of Pelasgus (date 7000 BC, place circum Mt Lycaon, Arkadia), don't let that scare you: I'm only trying to say how far bill WCW missed by not going behind Sam one Houston!" (The same criticism can be levelled against *The Maximus Poems* [1960], which deal mostly with New England in the seventeenth century, but in *Maximus Poems IV, V, VI* [1968] Olson greatly enlarges his temporal scope.) It is interesting that, as Olson would have expected, Williams was bewildered by the historical dimension of Olson's work; Williams scribbled in a note to Creeley that "the method" prescribed in "Projective Verse" is "Worth preserving. But what about the history? that is extension backward into TIME?"

The other problem Olson mentions is that Williams' conception of an American city is pastoral and outdated. Olson thought that the end of the First World War marked the death of Europe and the end of America's pastoral character; Pound's preoccupation with Renaissance history seemed to him as obsolete as Williams' attachment to nineteenth-century America: "that is, another reason why i don'tthink Ez's toucan works after 1917 is, that, after that date, the materials of history which he has found useful are not at all of use (nor are Bill's, despite the more apparent homogeneity: date 1917, not only did Yurrup (West, Cento, Renaissance) go, but such blueberry America as Bill presents (Jersey dump-smoke covering same) also WENT (that is, Bill, with all respect, don't know fr nothing abt what a city *is*)."

This criticism of Williams raises an important problem. In *The Maximus Poems* Olson is looking back to the time when Gloucester was a village, free of super highways and traffic jams, and clearly he likes much of what he sees. For example, in **"Letter 5"** Maximus says to Ferrini:

> . . . you
> are more like Gloucester now is
> than I who hark back to an older polis,
> who has this tie to a time when the port
>
> (I am not named Maximus
> for no cause
>
> when blueberries

But when Olson looks back "to an older polis," he points out those values—fineness, firmness, sureness, and vulnerability—which were pure in the past but which still happily survive, though in a corrupted and threatened form. Later in **"Letter 5"** he says:

> I'd not urge anyone back. Back is no value as
> better.
>   That sentimentality
> has no place, least of all Gloucester,
> where polis
> still thrives
>
> Back is only for those who do not move (as future
> is,
> you in particular need to be warned,
> any of you who have the habit of
> "the people"—as though there were anything / the
> equal
>   of / the context of / now!

Olson's retrospection is more normative than Williams': Olson defines for Gloucester (and always, by extension, for America) its heritage of values and conflicts; he cautions a firm grip on those values and a sharpened understanding of those conflicts in the present time of national slide and decadence. Williams mines the records for tableaux, graphic episodes which enter his poem as much by their inherent curiosity as by their significance for the present. Olson's "moral history of Cape Ann" more closely resembles in intent Williams' *In the American Grain* than *Paterson:* in 1925 Williams discerned in American history a recurrent pattern, which he must have hoped would

instruct his contemporaries; but in the forties and fifties, when writing *Paterson,* he preferred to open his poem to more disparate and eccentric historical episodes, whose meaning for the present would not overshadow their specificity in the past.

Williams' picture of Paterson struck Olson as unrealistic on still another count. The clutter of urban life gets into *Paterson,* but not the violence:

> . . . the watching of, the Passaic of
> orange peels?
>   . . . The dyes
> of realism? (Cats,
> & industry, not even
> violence
>
>   Why not the brutal, head on?
>   Fruits? beauty? to want it
>   so hard? Who . . .
>   has misled us?
>
> . . . what we needed most
> was something the extension of
> claritas: what do we have
> to report?
>   ("ABC's [3—for Rimbaud]")

With the six homicides, four drownings, two suicides, two decapitations, two executions, two rapes, the infanticide, the Indian massacre, the gang-fight, the dog killed in the Indian funeral, and the child burned to death, *Paterson* appears not to lack violence at all. Yet Williams gets these incidents into his poem largely on the level of anecdote: most of them are yanked out of old newspapers, or history books, and their contexts and causes have been left behind. By comparison, *The Maximus Poems* are far less violent. But there is nothing enigmatic about the violence in Olson's poem. In **"History is the Memory of Time"** Olson tells the story of a confrontation between Captain Hewes of the Dorchester Company and Miles Standish, representing the Puritans, as though it were a Saturday morning showdown, but he ends the story seriously, by explaining the significance of the incident:

> Which fight tells
> what heat there was
> in sd Harbour when
> was site of
> commerce
>
>   real bucks not
>   each man and woman
>   and child living off
>   things paid on
>   33 year schedule
>
>   credit out ahead,
>   each generation
>   living 33 years
>   of shoddy &
>   safety—not at all

living. Not all late
conantry (for which read
a nation fizzing itself
on city managers,
mutual losing banks,

how to send yr child
$100,000 more a
lifetime than
poor old
dad

The violence surrounding this conflict between the Dorchester Company men and the Puritans occurs only when human experience remains human, when economic forces confront each other in the flesh. Given the opportunity, Americans have avoided this violence by shaping anonymous institutions to channel and anaesthetize human relationships. It is true that these institutions—because they promote nonviolence—are normally cited as important achievements of civilization; we usually proclaim as civilized those institutions which eliminate brutality and violence from human intercourse. Olson did not advocate barbarism, but these institutions, far from being monuments of civilization, appeared to him as inhuman and ultimately irresponsible. This was no novel insight on Olson's part since at least the eighteenth-century anarchists have cast suspicious eyes on institutionalized civilization. Olson, however, cannot without doing violence to his work be enlisted in the anarchist tradition represented and extolled by Kenneth Rexroth. Shortly after he left his career in government, he set out to write a long poem that explores in fascinating detail the history of those economic and social institutions which retain what Olson called "polis."

Olson's sense of a city, a polis, has nothing directly to do with a large number of people living in a relatively small area of space. It has more to do with the quality of the relationships between people. When asked about Black Mountain College, he could call it "the largest city I'll ever know, the swiftest." [*Maps* 4, 1971]. By this standard it is understandable that Olson would question Williams' configuration of Paterson, New Jersey. *Paterson* is less a poem about the relationships between the people of a city, though of course these relationships do figure into the poem, than about the relationship between the American poet and his particularly American background. Olson, however, was intent on getting the interpersonal relationships down as precisely as he could, even to the point of allowing his language to turn in on itself in the face of the intricacies of human relationships:

Exactly what the status
of Thomas Morton was
at Cape Ann, or thereabouts,
and when—

he was the friend
of Ambrose Gibbons
& conceivably was acting
on John Mason's part?

Anyhow John Watts took salt
he said Morton said
was his, or was committed
to his charge

Morton, to New England, is as
Hastings was to California
(misled the Donner Party) a
wide fool but not vicious

as the Pilgrims put him
down.

Olson's city is above all else a society of people, and, like Pound, he aspired to his own luminous city: "That is my dream of creating a city which shall shine as such. And this is only what I am, is the builder of that dome" [*Reading at Berkeley*, 1966].

The most fruitful lesson Olson took from Williams is the idea of a long poem centered on a single city. Olson made this plain in a letter to Cid Corman late in 1953:

That is, if i think EP gave any of us the methodological clue: the RAG-BAG; bill gave us the lead on the LOCAL. Or put it that pat: EP the verb, BILL the NOUN problem. To do. And who, to do. Neither of them: WHAT. That is, EP sounds like what, but what his is is only more methodology, in fact, simply, be political. Politics—not economics—is him. And validly. For (1) politics is a context as wide as nature, and not only what we call "politics"; and (2) its essence is will. Which latter—will—is what EP cares abt.

Localism and politics are happily wedded in Olson's literalist imagination. When he speaks of politics he thinks of the Greek *polis,* the city-state. Politics, for Olson, means the public life of a city. And "life" implies that a city is a vital organism. When he says that in Gloucester "polis / still thrives," he is celebrating his city as a living and still healthy organism. But Williams' "lead on the LOCAL" runs still deeper in Olson's thought. In an essay on Herodotus, Olson went so far as to say that without roots in a locality one is without an identity altogether: "You are thus suddenly without a place. And you are thus anonymous, you are without a face, a name, clothes, set down in the midst of the city a no-face" [*Human Universe and Other Essays*].

But "localism" is the wrong term for Olson, because historically it has sentimental connotations. Olson did not countenance the popular nostalgia for village life:

As the people of the earth are now, Gloucester
is heterogeneous, and so can know polis
not as localism, not that mu-sick (the trick
of corporations, newspapers, slick magazines, movie
houses,
the ships, even the wharves, absentee-owned
they whine to my people, these entertainers, sellers

they play upon their bigotries (upon their fears)

Localism is "mu-sick" to Olson. And "mu-sick" is one of those terms which will bear some definition. In *The Special View of History* he writes at length about the division between *muthos* and *logos*. Olson prefers *muthos* to the more usual transliteration *mythos,* meaning word or story, because the former suggests a connection with the Old English *muth,* meaning simply mouth. Referring to Homer, Olson says: "but Muthos with him means 'what is said' in speech or story exactly like Logos in its primary sense". "Mu-sick" seems to mean, then, that what is said is sick, that it's a sick story or sick word which comes from a sick mouth. It also sounds like "muzak," the brand name for mechanized, prepackaged music. Olson found it a handy word for describing the effect of the mass media on the language.

The "lead on the LOCAL" became in Olson's hands more than a clue to subject matter; in *The Maximus Poems* the locale is a major structural device. Olson explains how this works in a letter to Cid Corman: "I figure, tho, that all i have to do is to keep answering my own lead—to toe in. And that the bending back to G ought always, actually, to give any reader a 'shape.'" Williams' lead is an Ariadne thread through the wayward serial structure Olson took from the *Cantos.* Yet Olson's serial structure is far from Pound's, partly because letters just aren't cantos. Cantos lay claim to comparison with the *Divine Comedy,* especially in terms of overall structure; letters are less presumptuous. Olson told Gerard Malanga: "I couldn't write a canto if I sat down and deliberately tried. My interest is not in cantos. It's in another condition of song, which is connected to mode and has therefore to do with absolute actuality. It's so completely temporal." Letters are casual and distinct from one another; they suggest a friendly and familiar relationship between writer and reader. Olson writes directly to his reader ("o my people," often with a nineteenth-century earnestness. A letter—Olson does not say "epistle"—is not normally an art form; it is a form of communication, a means of transmitting information.

Like Pound—and to a lesser extent like Williams—Olson thought the poet important as a teacher, one who conveys information: "the poet is the only pedagogue left, to be trusted" [*Human Universe and Other Essays*]—a questionable notion at best. But unlike Pound, Olson did spend much of his time from 1948 to 1956, from 1963 to 1965, and the year before his death in January 1970 actually teaching college students, which may account for his greater explicitness about the "lessons" he teaches. For example, near the end of **"The Song and Dance of"** he says: "Venus / does not arise from / these waters. Fish / do." The largest portion of the historical material in *The Maximus Poems* demonstrates that from the outset there was a conflict (a "moral struggle" Olson calls it in **"Letter 14"** between those who came to New England to make a living by fishing and those, like John Hawkins, who came to take treasure or to make a fortune. What Olson decries is the movement away from labor, the development of capitalism. Parasitic absentee ownership is the source of corruption in **"Letter 3."** In **"Letter 10"** Puritanism is

responsible for the removal of Conant's house to Salem; Olson remarks: "It was fishing was first. Only after (Naumkeag) was it the other thing, and Conant / would have nothing to do with it, went over to Beverly, to Bass River, to keep clear."

What makes Olson different from Pound in his handling of such material is his willingness to make—actually, his insistence on making—his point as directly and explicitly as possible, only too often at the expense of flat and uninteresting language. After briefly describing Nathaniel Bowditch's activities as an insurance executive and as a member of the Corporation of Harvard, for instance, Olson draws his conclusions in a prosaic, almost textbookish manner:

> He represents, then, that movement of NE monies
> away from primary production & trade
> to the several cankers of profit-making
> which have, like Agyasta, made America great.
>
> Meantime, of course, swallowing up
> the land and labor. And now,
> the world.

Olson has no commitment to the ideogrammic method, nor to any method that would prevent him from making his didactic purposes as explicit as possible:

> What we have in this field in these scraps among these
> fishermen, and the
> Plymouth men, is more than the fight of one colony
> with another, it is the
> whole engagement against (1) mercantilism (cf. the
> Westcountry men and
> Sir Edward Coke against the Crown, in Commons,
> these same years—
> against Gorges); and (2) against nascent capitalism
> except as it stays the
> individual adventurer and the worker on share—against
> all sliding statism,
> ownership getting in to, the community as, Chamber
> of Commerce, or
> theocracy; or City Manager

He justifies to his reader the inclusion of what might seem insignificant historical information and makes the take-home message absolutely unavoidable:

> . . . one's forced,
> considering America,
> to a single truth: the newness
>
> the first men knew was almost
> from the start dirtied
> by second comers. About seven years
> and you can carry cinders
> in your hand for what
>
> America was worth. May she be damned
> for what she did so soon
> to what was such a newing. . . .

His didactic clarity shows itself even in the organization of individual letters. Pound's ideogrammic method calls for the juxtaposition of distinct elements; this juxtaposition, when successful, leads to a perception of the unity behind the distinctions, or of the relationships between the distinct elements. Canto 4 works this way. But Olson is less oblique; **"Letter 20: not a pastoral letter"** is a good example. As usual, Olson has separated and enumerated the separate movements of the letter. The first section announces the letter's organizing principle: ". . . how it is honor / is the measure of, when the squeeze / is on." Section 2 describes how one Marine commando, Red Hanna, distrusts another's "yack-yack" about honor; a test of honor with automatic rifles follows. The next section deals with Olson's shame over not honoring a rent contract; and the fourth section shows that the landlord Olson deceived was an honorable man. The next section tells how Newman Shea, a Gloucester fisherman who sailed with Olson in 1935, dishonored himself in his own eyes and in the eyes of others; also in this section is the principle exemplified by sections 3 through 6: ". . . it is not the substance of a man's fault, / it is the shape of it / is what lives with him, is what shows / in his eyes (in our eyes." Section 6 explains that Shea has been an honorable man since his transgression. The following section is a major turn in the poem; Olson calls attention to the turn by using the roman numeral II for this section. Here he leaves off description and states directly that the nineteenth-century forms of honorable behavior, such as the wild west showdown, are obsolete now, but that lament is not his business:

> Not that the state of it
> needs crying over. The real
>
> is always worth the act of
> lifting it, treading it
>
> to be clear, to make it
>
> clear (to clothe honor
> anew

The last little section is numbered 1, which suggests that it is the start of a new series of sections left uncompleted. But the enumeration is misleading in a characteristic way, because it implies an asymmetry which is simply not present; Olson's tendency is to cultivate apparent disorder. The poem closes in a very conventional way, with a coda celebrating Olson's unclothed daughter who is transformed into a personification of potential but unformed honor "in all her splendor." To make a paradigm of it, we can say roughly that the first section announces the theme; the second shows how absurd received forms of honor have become in the present context; the third and fourth describe a contemporary example of dishonor; the fifth and sixth show how one dishonorable transgression can lead to an honorable life; the seventh section celebrates a naked little girl as a personification of honor. What a schema like this can show is simply that, despite appearances to the contrary, Olson arranged the parts of his poem in an order which is logical—in this instance, inductive—and which has little to do with Pound's ideogrammic method.

The continuity of *The Maximus Poems*, though, does owe a good deal to Pound's *Cantos* as well as to *Paterson*. Olson could not content himself with the continuity achieved either by Pound's "EGO-POSITION" or by Williams' fix on the local: "For if one won't (as I can't!) proceed by 'story' (in the Homeric, and Shakespearean size); and one can't (as I won't—don't) buy EP's 'history-plus-ego,' the morality of, the 'Good State' (the Confucian 'process'), or WCW's false-organism, a 'City' (the false-relativism to either of the above absolutes: the 'story,' or 'society')—then, one is in trouble!" [*Origin*, January 1971] Olson resolved this dilemma by constructing a history centered on a locality, Gloucester; but he remained sceptical of his choices and aware that this history would be only as good as he was wise:

> And narrative, (for me in these Max letters), is, I believe, *the authority* which the case (of the form as of 125—or 250 pages—) must rest on:
>
> the building-up, over the space & shape of it, of individuals & events so crucial
>
> (they need not be, I take it, "significant" people or happenings, or "intelligent", or necessarily "natural" (common, or whatever is WCW's guide to choice)—
>
> it is not the fall of a prince who is proud, or of a dope who gets tangled (American naturalism), or the peacocks of history (either of my own, or of any chosen time—like the Quattrocento, say)
>
> it is any of them, whom, in my "wisdom", I come to know. And use. (And it is just here, like I say, that the burden of being "right" is suddenly "fell" upon one! One then is an edge (a butter-knife) of life so sharp (has to find out how to be so sharp), that it is hell to pay, to pay oneself out at such intensity—to achieve such inevitability!

To depend upon one's own wisdom—quotation marks or no—is surely the "EGO-POSITION." But to gather individuals and events from one city is closer to Williams' method. Compromises are out of fashion these days, so it is probably best to say that Olson synthesizes Pound's and Williams' methods for achieving a measure of continuity in the long poem.

And although Olson, like Williams, gathered events and people from one city, his manner of gathering was much different from Williams' and deserves some discussion. In this context "manner of gathering" means nothing short of historical method. Olson rightly thought of Williams as a democratic kind of gatherer: "Williams is like Melville, a man who registers the going-ons of all of the human beings he lives among. He sees charge in them, worth in their fires, also a fire his own burns in, as against Ezra Pound, with that selection out of, that 'the light in the conversations of—the letters of—the intelligent ones,' or at least the literate ones . . ." [*Human Universe and Other Essays*]. Olson follows Williams to the extent he includes in *The Maximus Poems* "common" people like Ben Frost, Frank Miles, and Lew Douglas, the people Olson lived among. And yet the historical figures who are most crucial to Olson's major theme—the ownership v. fishing theme—cannot be thought of as common. They are political leaders like John White, Roger Conant, John Endecott, and Miles Standish, the figures important to most historians of colonial America.

Olson assumes that the important history of Gloucester has more to do with the uncommon political leaders than with the common people. Williams was another kind of local historian altogether: when he looked through history books he came up with people like Sam Patch, David Hower, Peter VanWinkle, Mrs. Cumming, Cornelius Doremus, Leonard Sandford, Officers Goodridge and Keyes—not the political leaders. The limitation of Williams' approach is that the historical incidents which get into *Paterson* remain anecdotal; no one is asked to believe that Sam Patch's leaps are significant in terms of the history of Paterson, or of America. (No doubt a more generous critic of Williams would advance the argument that *Paterson* challenges the standard categories of historical understanding, that it embodies a history of Paterson, and of America, which has little to do with political forces and economic relationships.) Does this distinction between Olson and Williams indicate that Olson was more elitist in political and historical matters—more like Pound in this regard—than Williams? To some degree, it does, but degrees are especially important in such matters.

Not only did Olson believe that the history of New England could be understood by looking at a few important individuals, he further thought that the future would be changed by an elite. Wisdom, he thought, can only be preserved by a small group: "I do not myself believe that symbols and signs are forced on sectaries, out of a necessity to be secret, but that wisdom itself, or at least the cultivation of energy-states per se, thrives on secrecy, on sect, and—at exactly the time we are in—finds its pleasure in conspiracy (*'épater tout le monde'*)" [*Human Universe and Other Essays*]. But to understand Olson's elitism properly, to understand how different it is from the Poundian variety, it must be realized that Olson romantically believed all men capable of the vision exercised by extraordinary individuals. At the end of **"Letter 6"** he makes this point:

> So few need to,
> to make the many
> share (to have it,
> too)
>
> but those few . . .
>
>> What kills me is, how do these others think
>> the eyes are
>> sharp? by gift? bah   by love of self? try it
>> by god?
>>   ask
>> the bean sandwich
>
> There are no hierarchies, no infinite, no such many
>   as mass,
>   there are only
> eyes in all heads,
> to be looked out of

All men have the capability of seeing accurately, though they do not know it, and may not even care. It takes only a few—more a vanguard than an elite—to show the many of what they are all capable; but those few are sadly absent.

Readers of Williams' poetry are bound to feel that *The Maximus Poems* have more in common with Williams' work than the focus on the local. For one thing, both these poets write poems about how to write poems. In 1952—after the first four books of *Paterson* had been published—Olson thought "The Desert Music," not *Paterson*, Williams' best work. What is vulnerable about that poem is its obvious self-consciousness. It is a program poem:

> How shall we get said what must be said?
>
> Only the poem.
>
> Only the counted poem, to an exact measure:
> to imitate, not to copy nature, not
> to copy nature
>
> NOT, prostrate, to copy nature
>   but a dance! to dance . . .

Williams knew that what life a poem like "The Desert Music" has is foetus-like: its life is a struggle to survive long enough for the slow process of formation to move forward. At any one point in this process the poem can never be fully alive. This kind of poem is born at its conclusion, not at its inception. The movement of the verse is nervous, nervous that the poem will not make it through the process. The line is not allowed to complete itself; it comes up against emptiness, its own incompleteness, and has to start again:

> Her cold eyes perfunc-
> torily moan but do not
> smile. Yet they bill
> and coo by grace of
> a certain candor. She
>
> is heavy on her feet.
> That's good. She
> bends forward leaning
> on the table of the
> balding man sitting
> upright, alone, so that
> everything hangs for-
> ward.

In a 1956 lecture at Black Mountain College Olson spoke of the poem as a struggle: "I mean, discords. The discordant. The want of agreement. The want of concord or harmony. Variance, dissension, contention, dissonance. Contest. The *agon* as well as the *pathos* and the *epiphany*. (The name of the actor in Greek tragedy was *agonistes*, contester.) The shift, from sorrow to joy." Poetry based on a principle of the poem as contest is likely to share more with Williams' later work than with Pound's. Most of Pound's

Cantos are about Venice, the Renaissance, Confucius, Jefferson, Adams, Van Buren, China—not about the struggle to write poetry. Pound's manner is more self-assured than Williams'. The characteristic movement of his verse is slow, steady, and incantatory; the line in the *Cantos* is a distinct and secure unit. But as Cid Corman has noted, Williams did notuse the line as a poetic unit until late in life, when he discovered the triadic line (which resembles three of his earlier lines). His lineation keeps the reader's eye moving from one short line to another; the movement of the verse is a constant flux of fragments: most resting places are suppressed. Olson's most characteristic verse moves with a similar nervousness; but, in fact, it is a good deal more jumpy, because it moves faster and with more frenetic force than Williams'. The last section of **"I, Maximus of Gloucester, to You,"** for instance, begins:

> in! in! the bow-sprit, bird, the beak
> in, the bend is, in, goes in, the form
> that which you make, what holds, which is
> the law of object, strut after strut, what you are,
>   what you must be, what
> the force can throw up, can, right now hereinafter
>   erect,
> the mast, the mast, the tender
> mast!

This strophe moves with great difficulty after struggling with the obstacles planted in its path. The first line, as I read it, includes five syllables which receive primary stress, one which gets secondary stress ("sprit") and the two articles which are unstressed, and the four caesuras keep these hammerings pretty well separated from each other. The second line loosens the movement by introducing more unstressed syllables, four by my count (the second, fourth, seventh, and eighth syllables). But still there are four caesuras in the line, like hurdles in the path of a runner. The third line retains only two caesuras and after an initial trochee slips into an iambic rhythm. The fourth line lengthens out far enough to include four separate phrases, each with two strong beats, and the beginning of a fifth; each phrase is a sizable stride forward. The fifth line remains long (a hexameter), and its rhythm tries to rise in iambs and anapests:

> x   ,   x   x   ,   ,   ,   x   , x , x
> the force can throw up, can, right now hereinafter
>   x   ,
>   erect,

After the first end-stop in this strophe comes the transparently iambic sixth line. Olson placed the two caesuras— after the first and second feet—so as to emphasize the regularity of the line. The last line, a single accented syllable, is enjambed with the sixth, and together these two lines read as, and close the strophe with, an iambic tetrameter.

Olson appears to have felt that he had to earn the formal regularity of the last two lines by struggling with the tough, discrete syllables of the first two lines. The last two lines are the achieved, triumphant denouement of a process of struggle, a struggle with dissonance, much like Williams' struggle in "The Desert Music," which ends in the jubilant and basically iambic (the play on "I am" as iamb could just conceivably be deliberate) proclamation of achievement: "I *am* a poet! I / am. I am. I am a poet, I reaffirmed, ashamed". And Williams, too, liked to measure his own dissonance against traditional metrical forms. This passage from "The Desert Music," for instance, embodies two not quite separate measures:

> ,   x   x   ,   x   ,
> I am that he whose brains
>   x   ,   x
>   are scattered
>   ,   x   ,
>   aimlessly

Williams' lineation makes the iambic trimeter (the initial inversion is well within the bounds of convention) of the first line seem to dissolve—or scatter—in the second and third lines. But the scattering is self-discipline. Williams would not allow himself the too easy iambic trimeter of

> ,   x   x   ,   x   ,
> I am that he whose brains
>   x   ,   x   ,   x   ,
>   are scattered aimlessly

Instead, he spaced out the words to make them seem asymmetrical. Similarly, the rhyme between "he" and "aimlessly" is off center, because "he" is buried in the middle of the first line. These are the techniques of a poet self-consciously testing out his language; the style is a distinctive but still a tentative one. But the tentative quality of Olson's verse comes from halting before and then banging against obstacles, such as commas, exclamation points, appositions, and parentheses; whereas Williams' line pauses before the emptiness at its end, then begins again, this time more cautiously, with a new line.

Pound's prosody had less to offer Olson, for one reason because Olson paid less attention to the integrity of the poetic line than did Pound; Olson preferred to work with units smaller than the line: "Let's start from the smallest particle of all, the syllable" [*Selected Writings*]. If one is constructing lines of verse, syntax—the ordering of words to form larger units of meaning—is a constant concern. Both Pound and Williams set precedents for disrupting conventional units of meaning. Williams, most characteristically, stretches syntactic units across the space between lines or suspends their completion way beyond conventional expectations: large units of meaning accrue only after tested patience has sharpened attention and disrupted conventional expectations. Pound made it part of his program to substitute his own theories of the ideogram for the principles of conventional prose syntax, but his intent was nonetheless to construct larger units of meaning. Olson, however, did not want to think much about larger units of meaning: "Word writing. Instead of 'idea-writing' (ideogram etc). That would seem to be it" [*Proprioception,* 1965]. He appears to have thought that conventional syntax expresses essentially conventional—logical—patterns of meaning: "the conventions which logic has forced on syntax must be broken open as quietly as must the too set feet of the old line" [*Selected Writings*]. Olson was impatient with logic (even though his poems are often logically structured), because he thought it responsible for that unhealthy distance between subject and object, between man and objective reality: "the rational mind hates the familiar, and has to make it ordinary by explaining it, in order not to experience it . . ." [*Special View of History*]. The implication seems to be that by avoiding conventional syntax a poet can reacquaint his readers through concrete images with the objective reality.

The other reason why Olson departed from conventional syntax is related to the whole matter of open-form poetry. He felt that his poetry must engage the flux of reality. He believed—and found confirmation of this belief in Heraclitus and Whitehead—that reality is an unceasing process which undermines all static achievements. Hence, all preconceived forms, in fact all closure, is unfaithful to reality. Olson engaged this matter in moral terms: in order to fulfill its moral obligation, art must commit itself—no matter the painful uncertainty—to process, to open form: "the morality any of us is led to, if we stick it, is by tales, to reveal anew, the humanism that art is the morality of[.] And that it is only to be discovered in the medley of one's own event by driving that content toward a form unknown even to the maker in the making[.] In other words I don't know what I am up to! And must stay in that state in order to accomplish what I have to do. Which is the weather, I guess, which makes this fierceness I speak of [*Origin,* January 1971]".

This commitment obviously contributed to the overall serial, open form of *The Maximus Poems*; but it operates as well on the stylistic level. It encourages repetition, parenthesis, and apposition. Because nothing can be stated exactly and finally, one must try to say something once, be dissatisfied at the incompleteness of expression, try to say it again more completely, be again dissatisfied, and so on, in theory at least, *ad infinitum*. These stylistic effects can be seen on almost any page of *The Maximus Poems*; take as an example this description of the Madonna on top of the Church of Our Lady of Good Voyage in Gloucester:

> (o my lady of good voyage
> in whose arm, whose left arm rests
> no boy but a carefully carved wood, a painted face,
> a schooner!
> a delicate mast, as bow-sprit for
>   forwarding

Her arm is referred to twice, the second time with more precision; and no fewer than six nouns, each quite distinct, form the description of what her bent arm carries.

One normally expects a poet to blot his first thoughts after they have led him to subsequent, more precise and refined, formulations, in the name of craft and artistry, not to mention brevity. But this expectation grows from a long-respected aesthetic theory of the artifact as achieve-

ment and result, which has little to do with Olson's poetics. "Artifact" is not even an adequate term for discussing *The Maximus Poems*: they are not the result of Olson's labors; they are his labors. They enact the process of composition. When Olson discovers in his historical research that he has admitted erroneous information into **"Letter 2"** concerning Nathaniel Bowditch's ship, he does not go back and revise because that would falsify the process of composition; instead he corrects his error in **"Letter 15."** Analogues to this practice can be found in the *Cantos,* especially in those which most concern the flux of historical events. In the Malatesta Cantos, for example, Pound uses pronouns with unclear antecedents:

> And Roberto got beaten at Fano,
> And he went by ship to Tarentum,
> I mean Sidg went to Tarentum
> And he found 'em, the anti-Aragons,
>   busted and weeping into their beards.
> And they, the papishes, came up to the walls. . . .

The self-corrections give the sense of Pound harried by the chronicler's unending task but trying to do his best to keep up with the flux and to report events accurately if not elegantly.

When it comes to matters of diction, Olson lines up with Pound, against Williams. Williams' statements on this subject are only too well-known. In an essay on Pound and Gertrude Stein, for instance, he wrote: "It's the words, the words we need to get back to, words washed clean. Until we get the power of thought back through a new minting of the words we are actually sunk. This is a moral question at base, surely but a technical one also and first. . . . Stein has gone systematically to work smashing every connotation that words have ever had, in order to get them back clean." Younger poets, like Robert Bly, appear to have taken Williams at his word in this regard. But Olson was an exception. He had little sympathy with Williams' pronouncements on language. Although he advocated getting in back of the word as name to the thing itself, he stopped short of nominalism: "I suspect Bill's nominalism is so thorough he lost his game—at least that *after* Grain the nominalism stayed fixed. And thus he went the opposite path from that one which Grain showed him" [*Letters for Origin,*]. Williams' chafing at the historical dimension of language held no attraction for someone like Olson who believed that the history of words is one of the most telling and accurate histories of civilization.

Williams' declarations about diction are the sort to be expected from a nominalist who distrusts the capacity of language to convey reality accurately. For the nominalist, the word and its referent can be conjoined only tentatively by a willing suspension of disbelief: the categories of language are too generalized to express the particularity of things. For Williams, driving the word back to its etymology is a means of dusting off verbal categories that have been allowed to accrue too many senses. Language remains suspect; it cannot be for long a precise and reliable measure of the real objects and events it refers to. The best the poet can achieve is a temporary consonance, a parallel movement of two systems, language and reality, which can never embrace: "The vague accuracies of events dancing two / and two with language which they / forever surpass . . ." [*Paterson*]. But Pound and Olson pick up accrued senses of words as clues to a more accurate perception of reality, a reality that inheres in the language almost magically. This conviction about language lies behind the wonder and enthusiasm with which Olson pursued philology, archaeology, and anthropology. But even though he was critical of Williams' antihistoricism, Olson gave Williams credit for the substantive shift of his linguistic declarations; Williams, like Olson, intended to reweld that connection between the word and its referent: "mr bill, gettin 'em fr the scrupulousness of his attention to the objects of which words are to him the nouns (he is in this sense a beginner, gets back to, the naming force/ function of language. . . ."

Unlike some of the poets influenced by Olson, Olson himself took etymological matters with absolute seriousness. There is little of that playfulness in Olson's diction that one comes across occasionally in Williams:

> I cannot say
> more than how. The how (the howl) only
> is at my disposal (proposal). . . .
>   with the roar of the river
> forever in our ears (arrears). . . .

What for William Carlos Williams was an occasional flight of fancy is a *modus operandi* for younger poets, like Jonathan Williams, who toy with words until they yield some slight pattern. Jonathan Williams' short poem, "Everybody Twist!," is an example:

LAWLESS WALLACE ÜBER ALLES

all ass, alas,
no arse-
nic, no

lace,
as well as no
solace

no Ace Carter, no Bull
Connor

LAWLESS WALLACE ÜBER ALLES

The word-play proclaims the poem a sophisticated game, but the symmetry of the refrain outlines the limits of the game's effects. When Johan Huizinga defined the nature of play, he called special attention to its spatial boundaries: "More striking even than the limitation as to time is the limitation as to space. All play moves and has its being within a playground marked off beforehand either materially or ideally, deliberately or as a matter of course" [*Homo Ludens: A Study of the Play-Element in Culture*, 1955]. E.E. Cummings, the American poet of this century most influential in this direction, could rejoice over the

separation between his poetry and actuality. In the "Foreword" to *is* 5 in 1926, when numerous American critics were promoting an autonomous poetry, he wrote: "Ineluctable preoccupation with The Verb gives a poet one priceless advantage: whereas nonmakers must content themselves with the merely undeniable fact that two times two is four, he rejoices in a purely irresistible truth (to be found, in abbreviated costume, upon the title page of the present volume)." Despite his acknowledgement in "Projective Verse" of Cummings' experiments with lineation, Olson, who thought of himself as a poet-pedagogue, could never have agreed that for the poet two times two is five.

Olson was wary of word-play and puns because of the inaccuracies they might perpetrate. He wrote to Larry Eigner in 1956 about his impatience with Robert Duncan, who evidently advocated what Olson took to be playfulness concerning etymology:

> What that Duncan means by arbitrary etymologies is a part of his department of misinformation =s "invention". . . . He means etymologies *one makes up*! Wow! You will imagine how I don't figure that one, being, as you sd (Gloucester) a hound for meaning! Comes any word I go the other way, and what's most needed right now is an *Indo-European* Dictionary— roots, so one can feel that far back along the line of the word to its first users—what they meant, in *inventing* it, not any one of us at the most freewheeling drag-race time in man's guesses.

Olson's attempt to reorient poetry toward the quantitative and syllabic led him to see new formal possibilities for rhyme and pun, but in an essay written as a sequel to "Projective Verse" he expressed more apprehension than hope concerning word-play: "that aspect of language which the word 'pun' fairly covers is raised up anew—as something, in fact, to be damned careful of, that words have this duplicity that, because sounds play on each other, the words or parts of those sounds slide into & upon each other, melt, and thus lose their structures, & the structure of any saying." Word-play was just too frivolous a method for Olson: "What struck me was, that the reason [word-play] isn't interesting—Duncan's, I mean—is that it is merely broad. And thus is palpably smart, is not serious. . . ."

Discussions of poetic influence are destined to be delicate and dangerous, even in the case of a poet like Olson, who forthrightly proclaims his literary ancestors. Arguments for influence, not just affinity, come right up against the fact that every poet has numerous avenues of access to most stylistic techniques and nearly all themes. Certain styles and techniques are in the air for a year, two, a decade, or whatever. And this has been and continues to be the case concerning many of Pound's and Williams' techniques. Then, too, a poet can arrive by his own course at stylistic devices over which older poets claim to preside. But Olson definitely went to the sources of the poetic innovations he tapped, and in his writing and during his term of office as Rector of Black Mountain College

But no matter how often he praised Pound and Williams, he remained sensitive and sometimes ambivalent about his relationship to them. In 1953 he wrote a nasty and bitter letter to Cid Corman about a comparison Corman seems to have made between *Paterson,* the *Cantos,* and *The Maximus Poems*; Olson's letter indicates that he did not want to be reminded of the similarities between these poems:

> Or maybe this is rage, at having maximus measured outside itself. And i shld fall back on what i have sd to you before, that you are not at home to yourself, are not simply simple, as any man is who looks after his self.

> For you impose on me a hierarchical system which is only yr own, is no part of my life or work. (In fact, I read exactly the passage you put between the Pat quotes & the Cant as *distinct* from either. And that makes me feel very damn good, thank you. . . .

> Christ, to say i leave the music in the things! You, who have seen that it was published! And now, by god, you use the very virtu of the practice to mouth WCW and Eppie at me, as, superior. Fuck em, even if they are. It's none of our bizness.

Twelve years later, during the reading at Berkeley, Olson had become confident enough of his own accomplishment to admit his impulse to imitate at least Pound:

> I mean I wrote a—a flagrant autobiography of myself, which is in—uh—imitating Ezra Pound, trying to make myself—You can't do it. There's no arbit—There's no artificial way to be arbitrary. There's only one way—moral. Then you are. But every imitation stinks. And it (?leaves) you wrong. . . . I mean Ezra Pound long years ago returned the presentation copy of Finnegans Wake to himself, with the word *décadence* written over the autograph, or written over the cover. I mean that takes guts. The same guts that led him to say, "I thought I knew something." If he hadn't said it I wish I could say it to you, I thought I knew something. I'd be proud to have been the in—man in this century—And like, here I am, dragging my ass after Ezra.

But on the same occasion, his statement about Williams appears to be in part a defensive reaction to some adverse criticism Williams made of Olson: "poor Bill . . . really never really was my man. I mean he never—I mean, Bill don't believe in me. I mean, he really included Allen because Allen was different. And he really believes in that guy. I mean, it's on the record." This is a puzzling statement, because in 1961, during an interview with Walter Sutton, Williams said of *The Maximus Poems*:

> And how he wrote the poem down on the page was very interesting to me. And the shorter lines. Anti-Whitman. It's a good example of what has happened to Whitman. Olson's line is very much more in the American idiom. A shorter division of the lines, not the tendency of Ginsberg. He went back. His longer

lines don't seem to fit in with the modern tendency at all. Retrograde. I didn't like them at all in *Howl!* If he had paid attention to what Olson was doing it would have been more successful. . . .

Olson was consistently more dubious of his relationship to Williams than of his relationship to Pound. And yet he took much from both poets. It is neither possible nor meaningful to say that he owes more to Pound than to Williams, or vice versa; such matters do not take to quantification. What is important is that Olson was right about *The Maximus Poems* being quite distinct from either *Paterson* or the *Cantos.* Olson's work contributes to a strain of American poetry that is well represented by Williams' and Pound's work and a strain that has continued after Olson. Robert Duncan makes this last point about *The Maximus Poems* in tersest Olsonese:

> close to Paterson? yes—and there be a root
> in the *Cantos,* in *Paterson* that is hardy stock
> —direction in poetry—

Sherman Paul (essay date 1975)

SOURCE: "In and About the Maximus Poems," in *Iowa Review,* Vol. 6, No. 1, Winter, 1975, pp. 118-30.

[*In the following excerpt, Paul presents a critical overview of the first volume of* Maximus Poems.]

Chronological order is implicit in the practice of projective verse. As William Carlos Williams said of *The Maximus Poems,* "This is a story of the events of a man's experience and the particular events of a man's experience. . . ." Williams, also indebted to Whitehead, perhaps appreciated the accuracy of "events"; a poem is an event, the actualization of its occasion. Set out chronologically, the poems tell that story, in this simple sequential way are narrative. We search for other modes ofcoherence, for themes, perhaps for historical narrative, but most essential to understanding *The Maximus Poems* is Olson's adherence to the method of field composition in which stance toward reality is all-important and the poems that issue from the poet's participation in the field of his life enact the movement of his attention. Williams' comment on the first two volumes—"categorically this book [*Maximus 11-22*] is much better than the first [*Maximus 1-10*] by which I was often defeated"—also reminds us that the poems were, and remain, work-in-progress, appeared in installments, chronologically, and that we, too, might consider them in this way.

Williams doesn't tell us why he was defeated by the first and not also by the second installment of poems. Perhaps familiarity is accepting, for his central criticism of both volumes is the same—that too often too much that is essential is left out and too much that is inessential is included. This is not, I think, the case in any acceptable sense of "essential," and it is not now the case because there is annotation enough to make the poems readily accessible. The most "difficult" poem, **"Tyrian Businesses"** (**"Letter 8"**), is a part of the occasion that included "A Syllabary for a Dancer," an essay published in *MAPS*, in 1971, that the poem itself takes up, that glosses its allusions as well as the meaning of its activity.

Maximus is a big poem, the "sort . . . of epic" Olson mentioned in "Projective Verse"—a demonstration, in fact, of his belief that the practice of projective verse might solve the "problem of larger content and of larger forms. . . ." The numbers indicate the limits of the present volume and promise subsequent poems, and the initial poem addresses us (intimately: Whitman's you whoever you are) at a pitch of high resolve, with unusual verbal force, and with a didactic, moral insistence as reminiscent of Pound, perhaps his most conspicuous teacher, as of Maximus of Tyre, a mediator or model of the self Maximus of Gloucester sometimes assumes and Olson assumed when he introduced himself with this poem in *Origin 1*, the issue featuring him. "Charley," Fielding Dawson says in *The Black Mountain Book*, "was possessed by his voice," and he counsels later in this valuable emotional memoir of Olson during the years these poems were written, "If you want to understand Charley's poems, he's talking." Like Apollonius of Tyana, whose life fables Olson even more than that of Maximus of Tyre, he "talked to live. . . ." He was a man of voices—sometimes disconcertingly theatrical, as in the NET film in which he reads **"The Librarian."** But the voice of **"I, Maximus of Gloucester, to You,"** is modulated, not always pitched to passion, personal, always, in its public task, leaving the impression, appropriate to what in epic poems would be the invocation, of largeness. That the task he set himself was large is evident in the evocation not only of Pound but of Williams, Eliot, and Hart Crane, poets whose long poems challenged his own maximum effort. And it is evident too in the epigraph, which Olson, characteristically, employs as a text to be unfolded by meditative enactment. This text is an obstructive element, at least to those who must fully gloss it before entering the poem. What is most immediately available is Maximus' position in respect to Gloucester and to us (assuming, as I think the reader does, that the "you" he addresses is the reader, that he too belongs to those "islands / of men and girls" whom the equally isolated Maximus, concerned with creating a polis, elects to address in **"Letter 3"**; the poems, after all, are letters, communications; Williams is right to note the poet's loneliness). Maximus is "off-shore," which permits him, as in **"The Librarian,"** to observe Gloucester in overview and as Olson's private landscape; and his off-shore position evokes a discoverer (public task) and a voyager returning home (private need) as well as the fisherman, summoned by "lance," the striking-iron, who are the heroes of Gloucester he most often celebrates. The difficult phrases are "hidden in the blood"and "a metal hot from boiling water," the first suggesting the equation of sea and blood, outer and inner waters, self and world, double, inseparable dimensions of the poem, and the second, calling up, with the help of "lance," the urgency, even aggressive force, of his purpose—in this he is like Ahab, though his purpose otherwise—a purpose not altered by but complexly elaborated by Olson's own remarks:

> Maximus, Hero, a metal hot from boiling water, born in the winter, 1949-50, age 38-39. Sprang easily into anything, including busses; and in the spring, year 1952, succeeded easily in walking through New York City in one day, to the tune of $2,500. A day.

Not himself a partisan of conventional heroes, Olson may be excused the tall-tale exuberance with which he responds to the emergence of the central figure of the poems. It is a great moment, like the watershed he notes in Apollonius' life: "He is now 40 years old, and at last aware of the dimension of his job. . . ." It is the moment, as the allusion to Whitman's emergence reminds us (Emerson had brought the simmering Whitman to a boil), of confirmation and resolution, the outsetting bard hoping to cease only with death. What follows this is not of immediate referential importance but provides a clue to the Oedipal motive of the work:

> O.K. That took care of Ma. The Hero though has also to be the King's son. This is very difficult in a democratic society. In a democratic society all men are fathers, like all women are mothers. This is not the same as being the King. By no means. The old man has to die, you have to succeed and not that one, here, of success: it has to be rule. You are omnipotent. Thus you do be what you were which you were born for. . . .

Olson acknowledges, in an autobiographical statement, that, at 40, he was still "hugely engaged with my parents," that their presence in him constituted part of the "live past" he explored.

The key words in Maximus' message to us are "lance," "obey," "dance." They involve a crucial matter of the poem, the crucial matter of Olson's desire to "restate man . . . repossess him of his dynamic," the matter of stance first treated in "Projective Verse"—how to stand a thing among things in a world in process, how, in Olson's reminiscently Thoreauvian words, to front reality—and they apply to, are exemplified by, both fishermen ("how shall you strike, / o swordsman, the blue-red back") and poet (for the lance is also a pen and the figures of the dance are syllables). Both fisherman and poet are men of skill, of attention and care ("eyes"), and are assimilated to each other throughout the poems, explicitly in **"Letter 6."** Their stance is creative, for it is the readiness, the responsiveness to the field in which one finds oneself, the quick attentiveness to change, to the moment, the possibility that summons one and defines "that which you can do!" It is creative, according to Olson, because in this participant action one is himself the "mover of the instant. . . ." Moreover, stance may be accompanied by love because, as Olson taught Fielding Dawson, love is a verb, an action; "love is form," is what is done in the world, is "to make things," as he says of William Stevens, the colonial carpenter, the "first Maximus"—to make necessary things, nests, houses, poems.

The initial verses situate the poet in the field of his endeavor and call him to his task. They also introduce us to Gloucester, place us in space, in a "culture of immediate references" (Williams'phrase in "The American Back-ground"). We are in the harbor-section, the old, preferred, still virtuous part of the poet's city, itself bowl-like, a nest, dominated in this poem, as in no other, by the gulls, tutelary birds, immemorial presences of place, exemplary, too, nest-builders, form-creators, weaving from miscellaneous materials, as the poet himself is doing and will do, and, what is more, of all creatures, for Olson, most wonderfully equilibrated in the field, paragons of stance. (We remember Olson's excitement over the chii-mi at the beginning of *Mayan Letters* and his admiration, in **"A Round & A Canon,"** for a bird in "his own world, his own careful context, those / balances.") And these verses initiate themes—they are insistences of the field, issuing from it, not imposed on it—and in them the poet begins to chart the moral geography of place.

The most important theme, subsuming stance and love, is self-action—"those self-acts," "the tasks / I obey to" treated in **"Letter 9."** It is treated here most explicitly in section 4, which resumes and modifies "love is form" in section 2:

> one loves only form,
> and form only comes
> into existence when
> the thing is born
>
> > born of yourself, born
> > of hay and cotton struts,
> > of street-pickings, wharves, weeds
> > you carry in, my bird
> > > of a bone
> of a fish
> > > of a
> straw, or will
> > > of a
> color, of a bell
> > > of
> yourself, torn

Olson especially liked these quatrains so admirably woven of the previous materials of the poem and brought to coherence by vowel-modulation, consonance, anaphora, internal rhyme, and rhythmic movement. Their theme is particularly his own, connected, as we will see, with *tropos,* with the self's answering growth to the petitioning energies of the world. What concerns him here is that created things are born of the self, of its own psychic travail and the materials it brings in in its forays on its immediate environment, and, as the placing of the quatrains indicates, that the act of creation is assertive, resistant. A resistant stance is one of the notable things about Olson: his verse is not only percussive (as in section 6) and prospective (open to what lies "around the bend"), but projectile. In *Maximus IV* he gives us his acute sense of environmental pressure and the necessity he feels he is under to push against it:

> . . . forever the geography
> which leans in
> on me I compell
> backwards I compell Gloucester

to yield, to
change

And since "Polis / is this," he is at the very start about this work, about the difficult task of making a poem—creating the polis, refounding Gloucester in its verbal space—when its very materials are not, as he says, easy to love. His revulsion at Gloucester, at the city beyond the harbor—its streets are immediately explored in **"Letter 2"** and the moral geography of sea and land, perhaps derived from Melville, made explicit—is similar to the revulsion at contemporary culture of Williams and Pound. And they are very much present to him, as the echo in "but how shall you know" of "But how will you find" from the preface to *Paterson,* where a similar issue is confronted, and the borrowing of "pejorocracy" from Pound, tell us. Pound is the dominant presence in this poem, not only in the "rhythmic assemblies" Williams complained of, but in the "violent prejudices" he also noted, prejudices that, as in the present instance of harbor vs. city, take the form of either-or, melodramatic, perhaps even conspiratorial oppositions. "Pejorocracy" and "musick," conspicuous thematically, are certainly unlovely, as are the worse rule and false language and the sick music and muzak they name. But is the case so extreme, or only the poet's revulsion, a revulsion that finds expression in Lear's outraged "o kill kill kill kill kill," an expression, too, of one of the poem's major themes:

> o kill kill kill kill kill
> those
> who advertise you
> out

Out-in, another opposition. Against those who betray his "sea-city," who neither look to sea nor reverence "my lady of good voyage," the guardian, the tutelary deity, of the fishing community, and who do not know, as he says in **"Letter 2,"** that

> it is elements men stand in the midst of,
> not these names supported by that false future she,
> precisely she,
> has her foot upon

—against these he enjoins the "in! in!" of creative action, the raising of the mast that establishes the center of the new-found polis. The argument may be said to be phallic, like Whitman's, and Williams' too, who links going-in with discovery. It has unusual physical force.

"I, Maximus of Gloucester, to You" opens the world and themes of what follows. In this, it reminds one of "Proem: to Brooklyn Bridge." And like Crane's poem, for all that is dismaying in what it surveys, it is optative, a summons to creative work. Placed as he is, Maximus is not subdued by musick. He "can still hear." He has the power of listening Olson treated in "Projective Verse," and he knows how to play (it) by ear, both attend the syllables and play things in the field as they come. For him the commonplace is wonderful, and "life as spirit," as Olson says in **"Apollonius of Tyana,"** "is in the thing, in the instant, in this man." The universe is open, we are equal to its occasions, and meeting the instant may, in Williams' words in *Paterson,* "begin to begin again."

The Maximus Poems 1-10 is a much better book than Williams thought it to be. It is coherent, having the intrinsic order-tension demanded by field composition. The poems vary in immediate difficulty but, as with *Paterson,* may be quickly read through with pleasure. Since composition is by field, the poems have the shapes of the poet's activity of thought; their forms are the extension of their contents. Yet in the way the themes are woven together the poems appear to follow a track, and Olson's practice of gathering various themes together in concluding sections (at the end of **"Letter 1,"** for example) seems artful rather than spontaneous. The art of projective verse, however, is in minding spontaneity, and one finds this skill in Olson's letters where he follows the thread of thought over pages of seemingly digressive movement. Certainly in an enterprise involving him as intensely and continuously as these *Maximus* poems he would have been equal to the need for coherence.

There is no narrative line in these poems. They do not advance, have no particular forward direction. Instead they get the large work under way, begin to move in place, to take possession of place. Olson follows his advice to Ed Dorn to dig (in) one place, though he has not yet consulted in the poems any documents, and the colonial and precolonial history of America, prominent in the later poems, becomes foreground only in **"Letter 10."** These poems involve the present time, Gloucester now, and the poet's need to move, to work in, and to establish the terms that chart the field and enable him to tell "the Fables and the Wills of man. . . ."

The terms, of course, have thematic importance and, as we have seen, are binary, composed of opposing elements, each pair clustering with others to develop the range of the poet's values. Of primary importance is the geographical pair, sea vs. land; to which one adds the directions, outward vs. inward; the occupations, fishing (and poetry) vs. capitalism (slaving, advertising, etc.); the polities, polis vs. pejorocracy; the economies, local vs. absentee; the stances, the "old measure of care" (of eyes, of ears) vs. carelessness (abstraction); the applications, work vs. sloth; and the goals, eudamia vs. euphoria. These values, moreover, are told by the senses: by sight (the white vs. black, for example, of **"Letter 2"**), by smell (tansy vs. gurry and the slime of ownership), by hearing (bells vs. musick), by touch (contact vs. withholding). In charting the field, they dramatize what Olson called "the binary problem"—"that at any moment of essential experience you are making a choice. . . ."

The most prominent concern of these poems—it is prominent also in subsequent installments—is "the practice of the self." As in the earliest poems in *Archaeologist of Morning* and in the writing that culminates in *The Special View of History,* Olson is preoccupied with a question of both public and personal urgency: how to act? He is preoccupied with the "actual willful man" who must do "some-

thing about [with?] himself," who, perforce, asks, "what act? what shall we do with Papa's shovel? what shall we do? . . ." In **"The Songs of Maximus"** (**"Letter 3"**) he writes:

> And I am asked—ask myself (I, too, covered
> with the gurry of it) where
> shall we go from here, what can we do

The question specifically relates to art as an action and finds an answer in **"Letter 5,"** the longest, most reproving and scornful poem of this installment. In this letter, Olson addresses Vincent Ferrini, a poet and the editor of *Four Winds* (where Olson published three of the *Maximus* poems!), a man, he feels, who has misconceived his task, has bungled it as badly as the skipper who in a storm abandoned two men at sea. A little magazine, like *Origin,* whose policy Olson did much to shape, might be a polis, a "place we can meet," but Ferrini has betrayed that possibility by seeking guidance everywhere except in the "context of / now," in the elements of the local place, the very Gloucester Olson knows intimately; with recollections of it he salts his disapproval and claims his nativity. In terms of the issue of language set forth in pejorocracy and musick (song, or poetry, is an alternative), Ferrini's act is equivalent to that of the absentee owners who advertise us out. He has failed at "men's business," that which confronts the elements and requires the "old measure of care." Not only has he failed to see out of his own eyes, which is a privilege Olson restores in **"Letter 6"** ("There are no hierarchies, no infinite, no such many as mass, there are only / eyes in all heads, / to be looked out of"), he has not had "the polis / in [his] eye. . . ."

Olson himself is as much the proper model in respect to Ferrini as are the fishermen he holds up as exemplary. But in respect to Marsden Hartley, another artist treated in these poems, the exemplary figure is his father. The issue in this letter (7), which continues the treatment of eyes, attention, and care in terms of "hands" ("hands are put to the eyes' commands"), is unmediated contact with things. Hartley, a painter connected with Gloucester only because in the 1930's he painted her landscape and chiefly that of Dogtown, the uninhabited moraine north of the town, is not contemned. Olson acknowledges his "many courages." What he disapproves of is his "transubstantiations," the way in which he transformed all things to cloth, made the Whale's Jaw, the particular instance related to his father, a "canvas glove." This is as much as to say that Hartley engaged reality with his gloves on, that he did not follow the way of objectism, proposed by Olson in "Projective Verse," but rather that of the egotistical sublime:

> Such transubstantiations
>
> as I am not permitted,
> nor my father,
> who'd never have turned the Whale Jaw back
> to such humanness neither he nor I, as workers,
> are infatuated with

This passage is of interest also because Olson identifies with his father and defines the artist—the carpenter prefigures this—as a worker. His father, he says, took the Whale's Jaw "as he took nature, took himself. . . ." He was a man of attention and care, dealing directly with things, and Olson, in the excellent short story "Stocking Cap," depicts him with an admiration that measures his own incapacity. Here, he is Jehovah!

> Jehovah, he looks that strong
> he could have split the rock
> as it is split, and not
> as Marsden Hartley painted it
> so it's a canvas glove

But why did Hartley do this? Why transubstantiate? Because he refused "woman's flesh." The remark—the disclosure, in the concluding line, shocks us—is unkind but may be justified because its truth had already been revealed in Paul Rosenfeld's study of Hartley in *Port of New York* and Williams' account of Hartley's homosexuality in the *Autobiography*.

Of course the most conspicuous example of behavior is Olson himself, for *The Maximus Poems* provide him the satisfaction he speaks of in *The Special View of History*: creating the history of one's self. The entire poem is his act, and much in these early poems involves his stance and preparatory enabling acts. We learn, for example, that he has adopted voluntary poverty. **"The Songs of Maximus"** (**"Letter 4"**), in which he tells of the "blessings" of the leaky faucet and the faulty toilet—this particular song recalls Williams' "Le Médicin Malgré Lui"—are themselves repudiations of the wanting encouraged by advertising. He sings because he "wants" something else, because "wondership," as exemplified in the account of recognizing Nike, moves him more than "ownership." There is bravado here as there is in **"The Green Man,"** an early poem originally entitled **"In Praise of the Fool,"** in which he advises the fool to turn from the way of politics ("chase a King") to the way of poetry ("furiously sing!"). Prompted by outrage at contemporary culture, these songs are his furious singing. We learn too in **"Letter 6"** what he confesses later in **"Letter 12"**: that the sea was not his trade, that he lacks the skills of professionals, wastes his eyes. He admits that "I have suffered since, / from that enthusiasm," but it's as much competitiveness as enthusiasm, as the subsequent anecdote of mountain-climbing tells us. He acknowledges the folly, but is proud of the fact that his sharpness comes of "pushing . . . limits." In the context of **"Letter 5"**—"Limits / are what any of us / are inside of"—the implied injunction is to move outward beyond them. The Olson of these poems is an adventurer; he risks himself.

There is nothing conspicuous in this, and the letters that address it, reaching deeply to the speculative sources of Olson's work, are the meditative center of these poems. In **"Tyrian Businesses"** (**"Letter 8"**), the poem under hand is his "exercise for this morning," an example of "how to dance / sitting down"; in **"Letter 9,"** which develops the idea of *tropos* in the previous letter, the concern is "self-acts" and "self-things," intrinsic growth and the making of poems. Olson tells us in "A Syllabary for a Dancer," the essential gloss on **"Tyrian Businesses,"** that man is "a thing which simultaneously thinks and dances," that he is concerned with using himself, with self-originating action, with "the kinetic as the act of life," the movement that engages things and makes them yield "that life which matter is so astoundingly capable of anew each day in each new human hand." For Olson, himself a dancer, movement is the basis of renewal: only get under way, begin the work by which one attacks chaos. But it must be movement of the kind exemplified here, vertical movement, having its origins, its *tropos,* in the chaos within oneself, in what is "implicit in himself, inside himself, what he is and what he is impelled to do, that is, how to move." The distinction between vertical and horizontal movement is crucial, and of historical import. For Olson connects the horizontal with the American westward movement, with "frontierism" and dispersion. American history follows the pattern of post-Sumerian history traced in **"The Gate at the Center"**: dispersion, loss of center, of coherence. Horizontal movement, accordingly, no longer serves "the last first people," Olson's characterization of the Americans in *Call Me Ishmael* ("We are the last 'first' people. We forget that. We act big, misuse our land, ourselves"). The business of **"Tyrian Businesses"** is indeed Tyrian, that of a Maximus concerned with, prescribing for, his country, "my countree," he says in **"Letter 10,"** the true, still to be discovered, America. And in these poems, as in the "Syllabary," he is still hopeful for America. With dispersion behind them, the Americans, he says, are "green again"; at last they have discovered "physicality" (that they are things among things) and "know what the earth is. . . ." Now they need only learn to sit.

Section one of **"Tyrian Businesses"** transposes the "Syllabary," and section two continues the poet's morning work, much of it his seemingly casual consulting of the dictionary. It is proper morning work, answering to Olson's stirring affirmation of himself as an "archaeologist of morning": "This is the morning after the dispersion, and the work of the morning is methodology: how to use oneself, and on what. That is my profession, I am an archaeologist of morning." *Heart, metacenter, tropaeolum, eudaemonia*—the definitions of these words, among others, provide the substance of a meditation on *tropos,* the inward-arising motion, the twisting and turning common to organic growth and verse. *Tropos* is self-action and its linguistic complement is the middle voice, mentioned here and in the "Syllabary" and defined later in *Proprioception* as the voice of "*proprious*-ception / 'one's own' -ception." In the middle voice, Olson explains, the subject is represented as acting on himself, for himself, and on something belonging to oneself—actions, incidentally, that yield him articles of faith: will, believe, be graceful, obey, accept self-responsibility.

Here, too, beginning proprioceptively with the contractions of the heart, he ponders the courage needed to live in a process world, a world of change. He considers his flower, the nasturtium, "my nose twist, my beloved, my / trophy"—a flower of the genus *Tropaeolum,* a kind of cress, pungent like tansy, associated by him with the "Tansy from Cressy's / I rolled in as a boy" (**"Letter 3"**). Flowers and flowering, as the subsequent poem bears out, are primary images of *tropos,* as important to him as they are to Williams; when he speaks in the "Syllabary" of vertical kinetics his example is "growing, and waving from the spine, like flowers are, or branches, on a tree." And since knowing how to dance sitting still is a "gravity question," he is properly concerned with the relations of M to G, of metacenter to gravity. A buoy or ship, after all, must be self-righting in any weather; must, as he shows in defining "felicity," move in accord with reason or nature. *Futtocks* and *fylfot* complete the logic of these definitions: felicity is a strong, lucky ship, able to survive storm and accident, or, in human terms, the lucky reward of those who are courageous, know how to grow, and move gracefully.

Or, as he declares in **"Letter 9,"** the splendid poem of spring following on this poem of morning, felicity comes of obeying what Emerson called the soul's emphasis, the tropic insistences of the self. The analogue of the self is the flower; the "likeness," he says, "is to nature's"; and "there are these necessities [natural process itself] / are bigger than we are." The poem celebrates a double flowering, that of "the flowering plum" and of his book of poems, ***In Cold Hell, In Thicket,*** just published in Mallorca. And since the latter reminds him of the fate of an earlier book, *Call Me Ishmael* ("as, in another spring, / I learned / the world does not stop / for flowers"), it raises for him the always disturbing question of contemplation vs. action, of the way of art vs. the way of acceptable public usefulness. Though Olson turned from politics to art, he did not abandon public ends: he says here that he wished that his book of poems "might stop / the workings of my city." And that it doesn't disturbs him:

> it puts a man back
> to find out how much
> he is busy, this way,
> not as his fellows are
> but as flowering trees

It disturbs him, and makes him defensive. Yet the intrinsic success of flowering is, as it had been for Thoreau in "Wild Apples," his chief argument, rehearsed here, one feels, to earn again and reaffirm his choice. Flowering, whether in the growth of the self or in the publication of books, is an end in itself ("these things / which don't carry their end any further than / their reality in / themselves"). And what interests him now, he says, is not extrinsic success but rather his own springlike condition, what he had referred to in the previous poem as "the seedling / of morning: to move, the problems (after the night's presences) the first hours of . . .":

> It's the condition in men
> (we know what spring is)
> brings such self-things about
> which interests me
> as I loll today
> where I used to
> atop Bond's Hill

His posture recalls Whitman's in "Song of Myself" and his survey of Cape Ann recalls Thoreau, in *Walden,* the monarch of all he surveys—the only monarch Olson chooses to be. And one element of the condition in men that accounts for such self-things as this poem is resistance, the *versus* the poem insists on as Olson opposes himself ("myself") to King Alfred, to history ("tempestuous / events"), to the tasks of the nation ("men's affairs"). To borrow the opposing Keatsian terms of *The Special View of History,* he would be a man of achievement, not a man of power, and he would obey the imperatives of his own being:

> versus
> my own wrists and all my joints, versus speech's
>   connectives, versus the tasks
> I obey to

He obeys his own turnings and twistings, and verse, itself a turning, is his opposing force. He is assertive; at the close of the poem the self is the measure of itself, and like the bee, whose buzzing also occurs elsewhere in the poem, he is angry at failure yet moved by it to poetic action.

The task for which all of this prepares is stated, finally, in **"Letter 10,"** which both concludes this installment and opens into the subsequent poems:

> on founding: was it puritanism,
> or was it fish?
>
> And how, now, to found, with the sacred & the
>   profane—both of them—
> wore out
>
> The beak's
> there. And the pectoral.
> The fins,
> for forwarding. [These images resume **"Letter 1"**]
>
> But to do it anew, now that even fishing . . .

Past and present juxtapose. Founding *and* refounding. The past begets the present, and the way its possibilities were dispossessed is repeated, the destructive agents, like Endecott (later associated with J. B. Conant of Harvard), destroying the beneficent founders, like Roger Conant, whose Tudor house, the first house built in Gloucester, "sat [at Stage Fort] / where [Olson says] my own house has been (where I am / founded." The history to which this poem may be taken to be prologue is of battle and destruction, of fierce oppositions, and it is still alive for Olson because historical dispossession is also a personal dispossession. Olson's concern with origins—with the founding—is prompted by the present need to refound. "The green republic now renewed": this entry in early notes on "Man is Prospective" states his public theme. The correlative private theme involves what is often a reverie toward childhood—an imaginative repossession of place, as the true place, the "my countree" of being and well-being with which he closes.

Paul Christensen (essay date 1977)

SOURCE: "Charles Olson's 'Maximus': Gloucester as Dream and Reality," in *The Texas Quarterly,* Vol. 20, No. 3, Autumn, 1977, pp. 20-9.

[In the following essay, Christensen discusses the major themes of The Maximus Poems.]

Charles Olson's distinguished long poem, the *Maximus* sequence, achieved final form with the publication of its closing book, *The Maximus Poems: Volume Three* in the early fall of 1975. Olson worked on the sequence for the last twenty years of his life; it is an intimate record not only of his passionate ideals but of the leaps and changes of his mind throughout that period. Like all works of high moral ambition, its appearance in final form has provoked mixed, even highly skeptical, reviews from critics who have had to judge its grand assertions. The *New York Times* described it as "a huge, angelic, failed effort"; Charles Altieri, writing a review for the *Washington Post,* called it "an ambitious failure." All the long poems written in this century—from Pound's *The Cantos* and Hart Crane's *The Bridge* (his hymn to the mysterious technology that created Brooklyn Bridge) to William Carlos Williams's *Paterson* and now Olson's *Maximus*—have been received similarly upon first public appearance, as though it were ritually necessary to attack poets who dare to inquire into the heart of a culture's mysteries and gods. In that ritual act of critics, the mythos of an age is fitfully revealed, as it more grandly is in the poems they judge. But what these poems illuminate of actual human nature and experience lies outside the purview of these preliminary assessments. I believe the more discerning criticism is that which asks of a poem like Olson's, What binds and unifies his work, what did he *make,* even if he fell short of his highest intentions?

Charles Olson's sequence, the *Maximus* poems, celebrates human community, as an ideal condition presently beyond the reach of mass man and as it may be achieved by the restoration of individual consciousness. Maximus himself, the speaker of this poem, is the primary example of how man struggles to transcend the alienation he suffers. In the slow unfolding of the poem we are intimate observers of the process by which this particular mind learns to break down its torpid subjectivity to become an active participant of reality again. And the implicit argument of the poem is that if each man were to achieve a similar openness, human community would again be a determinable possibility.

Olson came late to poetry; his first published poems appeared in 1946 when he was thirty-five years of age. Before turning to poetry he had successfully launched himself into politics. When he left Harvard University with all but his dissertation to write, he began working for the American Civil Liberties Union, and from there he went to the Common Council for American Unity. With the outbreak of World War II, he entered the Office of War Information, specifically to protect citizens of foreign nationality from slander or other abuse as the nation's

mood grew militant. Olson was an ardent idealist of those years, among the bright young men Roosevelt had attracted to government service. When he left the OWI over a dispute with his superiors, Roosevelt promised him a high post in the Treasury after his reelection, but Olson refused and quit politics to become a poet.

Even in those early political years, it is possible to see the ruling ideal of Olson's life: the desire to preserve a union of diverse nationalities, races, and creeds against the oppressive force of a single domineering majority. The son of a letter carrier of Swedish ancestry, he watched how his father was systematically persecuted by his employers as he struggled to establish a postal union. The bitterness and despair of those years enter into the *Maximus* sequence as one of its moving themes.

When Olson turned from politics to poetry, he renounced his liberalism and his belief in the power of government to improve or protect life in the nation. He believed that only art could change man's mind: not by its precepts and revelations, but by the example of the artist's awareness. The poet, when he is fully awake to the world and to his own responsiveness, demonstrates the force and excitement of his mind in the poem he writes. The reader who takes up such work will have before him the measure of human intensity. The poet will have shown him the paradise life is when the mind is held open to take in the world, and the reader will, either in envy or in admiration, allow his own faculties to relax and let more of earthliness register on him.

In a number of essays written during the 1950s—"Human Universe," "The Gate at the Center," the famous "Projective Verse" essay, collected in *Human Universe and Other Essays*—Olson attacked the state of contemporary American writing. His essential argument was that modern writers presented an abstract conception of reality in their work. They make their stories and poems, he said, "by selecting from the full content [of reality] some face of it, or plane, some part." The result: "It comes out a demonstration, a separating out, an act of classification, and so, a stopping, and for all that I know [the reality] is not there, it has turned false." For the artist, Olson wrote several years later, "There is one requirement, only one requirement, anywhere—the clue: open, stay OPEN, hear it, anything, really HEAR it. and you are IN." [sic] Taking his cue from a writer he deeply admired, D. H. Lawrence, Olson wrote in a review, "Nothing is so marvelous as to be done alone in the phenomenal world which is raging and yet apart," as was Lawrence's protagonist in *The Man Who Died.* Writers, in other words, who abstract from reality some fragment of details unwittingly reinforce the state of alienation that art should oppose and transcend. The only alternative to this shrinking reality of the arts and of thought in general was to step out of the bounds of Western humanism to engage the world freshly again.

The primary task of the *Maximus* sequence is to thrust a mind into the disarrayed particulars of Gloucester, Massachusetts, a seacoast town, to show that it could indeed absorb all the impingements of reality and render up fresh, often beautiful perceptions of its true nature. Gloucester had been Olson's summer residence as a child when his parents annually rented a small cottage in a modest section of this coastal resort. Not only was it among the largest fishing ports in the world, it was among the oldest settlements of the New England coast. As early as 1623, Dorchestermen were subsidized in a venture to establish a fishery in Gloucester; although it failed economically, this experiment led to the founding of the Massachusetts Bay Colony in 1630. English Puritans under John Winthrop succeeded in establishing a settlement, but Winthrop's dream of making a "City upon a hill," or what Olson calls a *"polis,"* failed when the settlers stepped from the *Arabella* and scattered to the distant countryside. Community, then, was a dream that perished on contact with American soil, and Olson's Maximus returns to it again and again as he surveys the limits and conditions of the town he inhabits.

The *Maximus* sequence, which is composed of three volumes and runs to nearly six hundred pages of text, has, among its many skeins of development, an epistemological plot: the poem moves forward by the leaps of Maximus's perceptions. Maximus begins his thought in the alien condition of the average citizen; he drifts over the rooftops of Gloucester like a bird, observing the configuration the city makes in his mind: it is a totality his sensibilities have not yet absorbed. The city is a congeries, a sum of things, which he enters bearing the blade of his discriminating intelligence. That blade shall be added to the form of Gloucester, as a bird adds his straw or twig to the nest he builds. "The nest, I say, to you, I Maximus, say/ under the hand, as I see it, over the waters from this place where I am, where I hear,/ can still hear." The form of Gloucester shall emerge in the poem that results as all the minutiae of the external world rush in and cohere in the perceptions of Maximus's mind.

Most of the ideas Olson uttered in his tensely written pronouncements on the state of poetry in the 1950s were intended to lead the poet away from the rigid conventions of traditional poetry toward an open stance he called Projectivism. This poetic charges the poet to explore his consciousness on paper in a language faithful to the events of his mind. The atrophy of awareness in modern technological society could be partly attributed to the distortions that traditional usage and convention have imposed upon consciousness. If the poet were free to simply cast his mind into language without falling into generality or abstraction (the universalizing tendencies of Western discourse that Olson fought against), it might be possible to make a true account of the nature of experience and of the human perception of it as it enters into the labyrinth of cognition. Hence, in the *Maximus* poems, we have before us the mind's processes reenacted typographically and linguistically. We are placed in the mind of Maximus among his most intimate dreams and thoughts as he bears us along in his deepening awareness of Gloucester.

But if the poetry is open in technique, the first volume, *The Maximus Poems* (1960), follows an orderly investigative procedure. Even this is part of the psychological realism of the poem: Maximus is careful and cautious in his first stages of contact with Gloucester. The first ten poems are really a reconnoitering by Maximus, an effort to attain some exact knowledge of the condition of Gloucester, the state of its fragmentation. The individuals that comprise Gloucester are buried over, he remarks, by the culture of the nation, with its vulgar advertisements and the deafening racket ofcorporate prosperity. The singing that Whitman once heard in America has turned into a deafening screech of product hawking, and the poet fears his citizens have lost the keenest sense of all, to hear, to hear clearly. The word *hear* is reiterated throughout these early poems almost incantatorily, in his plea for a restoration of that faculty. Maximus begins his penetration of the mysterious unities of the town in full self-consciousness, and he struggles unsuccessfully to take down those barriers that exclude him from fully sharing life with his fellowman; he aspires to be not poet, but poet-citizen, in order to transform Gloucester into his communal ideal, the *polis*.

In Letters 11-22 (the poems are called letters throughout the sequence), Maximus examines the social and economic history of Gloucester, where the early semblance of communal life was undermined by the first signs of capitalism and the consequent regimentaion of working life. Maximus sifts through the documents which reveal the turmoil of the early settlement as it is torn between two fates: to become the *polis,* that condition in which men live freely and share common beliefs, and a pejorocracy, a term Pound first coined in *The Cantos,* which translates to government by the worst. In Olson's poem, the pejorocracy was composed of all those who sought control of the community but who had no special wisdom or virtue, only the willfulness of their greed to drive them, and who finally accede to power. Olson was deeply opposed to capitalism as an economic principle; throughout his life he regarded capitalism as a consequence of the shift from a communal ethos to the ruthless philosophy of individualism. Like Pound and Williams before him, Olson rejected capitalism on the basis that it had merely fostered a hierarchy of ownership and servitude that continued the feudalism of the Middle Ages. Thus, in the poem's history of Gloucester, which is also the nation's history, the individual who once fulfilled himself through self-employment gradually became the means of another man's fulfillment, and his pleasure in the world shriveled to mere survival.

The heroic ideal of men happily self-employed is evanescent in early American history, and although he does not take up the theme in the *Maximus* sequence, Olson seems to have discovered its more durable equivalent in the civilizations of the ancient Sumerians and the more recent Mayans of the Yucatán Peninsula. Both grew up and prospered by virtue of their rational technologies and their keen preservation of individual autonomy within their communal systems. Olson comments at length upon each of them in "The Gate and the Center" and "Human Universe," but more importantly, it is in his poem **"The Kingfishers,"** an elegy of sorts, that he rejects the whole of Greco-Roman inheritance that led to the sacking of Mayan culture by the Spanish and vows his heartfelt allegiance to the wholeness of life he finds among the ruins and artifacts of Mayan experience. Olson wrote of the early Gloucester as though it had made fitful promise to become the likeness of a new Sumer or a second Mayan Empire, only to be dashed by the same forces that overtook its predecessors.

The *Maximus* sequence celebrates a heroic past as much as it does the vision of a redeemed future, and in this sense it is very similar to the mythopoeic poems of Pound and Williams. Olson's heroic fishermen, brave, thrifty, expert about the sea, are overthrown by men who know nothing about their craft but only of accounts and the profitable distribution of fish produce. Pound's *Cantos* also look back to a heroic past, the enlightened leadership of the Italian Renaissance and, even earlier, to Confucian China. Williams similarly celebrates what Olson once derisively characterized as "blueberry America," the simpler past of American small towns which the industrial city of Paterson had been at one time. Olson closes the first volume of *Maximus* with a moving description of how Gloucester fishermen were transformed from heroic seafarers to corporate drudges. His examination of a lost heroic ideal is very much a part of the form of the American long poem of this century.

The second volume, *Maximus IV, V, VI* (1968), is more boldly executed. The orderly progression of the first volume is abandoned as we enter into the "field" of consciousness that is now Maximus's mind. In 1956, Olson began reading *Process and Reality,* a forbidding essay on cosmology that perceives among the swarming particulars of the atomic universe some dialectical process of formation by which things come into existence. To perceive these myriad unfinished processes of particulars in the kinetic field is to view reality, according to Alfred North Whitehead, the British philosopher who wrote the essay. It was this cosmological perspective that Olson radically simplified and brought into his poem to represent the particulars of Gloucester that swarmed over the surface of Maximus's mind. Gloucester was now to be viewed by Maximus as a fragment of atoms in the whole potential field of matter. Its time was merely part of some vast eternity of processes. Hence, from the first poems of the second volume we are made to regard Gloucester and the nearby Dogtown as clustered particulars in a swirling cosmos. The eternal objects of Whitehead's cosmology, those forces that enter and disperse forms throughout time, are discovered in the casual events of Dogtown's past. An unfortunate prank by a drunken sailor becomes the vortex of various Greek and Egyptian myths relating to the creation of the world. And this same sailor who perished on the horns of a bull is absorbed again into the mothering earth by the same principles by which everything else forms and dissolves.

But a subtle development of themes emerges among the three books of this volume. Book IV is concerned with various creation myths and their contemporary Dogtown analogues. Book V charts in detail the stages of human migration that led to the settlement of the New England coast. The death and unification of the sailor with earth in an early poem of Book IV foreshadows the subject of Book IV, with its visions of a unified and harmonious cosmos at the center of which stands Gloucester. It is likened to a jewel in the hair of the earth goddess: "The earth with a city in her hair/ entangled of trees."

The second volume of the *Maximus* poems creates a mythic context in which Gloucester and Dogtown achieve their ultimate significance. It is in mythology, Olson insisted time and again, that the true primordial origins of man's consciousness are recorded—and the mythic imagination contains for him the most durable visions of a cosmic unity. The intense concentration upon migratory patterns makes history itself a process leading, for Maximus, to the founding of a new center of civilization. Civilization sprang up in the fertile ranges of Mesopotamia, and Sumer became the first center around which humanity densely gathered and began to express itself. The pattern of human migration was away from this primal center and westwardly—as it would be with the earth turning east—and humanity was scattered like a pod of seeds. Wherever these early explorers ventured, they forever tended toward America, toward the coast of Gloucester, and in Maximus's thought there is the constant implication that once the earth is fully girdled, man spread over the whole of the globe, and the traveling over with (the traveling that gave rise to the false sense man had of himself as alone, an individual responsible only to himself), Gloucester and the abandoned Dogtown shall be the epicenter of the new world community, its navel, the bud of the world rose. A new Sumer will arise if Maximus can inspire his fellow citizens to fight against the dissolution of Gloucester, prevent it from being devoured by Boston and the all-leveling culture of the nation.

In the third and final volume, *The Maximus Poems: Volume Three*, the poet falls back from the heady mythology of the previous three books to move among familiar objects again, the simple, elegant concreteness that composes Gloucester from day to day, season to season. The poet has earned an entirely believable omniscience about the town, a knowledge that includes the subtlest hue of sunset to the archival data of leases, wills, old account books, the exact and complex history of the ownership of certain city lots, the architectural details of houses long demolished. This preoccupation with close detail is a true reflection of Olson's own life. In the apartment at 28 Fort Square, Gloucester, where he lived from 1957 to 1969, the window frames are scrawled over with the penciled times of sunrise and sunset and other observations made while overlooking the harbor and fisheries. The poet contains in his own head what is missing in the actual Gloucester of the present; he has committed the life of the city to his memory. As he wrote in volume two, "My memory is the history of time."

It seems to me that here is the unique property of the long poem as a form: as he accumulates the material of the poem, the poet is gaining more and more of a context in which to rest his thought, until it would seem that the mere utterance of a word is enough to start chains of association through the reader's mind, as he recalls the different instances in which this word has already been used in the poem. At a certain point, the poet can depend upon what he has already written to express the connections, the significance of much that he says later. It frees him, in other words, to elaborate his thought in sudden fragments of language; at times no more than a word or two can function as a total poem. It is toward the end of a long poem that the poetry becomes almost unbearably rich with connotation. The final poem of **Volume Three**, for example, terminates the whole six-hundred-page poem with a list of eight words: "my wife my car my color and myself." Indeed, it is the last which so crowds the screen of the reader's attention that it almost calls up the whole of the poem by its mere mention.

The mood of the final volume is difficult to name precisely. It is a departure from the tone and dimensions of volume two, but the greater problem is that Olson left few notes or directions as to how the work was to be finally organized. George Butterick and Charles Boer, former students and close friends of the poet, arranged the poems in an order they felt best represented the implicit development of individual poems. Their editing has been scrupulous, but as Donald Byrd remarked in a recent review of **Volume Three**, it is likely that the work under Olson's hands would have been different, perhaps more jagged and with more of the astonishing leaps of thought he had achieved in volume two. Nonetheless, a clear extension of the work is visible in **Volume Three**, and the whole poem manages to sustain its overall integrity. Maximus seems to have found real contentment in his life as he roams the streets of Gloucester, day or night, recording the dawn light on the offshore rocks or the odor of an old garden while resting from a walk. He is the village sage, in a way, and he takes satisfaction in having mastered the knowledge of a culture and a local terrain. But we must also remember that this is Maximus after volume two, where the reach of thought is so extraordinarily broad. Few poets of the twentieth century have attempted so rigorous an expression of high ideals as Olson achieves in volume two. Not even Pound offers so densely clustered a set of ideas to convey his own vision in *The Cantos*. Even Yeats's system, really an astrological psychology, hasn't the reach of speculation that Olson forces into some ragged state of clarity. When we consider the mood of **Volume Three** it is almost inevitable there would be a sinking down to ordinary experience again, a falling off from the strain of his conceptions.

But throughout these poems there is the developing fear that not only is Gloucester doomed to become no more than a Boston suburb but that the nation will become some monstrous one-dimensional society premised on consumption and brute survival. Maximus frequently interrupts his musings on the manifest landscape of Gloucester to dread the tide of events he feels the city and the age itself are caught in. In one bitter lamentation he ends with this threat to the nation: If America cannot aspire to be an earthly paradise, "we will leave her/ and ask Gloucester/ to sail away/ from this/ Rising Shore/ Forever Amen." It is the angry threat of a child, but a visionary child at the very least. Maximus is really becoming aware of his own solitude, the state or condition he intended to transcend in the first poems of this long sequence. Without naming his condition he moves toward the consciousness of his isolation. Even his mastery of Gloucester has cost him his dearest connections: "I've sacrificed everything including sex and woman/—or lost them—to this attempt to acquire complete/ concentration." In a way, the last poem of the volume, with its eight words, seems the final, essential subtractions from the consciousness of Maximus, until, with the last, "myself," there is nothing left. "My wife" and "my car" refer to Olson's second wife who died in an auto accident, an experience so bitter for Olson that he was indelibly changed by it. "My color" may refer to Olson's painful last months, when he suffered cancer of the liver, from which he died in 1970. Maximus has thus moved from the earliest poems of **Volume Three** toward increasing loneliness, borne forward with the vision of an immense potentiality that his age squanders and destroys each day of his life. The great vision of volume two becomes the passing dream of the older Maximus of this final volume.

The communal ideal—this is the heart of the poem, what the poet finally captured in language, even though the poet failed to inspire a transformation of Gloucester itself. The *poem* is a failure if we can only perceive it as having an epic intent, in which the protagonist, for all of his vauntings, is unable to subdue his adversary. But there is no clear adversary, and if Maximus is a hero, he lays down his sword the moment he enters Gloucester. And his battle is with ghosts in a mist. He has come with a luminous ideal in his eyes, and after much travail and thought, that ideal passes, leaving the distinct, hard shape of the town as it is. If we can perceive the poem to have aspired to these facts, then we have a romance, not an epic, and *Maximus* may be seen as a great testament of the ethical imagination. It is a romance in the full sense of that term, just as Pound's *The Cantos*, Crane's *The Bridge*, Williams's *Paterson*, Robert Duncan's *Passages*, and Ed Dorn's *Gunslinger* are themselves romances. Epics, as W. P. Ker wrote at the end of the nineteenth century, an age of heroic tycoons, are for heroic times and heroic people. Romance is the natural antithesis of epic—it seeks a new ideal from which future heroes might emerge. John Stevens, in a recent study entitled *Medieval Romance*, complained that epic heroes do not have the word *dilemma* in their vocabulary and know nothing of spiritual or emotional difficulty; they only want to do battle against some enemy clearly marked on the horizon. Romance springs up in an age of confusion, when the coherence of faith is so eroded that the great ideals on which the civilization is predicated suddenly come into view again and compel attention. The great romances of the Middle Ages are the voluptuous portrayals of sexual love, raised to the austerity of a religion, sanctifying our most animal passions during the Hundred Years War.

The communal ideal is the stress of our own time, the sanctity of human relationships is our profound desire. It is an age, consequently, of political romances. Pound sought out the enlightened ruler who could unite us; Williams attempted to wring a village life out of the sprawl of Paterson; Olson wanted Gloucester to be the center of a new earth of relatedness, not only man and man, but man and the world around him, the world intimately related to its surrounding universe. The romance of *polis* comes in an age of deepening alienation, when all the known modes of relation are dissolving, including the ancient form of the family. It has become one of the most insistent themes of social theorists that the structure of society is beginning to simplify itself from within; it is sloughing off ethnic, racial, sexual, and age differences, as well as familial unities, and, as it does so, it is creating a more uniform population, a work force, that is increasingly more dependent on the economic system for its survival. Old forms of group protection are giving way, it seems, to individual rivalry for work and security, even within the family itself. As these profound changes erode traditional values, the fundamental ideals of Western civilization have loomed before poets again, to be examined anew, hoped for all over again, as we are swept into the disarray of the future.

Geoffrey Thurley   (essay date 1977)

SOURCE: "Black Mountain Academy: Charles Olson as Critic and Poet," in *The Academic Moment,* St. Martin's Press, 1977, pp. 126-38.

[*In the following excerpt, Thurley faults Olson for what he perceives as superficial and erroneous elements in his poetics.*]

A number of distinguished poets in the 1950s . . . received stimulus and direction from Black Mountain College. Although it's hardly possible to define a very clear Black Mountain style, it is possible to use the label to indicate a rough area of preoccupation in postwar American poetry. America has traditionally lacked—it still lacks—a literary centre on the scale of London or Paris, and it is interesting that at least two important poetic movements have originated in, or centred in, the South. Black Mountain may have owed something of its persistent ruralism to its location in Georgia, but it was never a regionalist movement, like the Fugitives. On the contrary, Black Mountain College was internationalist—*avant garde,* indeed—from the time Josef Albers crossed the Atlantic in 1932, to the time of its dissolution under Charles Olson in 1955. What Black Mountain stood for, as far as poetry was concerned, was the perpetualization—almost, we might argue, the institutionalization—of the poetics of imagism. . . . Phenomenalist modernism . . . found a home in Black Mountain College, and there, I should like to suggest, it became academic. In word progressivist and modernist, Black Mountain had become a retarding force in the development of poetry before it was dissolved. It encouraged an elitist exclusiveness, concerned all too often with the display of learning rather than with its spirit, and with erudition rather than with learning. The poetry it fostered tended to be refined rather than energetic, esoteric rather than refined. As an outpost of modernist prosody in the neo-metaphysical 1930s and 1940s, Black Mountain was positive; as a bastion of ideas that were at their most fertilizing in the years just after the First World War, it was negative. Black Mountain poetics had two important sources, Pound

and Carlos Williams. As a poetic influence, Williams was, I believe, negligible. But his prose work *In the American Grain* had an effect second only to that of Pound's seminal critical works—*Guide to Kulchur, ABC of Reading* and *How to Read.* From this point in time, *In the American Grain* seems a classic of proud provincialism—a bullheaded asseveration of cultural independence, like Twain's fiction and Sandburg's verse. As far as Black Mountain was concerned, its most important contention was that the Puritan forefathers served America badly by failing to see the great new continent as a "place": they saw it ethically, and everything that followed was their fault. Now this is clearly naïve ahistorical day-dreaming, a projection of twentieth-century thought onto seventeenth-century actions, not so much wise as stupid after the event. The fact is that all civilizations, all cultures, were founded by men with "vision" of some kind—Roman Catholic, Protestant Low Church, Buddhist, Vedic, Aztec, Inca. It is only our time that is stripped of vision. In its disavowal of all myths, Williams's book stands revealed as a piece of outrageously Romantic mythopoeia—a late instance of American new-Adamism. Such a capacity for "dreaming" has often been presented as an American strength; but in this case, as in many others, it seems more likely to have kept Americans from accepting themselves as they really are. And what they really are is not a nation of pioneering Boones or open-hearted Whitmans but an energetic hardworking European nation descended from seventeenth-century Englishmen with strict notions of conduct and a need for political freedom, who would never have established a society at all if they had tried to wander through the land, as Williams seems to have imagined Daniel Boone did. The Puritans were bad about their witches, but there is no instance of a civilization without some such "flaw"—as witness the elaborate tortures of the Sioux, for instance, the Aztecs' daily human sacrifices, or the bloodbaths in the Roman Colosseum. To blame "everything" on the Puritans, as Williams in effect does, is itself outrageously puritanical: the Puritan refuses to accept himself as he is, with his flaws and vices, but must continually excoriate himself, trying feverishly to sponge himself clean. We can see this spirit at work in the American intellectual's migrations to Paris in the 1920s, we see it at work today in his violent denunciation of America as she really is—a strange mixture of idealism and cynicism, ruthlessness and generosity, power and weakness, perspicacity and myopia.

Much of this distraught puritanism reappears in Black Mountain poetry and poetics, most notably in the work of Charles Olson. It is from Williams, in the first place, that Olson takes the notion of "place." We saw in the case of imagism that a particular openness of the sensibility, an active awareness, a vigorous patience with phenomena, was an important part of the poetic enterprise. This awareness was largely absent from Williams's somewhat inert "concreteness," and the reason may well be related to the poet's tendency to erect "place" itself into a concept, so that the actual vigilance of the sensibility was sacrificed to a faintly chauvinistic cult of "America." Williams dramatized this cult in *Paterson,* a long poem which has had many descendants in America. Taken in conjunction with

Pound's *Cantos, Paterson* has, I think, helped to slacken the muscles of American writing in the postwar period. In the absence of any precise aim, the poet tends to diffuse himself in images: the mystique of "place" encourages mere notation, observation without meaning, evidently noted down in the belief that the absence of any "poetic" or metaphysical dimension somehow justifies them.

This general slackness is, to be sure, disguised by Olson in the quasidynamic theory of "projectivism": "get on with it, keep moving, keep in, speed, the nerves, their speed, the perceptions, theirs the acts, the split seconds acts, the whole business, keep it moving as fast as you can citizen."

Stephen Spender is inclined to accept this at its face value, but in fact it runs counter to the rest of Olson's theory, to his own verse practice, and to the tradition from which it stems. Now the same paradox appears between Pound's poetry and theory. Yeats called Pound's verse "tapestry-like," that is to say, static and flat, a thing of texture and colour with little depth or drive. Yet there is a striking contrast between this (I think correct) conception of Pound's poetry as aesthetic and decorative, and the emphasis of Pound himself on the poetic image as essentially active and dynamic. This was a central idea of Ernest Fenollosa's, taken over first by Pound, then by Olson. Olson paraphrases Fenollosa so closely, in fact, that we can use his words without referring to Fenollosa's text directly at all: the sentence Olson sees as "first act of nature, as lightning." Now this account of the sentence, based upon Fenollosa's use of the Chinese ideogram as an "idea in action," has usually been accepted as an essential part of imagist poetry. Pound, in fact, introduced the idea for the first time in his Gaudier-Brzeska monograph of 1915, that is to say, two years after he had received the manuscript of Fenollosa's essay "On the Chinese written character" from Fenollosa's wife. The imagist manifesto of 1912 concentrates its attention exclusively on the image, which must be "hard, clear." The manifesto makes no reference to the necessity of using transitive verbs or of avoiding similes and the copula. As a matter of fact the original imagist emphasis is true to Pound's own practice, which is closer to the "exquisite" aesthetic textures of Lionel Johnson and Oscar Wilde than to the "transitive" drive of Marinetti or Mayakoswky. The entire imagist movement, in fact, from Pound and Amy Lowell down to the Black Mountain group, has never done more than pay lip-service to the idea of the transitive verb in action. An intentness on the image naturally led to a static poetry in the first place; and in the second, action was—as the strident vulgarity of the English vorticists and the Russian and Italian futurists showed—geared to a worship of the machine, and therefore to the idea of social change. Pound later came to envisage a social revolution, based upon the redistribution of capital and the establishment of a dictatorship. But it was essentially a retrospective conception, reactionary, conservative, based upon an idyllic vision of feudal contentment, with each man knowing his place. To embrace futurism—or indeed vorticism—the artist had to be prepared to cut his links with the aesthetic values of the immediate past and to throw in his lot with a raucous and raw future, egalitarian and "progressive" in precisely the sense hateful to Pound. If the criticism talks of action in language, the poetry fondles the past and the unchanging idyll of "aesthetic" feeling.

In fact, Fenollosa did poetry a disservice by making his famous parallel between the Chinese written character and the language of poetry. Chinese happens to be ideographic, not phonetic; hence, it appears, to the outsider accustomed to a phonetic language, to have preserved primitive pictural events in its signs for objects and processes which in Indo-European languages are referred to by symbols divorced from the prephonetic origins of language. To an enthusiastic but naïve Westerner, such an ossified ideographic language may appear a miracle of poetic vividness. In fact, Chinese is obviously just as threadbare to those that use it as our own languages are to us: from every cultural and literary point of view the ideogram is a disaster, which has—if this is not to put cart and horse wrong way about—kept the Chinese insulated from world history, as impervious to intellectual "progress" as the Boxers thought they were to the effects of small-arms fire. A Chinese proverb has it that "A picture is worth a thousand words": why, if the language is a running poetic performance, with detonations of active and concrete imagery every time a peasant opens his mouth to ask the time of day? It was Fenollosa's error initially, but it was wholly characteristic of Pound to accept uncritically his diagnosis of a general degeneracy of European language, with no attention to the facts of political or linguistic history.

Charles Olson transfers the Fenollosa fallacy to Mayan hieroglyphs in a later essay, "Human Universe": "They retain the power of the objects of which they are the images," he observes. The implication is that our own verbal icons lack this sort of vividness and that we ought to learn from this ancient culture how to refurbish our language. But the parallel is quite factitious. Olson is regarding the hieroglyphs as visual art. To *use* these symbols (pictural as they may be) is at once to sacrifice their mimetic quality, which becomes irrelevant to the needs of the sentence. And we should remember that *qua* hieroglyph the hieroglyph was not intended to have "power of the object." To believe that it was, again, is just the outsider's awe. To the Maya, it was a sign, and its visual quality hardly mattered. Certainly it can have no relevance to our own cultural needs. Granted that it may in certain circumstances be desirable to strive after clear imagery in poetry, it's by no means certain that the way to achieve this end is to concentrate on the 'concreteness' of language. Language evokes by naming, not by representing, and the events of language are quite different from those of visual media. Now in fact, every poet using his language well does charge his imagery with just the sort of trenchancy Olson found in the Mayan hieroglyph. And here we encounter the fundamental circularity of Olson's criticism: the apparently descriptive (and therefore helpful) criterion turns out to be merely an approval-word, a value judgement. Lawrence was a poet who found little favour with Pound; but don't Lawrence's animal poems precisely "retain the power of the objects of which they are the images"—granted only that the word "image," in relation to poetry, must be taken to refer to the combined capacities of several signs, not to single iconic vocables? What about this, for instance:

> Till he fell in a corner, palpitating, spent.
> And there, a clot, he squatted and looked at me.
> With sticking-out, bead-berry eyes, black,
> And improper derisive ears,
> And shut wings,
> And brown, furry body.
>
> Brown, nut-brown, fine fur!
> But it might as well have been hair on a spider;
>   thing
> With long, black-paper ears.
>   (D. H. Lawrence, "Man and Bat")

There is no twentieth-century volume of verse—there are few enough from any century—in which there are more verbal signs which "retain the power of the objects of which they are the images" than *Birds, Beasts and Flowers.* Yet the instance only makes us understand that the programme of transitive verbal power is, in the imagist theorists and poets, pure lip-service. What we must pay attention to in their poetry is the purpose of the imagery. Imagism, like projectivism, has a specific *Weltanschauung,* and the apparently practical methodological side of the movement is spurious, a smokescreen to conceal a detached, elitist, basically passive philosophy of life and society.

As far as "life" is concerned, Olson dutifully embraces a "dynamic" theory of the emotions, a theory which partakes equally of D. H. Lawrence and Ezra Pound. Olson indicates the Poundian bias of his thought by aligning himself with the Keatsian negative capables against the sublime egotists. This view of things is not backed up, in fact, by the poetry: Keats was no less concerned than Wordsworth with metre and regular stanza form, and the subjective coloration is if anything more pronounced than it is in Wordsworth. But it gives us an idea at least of where Olson is going. For the remark is followed by the repudiation of the "subject"—what Pound had rejected as 'the obscure reveries of the inward gaze.' "Objectism," Olson says, "is the getting rid of the lyrical interference of the individual as ego, of "the subject" and his soul, that peculiar presumption by which western man has interposed himself between what he is as a creature of nature (with certain instructions to carry out) and those other creations of nature which we may, with no derogation, call objects." ["Projective Verse," in *Selected Writings,* 1974]. Now the general evolution of European thought and literature over the past two hundred years has been in the direction of what we might call object-dominance. Europe has moved away from what is in fact a determinate historical phenomenon: that "under consciousness of a *sinful* nature" of which Coleridge spoke—and which Olson wants to castigate as an aberration, a wilful truancy of the mind away from "objectism." Once again we witness the ahistorical bent of Poundian thinking, reducing all ages to the same condition, with no consideration of the peculiar relations which dictate certain ranges of content and attitude in

some periods, and outlaw them in others. The basic problem still remains: man is an object, as Olson reminds us, but he is also (and perhaps more importantly) a subject. It is the subjective experience of things which is recorded in poetry. The subject-consciousness of man creates the world he has to live in, in Kantian terms; and the question of what he is to do with himself in it, and how he is best to live there, would not be answered by simply "recording" the world-as-object, even if this were possible. The rise of object-dominance was a historically governed development, not the sloughing-off of blindness. Man remains a "soul," and still has a responsibility for himself which cannot be honoured by abdicating from the subjective. The rise of object-dominance records Western man's changing relations with his world, not his gradual emergence out of a subject-self which egotistically blocked his "vision": this conception of externally existent reality, just waiting to be snapped by the alert eye of the poet, is one of the root-fallacies of imagist theorizing. Neither of its oriental models—neither the T'ang poetry of China, nor the Japanese *haiku*—abjured the subjective, as Olson suggests poetry can. The most engaging quality of Golden Age poetry in China was, as A. R. Davis observes, "its intimate expression of personal feeling." The greatness of Bash , similarly, was based upon his ability to express the profoundly subjective without mentioning or labelling the emotion; the *haiku* was the marriage of the inner and the outer, not the triumph of the outer over the inner. Moreover, the T'ang poets were profoundly influenced by the only alien cultural force before Marxism to make any impact on Chinese intellectual life—Buddhism; and Buddhism was the pervasive presence that made the *haiku* possible. Davis notes that Confucianism, the identifyingly practical social philosophy of China, was superseded during the T'ang dynasty by both Buddhism and the T'ao. Significantly, Pound himself ignored the deeper spirituality of Chinese poetry, and concentrated his attention on the 'unwobbling pivot'—Kung, the social rule-maker. Thus, once again, we see imagism, and its projectivist offspring, as deficient in depth and hinged upon nothingness.

Such philosophy as Olson himself articulates to back up his poetics is crudely naturalistic. If man "stays inside himself," Olson says, if he is contained within his nature as he is participant in the larger force, he will be able to listen, and his hearing through himself will give him secrets objects share. And by an inverse law his shapes will make their own way" ["Projective Verse"]. This seems a strangely arcane departure for the disciple of Poundian objectism. But it is of course the old symbolist lore, part Baudelairean *correspondance,* part Nervalesque animism, part Keatsian negativecapability. It echoes, too, dimly and confusedly, the ideas of the *haijin:* Bashō's advice to the poet was to recognize in great art the working of the spirit:

> It is a poetic spirit, through which man follows the creative energy of the universe and makes communion with the things of the four seasons. For those who understand the spirit, everything they see becomes a lovely flower, and everything they imagine becomes a beautiful moon.

But this is backed up by Buddhism, it is logical and wholly

consistent. It is Buddhism that breathes through Bashō, and the doctrines are senseless without the deep faith.

In the case of projectivism, we are left simply with the shallow dogma of objectism, the cult of which has left a great hollowness in American poetry in the postwar period. Projectivism makes a convenient target, merging, as it does, different strands of modern thought in their movement towards a common end of pseudo-primitivism. The *faux-naïf* primitivism, of which Marshall McLuhan was the leading exponent in the 1960s, was the fashionable form of the trend towards object-dominance in the late postwar period. Like McLuhan and William Burroughs, Olson rejects symbol, metaphysics, linear thought, causation, abstraction, logic, etc., all or any of the elements which make up the Western intellectual tradition initiated by the Greeks. We have witnessed this already in Olson's dream of returning to the semantic innocence of the Mayas. The great influence on this kind of thought in the twentieth century is Henri Bergson: nothing Olson writes is free from Bergsonian metaphysics, which lies also behind the thought of T. E. Hulme and Ernest Fenollosa: language with its symbolizing, abstracting, comparing functions, we are to understand, keeps us from "the active intellectual states . . . analysis only accomplishes a *description,* does not come to grips with what really matters" ["Human Universe"]. And so on. Bergson had some excuse for his error, of trying to destroy metaphysics with metaphysics. In indicating the "weakness" of intellectual descriptions of reality which merely "distort organic synthesis," Bergson failed to appreciate that when we describe a thing in intellectual terms it is our conception of the thing we are getting clear in propositions which mirror the logical fact; we do not pretend to represent the organic thing itself. Now that Wittgenstein has done the job of sorting out the different functions of language, there is no excuse for repeating Bergson's error. Olson distinguishes the "bad" abstractive processes of traditional "symbology" from some life-giving variety, in which metaphor or idea enters in at the pores of the skin—how, or under what dispensation, is never made clear. Olson provides the perfect example of the inevitably self-contradictory, self-destructive kind of alienation that has accompanied and proceeded from the evolution towards objectivity. Using a language composed of the general terms he pretends to disavow, Olson patronizes the primitive and assumes the mantle of prophet, and so obscures the nature of the difficulties that confront us today. If the present impasse in thought is to be evaded, it is not through the abrogation of thinking. We must think, and continue to think, acknowledging that the "universe of discourse," which is nothing but the world of our awareness (or the world we are aware of), comprises a stratification of hierarchical realms, from base matter itself up to the refinement of music and poetry. This means, though, also understanding that in so far as we are conscious of the universe, it is part of our consciousness, and that no matter how hard we try to deny abstraction, merely to refer to matter itself in the simplest terms is to commit ourselves to abstraction; it is useless pretending that in doing so we can somehow return to a Rousseauesque realm of intellectual innocence. As soon as we use language we are already committed to thinking, with all the linear constructs that that implies.

It was this paradox that Bergson's metaphysics, with its characteristic dichotomies of intensive and extensive manifolds, was intended to solve. It is true, as Lawrence saw so clearly, that an estrangement of mind and instinct accompanies the process of civilization, and that it behoves us to re-feel our consciousness, to regain contact with the life of the body and of the instincts. But he knew that this was not to be accomplished by trying to turn the clock back, by "going native," by ceasing to think. On the contrary, as he observed of Melville's *Typee,* nothing stinks like rotting civilized man, and civilized man rots if he does not exercise his mind, soul, awareness to its maximum extent. Man will grow by expanding his mind, not by contracting it.

The relative success or failure of poetry is not to be equated with intensity of belief. In the first place, belief, though it can pick itself up from nowhere—irrespective of the political or general spiritual atmosphere—can also be blinded by a single mote in the eye, or simply by nothing; it can fall away, and a man is dead even in the act of saying, *I believe.* But the imaginative daring that is required to give depth, weight and permanence to the poet's professional "openness" to experience, is all too often lacking in mid-century poetry. In England, this took the ideological form of a care for self-criticism and sobriety; in America, often, of a mistaken cleaving to the worn-out ethics of imagism. Donald Hall's introduction to his anthology of contemporary American verse, with its characteristically ironist emphasis on colloquial diction, also shared the general post-Poundian bias in favour of the "good" image against the "bad" abstraction:

> People talk to each other most deeply in images. To read a poem of this sort, you must not try to translate the image into abstractions.

Whoever would, or did? we might ask. And is it really true (if plausible) that "people talk to each other most deeply in images?" Don't we need a particular context of expectations and directives to be able to know what they mean, in the simplest terms, and to interpret the images?

In point of fact, this is not really the way either poetry or literature works. And the point seems worth labouring, not in order to condemn Mr. Hall of failing to understand its workings properly (we all fail in that task), but because it is a sign of an academicism which has probably gained rather than lost prestige since Hall wrote this preface in 1961. What we might call the imagist academy sponsored a poetry really no less circumscribed, no less in need of spiritual regeneration, than the neometaphysical academicism it was supposed to have replaced.

Hand in hand with the cult of the image goes the *breath* fallacy. Olson was a somewhat confused polemicist, but in so far as one can understand his notion of breath, it seems to be equivalent to Pound's notion of *music,* that is to say, the soul of poetry itself. (The same word is used for both *breath* and *spirit* in many languages of course.)

Basically, both critics want to distinguish poetry which is merely metrical from poetry which is alive through its rhythm. The underlying relations between metre and rhythm have been part of the English tradition since *Beowulf,* at least, and the reader wishing to understand them more formally will be better off reading Hopkins's introduction to his poems than wandering through Pound or Olson, who really throw no light on the subject at all. *Music* in Pound and *breath* in Olson are simply value terms, conferred on or withheld from oetry as it is considered good or bad, with no other reason given. We know, of course, from reading Pound, which poets Olson will approve of: approved of are the impressionists and the image-notchers of the nineteenth and twentieth centuries, the Elizabethan song-writers, the Romance poets of Provence, and Homer. Disapproved of are the soulful men, the Blakes, Whitmans, Hopkinses and Lawrences. What we have, in fact—clearly in Pound, confusedly in Olson—is a particular psychological type (what we might call the impressionist or the extroverted) erected into an universal norm. Back of the enterprise in Olson's case is Carlos Williams's pan-Americanism:

> Where else can what we are seeking arise from but speech, American speech as distinct from English speech. . . . In any case from what we hear in America ['The Poem as Field of Action,' *Selected Essays,* 1961].

This is crude but clear, and in its way sensible. Olson obscures the issue by adding to breath and speech his own notion of "syllable": "It is by their syllables that words juxtapose in beauty, by these particles of sound as clearly as by the sense of the words which they compose ["Projective Vorse"]. But it is equally by their syllables that words juxtapose in their ugliness or their banality (whatever the phrase "juxtapose in" actually means). Any good poetry will be syllable- and sound-responsive. Once again a value-word has been offered as if it helped us actually describe poetry. Olson quotes the opening lines of *Twelth Night* and a stanza of "Westren Wynde" as instances of syllabic poetry, but we are none the wiser: lines from Milton or Whitman could have been substituted without alteration of meaning. It is a waste of time asking what Olson means by saying that the syllable "dropped from the late Elizabethans": he merely relies on the reader's vague acceptance of the Pound/Eliot dissociation theory to guarantee agreement on a general decline.

The most striking feature of Olson's own verse seems now to be a curious amalgam of imagist notation and wide abstract generality. **"La Torre,"** for instance, begins with the approved sort of notation:

> The tower is broken, the house
> where the head was used to lift,
> where awe was . . .

Soon enough Olson is paraphrasing Fenollosa:

>   Lightning
> is an axe, subject to object to
> order: destroy!

This leads to a sinisterly fascistic tone a little later:

> To destroy
> is stand again, is a factor of
> sun, fire is
> when the sun is out, dowsed . . .

What is "dowsed" doing here? Somehow the usage epitomizes the Black Mountain style, falsely vernacular, awkwardly "concrete." Now "dowsed" is there, of course, because it is an *action* word: it is as if Olson had caught himself napping with "out," and added a suitably concrete word to keep up the Fenollosa programme. In fact it only clumsily distinguishes itself from "out" and so blurs the required contrast between the sun's shining and the fire's neutralized burning. This emphasizes yet again that language is often most effectively "concrete" when allowed to do its work invisibly. "Concreteness" in fact is a notion that relates to intension (and intention) rather than to any series of verbal procedures: an intentness on saying something, or rather on the something that needs to be said, is more likely to lead to an impression of concreteness or action in poetry than any imagistic programme of strong verbs and no copulæ. When he is set a "subject," a bit of "field" to do, to crystallize, Olson is no more successful than Williams:

> The sheep like soldiers
> black leggings black face
> lie boulders
> in the pines' shade
> at the field's sharp edge:
> ambush and bivouac
>
> A convocation of crows overhead
> mucks
> in their own mud and squawk
> makes of the sky
> a sty
>
> ("Lower Field—Enniscorthy")

It would be no defence of this to say that it was not intended to "crystallize." He is "doing" something here—sheep, crows—and doing it limply and inertly, with neither spring to the language nor point to the observations, which are mainly of the old-fashioned analogical variety (the sheep's legs are *like* soldiers' leggings, etc.). In **"The Moon Is the Number 18,"** we find this:

> the blue dogs paw,
> lick the droppings, dew
> or blood, whatever
> results are. And night,
> the crab, rays round
> attentive, as the ear to catch
> human sound

These lines again lack internal spring, aptitude of image, and sound pattern. One remembers Olson's advice to the poet to listen "to his own speech," and wonders how anyone aware of the question of sound at all could write so flatly:

The blue dogs rue
as he does, and he would howl, confronting
the wind which rocks what was her, while prayers
striate the snow, words blow
as questions cross fast, fast
as flame, as flames form, melt
along any darkness

("The Moon Is the Number 18")

Here is a syntactical movement begging for support from the sound: repeated verbs, complex sentence structure, and it would seem hard *not* to make the sound interlock here. But examination of any given moment or of the whole unit shows Olson to be incapable of making sound work for him. Such sound-play as there is is confined to premature repetition—"blue" and "rue," "snow" and "blow," "fast, fast," "flame, as flames." Like the examples in the previously quoted stanza—"paw" and "dew," "round" and "sound"—these assonances are timed mechanically, and the result is the opposite of what, as critic, Olson seems to have meant by "breath." He is reduced to front-office words like "striate," and tries to lose the reader in a show of complexity: first dogs howl, then the wind rocks what something feminine (the moon, presumably) *was*, prayers do something to the snow, then everything melts into everything else. Hardly a demonstration of projectivist virtues: rather a heavy piece of expressionism. Not surprisingly—to anyone familiar with Pound and the *Active Anthology* poets, that is—the show of projectivist method is then given away in a characteristically knowing use of the copula:

Birth is an instance as is a host, namely, death. . . .

As critic, Olson had laid great emphasis on the incising of images so that they "retain the power of the objects of which they are the images." Yet his verse is either inertly notational in the Carlos Williams manner, or extraordinarily general: few poets of the time sprinkle their verse with quite so many abstract generalizations, ethical injunctions and random *obiter dicta* as Olson.

It will be important for me often enough to distinguish between the poetics of a poet and his poetry, and I wish to make no simple causal relation here between Olson's shaky theorizing and his inert poetry. Yet it does seem that the poetic programme here must take some responsibility for the *kind* of poor performance we get. We could put him down simply as a middling poet. But the pretentious allusiveness, the arrogant tone, the passive pseudo-concrete notation (eschewing a more poetically authentic empathy with the object as somehow datedly Romantic), the sluggish reliance upon ponderous generalities—all these vices of Black Mountain poetry seem predictable from the Poundian foundations of the academy. This is especially true of the superior stance inherited from Pound, the esotericism more interested in displaying its knowledge than in the knowledge itself, which was, I believe, a definite brake on American poetry in the 1950s. Pound's frequent concern with manner and his lack of awareness of deeper matter, along with his pretentiousness, made for a knowing yet oddly superficial poetry. It was not until

Allen Ginsberg and Jack Kerouac made the crossing from East to West Coast, I think, that Black Mountain prosody made its biggest contribution. It was new spiritual synthesis that America needed then, not esotericism: the esotericism of Black Mountain encouraged an aloofness the exact opposite of the openness to experience advocated in its theory.

Robert Creeley   (essay date 1980)

SOURCE: "'An Image of Man . . .' Working Notes on Charles Olson's Concept of Person," in *Iowa Review,* Vol. 11, No. 4, Fall, 1980, pp. 29-43.

[*In the following essay, Creeley discusses Olson's concepts of history and identity.*]

Talking to a gathering of student writers (S.U.N.Y. College at Cortland, N.Y., October 20, 1967) Olson again tried to make clear that he was not involved in some self-aggrandizement and that *The Maximus Poems* were not therefore a backdrop for himself as quondam hero. He then read **"Maximus of Gloucester"** (*The Maximus Poems,* Volume Three)—the date for which he notes as "Friday November 5th/ 1965":

Only my written word
I've sacrificed every thing, including sex and
    woman
—or lost them—to this attempt to acquire complete
concentration . . .

                    . . . . .

                    It is not I,
even if the life appeared
biographical. The only interesting thing
is if one can be
an image
of man, "The nobleness, and the arete."
(Later: myself (like my father, in the picture, a
    shadow)
on the rock

One might expect to hear this plea from two other American poets, who are felt, I think reasonably, to be Olson's predecessors, Ezra Pound and William Carlos Williams. Paradoxically T.S. Eliot, whom Olson uses as a significant antagonist in **"ABCs,"** is not usually presumed to be *personally* present in his longer poems, although he said of "The Wasteland" that it was, after all, "the relief of a personal and wholly insignificant grouse against life. . . ." In contrast, Whitman's "Song of Myself" is read as an intimate relation with the factual poet himself, although the reader discovers remarkably little about Whitman literally. What Whitman depends on is the authenticity of the personal, that the fact on an 'I' 'feels' this or that emotion confounds all 'authority' of an otherwise abstract or general order. Both Pound and Williams make use of this fact. As Olson writes (*Mayan Letters,* 1968), "Ez's epic solves problem by his ego: his single emotion breaks all down to his equals or inferiors . . ." and, of Williams, "Bill HAS an emotional system which is capable of extensions and comprehensions the ego-system (the Old Deal, Ez as Cento Man, here dates) is not. . . . "

It is ironic that what I call so loosely 'the personal' is both our *subject* (which only an ego can determine as existing) and our *object,* "having to do with a material object as distinguished from amental concept, idea, or belief. . . ." It must be that Olson's own physical size (he was six foot seven) made the latter situation of person most insistent. One of his last wry points in hospital was upon his own pleasure that 'the fundament stayed as put as the firmament. . . .' The body did not go away, in short, forever lost among the stars.

Returning to Eliot, Olson again qualifies him in the second part of "Projective Verse" (*Human Universe and Other Essays,* 1967)—and it is the second part of this essay he felt especially valuable, as against the first part, which proved the most read:

> ——it is because Eliot has stayed inside the non-projective that he fails as a dramatist—that his root is the mind alone, and a scholastic mind at that (no high *intelletto* despite his apparent clarities)—and that, in his listenings he has stayed there where the ear and the mind are, has only gone from his fine ear outward rather than, as I say a projective poet will, down through the workings of his own throat to that place where breath comes from, where breath has its beginnings, where drama has to come from, where, the coincidence is, all act springs.

What Olson means by the statement, "down through the workings of his own throat to that place where breath comes from . . . ," can be found most clearly in his brief but remarkably helpful text, "Proprioception," for example, on the first page:

> the data of depth sensibility/the 'body' of us as object which spontaneously or of its own order produces experience of, 'depth' Viz SENSIBILITY WITHIN THE ORGANISM BY MOVEMENT OF ITS OWN TISSUES

It's to the point that Olson had wanted to compose a "Book of the Body," which would be an extensive study and report of the material, presumably, the "Proprioception" text so brilliantly graphs and/or outlines. This preoccupation is very frequently evident in his work, as in the short, initial statement, "The Resistance" ("It is his body that is his answer, his body intact and fought for, the absolute of his organism in its simplest terms, this structure evolved by nature, repeated in each act of birth, the animal man . . . ,") or, at more length, the proposal of human event found in "Human Universe":

> What happens at the skin is more like than different from what happens within. The process of image (to be more exact about transposition than the "soul" allows or than the analysts do with their tricky "symbol-

maker") cannot be understood by separation from the stuff it works on. Here again, as throughout experience, the law remains, form is not isolated from content. The error of all other metaphysic is descriptive, is the profound error that Heisenberg had the intelligence to admit in his principle that a thing can be measured in its mass only by arbitrarily assuming a stopping of its motion, or in its motion only by neglecting, for the moment of its measuring, its mass. And either way you are failing to get what you are after—so far as a human being goes, his life. There is only one thing you can do about the kinetic, re-enact it. Which is why the man said, he who possesses rhythm possesses the universe. And why art is the only twin life has—its only valid metaphysic. Art does not seek to describe but to enact. And if man is once more to possess intent in his life, and to take up the responsibility implicit in his life, he has to comprehend his own process as intact, from outside, by way of his skin, in, and by his own powers of conversion, out again.

Recognize, then, that surely *one* insistent human dilemma is lodged in the abstraction which consciousness permits, *if* that marvellous function be employed only to gain an "objective correlative" to that very existence any one of us is fact of. Olson's respect for the mushroom, specifically for the experiments which Timothy Leary was conducting in the early 60s, has obvious bearing. Talking to an informal group at William Gratwick's home in Pavilion, N.Y., November 16, 1963, he emphasized the apparent fact that hallucinogenic agents, LSD in particular, ". . . puts you on your own autonomic nervous system—as against the motor."

> And certainly the human race has been so bereft of its autonomic system for so long that you can practically talk that we're green. In fact I would think almost that you have to talk about the species today as *green,* individually and socially. Not all—how you say it—the way we tend to talk from our progressive or evolutionary or developmental past as though we've now got to take this step. It's not some step that you take easily, or that even to take the step, if you stop to think about it. You're just who you are; what you do, if it's any good, is true; and you are capable of being alive because of love. I mean it's about as simple—it's like those simplicities operate. And that's it. Well, it's not so easy to come to believe as absolutes, imperatives and universals. In fact, on the contrary, we've been encouraged to think there is some universal, absolute or imperative we seem to be missing out on. But the autonomic thing is very crucial. (*The Maximus Poems, Volume Three*)

In the same discussion he speaks of the triad of politics, theology, and epistemology, the three intensive-extensive patternings of human 'content,' and of how crucial it is that they be examined in present situation. Because once there is the human belief, "the idea that there is such a thing as knowledge . . . ("invented by a man named Plato. *Episteme* is his invention and it's one of the most dangerous inventions in the world . . ." the dislocation of mind and body is immediate. George Butterick's "notes from class, 15 September 1964" make a further clarification of Olson's emphasis:

Olson began his Modern Poetry course at Buffalo the following fall with the same triad, which he identified as "Augustinian," saying that it was "dogmatically true." He related the term politics, or the Greek *physics* 'nature,' to "necessity"; epistemology, or *nous* 'mind,' to "possibility"; and religon, or *theos* 'God,' to the "imaginable."

"Soul" also can be an obvious distraction, but only if you let it get away from you so to speak. I find, somewhat sadly, that the *OED*'s first listing of this word's definition, "The principle of life in man or animals; animate existence," is noted as obsolete, while the second definition not only survives but defines our problem entirely: "The principle of thought and action in man, commonly regarded as an entity distinct from the body. . . ." One can make a simple measure of the dangers inherent in abstraction by recognizing how removed the valued factor in existence, the soul, has become from that which it inhabits, the body—and, equally the life, the process, of which it is literal instance. Nonetheless the dilemma is clear, apart from this particular resolution: how is that which we are, as "thought," "action," "soul," what we also are as in Olson's phrase, "what gets 'buried,' like, the flesh . . . bones, muscles, ligaments, etc., what one uses, literally, to get about etc. . . ." But, he says, "the soul is proprioceptive . . . the 'body' itself as, by movement of its own tissues, giving the data of, depth . . . that one's life is informed from and by one's own literal body. . . . that this mid-thing between . . . that this is 'central,' what is—in this 1/2 of the picture—what they call the SOUL, the intermediary, the intervening thing, the interruptor, the resistor. The self.")

The gain: to have a third term, so that *movement* or *action* is 'home,' Neither the Unconscious nor Projection . . . have a home unless the DEPTH implicit in physical being—built-in spacetime specifies, and moving (by movement of 'its own')—is asserted, or found out as such . . .

The 'soul' then is equally 'physical.' Is the self. its own is such, 'corpus.' Or—to levy the gain psychology perception from 1900, or 1885, did supply until it didn't (date? 1948?)—the three terms wld be:

surface (senses) projection cavity (organs—here read 'archetypes') unconscious the body itself—consciousness: implicit accuracy, from its own energy as a state of implicit motion.

Identity, therefore (the universe is one) is supplied; and the abstract-primitive character of the real (asserted) is 'placed' projection is discrimination (of the object from the subject) and the unconscious is the universe flowing-in, inside.

Again and again one finds in Olson's thinking an insistence upon the *authority* of one's own life as initial. Whether it be "that all start up/to the eye and soul/as though it had never/happened before" or "That a man's life/(his, anyway) is what there is/that tradition is//at least is where I find it,/how I got to/what I say," ("**Letter 11**") there is no otherwise, or where.

It would be of point, clearly, to consider the way in which "history" is present in *The Maximus Poems*, and to say again, as he did constantly, that Olson

   . . . would be an historian as Herodotus was,
     looking
for oneself for the evidence of
what is said: Altham says
Winslow
was at Cape Ann in April,
1624

Characteristically, one is tempted to type, in the third line, "was" for "is," and "said" for "says"—but it is as much to the point that the present *is* "historical," as that there is, therefore, an "historical present." Or as answer to the question I had then asked, literally, "what is 'history'?" Olson's answer, the poem "**Place; & Names**":

a place as term in the order of creation
& thus useful as a function of that equation
example, that the "Place Where the Horse-
   Sacrificers Go"
of the Brihadaranyaka Upanishad is worth more
   than
a metropolis—or, for that matter, any moral
concept, even a metaphysical one
        and that this is so
for physical & experimental reasons of
the *philosphia perennis,* or Isness
of cosmos beyond those philosophies
or religious or moral systems of
rule, thus giving factors of naming
—nominative power—& landschaft
experience (geography) which stay truer
to space-time than personalities
or biographies of such terms as specific
cities or persons, as well as the inadequacy
to the order of creation of anything except
names—including possibly mathematics (?)

the crucialness being that these places or names
be as parts of the body, common, & capable
therefore of having cells which can decant
total experience—no selection
other than one which is capable
of this commonness (permanently
duplicating) will work

"Story" in other words as if not superior
at least equal to ultimate mathematical
language—perhaps superior because of
cell-ness (?) In any case history
(as to be understood by Duncan's Law
to mean a) histology & b) story)
applies here, in this equational way
& severely at the complementarity of
cosmos (complementary to individual
or private) and not to cities or

events in the way it has, in
a mistaken secondary way, been
understood

Duncan had written him (18 Dec. 61):

But 'history'?—couldn't we throw that word out and
establish histology: the tissue and structure, weaving,
of what [it] is we know.

story: what we know from the questions we asked.
This thing is made-up, or an answer—but is, also, the
only thing we knew to answer:oracle or sphinx-demand

That: we *do* hold by histology and story having to do
with one *gnosis*. And the art, the story, seeks out
histology or lapses into the cult-sure . . .

It's also to the point to remember, that Olson's favorite
definition of the word "history" was, finally, John
Smith's (despite, as he remarked, its curious faintness):
"History is the memory of time. . ." In an autobiographical note ("The Present Is Prologue"), published
1955, he writes:

There are only two live pasts—your own (and that
hugely included your parents), and the one other we
don't yet have the vocabulary for, because the West
has stayed so ignorant, and the East has lived off the
old fat too long. I can invoke it by saying, the
mythological, but it's too soft. What I mean is that
foundling which lies as surely in the phenomenological
'raging apart' as these queer parents rage in us.

I have spent most of my life seeking out and putting
down the 'Laws' of these two pasts, to the degree I am
permitted to see them (instead of the boring historical
and evolutionary one which the West has been so busy
about since Thucydides) simply because I have found
them in the present, my own and yours, and believe
that they are the sign of a delightful new civlization of
man ahead.

There is a sweetness, in that last phrase, and a 'progres-
sivism'—a sense that one is going to get somewhere
'ahead'—one does not find usually in Olson. But again,
it's of use to recognize that the 'history' of *The Maximus
Poems* is initial tracking ("mapping," as he would call it)
and is as much the form of the *agent* (the person acquiring
the 'history,' in this case Olson) as it is the events and/or
persons so examined. Lest one presume that is an extraordinary distortion of 'the facts,' that is, some body of information that might be 'objectively' the case, remember
that any response to and/or statement of such data will
presume a context and a meaning. It is the false face of
the 'objective' or the 'general' or the 'abstract' that Olson
finds comtemptible, as in **"Letter for Melville"**—"written
to be read AWAY FROM the Melville Society's "One
Hundredth Birthday Party" for MOBY DICK at Williams
College, Labor Day Weekend, Sept. 2—4, 1951":

Timed in such a way to avoid him, to see
he gets a lot of lip (who hung in a huge jaw)
and no service at all (none of this chicken, he

who is beyond that sort of recall, beyond
any modern highway (which would have saved him
from sciatica? well, that
we cannot do for him but we can
we now know so much, we can make clear
how he erred, how, in other ways
—we have made such studies and
we permit ourselves to think—they
allow us to tell each other how wise
he was

As though one could tidy up the *real,* or find another
place for it, or understand it apart from its enactment. . . .

Possibly the most active rehearsal of Olson's "methodology" is *"A Bibliography on America for Ed Dorn"*,
which George Butterick has called "a fusion of Whitehead's notion of *process* with an *Herodotean* sense of
history. . . . " It was written in January 1955 as a letter—
actually two letters—to the poet Edward Dorn, then a
student at Black Mountain College. . . . " The qualification there of *person* is very useful. In fact, the "Working
premises" given at the outset should make much clear:

I That *millennia:* & II *person /* are not the same as
either time as history or as the individual as single

And a little later, same page:

Results, as of historical study:

(a) it is not how much one knows but in what
field of context it is retained, and used (*millennia, &
quantity*)

(b) how, as yourself as individual, you are
acquiring & using same in acts of form—what use you
are making of acquired information (*person, & process*)

It's Olson's intent in these letters to define both the *nature*
of that attention he values, and the *method* which most
proves its use. Because he feels it absolutely required that
one move beyond any humanistic evaluation of data "BE-
CAUSE THE LOCAL AND THE SENTIMENTAL IS
HOW HUMANISM COMES HOME TO ROOST IN
AMERICA"—as instance, "*sociology,* without exception,
is a lot of shit—produced by people who are the most
dead of all, history as politics or economics each being at
least events and laws, not this dreadful beast, some average
and statistic . . ."

In contrast, his proposal is as follows:

millenia

person

Process

quantity

Continuing:

Applying all four of these at once (which is what I mean by *attention*), the local loses quaintness by the test of person (how good is it for you as you have to be a work of your lifetime?); itself as crutch of ambience, by test of ambience [to which one might add as plaintive parallel, "how long, oh Lord, how long . . ."] its only interest is as process (say barbed wire, as attack on Plains husbandry) or as it may be a significant locus of quantity (in America how, say, prairie village called Chicago is still, despite itself, a prairie village. . . .

If, in fact, by *person* one means "what, in fact, the critter, homo sap, is, as we take it, now . . . ," then, as Olson says, "our own 'life' is too serious a concern for us to be parlayed forward by literary antecedence. In other words, 'culture,' no matter how great . . ." "So far as 'scholarship' might, it will disclose the intimate connection between person-as-continuation-of-millenia-by-acts-of-imagination-as-arising-directly-from-fierce-penetration-of-all-past-persons, places, things and actions-as-data (objects)—not by fiction to fiction—." There follows, at this point, a lovely homage to Alfred North Whitehead, who is then used to define the principle at work here— "we should start from the notion of actuality as in its essence a process" (Whitehead, *Adventures of Ideas*). . . .

I think I might, more responsibly, now enter this discussion as a person, literally—and not as a commentator, editor, scholar, or however one may care to qualify what has been said thus far. Just as Olson had said to Ed Dorn, "Best thing to do *is to dig one thing or place or man* until you yourself know more about that than is possible to any other man . . . ," for me the crux was to be "the NARRATOR IN, the total IN to the above total OUT ["what I call DOCUMENT simply to emphasize that the events alone do the work"], total speculation as against the half management, half interpretation, the narrator taking on himself the job of making clear by way of his own person that life *is* preoccupation with itself, taking up the push of his own single intelligence to make it, to be—by his conjectures—so powerful inside the story that he makes the story swing on him, his eye the eye of nature INSIDE (as is the same eye, outside) a light-maker." Always in my own situation, there was tacit fear some essential information was lacking, that one was dumb, in some crucial sense, left out of the 'larger picture.' So that this possibility, as a *method*, was extraordinarily moving to me insofar as it exchanged a concept of social limit (again 'culture,' in its most pernicious sense) for the active potential and authority of a human life, *lives,* literally being lived. I had known, certainly, what Olson elsewhere proposes as "There are no hierarchies, no infinite, no such many as mass, there are only/eyes in all heads,/to be looked out of." So too, in somewhat parallel sense, Pound's insistence: "What thou lov'st well shall not be reft from thee/What thou lov'st well is thy true heritage . . ." (*Pisan Cantos*). But the condition, the law, so to speak, of this situation I took time to trust.

Why? That question seems to me intimately involved with all the familiar senses of enclosure and self-limit, what Louis Zukofsky wryly put as "born very young into a world already very old. . . ." It is hard to change the system, like they say—the more so, paradoxically, when it is, by virtue of consciousness, so very simple to. Think of what's become of the various significant patterns of "history" even in our own lifetime. But my point is really that significant aspects of Charles Olson's thought and work have been confusing to its critics insofar as the *model* of 'world' in mind, in each case, was very different, if not altogether antithetical. In short, there is often a disposition to read *The Maximus Poems* as if they were a symbolic representation of the forces of history, in the abstract, and that the unremitting emphasis upon "the facts," as he would say, whether of dreams or Gloucester records or his own daily existence, are somehow there to 'describe' or otherwise 'stand for' a 'reality' of general kind. They are not. Let me, in fact, make an absolute emphasis: *they are not.*

No, the "cause" is otherwise, "It is the cause the cause, still, it is (and she, still/even though the method be/new, be/the rods and cones of a pigeon's or, a rabbit's/eye, or be/who, man, is that woman you now dream of, who/ woman, is that man. . ." (**"by 3/6/51"**). In his lecture at the Berkeley Poetry Conference (July 20, 1965), Olson makes the point very flatly, "You're simply stuck with the original visionary experience of having been *you,* which is a hell of a thing. [Laughter] And, in fact, I assume that the epigraph that I've offered today is my only way of supporting that, which is [he writes on the board]: *that which exists through itself is what is called meaning. . . ."*

> I believe there's simply ourselves, and where we are has a particularity which we'd better use because that's about all we got. Otherwise we're running around looking for somebody else's stuff. But that particularity is as great as numbers are in arithmetic. The literal is the same as the numeral to me. I mean the literal is an invention of language and power the same as numbers. And so there is no other culture. There is simply the literal essence and exactitude of your own . . . Truth lies solely in what you do with it. And that means *you.* I don't think there's any such thing as a creature of culture . . . The radical of action lies in finding out how organized things are genuine, are initial, to come back to that statement I hope I succeeded in making about the *imago mundi.* That *that's* initial in any of us. We have our picture of the world and *that's* the creation.

There is, finally, a late text ("Gloucester, 28 Fort Square Feb. 15th (LXIX)") which makes an intensive compact of a great range of Olson's thinking, and since one cannot, responsibly, undertake all the materials and situations of his work in such "working notes" as these, let it serve as center for our own ending here. (Regretfully, in some respects, since much dear to my own heart, **"Apollonius of Tyana,"** for example, or the specific relations with Jung, Corbin, and that primary man, Alfred North Whitehead, have barely been touched upon, if at all. But one takes heart in Whitehead's insistence, dear indeed to Olson: "There is nothing in the real world which is merely an inert fact. Every reality is there for feeling: it promotes feeling; and it is felt." (Whitehead, *Process and Reality*,) So we won't miss 'it' insofar as it is 'here.')

The text, then, is "The Animate Versus the Mechanical, And Thought." He begins, "Gravity, in fact, but pre- or post-mechanics. That is, not effect (Newtonian) nor proof (Recent) but experiential: phenomenological, perceptional, actionable." In short, that this fact of being, in any given instance, not be taken *outside,* so to speak, but be recognized as the "Dogmatic Nature of Experience," which it is. He notes the situation of a plant, which "has at the tips of its leaves and the ends of its roots "standing-growing-responding" actions . . . and has, if and as 'weight,' gravitational 'history.'"

> In fact 'history,' as, in that sense, difference from "astronomy" [which relies, perforce, on 'mechanical' measure]: that event (in Merleau-Ponty's sense—narrative) is a perceptual—that wld be *primordial*—element of experience so much so that it 'carries' through-out the system—the system being 'Creation'—as 'element' (or 'weight') as profound as any mechanically measurable or demonstrable 'truth'; that even in short—or here decisively 'history'—as *must* [as necessity, as what has to happen]—is a condition of organism. (Above 'Animate.') . . . now I am proposing an even more fundamental 'tropism' ["Tropism, I think, is actually the riddler of the lot. Or it's the management, or it's the manueverer, or it's then . . . it's ourselves."]: that one cannot 'think' even—because one cannot 'act' even—without such limits as the 'lines' of being, both in the plant and the animal 'meaning,' 'animate' . . . So I am back to animate, plant-or-animal—'perception' sense—of the freshness in time of the narrative or history as a tone or mode and so activeness of, for a human being, 'Creation': that there is no 'knowledge' of the crucial (axial-tropistic) sense of *anything,* including the "Universe" or the "Self," except by this 'Time' phenomenon of freshness which Animateness, *in and by itself,* as initial *of* experience.

You will recall the frequency with which Olson quoted Heraclitus, 'Man stands estranged from that with which he is most familiar'—literally, that fact, that living organism, of him/herself, and the crisis, persistently, in the situation is that all else is affected by such a powerful 'unit of meaning' so intensively awry. It is as if we have entered the 'inside' of this animate 'content' with the same terms of measure and their related agency, the mechanical, with which we had presumed our mastery over the 'outside,' that "geography" also so insistently present and which "forever . . . leans in/on me . . . ." In contradiction, Olson proposes:

> The animate—plant or animal—is the aboriginal instance of our occurence and is therefore the aboriginal condition which qualifies—defines both in fact and act, including the form-making usefulness of—our action.

> . . . . .

> The import of this can be quickly stated: man as Love (plant, heliogeotropic) grows up and down, man as separateness (animal) disposes of himself by *sitio*—chooses his place but which even though it gives him

> freedom disposes him likewise by gravity (statolith)—starch, turgor—'weight'-of-mass)—
> equal tropistically. Heaven and Earth.

What's to be made of that, with that, is all that any human life or the acts that make it life can constitute:

> an actual earth of value to
> construct one, from rhythm to
> image, and image is knowing, and
> knowing, Confucius says, brings one
> to the goal: nothing is possible without
> doing it. It is where the test lies, malgre
> all the thought and all the pell-mell of
> proposing it. Or thinking it out or living it
> ahead of time.

George F. Butterick (essay date 1982)

SOURCE: "Charles Olson and the Postmodern Advance," in *Iowa Review,* Vol. 11, No. 4, Fall, 1980, pp. 4-27.

[*In the following essay, Butterick examines how Olson attempted to break with traditional western rationalism.*]

Charles Olson was always very pleased by the fact that the only time he was ever given a psychological test—when he was invited to participate along with twenty-three other poets, including William Carlos Williams, Robert Lowell, and the like, as part of an examination of creativity conducted by a Harvard graduate student—the results of the test confirmed that he had a "high tolerance of disorder." The experiment was administered in 1950 by Robert N. Wilson, working under Olson's friend and fellow Melville scholar, Henry A. Murray, father of the widely known Thematic Apperception Test (TAT), and consisted of an interview and modified form of the TAT, in which visual patterns are explored and narrated. Not insignificantly, it is also known as a "projective" test although Olson experienced it after his well known "Projective Verse" essay was already in press, so there probably was no connection. But this quality—a "high tolerance of disorder"—I would offer, may be one of the chief characteristics of the poetry written since the Second World War which we know as "post-modern."

Postmodernism is a critic's term; it has no popular use or necessity. It has its limits, as most descriptive terms of its order do—to such an extent that I recently came upon an interviewer asking Amiri Baraka about a "post-postmodern" art! It is, like the designation Black Mountain Poets, a term of convenience that has no absolute bearing on reality. It is like the Middle Ages—or even middle age, for that matter—unlikely to be defined with satisfaction to all. I introduce it into the present discussion only because it may be useful in order to distinguish Charles Olson from his immediate predecessors, and, most importantly, because Olson himself used it, and used it about himself.

Most generally, "postmodern" (with or without the hyphen) is used to distinguish the new energies appearing in

American culture following World War II, from an exhausted modernism which had outrun its course. The term itself has gained increasing critical acceptance in recent years, until by this date it seems to be a fixity in literary history. A prominent literary periodical declares itself in its subtitle to be a "journal of postmodern literature," and there have been any number of essays and symposia on the subject. The writings of critic Ihab Hassan and David Antin's essay "Modernism and Postmodernism: Approaching the Present in American Poetry" in *Boundary 2* come most readily to mind. Even a California bookseller specializing in recent American writing offers his wares in catalogues designated "Modern & Postmodern Literature." The term has been surveyed with all desired thoroughness in two recent articles in the journal *Amerikastudien,* published in Stuttgart for the German Association for American Studies, so there is no need to do that here, even if there were time.

The term was first used, apparently, by the historian Toynbee, although Olson—and this is not generally known—may have actually been the first use it in its current application, and the first to use it repeatedly if not consistently. I will take the time to document this because in so doing we can have a better understanding of what it might mean to be a "post-modern" poet.

As Olson uses it, the designation serves not merely to advance beyond an outmoded modernism, but it seeks an alternative to the entire disposition of mind that has dominated man's intellectual and political life since roughly 500 B.C. As early as *Call Me Ishmael,* published in 1947, Olson felt that logic and classification betrayed man. "Logic and classification had led civilization toward man, away from space." Now Olson sought to restore man from his egocentric humanism to a proper relationship with the universe, in the same way he says Melville had, and, before that, early man: "Melville went to space to probe and find man. Early man did the same: poetry, language and the care of myth." His classic statement is in "Human Universe," his finest piece of theoretical prose, the one he called the "base" of his cultural position and "the body, the substance, of my faith." There he explains how logic and classification intervene between man and the universe, "intermite our participation in our experience." And the only way out is to restore mythological participation in the laws of nature through a language which is "the act of the instant" rather than "the act of thoughtabout the instant." The result is an intensified syntax which fuses man with natural processes. In an effort to break free, postmodern poetry requires almost a total and systematic disordering or disorientation—not so much of the senses, as Rimbaud proposed—but of syntax, at the same time accompanied by a demand for a re-orientation to a new, a "human universe." As we shall see, the expanded syntax is a manifestation in language of the postmodern demand out of which any advance is made.

The earliest occurrence of the term "postmodern" I am yet aware of in Olson's writing comes amid a discussion of the modern era as "the age of quantity" in a letter to Robert Creeley, 9 August 1951, where he writes without further definition or elaboration: "I am led to this notion: the post-modern world was projected by two earlier facts," and goes on to cite the voyages of discovery of the fifteenth and sixteenth centuries which made "all the earth a known quantity" and the development of the machine in the nineteenth century. The term, however, appears more elaborately and significantly in another letter to Creeley some days later, on August 20, where Olson distinguishes "modern" man from the "post-modern" in the following manner: "the *modern* . . . feel[s] he does *not* belong to . . . just, quick, call it, the universe." In other words, he is in familiar terms, alienated, or "estranged from that with which he is most familiar." Whereas, Olson continues, "my assumption is any POST-MODERN is born with the ancient confidence that, he *does* belong." It is this same "ancient confidence" that enables Olson to begin "Human Universe" with "There are laws," or to write those words which Allen Ginsberg said first attracted him to Olson: "I am one/with my skin." Indeed, it is the same confidence that enables Olson to name his hero, Maximus.

Olson continues to use the term "post-modern" in his letters to Creeley and to Cid Corman from this time (1951-52), in his "Special View of History" lectures from 1956, and in essays like "The Law," which he saw as a sequel to "Human Universe" ("Human Universe" itself was almost entitled "The Laws"), from 3 October 1951. In it he explores the question, "how did other men than the modern (or Western) ground the apprehension of life," and in response, he writes of the first half of the present century as "the marshalling yard on which the modern was turned to what we have, the post-modern, or the post-West." Earlier in the piece, he had summarized what for him are the characteristics of the Western inheritance which makes up modern man. First of all, our history can be viewed as a closed "box," from roughly 500 B.C. to 1950 A.D. As in "Human Universe," the fault lies with the three "great Greeks," Socrates, Aristotle, and Plato, who together invented the reason which has dominated man and "from whom," writes Olson, "it is always my argument, the 'West' followed." As a result of the development of abstract thought by the Greeks, the poet writes, "it is my impression that intellectual life in the West has been and still to a great degree stays essentially *descriptive* and analytical." His conclusion is a general renunciation of the West in its roots: that Socrates (the generalizer) and Thucydides (the proponent of history as "truth," an abstract) "date exactly together," and that "the division of FORM and CONTENT . . . follows" therefrom. And in this essay "Definitions by Undoings," from as early as 1952, it is clear that the "post-modern" is likewise opposed to "the Western tradition," for much the same reasons.

Now, it is nothing new to reject Western culture. It goes on all the time—and to such an extent that the time has certainly come to reaffirm its accomplishments. Indeed, Olson himself—in railing against . . . this time it was the East, or those contemporaries who sought their practice or ecstasy principally in the East (he railed at whatever gave him energy, of course, as any high-spirited man)—pointed out that anything the East had to offer, whether it was calm or selflessness or a sense of the kalpa (an end-less but measurable eon) the West also, or already, had. (I believe the subject under discussion was self-efface-ment as an exercise in spiritual discipline.) But it is also true that the post-modern demand is that the West curb its excesses and interferences which divide man from nature and from himself.

"Post-modern" occurs again in Olson's writings in the review "The Materials and Weights of Herman Melville," written for the *New Republic* in August of 1952, where Olson writes of D. H. Lawrence as "the one man of this century to be put with Melville, Dostoevsky and Rimbaud (men who engaged themselves with modern reality in such fierceness and pity as to be of real use to any of us who want to take on the post-modern . . ."). The term and the same four authors, as precisely those who make possible our or any "post-modernism," occur again a short while later in an important autobiographical statement written on Election Day, 1952, while awaiting the returns of the national elections in which Adlai Stevenson would lose to Eisenhower—a time when a former politico and New Dealer might very well reconsider his own identity! It comes in the piece in which his famous phrase, "archeol-ogist of morning," used to title (post-humously) his col-lected poems, also occurs:

> . . . I find it awkward to call myself a poet or a writer. If there are no walls there are no names. This is the morning, after the dispersion, and the work of the morning is methodology: how to use oneself, and on what. That is my profession. I am an archeologist of morning. And the writing and acts which I find bear on the present job are (I) from Homer back, not forward; and (II) from Melville on, particularly himself, Dostoevsky, Rimbaud, and Lawrence. These were the modern men who projected what we are and what we are in, who broke the spell. They put men forward into the post-modern, the post-humanist, the post-historic, the going live present, the "Beautiful Thing."

As a final example of the extent of Olson's use of the term (there are many others that can be documented) and for some further sense of Olson's own understanding of how far the term could take him, he writes in a note from the time of his New Sciences of Man lectures in early 1953: "we are now in a stage which may best be called 'post-modern,' in order that the theory of *openness* may be free even from the very gains which made the open-ness possible—free from all argument, & thus already into that stage of *will* (which is *after,* or at least *more necessary* even than understanding) from which LAWS can come into existence. . . ." The term thus had a cur-rency for the poet, like those terms *archaic 'istorin,* and *myth,* among the others we will touch upon briefly in order to delineate his accomplishment, his advance into the post-modern.

In his admirable survey of the term in American cultural history, Michael Köhler points out that "post-modern" appears to have been first used by Toynbee in a chart in the 1946 abridged edition of his famous *Study of History.* There Toynbee assigns the date of 1875 for the beginning

of the new era he calls "Post-Modern," that following the "Modern" period of 1475-1875. Köhler also notes that this is exactly the date that Olson cites when he writes in "A FIRST DRAFT of a READING list in the new SCIENCES OF MAN" from 1995, "It is not yet gauged how much the nature of knowledge has changed since 1875. Around that date man reapplied known techniques of the universe to man himself, and the change has made man as non-Socratic (or non-Aristotelian) as geometers of the early 19th century made the universe non-Euclidean." And indeed Köhler is quite right in noticing the similarity, for—although he does not say this, does not fully make the connection—the year 1875 is precisely the same one Olson chooses to identify the begin-nings of what he calls the New Sciences of Man, those same sciences he believed provided the methodological alterna-tive to humanism and modernism.

The coincidence is too great to be overlooked, and led Köhler to wonder if there wasn't some indication that Olson had drawn the term "post-modern" directly from Toynbee. There is, however, no such evidence. *A Study of History,* whether in its original multi-volume form or its more popular abridgement, was not among the books in Olson's library, and Olson mentions Toynbee only three times, to my knowledge, in his writings, in each case disparagingly, as a type of historian to be avoided. Of course, Olson might have read Toynbee early—though not in college, as many had done, since the first volumes of *A Study of History* were not published until 1934, the year after he had received his MA from Wesleyan; and there is no indication the work was part of the assigned or recommended reading in his graduate courses in history at Harvard. Still, it is odd, even uncanny, that of all the dates available to mark the beginning of an era, the two earliest users of the term "postmodern" in English should choose the same one to accompany or illustrate their term. Another observer might have chosen 1914; or 1863, the date of the Salon des Refusés in Paris, which some give for the birth of the Avant Garde; or, as Olson himself elsewhere, 1897, Brooks Adams' date for the beginning of the New American Empire. But 1875? That's an ex-traordinary coincidence, inescapably close.

Although it would seem at first a coincidence too highly improbable, both writers hold different reasons for choos-ing the same date. Toynbee, as explained in his *Study of History,* offers the date exclusively in political terms, for the general onset of nationalism and the spread of in-dustrialism. Now, Olson may have been *encouraged* by Toynbee (if at all), but he gives his own reason as—with a specificity so typical of him—the date for the founding of the science of archeology, the core of the so-called New Sciences of Man, which he identifies as having had its start with the excavations at Olympus under the German archeologist Wilhelm Dorpfeld, Schliemann's collaborator and successor at Troy—the first, apparently, to exercise the rigors of classification while preserving the larger context, and thus, the first to apply the methods of exact science to man himself. It is not that Olson uses the year 1875 to mark the birth of postmodernism as such, but of the tools that make possible a post-modern advance. He writes in his plan for Black Mountain College in 1956:

It was archeology . . . which broke loose the birth of new knowledge around 1875, it was the digging up of the past not the mere recording or repeating the history of it. It was the objectification, the literal seeking and finding of *the objects* of the past of man which took down all generalization with it, made the specific pin or gold piece . . . *the evidence* of the oral existence of man. For example: the mythological as the matter will remain nothing but removed tales of somebody else unless any one of us achieves a means to take seriously what goes on inside ourself. And you can't do that by simply sitting around in wonder and fantasy and trouble over what happens to one or what one dreams. You have to have the experience of hard objects, of panning, of what does wash out when all the water is out of it.

So that although Toynbee may have used the term "postmodern" as early as 1946, it appears Olson came to the designation independently in 1951, through his own observation and understanding of the world.

But before exploring further the grounds for his rejection of modernism and suggesting the qualities of post-modernism which characterize Olson's poetry, let me first say a bit more about what these New Sciences of Man were, that he saw as the means to advance man into post-modernism.

Recognizing that the occasional summer sessions at Black Mountain in the past had elicited far more support in terms of tuition-paying students than the regular program, the total enrollment of which at that time wavered at 35, Olson, in an attempt to save the foundering school, proposed in 1952 a series of what he called "institutes." These were to be in the crafts, pottery, theater, the natural sciences, along with his own special child, an institute in what he called the "New Sciences of Man." This was to be held at the college in the early spring of 1953, and was originally to include geographer Carl Sauer, who Olson invited to be the "governing lecturer" of the series, ethnobotanist Edgar Anderson, archeologists Robert Braidwood and Christopher Hawkes, and Carl Jung, although only Braidwood and Marie Luise von Franz, sent by Jung in his place, finally came, for a week apiece that March. In inviting Christopher Hawkes to come—whose book *The Prehistoric Foundations of Europe* he found not only informative but methodologically valuable—Olson summarizes his intentions regarding the Institute: "this Institute is planned as as thorough an attack upon the state of real knowledge now as the few of us who stand on such grounds can make it. What I want to do is to bring together here three or four men who can, together, and for such as attend, examine three sciences simultaneously—what I think you, of all men, will follow me in, if I put them this way: (1), the science of place, or what Sauer had called 'the morphology of landscape' . . . ; (2), the science of culture, or, the morphology of same [defined in a similar letter to Braidwood as "that discipline man displaced evolution by"]; and (3), the science of mythology," about which he adds: "the least familiar, perhaps, but you will know Jung and Kerényi's attempt to give circulation to it: it might vastly & quickly be said to be what art and religion have previously divided between themselves" (letter to Hawkes, 3 January 1953).

Olson himself was to pave the way by delivering a series of at least eight background lectures in the five weeks of February and March before the invited speakers came. He gives the titles in another letter to Christopher Hawkes, 2 February 1953 (also in one to Corman the same day, and to Creeley on February 23):

> The Cave, or, Painting
> The Cup, or, Dance
> The Woman, or,
> Sculpture
> The
> Valley, or, Language
> The Plateau, or the Horse, or, War
> Lagash, or, the Hero
> Thebes, or, the City
> The Sun,
> or the Sum, or, Self

—although all do not seem to have survived, or survived intact. But what we do have of the lectures—which Olson describes to Creeley, 23 March 1953, as "a sort of researching made public"—reveal the enormous labor he put into the program (nowhere hinted at in Martin Duberman's brief account in his *Black Mountain: A Study in Community*). Everywhere present in the lectures is Olson's energy and capacity for research, his Goethian scope and wide grasp of information, the sheerboldness to attempt such a venture. Not least, there is displayed Olson's belief in the New Sciences themselves. He tells his audience at the beginning of his third lecture, "my joy of science is such, I am apt to forget most people have a double-trouble: they are either captive of its mechanisms (unable to see how Heisenberg restored science to man) or they are full of the old religion-art suspicion of it as robber of the lustre of the daydreams of man . . . My joy of the sciences of this Institute is this: that it enables any of us to inhabit man in his story backward & forward as close to exactly as any of us actually inhabit ourselves." It is of consequence that Olson does not shy from or reject science like a romantic humanist, but freely acknowledges its usefulness as a "tool." He never had any objection to the scientific method, so long as that was understood to be "a stage which man must master and not what [it is] taken to be, final discipline." Logic and classification are only means to an end not "ways *to* end, END, which," he insists, "is never more than this instant, than . . . you, this instant, in action." (*Human Universe*).

The resulting series of lectures Olson hoped to publish as a book, as he wrote Jonathan Williams on 1 March 1953, under the title, *The Chiasma* (or intersection). They were his most ambitious attempt to be comprehensive in prose after "Human Universe" and prior to *A Special View of History,* and in many ways go beyond those later lectures in scope and clarity of address. The lectures push back to Cro-Magnon man (they are continued almost fifteen years later in Olson's letters to John Clarke, published as *Pleistocene Man*), and while many readers are aware of Olson's interest in the Maya or Sumerians, far more profound is this interest in the origins of man himself, in an effort to bring him beyond the modern. The formula seems inescapable: the deeper man returns to his archaic, primordial, pre-rationalist condition, the further beyond modernism he advances.

The science that Olson discovered to take him beyond modernism was mythology, assisted by Jung and Kerényi's suggestion in the title of their book together, *Essays on a Science of Mythology,* that mythology could indeed be a *science.* The term or the notion stopped Olson at first; he resisted it, as evidenced in a letter to Creeley from 25 October 1950, where he rejects the phrase, "science of mythology," as "crap." But what he could not reject was that myth, in the definition he found in the introduction to the Jung and Kerényi book, from Malinowski's *Myth in Primitive Psychology,* was a "reality lived." Mythology, as Malinowski saw it, was "the assertion of an original, greater, and more important reality" through which a man's "present life, fate, and work" were governed, and the knowledge of which provided him "on the one hand with motives for ritual and moral acts [or for the poet, poems], on the other hand with directions for their performance [his poetics]."

This was followed by Olson's discovery around the same time of classical scholar J. A. K. Thomson's identification of mythology as "muthologos," or "what is said (of what is said)," which also had the advantage—in Thomson's presentation—of linking that with the "history" Olson had always been interested in, and being at the same time a definition that corresponded to the one he knew from Jane Harrison (myth as mouth, *mythos* as *muthos*)—which got in narrative, the story, the spoken equivalent of act, art as *dromenon* or enactment—so that his aesthetics of the "instant" could emerge intact.

These, then, are the principal sources for Olson's understanding of myth, in addition to Freud and Frazer earlier, and what he knew genetically, instinctively, in his blood (his mother was said to believe in leprechauns—although that has been said in America about most Irish mothers or grandmothers). These sources of understanding supply and support him until the end. In an essay entitled, directly, "The Science of, Mythology," written 15 January 1953 in anticipation of the New Sciences of Man institute, Olson says: "I propose that mythology is a word to use for the present to characterize an observable series of phenomena as decisively as physiology is taken to cover the matter of our body's functioning . . ." He continues: "the care of myth is in your hands—you are, whether you know it or not, the living myth—each of you—which you neglect, not only at your own peril, but at the peril of man. For when men lose their mythology, they are as dead—simply, that it is what used to be called the soul of them, and, by the law of the soul (the palpable force of it), if you lose it—like if you lose your body—you are not alive." Later, Olson will insist that mythology is the same "hard" science as any of the taxonomic sciences such as physics. Some ten thousand pages of his own notes survive as evidence of just how rigorous a study mythology could be and the demand he made of it.

In speaking of the New Sciences to his audience at Black Mountain, Olson says his own specialty is the "science of image." Image—and image in its narrative form, story—is the alternative to logic and classification—which is why the poet concludes "Human Universe" on a myth. Image is unique and indivisible, it defies comparison, which, Olson writes in a first version of his "Human Universe" essay, "has lain . . . at the root of humanism as one of its most evil characteristics." "Image," he says further, "denotes a much more active process, deriving as it does from the root of the Latin verb 'imitare,' to imitate, and thus is closely joined to the implicitly dramatic action of the concept 'to mime,' and bears always in the direction of direct representation of an original object or act, not, as symbol goes, in the contrary direction, toward generalization, towards an abstract sign, figure, or type to stand in the place of . . . the original object or act." Olson had become a "specialist" very much like he says Ahab had (*Call Me Ishmael*), concentrating all space, not into "the form of a whale called Moby Dick" like Ahab, but into Gloucester. Gloucester is an image of possibility for a city the way Maximus is the image of possibility for man.

In many ways Olson was his own myth and his own image. He was, as many know by now, a man of unavoidable physical presence. It might be said he was obsessed, preoccupied with size, ruled by it, for there was no place he could go without his own. One can readily imagine the mixed feelings of the young Olson reading Thomas Wolfe's story, "Gulliver: The Story of a Tall Man," in a June 1935 *Scribner's* magazine, which begins: Some day some one will write a book about a man who was too tall—who lived forever in a dimension that he did not fit, and for whom the proportions of everything—chairs, beds, doors, rooms, shoes, clothes, shirts, and socks, the berths of Pullman cars and the bunks of transatlantic liners, together with the rations of food, drink, love, and women which most men on this earth have found sufficient to their measure—were too small." And that man, that Gulliver, was only six foot six! In his notebook (entry for 9 July 1935), Olson records his reading so far that summer: Malraux's *Man's Fate,* Auden's *Poems,* Dorothy Sayers' *Nine Tailors,* Hemingway, etc., and adds: "Of all this the most important is an unmentioned short thing—Thomas Wolfe's 'Gulliver—The Story of a Tall Man,'" which he describes as "achingly true in exposing the hell of a tall man's life."

Jonathan Williams tells a story of going to a movie theater one night with Olson in Asheville, N.C., the city outside Black Mountain—the Isis Theater, no less—to see a film called, yes, "The Bride of Frankenstein." And at the end, as the screen went dark and the lights came on, and he and Olson stood up in the center of the theater preparing to go, Williams noticed the rest of the audience, good Asheville citizens, tradesmen and their wives, farmers from the hills, were eyeing Olson peculiarly. Wide-eyed, unable to take their eyes off him, they inched further and further away, making their way without further hesitation to the doors. It was as if they were witnessing—and suddenly participating in—a continuity of the movie, the image from the screen become live in their midst!

Or the picture of Olson moving through the vast enclosed space of a crowded airline terminal, every head turned to follow him, with his top-knot and overcoat cloaking his shoulders like a giant Samurai, head after head, looking up from newspapers, schedules, mother's laps. No wonder he responded to Eric Havelock's description of the Mycenean hero, the model for the oral prince, as a "conspicuous" public figure.

It was not an unattractive sight, his size in person, just strange and awesome, and Olson took advantage of it as he did the size of his voice. Certainly the poems reflect this quality and this authority. It would be all too peculiar, too precious, almost too perverse a thought, for so large a man to incise only haikus, a sonnet, a rondeau. How well he responded to Melville's cry, "Give me a condor's quill! Give me Vesuvius' crater for an inkstand! . . . Such, and so magnifying, is the virtue of a large and liberal theme! We expand to its bulk." (*Moby Dick*) Maximus was an attempt to live up to his full potentiality in size.

It was perhaps only a fluke that one of Maximus's manifestations, James Merry who wrestled a bull on Dogtown Commons, was exactly 6'7", Olson's size. But there can be little doubt that Maximus himself is named in part autobiographically. There were indications all along that this might be so. Who else does Olson seek to begin his story of America with, when taking his first steps toward the proposed narrative (alternatively a long poem) to be called *West*—which itself evolved into **The Maximus Poems**—but Paul Bunyan. And how uncomfortably obvious is the name Bigmans for a hero, prototype of Maximus, from a man who bought his clothing by mail from an outfitter called King Size. How immoderate, then, is the name Maximus itself, how immodest? With a name like that, how is a hero to avoid all the worst qualities of a Mohammed Ali, who also called himself "The Greatest"?

It should not be imagined that Olson, a man who could "lift an arm/flawlessly" and who walked with a spring, would feel because of his unusual size alone that "man is estranged from that with which he is most familiar." Nor would he be so overweening as to think that a writer's subject is his single human life alone. Instead, "size" is something all men might be capable of. He asks his audience at Black Mountain in one of his New Sciences of Man lectures: "What is your experience of your size? do you, or not, move among the herd of men with the sense of yourself as not yet filling out your size? do you, thus, have the feeling of being smaller, both than yrself and than how others appear to you? . . . am I right that most of our time we take ourselves to be smaller than others, to be smallness in face of the world?" Of course he does not mean mere physical size. Again, to Melville scholar Merton Sealts he writes (7 March 1952): "one of the central preoccupations of man today—one of his central necessities—is exactly this problem of *hero:* which is, any time, man's measure of his own *possibilities*—how large is he?" With Maximus, Olson allows his possibilities to stay enormous. "I am not named ['The Greatest'] /for no cause."

Olson had already discussed this matter of size in "Projective Verse," how the content of the poem changes for the poet, "the dimension of his line itself changes" (as we will see in our discussion of syntax to come), and how the "projective act . . . leads to dimensions larger than man," leads to, indeed, a Maximus. And could he have been speaking of anything but his own hero when he writes in "The Gate and The Center" of the *size* of the earliest Sumerian kings, saying: "I have this dream, that just as we cannot now see & say the size of these early HUMAN KINGS, we cannot, by the very lost token of their science ["the old human science of archetype figures and archetype event"]," we cannot, he says, "see what size man can be once more capable of, once the turn of the flow of his energies that I speak of as the WILL TO COHERE is admitted, and its energy taken up." This is precisely the will Maximus exercises when he "compells" Gloucester to "yield" itself, to be a polis once again, a "coherence not even yet new." Maximus, it must be granted, is Olson's attempt at a post-modern hero.

Maximus fulfills Olson's mythic ambitions. He absorbs the disorder, grows large on it. Maximus is saved from the presumption of his name by his ties to Gloucester and to an historical namesake, Maximus of Tyre, that both relieves him of egotism and allows him to participate in the past. He is a man, not an allegorical Everyman or Red Cross Knight; or if allegorical only in Keats's sense that a man's life, to be of any worth, must be a "continual allegory." It is Gloucester that gives Maximus dimension, a Gloucester of his own creation. Maximus is a proposition, a proportion to be filled, a challenge thrown ahead from the moment of its naming. Maximus is the sum of man; he grows by what all men—Lou Douglas, John Smith, John Winthrop, Enyalion and the other heroes of the poem—contribute to him. He is a model not a mirror; an "image," not of *a* man, but—the poem **"Maximus of Gloucester"** is careful to say—"of man." He is a magnification, a metaphor for human possibility. All men can be Maximus if they practice themselves like William Stevens, if they "make things,/not just live off nature," if they resist.

And he succeeds, even though in the final poem of the series—"my wife my car my color and myself"—the forces are finally equal to the hero, have caught up with him. Maximus yields back to the man, the heroic is pinched down to the human by the pain of having been alive and the bewilderment of being about to lose that life. The components of the poet's life are put to rest, at ease in their simplicity. This does not mean any need to bemoan like a sad trumpet the poems as a failure. It is such a commonplace that *all* modern long poems have been failures, including *The Wasteland, The Bridge, The Cantos, Paterson, A*—if that is ever a helpful way to talk about them. They are only failures because we no longer know what success is.

Maximus is a creature of language; the "Man in the Word," Jonathan Williams' editorial note to the first volume calls him. He has no life outside the poem and our memories of it. Among the six thousand or so pieces of mail preserved among Olson's papers, not one addressed simply "Maximus, Gloucester," ever reached him. Maximus is only as large as the language he can speak. He remains unbound by the fallacy of the sentence as a "completed thought." Instead, he extends the sentence—or the poetic line—increasingly onward until what must be said *gets* said, completes itself—often with another sentence (a sentence within the "sentence"), as in **"A Later Note on Letter # 15."** It may help if we think of the grammatical sentence, the one of words, in terms of a prison sentence—a time-conditioned event, "doing time," a stretch, not of the pen, but in the "pen." The reader is released from the sentence, that cell of language, only when his "time" is up, when the meaning has been fully served. Thus the many unclosed parentheses, the proliferation of commas and relative clauses, dashes, colons in the poems (in **"A Later Note,"** three open parentheses and three colons in eighteen lines propel the poem). The syntactical unit is as large as needs be. "The lines which hook-over should be read as though they lay out right and flat to the horizon or Eternity," Olson advised the readers of his *Selected Writings*.

This is no longer a condition or question of traditional syntax but of parataxis, the recording of the order of events as they occur in nature, even mimetically, as in the **"Hotel Steinplatz"** poem we will shortly look at in greater detail, tracing the fluctuations of the falling, blowing snow, at the same time the poet reveals his interiority through a meditation told in terms of the Norse "End of the World." Or the wonderful example of the late *Maximus* poem snatched from the flow of event, written between one o'clock and three one June morning in a checkbook, all the poet had in his pockets at the time, while standing under streetlights near the Blynman Canal or "Cut" in Gloucester, being inspected by prowling police cars curious as to the great shape in the shadows.

Syntactic strain forces the reader to perceive the world as Maximus does, to make his discoveries. It compels (his verb) us to participate in his world of language until Gloucester, too, is our own. Not of course the Gloucester of the Massachusetts coast which this very day may be having intermittent showers over its narrow streets and wharf pilings and back-lying hills, or where the smell of the frying batter General Mills developed for its Gorton's fishsticks is as pervasive in the air over Main Street as the gulls. That Gloucester might be for many just as Edward Dorn writing in 1959 thought he'd find it: "I would be bored to sickness," he predicted, "walking through Gloucester." But the Gloucester of which I speak is a polis of the mind, built and preserved by the rhythms of knowing. The obsessiveness of Olson's syntax holds to the turns of his mind as closely as that mind does to Gloucester, archeologically, exhaustively.

Much of the difficulty in Olson's poetry—and who would have it any other way—derives from just this torsion. This is not the occasional practice of ellipses or enjambment or syncopation that Olson—like most poets, even the most formal—is *also* capable of. It is an effort to drive against the limits of reality itself, where the language is done violence to, and with it, inherited, conformist linearity. Syntax yields or gets broken, broken through, as in the "Footnote" to **"John Burke"**: "And past-I-go/ Gloucester-inside/

being Fosterwise of/Charley-once-boy/ insides," (*Maximus I*) or in **"AN ART CALLED GOTHONIC"**: "We trace wood or/path/will not/hasten/our/step-wise ad-/vance"—where there are conscious attempts to write Yana and Gothonic in English, to press for an alternative.

But also the English—or American, actually—itself is stretched, the words written practically on top of one another in their tumble forth to get free: "I said to my friend my/life is recently so hairy honkie-/hard & horny too to that ex/tent I am far far younger/now than though of course I am/not twenty any more, only/the divine alone interests me at/all and so much else is other-/wise I hump out hard &/crash in nerves and smashed/existence only" (*Maximus III*). Or the episode of the toy steam shovel (or any modern toy or goods or product) in the poem for Jack Clarke, **"Golden Venetian Light"**:

> that model toy steam shovel I bot the Waiting
>   Station for Chas Peter's
> 1st Christmas Gloucester (age almost 3) and I stood
>   naked in a
> rage both fr. tiredness (& from damn) and the
>   goddamn toy
> it wasn't one it was a goddamn literally practically
>   *exact*
> model crank-crank & all that shit in the world: it
>   was too much
> both for him and myself, and his mother like any
>   mother
> doing that thing all from love, that somehow
> the goddamn thing might satisfy. Bullshit, it won't
>   if it don't, and
> forever!

Now, *that's* speech! (Is that, by the way, what Wordsworth meant by "the real language of men in a state of vivid sensation"?) It is not, of course, where the poetry, sheer poetry, lies—and there is control, masterful control and lightness otherwise—but the point is, the verse is open enough, at any given point, to include the sudden warps or excrescences or rages of being.

At the same time, Olson's language gives up neither its commonality nor its semantic intent. There is no instance in Olson I am aware of where the words do not "mean" something. To achieve a more accurate view or reality, word order is dislocated, the troops (I use military terminology here, conscious that not only "parataxis" but "avant garde" originally had that usage), the troops of words are ordered to fall out or are deployed in guerrilla position to wage a revolution of language closest to man's given shape, where language itself is a double helix. Indeed, there is that late *Maximus* poem written in a swirl on the page, literally, visually, until, totally caught up in itself as the poet by his own cares, it ends in a snarl of woe. In another poem, two lines of language are crossed over one another, demanding a simultaneity, and were it not for an initial capital on one, there would be some question which to read first.

I do not mean to suggest that this heightened, strained condition is unrelieved throughout Olson's long serial poem, or that such is most naturally satisfying to man. We lead lives of sufficient regularity to sleep once every 24 or 36 hours, eat while awake, have a pulse, and the like. It's just that reaches are called for that the old grasps or forms can not allow.

Olson himself repeatedly uses images of strain and contortion in speaking of how poems got written. In "Poetry and Truth" he describes a block of moveable type, with the printer as "under your words in order to make the letters of them. Which always delights me," he continues, "as a problem of creation. In fact . . . I would go so far— if you will excuse my Americanism—to think that you write that way. That you write as though you were *underneath* the letters. And I take that a hell of a lot larger. I would think that the hoof-print of the Creator is on the bottom of Creation, in exactly that same sense." (*Mythologos*, II). He describes the Rose of the World poem, reproduced in its holograph spiral in *Maximus III*, as an attempt to "go widdershins [i.e., counter-clockwise], & write both inside in . . . & R[ight] to L[eft]," and another late *Maximus* poem as "written as though *below* low water." Paul Blackburn had long ago accused him of twisting the issue: "He sd, 'You go all around the subject.' And I sd, 'I didn't know it was a sub-/ject.' He sd, 'You twist' and I sd, 'I do.' He said other things. And I didn't say anything." The point is, it is not a subject until the poet makes it one. There are no preconceived, predetermining forms to be accommodated, no preferred categories. Forms reveal themselves only by the act of the poem: "nothing is possible without/doing it. It is where the test lies, malgré/ all the thought and all the pell-mell of/ proposing it. Or thinking it out or living it/ahead of time" (*Maximus III*). It is a *willed* organicism.

Often the poem contorts and twists itself, enters into digressions, all to escape anticipated patterns which are simply too facile and belie the complexity the poet knows to be in the world. It might be said that such a poem creates its own difficulties, which it then must seek to resolve, Harry Houdini-like. For example, in one not necessarily successful but somewhat curious and noticeable late poem—the next to last poem in *Archaeologist of Morning*—even something so egregiously ungrammatical and confusing as a double negative is allowed and sought advantage of. The double negative appears to sustain a paradox raised earlier in the poem: that neurosis, termed characteristic of the old Norse, the pre-Hesiodic Greeks, and the earliest Celts (and this must surely be an irony, further throwing the poem into complexity), is (such neurosis is) a prerequisite for what the poet calls, probably with further irony, "modern Non-Neurotic Man, the Neue Klasse of/ freedom." And as proof or illustration, quotes "a lady/Poet who calls herself/an Artist," who, by the very stridency of her protest—"I *am* free, I *am* an Artist, I am the/ Poetry"—reveals her chains. Her claims—ordinarily, altogether attractive, and actually, in her original poems, basic feminist outcry—are rendered shrill and unconvincing and, indeed, in terms of what seems to be the subject of the poem, at the least, high-strung. But the point is, it is only the totally absorbing sweep of these last lines that offers the poem (all that has gone before)

any integrity and resolves the uncertain paradox proposed by the opening stanza. So much is held in abeyance, suspended, until the poem—by an accumulated argument of images and facts—has the authority to reveal, and only then, the truth it bears.

Such syntax is what in Donald Davie's terms might be called "subjective," that is, one "whose function is to please us by the fidelity with which it follows the 'form of thought' in the poet's mind," but goes beyond Davie's definition in one decisive sense, because the "form" may not yet be in the poet's mind. "Who knows what a poem ought to sound like? until it's thar?" It is still a question of where the poet acquires "form" for his thought. Postmodernist poetry does not accept preconceived forms, like fourteen lines, into which its cement is poured. Rather, it is intent, like all time arts, upon discovering the space of the world for itself. As early as 13 July 1953, Olson wrote to English author Ronald Mason: "The quarrel is with discourse—and thus, up to a certain, but extreme point, with traditional syntax. Because it is not possible to say everything at once, is no reason, to my mind, to lose the advantage of this pressure (or compression) which speech is [,] which it wants to be: that it rushes into the mouth to crowd out to someone else what it is is pressing in the heart & mind to be said."

Syntactic flexibility occasionally yields sprightly economies and syncopations, such as this syntactical sharing in lines from **"Letter # 41"**: "I run back home out of the new moon/makes fun of me in each puddle on the road" (*Maximus II*), where instead of subordination into clauses, there occurs a "Siamese" sentence, joined head to tail, the object of the prepositional phrase in the previous sentence becoming the subject of the subsequent one. Although sometimes the openness leads to periphrasis, and eventually, perhaps, to a mannerism. Occasionally it is only the poet's great will or vivaciousness that creates a gravity enough to hold meaning in sway, or where the wheels do leave the road, pulls them back on, as in this passage from **"Poem 143. The Festival Aspect,"** speaking of the god Ganesha: "Through the mountain/through the bole/of any tree through the adamantine/he passes/as though it were nothing. Only the God himself/of whom he is the frazzled stalk/in each of the coolness, and ease, of his power/is more than water . . ."—which Olson then saves by saying, "Water is not equal/to the/ Flower etc. (*Maximus III*), bringing the poem to a satisfying end. Of course, some of the poems don't make the turn. They end in a heap and rust there. Most notable isthe mightily ambitious, cosmogonic ["**Maximus, From Dogtown—IV**"], an attempt to bring Hesiod into American (with some Old Norse support). The poet exhausted himself by the time he got to Love in the poem.

Individuated syntax is the linguistic consequence of '*istorin*. Maximus, as a verb—as the verb Olson once said he was—is the '*istorin* of the sentence. In **"Letter, May 2, 1959"** there is the actual pacing out and recording of the distances on the old Meeting House Plain of Gloucester, now covered by modern settlement. The poet jots the figures on an air-letter from a Scottish editor he pulled out of his pocket, and writes them in the poem along with soundings from the earliest known chart of Gloucester Harbor by Champlain, both as examples of mapping as narrative and of "finding out for yourself." This is truly physiological writing; not only the famous "breath" of the projective poet, but the total body of man gotten back into his composition, making of his verse a "human universe." Poems are written with our bodies, not our tongues, our calloused thick or uncalloused tapering fingers, or rhythmically bobbing heads alone. Olson wrestling the lectern at Beloit is a metaphor for the act of writing itself. If there are roughnesses, they are not only non-Euclidean, but because creation is a spasm. To live second upon second, as Olson well knew, added up to "40 hours" each day.

This brings us once again to the postmodern demand. Postmodern poetry categorically includes more—dream data, imparted messages, chance occurrences (and reoccurrences), fortuitous rhymes, misspellings, frustrations, the blanks Pound said should be left in for what we don't know, stanzas, vulgarity, allusions, direct confessions, philosophical waxings, personal waning, aesthetic gossip. It demands more of the reader, proportionally. The syntax itself exhibits the postmodern "high tolerance for disorder." Such poetry is not to be mistaken for gross randomness, pilings, that abuse our trust. It is even intended to test our faith in the representative power of language. One practices the '*istorin* of the sentence—to find out for oneself. The meter is the measure of the man not of the line.

A late *Maximus* poem written in the Hotel Steinplatz while in Berlin on a visit to give a reading, will serve as a last illustration (*Maximus III*). The poet, in full loneliness on Christmas Day, two days before his fifty-sixth birthday, and having recently suffered a minor heart attack, watches the falling snow outside his window. The observed external phenomenon mirrors the poet's internal condition, the snowswept, noble anguish of it, extending to the archaic depths of the mythological. Even there, gazing out the window, it is not all a fixed flow: the snow hesitates, is blown about and transformed into rain, before thickening back to snow again. It is an astoundingly rich occasion, and all of it cinematically captured—but not frozen—by the poem. Before the gloomy winter afternoon, the poet stands as Odin, who had sacrificed himself for poetry by hanging nine days on Yggdrasill, the World Tree, his side pierced by a spear, like Christ on the cross. The pain in the poet's side from his overstressed heart recalls both Odin's wounded side and that of Christ, from which blood and then water ran, a sure sign of his death (on this day commemorating his birth). The wet snow evokes the dew sprinkled on Yggdrasill, itself constantly gnawed and torn by the animals of creation. Above all, there is no self-pity, only the grandeur of the mythic reenactment.

There are two simultaneous tracks in the poem—a technique that appears already in **"To Gerhardt, There, Among Europe's Things,"** although here more interwoven. There is a twin reel of syntax that not only allows the time element in—the archaic time of the Norse Eddas concurrent with the suffering, snowing present—but "proprio-

ceptively" fuses external and internal conditions. That is, we have "the universe flowing-in, inside" (*Additional Prose*). Description banished, uniqueness is restored. It is a total mythological experience.

The internal conditions are the poet's feelings, but also the primordial recesses where the myths from the Eddas remain active. The poet's feelings are both bodily (the pain of recent illness) and psychological (alone on Christmas in a strange city, his health uncertain, the death of his wife less than three years before still haunting him). But it is from other depths—call it the archaic, or the unconscious, if one wants to use so boring a term—that the poet speaks and that Maximus lives. The narrative moves to incorporate the words of a seeress whose story is told in the old Norse *Baldrs Draumar*. Sought by Odin, called up from the dead and forced to answer his questions, she cries, just as the poem has it, "who is this man who drives me all the way/ who drives me on down this weary path?/ Snowed on by snow, beaten by rain [no wonder the poet recalls her and identifies with her] /drenched with the dew, long I lay dead." Her identity is taken over wholly by Maximus, without further differentiation, making him an Odin to himself, yielding the anguish of the cry, this poem itself. At that moment the snow gives way.

The narrative, although it progresses—both syntactically and semantically—remains non-linear. The shifting, mimetic syntax carries the poem, allows Maximus another manifestation of his nature. The poet is fully absorbed by the scene, and merges—without differentiation of voice—into the mythic, chanting words of the seeress, assuming her experience as his own. At that moment, in the grip of that power, with the realization of what has been wrung from him—as abruptly as it all began, he emerges, like Rimbaud, "on the other side of despair"—the snow having suddenly ceased. Here at last we have the true "mythological man" in an "archeological present," a post-modern man completely possessed by myth, completely repossessed of his mythic life, his mythhood (and his method).

There will always be Battles of the Books, and the battle of the Ancients and the Moderns, the struggle of any age or individual to gain self-identity. Postmodern, then, is rather an assertive term. It seeks to put distance between the preceding generation (as what cultural generation does not) at the same time to adequately engage the problems of one's own lifetime. When Olson taught a course at Buffalo designated in the catalogue as "Modern Poetry," I for one was curious to see who he would include. Would he begin with Whitman or Pound, would he have anything to say about Lowell or Roethke or would he include only his friends, Duncan, Creeley, Dorn, would there be a new orthodoxy? I was greatly satisfied when he announced, "modern is how far any of us in this room has gotten." He meant, of course, modern in the sense of contemporary, in its etymological sense of "right now." It was clearly another form of "you, this instant, in action," which is the essence of "Human Universe" and indeed of Olson's entire philosophy. It was probably then he drew so hard on his Camel that there was left an inch of ash, or tucked his tie into his shirt so it wouldn't interfere, or tied his sweater around his waist, or swiped at his nose like a boxer, or wagged his eyebrows, or any of the characteristic gestures that meant we were going forward, that we were making the advance.

Thomas F. Merrill (essay date 1982)

SOURCE: "The Grammar of Illiteracy," in *The Poetry of Charles Olson: A Primer,* Associated University Presses, 1982, pp. 38-63.

[*In the following excerpt, Merrill examines the principles underlying Olson's unorthodox use of language.*]

> These Days
> whatever you have to say, leave
> the roots on, let them
> dangle
> And the dirt
>   just to make clear
>   where they came from
>   —*Archaeologist of Morning*

Once at a poetry reading at Brandeis Charles Olson "got so damned offended" that he screamed at his audience, "You people are so literate I don't want to read to you anymore." To underscore the seriousness of his point, he added, "It's very crucial today to be sure that you stay illiterate simply because literacy is wholly dangerous, so dangerous that I'm involved everytime I read poetry, in the fact that I'm reading to people who are literate—and they are *not* hearing. They may be listening with all their minds, but they don't hear."

It is hard to hear someone when he is shouting all the time, Cid Corman once observed of Olson, but it is not just the volume, the content, nor the dogmatism of Olson's utterances that dismay even his most sympathetic listeners; it is his conviction—a rigorously practiced one—that language should never surrender the fullness of experience for the sake of logical tidiness.

Capturing the fullness of experience is a creative ambition that can hardly be challenged, but how much untidiness can an audience of listeners or readers tolerate? Chad Walsh, a sympathetic but "literate" listener at an Olson performance at Beloit College, responded to the experience perhaps as many baffled readers have responded to Olson's work at large:

> Once in a while some brief remark would seem to press a button in my mind and a light would gleam, very briefly. I would seem to have a precious insight, though afterwards I could never recall what it was. Mainly, though, I found myself vainly trying to discover a topic sentence somewhere, or discern the connection of anything to anything. . . . I suspect that Olson was already living in the world of complex simultaneity, with its own and different rules of logic.

Walsh is considerably more gracious than other detractors who have found Olson's roots-and-all style "pretentious," "more manner than matter," "unspeakably sentimental," and "a rhetoric not easily distinguished from bluff." To such critics Olson's unabashed "illiteracy" is a cultural offense that is pathetically but irresistibly vulnerable to patronizing sneers and elegant put-downs.

Walsh's patient dismay, however, ought perhaps to be gauged against Frank Davey's ardent apology for the same Beloit lecture-reading: "Somebody tries to toss the universe in your lap. You duck. Hell, it's heavy, no handles. But on Olson's side not that easy to throw." Handles (and here Davey surely has in mind topic sentences, connectives, and the other amenities of "literate" grammar) certainly would make the world easier to toss, but would such a domesticated missile, so accommodated with handles, be the one of "complex simultaneity" that Olson experienced? Would not the handles distort the configuration, alter the trajectory? Would not such a universe so equipped become the captive of its own equipage and evolve as a universe of discourse rather than a universe of experience? Such is Olson's position and the basis of his defense of illiteracy.

Both Davey and Walsh seem instinctively to respond to Olson's style in cosmological terms—a *world* of "complex simultaneity," a handleless *universe*—and for very good reasons, because the real underlying issue to their debate goes well beyond literacy, well beyond style, to the very ontological foundations upon which language rests. They are arguing the nature of "being" that language attends. Is that world of "complex simultaneity" without handles the familiar kind of Euclidean reality to which the grammar and syntax of our conventional language has been accommodated, or is it a new conception of "being" so remote from Euclid's orderly universe that it renders traditional expressive structures obsolete? In other words, is reality substantial, discrete, and vulnerable to forces, or is it force itself, a continuous flow of constantly changing energy concentrations much like changes in an electromagnetic field? How do such ontological alternatives affect the conduct and the structure of language?

Olson's position is implicit in the famous opening line of his poem **"The Kingfishers"**:

> What does not change / is the will to change

Not only does this utterance brand him as an unabashed neo-Heraclitean, but it also heralds his growing ontological conviction that a "contrary Renaissance" had occurred in the mid-nineteenth century that had corrected the "error on matter" that, since Aristotle, had kept man "estranged from that with which he is most familiar." The initiators of that "contrary Renaissance" were the non-Euclidean mathematicians Bolyai, Lobatschewsky, and ultimately Bernard Riemann, and their work, as Olson was to put it, "redefined the Real." Having been lured by the Greeks into believing that reality was made of "substance" that possessed "properties" and was passively subject to "causes" of which it became the "effect," we became epistemologically and linguistically estranged from the immediate experience of things. We were, Olson believed, imprisoned in an artificial "universe of discourse" that the very syntax and grammar of our language seemed to validate.

Riemann, in particular, showed how man could regain his world by developing an alternative to the rigid Euclidean way of regarding the universe. Riemann, Olson explains, "distinguished two kinds of manifold, the discrete (which would be the old system, and it includes discourse, language as it had been since Socrates) and, what he took to be more true, the continuous." The "continuous" conception of reality exposed the Greek "error on matter" by presenting a world characterized by process and change rather than inert substance and properties. Thanks to the non-Euclideans, the world had been liberated from its Greek stranglehold. Man was no longer estranged. "Nothing was now inert fact," Olson chortled,

> all things were there for feeling, to promote it, and be felt; and man, in the midst of it . . . was suddenly possessed or repossessed of a character of being, a thing among things, which I shall call his physicality. It made a re-entry of or to the universe. Reality was without interruption, and we are still in the business of finding out how all action, and thought, have to be refounded.

The poem **"La Torre"** vividly pictures what re-entry to the universe really means by characterizing it as a liberation from a prison of Hellenism. The tower itself is constructed of Greek epistemological presuppositions in which "the head" and the "the hands" are established as distinctions that separate man from the universe surrounding his stony bastion. He is defined as a rational animal (the head) and a maker (the hands). By virtue of these superior attributes he manipulates Nature for his purposes and exiles himself from Her. His tower is testament to his denial that he is a "thing among things." It is Hellenism itself and it effectively dramatizes how Greek tradition has "estranged us from that with which we are most familiar."

But the tower is also language. It is a Babel of architectural rigidity that blocks out light. Its destruction necessitates a grammatical reconstruction:

> To begin again, Lightning
> is an axe, transfer
> of force subject to object is
> order: destroy!

Olson's phrasings here are virtually lifted from Fenollosa's *The Chinese Written Character as a Medium for Poetry*," and that essay's attack on the artificiality of "the sentence" as a "complete thought" helps us to appreciate the full measure of Olson's call for a linguistic "re-entry to the universe." Fenollosa's position is simple. "Nature herself has no grammar," he argues, and so the classical grammarians' definition of the sentence as "a complete thought" or as a construction "uniting subject and predicate" is simply at odds with reality. There is no completeness in Nature and therefore there should be no completeness

in the sentence. The notion of subject and predicate forces an unnatural subjectivity onto man's relationship with his universe. The sentence requires that he view himself as an "I" that does something to an "it." Thus, concludes Fenollosa, "The sentence . . . is not an attribute of nature but an accident of man as a conversational animal."

In place of the syntactically defined sentence Fenollosa would have a *"transference of power . . . a flash of lightning."* In other words, the sentence is not grammar; it is power.

The destruction of the tower means the destruction of the sentence, but it also has a physical effect on man. It causes his "jaws to grind" and his nostrils [to] flare / to let the breath in." A linguistic complement to "discourse" enters—speech. What had been in the tower a "universe of discourse" now becomes a language that accommodates both "discourse" *and* speech. **"La Torre"** poetically renders what Olson argues in the "Human Universe":

> We have lived long in a generalizing time, at least since 450 B.C., And it has had its effects on the best of men, on the best of things. Logos, or discourse, for example, has, in that time, so worked its abstractions into our concept and use of language that language's other function, speech,seems . . . in need of restoration.

Speech is the linguistic mode of physicality, just as "discourse" is the mode of the mind. When breath links them together, a new epistemological foundation for man results. He is no longer locked in a tower to which his five senses condemn him; he now experiences an openness to the world that his body affords him. "Physicality," we recall, is a bodily "depth sensibility" that is tantamount to what Olson's favorite metaphysician, Alfred North Whitehead, calls "causal efficacy." The essence of the idea is that the body, as distinct from the five senses, is itself an epistemological instrument. It "feels" reality in addition to the sense perceptions that the five sense supply. Olson's recurring stress on the vital importance of breath stems from a conviction that breath liberates the "self" from its traditional seat in the mind and reestablishes it in its proper place—the body. Thus, our knowledge of the world and our expression of that knowledge through speech comes from inside us. "One's life," says Olson, "is informed from and by one's own literal body, . . . the intermediary, the intervening thing, the interruptor, the resistor. The self."

The fall of the tower naturally precipitates a sense of vulnerability, for

> Where there are no walls
> there are no laws, forms, sounds, odors
> to grab hold of

It takes a while to adjust to freedom and accept the challenge that Olson poses in this poem and in the "Human Universe" as well:

> We stay unaware how two means of discourse the Greeks appear to have invented hugely intermit our

participation in our experience, and so prevent discovery. They are what followed from Socrates' readiness to generalize, his willingness . . . to make a "universe" out of discourse instead of letting it rest in its most serviceable place. (It is not sufficiently observed that logos, and the reason necessary to it, are only a stage which a man must master and not what they are taken to be, final discipline. Beyond them is direct perception and the contraries which dispose of argument. The harmony of the universe, and I include man, is not logical, or better, is post-logical, as is the order of any created thing.) With Aristotle, the two great means appear: logic and classification. And it is they that have so fastened themselves on habits of thought that action is interfered with, absolutely interfered with, I should say.

The toppling of the walls (and with them "laws, forms, sounds, odors") literally creates an open space where "FORM IS NEVER MORE THAN AN EXTENSION OF CONTENT."

> Let the tower fall!
> Where space is born
> man has a beach to ground on

The overriding intent of **"La Torre,"** then, is to celebrate man's reconciliation with his immediate experience—to end his estrangement from "that with which he is most familiar." To accomplish the reconciliation, Olson believed that "particularism has to be fought for anew" and **"La Torre"** demonstrates the strategy vividly:

> We have taken too little note of this:
> the sound of a hammer on a nail can be as clear as
> the blood a knife can make spurt from a round taut
>   belly

These pure, immediate acts that the passage documents— creation, ritual and death—are particulars that must be fought for with weapons that are not likely to be found in the tower. Different tools and materials are required, and as Olson has us stand grounded on the beach he directs our attention out to the sea where

> rafts come towards us lashed of wreckage and
>   young
>   tree.
> They bring the quarried stuff we need to try this
>   new
>   found strength.
> It will take a new stone, new tufa, to finish off this
>   rising tower.

The "new tufa" of which the new tower will be made will be the stone of the Mayan glyphs that so excited Olson's imagination in Campeche—glyphs that on their "very face" are "verse" with the signs "so clearly and densely chosen that, cut in stone, they retain the power of the objects of which they are images."

Particularism and *physicality* are just two of the terms that Olson uses to suggest the configuration of the new tower. *Topos, place, objectism, complementarity,* and, of course, *projective* all address that stance which Olson insists will return man's universe to him and render him once again privy to the "secrets objects share." The perspective from the old tower sees this as illiteracy; after all, denizens of the old tower are accustomed to a discrete rather than a continuous world. They prefer their discourse to be representational and mimetic and therefore invariably "referential to reality." The grammar of literacy, as Olson sees it, fails because it is merely *about* experience. The grammar of illiteracy succeeds because it is *of* it. "If anybody wants forever never to enjoy language," Olson once counseled (resolutely practicing what he preached), "they will remember grammar as it was taught from those abhorrent Alexandrians down to probably every poor school kid right now."

But in a very practical sense, what is it about Alexandrian grammar and the "universe of discourse" that is so abhorrent to Olson? Has not its generalizing capability, in spite of its subversion of the "familiar," actually served both western science and humanism rather handsomely since Aristotle? Does it really make any practical difference if a disparity exists between language and the ontology that underlies it? If man's thoughts, feelings and commands are reasonably well served by "discourse"—if our language "works"—is it not impractical, no matter what theoretical sense it might make, to "refound" it upon another basis?

Olson's reply would be that "discourse" has nothing to do with humanism; in fact, it is humanism's antithesis. Not only does it estrange man from that which is most familiar, it creates a new universe in which he has no part. It accords science, for instance, an autonomous, humanly *un*related existence, ignoring the fact that reality is never more than "as much nature as man is engaged with." In other words, "discourse" artificially inflates reality by extending it beyond human limits, and for this reason Olson vigorously contends that Art is a much superior epistemological tool than Science:

> The flopping around, in whatever order, of the galaxies and that infinite out beyond, now that it's home, in light, and signals and mass points are the best narration physics can manage. Men say Hoogh to that Honey. . . . This is no knowledge superior to an arts action when it is superior.

What he means is that once we acknowledge that we live in a "human universe" with boundaries set in terms of "as much nature as man is engaged with," then Art is a more appropriate tool than Science simply because it respects the built-in limits of humanism—that it is human. The seat of reality is in the human physiology:

> It's a matter of where the music and the color and the words are. They are in the body and the motion and that's where they and the real become one, in the passings and intersections of a physicality which talks and runs and wears what it does.

Illiteracy, or to use its more respectable name, the "projective," is no mere peevish kicking of syntax in the teeth to spite Aristotle; it is a humanist attempt to subvert the inhuman rigidities and inflations of reality that lie embedded in classical "humanism" itself. The specific rigidities and inflations it seeks to purge are: forms, classes, ideals, conventions, similes, symbols, allegories, comparisons, and descriptions—all things, in short, that betray "particularism" by remaining *referential* rather than *of* reality. Again, "FORM IS NEVER MORE THAN AN EXTENSION OF CONTENT."

"Projective Verse," which first appeared in *Poetry New York* in 1950, was Olson's first public defense of the grammar of illiteracy. This essay was probably what Hugh Kenner had in mind when he observed that "if Olson's expositions seem messy, it is because they are less composed than talked about." In a broad sense, the grammar of illiteracy is the grammar of talk, and "Projective Verse" is Olson talking—talking rapid-fire, urgently, and with more concern for the act of his *own* engagement with his material than with his comprehensibility to a general audience. It is full of "difficulties" and "proper confusions" that are not limited to the infamous violations of "correct usage and form" that Olson's critics wince at with regularity. The essay *assumes* rather than creates its context. The uninitiated reader feels as though he is entering an ongoing conversation late after the terminology has been established and the issues already defined. A blurb on Olson's style from *The Floating Bear* says it all: "Solid, declamatory prose, though he, like Pound, expects you to know his subject as well as he does. Many times like notes to himself, you are infuriated that you don't know what he's talking about because you didn't read a certain book."

Olson's enormous and diverse reading, combined with the fact that he "reads to write," virtually assures many bewildered and infuriated critics. With little contextual assistance from Olson, and thus thrown on their own resources, these critics understandably assume their own contexts for "Projective Verse," which are usually much, much narrower than Olson's, and which inevitably confine his dogmas exclusively to the Pound-Williams objectivist axis. The result is usually a plausible critique of a misleadingly "reduced" Olson.

Some examples: "What Olson's notion of 'open' verse does is simply to provide creative irresponsibility with the semblance of a rationale which may be defended in heated and cloudy terms by its supposed practitioners" (James Dickey); "'Projective Verse,' . . . though it has been very influential, it would not be unfair to describe as the worst prose published since *Democratic Vistas*. . . . 'Put down anything so long as you keep writing' would be a fair enough paraphrase" (Thom Gunn); "Olson consistently insinuates . . . that his theory of poetry is revolutionary. Yet his main deviation from the Pound-Williams aesthetic is that he muddles their concepts" (Marjorie Perloff). On the other hand, Williams himself wrote to Robert Creeley after reading the essay, "I share your

excitement, it is as if the whole area lifted. It's the sort of thing we are after and must have."

The problem is that Olson regarded "Projective Verse" as merely the literary tip of a metaphysical iceberg. His detractors tended to see it as an autonomous poetics. Consequently, Olson's dogmas, some new, many borrowed, seem derivative rather than revolutionary when they are extracted from their larger context. Consider dogma one, for example:

> (1) the *kinetics* of the thing. A poem is energy transferred from where the poet got it . . . by way of the poem itself to . . . the reader. . . . Then the poem itself must, at all points, be a high energy-construct and, at all points, an energy-discharge.

Certainly this is little more than Fenollosa's concept of the sentence as a "transference of power" applied to verse. Defining the poem as an "energy-construct" is hardly innovative either; Williams and Pound had been saying as much for years. But the intensity with which Olson urges the perhaps tired dogma overwhelms an important qualification that follows it and that at least suggests a philosophical depth to Olson's version relatively absent in Pound and Williams:

> From the moment he ventures into FIELD COMPOSITION—puts himself in the open—he can go by no track other than the one the poem under hand declares, for itself. Thus he has to behave, and be, instant by instant, aware of some several forces just now beginning to be examined.

This is less poetics than epistemological position and when it is viewed against the context of Olson's complete "stance towards reality," it reveals inchoate hints of the influence of Whitehead, Jung, and even Merleau-Ponty to come. In other words, the dogma can be seen as merely the poetic facet of the larger philosophy of obedience that so significantly informs Olson's work as a whole.

Dogma number two similarly emerges from an underlying epistemology:

> (2) . . . the *principle*, . . . FORM IS NEVER MORE THAN AN EXTENSION OF CONTENT

As a principle of poetics, this statement yields little more than the commonplace notion that subject matter should be allowed to discover its own natural form, but again, from the perspective of Olson's comprehensive stance, it involves the status of a man (be he poet or not) in relation to his environment. Man should resist imposing his forms egotistically upon Nature as a matter of perceptual propriety. The very urge to impose form upon Nature creates "lyrical interference" both in poetry and life.

Dogma three reads:

> (3) the *process* of the thing, how the principle can be made *so* to shape the energies that the form is

accomplished. . . . ONE PERCEPTION MUST IMMEDIATELY AND DIRECTLY LEAD TO A FURTHER PERCEPTION.

Here we see once again the poetical application of an ontological truth. If reality, as Riemann and Olson both believed, is a continuous rather than a discrete manifold, the expression of that reality accordingly should be continuous and not discrete. Thus the dogma proposes a poetic process consonant with the natural process of the universe. Olson's notion here is somewhat less naive than Thom Gunn's characterization of it: "Put down anything so long as you keep writing."

The genuine originality of "Projective Verse" cannot be appreciated from the dogmas, which, like gaudy blossoms, inevitably steal the show, but must be savored at the roots that lie deep in the soil of an alternative humanism. In "Projective Verse" this alternative humanism is dubbed "objectism." Olson is obviously nervous about that term and goes to some lengths (vainly, as it turns out) to distinguish it from the "objectivism" of Pound and Williams. He defines it as

> a word to be taken to stand for the kind of relation of man to experience which a poet might state as the necessity of a line or a work to be as wood is, to be as clean as wood is as it issues from the hand of nature, to be as shaped as wood can be when a man has had his hand to it. Objectism is the getting rid of the lyrical interference of the individual as ego, of the "subject" and his soul, that peculiar presumption by which western man has interposed himself between what he is as a creature of nature (with certain instructions to carry out) and those other creations of nature which we may, with no derogation, call objects. For a man is himself an object, whatever he may take to be his advantages, particularly at that moment that he achieves an humilitas sufficient to make him of use.

That this definition can be taken as "merely Pound's 'objectivism'" in not very new dress, as Marjorie Perloff does, is a good example of how easy it is for the parochial literary mind to bend all to its own presuppositions. Perloff backs up her assertion with Pound's famous remark from "Retrospect": "I believe that the proper and perfect symbol is the natural object, that if a man use 'symbols' he must use them so that their symbolic function does not obtrude." Undoubtedly, Olson's analogy of poetic creation to wood draws Perloff's charge, but the fact is that Olson isn't talking about symbols here nor is he even talking about perception; he is simply once again outlining that epistemological posture that he ubiquitously calls the proper "stance towards reality." "It comes to this," he continues,

> the use of a man, by himself and thus by others, lies in how he conceives his relation to nature, that force to which he owes his somewhat small existence. If he sprawl, he shall find little to sing but himself, . . . But if he stays inside himself, if he is contained within his nature as he is participant in the larger force, he will be able to listen, and his hearing through himself will give him secrets objects share.

In a letter to Creeley, he comes at "objectism" from a slightly different but more succinct direction:

> man as object in field of force declaring self as force because is force in exactly such relation & can accomplish expression of self as force by conjecture, & displacement in a context best, now, seen as space more than a time such:

> which I take it, is precise contrary to, what we have had, as "humanism," with, man, out of all proportion of, relations, thus, so mis-centered, becomes, dependent on, only, a whole series of "human" references which, so made, make only anthropomorphism, and thus, make a mush of, *any* reality, conspicuously, his own, not to speak of, how all other forces (ticks, water-lilies, or snails) become only descriptive objects.

Obviously "objectism" is no mere literary bias; it is a way of life. It is *humilitas*, a rejection of the "Egotistical Sublime," a denial of the subject-object predication of Alexandrian grammar and Western epistemology, a "contrary Renaissance," and a useful creative attitude. Why useful? Because when it is employed as "the artist's act in the larger field of objects, [it] leads to dimensions larger than the man."

Those dogmatic blossoms of "Projective Verse" (the "*kinetics* . . . the *principle* . . . the *process* of the thing") are vulnerable to the worst kind of *reductio ad ordinarium* when they are lopped from the plant that nourishes them. The same is true of other corollary points. Olson's comments on "breath," for example: "the line comes (I swear it) from the breath, from the breathing of the man who writes, at the moment he writes . . . for only he, the man who writes, can declare, at every moment, the line, its metric and its ending where its breathing shall come to termination."

A poem that is act itself, not thought about act, is beholden to that authority that issues through the breath from where "all act springs"; that is, the physiology of the poet. Lest one think this a mere "heated and cloudy" theory rather than practical methodology, note the results of the experiments of Marcia and Philip Lieberman. The Liebermans compared the "breath-grouping" of Olson's reading of his own poems with those of Keats. They discovered that the distinctiveness of Olson's poems was that they used "breath-groups to delimit and emphasize lines in violation of grammatical restraints." In the Keats poems, on the other hand, breath-groups tended to play a "syntactical role." In total fidelity to his assertions in "Projective Verse," Olson seems to permit the rival delimiting authorities, syntax and breath, to coexist in his poems, which has the effect of breaking down the rigid tyranny of the "logical" sentence and allowing an expansive breath-group flexibility continually to offer interpretive alternatives. In other words, the Liebermans empirically demonstrate that Olson's own poetry in fact does restore "speech-force" to the language. Breath demonstrably "rights the balance" by asserting its partnership with syntax. Commenting upon their findings from an oral reading of **"Maximus, at the**

Harbor," they ask that we "note that the logical—that is, syntactical—function of the breath-group is still manifested in this reading, even though individual lines are then set apart by individual breath-groups. The disturbance of the listener's expectations that occurs when a breath-group terminates a line in violation of syntactic constraints gives emphasis to the line. The listener has to attend more closely to the line to reach a semantic interpretation."

The "projective" poet, Olson maintained, was one who "manages to register both the acquisitions of his ear *and* the pressures of his breath." In terms of his "stance toward reality," this complementarity of breath and ear is the poetic counterpart to the principle of "physicality," that is, bodily depth sensibility, the notion of the "body-subject." The ear, Olson insists, "is so close to the mind that it is the mind's," just as the breath is so obviously of the body. From the "union of the mind and the ear . . . the syllable is born," Olson tells us, and accordingly, "the line comes (I swear it) from the breath." The poem therefore becomes the uniting act of mind and body achieved through the creative coalition of ear and breath as they spontaneously merge syllable into line. Hence, Olson's much-maligned formula:

> the HEAD, by way of the EAR, to the SYLLABLE
> the HEART, by way of the BREATH, to the LINE

Breath, as Olson means it, then, is the instrument of the larger stance towards reality that he has identified as "physicality," but it also serves as means for restoring "speech" to discourse: "breath allows *all* the speech-force of language back in (speech is the 'solid' of verse, is the secret of the poem's energy), because, now, a poem has, by speech, solidity, everything in it can be treated as solids, objects, things." Breath reifies experience by creating an awareness of bodily "depth sensibility" that assures its being felt in addition to its being observed, but it also, Olson claims, reifies the elements of verse. This certainly sounds like standard Objectivist logic: "No ideas but in things" (Williams); "The World must be measured by the eye" (Stevens); "the rock crystal thing" (Marianne Moore); but the difference in Olson's "objectism" is breath. Breath shifts the basis of objectivist reification from perception to physical "depth sensibility" and this is why Olson insists that his position be called "objectism." "Objectism" is no perceptual attitude toward things; it is a comprehensive stance that man assumes toward the world that deliberately humiliates his epistemological status by insisting that he be merely a "thing among things." It is, Olson explains, "the getting rid of the lyrical interference of the individual as ego, of the 'subject' and his soul, that peculiar presumption by which western man has interposed himself between what he is as a creature of nature and those other creations of nature which we may with no derogation, call objects."

In a very real sense, then, breath liberates the self from the mind (or soul) and places it physically in the body so that our knowing of the world, our experience and discovery, comes from "inside us/ & at the same time does

not feel literally identical with our own physical or mortal self." In other words, "one's life is informed from and by one's own literal body, . . . the intermediary, the intervening thing, the interruptor, the resistor. The self."

From the point of view of one who considers the poet a "maker" or craftsman of "discrete" poems that thereupon become available for analysis, interpretation, and criticism, projective verse will inevitably seem perverse, for it rejects the overt manipulation of reality that such words as "craft" and "art" imply. Fealty to the real is the overriding criterion. Time and again, Olson and his disciples allude to Werner Heisenberg's "uncertainty principle" as a kind of scientific rationale for avoiding artifice, pointing out that just as the instruments of observation in physics distort the reality of the observed phenomenon (we must "freeze" mass to weigh it, and mass is actually never in repose), so in verse the intrusion of literary "devices" artifically stops the ongoing process of "continuous" reality. In short, the "projective" mode asks the poet to assume an attitude of passive obedience to the inner and outer experiences that he registers.

Perhaps the greatest burden of patience falls on the readers of projective literature, for they, even more than the projective writer (who at least has the guidance of his own experiences to assist him) are truly "naked" in the open field. They are advised that a projective poem is a reen-actment rather than an artifact and that they should concern themselves with absorbing the energies (rather than substance) that are "held" in a kind of dynamic tension within the field of the poem. The images of the poem, by virtue of the solidity that breath gives them, are allowed the free play of their individual energies, they are advised, even while, through juxtaposition with other images, they create an energy field. The character of the engagement that readers are expected to have is radically different from what they are accustomed to. They are asked to "avoid all irritable reaching after fact and reason" and to remain "in the absolute condition of present things,"—that is, in the poem itself.

And yet, is this projective nakedness in the open field, this remaining "in the absolute condition of present things" all that unfamiliar? So many times Olson's art is characterized as mere conversation—Olson talking—and there is more than just a ring of truth to such observations. Talk *is* the template of Olson's style and it is talk that links his style to its underlying ontology. Talk, as opposed to frozen discourse, is spontaneous, ongoing, irreversible, verbal act. The flexibility of conversational talk—its toleration of inconsistencies and logical imprecision—makes it an effective net for gathering particulars even though this advantage may be bought at the expense of vagueness. But what of vagueness? Must it necessarily be a liability? May it not in fact be the only possible mode of expressing "direct perception and the contraries that dispose of argument" that, Olson insists, are "post-logical" and beyond "the irritable reaching after fact and reason"?

Interestingly, the structure of nonwestern languages bears striking resemblance to English informal conversation. By way of accounting for a pervasive, annoying vagueness in the work of the Chinese philosopher Mencius he was attempting to translate, I. A. Richards was struck by how similar that "vagueness" seemed to

> the successive attempts that a speaker will sometimes make to convey a thought which does not fit any ready formulation. He may intimate as he switches (with an "or rather" or a "perhaps I ought to say") over from one statement to another, that he is "developing" his thought. Those with a taste for clear, precise views (itself a result of special training) will accuse him of not knowing what he wants to say, or of having really no thought yet to utter. But there is another possibility— that a thought is present whose structure and content are not suited to available formulations, that these successive, perhaps incompatible, statements partly represent, partly misrepresent, an idea independent of them which none the less has its own order and coherent reference.

Is what Richards describes really much different from projective "open" form? Both are unusually supple modes that are immediately reflexive to the "condition of present things." Both function admirably "in uncertainties, Mysteries, doubts, without any irritable reaching after fact and reason." Can it be that the aggravation some feel toward projective verse is simply that it embarrasses them with the fact that our most meaningful experiences occur not in lofty elegies, majestic odes or symmetrical sonnets but in the halting, inconsistent, difficulties and proper confusions of you and I in urgent talk.

Can we, though, seriously regard "you and I in urgent talk" as Art? What happens in talk? Is it a mimetic activity? Does it hold up a mirror to Nature, as Plato insisted Art does? Or, if that claim seems irrelevant, can we hold that talk "improves" on Nature, idealizes it? Obviously, none of the classical approaches touch even near the actuality of Olson's enterprises, for they are mesmerized by the metaphor of artist-as-maker and Art as the-object-made. Talk, however, is an activity, a process, an event. True, it can be notated on a printed page, but its essential value is its movement. Its shifts, its false starts, its indecisions, its non sequiturs—Olson's intensified stammerings, juxtaposings, indirect guesses—these are participatory events that rise to Art when, through heightened intensity and sense of collective experience, they become the requickening of a previous or anticipated emotion through rite, what the Greeks called *dromenon*, "the thing done."

It is the "doing," the acting, that sets the value to Olson's "talk." As Olson's favorite mythologist, Jane Harrison, explains it,

> The Greeks had realized that to perform a rite you must *do* something, that is, you must not only feel something but express it in action, or, to put it psychologically, you must not only receive an impulse, you must react to it.

This kind of "doing" applies not only to the poet but to the reader as well. Talk is a social, collective activity. We may only nod our head occasionally, widen our eyes in surprise, grimace in exasperation or simply sigh, but we are called upon to "do," to react, to engage our energies with those of the poem in urgent conversation.

One final dimension of Olson's "illiteracy" ought to be savored if for no other reason than to appreciate how comprehensively the poet applies and translates his notion of the projective to the whole front of reality. It is his willingness to expose writing to the same ontological challenge that has faced mathematics and physics—that is, how to make it "Equal, That Is, to the Real Itself."

That last phrase is the title of Olson's important review-essay of Milton Stern's *The Fine Hammered Steel of Herman Melville* in which Olson spells out in remarkable detail, although in the confusing technical jargon of space-age physics, how he regards projective writing as an inevitable consequence of the same non-Euclidean "redefinition of the Real" that gave birth to relativity theory, quantum physics, and the whole conception of a continuous, as opposed to a classically discrete, universe. This new ontological premise excited Olson because he saw it as a reaffirmation of Heraclitus's view of reality: "All things flow."

"Equal, That Is, to the Real Itself" is a difficult essay partly because so much of it is eclectically wrenched from an unacknowledged source text, Hermann Weyl's *The Philosophy of Mathematics and Natural Science,* and partly because it undertakes to talk of fundamental literary problems in an unfamiliar idiom and from an unfamiliar perspective. Still, it affords perhaps the most mature, most sophisticated rendering of the "stance towards reality" and its impact upon "literacy" that Olson leaves us. The essential argument is that adjustments have to be made to the way in which we "know and present the real" (writing) in order for it to "equal" a continuous rather than a discrete reality. The first obstacle to effecting these adjustments is the "error on matter" that previously was the means by which "one can avoid the real." In a discrete universe the norm for evaluating experience is inert matter. Things are regarded as constant and autonomous, sufficiently so that they are perceived as "substance" that possesses classifiable "qualities." In a continuous universe, however, time, as a fourth dimension, forces us to perceive things no longer as inert "substances," but as "events"— "All things flow." Consequently, projective writing characteristically eschews "qualities" (it is rarely descriptive) and stresses instead the intensive "quantities" of things; that is, their "velocity, force and field strength" within the continuous manifold.

An apt metaphor for such a continuous reality is the electromagnetic field in which interrelated transformations of energy points take place. In such a field discrete formulations, such as subject-object, cause-effect, and even mind-body, give way to the notion of flexible interplay between "things among things." Indeed, Olson eventually underscores this "field" assumption at the end of his essay by a quotation from the mathematician Bernard Riemann, which he assesses as the most "relevant single fact to the experience of *Moby-Dick* and its writer":

The inertial structure of the world is a real thing which not only exerts effects upon matter but in turn suffers such effects.

What Riemann documents here is a shift from the mechanical view of the world's processes to an organic one. If the world's structure is "give-and-take"—both exerting and suffering effects—this means that matter itself can no longer be considered inflexibly inert; it too gives and takes. The old Euclidean view of a reality in which inert particles of matter are passively pushed about by arbitrary forces is replaced by the more appropriate notion of fluid interplay. Once again, "All things flow."

But perhaps the most important adjustment projective writing strives for has to do with measurement, for "art is measure." Olson quotes Riemann's corollary to the previous statement on the inertial structure of the world, showing how it affects measurement as well:

> . . . the metrical structure of the world is so intimately connected to the inertial structure that the metrical field . . . will of necessity become flexible . . . the moment the inertial field itself is flexible.

Euclidean measuring techniques are obsolete in a continuous reality because they depend upon the assumption that rigid bodies can move freely in space in order to determine congruence. "What is measure," Olson asks, "when the universe flips and no part is discrete from another part except by the flow of creation itself, in and out, intensive where before it seemed qualitative?" The constant transformations of the continuum cannot be artificially halted to accommodate a yardstick. Reality, Olson concludes, is "a pumping of the real so constant art had to invent measure anew."

Of course the problem of a new measurement was not merely art's, but the problem of all mathematics and science. The unassailable organic integrity of sheer process, which characterizes the continuous manifold, is simply inaccessible to "additive" measurement. As Riemann himself puts it, "for a discrete manifold the principle of measurement is already contained in the concept of this manifold, but for a continuous one it must come from elsewhere."

The "elsewhere" for Olson was "the new world of atomism" that, he claimed, "offered a metrical means as well as a topos different from the discrete." That means was "congruence," but not the congruence "which had been the measure of space a solid fills in two of its positions" (Euclidean congruence), but a "point-by-point mapping power of such flexibility that anything which stays the same, no matter where it goes and into whatever varying conditions (it can suffer deformation), it can be followed, and, if it is art, led." This non-Euclidean (topological) definition of congruence made it possible to effect the measurement of things in motion, things undergoing the normal transformations characteristic of the continuous manifold. It demanded no reference to metrical absolutes "outside" the continuum or, for that matter, outside the thing itself.

Instead of depending upon a principle of free mobility of rigid bodies in space, topological congruence concerned itself with "automorphic transformations," that is, a "one-to-one mapping $p \rightarrow p'$ of the point field into itself which leaves the basic relations undisturbed." In short, what determines congruence is not similarity of metrical lengths but simple connectedness. The object in the process of transformation within the continuous manifold carries its own congruency standard with it; its point field can be mapped continuously and will always maintain the single invariance of connectedness so long as it does not violate the continuum. As one topologist describes the rules of this form of congruence,

> Arbitrary deformations of curves, surfaces and figures are allowed as long as connectivity is maintained. Therefore, distortion, bending, battering, etc., is allowed, but tearing, cutting, breaking, joining or sticking together, welding, cementing, disregarding of holes, etc., is forbidden. In this type of geometry square and circle, cuboid and sphere are equivalent. [H. Graham Flogg, *From Geometry to Topology,* English Universities Press, 1974].

All fine and good. But how does all this affect the projective mode? "Taking it in towards writing," Olson explains,

> the discrete, for example, wasn't any longer a good enough base for discourse: classification was exposed as mere taxonomy; and logic (and the sentence poised on it, a completed thought, instead of what it has become, an exchange of force) was as loose and inaccurate a system as the body and soul had been, divided from each other and rattling, sticks in a stiff box.

Classification, logic, separation of body and soul, and the "complete" sentence are rejected from the projective on the basis of their ontological inconsistency with *continuous* reality; each, in its way, interrupts the connectedness of the transformational process of the field.

Olson calls such interruptions of connectedness "discontinuous jumps." In writing these jumps take the form of allegories, symbols, comparisons and all other devices that take us out of the continuum altogether or disturb our equality with it. Citing the prose in *Moby-Dick* as an example, Olson points out that Melville

> was not tempted . . . to inflate the physical: take the model for the house, the house for the model, . . . using such sets as the mirror image. . . . he was essentially incapable of either allegory or symbol for the best of congruent reason, mirror and model are each figures in Euclidean space, and they are *not* congruent.

Mirror and model (allegory and symbol) are *not* automorphic mappings of their originals; therefore, they violate the topological invariance of connectedness. They are "tears" or "cuts" in the narrative continuum. But more than that, they also violate the epistemological stance that "objectism" dictates by promoting, rather than suppressing, the "lyrical interference of the ego." For example, Melville, according to Olson, "couldn't abuse object as symbol does by depreciating it in favor of subject. Or let image lose its relational force by transferring its occurrence as allegory does. He was already aware of the complementarity of each of two pairs of how we know and present the real—image & object, and action & subject." By forcing a subjective significance on images and objects, symbol and allegory demean their "self-incidence" and artificially elevate the human ego to an uncomely status above other objects.

The grammar of illiteracy, then, is really the grammar of life—life in all its ongoing continuity and unremitting process. It is a grammar that forbids "sprawl," forbids existence outside the "human universe." But for all that, it is a grammar committed to man's physical being, dictated by the heart's "pumping" of the real and, most of all, by the breath that has its beginning in that place from where "all act springs."

David Kellogg   (essay date 1991)

SOURCE: "Body Poetics, Body Politics: The Birth of Charles Olson's Dynamic," in *Sagetrieb,* Vol. 10, No. 3, Winter, 1991, pp. 63-82.

[*In the following essay, Kellogg examines Olson's shorter poems in light of the poet's own principles of direct experiential knowledge.*]

> It's going to be somebody else's business to say, see, hear, eventually, what's been done.
>
> -Charles Olson to Robert Creeley

Twenty years after his death, Charles Olson's 1950 statement to Robert Creeley still applies as much to the content of Olson's writing, a great deal of which remains unpublished or only narrowly available, as to questions of meaning or interpretation. If, as there is reason to believe, Olson's writing significantly challenges our conceptions of meaning in the first place, we may be tempted to wait until the drama of textual recovery is complete before attempting thoroughly to revaluate Olson's contribution to contemporary poetry and poetics. However, with the death of Olson's heroic editor George Butterick we have reached an impasse, and who will pick up the torch is unclear. Furthermore, recent publication of the *Collected Poems* (one of Butterick's last and most important editorial accomplishments) presents a less somber reason to pause and consider Olson's achievement. Unencumbered by the large architecture of *The Maximus Poems*, Olson's shorter poetry allows more direct access to his poetic than does the *Maximus* sequence, thus providing an interesting point of departure.

In this essay I would like both to examine the dynamic of some of Olson's short poems, particularly as a way of revising often rather simplistic discussions of his poetic,

and to consider this poetic asa critique of Western metaphysics. While there is not space fully to examine the implications of this critique, I find that Olson's poetic has significant affinities with recent philosophical discussions of the role of the body in, as one writer has put it, "the making and unmaking of the world" (Scarry); mapping some of these affinities may allow us to rethink the radical nature of Olson's poetic theory and practice. Indeed, it may be that Olson's work comes to us as part of a larger, and ongoing, reconsideration of the role of the body in knowledge and human creation. By understanding one, we contribute to our knowledge of the other.

Olson's poetry stands at the border, or perhaps the rupture, between what are somewhat misleadingly termed modernism and postmodernism, terms which, in discussions of English-language poetry at least, often revolve around the figure of Ezra Pound. Olson freely admitted in his 1950 essay-manifesto "Projective Verse" to being one of the "sons of Pound and [William Carlos] Williams"; [*Selected Writings*]; to that degree, Olson might be viewed as carrying on the imagist, vorticist, or objectivist traditions they began. In his emphasis on speech, in his use of free verse and "unpoetic" language, indeed in his very idiom, Olson obviously has strong affiliations with Pound and Williams. He is distinctly *not* of the Eliotic school, in spite of his New England education. As his poem "ABCs" puts it:

> The word
> is image, and the reverend reverse is
> Eliot
>
> Pound
> is verse
>
> [*Collected Poems*]

Clearly, and as many (Olson not least of these) have remarked, Olson learned much from Pound.

Yet this attribution is misleading, for Olson's differences from his masters outweigh his affinities. Influence is a difficult beast to track; while Olson's *idiom,* especially in his early writings, sprang directly or indirectly out of the imagist mode, his thinking was always his own. Olson came to poetry late, many of his views already formed; his "influences" were wide-ranging: Melville, Whitehead, the Gloucester community, F. D. R. Though it is helpful to place Olson in a Poundian line, his differences from Pound are greater than many of Olson's proponents, to say nothing of his detractors, would allow. Hugh Kenner, for instance, in *A Homemade World,* finds Olson interesting only insofar as he carries on the Poundian tradition; his low appraisal of the later Olson suffers from a narrow Poundocentric orthodoxy that refuses to take Olson on his own terms. Thus, Olson's radicalism gets dismissed as bluff.

Indeed, in spite of surface similarities, Olson's verse flies in the face of the simplicity and clarity we associate with Imagism, and the observer or speaker of Olson's poems is regularly implicated in the act of observation in a way that an Objectivist poet like Louis Zukofsky would find both careless and alarming. Olson's abstraction, as well as his interrogation of referentiality, also distance him from both Imagism and Objectivism. The confusion must lie partly with Olson himself, whose term *objectism* too easily slides into objectivism, and whose comments on technique often overplay the role of Pound. Still, more than idiom or technique are at stake here, as Olson knew full well: "the projective involves a stance toward reality outside a poem as well as a new stance towards the reality of a poem itself" [*Selected Writings*]. It is this stance which I would like to examine here, especially as it relates to the concept of reference.

Even a short survey of scholars reveals that the question of Olson and reference is by no means resolved. Robert von Hallberg, for example, in his book on Olson's poetics, claims that Olson's "is first of all a referential poetics," and criticizes Olson accordingly, in a disparaging comparison with Pound:

> What makes Olson different from Pound in his handling of such material is his willingness to make—actually, his frequent insistence on making—his point directly and explicitly, only too often at the expense of flat and uninteresting language.

It is unclear whether von Hallberg means by this that Pound is never explicit, or for that matter never flat and uninteresting; perhaps he never read the Adams Cantos. In any case, as we shall see, Olson's revisions of Pound are at once more radical and more interesting than von Hallberg knows.

Thomas F. Merrill, on the other end of the spectrum, claims rather broadly regarding Olson's poetic:

> [S]uch constructions of the ego as metaphysical systems, logic, classification, abstractions, ideal forms, symbols, similes, allegory, comparison—all that is *referential* to reality rather than *of* it—must be purged.

While Merrill grasps much of Olson's poetic, his obliteration of the concept of reference in a single sentence is as striking as von Hallberg's pithy affirmation of it, not least because Merrill admits such "constructions of the ego" into his own dissection of Olson's poems. Obviously the question of reference has to be reassessed, and we might well begin by moving beyond the Romantic paradigm of mirror v. lamp proposed by M. H. Abrams, a paradigm which hamstrings both von Hallberg and Merrill. Abrams's formulation attempts to account for the "radical difference between the characteristic points of view of neoclassic and romantic criticism," and his models for these—the mimetic mirror and the expressive lamp—have had enormous impact upon subsequent readers, including von Hallberg and Merrill. Both of these critics, caught in a vocabulary which distinguishes only between a poetry of mimesis and a poetry of expression, find themselves unable fully to account for Olson's procedure, one of the major achievements of which is its interrogation of those distinctions themselves. For the mirror/lamp paradigm

assumes an easy separation of subject and object, of self and world, that Olson repeatedly calls into question.

Many critics and poets have remarked on Olson's somatic focus. Everywhere in Olson's writings are references to the material of the body, as well as to its poetic extension in the breath. Poet Michael McClure contrasts Olson's complex poetics of the body, which McClure relates to action painting, with the "overabstracted [type of] nature that does not see the complexity, or feel the complexity, of the body." Charles Altieri, in a perceptive discussion of Olson's postmodernism, uses similar terms to summarize much of Olson's practice:

> But if we can't trust the synthesizing imagination [*cf* Pound], how do we apprehend the unity inherent in the event? Olson turns to the most physical aspect of the poem—its rhythm—and redefines [it]. . . . Our bodies are the place where the fullest union of man and world takes place, and it is within them that the unity of experience can be grasped. Discussion of rhythm must be taken out of formalist contexts and related explicitly to the acts of the body.

I would question Altieri's use of the term *union*—Olson's poetic seems to me far more contingent, fluctuating, and thus radical—but his summary is the best I know, and what follows largely extends his formulation to contemporary discussions of the body.

Olson puts it bluntly:

> [A] man is himself an object, whatever he may take to be his advantages, the more likely to recognize himself as such the greater his advantages, particularly at that moment that the achieves an humilitas sufficient to make him of use.

This observation (some of the terms of which need fuller examination) is central to Olson's practice. It leads Olson to propose, in his still underread essay "Human Universe," the Heisenberglike axiom that "we are ourselves both the instrument of discovery and the instrument of definition." Rejecting summarily the metaphysical tradition beginning with the Greeks, Olson asserts against all idealisms that "[i]f there is any absolute, it is never more than this one, you, this instant, in action."

This assertion sounds dangerously close to subjectivism, as Olson knows full well, but he will make the case for a more positive relativism based on the self-evident fact that "any of us, at any instant, are juxtaposed to any experience, even an overwhelming single one, on several more planes than the arbitrary and discursive which we inherit can declare." Rather than an idealistic, static world, Olson sees a post-Einsteinian universe in which matter and energy exchange, in which *object* metamorphoses into *act*. Thus, Olson sees the regaining of a sort of epistemological dynamism as the way out of subjective despair, indeed as the door to a truer knowledge than is possible in the static separations of subject and object typical of Western thought.

Later in the same essay, he asks whether it is possible to "restate man in any way to repossess him of his dynamic." As one answer to this question, he makes an interesting proposition, which has considerable importance for his poetry:

> [M]an at his peril breaks the full circuit of object, image, action at any point. The meeting edge of man and the world is also his cutting edge.

Olson would recenter our knowing in the dynamic material body rather than in a disembodied mind; seeing the human as material object opens the door between subject and object, or shatters the wall that divides them. When "man [is] at his peril," he is most aware of his body, most fully somatic. This formulation, the radicalism of which is rarely appreciated, resembles some of thepropositions of Mari Soori and Jerry H. Gill in their recent book, *A Post-Modern Epistemology*. Extending some observations of Maurice Merleau-Ponty, Ludwig Wittgenstein, Michael Polanyi, and others, they propose that

> [A] more somatic understanding of cognitive activity, one which takes human embodiment as crucial to knowledge, both avoids the traditional difficulties of Western epistemology and clears the way for more fruitful dialogue with other fields of investigation and with everyday experience.

Obviously such an understanding, if fully developed, would revise our view not only of cognitive activity but of our more immediate concern, Charles Olson, whose poetic bears striking resemblance to the project of Soori and Gill.

Finding the locus of poetic action, the "cutting edge" of man, at the "meeting edge" of the body and the world, Olson in "Human Universe" approaches a poetic of pure expression, pure "lamp" in Abrams's terms, when he claims that "[a]rt does not seek to describe but to enact." However, this needs to be qualified; art enacts *in* the world, as Olson realized: "his [that is, man's] door is where he is responsible to more than himself." The dynamic of Olson's poetry at its best enacts a dialectic of mimesis and expression, a meeting of world and body which becomes (one might say *enables*) a radical critique of Western metaphysics. If our examination of Olson's poetry focuses on poems of birth and origin, it is because here Olson's formulation of body poetics relates explicitly to his own physical body, its birth and dynamic action.

Olson's poem **"La Préface"** is rightly regarded as his first attempt at what he would later define as *projective verse*, verse which explores the meeting-point, the cutting edge of body and world through the medium of the breath. One of the first poems in English to face the reality of the Holocaust, **"La Préface"** is also one of the first poems fully to earn the name *postmodern*. Von Hallberg notes that in **"La Préface"** "[h]istory . . . has left poets only bare bones"; his metaphor, though apt, obscures in its allusion to Eliot. **"La Préface"** sees modernist searches for closure and explanation through delving into a mythic,

religious, and usually valorized past as escapist, and demands a greater life in the "space" of the present. It asks the reader to "Put war away with time, come into space." Soori and Gill, in their discussion of the epistemological dynamic of the body, argue that "space *becomes* space as we interact and move within it," and also that "our body is not a neutral object in abstract space, it is our way of being-in-the-world." Surely Olson's admonition to "come into space" serves partly an invitation to a fuller "being-in-the-world"; who does not live in space exists in a state of non-being, dead.

Indeed, the ancient dead—the subject of so much modernist speculation à la Eliot—are, as an early line of **"La Préface"** states, "in via," in the way, and must be pushed aside. Why? Because this is a "vita nuova"; the speaker of the poem, like Dante's narrator, confronts a recent and overpowering death. The ancient dead obstruct the path to a proper dwelling in the space of the present, a space inhabited by the "unburied dead"—the new dead of the new life, of the Holocaust. Methods of describing this fresh horror are, of course, not yet worked out:

> "I will die about April 1st . . ." going off
> "I weigh, I think, 80 lbs . . ." scratch
> "My name is NO RACE" address
> Buchenwald new Altamira cave
> With a nail they drew the object of the hunt.

Faced with such a reality, old methods of articulation get nowhere. The poet must find models in his own time.

Olson in this poem finds one in his friend, the Italian artist Corrado Cagli. As von Hallberg and others have noticed, the line "It was May, precise date, 1940" refers both to the German invasion of France (and thus the effective expansion of the war) and to Olson's first meeting with Cagli, who was to illustrate Olson's volume *Y & X*. Cagli and Olson begin a conversation without words, in object-language:

> He talked, via stones a stick sea rock a hand of
> earth.

In a marvelous act of poetic *hubris*, Olson dates the beginning of the postmodern era 1910, the year of his own (and of Cagli's) birth, placing closed parentheses before, and an open parenthesis after that year. The poem sees the "root" of the matter not in another world (as in Eliot) or in Pound's search among the heros of the past in *The Cantos*, but in the material fact of the body itself, seen as more fluctuating but more communal than the escapist solipsism of modernism: "It is the radical, the root, he and I, two bodies." In von Hallberg's phrase: "1910 . . . marks a new, postpastoral epoch of documentation." When Olson writes that new method entails "no parenthesis," he means that the ego must refrain from constructing some sort of rational validation for the horror of Buchenwald. The new method forces not justification but witness: "We put our hands to these dead." The act centers not in the reasoning mind but in the witnessing body, seen here in a community of two.

Rejecting Eliot and Pound, Olson rejects also any valorization of the past:

> The closed parenthesis reads: the dead bury the
> dead,
>   and it is not very interesting.

The postmodern poet puts himself in the open, and declares that "we are the new born." Furthermore, while concerned, even obsessed with death, the new poets as Olson conceives them encounter the deaths of their own time—"these unburied dead" of Auschwitz, Buchenwald—rather than the ancient dead, who are already buried. When at the end he declares his generation

> The Babe
>   the Howling Babe

it is a birth without explanation in the past, without metaphysical meaning or purpose, into an inexplicable, horrifying present.

Though much of Olson's verse explores the past, it does so without the search for ultimate grounding in another world. In many ways a materialist poetic, Olson's search for ground remains shifting, contingent, moving forward, without ultimate explanation of the kind sought in Pound's *The Cantos* or Eliot's *Four Quartets*. Furthermore, it locates knowledge not in the mind's unifying force, but in the physical body and its acts of forceful witness. The witness, who puts his hands to the dead, becomes part of the scene witnessed: he is a body among other bodies, caught in a web of implication and possibility. Observation is participation; the poem's confusion of reference enters the realm of common implication we find, for instance, in the recent Holocaust documentary film *Shoah*:

> He put the body there as well as they did whom he
> killed.

This is the postmodernism of projective verse.

Recently, Elaine Scarry's brilliant *The Body in Pain* has taken up issues paralleling those raised by Olson: specifically, the development of a somatically focused theory of human creation. Part of the continuing reexamination of the role of the body in our knowing, Scarry's project does not, like the work of Soori and Gill, trace the philosophical dismissal of the body in Western thought. Rather, she uncovers a more harrowing phenomenon—the way the body "disappears from view" in our descriptive language precisely at those points when it ought to be most visible: when being tortured, when in war, when performing physical labor. Scarry tracks human experience along a line, the end-points of which are body and voice, or pain and imagination. As she puts it:

> Physical pain . . . is an intentional state without an
> intentional object; imagining is an intentional object
> without an experienceable intentional state. Thus, it
> may be that in some peculiar way it is appropriate to
> think of pain as the imagination's intentional state,

and to identify the imagination as pain's intentional object. . . . "[P]ain" and "imagining" constitute extreme conditions of, on the one hand, intentionality as a state and, on the other, intentionality as self-objectification; . . . between these two boundary conditions all the more familiar, binary acts-and-objects are located. That is, pain and imagining are the "framing events" within whose boundaries all other perceptual, somatic, and emotional events occur; thus, between the two extremes can be mapped the whole terrain of the human psyche.

There is not space in this paper adequately to explore the implications of Scarry's powerful project. It should be obvious from this excerpt, though, how Scarry attempts to "repossess" the human "dynamic," to use Olson's words, in a strikingly somatic fashion. By proposing a dialectic of pain and imagination, of body and voice, Scarry has opened the door to a positive and body-centered theory of human creation. As Yeats came slowly to realize, "In dreams begins responsibility."

Returning to Olson, we find that **"The Babe"** both anticipates Scarry and extends the questions of **"La Préface,"** again locating the crucial point in the material body, as its opening lines express:

> Who is it who sits
> behind the face,
> who is it looks out by both,
> by beauty and by truth,
> those cheeks . . .

The question is the identity of the human, the answer sought through perception, eyes searching the eyes of others for a reality outside the self. Realizing a somatic poetic, **"The Babe"** accepts Keats's equation of beauty and truth but amplifies both, having them participate in a dynamic material space. The word is responsible to the world. There is no question here of deep calling unto deep, of soul-to-soul conversation; the material body steps between. Thus the act of the poem finds its way out of solipsism through recognition of the somatic other. The search is anti-lyric—"not by lyric, not by absolute"—and grounds itself in something

>   more
> than beauty or than truth, be
> the recognition that you are
> of use

Of use: the poetic act as communal, fluctuating, dynamic. Olson uses the same phrase in "Projective Verse," as we have seen, and the term deserves examination. It is perhaps clarified by Olson in a playful letter to Creeley which, though it does not use the term *use,* raises the issue in another context:

> what, at root, is the reality contemporary to us, &
> which we are, which is, therefore, the CONTENT (the
> contest leading to issue arriving at CHANGE)
>
> is NO LONGER, THINGS, the TERMS, but WHAT
> HAPPENS BETWEEN THINGS

In the world since Heisenberg (whom Olson mentions earlier in the same letter) the verb is a form of the noun. Truth does equal Beauty, yet both are involved in participating action. The point is "CHANGE," or the opening of possibility. Indeed, Olson's use of the word *issue* in the letter brings the language full circle, back to the birth-giving body, and inscribes another sense of action into the birth-imagery and title of **"The Babe."**

The end of that poem deserves full quotation, expressing as it does the communal quest of Olson's best poetry:

> one to another separate, but
> the form we make by search, by error, pain
> be seen by eyes other than our own
>
> dedicate, thus, one to another, aid:
> to offer, able to offer the just act, the act
> crying to be born!

The search of the poem comes out of pain, "man at his peril" as Olson had put it previously. The form is found not in the synthesizing ego but rather "by search, by error," in the flawed trajectory of the quest. Approaching an ethic of shareable pain, it recognizes a fact Elaine Scarry finds crucial:

> [Pain] achieves its aversiveness in part by bringing about, even within the radius of several feet, [an] absolute split between one's sense of one's own reality and the reality of other persons.
>
> Thus when one speaks about "one's own physical pain" and about "another person's physical pain," one might almost appear to be speaking about two wholly distinct orders of events.

"[T]he just act" of **"The Babe"** is seen in witness as a form of aid: that "pain / be seen by eyes other than our own." Pain is first witnessed, then expressed not privately but in the shared context of a community.

Olson's poetic is activist not because it takes up a certain political cause (though it does, and often), but because the poetry itself is *act* as much as object. We find, as Olson writes to Creeley, "RE-ENACTMENT displacing REPRESENTATION." As Soori and Gill argue, "truth is better construed as a process than as a static quality; it is . . . *a way of being.*" Or, in an observation relating more directly to **"The Babe,"**

> the human being is a subject-object phenomenon, not a purely objective being. . . . The subjects interlace with each other because they are *mediated to* each other rather than . . . *separated from* each other by their bodily dimension.

Coincidentally, Soori and Gill use one of Olson's favorite terms when they speak of our moving in "a diffuse *field* of unknown particulars" (emphasis added)—that is, in space. Olson sees the space of **"La Préface"** and **"The Babe"** not only, as he once wrote of one of his favorite maxims, as "at once aesthetic and metaphysic," but also

as political, "the act / crying to be born." Olson's somatic poetic thus becomes a complex *politics* of the body, the articulation of pain in a field of empathy, a shared dwelling in a bodily space.

We can explore some of the implications of bodily pain for Olson's postmodern project by examining Olson at his most perilous, encountering his own new birth through facing the loss of his mother. Though not directly political, Olson's mother-poems confront the issue of the unburied dead in a forceful manner, and thus impinge upon the politics of the poetic. In fact, by admitting the self back into the poem, they move beyond the impersonal poetics of modernism and powerfully raise the issue of personal (and, by implication, political) responsibility.

The loss of a parent is for anyone a highly traumatic experience, destabilizing in the most fundamental sense. As the loss, quite literally, of origin, the parent's death holds a special place in the chronicle of losses that make up a life. One might say it makes people aware of their own bodies, which is in fact the way Elaine Scarry defines bodily pain. While not wanting to construct a monomyth of origin which sees woman as some transcendant, Jungian Other and thus not quite human, we need to see how Olson's poetic both raises the issue of such myths and finally surpasses them. For Olson, highly indebted to Jung as well as to modern science, the time in the womb might be seen as the beginning of art as well as the state in which "space" is most fully inhabited, subject and object are at one. The mother's death, then, assaults and shatters idealistic notions of return; the survivor is forced to live in a radically contingent space. One might say that the death of the mother is the last casualty in the war with time. Olson's mother, to whom he remained extremely close until the time of her death, remains for him one of the unburied dead, preying upon him, existing beyond her death in and through his consciousness of loss. Paradoxically, it is through reenacting that loss that Olson makes some of his own most significant poetic gains.

One can only speculate on why Olson wrote **"Tanto e Amara"** when he did, over two years before his mother's death in 1950. Perhaps in part a rehearsal, **"Tanto e Amara,"** whose title is stolen from Dante, prepares for the bitter loss to come. The poem presents itself as anti-Platonic, countering the idealistic statement that "nothing dieth / but changing as they do one for another show / sundry formes" with what the speaker knows: "I cannot have back my mother." Still, the language is Platonic insofar as it remains idealized, a state rather than an activity. While in some ways a moving poem, **"Tanto e Amara"** evokes sympathy rather than empathy, pity rather than shared pain. Olson does not in this poem realize the potential of a somatic poetic, perhaps because he has not yet had the experience described. His song is stunted, and ends by questioning its own possibility:

> And what shall I be, which forms will plague me then
> where shall I go, in what ditch pour what blood to hear

her voice, the love I hear, that voice now mingled
in the song,
the song of the Worms?

Anticipating the loss of his mother, the speaker realizes that the problem of new forms of articulation must be raised sooner or later. It is fundamentally a problem of language: how will he communicate with his dead mother, how can he construct a communal poetic when the other end of the line goes silent?

Though Olson composed a draft of **"The Moon is the Number 18"** in late 1946, he revised it radically on 8 January 1951, just weeks after his mother's death on Christmas day 1950. As Richard G. Ingber has noted, the poem focuses on "the possibility of . . . a spiritual initiation" which is incomplete; the poem ends literally in "conjecture." The tarot definition of the moon in the title is modified throughout the poem: the moon becomes "a monstrance," while later it "is a grinning god, is / the mouth of, is / the dripping moon"—it comes back to itself. **"The Moon is the Number 18"** exists, as it were, in its ebb and flow.

Though "the son sits, / grieving" outside the tower with the blue dogs, there is no explicit *I* in the poem. Rather, the reader proceeds through the poem in the same manner as the grieving son watches the metamorphoses of the moon: tentatively, alert to the swift changes that alter perception and meaning. Ingber, analyzing the poem in terms of its Tarot allusions, finds in the speaker a sort of motherless Christ figure. Without parents, the speaker identifies himself with the blue wolfish dogs who feed on the waste of grief:

The blue dogs paw,
lick the droppings, dew
or blood, whatever
results are.

Thus, the poem is a sort of secular pilgrimage.

While not wanting to discount the religious imagery in the poem, I would relate Ingber's concept of "spiritual initiation" here to a more Jungian possibility, the devouring of unconscious shadow energies. "Spiritual" seems to admit a finality which I simply do not find in the poem, while *shadow* as a term keeps the movement tentative:

. . . he would howl, confronting
the wind which rocks what was her, while prayers
striate the snow, words blow
as questions cross fast, fast
as flames, as flames form, melt
along any darkness

The poem inhabits a Heraclitean universe of flux as against a Christian or even post-Christian stasis. The religious imagery serves merely as a rung on the psychological ladder.

Finally, the speaker absorbs his shadow through recognizing the materiality of the body. When the speaker accepts his mother's absence ("wind . . . rocks what was her"), he finally moves from prayer and the moon. The poem walks away from symbolism toward a confrontation with the actual:

in that tower where she also sat
in that particular tower where watching & moving
    are,
there,
there where what triumph there is, is: there
is all substance, all creature
all there is against the dirty moon . . .

Hardly an epiphany, such an end is powerfully anti-idealistic.

"As the Dead Prey Upon Us," a much later and longer poem, reexamines some of the problems involved in **"The Moon is the Number 18"**'s lack of resolution. Robert J. Bertholf has said that "[t]he poem attempts to show the complexity of the process of the mind viewing, in an instant, the unity of the past and the present—the breakage, whole," a formulation both memorable and inaccurate, as the body, which I take to be a central fact of the poem, goes undiscussed. Though there is not space exhaustively to consider this extraordinary poem, we can briefly examine it as it relates to the issues we are pursuing. Opening with an invocation, it seeks at first a resolution of the problem of the unburied dead:

As the dead prey upon us,
they are the dead in ourselves,
awake, my sleeping ones, I cry out to you,
disentangle the nets of being!

The unburied dead are "the dead in ourselves," those dead who coinhabit the space of our consciousness. Unlike the ancient buried dead, about whom we read in books, the dead who "prey upon us" are the dead of our own time, the dead who live in personal memory (though they need not be personally known, as **"La Préface"** shows).

From this invocation we move suddenly to Olson trapped under his car, which has rolled over him as he tried to push it—underneath the vehicle, he is suddenly faced with a vision of his mother, alive. What had seemed solvable problems, both with the car, which the poet thought "only needed air" in the tires, and with his mother, whom he had thought was dead, now present themselves as deeply entangled with his own body. They literally invade and threaten his space.

It's a comic moment, to be sure, but terrifying as well. "[T]he nets of being," the contingencies of existence, entangle and trap the poet, and escape seems impossible. In addition, the nets are not only difficult to get out of, they are inextricable from each other. The psychological and the physical are equally involved with the poet's space. Thus the associative technique of the poem diverges widely from that of Eliot in *The Waste Land* and Pound in *The Cantos*. Instead of the dance of the intellect among words or the search of the past for meaning, we find the pose of the body in material space:

But suddenly the huge underbody was above me,
    and the rear tires
were masses of rubber and thread variously clinging
    together

as were the dead souls in the living room, gathered
about my mother . . .

Olson converses with them all, who are "all of them / desperate with the tawdriness of their life in hell." Faced with this tragicomic technological *Inferno,* Olson discovers that his mother "returns to the house once a week" and that he can talk to the dead, among them a blue deer. Things of this world exchange with the other world: the automobile metamorphoses into a chair at the edge of the yard, at the farthest reaches of his "space":

Walk the jackass
Hear the victrola
Let the automobile
be tucked into a corner of the white fence
when it is a white chair. . . .

He wants his mother to rest easy (meaning away from him):

O peace, my mother, I do not know
how differently I could have done
what I did or did not do.

As the language of this passage indicates, the poet is confronted here with his own guilt, sins of commission and omission. The poet's invocation to his mother changes into a prayer to the self:

                                        Awake,
my soul, let the power into the last wrinkle
of being, let none of the threads and rubber of the
    tires
be left upon the earth. Let even your mother
go. Let there be only paradise

However, this Poundian prayer is immediately qualified by what Olson elsewhere calls "the sliding present":

The desperateness is, that the instant
which is also paradise (paradise
is happiness) dissolves
into the next instant, and power
flows to meet the next occurrence

At this point the speaker comes to realize that he will not be rid of his mother in this life: "Is it any wonder / my mother comes back?" Projecting his own guilt onto his mother, he decides that she comes to relive her life. He would prefer escape from his own entanglement in being:

The vent! You must have the vent,
or you shall die. Which means
never to die, the ghastliness

of going, and forever
coming back . . .

He prefers the purity of death: "I want to die. I want to make that instant, too, / perfect."

This is the poem's lowest point. To release himself from his mother, the speaker attempts to reassure himself that it was only a dream, but that effort, too, is thwarted:

The car did not burn. Its underside
was not presented to me
a grotesque corpse. The old man

merely removed it as I looked up at it,
and put it in a corner of the picket fence
like it was my mother's white dog?

or a child's chair

Back in reality, the speaker remains oddly confronted by the presence of his mother and the fluctuating terms of reality. He cannot escape their force; they *do* prey upon him.

The scene immediately shifts to an embarrassing encounter with a neighbor, a meeting which only heightens the narrator's emotional instability. He comes back to the house to find "my mother sitting there / / as she always had sat, as must she always / forever sit. . . ." One can almost see the narrator being scolded by the mother. At this point, there is no choice; seeing her there, he comes to a final recognition, an acceptance of the nets of being, an affirmation of this-worldly transcendence:

        . . . We have only one course:

the nets which entangle us are flames

The nets, the knots, the skin of bodily existence, are the stuff of poetry.

At the end of the poem the narrator asks his dead mother "to stay in the chair"; by this he means the chair "in the corner of the fence," at the edge of his space. But by now she's the one in control, and takes a seat at the center of his being, "by the fireplace made of paving stones." By affirming the material life of this world, the poet can accept death wholly, can allow the unburied dead to live with him. Rather than push her off, he accepts the reality of her death and his implication of her life. The poem's conclusion—

And if she sits in happiness the souls
who trouble her and me
will also rest. The automobile

has been hauled away

—is one of the most positive ends anywhere in Olson's poetry, a ringing affirmation of the complex, entangled life of the body.

If in **"Moonset, Gloucester, December 1, 1957, 1:58 *am,*"** written years later, Olson has not yet come to the end of his dialogue with his mother nor to the end of his anguish, he has found the source of a new type of poetic, a poetic of the body in pain, a struggling through experience at the edge, at the painful, cutting meeting-point of the body and the world. Again in this poem the mother invades the speaker's space; again he must free himself from her. Olson was born December 27, so his mother was buried some time around his birthday; the line "you set I rise" admits not only his freedom from origin, living in the space of the present, but his continual feeding on her death:

> you set I rise I hope
> a free thing as probably
> what you more were . . .

The end of the poem, though forceful and startling, recognizes the complex entanglement of the body, the inhabiting of bodies in a common space, the continuing encroachment of painful memory, and the need for repeated exorcism:

>   Rise
> Mother from off me
> God damn you God damn me my
> misunderstanding of you
>
> I can die now I just begun to live

While **"As the Dead Prey Upon Us"** affirmed that the mother, though dead, would not leave, **"Moonset, Gloucester"** takes it a step further: her death is necessary for his life. If **"As the Dead Prey Upon Us"** concluded with the dead still preying on the living, **"Moonset, Gloucester"** reverses the process. He, the living, feeds on her, the dead. As in **"La Préface,"** where the speakers are implicated in the very acts of witness, Olson's poems about his mother widen the notion of common space and common implication to include the realm of the personal dead. The poetics of the body become political; the poem is a shared expression of implication and opens the door to a political poetics of responsible action.

FURTHER READING

Biography

Duberman, Martin. *Black Mountain: An Exploration in Community.* New York: E. P. Dutton and Co., 1972, 511 p.
  Historical survey of the experimental college, including discussions of Olson's dominant presence and vital contributions as a teacher there.

Du Plessix Gray, Francine. "Charles Olson and an American Place." *The Yale Review* 76, No. 3 (Spring 1987): 341-52.

Recollections by a former student of Olson's at Black Mountain College.

Criticism

Bertholf, Robert J. "Righting the Balance: Olson's *The Distances.*" *Boundary 2* 2, Nos. 1 and 2 (Fall 1973-Winter 1974) 229-49.
  Discusses Olson's efforts to conceptually unite thought and action in *The Distances.*

Bollobás, Enikő. *Charles Olson.* New York: Twayne Publishers, 1992, 150 p.
  Critical survey of Olson's writings.

Byrd, Don. *Charles Olson's* Maximus. Urbana: University of Illinois Press, 1980, 204 p.
  Discussion of *Maximus* poems, focusing on Olson's theoretical expansion of poetic space.

Carter, Steven. "Fields of Spacetime and the 'I' in Charles Olson's *The Maximus Poems.*" In *American Literature and Science,* edited by Robert J. Scholnick, pp. 194-207. Lexington: The University Press of Kentucky, 1992.
  Appraises Olson's attempt to discover "the poetics of a cross-pollination of scientific epistemologies and the language of verse."

Christensen, Paul. *Charles Olson: Call Him Ishmael.* Austin: University of Texas Press, 1979, 243 p.
  Overview of Olson's life and work as a poet and theorist.

Hatlen, Burton. "Kinesis and Meaning: Charles Olson's 'The Kingfishers' and the Critics." *Contemporary Literature* 30, No. 4 (Winter 1989): 546-72.
  Analyzes the poem as a "kinetic event."

Merrill, Thomas F. *The Poetry of Charles Olson: A Primer.* London: Associated University Presses, 1982, 228 p.
  Essays dealing with Olson's major poetic works, his literary theories, and his tenure at Black Mountain College.

Rosenthal, M. L. "Olson/His Poetry." *The Massachusetts Review* 7, No. 1 (Winter 1971): 45-56.
  Examines Olson's poetry and defends it from its detractors.

Interviews

Malanga, Gerard. "Charles Olson: The Art of Poetry." *The Paris Review* 13, No. 49 (Summer 1970): 176-204.
  Olson reflects on his own work and influences and the state of contemporary American poetry.

Additional coverage of Olson's life and career is contained in the following sources published by Gale Research: *Contemporary Literary Criticism,* Vols. 1, 2, 5, 6, 9, 11, 29; *DISCovering Authors: Poets Module; Contemporary Authors,* Vols. 13-16; *Contemporary Authors Biography Series,* Vol. 2; *Contemporary Authors New Revision Series,* Vol. 35; *Dictionary of Literary Biography,* Vols. 5, 16; and *Major Twentieth-Century Writers.*

Wilfred Owen
1893-1918

(Full name Wilfred Edward Salter Owen) English poet.

INTRODUCTION

Considered the leading English poet of the First World War, Owen is remembered for realistic poems depicting the horrors of war, which were inspired by his experiences at the Western Front in 1916 and 1917. Owen considered the true subject of his poems to be "the pity of war," and sought to present the grim realities of battle and its effects on the human spirit. His unique voice—less passionate and idealistic than those of other war poets—is complemented by his unusual and experimental technical style. He is recognized as the first English poet to fully achieve pararhyme, in which the rhyme is made through altered vowel sounds. This distinctive technique and the prominent note of social protest in his works influenced many poets of the 1920s and 1930s, most notably W. H. Auden, C. Day Lewis, and Stephen Spender.

Biographical Information

Owen was born in Oswestry, Shropshire, the eldest son of a minor railroad official. A thoughtful, imaginative youth, he was greatly influenced by his Calvinist mother and developed an early interest in Romantic poets and poetry, especially in John Keats, whose influence can be seen in many of Owen's poems. Owen was a serious student, attending schools in Birkenhead and Shrewsbury. After failing to win a university scholarship in 1911, he became a lay assistant to the Vicar of Dunsden in Oxfordshire. Failing again to win a scholarship in 1913, Owen accepted a position teaching English at the Berlitz School in Bordeaux, France. There he was befriended by the Symbolist poet and pacifist Laurent Tailhade, whose encouragement affirmed Owen's determination to become a poet. In 1915, a year after the onset of the Great War, Owen returned to England and enlisted in the Artist's Rifles. While training in London, he frequented Harold Monro's Poetry Bookshop, where he became acquainted with Monro and regularly attended public poetry readings. At the end of his training, he was commissioned as a lieutenant in the Manchester Regiment; in late 1916 he was posted to the Western Front where he participated in the Battle of the Somme and was injured and hospitalized. Later sent to Edinburgh's Craiglockhart Hospital for treatment of shell-shock, he met fellow patient and poet, Siegfried Sassoon, an outspoken critic of the war, who encouraged Owen to use his battle experiences as subjects for poetry. Owen wrote most of his critically acclaimed poems in the fifteen months following this meeting. After being

discharged from the hospital, Owen rejoined his regiment in Scarborough. He returned to the front in early September 1918 and shortly afterwards was awarded the Military Cross for gallantry. He was killed in action at the Sambre Canal in northeast France on November 4, 1918—one week before the Armistice. He is buried in Ors, France.

Major Works

Owen's early poetry is considered to be derivative and undistinguished, influenced by his interest in romantic themes, particularly beauty, much as Keats had been. The emergence of war shattered his idealistic vision of life and caused Owen to rethink his philosophy. He came to believe that war could not be described in an heroic, idealized manner, but should be treated with a realism that could describe the impact warfare has on human lives. The maturation of his poetic style can be traced to his encounter with Sassoon, from whom he learned to adapt his technique to nontraditional war subjects, allowing him to express more fully his emotions and his experiences. Owen strove to give voice to the feelings of the common foot soldier, whose experiences were not represented in the conventional war poems that spoke of heroism and patriotism instead of fears and death. As he stated in the introduction to the collection of poems he began to assemble for publication before his death, Owen's goal was not to glorify conflict or soldiers dying for their country, but to express the "pity of war," and to offer a more complex emotional response to fighting, one that allows for a greater understanding of war itself.

At the time of Owen's death, only a handful of his poems had been published. Among his best-known poems are "Dulce et Decorum Est," "Anthem for Doomed Youth," and "Strange Meeting," an uncompleted elegy that is considered by many critics to be the finest poem written about the First World War. "Strange Meeting" presents historical, humanistic, and mystical themes, while considering the conflict between ego and conscience in war. In a dreamlike vision, the narrator of the poem encounters a soldier whom he has killed, and the ensuing dialogue presents Owen's protests on the futility of war. By not specifying the nationalities of the two soldiers in the poem, Owen achieved an ambiguity that allows the verses to be viewed as both a commentary on World War I and on the universal nature of war and suggests analogies between the soldier and Christ and between the enemy and oneself. In this and other poems, the Christian ethical principle of "greater love," based on the New Testament teaching "Greater love hath no man than this, that a man lay down his life for his friends" (John 15:13), is considered highly significant. Many critics have noted that while Owen rebelled against the strict institutional religion of his mother, he retained a deep love of Christ, who often appeared in his poems as a symbol for the young men sacrificed on the battlefields.

Critical Reception

Owen's reputation was established posthumously with the 1920 publication of a collection of his poems edited by Sassoon. His poetry subsequently gained a wide audience as a result of collections compiled by Edmund Blunden and C. Day Lewis; however, critical attention developed more slowly, due to a lack of biographical information, which led to confusion over the dates of various poems and the progress of Owen's development as a poet. Generally, critics have come to agree that Owen's verses represent a unique emotional response to war and a masterful technical achievement. This consensus was challenged by W. B. Yeats, who omitted Owen's poetry from his anthology *The Oxford Book of Modern Verse* (1937), commenting that "passive suffering is not a theme for poetry." However, the exclusion of Owen's verses was itself challenged by numerous commentators, who questioned Yeats's selection criteria. Perhaps the greatest indicator of Owen's importance lies in the influence he had on poets of the next generation, including Day Lewis, who noted that Owen created "poems that will remain momentous long after the circumstances that prompted them have become just another war in the history books."

PRINCIPAL WORKS

Poetry

Poems   1920
The Poems of Wilfred Owen   1931
Thirteen Poems   1956
The Collected Poems of Wilfred Owen   1963
Wilfred Owen: War Poems and Others   1973
The Complete Poems and Fragments   1983

Other Major Works

Collected Letters   (letters)   1967

CRITICISM

J. Middleton Murry   (review date 1921)

SOURCE: "The Poet of War," in *Nation and the Athenaeum*, Vol. XXVIII, No. 21, February 19, 1921, pp. 705-07.

[*In the following excerpt, Murry lauds Owen's* Poems *and argues that the author was the greatest poet of World War I.*]

The name and the genius of Wilfred Owen were first revealed by the publication of his finest poem, **"Strange Meeting,"** in the anthology *Wheels* a year ago. I still remember the incredible shock of that encounter, the sudden, profound stirring by the utterance of a true poet. Since that time other fragments of Owen's work have been made known, and if none so evidently bore the impress of poetic mastery as **"Strange Meeting,"** they were a part of that achievement. We could be sure that when the promised volume of his poetry appeared it would be single, coherent, and unique.

And so it is. Here in thirty-three brief pages [*Poems*] is the evidence that Wilfred Owen was the greatest poet of the war. There have been war-poets; but he was a poet of another kind. He was not a poet who seized upon the opportunity of war, but one whose being was saturated by a strange experience, who bowed himself to the horror of war until his soul was penetrated by it, and there was no mean or personal element remaining unsubdued in him. In the fragmentary preface which so deeply bears the mark of Owen's purity of purpose, he wrote: "Above all this book is not concerned with Poetry. The subject of it is War, and the Pity of War. The Poetry is in the pity."

"The Poetry is in the pity." Whatever the new generation of poets may think or say, Owen had the secret in those words. The source of all enduring poetry lies in an intense and overwhelming emotion. The emotion must be overwhelming, and suffered as it were to the last limit of the soul's capacity. Complete submission is an essential phase in that process of mastering the emotion with which the poet's creation begins, for the poet himself has to be changed; he plunges into the depths of his emotion to rise mysteriously renewed. Only then will the words he utters bear upon them the strange compulsion of a secret revealed; only then can he put his spell upon us and trouble our depths. For the problem of poetry is not primarily, or even largely, a conscious problem; true poetry begins with an act, a compelled and undeliberate act, of obedience to that centre of our being where all experience is reconciled.

And the further process of poetry is also an instinctive adjustment rather than a conscious seeking. The poet's being, changed by the stress of its overwhelming experience, gropes after a corresponding expression. Learning and the intellect are no better than tentative guides. The correspondence toward which the poet moves is recognized and ratified by other powers than these. And Owen's search after some garment for his new comprehension more closely fitting than the familiar rhyme arose, not from any desire to experiment for experiment's sake, but from the inward need to say the thing he had to say most exactly and finally. Consider the assonances in the opening lines of **"Strange Meeting"**:

> It seemed that out of the battle I escaped
> Down some profound long tunnel, long since
>   scooped
> Through granites which Titanic wars had groined.
> Yet also there encumbered sleepers groaned
> Too fast in thought or death to be bestirred.
> Then as I probed them, one sprang up and stared
> With piteous recognition in fixed eyes,
> Lifting distressful hands as if to bless.
> And by his smile I knew that sullen hall;
> With a thousand fears that vision's face was
>   grained;
> Yet no blood reached there from the upper ground
> And no guns thumped, or down the flues made
>   moan.
> 'Strange friend,' I said, 'there is no cause to
>   mourn.'
> 'None,' said the other, 'but the undone years,
> The hopelessness. Whatever hope is yours,
> Was my life also; I went hunting wild
> After the wildest beauty in the world,
> Which lies not calm in eyes, or braided hair,
> But mocks the steady running of the hour,
> And if it grieves, grieves richlier than here.
> For by my glee might many men have laughed,
> And of my weeping something has been left
> Which must die now. I mean the truth untold,
> The pity of war, the pity war distilled . . .'

I believe that the reader who comes fresh to this poem does not immediately observe the assonant endings. At first he feels only that the blank-verse has a mournful, impressive, even oppressive, quality of its own; that the poem has a forged unity, a welded and inexorable mas-

siveness. The emotion with which it is charged cannot be escaped; the meaning of the words and the beat of the sounds have the same indivisible message. The tone is single, low, muffled, subterranean. The reader looks again and discovers the technical secret; but if he regards it then as an amazing technical innovation, he is in danger of falsifying his own reaction to the poem. Those assonant endings are indeed the discovery of genius; but in a truer sense the poet's emotion discovered them for itself. They are a dark and natural flowering of this, and only this, emotion. You cannot imagine them used for any other purpose save Owen's, or by any other hand save his. They are the very modulation of his voice; you are in the presence of that rare achievement, a true poetic style.

Throughout the poems in this book we can watch Owen working towards this perfection of his own utterance, and at the same time working away from realistic description of the horrors of war towards an imaginative projection of emotion. The technical refinement works parallel with the imaginative sublimation. But even the realistic poems are hard and controlled, and completely free from the weakness of emotional dispersion; while on Owen's highest plane no comparison at all between him and the realistic poets is possible. He speaks to the imagination; his poems evoke our reactions, not to a scene of horror played again before our eyes, but to words spoken in silence when all material tumult has died away; they are the expression of that which remains in the soul when the nightmare of the senses is over.

His poems are calm. In spite of the intense passion which is their impulse, they have a haunting serenity. For the poet has, at whatever cost, mastered his experience; his emotion has become tranquil. In these poems there is no more rebellion, but only pity and regret, and the peace of acquiescence. It is not a comfortable peace, this joyless yet serene resignation; but it is a victory of the human spirit. We receive from it that exalted pleasure, that sense of being lifted above the sphere of anger and despair which the poetic imagination alone can give. Listen to this **"Anthem for Doomed Youth"**:

> What passing-bells for these who died as cattle?
>   Only the monstrous anger of the guns.
>   Only the stuttering rifles' rapid rattle
> Can patter out their hasty orisons.
> No mockeries for them; no prayers or bells,
> Nor any voice of mourning save the choirs,—
> The shrill demented choirs of wailing shells;
> And bugles calling for them from sad shires.
>
> What candles may be held to speed them all?
>   Not in the hands of boys, but in their eyes
> Shall shine the holy glimmers of good-byes.
>   The pallor of girls' brows shall be their pall;
> Their flowers the tenderness of patient minds,
> And each slow dusk a drawing-down of blinds.

There the calm is unmistakable, and indeed so evident that one might describe the sonnet as being in the familiar sense beautiful. Beauty of this kind is not to be found in the ghastly poem called **"The Show"**; but a still deeper calm is there. The poem is in Owen's later style, though the complex scheme of assonances is somewhat obscured by the arbitrary manner in which it has been printed. It opens thus:

> My soul looked down from a vague height with
>   Death,
> As unremembering how I rose or why,
> And saw a sad land, weak with sweats of dearth,
> Gray, cratered like the moon with hollow woe,
> And fitted with great pocks and scabs of plaques.
> Across its beard, that horror of harsh wire,
> There moved thin caterpillars, slowly uncoiled.
> It seemed they pushed themselves to be as plugs
> Of ditches, where they writhed and shrivelled,
>   killed. . . .

He sees the caterpillars advance upon each other, brown against gray:

> Whereat, in terror what that sight might mean,
> I reeled and shivered earthward like a feather,
> And Death fell with me, like a deepening moan.
> And He, picking a manner of worm, which half
>   had hid
> Its bruises in the earth, but crawled no further,
> Shewed me its feet, the feet of many men,
> And the fresh-severed head of it, my head.

There is horror at its extreme point, but horror without hysteria, horror that has been so overcome that it can be communicated direct from the imagination to the imagination. Hence there is calm.

It may be true, as Mr. Sassoon suggests in his introduction, that the majority of war poets wrote for the sake of the effect of a personal gesture, and that Owen did not. But the important difference between Owen and the rest is a difference in the power and quality of the imagination, which seems to arise in a difference in the power and quality of the kindling experience. So profound is this that we can hardly refrain from calling Owen a great poet. He had, more surely than any other poet of his generation, the potentiality of greatness; and he actually wrote one great poem. **"Strange Meeting"** is complete, achieved, unfaltering, and it is not solitary, for although Owen wrote no other poem which is wholly on this secure imaginative level, we cannot but regard it as the culmination of poems hardly less achieved. **"Exposure"** is charged with the same sombre mystery, and the unity of technique and emotional intention is almost as close. **"Greater Love,"** which seems to have been written before Owen's final period had begun, will reveal the purity of the poet's emotion to those who may be disconcerted by his later work:

> Red lips are not so red
>   As the stained stones kissed by the English dead.
> Kindness of wooed and wooer
> Seems shame to their love pure.

> O love, your eyes lose lure
>   When I behold eyes blinded in my stead!
> Your slender attitude
>   Trembles not exquisite like limbs knife-skewed,
> Rolling and rolling there
> Where God seems not to care;
> Till the fierce love they bear
>   Cramps them in death's extreme decrepitude.

> Your voice sings not so soft,—
>   Though even as wind murmuring through
>   raftered loft,—
> Your dear voice is not dear,
> Gentle, and evening clear,
> As theirs whom none now hear
>   Now earth has stopped their piteous mouths that
>   coughed.

> Heart, you were never hot,
>   Nor large, nor full like hearts made great with
>   shot;
> And though your hand be pale,
> Paler are all which trail
> Your cross through flame and hail:
>   Weep, you may weep, for you may touch them
>   not.

But it is not this poem, beautiful and poignant though it is, which will vindicate the claim that Owen is the greatest poet of the war; it is **"Strange Meeting"** and certain fragments of other poems which are lifted up by a poetic imagination of the highest and rarest kind—the sad serenity of the closing stanza of **"Insensibility"**:

> But cursed are dullards whom no cannon stuns
> That they should be as stones.
> Wretched are they, and mean
> With paucity that never was simplicity.
> By choice they made themselves immune
> To pity and whatever mourns in men
> Before the last sea and the hapless stars;
> Whatever mourns when many leave these shores;
> Whatever shares
> The eternal reciprocity of tears.

And the magical metaphors of the last five lines of this concluding passage of **"A Terre"**:

> Friend, be very sure
> I shall be better off with plants that share
> More peaceably the meadow and the shower.
> Soft rains will touch me,—as they could touch
>   once,
> And nothing but the sun shall make me ware.
> Your guns may crash around me. I'll not hear;
> Or, if I wince, I shall not know I wince.
> Don't take my soul's poor comfort for your jest.
> Soldiers may grow a soul when turned to fronds,
> But here the things best left at home with friends.

> My soul's a little grief, grappling your chest;
> To climb your throat on sobs; easily chased

On other sighs and wiped by fresher winds;
Carry my crying spirit till it's weaned
To do without what blood remained there wounds.

After all, it may be asked, even if we admit that Owen
was a poet of unusual imaginative power, why is he the
only poet of the war? Other poets—true poets some of
them—have written of the war. Why are they less than
he? For this single reason. The war was a terrible and
unique experience in the history of mankind; its poetry
had likewise to be unique and terrible; it had to record
not the high hopes that animated English youth at the
outset, but the slow destruction of that youth in the sequel; more than this, it had to record not what the war
did to men's bodies and senses, but what it did to their
souls. Owen's poetry is unique and terrible because it
records imperishably the devastation and the victory of
a soul.

I. M. Parsons (essay date 1931)

SOURCE: "The Poems of Wilfred Owen," in *The Criterion*, Vol. X, No. 41, July 1931, pp. 658-69.

*[In the following excerpt, Parsons praises Owen's fine
sensibility and rich imagination as a realist poet.]*

Only two poets, Wilfred Owen and Siegfried Sassoon,
attempted in any wholehearted sense the realist method
. . . and endeavoured to interpret their reactions to War
primarily in terms of objective experience. Of the former
Owen's is unquestionably the more compelling voice,
not only because the twenty-four poems which comprised,
till the recent appearance of [Edmund] Blunden's en-
larged edition, his one published book of verse, constitute a complete and altogether unique corpus of war
poetry, but because in the main his sensibility is finer
and his imagination richer than Sassoon's. Sassoon,
moreover, is primarily a lyric poet and a satirist: his
realism is only an indirect implication of his satire.
Expressing essentially the same attitude as Owen, he
writes with a certain subjective bias which gives to his
work a rather consciously intellectualized flavour. It is
as though the poems, composed in part retrospectively,
demanded a recapitulative effort of the imagination incompatible with complete spontaneity. With Owen on
the other hand, whatever the actual fact may have been,
the impression left on the reader certainly suggests composition while the visual image was still clear in the
mind's eye. It is, indeed, a kind of sublime indignation
consequent upon present experience which is one part of
the essence of his poetry. He was emphatically not among
those of whom he wrote:

Happy are men who yet before they are killed
Can let their veins run cold.
Whom no compassion fleers
Or makes their feet
Sore on the alleys cobbled with their brothers.

Far otherwise. His extra-sensitive mind reacted with
extreme urgency to the welter of promiscuous sensations
with which it was confronted, discriminating unerringly, and laying bare every implication which the circumstances involved. He saw, as few saw clearly while the
War was still actually in progress, the forces really at
work behind the multitude of conflicting noises—the
prayers and exhortations, religious and patriotic, the
explanations and justifications—indeed, the whole gam-
ut of self-deception which inevitably accompanies war
on a large scale. He saw also the extent of the sacrifice
that was to be incurred. It is thus that pity struggling
with indignation, or perhaps indignation chastened and
restrained by pity, emerges as the dominant emotion of
his verse. This conflict, more or less resolved as the case
may be, is implicit in one form or another in every poem
which came from him. It is responsible for the crude,
hard, astringent quality of so much that he wrote. It is
expressed again simply, disjointedly, but with perfect
precision, in the fragment of a Preface to the poems,
which was found among his papers after he was killed.

> Above all, this book is not concerned with Poetry.
> The subject of it is War, and the pity of War. The
> Poetry is in the pity.
> Yet these elegies are not to this generation,
> This is in no sense consolatory.

"These elegies are not to this generation," and again
later: "they may be to the next." In the light of these
statements it is not necessary to look further for evidence of Owen's attitude towards war. The Preface speaks
for itself. It is not surprising that the poetry which
emerged as the fruit of such experience bore so bitter a
flavour with its sweetness.

This full-blooded squaring-up to reality, moreover, inevitably carries with it some measure of surprise when
crystallized into verse. It occasions, like nearly all poetry which even approximates to the highest, a complete
orientation of the mind, a screwing round of the head,
as it were, to look the thing full in the face. The effect
of this readjustment is primarily a sense of release, as
from some clogging mental medium into a cleaner and
more firmly grasped state of mind. Stripped of our habitual mental make-up, with all the prejudice and irrelevance with which the latter is invariably loaded, we
react intuitively, if we react at all, to the stimulus of the
poet's emotion. In Owen's case this stimulus is so fiercely
and uncompromisingly direct that it tends, more often
than not, to embarrass by its very frankness. For that
reason Owen is less easy of approach than most poets
who have found in war, and the pity of war, the inspiration of their work. He is, as Mr. Eliot has remarked of
Blake, too terrifyingly "honest" to be comfortable. His
eye blinks at nothing; conceals and equivocates over
nothing. Take this, the last stanza from a poem written
round a gas attack:

> If in some smothering dreams, you too could pace
> Behind the wagon that we flung him in,
> And watch the white eyes writhing in his face,

His hanging face, like a devil's sick of sin,
If you could hear, at every jolt, the blood
Come gargling from the froth-corrupted lungs
Bitten as the cud
Of vile, incurable sores on innocent tongues,—
My friend, you would not tell with such high zest
To children ardent for some desperate glory,
The old Lie: *Dulce et decorum est*
Pro patria mori.

There is nothing pretty or elevating about that, nothing
which the most ingenuous critic could call "charming."
It is, in fact, necessary to acclimatize oneself to this
honesty and directness of attack, before one can appreciate fully the quality of the emotion which lies behind
it. One is even in danger of mistaking it, in some cases
at least, for technical immaturity. And in this connection it is interesting to note a remark, made by Sassoon
himself, in the short introduction which he contributed
to the original edition of Owen's poems. Speaking of the
latter's technical innovations, he writes: 'The discussion
of his experiments in assonance and dissonance (of which
"Strange Meeting" is the finest example) may be left to
the professional critics of verse, the majority of whom
will be more preoccupied with such technical details
than with the profound humanity of the self-

revelation manifested in such magnificent lines as those
at the end of his **"Apologia pro Poemate Meo."'** The
author of *Satirical Poems* and *The Heart's Journey* doubtless had his good reasons for making this very arbitrary
statement; but it is surely erroneous to suggest, as he
does, that a desire to investigate details of technique
precludes, in a critic, any intelligent appreciation of what
a poet has to say; and it is certainly misleading to imply
that in Owen's case such an investigation would be
wasted. Owen himself, as Mr. Blunden tells us, was
never in any doubt "whether a poet should be a curious
designer of verses or not." In point of fact, though, interest in a writer for the emotive experience which he is
expressing invariably precedes interest in technicalities
per se. It is only after one has "got" a poem, to use a
convenient shorthand term, that one begins to enquire
how exactly the poet succeeds in communicating his
experience to the reader. There is, moreover, much to be
learnt from a study of Owen's methods.

In the first place, his use of alliteration. In Swinburne,
where sound and sense are so closely identified, and,
more often than not, the sound forms the major part of
the content of a poem, alliteration becomes almost an
organic quality approximating more and more closely to
a kind of (tonic) onomatopœia. Since Swinburne's death
the practice of alliteration has been so vulgarized in the
Press that it has degenerated, in popular idiom at least,
into a facile means of emphasis—a mere verbal trick—
and in literature has now to struggle hard to escape the
inevitable associations which such a debasement involve.
It is interesting, therefore, to find a poet like Owen
openly embracing the alliterative convention, and by
virtually inventing a new alliterative method, or at least
imparting a fresh significance to his own, transcending

the limits of its general application. In Owen's verse the
repeated letter or group of letters affects not only the
cadence of the poem as a whole, but each individual
stressed syllable derives an added value both from its
isolated emphasis and from the relation in which it stands
to previous or subsequent alliterated words. It is easy
enough to see the difference between:

Though one were strong as seven,
He too with death shall dwell,
Nor wake with wings in heaven,
Nor weep for pains in hell.

and:

Red lips are not so red
As the stained stones kissed by the English dead.
Kindness of wooed and wooer
Seems shame to their love pure.
O love, your eyes Lose lure
When I behold eyes blinded in my stead!

It is not only that in the Swinburne the alliteration is so
glib, the rhythm so regular, that almost all trace of
emphasis is lost in the liquid evenness of the lines; but
that Owen, using emphasis with careful intent, manages
to achieve perfect cross-references of sound and stress,
little echoes and anticipations of tone, which are too
subtle to be analysed. Such effects cannot be obtained in
the manner of newspaper headlines. In each case the
alliteration, far from being an external ornament, has
become, as Dryden insisted that it should be, an integral
part of the emotional content of the poem; though while
in Swinburne this content is primarily expressed by
sound, and the alliteration is therefore in a sense ono-
matopœic, in Owen the sense-value of the poem imparts
a certain intellectual significance to the alliteration. It is
this intellectual connotation which distinguishes Owen's
use of alliterated words.

His use of assonance, and dissonance, is more straightforward; though the fact that he employed such a comparatively unknown form of line-ending in so many different poems compels some comment. The first point to
notice is that Owen avoids the stock pitfall of cacopho-
ny, and that curious sense of *frustration* consequent
on an uncompleted rhyme, which has hitherto frightened
most poets away from this particular termination. There
is never any hint of a tortured vowel sound, nor any
suggestion of bathos through a line being left hanging
"in mid-air." Inevitably lacking the conclusiveness of
rhyme, assonance has, when used skilfully, certain positive qualities of its own. It has, for example, rather
striking affinities with the elaborately ingenious conceits so generously exploited by the metaphysical poets
of the seventeenth century. Thus it combines an element
of *surprise* with a subsequent sense of satisfaction or
assent. Surprise that what should, seemingly, have been
a rhyme, is in fact not a rhyme; and satisfaction, when
the initial unexpectedness of the effect has been assimilated, at the added pungency given to the termination
by this piquant divergence from the normal. Again like

the conceit it frequently involves what might be called a *burlesque* factor—a burlesque of rhyme of course but without any comic implication—which serves to produce in the reader a sense of belittlement, and provides in this instance a technical equivalent, along a different line, to the disquieting, humbling purgation already remarked as characteristic of Owen's work.

Lastly, something at least should be said of the rhythmical structure of the poems. Regarded collectively, the latter exhibit two particular and largely individual effects of rhythm. The first occurs at regular intervals throughout the poems and can only be described, clumsily enough, as the resolution of a conflict between extreme verbal emphasis on the one hand and extreme rhythmical restraint on the other. An example may make this clearer.

> Who are these? Why sit they here in twilight?
> Wherefore rock they, purgatorial shadows,
> Drooping tongues from jaws that slob their relish,
> Baring teeth that leer like skulls' tongues wicked?
> Stroke on stroke of pain—but what slow panic,
> Gouged these chasms round their fretted sockets?
> Ever from their hair and through their hand palms
> Misery swelters. Surely we have perished
> Sleeping, and walk hell; but who these hellish?

In the above stanza, taken from a poem entitled **"Mental Cases,"** the verbal texture of the lines is so consistently emphatic, quite apart from any forcefulness of diction, as to be almost rhetorical; while the rhythm, in direct contrast, is so markedly *un*rhetorical as to be virtually colloquial. The result is a groping, jolting, clutching effect, magnificently appropriate to the subject, in which one can almost feel the convulsive vitality of the words struggling to become articulate through the quiet, choking, ironic monotony of the rhythm. This effect recurs mainly when Owen is describing specific episodes, either of actual fighting or the immediate results of fighting, and not in the more general poems, abstract or philosophical. It seems clear that in the former case something of the horror of such scenes remained fiercely alive in his memory, goading him into frantic efforts at depiction, efforts which he recognized intuitively could only attain artistic expression through the controlling medium of the strictest rhythmical restraint.

The second example is, in a sense, less complicated and less individually peculiar to Owen. It is, ultimately, only a modification of the "suspended" or "arrested" rhythm effect common to much English lyrical poetry. In it the rhythm is caught up and held, as it were momentarily above a precipice, before it topples over and descends precipitately in a swift cascade of sound. A poem named **"Futility,"** which opens with the lines:

> Move him into the sun—
> Gently its touch awoke him once,

furnishes a striking example of this in the second and concluding verse, which runs as follows:

> Think how it wakes the seeds—
> Woke, once, the clays of a cold star.
> Are limbs so dear-achieved, are sides
> Full-nerved—still warm—too hard to stir?
> Was it for this the clay grew tall?
> —O what made fatuous sunbeams toil
> To break earth's sleep at all?

Here the gradual retardation of cadence in the first four lines, leading up to the rhythmical climax of line five, enhances the reader's emotional reaction by delaying the stimulus for complete response until the latest possible moment, then flinging open the floodgates of the rhythm for the latter to rush with redoubled speed to its inevitable conclusion. Nowhere else does this effect occur in such entire formal perfection, though it is approached periodically in such lines as:

> One Spring! Is one too good to spare, too long?
> Spring wind would work its own way to my lung,
> And grow me legs as quick as lilac-shoots.

And also appears in embryo in single lines such as "Lend him to stroke these blind, blunt, bullet-heads," which recur regularly throughout the poems, in conjunction with more normal rhythmical structures which it is not necessary to consider here.

The intellectual and emotional content of Owen's verse is valuable because it expresses, in terms of poetry, a personal reaction to experiences which, at the time of their incidence at least, left most men hopelessly inarticulate.

—*I. M. Parsons*

So short an interval as twelve years does not appreciably lessen the difficulties always inherent in assessing the work of a young poet, more especially one who did not live to see the conclusion of the catastrophe which provoked his writings, and died leaving many of them fragmentary or unrevised. Yet in Owen's case the attempt is worth while if only in the hope of increasing, by however slight a margin, the number of people at present familiar with his work. That this number should still be comparatively small may be due to several causes: to his uncompromising honesty, to his many crudities of imagery and technique, or to the fact that it is the fashion among some critics to-day to ignore recent or contemporary poetry not susceptible of facile classification in some "school." Owen neither followed nor founded any school. Mr. Blunden rightly emphasises his early indebtedness to Keats, but seems unwitting of how swiftly Owen developed once the War had possessed his imagination. The influence of other poets is traceable in the later poems, but difficult to specify, and certainly few have since attempted to imitate his methods. Fortunately they do not lend themselves easily to imitation; they provided the vehicle for the communication of an entirely individual experience and are themselves stamped with the same individuality.

But Owen's importance does not rest finally in individual methods nor yet in any formal innovations which he employed. His significance is primarily one of purpose rather than of form. The intellectual and emotional content of his verse is valuable because it expresses, in terms of poetry, a personal reaction to experiences which, at the time of their incidence at least, left most men hopelessly inarticulate. It is only recently, under the influence of what might be called a tacit agreement on both sides to regard the War in the light of history, that the latter has begun to find permanent artistic record in prose. It is probably too much to hope that anything further will be added to the existing body of verse. Had Owen himself survived it is questionable whether he would have written finer poems, either on the subject of the War or outside it. Without the incentive of immediate experience, and away from the latter's inevitable environment, it is difficult to conceive of any retrospective experience providing a sufficient stimulus to force his latent emotions into renewed articulation. It is, accordingly, all the more significant that the burden of his poetry is substantially the same as that of the prose writers, German and English, whose work has received so much attention during the last two years. That side of war which they were so busy expressing then, he, ten years further back and through the distorting mirrors of the actual events, saw and felt with equal clarity. Like them, like all poets worth the name, he too is a propagandist. Not subversively like Shelley, nor ecstatically like Blake, nor yet didactically like Tennyson in his less inspired moments. There is neither creed nor dogma overtly expressed in these verses. Owen's propaganda is more subtly clothed, his metaphysic more modestly expressed. *"All the poet can do to-day is to warn."* Implied rather than stated it is none the less positive for that; and its implications are as sane as they are unequivocal. They embody, first, a calm realization of the inevitability of his position:

> Since we believe not otherwise can kind fires
>   burn;
> Nor ever suns smile true on child, or field, or
>   fruit.
> For God's invincible spring our love is made
>   afraid;
> Therefore, not loath, we lie out here; therefore
>   were born,
>   For love of God seems dying.

The sincerity of that verse alone, despite the rather disappointing portrait of Owen which Mr. Blunden's memoir provides, suffices to dispel any suspicion of an hysterical or sentimental brand of pacifism latent in the passionate utterance of some of the other poems. "He pitied others," writes Sassoon, "he did not pity himself." Indeed the complete impersonality of his work, includ-

ing those poems in which he wrote of himself, presupposes a hard objectivity which denies utterly any trace of sentimentality or morbid introspection. Even in **"A Terre,"** the most personal and in many ways the most poignant of his poems, it is a universal rather than an individual "I" who speaks, and the sub-title "Being the Philosophy of Many Soldiers," is amply justified.

But Owen's philosophy does not stop short at anything so negative as this calm acceptance of fate. Beyond it there exists always that fund of burning resentment against the ugliness of war—against the brutality, and hypocrisy, and futility and waste of it all—which remains, at bottom, the paramount incitement of his verse. Without that bitter indignation within, demanding utterance, these poems could not have been written. Nor, had that emotion constituted their sole source, would they have emerged the things of beauty which they are. It is only because the poet in Owen was stronger than the humanitarian, because his sense of values was keen enough to temper and control his indignation, that the latter could be directed successfully into a creative channel. But for that emotional equilibrium the result might still have been tragic or terrible, but not beautiful. As it is, the poems evidence not only his clear perception of the real issues involved, but the vital humanity which was so essential a part of his philosophy of life: *"I am the enemy you killed, my friend."* And there faces us on every page just that sense of pity, which is neither maudlin sentiment nor petty self-commiseration, which he himself once summed as "the pity of war, the pity war distilled."

Dylan Thomas (essay date 1946)

SOURCE: "Wilfred Owen," in *Quite Early One Morning,* New Directions, 1954, pp. 117-33.

[*In the following excerpt from an essay that was written in 1946, Thomas hails Owen as "a poet of all times, all places and all wars."*]

[In a volume of his poems, Wilfred Owen] was to show, to England, and the intolerant world, the foolishness, unnaturalness, horror, inhumanity, and insupportability of War, and to expose, so that all could suffer and see, the heroic lies, the willingness of the old to sacrifice the young, indifference, grief, the Souls of Soldiers.

The volume, as Wilfred Owen visualised it in trench and shell hole and hospital, in the lunatic centre of battle, in the collapsed and apprehensive calm of sick-leave, never appeared. But many of the poems that were to have been included in the volume remain, their anguish unabated, their beauty for ever, their truth manifest, their warning unheeded. . . .

[He] was the greatest poet of the first Great War. Perhaps, in the future, if there are men, then, still to read—by which I mean, if there are men at all—he may be regarded as one of the great poets of all wars. But only War itself can resolve the problem of the ultimate truth of his, or of anyone else's poetry: War, or its cessation. . . .

[The] voice of the poetry of Wilfred Owen speaks to us, down the revolving stages of thirty years, with terrible new significance and strength. We had not forgotten his poetry, but perhaps we had allowed ourselves to think of it as the voice of one particular time, one place, one war. Now, at the beginning of what, in the future, may never be known to historians as the "atomic age"—for obvious reasons: there may be no historians—we can see, rereading Owen, that he is a poet of all times, all places, and all wars. There is only one War: that of men against men.

Owen left to us less than sixty poems, many of them complete works of art, some of them fragments, some of them in several versions of revision, the last poem of them all dying away in the middle of a line: "Let us sleep now . . ." I shall not try to follow his short life, from the first imitations of his beloved Keats to the last prodigious whisper of "sleep" down the profound and echoing tunnels of **"Strange Meeting."** Mr. Edmund Blunden, in the introduction to his probably definitive edition of the poems, has done that with skill and love. His collected poems make a little, huge book, working—and always he worked on his poems like fury, or a poet—from a lush ornamentation of language, brilliantly, borrowed melody, and ingenuous sentiment, to dark, grave, assonant rhythms, vocabulary purged and sinewed, wrathful pity and prophetic utterance.

Who wrote [**"Exposure"**]? A boy of twenty-three or four, comfortably born and educated, serious, "literary," shy, never "exposed" before to anything harsher than a Channel crossing, fond of *Endymion* and the open air, fresh from a tutor's job. Earlier, in letters to his mother, he had written from the Somme, in 1917, in that infernal winter: "There is a fine heroic feeling about being in France, and I am in perfect spirits . . ." Or again, he talked of his companions: "The roughest set of knaves I have ever been herded with." When he heard the guns for the first time, he said: "It was a sound not without a certain sublimity."

It was *this* young man, at first reacting so conventionally to his preconceived ideas of the "glory of battle"—and such ideas he was to slash and scorify a very short time afterwards—who wrote the poem? It was this young man, steel-helmeted, buff-jerkined, gauntleted, rubberwaded, in the freezing rain of the-flooded trenches, in the mud that was not mud but an octopus of sucking clay, who wrote [**"Anthem for Doomed Youth"**]. . . .

There is no contradiction here. The studious, healthy young man with a love of poetry, as we see him set against the safe background of school, university, and tutordom, is precisely the same as the sombre but radiant, selfless, decrying and exalting, infinitely tender, humble, harrowed seer and stater of the **"Anthem for Doomed Youth"** and for himself. There is no differ-

ence. Only, the world has happened to him. And everything, as Yeats once said, happens in a blaze of light.

The world had happened to him. All its suffering moved about and within him. And his intense pity for all human fear, pain, and grief was given trumpet-tongue. He knew, as surely as though the words had been spoken to him aloud, as indeed they had been though they were the words of wounds, the shape of the dead, the colour of blood, he knew he stood alone among men to *plead* for them in their agony, to blast the walls of ignorance, pride, pulpit, and state. He stood like Everyman, in No Man's Land. . . . And out of this, he wrote the poem called [**"Greater Love"**]. . . .

It was impossible for him to avoid the sharing of suffering. He could not record a wound that was not his own. He had so very many deaths to die, and so very short a life within which to endure them all. It's no use trying to imagine what would have happened to Owen had he lived on. Owen, at twenty-six or so, exposed to the hysteria and exploded values of false peace. Owen alive now, at the age of fifty-three, and half the world starving. You cannot generalize about age and poetry. A man's poems, if they are good poems, are always older than himself; and sometimes they are ageless. We know that the shape and the texture of his poems would always be restlessly changing, though the purpose behind them would surely remain unalterable; he would always be experimenting technically, deeper and deeper driving towards the final intensity of language: the words behind words. . . . Owen, had he lived, would never have ceased experiment; and so powerful was the impetus behind his work, and so intricately strange his always growing mastery of words, he would never have ceased to influence the work of his contemporaries. Had he lived, English poetry would not be the same. The course of poetry is dictated by accidents. Even so, he is one of the four most profound influences upon the poets who came after him; the other three being Gerard Manley Hopkins, the later W. B. Yeats, and T. S. Eliot.

But we must go back, from our guesses and generalisations and abstractions, to Owen's poetry itself; to the brief, brave life and the enduring words. In hospital, labelled as a "neurasthenic case," he observed, and experienced, the torments of the living dead, and he has expressed their "philosophy" in the dreadful poem **"A Terre."** . . .

To see him in his flame-lit perspective, against the background now of the poxed and cratered warscape, shivering in the snow under the slitting wind, marooned on a frozen desert, or crying, in a little oven of mud, that his "senses are charred," is to see a man consigned to articulate immolation. He buries his smashed head with his own singed hands, and is himself the intoning priest over the ceremony, the suicide, the sunset. He is the common touch. He is the bell of the church of the broken body. He writes love letters home for the illiterate dead. Ignorant, uncaring, hapless as the rest of the bloody troops, he is their arguer shell-shocked into diction, though none may understand. He is content to be the unhonoured prophet in death's country: for fame, as he said, was the last infirmity he desired.

There are many aspects of Owen's life and work upon which I haven't touched at all. I have laboured, in these notes . . . , only one argument, and that inherent in the poems themselves. Owen's words have shown, for me, and I hope (and know) for you, the position-in-calamity which, without intellectual choice, he chose to take. But remember, he was not a "wise man" in the sense that he had achieved, for himself, a true way of believing. He believed there was no one true way because all ways are by-tracked and rutted and pitfalled with ignorance and injustice and indifference. He was himself diffident and self-distrustful. He had to be wrong, clumsy, affected often, ambiguous, bewildered. Like every man at last, he had to fight the whole war by himself. He lost, and he won. In a letter written towards the end of his life and many deaths, he quoted from Rabindranath Tagore: "When I go hence, let this be my parting word, that what I have seen is unsurpassable."

Joseph Cohen (essay date 1956)

SOURCE: "Wilfred Owen's Greatest Love," in *Tulane Studies in English*, Vol. VI, 1956, pp. 105-17.

[*In the following excerpt, Cohen explores the spiritual source of Owen's poetry.*]

Here in thirty-three brief pages is the evidence that Wilfred Owen was the greatest poet of the war. There have been war-poets, but he was a poet of another kind." Thus wrote John Middleton Murry in reviewing the 1920 edition of Wilfred Owen's *Poems*. Between Murry's pronouncement and a statement by Dylan Thomas in 1954 that Owen was "the greatest of the poets who wrote in and of the Great War, and one of the greatest poets of this century," many similar laudatory comments have appeared in print. But the commentators, however lavish in their praise, have been sparing in their criticism. Surprisingly few really perceptive studies of Owen's poetry exist, although appreciative remarks appear frequently.

Those who have sought to explain critically the phenomenal regard for Owen's work—apparently he has had no more than two detractors of international reputation among hundreds of published admirers—have suggested that he merits attention either for his aesthetic and technical accomplishments or for his political attitude toward war. At the same time they all acknowledge the presence of a distinguishing *spiritual* element in the poetry. It goes by various descriptions. A *New York Times* reviewer called it "divine understanding," Ifan K. Fletcher termed it "a state of spiritual awareness," Cecil Day Lewis said that it was "unsentimental pity and sacred imagination," Stephen Spender referred to it as "an attitude of mind, for instance, love or pity"; W. B. Yeats thought of it as "passive suffering" and David Daiches

defined it as an "eternal plangent appeal." Further, V. de Sola Pinto, in a discussion of Owen as a political prophet recognized the poet's "profoundly religious mind"; and Edmund Blunden, whose edition of Owen's poems is the only one now in print, described him as one who possessed "the dignity of a seer."

None of these writers deemed the distinguishing spiritual element of sufficient meaning, however, to give it their full critical attention. Yet I believe it is important enough in Owen's mature poetic thought to warrant equal if not more attention than that given to either his aesthetic accomplishment or his political conviction. In the subsequent discussion I seek to establish the point of view that Owen was above all a spiritual poet, and that the distinguishing spiritual element in his poetry is a thoroughly developed religious concept which he called the greater love. Its source, I believe, is to be found in the impact on his thinking made by the life of Jesus. . . .

> Owen was above all a spiritual poet, and the distinguishing spiritual element in his poetry is a thoroughly developed religious concept which he called the greater love.
>
> —*Joseph Cohen*

One of Owen's last prose utterances contains an emphatic but apparently incomplete statement of the spiritual force which the concept of the greater love gave to his poetry. . . . The meaning of [Owen's preface, for his first volume of poems] now heralded as one of the significant poetic documents of the twentieth century, has been widely and variously interpreted. In practically every case it has been described as a statement of either artistic principle or political belief. These it may contain, but it is essentially an early draft of a detailed definition of the greater love in time of war:

> This book is not about heroes. English poetry is not yet fit
> to speak of them.
> Nor is it about deeds, or lands, nor anything about glory, honour,
> might, majesty, dominion, or power, except War.
> Above all I am not concerned with Poetry.
> My subject is War, and the pity of War.
> The Poetry is in the pity.
> (If I thought the letter of this book would last, I might have
> used proper names; but if the spirit of it survives—survives Prussia
> —my ambition and those names will have achieved themselves

fresher fields than Flanders. . . .)
> Yet these elegies are to this generation in no
> sense consolatory.

They may be to the next. All a poet can do to-day
> is warn. That
is why the true Poets must be truthful.

The preface, it will be observed, closely follows Owen's spiritual point of view. The concern for the divergence between spiritual principle and practice is immediately seen. In practice the poetry of the war failed, Owen thought, because it concentrated on those same interests which were undermining the church. The two were so closely identified in Owen's mind that he was able to describe the failure of one by using the language of the other. Poetry had spoken of deeds, lands, glory and all the rest; and like the words of the "pulpit professionals," it said nothing of the pity of war on a grandly spiritual scale, or of sympathy for German combatants as well as British. In its patriotic selfrighteousness it stressed little of the necessity of God's justice for all men or the meaning of Jesus' sacrifice. It was therefore unfit to speak of heroes, Owen suggested, because in his opinion the only heroes were those who put the principles of Jesus into practice. They lived without hate and died with the greater love, not in patriotic sacrifice but in spiritual affirmation. The preface itself is Owen's spiritual manifesto of his poetic purpose, and as such it serves, incomplete though it may be, as an adequate introduction to his fundamentally spiritual poetry.

Over one half of the fifty-nine poems printed in the Blunden edition are devoted to Owen's spiritual pronouncements. Taken as a whole, they illustrate the poet's conscientious retreat into the "pure Christianity" of his early youth in an attempt to repudiate the "pure patriotism" of the state church. De Sola Pinto has said that Owen "was unable to retain his belief in orthodox Christianity." Indeed, it was this orthodox Christianity the poet sought to get back to. The clearest indications of his effort are in his poetic treatment of God, the sacrifice of Jesus, and the relationship of that sacrifice to the greater love. . . .

Owen's training emphasized the somewhat narrow but strongly entrenched Old Testament concept of God as a disinterested though jealous, sternly just, tribal Deity. His poetry reflects that training. God is, in Owen's words, the "Field-Marshal" whose strategy is carefully planned. To worship Him is to compound love with the fear the soldier feels toward his commanding general. In the poem **"Exposure"** this fear finds expression through discipline in the face of death: "To-night, His frost will fasten on this mud and us, / Shrivelling many hands, puckering foreheads crisp." Through the winter stalemate the soldier sustains his faith, but when that season ends the fear clearly predominates: "For God's invincible spring our love is made afraid." War has, for the poet, halted the incarnation of divine love, since the invincibility of spring referred to here is no longer the renewal of life in the Adonis-Osiris-Christ tradition: "Nor ever suns smile true on child, or field, or fruit," but the stern judgment of death by fire for those sojourning in the new Sodom and Gomorrah.

Yet the poet knew God's manifestations were infinite. In **"Spring Offensive"** he records the increased casualties, but he makes a point of mentioning that God is not oblivious to these deaths. Of those whose lot it is to die, he writes that "Some say God caught them even before they fell." In **"Apologia pro Poemate Meo"** Owen begins on a different tack with the line, "I, too, saw God through mud," developing forthwith the divinity in man; and in **"To My Friend with an Identity Disc"** and **"The Chances"** God is thanked for specific blessings.

He remains, however, essentially the "Jahveh" of the Old Testament, mysterious, taciturn, silent. Owen could not conceive of Him as an informal ally, and he consistently refused to sanction the pat, comforting assurance from many pulpits that God was "on our side." Nor could Owen accept explicit assurances of a reward from Him in the next world for making the supreme sacrifice in this one. In **"The End"** he first posed the query:

> Shall life renew these bodies? Of a truth
> All death will He annul, all tears assuage?—
> Fill the void veins of Life again with youth,
> And wash, with an immortal water, Age?

He answered it thus:

> When I do ask white Age he saith not so:
> 'My head hangs weighed with snow.'
> And when I hearken to the Earth, she saith:
> 'My fiery heart shrinks, aching. It is death.
> My ancient scars shall not be glorified,
> Nor my titanic tears, the sea, be dried.'

Owen's experiences . . . were bringing him closer to a structure of belief centering around Jesus. When war came Owen saw its solution not in the love based on fear but in a love based on sacrifice. As an officer in a combat infantry regiment he was in constant anxiety for the welfare of his men, and his poetry expounded and reiterated that responsibility in terms of Christian sacrifice rather than in terms of military discipline or patriotic duty. **"At A Calvary Near the Ancre"** is one of several poems which deals with this theme:

> One ever hangs where shelled roads part.
> > In this war He too lost a limb,
> But His disciples hide apart:
> > And now the Soldiers bear with Him.

> Near Golgotha strolls many a priest,
> > And in their faces there is pride
> That they were flesh-marked by the Beast
> > By whom the gentle Christ's denied.

> The scribes on all the people shove
> > And bawl allegiance to the state,
> But they who love the greater love
> > Lay down their life; they do not hate.

The poem is undated, like many of Owen's other poems, but its title provides a clue to its composition. The Second Manchesters, to whom Owen was attached, were stationed in the vicinity of the Ancre (now the Albert River) around February, 1917. His mentioning the greater love indicates that he had worked out the concept by that time, five months before he wrote of it from the hospital on the Somme. I think it can thus be safely assumed that Owen reached his final spiritual position at least twenty-one months before he died. Having worked out this position, he did not go beyond it. He sought merely to test it by examining the relationship between the greater love and other kinds, namely, paternal, sexual and brotherly love. The first relationship he worked out in **"The Parable of the Old Men and the Young,"** the second in **"Greater Love,"** and the third in several poems of which **"Strange Meeting"** was the last and most important.

"The Parable of the Old Men and the Young" compactly and succinctly retells in sixteen brief lines the Old Testament story of Abraham's near-sacrifice of Isaac. Owen's version, however, ends with Isaac's murder:

> Behold
> A ram, caught in a thicket by its horns;
> Offer the Ram of Pride instead of him.
> But the old man would not so, but slew his son—
> And half the seed of Europe, one by one.

In the biblical treatment Abraham's love for his son is never impugned. Neither is his greater love for God, which is made manifest in his willingness to sacrifice his child. He is called upon, however, to relinquish one love to demonstrate the other. Torn between these two loyalties he gives more meaning to paternal affection by remaining steadfast to the greater love. Like Isaac, he is the child obeying the father. His test of faith is one of ancient Hebrew justice. The modern Abraham's test is in a different tradition, that of Christian mercy. Yet the terms remain the same: The father must acknowledge the greater love in order to give meaning to his role as parent. The only difference is in the nature of the sacrifice. The biblical Abraham was called upon to give his son, whereas the modern Abraham had only to exorcise his pride. The former's test was harder, yet he passed it because he possessed the greater love; the latter's was easier, but he lacked both the greater love and mercy, and his failure was more profound and more shameful. Owen saw this failure as the result of his countrymen's confusion of political and economic ambitions with spiritual values, which he symbolized in the Ram of Pride.

The moral of Owen's parable is that parental affection is valueless without the greater love. When it is absent catastrophe, as in Isaac's case, follows. If this is possible with a close blood relationship, what values, Owen asks, can sexual love sustain in a time when the greater love is manifestly unpopular? His answer, in the poem he chose to entitle **"Greater Love,"** is that it can sustain none. Herein the lover, who has been to war, contrasts his beloved's erotic charms (found in the physical

referents: lips, eyes, limbs, voice, heart and hands), with his own spiritual reflections, produced by his experience in combat. Through this juxtaposition Owen emphasizes—somewhat in the manner of John Donne—the absence of spiritual sustenance in physical attraction as opposed to the eternal value of spiritual reflection. The extracted juxtapositions are as follows:

> Red lips are not so red
> As the stained stones kissed by the English dead.
> O Love, your eyes lose lure
> When I behold eyes blinded in my stead.
>
> Your slender attitude
> Trembles not exquisite like limbs knife-skewed. . . .
>
> Your dear voice is not dear . . .
> As theirs whom none now hear.
>
> Heart, you were never hot,
> Nor large, nor full like hearts made great with
>   shot. . . .
>
> And though your hand be pale
> Paler are all which trail
> Your cross through flame and hail.

In addition to the father-son and the lover-beloved relationships Owen examined the presence of the greater love, or its more frequent absence, in the relationships between civilian and soldier in **"Apologia pro Poemate Meo,"** between officer and enlisted man in **"Inspection,"** and between the British and the Germans in **"Strange Meeting."** These poems are concretely religious in their imagery, and each contributes something to the view of Owen as spiritual poet. But of all the poems Owen composed on the theme of the greater love **"Strange Meeting"** may be singled out as the most accomplished of his attempts to express the practice of his dominant spiritual principle.

Owen argued in **"Strange Meeting"** that the full meaning of the greater love was to be found in its application to life, rather than in its expression through death. In wartime, or prior to the outbreak of hostilities, that application meant putting into practice Jesus' words in the "Sermon on the Mount" to "love your enemies" (Matt. 6:44). The fundamental message of **"Strange Meeting"** is that brotherly love must be learned not in the death struggle between enemies but before such a struggle can come about.

From the discussion between the two dead soldiers in hell—one British, the slayer, the other German, the slain—"the truth untold, / The pity of war, the pity war distilled," comes out. It is that the greater love can be achieved only through the recognition of the meaning of sacrifice prior to death. If a man is willing to lay down his life for his friend then he must learn earlier to live for that friend, with whom he shares a common brotherhood. When the British soldier tells his strange friend "here is no cause to mourn," the latter voices his despair in being made an inheritor of unfulfilled love: "For by my glee might many men have laughed, / And of my weeping something had been left, / Which must die now." Without recognizing the full value of this lost contribution there can be only spiritual dissolution: "Now men will go content with what we spoiled. / Or, discontent, boil bloody, and be spilled." For those who do learn in time, there is not only salvation but fulfillment in this life: "Courage was mine, and I had mystery, / Wisdom was mine, and I had mastery." Thus in its final application Owen's spiritual philosophy taught not only the value of life but that sacrificial love was involved in obtaining and keeping it. It is the same lesson Jesus taught by word and example nineteen centuries ago.

In spite of this obviously spiritual content and the presence of even more literal references of a religious nature in **"Strange Meeting,"** such as the biblical allusion to the swiftness of the tiger (Second Samuel 1:23), some critics have been inclined to regard the poem as prophetic in a limited political context. It seems more likely, however, that Owen meant it to be spiritually apologetic in the fullest orthodox sense.

The significance of the greater love in Owen's central spiritual philosophy does not need, it seems to me, further exegesis. Without question, it was his one most important belief. But it may be useful to document further for the general reader my assumption that Owen was primarily a spiritual poet. This may be accomplished first by taking cognizance briefly of religious allusions in poems not mentioned heretofore; and secondly, by extracting, as it were, a spiritual credo implicit in Owen's works.

Keeping in mind the multiple references to God, Jesus and the greater love cited already, we may observe that allusions to heaven and hell appear with frequence, particularly in **"Mental Cases," "Winter Song," "The Show," "Cramped in That Funnelled Hole,"** and **"A Farewell."** In **"All Sounds Have Been as Music"** Owen writes of the country church bells clamoring; and in **"Music"** he speaks of having "hurled / Thuds of God's thunder." His key words in **"Anthem For Doomed Youth"** are "prayers," "bells," "choirs," "candles," and "holy glimmers." The third stanza of **"The Calls"** describes the church bells pealing in the background as services begin. In **"A Terre"** a multiple amputee begs God for the spring wind, while in **"Disabled"** the soul of another is inquired after. In **"My Shy Hand"** Owen speaks of holding a love there where "Life . . . is sweeter held than in God's heart." **"Arms and the Boy"** discusses man's inventing weapons alien to his nature since "God will grow no talons at his heels / Nor antlers through the thickness of his curls." In **"Asleep"** the heavens are "High pillowed in calm pillows of God's making." The **"Sonnet On Seeing A Piece Of Our Artillery Brought Into Action"** closes with a prayer that God will curse the great gun, just as the gun curses heaven whenever it is fired. **"The Promisers"** portrays the poet's searching through the city for Jesus whom he thinks he will locate easily; and **"Training"** reproduces some of those same images of Jesus which Owen used in his letter to Osbert

Sitwell. Lastly, **"Le Christianisme"** deals with the irony in the destruction of a Christian house of worship by Christian soldiers.

From all these poems plus the letters it is possible to extract what I believe to be the poet's spiritual credo. It is not complete, and it is highly unlikely that it can ever be positively verified, but it is nonetheless valuable for that. The main tenets of this credo are as follows: (1) God created the universe and man out of love, which finds its expression in the dispensation of divine justice. (2) Jesus is the Son of God who, out of love, sacrificed Himself for the redemption of mankind. In so doing He established an identity with man which makes it possible for the latter to understand and pursue spiritual goals. (3) The *Bible* contains the revealed word of God. (4) Faith is sufficient unto itself. (5) Immortality, if it does exist, is probably quite different from the conventional interpretation of the church. (6) War as an instrument of national policy and human activity is incompatible with the principles set forth by Jesus. (7) True happiness can be achieved only in spiritual terms. (8) The brotherhood of man will come only through the individual expression of the greater love. (9) Evil in our time often expresses itself in political ambition and pride, reaching even into the church itself. (10) The church, before it can do God's work, needs to divest itself of much corruption, diversion and ornamentation. (11) Man is his brother's keeper. (12) Only through temptation and its rejection can man determine his true spiritual strength. (13) True repentance, if it takes the form of putting into practice the principle it teaches, is its own reward. It is significant that neither an extensive aesthetic statement of principles nor a political one can be similarly taken from Owen's work. . . .

[It] is my belief that Owen's ultimate status, whatever it may be, must rest primarily on his orthodox evocation of the greater love. It was the expression of this distinguishing spiritual element which made him not merely a war-poet, but as John Middleton Murry first described him, "a poet of another kind."

Edmund Blunden (essay date 1958)

SOURCE: "Mainly Wilfred Owen," in *War Poets, 1914-1918*, Longmans, Green, 1958, pp. 32-9.

[*In the following excerpt, Blunden explores the influences on Owen's poetry and characterizes his poems as richly imaginative and distinguished by a "spiritual and mental dignity."*]

The poems of Owen on war express many aspects, as his own attempted classification shows, but perhaps pity is the one he felt most. In **"Strange Meeting"** the ghost of the enemy soldier whom he has bayoneted, calling him friend in the world of shades, says that he might otherwise have made a gift to posterity. But:

It seemed that out of the battle I escaped
Down some profound dull tunnel, long since
   scooped
Through granites which titanic wars had groined.
Yet also there encumbered sleepers groaned,
Too fast in thought or death to be bestirred.
Then, as I probed them, one sprang up, and stared
With piteous recognition in fixed eyes,
Lifting distressful hands as if to bless.
And by his smile, I knew that sullen hall;
With a thousand fears that vision's face was
   grained;
Yet no blood reached there from the upper
   ground,
And no guns thumped, or down the flues made
   moan.
'Strange, friend,' I said, 'Here is no cause to
   mourn.'
'None,' said the other, 'save the undone years,
The hopelessness. Whatever hope is yours,
Was my life also; I went hunting wild
After the wildest beauty in the world,
Which lies not calm in eyes, or braided hair,
But mocks the steady running of the hour,
And if it grieves, grieves richlier than here.
For by my glee might many men have laughed,
And of my weeping something had been left,
Which must die now. I mean the truth untold,
The pity of war, the pity war distilled . . .

The conclusion of **"Insensibility"** is a solemn condemnation of those with no compassion for the victims of the fighting:

By choice they made themselves immune
To pity and whatever grieves in man
Before the last sea and the hapless stars;
Whatever mourns when many leave these shores;
Whatever shares
The eternal reciprocity of tears.

Again, preparing a preface for the book that he designed, Owen insisted, "Above all, this is not concerned with Poetry. The subject of it is War, and the pity of War. The Poetry is in the pity." Be it noted that Owen had no tolerance for amateurish elegies such as the time teemed with—calling them "poets' tearful fooling." Finally a true word on Owen's quality of pity is found in his friend's introduction to the selection of poems published in 1920. "He never wrote his poems (as so many war poets did) to make the effect of a personal gesture. He pitied others; he did not pity himself. . . ."

In 1914, when he was aged only twenty-one, his immature verse at any rate spoke for his breadth of vision and his ability to sum things up. After 1914 when as poet he had shed a certain weak luxuriousness through his ordeal by battle, with intervals for reflection and analysis, his intellectual advance was swift. In many respects Owen was what is called a typical young officer, well in control of his duties, meeting emergencies with good sense, at the same time ready with the usual dry comments on the daily round and idle authority. But very few young officers had also his profound interest in the great subjects of the world's destiny. We meet with a spiritual and mental dignity, with a solitariness of imaginative purpose, in many of his poems; by that quality, it may be, his individual genius is most clearly distinguished.

"The Show" is one of the poems referred to, with its opening line "My soul looked down from a vague height with Death" and its unveiling of a stupendous, automatic, painful scene of modern war—almost the hieroglyph of the end or the denial of our civilization. This is of the order of those panoramas in Thomas Hardy's *Dynasts,* or of the Vision of Dante. The poet's high imagination is voiced with a clear certainty. Such compositions might justify wonder even in a critic when it is remembered what the author's situation was, either involved in the mud-pits and barrages he describes or about to be among them. Imagination triumphs.

But it is not only in such allegorical pieces that Owen the poet is seen above the battle in which as a soldier he was desperately engaged. A number of original and understanding essays or does on human nature—for instance, **"Insensibility."** **"Greater Love"** or the more pictorial **"Spring Offensive"**—were written with singular devotion. Wisdom and art in them were united while the poet as his first editor remarks quite forgot his own case. This richness of thought and word reminds us always that Keats was his idol, and if Keats could know that he had a worshipper so congenial and so equally capable of taking his themes far beyond his own actual afflictions he would be happy. In Keats's lines on negative capability in "Hyperion" something very like the selfless power of Owen's war poems is defined:

to bear all naked truths,
And to envisage circumstance, all calm,
That is the top of sovereignty.

It is true, of course, that some of the poems are not calm, but imprecatory and scalding; it could not have been otherwise, the urgency being that of a cry from the depths, as one devastating day or night seized the humble heroes or conscripts.

Nothing has yet been said here of the radiant art of poetry which Owen practised, and which was progressive. It is not out of place to glance at it, for deeply considered technique itself was part of the offering that this soldier-poet made to eventual peace and mercy. He was what Wordsworth called Coleridge, "an epicure in sound," he gathered a copious and various vocabulary partly because of the musical values of words. With Keats he delights in slow movements, full tides of stresses. He plays with alliteration finely, and with internal rhyme. Owen's assonances in place of rhymes have made him a name among later poets and prosodists. Verlaine, whose poems like many others by French writers were part of his inner life, may have helped him to think over this novelty of assonances, which in **"Strange Meeting"** especially is so integral. The bitterness of his heart required some discord in the utterance. Lastly, what an excellent writer of sonnets he became! To concentrate meaning and metaphor within that enduring form was no doubt a pleasure to him, a son of art, even if the topic was pain and grief.

Hilda D. Spear (essay date 1958)

SOURCE: "Wilfred Owen and Poetic Truth," in *University of Kansas City Review,* Vol. XXV, No. 2, Winter 1958, pp. 110-16.

[*In the following excerpt, Spear explores Owen's concept of poetic truth, which she believes was arrived at through disillusion with his own earlier poetry.*]

Although many writers have glanced at Wilfred Owen's ideas of poetic truth, no one has fully defined and documented them; no one has followed him through the profound mental and spiritual struggles in which he was led to reject the kind of poetry which he had once most admired; no one has succeeded in fully correlating his final concept of truth, arrived at through agony and disillusion, with the concept found in his earlier poems. . . .

Owen's early poetry appears to be far removed in spirit from his later work. As a young man he was a natural romantic. His poetic idol was Keats and his first poetic effusions reflect his idolatry. From the age of ten he believed in his vocation as a poet, and year by year he steeped his mind and thoughts in poetry, particularly romantic poetry, and especially that of Keats, although his constant references to and quotations from Shelley suggest that Shelley too had a considerable place in his affections. When he was seventeen he celebrated the memory of Keats in a sonnet; at eighteen he went on a pilgrimage to Keats' house in Teignmouth; at nineteen the sight of a lock of Keats' hair moved him once more to laudatory verse. Yet he himself was, above all, a poet, interested in the art of poetry and in poetic truth.

It may be expected that to the youthful admirer of Keats the famous dictum, "Beauty is truth, truth beauty," would be his accepted creed. And there is every evidence that this was indeed so, for the sensuous perception of beauty is very strong in his juvenilia, and the rich, somewhat lush imagery would have justified Yeats' gibe in his letter of December 21, 1936, to Dorothy Wellesley about the "sucked sugar-stick" in Owen's poetry, if Yeats had had no opportunity to read the mature work of Owen's last years.

The subjects which Owen chose for his early poetry were closely connected with the conventional, romantic idea of beauty—golden hair, autumn, perfect beauty; he wrote of these subjects with a richness of vocabulary which almost dazzles in the brightness of its colors and the sparkling resplendence of its imagery. One has only to read his sonnet on **"Golden Hair"**:

> This is more like the aureoles of Aurora,
> The leaves of flames, the flame of her corona.
> Not Petrarch wore such coronals, nor Laura,
> Nor yet his orange-trees by old Verona,
> Nor gay gold fruits that yellow Barcelona.

or the even more lush version of this sonnet in the British Museum—or, among the same manuscripts, many other passages rich with the names of precious stones and bright colors—to realize how deeply Owen was impressed by the sheer sensuous beauty of language, and how he became carried away by what he once described as "language sweet as sobs."

The idea of beauty which pervades this early poetry is a purely external one, finding its origin in physical sensations—principally in appeals to the eye or the ear. An excellent illustration of the receptiveness of Owen's mind to such appeals is the poem **"From My Diary, July 1914,"** in which not only is his subject-matter drawn from visual and aural impressions, but also the poem itself is given a visual pattern to enhance the rhythmic pattern and to emphasize the experimental use of half-rhyme:

> Leaves
>   Murmuring by myriads in the shimmering trees.
> Lives
>   Wakening with wonder in the Pyrenees.
> Birds
>   Cheerily chirping in the early day.
> Bards
>   Singing of summer scything thro' the hay.

This poem with its stamp of immaturity and of conscious artistry was written a week or so before war broke out. At that time Owen was in France. He was twenty-one years old. For him the pleasure of such simple joys and beauties in life were still the truth and could be interpreted in poetry.

When war descended with terrible suddenness on Europe, Owen was in France. In England a great wave of war eagerness swept over the country: *The Times* for 5 August 1914 reported that the London crowds were "filled with the war spirit"; in December Ben Keeling was writing, "I may possibly live to think differently, but at the present moment, assuming this war had to come, I feel nothing but gratitude to the gods for sending it in my time." Bertrand Russell remembers that "average men and women were delighted at the prospect of war." But in France there was no excitement, only a grim determination to protect the country from the threat of the German army. . . .

Wilfred Owen was immediately faced with the negation of beauty as he had seen it:

> The cyclone of the pressure on Berlin
> Is over all the width of Europe whirled,
> Rending the sails of progress. Rent or furled
> Are all art's ensigns. Verse moans. Now begin

Famines of thought and feeling. Love's wine's
thin.
The grain of earth's great autumn rots, down-
hurled.

The idyllic beauty of the Pyrenees was threatened with
desecration. What had seemed the simple truths of life
were not large enough to take in the threat of war.

When Owen returned to France in January 1917 as an
officer attached to the 2nd Manchester Regiment, he
was briefly moved by the spirit of excitement which had
seized nearly every young man going to war for the first
time: "There is a fine heroic feeling about being in
France," he wrote to his mother but this feeling was in
no way a reflection of his poetic beliefs which were finally shattered by his first contact with trench warfare. A
month after the letter to his mother quoted above, he was
writing to her again, "I suppose I can endure cold and
fatigue and the face-to-face death as well as another; but
extra for me there is the universal pervasion of *Ugliness*.
Hideous landscapes, vile noises, foul language . . . everything unnatural, broken, blasted." This was the new truth
with which he had to come to terms, and for which he
strove to find expression. In 1917 Wilfred Owen was not
quite twenty-four years old, but maturing "with terrible
rapidity" he became convinced of the inadequacy of his
former poetic creed to express contemporary experience.
Amidst the physical ugliness and horror of the trenches
he saw beauty and truth emerge as spiritual qualities. The
ephemeral exterior was unimportant; it could be rough as
"the hoarse oaths" which hid the soldiers' courage; it
could be as silent as the steadfastness of sentries on duty.

> **The experience of war had given to
> Wilfred Owen a new set of values; he
> knew the power of poetry, and as a poet
> he believed that he could and should
> express the horror and pity of war.**
>
> —*Hilda D. Spear*

Having come to a new realization of truth, Owen was
ruthless with his own poetry: sentimentalism could have
no place in a world at war, and it seems probable that
had he lived, there would have been little trace of the
romantic and conventionally "poetic" in his work, for
with the sureness of the true artist he was expunging
everything that was not meaningful from his writing.
His mother told how he asked her to burn a whole sack-
ful of his work; the extant manuscripts are full of can-
cellations and corrections; manuscripts of many of the
published poems show with what care he sharpened and
made more exact the language that he used. In addition
to all this he looked upon poetry with a new eye, with
mockery for the "poetic" epithet and the euphemistic
metaphor, with irony for the subjects that were usually

the stuff of poetry: women, love, nature, patriotism. To
write romantically of war was to encourage the prolongation of horror and ugliness, to belie the reality.

He had not renounced the poetry of the past, but he had
come to believe that it could not be an adequate expression for the contemporary scene. There was a whole area
of experience which had not been explored by earlier
poetry, for past poets had not comprehended the truths
of twentieth century warfare. Owen placed a constant
emphasis upon the perfection, or completeness, of the
experience afforded to him and his contemporaries.
Absolute happiness, absolute misery, absolute serenity,
absolute identification with nature, were within the grasp
of all men as they had never been before. . . .

Of Shelley he wrote to Siegfried Sassoon, "Serenity
Shelley never dreamed of crowns me," and again in his
poem, **"A Terre,"** he refers with slight irony to Shelley's expression of pantheism in the forty-second stanza of "Adonais":

"I shall be one with nature, herb, and stone,"
Shelley would tell me. Shelley would be stunned:
The dullest Tommy hugs that fancy now.
"Pushing up daisies" is their creed, you know.

War was making a mockery of Shelley's philosophy,
and Owen believed that the common man had gone
beyond the experience of the romantic poet. The true
poet had to interpret things afresh in the face of new
and larger demands.

It was an effort to push the Keatsian romantic behind
him; the old poetic phrases sprang uncalled to his mind;
the conventional epithet was written before it could be
recalled. Yet the experience of war had given to Wilfred
Owen a new set of values; he knew the power of poetry,
and as a poet he believed that he could and should express the horror and pity of war:

For leaning out last midnight on my sill
I heard the sighs of men, that have no skill
To speak of their distress, no, nor the will!

The ordinary soldiers responded to the demands made
upon them; it was for the poet to watch "their sufferings
[and] speak of them as well as a pleader can." Above
all, it was for those who had the skill, to tell the truth
about war—not the simple factual truth of loss and gain,
of victory and defeat, but the whole complex truth which
would never find its way into official accounts or published history-books. . . . For this reason Owen could
not relax his vigilance: his subject was to be "War, and
the pity of War":

Not this week nor this month dare I lie down
In languor under lime trees or smooth smile.
Love must not kiss my face pale that is brown.

His reaction to conventional and romantic poetry was to
take its subject-matter, its imagery, and its epithets, and

use them to give added pungency to his own message. Owen was "not concerned with poetry" until poetic values were readjusted. Earlier poetry with its partial picture had helped to misrepresent war, because it repeatedly displayed only one aspect of battle, and that an aspect that soon lost its appeal to men who had to endure days, weeks, or months in the trenches. . . . In his poetry Owen tried to "cut out the rot." Because poetry had used the romantic image and the euphemistic description, he adopted a deliberately "anti-poetic" attitude. Describing in a letter the unburied dead strewn about the battlefield, he wrote that they were "the most execrable sights on earth," and immediately added, "In poetry we call them the most glorious." This cynical strain is repeated in his poems. In **"A Terre"** the dying soldier says

> My glorious ribbons?—Ripped from my own back
> In scarlet shreds. (That's for your poetry book.)

In **"Insensibility,"** the most powerfully condemnatory of all war poems, he uses the poetic euphemism, "The front line withers," but this is followed by the realistic retort,

> But they are troops who fade, not flowers
> For poets' tearful fooling.

The "anti-poetic" element which was developed in Wilfred Owen's work was the more forceful because he was conversant with the terms and themes of romantic poetry; these he interpreted in his own way. The "pathetic fallacy" of nature was exposed; the soldiers could "only know war lasts, rain soaks, and clouds sag stormy." The sympathies they attributed to nature were in themselves antiromantic, for they were alien sympathies: dawn "mass[ed] in the east her melancholy army" and, like the opposing forces, "Attack[ed] once more in ranks on shivering ranks of gray"; heaven was "the highway for a shell"; the air "shudder[ed] black with snow" which was more deadly than the flights of bullets; to the war's **"Mental Cases,"**

> Sunlight seem[ed] a blood-smear; night [came] blood-black;
> Dawn [broke] open like a wound that bleeds afresh . . .

the "fatuous sunbeams" no longer awoke the dying. Poetic imagery was reversed and nature served to illustrate metaphorically the truths of war: a soldier's death was described in terms of a sunset,

> I saw his round mouth's crimson deepen as it fell,
>   Like a Sun, in his last deep hour;
> Watched the magnificent recession of farewell,
>   Clouding, half gleam, half glower . . .

Bullets were "these clouds, these rains, these sleets of lead"; gas was a "green sea"; No Man's Land was "Gray, cratered like the moon with hollow woe."

With poetic terms, as such, Owen had no quarrel. It was the sentimental falsification of the searing truths of war experience that made him claim that "English Poetry is not yet fit to speak of [heroes]." He described as "the old Lie" the words "Dulce et decorum est / Pro patria mori"; his irony lit upon the hackneyed poeticisms, "our undying dead," or "Death sooner than dishonour." His own poetry spoke not of heroes, but of suffering men,

> You shall not come to think them well content
> By any jest of mine. These men are worth
> Your tears. You are not worth their merriment.

Owen's attitude was not a negative one, however; he was not a mere iconoclast, destroying the old values and putting nothing in their place. Going beyond anti-poeticism he created a new concept of poetic truth and beauty. His emphasis upon the perfection of experience is important. Nothing could be complete truth or complete beauty which was unable to stand up to the test of all human experience. Love in the context of sexual desire—"the binding of fair lips," "the soft silk of eyes that look and long," the red lips, soft voice and pale hands of the beloved—all this was not sufficient for every human situation. And in the midst of war its failure was apparent. Fellowship was true when,

> . . . wound with war's hard wire whose stakes are strong;
> Bound with the bandage of the arm that drips;
> Knit in the webbing of the rifle-thong.

> **For Owen, poetic truth could not be separated from spiritual truth, for they were the same. He wrote anti-war poetry because truth as he comprehended it was unremittingly at variance with the pursuance of war.**
>
> **—Hilda D. Spear**

Love was beautiful when a man was willing to sacrifice everything that others should live—that is, the "greater love" of the New Testament. The ordinary shows of religion—"the church Christ," the candles, prayers and bells—were not enough. Religion was true when it endured the experience of war; God could be seen through "the mud that cracked on cheeks when wretches smiled." True Christianity was to be found, not among those who preached, but among those who fulfilled.

> They who love the greater love
> Lay down their life; they do not hate.

For Owen, poetic truth could not be separated from spiritual truth, for they were the same. He wrote anti-war poetry because truth as he comprehended it was unremittingly at variance with the pursuance of war: "one of Christ's essential commands was: Passivity at any price! . . . Be bullied, be outraged, be killed; but do not kill . . . Christ is literally in 'no man's land.' There men often hear His voice: 'Greater love hath no man than this, that a man lay down his life for a friend.' Is it spoken in English only and French? I do not believe so." He fought because he believed that, under conditions of war, it was only thus that he could fulfil the demands made by the "Greater Love"; yet it was with a "very seared conscience" that he went into battle. His second return to France, in September, 1918, was the determination of a profound spiritual dilemma, but it was a dilemma that many sincere and sensitive men who fought in that war had faced. . . . So Owen knew that only there, in France, was he "able to cry [his] outcry," and express his beliefs in the "greater love" not only in words but also in deeds. . . . Owen faithfully accomplished this duty until his death on November 4, 1918. What he had to say was uncongenial to men and women at home in England; it was not about the conventionally "heroic," but about the true heroes, those who love the "greater love" and "lay down their life," without hate. It was incompatible with "glory, honor, might, majesty, dominion, power" for it was the pity and futility, the truth—as it seemed to him—of war.

D. S. R. Welland   (essay date 1960)

SOURCE: "The Very Seared Conscience," in *Wilfred Owen: A Critical Study,* Chatto & Windus, 1960, pp. 84-103.

[In the following excerpt from his book-length critical study, Welland examines the conflict between patriotism and Christianity in Owen's poetry.]

In all Owen's writing no phrase is more revelatory than his description of himself as "a conscientious objector with a very seared conscience," which occurs in the important letter where he records poignantly his realisation that "pure Christianity will not fit in with pure patriotism." [In his earliest poetry we see] an uneasiness over religious belief finding expression in a somewhat derivative idiom that detracts from its spontaneity, but of the intensity of the spiritual crisis into which his participation in the war plunged him there can be no doubt. [A] sense of guilt and of divided responsibility [can be found] in **"Mental Cases," "Spring Offensive,"** and elsewhere. . . . [The writer] in every instance betraying the Christ-soldier and thus alienating himself from the mercy of Christ.

Such popularly-accepted phrases as "the supreme sacrifice" illustrate how readily the soldier came to be thought of in a role similar to that of the crucified Saviour. One of the few successful poetic versions of this identification is Sassoon's "The Redeemer," but too many poems of . . . "the personal phase" of Great War poetry suffer by the overfrequency of analogies with the Crucifixion. The 1914 certainty that God was on our side survives in the work of many of these young men in the form of an emotional religiosity and a sense of personal kinship with Christ; this may have been of value of them as individuals but not as poets, since it has the effect of shutting their eyes to the real significance of what is happening around them without correspondingly increasing their powers as meditative or religious poets. The basis of this identification is, of course, the scriptural text which Owen quotes in the following form in the letter speaking of his seared conscience, and again at the end of **"At a Calvary"** (it also gave him the title for one of his most deeply-felt poems): "Greater love hath no man than this, that a man lay down his life for a friend"; but the same letter contains the realisation that the soldier who makes this sacrifice may in the course of so doing disobey "one of Christ's essential commands . . . do not kill." This paradoxical concept has been memorably defined by Alex Comfort: "The Promethean Infantryman, both Christ and Crucifier"; and the greatness of **"Strange Meeting"** lies, in part, in the success with which it (like **"The Show"**) develops the *doppelgänger* theme as a perfect symbol of this dichotomy. Since this religious problem underlies so much of Owen's poetry it is not extravagant to see a possible reference to Christ in the sun "whose bounty these have spurned' in **"Spring Offensive,"** for ignoring the "essential commandment" is tantamount to spurning the salvation Christianity offers.

This is not to attribute to Owen in these poems a wholly orthodox Christian view. In **"At a Calvary near the Ancre"** he is as much at odds with the "pulpit professionals" as in the letter on pacifism, but in both cases his accusation is that Christ has been betrayed by His Church. In **"Le Christianisme,"** a more balanced, ironic poem, the inadequacy and remoteness of the Church is neatly epitomised in the lines

> In cellars, packed-up saints lie serried
>   Well out of hearing of our trouble.

In this sentiment Owen was by no means alone. The religious assurance of earlier was poets was dying out by 1917: Christ in Flanders was too much of a paradox to be easily accepted any longer. . . .

[Whereas] the "bardic" poets had usually invoked God in their patriotic poetry, it is to Christ that the later poets more frequently appeal.

The significance of this is nowhere better illustrated than in Owen's unpublished **"Soldier's Dream,"** a pungent eight-line poem of 1917 in which a soldier dreams of the war ending by the personal intervention of "kind Jesus" in putting all weapons out of action. The peace, however, is shortlived:

> But God was vexed, and gave all power to
>   Michael;
> And when I woke he'd seen to our repairs.

God, that is, has been identified with Jahveh, the Old Testament God of battles and of wrath, whose interest in the perpetuation of the war is sharply contrasted with the compassion of Christ who, as Divinity incarnate, can sympathise with the human suffering war involves. In the face of this prolongation of suffering neither victory nor death has any great significance. The war that Jahveh wishes for is death, the death of the spirit, whereas the compassion represented by Christ is life-giving and kind, like the sun in **"Futility"** and in **"Spring Offensive"** where the antithesis between the sun, "the friend with whom their love is done," and the "stark, blank sky" full of incipient menace and hostility may be a reflection of this antithesis between Christ and God.

Questionable as its theology may be, Owen's position here is one to which many must, in varying degrees, have been attracted . . . , and it is one for which the Church was itself partly to blame because of the ardent and uncritical support it appeared to give to the continuance of the war. . . . It is hardly surprising that Owen's poetry should contain such statements as "God seems not to care" and "love of God seems dying," though his refusal to word either of them more dogmatically indicates the strength of the religion in which he had been brought up. . . .

The only call to which Owen answers is not that of the church but of human suffering. It is human sympathy rather than abstract morality that determines his ethical position, and he reaches that position by a decision as independent, as courageous, and in some ways as theologically debatable as that of a fictitious character with whom Owen would at first sight seem to have little in common. In a situation where the social and religious codes of his day appear to be at variance with his own instinctive loyalty to his friend, Huckleberry Finn puts the humanitarian consideration before the abstract by a choice, the momentousness of which he expresses to himself in the words "All right, then, I'll go to hell!" Confronted by a moral problem considerably more complex in its implications but not necessarily any more intensely-realised for that reason, Owen came in effect to a very similar decision, as his letters show time and again. From very different circumstances he learned, like Huck, that "Human beings *can* be awful cruel to one another." . . . In neither case, however, is there anything sentimental about this precept of love and solidarity; *Huckleberry Finn* ends with its hero's despairing withdrawal from a civilisation whose true nature he has come painfully to recognise, just as in **"Strange Meeting"** the dead soldier has the courage and the wisdom necessary "To miss the march of this retreating world."

The lonely independence of which Huck is the fictional symbol becomes increasingly dominant in Owen's poetry in direct proportion to the increase in his dedication to the task of speaking for "these boys . . . as well as a pleader can." His sense of comradeship and solidarity leads to no sentimentally Whitmanesque merging of identity with them, but at the same time his awareness of isolation is more firmly grounded and poetically more

valuable than the uneasy Romantic pose of the juvenilia to which it is directly related. [In] the ten-stanza poem, of which **"This is the Track"** originally formed the three last (and only revised) verses, . . . he aspires to be a solitary meteor awakening in men premonitions and intimations of eternity. The published stanzas illustrate a similarly purposeful self-sufficiency coupled with an almost messianic belief in the poet's responsibility, the exercise of which may even "turn aside the very sun," but another and rather better poem of probably similar date puts the other side.

"Six o'clock in Princes St" is just as Tennysonian in origin as is the contemporaneous **"Hospital Barge"** sonnet which he described as "due to a Saturday night revel in 'The Passing of Arthur,'" but it is more critical of that revel than is **"Hospital Barge."** A half-envious watching of the home-going crowds creates dissatisfaction with his own loneliness and the reflection:

> Neither should I go fooling over clouds,
>   Following gleams unsafe, untrue,
> And tiring after beauty with star-crowds,
>   Dared I go side by side with you.

A letter to Sassoon of 27 November 1917 had parodied Tennyson's "Merlin and the Gleam":

> I am Owen and I am dying,
> I am Wilfred; and I follow the Gleam

so that the 'gleams unsafe, untrue' may be associated not only with the failing vision of beauty but also with the weakening of religious belief. Certainly the mood is antithetical to that of **"The Fates,"** written less than six months earlier, with its Georgian confidence in beauty and art as an escape from "the march of lifetime"; and the choice of the verb "dared" in the last line shows an honesty of self-knowledge. . . . The real quality of this poem is most apparent in the final stanza where the poet's isolation is embodied in the wish that he might

> . . . be you on the gutter where you stand,
>   Pale rain-flawed phantom of the place,
> With news of all the nations in your hand,
>   And all their sorrows in your face.

The newsboy is more than a feature of the Princes Street scene: he is symbolic of the human condition as well as of the war-torn world and, in the pity of the final line, a projection of Owen himself. The effectiveness of the unusual "rain-flawed" is a reminder of Owen's fondness for and success with elemental imagery and of the progress he has made since the juvenilia in compressing into one line a wealth of association and suggestion.

If this is a poem of which he might have said, as he did of **"Miners,"** "but I get mixed up with the War at the end," it resembles **"Miners"** also in its development of a symbolist technique as a means of communicating a sense of isolation. There is a richness and complexity about **"Miners"** that is quite absent from, for example, so slight a piece as **"The Promisers"** and even from **"Winter Song."** The burning coal becomes a symbol for, in turn, the remote past, the miners who dug it, and, by a well-managed and apparently easy but none the less effective transition, the war dead. The atmosphere of the opening stanzas with their leaves, frond forests, ferns, and birds is reminiscent of **"From My Diary"** and the **"Sonnet: to a Child,"** but where **"From My Diary"** contents itself with the creation of that atmosphere and the sonnet associates it pleasantly but conventionally with the ideas of anamnesis and growing old, **"Miners"** contrasts it with the "sourness" of the sacrificed lives (to use Owen's own word for the poem's quality). Out of the oxymoron of this fusion comes a new strength, while the end of the poem gains in emotive force by the unexpected identification of the poet with the suffering of the lost which he has hitherto described detachedly. (It is of course the same device that he uses so effectively in **"The Show," "Mental Cases,"** and **"Strange Meeting."**

> Comforted years will sit soft-chaired
>   In rooms of amber;
> The years will stretch their hands, well-cheered
>   By our lives' ember.
>
> The centuries will burn rich loads
>   With which we groaned,
> Whose warmth shall lull their dreaming lids
>   While songs are crooned.
> But they will not dream of us poor lads
>   Lost in the ground.

The skill with which these two stanzas build up an impression of relaxed luxury, physical ease, and opulent, unquestioning well being, is epitomised in the phrase "rooms of amber," where the one word "amber," apart from its richness of sound, carries immediate associations of wealth and of the warm, golden light suffusing a fire-lit room. But amber, being fossilised resin, is doubly relevant here, for it is produced by the same process as the coal which makes possible all the luxury; this may suggest a secondary association with the insects frequently found imprisoned in amber—cut off, in fact, from the outside world by the amber as effectively as the "comforted," "soft-chaired" occupants of these rooms are isolated from reality by the opulence that "amber" symbolises in this stanza. Thus not only is amber the perfectly appropriate symbol here, but it grows organically out of the rest of the poem. The "frond-forests" become fossilised into two products: the utilitarian coal, the luxurious, hard amber; so the post-war stability and also the hard-hearted luxury that will again be possible in those more stable conditions are both produced by the war-dead "lost in the ground." An exactly parallel idea is sketched in the fragment **"The Abyss of War"** but there the pearl imagery is less integrally related to the bronze. **"Miners"** moves from the remote past of the forests, emerging from underground into the present, and passing on (by the unobtrusive gradation "the years . . ." "the centuries") to the remote future as it returns underground. In other words it has a unifying shape indispensable to the conveying of

the total effect, and it uses imagery not decoratively but integrally and functionally with a flexibility and evocative subtlety in the manner of the Symbolists.

Edmund Blunden's observation that Owen "is, at moments an English Verlaine," becomes most meaningful in relation to such a poem as **"The Roads Also"**:

> The old houses muse of the old days
> And their fond trees leaning on them doze,
>
>   . . . . .
>
> Though their own child cry for them in tears,
> Women weep but hear no sound upstairs.
> They believe in loves they had not lived
> And in passion past the reach of the stairs
>   To the world's towers or stars.

This is reminiscent in mood and manner of "Chanson d'Automne":

> Je me souviens
> Des jours anciens
>   Et je pleure

and even more of Verlaine's lyric from *Sagesse* 'Le ciel est, par-dessus le toit." (In **"The Unreturning"** there is a verbal echo from "Mon Rêve Familier" of the reference to the dead as "ceux des aimés que la Vie exila.") . . .

Essentially a poem of trench warfare, realistically based on the First World War, "Strange Meeting" is a fine statement of Owen's moral idealism, but it is also a poem that shows his true relationship to the Romantic tradition as something much more positive and creative than his earlier aestheticism suggests.

—D. S. R. Welland

[From] Verlaine's "Art Poètique" is a good description of **"The Roads Also"** where the clear definition of images in the earlier part of the poem melts into the frustrated, uneasy melancholy of the last nine lines with their symbolist evocation of a loneliness so complete that even communication is no longer possible. Much of the mood of this poem depends upon its lyrical dream-like movement which again recalls Verlaine.

Though not specifically war-poems, these, like **"The Kind Ghosts,"** illustrate Owen's range and may offer some indication of how his poetry might have developed had he lived, but they are important also as examples of the positive though indirect influence on his poetry of the compassion and the sense of isolation induced by his "very seared conscience."

[There are] two types of poem with which Owen experiments: his poems of dramatic description (such as **"The Chances"**) and the more subjective lyrics of personal response (such as **"Greater Love"** or **"Apologia"**). Both have their advantages and their limitations but what Owen needed for the full attaining of his purpose was a poetry where the more objective detachment of the one could be harnessed with the emotional intensity of the other. He often achieved this in his poems of imaginative description such as **"Spring Offensive"** but he also accomplished it in . . . poems of visionary description; of these **"The Show"** is a good example, but **"Strange Meeting,"** the poem that Sassoon once called Owen's "passport to immortality, and his elegy to the unknown warriors of all nations," is the best, especially for the way in which it brings together so many strands of his work already discussed. Essentially a poem of trench warfare, realistically based on the First World War, it is a fine statement of Owen's moral idealism as well, but it is also a poem that shows his true relationship to the Romantic tradition as something much more positive and creative than his earlier aestheticism suggests.

This may most readily be seen if . . . Shelley's *Revolt of Islam* (Canto V stanzas ix to xiii inclusive) be examined with Owen in mind. Wounded in battle, the protagonist hails the flow of blood with rapture because of its "eloquence which shall not be withstood" and its demonstration to his comrades of "the truth of love's benignant laws." He seizes the opportunity to reveal to his fellow soldiers the awful significance of what they have blindly done:

> And those whom love did set his watch to keep
> Around your tents, truth's freedom to bestow,
> Ye stabbed as they did sleep—but they forgive ye
>   now.

> Oh wherefore should ill ever flow from ill
> And pain still keener pain for ever breed
> We all are brethren—even the slaves who kill
> For hire, are men.

The closeness of this to **"Strange Meeting"** and other poems of Owen's is apparent enough; but it becomes unmistakable when the speaker, having swooned from loss of blood, awakens to find himself "mid friends and foes":

> And one whose spear had pierced me, leaned
>   beside,
>   With quivering lips and humid eyes;—and all
> Seemed like some brothers on a journey wide
>   Gone forth, whom now strange meeting did
>   befall
>   In a strange land, round one whom they might
>   call
> Their friend, their chief, their father, for assay
>   Of peril, which had saved them from the thrall

> Of death, now suffering. Thus the vast array
> Of those fraternal bands were reconciled that day.

The reconciliation of enemies, the sense of the brotherhood of man, and of the ultimate conquest even of death, as well as the title phrase **"Strange Meeting"** are common to both poems, though Owen's is the more closely-knit and the more intensely visualised.

Another parallel may be found towards the end of Keats's *Endymion:*

>   or when in mine
> Far under-ground, a sleeper meets his friends
> Who know him not. Each diligently bends
> Towards common thoughts and things for very
>   fear;
> Striving their ghastly malady to cheer.

The imaginative force of **"Strange Meeting"** . . . resides in the fact that it is not a friend or an enemy that the soldier meets so much as an *alter ego.* The fascination that this idea had for the Romantic imagination is illustrated in Rossetti's drawing "How They Met Themselves"; it recurs in Poe's "William Wilson" and in other tales; and it receives a particularly interesting form in Emerson's assertion "that should he ever be bayoneted he would fall by his own hand disguised in another uniform, that because all men participate in the Over-Soul those who shoot and those who are shot prove to be identical." The extent of Owen's familiarity with American literature is no more capable of verification than is the relationship between his pacifism and Shelley's "Mask of Anarchy"; these parallels are cited not as authenticated sources, but as analogues indicative of a body of nineteenth-century thought to which Owen is in spirit related.

From his echoing of it in an unpublished poem, we may be certain that he knew Wilde's line "Yet each man kills the thing he loves" and this too lies at the back of **"Strange Meeting."** The point is well made by the enemy's identification of himself with his killer in lines that are in effect Owen's own elegy, the final comment on his spiritual progress from the artificial aestheticism of the early years to the altruistic, splendid pity of these last poems:

>   Whatever hope is yours
> Was my life also; I went hunting wild
> After the wildest beauty in the world,
> Which lies not calm in eyes, or braided hair,
> But mocks the steady running of the hour,
> And if it grieves, grieves richlier than here.

The enemy Owen has killed is, he suggests, his poetic self, and "the undone years, The hopelessness" of which the enemy speaks are in one sense very personal to Owen, while in another sense they are tragically universal. Other poets had mourned the cutting-off of youth before its prime, but usually in terms of the loss to the individuals themselves or to their friends; if they envisaged the world becoming poorer they did not envisage it becoming actually worse, because tacitly or explicitly they assumed that the progress which the war had interrupted could be resumed by the survivors when it ended. Owen's vision is more penetrating and less comfortable. The war has not merely interrupted the march of mankind; it has changed its whole direction and done incalculable and irreparable damage. It is this terrible prophetic vision of a dying world embodied in this and other poems that gives Owen's work abiding relevance, but what he mourns is not merely the men themselves. Not only "the old Happiness" but the potentialities offered by the past are unreturning, and there is truly no sadness sadder than the hope of the poet here foreseeing the disintegration of values, the retrogression of humanity, involved in this second Fall.

> Now men will go content with what we spoiled.
> Or, discontent, boil bloody, and be spilled.
>
> . . . . .
>
> None will break ranks though nations trek from
>   progress

a wise comment on history since 1918. Only the men who fought in that war had, in Owen's belief, been vouchsafed an insight into the Truth, but it was too late to put that knowledge to any constructive use. If only they could have held themselves apart from the process of disintegration, had they only had the opportunity

> To miss the march of this retreating world
> Into vain citadels that are not walled

they might, in the fullness of time, have been empowered to arrest that march and to restore the truth:

> Then, when much blood had clogged their chariot
>   wheels,
> I would go up and wash them from sweet wells,
> Even with truths that lie too deep for taint.

Here perhaps is the last flourish of that messianic impulse which Christianity and Romanticism had combined to implant in Owen in the dedicated ideal of service to humanity that these lines express:

> I would have poured my spirit without stint
> But not through wounds; not on the cess of war.
> Foreheads of men have bled where no wounds
>   were.

But the opportunity for such service is gone, and characteristically in one of his simplest but most effective phrases Owen indicts himself as much as anyone else for the destruction of that opportunity: "I am the enemy you killed, my friend."

Despite the technical maturity with which this rich complex of ideas is developed, despite the creative genius that evolved so superb a myth for its poetic purpose, it is more than the loss of a poet that one laments after reading "**Strange Meeting.**" The sleep to which the dead enemy invites him is certainly

> less tremulous, less cold,
> Than we who must awake, and waking, say Alas!

for "**Strange Meeting**" carries its own conviction of the irreparable loss to humanity of "us poor lads / Lost in the ground"—irreparable not for what they were but for what they would have been, not for what they gave but for what they would have given. . . .

C. Day Lewis   (essay date 1964)

SOURCE: Introduction to *The Collected Poems of Wilfred Owen,* edited by C. Day Lewis, Chatto & Windus, 1964, pp. 11-29.

[*In the following excerpt, Day Lewis admires the poetic maturity evident in Owen's war poems.*]

Wilfred Owen must remain, in one respect at least, an enigma. His war poems, a body of work composed between January 1917, when he was first sent to the Western Front, and November 1918, when he was killed, seem to me certainly the finest written by any English poet of the First War and probably the greatest poems about war in our literature. His fame was posthumous—he had only four poems published in his lifetime. The bulk of his best work was written or finished during a period of intense creative activity, from August 1917 (in one week of October he wrote six poems) to September 1918—a period comparable with the *annus mirabilis* of his admired Keats. The originality and force of their language, the passionate nature of the indignation and pity they express, their blending of harsh realism with a sensuousness unatrophied by the horrors from which they flowered, all these make me feel that Owen's war poems are mature poetry, and that in the best of them—as in a few which he wrote on other subjects—he showed himself a major poet.

The enigma lies in this maturity. Reading through what survives of the unpublished poetry Owen wrote before 1917, I found myself more and more amazed at the suddenness of his development from a very minor poet to something altogether larger. It was as if, during the weeks of his first tour of duty in the trenches, he came of age emotionally and spiritually. His earlier work, though an occasional line or phrase gives us a pre-echo of the run of words or tone of thought in his mature poetry, is for the most part no more promising than any other aspiring adolescent's of that period would have been. It is vague, vaporous, subjective, highly 'poetic' in a pseudo-Keatsian way, with Tennysonian and Ninety-ish echoes here and there: the verse of a youth in love with the *idea* of poetry—and in love with Love.

And then, under conditions so hideous that they might have been expected to maim a poet rather than make him, Owen came into his own. No gradual development brought his work to maturity. It was a forced growth, a revolution in his mind which, blasting its way through all the poetic bric-à-brac, enabled him to see his subject clear—"War, and the pity of War." The subject made the poet: the poet made poems which radically changed our attitude towards war. The front-line poets who were Owen's contemporaries—Sassoon, Rosenberg, Graves, Blunden, Osbert Sitwell—played a most honourable part, too, in showing us what modern war was really like; but it is Owen, I believe, whose poetry came home deepest to my own generation, so that we could never again think of war as anything but a vile, if necessary, evil. . . .

What Wilfred Owen's future as a poet would have been, had he survived the war, it is impossible to say. War is the subject of nearly all his best poems, and a reference point in others, such as **"Miners."** It is true that he wrote a few poems of great merit on other subjects. But when, during the great productive period, he sought to write or finish such poems, we often notice in them a regression to his immature manner. It is interesting to speculate upon what subjects might have fired his imagination and possessed his whole mind, as did the war experience. Would the vein of savage indignation prove exhausted, or might Owen have found it renewed in the struggle against social injustice which animated some of his poetic successors? It seems possible; but his honesty, fervour and sensuousness might have been directed elsewhere to produce a Catullan kind of love-poetry. My own conviction is that, whatever poetry he turned to, he would have proved himself in it a poet of a high order. His dedication was complete: he passionately wanted to survive the war, so that he might continue to write poetry.

Certainly, in the writings of his last two years, he showed himself both a serious poet and an increasingly self-critical one. If we follow the successive drafts of the poems over which he worked longest—**"Anthem for Doomed Youth,"** for instance—we can see how admirably he kept sharpening the language, focusing ever more clearly his theme. Clumsiness there sometimes is, in these later poems; but nothing facile, and no shallow amateurism. Even his juvenilia, undistinguished though for the most part they are, present one promising feature—a gift for sustaining, in the sonnet form particularly, what musicians call *legato;* for keeping the movement of the verse running unbroken through an elaborate syntactical structure.

The language and rhythms of Owen's mature poetry are unmistakably his own: earlier influences have been absorbed, and we recognize in the style an achieved poetic personality. But it was achieved not solely through the impact of war: the seeds of it can be found in such early lines as

> . . . the lie
> Of landscapes whereupon my windows lean

or

> I kissed the warm live hand that held the thing

or

> For us, rough knees of boys shall ache with
>   rev'rence

or

> I shall be bright with their unearthly brightening.

Although his later work was largely cleared of derivativeness and false poeticism, Owen was not a technical innovator except in one respect—his consistent use of consonantal end-rhymes (grained/ground; tall/toil). Consonantal rhyme, and other forms of assonance, are common in Welsh poetry and had been used previously in English by Vaughan, Emily Dickinson and Hopkins. There is no evidence that Owen had read any of the three last; nor could he read Welsh—his parents were both English and he was born in England. The first surviving poem in which he experiments with consonantal rhyme is **"From My Diary, July 1914,"** while **"Has your soul sipped?"** may be another early experiment. . . .

Again, it has been noticed how Owen tends to have a lower-pitched vowel following a higher one as its rhyme; and this has been explained as a method of stressing the nightmare quality or the disillusionment of the experience about which he was writing. It may be so. But, lacking a theoretical statement by Owen about his rhyme, we should be cautious in attributing its workings to any *methodical* practice. Poets, when they have such urgent things to say as Owen had, seldom attend so consciously to musical detail; the harmonies of the poem, and its discords, are prompted by the meaning rather than imposed upon it. Nevertheless, Dr. Welland is justified in saying that Owen's consonantal rhyming "is right for this poetry because its note of hunting uneasiness, of frustration and melancholy, accords perfectly with the theme and the mood."

The language and rhythms of Owen's mature poetry are unmistakably his own: earlier influences have been absorbed, and we recognize in the style an achieved poetic personality.

—*C. Day Lewis*

By temperament and force of circumstances, Owen had led a solitary life, cut off from any close fraternity with other men, out of touch with the cultural movements of pre-war England. Shy and diffident as he was, this previous isolation must have heightened the sense of comradeship he felt when, in the army, he found himself accepted by his fellows and able to contribute to the life of a working unit. The old solitude was fertilized by the new fraternity, to enlarge his emotional and imaginative scope. Laurent Tailhade's eloquently uttered pacifist beliefs had, no doubt, impressed themselves upon the young Owen; but I can find no evidence that Owen was influenced by his poetry. At the Craiglockhart War Hospital, Owen met a man whose poetry and pacifism appealed to him alike. Siegfried Sassoon brought out, in a way almost embarrassing to him, all the younger poet's capacity for hero-worship: he had been a most gallant Company commander; he had written poems and a prose manifesto condemning the war in an uncompromising manner. No wonder Owen felt at first like a disciple towards him.

It was a sign of Owen's integrity and growing independence as a poet that his work was not radically affected by his admiration for this new friend. In a few satirical or colloquial poems, such as **"The Letter," "The Chances,"** or **"The Dead Beat,"** we may perceive Sassoon's influence; but Owen must have known that Sassoon's ironic and robust satire was not for him, and he continued in the tragic-elegiac vein which he had started working before he met the other poet. What Sassoon gave him was technical criticism, encouragement, and above all the sense of being recognized as an equal by one whose work he respected: it meant the end of his isolation as an artist. . . .

Wilfred Owen described himself as "a conscientious objector with a very seared conscience." He had come to see the war as absolutely evil in the agonies and senseless waste it caused: on the other hand, only as a combatant could he conscientiously and effectively speak for the men who were suffering from it. This conflict within himself . . . was a basic motive of the war poems. It is a conflict every honest poet must face under the conditions of modern total war; for, if he refuse to take any part in it, he is opting out of the human condition and thus, while obeying his moral conscience, may well be diminishing himself as a poet. This conflict is seldom overt in Owen's war poetry, which, although it makes use of his personal experiences, is remarkably objective: his 'seared conscience' and his inward responses to that experience provided a motive power, not a subject, of the poetry.

Looking once again at this poetry, thirty-five years after I first read it, I realize how much it has become part of my life and my thinking—so much so that I could hardly attempt dispassionate criticism of it. Now, as then, I find Owen's war poetry most remarkable for its range of feeling and for the striking-power of individual lines. "He's lost his colour very far from here" would stand out even in a play by Shakespeare or Webster: "Was it for this the clay grew tall?" has a Sophoclean magnificence and simplicity. Ranging from the visionary heights of **"Strange Meeting"** or **"The Show"** to the brutal, close-up realism of **"Mental Cases"** or **"The Dead Beat,"** from the acrid indignation of such poems as

"Dulce Et Decorum Est" to the unsentimental pity of **"Futility"** or **"Conscious,"** and from the lyricism of **"The Send-Off"** to the nervous dramatic energy we find in **"Spring Offensive,"** the war poems reveal Owen as a poet superbly equipped in technique and temperament alike. He was not afraid to be eloquent; and because he was speaking urgently for others, not for self-aggrandisement, his eloquence never ballooned into rhetoric. The war experience purged him of self-pity and poetic nostalgia. During his great productive year, the pressure of his imaginative sympathy was high and constant, creating poems that will remain momentous long after the circumstances that prompted them have become just another war in the history books. They, and the best of his poems not directly concerned with war, are in language and character all of a piece.

A. Banerjee (essay date 1977)

SOURCE: "Wilfred Owen—A Reassessment," in *The Literary Half-Yearly,* Vol. XVIII, No. 2, 1977, pp. 85-100.

[*In the following excerpt, Banerjee supports Yeats's controversial negative view of Owen's poetry and concludes that Owen is overrated as a poet.*]

[Wilfred Owen has] received sufficient critical attention (mostly favourable) . . . and there have been numerous critical articles on him or about him. He can also claim to have influenced later poets (e.g. C. Day Lewis held Owen up as one of the literary ancestors of the poets of the thirties in his *A Hope For Poetry* (1934), and Philip Larkin has mentioned Owen as one of the poets he has, "enjoyed" and he has been "associated with"). Indeed, it is a measure of the esteem in which Owen is held by his admirers and critics that Yeats's strictures on him have generally been taken as evidence of blind-spots in Yeats as critic rather than valid criticism of Owen as poet. That Owen wrote some remarkable poems—even a few perfect poems like **"Insensibility," "Futility"** and **"Greater Love"**—can hardly be denied. But I think he has been over-rated as a poet and a typical example of this fact is Roy Fuller's assertion in one of his Oxford Lectures, that Owen was "a major poet"—an accolade which very few poets since Yeats would seem to deserve.

Owen's critics and editors have tended to be bowled over by his compelling subject-matter—suffering and waste of war—and his poignant and compassionate treatment of it. His poetry has a special appeal for people of this century who have been, directly or indirectly, affected by the terrible devastations caused by the two World Wars, and who have come to loathe and denounce wars of any kind anywhere in the world. It is not surprising, therefore, to find that so many of the critics and readers have failed to notice the limited nature of Owen's poetic achievement or see the extremely narrow conception of poetry ("The poetry is in the pity," "All a poet can do today is warn") that he propounded. But I think one must now recognize Owen's severe limitations as a poet in order to see his achievement in a right perspective, and this is possible now more than ever before because many of the biographical details about the poet and his unpublished writings have been recently made public for the first time.

I propose to examine some of these limitations . . . taking Yeats's criticism as my starting-point. However, before doing so, I should point out the fact that before Yeats excluded Owen from *The Oxford Book of Modern Verse,* and indicated in the Introduction his reasons for doing so, at least two important reservations were made about his poetry, one in a private letter and another in a published book. Ironically, a self-confessed Imperialist like Sir Henry Newbolt was among the first to pinpoint the characteristic weakness in Owen's attitude to war and poetry. In a letter written on 2 August 1924, he remarked. . . .

> Owen and the rest of the broken men rail at the Old Men who sent the young to die: they have suffered cruelly but in the nerves and not the heart—they haven't the experience or the imagination to know the extreme human agony. . . .

And Stephen Spender, though he made some appreciative comments on Owen's poetry, did admit in the course of his discussion of Owen's **"Miners"** (in *The Destructive Element,* 1935); "His one emotion is a passive grief for the men and boys. The difficulty is, that poetry inspired by pity is dependent on that repeated stimulus for its inspiration." Without quite intending to do so, Spender made the central criticism of Owen's poetry.

Yeats's objections to Owen's poetry include the criticisms made by both Newbolt and Spender but his overall judgement has the backing and force of a belief that poetry should deal with something stable and permanent, that while it can, and does, encompass particular experiences of a given time, it should be able to look to those experiences from a larger perspective of human life as such. Yeats's complaint against war poetry (the kind that Owen wrote) was directed against various aspects of that poetry, but the tendency among critics has been to seize only the pronouncement "passive suffering is not a theme for poetry." This is, of course, one of Yeats's main charges but it can be better appreciated in the context of the other points that he makes. . . . Yeats was convinced that a poet ought not to take up a subject of merely topical import (however "intense" or "urgent" his feelings about it) unless he can deal with it in terms of something fixed and eternal, life itself. When Yeats remarked that "ten years after the war certain poets combined the modern vocabulary, the accurate record of the relevant facts learnt from Eliot, with the sense of suffering of the war poets, that sense of suffering no longer passive, no longer an obsession of the nerves: philosophy had made it part of all the mind," he was criticizing, by implication, the war poet's attitude to suffering which was "passive" and was marked by "an obsession of the nerves," and also his inability to transmute the suffering into "part of all the mind." That is to

say, the war poet was so totally overwhelmed by the physical actualities of the war that he was not able to transform them into "the realities of the mind." Yeats made this point more succinctly when in the same year as his *Oxford Book* was published, he said in a BBC talk that the war poets "were too near their subject-matter to do, I think, work of permanent importance," Secondly, Yeats said "much of the war poetry was pacifist, revolutionary, it was easier to look at suffering if you had somebody to blame for it . . . No matter how great a reformer's energy a still greater is required to face, all activities expended in vain, the unreformed." Here again, Yeats view seems to be that in dealing with the tragedy of war, the war poets found it easy to blame someone (callous civilians and politicians) for it. But Yeats believes, a poet in such a situation should concern himself with the greater tragedy—the tragedy of life for which "there is no remedy." The main target of these criticisms was, of course, Wilfred Owen. Yeats was and has since been roundly attacked, sometimes quite venomously, for this judgement. Yeats had anticipated such a reaction, and remarked in a letter to Dorothy Wellesley: "Most of my critics are very vindictive, a sure sign that I have somewhere got down to reality."

Yeats had certainly "got down to reality" and we can appreciate this fact better if we start by seeing the younger poet's achievement in the light of his early attempts at writing poetry. Anyone who is already familiar with Owen's mature poems is somewhat astonished by the unpromising nature of his pre-war poems—poems which are marked by pseudo-Keatsianisms and debilitated ninetyishness. A comparison in this respect with his contemporaries, Isaac Rosenberg or Charles Sorley, or with the major poets of the Second World War, serves to show how Owen started his poetic career as a naive adolescent, with little understanding of his poetic destiny and less real faith in himself as a poet. In fact, he never seems to have had any mature conception of poetry, and even in his later utterance on the subject, like "I am not concerned with Poetry" (Preface) and "poets' tearful fooling" (**"Insensibility"**), tend to confirm such a suspicion. Yet a claim has inevitably been made (as it is likely to be made for "a major poet") that the seeds of Owen's mature work are to be found in his early life and work. . . .

It can hardly be seriously denied that the war made Owen a poet by giving him the subject-matter and material for his poetry, and Anthony Thwaite is right in surmising that once the war was over, Owen (had he survived) would have had nothing to write about. This point needs to be stressed because in the absence of war as *the* subject, his poetry was generally unremarkable. Speaking of Owen's later poems which deal with non-war subjects, C. Day Lewis has pointed out that "when, during the last great productive period, he sought to write or finish such poems, we often notice in them a regression to his immature manner."

It was the war, or rather his war experiences that led Owen to formulate his own ideas about a poet's "duty" in times of war. He came to believe that poetry was essentially a matter of experience: "I think every poem, and every figure of speech should be *a matter of experience*" (Owen's italics). Though it would be generally agreed that "*every* poem" (my italics) is not a matter of experience, many (like Lawrence's, for instance) are. But the success of such poems as poems depends on the extent to which the poet is able to relate his particular experiences to life in general. In simple words, one of the challenges this kind of a poet faces is how to universalise his experiences. Owen has had the advantage of dealing in his poetry with sentiments to which, to borrow Dr Johnson's words of praise for Gray's *Elegy,* "every human bosom returns an echo"; especially in this century. But despite this advantage, the appeal of Owen's poetry is limited and limiting because it neither goes nor seeks to see beyond personal experiences.

It may be argued that Owen was not concerned with his personal experiences so much as with his reactions to, and understanding of, his fellow-soldiers' experiences. But such an attitude presented its own problems, and one such problem was that he felt more and more impelled to describe the ghastly actualities of war, and thus was reduced to writing poetry some of which, at any rate, cannot avoid being labelled 'reportage'. Owen was aware of this and, in fact, he wanted to report to the civilians about the terrible plight of the fighting soldiers. And this was his attitude right from the start of the war, even before he became actively involved in it. . . .

[It] is clear that there was a strong sado-masochistic streak in his personality and this fact can explain such behaviour on his part. Further, I feel that this had a damaging effect on his poetry. Already in his early poems, [Jon Stallworthy, in his *Wilfred Owen*] has detected "a masochistic note" which he associates with feelings of sin as a result of the poet's homosexual leanings. And in his later poems and writings too, his obsession with the physical wounds of boys and men can perhaps be explained in terms of his homosexuality.

It may be argued that Owen was not concerned with his personal experiences so much as with his reactions to, and understanding of, his fellow-soldiers' experiences, and felt more and more impelled to describe the ghastly actualities of war, and thus was reduced to writing poetry some of which, at any rate, cannot avoid being labelled "reportage."

—A. Banerjee

To give in his poetry descriptions of actual and physical wounds and mutilations on soldiers' bodies became for Owen some sort of poetic creed. . . .

Such an attempt at giving "photographic representation" of the soldiers' plight in his poetry made Owen open to the charge, which Yeats made, that he was "all blood, dirt . . ." One would suspect that Owen had not learnt from his master Keats the lesson "the excellence of all art is its intensity, capable of making all disagreeables evaporate . . ." To this, Owen's rejoinder could have been (was?) that he was not "concerned with Poetry" (or art), that he wanted to shock the civilians and his readers into a recognition of the brutal realities of war. The whole concept of poetry, Owen felt, needed a drastic revision in the context of war. His poem **"Apologia pro Poemate Meo,"** written in November 1917 (exactly a year before he died), sets out the standards that he had discovered through his war experiences. He handles the age-old human feelings in this poem, but the sources of his emotions are different:

> I, too saw God through mud—
>   The mud that cracked on cheeks when wretches
>   smiled.
>   War brought more glory to their eyes than blood,
>   And gave their laughs more glee than shakes a
>   child
>
>   . . . . .
>
> I have perceived much beauty
>   In the hoarse oaths that kept our courage
>   straight;
>   Heard music in the silentness of duty;
>   Found peace where shell-storms spouted reddest
>   spate.

There is nothing new as such in the ideal which guides these lines because every poet has to realize his emotions in the context of the realities and conditions of the age in which he happened to live. What is disturbing about the poem is the series of rejections of human values on which it is based (for God, joy, beauty etc. do not, according to the poem, really exist). But, one may say, this was the reality that Owen found and experienced. As his poems show, and his Preface makes clear, Owen felt that a poet in his situation must express pity for the people in such a plight, and should see his poetry as a warning to future generations:

> My subject is War, and the pity of War.
> The poetry is in the pity.
> Yet these elegies are to this generation in no
>   sense
> consolatory. They may be to the next All a poet
> can do today is warn. . . .

Thus, Owen's central objective in writing the "elegies" was to express grief and pity for the victims of war in order to prevent the recurrence of such horrors in the future. In the event, however, another devastating war came and bitterly demonstrated how right Yeats was in saying that—

I think it better that in times like these
A poet's mouth be silent, for in truth
We have no gift to set a statesman right.
        ("On Being Asked for a War Poem")

I am not suggesting that Owen's poetry ought to be judged in terms of the failure/success of his political/ social ideals. But it must be remembered that he himself had set up such an ideal, and it is my contention that this ideal vitiated his poetic achievement.

One inevitable result of such an ideal was that Owen's poetic range had to be limited. Though he wrote a few highly impressive poems, his poetry when taken as a whole, does seem to be "all on one note" as Newbolt had complained. But, as Yeats had indicated in his Introduction, there are different ways of looking at war, and as he showed from his own example ("Easter 1916") it is possible for a poet to discover both 'terror' and 'beauty' in the midst of war's carnage. Owen's poetry was much too exclusively rooted in a particular experience which, in the absence of a larger vision and experience on the part of the poet, does not yield anything freshly illuminating after the initial crop. Secondly, it seems to me that Owen would not have denied, and therefore his critics should not try to deny either, that his poetry was most deliberately concerned with "passive suffering." He was sufficiently influenced by the fatalistic faith that his mother had to make the categorical assertion that Christ had advocated "Passivity at any price!" He saw the soldiers suffering "passively" and evidently there was no room for "tragic joy" in such a predicament where men were dying "as cattle." In fact, these two elements— "passive suffering" and "joyless tragedy"—constituted *raison d'etre* of his mature poetry. His letter to his mother, written exactly a month before he was killed, confirms such a view: "I came out in order to help these boys—directly by leading them as well as an officer can and indirectly, by watching their suffering that I may speak of them as well as a pleader can." He could hardly have maintained this role as a "pleader" had he not watched his fellow-soldiers suffering and dying "passively" and "without joy." . . .

In spite of Owen's great compassion and pity, his poetry is apt to strike one as "monotonous" and "painful"— "almost unbearably painful" as D. J. Enright has admitted. To argue that, well the war was like that, and that Owen was being just truthful about it is to betray a confusion between "poetic truth" and "photographic representation." Robert Nichols, himself a poet of the First World War, made the acute point that the poetry of that war was essentially a recreation of the catastrophic events, without the force and interpretative power of a tragic vision. . . .

This criticism is particularly true of Owen's poetry because he was not able to see war suffering as part of human suffering in general. As for the contention that in the face of unprecedented brutalities of war (in which he was personally involved), a poet (Owen) was not able to maintain such an artistic stance, one may turn to

another poet of the same war, Isaac Rosenberg. Rosenberg spent about twenty months in and around the trenches (as compared to about six months spent by Owen) and that too as a private. Rosenberg, therefore, can claim to have personally experienced the "reality" of war. But his **"Trench Poems"** seem to display a wider range both in vision and technique. Critics have tended to believe that because Rosenberg came from a background of poverty and deprivation, he was not too greatly shocked by the atrocities of war. That may be true, but only to a limited extent. Rosenberg's poems show that he had an important faculty, namely, poetic imagination which Owen did not seem to have possessed in adequate measure— hence Newbolt's criticism that Owen did not have "the experience or the imagination to know the extreme human agony 'Who giveth me to die for thee, Absalom, my son, my son'". . . .

> **Owen's poetry was much too exclusively rooted in a particular experience which, in the absence of a larger vision and experience on the part of the poet, does not yield anything freshly illuminating after the initial crop.**
>
> **—A. Banerjee**

Surely, it is wrong to blame a poet for not having a particular kind of experience, though one may perhaps legitimately criticise him for not having the imagination to *realize* a significant human feeling or predicament. Stephen Crane possessed this quality so that even without personal experience of wars, he was able to write a powerful work of art on the subject. Rosenberg apparently had both experience and imagination. . . .

Owen was too overwhelmed by the war to prevent it from mastering his "poeting." No wonder it was not Owen but Rosenberg (and Edward Thomas) whom poets of the Second War (e. g. Douglas, Lewis) found inspiring.

Yet, paradoxically enough, Owen *needed* war experiences for writing his kind of poetry. Sassoon had told him that "it would be a good thing for (his) poetry if (he) went," and Owen himself knew it. . . . One cannot help detecting . . . Owen's abnormal need for, and an obsession with, physical horrors. The sado-masochistic streak in his personality (which was probably the result of his guilt feelings as a result of his homosexual leanings) seemed to have fed on the slaughter of war. Newbolt, therefore, was remarkably acute and accurate in his appraisal of Owen the poet and man:

> . . . they (Owen's poems) are terribly good, but of course limited, almost all on one note . . . there are more than two sides to this business of war, and a man is hardly normal any longer if he comes down to one.

Thorpe Butler (essay date 1983)

SOURCE: "Wilfred Owen: World War and Family Romance," in *University of Hartford Studies in Literature*, Vol. XIV, No. 2, 1983, pp. 63-74.

[In the following excerpt, Butler examines Owen's unconscious personal conflicts as a source of his poetry's power.]

Wilfred Owen's poems are generally considered the finest written about the First World War in English by a participant. Yet no study I am aware of has developed an adequate synthesis of all three of the most crucial aspects of his achievement: his astonishingly sudden and complete maturation as a poet; his rapid and profound assimilation of the overwhelming experience of modern warfare; the continuity as well as the differences between his juvenile and mature work. I think it was Owen's ability to perceive significant continuity between his pre-war and war-time experiences that made his remarkable achievement possible. War experience similarly galvanized his friend Siegfried Sassoon from a very minor Edwardian versifier to England's most powerful verse satirist since Byron. But while Sassoon could exploit the incongruities between war and peace brilliantly, he could not resolve or transcend them, and after the War he declined again to minor status. Owen was able to counterpose nineteenth-century Romantic thought and his war experience in such a way that each illuminated and judged the other. Furthermore, he perceived the War among the family of nations as analogous to conflict within his own family, especially to aspects of his relations with his parents. How conscious he was of the hidden content in his poetry poses a tantalizing question. In the poetry, however, World War I seems to become a stupendously magnified reflection of his family romance. . . .

Joseph Cohen [in "Owen Agonistes," *English Literature in Transition* 8, 1965] has argued (perceptively, I believe) that [Owen's] relationship with his parents was probably a primary source of the homoeroticism, the misogyny, and the representation of the War in terms of generational conflict which appear in his poems.

It seems likely that one important source of the erotic sensuousness of his verse is displaced erotic feelings for his mother. Wilfred, Harold, and their mother concur independently that Wilfred's development as a poet began about his tenth year during a vacation of several weeks which she and Wilfred spent alone together in idyllic rural surroundings. Wilfred refers to "the weeks at Broxton, by the Hill, / Where first I felt my boyhood fill / With uncontainable movements; there was born / My poethood." The covert eroticism of these lines echoes the more overt eroticism of some of his behavior toward his mother, who incidentally had been a locally celebrated beauty in her youth. At the age of nine, Wilfred delighted in having his mother feign sleep on a couch while he covered her with flowers, and he also liked to strew her pathway with flowers, like a gallant

lover in a poem. She did not discourage such attentions and never displayed uneasiness about her possessive intimacy with her oldest son.

His early enthusiasm for poetry probably stemmed partly from his need to escape from and compensate for the stifling bleakness of his surroundings and prospects. In his "Memoir" [in Owen's *Collected Poems,* ed. C. Day Lewis, 1963] Edmund Blunden describes Owen's juvenile verse as an obvious attempt to "build up his own House Beautiful." Owen had a particular relish for sensuous images and sounds:

> This is more like the aureoles of Aurora,
> The leaves of flames, the flame of her corona.
> Not Petrarch wore such coronals, nor Laura,
> Nor yet his orange-trees by old Verona,
> Nor gay gold fruits that yellow Barcelona!

As Blunden points out, the horrid intrigued him as much as the sweet:

> A tinge
> Curdles the sea, like mingling oil and ink. . . .
> The witch's den! Around was filthy quag,
> In whose soft mire slow-wallowed water-slugs,
> Large, fat and white. There sat the fishy hag,
> Beneath her hut of bones. . . .

Owen's juvenile eroticism has a strong Decadent flavor, probably indebted as much to Swinburne and Wilde as to Keats, whom he frankly idolized. A displaced fixation on his reputedly beautiful mother may account partly for the eroticized "fusion of beauty and sin" which marks so much of his non-war poetry [D. S. R. Welland, *Wilfred Owen: A Critical Study,* 1963]. For instance, his use of the *femme fatale* motif in **"Long Ages Past"** (1914) may have been rooted in that fixation on his mother as the woman whom it was dangerous for him to love. The female figures in the poem rejoice in the blood of their male and female victims. The association of erotic beauty with pain and death culminates in the sadomasochism of the last four lines:

> Thou are the face reflected in a mirror
> Of wild desire, of pain, of bitter pleasure.
> The witches shout thy name beneath the moon,
> The fires of hell have held thee in their fangs.

The linking here of the witches with perverse sexuality encourages a sexual interpretation of the "water-slugs, / Large, fat and white" lurking around the witch's cave in the earlier passage cited above. If Owen did indeed unconsciously associate these menacing female figures with his mother, then his feelings about her were considerably more ambivalent than his overt devotion suggested.

Another kind of sexual ambivalence manifested in both his juvenile and later poetry is homoeroticism. There is no definite evidence that he was ever an active homosexual (Cohen calls him an "inverted" homosexual), and it is difficult to discern to what extent he was merely conforming to the "British homoerotic tradition" as described by Paul Fussell [in *The Great War and Modern Memory,* 1975]. Homoerotic elements can be discerned fairly clearly in only three of the non-war poems in C. Day Lewis' edition, but Jon Stallworthy's biography [*Wilfred Owen: A Biography,* 1974] includes several previously unpublished verses with fairly clear homoerotic implications. The homoerotic poems in Lewis' edition are **"To Eros," "To the Bitter Sweetheart, a Dream," "To—."** and **"Maundy Thursday."** In the first it is the "Boy," Eros, whom he "worshipped." In the second poem Eros seduces the speaker while transporting him in a dream to his girl friend: "Feeling my empty hand fulfilled with His, / I knew Love gave himself my passion-friend." At the end of the poem the lover dismisses the girl. In **"To—"** two boys running together in play fall, apparently into sexual awareness of one another. In **"Maundy Thursday"** when the speaker's turn comes to kiss the crucifix held up for adoration by an acolyte, he kisses instead "the warm live hand that held the thing." This homoeroticism was no doubt partly a revolt against the severe constraints in his own life, including his mother's extreme puritanism. On a deeper level, however, it probably stems also from his intense, unbroken fixation on his mother, which apparently never underwent the normal Oedipal process of frustration and renunciation that later culminates in a heterosexual orientation. Owen's sexual orientation is a matter for our concern because it is an important element in the intense elegiac compassion for his dead and doomed comrades that is a hallmark of his finest poetry.

The linked themes of beauty, erotic love, suffering, and death underwent drastic transformation in the war poetry, but they were also a basis of continuity between the earlier and the mature works. That knot of preoccupations enabled him to relate to his past experience the novel, alien, menacing experience of mass mechanized warfare, which presented a massive challenge to his imaginative capacity.

His increasing concern with the nature and function of art and the artist also stimulated his desire to cope with the War in his poetry. From the Romantics Owen had inherited a paradoxical concept of poetry. On the one hand the poet yearned to create what Northrup Frye [in *Anatomy of Criticism,* 1967] calls the "world of desire," a beautiful imaginary world more satisfying to the mind than the one we grudgingly acknowledge as "real." On the other hand he felt a responsibility to use his superior mental powers to explore the nature of reality more fully than the common man can or wishes to and also to lead the rest of mankind toward the realization of the ideal within the actual. In its preoccupation with erotic beauty in a purely private, imaginary context, Owen's early Decadent style reflects the increasing subordination of the second concern to the first throughout the nineteenth century, so that in the first decade of the twentieth century few British poets made serious attempts to treat the urban, industrial, imperial culture in which they lived. Even before the War Owen had shown some vague signs

of desiring to expand the scope of poetry to include more than lurid fantasies or rural retreats. In **"O World of many Worlds"** [sic] Owen compares himself to a

> meteor, fast, eccentric, lone,
> Lawless; in passages through all spheres,
> Warning the earth of wider ways unknown
> And rousing men with heavenly fears—.

In January 1913 he wrote, "I am convinced that I hold under my tongue, powers which would shake the foundation of many a spiritual life." The War gave him a subject worthy of his ambition and assumed powers.

Because of obligations as a private tutor in France, Owen did not enter the trenches until the beginning of 1917; he had also become friends with the pacifist poet Laurent Tailhade. Partly for these reasons he never passed through the phase of intense patriotic enthusiasm that so few of his contemporaries throughout Europe escaped. His first poetic response to the War, **"1914"** (written in that year), regards it as a "foul tornado" ushering in "the Winter of the world" and requiring "blood for seed" for the next millenial cycle. His primary concern in the poem seems to be the deleterious effect of the War on the arts, especially his own. He did not write explicitly about the War in verse again until he became a participant in 1917.

When he did at last encounter war directly, his adjustment as a poet to the new experience was extremely rapid but not smoothly linear. At least through 1917 he continued to write poems in his prewar style; some of those were about war, e.g. **"Fragment: I saw his Round Mouth's Crimson . . ."** (except for the last line), **"Fragment: As Bronze may be much Beautified,"** and **"Has Your Soul Sipped?"** However, neither aestheticism nor patriotic platitudes proved appropriate to the new situation, at least not in their conventional forms. Partly under the influence of the poetry and then the person of Sassoon, Owen began to emphasize the evil, ugly truth of the War as experienced by combatants.

Correspondingly, in these poems and the preface he wrote to introduce them, he emphasized the truth and rejected "poetry," which he associated with beauty divorced from actuality. Fortunately for his own poetry, he sought more than circumstantial truth about the War, though his poems contain plenty of that. Owen reassumed the prophetic role that the early Romantic poets had claimed for themselves; his truth would be ultimately spiritual. The meanings of love and beauty were for him transformed by the pressure of immanent death and chaos on a universal scale.

He did sometimes emphasize the physical ugliness of war as an aspect of the truth generally concealed from noncombatants. Soon after his arrival in the trenches he wrote home about "the universal pervasion of Ugliness. Hideous landscapes, vile noises, foul language . . . everything unnatural, broken, blasted; the distortion of the dead, whose unburiable bodies sit outside the dugouts all day, all night, the most execrable sights on earth. In poetry we call them the most glorious." Owen's poetry did not, at least not on that level. His description of a soldier dying from gas poisoning in **"Dulce et Decorum Est"** is deliberately revolting, as is the description of the appearance and behavior of those whom war has driven insane in **"Mental Cases." "The Show"** consists entirely of a hideous analogy between the battlefield and a death's-head being devoured by worms. Actually, however, relatively few of his poems dwell much on the physical ugliness of war; he seemed more concerned to emphasize the moral and spiritual ugliness caused, or revealed, by the slaughter, as in the middle stanza of **"Mental Cases"**:

> —These are men whose minds the Dead have
>   ravished.
> Memory fingers in their hair of murders,
> Multitudinous murders they once witnessed.
> Wading sloughs of flesh these helpless wander,
> Treading blood from lungs that had loved
>   laughter.
> Always they must see these things and hear them,
> Batter of guns and shatter of flying muscles,
> Carnage incomparable, and human squander
> Rucked too thick for these men's extrication.

Such horror challenges traditional concepts of poetry as well as of war.

What beauty Owen did perceive in war was founded no longer upon sensuous gratification enhanced by the imaginary prospect of death, but upon spiritual transcendence of the hideous perversion and deformation of all things, including humans, which in the trenches seemed the only reality: "Faces that used to curse me scowl for scowl, / Shine and lift up with passion of oblation, / Seraphic for an hour; though they were foul . . . I have perceived much beauty / In the hoarse oaths that kept our courage straight" (**"Apologia Pro Poemate Meo"**). In **"Greater Love"** a point-for-point comparison proclaims a beautiful woman's charms—lips, eyes, figure, voice, hand, etc.—inferior to the corresponding men's features destroyed by war. The men's former physical beauty has been distorted into ugliness, but the spiritual splendor of their sacrifice creates a new dimension of beauty. This "terrible beauty" in no way justifies the War or denies its morally and spiritually degrading effects on combatants and noncombatants alike; those effects were among his major themes. Rather, the beauty is all he can salvage from the general havoc. This new concept of beauty is of a qualitatively different order from Owen's earlier Decadent concept, because the beauty is spiritual rather than sensual and because the suffering and death associated with beauty are palpably real on an enormous scale, instead of being private and imaginary.

Owen's understanding of love and death and of the relations between them was likewise transformed by his experience of international conflict. The homoeroticism in **"Greater Love"** and other war poems is sublimated as a solemn, mournful compassion for the myriads of young men being slaughtered in the trenches; nevertheless, the erotic implications in **"Greater Love"** of the detailed contrast between dead men's mangled features and the charms of a beautiful woman are fairly apparent. In **"Spring Offensive"** a sexualized Nature manifests an ambivalent love/hate attitude toward soldiers about to enter battle: ". . . the buttercup / Had blessed with gold their slow boots coming up, / Where even the little brambles would not yield, / But clutched and clung to them like sorrowing hands." When the soldiers reject both the earth's pleas and the "sun, like a friend with whom their love is done," both turn against the men with the fury of the scorned: ". . . And instantly the whole sky burned / With fury against them; earth set sudden cups / In thousands for their blood; and the green slope / Chasmed and steepened sheer to infinite space." As in others of his war poems, the cosmos itself becomes embroiled in the human conflict. In this poem the soldiers' relations with the sun and earth may dimly reflect Owen's fantasized relations with his parents. The sudden hostility of sexualized personifications of the earth and sun, traditionally represented as Mother Earth and Father Sun, may adumbrate Owen's guilty expectation of retaliation for breaking away from his parents. He had been rejecting his father's love for years, and, especially after he left home, he had increasingly rejected his mother's narrow, rigid Calvinism. Such a reading seems more plausible considering the recurrent theme of paternal hostility in the war poems.

The *Doppelgänger* motif noted by Gose and Welland in **"Strange Meeting"** also manifests Owen's internal ambivalence about his parents and about himself [Elliott B. Gose, Jr., "Digging In: An Interpretation of Wilfred Owen's 'Strange Meeting,' *College English* 22, March 1961]. Gose and Welland regard the main speaker of the poem as a split-off aspect of the narrator, in which case the bonds of enmity and love between them are partly projections of self-love and self-hatred by the narrator, and ultimately by Owen himself. By extension, Owen's homoeroticism and its sublimation, his compassionate mature love for the millions of doomed soldiers, are also partly rooted in projected self-love. Conversely, the enmity which made one character kill the other is to some extent a projection of Owen's self-hatred, resulting partly from his contradictory roles as warrior and pacifist poet; as he indicated elsewhere, "Am I not a conscientious objector with a very seared conscience?"

Owen's deepest conflicts, however, had to do with his relations with his parents. Correspondingly, in the war poems he directs his animosity not against German soldiers, nor even the militarist German state, which he deplored, but primarily against those in England he considered responsible for the unnecessary continuation of the War. In his poems the War is ultimately a conflict between generations, particularly between fathers and sons. Sassoon also develops this theme but not as overtly or persistently as Owen. It is not entirely confined to the war poems. In **"Storm,"** written two months before Owen entered the trenches in early 1917, the speaker compares himself to a tree threatened by lightning from a storm cloud. He is both frightened and extremely aroused by the "brilliant danger"; he feels he "must . . . tempt that face," with its "beauty lovelier than love," to "loose its lightning." If he is indeed struck, he will become "bright" with the "unearthly brightening" of the laughing "gods, whose beauty is death." He yearns for the blow as a lover yearns for sexual consummation. Owen elsewhere wrote, "Consummation is Consumption," and here he identifies consumption with ecstatic glorification. The ambiguous, threatening figure could represent war, fame, or death; it could also represent his father. The threatening figure is clearly masculine and dominant, the speaker passive and "feminine," at least in attitude. Under the circumstances it seems plausible that Owen may have used the trope to express and conceal simultaneously his yearning for a relationship, even a sexual one, with a father whose hostility he fears. Such a masochistic yearning might be the submerged counterpart to his expressed disdain for his father, as his hostility towards women in general may have been the other face of his apparently unclouded adoration of his mother. The poem can be read as Owen's anticipation of death just as he achieved brilliance as both warrior and poet, the death an expiation for successful rivalry with his father in both love and their careers (his father was a frustrated seaman). The death might also be a means of (sexual) reunion with the father, as it is a possible means of reunion with God in **"Spring Offensive."**

Still submerged, the theme of generational conflict appears in a form unique for Owen in **"Antaeus: A Fragment,"** apparently written in 1917. In Owen's version of the wrestling match between Hercules and Antaeus, the latter is a "slim" stripling instead of a giant. In a note about the poem to a friend he remarked, "Antaeas [sic] deriving a strength from his *Mother* Earth nearly licked *old* Herk" [emphasis mine]. In no other poem does Owen represent such an alliance between mother and son against a father figure; he usually rejects women when he includes them at all in his poems, e.g., **"Greater Love," Apologia Pro Poemate Meo,"** and **"Disabled."** Both **"Storm"** and **"Antaeus"** manifest his conviction that he would die young, like his hero Keats, and furthermore suggest that he expected to die at his father's hands.

In the war poems themselves the generational conflict is often explicit. Even in partial exceptions like "Inspection," in which it is the "world" that is "washing out its stains" by sacrificing its young and then despising their blood as dirt, the generational factor is covertly present. "World" is clearly a euphemism for older adults, and "Field-Marshall God," who presides over the slaughter, is implicitly paternal. In **"Smile, Smile, Smile,"** Owen's version of a newspaper editorial advocating the continuation of the War, he satirizes the sometimes frankly exploitative attitude of the Nation at Home. The proximity of the words "victory," "glory," and "integrity" to such mercantile terms as "bought," "indemnified," and "something lasting in their stead" suggests that the "sons we offered" are not just being too readily sacrificed but frankly traded like commodities in a cold-blooded business deal. The maimed soldiers reading the editorial react, not with bitterness like the speaker in **"Inspection,"** but with

quiet, ironic smiles concealing their secret conviction that only they and their slain comrades—not aging civilian warmongers—truly represent England. Like the other soldier-sons in Owen's poems, they do not revolt but passively submit to their immolation by their fathers, just as Owen's resistance to his own father was mostly passive.

The relationship between hostile fathers and submissive sons emerges most clearly in **"The Parable of the Old Man and the Young,"** Owen's war-time version of the story of Abraham and Isaac. The angel tells Abraham to "Offer the Ram of Pride instead of him. / But the old man would not so but slew his son, / And half the seed of Europe, one by one." The son in **"S. I. W."** carries passive submission to the extreme of executing his father's murderous wishes on himself by committing suicide when he can no longer stand the strain of the trenches. He rejects self-mutilation for the purpose of getting himself sent out of the trenches, because those who did so "were vile" according to his father's injunction: "'Death sooner than dishonour, that's the style!'." The repetition and phrasing of the father's admonitions to his son convey the sinister implication that the father simply, if unconsciously, wanted him dead: "Father would sooner him dead than in disgrace— / Was proud to see him going, aye, and *glad*" [emphasis added]. Concern for honor seems a mask for deadly hostility, so that the boy's dilemma in the trenches is a grotesquely magnified and distorted reflection of the situation he felt he had long faced at home.

Owen's preoccupation with father-son relationships informs the religious concerns expressed in some of his poems, where God is an ambiguous father figure whose love Owen sometimes seeks despite apparent rejection or persecution. "Field-Marshall God" in **"Inspection"** has already been mentioned. The speaker in **"Arms and the Boy"** ironically recommends tempting a boy with deadly weapons because he seems innocent and because "God will grow no talons at his heels, / Nor antlers through the thickness of his curls." Since boys are indeed transformed into murderous monsters when given weapons and trained to use them, God may be ultimately responsible for that change. On the other hand, in **"The Parable of the Old Man and the Young"** God requires the sacrifice of pride, not progeny; it is the earthly father who insists on killing his son. Despite his skepticism Owen twice expresses a heavily qualified yet poignant hope for an ultimate reconciliation between the slain soldiers and their heavenly Father. In **"Spring Offensive"** the hope is expressed as a dubious speculation: "Some say God caught them even before they fell." In **"Asleep"** Owen wonders of a boy just slain "Whether his deeper sleep lie shaded by the shaking / Of great wings, and the thoughts that hung the stars, / High pillowed on calm pillows of God's making." He considers the alternative that the corpse will merely decompose in the ground, then dismisses both possibilities as irrelevant compared to the sufferings of the soldiers still alive. Owen apparently could not imagine a reconciliation even with a heavenly father without first suffering death as expiation.

Owen's soldiers consistently seem to be the innocent victims of motiveless parental hatred. Yet the soldiers do bear a terrible guilt for their deeds:

> For power was on us as we slashed bones bare
> Not to feel sickness or remorse of murder.
> > ("Apologia Pro Poemate Meo")

> And there out-fiending all its [Hell's] fiends and
> > flames
> With superhuman inhumanities,
> Long-famous glories, immemorial shames—
> > ("Spring Offensive")

> Have we not wrought too sick and sorrowful
> > wrongs
> For her [Mother's] hands' pardoning?
> > ("Happiness")

In "Strange Meeting" the narrator's slaying of an enemy soldier who turns out to be his double amounts to fratricide, almost suicide, and blights the future of civilization. Owen himself killed at least one enemy at close range. Thus the immediate reason for that sense of guilt is obvious. However, his emphasis on unprotesting submission to slaughter suggests the possibility of other, unconscious sources of guilt as well. The homoerotic undertones of his love for his comrades, his too-successful rivalry with his father, and his implicitly incestuous emotional intimacy with his mother gave him special reasons to associate conflict and guilt with love. His conviction since adolescence that he would die young was not justified by external circumstances before the War and must therefore have been a product of internal fantasy, which probably involved a combination of Oedipal guilt and consequent fear of, and longing for, paternal retaliation. His passionate protest against war is the other side of the passive submission.

Owen regarded both his personal crisis and the crisis in Western civilization as terminal; their imaginative fusion in his poetry is apocalyptic: ". . . on their sense / Sunlight seems a blood-smear; night comes blood-black; / Dawn breaks open like a wound that bleeds afresh" ("Mental Cases"). From an aerial viewpoint the battlefield itself resembles a death's head being consumed by worms ("The Show"). In "Insensibility" the speaker "mourns . . . Before the last sea and the hapless stars." In "Strange Meeting" Owen implies that unrestrained conflict destroys the sympathetic creative imagination in both individuals and civilizations. The cosmic reverberations of that conflict imply that the cosmos itself may be sustained by the human imagination.

Owen's best poems constitute a triumph of the imagination over the deadly conflicts that were rending both him and the world. He could not resolve or escape these, but in the middle ground of his poetry he could integrate his inner and outer worlds as manifestations of a single fundamental struggle, a side of which helped him to realize and articulate the other. His unconscious personal conflicts are most fully and clearly developed in the war poems and, at the same time, are a primary source of the poetry's power and depth.

Caryn McTighe Musil (essay date 1986)

SOURCE: "Wilfred Owen and Abram," in *Women's Studies*, Vol. XIII, No. 1, 1986, pp. 49-61.

[*In the following excerpt, Musil examines Owen's challenging of patriarchal notions of nationalism, masculinity, and sexuality in his poems.*]

A week after World War I broke out, Wilfred Owen wrote to his brother, "After all my years of playing soldiers, and then of reading history, I have almost a mania to be in the East, to see fighting, and to serve." He resisted his "mania" for another sixteen months, but by January, 1917, he found himself a commissioned officer at the Front. At first his early enthusiasm for the war survived. "There is a fine heroic spirit about being in France," he wrote in early January and after hearing the guns for the first time reported, "It was a sound not without a certain sublimity." Two days later he wrote home, "There is nothing in all this inferno but mud and thunder," and within ten days confessed, "We were wretched beyond my previous imagination." Out of such wretchedness some of the greatest anti-war poetry in the English language was written. As Owen came to repudiate the war, he bitterly condemned with all the ferocity of a son's disillusionment the fathers who were orchestrating the meticulous slaughter. Like other modernists, Owen was not merely railing against the carnage he witnessed; he was, finally, profoundly opposed to the patriarchal culture that seemed to make war such an inevitability and the stubborn continuation of it so imperative.

The values of this culture were carefully inscribed by a powerful male tradition in texts that taught young boys how to become men. These tablets contained inherited masculine wisdom about how to perpetuate a world where male political and sexual dominance would continue. . . . His assaults on those male-authored books permeate the letters and poetry of the posthumously decorated warrior. To subvert his male legacy, Owen provides us with a text of his own in which he tells the truth about what it means to be a man. "The true Poets must be truthful," he says in his Preface. In speaking truth, Owen violates the secret conspiracy between fathers and sons to remain silent about failure, inadequacy, or disagreement. Despite Freudian theories, there is no reconciliation with the father, at least not for Owen. The son does not eventually assume his throne in the patriarch's kingdom. Instead Owen rejects the king and kingdom outright.

While fathers have sent their sons to die in other wars, the casualties of World War I were so staggering that the usual generational cycles were shattered. . . . Owen was constantly assaulted by visual evidence of fathers literally sending boys to die. Rather than be silently sacrificed to his father's sentence, Owen uses his voice to challenge the authority and veracity of inherited notions from his father's culture of nationalism, masculinity, and sexuality. Trying to sever his traditional loyalties, he seeks an alternative model of manhood by embracing forbidden female qualities in himself.

Owen uses his voice to challenge the authority and veracity of inherited notions from his father's culture of nationalism, masculinity, and sexuality.

—*Caryn McTighe Musil*

Reflecting his re-defined role as an outsider who disdains his father's lineage, Owen assumes a poetic identity with the prophets, outcasts from existing social orders who speak truths to an unreceptive populace. "All a poet can do today is warn," Owen claims in his Preface. Like all prophets, Owen warns primarily by telling the truth despite the fact that World War I was the most heavily censored war in history. The most dangerous and subversive truth Owen tells is that fathers are murdering their sons, and doing so consciously. Many critics, from [Arthur E.] Lane to [Jon] Stallworthy to [Paul] Fussell, have commented on how Owen deliberately refers to soldiers as "boys," "youths," and "lads" to reinforce the sense of their innocence as they are subjected to war's obscene horrors. Such commentaries miss, however, Owen's implicit bitter attack against the father figure who is responsible, according to Owen, for the death and mutilation of his own "boys." **"The Parable of the Old Man and the Young"** is Owen's most explicit poem about such inter-generational murder.

Using the Old Testament story of Abraham and Isaac as his literary analogue, Owen transformed the father, Abram, into the one who is willingly the military architect for his son's doom:

> Then Abram bound the youth with belts and
>   straps,
> And builded parapets and trenches there,
> And stretchèd forth the knife to slay his son.

The biblical story has an angel intervene to save Isaac at the last moment since Abraham has proven his willingness to obey God's orders. When a similar angel appears in Owen's poem, however, the scenario is radically different:

> When lo! an angel called him out of heaven,
> Saying, Lay not thy hand upon the lad,

> Neither do anything to him. Behold,
> A ram, caught in a thicket by its horns;
> Offer the Ram of Pride instead of him.
> But the old man would not so, but slew his son,
> And half the seed of Europe, one by one.

The patriarch Abram, like the patriarchs in power during Owen's life, breaks the covenant, ignores the divine voice, and establishes instead *his* male supremacy, his own version of the truth. In so doing, he creates the ritual that demands the endless yet meticulous slaughter of innocent male lambs rather than the single and redeeming sacrifice of the matured, arrogant male ego, "the Ram of Pride." Like Sir Douglas Haig, Commander-in-Chief of the British Forces, and Lloyd George, Prime Minister, the father stubbornly refuses to deviate from his chosen course, opting rather to slay his son and all sons in order to guarantee his pride. He thus enshrines a male rite for authority that demands awful and fatal initiations for sons.

In describing patriarchs as the real enemy of civilization and of God's kingdom, Owen, like D. H. Lawrence, offers a critique of the patriarchal institutions that had dominated western culture. By revealing murderous manipulations, Owen joins with other modernists who understood part of the social dynamics of the early twentieth century as hinging on the ferocious battle of the fathers against the sons. Owen appropriately uses Christian analogues to describe that bitter antagonism. In **"The Parable"** Isaac is described as a "lamb" and therefore is linked with Christ, another son who feels betrayed by his father and murdered that his father might have greater glory. That same struggle for dominion with the same defeat of the son occurs tellingly in **"Soldier's Dream."** There, too, Jesus, the peacemaker, is seen in opposition to his Father, the god of war.

> I dreamed kind Jesus fouled the big-gun gears;
> And caused a permanent stoppage in all bolts;
> And buckled with a smile Mausers and Colts;
> And rusted every bayonet with His tears.
>
> And there were no more bombs, of ours or Theirs,
>
>   . . . . .
>
> But God was vexed, and gave all power to
>   Michael;
> And when I woke he'd seen to our repairs.

God the Father, vexed with his son's audacity in stopping the war, reasserts power by reassembling the machinery of war. General Abram reigns once more. In another poem, **"Inspection,"** the Abram-Haig-Lloyd George-God the Father figure reappears literally as "Field Marshall God." Owen continues to describe in a religious paradigm the generational warfare he witnesses. What he has salvaged from his shattered faith is not his reverence for God the Father, but for God the Son.

In pitting himself against Abram and his legions, Owen subverts, among other things, Abram's sacred book of

nationalism by writing the truth about war, not the father's fictions. The dramatic impact of much of Owen's
poetry depends on the juxtaposition of public claims or
abstractions about war with the concrete, lived experience of war. "They are troops who fade, not flowers /
For poets' tearful fooling," he writes in **"Insensibility."**
And the soldiers "Bent double" "Knock-kneed," cursing
and "coughing like hags" or "beggars" hardly match the
shining, erect, smiling Tommies of World War I post-
ers. **"Dulce et Decorum Est"** most effectively undermines the heroic code of yet another male text whose
origins go back as far as Horace, claiming, "It is sweet
and honorable to die for one's country." By forcing the
reader to witness in minute, concrete detail just one
soldier's gruesome death, the soldier persona in the poem
shatters easy nationalistic slogans that lure innocent boys
to war.

In a less well-known but still compelling poem, **"Smile,
Smile, Smile,"** Owen similarly undermines the patriarchs' banner of nationalism. The setting of the poem is
a hospital for "half-limbed," "sunk-eyed wounded" vet-
erans who are reading yet another text in the *Mail*. They
are smiling ironically as they read the paper's lies and
see exposed their fathers' motivations:

> The sons we offered might regret they died
> If we got nothing lasting in their stead.
> We must be solidly indemnified.

Just as the above lines suggest the attention is on reim-
bursing and protecting the safe instigators of war rather
than the unsafe enactors of war, so the following lines
point to a similar obsession with self-interest clothed as
nationalism:

> We rulers sitting in this ancient spot
> Would wrong our very selves if we forgot
> The greatest glory will be theirs who fought,
> Who kept this nation in integrity.

But where is the nation? And what is the attitude toward
it of soldiers whose bodies were mutilated on its behalf?
We are told they "smiled at one another curiously /
Like secret men who knew their secret safe." The secret is that
the "nation" resides *in* the sons themselves whom the
"rulers" in their "ancient spot" have forfeited long ago:

> (This is the thing they know and never speak,
> That England one by one had fled to France,
> Not many elsewhere now, save under France.)

Although the wounded soldiers keep their silence, their
companion soldier Owen breaks it when he writes this
poem. In attacking the manipulative use of nationalism
as an excuse for continuing war, Owen speaks for the
silent soldiers for the last time. It seems from all records
to be the last poem Owen ever wrote.

Another script of the patriarchs which Owen subverts in
addition to nationalism is the traditional definition of
masculinity. In a number of poems he questions the so-

cialization of young boys which seems to lead them inevitably to becoming soldiers. The officer in **"A Terre"**
who is dying of wounds still says to his orderly:

> Little I'd ever teach a son, but hitting,
> Shooting, war, hunting, all the arts of hunting.
> Well, that's what I learnt,—that, and making
>   money.

The male tradition of sports also carried into the war the
same skills and attitudes as those used on the playing
fields. War was simply a more strenuous contest. . . .

Owen's response to such male socialization that makes
sports, war, and life simply a contest of physical prowess and endurance is evident in one of his most moving
poems, **"Disabled."** The veteran in this work, a boy not
yet twenty, was a soccer player who internalized his
culture's equation of sports and war:

> One time he liked a blood-smear down his leg,
> After the matches, carried shoulder-high.
> It was after football, when he'd drunk a peg,
> He thought he'd better join.

Less than a year after joining, he is sitting "in a wheeled
chair, waiting for dark" "in his ghastly suit of grey, /
Legless, sewn short at elbow." The women around him
no longer cheer him on but "touch him like some queer
disease."

For Owen, traditional notions of manhood included two
important rites: initiation into the warrior myth and sexual initiation. The two intertwine and Owen refuses both.
Though a warrior himself, Owen redefines what that
really means. The young amputee veteran in **"Disabled"**
originally imagined what being a warrior would be like
through the language of other men like Tennyson or
Morris or Kipling:

> He thought of jewelled kilts
> For daggers in plaid socks; of smart salutes;
> And care of arms; and leave; and pay arrears.

"S.I.W." (Self-Inflicted Wound) dramatizes the suicidal
imperative of the warrior myth for a young soldier who,
filled with false rhetoric about male valor, shoots himself when the war deprives him of his own glorious
death. The worst perpetrator of the myth in **"S.I.W."**
significantly is the father.

> Patting good-bye, doubtless they told the lad
> He'd always show the Hun a brave man's face;
> Father would sooner him dead than in disgrace,—
> Was proud to see him going, aye, and glad.

> "Death sooner than dishonour, that's the style!"
> So Father said.

When the son, whose "Courage leaked, as sand / From
the best sandbags after years of rain," finally plants the
bullet in his own body which the enemy refused to, "It

was the reasoned crisis of the soul." Indeed, the ethics of the father demanded the son's suicide.

One of Owen's better known poems, **"Arms and the Boy,"** continues his critique of the male warrior myth. It is a poem that describes the corruption of innocence in a boy seduced by weaponry. The alluring arms of war however, associate his maturation with the loss of Eden, "For his teeth seem for laughing round an apple." That the warrior myth is superimposed upon the youth's normal development is clear when we learn that he was not naturally equipped with weapons:

> There lurk no claws behind his fingers supple;
> And God will grow no talons at his heels,
> Nor antlers through the thickness of his curls.

As the boy is transformed into a warrior, his mouth is filled with "cartridges of fine zinc teeth." The soldier fully armed is, in fact, transformed into the terrifyingly monstrous figure of the arms themselves: "Blue with all malice, like a madman's flash: / And thinly drawn with famishing for flesh."

In addition to rejecting fictions about the warrior myth, Owen rejects traditional male sexual initiation as well. In *The Great War and Modern Memory* Paul Fussell brilliantly describes Owen's homoerotic writing and places him in a larger cultural and literary tradition that extends from Whitman to Hopkins to Symond, all of whom celebrated the beauty and body of men or boys and honored the passionate bonds between them. Fussell uses the term homoerotic "to imply a sublimited (i.e. chaste) form of temporary homosexuality." He argues that Owen's mind was "feeling always towards male particulars." Consequently, his poetry is dominated by lads and boys and by parts of the body: mouths, limbs, hair, chest, hands. While it is true, as Fussell claims, that sexuality behind the lines provided a necessary counterbalance to carnage on the front, Owen's identification with the tradition of the homoerotic has at its roots a repudiation of the father's traditional heterosexuality. The latter eventually comes to be linked in Owen's mind with the rape and violation of war, for Owen sees soldiers as the surrogate female rape victims.

Phallic symbols of the gun, especially in **"Arms and the Boy"** are described as frightening, vicious, seductive, and blood-thirsty. The sexual stimulation when the boy is lured "to stroke these blind, blunt bullet-leads" results in the boy's murder: the phallic bullets "long to nuzzle in the hearts of lads." The "arms" in the poem thus bring death not love. To avoid being a warrior / ravager, Owen rejects sexual initiation completely. A juvenile poem, **"The Sleeping Beauty,"** has the prince kiss the sleeping princess, but without affect, presumably for either of them. He draws back since it was clearly "not my part, / To start voluptuous pulses in her heart." Owen continues to draw back from the role of the prince and in rejecting heterosexuality seems to reject practicing homosexuality as well. Though sensuous in his poetry,

Owen remains above all chaste and in so doing claims identity with that chaste son, Jesus.

Assuming Christ's very words in **"Greater Love,"** "Greater love hath no man than he lay down his life for his friends" (*John* 15:13), Owen posits a detailed rejection of male heterosexuality. What he rejects is the male creation through Petrarch and others of the appropriate female love object. He mocks Petrarchan red lips, luring eyes, slender body, soft gentle voice, full heart, and pale hands. All of these male designated female attributes are diminished next to the genuine love object—dying male soldiers. The new love object is, by contrast, curiously grotesque, violated, murdered. Still, it attracts Owen by its very victimization: "eyes blinded in my stead," "limbs knife-skewed / Rolling and rolling there," "cramp[ed] . . . in death's extreme decrepitude," "hearts made great with shot." Owen echoes Christ's words at the end of the poem, this time on the cross when Jesus says, "Woman why weepest thou? . . . Touch me not" (John 20:15-17). The woman in the poem may weep but the male sacrificed figure is now sanctified and beyond her reach. Thus Owen makes the greatest love of all that between men; woman may only watch and weep. In this poem Owen's very complicated sexual identity surfaces. He rejects father figures and heterosexuality, is drawn to traditional female qualities, yet clearly prefers men in arms to women's arms.

Raised in a world of boys' schools and surrounded only by men in the trenches, Owen has sensual antennae only for other men. Even in the early **"Maundy Thursday,"** the persona reluctantly kneels at the altar to take the Eucharist. Instead of revering the Christ there who "was thin, and cold, and very dead," he kisses—even has his lips cling to—"the warm live hand" of the "server-lad." A later 1917 poem, **"To My Friend,"** sustains a similar passion between two men. In it the persona is wondering what sort of monument he yearns for after death and prefers to be remembered only by his soldier's identity disk, one worn by his "sweet friend."

> Inscribe no date nor deed
> But may thy heart-beat kiss it, night and day,
> Until the name grow blurred and fade away.

His sexual attraction for his friend is acknowledged but not acted on. The orgasm he would normally experience comes after his death as he fades away under his lover's kisses night and day.

More subversive of Abram's authority than his rejection of the warrior myth or male sexual initiations is Owen's acknowledgement and embrace of the "woman" in himself. While his locus is usually an exclusively male world, Owen recognizes the deadness and deathliness of traditional male legacies. Thus he turns to women's legacies for inspiration as he had turned to his own mother so often in his lifetime. . . . Unabashedly his mother's favorite child, Owen was profoundly attached to his mother. His relation with his father was more distant. . . .

His mother was the major influence in the poet's life, and according to Owen's brother Harold, responsible for his poetry. . . .

In appropriating a matriarchal not a patriarchal tradition, Owen cultivates feelings, tenderness, and sensitivity. Most miraculous of all, he risks doing so in the most brutalizing and numbing of experiences. . . . Owen's war experience also subjects him to situations that parallel many women's lives, especially in relationship to power and authority. More powerful figures or forces typically impose self-division. In **"The Show,"** for example, the soldier in the poem is literally divided, first from the Earth and then from his body as Death shows him a worm and "the fresh-severed head of it, my head." Similarly in **"Strange Meeting,"** set in a hellish underworld, the soldier meets an enemy he has killed. The enemy, however is not only a German but also that part of the English soldier who dreams of healing wounds, ending war, and shedding his uniform. The enemy maps out what he would have liked to have done had he lived:

> Then, when much blood had clogged their chariot
>   wheels,
> I would go up and wash them from sweet wells,
> Even with truths that lie too deep for taint.
> I would have poured my spirit without stint
> But not through wounds; not on the cess of war.

The gesture of washing from a well is both biblical and female as is the expending of self not as warrior but as a peacemaker.

In curious ways, Owen seems deliberately to take the stance in his poetry, too, of an observer rather than a participant. One is, then, falsely led at times to think of him as vicariously experiencing the war as an empathetic woman might, not as a commissioned officer. . . . One could almost forget that Owen was a soldier himself and not a nurse. A number of poems, **"Dulce," "Greater Love," "Asleep," "Futility," "A Terre,"** and **"Mental Cases,"** also have the persona record events other soldiers suffer. As witness and scribe of a new text other than Abram's, he constantly identifies with the innocent victims acted upon by those far more powerful. Likewise he repeatedly turns his men into boys, into children whom he nurtures and cares for much as his influential mother nurtured him.

In subverting the father figure and his current reign, Owen will appropriate sources of female power, but he carefully excludes women from any but the most marginal existence in his re-visioned world. Like other male modernists, such as Lawrence, Eliot, and Joyce, Owen establishes a paradise populated and dominated by men. Like them, too, his passionate and most genuine bonds are with other men, but with sons, not with fathers. In critiquing the patriarch's kingdom which ostensibly he should inherit, Owen defines the king as murderous, refuses initiations into several socializing male rites, and transforms men into boys, thus recapturing their less gender-differentiated pre-pubescent state. In so doing,

Owen undermines the power of Abram whom he credits with causing such carnage in the world. Although some other officer had to write "Deceased" across Owen's name on November 4, 1918, Owen's poetry, life, and letters still testify to the ways he himself sought to scrawl "Deceased" over Abram's death-laden books.

Paul Norgate (essay date 1989)

SOURCE: "Wilfred Owen and the Soldier Poets," in *The Review of English Studies,* Vol. 40, No. 160, November, 1989, pp. 516-30.

[*In the following excerpt, Norgate commends Owen's poetic need to "break out of the closed circle of meaning guarded by the Soldier Poets."*]

It is . . . almost a critical commonplace that Wilfred Owen's poetry is full of echoes—he was, as he described himself, "a poet's poet." Innumerable allusions bear witness to his wide reading in the Romantic/Victorian tradition, and the influence of Georgian contemporaries is also evident—Monro, Gibson, and Graves, as well as (obviously and pre-eminently) Sassoon. Similar uses and transformations have been observed of material from classical literature and from the Bible. In Owen's war poetry, reference and allusion has almost always an ironizing function. The primary thrust of this irony is generally in one of two directions—towards the situation of war itself, or towards the source of the allusion. In the first, more frequently recognized, usage, Owen's source material is employed as it were approvingly, unequivocally: adding depth and resonance as a means of exposing the horror or futility of present circumstances. Of this kind are, for instance, the allusions to Dante in **"Mental Cases"** or to Shelley in **"Strange Meeting."**

On the other hand, the allusion itself may be deployed ironically by Owen, in order to demonstrate the inadequacy of his "original" as a source of understanding, of reassurance, or of values by which to interpret the war; in such cases the allusion itself becomes in effect a "subject" of the poem. Irony of this kind is most typically directed by Owen at contemporary targets—at the failure of organized religion, for instance, as in **"Parable of the Old Man and the Young"**; at the pronouncements of wartime statesmen, as in **"Smile, Smile, Smile"**; or at such writings as those of the Soldier Poets.

In the drafting of one of his earliest war poems, **"Dulce et Decorum Est"** (completed in October 1917), Owen had at one stage identified a specific contemporary target, subtitling the poem "To a Certain Poetess." This was Miss Jessie Pope, whose jingoistic doggerel appeared frequently in newspapers and magazines; **"Dulce et Decorum Est"** is in fact generally read as an attack upon the ignorant belligerence of civilian non-combatants. In the process of rapid revision and redrafting, however, this "dedication" was abandoned: in its bitter excoriation of "the old lie," the energy of Owen's poem encompasses more than a single "liar," just as its barbed reference to the Horatian motto signals the rejection of something more immediate than a merely traditional philosophy of battle.

For, prior to Owen, more than one piece of Soldier Poetry retailed this same Latin tag entirely unironically, as a text of current relevance and value. (It had been inscribed above the chapel door at Sandhurst in 1913.) Cpl. H. J. Jarvis's "Dulce et Decorum Est pro Patria Mori," for instance, appeared first in the *Poetry Review* and then in *More Songs by the Fighting Men;* a piece under the same title by Major Sydney Oswald was also published in the *Review,* and reprinted in *Songs of the Fighting Men.* Oswald celebrates deeds of combat in the line, and the impulse to invest such action with significance is clearly evident in his concluding lines:

> Glory is theirs; the People's narrative
>   Of fame will tell their deeds of gallantry,
> And for all time their memories will live
>   Shrined in our hearts.

Owen's "narrative," by comparison, is of people who suffer and die, not "the People" who applaud and sanctify. With persistent emphasis on its degrading, nightmarish setting, Owen's **"Dulce et Decorum Est"** images a random and futile death, far removed from any meaningful "action" and whose memory offers no comfort or heroic reassurance.

Read thus in the context of Soldier Poetry, the emphasis in the second half of Owen's **"Dulce et Decorum Est"** may be seen to fall not merely on "you," with the implication of ignorant *non*-participation, but also on those verbs which stress participation: "if you could pace . . . and watch . . . if you could hear . . ." It is a reading which unleashes a sharper, more unexpected irony, Owen's poem now speaking also to those who *have* participated, who must have watched and heard, but who apparently still do not really *see;* those—such as the Soldier Poets—who, having experienced warfare in the trenches, can still (for whatever reason) "lie" about it.

The rhetoric of Soldier Poetry, clearly, articulates a tradition in which battle can only be idealized, and the collision of Owen's first-hand experience with this heroic rhetoric—the "execrable" as against the "glorious"—may be traced in further juxtaposition:

"Anthem For Doomed Youth"

> What passing-bells for these who die as cattle?
>   —Only the monstrous anger of the guns.
> Only the stuttering rifles' rapid rattle
>   Can patter out their hasty orisons.
> No mockeries now for them; no prayers nor bells;
>   Nor any voice of mourning save the choirs,—
> The shrill, demented choirs of wailing shells;
>   And bugles calling for them from sad shires.

> What candles may be held to speed them all?
>   Not in the hands of boys but in their eyes
> Shall shine the holy glimmers of goodbyes.
>   The pallor of girls' brows shall be their pall;
> Their flowers the tenderness of patient minds,
> And each slow dusk a drawing down of blinds.

"Anthem" was written in September 1917, and as Jon Stallworthy has observed, one stage in the crystallization of this poem was probably Owen's reading of the "Prefatory Note" to another contemporary anthology, *Poems of Today* (1916), which speaks of "the music of Pan's flute, and of Love's viol, and the bugle-call of Endeavour, and the passing-bells of Death." However, for a further insight into the "context" of Owen's poem we may turn to this—by a Soldier Poet:

"A Soldier's Cemetery"

> Behind that long and lonely trenched line
> To which men come and go, where brave men die,
> There is a yet unmarked and unknown shrine,
> A broken plot, a soldier's cemetery.
> There lie the flower of youth, the men who
>   scorned
> To live (so died) when languished Liberty;
> Across their graves flowerless and unadorned
> Still scream the shells of each artillery.
> When war shall cease, this lonely unknown spot
> Of many a pilgrimage will be the end,
> And flowers will shine in this now barren plot
> And fame upon it through the years descend;
> But many a heart upon each simple cross
> Will hang the grief, the memory of its loss.

Cpl. (later Sgt.) J. W. Streets was one of the most popular of the Soldier Poets, widely anthologized and with a memorial volume of his verse published posthumously in 1917. "A Soldier's Cemetery" is representative of both his own writing and that of the Soldier Poets generally. . . .

Surface similarities between the two sonnets are probably no more than coincidental, but one of them provides a useful starting-point for comparison: the intersection of imagery at the centres of the poems. "Across their graves . . . / Still scream the shells of each artillery" strives merely to intensify the brave pathos of Streets's "lonely unknown spot"; but in Owen, "The shrill, demented choirs of wailing shells" inscribes the madness of no man's land where the "monstrous anger of the guns" and the "wailing shells" are metonymic of a war that is become its own cause for continuing. Owen's sonnet bitterly contradicts the central premiss of "A Soldier's Cemetery," which (for all its reiteration of "lonely" and "unknown") comprises a series of essentially positive statements: "there *is* a shrine . . . war *shall* cease . . . ," the cemetery *will* be found, "fame [*will*] descend," and so on. All such consolatory possibilities are dismissed as mere 'mockeries' by the relentless sequence of questions, negatives, and quasi-negatives in **"Anthem."** Owen's comprehension of the war discovers no "plot" (of any kind), however "broken," to offer the reassurance of ultimate meaning or significance—"What passing-bells for these who die as cattle?" Streets's final couplet elevates "each simple cross" into a heroic memorial to many losses, and thus effectively obscures the true implications of the disparity between the (small) number of marked graves and the (unspecified, unimaginable) number of dead. But in **"Anthem"** the enormity of the slaughter precludes any of the traditional rituals of consolation or mourning; all that remains is the suffering of unfocused grief down an endless recession of time, and "each slow dusk a drawing down of blinds."

An attempt to emulate Siegfried Sassoon is characteristic of many of Owen's early war poems, but **"Anthem for Doomed Youth"** (although Sassoon's presence is evident in manuscript corrections) is more usually cited as an example of Owen's debt to the Romantic tradition. However, comparison with Soldier Poetry, as exemplified in "A Soldier's Cemetery," reveals how "Sassoonish" **"Anthem"** may in fact be, refusing not only the memorializing rituals of organized religion itself but also the rhetorical tradition which offers poetic memorials as either complementary to, or a substitute for, religion. Reaching beyond mere polemic or specific parody, Owen's poem begins to envisage the chaos of war as an unending condition of modern existence, every individual bearing somewhere ("in their eyes . . . brows . . . minds") its scars.

Siegfried Sassoon's war poetry had already set itself in contention with Soldier Poetry; Owen, however, went on to develop a subtler, more complex response to war, incorporating dialogue with both Soldier Poetry and Sassoon. It is instructive to compare Owen, Sassoon, and Soldier Poetry at work, by drawing together three poems which—to use an apt metaphor—"bleed into" one another. Like **"Dulce et Decorum Est"** and various other of his poems, Owen's **"Conscious"** (completed early in 1918) refers to specific elements of his personal experience—here, to the several spells which he had spent in hospitals and Casualty Clearing Stations during 1917:

"Conscious"

His fingers wake, and flutter; up the bed.
His eyes come open with a pull of will,
Helped by the yellow may-flowers by his head.
The blind-cord drawls across the window-sill . . .
What a smooth floor the ward has! What a rug!
Who is that talking somewhere out of sight?
Why are they laughing? What's inside that jug?
'Nurse! Doctor!'—'Yes, all right, all right.'

But sudden evening muddles all the air—
There seems no time to want a drink of water.
Nurse looks so far away. And here and there
Music and roses burst through crimson slaughter.
He can't remember where he saw blue sky.
More blankets. Cold. He's cold. And yet so hot,
And there's no light to see the voices by;
There is no time to ask—he knows not what.

Reference to biographical detail is, however, less helpful to our understanding here than is a knowledge that the poem belongs to a popular "sub-genre' of war poetry—the hospital poem. The following example is by a Soldier Poet, Lt. Gilbert Waterhouse:

"The Casualty Clearing Station"

A bowl of daffodils,
A crimson quilted bed,
Sheets and pillows white as snow,
White and gold and red—
And sisters moving to and fro
With soft and silent tread.
So all my spirit fills
With pleasure infinite
And all the feathered wings of rest
Seem flocking from the radiant West
To bear me thro' the night.

See how they close me in,
They, and the sisters' arms,
One eye is closed, the other lid
Is watching how my spirit slid
Toward some red-roofed farms,
And having crept beneath them, slept
Secure from war's alarms.

Between this and **"Conscious"** there are similarities of setting and some surface detail (yellow flowers, "crimson"), but what is thrown most sharply into focus by the juxtaposition of texts is, again, Owen's refusal to conform to the conventional responses to war as represented in Soldier Poetry. Waterhouse's casualty drifts into peaceful sleep, lulled by the soothing calm of the hospital (and incidental echoes from Wordsworth's "Daffodils") into "pleasure infinite." Conflict and injury—the reasons, presumably, for being there—are reduced to mere echoes in that reassuring final phrase, "secure from war's alarms." "The Casualty Clearing Station" contrives an image, virtually, of paradise regained, whether read as the prelude to safe awakening on the morrow, and the road to recovery; or, possibly, as the moment of happy release into a serene death. From its ironic title onwards, Owen's **"Conscious"** comprehensively undercuts any such expressions of hope. This casualty must awake, but only to a disjointed sequence of sense-impressions: the polished silence of the hospital enforces alienation rather than comfort; his memories are of "crimson slaughter," not "red-roofed farms," and he is **"Conscious"** only of his inability to hold on to the world of consciousness. As becomes characteristic in Owen's war poems, the 'narrative' is unresolved; both casualty and reader are here left suspended amidst incoherence and fragmentation.

"The Death-Bed" by Siegfried Sassoon—which Owen had earlier much admired, according to his letters—similarly describes the case of a wounded soldier in a hospital bed, but (as its title indicates) in a far less ironically ambiguous fashion than **"Conscious."** Sassoon's soldier *must* die, in order to provide the occasion for overt polemic, moralizing:

"Speak to him; rouse him; you may save him yet.
He's young; he hated War; how should he die
When cruel old campaigners win safe through?"

Owen's **"Conscious"** thus suggests a 'reading' both of Soldier Poetry and of his mentor, Sassoon. The naïve optimism of Waterhouse is rejected in a series of negatives reminiscent of **"Anthem for Doomed Youth"**: "he can't remember . . . no light . . . no time . . . he knows not what." But significantly, the limitations of Sassoon's "propaganda" are also exposed, as Owen's poem struggles to resist the drawing of *any* supposed "conclusion" from the situation of the soldier.

The need to invest every action of the ordinary soldier with positive significance is, as we have seen, characteristic of the Soldier Poets, and, not surprisingly, religious symbolism was enlisted to the cause. The identification of the soldier with Christ himself was in fact a motif so common in contemporary writing about the war as to be almost a cliché—and generally, of course, presented without the ironic perspective of Owen's **"At a Calvary Near the Ancre,"** which dates from late 1917/early 1918:

"At a Calvary Near the Ancre"

One ever hangs where shelled roads part.
  In this war He too lost a limb,
But His disciples hide apart;
  And now the soldiers bear with Him.

Near Golgotha strolls many a priest,
  And in their faces there is pride
That they were flesh-marked by the Beast
  By whom the gentle Christ's denied.

The scribes on all the people shove
  And bawl allegiance to the state,
But they who love the greater love
  Lay down their life; they do not hate.

Owen's allusions to the crucifixion story are consistent and to the point, exposing the continuing inadequacies of organized religion: the poem is usually discussed in terms of an attack on the hypocrisy of conventional pieties. Thus, the sacrifice of "the gentle Christ" is paralleled in war by the sacrifice of the ordinary soldier, but both are equally undervalued, misunderstood, or simply ignored. Knowledge of Wilfred Owen's religious upbringing, and of his rejection of the orthodox Christian creed, has led to a clearer understanding of the biblical allusions in **"At a Calvary,"** but here again reference to the work of the Soldier Poets illuminates the more specifically literary context of Owen's poem. Cpl. H. J. Jarvis's "At a Wayside Shrine" (in *More Songs by the Fighting Men*) typifies the unquestioning—and selective—appropriation of the soldier/Christ analogy to blatantly patriotic purposes; there is perhaps more than a passing similarity of titles to suggest that in **"At a Calvary Near the Ancre"** Owen seeks once more to fracture the conventions of popular war poetry:

"At a Wayside Shrine"

The column halts before a wayside shrine
To change formation into battle line
From double file. 'Tis even, and the sun
Its daily circling race has wellnigh done.
Behind me in the West, a dying glow
Of gold still gleams, to cast a pale halo
Upon the shrine . . .

    . . . And now the line will pass
The shrine—itself as steady as the mass
Of England's sons slow-moving to the fray,
Their destiny now in the hands of—say,
The dim Divinity within that shrine—
A loving God (the stricken Christ His sign
Of Love)—or what? . . .

    . . . So have some died
For right—bravely as Christ Crucified
And just as sacrificially. To save
The world He died, or so the worn-out creeds
Of church would teach—but they, but men, dared deeds
And died as men . . .

    Because of Greater Love—
That Love of Loves, all other loves above—
The love of Home and Friends and Native Soil.
That these might never be the Foeman's spoil,
They gave their lives, their youth, their golden dreams
And airy castles, built where Sunlight gleams,
And Roses bloom . . .

    And ere I leave the shrine
I look upon the Christ—then at the line
Of men . . .
    . . . —these other Christs in thin disguise
Of Khaki-brown.

As in the previous comparisons, Owen's style is bleaker, more oblique. The terse quatrains of **"At a Calvary"** point up an almost embarrassing prolixity in "At a Wayside Shrine": from the "dying glow / Of gold . . . a pale halo / Upon the shrine," through the shrine itself which is "rent and drilled with bullets," to the soldiers' uniforms, a "thin disguise / Of Khaki-brown," virtually every detail in Jarvis's poem is heavily overlaid with significance. For all the "haloesque" rhetoric that surrounds it, however, the identification of Christ and soldiers which is central to "At a Wayside Shrine" is circumscribed by assumptions which render it ultimately as unsatisfactory as those "worn-out creeds / Of church" with which Jarvis—consciously daring, one feels—seeks to contrast it. Jarvis's shrine, though "rent," is "steady as the mass / Of England's sons slow-moving to the fray": if the soldier is Christ-like, Christ is specifically an Englishman. If the soldier acts "because of Greater Love," it is a nationalistic "love of Home and Friends and Native Soil"; he may love his neighbour, but he must definitely hate his "Foeman."

Caught between the institutionalized exhortations of Church and State and the sentimentalized patriotism of the civilian population, the soldiers in Owen's **"At a Calvary"** die less for creed or nation than for comrades; they "bear with Him" and are thereby the more truly Christ-like. While Soldier Poetry, as in "At a Wayside Shrine," continues to further the notion of significant sacrifice, Owen implies that where it matters—in the political arena, where "The scribes on all the people shove / And bawl allegiance to the state"—the soldiers' deaths are probably a virtual irrelevance.

The closing lines of **"At a Calvary"**—

> But they who love the greater love
> Lay down their life; they do not hate

—do not signal any endorsement of the popular conception of patriotic sacrifice by the soldier/Christ, as typified in Jarvis's poem. Rather, they frame a rebuke to those who seek to replace the "worn-out creeds" of one partial version of Christianity with the even more tendentious creed ("So have some died / For right . . .") of another. "At a Wayside Shrine" enlists the Christ-figure as a convenient (and retrospective) justification and encouragement for men moving down a road they have already chosen. **"At a Calvary"** confronts the implications of true sacrifice and recognizes the war as continuing evidence of man's inability to comprehend "the greater love." The soldier-Christ, for Owen, "ever hangs where shelled roads part," mutely symbolic of humanity forever at a crossroads amidst its own destructiveness.

Wilfred Owen's experience of war on the Somme was of conditions and circumstances which conformed to no "meaning" or "plot" such as might be conceived in traditional or conventional terms. It was an experience which at first all but paralysed Owen's writing of poetry and, in shell-shock, threatened his very sanity. The Soldier Poets' continuing ability to sustain their positive statements in the face of such destructive experience was managed by reference back to the terms—religion, nation, duty, sacrifice, etc.—by which earlier wars had largely been defined and given "meaning" in a dominant social and literary culture. This circumscribing of language in First World War popular poetry effectively produced a circumscription of experience, whereby understanding of the war could be 'held in' and limited to what was acceptable or could be coped with. Siegfried Sassoon's satirical verse sought to counter this by a direct inversion of Soldier Poet rhetoric: for the motifs of religion, nation, duty, and sacrifice, Sassoon simply substituted hypocrisy, arrogance, stupidity, and futility. But the powerful initial shock effect of this tactic, when repeated, works rather to exclude than to include—you either agree with Sassoon, or you don't see his point. This in effect tends to produce its own "closed circle" of meaning, its own kind of oppositional "closure" which, as a minority voice in 1914-18, was too easily marginalized.

However, it was through his fortunate encounter with Sassoon's satirical polemic that Owen had gained access

to perhaps the one form of discourse which could at that point contain his own sense of alienation and his impulse to bitter denunciation and rejection of war experience. In his earliest war poems from Craiglockhart Hospital, those who would falsify or misrepresent the experience of the trenches are vilified and rejected, if anything more vehemently than is the experience itself. **"Anthem for Doomed Youth"** and **"Dulce et Decorum Est"** exemplify this phase: written within weeks of meeting Sassoon, they clearly rehearse the Sassoonish tactic of inversion and counter-assertion.

But Owen's own writing could not rest merely in the refusal of others': "I think every poem . . . should be a matter of experience." His poetry must go on to seek whatever "reality" might be found in war experience—or, if necessary, to confront the absence of it: poems such as **"Conscious"** and **"At a Calvary"** mark early stages in the development of a more subtly provisional discourse which might attempt this. Comparison with the writings of the Soldier Poets here highlights a characteristic which becomes increasingly important in the relatively small Owen corpus—his war poetry coming more and more to resist the "closure" so confidently, so regularly achieved by the writings of his contemporaries. Recognizing how their language essentially pre-dates the experience of the Somme (where the values it signals are not merely under threat but now hopelessly disconnected from the conditions of existence), Owen's poetry must break out from the "closed circle" of meaning guarded by the Soldier Poets, and confront the no man's land that lies outside it.

Mark Graves (essay date 1994)

SOURCE: "Wilfred Owen's 'The Letter' and the Truth of War," in *English Language Notes,* March, 1994, pp. 59-66.

[In the following excerpt, Graves focuses on the issues of wartime censorship and propaganda revealed in Owen's "The Letter."]

As an officer at the front editing soldiers' letters home, [Wilfred] Owen acted as a cog in the British propaganda machine during World War I. British propaganda, and the subsequent censorship of wartime correspondence, hoped to serve two purposes: first, to insure national security in Britain, and second, to keep up morale on the homefront by sheltering civilian sensibilities from the devastation on the Western Front. As Owen reveals in his poem **"The Letter,"** however, wartime censorship and propaganda, and the sense of patriotism which encouraged both, accomplished neither. Instead, they distanced the soldiers witnessing the atrocities of the Western Front from civilian England, just seventy miles away, and they offered a false sense of a loved one's security to millions at home clamoring for news about the war.

Little critical attention has been focused on this gem in Owen's literary repetoire, perhaps because critics disagree on when Owen actually wrote the poem. Some critics attribute its composition to a two-month period between January through March, 1917, because the manuscript's watermark matches that of letters Owen wrote home in the period. What some critics call Owen's "Sassoonish style" in the poem—his harsh, direct political onslaughts presented in a loose structure—suggest that he began the poem months later during his convalescence from nervous exhaustion at Craiglockhart War Hospital in Edinburgh, Scotland, where he met Sassoon. Owen's poems of this period reflect his admiration for Sassoon's work, and Owen seems to draw the letter format used in his poem from the first two lines of Sassoon's poem "In the Pink":

> So Davies wrote: "This leaves me in the pink."
> Then scrawled his name: "Your loving sweetheart, Willie."

But many of the poems Owen wrote in this "Sassoonish style" he repeatedly revised, often well into 1918. This awareness, along with the confusion over watermarks, accounts for the difficulty in arriving at a precise date of composition for **"The Letter."**

Regardless of when Owen actually composed it, the poem springs from essentially the same impulse which produced his more well-known works such as **"Dulce Et Decorum Est,"** namely a need to proffer realistically the futility of war. In a tone of irony and understatement. Owen presents a middle- to lower-class Englishman writing a brief, superficial letter expressing a nostalgic longing for reminders of home, probably all the censors and his British pride will allow, we assume. Ironically, just after the soldier pacifies his wife with lies about his well-being, an incoming round mortally wounds him.

As Owen's representation of an infantryman's wartime existence, the poem serves two functions: as a social satire on British stoicism and propaganda and as a statement in colloquial dialect on the common infantryman's predicament in the trenches which he alone cannot articulate. In the combat zone, British propaganda and censorship policies, which Owen parodies here, sought to provide the homefront with information about the steady progress of the war and of a loved one's well-being while simultaneously saying nothing, speaking of the war as if it were entirely "normal and matter-of-fact." Owen himself wrote to his mother, "[E]verything is toned down. . . . Nothing is 'horrible.' The word is never used in public. Things are 'darned unpleasant,' 'Rather nasty,' or, if very bad, simply 'damnable'." . . .

Emerging from this context of propaganda and censorship, . . . Owen's **"The Letter"** creates two levels of reality: the first, and what I call "primary" text, upholds the "official" view of the war, and the second tells Owen's truth of war in a soldier's vernacular. In the primary text, Owen captures the tragic great lie about the glories of war by satirizing the formulaic Other Rank's letters with their pat, empty cliches which characterize the genre. [The] protagonist writes, "I'm in the pink at present, dear, I think the war will end this year? . . . We're out of harms way, not bad fed"—all cliched, standardized reassurances designed to ease fears at home. In combination with the generic title **"The Letter,"** these images evoke a sense of anonymity, of a blind unquestioning loyalty to the British cause. But, Owen believes, the promoters of British propaganda policies failed to consider the humanity of these fighting men, individuals with distinct needs, desires, feelings, and, most important, fears that no amount of flag-waving or "stiff upper lip" could eradicate.

One cliche, "in the pink," particularly evokes the sense of blind faith in the righteousness of the war which Owen rejects. An examination of the British associations embedded in the phrase fully reveals its usefulness as a tool of propaganda. Two definitions from the *Oxford English Dictionary* seem relevant here:

> 1. The "flower" or finest example of excellence . . . the most perfect condition.

> 2. A small flower with pale pink florettes.

In Owen's poem, and in its use in any number of soldiers' letters home during World War I, the significance and applicability of the first definition is obvious: "pink" merely describes an exalted sense of well-being. It meant "I'm fine," or more specifically, "I'm not badly wounded or dead."

The second definition draws on much more subtle associations, relying on the long-standing English reverence for the pastoral. Pinks, as a flower growing wild in the English countryside and in gardens in a domestic variety similar to the American Sweet William, symbolized England and the rusticity and beauty of its countryside. In this respect, "in the pink" could be literally interpreted as "in the pinks," in a condition similar to the simplicity and safety of an English garden. Owen objects for propaganda purposes to the use of an icon evoking a particular English state of mind which could not be duplicated in the melee of war.

In contrast to the "official" picture he presented in the primary text, Owen combines both colloquial language and a definite structure in the narrative interruptions found in the parenthesis to create a second, more immediate, truthful wartime reality. He juxtaposes the typical British cliches with the common man's vernacular and psychology to disclose the disparity between the "official" appearance of the war and the reality of the situation. In these narrative intrusions, Owen reveals the fragility and vulnerability of common fighting men facing death once the bravado and patriotic cliches have been stripped away. The tone in the phrases evokes the terror of the trenches; the actions, the great anxiety of men laboring under unlikely odds for survival. The first narrative interruptions, for example, present Owen's reinterpretation of the camaraderie which existed among soldiers who found themselves in a similar crisis. Far from the highly idealized portraits of noble comrades perilously united against a bitter "foe," the soldiers in Owen's poem depend upon one another for simple sustenance and survival. For example, the protagonist asks his comrades for a knife to sharpen his pencil, his only means of communication to the outside world, and for a bit of food perhaps to soothe his aching stomach. "O blast this pencil," he remarks, "Ere, Bill, lend's a knife." And to another, he entreats, "Say, Jimmy, spare's a bite of bread." Despite their mutual dependence, in their anxiety and in their uncertain circumstances, the comrades squabble among themselves as a method of relieving tension. Retrieving a cigarette becomes as important as advancing on a battlefield or capturing enemy territory. The troop struggles for this simple pleasure with the same level of aggression exhibited in battle. "Yer what? Then don't, yer ruddy cow!" the tommy exhorts. "And give us back me cigarette!"

But besides physical deprivation, Owen suggests that perhaps the ever-present possibility of his own death was the most difficult hardship with which the average soldier had to cope. In the poem, the protagonist's fear and tension mounts as shelling begins, and he is caught off guard by the chaos surrounding him. "Eh? What the 'ell! Stand to? Stand to!" he cries, but it is too late. His worst fear materializes: he is hit. In the final lines of the poem, we see and hear the panic and terror in the man's words when he recognizes the severity of his wound and the certainty of his death. He gurgles, "Guh! Christ, I'm hit. Take 'old. Aye, bad." All the cliches about the war cannot now staunch the blood pouring from the soldier's wound, not literally and not figuratively. For while the British government concerned itself with preventing any emotional or political abscesses at home, it failed to provide its fighting men with the aid and comfort they need. Owen's soldier shrugs off any attempts to dress his wound, bellowing, "No, damn your iodine." His wound cannot benefit from frontline medical attention. An acute awareness of one's own mortality and an inability to prevent the inevitable are perhaps the most difficult truths about war to accept, Owen suggests.

Sadly, when dying, the man concerns himself ultimately with guaranteeing the sanctity of the lie about the war which brought him to the brink of death in the first place, not with his own mortality. With his dying breath, the tommy asks his comrade, Jim, to write to his "old girl" a letter destined to contain cliches and euphemisms cloaking the truth about his demise.

Interestingly, in the original table of contents and preface to the collection of poems Owen began to compile while convalescing in 1917, he included the title of the poems he chose for the volume and his motives for choosing them. Although not published along with the titles, Owen's motive for including **"The Letter"** in his collection he called "Heroic Lies." If they were indeed lies, then one wonders why Owen himself, like the soldier in his poem, believed them enough to endure the kind of

hell under fire which probably even his own words fell short of describing. One can only speculate, since Owen was a victim himself of the very falsehoods which he denounced British propaganda for furthering and British stoicism for accepting. Perhaps he felt compelled to record the "real" war for posterity. And only by exploding patriotic myths in poems such as **"The Letter"** and **"Dulce Et Decorum Est"** could Owen expose where the "real" war was fought, in the hearts and minds of the common soldier at the front for whom he was a spokesman.

Jahan Ramazani (essay date 1994)

SOURCE: "Wilfred Owen," in *Poetry of Mourning: The Modern Elegy from Hardy to Heaney,* The University of Chicago Press, 1994, pp. 69-96.

[*In the following excerpt, Ramazani examines Owen's challenge to received notions of elegiac conventions in his poetry.*]

Much as [Thomas] Hardy instilled his personal and public elegies with the intensified skepticisms of modernity, Wilfred Owen forged a new kind of elegy upon the anvil of modern industrialized warfare. One of Hardy's most capable admirers, Owen considered entitling a projected collection of his war poems *English Elegies* or, in a phrase from Shelley's elegy for Keats, *With Lightning and with Music.* But critics have not pursued the implication that Owen's poems should be read generically as elegies. This reluctance is understandable, since Owen's poems challenge received notions of elegiac convention, structure, and psychology. In poems such as **"Anthem for Doomed Youth," "Futility," "Mental Cases,"** and **"Miners,"** Owen exemplifies the paradox of many modern elegies: that the best are frequently the most anti-elegiac. In his draft Preface, Owen states, "these elegies are to this generation in no sense consolatory." Owen's melancholic elegies, like Hardy's, make it harder to interpret the elegy solely under the aegis of the pleasure principle, harder to maintain normative explanations of the genre as psychic remedy. Resisting the traditional drive toward solace, his elegies magnify the masochism latent in the genre. Critics have noted the "sadomasochism" of Owen's prewar poems; this quality may suggest that we should think of Owen's poetic sensibility not only as a by-product of the painful facts of war but as a sensibility in search of such facts. If even Owen's apparently realistic work is symbolically implicated in the production of the horrible pain and death it laments, then another key assumption about the elegy as a genre and the war elegy as a subgenre becomes problematic: that they are irreducibly "occasional" forms of poetry. Owen's work helps us to rethink the elegiac triad of mourning poet, mourning reader, and mourned victim, eerily suggesting that, even in war elegies, both poet and reader may partly create the victimization they mourn.

Although Owen claims to write nonconsolatory elegies, his best-known poem has been attacked precisely for being consolatory. Following Geoffrey Hill and Peter Dale, Jon Silkin accuses Owen of "consolatory mourning" in **"Anthem for Doomed Youth."** According to this critique, Owen participates in the religious and nationalist ideology of compensatory exchange, urging us to accept memory as a substitute for human lives. Certainly the elegy is more consolatory than such self-excoriating war elegies as Hill's "Two Formal Elegies" written *"For the Jews in Europe"*—later poems that scrutinize their complicity in the repellent exchange of "song" for lost life. . . .

Against the severe standard of a later generation, Owen's poetry does fall short, particularly the sestet of **"Anthem for Doomed Youth."** But "consolatory" and "nonconsolatory," like "mourning" and "melancholia," should be regarded as matters of degree and not of kind: Owen's poetry is less melancholic, less anti-consolatory than Hill's, but much more so than the poetry of most predecessors and contemporaries. Whereas Hill, Silkin, and other postwar writers must mourn in the shadow of the Holocaust and must disentangle their elegiac work from the vast commercial industries of the visual media, Owen's poetry precedes this historical cataclysm and the subsequent mass-marketing of atrocity for profit—films, shows, documentaries that, from Hill's perspective, ultimately make "their long death / Documented and safe" and leave us "witness-proof." Writing long before the ascendancy of such commercial genres, Owen responds to a different set of cultural intertexts. Notoriously, Rupert Brooke in "The Soldier" finds compensation for the loss of his life in the consequent expansion of England, literalizing imperialist ideology:

> If I should die, think only this of me:
>   That there's some corner of a foreign field
> That is forever England.

Brooke wagers his death for England's continued life. Unlike the victims in this patriotic war elegy and many others, Owen's dead never achieve apotheosis in the ideal of the state. Casting aside such consolations, Owen's elegies reject the broad current of patriotic verse and join the countercurrent not only of war poems by Siegfried Sassoon, Ivor Gurney, and Isaac Rosenberg, but also the international melancholic mode of Hardy's *War Poems,* Stevens's "Death of a Soldier," and Yeats's "Reprisals." Together with the authors of such poems, Owen helped to make the elegy a more disconsolate and discordant genre—a genre less contaminated by its likeness to the compensatory discourse of patriotic propaganda.

To the experience of modern warfare, Owen brought a profound but skeptical understanding of the resources available to the mourning poet. In the sonnets **"Anthem for Doomed Youth"** and **"Futility,"** he powerfully resists and revises the traditional tropes, conventions, and economics of elegy. **"Anthem"** is a collective elegy for the nameless many, **"Futility"** an elegy for a single man.

"Anthem" is consolatory in its ending, **"Futility"** resolutely anti-consolatory. Silkin objects that **"Anthem"** ends in the mode of pastoral elegy, falsifying the deaths of the soldiers; but we can appreciate the poem's overall transformation of pastoral elegy only if we take into account its initial bleak joke on the genre. Whereas the death of an individual shepherd traditionally moves animals to mourn, many die here, and their deaths cannot be sorrowful to the animals since the dying soldiers are themselves the herd:

> What passing-bells for these who die as cattle?
>   —Only the monstrous anger of the guns.
>   Only the stuttering rifles' rapid rattle
> Can patter out their hasty orisons.
> No mockeries now for them; no prayers nor bells;
>   Nor any voice of mourning save the choirs,—
> The shrill, demented choirs of wailing shells;
>   And bugles calling for them from sad shires.

The dead strangely resemble not only the "unhonored dead" of Gray's collective elegy but also that poem's "lowing herd." Confounding the categories of pastoral elegy, the first line prepares for the bizarre metamorphosis of the genre's central trope—the pathetic fallacy. As part of the genre's compensatory economy, the pathetic fallacy traditionally functions as a point of exchange, converting human loss into nature's gain of humanity. Owen interrogates the trope in **"Anthem,"** **"Futility,"** and his other successful elegies, though he adopts it uncritically in a few poems, producing dismal failures like **"Elegy in April and September."** Earlier elegists had consoled in part by personifying a nature that sympathetically mourns; in **"Anthem"** Owen personifies machines instead, and these machines cannot assuage grief since they have helped to cause it. Although some consolation might seem to lie in his projecting "anger," "mourning," and "wailing" onto an external world, he checks this possible solace by suggesting the absurdity of this projection: the idea that the guns, rifles, and shells might be sympathetic is deliberately forced and artificial, since they are also slaughtering the soldiers like cattle. Whereas the pathetic fallacy had assuaged grief by converting, magnifying, and elevating it, the trope now short-circuits: the object-world onto which the elegist projects his feelings turns out to be the very engine of destruction rather than an alternative though mirroring reality.

Along with the pathetic fallacy, all other devices prove impotent to mourn death on such a scale: "prayers" and "bells" would be mere "mockeries," futile attempts to lend meaning and consolation to atrocities beyond meaning or consolation. While the poet suggests that neither he nor anyone can provide a soothing "voice of mourning," the weapons instead are vocal: the rifles are "stuttering" as they "patter out" prayers, and the "wailing" shells are "shrill, demented choirs"—tropes that Owen will stretch even further in **"The Last Laugh,"** where the armaments chirp, chuckle, guffaw, hoot, and groan. This chiastic reversal of poet and machine, voice and voicelessness, indicates the poet's resistance to the consolatory role he must partly assume. His own "voice" seems overwhelmed by the sounds of destruction, as represented by the alliterated *t*'s and *r*'s and by the dissonant echoes in phonemic sequences like "stuttering," "rattle," and "patter," or "shrill," "shells," and "shires." Letting these sounds jar against one another, Owen suggests his reluctance to adopt the more continuous and comforting voice of traditional elegy.

Although Owen subverts consolatory fictions in the octave, he attempts to reinstate them in the sestet, as Silkin and others have shown. In a consolatory chain of substitutions, he replaces candles with the inner light of sorrowful eyes, pall with the whiteness of grieving foreheads, flowers with the tender memories of mourners, whereas gun-rattle and shell-wail had earlier been the nonconsolatory replacements for prayers and choirs. Writing at a time when many mourners were turning away from traditional mortuary codes, the poet in the second stanza takes over the ritual role, offering in place of real "flowers" the memorial flowers of his verse, in place of social ceremonies the ceremonies of elegiac poetry. As Owen's harshest critics imply, his compensatory economy offers a poetic equivalent to religious and nationalist systems: the dead live on neither in heaven nor in the nation but in the imaginations of the bereaved. Having grimaced earlier at the fiction of a sympathetic nature, Owen obliquely revives the trope in the final line, "And each slow dusk a drawing-down of blinds": as the poem draws down its own blinds, it suggests the resemblance among the nightly descent of the sun, the nightly drawing down of blinds, and the closure of the poem itself with every reading. Nevertheless, the earlier stanza more strenuously disrupts elegiac norms than critics have recognized, making this stanza's recuperative effort fall short of consolatory closure. The poem cannot suppress its dissonances by ending on a major chord. The compensatory claims of the sestet seem so weak after the iconoclastic octave that the division between the parts of the poem betokens an unhealable grief. Though based on the elegy's usual split between initial despair and subsequent affirmation, the poem's structure is more radically discontinuous, replacing the traditional "turn" with a conspicuous tear in the fabric of elegy.

In the later sonnet **"Futility"** Owen resumes his revisionist approach to the pathetic fallacy and compensatory economics, but now he carves out of the inherited language of elegy a poem more persistently evocative of abject loss. The stock elegiac figure of the sun—alluded to at the end of **"Anthem for Doomed Youth"**—is the poem's dominant trope. Whereas **"Anthem"** begins with an overhaul of the pathetic fallacy and then softens the critique, **"Futility"** moves in the opposite figurative direction, first personifying the sun and then subverting this personification. **"Futility"** takes its title from the famous depiction of an indifferent nature in Tennyson's tetrameter elegy *In Memoriam,* but Tennyson, after responding "O life as futile, then, as frail!" retracts his "song of woe," while the woe of Owen's song only intensifies. Elegizing one soldier rather than the anonymous multitude of **"Anthem,"** Owen seems to restore

intimacy to the form of the sonnet, though it soon turns out that the poem's tender tone and tropes are irrelevant to the soldier's condition:

> Move him into the sun—
> Gently its touch awoke him once,
> At home, whispering of fields half-sown.
> Always it woke him, even in France,
> Until this morning and this snow.
> If anything might rouse him now
> The kind old sun will know.

The sun, a familiar image of desired renewal in elegies like "Lycidas" and *In Memoriam,* loses here its sympathetic responsiveness and its regenerative power. Although the poet personifies the sun as touching, whispering, waking, these pathetic fallacies become ever more overtly fallacious, until the gap between tenor and vehicle opens into the broad irony of the mock-assurance, "The kind old sun will know." Unlike Donne's playfully ironic apostrophe in "The Sun Rising," Owen's bitterly ironic line deflates the earlier projections of a tender power onto the sun. This sun can neither rouse the soldier nor know whether anything else might rouse him. The personifications are deliberate failures, triggering expectations of sympathy and renewal only to thwart such hopes. Other elegists writing during the same decade turn with similar harshness against the image of compensatory light, Hardy watching the "morning harden upon the wall" in "The Going," Stevens letting the indifferent "lamp affix its beam" in "The Emperor of Ice-Cream." For such poets, the elegiac image of a renewing light had come to seem a sentimental evasion of the reality principle.

In the three concluding questions of **"Futility,"** the anger at the impossibility of renewal mounts:

> Think how it wakes the seeds—
> Woke once the clays of a cold star.
> Are limbs, so dear achieved, are sides
> Full-nerved, still warm, too hard to stir?
> Was it for this the clay grew tall?
> —O what made fatuous sunbeams toil
> To break earth's sleep at all?

The three questions widen in scope, asking why the sun can't instill life in this dead body, why humans developed, and why life at all? The first question—are limbs and sides too hard to stir?—has embedded within it subsidiary questions that indicate the speaker's growing passion and bewilderment: are his limbs so dear achieved? are his sides full-nerved? are his full-nerved sides still warm? Elegiac questions, directed at nymphs and felon winds, had long been angry, but seldom had they been so chaotic and sweeping. Nor does Owen move from accusatory questions toward a comforting resolution, as had Milton. In its use of the figure of the sun, the poem summons the traditional compensatory hopes of elegy but turns against them, transforming the sun from a parent with a gentle touch into inane rays of light. In the phrase "fatuous sunbeams" Owen plays on *ignis fatuus* (will-o-the-wisp or jack-o'-lantern), suggesting that any elegiac hope we might project onto sunlight is self-deceptive and deluded. Intermingling the scientific story of evolution with the biblical story of Adam's genesis from clay, he turns to narratives of origination not, as earlier elegists had, to locate a primordial force that gave and thus can restore life, but to mock such fictions of rejuvenative return to a source. Life reverts neither to the mystic One of Shelley nor to the benevolent deity of Milton and Tennyson but to the inert earth.

It was partly in response to the First World War that Freud developed his controversial theory that "all instincts tend towards the restoration of an earlier state" and that *"the aim of all life is death."* Freud's theory and Owen's poetry engage in a parallel questioning of the pleasure principle as the sole law of psychological economics. Repudiating the compensatory tropes of elegy, Owen writes poems that, instead of exchanging new life for death, envision the irreversible dwindling of life into death. Among Owen's war elegies **"Futility"** is hardly alone in portraying life's cyclical reversion to matter. After another soldier's death in **"Asleep,"** the poet asks

> whether yet his thin and sodden head
> Confuses more and more with the low mould,
> His hair being one with the grey grass
> Of finished fields, and wire-scrags rusty-old. . . .

Owen echoes the "Whether . . . / Or whether" passage of "Lycidas," in which Milton reflects on the water-hurled body of the drowned man, and he alludes to the fate of Adonais, who "is made one with Nature." But Milton rescues Lycidas from the "watery floor" to raise him high, and Shelley makes Adonais a shaping "presence" in the natural world he joins, whereas Owen imagines the soldier's return to earth as a messy confusion without transcendence. Changing the traditional elegiac synecdoche of the immortal head into an emblem of mortality, Owen plays on the verb *confuses,* as if the mingling of brain with matter were also an intellectual muddle—a secondary meaning whose defeat wryly confirms the sheer physicality of this head. Milton's sun, like Lycidas, "repairs his drooping head, / And tricks his beams," but the head of Owen's soldier droops without repair, its hair not like sunbeams or nectar-soaked locks but like dead grass and rusting wire.

In his resistant adaptation of elegiac tropes and phrases, Owen takes from *Adonais* the title of a sonnet, **"The One Remains,"** and he again quotes Shelley's poem in **"A Terre,"** updating Shelley's representation of a paradoxically natural immortality. Owen repeatedly echoes the most melancholic elegy in the English canon, though he would outdo his predecessor with a still darker mood. The self-pitying speaker of **"A Terre"** muses that

> Dead men may envy living mites in cheese,
> Or good germs even. Microbes have their joys,
> And subdivide, and never come to death.
> Certainly flowers have the easiest time on earth.

> 'I shall be one with nature, herb, and stone,'
> Shelley would tell me. Shelley would be stunned:
> The dullest Tommy hugs that fancy now.
> 'Pushing up daisies' is their creed, you know.

The pun on stunned—slang for "shell-shocked"—further associates Shelley with the "dullest Tommy." Such soldiers long for the final release from pain—a return *à terre,* to the insensate state from which human clay emerged. Writing at about the same time, Freud also correlated shell shock with the drive of all life to restore a simpler, earlier state of being. He was puzzled that dreams occurring in such traumatic neuroses as shell shock "have the characteristic of repeatedly bringing the patient back into the situation of his accident," and so, recognizing the insufficiency of the pleasure principle to explain such dreams, Freud posited the repetition compulsion and the death drive. Owen's officer ironically quotes the soldiers' diminished "creed" of postmortem life, the daisy being a mundane version of elegy's more spiritualized flowers. He distinguishes the mortality of humans from the apparent immortality of simpler organisms like microbes. For Freud too, "higher organisms" like humans instinctually desire a return to oblivion, and "germ-cells, therefore, work against the death of the living substance and succeed in winning for it what we can only regard as potential immortality, though that may mean no more than a lengthening of the road to death." More than coincidental, the resemblance between Freud's and Owen's work is rooted in a common if divergent historical experience of war neuroses and a shared disbelief in spiritual immortality. From the wartime essays "Thoughts for the Times on War and Death" (1915), "Instincts and Their Vicissitudes" (1915), and "Mourning and Melancholia" (1917) to subsequent works like "A Child is Being Beaten" (1919), *Beyond the Pleasure Principle* (1919), and "The Economic Problem of Masochism" (1924), Freud's meditations on the death drive, melancholia, and masochism bear the imprint of the Great War.

Owen wrote most of his major poetry after his evacuation from the front with shell shock. **"Mental Cases"** is his most powerful elegy for the shell-shocked victims of the war—the living dead or "purgatorial shadows" that inhabit a "hell" in which the Dantean poet walks. With "jaws," "skulls' teeth," and "fretted sockets," they seem skeletons. The hell they live in is memory. "Stroke on stroke of pain," they compulsively review the events that destroyed them:

> —These are men whose minds the Dead have
>   ravished.
> Memory fingers in their hair of murders,
> Multitudinous murders they once witnessed.
> Wading sloughs of flesh these helpless wander,
> Treading blood from lungs that had loved
>   laughter.
> Always they must see these things and hear them,
> Batter of guns and shatter of flying muscles,
> Carnage incomparable, and human squander
> Rucked too thick for these men's extrication.

As Desmond Graham states in his excellent close reading of Owen's work, here "we are at the extremity of poetry's rhetoric." Owen is no "objective" reporter of war. What we call the "realism" of his war poetry is a rich intertextual effect; this stanza appropriates the topography and repetition of *Inferno,* the gore and guilt of *Macbeth.* The suffering victims become "real" precisely because of, not in spite of, the literary intertexts, for the poem's extremity and intertextuality self-consciously intimate a "real" horror in excess of the poem—in excess of its rhetorical excess. If the poem pretended to hold a mirror up to war alone, it might give the reader the pleasing illusion of having "understood" such suffering, but it also holds a mirror up to itself, echoing its own sounds and parading its allusions and figurations. Owen's intense engagement with literary tradition enables, not inhibits, his articulation of a new historical reality of untold psychic trauma. The soldiers habitually reenact painful scenes on the screen of memory, but instead of mastering by rehearsing them, the men sink ever deeper into their pain, much as the poem's language sinks ever more indulgently into its own excesses. Masochists, they reinflict the torments they endured earlier. Their world is flesh, blood, and muscle, a vast body turned inside out. Compulsively repeating its alliterations and biblical cadences, the poem's language also seems corpselike, an aural body of irrepressible materiality; turning and turning in its own resonances, it is a phonemic pattern rucked too thick with iteration, inversion, and allusion to be read transparently. Its language is an allegory of the war-inflicted pain it evokes by impeding realistic representation.

Owen is no "objective" reporter of war. What we call the "realism" of his war poetry is a rich intertextual effect. The suffering victims become "real" precisely because of, not in spite of, the literary intertexts.

—Jahan Ramazani

Hammering the reader with bilabial stops, the next stanza savagely parodies the elegiac apotheosis of the dead as the returning sun:

> Therefore still their eyeballs shrink tormented
> Back into their brains, because on their sense
> Sunlight seems a blood-smear; night comes blood-
>   black;
> Dawn breaks open like a wound that bleeds
>   afresh.

Its figures becoming ever more extravagant, the poem persists in blocking the pleasures of transparency. Once again Owen aggressively personifies the sun, but the sun's human properties do not prove the human power to transcend death and loss, to sink low but mount high.

The opposite of Milton's "opening eyelids of the morn," this dawn opens like an incurable wound. "The complex of melancholia," we remember from Freud, "behaves like an open wound." Owen turns an emblem of consolatory promise into an emblem of inconsolable grief. The melancholic psychology of the poem operates at more than one level: the men ironically labeled "mental cases" perpetually grieve over "the Dead," and the poet and reader in turn grieve over the soldiers' mental death. Mourners mourn mourners mourning the dead and themselves.

Lest we think the only masochists in this chain of mourning are the soldiers, the poet suggests that he torments himself with the "hellish" scene he relates, and this in turn implicates the reader in Owen's self-punishing fascination. At first the poet marks his distance from the damned, asking as Keats asks of the Grecian urn "Who are these?" But soon he confesses that to observe the damned "we" too must "have perished." At the end of the poem he clarifies this "we," accusing himself and the reader of being the tormentors of the living dead. The soldiers are

> Snatching after us who smote them, brother,
> Pawing us who dealt them war and madness.

In this elegy the poet is "purgatorial," halfway between the hell of the waking dead and the ignorant bliss of the civilians, identifying with the pitiable victims but also with their murderers. Though often represented as an unambiguous victim, Owen is poised in his poems between mourner and mourned, voyeur and victim. He and the reader have been more destructive than the former soldiers: we "smote them" (originally "*scourged* them"), but a panic "Gouged" the hollows of their eyes, and the recollected dead "have ravished" their minds. Like the slaughter in **"Anthem for Doomed Youth,"** the "murders" and "Carnage" have no human agents at first: the men recall not murders they committed but "murders they once witnessed." Despite the Dantean intertext, Owen attributes no guilt to the sufferers: they only look "like" the "wicked." Suddenly the last lines of the poem assign all guilt to poet and reader—a gesture that again disrupts the assumption that reading or writing the elegy is reducible to the psychic economy of pleasure.

This surprising ending should be understood in the larger context of the political vision of Owen's war elegies, particularly the elegies that map the complex relations among soldier, poet, and civilian reader. In **"Insensibility"** Owen similarly assigns blame to the civilians. Because "dullness" defends soldiers against the forced pain they must endure, they differ from civilian "dullards," whose insensibility was chosen: "By choice they made themselves immune / To pity." One critic faults Owen for side-stepping the fact "that he, and many of his fellow soldiers, volunteered"—a view that fails to appreciate not only Owen's self-accusations but also the question of relative "choice." Elsewhere, Owen reveals the ideological pressure that made the "choice" of combat less free than it may seem. In **"S.I.W."** a boy remains trapped by his father's dichotomous cant even after experience at the front might have nullified it. "Father would sooner him dead than in disgrace," and so the boy, still possessed by his father's words, still seeing soldiers who shirk combat as only "vile," yet tortured by shells and fire, shoots himself through the mouth. The boy's father is the ideological representative in the poem of "this world's Powers who'd run amok." He resembles the still more allegorical father of **"The Parable of the Old Man and the Young,"** a generation of Abrahams who sacrifice a generation of Isaacs: the old man "slew his son, / And half the seed of Europe, one by one." For Owen, the guilt of parent, patriarch, and state far outweighs the guilt of those whom they manipulate into combat.

Owen states only half of his paradoxical aesthetic when he writes: "My subject is War, and the pity of War. The Poetry is in the pity." "Pity" is Owen's term for emotional identification with the victims of war. But Owen's poetry suggests that "pity" cannot erase the boundary that separates victim from onlooker. Using an overwrought rhetoric in poems like **"Anthem for Doomed Youth"** and **"Mental Cases,"** Owen signals through verbal excess his inevitable failure to erase the boundary. His subject is also the incomprehensibility of war; the poetry is also in the alienation. Having roused pity, Owen often forces the reader back, warning that pity cannot bridge the chasm separating spectator and victim. At the end of **"Apologia Pro Poemate Meo,"** as at the end of **"Mental Cases"** and **"Insensibility,"** he points an accusing finger at the civilian reader: "These men are worth / Your tears. You are not worth their merriment." Similarly, at the end of **"Dulce et Decorum Est,"** he confronts civilians not only with their responsibility but also with their inability to "watch" or "hear" the physical details of inglorious death. If they could experience such death, they would not tell the old Horatian lie, and yet they would tell a different lie if they thought they could know suffering beyond the range of their experience. In these poems Owen recasts the elegy's typical configuration of mourning audience, mourned dead person, and mourning poet. For Owen, the audience is often guilty, the dead person innocent, and the poet split between the two poles. Elegists had usually attributed guilt to someone or something beyond the poetic triangle—a "fatal and perfidious bark" sinking Lycidas, a "nameless worm" killing Adonais. The primary target of Owen's anger is the civilian audience.

But, as has already been indicated, Owen also blames himself for the deaths he laments. Earlier elegists had punished themselves. Having called down the curse of Cain on the murderer of Adonais, Shelley reveals a brand on his brow that may also be Cain's (stanza 34). But Owen's blame-taking, even more than such self-accusations, is sometimes disarmingly direct. In **"Strange Meeting"** the poet accuses himself of murdering his double, who says, "I am the enemy you killed, my friend." This "conscientious objector with a very seared conscience" writes poems of melancholic or so-called "pathological" mourning, exemplifying what Freud calls the splitting of the ego, the narcissistic identification with a double, and "self-reproaches to the effect that the mourner him-

self is to blame for the loss of the loved object, i.e. that he has willed it." We have already seen that Owen tends to divide himself between the positions of guilty audience and innocent victim. Much as in **"Mental Cases"** the poet is halfway between deranged soldier and guilty onlooker, so too in **"Dulce et Decorum Est,"** he is one with both the victims and the voyeurs. Although he affirms at the end of the poem the authenticity of his inaccessible war experience, he earlier plays the role of the guilt-ridden, passive spectator. Helmeting himself at the cry of "Gas! Gas!" he watches as someone yells and flounders:

> Dim, through the misty panes and thick green light,
> As under a green sea, I saw him drowning.
>
> In all my dreams, before my helpless sight,
> He plunges at me, guttering, choking, drowning.

Owen uses the underwater imagery in part to emphasize the ontological divide that inevitably separates this observer, like any survivor, from the dying. Such a survivor may extend his pity across the spectatorial gap, but the pity would be a defensive reaction to the more fundamental guilt. "Pity," according to Freud, is really a *"reaction-formation"* against the sadistic drive. In his sole aggressive act, the dying victim figures the poet's self-accusation: he "plunges" at the poet in dreams, much as the insane were "Snatching after us" at the end of **"Mental Cases."** The speaker's latent thought seems to be, "I lived, he died; therefore I caused his death." But as Desmond Graham observes, Owen "makes from what is a poem of guilt, a poem of protest." He appropriates the anger initially directed against himself and turns it outward, transforming masochistic self-reproach into a sadistic attack on the civilian reader. The alienated reader, guiltily and helplessly looking on at incomprehensible suffering, mirrors the poet, voyeuristically peering through the gas at his convulsed double. As in **"Mental Cases,"** the poet inhabits a terrible no-man's-land between victim and reader.

More than any other of Owen's poems, the elegy **"Miners"** is wracked by the instability of this intermediary position, possibly because Owen attempts to write not about the war he knew at close range but about dead miners, making him all the more conscious of the inevitable gap between spectator and sufferer. In the course of the elegy, the poet modulates from an observer at his hearth to one of the dead men in the ground. As observer, he listens to the coals, first thinking they "recall" the vanished primeval world to which they once belonged. He projects his exercise of poetic memory onto the coals, as if they were the mourners of their pastoral origins. But he discovers he has misinterpreted their sounds: "the coals were murmuring" not of themselves but of the men and boys killed in the mine, "Writhing for air," like the gassed man's eyes that were "writhing" accusingly in **"Dulce et Decorum Est."** Seeing bones in his cinder-shard, the poet becomes a miner himself—he digs deep to uncover what "few remember"—just as the miners come to resemble "all that worked dark pits / Of war." As in other poems, Owen first depicts the plight of the victims and then attributes responsibility to the benighted civilians:

> Comforted years will sit soft-chaired,
>   In rooms of amber;
> The years will stretch their hands, well-cheered
>   By our life's ember. . . .

The sudden metamorphosis of the singular pronoun "I," representing a person sitting by the hearth, into the plural pronominal adjective "our," representing the many lost in the ground, suggests that the poet has changed positions through identification with the dead, moving to the other side of the hearth. But the darker reason for this shift becomes clear as the elegy comes to its close:

> The centuries will burn rich loads
>   With which we groaned,
> Whose warmth shall lull their dreaming lids,
>   While songs are crooned;
> But they will not dream of us poor lads,
>   Left in the ground.

Among the songs crooned beside the hearth is this very song about the miners. Owen glances nervously at his complicity in the exploitation of the miners by bourgeois consumers, though he also distinguishes his memorial act from their amnesia. His own song, like the other songs and like the comfortable civilian world, is born of death; its elegiac fuel is loss. To suppress this latent recognition, Owen crosses over to the position of the dead, leaving behind the cozy room in which he began the poem. As poet, Owen is implicated in the space of middle-class leisure, and he is at an inevitable remove from the deaths he mourns. As victim, he is one of the exploited and oppressed, but to maintain this stance, he must evade his own indirect confession that he uses the dead for poetic gain.

This ambiguity leads into difficult and insoluble questions about the psychology of Owen's war elegies, particularly about their sadomasochism. In "A Child is Being Beaten" (1919), one of several meditations on sadomasochism that Freud published soon after the war, he analyzes childhood fantasies in which either someone else is being beaten, leaving the child merely to look on, or the child himself is being beaten. That one form of the fantasy turns into the other suggests the indeterminate relation between sadism and masochism—an indeterminacy reflected in Owen's work. Freud interprets the being beaten in these fantasies as a distorted expression of being loved—being loved by the father in particular. We have already seen that Owen sometimes imagines himself the victim, sometimes the onlooker; we have also seen that he often represents the punishing sadist as the father. On Freud's view, some of these poems could be said to represent an incestuous, homosexual love for the father, but they represent it as the father's violence against his passive, "feminine" son. From this perspective, Owen's panoramas of death and ruin could be seen as in some sense homoerotic, the poet identi-

fying masochistically with the men who are passively victimized. In poems of "passive suffering" (Yeats's phrase), the poet looks on as others endure what Owen calls in **"S.I.W."** the "torture of lying machinally shelled." It is possible to read these poems as objectifying the kind of fantasy characteristic of Owen even before the war. Compare, for example, the soldier's *torture* in **"S.I.W."** with the poet's avowal in **"Lines Written on My Nineteenth Birthday"**:

>   For there have been revealed
> Heart-secrets since the coming of this day,
> Making me thankful for its thorn-paved way.
> Among them this: 'No joy is comparable
> Unto the *Melting*—soft and gradual—
> *Of Torture's needles in the flesh.*'

At once a Christ and a St. Sebastian (a saint often associated with homosexuality at the time), Owen displays what Freud paradoxically calls the "pleasure of unpleasure." Pain here is unmistakably sexualized. Some of the early poems take the "unpleasure" further, rehearsing in Keatsian fashion the poet's premature death. Bathetically, Owen even stages the final moment itself:

>   My heart stops—it is well . . .
> O Light, which art but darkness,
> O cruel world . . . O Men . . . O my own Self . . .
> Farewell!
>
>   (**"Science has looked . . ."**)

It may be unfair to Owen's mature aesthetic to discuss it in the context of such pieces, but this should not distract us from the brief career's psychological continuities. We have seen that Owen's mature work is melancholic in its refusal of traditional consolations, its identification with obsessional neurotics and the dead, and its division of the poet between two psychic positions; we have also seen that it is melancholic in its proclivity for self-punishment. Although we are accustomed to thinking of Owen as writing melancholic elegies entirely in response to the brute facts of war, we might also think of him as writing such elegies partly in response to his own masochism—a masochism in search of such painful facts as those provided by the war. Reviewing Owen's early letters, Adrian Caesar argues that Owen was drawn to the experience of warfare because he hoped it would make him a better poet. His first letter from France is full of "excitement" over the pleasure of unpleasure: "This morning I was hit! We were bombing and a fragment from somewhere hit my thumb knuckle. I coaxed out 1 drop of blood. Alas! no more!!" Poems of rhetorical excess, the war elegies indulge a similar excitement over the slaughter they evoke but occlude. In such self-berating poems as **"Mental Cases," "Dulce et Decorum Est,"** and **"Strange Meeting,"** Owen implicates himself in the murders he mourns. Perhaps we should take more seriously his suggestion that he "smote" and "killed" the soldiers whom he pities—smote and killed them, that is, in the symbolic act of writing their elegies, of reaping poetic gain from their loss. On this view, his war elegies are not merely occasional; rather, they are also metaleptic, partly creating the occasion that engenders them. And on this view, Owen's pity is no simple affect; rather it is also a reaction-formation, as Freud suggests, against the sadomasochistic drive.

Rereading English elegiac tradition in the light of Owen's elegies, . . . we become more aware of the masochistic trend embedded in the form throughout its development. This trend becomes especially salient toward the end of the nineteenth century, when Swinburne, for example, luxuriates in Baudelaire's flowers of sickness, sin, and poison. It is already apparent as far back as "Astrophel," where Spenser mirrors his own grief in Stella's self-destructive rage. . . .

Tearing her hair and breast, she wounds herself in imitation of him, a mimetic masochism that ultimately leads to her death. Yet, the poet checks his similarly self-destructive sympathy by imagining Astrophel and Stella reborn in a flower. By means of this consolatory substitution, he tries to override the pain with a yield of pleasure. Other examples abound in the history of the elegy. In "Lycidas" Milton figures self-contempt as a destructive assault on his own craft, from plucking berries and shattering leaves to subverting the false surmises of poetic tradition. But once again, these episodes of reality-testing serve to make credible the poem's final consolation. Accusing himself of being "drunk with loss," Tennyson occasionally glimpses an extreme solution to his pain, but he fends off the temptation of "vacant darkness" with religious reasonings. Even Shelley, whose *Adonais* is melancholic in its ending, beckons death not as a final cessation of vitality but as a rejoining of the radiant One. The more fully articulated masochism of Owen's poetry throws into relief these episodes of self-punishment, though Owen transforms what had been episodes into a major impulse of his elegies.

Freud developed his theory of the death drive partly to explain the behavior of recalcitrant patients. The guilt of such patients demanded satisfaction, thus holding them back from cure: "the suffering entailed by neuroses is precisely the factor that makes them valuable to the masochistic trend." Freud goes on to note that such patients have what he calls a "need for punishment." What matters to them, he says, is that they maintain "a certain amount of suffering." Critics often treat the elegy as a therapeutic device: working through grief, creating an aesthetic substitute for loss, the elegist masters or at least manages pain. Many of Owen's elegies do not fit this therapeutic model. Their task is to maintain a certain amount of suffering, not to effect a cure; they produce not a yield of pleasure but an aggravation of pain. The guilty self-divisions in many of the poems suggest a delight in self-torment, the poet occupying a dual position as both victimized soldier and performer of the victimization. The reader's position in the elegies is similarly dual. As object of the poet's accusations, the civilian reader is pawed and plunged at, the target of the poetry's aggression; further, as pitying subject, the reader identifies with the victimized soldier, the target of war's aggression. But as performer of the act of reading,

the reader is also complicit in producing the pain and death that she or he laments. "I am the enemy you killed, my friend"—addressed to the poet-speaker, this apostrophe extends beyond him to the reader, who symbolically kills the soldier in reading the poem, and who is therefore not only his pitying friend but also his destructive enemy.

FURTHER READING

Bibliography

White, William. *Wilfred Owen (1893-1918): A Bibliography.* Kent, Ohio: Kent State University Press, 1967, 41 p.
 Bibliography of and about Owen and his work.

Biography

Hibberd, Dominic. *Owen the Poet.* Athens: The University of Georgia Press, 1986, 244 p.
 Critical biography of Owen with bibliography.

Owen, Harold. *Journey from Obscurity: Wilfred Owen 1893-1918. Memoirs of the Owen Family.* 3 Vols. London: Oxford University Press, 1963-95.
 Complete biography of Wilfred Owen and his siblings by his brother.

Stallworthy, Jon. *Wilfred Owen: A Biography.* London: Oxford University Press, 1974, 333 p.
 An appreciative biography intended as a complementary volume to existing biographical sources, including Harold Owen's *Journey from Obscurity* and *The Collected Letters.*

Criticism

Bäckman, Sven. *Tradition Transformed: Studies in the Poetry of Wilfred Owen.* Lund, Sweden: C. W. K. Gleerup, 1979, 204 p.
 Examines Owen's relationship to poetic tradition and assesses his technical innovations.

Blunden, Edmund. "The Real War." *Athenaeum,* No. 4728 (December 10, 1920): 807.
 Appreciative review of *Poems.* Blunden maintains that "in Owen we lost a poet of rare force."

Caesar, Adrian. "The 'Human Problem' in Wilfred Owen's Poetry." *Critical Quarterly* 29, No. 2 (Summer 1987): 67-84.
 Offers a modern assessment of Owen's response to war.

Cohen, Joseph. "Wilfred Owen in America." *Prairie Schooner* XXXI, No. 4 (Winter 1957): 339-55.

Discusses Owen's critical reputation in America.

———. "Wilfred Owen: Fresher Fields than Flanders."
English Literature in Transition VII, No. 1 (1964): 1-7.
    Examines the various editorial approaches to Owen's
poetry, including those of Siegfried Sassoon, Edith
Sitwell, Edmund Blunden, and C. Day Lewis.

———. "Owen Agonistes." *English Literature in Transition*
VIII (1965): 256-57.
    Argues that a form of homosexuality dominated Owen's
sexual nature and that it provides the key to
understanding his poetry.

Daiches, David. "The Poetry of Wilfred Owen." In *New
Literary Values: Studies in Modern Literature*, pp. 52-68.
Edinburgh: Oliver and Boyd, 1936.
    Calls Owen's greatest achievement his ability to bring
"suffering into his poetry sufficiently to make it genuine
but not so that it warped his sense of truth."

Deutsch, Babette. "Wars and Rumors of Wars." In *Poetry
in Our Time*, pp. 348-77. New York: Henry Holt and
Company, 1952.
    Finds Owen's poems technically flawed. According to
Deutsch, Owen was "a very conscious craftsman . . .
[who] spent pains on form in a manner that was apt to
draw attention away from the poem to its technical
details."

Draper, R. P. "Wilfred Owen: Distance and Immediacy." In
Lyric Tragedy, pp. 162-77. London: The Macmillan Press,
1985.
    Discusses the reconciliation of objectivity and
subjectivity in Owen's verses.

Enright, D. J. "The Literature of the First World War." In
*The Pelican Guide to English Literature, Volume 7: The
Modern Age*, ed. Boris Ford, pp. 154-69. Harmondsworth,
Middlesex: Penguin Books, 1961.
    General discussion of the work of Owen and his
contemporaries.

———. "The Truth Told." *New Statesman* LXVI, No. 1698
(September 27, 1963): 408, 410.
    Discusses textual revisions in *The Collected Poems of
Wilfred Owen*, edited by C. Day Lewis, and favorably
assesses *Journey from Obscurity*, the first volume of
Harold Owen's biography of his brother.

Fairchild, Hoxie Neale. "Toward Hysteria." In *Religious
Trends in English Poetry, Volume 5: 1880-1920—Gods of
a Changing Poetry*, pp. 578-627. New York: Columbia
University Press, 1962.
    Compares the war poetry of Siegfried Sassoon, Osbert
Sitwell, Herbert Read, Isaac Rosenberg, and Owen.

Freeman, Rosemary. "Parody as a Literary Form: George
Herbert and Wilfred Owen." *Essays in Criticism* XIII, No.
4 (October 1963): 307-22.
    Discusses Owen's parodic use of love imagery in
describing war scenes.

Fussell, Paul. "Soldier Boys." In *The Great War and Modern
Memory*, pp. 270-309. London: Oxford University Press,
1975.
    Considers the "homoerotic sensuousness" of Owen's
poetry, comparing his works to those of Gerard Manley
Hopkins and A. E. Housman.

Graham, Desmond. *The Truth of War: Owen, Blunden and
Rosenberg*. Manchester: Carcanet Press, 1984, 168 p.
    Discusses the experiential nature of Owen's poetry.

Hibberd, Dominic, ed. *Wilfred Owen: War Poems and
Others*. London: Chatto and Windus, 1973, 158 p.
    Includes a biographical and critical sketch, notes on
Owen's poems, Owen's own Preface to his poetry, a
bibliography, and an index of first lines and titles.

———. "Wilfred Owen and the Georgians." *Review of
English Studies* XXX, No. 17 (February 1979): 28-40.
    Emphasizes the influence of Georgian poets Harold
Monroe, Siegfried Sassoon, and Robert Graves on the
development of Owen's poetic style.

Hoffpauir, Richard. "An Assessment of Wilfred Owen."
English Literature in Transition: 1880-1920 28, No. 1
(1985): 41-55.
    Offers a negative assessment of Owen's poetry, finding
"the didactic demands of his poetic situations are rarely
met by his poems."

Johnston, John H. "Poetry and Pity: Wilfred Owen." In
*English Poetry of the First World War: A Study in the
Evolution of Lyric and Narrative Form*, pp. 155-209.
Princeton, N. J.: Princeton University Press, 1964.
    A survey of Owen's later war poetry and discussion of
Owen's concept of "greater love."

Kerr, Douglas. "Wilfred Owen and the Social Question."
English Literature in Transition XXXIV, No. 2 (1991):
183-95.
    Discusses the debate in Owen's poetry about the proper
attitude of Christians, and especially of the clergy, to
social misery and injustice.

———. "Brother in Arms: Family Language in Wilfred
Owen." *Review of English Studies* XLIII, No. 172 (November
1992): 518-34.
    Discusses the language of family in Owen's poetry.

Lane, Arthur E. *An Adequate Response*. Detroit: Wayne State
University Press, 1972, 190 p.
    Examines the artistic milieu in which Owen and
Siegfried Sassoon worked, their poetic responses to
war, and their relationship to Rupert Brooke, Charles
Hamilton Sorley, and others who produced more
traditionally patriotic verse.

Norgate, Paul. "Soldiers' Dreams: Popular Rhetoric and the
War Poetry of Wilfred Owen." *Critical Survey* II, No. 2
(1990): 208-15.
    Notes that "Owen's writing, rather than being the voice
of some universal moral absolute, or 'truth' . . . is in

fact deeply rooted in a struggle against the popular rhetoric of war."

Sergeant, Howard. "The Importance of Wilfred Owen." *English* X, No. 55 (Spring 1954): 9-12.

Finds Owen superior to Siegfried Sassoon and maintains that "of all the poets who wrote of the First World War, Owen constitutes the strongest link between the poetry of the nineteenth century and that of today."

Silkin, Jon. "Wilfred Owen." In *Out of Battle: The Poetry of the Great War,* pp. 197-248. London: Routledge & Kegan Paul, 1972.

Discusses Owen's poetic responses to nature and examines his treatment of warfare using anger and satire.

Spear, Hilda D. "'I Too Saw God': The Religious Allusions in Wilfred Owen's Poetry." *English* XXIV, No. 119 (Summer 1975): 35-40.

Detailed examination of the religious references in Owen's poems showing how Owen "adapted the Christian myth to the circumstances of twentieth-century warfare."

Tomlinson, Alan. "Strange Meeting in Strange Land: Wilfred Owen and Shelley." *Studies in Romanticism* XXXII, No. 1 (Spring 1993): 75-95.

Discusses the romantic mannerisms of Owen's style and the influence of Percy Bysshe Shelley on his poetry.

Walsh, T. J., ed. *A Tribute to Wilfred Owen.* Liverpool: Birkenhead Institute, 1964, 62 p.

Includes biographical sketches and critical essays, as well as tributes by Siegfried Sassoon, Benjamin Britten, Edmund Blunden, Herbert Read, Stephen Spender, C. Day Lewis, and T. S. Eliot.

Welland, Dennis S. R. "Half-Rhyme in Wilfred Owen: Its Derivation and Use," *Review of English Studies* n.s. I, No. 3 (July 1950): 226-41.

Suggests literary and folk poets who may have inspired the use of half-rhyme by Owen and comments on the use of the device by poets who succeeded Owen, including C. Day Lewis and Louis MacNeice.

White, Gertrude M. *Wilfred Owen.* New York: Twayne Publishers. 1969, 156 p.

Studies Owen and his poetry, discussing his poetic craftsmanship and the posthumous growth of his critical reputation.

Yeats, W. B. *Letters on Poetry from W. B. Yeats to Dorothy Wellesley.* London: Oxford University Press, 1964, 202 p.

Contains two letters in which Yeats disparages Owen's abilities as a poet. Of one poem, Yeats declares, "I cannot imagine anything more clumsy, more discordant."

Additional coverage of Owen's life and career is contained in the following sources published by Gale Research: *Concise Dictionary of British Literary Biography, 1914-1945; Contemporary Authors,* Vols. 104, 141; *Dictionary of Literary Biography,* Vol. 20; *DISCovering Authors; DISCovering Authors: British; DISCovering Authors: Canadian; DISCovering Authors—Modules: Most-Studied Authors Module; DISCovering Authors—Modules: Poets Module; Twentieth-Century Literary Criticism,* Vols. 5, 27; **and** *World Literature Criticism, 1500 to the Present.*

Pindar

518 B.C.-c. 438 B.C.

Greek poet

INTRODUCTION

Pindar has been admired as the supreme lyric poet of Greece since ancient times. His surviving works consist primarily of choral odes celebrating the athletic prowess of victors at the four great Panhellenic games; each displays bold imagery coupled with dazzling verbal virtuosity. Scholars imperfectly understood the epinicion genre, or victory ode, until the 1960s, when they recognized that the treatment of mythological and ethical themes in Pindar's odes derives from an established tradition which reflected the culture and religion of his times. As the most eloquent and original representative of the Greek archaic age, Pindar has been a wellspring of poetic inspiration for centuries.

Biographical Information

Little is certain about Pindar's life. He was born in the city of Thebes in the province of Boeotia, where his family belonged to the aristocracy. As a young man, Pindar received training in music and song at Athens, and he wrote his first poem, "Pythian 10," in 498 B.C. for a powerful Thessalian family. During his fifty-year career as a professional poet, Pindar traveled throughout the Greek world and developed a Panhellenic attitude, witnessing the Persian threats to Greek independence in the early fifth century B.C. and the subsequent rise of Athenian democracy and power. Consequently, Pindar achieved renown for his verse; numerous aristocratic patrons regularly commissioned his poetry, most notably Hieron I of Syracuse, members of Sicily's ruling family, and the nobility of the island of Aegina, for which he seemed to have a particular affection. Pindar also immortalized in verse the victors of the Olympic, Nemean, Pythian, and Isthmian games. These events featured athletic competitions and religious festivals, during which a sacred truce was observed throughout the Greek world. Pindar's last surviving work "Pythian 8," which honors the victory of a wrestler from Aegina, was written in 446 B.C. Pindar is said to have died in Argos about 438 B.C. at the age of 80.

Major Works

Pindar's body of lyric poetry is among the best-preserved of ancient Greece. Although the great library at Alexandria had poems by Pindar of many types, including encomia, hymns, dirges, and paens, only his epinician odes survive intact. These are grouped as Olympian, Nemean, Pythian,

and Isthmian, according to which games the various odes relate. Epinician odes were originally performed to musical accompaniment by a trained chorus who sang and danced, although some recent critics claim that the odes were intended for a soloist. These choral odes feature an intricate metrical and syntactical structure, based on aeolic and dactylo-epitritic rhythms, and follow a conventional pattern of praise (although Pindar so mastered the form their variety is remarkable). Pindar's epinician odes espouse an essentially religious viewpoint, underscoring the poet's belief that talent and success are god-given. Notable among Pindar's forty-four extant odes are the "Olympian 1," which celebrates the victory of Hieron's horse Pherenikos in 476 B.C.; "Olympian 2," which is unique among epinician odes for its theme of reincarnation and judgment after death; and "Olympian 7," which honors Diagoras of Rhodes, an athlete who claimed victory at all four games. "Olympian 8," "Pythian 8," "Nemean 3-8," and "Isthmian 5, 6, 8" relate the heroic stories of Aeacus and his descendants, the mythological forebears of Aegina, while "Isthmian 7" describes the mythical grandeur of Pindar's native Thebes. In addition, a number of fragments of poems survive, including parts of a hymn to Zeus and a paean for Thebes to Apollo.

Critical Reception

Highly regarded during his lifetime, after his death Pindar was referred to as an authority by the classical authors Herodotus and Plato. Perhaps a more remarkable indication of Pindar's fame in the ancient world occurred when Alexander the Great ordered his troops to spare Pindar's house during the destruction of Thebes in 335 B.C. His status as the preeminent lyric poet of Greece persisted during the days of the Roman empire, when the poet Horace attempted to imitate Pindar's "Olympian 2" in his *Odes,* and Vergil imitated "Pythian 1" in his *Aeneid.* During the Middle Ages Pindar's poems were unknown except in Byzantium. After Aldus Manutius published the first modern edition of the poet's works in Venice in 1513, Italian imitations appeared later that century. Pindar's most eminent Renaissance imitator was the French poet Pierre de Ronsard, whose synthesis of French and Greco-Roman poetry inaugurated a school of elevated lyric verse on the Continent similar to the development of the Pindaric ode in English poetry by such seventeenth-century poets as Abraham Cowley and John Dryden. By the eighteenth and nineteenth centuries Pindar's odes influenced many European poets, notably Thomas Gray, Percy Bysshe Shelley, Friedrich Holderin, and Victor Hugo. Nineteenth-century German scholars elucidated many historical and philological complexities of Pindar's works in an attempt to discover thematic unity in individual odes. By the 1960s the conventions of choral poetry were better understood, and American and English scholars have demonstrated the nature of Pindar's religious outlook, his handling of myth, and the social context of the athletic victors for whom his odes were written. By analyzing individual odes with reference to their social and religious underpinning, late twentieth-century scholars have fostered a new appreciation of Pindar's worldview and imaginative power.

PRINCIPAL ENGLISH TRANSLATIONS

Poetry

Pindaric Odes (translated by Abraham Cowley) 1656
Pindar in English Verse (translated by Henry Francis Cary) 1823
The Extant Odes of Pindar Translated into English, with an Introduction and Short Notes (translated by Ernest Myers) 1874
The Odes of Pindar (translated by John Sandys) 1915
The Odes of Pindar (translated by Richmond Lattimore) 1947
The Odes of Pindar (translated by C. M. Bowra) 1969
Pindar's Victory Songs (translated by Frank J. Nisetich) 1980

R. W. Livingstone (essay date 1912)

SOURCE: Two Types of Humanism: Pindar and Herodotus." In *The Greek Genius and Its Meaning to Us,* pp. 139-159. Oxford: Oxford University Press, 1912, pp. 139-59.

[In the following excerpt, Livingstone comments on Pindar's thought as representative of Hellenism.]

Pindar is writing for the society that existed in the early part of the fifth century; for the society that fought and beat the Persians, conceived the ideal of a united Greek nation, made a few generous, unpractical efforts to achieve it, failed and resigned the attempt. It was a society in which aristocracies were supreme; but Pindar saw democracy arise in one state after another, in some dispossess its hereditary lords, in almost all wage against them internecine war. Of these two great movements, the national and the democratic, there is hardly a trace in him. He has no interest in politics, either at home or abroad; he has no interest in the masses; if anything, a dislike for them. He writes for the rich, the noble, the 'upper classes'; and even here he is limited; his masterpieces were written for those who won athletic victories. It is as if a modern poet should confine himself to Oxford and Cambridge—indifferent to newer universities, indifferent to socialism and the working classes, indifferent to imperialism, to India, Egypt, or the Colonies; and in Oxford should celebrate mainly the exploits of 'blues'. It may seem a narrow field and typical of a narrow mind, and Pindar may appear a bad example of the Greek manysidedness. Yet on the other hand, just because he is not a very profound thinker, he probably represents the way in which an ordinary Greek looked at life, better than any of the great writers except perhaps Herodotus; and the peculiar Hellenic virtues stand out the more vividly against a background of convention.

He leaves us in no doubt as to what he thinks to be the highest happiness, and the enthusiastic Hellenist is apt to be shocked when he comes to Pindar's view of the ideal life. What Pindar covets and admires is no mystic vision of supersensual beauty, no intellectual grasp of abstract truth, but an earthly, tangible, profitable good. To start with, a man should be young and tall and handsome, and have those natural gifts which attract friends, help him to win races at Olympia, put him in a position to enjoy the good things of life, and make him, in a word, a success. He must have ἀγλαόγυιος ἥβη—'glorious-limbed youth'—you could not parallel the phrase outside Greek. The picture of Jason, as he comes down from the Centaur's cave among the forests of Pelion to claim the kingship which was his due, gives a clear notion of Pindar's, and indeed of the Greek, ideal of man. 'So in the fullness of time he came, wielding two spears, a wondrous man; and the vesture that was on him was twofold, the garb of the Magnetes country close fitting to his splendid limbs; but above he wore a leopard's skin to turn the hissing showers; nor were the bright locks of his hair shorn from him, but over all his back ran rippling down. Swiftly he went straight on, and took his stand, making trial of his dauntless soul, in the market-place when the multitude was full.' This is the sort of man Pindar would like you to be.

Then, if you can choose your station in life, be a king—that is the crown and summit of human good. But in any case be rich, and wealth joined to—or in Pindar's expressive phrase, 'enamelled with'—the gifts of nature will make you as secure as a man can be. It will give you chances which the ordinary man has not, it will suppress the deeper cares, and in the end it will bring you to the Paradise of the Just. So at least Pindar implies. A strange key it seems with which to open heaven. And yet there is some sense in Pindar's view; for the possession of wealth puts a man beyond the vulgar temptations of poverty, and it is a law of life that to him that hath more is given. Be rich, be strong, be handsome. This is the Greek grasping after facts, after hard, concrete, physical facts.

But supposing Nature has done her duty, and made you an athlete and a rich man, what of the world into which you are born? It seems a bad world on the whole. Any one glancing through a collection of Pindar's sayings might think them predominantly gloomy. Everywhere death is seen closing up the avenues of prosperity and success which these athletic triumphs open, and Pindar will not let the victor forget that he is putting his festal robes on a body which is mortal, and that at the last he will clothe himself in earth. Even life itself is a dark thing. The poet is oppressed by thoughts of πόυς and λήθη, the hard work which is necessary to success, the oblivion which so soon and so remorselessly devours it. For man is 'a creature of a day, the dream of a shadow. Then, too, there are the ordinary misfortunes of human life, which Pindar thinks so many that 'heaven allots two sorrows to man for every good thing. Even his heroes are not exempt. Some one of these brilliant victors is in disfavour, or in exile, or has been disappointed of some hope. Perhaps there has been death in his house, or illness is sapping his strength, or old age has ended his triumphs and warns him of the approach of death; and 'there is no work, nor device, nor knowledge, nor wisdom in the grave whither he goes.' Then, too, there are all those unnumbered hindrances, accidents, and checks to ambition, summed up in the bitter words of the fourth Pythian: 'now this they say is of all griefs the sorest, that one knowing good should of necessity abide without lot therein.' Pindar never holds his tongue about these things, and, if he were a modern, we should call him a pessimist. But he is Greek, and so a page or a line further on, and we are deep in one of those brilliantly coloured, 'purple' descriptions of joy or feasting or adventure of which he is a master, 'moving among feasting and giving up the soul to be young, carrying a bright harp and touching it in peace among the wise of the citizens.

Here is the Greek, determined, as far as he can see it, to tell himself the truth. There is no shirking facts, no pretending that evil is good and death pleasant; there is no attempt even to conceal the fact that such things exist. Yet the existence of evil is no argument for pessimism in Pindar's eyes. The skeleton is indeed brought out to fill his place; but he is only one among the guests at the banquet of life. If the dark days are many, so are the bright, and the wise man enjoys or endures each as it comes.

Many people would criticize Pindar's view of life as earthy, and find fault with a poet who seems to place man, not a little lower than the angels, but rather a little higher than the brutes. Yet no one could call Pindar sordid,

for he has the Greek gift, to repeat a phrase, of spiritualizing material things. The joys of feasting, for instance, play some considerable part in him (they were, then as now, the sequel to athletic contests). But they are viewed in a glory of ideal light, not as the mere filling of the belly, but as εὐφροσύνη, 'cheerfulness,' as ἱερὸυ εὐξῴας ἄωτον, 'the sacred blossom of joyous living.' English keeps traces of the same thought in phrases like 'good cheer' and 'good living,' but they have long since sunk into synonyms for gluttony; in Pindar the good fellowship remains more than the good food, as we see in the description of the brilliant company of poets and statesmen at the table of Hiero. 'They celebrate the son of Kronos, when to the rich and happy hearth of Hiero they are come; for he wieldeth the sceptre of justice in Sicily of many flocks, culling the choice fruits of all kinds of excellence; and with the flower of music is he made splendid, even such strains as we sing blithely at the table of a friend.

No, it is not sordid, nor, if life is to be regarded from a purely human point of view, is it wrong. At any rate even the most aspiring idealists have at times their human moments, and there are few who will not find it refreshing after reading Carlyle or some other mystic prophet, till the head grows dizzy and numb with the thought of the mystery of life and of man wandering between two eternities, to take up Pindar and read, set out in a flaming glory of language, this sober, commonplace philosophy of the earth on which we live.

Probably the more we have said about Pindar, the more unfitted he has seemed to illustrate the view of Hellenism. . . . [:] the Greek united to his love of physical excellence a love of, and respect for, the things of the mind. And now, to illustrate this theory, we have hit upon a poet, who has the Greek truthfulness and the Greek love of personal beauty and of concrete things, but who has so far shown no sign of the Greek love of reason. Pindar, to judge from what we have seen of him, appears to have had a very commonplace intellect, and to have compensated for intellectual commonplaceness, as a man by a passion for athleticism, as a poet by a rich sense of beauty.

True Pindar has not a first-class intellect; he has no speculative power at all; and though much of his poetry is sudden and dazzling like lightning, its flashes do not illuminate the depths of human nature. Yet Pindar is more philosophical than at first appears. He has an elaborate intellectual theory of life, is clearly very pleased with it, and loses no opportunity of preaching it. He may not be speculative in the sense in which Plato and the dramatists are speculative, but like all his race he felt the need for some rational account of things. Hence a philosophy. Its catchwords sound meaningless (so do Election, Reprobation. Justification by Works or by Grace); but that is only because we have outgrown the phraseology, and use clearer or ampler language to express our meaning. The meaning is modern, if not the words.

Let us take a fragment of this philosophy—Pindar's account of evil. Our misfortunes, he thinks, are due to three causes. First comes the nature of the universe, in which death and old age are inevitable, and some people are born weak or sickly; in which accidents happen that no one can foresee or avert. That is Μοῖρᾳ, Fate, which sends evil not of our seeking and beyond our control. It is no use our complaining or rebelling against it. Death and old age have to be frankly accepted—as the tyrant of Syracuse had to accept them; ἀσθενεῖ μὲν Χρωτὶ βᾳίνωνε ἀλλὰ μοιρίδιον νῇ, 'walking with sick body, yet so it was fated to be. Then there are the evils which we bring on ourselves, by arrogance or vice or some other sin; and these are due to Ὕβρις, the Insolence of man. Finally there are the evils which cannot be put down to either of these causes, which are not of God, yet for which we can hardly blame ourselves. An upright, patriotic citizen is banished; his very virtue makes it impossible for him to live peaceably with his neighbours, and keeps him out of office and power. What is the malign influence which works against him but Φθόνος, Envy; Μοῖρᾳ, Ὕβρις, Φθόνος, the three sources of our misfortunes; how could we improve on the definition, except by a change of words? What is the remedy for these evils? For illness? doctors, medicine: but there are many evils which they never cure. For Ὕβρις? repentance and amendment: but the evil done may be irreparable. For Φθόνος? it is difficult to find any remedy for that, except Pindar's general remedy for them all, Χρανος, Time. A slow remedy and one sometimes overtaken by death; but is there any other which is effective? S. Paul, perhaps, might have said ὑπομονή, 'patient endurance'; but that is only putting the same idea in a profounder and more personal way.

So, after all, Pindar serves to illustrate our point; a commonplace intellect; interests which might well have crowded out intellectual things, and certainly do not encourage them; yet a complete philosophy; not profound, in some ways crude, but carefully thought out, elaborately rounded off, and perhaps not so very inadequate or contemptible.

Lawrence Henry Baker (essay date 1923)

SOURCE: "Some Aspects of Pindar's Style." *The Sewanee Review,* Vol. 31, No. 1, January-March, 1923, pp. 100-110.

[*In the essay below, Baker discusses the figurative language, meters, rhetoric, and myths that comprise the style of Pindar's odes.*]

There was once a time when Pindar was regarded by moderns as a queer jumble of contests, of gnomic sayings, of myths, and of almost arrogant self-esteem. The blending of all these elements—if not the very reason for presenting them in poetry at all—was not easily to be explained; and men long held, therefore, that Pindar was not only difficult but also of questionable value. The discovery of the works of Bacchylides, in 1896, however, helped greatly to change this feeling. Bacchylides is far easier to follow than is Pindar, and very much more translucent; therefore he furnished a simpler model whereby to study Pindar's department, namely that of Choral-Lyric— the lyric written for the song and the dance. A comparison of the two poets has thrown much light on what was not so clear before, and has proved what was previously suspected—that many of the striking peculiarities of Pindar are manifestations of the tradition and precedent of his department.

But the removal of the departmental difficulties could not sufficiently lighten the task of reading Pindar to make him more generally studied. The individualistic and personal difficulties remained behind; so that we may call Pindar one of the infrequently read classical authors, and one who beyond a limited circle of Greek students is to-day practically unknown.

Pindar's fame in Greece was unquestionably greater, and his circle of readers larger than it is in the modern world, although we can hardly ascribe to him all the popularity which Plutarch, whose frequent quotation from Pindar, a fellow-citizen of Bœotia, would lead us to think he had. The very nature of his choicest compositions, the *Epinicia*, or *Songs of Victory*, which were written to celebrate the rewards of success in contests at the great national festivals at Olympia, Delphi, Corinth, and Nemea, was such as to preclude the possibility of very wide circulation. Admirable works of art though they are, the epinicia were not entirely floods of poetic inspiration which burst the gates of the poet's restraint and demanded expression merely for expression's sake. Inspired they were; but unfortunately the inspiration was often the yellow light of gleaming gold, or the exultant hope of favor and patronage. Each epinicion was written to celebrate a given man's success. It was of particular interest, therefore, to him and his immediate circle alone; and if we add to this fact that in each instance the man celebrated was a member of the Greek aristocracy, we can see an even greater limitation placed upon the number of Pindar's hearers or readers. Much has been written about the poet's art of making a national event out of a given patron's victory; but the personal theme of his poetry certainly made for narrowness of appeal, even though we must admit that Pindar's treatment of a specific victory proceeds on broad and general lines calculated not to end in the immediate family of the victor.

The ancients have agreed with the moderns as to the problem which Pindar presented to the reader. To the writers on Greek rhetoric who flourished in the post-classical period, when men were too busy learning the intricacies of classical Attic to write anything original, he stood largely as a representative of the rugged style of composition— merely a specimen to be collected and put into the same preserving-jar with Thucydides, his counterpart in prose. Some modern critic dubbed Pindar "the scholar's poet"; and the evil effects of this name he has never been able to live down. Few people now read him, and fewer still are intimately familiar with him, largely, perhaps, because of the fact that he has come to be surrounded in the minds of most modern students with an aura of exoticism which they fancy requires for its penetration too much of the primitive element that Hesiod prescribed for the ascent to Arete—namely, hard work.

That Pindar is difficult to read is not to be denied; for the student who has been reading the carefully constructed, smooth, easily-flowing sentences of Lysias, for example, would find a decidedly painful contrast in Pindar. These two are—in addition to the fact that one is a prose writer, the other a poet—quite widely removed in their positions in Greek style. Lysias is perhaps the world's finest master of the art that conceals art; and in his works will be found passages that read along as smoothly and easily as the imperceptible current of a mighty river—passages that for all their apparent guilelessness are the despair of imitators. Lysias is a strikingly excellent illustration of clear, transparent writing; whereas Pindar typifies the style which the ancients themselves regarded as harsh—the ἀὐστηρὸς ἁρμονίᾳ, or the severe style.

The troublesome characteristics of Pindar could perhaps be best described by giving an account of the ἀὐστηρὸς ἁρμονίᾳ. This is a style in which the virile, concept-bearing noun predominates at the expense of the lighter, more unifying verb. Juxtaposition of ideas is far more frequent than a predication facilitated by means of the copula; and a rugged massing of substantives almost beats into our minds the thought that seems to lie under, through, and over them all, yet not in any single one of these substantives.

Dionysius of Halicarnassus, a writer of the time of Augustus, and perhaps the greatest student of literary style in all ages, has made an unsurpassable analysis of this severe manner of composition. In elucidation I quote him as follows:—

> It [the austere style] requires that the words should be like columns firmly planted and placed in strong positions, so that each word should be seen on every side, and that the parts should be at appreciable distances from one another, being separated by perceptible intervals. It does not in the least shrink from using frequently harsh sound-clashings which jar on the ear; like blocks of building-stone that are laid together unworked, blocks that are not square and smooth, but preserve their natural roughness and irregularity. It is prone for the most part to expansion by means of great spacious words. It objects to being confined to short syllables, except under occasional stress of necessity.

> In respect of the words, then, these are the aims which it strives to attain, and to these it adheres. In its clauses it pursues not only these objects, but also impressive and stately rhythms, and tries to make its clauses not parallel in structure or sound, nor slaves to a rigid sequence, but noble, brilliant, free. It wishes them to suggest nature rather than art, and to stir emotion rather than to reflect character. And as to periods, it does not, as a rule, even attempt to compose them in such a way that the sense of each is complete in itself: if it ever drifts into this accidentally, it secks to emphasize its own unstudied and simple character, neither using any supplementary words which in no way aid the sense, merely in order that the period may be fully rounded off, nor being anxious that the period should move smoothly or showily, nor nicely calculating them so as to be just sufficient (if you please) for the

speaker's breath, nor taking pains about any other such trifles. Further, the arrangement in question is marked by flexibility in its use of the cases, variety in the employment of figures, few connections; it lacks articles; it often disregards natural sequence; it is anything rather than florid, it is aristocratic, plainspoken, unvarnished; an old-world mellowness constitutes its beauty.

Other critics, men who have been farther removed in time from Pindar than was Dionysius, and who, accustomed from childhood to other tongues, knew far less Greek than didhe, have substituted the term *archaism* for his *old-world mellowness;* but the substitution has brought a loss rather than a gain. To call Pindar archaic is to admit an ignorance of the conventions of his department, or to overlook the fact that he post-dates Homer, who is always modern, and that he is the contempory of Aischylos, who stands at the bud and flower of Greece's prime. The term archaic, in plastic art, has come to be applied to works characterized by adherence to the law of frontality and by the 'type' manner of production prevalent before the work of Myron. It is doubtful whether Pindar fits in this category; for, although his extant poems are types of epinicia, they are not the whole of his productions. Besides, their language and metres are greatly diversified; and this term which fills a prominent place in material art, has but doubtful significance when applied to literature.

The language of Pindar is somewhat responsible for the "old-world mellowness" that is to be found in his works. It is not Theban, as a recent author seems to imagine, who asserts that Bœotia developed stiffness and bombast, whereas Athens produced grace and ease. It is not bombastic language, nor yet is it characterized by Athenian fluency. It is, rather, a language remotely comparable to that of Spenser, a literary vehicle, and no spoken speech at all. Aischylos has said that his dreams were the τεμάχη, or scraps, from the feast of Homer; and Pindar, as well as all the other poets—and not a few prose writers of Greece—partook heavily of the fare of their blind host. Pindar's language is a mixture of the Epic, Æolic, and Doric dialects, each of these elements varied according to the mood of the particular poem. Perhaps the Doric seems more in evidence than the other dialects; but this predominance can be naturally explained as caused by the handling of Stesichorus, the Doric pioneer in choral-lyric.

To the variations according to mood must be added the variations according to the personality of the poet. It is to be remembered that Pindar was a member of the aristocracy, who would, on the one hand, feel the right to assume a lofty and terse diction, and, on the other, would feel himself not bound to avoid giving offence. He is conscious of the security of his position, and for that reason does not recoil from expressing the commonplace, even the unseemly.

Another matter which has contributed to the difficulty of reading Pindar is the intricacy of the metres which he uses. The division of his works into their metres and cola has come down to us in a long tradition based upon metrical scholia which show the influence of Hephæstion and Aristoxenus. This tradition was discarded by the scholar Boeckh (1811-21), who in turn was followed by Schmidt, with his neat systematization of the poems. Schmidt is perhaps best known to students to-day through John Williams White's translation of his *Rhythmic and Metric,* in 1878. Probably the latest scansion of Pindar which has sought authenticity by publication is that of Schroeder, 1908. That none of these treatments has been universally accepted *in toto* is attested by the fact that Professor Wilamowitz has what he considers some improvements upon them in his latest work on Greek metrics. We may say that the odes of Pindar are composed in dactylo-epitrite, logœdic, and paionian rhythms; but unfortunately the former two of these terms are now involved in dispute, so that our information is not as enlightening as it seems. Whatever may be the technical term applied to his rhythms, however, a sympathetic reading of the poems, with due regard for long and short syllables, will make one feel their movement; and it will do more than this—it will bring out the *mood* of each poem.

Possibly Pindar's metres, possibly the dictates of his department, and possibly his personality alone will account for the characteristics of his poems. Of any one of these we know less than we might wish; but we can draw our inferences from his works. We have said that his personality was aristocratic. The conventions of his department have been surveyed by Dornseiff, who seems to think that the purpose of choral-lyric was largely to convey the effect of turgidity and bombast. This, however, can hardly be considered a sympathetic view. We should be fairer to Pindar if we adhered more closely to the information given by Dionysius of Halicarnassus. In Pindar we find a large rhetorical element; but this element is in keeping with the ἀὑστηρὸς ἁρμονίᾳ. It is not the art which smooths away all difficulties from the path of the reader; but it is the art in which the author solicits the help of the reader and makes him a co-worker in the elaboration of his ideas.

The diction of Pindar is lofty and elevated, with much fullness. As would be expected, circumlocution occurs very frequently. There is seen in it an influence of the speech of the Delphic priests, who, more because they were guided by traditional and religious impulses than because they sought to insure a means of escape, if their prophecies failed, refrained from calling a spade a spade, but resorted to giving descriptions of the objects meant in their divinations.

As in sentence structure Pindar shows a fondness for coördination, so in his arrangement of words, coördination prevails. The chief indication of its presence here is a large use of apposition, which often comes to equal the use of a comparison without ὡς, or some sign of the simile.

Similes and perhaps all the figures known to rhetoricians are present in the odes of Pindar; and his diction may be called highly figurative and imaginative. Manifold are the objects which serve as the basis for these figures; but the very first strophe of the **"First Olympian Ode"** will present the best epitome of Pindar's favorite objects of comparison. Here we find water, gold, gleaming fire, lordly

wealth, the sun that shines by day, the stars that gleam at night, the broad expanse of the sky or the ether. Pindar's love for figures which portray flashing brilliance and masterly swiftness has been the subject of much consideration, the outcome of which has been to attribute this predilection to his aristocratic inheritance. The aristocrat must be rich and strong; and brilliant display and swiftness are manifestations of wealth and strength.

The *Odes* of Pindar are so strongly ornamented with figures that their author has often been charged with mixing his metaphors. Dornseiff seems to find in him figures that coil and uncoil about one another, and are extremely difficult to follow:—

> Pindar is continually mingling picture and reality, or is continually hovering back and forth between the concept and the portrayal, between the object itself and a pretty veil for the object. The archaic tendency to strong metaphorical speech is so intensified in Pindar that his figures cross each other so frequently as to make it difficult to see the end of his flourishes.

To me, the term *archaic* used here is odious; and I feel that we should do better to maintain toward this apparent shortcoming of the poet the attitude stated by Professor Gildersleeve. Pindar slides from view to view with great rapidity; and his quick succession of figures is but another objective indication of his love of swiftness. Perhaps, too, his readers have read into him a fault by taking his asyndeton as the result of omission rather than of commission.

In considering Pindar's work, we must not pass over the general form of the epinicion itself. Each of these songs of victory was merely another variation of the same theme, in which the conventions of the department seemed to dictate that there should be four elements—namely, the personal, the hymnic, the gnomic, and the epic-mythical.

The personal element, of course, consisted in the giving of publicity and praise to the victor who commissioned the poet. This element certainly must have severely menaced the artistic perfection of the whole poem; but if the given hero were sufficiently famous, or traced his genealogy back to a member of the Pantheon, as most of them seem to have done, then this element furnished an approach to the poet's business of making the poem rise to the height of general and abiding interest.

The holding of the games was not merely Greece's means of surmounting the difficulty caused by the absence of modern clocks to mark the flight of time, as I was once told by a freshman studying Ancient History; but it was the expression of religious impulses. Back of the pleasure, joy, or fame that either the spectator or contestants gained, there was the feeling that all present were convened to do honor to some potent patron and deity. The poem which celebrated a victory won at any of these games must not entirely overlook the rendering of honor to the god whose worship gave the victor the opportunity to cover himself with glory. For this reason, we find scattered through the poems words of praise for the gods—for Zeus, Apollo,

Poseidon, and Heracles. Sometimes the hymnic element takes the form of a proemium.

Pindar is particularly rich in gnomic expression; but in this respect he merely emphasizes the general tendency of ancient literature, which is rarely free from the morally didactic strain. According to him, "If any man hopeth to escape the eye of God, he is grievously wrong"; "Few have gained pleasure without toil"; "Wealth adorned with virtues is the true light of man"; "The truly wise is he that knoweth much by gift of nature"; "Praise is attacked by envy." Sometimes the outlook on life is somewhat melancholy, for the **"Second Olympian"** tells us:—

> Verily, for mortal men at least, the time when their life will end in the bourne of death is not clearly marked; no, nor the time when we shall bring a calm day, the Sun's own child, to its close amid happiness that is unimpaired.

And the **"Eighth Pythian"** adds to this the mournful reflection that "man is but the dream of a shadow", a statement which Shakespeare seems to echo in *Hamlet*, in the form, "Man is but the shadow of a dream." We are given the consolation, however, that "Under the power of noble joys, a cruel trouble is quelled and dieth away, whenever good fortune is lifted on high by a god-sent fate." The melancholy is that of the man who sees life as no bright, sweet dream; but who, on the other hand, is willing to take the bitter with the sweet and to stand up like a man against the trial that will prove his true genuineness. There is in Pindar nothing that approaches the morbid, sentimental melancholia which Thomson shows in his *City of Dreadful Night*.

The mythic element of the epinicion is perhaps that which gives cohesion to the whole structure, and for most people adds the strongest touch of beauty. The tendency used to be to ascribe the presence of the myth to the epic influence; but now we reverse the process because we think that there can be detected in choral-lyric the rudiments of the old heroic sagas which must have preceded the epic. In the growth of poetry, lyric must have preceded the other departments; but our evidence shows that the order of *crystallization* of the departments must have been epic, lyric, drama. Hence there may be some truth in the above statement; and the epic, instead of affecting, shows effects itself.

The **"Fourth Pythian"** is Pindar's greatest poem, both in size and in Æsthetic appeal. It deals with the Argonautic expedition, and is a famous handling of an epic theme in a lyric manner. Next to this I personally like the **"Second Olympian,"** the **"Eighth Pythian,"** and the **"First Olympian,"** in the order named.

The appreciation of Pindar has varied somewhat with the ages. Dionysius of Halicarnassus remarks apropos of a dithyrambic fragment of Pindar's:—

> These lines are vigorous, weighty, and dignified, and are marked by much severity of style. Though rugged,

they are not unpleasantly so, and though harsh to the ear, are only so in due measure. They are slow in their rhythm, and present broad effects of harmony, and they exhibit not the showy and decorative prettiness of our own day, but the severe beauty of a distant past.

Horace says of Pindar that he—

> is like a river rushing down from the mountains and over-flowing its banks. He is worthy of Apollo's bay, whether he rolls down new words through daring dithyrambs, or sings of gods and kings, or of those whom the palm of Elis makes inhabitants of heaven, or laments some youthful hero and exalts to the stars his prowess, his courage, and his golden virtue.

And Quintilian declares that—

> Of lyric poetry Pindar is the peerless master, in grandeur, in maxims, in figures of speech, and in the full stream of eloquence.

Ronsard, 1550, wrote a number of odes to show *le moyen de suivre Pindare*; and this action was followed by a long succession of English poets who adopted what they considered to be the Pindaric method of constructing odes,—Cowley and Shadwell in the seventeenth century, and Congreve and Gray in the eighteenth.

In his *Progress of Poesy* Gray, indeed, speaks of the *pride* and the ample pinion—

> That the Theban eagle bear
> Sailing with supreme dominion
> Thru the azure deep of air.

Matthew Arnold had a high opinion of Pindar, and paid him the compliment of imitating him in passages. "Pindar," he says, "is the poet above all others on whom the power of style seems to have exercised an inspiring and intoxicating effect." His *Merope* is a copy of Pindar's [**"Olympian VI"**] and his eagle who—

> Droops all his sheeny, brown, deep-feathered neck,
> Nestling nearer to Jove's feet,
> While o'er his sovereign eye
> The curtains of the blue films slowly meet,

is from the **"First Pythian"** of Pindar.

Tennyson said of Pindar: "He is a sort of Australian poet; has long tracts of gravel with immensely large nuggets imbedded." Voltaire thought of Pindar only as "the inflated Theban"; but even these characterizations were less unkind than the remarks of those who saw in Pindar's lyric flights the crude gambols of a mastodon.

Fortunately, however, some scholars and critics—unprofessional as well as professional—have found Pindar to possess charm and grace in his massive gambols. Delicacy, smoothness, ease are not his; but he has a satisfying substantiality which is at once welcomed by the mind capable of understanding him. Translation of him is, at best, but a travesty; but a reading and re-reading of him in the original Greek is like successive hearings of Wagnerian music—one thinks it strange at first, but finds in it new enjoyment at each successive hearing.

Edith Hamilton   (essay date 1930)

SOURCE: "Pindar, the Last Aristocrat." In *The Great Age of Greek Literature*, pp. 85-103. New York: W.W. Norton & Co.

[*In the following essay, Hamilton relates Pindar's poetic achievement as the greatest interpreter of the Greek aristocracy at its greatest moment.*]

"Pindar astounds," says Dr. Middleton in *The Egoist*, "but Homer brings the more sustaining cup. One is a fountain of prodigious ascent; the other, the unsounded purple sea of marching billows."

The problem anyone faces who would write about Pindar is how to put a fountain of prodigious ascent into words. Homer's unsounded purple sea is in comparison easy to describe. Homer tells a great story simply and splendidly. Something of his greatness and simplicity and splendor is bound to come through in any truthful account of him; the difficult thing would be to obscure it completely. The same is true of the tragedians. The loftiness and majesty of their thoughts break through our stumbling attempts at description no matter how little is left of the beauty of their expression. Even translation does not necessarily destroy thoughts and stories. Shelley's poet

> hidden
> In the light of thought,
> Singing hymns unbidden
> Till the world is wrought
> To sympathy with hopes and fears it heeded not—

could be turned into another tongue without a total loss.

But this kind of poetry is at the opposite pole to Pindar's. Hopes and fears unheeded by the world he lived in were never his. The light of thought shed no glory of new illumination upon his mind. Such thinking as he did went along conventional, ready-made channels and could have moved no one to sympathy except the most stationary minds of his day. Nevertheless he was a very great poet. He is securely seated among the immortals. And yet only a few people know him. The band of his veritable admirers is and always has been small. Of all the Greek poets he is the most difficult to read, and of all the poets there ever were he is the most impossible to translate. George Meredith with his fountain of prodigious ascent gives half of the reason why. So, too, does Horace, who paints essentially the same picture of him:

> Like to a mountain stream rushing down in fury,
> Overflowing the banks with its rain-fed current,

> Pindar's torrent of song sweeps on resistless,
>   Deep-voiced, tremendous.
> Or by a mighty wind he is borne skyward,
>   Where great clouds gather.

Pindar is all that. One feels "life abundantly" within him, inexhaustible spontaneity, an effortless mastery over treasures of rich and incomparably vivid expression, the fountain shooting upward, irresistible, unforced—and beyond description. But in spite of this sense he gives of ease and freedom and power, he is in an equal degree a consummate craftsman, an artist in fullest command of the technique of his art, and that fact is the other half of the reason why he is untranslatable. His poetry is of all poetry the most like music, not the music that wells up from the bird's throat, but the music that is based on structure, on fundamental laws of balance and symmetry, on carefully calculated effects, a Bach fugue, a Beethoven sonata or symphony. One might almost as well try to put a symphony into words as try to give any impression of Pindar's odes by an English transcription.

We ourselves know little about that kind of writing. It is impossible to illustrate Pindar's poetry from English poetry. Metre was far more important to the Greeks than it is to us. That may seem a strange assertion. The rhythmic beauty and lovely sound of the verse of countless English poets is one of the characteristics we think most of in them. Even so, it is true that the Greeks thought more of metrical perfections. They would have in their poetry balanced measure answering measure, cunningly sought correspondence of meaning and rhythm; they loved a great sweep of varied movement, swift and powerful, yet at the same time absolutely controlled. The sound is beautiful in

> Bare ruined choirs where late the sweet birds sang

and in

> Under the glassy, cool, translucent wave

Nevertheless Shakespeare and Milton are painters with words more than they are master craftsmen in metrical effects. "A poem is the very image of life," Shelley said. No Greek poet would have thought about his art like that, hardly more than Bach would about his. The English-speaking race is not eminently musical. The Greek was, and the sound of words meant to them something beyond anything we perceive. Pindar's consummate craftsmanship, which produces the effect upon the ear of a great sweep of song, cannot be matched in English literature.

But Kipling has something akin to him. The swift movement and the strong beat of the measure in some of his poems come nearer than anything else we have—if not to Pindar himself, at any rate to what an English reader unversed in the intricacies of musical composition can get from him. Compare

> That night we stormed Valhalla, a million years
>   ago—

with the two lines just quoted from Shakespeare and Milton, and Kipling's characteristic speed of movement and strength of stress become evident. Pindar could be as stately as Shakespeare and Milton on occasion; he could do anything he chose with words, but the measures he preferred have the sweep and lift Kipling shows so often:

> Follow the Romany patteran
> Sheer to the Austral Light,
> Where the besom of God is the wild South
> wind,
> Sweeping the sea-floors white.
>
> The Lord knows what we may find, dear lass,
> And the Deuce knows what we may do—
> But we're back once more on the old trail, our own
> trail,
> the out trail,
> We're down, hull-down, on the long trail, the trail
> that is
> always new.

In such lines the rhythm is of first importance. What they say is not of any especial consequence; the great movement holds the attention. The lines stay in the mind as music, not thoughts, and that is even truer of Pindar's poetry. His resources of vivid and beautiful metrical expression are immensely greater than Kipling's, and the compass of his music, too. The mirror Kipling holds up to him is a tiny thing; nevertheless we shall not find a better. It is worthy of note that Kipling himself declared that he was one of the little band of Pindar's lovers:

> Me, in whose breast no flame hath burned
> Life-long, save that by Pindar lit.

If Pindar's poetry is, when all is said and done, indescribable and his thoughts merely conventional, it would seem superfluous to write about him. It is anything but that to one who wants to understand Greece. Pindar is the last spokesman for the Greek aristocracy and the greatest after Homer. The aristocratic ideal, so powerful in shaping the Greek genius, is shown best of all in his poetry.

He was an aristocrat by race and by conviction, born in the late sixth century when aristocracy in Greece was nearing its end. The first democracy in the world was coming to birth in Athens. Pindar was the figure upon which much romantic pity and sympathy have been expended—the champion of a dying cause. The man who fights for a new cause does not receive that tribute. He is up against the immense force of stubborn resistance the new always arouses. He must give battle without trumpets and drums and with the probability that he will not live to see the victory. Indeed he cannot be sure that there will ever be a victory. Nevertheless he is far more to be envied than the man who tries to turn the tide back; and that is what Pindar did.

To judge him fairly one must consider what the ideal was that produced the aristocratic creed. It was founded upon a conception altogether different from the one behind

tyranny, of all power in the hands of a single man. The tyrants departed from Greece unlamented, and never to be revived again even in wishful thinking, except for Plato's rulers who were to be given absolute power only upon the condition that they did not want it, a curious parallel to the attitude prescribed by the early Church. A man appointed to the episcopacy was required to say—perhaps still must say, forms live so long after the spirit once in them is dead—"I do not want to be a bishop. *Nolo episcopari.*" To the Fathers of the Church as to Plato, no one who desired power was fit to wield it.

But the case for the aristocracy was different. In the aristocratic creed, power was to be held by men who alone were immune to the temptations that beset, on the one hand, those struggling to be powerful and, on the other, those struggling to survive. The proper leaders of the world, the only ones who could be trusted to guide it disinterestedly, were a class from generation to generation raised above the common level, not by self-seeking ambition, but by birth; a class which a great tradition and a careful training made superior to the selfish greed and the servile meanness other men were subject to. As a class they were men of property, but position was not dependent upon wealth. The blood ran as blue in the veins of the poor noble as in the rich, and precedence was never a mere matter of money. Thus, absolutely sure and secure, free from the anxious personal preoccupations which distract men at large, they could see clearly on the lofty eminence they were born to, what those lower down could not catch a glimpse of, and they could direct mankind along the way it should go.

Nor was their own way, the aristocratic way, by any means a path of ease. They had standards not accessible to ordinary men, standards well-nigh impossible to men obliged to fight for their daily bread. An aristocrat must not tell a lie (except in love and war); he must keep his word, never take advantage of another, be cheated in a bargain rather than cheat by so much as a hair's breadth. He must show perfect courage, perfect courtesy, even to an enemy; a certain magnificence in the conduct of his life, a generous liberality as far as his means could be stretched, and he must take pride in living up to this severe code. Aristocrats subjected themselves as proudly and willingly to the exacting discipline of the gentleman as they did to the rigid discipline of the warrior. High privilege was theirs, but it was weighted by great responsibility. The burden of leadership lay upon them; they must direct and protect the unprivileged. Nobility of birth must be matched by nobility of conduct.

This was the creed of the aristocracy. Theoretically it is impeccable. Men placed by birth in a position where disinterestedness was easy were trained from childhood to rule other men for their greater welfare. Purely as a theory there is not another that can compete with it, except the one that all men are to be enabled to be disinterested, trained to be rulers, not of others, but each of his own self, and all interdependent, equally bound to give help and to accept it. This utopia, the merest dream so far, is the only conception that surpasses or even matches the conception of authority in the hands of the disciplined best. But most unfortunately for the world it did not work. There was no fault with the idea, only with its supporters. It was never allowed to work by those who upheld it. That is beyond dispute to us to-day. From the first moment that we catch sight of it in history it is a failure. Class privilege has become class prejudice, if it had ever been anything else; inherited power creates a thirst for acquiring more power; nobility of birth has no connection with spiritual nobility. The aristocrats always failed every time they had their chance. Their latest embodiment, the English House of Lords, endowed by birth with all the best the world could give—power, riches, reverential respect—fought throughout the nineteenth century with almost religious resolution every attempt to raise the condition, the wages or education, of the agricultural laborer.

We all know that by now; but Pindar did not. He believed that the great had and would use their power for the benefit of others. His poems express to perfection and for the last time in Greek literature the class consciousness of the old Greek aristocracy, their conviction of their own lofty moral and religious value. It has often been pointed out that the perfect expression of anything means that that thing has reached its culmination and is on the point of declining. *La clarté parfaite, n'est elle pas le signe de la lassitude des idées?* The statue of the man throwing the discus, the charioteer at Delphi, the stern young horsemen of the Parthenon frieze, and the poetry of Pindar—all show the culmination of the great ideal Greek aristocracy inspired just before it came to an end: physical perfection which evokes mysteriously the sense of spiritual perfection.Every poem Pindar wrote is a tribute to that union.

The games, the great games, had belonged time out of mind to the aristocrats. Only they had money enough and leisure enough to undergo the strenuous discipline of the athlete for the reward of a crown of wild olives. When Pindar lived, the bourgeois were beginning to take part in them, but professionalism had net yet come into being. Almost all his poems that we have are songs in honor of a noble victor at one of the four chief games—the Pythian near Delphi, the Isthmian at Corinth, the Nemean in Argolis, and, most glorious of all, the Olympic at Olympia. These triumphal odes are written in a way peculiar to Pindar. No other poems that praise physical achievement, poems of battle and adventure and the like, bear the least resemblance to them, and it is Pindar's creed as an aristocrat that marks them out. Anyone who has not read him would expect his songs to centre in the encounter he celebrates, to describe the thrilling scene when the chariots went whirling down the race course, or the light flashing feet of the runners carried them past the breathless crowd, or two splendid young bodies locked together in the tension of the wrestling match. Nothing light was at stake. A victory meant the glory of a lifetime. The soul-stirring excitement together with the extreme beauty of the spectacle would seem to give a theme fitted to the heart's desire of a poet. But Pindar dismisses all of it. He hardly alludes to the contest. He describes nothing that happened. A good case could be made out for his never having been present at a game. He sings praises to a victor and he disdains to mention a detail of the victory. His attention is fixed upon the young hero, not upon his achievement. He sees him as the noble representative of the noble, showing in himself the true ideal for humanity. He sees him as a religious figure, bringing to the god in whose honor the game was held the homage of a victory won by the utmost effort of body and spirit. What did this or that outside event matter—the way a horse ran or a man, or the way they looked, or the way they struggled? Pindar was glorifying one who had upheld the traditions of the great past upon which all the hope of the world depended.

In all his odes there is a story of some hero of old told with solemnity. The hero of the present, the victor, is pointed back to what men in other ages did and so shown what men in future ages could do. Pindar gives him a model upon which to form himself and make himself fit to join the august company of the noble dead. Pindar in his own eyes had a mission to the world lofty enough to employ worthily the great endowments of genius and noble blood he had been born to. He was the preacher and the teacher divinely appointed to proclaim the glory of the golden past and to summon all the nobly born and the highly placed to live their own lives in the light of that glory. This was his great charge, and no man on earth, however powerful, could make him think himself inferior. He felt not the slightest degree of subserviency. He spoke to his patron invariably as one equal to another. So they were in his eyes. In point of birth, they were both aristocrats; in point of achievement, the glory of an Olympic victory did not surpass the glory of his poetry. When summoned to Sicily to make an ode in honor of one or another of the mighty tyrants there who often competed in the games, he would admonish him and exhort him exactly as he would any lesser noble. Indeed, in the many poems he wrote to Hieron the Magnificent, the tyrant of Syracuse, he speaks more plainly even than elsewhere. "Become what you really are," he bids the great ruler. Pindar will show him his true self and spur him not to sink below it. "Be straight-tongued"—in the old aristocratic tradition, which is ever "in harmony with God, and shoulder the yoke which God has laid upon you."

There is nothing quite so unique in literature as these solemn admonitory poems dedicated to the praise of a powerful ruler and a popular hero crowned in an athletic victory, and written in a way that is the very reverse of the popular, never condescending to one word of flattery. "Wherefore seeing we are compassed about with so great a cloud of witnesses, let us run with patience the race that is set before us." Something like that Pindar said to his victorious athletes, and no other poems written to praise an exploit, athletic or military or of any sort, ever said anything in the least like that—as witness all the poets laureate.

He is different from them all. His subjects were chosen for him just as theirs were, and no doubt he too was paid for his poems; but these were matters of no importance to him. The thing that mattered was that he always would and could write exactly as he pleased. His odes were written at command, but how they were written was his affair alone. He was loftily sure of his own position. There never was a writer more proudly conscious of superiority. He is "an eagle soaring sunward," he declares, while below him the other poets "vainly croak like ravens," or "feed low like chattering crows." His odes are "radiant blossoms of song"; "an arrow of praise that will not miss the mark"; they are "a torch, a flame, a fiery dart"; "a golden goblet full of foaming wine."

"I will set ablaze the beloved city with my burning song. To every quarter of the earth my word shall go, swifter vale I build a treasure-house of song. No rain of winter sweeping to the uttermost parts of the sea upon the wings of the wind, no storm-lashed hurricane, shall lay it low, but in pure light the glorious portal shall proclaim the victory."

Such poetry proves its sublime descent. The power to write it, Pindar says in many an ode, comes from God alone. It is no more to be acquired than noble blood by the baseborn. Can excellence be learned? Socrates was to ask the Athenians that question again and again in a later day, but Pindar first propounded it and his answer was, No. "Through inborn glory a man is mighty indeed, but he who learns from teaching is a twilight man, wavering in spirit." That is the *ne plus ultra* of the aristocratic creed, and so stated it cannot be refuted. To us to-day the theory of the aristocracy has almost ceased to be. The fact that there are aristocrats remains. Power, of poetry or anything else, comes to a man by birth; it cannot be taught in the public schools.

The Greeks put Pindar with Æschylus and Thucydides, in the "austere" school of writing, the severe and unadorned. It seems a curious judgment in view of his power of rich and vivid expression, which is one of his most marked characteristics, but there is much truth in it. Pindar is austere. Splendor can be cold, and Pindar glitters but never warms. He is hard, severe, passionless, remote, with a kind of haughty magnificence. He never steps down from his frigid eminence. Aristocrats did not stoop to lies, and his pen would never deviate from the strict truth in praising any triumph. He would glorify a victor so far as he was really glorious, but no further. As he himself puts it, he would not tell "a tale decked out with dazzling lies against the word of truth." Only what was in actual fact nobly praiseworthy would be praised by him. "Now do I believe," he says, "that the sweet words of Homer make great beyond the fact the story of Odysseus, and upon these falsities through Homer's winged skill there broods a mysterious spell. His art deceives us. . . . But as for me, whoever has examined can declare if I speak crooked words." Again, "In ways of single-heartedness may I walk through life, not holding up a glory fair-seeming but false." And in another ode:

> Forge thy tongue on an anvil of truth
> And what flies up, though it be but a spark,
> Shall have weight.

Nevertheless, also strictly in the aristocratic tradition, he would leave the truth unsaid if it was ugly or unpleasant,

offensive to delicate feeling. "Believe me," he writes, "not every truth is the better for showing its face unveiled." He adds:

> That which has not the grace of God is better far in silence.

The reserve which has always been held to characterize gentlefolk is stamped on everything he wrote. "It is fitting," he writes, "for a man to utter what is seemly and good," and in one way and another the idea is repeated throughout the odes. Essentially the same feeling makes him unwilling to touch with his pen the torments of the damned in hell which so many great writers have loved to linger on. The joys of the saved, yes:

> Their boon is life forever freed from toil.
> No more to trouble earth or the sea waters
> With their strong hands,
> Laboring for the food that does not satisfy.
> But with the favored of the gods they live
> A life where there are no more tears.
> Around those blessed isles soft sea winds breathe,
> And golden flowers blaze upon the trees,
> Upon the waters, too.

But as for the others, "those bear anguish too great for eye to look upon." A gentleman will not join the staring crowd. Neither Virgil nor Dante would have tempted Pindar to journey in their company.

If Pindar had lived where he belonged by all his convictions and ideas—in the sixth century, or the seventh, instead of the fifth, he would be that not uncommon figure among men of exceptional gifts, a man of genius moving with the tide and not great enough to perceive that the flow is feeble and the ebb is near. But Pindar's life was lived when the tide of Greek achievement was at fullest flow, and he withstood it. Marathon, Thermopylæ, Salamis—he had no part in them nor in the exultant and solemn triumph the land felt when the Persian power was broken. Not an echo of these heroic events is in his poetry. His city, Thebes, did not join in the glorious struggle. She refused to help, and her poet took his stand with her. He acted as the aristocrats always act in the face of whatever threatens to disturb things as they are. He did concede praise to the chief defender of Greece, Athens, in two famous lines,

> O shining white and famed in song and violet-
> wreathed,
> Fortress of Hellas, glorious Athens, city of God,

but that was the utmost he could do for the new cause. What was dawning in Greece would give light to the world for all ages to come, but Pindar would not look at it. He kept his eyes fixed on the past. He used his genius, his grave and lofty spirit, his moral fervor, to defend a cause that was dying through the unworthiness of its own supporters. And that, not the difficulty of understanding his poetry, is at bottom the reason why he has not meant more and has become to the world a name without a content. What has the man who is bent wholly on the past to say to those who come after him? Æschylus, also an aristocrat, was able to discard the idea of being set apart by noble birth and become the spokesman for the new freedom which after Salamis leveled old barriers. His poetry is permeated with aspiration toward a good never known before, and with insight into loftier possibilities for humanity than had ever yet been discerned. He saw Athens no longer divided into ruler and ruled, but the common possession of a united people. To compare this spirit with Pindar's is to see why with all his great gifts Pindar essentially failed. Æschylus is greatly daring as the leader to new heights must be; Pindar is cautious and careful, as the defensive always must be. Stay within safe limits, he constantly urges. The aristocrats must attempt nothing further if they are to keep what they have. He warns them solemnly not only against ambition, but against aspiration as well. It is dangerous; it tempts a man to stray from the old roads to the unknown. Be content, he tells the victor in the games. Seek nothing further. Man's powers are bounded by his mortality; it is sheer folly to think that that can ever be transcended. "Strive not thou to become a god. The things of mortals best befit mortality." And again, "Desire not the life of the immortals, but drink thy fill of what thou hast and what thou canst." "May God give me," he prays, "to aim at that which is within my power." An Olympic victory is the height of human achievement, as is also in a different sense the splendor and dignity and remoteness from all things vulgar of a great prince's court, as Hieron's in Syracuse. That height once gained, all that remains is to defend it and keep it inviolate for nobles and tyrants forever.

As a result, Pindar is often sad. The brilliant odes of victory have an undercurrent of dejection. It is a discouraging task to defend in perpetuity. Hieron's festal board is spread; the wine sparkles in the golden cups; the high-born gather to celebrate; they chant the praise of driver and steeds that won the glorious race—and the mournfulness of all things human weighs down the poet's heart. That terrifying page has been reached in the book of man's destiny which Flaubert says is entitled "Accomplished Desires." There is nothing to look forward to. The best has been achieved, with the result that hope and endeavor are ended. Then turn your eyes away from the future. It can bring nothing that is better; it may bring much that is worse. The past alone is safe, and the brief moment of the present. This point of view has no especial distinction; it is not profound, neither deeply melancholy nor poignantly pathetic. It is hardly more than dissatisfaction, a verdict of "Vanity of vanities; all is vanity." "Brief is the growing time of joy for mortals and brief the flower's bloom that falls to earth shaken by grim fate. Things of a day! What are we and what are we not. Man is a shadow's dream." That is Pindar's highest contribution toward solving the enigma of human life.

Only in a very minor capacity does he still speak to the world as the greatest interpreter of the Greek aristocracy at its greatest moment. In his true and sovereign capacity as a mighty poet he has almost ceased to speak. It is our irreparable loss that his peculiar beauties of language and rhythm cannot ever be transferred in any degree into English. It is our still more irreparable loss that this man of genius used his great gifts to shed light only upon the past and turned away from the present which was so full of promise for the future of all the world to come.

Kathleen Freeman (essay date 1939)

SOURCE: "Pindar—The Function and Technique of Poetry." *Greece and Rome,* Vol. 8, No. 24, May, 1939, pp. 144-159.

[*In the essay below, Freeman surveys Pindar's odes for the poet's own views about his art in many of its aspects.*]

All writers are to some extent consciously interested in the technique of their art; many of them fare more so than is generally realized. The majority follow the principle *Ars maxima celare artem*, and do not allow us more than a glimpse into their workshop; many a lyric that delights us by its apparent spontaneity has been hammered out slowly and shaped and altered until its final form contains hardly a trace of the original creation. The late W. B. Yeats in his *Autobiography* says:

> Metrical composition is always very difficult to me. Nothing is done upon the first day, not one rhyme is in its place; and when at last the rhymes begin to come, the first rough draft of a six-line stanza takes the whole day. Sometimes a six-line stanza would take several days, and not seem finished even then.

We should not have guessed this even from his more ambitious pieces, much less from his lyrics.

I quote this statement of Mr. Yeats, not as being typical of the methods of a lyric poet—I do not think that it is—but as an example of the surprising information about their own craftsmanship that poets can give us if they will. They sometimes will, if they are deeply interested in their own processes. Nowadays, there is the convenient separate manifesto, the autobiography or the explanatory preface, in which the information can be given. But when studying the ancient writers we have to look for such information in the works themselves. In almost every poet we find a few passages on poetry in general, and scattered remarks on himself and his own methods in particular. There are famous testimonies to the power of the Muse, and frequent personal claims to immortality, such as Sappho's μνάσεσθαί τινά Ϙᾶμι καὶ ὕστερον ἄμμεων; but where will you find anything comparable to the above passage in Yeats's autobiography? Nowhere an exact parallel; the nearest approach to it, I maintain, is in Pindar, and in Horace when he was imitating Pindar.

The great *Victory Odes* of Pindar follow a fairly consistent plan. There is an opening address, generally containing the name of the victor whose success in the Games is being celebrated. Then there is the body of the Ode, the Myth, a story of god or hero having some connexion with the victor's family, country, or fortunes; and the conclusion, which usually returns to the mention of or address to the person celebrated. Somewhere in the Ode, if it is required, there is an enumeration of all the victories won by members of the house; and there are digressions, moral reflections, advice, sometimes veiled, and personal allusions often difficult to understand. When we consider the demand on Pindar, to write to order an Ode to be sung on a triumphal occasion, in celebration of a victory won in the chariot-race or the pancration, or in racing, boxing, wrestling, and so on, we feel that his task was difficult, and we think of him as bedecking with all his own wealth of colour and imagery a subject that might easily become tedious and prosaic; escaping from it as soon as may be into the romantic region of the Myth, and hurrying lightly over, or compressing by a *tour de force* that tiresome necessity, the Enumeration.

It was all very well when the client was a King Hiero of Syracuse; but what of an order such as that which must have been the occasion of the **"Thirteenth Olympian"**? The client is Xenophon of Corinth, victor at the Olympian Games in the pentathlon and the foot-race; his other victories are two at the Isthmian Games and one at Nemea. His father Thessalus has won the following victories: one in the foot-race at Olympia; two on the same day in foot-races at the Pythian Games; three similar successes at Athens, and seven at Corinth. His grandfather Ptoeodorus, his great-uncle Terpsias, and his father's cousin Eritimus have also won victories. The house boasts three Olympian crowns, and many at less notable gatherings. Pindar is commissioned to writean Ode for the present occasion, bringing in all the family triumphs of the past. At another time, the client is Timodemus of Athens, victorious in the pancration at Nemea; other victories of the family are: four at Delphi, eight at the Isthmus, seven at Nemea, and many local successes. Who would have expected that with material like this a lyric poet could have written a song that not only satisfied the requirements of the client, but charmed and delighted the hearers of all ages, impressing them with a sense of majesty and power? Whence comes the energy, the passionate interest and vitality, with which the poet sweeps up all these odds and ends, and bears them along in the tremendous volume of his inspiration, as easily as the mighty river to which Horace compares him carries along the pebbles to which Pindar himself compares facts such as these?

It is not enough to speak of the place held by the Great Games in the minds of the Greeks, the importance and dignity and the religious and social significance of the festival. It does not follow that because a theme in itself is magnificent or socially important, the use of it results in a splendid poem, as a consideration of the works of Poets Laureate will show. The theme must appeal to the interest of the poet, claiming his fullest energy; he must be not only impressed, but personally stimulated. In what way did the Games appeal to Pindar? Where exactly did they touch him? The answer is, I think, that they appealed to him as an artist, not externally by their beauty and splendour only, but personally; that when he wrote of the victor and his progress through difficulties to success, he was thinking of himself as the champion of the Muses,

and his own progress in his art. His chief interest lay just there, in his own view of himself as poet; and his poems are full, not only of the implied comparison, but of detailed and direct statements of his own methods, his differences from his predecessors and contemporaries, and the work he conceived himself as destined by nature to perform.

If all these passages be collected, it is surprising to find the bulk to which they attain, and the wealth of precise information they afford. To see them as a whole, it is necessary to collate them in various ways, chronological and other. But that would require a volume; here I shall attempt only a brief survey.

In the first place, Pindar is perfectly conscious of himself as poet, and of the function of poetry. He really is, as the Platonic epigram calls him, εὐφώνων Πιερίωλ πραπολος, and he calls constantly upon the Muses, the Graces, the Hours, Apollo and Zeus, not merely rhetorically, but with prayer containing definite requests for aid in his task. The Muses are the daughters of Memory; the function of poetry is the preservation of the names and deeds of the great from oblivion; his songs give fame, without which success is a poor thing, shortlived and worthless. In this he is at one with all poets. We have this in his own words in the **"Tenth Olympian,"** where he says:

> O Agesidamus, a man may have done glorious deeds, and yet if he goes down to the realm of Hades without a song, his panting struggles are vain, and brief is his delight. But upon thee the sweet-voiced lyre and the tender flute shed radiance; and the nurses of thy fame that shall go far and wide are the Muses, the Pierian daughters of Zeus. I, their eager helper, have fallen upon the noble Locrian people, like a shower of honey raining down on that land of heroes; and I have acclaimed the charming son of Archestratus, whom I saw winning a victory with the might of his arm beside the altar of Olympia on that day—beautiful of face, and wedded to that bloom of life which once by the aid of the Cyprus-born warded off hateful doom from Ganymede.

And again, in the **"Fourth Nemean"**:

> Speech has a life longer than deeds, when by the favour of the Graces the tongue has given it utterance from the depths of the mind.

Over and over again he thus insists on the power of song to save deeds from oblivion. There are two 'blossoms of life.'

It follows from this that poetry must have a strict regard for truth; and here we come to one of the differences which Pindar believed to exist between himself and his predecessors. In these differences he is much interested, and he speaks of them frequently and in detail. Over none of them is he more deeply concerned than over his claim to be truthful, and further, to rectify errors made by poets in the past. Thus he takes a place in the forefront of the great controversy between poetry and philosophy, and anticipates the criticism of Plato's *Republic*. The line Pindar takes is uncompromising: he is on the side of truth. None knows better than he the power of poetry to make acceptable whatever, true or false, probable or improbable, it chooses to adorn. But he will adorn only what is true and noble. In the **"First Olympian"** he says:

> Truly, marvels are many, and I doubt not, the report of mankind passes somewhat beyond the true tale. It is legends embroidered with many-coloured falsehoods that utterly deceive; and the Grace, she who fashions all sweet things that mortals know, often crowns the unbelievable with honour and a semblance of belief by her skill. But the days which come after are the surest witnesses. It is proper that one should speak what is fair concerning the gods; for the blame is less.

And then he goes on to give a revised version of the story of Pelops, who in the legend was supposed to have been devoured by the gods. He says:

> To call one of the blessed gods a cannibal is beyond my power; I shrink back.

And he so alters the story as to get rid of this horrible idea, giving another explanation.

In the **"Seventh Nemean,"** after testifying to the power of poetry, he makes a direct attack on Homer. He says:

> If a man's labours meet with success, he has flung a honeyed theme into the streams of the Muses. Mighty valour stays in the deep darkness, if it be not endowed with a song. One only is the way by which we know the reflected image (ἔσοπτρον) of noble deeds, if by the will of Mnemosyne of the shining snood a man win recompense for toils in the singing of his story, which gives fame. The gifted know the wind that is to blow three days hence, and they are not misled by greed. Rich and poor alike are marching towards the bourne of death. Now I believe that the tale of Odysseus exaggerates his experiences, through the sweet words of Homer; for upon Homer's falsehoods and his winged skill there broods a mysterious sacred spell. His art deceives us, leading us astray by its tales, and a concourse of men has for the most part a blind understanding.

The whole of this Ode is a passionate vindication of Pindar's truthfulness. 'Any man who has examined,' he says, 'can declare whether my going is inharmonious, and my utterance a crooked discourse.' He speaks almost as if he were on his defence; and elsewhere scattered throughout the Odes are tributes great and small to the Truth, and claims that he is a witness toit under oath. In the **"Eighth Nemean"** he prays to Zeus to be kept pure from deceit:

> It seems that hateful guile in speech lived even in the days of old, the companion of flattering words, the deviser of deceit, the worker of harm through calumny, she who brings injury upon the brilliant, and holds up for the obscure a glory that is rottenness. Never, O Father Zeus, may my heart be such as this, but in

ways of single-heartedness may I tread through life. Some pray for gold, others for a wide estate; but I, that I may have the love of my fellow-men until I hide my limbs below the earth, in that I gave praise to the praiseworthy, and shed condemnation on the wicked.

In the **"Tenth Olympian"** he prays to the Muse and to Truth, daughter of Zeus, together, linking their names in the dual number; and he prays to Apollo, not only as the god of inspiration, but as the god who 'does not touch a lie.'

He does not mean that poetry must tell the whole truth. He expressly says that there are some things better kept silent. In the **"Fifth Nemean"** he changes his subject with the words:

> A sense of seemliness restrains me from speaking aloud a deed perhaps hazarded wrongly. I will stay my steps. Believe me, not every truth is the better for showing its face unveiled, and silence is often the wisest plan for a mortal.

The criterion is of course Due Measure; and the artistic gift is the recognition of it. Pindar claims that he has this gift more certainly than any of his contemporaries; he is ἴδιος ἐν κοινῷ, unique.

This view of the function of poetry is marvellously in harmony with the demands of Greek philosophy. Art is to be truthful in the sense that it is not to adorn the false so as to give it credence, and therefore not to make the bad look good, or the good bad, or to attribute the properties of the one to the other. It is to go a step farther in its service to morality, and to leave the truth itself unsaid when it passes a certain limit of vileness. In my opinion these declarations of Pindar, this unmistakable definition of his position as opposed to that of many of his predecessors and contemporaries, are the direct result of the philosophical criticism of his day, and in particular of that of Xenophanes and his adherents. Xenophanes, himself primarily a travelling bard, was a great opponent of anthropomorphism, and he made a violent attack upon the earlier poets, especially Homer and Hesiod, because, as he says, 'they have ascribed to the gods all things that are a shame and a disgrace among men—theft and adulteries and deception of one another.' Xenophanes was born in about 570 B.C., and died about 480; Pindar, born about 520, must have been acquainted with his views. Xenophanes visited Sicily, and was actually called by one historian (Timaeus) the contemporary of Hiero of Syracuse; this is probably not correct, since Hiero did not begin to reign till 478 B.C., but his views must have been current at the time, especially in Sicily. He would naturally attract Pindar's interest because he was unfavourably impressed by the Sicilian passion for the Games, and wrote a poem, of which a long fragment survives, in which he asked:

> Why do cities reward prowess in the Games—fleetness, skill in wrestling, boxing, chariot-racing, in the pentathlon and the pancration—more highly than my own gift of song? Why do they rejoice excessively at an Olympian

victory? This will not fill their warehouses or improve their laws.

It would be natural that Pindar, addressing the **"First Olympian Ode"** to Hiero of Syracuse in 472 B.C., should include in it an answer to some of these charges, which came home to him so nearly. In his prooemium he glorifies the Olympian Games that are his theme—ἄριστον μὲν ὕδωρ, and the rest—and in the foreword to the Myth he represents himself as a poet who sings 'in opposition to his predecessors,' correcting that evil story which depicts the gods as cannibals; he is the poet of truth and morality, a poet, in fact, with whom not even the sternest philosopher could find fault. Μείων γὰρ ἀιτίᾳ, he says; and we find elsewhere in his poems that he is extremely sensitive to criticism from any quarter. For example, he resents the slur on his countrymen that was expressed in the current gibe, 'Boeotian swine,' and he frequently refers with bitterness to the spite and envy and calumny from which no prominent man escapes. In several Odes he is at pains to apologize for an offence unwittingly given. This being so, he would be peculiarly susceptible to the criticisms of Xenophanes and his followers; and I believe that the position he takes up as the servant of Truth in art is a direct attempt to meet that criticism. This explains why his attitude anticipates so strikingly the demands of Plato in the second and third books of the *Republic*; for the whole of that section, on the function of poetry in education, is undoubtedly based on the earlier criticisms of Xenophanes.

But Pindar's views on his own art are not merely negative and apologetic; nor are they confined to its subject-matter. His delight in it is active and unceasing, and is aroused by its every aspect and manifestation. There is scarcely an Ode which does not contain a direct expression of this. He is constantly speaking of his song, and he clothes it in innumerable metaphors. He likens it to a flower, to a garland; to a building with shining façade, to a column or a statue (though elsewhere he says that he is no maker of statues: his songs are not made to stand at ease on a pedestal, but to move all over the world). He calls it a torch, a flame, a wave, a breath of wind; a ship, a bale of merchandise; honey, a bee that darts from flower to flower; a garment with beautiful folds, a sandal, a Lydian chaplet; a javelin, an arrow, a race-horse or chariot. Often he personifies it, and incidentally describes the experience of poetic inspiration: it comes and beats on the doors of the poet's mind, saying 'Sing!'; it places the mind under the yoke of sweetest pleasure. It is honey-voiced, and brings charm that gives healing. These many and varied metaphors are frequently repeated; sometimes they are worked out at length, sometimes indicated by a word, sometimes linked together in rapid succession, as in the **"Eleventh Olympian,"** where he sings:

> Oft-times have mortals joy in the winds,
> Oft-times in the heaven-sent rain,
> Moisture that falls from the womb of the cloud.
> Yet if a man with toil and pain
> Fair fortune finds,
> A choir of honey-voiced songs arise,

> And lay the stone of his future fame,
> Attest aloud
> And in truth proclaim
> The might of his glorious victories.

> No power hath envy to overthrow
> This moment to his praise,
> The Olympian victor's song. 'Tis mine,
> Sweet task of my lips to tend and raise
> This song below.
> But heaven alone can give wisdom's flower.
> See then, Agesidamus, won
> Is this prize of thine,
> Archestratus' son,
> The song of the boxer-victor's power.

These metaphors are not merely rhetorical and fanciful; they contain definite views of his craft, and each one if examined will be found to yield a precise meaning which fits in with and contributes to the understanding of his more direct statements. Here I must limit myself to the discussion of only one class of them. In the list given above I mentioned those in which his song is likened to a javelin or an arrow, and to a race-horse or a chariot. The javelin-and-arrow metaphors are among the most numerous and interesting. He likens himself to an archer, saying, 'Many are the swift arrows at my elbow within the quiver; they have a message for those who understand, but for the mass they need an interpreter,' and, 'For me my Muse is cherishing a dart yet mightier in strength.' He speaks of tending his bow upon the mark, and shooting arrows that bring not death but the immortality of fame. 'My tongue', he says, 'is ready with words, and has many arrows.' And when he shoots an arrow of praise, 'I think,' he says, 'I shall not miss the mark.' Similarly he likens himself to a javelin-thrower in the Games, and his tongue to the javelin. A good theme is a vantage-ground on to which he steps to fling missiles with truthful aim. He does not break any of the rules: 'I swear, Sogenes, that my foot was not before the line when I hurled my swift tongue like a brazen-checked javelin. His cast does not go wide: 'I am confident that in my zeal to praise this man, I shall not throw my brazen-cheeked javelin beyond the course, when I whirl it in my hands, but shall make a long cast that will out-distance my adversaries.'

There are many other such metaphors, the most remarkable of which is that in the **"Sixth Olympian,"** where he says:

> I have on my tongue the sensation as of a shrill whetstone; it draws me on unresisting, with its sweet-flowing breaths.

The change of metaphors is so sudden that attempts have been made to emend away the whetstone (ἀκανὰς) and substitute something that leads on more gently to what follows, as for example Bury's ' λκύονος. But that the whetstone is genuine is made probable by comparison with Pindar's other metaphors for the tongue. In the **"First Pythian"** he bids Hiero, 'Forge thy tongue on an anvil of truth; whatsoever flies up, though it be but a spark, has weight since it comes from thee.' So, too, in the **"Sixth Olympian"** the tongue is the brazen-cheeked javelin, which is sharpened on the whetstone and gives out a shrill cry as it is prepared for its flight through the air; and this feeling draws the poet on with sweet breaths of inspiration. He is in fact drawn on so swiftly by a rapid succession of images that we can scarcely keep up with him; and that is his usual method of working, both in narration and in thought and imagery—to let the association of ideas have free play, and to follow the course they take, however rapid and involved it may be.

In these javelin-metaphors, and in those in which the song is likened to a race-horse or a chariot, he is reversing the process one might expect in a poet of the Games; instead of using his song to bedeck the Games with metaphors drawn from other spheres, as he does elsewhere, he is here using the imagery of the Games to adorn his own art, and to express its nature. He is regarding himself, the poet, as a contestant, with an end to attain, a prize to win, adversaries to surpass, and a prowess of his own that makes him one in spirit with the athletic competitor. He has his craft,they have theirs. We are all strivers after different things, linked to one vocation by the law of fate; but there are some rules that hold true of all forms of activity. Thus is revealed one of the chief sources of his interest in the Games, and the celebration of successful effort therein. He can compare himself as artist with these artists in another sphere, and sympathize with their efforts, their difficulties, their successes, their victories over opponents, their openness to assault from the envious obscure.

Often we can clearly see him identifying himself with the victor he is celebrating, or with one of the heroes whose story he tells in the Myth; and he constantly uses the opportunity to refer to himself and his work. It would be a fascinating task to work out this idea in the great Myths; here one or two examples must suffice. In the **"Ninth Olympian,"** after recounting the many victories of Epharmostus to whom the Ode is addressed, he passes on to generalizations which apply to athletic prowess, but even more to artistic power, of which he is primarily thinking:

> The inborn gift is ever the victor; but many rush forward
> to seize glory by a prowess acquired by teaching.

This is a favourite contention of his, that training is useless without natural gifts, though he does training and trainers full justice. He goes on:

> Everything that has not the grace of God is better kept
> silent. Of paths there are some which stretch beyond
> others, and not all of us will the same pursuit cherish.
> Art is a rugged way.

Thus we see the transition by stages from the contemplation of the prowess of the athlete to the thought of his own gifts and their progress, a thought to which he is ever returning. On two other occasions, when a victory comes to a family which for a period has gained no such distinction, he uses the opportunity to enunciate the law of productivity that applies to all art: production is not continuous, but alternating, like the fields which one year bear harvest, another year lie fallow, seeking fresh strength.

Pindar, therefore, regarded himself as a combatant, with adversaries whom he excelled by his skill. Hence the career of the athlete or any other striver after fame and excellence can be compared with that of the poet. But there are of course differences. Pindar rates his own vocation very highly, and would not change it, even for the destiny of a prince like Hiero. He is not only proud of it; he has the keenest personal pleasure in it. His poems abound with such phrases as 'the delightful blossom of my song'. Poetry is divine inspiration, and he is sure that he has it in abundant measure. In the **"Ninth Olympian,"** celebrating Epharmostus of Opuntian Locri, he says:

> I will set ablaze a beloved city with my burning songs,
> and send this news to every quarter, swifter than noble
> horse or winged ship, if indeed with a hand gifted by
> fate I till the choicest garden of the Graces—for they
> it is who give the things of beauty. It is by divine
> genius that men prove themselves excellent or gifted.

And in the **"Third Pythian"**:

> I will serve as best I may the fleeting genius that attends
> me; and if Heaven grant the luxury of success, I have
> hope to win a lofty glory for future time. Nestor and
> Sarpedon are names on men's lips. It is from poems of
> praise, framed by skilled craftsmen, that we know
> them.Excellence lives long in glorious songs; but to
> few is given the making of them.

The Graces, then, who preside over all excellence and all delight, have given Pindar one of their choicest gifts. Moreover, it has been granted him not only to excel, but also to be an innovator, in his craft. We have seen how he believed that he had improved on his predecessors in the actual content of his work; he considered himself to be a pioneer and leader in technique also. He makes the explicit claim that he has discovered a new method of narration—the lyric method as opposed to the epic; and he shows us what this is. The **"Fourth Pythian,"** addressed to Arcesilaus King of Cyrene, is by far the longest of the *Victory Odes*; in it he narrates the epic story of Jason and Medea, and the voyage of the Argonauts. An analysis of this narrative will show clearly enough Pindar's method at work. The arrangement is neither epic nor dramatic; the chronological sequence of the events is disregarded. We begin with a scene in which Medea prophesies to the Argonauts on the homeward voyage; we end with the scene in which Jason masters the fire-breathing bulls; and in between these, the narrative doubles back on itself to present other striking scenes, connected with the coming of Jason to Iolcus *before* the setting out of the heroes. These expanded scenes are presented with consummate skill as pictures; they are lightly introduced and linked together by references to the royal house of Cyrene; and the narrative closes with a rapid summary of the rest of the Argonautic story compressed into a few lines, bringing it down to the events leading to the foundation of Cyrene.

Now between the last 'expanded scene', and this closing summary, Pindar gives a brief explanation of his method:

It is too long for me to go by the high road; for time is closing in, and I know a special short path. I am the leader of a large band in the region of art.

We may set beside this another pronouncement, from the **"Fourth Nemean."**

'That I should tell the tale in all its length and detail is forbidden me by the law of my art, and by hastening time. But my heart is whirled by a new-moon spell of desire to touch upon it;'

and this from the **"Ninth Pythian":**

Great deeds ever bring much speaking; but the pleasure of cultivated hearers is the adornment of a few things in a long theme. Seasonableness invariably takes pre-eminence.'

It is this technique of choosing out a few things and expanding them, and condensing the rest, that is Pindar's peculiar gift. He works by the pictorial method, the presentation of a few great scenes depicted with minuteness and clarity and brilliant colouring. These he links together very lightly by a few apothegms, or by the association suggested by a single word or detail of the picture. He refers to this technique in metaphors, as when he describes his song 'darting like a bee from theme to theme,' and himself as 'poised on tip-toe, taking a breath before I speak a word.' It is because he uses this method of association that he finds his craft easy, a 'light gift.'

There was one part of his task, however, that he did not find easy, and that was the Enumeration—the setting-forth, when required, of the victories won by the client and his house. It is here that Pindar calls most strenuously into play his gift of condensation. He does not conceal the difficulty he experiences; on the contrary, he expresses it in all manner of ways, directly and metaphorically. His favourite method is to give as the reason for brevity the fact that excess of anything brings satiety, and in particular, excessive praise breeds envy in the hearers. A mass of words hides rather than magnifies excellence. He says in the **"Eighth Pythian."** I have not the time to set up all the long story in the mingled strains of lyre and tender voice, lest Surfeit draw near and annoy'; and in the Ode placed tenth among the Nemeans: 'My tongue is not strong enough to narrate the whole succession of brave deeds which are the lot of the Argive realm; and there is the satiety of men besides, a heavy foe to withstand.' At other times, he turns the condensation into a compliment to his client: the victories or virtues are too numerous to be counted, like the sands of the sea, or like a heap of bronze pieces.

But though he insists on applying his method of condensation, he does not neglect the Enumeration. It was required by his clients and he gives it, often with marvellous variety and skill. I will quote in full the enumeration from

the **"Thirteenth Olympian,"** to which I referred at the beginning. The client is Xenophon of Corinth, victor in the foot-race and the pentathlon.

O thou Highest, ruler far and wide of Olympia, be thou for all time without envy at my words, Zeus the Father. Guide this people in safety, and make straight the fair breeze of Xenophon's good genius. Receive the ceremony in honour of the garlands, the procession which he leads from Pisa's plains, victor in the foot-race and the pentathlon; these honours no mortal before him has attained. Two twined wreaths of parsley crowned him for his pre-eminence in the Games of Isthmus; and Nemea is no adversary of his. For his father Thessalus the bright fame of fleetness is stored up by the streams of Alpheus, and at Pytho he holds the victory of the straight race and the double race, gained both in one sun's passage. Within the same month, at craggy Athens, one fleet day set three glorious deeds upon his hair. Seven times the Hellotian festival crowned him. In the sea-girt realm of Poseidon, too long to sing are the songs that will attend upon his grandfather Ptoeodorus, along with Terpsias and Eritimus. How great is the number of your victories at Delphi, and in the lair of the Lion! I war with many about the number of these glories, just as I cannot surely tell the number of the sea-pebbles. There is a measure to everything. The right moment is when that measure is realized.

This account, however, does not exhaust the list of victories given by the client; so Pindar leaves it there for the present, and goes on to the Myth, the story of Bellerophon and Pegasus. At the end of the Ode he returns to the Enumeration, bringing in the remaining items:

But I, who fling straight my whirring javelins, must not send beside the mark these many missiles sped by my two strong hands. With all my heart I have come as an ally to the bright-throned Muses and the family of the Oligaethidae; for with brevity of speech I shall pile up clear to the view the heap of garlands won at Isthmus and Nemea; and there shall support me the true voice attested by oath, the sweet cry of the noble herald, with its sixty-fold message from both sides. As for their Olympian victories, these, I think, have been already told ere this; those to come in the future I may truly tell when they arrive. To-day I am full of hope; the fulfilment rests with Heaven. If the genius of the house goes onward, we will submit realization into the hands of Zeus and Ares. The victories won beneath the brow of Parnassus, those many prizes at Argos and Thebes, and those to which the King-Altar of Zeus Lycaeus, that rules the Arcadians, will bear witness; and Pellene and Sicyon and Megara and the fair-fenced precinct of the Aeacidae, and Eleusis and shining Marathon, and the rich cities beneath high-crested Etna, and Euboea—throughout all Greece you will find them, if you seek, in greater numbers than I can recount. Up, swim forth with nimble feet! O Zeus, giver of fulfilment, grant honour and a fortune sweet with delights!'

Here I must end this account. I have been able to touch upon a few main points only: the κεφάλαια λαγων, as Pindar would say. But I hope to have demonstrated the thesis with which I began—Pindar's all-pervading interest in his own art, and the presence in his own poems of his views about it in all its aspects. A Pindaric Handbook, if not a Poet's Calendar, could be compiled from the Odes. And yet, though he of all poets gives us the fullest information about his methods, he of all poets is the most difficult to imitate, and the praise of Horace still holds good:

> He who would strive to rival Pindar
> Shall be like him who vainly gave
> His trust to Daedal's waxen pinions,
>   And named a watery grave.
>
> As, swoll'n by showers, his banks o'erflowing,
> Down from the mountains rolls along
> The river, rush the foaming torrents
>   Of Pindar's mighty song.

Raymond V. Schoder (essay date 1943)

SOURCE: "The Artistry of the First Pythian Ode." *The Classical Journal,* Vol. XXXVIII, No. 7, April, 1943, pp. 401-412.

[*In the excerpt below, Schoder analyzes the "First Pythian," highlighting the structure, myths, and imagery of the ode.*]

When Pindar was a child, a swarm of bees from Mt. Helicon fashioned about his tiny lips a fragrant honeycomb. So at least it is reported, and no one who has fought his way up the sheer peaks of Pindar's odes to pluck at last the "outpoured nectar, the Muses' gift, the sweet fruit of the poet's mind" will wish to disbelieve it. For Pindar's songs have a charm, a vigorous, soaring, brilliant power which no other steward of Pierian treasures has merited to wield. The universal reaction to his genius has been an awed amazement at such virtuosity of fancy, of language, and of rhythm. His words reveal such taut explosiveness of content, his imagery sweeps on in such charged opulence, his thought weaves in and out of its symmetrical framework in so intricate a fugue formation that protests of helpless bewilderment have been wrung from many a student of his works:

> An eagle, soaring in the lonely sky,
> Proud favorite of the gods and sport of Kings,
> Despising earth, aloft to heaven springs
> Where gentle feathered carolers dare not fly,
> A bird of wonder to delight the eye
> (Could eye so far discern): so Pindar sings
> In lofty tone far-off, majestic things—
> Ah! earth-born scarce can hear, so far, so high!

It is a hardy task, consequently, to essay an analysis of Pindaric technique and genius at its zenith of achievement in the **"First Pythian"** ode, "the highwater-mark of Pindar's inspiration, and one of the masterpieces of the world's lyrics." Certainly ἄναλκιν οὐ φωτᾶ λαμβάνει. But let us draft courage and make the attempt. It will be worth it!

Without hoping for complete capture of the prey in our pursuit, we shall profit at least by whatever specimens the "many-eyed net" of modern scholarship may help our eager searchings to ensnare. For not only will the catch be fair to gaze on, but it will typify the other multitudinous denizens of that rich sea of song. Because, as Wilamowitz points out, "Pindar has a set style which scarcely changed all through his long life." Most of his special characteristics appear in this ode. If elsewhere they are less brilliantly present, they are still present. It is not only of the **"First Pythian"** that Jebb [in his *The Growth and Influence of Classical Greek Poetry*] is thinking when he states that "The impression given by Pindar's style is that he is borne onward by the breath of an irresistible power within him, eager to find ample utterance, immense in resources of imagery and expression, sustained on untiring wings." But it is this poem especially which proves him right.

The occasion of this ode is noteworthy. Hiero of Syracuse, the most splendid and powerful ruler in the fifth-century Greek world, had added to his triumphs in the great battles of Himera (480 B.C.) and Cumae (*c.* 474) the glory of founding a new city, Aetna, at the base of the great volcano of that name, in addition to the international distinction of a victory in the chariot-race at the Pythian games. This was in 470 B.C. (or, less probably, in 474), and Pindar had been living on intimate terms with Hiero for several years, including a considerable stay at his court. It seems that Hiero wished to celebrate this double glory—founders of cities received heroic honors in the Greek world—by a splendid musical festival at which the greatest Greek lyrists were to vie in singing his achievements. This challenged Pindar to exert to the utmost his great genius and outshine all his rivals (ἔλπομαι. . .ἀμεύσασθ᾽ ἀντίους, as he says in verse 45), to settle once and for all the truth of his boast that he was the greatest poet in Greece: πολλοῖσι δ᾽ ἄντημαι σοφίας ἑτέροις, or to repeat it: ἐμὲ. . .πραφάντον σοφίᾳ καθ᾽ Ἑλλανὰς πᾶντα. Settle it he did!

The task before him was not easy. He had to praise a great prince for physical prowess, for his prosperity and beneficence, and above all, by the terms of his commission, for founding the new city and crushing the barbarian foe. Yet Pindar's own poetic genius exacted that all this be raised to the plane of high poetry with undying significance and interest. He had, in short, to make "an eternal event out of a client's career [David M. Robinson, *Pindar, a Poet of Eternal Ideas* (1936)]. But he had developed a technique for achieving this—by bringing in the eternal truths of religion and of human wisdom, by associating the event with some parallel achievement in his nation's mythical past, by lifting the temporary victory to the level of the eternal prevalence of good over evil and the beautiful over the base, by transfiguring the victor into a glorious personification of his race by reflecting, magnifying, and illuminating the present in the mirror of the past, and by raising the real to the ideal order, the particular to the universal. This would also give him the opportunity of "speaking as a hierophant, with a touch of priestly majesty." For by pointing out to his patron that, for all his enjoyment of supreme prosperity, his limbs will one day decay, and his power pass to another; that he must not think to become a god, but rather give to the gods his glory; that he must think moral thoughts and walk in the ways of justice and moral preeminence, he could from this starting-point moralize on the great issues of life and turn the occasion to the uses of supreme and immortal poetry. As usual, then, as Symonds remarks, "the whole poetic fabric is so designed as to be appropriate to the occasion and yet independent of it. Therefore Pindar's odes have not perished with the memory of the events to which they owedtheir origin [John Addington Symonds, *Studies of the Greek Poets*]. With consummate skill, Pindar has worked out this, his usual procedure, with a variation in details and a pervading brilliance which give the **"First Pythian"** ode a beauty all its own.

This appears, first of all, in the general structure of the ode. It displays, as Jebb says of all Pindar's odes, the features of an oratorio, with its "rapid transitions from one tone of feeling to another, from storm to calm, from splendid energy to tranquillity, from triumphant joy to reflection or even to sadness . . . [transitions] held together by massive harmonies of rhythm and language." We must not look in Pindar for rigid structural divisions of the thought, such as ruled over the Terpandrian νσμος, or for the fixed articulation of an oration of Demosthenes, or even, within such a framework, for the orderly development of a rhetorical period. Pindar's thought is guided, not by strict logical order, but by the rushing impulse of his crowded imagery, one thought suggesting another through association in object or coloring or symbolism or even in the very music of its sounds. Pindar is a poet, a man of visions and sudden intuitions, of soaring fancy and delight in splendor (φιλάγλαος), not a solemn, regularized panegyrist. . . .

Another phase of Pindar's artistry is his handling of the customary myth. In this ode it is very brief, but skilfully fitted to its counterpart *ad unguem*. It comes in at exactly the middle of the poem—line 50 out of a total 100—in the very center of the central triad. It delicately consoles Hiero for his illness (gallstones), pictures him as a new hero, points out the parallel with Philoctetes in the humiliation of the haughty petitioners, and both men's position in the divine plan. Moreover, the words "fauning petitioners" seem to refer to the citizens of Cumae, which is thus alluded to at the beginning, middle, and end of the poem. And Philoctetes is not only appropriate as the type of suffering hero, but also because there was a famous statue of him in Hiero's city. Pindar, as usual, misses no associations or local details. Everywhere, as it has been said, "He reveals an extraordinary intimacy with the old traditions of the land, and an amazing, even at times overdone, dexterity in linking up the myth with the victor."

Admirable technique is also manifested in the transitions from one part of the ode to another. The praise of music's power flows from men, to nature, to heaven, to the gods, then ebbs into the thought of regions where it is negated, thereby introducing the suggestion of moral harmony as a requisite for men, lest one suffer Typhon's fate, or fall under his erupting fury with no protection from Zeus. This mention of Aetna prepares for the praise of its namesake city; this for the praise of its founder Hiero; this for

the stress that human glory yet depends on the gods, and so forth through all the varied involutions till the final conjunction in prayerful praise. Grammatically, this *callida iunctura* is achieved by unobtrusive particles (δέ, δὲ, μή, γάρ, τοι), relative pronouns, careful position of words, and sudden dashes of thought into new directions too clear to need synapses. "The hearer slips from phrase to phrase almost without noticing it," as Croiset justly remarks.

The metre, too, is a marvel of art. It is in the Dorian mood, "of which," as Farnell says, "the rhythm lifts us and takes possession like melodious thunder." The musical phrases (κῶλα) within the larger rhythmic periods of the strophe and antistrophe are uniformly balanced off against one another, in point of constituent metrical feet, in the pattern: I 2.5; 4; 5.2; II 4.2; 3.4.3; 4.2; III 5.3.5; but in the epodes somewhat differently; I 5.2.5.3; II 4.4; III 3.2; 2.3.2; 2.3; IV 4.4; 3; 4.4. The individual feet in corresponding recurrences of the pattern are very seldom dissimilated through substitution, and the substitution allowed only serves to introduce the bit of "play" or "entasis" needed to keep the impression of life and human touch, rather than of coldly perfect mathematical precision. Then too, the sense of the words is greatly enhanced by the skilfully controlled coloring imparted to their effect by their rhythmical value in themselves and in the pattern as a whole. One instance must suffice: beyond question there is a rich addition to the beauty of the fourth lines in the strophe-antistrophe groups when the metrical values are noted, bringing into prominence, as they do, the final words, when the slow, stately movement suddenly rushes forward and cloaks the strong, high-pitched last syllable with an echo of the whole line, as it were, trying to catch up with its soaring member. When Pindar describes the procedure, one thinks to hear the poet's golden lyre tremble softly at the idling brush of his fingers as he prepares to play, then suddenly swell out into echoing melody as he opens the overture to his song. . . .

So too, when he speaks of Aetna hurling rocks down into the sea far below, ear as well as mind perceives the poet's meaning. . . .

In like manner, the important thought of "harmonious peace" is made to reverberate in our attention by being placed at the close of this fourth line. Alas, that people still read Pindar in translation, or ignore this metrical charm even in the Greek! It is a music which penetrates and brightens the entire ode. Nor must it be forgotten that Pindar provided, in actual production of the ode, choral dancing and music.

Pindar's use of words is an important feature in his peculiar form of genius. He shows an artistry and power in their use which have no real parallel in other poets. The elements of his technique—compounds, word music, pregnant or special meaning, effective position, colorful coinage or choice of synonym—are common, but he has a fusion and sublimation of them all his own. To illustrate this properly would mean an appreciative analysis of every word, and in context. Some typical cases may, however, hint at the full truth. The end of the first line sings, in picture as in sound, of the Muses as ἰοπλοκάμων, a word to compel anyone's awed delight. At the close we hear of ὀπιθβμβροτον αὔχημᾳ, an original compound, which, as usual with Pindar, "shows no rivets," and, moreover, as Gildersleeve says, "resounds as if the words themselves echoed down the corridors of Time." This opalescence of language is a commonplace in Pindar. He is forever startling one with the gleaming freshness and melody of his words. "In the fine feeling of language few poets can vie with Pindar . . . like a true artist he delights in the play of his own work . . . he is a jeweller, and his chryselephantine work challenges the scrutiny of the microscope . . .—invites the study and rewards it." Most remarkable of all is his wholly unparalleled power. His words seem to strain and rock with the richness of implication he has forced into them under the high pressure of his world-encompassing visions. The pride of Hiero's foes becomes, in a bold expression, the war-boast personified (κατ᾽ οἶκον ὁ Φοίνιξ . . . ἀλαλατᾳς ἔχη). The fierce fury of erupting Aetna roars in the very description, as its παγᾳὶ of unapproachable fire ἐρεύγονταῑ . . . ἐκ μυχῶν, and its ποταμοὶ . . . προχέοντι ῥαον καπνοῦ᾽, and it jets forth Ἀφαίστοιο κρουνοῦς . . . δεινοτάτους. Was ever natural violence echoed more powerfully in words? This tension and energy is so pronounced everywhere in Pindar that it is aesthetically exhausting to read more than an ode or two at a sitting—even when repetition has removed the physical prostration of first working out his meaning.

A final aspect of Pindar's artistry is the most admirable and Pindaric of all. In imagery and concept he is unique, alone, awesome. Not that Homer, or Dante, or Pindar's friend Aeschylus are inferior to him, but that they are not like him, they never trespass on his peculiar domain. The critics speak as though beside themselves at his genius: ". . . his fierce and calm grandeur, his loftiness and flash," "His work is strained, audacious, fantastically high-pitched, yet fiery and swift—'hot with speed'—like work done with intense force on a glowing anvil"; "The detail of Pindar's odes produces . . . an irresistible effect of opulence and elevation—of wealth that makes itself felt, that suggests, almost insultingly, a contrast, and that contrast is indigence. . . . Pindar is a lover of swiftness . . . and of concentration—the gathering of energy to a point, a summing up of vitality in a word"; "One must admire his instinct for grandeur, delight in strong thoughts . . . splendor of imagery . . . quick flashes of light thrown on the mystery of life"; ". . . the quality peculiar to Pindar among all the poets of the world—splendor, fire, the blaze of pure effulgence . . . the stormy violence of his song, that chafes within its limits and seems unable to advance quickly enough in spite of its speed . . . while he is pursuing his eagle-flight to the sun, or thundering along his torrent-path." To Horace, he is inimitable, an overflowing mountain torrent seething and rushing in a vast flood of deep speech, or a swan soaring on strong blasts of inspiration as he launches up toward the clouds—often to disappear in them from our sight, as Merlet adds [in his *Études littéraires sur les grandes classiques Grecs*]. Yet amid all this rush of thought and play of words Pindar manages to adhere with consummate skill to the minute demands of his intricate metrical pattern. Never was genius more cruelly misrepresented than when Horace goes on to explain Pindar's sweeping progress of thought as made possible by an arbitrary defiance of metrical restrictions: *numerisque fertur lege solutis.*

In the great prelude to this ode all these enthusiastic statements find their fullest justification. Only the entire passage in the Greek can really show why; it would be treachery to "translate" it here. But one can point out, perhaps, what splendid visions and metaphors are to be found there—the foot poised for the gala dance, listening for the directions of the poet's lyre; the vivid sketch of the thunderbolt, daringly personified as spear-man of unflagging fire; the magnificent image of the eagle sleeping atop the sceptre of Zeus, relaxing his swift pinions and heaving his back like a rippling sea under the sweet spell of the gales of song; the very war-god succumbing in gentle slumber to the poet's shafts. Then follows that volcanic, awesome vision of the rebel Typhon, whose shaggy breast the vast weight of Sicily's and Cumae's sea-restraining cliffs scarce can constrain, or even that pillar of the heavens, snowy Aetna, eternal nurse of biting snow, from whose secret depths well forth the unapproachable rivers of fire and gleaming freshets of smoke, while the black night is pierced by flashing swirls of fire, as mighty rocks plummet with a roar into the smooth sea far below.

How admirable too the fancy which thus personifies in the savage foe of Zeus the unrestrained fury of nature, and at once makes him symbolize domestic disorder (Σικελίᾳ) and foreign violence (Κύμη)! Actna itself becomes for Pindar, in a striking figure, εὐκάρποιο γαῑᾳς μέτωπον. His own song of praise is a bronzecheeked spear speeding unerringly to its goal from his whirling hand. Hiero "plucks" his wealth and glory as a flower (δρέπε). The "deep gloried" Dorians' fame "blooms on their spearpoints." Pindar "climbs up to Himera by parallels, as is his wont," when carrying out his commission to glorify that great triumph of his patron. His encouragement of Hiero to grow yet in virtue is bright with vigorous images—the rudder of justice, the tongue's anvil of truth amid the flying sparks of each royal pronouncement, the "flowering-tide of soul," the bellying sails of state emprise, the good man's society with the soft warbling of boys, and the sound of lyres beneath the festive roof. Thereupon Pindar, as he says in another ode, with a swift thrust of his feet swims out of the deluge of glory which his song has loosed upon the gathering, for fear lest even he may get lost in its swirling.

His wisdom deserves to be imitated. *Sufficit.* Golden glories enough have been brought out from the endless store to justify our willingness to accept Quintilian's judgment on Pindar: *Novem vero lyricorum longe Pindarus princeps spiritus magnificentia, sententiis, figuris, beatissima rerum verborumque copia et velut quodam eloquentiae flumine: propter quae Horatius eum meritocredidit nemini imitabilem.* But perhaps a modern poet has best stated, in a more Pindaric fashion, our final impression of Pindar's genius—the

. . . Ample pinion
That the Theban eagle bare,
Sailing with supreme dominion
Through the azure deep of air
         [Thomas Gray, *The Progress of Poesy*].

Paolo Vivante (essay date 1971)

SOURCE: "On Myth and Action in Pindar." *Arethusa*, Vol. 4, No. 2, Fall, 1971, pp. 119-35.

[In the excerpt below, Vivante examines action in Pindar's odes as expressing fulfillment of mythic forms rather than individual feats.]

. . . If . . . we turn to ancient Greece, we find a very peculiar situation. Right at the beginning of its civilization there is a pervasive mythology whose roots, as Nilsson showed, sink deep into the Mycenaean past. And, what is more, this mythology has a strong hold on literature. The poets drew from it, generally, their material for the portrayal of human action. Whereas in the European Middle Ages historical events were consciously transformed into legends, the reverse process seems to have occurred in early Greece: legends were brought down to a human measure. Recorded memory had receded; but a powerful mythical imagination had reduced into a series of lifelike representations the compact mass of tribal history and religious belief.

How did this happen? We shall never be able to recover the origin and the formative moment of the Greek myths, but we can say something about their relevance to literature. What is mythology in this respect? It is, I would say, a sort of symbolic language, a system of hieroglyphs whereby modes of being and of action are condensed into typical hallowed forms mysteriously removed from the world of everyday life and yet somehow reflecting it. Here are concretions of thought and expression, natural phenomena dramatized into words and acts, actions and events crystallized into phenomena—a whole paradigm of existence laid over existence itself. If mythology were developed into a complete system, it would be tantamount to a real language—having instead of single words clusters of words, each cluster forming a self-contained whole and carrying its own message. It is easy to imagine what strong effect this would have on the mind of a writer: he would have to come to terms with such a system just as we see him coming to terms with single words.

There are mythologies of many kinds—some heavily symbolical, others hardly risen above the sensuous material of magic and superstition, others again quite absorbed into the sphere of a higher religion. Greek mythology appears singular in many ways, above all in the predominance of aesthetic plastic values. I will not deny, of course, that deep moral ideas may be found in Greek myths, but wherever present, they were quite embedded in the sensuous relevance of the image. Heracles, for instance, locked in a life and death struggle with the Nemean lion is far more striking to our imagination than the idea of the hero as a liberator of the world from monsters; Prometheus nailed to his rock far more than his role as a martyr for mankind; the delicately beautiful myth of Demeter, Persephone, and Pluto far more than the symbolism of Winter and Spring. Look at some of the earliest Greek sculpture portraying action—Perseus and Medusa from Selinus, or Heracles and the Erymanthian boar at Paestum: there is no softening, idealizing, narrative interpretation; everything is a feeling of sheer mysterious vitality craving for a shape, for a sensuous form.

Greek myth thus presented itself with a full-blown imagery that embodied all sorts of situations—birth, death, victory, defeat, the winning of a bride, adultery, etc. The absence of a clearly defined moral idea or symbolism left the artist relatively free as to the treatment of factual details, but the sensuous charm cast a spell over his mind, conditioning him to the habit of conceiving action in a mythical form. The myth could be transformed, but the mythical mold remained shutting off the rendering of everyday experience. This is quite different from what happens when the moral symbolism stands supreme, quite different from Dante, for instance: he could not but accept the biblical mythology as an article of faith, but, at the same time, he could admit into his Divine Comedy the people whom he personally knew.

The effect of mythology on literature and art was not, therefore, a mere influence: not the attraction of a model, nor the impact of certain ideas. It went much deeper, affecting the artistic temperament itself. It came as an elusive but compelling power of suggestion, a force that at once constrained and stimulated the imagination. Mythology, says F. Solmsen in his book on Hesiod and Aeschylus, was at once the inspiration and the enemy of Greek Poetry. In some such way, a recurring dream or a distant memory haunts our mind; it baffles and charms us; it is suggestive of familiar and yet mysterious things; we struggle to make some sense out of it; and can never get rid of it.

Now, insofar as a myth portrays action, it implies important relations between the actors of that action. These relations, in order to be intelligible, must bear a human contents; but at the same time a myth also posits mysterious, divine forces. The human inevitably yields to the superhuman. Here lies a basic contradiction. It thus happened that the Greek poets, at least those that still speak most clearly to us, were deeply involved in a great struggle to humanize the myths or at least to naturalize them in the world of feeling and thought. Right at the beginning Homer achieved this task most effectively and beautifully, passing over the many oddities of myth, eliciting out of the mythical material all that could accrue to his theme, engrossed as he was upon a certain action that moved from its dramatic beginning to its dramatic end. After Homer, Hesiod and even more the tragedians grappled with the moral and theological difficulties of myth, extracting from it, each in his own particular way, a certain plan or a certain action. The myth was thus attuned to the requirements of a philosophical and poetic thought: for instance, in the figure of Prometheus in Hesiod and Aeschylus. Other poets, however, accepted the myths more or less as they stood in their traditional form, captured as they were by the sensuous mythical imagery. Foremost among them appears Pindar. If he does sometimes alter certain uncanny features of a myth, he does so out of a pious concern, not out of any creative need to humanize the material from within and resolve its inherent complexities. He simply declares that a certain story is not true, as when about Tantalus treating the gods to a banquet made up of the flesh of his son Pelops he says (**"First Olympian"**):

> No, I will never say that any of the gods is a
>   cannibal;
> ill fare those who have evil tongues.

In the same spirit, he mentions cursorily or does not mention at all those myths that absorbed the mind of the tragedians—Oedipus, the House of Atreus, Prometheus . . . His mind rested at ease upon those in which the action seemed to take place in its own right, as a force of nature, unimpeded by problems of individual responsibility.

Let us look more closely at these two different imaginative approaches.

If—as it is in Homer—the myth is to be transformed into terms of human action, the first condition is to see it objectively, as an event that might have developed otherwise or not have taken place at all. It must not be taken for granted, but rendered with a sense of that relativity which is inherent in any process. It must be dramatized, seen as the effect of feelings that have their own variable reality. That is to say, it must as much as possible be severed from the primitive mold which held together the imagery in a powerful but opaque symbolism.

If, on the other hand—as in Pindar—the myth is rendered *qua* myth, in its primitive force, the human action as a characterizing experience falls into the background. Here each material element is just as relevant. The skin of the Nemean lion, for instance, or Jason's sandal, or the bridle of the horse Pegasus: such objects are imbued with power, are signs, terms of reference, essential to the heroes and their actions. Through them the action follows its course, quite sunk into an inevitable pattern. The poet is thus presented with a series of focal points which exert their own spell. Rather than discourse, we have imagery; rather than a real story, a revelation or consummation. Myth must have been originally just this: not a story *about* a certain action or event, but an action or event embedded into a certain form—rehearsed or expressed in language, as a prophecy or a celebration or a message.

If now we turn to the Odes of Pindar, we shall find evidence of what we may call the mythical representation of action. Pindar never lets the action develop into moods and passions that have their own immediate justification. There is no such scene, for instance, as that between Paris and Helen in the third book of the *Iliad*. Even Simonides and Bacchylides leave far greater room for a certain pathos.

No, for Pindar the action is far more important than its actors, it is a divine fulfillment taking place outside the domain of individual responsibilities.

Let us take the **"Fourth Pythian,"** the longest Ode, the one that presents action at its fullest. It is addressed to Arkesilas king of Cyrene, winner at the chariot race in 462 B.C., descendant of Battus, founder of the city, who was in turn descended from Euphamus, one of the Argonauts. On the meandering journey of the Argonauts from Colchis, he received, in Libya, from a god, the gift of a clod of earth that predestined him to the colonization of that land. Thus the whole story of the Argonauts with the heroic action of Jason is introduced as a prelude to a future destiny. It is Medea that predicts this destiny right at the beginning of the poem.

Battus, we are told, was prompted by the oracle of Delphi to found Cyrene

> so that he might summon up to fulfillment
> . . . . the word of Medea
> once spoken at Thera,
> the word which Aietes' spirited daughter
> breathed forth from her immortal mouth. . . .

It will be noticed that not only does Medea predict, but her prophecy is so rendered that it seems to bring about the future event. Pindar loves such a notion. In **"Pythian 5,"** we read that lions fled away before Battus "so that the oracle might not go unfulfilled for the lord of Cyrene." In a fragment of **"Paean 8"** we read something about "a word that will accomplish its task in justice." Such an expression as "words brought to fulfillment" is typically Pindaric, compare **"Olympian 7"**; **"Olympian 1."** The relevance of all this to my point is clear. The action is visualized as an outcome—a preconceived event, something present in the mind that prophesies or utters a revelation. The passage I have quoted from **"Pythian 4"** is characteristic. The image of Medea stands out impressively on the strength of her utterance.

Let us continue our reading of the Ode in the same spirit. The Argonauts are in the island of Thera, on their return journey. Medea foretells how a descendant of Euphamus will found a glorious city, Cyrene. We might expect her to rehearse future facts, like a *deus ex machina* in Euripides. But no; the action of men founding a city is a matter of no interest to Pindar. What concerns him is the foundation as an outcome prodigiously inscribed in some sign, in some portent; and the speech of Medea dwells mostly upon that mysterious clod of earth given to Euphamus:

> That omen will bring it to pass
> That Thera one day become
> a mother of cities—
> that omen, that gift, that clod of earth
> from the hands of a god in semblance of man;
> Euphamus received it as he sprang down from the
>   prow
> at the mouth of the Lake Tritonian;

and for the portent's sake
Zeus son of Cronos rang out with thunder.
The moment it was when we hung up aloft
the bronze-jawed anchor, swift Argo's bridle.
For twelve whole days before that,
from the banks of Ocean across desert strands,
had we carried the sea-faring timber,
dragging it on with our arts.
Then the lonely god came upon us,
taking the bright face of a man beloved and
    revered.
With friendly words he began,
such words as invite you to stay, to take food,
as guests just arrived in the land.
But no, sweet return was the reason
preventing our stay.

       . . . . .

He understood why we hasted; and all of a sudden
he seized of the soil what fell to his hand,
wishing the earth as his gift.
Euphamus refused not; he jumped on the shore,
and pressing hand against hand
he received the clod possessed of a daemon.
But—I am told—of an evening,
away was it washed from the ship,
away in the midst of the brine,
driven on by the drifts of the sea.
I did urge the seamen to watch it,
each man in his turn;
but they forgot; and so is it that now,
out of season,
the seed of vast Libya is thrown
On the shores of this island.

Medea then explains the complications entailed by this loss: it is as if the extraordinary wanderings of the clod and its final rest foreshadowed the migration of men and their settlement.

What stands out above all is the picture of the god picking up the clod of earth and Euphamus receiving it. It is quite central, a term of reference to past and future; but, in point of human action, it is something quite trifling—nothing but the handing of a clod. All the more we admire the way in which Pindar has set it in high relief. Each movement, in its suddenness and decisiveness, seems sustained by fate; and Zeus sanctions it with his thunder. Here we have then a scene which is essentially mythical—poor in its human contents, but suggestively symbolical and impressive in its plastic vigor.

I shall pass now to the account of the Argonauts in quest of the Golden Fleece, which comes naturally a little after Medea's speech. Here again the mythical spirit overshadows the rendering of action in the human sense. See how the narrative begins:

    What first movement of sea-journey encompassed
       them?
    What peril bound them with strong bolts of steel?

"What first movement of sea-journey encompassed them?" The Greek is τίς γὰρ ἀρχὰ δέξατο ναυτιλίας; This is difficult to translate. In default of anything better I have tried to do it literally. Sandys has: "Tell me what was it that first befell them in their seafaring." Lattimore: "What then was the beginning of their adventure?" Burton: "What motive for the voyage welcomed them?" Sandys and Lattimore seem too matter-of-fact; Burton seems to solve the difficulty rather blandly. The words are untranslatable unless we find an equivalent image. For *archa* is in Greek at the same time "beginning," "cause," "principle," "rule." Conceived as it is by Pindar, the *archa* or "beginning" appears as an active force which, in its first movement, "receives," that is to say "takes over," "encompasses," "drags on with it," the participants in the expedition—this much, at least, seems implied by the verb *dexato*.

Right in the opening words the action is thus visualized in its totality, as a destiny. Pindar does not invoke the Muse to open up the avenues of memory. Nor does he lead us *in medias res*. Facts with their pertinent human motives hardly interest him at all. What haunts him is an action which speeds to its great conclusion.

The way in which the expedition of the Argonauts is told fits in with this opening. It is preceded by premonitions and oracles. First, Pelias, king of Iolcus, must beware of the "one-sandaled" man at the risk of his life; and Jason, his nephew, with just one sandal, appears before him asserting the claims to the kingdom. Secondly, the same Pelias is troubled by the ghost of his ancestor Phrixus who demands the recovery of the Golden Fleece, seconded by the Delphian oracle; Pelias will yield to Jason's claims, if he sets out on this quest. Jason accepts. The enterprise is thus seen as the fulfillment of a destiny. Now these preliminaries must have been handed down in the traditional myth; but Pindar makes the most of them. The interviews of Jason with Pelias and his kin, fraught with a sense of things to come, run for about a hundred lines; they are longer than the account of the expedition itself. Just as in the episode of Euphamus and the clod of earth, the anticipation of the outcome appears more important than the factual developments.

But it is in the actual rendering of the journey that the mythical touch appears most revealing and original. Take first the assembly of the heroes about to sail. They are not prompted by any overriding personal issue, but:

    Hera it was that inflamed them
    with a sweet all-persuasive desire
    for the ship Argo,
    lest any remain with his mother at home
    unnerved in a life of ease—
    that each one, along with the others,
    should, even in death,
    find a charm, a release for his strength.

Here is a sort of collective passion, "a sweet all-persuasive desire for the ship Argos"— an emotion which is very intense, and yet quite irrational, narrowly limited in its aim. What we would like to imagine as the infinite longings of restless youth is nothing but an elixir: *phar-makon* is the Greek word, which literally means "drug." This is subtly mythical in the very mode of expression. The action follows as an effect rather than an initiative.

The vicissitides of the journey are mentioned most cursorily. What stands out instead is Jason's prayer, preceding the departure:

> With a golden goblet in hand, at the stern,
> the leader
> called on the father of gods, on Zeus whose spear
>   is the lightning;
> he called on the swift-coursing sweep of the waves,
> on the winds, on the nights and the paths of the
>   sea,
> on kindness of days and on the dear chance of
>   return.
> Out of the clouds there came in reply
> a peal of thunder in unison;
> and bright sparks of lightning burst forth.

Again, the prefiguring stands foremost; the utterance, in this case, is laid over the concrete world of experience. Pindar would rather evoke winds and waves in a prayer than render them in their actual movement as Homer so often does.

The only adventure mentioned in the journey is the passage through the Symplegades, the Scylla and Charybdis of the Bosporus:

> speeding now into deep danger
> they prayed the God lord of ships
> for escape from the relentless movement
> of the Clashing Rocks—
> two of them, creatures alive
> that rolled more swiftly
> than the rows of deep-roaring winds;
> but that sailing of demigods
> now reduced them to a standstill.

It is the prayer, once more, that comes first. There is only prayer and fulfillment; nothing about the human reaction to the danger. The episode is turned into an aetiological myth.

In Colchis at last, the love of Medea and Jason is an essential development. Pindar understands this love as the effect of a charm embodied in a magic bird, the *Iynx*, or wryneck, sent by Aphrodite:

> Then was it that first
> the Queen of sharpest arrows,
> the goddess of Cyprus,
> did bring the dappled wryneck
> fast bound to a four-spoked wheel—
> a maddening bird among men;
> and she taught Jason the incantations of prayer,
> to rid Medea of all her filial devotions,
> so that Hellas be for her a passion,
> burning her mind and driving her on with the whip
>   of Seduction.

As in the other instances, things are bodied forth in advance rather than represented as they are: we have here the incantations, not the acts, of love. Moreover, narrowed down as it is into a charm rather than interpreted as an emanation of the goddess, this love gains in effectiveness what it loses in depth. It is a mythical force working its way. What follows—the action of Jason in recovering the fleece and sailing back—is very brief. With Medea's arts everything becomes easy, each movement of Jason coming as a manifestation of power without effort. So the story draws full circle, sweeping back to the point of Medea's initial speech.

The **"Fourth Pythian Ode"** is characteristic of Pindar. In all the other Odes—in those, at least, which present the narrative-mythical part most fully—we find the same imaginative principle: the actual narrative is preceded or accompanied by a vision of the myth as a whole, whether the vision be contained in a prophecy, or a prayer, or a dream, or some kind of message.

Sometimes the action itself is quite contained in the preceding vision, and then the poet simply tells us that it actually took place. So, in the **"First Olympian,"** Pelops prays Poseidon for the winning of Hippodameia giving details of that dangerous suit; and the actual exploit, interesting as it is, follows in one brief line. Or, in the **"Sixth Olympian,"** the future of Iamos as a seer and his establishment in Olympia is all contained in his prayer to Poseidon and in the Delphic oracle; there is little about his actual achievement.

Elsewhere the action grows out of the vision at some length. In **"Olympian 13"** the exploits of Bellerophon with Pegasus are fore shadowed in the dream in which Athena appears to him. In **"Pythian 9"** the consummation of Apollo's love for Cyrene is accounted for beforehand in Cheiron's prediction. In **"Isthmian 8"** the marriage of Peleus and Thetis and the birth of Achilles are traced beforehand in the designs of fate and the conversations of the gods. In other instances the happening itself is surrounded with an atmosphere of prophecy—as the birth of Iamos in **"Olympian 6,"** that of Heracles in **"Nemean 1,"** that of Ajax in **"Isthmian 6."** Or it is a principle of divine retribution which is enforced like an oracle, as in the plight of Coronis in **"Pythian 3."** In **"Nemean 10"** the Dioscuri fight with the sons of Aphareus; but it is a sense of their alternate immortality which occasions the story, opening it and concluding it.

In the Odes which I have mentioned the action is not really told, but delivered, accounted for. It does not take the form of a straight narrative, nor of an apologue. It is not described, but molded into the pattern of its delivery, in the way in which a certain act is stated in an oath or a promise.

Such a mythical view of events was perfectly fitted to Pindar's mind. What struck him was the wholeness, the culmination of achievement. Word and phrases which mean consummation, crowning touch, acme, summit, abound in his poetry. . . . Everything must be presented in a sort of finality and fullness. Now a myth aims precisely at this. Take again the toils of Heracles as an example. They are not really actions, but in the Greek word that describes them, *athloi*—that is to say, tests only carried out in view of the outcome. A sense of the outcome precedes the beginning itself. The ups and downs of action are minimized. Pindar, in this sense, is quite mythical—not because he goes into fantastic details, but because he stresses a sense of mysterious and powerful destination even in the simplest deeds, and subordinates to it everything else. This appears not only in the general pattern, but in the details of the representation. Look, for instance, at the way situations are dramatized through dialogue: the characters hardly ever talk to one another about an immediate issue or about mutual feelings, but their conversation turns to some future event which by far transcends the present—as in the case of Pelias and Jason in **"Pythian 4."** But the dialogue is most often left out. The implications of this are clearest in the love scenes. Pindar's women—Evadne, Cyrene, Coronis—do not speak at all. They are lovely fruits to be plucked and enjoyed for the sake of a secret destiny; and all feelings, all unspoken words are gathered in the divine imagery of Aphrodite and desire.

Now this mythical conception leads to a certain form of narrative style. As the action is first viewed in its completion, we find it ordered in a pattern that seems to contradict the ordinary time sequence of experience. It is as if the story started from the end. So we are shown Cyrene landing with Apollo in Libya before we are shown their first encounter; and then again the flight to Libya is mentioned. We thus have a circular motion: end-beginning-end. This is known as *ring composition*, thanks to L. Illig who dealt with it in his book on Pindar's narrative form. It is now common knowledge. But scholars seem to look at it simply in terms of style. Burton points out that through this type of composition "the outlines of the story are sketched at the beginning in such a way as to arouse curiosity about the details." H. and A. Thornton, in their book *Time and Style,* treat the whole subject as part of the appositional mode of expression. Van Groningen points to the same form of composition as something peculiar to archaic Greek. I should like to stress, instead, the mythical implications. There is something inevitable, predetermined, in a myth. The premises project over the outcome, and the outcome is somehow given in the premises. The dénouement is known in advance. It is so even in Homer and the tragedians; though they spiritualized the myths, the material skeleton remained: that is why their transitions and developments are so full of human tension—as if the spirit of each passage labored against a superimposed pattern. But in Pindar there is no such break. The actions he portrays hardly rise above the basic mythical element into a sphere of their own. They are manifestations rather than individual exertions. They necessarily proceed by fits and starts, propelled by the same force that spells out the beginning and the end. Their movement is wayward and predetermined at the same time. The various stages are really shifts of position revolving around the same center. The mythopoeic spirit presents itself in a cyclical form.

The so-called ring composition, I imply, characterizes a mythical view of action. But let us look at it in itself and by itself, outside any historical frame of reference. Let us abandon, therefore, the technical term *Ring-composition.* What is the meaning of it in general terms? It is that an action is viewed as an outcome rather than as a development from beginning to end. The feeling for the outcome stirs the mind to inquire after the beginning and quickly survey the actual course of action, returning to the outcome. We have a sort of circular movement, as in Pindar's myths.

Now such a notion is certainly not confined to Pindar or to certain archaic poets. It is deeply familiar to us. It is quite natural. It lies in our reaction to the announcement of any calamity or good fortune. What first looms to our mind's eye is, for instance, the image of someone triumphant or dead, a blessing or a curse; and only later do we inquire into how and why it happened, when we reassess the outcome with a clearer mind. This attitude is reflected in the newspapers: there are the headlines, then the subtitles, then the whole story. The same is true about many films, plays, novels, especially when the plot is all-important. Though they do not set forth the outcome in advance, yet it runs through them as a driving motive right from the beginning. In a thriller, for instance, is not the key to the whole situation an overriding point of interest, prepossessing to the author's mind? We are tempted to read the last pages, we might even read the book backwards.

Now I call all this mythical in a particular sense. A newspaper headline—just like a myth in Pindar—presents the action as an outcome, as a blessing or a curse. It leaves no room for contemplation. It renders nothing for its own sake. No act, no word, is given the full worth of its own spontaneous significance. As we read, we are surprised, baffled, curious; we are induced to admire or to reprove. In each case, the actuality of the event escapes us. We are given a message which we take for granted: something mythical—that is to say, crystallized, hypostatized, claiming recognition on the strength of what it purports and not through the transparency of its realization or identity.

Opposed to the mythical, I would say, is the representation of an action from beginning to end in its own inherent and intimate unity. Aristotle expounded it in his *Poetics,* dwelling on Homer and on Tragedy. We have here a poetic unity, not the impenetrable wholeness of myth. The stress falls on the process rather than on brute facts. Beginning and ending become the indispensable terms of an inner development, not landmarks of fate imposed from without. Such are the climax and anticlimax in the wrath of Achilles, but not, say, in the forebodings of Pelias. It follows that in a poem like the *Iliad* our mind rests upon inner themes rather than upon a certain pattern of events— upon Achilles' feeling of mortality rather than upon the doom that willed him to die young.

The action poetically conceived, rendered in the inner motives that span its development and sustain its unity, followed through its creative phases from beginning to end—this is what I would oppose to the mythical action, the action viewed as a compact uncontroversial event, powerful perhaps and mysterious, but taken for granted, whether brought about by divine agencies as the ancients believed or by a mechanical concatenation of factors, as we tend to believe today. I would say that the former conception—let me call it the poetical conception—is the rarer one, though at first sight it might appear the simpler and easier one. All too frequently do we lose sight of the delicate existential thread, and yield to the superstructures of myth, whatever that myth may be.

I am opposing, at this point, the terms "mythical" and "poetical," though I realize that the values they describe may overlap in the work of the same poet, and even within the same phrase. Poetry, I would say, apprehends the object directly, rendering it in a transparent imagery; while myth visualizes it in a certain function which it imputes to it *a priori*. Homer's "rose-fingered Morn" or Aeschylus' "numberless laughter of the sea," I would say, are no more mythical than Keats' "night's starred face"; but when Pindar calls rain "pitiless host born of the thundering cloud" (**"Pythian 6"**), I find in the expression a mythical strain. It is that myth endows objects with powers and properties which must be taken literally and are unrelieved by any idealizing metaphorical touch. This also applies to the treatment of action. In myth the rhythms of life are sacrificed to the downright sweep of what happens; there is no room for those solitary individual acts upon which Homer shed so much light with his similes.

Myths, however, are ultimately suggestive of life; and the mythical action, in its compact bulk, may well be awesome and inspiring. But the poetry that grows out of it contains an alien element; it has to rely for its effect upon preconceived notions of power. Pindar, at his best, recovers the poetic moment of a mythical action; and yet, at a certain point, the mythical mold arrests the poetic development—as, for instance, in the lovely passages about Apollo and Cyrene, whom the god (**"Pythian 9"**)

> carried away from the wind-echoing folds of mount Pelion,
> a wild virgin enclosed in his chariot of gold,
> and made her the queen of a land rich in sheep, rich in fruit,
> to dwell in the blossoming root of the earth's third portion.

> There she received them—Aphrodite of the silver feet,
> laying her hand on the god-built chariot
> with the lightest touch;
> and upon their sweet bedding she shed
> a spell of desire and coyness.

To appreciate this we must be attuned to the religion of Aphrodite, to the mythical imagery, to that massive sweep and that delicate touch. But what of Cyrene herself, what of Apollo? The heart-beat of experience is silenced in one magic movement, one gesture.

Whoever wishes to get a glimpse of the myth-making process must turn to Pindar. He naturally transforms even contemporary events into myths. **"Pythian 1,"** for instance, is a sort of hymn to harmony under the sway of Zeus whereby Typhon and all monsters are for ever defeated; then, later on in the Ode, we find Hieron, tyrant of Syracuse, and his victory over Carthaginians and Etruscans. Myth and history are thus presented on the same level. This is not done by way of similes, but by letting the tide of myth sweep up to the present. What about Hieron, the person, the cruel tyrant? In **"Olympian 1"** we find him.

> wielding the scepter of justice,
> plucking all the blossoms of virtue,
> rejoicing in the high strains of music.

It is the same with Pindar's victorious athletes. We hardly see them as persons; they rather appear as statues. And what about their action? Their athletic exploits were well suited to Pindar's mode of representation. Here were actions carried out in the contemporary scene but quite removed from ordinary human experience—shows of strength wholly converging towards success in a sacred atmosphere: all human complexities stolidly simplified in a present myth. Pindar does sometimes extract poetry from the figure of a young athlete, as in a famous passage of **"Pythian 8"**:

> A newly won splendid thing in his hands,
> in the luxuriance of youth,
> spurred by great hope,
> he rides on the wings of his strength,
> with thoughts that rise above fortune.
> Brief is joy's growth: the purpose shifts,
> and down is it dashed to the ground.
> Ephemeral creatures, what are we? What are we not?
> The dream of a shadow.
> But if a flash descends from heaven,
> a clear light rests upon men and life is sweet.

. . . These lines could be applied to life in general, and not only to an athlete. They have a clear resonance. And yet Pindar cannot help treating experience mythically, even outside the heroic age. That hope, that strength, that virtue, that light are conceived as external agencies, as presences that enshroud all particular feature; and they prevent us from getting closer to that young man, to that image of youth. Myth intervenes in the very paths of perception. Reality shimmers a moment and disappears.

Geoffrey S. Conway (essay date 1972)

SOURCE: The introduction to his translation of *The Odes of Pindar*, London: J. M. Dent & Sons, 1972, pp. xi-xxvi.

[*In the following excerpt, Conway presents an overview of Pindar's odes, including principal themes, structure, and historical background.*]

The Odes of Pindar were written in honour of victors in the events of the four great national athletic meetings of ancient Greece, held at regular intervals at Olympia, at Delphi (the Pythian Games), on the Isthmus of Corinth and at Nemea. These Games were in each case part of one of the four Panhellenic festivals, the most important of all the religious festivals of ancient Greece.

THE PANHELLENIC GAMES AND THE EPINICIAN ODE

Competitive athletic meetings had from early times been a regular part of Greek life, and by the time of Pindar, whose working years covered the first half of the fifth century B.C., these were widespread amongst the cities of Greece. Such local festivals however were far surpassed in importance by the four Panhellenic meetings, and superlative honour attached to those who were successful in these most eagerly contested of all Greek athletic competitions. On their return to their native city the victors were abundantly fêted and given distinctions and privileges of various kinds, sometimes including a free table at the headquarters of the local government. The fête in honour of the victor's success was held in combination with religious rites, and often followed by a banquet. Where an Ode in honour of the victory, known as an 'epinician' Ode, had been commissioned, its performance was an important part of this celebration. The epinician Ode was written for accompaniment by music and a dance, and was performed by a chorus of singers and dancers. Little knowledge has come down to us of the music and dances, but their composition was undertaken by the writer of the Ode and was held to be of no less importance than the words. The writer was also responsible for the training of the chorus, and if he attended the celebration, though this might involve him in a lengthy journey to the victor's city, he would also direct the performance of the Ode. Sometimes a triumphal march or procession took the place of the dance. A few of Pindar's short Odes, on those occasions when he had himself been an onlooker at the Games, as he not infrequently was, were written immediately on the victor's success and performed at the venue of the athletic meeting, at a fête, or procession to the temple, held on the evening of the contest or before the conclusion of the festival. Most of his Odes however were completed after an interval of time and delivered for performance at the home of the victor.

THE MYTHS

Pindar was the author of many different kinds of lyric poetry—he is credited with the composition of seventeen books of various types of poems—but except for his four books of epinician Odes, corresponding with the four Panhellenic festivals, which have come down to us in nearly complete form, his other works now consist only of fragments, few of them of any length. A feature of his Odes, written in conformance with rules for lyric poetry well established by Pindar's time, is the inclusion in each Ode, except the few very short ones, of a myth, a story chosen from the vast stock of Greek mythological legends with which most Greeks were familiar from childhood onwards. We thus find expressed in lyrical form a combination of epic and lyric material which adds no little to the interest and attractiveness of these poems.

THE EPINICIAN ODE AND THE PANHELLENIC IDEAL

The Panhellenic festivals and Games, which were open to all men of Greek birth, were attended by great numbers of pilgrims, competitors or onlookers drawn from all parts of the Greek world, including such distant places as the Greek cities in south Italy and Sicily, Cyrene in North Africa and the island of Rhodes in the eastern Aegean, as well as from all parts of the mainland of Greece and the Greek islands. They played an important part amongst those elements in Greek life which helped to foster the Panhellenic spirit, to strengthen the idea of a common Hellenic tradition and a unity of outlook in religious and cultural spheres. Other such elements were the bond of their common language, their common recognition of Delphi as the supreme oracle and centre of religious worship for all Greeks, and their common inheritance of the poems of Homer, held in veneration throughout the Greek world for many centuries both before and during the Classical era of Greece. The poems of Pindar can certainly be regarded as a further influence, by no means a small one, tending in the same direction. Though his Odes are concerned with particular achievements, his treatment of his subject-matter frees it from all local limitations, and his poetical genius raises the victor's achievement and the poem which celebrates it out of the sphere of every-day reality to the plane of the ideal. His myths, treating as they do of the legends of gods, heroes (demigods) and mortals of mythical antiquity and their more than human exploits, are in keeping with this idealizing tendency. The competitors in the 'Great Games,' for whom his Odes were written, were for the most part drawn from members of wealthy and aristocratic families who took pride in tracing their descent from the heroes of antiquity, and through them, often enough, from the gods themselves. It need not surprise us that his Odes became the treasured possessions of the families to whom they were delivered, or that one of his best-known Odes **"Olympic VII"** written in honour of Diagoras of Rhodes, is said to have been set up in letters of gold in the temple of Pallas Athene in Lindus, one of three main cities of the island.

The connection of the myth with the victory which the Ode celebrates is not always a close one, deriving sometimes from the reputed ancestral descent of the victor's family, sometimes from the mythical figures associated with the early legends of the victor's city, sometimes from some similarity in the nature or circumstances of the victory with the legendary tale. In some Odes the connection is more subtle and less easily defined. Pindar's handling of his myths appears to have been a special target for the criticisms of his rivals or adversaries, often jealous of the high reputation which his poetry achieved from fairly early in his career. His myths are rarely told in a conventional way, though they are no less effective for this, sometimes consisting of briefly told references rather than the full story, and on occasion telling the story back to front, the final outcome announced first, followed by the preceding incidents, e.g. the stories of Castor and Pollux, and of

Perseus and Medusa. To a Greek audience, to whom those legends were familiar, this would be of little account.

RELIGION AND ETHICS

The content of Pindar's Odes makes it quite clear that their purpose was much more than that of providing an attractive record of a joyful event. Descriptions of the victor's actual athletic achievement are not given, but the Odes find their main theme in extolling the fine qualities— the *aretê* or excellence of spirit—which have enabled the victor to rise to the heights of supreme skill; and the hard work of the preliminary training is frequently included as an additional mark of that merit. The Greek word *aretê*, in other contexts often translated 'virtue', has a much wider meaning than that English word, and can apply to high merit in almost any activity that is praiseworthy or skilful. It is also used by Pindar, more often in the plural than the singular, to mean the actual deeds, usually deeds of courage or heroism, which exemplify the spirit of the doer:

> Brave deeds, high merits are ever rich in story

This quality of excellence which has now proved itself in action, thus earning the praises which will give it immortality, 'For words live longer down the years than deeds', is the prevailing *motif* of the Odes, and this is combined with the theme that such qualities, and the successes they bring, derive from the will of heaven:

> For from the gods comes every skilled endeavour
>   Of mortal quality

> This path of glory where his sandals tread
>   Is given of heaven

Reverence for the gods is constantly emphasized, and that a man's aims, however great his capabilities, should be in keeping with divine law:

> God achieves all his purpose and fulfils
> His every hope

> But if a man shall hope in aught he does
> To escape the eyes of god, he makes an error

The need for humility in a man's outlook and the avoidance of acts of pride and insolence is equally stressed:

> Seek not to become Zeus . . .
>   For mortals mortal gifts are fitting.

> But violence brings to ruin even
> The boastful hard-heart soon or late

Many of his myths exemplify the theme of the punishment which attends failure to comply with the eternal laws, e.g. the myths of Tantalus **"Olympian I,"** of Ixion **"Pythian II,"** and of Asclepius and his mother Coronis **"Pythian III."** It will be clear to readers of the Odes that Pindar regarded his function as that of a preacher as well

as that of a poet. His poems give forceful and clear expression to the traditional beliefs and moral or ethical standards which over many centuries had helped the Greek people to reach the position they enjoyed by the beginning of the fifth century B.C., a position which enabled them, not without justification, to regard the Hellenic race as the possessor of gifts of a special kind, and encouraged them to look on other races as people of quite a different order.

> **"The content of Pindar's Odes makes it quite clear that their purpose was much more than that of providing an attractive record of a joyful event. . . . the Odes find their main theme in extolling the fine qualities—the *aretê* or excellence of spirit—which have enabled the victor to rise to the heights of supreme skill. . . .**
>
> —*Geoffrey S. Conway*

In general however Pindar does not attempt any analysis or close definition of what constitutes right or wrong action. He was a man of conservative mind and his poems were composed for people of a similar outlook. They assume that the principles of right and wrong are generally recognized and that the individual conscience will not have difficulty in deciding what actions are or are not in keeping. In these respects his poems have no direct share in the great outburst of liberalizing ideas which found its zenith in the latter half of the fifth century and the ensuing years of the fourth. Though the origin of many of these new ideas can be traced to the influence of writers of Pindar's time, notably to Aeschylus, Pindar's exact contemporary, and to Sophocles, his junior by twenty-five years, we cannot look to Pindar for an expression of the more considered philosophies and the attitude of enquiry and rational analysis which found their place in the world after his time. But his poems throw a bright light, probably more clearly than any other writer, on the beliefs and standards prevalent amongst the Greeks of his own earlier age. The Greek achievement and its pre-eminent influence on future civilizations is sometimes apt to be remembered mainly in respect of its later more intellectually diversified period. Pindar's poetry is a reminder of the splendid foundation on which that later development rested.

PINDAR'S POETRY

It is not however to Pindar's thought or philosophy that we look to find the qualities that have given his poems their unique reputation. It is as a master of language and a poet of supreme lyrical merit that his name has won such well-deserved fame. His poems show, amongst their more obvious characteristics, superb qualities of vigour and vividness and a mastery of metre and imaginative diction. Expressing, as has been suggested, much of what lay at the root of the Hellenic spirit, often in terms of impressive weight, they display a mind of marked individuality whose engaging idiosyncrasies are constantly felt, whether in his methods of expression or in the skill with which he laces together the various elements, often numerous and differing in kind, of a particular poem. In the choice and order of his words and in the magnificent sound of his lines Pindar reveals himself as a superb craftsman at the height of his technique, unfolding a lyrical beauty which a translation cannot reproduce. Nor can we reconstruct the music or the melodies and dances which were an integral part of the composition and production of the Ode.

It may be useful however to make brief mention of a few basic features of Pindar's style and method. His poems are marked by the swiftness of his transition from image to image and from thought to thought, and by an abundant and strikingly imaginative use of metaphor—it was Aristotle in his *Poetics*, written in the fourth century B.C., who referred to the use of metaphor as 'the token of genius.' Poetry becomes in Pindar's phrases:

> . . . the fine flower
> Of music's utterance

> A pillar . . . whiter than Parian marble

> . . . this gift
>   Of milk and honey blended,
> And the cream of the mixing crowns the bowl,
>   A draught of song
> Borne on the breath of flutes of Aeolis.

Many of man's activities contribute to the picture of poetry and its inspiration:

> Many a swift arrow my quiver holds
>   . . . . speaking to men of wisdom

> . . . my Muse in her array
> Nurses her strongest dart of all.

> Listen, I plough the meadow
>   Of Aphrodite of the glancing eyes, or of the
>   Graces

>   . . . that my hand may till
> The precious beauty of the Graces' garden.

Or the poem becomes a ship, while Pindar rebukes himself for straying off course:

> Oh heart of mine,
> To what far foreign headland
> Lead you my sail astray?

> About, my ship: to Europe's mainland
> Turn once again your sail

Sometimes his metaphors are mixed:

> Hold now your oar, and quickly from the prow
> Cast anchor to the deep sea-bed, to hold

> Our ship from the rocky reef.
> For like a bee flitting from flower to flower,
>   The rich strain of my songs of triumph
> Lights now on one tale now upon another.

In another passage Pindar suggests:

>   . . . maybe to souls below the earth
>   Great deeds are known,
> Sparkling in the soft dew of flowing songs of
>   triumph

Another feature of interest, one which again makes the meaning of some passages less easy to grasp at first sight, is his frequent habit of interspersing, at appropriate places in his text, comments or 'asides', usually quite briefly expressed, related more or less directly to the passage in which they occur. These 'asides' are always phrased in general terms and are of a general validity, as are our own proverbs; they usually serve to point the moral, briefly and pithily, to the theme or story which is being handled. Sometimes they appear to have the further purpose of providing a useful link passage to bridge over a change in the subject matter or in the flow of thought. In a few cases, where the 'aside' seems to be introduced with almost surprising abruptness, it is usually a sign that the passage which is to follow it is one on which Pindar wishes to throw special emphasis. The main interest however of these 'asides' is that they contribute with much else in Pindar's poetry to furnish us with a clearly cut picture of his lively convictions, whether on ethical or moral themes, or on various other aspects of human behaviour, or on topics such as the poet's inspiration and the importance of his art:

> Yet only of god's giving
> In a poet's heart is born the flower of song.

> The songs inspired of heaven

On occasion they supply us with forcibly expressed comments on his critics and rivals, amongst whom were often to be found, though they are never mentioned by name, the poets Simonides and Bacchylides, who were also composers of epinician Odes and other lyrical poetry. In two such passages he likens himself to an eagle compared with lesser birds:

> . . . taught skills, rough-hewn,
>   Gross-tongued, are like a pair
> Of ravens vainly chattering
> Before the divine bird of Zeus.

And with an apology for the late delivery of a poem:

> Though it comes late. Yet of all birds on wing
> Swift is the eagle, from the deep sky afar
>   Spying his mark,
>   Lo, suddenly hath he seized, swooping,
>   His tawny-dappled prey.
> But chattering daws have a lowly range.

Pindar makes clear his firm belief that the true poet was divinely inspired, and does not conceal his own justifiable pride in the excellence of his own art:

> Inborn of nature's wisdom
> The poet's truth
>
> . . . the task divinely given

In a metaphor from the long-jump, with another rapid change of image, he writes:

> . . . rake a long landing-pit
> Straightway for me; my limbs can muster
> A nimble spring; even o'er the main
>   Eagles can wing their way.
> Through all Hellas pride of the poet's art.

An aristocrat himself, and one whose work and friendships lay largely amongst people of his own kind, Pindar was fittingly a great believer in the value of inherited qualities. Many of his most forceful comments are intended to point the superiority of inborn genius over acquired or instructed skills, not only in the sphere of poetry but in many other of man's activities:

> . . . let him follow straight
> The paths appointed, striving with the skill
>   That nature's gift endowed him.
>
> His inborn fate decrees each man's achievement
>
> . . . By worth
> Of inborn talent a man
> Wins rich repute. Whose art is but instructed,
> An obscure feather-brain he

Pindar's conservative inclinations made him a respecter of established authority and of wealth and possessions, provided their possessors were aware of the responsibilities these entailed and used them with justice and generosity.

> The best that fate can bring
> Is wealth joined with the happy gift of wisdom.
>   . . . Wealth too,
> Be it with noble deeds inwrought,
>   Brings gifts of many a kind,
> Sustaining deep and troublous cares,
> A shining star, light of sure trust for man

This is followed by a warning that in the next world

> Hearts that were void of mercy
> Pay the due penalty

Frequently featured in his Odes are short and vividly expressed warnings to the victors whom he is praising against the dangers of pride and excessive ambition. The theme that success can only derive from the favour of heaven also finds frequent repetition:

> . . . Therefore forget not
> . . . to ascribe
> This glory to none other but the hand of god.
>
>   . . . For from thee,
> Great Zeus, only may mortal souls be given
> Worth of true excellence
>
> But success lies not in the power of men;
>   It is a deity bestows it,
>   Exalting one man now, another
>   Crushing beneath strong hands.

On occasion Pindar addresses remarks to himself, sometimes by way of an apology for a digression, or to explain a change in his theme:

> Be still my tongue; here profits not
> To tell the whole truth with clear face unveiled.
> Often is man's best wisdom to be silent.

After a digression, Pindar tells himself to return to his proper theme:

> Search nearer home. There you have fitting glory,
> Rich theme for song.

STRUCTURE OF THE ODES

The normal arrangement of the Pindaric Ode, though many Odes vary from this, is not difficult to follow. The athletic contest celebrated by the poem is not directly described, but it often colours the metaphors and similes used. Starting with a short invocation to one of the gods, or to the Muse or Muses, or some other appropriate deity, the poem proceeds to praise of the victor and his success, often including eulogies of his family and ancestors or of his native city. Then follows the myth, usually occupying the central and longest section of the poem, after which the Ode concludes with further eulogies of the victor. A due tribute to the tutelary god of the Games in which the victory was won—to Zeus, Apollo or Poseidon as the case may be—was always included by Pindar, often with repeated emphasis. Mention by name of the victor's father and of any other athletic successes gained by the victor appears also to have been a *sine qua non*, and it is clear from some of the Odes that the commission given to Pindar frequently included instructions or the mention of this or that relative or ancestor, and of any athletic successes, or sometimes other distinctions, gained by members of the family.

Of the forty-five Odes of Pindar which have come down to us, a minority, seven in all, consist of a succession of stanzas, known as strophes, of identical length and metre in any one Ode. This form appears to have been more suitable for performance in company with a triumphal march or procession, rather than a dance. The remaining thirty-eight Odes are made up of triads, each triad consisting of three stanzas, the strophe, antistrophe and epode. In any one poem the strophe and antistrophe are of identical length and metre, the epode slightly different. Subject to this arrangement of stanzas, each Ode has its own metre differing from that of any other. This is also the case in the seven Odes made up of a succession of strophes. The present translation conforms in these respects with the original Greek, but the English metres adopted are necessarily quite different from the Greek, which were governed by entirely different and far stricter rules of metrical scansion. The Odes vary considerably in length; those made up of strophes vary between two strophes and twelve; those made up of triads consist mainly of three, four or five triads; a few shorter Odes have only one triad, and one exceptional Ode **"Pythian IV,"** a notably fine one, has thirteen triads, i.e. thirty-nine stanzas.

ORDER OF THE ODES

Editions of Pindar's Odes, both of earlier years and of more recent publication, maintain the traditional order of the Odes in each book, though this is not the order of their dates of composition. . . .

Readers will notice that the last three Nemean Odes do not refer to victories won at the Nemean Games. The ninth Ode ["**Nemean 9**"] celebrates a victory won at the games of Sicyon, the tenth ["**Nemean 10**"] a victory at Argos, and the eleventh ["**Nemean 11**"] is not in honour of any athletic success, but celebrates the appointment of a Greek named Aristagoras to the presidency of the island of Tenedos, though, as the Ode mentions, he had won successes at various unnamed athletic meetings. The reason for this is that in the earliest manuscripts of Pindar's Odes, the four books were no doubt arranged in the order of importance in which the four festivals were regarded, that is, with the Isthmian book third and the Nemean book last. These three Odes, as they have a closer resemblance to epinician Odes than to any other category of lyric poetry, were no doubt tacked on as an appendix to the last book of the four. At some later date, in copies made of the earlier manuscripts, the Isthmian and Nemean books changed places, and as the earlier manuscripts disappeared, that has remained the traditional order of the books through later editions, leaving the three Odes to appear under the Nemean title.

THE PANHELLENIC FESTIVALS

The Panhellenic festivals and Games, and the order of importance in which they were held, were as follows:

1. The Olympian festival was founded, according to the earliest historical records which have come down to us, in the year 776 B.C. This year came to be adopted by Greek historians as the first in the Greek calendar, from which all subsequent events were dated. Olympia lies in the district of Elis in the north west of the Peloponnese, and was situated beside the river Alpheus not far from the city of Pisa. The festival was held every four years in honour of Zeus, king of the gods, and the prize awarded to victors in the Games was a wreath of wild olive.

2. The next in importance were the Pythian Games, held at Delphi once in every four years, two years after those of Olympia, in honour of Apollo, god of music, poetry and the arts, and of prophecy. The prize for victors was a wreath of laurel. The festival was founded (or put on a firmer footing in place of an earlier existing one) in the year 582 B.C.

3. The Isthmian Games were held every two years on the Isthmus of Corinth, in honour of Poiseidon, god of the sea of subterranean powers. Their establishment, or revival, is attributed to the year 582 B.C. The prize awarded was a wreath of wild parsley or of pine.

4. The Nemean Games were held every two years at Nemea, near the small town of Cleonae in the north-eastern part of the Peloponnese, about twenty miles south of Corinth. They were held in honour of Zeus and the prize was a wreath of wild parsley. The date of their foundation or revival was 573 B.C.

Greek legend attributed the foundation of the Panhellenic festivals to much earlier periods; the Olympian Games, for example, are pictured as founded by Heracles, and the Nemean Games by Adrastus, a legendary king of Argos, in times anterior to any historical records. It is significant of the importance in which the Panhellenic festivals were held throughout Greece, that on their approach a sacred truce was proclaimed by heralds sent to all Greek states. Even in a period of constant inter-state warfare the truce was rarely if ever broken, and the safety of travellers to the festival was assured. In the district of Elis in which Olympia lies, any soldier-in-arms who crossed the border of that state during the festival was treated as a prisoner of war who could not return to his own state until he had been ransomed.

THE GAMES

The competitive events which made up the Panhellenic Games were chariot-races, horse-races, foot-races (including the race for men in armour), the long-jump, boxing, wrestling, the pankration (a combination of boxing and wrestling, probably with a wide licence of rules), javelin-throwing, hurling the discus, and the pentathlon, an event combining the foot-race, the long-jump, the javelin, the discus, and a wrestling match. The four-horsed chariot-race enjoyed the highest prestige, and entailed the highest honour for the victor.

At Delphi, where musical programmes had been a feature of the earlier festival reorganized in 582 B.C., two competitions were added: singing to the flute and a solo on the flute. Playing on the lyre was added in 558 B.C. At Olympia a mule-chariot-race existed for a period of about fifty years until discontinued in 444 B.C.

The competitor whose name appeared as the official entrant for an event, and to whom in case of his victory the epinician Ode was addressed, did not always compete himself in the horse or chariot-races, but could delegate this to a subordinate. The powerful Sicilian rulers, Hieron and Theron, for whom several of Pindar's Odes were written, did not themselves ride in the races which gave them their victory, though Theron's young nephew Thrasybulus acted as charioteer for his father Xenocrates, the brother of Theron, in the race celebrated in Pindar's **"Sixth Pythian Ode,"** in 490 B.C. the majority of the victors addressed in Pindar's Odes were however actual participants in the events. The expense of entry, which involved not only the cost of training, the supply of horses and equipment etc., but sometimes of lavish contributions to the religious rites of the festival, was considerable.

There were three classes of event: for grown men, for youths (the 'beardless' class) and for boys. Professional trainers were employed, particularly for boy competitors, during the arduous training which preceded the competitor's entry. The Games and the religious rites were open only to males. Women were strictly excluded, even from participation as spectators. Only one noteworthy exception is recorded to this rule. A famous wrestler, Diagoras of Rhodes, celebrated in Pindar's **"Seventh Olympian Ode,"** won victories at all four Panhellenic festivals. His three sons were also Olympian victors, and two grandsons were successful at Olympia and Delphi. His daughter Callipateira was accorded the exceptional privilege of attendance at the Games, in virtue of her being the mother, the daughter, the sister or the aunt of six Olympian victors.

AEGINETAN ODES

No less than eleven of Pindar's forty-five Odes were written in honour of victors whose home was on the island of Aegina, where it is clear that Pindar had many friends and found a society sympathetic to his poetical and musical interests. For the subjects of his myths in the **"Aeginetan Odes"** Pindar drew naturally enough from the famous stories of the clan of Aeacus, the first mythical king of Aegina, whose descendants included such great names as Peleus, Telamon, Ajax and not least Achilles. Although the Aeacid clan became dispersed to other parts of Greece these mythical heroes continued to be regarded as part of the great heritage of Aegina. . . .

Mary R. Lefkowitz (essay date 1976)

SOURCE: "Pindar's Pythian 8." *The Classical Journal*, Vol. 72, No. 3, February-March, 1977, pp. 209-221.

[*In the following essay, Lefkowitz examines the vocabulary and diction of "Pythian 8," focusing on the proem, the encounter with Alcmeon, and the last stanza.*]

I ought to begin by explaining why I want to talk about this particular ode, which celebrates the victory of Aristomenes of Aegina in the boys' wrestling contest at the Pythian games in 446 B.C. There are many practical reasons: its date is known, so we don't need to speculate; it's short, so we can read through it in relatively little time and remember what the poet has been saying; and it presents numerous difficulties (challenge is one of Pindar's principal attractions). But in the end none of these reasons truthfully explains why I want to spend time on **"Pythian**

8." I am in fact interested in the ode because of what it says: this is the victory ode that mentions the poet's meeting with a (dead) hero; the poem devotes unusual space to the reactions of the defeated; and it contains the famous (though ostensibly depressing) statement that a human being is a dream of a shadow—all of which would appear (at least at first sight) to be peculiar means of celebrating a victory.

I should say at the outset that of course I accept the basic premise from which my colleages Professor Slater and Professor Young have begun all their discussions of this poet's work: that the odes are meant to praise the victor, that they do so in conventional patterns and with conventional elements of exposition that can be named and classified and recognized in whatever mutation they may occur. I shall call attention to these structures (and they are marked in the appended translation). But I don't think we should stop there. Vocabulary and diction also matter, the words and linguistic structures the poet chooses to talk about success and failure.

Of course we can find parallels in Pindar and elsewhere to the basic thought behind phrases like "placing insolence in the bilge," "throwing one man high, another underhand," "falling on four bodies," "flying by hope on winged manliness," "man is a dream of a shadow." For example, inscriptions about the ancient games tell us that falling on four bodies simply states that wrestlers competed in a tournament structure, with successive eliminative bouts. But in context "falling from *on high* on four bodies" also makes a qualitative statement about the nature of victory that goes beyond a simple denotation of tournament procedure, because of other falls that precede and follow it in the course of the poem. Specifically, in the first antistrophe, Calm, now harsh against her enemies, opposes them by putting insolence in the bilge; in the fifth antistrophe "joy" falls to the ground, struck by a back-turning intention. By stating each time the negative as well as the positive effects of victory, the poet prepares the victor and his friends for his concluding reflection on the inevitability of defeat for all victors, and for all human beings, and gives his message a general significance that goes far beyond this particular victory in wrestling.

I have mentioned instances of fighting and falling to warn that I am going to suggest, as I have in discussing other odes, that the language of this ode has some internal consistency. To describe the function of language within an ode I sometimes use contemporary terms that have no direct analogue in ancient rhetorical theory. I have found words borrowed from music criticism convenient for my purpose: repetition, reiteration, motif, theme, elaboration, development, but I intend these words as metaphors, not as scientific terminology. Internal coherence, interrelation of ideas within the poem, if they exist, will be apparent whatever we call them, provided that we are willing to look. Do not underestimate the difficulties confronting us in contemplating any ancient text: the barriers posed by our own language, by critical issues rightly or wrongly raised by scholars, ancient and modern.

Since space is limited, in the process of reading through the ode, I would like to concentrate disproportionately on the language of passages which have since antiquity elicited animated scholarly discussion: the proem, the encounter with Alcmeon, and the last stanza (beginning with the famous lines, "creatures of a day, what is someone? what is no one?"). A copy of a special working translation is appended. Its English will seem awkward and inelegant because it follows closely the grammatical structure of the Greek, and because it tries to express root meanings of words and to represent cognate words in Greek with cognates in English.

"Kind-thinking Calm, Right's daughter—" the relevance of Calm (*Hesychia*) to a victory celebration puzzled the ancient commentators and led them to suggest some historical hypotheses: "peace" after the Persian wars, or with more likely chronology, the domination of Aegina by Athens after 457. But rather than look outside the ode for answers, let's begin instead by seeing if the poet himself tells us why he chose to begin this way. We know that in other odes the opening lines deliberately pose riddles or make impressive statements that do not completely make sense until we have heard more of the ode. The opening lines of **"Olympian l,"** for example (the famous "best is water, and gold like blazing fire shines out in the night beyond great men's wealth") makes stunning (in the Gorgon's head sense) statements about superlatives in compressed and excited phrases. In **"Pythian 8"** the syntax is more relaxed, built of coordinated clauses rather than of staccato paratactic statements, but nonetheless its contents are vague and intricate: why (for example) the emphatic initial compound adjective "kind-thinking" Calm; why does the poet then go on to spend proportionately more time describing how Calm *fights* against her enemies?

The ode begins in a traditional pattern, with an invocation and description of a goddess: it is a prayer to kind-thinking Calm, holder of keys to plans and wars, to receive the victor. We hear first that she understands how to work and to experience what is soft with accurate timing, and then that—whenever someone fixes unsweet anger into her heart, she becomes (by contrast) harsh and opposes her enemies' power by putting their insolence in the bilge (which might seem suddenly to imply that she has become a hoplite fighting on shipboard). An example of her power follows: Porphyrion did not learn that he was rousing her to wrath beyond his destiny." The specific illustration prompts a general reflection: "gain is best when one takes it from the house of one who is willing."

A reference to insolence (*hybris*) would lead a Greek audience to expect a reminder of this sort, not to try to take what the gods do not want to give. But by phrasing familiar advice in terms of removing something from a household (ἐκ δαμων), the poet keeps us within the confines of the opening description of Calm's domain: like a priestess at a temple or *heroön,* she has the keys to the storeroom that contains the plans and wars.

The first epode restates—again in terms of fighting—that "force makes even the great-boaster slip in time: Typhos

the Cilician hundred header did not escape her" (again there is a postponed personal pronoun, like "calm whom" in the previous stanza [τάν]). Here again Porphyrion is cited as illustration: "certainly the king of the Giants did not escape force." A final sentence links him with Zeus' arch-enemy Typhos and adds, remarkably, that *Apollo* shot him (according to the usual story it was Heracles). Reference to Apollo serves as a transition back to the victory the ode is celebrating: Apollo, like Calm in the opening prayer, welcomes (ἔδεκτο, cf. δέκεν, "welcome,") the victor, Xenarces' son. The detail "with kindly mind," further associates Apollo with "kind-thinking calm," who understands how "to enact and experience what is soft." Reference to "Xenarces' son from Cirrha," namely the victor Aristomenes, "crowned with Parnassus' grass and a Dorian victory procession" moves us directly to the present moment, restating in concrete and visible terms the first general prayer to Calm to welcome Pythian victory honor for Aristomenes.

Granted then that this opening triad provides in the appropriate place the appropriate conventional information, the name of the victor, his father, the place of victory, an estimation of the value of victory (i.e., that it is an event analogous though not equivalent to the victories of the gods), a warning not to try for much more—nonetheless, the way all these things are expressed sets the pattern for language and action in the rest of the ode.

For example, at the beginning of the second triad, where Aegina, the victor's homeland, is described as "the island with her just city has fallen not far from the Graces having contact with the famous achievements of the Aeacidae"— here the first work, ἔπεσε could connote simply fate (itself a cognate word, πατμος, "falling out"), but θιγοῖσᾳ ("having contact with") a word more specific in its connotations than our "touch upon" again emphasizes that the collocation of Aegina and achievement has taken place as the result of a physical encounter. Later in the poem "falling" describes the victor's winning bout "you fell (ἔμπετες) from high above on four bodies."

Note, too, that the transition to the myth at the end of the second antistrophe is described not in terms of the traditional winged words but again in language that stresses contact: "my debt to you, child, the song that is running before my feet, may it go forth, newest of good (achievements), winged by my skill." Here, as often, the poet describes his task in terms of athletic competition, but it is interesting to observe that in this passage his words are not the traditional arrows or even missiles but rather "flying" about in a circular motion, as if emphasizing his proximity to them and his control over them.

This description of action involving close physical contact keeps within the frame of reference established in the first triad, but in a characteristically inexplicit way. It is the kind of metaphor Aeschylus uses in the *Agamemnon,* variously suggestive, inviting contemplation. The idea that the song, the poet's present debt to the victor, goes "running at my feet" (τὸ δ' ἔν ποσι μοι τράχον ἴτω τεὸν χρέος) may help explain why in the next stanza the poet speaks of the victor "in the wrestling match following the tracks of your mother's brothers," and not simply of emulating them. Concentration on motion stresses the similarities between poetry and athletics, so that one's achievement mirrors the other's and the poet can demonstrate his sympathy for andunderstanding of the victory he is celebrating.

Emphasis on the process and result of close combat emerges also in the myth. There are many ways to tell the story of the Seven against Thebes and of the Epigonoi, but Pindar's version in its compression concentrates on the victory that ultimately results from loss and conflict (i.e., Alcmeon triumphs where his father was killed), on inherited skill (Alcmeon even wields the snake that has forecasted disaster for his father Amphiaraus), and on the loss that results from victory (Adrastus loses his son). The proem similarly stated the ancestry of Calm (she is Right's daughter) and described her power in terms of her success against an adversary, whose fate claims our attention briefly toward the invocation's end: "force causes even the great-boaster to slip in time, Typhos the Cilician hundred-header did not escape her, nor did the king of the Giants. They were conquered by the thunderbolt and by the bow of Apollo." Significantly, the myth's ending, like the proem's concludes with a welcoming reception, "and in joyful greeting I also throw crowns at Alcmeon and shower him with a song of praise." In the proem Apollo with benevolent mind welcomed from Cirrha Xenarces' son crowned with Parnassus' grass and a Dorian victory procession.

The third epode closes with a remarkable affirmation of the relevance of the myth to the present time—this is one of the controversial passages that deserves our special attention. The poet concludes the myth and the epode by recounting that he (the poet) also had a prophetic experience involving Alcmeon: "because my neighbor and guard of my possessions opposed me as I was going to the sung-of navel of the earth and embraced his inborn arts of prophecies."

Let's discard (as we did in the case of the relevance of Calm in the proem) explanations of this passage that depend on determining the geographical location of Alcmeon's shrine, and look instead at the way the poet describes the encounter to see what he means by it (it's fair to assume that if he wanted us to be able to find the exact spot where Alcmeon met him he could have told us more explicitly, as, for example, in his description of Cyrene in **"Pythian 5"**). Alcmeon is called "neighbor," because the poet wishes to stress the friendly nature of the encounter. The hero-neighbor is also guard of his possessions. The neighbor-guard "opposes" the poet (ὑπάντασεν): in the proem Calm welcomes the victor Aristomenes, holds the keys to plans and wars, and opposes (ὑπαντιάξαισα, the terminology is virtually the same) her enemies. But since the poet comes (unlike Calm's enemies) without "fixing anger into his heart," "embracing prophecies" confers benefits on him: he knew that Aristomenes would win at the Pythian games. Aegina earlier in the poem has contact with the achievements of the Aeacidae. Now Alcmeon's encounter with the poet (like Aegina's with the achieve-

ments of her descendants) is a positive illustration of the conclusion drawn about Porphyrion in the opening triad of the ode: "gain is most dear when one brings it from the home of one who is willing."

References back to the language and action of the proem at the end of the third triad present an Alcmeon whose friendly actions stand in diametric contrast to the behavior of the Alcmeon of Amphiaraus' vision, the hero attacking Thebes: "I see clearly the many colored snake Alcmeon is guiding on his blazing shield at the gates of Cadmus," where the Greek word order briefly suggests an identity between the snake and Alcmeon, expressing the violent power of a chthonic deity. If we keep the special values of Greek hero cults in mind the praise the Theban poet lavishes on this enemy of Thebes seems less surprising. Other heroes are worshipped by the citizens they besieged (for example, Neoptolemus at Delphi, or cases of historical heroes noted by Herodotus, such as Onesilaus, besieger of Amathus, or Artachaeus, a Persian who died and was worshipped in Thrace). What makes a hero worthy of divine honors is his extraordinary power (for good or evil), not his politics. At the end of the narrative the poet, in the process of bestowing on Alcmeon a victor's honors, emphasizes his power to do good, to protect, to inspire. Apollo and Calm herself show the same ambidexterity in the proem, defeating their enemies with efficient violence, then welcoming and rewarding their friends.

The myth and its conclusion celebrate triumph, but not without an emphasis on loss. The natural result of this antithetical collocation is to make achievement appear to be an intermittent (i.e., not continuing) phenomenon. The last two triads of the ode restate these basic ideas in increasingly explicit terms. Immediately at the beginning of the fourth strophe, there is a second reference to Aristomenes' present and past victories, which are again described as gifts willingly bestowed by the god Apollo. A prayer for continued success necessarily follows, phrased in language that addresses the questions left unanswered in previous stanzas about the negative and positive results of violence: "o lord, with willing mind I pray that you look along some harmony about each event, however many times I return." The phrase "with willing mind" has an analogue in the "benevolent mind" of Apollo as he welcomed the victor and also in the "willing" giver in the general statement about gain that is most dear. As such, "with willing mind" establishes that Apollo also has gifts to give the poet. That the god's help takes the form of *looking* stresses the importance of vision in this ode. Amphiaraus *saw* the Epigonoi and Alcmeon's snake and prophesied victory; Alcmeon appeared to the poet.

The striking term "harmony" encapsulates the positive essence of all the preceding encounters in the poem, with their emphasis on close contact of limbs (Aegina grasping achievements; the song running at the poet's feet; the victor tracking his uncles' steps; Adrastus "held down" by an oracle; Alcmeon embracing prophecies). Homer in *Iliad* describes Odysseus and Ajax "taking hold of each other's arms in strong hands" in a wrestling match, "as when rafters [take hold of each others' arms], which a renowned carpenter has joined (ἤρᾱρε) of a high house, to keep out the might of winds." Thus engagement in conflict, like carpentry or music, involves "harmony," and can offer a constructive outcome, "to keep out the might of winds." The poet's duty demands that he praise the achievement which results from conflict, and to suggest from all the myriad events of the past analogues to present occurrences. The qualifier "some" (τιν'), reinforced by the indefinite, "however many times I return," stresses the difficulties involved in the attainment of achievement, be it athletic victory or song. The myth has already concluded by referring to the losses that result from gaining success (Amphiaraus, Adrastus' son).

The lines following comment explicitly on both the promise and the threat in the "harmony" of conflict. Victory cannot be gained without cost (only fools think otherwise). Greek poets from Homer on characteristically refer to the inevitable alternation in human life (e.g., Hesiod in the proem to the *Works and days*). But in **"Pythian 8"** destiny, like a wrestler, raising his opponent high and then throwing him down in a standard hold, enters the competition "at the measure." Calm also causes and experiences what is soft with a judge's unswerving timing. By stating a traditional thought in terms of the close contact of a wrestling match, the poet emphasizes what he had stated earlier in the myth, and in the gnomic statement about the need in life for divine support and long toil, that struggle precedes victory, though now the battle is not between fate and man in general, and the loser is not (cf. Porphyrion) guilty of *hybris*.

The second detailed description of victory continues to develop reflections about victory and defeat that are more directly applicable to the present celebration. A description of Aristomenes' successes provides an encouraging climax to the fourth triad. But this positive list of achievements is balanced in the opening of the next triad by a description of the effect of Aristomenes' victory on his opponents. In the course of conveying the straightforward information that Aristomenes won four bouts and accordingly the tournament, the poet emphasizes the degree of force involved in his victory, "you fell from on high" (ἔμπετες ὑψαθεν), instead of the more traditional ἔκλινε ("leaned on") or ἑλών ("took"). He also makes special reference to the victor's state of mind, "thinking evil thoughts" (κακὰ φρονέων)—in the myth Amphiaraus' first observation about the Epigonoi concerned their determination to defeat their fathers' enemies: "in their nature a *will* (λῆμᾰ) inborn from their fathers is recognizable." Violence, anger, a determination to value oneself above all others, despite consequences to them or to oneself, are the hallmarks of the Greek heroic character. For this reason κακὰ φρονέων ("thinking evil") is not derogatory, as it would be in terms of Anglo-American notions of good sportsmanship, but accurately descriptive of a hero attacking—Alcmeon against Thebes, as opposed to Alcmeon prophet, or to "kind-thinking" (φιλαφρων) Calm.

But then the focus shifts to the plight of the defeated: "for them all the same no happy return was judged in the Pythian festival, nor when they came to their mother did

sweet laughter raise joy all around. Down narrow ways borne from their enemies they fall back, bitten by their misfortune." In the proem, a reference to the fate of Porphyrion and Typhos followed the statement of victory, and the success of the Epigonoi is balanced by a reference to Adrastus' gathering the bones of his son, a personal loss then offset by a second reference to Alcmeon's triumph. Now in this last triad the fate of the defeated is explicitly contrasted to the victor's: "unhappy return to their mothers, down narrow street." Aristomenes was received by Apollo with benevolent mind as he returned crowned from Cirrha, and the goddess Calm was asked to receive Pythian honor on his behalf. Adrastus' unharmed army marched in triumph through "Abas' streets *broad for dancing*."

Why devote so much attention to the defeated in an ode that celebrates victory? The description of the losers' return economically conveys a traditional warning about the impermanence of victory. The thought is restated in the fifth antistrophe, "the man who wins a beautiful new thing on great luxury flies by his hope on his winged manliness and has ambition stronger than wealth. In a short time men's pleasure grows great; so it falls to the ground shaken by an intention that turns it aside." The conventional idea of the flight of deceptive hope is replaced here by a portrayal of a hopeful man flying on the wings of his own strength, only to fall in defeat. The reference to wings derives special impact from the poet's earlier description of his task, "flying winged by my skill" and from the wrestling terminology that follows, "falls to earth" and "shaken by an intention that turns it aside." The inverse image is familiar to us from the description of fate's holding his opponent high and throwing him down, and Aristomenes' triumph, "he fell on four bodies thinking evil thoughts."

The last triad of an ode characteristically turns attention back again to the present day. First what the preceding stanza implied about the transient nature of victory is applied to human experience in general: "men are creatures of a day. What is someone? What is no one? A shadow's dream is a man. But whenever Zeus given radiance comes, it is a shining light for men and life is sweet. These famous lines, so often quoted out of context, have a more affirmative meaning in context because of the many references to alternation that have preceded them Porphyrion, Amphiaraus, Alcmeon, the victor, the losers. σκιᾶς ὄναρ ἄνθρωπος, "man is a shadow's dream" describes insubstantiality, but at the same time it can be said to denote significant appearances that presage victory, Amphiaraus' vision of Alcmeon with his shield, Pindar's encounter with Alcmeon on his way to Delphi. σκιᾱ means both shadow and shade of the dead, a partial reflection of a living being. The following sentence about Zeus given glory reinforces the value even of temporary achievement, again with emphasis on gods as givers, and the sweetness earlier involved in success, the Mother's sweet laughter, and the unsweet rage of the gods' enemy Porphyrion.

A final prayer restates this general message in terms of Aegina's own history: "Aegina dear mother, with a free voyage bring home this city with Zeus and with king Aeacus and Peleus and good Telamon and with Achilles." This forceful reference to Aegina as mother, which puzzled the literal-minded scholiasts, makes perfect sense after the description of the defeated contestants' return: "nor when they came to their mother did sweet laughter rouse joy all around." Calm welcomes the victor at the beginning of the ode, her mother Right (*Dike*) stands by the victory procession. The concluding lines reinforce the significance placed on inheritance earlier in the ode (Aristomenes' following the tracks of his mother's brothers, and in the myth of the Epigonoi, especially Amphiaraus and Alcmeon): mother Aegina, Zeus father of Aeacus, Aeacus' sons Peleus and Telamon, Aeacus' grandson Achilles.

Significantly the ode ends with the strongest (and angriest) hero of all, Achilles. By returning to the pattern established in the opening lines, the female welcoming a male after a great victory, the poet concludes the ode by affirming the special qualities needed for positive achievement: force and repose. The hero is worshipped only after his death, when he is held (like Amphiaraus) within the earth, expressing his power only intermittently.

In this survey of **"Pythian 8"** I have tried to suggest that particular words and mythological references occur in this ode in distinctive, interrelated configurations, and to show why, for example, one cannot substitute at the end of this ode—no matter how generally it might seem to be expressed—the closing prayer from another ode, like **"Pythian 2"** In other words, the meaning and internal coherence of an ode does not derive solely from the traditional arrangement of its conventional parts, but from deliberate choice of vocabulary and syntax. No convenient composer's footnotes survive to explain why Pindar chooses in this particular ode to talk about encounters, welcoming and hostile, from Calm, to Alcmeon, to Aegina, and not, as for example in **"Pythian 2,"** about bestiality and taming. But if, as in other odes, the basic pattern of language is determined by the principal narrative section, we can look to the vision of Alcmeon as primary source of the special emphases in the rest of the ode. It seems particularly significant that in this, possibly the last of Pindar's victory odes, that the poet mentions traditional terms in the myth. It is interesting that the Alcmeon whom the poet encounters is no longer the combatant with the snake on his shield or the man who returned to murder the mother who was waiting to welcome him, but rather an established victor who can be greeted with joy, and whose function is to be neighbor and guard, and whose touch conveys inspiration. Brelich observes that heroes in their quiescent (i.e., subterranean form) are known by euphemistic epithets, "Crown-winner" (στεφᾶνηφαρος), "calm" (ἤσυχος), "silent" (σιγηλας) "whisperer" (ψιθυρας), "keyholder" (κλαϊκαφορος). Is this fundamental notion of constructive quiescence the source of the personification "Calm" (*Hesychia*) at the ode's opening, who also stands with her keys as guardian, and who can enact and experience "what is soft," and who *receives* the victor (δέκευ). "Receiver" also serves as a hero title; Sophocles in death was known as Δεξίων.

But whether or not the central narrative in fact sets the pattern for language elsewhere in the ode, it at least clarifies and restates in relatively straightforward terms the complex and highly metaphorical language that precedes it. It is important to recognize that and how diction varies in intensity within an ode, that later lines explain and elaborate on the striking and rather oracular statements at the ode's beginning. I would therefore caution against trying to pin down too precisely the meaning of the first stanzas of ode, or against trying to decide conclusively about particular connotation of metaphors and compound adjectives, until one has heard the myth and discerned the special emphases in the more plainly expressed praise in the ode's concluding section. Part of the listener's pleasure derives from not knowing precisely why the ode begins the way it does. The answer comes slowly, and indirectly, with reflections that develop every potential of what seems initially unrelated and even contradictory: why does Calm become violent? The end of the poem suggests reasons: combat and struggle precede success; repose and death offer a setting in which violence can have positive meaning.

The ode's various reflections on the nature of heroism in the end provide the ultimate justification for the time and effort spent (and blood shed) in our attempts to understand it. It is typical of Pindar to transform a particular event, in itself perhaps only locally and temporarily significant (like a victory in the boys' wrestling match at Delphi) into a general statement with continuing meaning. One need only compare this ode to any of the inscriptions or epigrams about wrestling victories to estimate the complexity and skill involved in Pindar's art.

Pindar's resources and techniques are in many ways similar to his dramatist colleagues' in Athens, who also used past to comment on the present, and who emphasized the general significance of particular mythical events. Like them he also is concerned with the motivations—anger, hatred, shame—that inspire men to achieve and ultimately also to fail in their endeavors. It is tempting, because this ode would have been composed toward the end of his life, to see in it some final message. Death and defeat seem more prominent in **"Pythian 8"** than in the early Hieron odes; there is no reference to healing, as in **"Pythian 3"** The comparisons of superlatives or of models of behavior characteristic of earlier odes are replaced here by unqualified statements. Even the question "what is someone? what is no one?" is answered. But I think it is a mistake, as some commentators have done, to see in the ode a sense of despair, either because the poet supposedly senses that aristocratic values are decaying, or because he resents Aegina's subjection to Athens, or because he is depressed in his old age. In fact he does not place any emphasis on any of these matters, but rather on the nature of heroism, and if any literary analogy is drawn, it should be to Sophocles' portrayal of Oedipus at Colonus. The drama has little appeal for contemporary students, and is seldom performed, but it expresses more clearly than any other extant tragedy, as Knox has shown, the distinctive nature of Greek heroism, the anger and violence that made Oedipus everything he was and is in the play, and the fame conferred on him by his final rest and death. Could the meaning of hero-cults have impressed Pindar also more strongly toward the end of his life? Possibly. But it is far more important to note (and here we no longer need to speculate) that he has compelled his audience to think about victory in its manifold connotations, and turned Aristomenes' wrestling victory at the Pythian games into a κτῆμα εἰς ἀεί.

Richmond Lattimore (essay date 1976)

SOURCE: "A Note on Pindar and His Poetry." In *The Odes of Pindar,* second edition, translated by Richmond Lattimore, pp. v-xiv. Chicago: The University of Chicago Press, 1976.

[In the essay below, Lattimore reviews Pindar's life and career.]

Concerning the life of Pindar we can be sure only of the bare outlines, together with certain general facts. There is no sound biographical tradition for his period. It will perhaps be best to ignore anecdotes, guesses, and combinations which cannot be confirmed, and to state briefly what seems to be established. Pindar was born a citizen of Thebes, the chief city of the Boiotian confederacy, probably in 518 B.C. The date of his death is unknown; but the last work of his for which we have a date is the **"Eighth Pythian,"** for a victory won in 446 B.C. His first dated ode is the **"Tenth Pythian"** of 498 B.C. Thus, he lived to an advanced age. We may be sure that he was of aristocratic birth. The simple list of his contracts indicates that he was a professional poet of great repute, and as such he must have earned a great deal. The rest of his biography must be pieced out from the contents and implications of his poems, many of which are dated.

Pindar lived through a period of crucial change in Greek history. His life is bisected by the great Persian invasion of 480-478 B.C., a war in which Thebes, split within by factional rivalries, played a difficult and unhappy part. Against the forces of Xerxes, the combined Greek command chose to defend central Greece by holding the mountain pass of Thermopylai and the sea pass of Artemision. The Persians forced them to give up both positions. Theban soldiers had fought beside Leonidas at Thermopylai—badly, according to Herodotus, but he is prejudiced and may be wrong. In any case, when the Greek armies fell back on the Isthmos of Korinth and the fleet on Salamis, Boiotia and all other states to the north were left open to the enemy; nor had the Thebans the opportunity, as did the Athenians, to evacuate their population by sea. Thebes gave in, the city was in the hands of the Persians and Persian sympathizers, and the Persian general, Mardonios, made it his base of operations. At Plataia, where the invaders were finally defeated and forced to withdraw, a Theban contingent fought on the Persian side. What part, if any, Pindar played in all this is not known; but for some years after Plataia he was a citizen of a dishonored state. Parallels from more recent wars are only too obvious, and it should be understandable if a certain

bitterness over this defeat and betrayal, and over the attitudes of more fortunate states with better war records, remained with Pindar. Of the cities which fought the Persians, Athens in particular emerged from the struggle with greatly augmented prestige and strength. Pindar is said to have studied at Athens and undoubtedly had many friends there; but his openly avowed admiration for Athenian achievement must have been tempered with resentment even before the Athenians, in or about 457 B.C., temporarily deprived the Thebans of their leadership in Boiotia.

As a professional poet, Pindar traveled much, and his acquaintance was singularly wide. His poems (including the fragments) show connections in all the leading Greek states of his day and with many small cities as well. Among these external relations there are several which are of particular importance. He wrote several poems in honor of Hieron, tyrant (that is, dictator) of Syracuse in Sicily, and considered that ruthless, gifted, successful ruler to be his friend. In Greek history aristocrats are not regularly found on the side of tyrants; but Pindar thought he saw in Hieron a champion of Greek civilization against the dark forces of barbarism [**"Pythian 1"**] and a ruler intelligent enough to use his vast power toward ultimate good. Pindar himself visited Sicily, and his works show acquaintance with other prominent Sicilians, including Theron, tyrant of Akragas and, in particular, Theron's nephew, Thrasyboulos.

Another important external connection is Pindar's friendship with various noble families in Aigina, a Dorian island-state across the water from Athens. The friendship between Thebes and Aigina was close, and in legend the nymphs Thebe and Aigina were said to be sisters. Pindar has left us eleven odes for Aiginetan victors—almost one-fourth of the total number—and did not weary of singing the praises of their special heroes, the Aiakidai: Aiakos and his sons, Peleus and Telamon, and their sons, Achilles and Aias (Ajax). The Aiginetans, famous seafarers who distinguished themselves at Salamis, were also victims of Athenian imperialism (their state was liquidated by Athens during the Peloponnesian War), and it is tempting to see in **"Pythia 8"** a protest against the pretensions of the Athenian democracy led by Perikles. Yet, if this is true, toomany conclusions concerning Pindar's political views should not be recklessly drawn. Despite certain aristocratic prejudices, he belonged (apparently) to no faction; when he speaks of states, he generally speaks only to praise; and he considers himself to be in sympathy with all intelligent and well-meaning men, whatever their city.

Of Pindar's works, only the epinician, or victory, odes have survived almost intact, although the fragments show that he wrote much besides. The victory odes commemorate the success of a winner in the games or athletic meets held at regular intervals from very early times down to the Roman period. There were four great games: the Olympian, at Pisa in Elis, sacred to Zeus; the Pythian, at Pytho (Delphoi), sacred to Apollo; the Isthmian, at the Isthmos of Korinth, sacred to Poseidon; and the Nemean, at Nemea in the Peloponnese, sacred to Zeus. Of these, the Olympian games were the oldest and most honorable. In addition, there were numerous local games, in which success also brought considerable acclaim; many of these are named in poems for famous champions, such as Diagoras of Rhodes or Xenophon of Korinth. The events included races for four-horse chariot, mule chariot, and single (ridden) horse; foot races at various distances; contests in boxing, wrestling, and the pankration (a combination of the two); and the pentathlon, a complex event which involved racing, jumping, throwing the discus and javelin, and wrestling. It must be understood that in all horse and chariot races the "victor" was the person who entered horse or team; he was not required to ride or drive in person.

Pindar's peculiar excellence seems to have lain in the composition of victory odes; they may well have been his favorite form. The modern reader will always wonder why. There are several considerations. In the first place, the games were occasions of high sanctity, held in holy places, and protected by a truce of God, invoked to secure free competition; it will be seen that every epinician wears, in one place or another, the attributes of a hymn. Further, success meant a demonstration of wealth and power (particularly in the chariot races) or of superb physical prowess, shown through peaceful and harmless means. The very uselessness of these triumphs, which aroused the contemptuous anger of Xenophanes and Euripides, might have attracted Pindar. A victory meant that time, expense, and hard work had been lavished on an achievement which brought no calculable advantage, only honor and beauty. This may sound somewhat romantic, but competition symbolized an idea of nobility which meant much to Pindar; and in the exaltation of victory he seems sometimes to see a kind of transfiguration, briefly making radiant a world which most of the time seemed, to him as to his contemporaries, dark and brutal.

The occasion and circumstances of the ode must have been somewhat as follows: When a victory was won, the victor (or his family or some wealthy friend) commissioned the poet to write the commemorative ode. When this was complete, a choir of men or boys (probably amateurs and friends of the victor, in some cases) was trained to sing it. The true presentation of the ode was, then, a performance given for the victor and his friends some time after the event. (In the case of very short odes, such as **"Olympia 11"** or **"Pythia 7"** it has been commonly thought that they were composed immediately and presented before the festival was over, but for this I know of no actual evidence.) Pindar himself was not always present at the performance, nor did he always train the choir. In commissioning, some sort of agreement or contract was made. This contract may often have concerned not only the poet's fee but also various matters which the person who paid for the ode desired to have included, such as, for instance, mythical allusions to be made or details concerning the victor or his family. Thus, when we find Pindar being rather tediously exact about the exploits of brothers, uncles, cousins, or remote ancestors of his hero, we must remember that all this may have been stipulated in the contract. At other times he was doubtless given a free hand.

Concerning the form of the ode, there has been much discussion. This is not the place for me to set forth a thesis or to defend one in detail; I shall simply state what I take to be the general principles of composition. The poet had before him certain matters which must be included: the name of the victor, the place of the victory with some allusion to the protective deity of the place, one or more stories or episodes from heroic legend (in all but the very short odes), or any further elaboration which was called for in the contract or suggested itself to the poet. Above all, it was necessary to make a beginning. He may begin with an invocation addressed to a god or a city etc; with a comparison or simile with a wish [**"Pythian 3"**]; with a direct address to the victor or a statement of the poet's own position and obligations or with various combinations of the above motives. From such a formal opening he proceeds by way of compliment and acknowledgment to the rest of his material. The manner is that of an improvisation, so that (for example) a myth is generally introduced as if it were not foreplanned but suggested out of the immediate context. How much of this forward development represents actual method, how much means only a contrived appearance of improvisation, it is impossible to say, except for this proviso: good poems move of themselves, and the poet's combinations do surprise him into new combinations which he had not foreseen.

Since it is normal to speak of the victor at the beginning, either in or immediately after the invocation, and since it is natural also to end with the victor or with persons close to him, the natural place for the myth or episode out of heroic legend—that part of the material most remote from the present—is in the center. But here, as always, there is no hard-and-fast rule. In **"Nemea 1"** and **"10"** the myth runs from the middle of the poem right to the close. In **"Pythia 3"** and **"9"** we come to the myth at, or near, the beginning. Again, in **"Pythia 1"** (as also elsewhere) there is no one myth, but various mythical descriptions and allusions are scattered throughout the ode.

Nothing could be more deceptive than to emphasize too much the parts of the poem (invocation, personal compliment, prayer, moral, myth) as sharply distinct elements which must be bound together by transitional ties. It is better to admit that the transitional passages, such as moralities, wishes, comparisons, may grow directly out of what precedes and may generate what follows. Consider, first, for example, the beginning of **"Pythia 10,"** probably the earliest ode. Pindar's opening note is the happiness of Thessaly (and of Lakedaimon, a foil to show how happy Thessaly is). After brief self-adjuration, he gathers up the elements of the victory, in naming the winner, his home, the place of the contest; then proceeds, via the victory of Hippokleas' father and Apollo's favor, to prayer that such successes may continue unbroken and the gods' favor be constant. Yet no mortal can always be happy, though the success of father and son after him symbolizes such fortune as can be attained by men, beyond whose reach lies the almost superhuman happiness of the Hyperboreans. Through these moralities thought is swung against counterthought until the illustrative name, Hyperboreans, chimes the keynote of the myth, which follows. Here invocation, occasion, victor, prayer, moral, and myth are more or less discernible elements, though the development is so smooth that we pass naturally, even unconsciously, from one stage to another (here, as often, the return from myth to occasion and victor is less happily accomplished). Contrast, now **"Pythia 8,"** the latest datable ode. This opens with invocation of Hesychia, the goddess of peacefulness, tranquillity, or civic concord, who is besought to accept the song in honor of Aristomenes, the victor. But peace and justice evoke, by way of contrast, hatred and violence, as embodied in giant rebels, Porphyrion and Typhon. Their fall came about at the hands of Zeus and Apollo; and Apollo, lord of Pytho, brings us once more to the victory, the victor, and Aigina. Invocation, victor, myth, moral, and warning are inextricably intertwined. This is no fusion of parts but an organic development from the idea of Hesychia and the presenceof Aristomenes, compounded by the fact that Hesychia means, not only civic tranquillity, but also the calm of triumphant repose after a struggle.

There are also many mythical passages which were doubtless forecast in advance and which are to some extent self-subsistent entities. The best example is the story of Jason in **"Pythia 4,"** which opens formally and closes not through overlapping phrase but through an abrupt, conscious summary and an equally formal and conscious return to the victor, Arkesilas. Even in such "pure" myths, Pindar hardly tells a story, for he assumed that the outlines of legend were generally familiar to his listeners; rather, he lights up some intense moment, or series of moments, in a tale already known.

Further, although embarrassment over the terms of hire and the status of the poet as a paid entertainer may break to the surface, Pindar likes to appear as one who writes as he pleases, being the friend and equal of his patrons. These allowed the great man much liberty. Thus he feels free to moralize as he will, even in the middle of a myth; to correct himself in mid-progress; to talk to himself; to defend his own position and policies [**"Pythian 9, 11"**; **"Nemian 7, 8"**]; to make entirely personal acknowledgments. And here, perhaps, is one more reason for Pindar's devotion to the epinician ode; it gave him a starting point from which he could evolve, within certain limits, almost any sort of variation on the choral ode, and, at the same time, a firm point of reference to which he could always return.

Pindar's odes are generally cast in triads, each triad consisting of two identical stanzas, called "strophe" and "antistrophe," followed by a third which is different, called "epode." In any given poem, all triads are identical. In a few of the odes there are no triads but a series of identical stanzas. Such odes are called "monostrophic." The meters are exceedingly complex.

The obscurity commonly attributed to Pindar is partly due to his allusiveness, that is, his habit of plunging obliquely into legendary matter or personal compliment where we have lost the clues. Also, his work is at times formidably studded with proper names. These cannot be excised, and

the translator can only furnish a glossary and hope that his readers will be patient enough to use it when they need to. Another inherent difficulty is stylistic. Sentences are long, main verbs often hang fire, shifts of subject or emphasis may be sudden. Even so, Pindar is never quite so difficult as Browning, Shelley, or for that matter Thucydides can be; but where the new reader finds that he cannot make sense, he may feel sure that he is dealing with a passage which has perplexed scholars, and probably also the poet's own listeners. At his dazzling best, Pindar is perfectly clear.

Nancy Felson Rubin (essay date 1984)

SOURCE: "The Epinician Speaker in Pindar's First Olympian: Toward a Model for Analyzing Character in Ancient Choral Lyric." *Poetics Today*, Vol. 5, No. 2, 1984, pp. 377-98.

[*In the essay below, Rubin describes various roles played by the poet-persona of the "First Olympian," revealing a correlation between the mythic and non-mythic roles of the poet.*]

How does Pindar, fifth century B.C. composer of encomia for victors (epinicia), depict the actions of the figure of the poet in his odes? How do the depictions of this figure correspond to the actual activities of Pindar in the real world? What poetic argument is Pindar making by depicting the figure of the poet as he does?

These are some of the issues which I address in a longer treatment of the roles played and the rhetorical and linguistic devices used by what I call the Epinician (E-) speaker—the poet figure in the text, or poet-persona in the familiar phrase. In that work I distinguish social or external roles of the real poet, "Pindar," from those inscribed in the text for the E-speaker; and I analyze the language used, the enunciation, of that speaker.

This paper lays the groundwork for a portion of my study of the E-speaker in which I develop a model for describing the actions he performs, including his speech acts. In Part One I present my method for delineating the many roles that this figure assumes. Then, in Part Two, I apply this typology of roles to both the E-speaker and mythic figures within **"Olympian 1."** As a result of my study, extensive correlations between the mythic and non-mythic sections of the poet become clearly visible. These correlations, in turn, have an important bearing on the poetic argument: they allow Pindar to show a highly efficacious E-speaker attempting to alter reality for the victor he celebrates and commemorates and, in the process, for himself. He attempts this through his positive assumption of a diversity of speaker-roles. Of course, the way Pindar depicts the E-speaker in all his intensional roles has important implications for his own self-presentation in the real world; and in fact Pindar's composition of an ode is in itself a speech act having consequences in the extensional world.

I. DEVELOPMENT OF A MODEL: CONSTRUCTION OF SEVERAL INTENSIONAL SUBWORLDS

I begin by designating the traditional components of the epinikion: *encomium, myth* and *maxims.* In order to explore the relationship among these three components I first must constitute them from their dispersed manifestations in the text. From all the material that pertains directly to the victor and E-speaker I imagine a subworld of the text EnW (for Encomium World). In **"Olympian 1"** the inhabitants of this subworld are: the E-speaker, the victor Hieron, his horse Pherenikos, other poets around Hieron's table, and several divine figures (Zeus, the Muse, a guardian god). From the events of EnW I construct a skeletal narrative structure or plot line, having, in **"Olympian 1"** the following elements: Hieron wins a chariot-race with his horse Pherenikos; the E-speaker feels obliged to garland him with a song; he wishes to sing of contests and bids himself do so; he composes this ode for Hieron; he prays for Hieron's continued victories; he states his wish to mingle with winners and excel in poetry throughout Greece.

It is obvious that EnW resembles the real world, RW, the historical world in which the poet named Pindar lived and celebrated the victories of actual contestants in the games. Though reconstructing the RW is not my primary focus here, my findings, as we shall see, do shed light on the role of Pindar in that RW. (We recall that "Pindar" designates the extensional or RW poet, while the poet figure of EnW is the E-speaker.)

From the mythic portions of an ode we can even more easily construct a subworld MW, radically different from EnW in some respects yet parallel in others. MW is even in some sense a part of EnW, and the differences and similarities contribute to the meaning MW has for the entire epinikion.

MW differs from EnW because it occurs in a different time and because its action is completed.For MW events, since they are located in the mythic past, verisimilitude is a weaker consideration than for EnW events, many of which the performance audience would have witnessed or heard about first-hand: EnW audiences would tend to reject any claims or descriptions which were too far-fetched. Moreover, since mythic agents have lived out their lives and attained (or not attained) their ultimate as well as proximate goals, cause and effect is more traceable in MW than in EnW. MW agents attain what can often only be anticipated or avoided by EnW agents. Parallelism between MW and EnW allows an audience to feel what outcome might eventuate if EnW operates on the same principles as MW, but such principles are not themselves as retrievable from EnW as they are from MW.

As far as similarities between the two subworlds, they occur in plot structures, character configurations and semantic domains. In all the odes the plot lines of MW offer partial parallels and counter-parallels to the EnW plots. In numerous odes that I have examined the configuration of characters in MW reflects the configuration in EnW; and of course it is a primary goal of this paper to show that this is true for the mythic counterpart to the E-speaker. Moreover, semantically there is often an overlap between the two domains. For example, birth may occur as a motif in the plot of MW (Iamus' birth in **"Olympian 6,"** Athena's and the nesogony of Rhodes in **"Olympian 7,"** Ajax's birth in **"Isthmian 6"**), while the language of birth colors the figurative expressions of the EnW of those poems, or agonistic motifs and metaphors may suffuse both MW, usually in terms of heroic exploits seen as contests, and EnW. Correspondences between MW and EnW should not be forced: there is no reason to except a one-to-one relationship, especially since the myth which gives rise to the epinician myth, and hence to the MW, predates the poem and can only be molded up to a point.

Maxims, the third component of the epinikion, tend, among other functions, to enlarge the vision offered by EnW and MW. This function of maxims is the one which most concerns us here. Many of these universal statements pertain to the use of words and the winning of contests; hence the inhabitants of the Maxim Worlds (MaxWs) include, as in EnW, poets, victors, audiences, patrons, etc. Sometimes the reference is so general as to include epinician figures, but others as well; sometimes it is more restrictive. In either case, to apply the generalizations of MaxWs to EnW situations augments the meanings of those situations. Moreover, MaxWs, like EnW, have a mimetic relation to the RW. They pertain to the RW performance audience and to all subsequent audiences who may subscribe to the wisdom they offer. In addition, the E-speaker, who usually transmits these statements, tends to ground their wisdom in the past—in the tales of heroes. And so the principles of the maxims are compatible not only with those of EnW and RW but also of MW. All the maxims express the views of the E-speaker as he reflects on MW and EnW events. Consequently, once we construct MaxWs based on the maxims in a given ode we can also use the maxims in order to delineate roles taken up by the E-speaker in the EnW. Like MW, MaxWs become incorporated in the poetic argument of the whole epinikion.

So far, I have described the three traditional components of an ode and constructed from them three types of subworlds: EnW, MW and MaxWs. If we now compare EnW of **"Olympian 1"** with EnW of other odes, we find, as we might expect, many similarities. Such comparison enables us to expand the list of EnW inhabitants to include, for example, other competitors, the athletic trainer, audiences at the victory or at prior victories, the audience at the ode's performance, victor's family, the family member who commissioned the ode, etc. All these EnW inhabitants, including the E-speaker, engage in certain activities. From these activities we can abstract a list of roles played by inhabitants of the EnWs of a number of odes. If we consider only those activities engaged in by the E-speaker, we abstract the following speaker roles (those inquotes are metaphors):

a. celebrator: includes "garlander," "master of ceremonies"

b. commemorator

c. intercessor

d. interpreter

e. preceptor

f. advocate

g. accuser

h. competitor, "poet as athlete"

i. donor, transmitter of a gift and of gratitude to the gods

j. recipient of a gift and of favors from the gods

k. manipulator of words, or "poet" in an aesthetic sense; user of rhetorical devices

l. composer of this ode, "fabricator," "builder"

m. performer(s) of this ode

Undoubtedly, the number of roles would expand if we considered the whole corpus of Pindaric odes, and included (under appropriate headings) all roles expressed metaphorically for the E-speaker. Most of the thirteen roles are unmarked as to value, though all tend to be positive for the E-speaker himself; nearly all can be correlated to one or more marked negative roles. A list of roles that have a negative value and are contrasted to those usually taken up by the E-speaker would include:

neg. a. detractor, begrudger, withholder of praise

neg. b. obliterator

neg. c. improper intercessor or transgressor (of divine/human boundaries); misuser of divine connections

neg. d. misguided interpreter, or distorter of a divine message

neg. e. improper preceptor, corrupter

neg. f. improper advocate or defender of someone undeserving

neg. g. improper accuser or accuser of someone worthy

neg. h. unsuccessful competitor, non-competitor

neg. i. improper donor, inadequate host, withholder of gifts; one who forgets or refuses to give thanks to the gods

neg. j. improper (e.g. undeserving) recipient of gifts; non-recipient of gifts

neg. k. improper manipulator, or misuser of words and rhetorical devices

neg. l.—

neg. m.—

The same procedure whereby I abstracted these sets of roles from a number of epinicia could be used to generate roles filled by the victor, members of his family, the various audiences, etc. In fact, some of the roles assumed by the E-speaker, notably preceptor, donor and competitor, are at times also played by other epinician figures. For example, the victor as well as the speaker consistently takes up the role of competitor and frequently that of donor—whenever the victory is explicitly seen as the victor's gift to the speaker. The patron is always donor because he gives the poet a fee. And the role of preceptor can be played by the trainer as well as by the E-speaker.

In most of his roles the E-speaker is the desiring subject (in the sense of the one aspiring toward a goal), while the victor is the object (the target of the action, the one celebrated or commemorated) or the recipient of the action (the one interceded for or interpreted to or given a gift). But the speaker too can be the object or beneficiary of his own actions. He can be the recipient of favors from others, such as the victor (his victory or hospitality), the family (their patronage), the gods (his talents, their favor). Thus we can see that the roles are on a higher level of generality than the specific characters who fill them, and that some roles are filled by more than one specific character.

Most of the roles abstracted for the E-speaker are realistic in nature. That is, there are RW poetic functions to which these roles correspond, social functions of an epinician poet toward his patron and the victor and toward the divine and human audiences he is known to have addressed. In fact, of the thirteen positive roles enumerated, all but performer correspond to known RW functions of Pindar.

Thus we have observed two sets of correspondences— EnW from ode to ode, and EnW and RW for a given ode. At this point it is natural to wonder whether there are similar correspondences between EnW and MW, and especially between encomiastic and mythic figures. The logical way to organize any such correspondences is to ask if certain roles are shared by figures in these two discrete subworlds. My investigation of a number of odes has shown that there are indeed mythic figures who fill the same roles, or corresponding negative ones, as EnW figures. In particular, those roles enumerated for the epinician speaker are indeed evident in MW, as I will show in the following analysis of encomium and mythic figures in **"Olympian 1."**

II. ANALYSIS OF "OLYMPIAN 1"

Pindar composed this ode for Hieron, prince of Syracuse, on the occasion of his victory in a chariot-race at the Olympian Games of 476 B.C. As we proceed through the ode, following its textual order, we shall notice that occasionally the E-speaker departs from the diegetic mode and directly addresses mythic figures, just as he habitually addresses epinician figures in numerous poems. When he does this for a mythic character, he is entering MW linguistically in one of his many capacities (that is, as celebrator, commemorator, etc.). I describe his activities during these departures from diegesis within my analysis of E-speaker roles in **"Olympian 1."**

In his statements and his actions the E-speaker plays most of the roles enumerated above. After the opening priamel, he admonishes his own heart [*philon êtor*]: "if, dear heart, you wish to celebrate great games, look no further [. . .] for a contest mightier than Olympia." The address culminates with a focus on the loftiness of the Olympian games and of the victor Hieron, who "plucks the peak from all virtues." In all these lines the speaker occupies the role of celebrator (a).

The E-speaker has not yet begun his ode (Pindar has). He will do this in 18-19, "take down the lyre." He moves meditatively from generalities [*ariston men hud r*] to the present occasion. In doing so he is praising the victor, Hieron. He is thus occupying the role of celebrator (a). But since he is presumably meditating, not celebrating, he cannot call attention to his function, as he does in other odes where he speaks, for example, of pouring libations or serving as master of ceremonies at a banquet. As one who offers advice, he is also occupying the role of preceptor (e); we can say this even when, as here, he is advising himself.

The E-speaker's formal opening of his ode, the words "take down the lyre," are also self-admonishing and thus sustain the role of preceptor. They introduce two other roles as well, composer (1) and performer (m), here combined into one, as if the E-speaker were an oral-improvisatory poet (in ironic contrast to Pindar, whose previously written poetry is being performed by the Chorus). The E-speaker then refers obliquely to his social obligation (i), saying that the *charis* of Olympia and of his horse Pherenikos have "put his mind under the yoke of the sweetest thoughts." When he adds that Hieron "takes delight in horses, and his glory shines forth," he is celebrating and commemorating the victor by setting forth his *kleos* (a and b).

Next, in a maxim, the speaker observes that "tales embroidered with dappled lies deceive" [*dedaidelmenoi pseudesi poikilois exapat nti muthoi*] and he claims that Grace [*Charis*] "fashions all things soothing [*meilicha*] to mortals, and, adding honor besides, devises that often even the unreliable [*apiston*] is relied upon [*piston*]." This pessimism about the power of stories (especially charming ones) to mislead and this acknowledgment of mortal susceptibility to misleading words brings the speaker to affirm the proper and the safest way to speak of the gods: "it is seemly [*eoikos*] for a man to say noble things [*kala*] about the gods, for the blame is less" [*mei n gar aitia*]. This pair of maxims contains implicit self-instruction (e) and in fact the E-speaker proceeds to obey the principle he has just espoused, at the same time calling attention to his departure from earlier (improper and blasphemous) singers: "I shall sing you, son of Tantalos, differently from the earlier ones" [*se d'antia proter n phthegxomai*].

He implies that he will celebrate and commemorate Pelops (a and b), not blame him; in fact, his use of direct address to the dead Pelops produces the fiction that he is the poet "commissioned" to celebrate and commemorate the hero. By distinguishing himself from earlier tellers and by undermining his rivals the E-speaker appropriates the role of interpreter of this ancient tale (d), shaping and defining this role as he assumes it.

The prior version which he tells in order to repudiate it involved accusing the gods of cutting up, boiling, and devouring the human flesh of Pelops, in other words, of being gluttonous[*gastrimargon*]. The speaker, adhering to his own dictum to speak well of the gods, stands back [*aphistamai*] from this blameworthy account and explains Pelops' disappearance during the banquet in another way (d). In his next maxim he warns (e) that profitlessness [*akerdeia*] often befalls slanderers [*kakagorous*] (neg. f) who misinterpret events (neg. d). Condemning Tantalos (g) for not digesting his great success [*megan olbon*] but instead seizing ruin [*atê*] with satiety [*koros*], the speaker argues (g) that Tantalos deserved his double punishment—the torment of eternally longing to cast from his head the stone that hung over it, and his son's deprivation of immortality. For Tantalos exemplifies "a man" [*anêr tis*] who hopes in his actions to escape divine notice and who miscalculates [*hamartanei*].

The statement which returns us from MW to EnW is characteristically self-preceptive (e). "I must crown that man [*stephan sai keion . . . chrê*] to a horseman's tune" shows the social obligation to the victor (i). The E-speaker celebrates Hieron (a) in terms reminiscent of the proem: "I believe that we shall never embroider in the shining folds of song a host more familiar with noble things and more lordly in power." He then addresses the victor, as he had Pelops earlier:

> A god as overseer, having this as his care, tends your concerns, Hieron; and if he does not desert you soon, I hope for an even sweeter victory that, finding a helping pathway of words, I shall celebrate with my swift chariot as I come beside the brightest hill of Cronus. For the Muse nourishes with valor the strongest missile.

This hope for an even sweeter future victory is virtually an intercession (c), while the chariot metaphor suggests competition (h). The speaker, like Hieron, is a recipient of divine favor (j) whose connection to the Muse suggests a role of interpreter of the divine (d). In the ensuing maxim he asserts that the "ultimate culminates for kings" (i.e., a king's culmination is the farthest one can go toward blessedness) and follows this with the advice to "peer no further" (i.e., ask for no higher joy); he both asserts and advises as preceptor (e). "May you walk on high for this time" expresses further advice to Hieron (e) but perhaps also intercession (c). The wish to consort as a poet with prize-winning athletes [*nikaphorois . . . homilein*] emphasizes the social poet-victor bond, a bond of guest-friendship, of mutual giving and receiving (i and j). Finally, the poem closes with the speaker's further wish that he may consort with victors "while being foremost in song [*prophanton sophiai*] everywhere throughout Greece," and this brings forth his role as competitor in poetry (h).

Thus, as we see, the E-speaker fulfills all of the positive roles enumerated above. He also designates other EnW figures: "earlier ones" [*proteroi*] against whom he sings and, more specifically, "someone of the envious neighbors" whose account he refutes. The *proteroi* (who include the envious neighbor) misinterpret myths (neg. d) and also slander (neg. g). They blame the gods rather than praising them, for which the E-speaker characterizes them as blasphemers (perhaps neg. i).

We now turn to MW figures in "Olympian 1" to see whether any of them assumes speaker roles. According to the E-speaker's narration, Tantalos, father of Pelops, was a mortal most honored by the gods. He even hosted a banquet for the gods and dined with them. At that banquet Poseidon fell in love with Pelops and carried him off to Olympos to become his beloved. Later, Tantalos stole nectar and ambrosia and gave them to his drinking companions, probably intending to make them immortal. He was punished with a burdensome, helpless afterlife, in which he endlessly desired to cast a mighty stone from his head. As an additional penalty for his affront the gods returned his son Pelops to the "brief-fated race of men." Pelops, now grown to manhood, is contemplating marriage to Hippodameia, daughter of Oinomaos; but before entering a risky chariot race for her hand, he prays, alone in the darkness, to his divine benefactor Poseidon:

> If at all, Poseidon, the dear gifts [*philia dōra*] of Aphrodite count in my favor [*charis*], shackle [*pedason*] the bronze spear of Oinomaos, bring me [*poreuson*] on the swiftest chariot to Elis, and put me within the reach of power [*kratei [. . .] pelason*]; for he has slain thirteen suitors now, and so he delays his daughter's marriage. Great danger does not come upon the spineless man [*analkin [. . .] phōta*], and yet, for those who must die, why, sitting in darkness, should one pursue a nameless [*anonumon*] old age, with no share of nobility, for nothing? As for me, I will undertake this exploit [*aethlon*]. And you—give me my means [*praxin philan*].

Pelops grasps words that would not go unfulfilled [*oud 'akratois ephepsato epesi*]. As a means of victory Poseidon gives Pelops a golden chariot and winged, unwearying horses. With these gifts Pelops wins the race, defeating the violent father and taking Hippodameia as his wife. He achieves, in addition, undying glory, a heroic name, and a grave near a much-frequented altar. These ultimate attainments suggest his eventual status as an object of cult worship, a status realized by the time of this ode and recorded in it. His destiny is commensurate with the heroic values which we hear him espouse in his prayer to Poseidon—a just reward for his decision to enter the risky contest.

The sequence of Pelops' prayer, Poseidon's immediate and favorable response, and Pelops' ultimate blessedness and godlike stature is paralleled by events in EnW. A number of Pindarists have made interesting observations to this effect.

In a recent commentary on "Olympian 1" Gerber concisely and convincingly summarizes the analogies between Pelops and Hieron:

> Poseidon gives Pelops a golden chariot and timeless horses because of his love for him and a god acts as a guardian of Hieron because of his concern for him. Pelops and Hieron have a mutual knowledge of *ta kala*, i.e., of what is honorable and noble, and a mutual awareness that this knowledge must be combined with appropriate deeds, if heroic stature is to be achieved. Pelops knows what is at hand (*hupokeisetai*) is preferable to a distant and inglorious old age, and Pindar repeats this general outlook on life when he tells Hieron that the blessings which each day brings are best. Pelops realizes that darkness attends a life lived without danger and Hieron's fame shines forth because of his boldness in the games. Pelops prays that Poseidon may grant him victory and the language in which the prayer is cast reminds us of the victory which Hieron has just won. [*Pindar's Olympian I: A Commentary* (1982)]

All this parallelism suggests that, after his death, Hieron too will receive worship as a hero—an implied prophecy which was indeed fulfilled at Catana.

Thus the parallels between Pelops and Hieron are extensive. Using the life-story of Pelops, the E-speaker praises and commemorates Hieron, implicitly mediating with the gods and pleading with men on Hieron's behalf. It has, however, gone unnoticed by Pindarists, . . . that Pelops is also an analogue of the E-speaker. Like Pelops, the speaker uses a swift race chariot to find his "helping pathway of words" (thus both are competitors, h). His means is a missile [*belos*] from the Muse, Pelops' is a chariot from Poseidon. Like Pelops, who himself resembles Ganymede, the speaker is a recipient of divine favor (j) and he is gracious in serving deity (i). Both hero and E-speaker pray, and in a modest fashion—modest, in that the speaker in his future prayer (epode 4) merely seeks to mingle with victors and be included in their hospitality, while Pelops prays to Poseidon in a private setting, so as not to demean the god, nor display their former intimacy. Thus both Pelops and the speaker respect their reciprocal bonds with deity and are intercessors (c, Pelops on his own behalf). Knowledge of what is noble [*ta kala*] characterizes both Pelops, who chides one who would remain "sitting in darkness, not sharing in all things noble" [*hapant n kal n ammoros*] and the speaker, who remarks that "a man had best say noble things [*kala*] about the gods" (36). Both are therefore preceptors (e).

Pelops and the E-speaker both use words to construct their own "anti-parallels" or foil, whom they accuse (g) of inadequacies. The speaker *retells* the Tantalos story, mistold by an envious neighbor. Other "earlier ones" [*proteroi*] who also mistold the Tantalos tale are comparable, in the myth itself, both to the losers whom Oinomaos has caused to perish and to those who, sitting in darkness, do not bother to compete (neg. h). Pelops has distinguished himself from such inferior others, and so does the speaker—both assuming a competitor role (h). It is in his words [*epesi*] that Pelops is "not inefficacious, and the speaker too stands out from the others for his poetic and narrative skills. Both Pelops and the speaker pinpoint the anonymity of their flawed competitors by referring to them with the indefinite pronoun *tis* (Pelops stresses this by using *an numon,* "nameless," to describe their old age) and both associate their denigrated competitors with darkness (*kruphai* and *en skot i*).

Of all the parallels between Pelops in MW and the speaker in EnW, the most interesting and least noticed is their similar use of rhetorical devices to bring about certain desired effects. One such device is ring composition. Pelops frames his prayer to Poseidon with *philia d ra* and *praxin philan didoi.* The speaker frames the myth with *lampei de hoi kleos* and *to de kleos dedorke* and frames the whole ode with an array of comparatives and super-latives (*ariston, thalpnoteron, pherteron* in the proem and *glukuteran, karter taton, to d'eschaton koruphoutai, prophanton sophiai* in the closing epode).

Furthermore, in his argument on his own behalf Pelops uses two forms of persuasion characteristically used by the E-speaker: "history" (the fate of thirteen slain suitors; compare the speaker's use of the mythic past) and "philosophy" or earthly wisdom (the "great risk" maxim; compare the speaker's frequent use of maxims in all the epinicians).

Finally, in the sequence *pedason, poreuson, pelason* Pelops uses several rhetorical devices which mark his prayer as poetic: alliteration, homoteleuton, and grammatical ana-phora. Although no speaker in the epinicia can avoid speaking in poetry, still the accumulation of poetic devices in Pelops' prayer calls attention to his skill at manipulating words. Both Pelops and the E-speaker employ word-magic to attain certain ends, Pelops to intercede on his own behalf and the E-speaker to intercede for the victor and for himself.

The similarity between Pelops and the E-speaker become clearer when we contrast the two of them with Tantalos. Before his abuse of power, Tantalos was at the pinnacle of success, having connections with the gods and special favor (*charis*) from all of them. "If ever the watchers on Olympos honored any man, that man was Tantalos") (j). Even so, Tantalos misinterpreted his own greatness (neg. d), and never reflected upon the gods' munificence, never prayed to his benefactors (neg. c). He displayed no knowledge of what is honorable and noble [*ta kala*] and expressed no desire for heroic status.

In addition to all these general failings, Tantalos neglected to request permission from the gods to distribute nectar and ambrosia among his drinking companions, but simply took these immortalizing substances, hoping to escape divine notice (neg. c). This theft shows a misplaced desire to bring things beyond human grasp, lofty, ultimate goals, into mortal hands. Nor did Tantalos anticipate divine retaliation—a further misperception of divine principles (neg.

d). Most important, he had the wrong sort of *philia* toward his *sympotai;* and, while there is no indication that he literally misled humans (neg. e), this is implicit in his improper gift to them (neg. i).

Tantalos' crime is complex: it involves abusing his state of blessedness, his connection to the gods; giving mortals an inappropriate gift; and being gluttonous for the power to give this gift, the prerogative of the gods. Both his punishments suit this single crime. For his outrageous desires on behalf of himself, he is placed in a situation where there can be no desire and no future, no movement and no change. He is trapped in a static and burdensome afterlife. And for violating the boundary between humans and gods, he sees his son thrust out of Olympos. Part of a hero's ultimate attainment comes via his offspring, and Pelops' presence on Olympos indeed enhanced Tantalos' state of blessedness. Hence, deprivation of that immortality was as meaningful and as painful a punishment as the mighty stone.

Tantalos' career stands in three-fold contrast with the career of Pelops. They differ in their use of divine connections, in the appropriateness of their respective goals, and in the way the gods responded to their acts or requests (that is, in the quality of their respective after-lives). Both Pelops and Tantalos had power and access to the divine; Pelops felt more limited and hence prayed piously for aid, while Tantalos boldly stole, expecting to escape the gods' notice. Pelops sought proximate, modest goals, suitable to humans—victory in a chariot-race and marriage with Hippodameia. Tantalos, in contrast, sought to usurp divine power and to give mortals nectar and ambrosia. Pelops attained his goals (the victory leading to the marriage) and a generation of six sons excellent in their virtues, but also gained worship as a hero, a frequented tomb beside a much-visited altar. He is appropriately godlike after death, but not before. Tantalos, on the other hand, during his lifetime actively sought immoderate goals for himself (godlike power) and for his *sympotai* (the food of godlike existence); in contrast to Pelops he does not achieve his goals, but sees his son suffer loss of Olympos; and after death he is powerless and futile.

The E-speaker likewise has divine connections. But unlike Tantalos, he shows the proper *philia* in offering his gift of poetry, an appropriate form of immortalization, to the victor. And while Tantalos is ultimately reduced to help-lessness, since he cannot cast off [*balein*] the mighty stone [*karteron lithon*] which Zeus suspends over his head after death, the E-speaker is given during his lifetime, the "mightiest missile" [*karter taton belos*], which assures an accurate cast and hence a measure of power and control in contrast to Tantalos' helplessness.

The extensive contrasts between Tantalos and Pelops on the one hand, and Tantalos and the E-speaker on the other, accentuate the several points of similarity between Pelops and the E-speaker which we have already noted. Pelops and the E-speaker use their divine connections correctly through poetry and prayer. Their goals are appropriate to human beings. They want victory and glory, not stolen immortality. Their benefits are similar: the E-speaker is granted the missile of poetic power while Pelops is given the altartomb of the hero's power to bless.

To summarize the parallels between Pelops and the E-speaker, we can now say that they both fill the following speaker roles: c, e, g, h, i, j and k. Tantalos fills the positive role of j (and this aligns him with them) and three negative roles: neg. c, neg. d and neg. i. Neg. c and neg. i contrast with both Pelops and the E-speaker (the improper donor, neg. i, offering a more striking contrast to the E-speaker), while neg. d contrasts only with the speaker, in his role as interpreter.

What can we infer from the extensiveness of these correspondences between EnW and MW figures? As stated already, some major differences distinguish the epinician and mythic subworlds. Most important, in MW action is completed, in EnW not. In MW, with verisimilitudinal constraints relaxed, miracles (such as Pelops' transposition to Olympos) occur; EnW is, at least in its indicative statements, more realistic. Prayers in MW are regularly answered (Pelops' prayer to Poseidon, for example); in EnW they are not. In MW rules of causality become clearly visible and give rise to the E-speaker's assertions of universal principles; this is less true of EnW, where such assertions would, in any case, have less validity.

We have so far elucidated an elaborate metaphoric relation between two subworlds constructed (for analytic purposes) from the materials of the text. Now, having observed important differences between these two subworlds, we can examine their metonymic (that is, synecdochic) relation and ask: How do the analogies between MW and EnW, now made explicit, contribute to the poetic argument?

The E-speaker tells the myth digressively to an unspecified audience. He draws explicit inferences from it, such as expressed in the *anêr tis* maxim ("a man who hopes in his actions to escape divine notice miscalculates.") His inferences draw support from the mythic exempla. He can use MW as a source of wisdom, for he claims a continuity between MW and EnW, a sharing of certain principles.

One such principle is the principle of fairness [*dikê*], implied in the maxim just quoted—the E-speaker's explanation for Tantalos' downfall. He did evil and therefore was punished. Pelops, on the other hand, did noble things and behaved piously, and Pelops received the ultimate in human rewards. For Pelops too the principle of *dikê* is in effect, at least in the E-speaker's revised account. In the earlier account Pelops suffered undeservedly through the impiety of his father and the gluttony of a god; it is for that reason too, and not only because he wishes to speak well of the gods, that the E-speaker retells the tale as he does. He wants to illustrate the strength of the law of *dikê* in the mythic past.

The logic of the E-speaker's thinking becomes quite clear. If the law of *dikê* was true in MW, as he has shown, then Hieron, if his guardian deity stands by him and if he does not "peer beyond," will also attain ultimate rewards along

with future victories. This is implied already by the many analogies between Hieron and Pelops (see the passage quoted above from Gerber 1982).

But what about the E-speaker himself—the focus of my study? He has manipulated how we view mythic figures and how we view the victor: we see them just as he presents them. He, on the other hand, is less direct and outspoken in telling us how he is presenting himself. We see him taking down the lyre, standing back from telling a worthless false account, competing for honors throughout Greece. He is somewhat cagey in his poses, and does not communicate to us how seriously we are to take him. When, however, we examine the roles he plays in light of roles taken up by mythic heroes, it becomes clear immediately that a voice outside the consciousness of the E-speaker is making parallels and contrasts *to some purpose*. That is the voice of Pindar, RW poet. Because it stands outside the E-speaker, he becomes objectified even while being designated *"egó."* We (the audience) experience the E-speaker more as an object than as a subject. Pindar shapes him as he would any other epinician character, his identification with him notwithstanding.

Once we recognize that the E-speaker is objectified in the ode and is seen celebrating, commemorating, interpreting, instructing, competing, etc., then we can address an important question: For what purpose does Pindar objectify the *eg* in all its diverse roles? Naturally, it is in order to examine these roles, which mainly concern the use of words to effect changes in reality. One can examine each of these roles as a type of speech-act directed at a divine or human addressee. What, Pindar is asking, are the chances that the E-speaker will be efficacious in each of his diverse roles?

By setting the speaker up as an analogue of Pelops and Tantalos Pindar suggests an answer to that question: the speaker, like Hieron, will achieve his desires. His prayers, which followed self-prescribed lines ("to speak well of the gods"), will, like the prayer of Pelops, be favorably answered. Why? because of the principle of *dikê*. The speaker is just and deserving in his manner of praising, his choice of subjects, his use of his god-given poetic skills; therefore he will receive his due reward. Moreover, unlike the envious neighbor and other earlier story-tellers, *he* is setting the mythic record straight. He is thereby contributing to *dikê*, since mythic heroes like epinician ones deserve the proper credit, whether it be praise or blame. And what would be the just rewards for the speaker's efforts? Surely, for the victor he celebrates to win proximate rewards, such as future victories, and ultimate rewards such as blessedness and eternal acclaim; and for himself to gain proximate rewards, such as the opportunity to mingle with victors and shine in poetry throughout Greece, and perhaps such ultimate rewards as Pelops attained. The speaker will attain his immediate goals if his poetry, like Pelops' prayer to Poseidon, is efficacious. If his verse persuades human audiences (contemporary or subsequent), they may bestow on the E-speaker, as well as on the victor, everlasting acclaim [*kleos*]. Moreover, ultimate rewards may be in store for him if the gods grant him his pleas.

CONCLUDING REMARKS, THEMATIC IMPLICATIONS FOR THE POETIC ARGUMENT

From this study of **"Olympian 1"** it has become clear that frequently mythic personages partake of the same roles as the epinician speaker. When it is in efficacious or inefficacious use of words or of poetic actions that a mythic figure is engaged, this allows the speaker to augment his direct statements on the topic of poetic efficacy. Thus the way he characterizes and depicts mythic counterparts allows him to express feelings and beliefs and hopes about his own craft, his poetry, and its potential influence. These ideas would either not lend themselves to direct expression or, if expressed directly, would have less force than when presented via analogy. By using indirect expression, the speaker avoids hubris and a personal specificity which would reduce his statements as a desiring subject to the level of the trivial. The parallels with mythic counterparts enlarge the role of the E-speaker and allow an exploration of the whole theme of poetic efficacy.

To show that MW figures offer partial parallels to EnW ones and that this is true of mythic speakers as well as mythic victors is to argue that Pindar inscribes into epinician myth his own concerns with the efficacy of his poem. Thus myth functions as part of an elaborate argument on behalf of the victor's proximate and ultimate attainments, as several scholars have suggested, but myth also, in its obedience to the principle of *dikê,* has implications for the power of words to change reality in the epinician world of the epinician speaker.

Charles Segal (essay date 1985)

SOURCE: "Messages to the Underworld: An Aspect of Poetic Immortalization in Pindar." *American Journal of Philology*, Vol. 106, No. 2, Summer, 1985, pp. 199-212.

[*In the excerpt below, Segal elucidates the significance of sending messages between the living and the dead in Pindar's odes.*]

In a dithyramb for Thebes, Pindar calls himself an "outstanding herald of skilled verses" appointed by the Muse. At the end of the **"Fourth Pythian,"** he claims Homer's authority for his role as a "noble messenger" through whose "upright" skill the Muse gains in honor One of the tasks of a "messenger of song" is to establish communication: communication between the mortal victor and the timeless realm of the gods, between the present and the past (both actual and mythical), between the individual *laudandus* and the community as a whole, between his native city and the place of the victory. Pindar frequently uses concrete spatial metaphors to express this act of mediation. In **"Olympian 6"** he yokes the victor's chariot to travel into the land of myth. In **"Pythian 2"** and **"Nemean 5"** he sends his message of song like cargo across the sea. Frequently he makes a journey, real or imagined, to his patron's home city, even though this is as far as Sicily or Libya.

In establishing communication between realms separated by time and space, the poet also may send a message to the Underworld. The motif occurs several times in the Epinicia but has not received from interpreters the attention that it deserves. This message to Hades is symmetrical with the more familiar poetic task of suffusing mortal life with the radiance of Olympian eternity. When the poet addresses the deceased kinsmen of the victor, he momentarily illuminates even the realm of death with the light of song. At the end of **"Nemean 8"** for example, he speaks directly to the victor's deceased father of the impossibility of bringing back his life. By contrast, he can easily raise a "stone of the Muses" to memorialize the family's athletic prowess.

This sending of messages between living and dead is an important theme in classical literature. Plato's Er is to be a "messenger to men" of the things in Hades. In a later development of the poetic tradition, Virgil's Neoptolemus brutally sends Priam to Hades as a "messenger" of his deeds:

> referes ergo haec et *nuntius* ibis
> Pelidae genitori. illi mea tristia facta
> degeneremque Neoptolemum narrare *memento.*

This establishment of continuity between the separate spheres of existence is one of the gifts of the goddess Memory, Mnemosyne. As Jean-Pierre Vernant remarks, she confers on the poet "le privilège . . . d'un contact avec l'autre monde, la possibilité d'y entrer et d'en revenir librement." This motif is another form of the poetic Ἀλήθεια, the commemorative praise that bridges the gap between past and future and overcomes the power of time's oblivion to efface mortal achievement. Song enlists the positive value of time as preserver, instead of time as destroyer, to keep great deeds alive for future generations. Bacchylides provides a lucid statement of how the "truth" of this poetry of praise will defeat the darkness of blame and envy and overcome the "forgetfulness" or λήθη associated with them. . . .

On the whole, Pindar remains more concerned with death than Bacchylides. This insistent consciousness of death— as in his address to deceased kinsmen—results in the mixture of both funerary and triumphal imagery throughout the Epinicia.

The wish to span the distance between the living and the dead (as the poetic ἀλήθεια seeks to do) is typical of most societies' interest in reaching the departed and communicating to them the concern that the living still have for them. In archaic and classical Greece, an important duty of the men of the household is to attend to the funeral offerings for departed ancestors. Communication with the dead takes place particularly at the tombs, often through the pouring of ritual libations. The aural dimension of this communication also receives particular stress. We may recall, for example, Orestes' emphatically repetitive κλύειν ἀκοῦσαι in the prologue of the *Choephoroe,* a verse for which Euripides takes Aeschylus to task in the *Frogs.*

From the other side, the dead can be presumed to have a continuing interest in the affairs of the living. Despite the shadowy existence of the souls in the Homeric *nekyiai*, popular belief continued to endow them with some kind of vague sentience about the world above. The most influential literary paradigm is Achilles' meeting with Odysseus in *Odyssey*. The dead hero is eager for news about his father, which Odysseus cannot supply, but he strides off with joy at Odysseus' report of his son Neoptolemus. The great literary figures, of course, have special privileges; but even for ordinary mortals the rites of the dead and the cult of heroes probably contributed to the feeling that the deceased were somehow reachable beyond the grave. I have already mentioned Pindar's frequent address to dead ancestors; and throughout the Epinicia he also shows much interest in cult-heroes. A recent article by Jeffrey Rusten ["Ι ΕΙΤῪΝ ΗΡῪΟ̒: Pindar's Prayer to Heracles (*N.* 7.86-101) and Greek Popular Religion," *HSCP* 87 (1983)] reminds us of the poet's concern to stress his personal ties to local heroes, particularly through the proximity of their graves.

Ancestors are obviously not heroes, and the degree of their vitality in the Underworld is more obscure and more precarious. But several contexts in the Epinicia suggest that Pindar associates the figurative libations of song with the cult practice of pouring libations on the graves of the departed and that in both cases the poet is functioning as a "messenger" between the upper world and Hades. The associations, both in Pindar and elsewhere, between athletes and heroes perhaps also tended to strengthen the connection between the poet's offerings of song to departed kinsmen of the victor and the cult offerings to heroes. In a number of legends, analyzed by Joseph Fontenrose in an important article, ["The Hero as Athlete," *CSCA* 1 (1968)] athletes gain the status of cult heroes. From the eighth to the early fifth centuries B.C., these figures follow a remarkably consistent pattern: they display extraordinary athletic prowess at the panhellenic festivals, meet a violent and mysterious death often attended by homicidal madness, and after their mortal end roam the land as potent but ambiguous divinities, jealous and irascible, requiring honors, cult, and propitiation to end plague, barrenness, or famine that their wrath has brought upon the city. We are here far away from the luminous Olympian world which Pindar brings into association with the glory of the athletes celebrated in his odes; but it is clear that in the popular imagination and religious attitudes of his time it was easy to assimilate the victorious athlete's capacity for superhuman-appearing feats of physical strength to the aura of supernatural power that surrounds the hero and reaches out beyond the grave.

The best known of these Pindaric messages to the Underworld is the end of **"Olympian 14"**. . . .

Through the vivid personification of the sound itself, Acho, song crosses the barrier between life and death. But this oral/aural message also renews the sense of "sight" in Persephone's "black-walled" house. The lasting fame through song implied in κλυτάν and εὐδαξοις can, for a moment, penetrate the blackness and enclosure of Hades. The bold metaphor of "wings" or "feathers," πτερά, for the olive wreath with which the victorious son crowns his "young hair" also keeps in the foreground the upward movement toward the gods and Olympus. The end of the first strophe describes the Charites as the "stewards of all deeds in the heavens." The "wings" at the very end of the ode recall this skyward movement of eternizing song, in contrast to the subterranean gloom of Hades.

As the ode's opening lines tell us, this locale of Orchomenos is also the site of the Charites, who preside over the waters of the Cephisus. They are worshipped here as divinities of the fecundating, nurturing, and life-giving power of water. These, like the waters of Castalia, Dirce, or Tilphussa elsewhere in Pindar, are associated with birth and the immortalizing power of poetry. Here they strike an initial mood of vital energy, over against Hades at the end.

Pindar has prepared an elaborate foil to the subterranean darkness. The intricate word-order of his opening lines associates Orchomenos with both the radiance and the liquid vitality of poetry: the Charites who dwell there are the *songful* queens of *bright* Orchomenos. The reference to the "Minyans of ancient race" in the next phrase stresses the continuity of local habitation and the association between the people and their divinities, the Charites. The "hearing" that takes place here establishes an upward communication between the mortal realm (the singer and the Minyan ancestors) and the goddesses who also dwell on Olympus. The second strophe begins with another request for "hearing" and repeats the first strophe's association of radiance, song, and "hearing." We may note that all three of the imperatives in the ode are requests for hearing or telling.

This "hearing" between mortal and divinity, via the mediation of the poet's song, is symmetrical with the "hearing" that takes place in Hades in the ode's last lines. Hence the "everflowing glory of the Olympian father" that the Charites honor in the heavens contrasts sharply with the dead "father" underground who receives Echo's "message of glorious hearing."

The communicative power of song operates on a vertical (and temporal) axis that runs between Olympus, Orchomenos, and Hades and between past and present. It also operates on a horizontal (and spatial) axis, between Orchomenos and Olympia. The Minyans at the beginning are first mentioned in close association with their local setting; but when the name recurs, near the end, its modifier, "winning at Olympia," intertwines the "Minyan city" with the place of the victory. Acho's literal journey to Hades' "black-walled house" follows almost at once.

Several of these motifs in **"Olympian 14"** are thematically akin to the closing section of **"Isthmian 6,"** where the poet again connects the Charites, water, poetry, and the family of the victor: . . .

By including the victor's clan of the Psalychidae, Pindar may imply that the "light" of song extends beyond the individual *celebrandus* to the whole family. The reference to the whole clan will presumably include its dead members, but Pindar says nothing of the dead explicitly, perhaps because the old patriarch. Themistius, is still living. Hence his imagery here is all of upward movement.

In the **"Fifth Pythian,"** Pindar uses a different technique to interweave the motifs of dead ancestors, the locale of their burial, and the connection with the living through fame and the waters of poetic immortality. Praising the victory of King Arcesilaus of Cyrene, Pindar refers to his remote ancestor, Aristoteles or Battus I, who founded the kingdom. Battus' descendants, "coming forth as bearers of gifts, receive with sacrifices" the Trojan Antenoridae who reached Cyrene in the mythical past: . . .

> Coming to them as bearers of gifts, the men whom Aristoteles led in swift ships as he opened the sea's deep path receive with sacrifices the horse-driving race (of the Trojan Antenoridae).

Here Pindar links Cyrene's historical past to the great cycle of Trojan myths. The Cyreneans' sacrificial honors to these early Trojan settlers also parallel the rituals in which they honor their own Battus in his status as a cult-hero. As a "founder." Battus has his tomb "at the lower edge of the agora where he lies apart in death." The word "dead," θανών, the last word of the epode, leads into the reference to Battus as heroized founder in the following strophe. Instead of viewing death in terms of ending and rupture, Pindar sets it into the continuity that is one of his main poetic goals. He incorporates Battus and the other "holy kings" of the remote past into the traditions of the city which the poet himself revivifies through the commemorative power of song.

In this passage, then, the opening of the fourth strophe, Pindar tells how Battus and the other "holy kings" of the past dwell in death "apart, before their homes" and hear the celebration of the great deeds of the present. They share in the χάρις that Pindar now bestows on the present king. Arcesilaus. . . .

Here, as in **"Olympian 14"** and **"Isthmian 6,"** the present celebration binds together the living and the dead generations. By reminding us of the heroized founder's presence beneath the soil of the agora and of the old kings' graves each before his own house (whether or not these are now outside the city walls), Pindar evokes the favoring presence of the kindly dead in the earth, who now approximate the status of local divinities.

That communication with the past takes place through the aural resonance of the poet's song: the "holy kings" who "hear the good fortune" of their descendants in Hades are exactly parallel to the dead father who receives the message brought by Acho in **"Olympian 14."** To complete the analogy, Arcesilaus is here called their "son," as the victor of is **"Olympian 14"** is the "son" of the "father" who receives Acho's message.

Though these remote kings have their φρένες beneath the earth, they are able to participate somehow in the festive music of the present celebration. The adjective κοινάν in 102 and the filial bond between the remote founder and the living Arcesilaus in the next lines explicitly link the glory conferred by song in the present and the glory won by his ancestors and celebrated with cult and sacrifice at the festivals. The poet's "soft dew of song" freshens the old *arete* of the ancestors; and simultaneously they, like Achilles in *Odyssey* 11, rejoice in the present *arete* made manifest in the victory of their descendant, King Arcesilaus.

The sequence of thought in 85-103 places the poet's present offerings of "libations of praise songs" in the context of the city's cult-offerings to its heroes and ancestors. These songs are themselves a kind of libation—one of Pindar's favorite metaphors. They are both a freshening "dew" and a "libation" that might be poured on a hero's grave.

Encomiastic song, like the communal rituals, participates in what Mircea Eliade calls [in her *Cosmos and History: The Myth of the Eternal Return,* trans. W. Trask (Princeton 1954)] the renewal of time: it makes the past part of the living present in the ever-renewable time of myth. This renewal of time, time as continuity, stands out the more forcefully against the ravages of time in seasonal change and biological decay, the "wintry blast of winds" that brings withering and destruction at the end of the ode.

Recently, Gregory Nagy has elaborated [in his *The Best of the Achaeans* (Baltimore 1979)] for the epic hero the implicit equation between hero-cult and the "fame imperishable" conferred by song. A similar equation, far more explicit, pervades the Epinicia. Pindar's closest analogy between the cultic honor of heroes and the poet's encomium of the victor occurs in **"Olympian 1."** Hieron's radiance and "mingling" with the supremacy of victory corresponds to the "radiant sacrifices" with which the heroes at Olympia are "mingled" at Pelops' tomb and altar, where ἁιμᾱκουρίᾳι is the cult term for offerings to heroes. We may recall also the legends of heroized athletes studied at length by Fontenrose.

The finale of **"Olympian 8"**, like that of **"Olympian 14,"** deals with ordinary mortals rather than founding heroes or "sacred kings." Here Pindar makes explicit the power of poetic Memory to overcome old age and death. The young victor's athletic success at Olympia "breathed into his father's father the spirit that can wrestle against old age." When Pindar remarks that success in itself brings a "forgetting" of Hades, he is perhaps playing on the force of poetic ἀ-λήθεια, the negation of oblivion by the poetry of praise. In the next verse he will "awaken Memory" (Mnamosuna) to preserve the achievements of the victor's family.

The poet then turns from the living to the dead. . . .

Like Acho in **"Olympian 14"** the agent of his message is personified (Angelia). Pindar makes Angelia the daughter of Hermes, appropriate enough in view of the latter's role as "messenger of the gods." But may we also think of the mediating function of Hermes Psychopompos, the god who literally makes the passage between life and death and connects the two worlds? Nowhere do the Epinicia explicitly mention Hermes Psychopompos. The Hermes of the Odes is Hermes Enagonios. The psychopomp is presumably out of place amid the joy of victory. And yet the emphatic placement of "Hermes" at the beginning of the epode, coming between the description of the dead in 77-80 and the deceased relative in Hades hearing news from the living, makes one wonder if the god's funereal role is not also in the background.

As in **"Olympian 14"** too, the verbal component of the message is reinforced by a visual quality which helps counteract the darkness of the Underworld. The "brilliant adornment" that the dead kinsman Iphion will "hear" from Angelia and "tell" to his Underworld companion Callimachus contrasts with the "covering dust" of burial. The ode's message will in fact prevent this concealing dust from doing its work of hiding the glory of the present victory. What is not "hidden" is specifically the *charis*, the honor of the victory as a shared joy in the reciprocal relations of the family. The emphasis on family solidarity here parallels the motif of the "joy in common with their son" that the dead kings "hear of" in **"Pythian 5."**

The metaphor of 79 f. now marks the third defeat of the forces of oblivion: first the "wrestling" against old age, then the "forgetting" of Hades, and finally the dust's "not concealing." In these three instances the battle against time receives a negative formulation, and this negative statement is a foil to the positive statement of the poet's "awakening Memory" in 74.

In countering the darkness of death with this "radiant adornment"—a phrase that can refer both to the victory and to the poetry that celebrates it—Pindar not only restores communication between living and dead kinsmen, but also reestablishes communication among the dead themselves. He restores to the inhabitants of that silent realm the "hearing" and "speaking" of animated family life. One is reminded of the power of speech that the shades in Homer's Underworld regain when they drink the sacrificial blood poured out to them by living men.

The verb "speak," ἐννέπειν, in 82 occurs twice before in the ode. The victor "spoke forth" or "proclaimed" the name of his city in glory to living men at Olympia. Apollo "spoke" to Aeacus, a signal communication between god and mortal, in the mythical past. This emphasis on "speaking" builds up the communicative energy set into motion by the victory so that the reverberations may reach down to Hades and impel the shades to address one another.

Pindar frequently suggests analogies or parallels between the victor, the mythical hero, and the poet. The visit of the poet's song to the Underworld reflects one such parallelism. A journey to the realm of the dead to bring back knowledge of the Beyond is a common task of the hero, from Gilgamesh on to Odysseus, Aeneas, and Dante. Pindar and Bacchylides both describe such catabases of the hero Heracles, Pindar in a fragmentary **"Theban Dithyramb,"**

Bacchylides in his Fifth Ode. Pindar performs an equivalent journey, figuratively, and brings back consoling wisdom about the realm of death in his account of the Beyond in **"Olympian 2."**

The passages that we have examined in **"Olympian 8,"** **"Olympian 14"** and **"Pythian 5"** remain within the traditional "Homeric" conception of Hades: lifeless and bloodless ghosts moving feebly amid dim shadows. Pindar knew of happier possibilities in the hereafter: in a celebrated passage of **"Olympian 2"** he describes the Isles of the Blest, with their soft winds, golden flowers, and radiant trees. But even in the three odes under discussion, the poet lightens the darkness of death through his privileged access to what is hidden or closed off from ordinary mortals. By penetrating both time and space through Memory and through the mobile power of his poetry's sound (Acho, Angelia), he too is able to bring knowledge of the living to the Underworld, and vice versa. He makes the unforgotten dead participate once more in the fresh joy of the living, and thus he soothes the bleakness of Hades with the balm of consolation.

Anne Burnett (essay date 1989)

SOURCE: "Performing Pindar's Odes." *Classical Philology*, Vol. 84, No. 4, October, 1984, pp. 283-93.

[*In the following excerpt, Burnett argues that a chorus sang and danced Pindar's odes.*]

It has been suggested in several places recently that we have been wrong to suppose a choral production for all of Pindar's epinician odes. One scholar, in fact, now assures us that—barring evidence to the contrary—we should assume of any Pindaric ode that it was meant for the solo voice. Furthermore, "evidence to the contrary" is recognized only if it appears within the song in question, and it is found to be virtually nonexistent. Passages in which Pindar might seem to refer to the singing of his chorus are explained in two ways: they refer either to impromptu group activities that were associated with, but quite separate from, the performance of the epinician ode, or to the behavior of a group of dancers who participated in the performance but did not sing. A chorus of mutes is allowed to appear sometimes, dancing while the soloist sang; however, if Pindar ever seems to attribute voices to them, he refers only to some kind of rhythmical sound that they made—a humming, or the repetition of a nonsense sound. This, we are told, will have been "the most convenient arrangement," but the basis of this judgment is not revealed. An "arrangement" that set one singer's voice against a background of manifold vocal noises might well have seemed inconvenient, not only to a soloist who wished to be heard but also to a poet who valued his words. Surely some quality other than "convenience" will have to be urged before we can accept this as one of Pindar's chosen modes.

If we are to appreciate the odes, we need to know what sort of performance Pindar envisioned as he composed them. Did he expect a chorus to take part, and if he did, what did he ask it to do? Discussion of performance must now take account of the humming hypothesis, and so as a preface to a review of Pindar's own words it should be noted that the Greeks did indeed recognize the making of nonsense sounds as a possible human activity. To do so was τερετίζειν, literally "to twitter like a swallow," and anyone who used his voice in this way was apt to be thought disgraceful or funny. Diogenes, when he could not keep the attention of his audience by making sense, attracted them by uttering sounds that were not words, thus confirming their foolishness. Unintelligible gibber was the mark of someone crude or primitive, and the verbal noun τερέτισμα came to be used in denigration of remarks that were mere twaddle. In a musical context nonsense sounds were even more objectionable. For Theophrastus to chirp along with the flute-player was typical of ugly and boorish behavior, while twaddling an accompaniment to his own dance was what the late-learner did as he tried to show off. The author of the pseudo-Aristotelian *Problems* took the trouble to point out that though the human voice, when it sang words, was sweeter than the lyre or the pipe, it was inferior to those instruments when it eschewed sense and simply twittered. Most striking is the remark that occurs in Plutarch's *Table Talk*, where the conversation turns on the possibility of redeeming one whose taste has been debauched by vulgar art. According to an optimistic speaker, even those who have sunk into such gibberish and gambolings can be led back to the opposite pole, which is represented by the high art of Menander, Euripides, and Pindar. His Pindar, at any rate, knew nothing of nonsense sounds, and it is natural to wonder whether any poet who was bent on solemn praise would have asked for a practice that carried these low connotations. Or, in reverse, one must wonder whether, if Pindar had used voices that did not produce words, the sound of "twittering" would ever have fallen into such disrepute. Would it not rather have been established as a respectable form of vocalization?

This, however, is not the way to enter the current discussion of Pindar's performances. According to its rules, those who still believe in singing choruses must bring "direct evidence" in support of their view. Ancient opinions, and especially the scholia, are not to be trusted, for they are capable of error. Furthermore, we cannot draw conclusions from undoubtedly choral works like the Pindaric paeans and partheneia, even though diction, meters, and stanza forms are common to them and the epinicians. Formal structure, we are told, is no indication of performance mode, for the ancients did not recognize generic differences between choral and solo song. Triads, it is now said, could be sung by a lyre-playing soloist, and therefore no argument can be made from what had seemed to be choral tradition. Not one of these negative assertions is entirely valid, but for the sake of tidiness it may be best to take up the challenge as it is offered, and to consider only the words of Pindaric victory odes as we try to decide how Pindar wished them to be sung.

With all tradition and precedent ruled out, it is reasonable to start with Pindar's own models—the divine originals, in the likeness of which each separate production was formed. Were the heavenly songs that cast themselves over the minds of praise poets sung, in Pindar's ideal view, by one voice or by many? Were there dancers, and if there were, what did they do? Three passages provide a single answer to these questions.

The first is **"Nemean 5,"** where the Muses' praise of the Aeacids becomes the ode's own mythic praise of its victor. . . .

Here the work of the divine dancers is to sing; so also that of the mortals who imitate them, one would suppose.

Again, in **"Isthmian 8,"** it is a plurality of Heliconian virgins that pours forth a θρῆνος for Achilles, thus providing the pattern for all epinician ὕμνοι and specifically for the one now being sung. . . .

Obviously the earthly replica of these maidens is to be found, not in a single lyre-player, but in the κῶμος so artfully assembled at the beginning of the ode.

A third model performance occurs at the opening of **"Pythian 1,"** where Pindar shows us the ideal that informs all of his songs. . . .

The lyre strikes up the prooemium that leads out the chorus, who, as singers, obey while their dance-steps commence. Those who would deny choral performance assert that Pindar here breaks the Muses into two mutually exclusive groups, so that "the singers do not dance and the dancers do not sing." This would be to rob each Muse of half her power, and Pindar in fact does no such thing. What he says is that the lyre gives the impulse to both rhythm and melody; the distinction is thus not between dancers and singers, but between the feet and the throats of performers who answer the lyre's commands with both.

These, however, are only ideals. When the Pindaric odes describe the actualities of their own celebrations, the noun κῶμος, with related verbs and compounds, makes a frequent appearance. Since a κῶμος is a group of males who sing and dance, it is natural to suppose that the victory songs bear witness, with these terms, to the mode of their own performance. Those who believe in solo performance, however, counteract this easy supposition with the assertion (indemonstrable) that κῶμος-singing could only be impromptu, and that the κῶμος thus could not, by definition, sing a formal epinician ode. Then, since Pindaric odes can say "we, or I, will make a κῶμος" can speak of the victor as being in the κῶμος, and can point to "this present κῶμος, they are forced to argue that the reference in all these cases is to disorganized bands of revelers who perform in some unrehearsed and artless fashion, before or after the singing of the proper song of praise.

The obstacle to any such separation of the Pindaric κῶμος from the Pindaric ode is the fact that the poet's words again and again announce the interdependence of κῶμος and ὕμνος, which is what Pindar calls his own songs. The oldest example of epinician song is termed ἐπικώμιος ὕμνος at **"Nemean 8."** At **"Pythian 10,"** in a metapoetical passage and so with clear reference to the present song, praise is ἐγκωμίων ἄωτος ὕμνων. At **"Pythian 4,"** the Muse is asked to rouse up an οὖρον ὕμνων for Arcesilaus in κῶμος, and again the self-reference is clear, since the Muse does not inspire impromptu revels and this wind of song is to praise Delphi and thechildren of Leto "today." Moreover, at **"Olympian 3,"** the Muse inspires the poet to find a new way of combining the voice that is the glory of the κῶμος (or that finds its glory in the κῶμος, the φωνάν... ἀγλαακωμος) with the Doric rhythm; this can only mean that the κῶμος sings the poet's composition.

At **"Isthmian 7,"** the sweetly melodious ὕμνος is to be the implement of those who make this present κῶμος for Strepsiades: κώρᾳζ' ἔπειτεν ἀδυρελεῖ σὺν ὕμνῳ καὶ Στρεψιάδᾳ. And in return, the κῶμος borrows this same epithet from the ὕμνος at **"Pythian 8"** where it is itself ἀδνμελής. Surely this is worth thinking about. If the melody of the κῶμος has precisely the same quality as that of the ode, it cannot be that Pindar's κῶμος is using its voice to give out some accompanying whisper or rhythmic repetition: it is singing the tune that Pindar has composed.

So much for the melody of the chorus; now for its verbal equipment. **"Nemean 9"** specifies that words are a part of this choric hymn-melody. . . .

"We are going to make a κῶμος from Sicyon to Etna, so, Muses, . . . supervise the sweet hymn made of words!" Here the song is directed by the Muses, and so is related specifically to memory and to sense; it is a composition, not an on-the-spot pastiche of victory cries. And we find the chorus handling not just words but grand subjects in **"Nemean 3"**. . . .

The ὕμνος tosses Zeus' contest to the young men's voices as the object of their praise. They could not be said to "sing an ἀγών" if their song was limited to rhythmical backup sounds uttered when the soloist paused.

At the beginning of **"Nemean 3"** the victory ode explicitly assigns itself for performance to a chorus of young men. Here the audience is taken backstage, the fiction being that we have caught the production while it is still in preparation. The performers who will make up the κῶμος are ready and waiting at some Aeginetan Asopus-place, but they have not yet received their "voice," which is to come to them from the Muse, by way of the poet's cleverness. Once the Muse has given him his start, the poet scores a song for the voices of these youths and for an accompanying lyre. . . .

The song's depiction of itself as it comes into being is a choral practice known from Alcman, but we have been disallowed that sort of observation. The points to be noticed are more minute, but they are telling. First, this κῶμος sings, since its epithet is μελιγάρυς. Next, its voice is the sort that comes from a Muse, and so it deals with sense, not nonsense. This is a song that praises virtue, not

a "rhythmic accompaniment" or an informal jubilee. It is provided to the young men from the poet's mind and so it is Pindar's composition, and it is allocated for performance to two parties, not to three. The ὕμνος is made the common property of a plurality of human voices and a single musical instrument. Nothing suggests that it is portioned out among solo singer, instrument, and wordless, murmuring dancers.

As evidence that the chorus does not sing words, the term ὄαρος has been emphasized; we are told that it "does not denote a singing voice but rather the sound of quiet conversation," and that it consequently indicates whispered background sounds. This conclusion, however, is invalidated by Pindar's own usage, for the same word appears at **"Nemean 7,"** where it represents the song claimed by the ode's first-person singer—the lone singer, by the antichoral hypothesis! It also appears at the end of **"Pythian 1,"** where it is part of a generic description of praise performance. Pindar is there establishing a model: εὖ ἀκούειν at its most desirable, the sort of praise that the victor is at this moment receiving, but that Phalaris did not. . . .

In this paradigm, praise is the sweet common possession of lyre and of soft voices of boys; there is no other vocal element, and so, if these boys could only murmur nonsense, this perfect song would have no power over fame.

The important fact about the word ὄαρος (strongly associated with lovers' whisperings and so with voices that are youthful and dulcet) is that it does denote communication by means of words. Thus Jason's highly rhetorical speech can be called πραῢς ὄαρος because it was spoken in a winning voice and by a young man. Here, in **"Nemean 3,"** the term adds a whiff of erotic charm to the poem's description of itself as a δακιμος ὕμνος—a song made of words, time-tested and traditional in its form.

The fact that the chorus not only sings, but sings sense and sings the present ode, is once again made clear in **"Pythian 5,"** where buried kings listen and understand with their entombed minds, as the κῶμος sprinkles family deeds with the sweet dew of song. . . .

In the lines that follow **"Pythian 5"** is even more directly self-described as voiced by a group of young singers. Arcesilaus has commissioned it because, having received the καλλίνικος-song at Delphi, he ought properly to repay Apollo in kind—that is, with expression of honor in another song performed by young men. . . .

That the present ode is what is meant by this ἀοιδὰ νέων is indicated by a phrase that came earlier, where the visible chorus is described as Apollo's delight.

At the end of **"Nemean 2"** the members of a citizen chorus are asked to use their sweetly melodious voices as they lead out a victory celebration in Acharnia. . . .

In this case we cannot be absolutely sure that the ode is describing its own performance, but the current song is safely placed in the mouths of another such chorus by the phrasing of **"Pythian 10."** Those who commissioned the ode wished to lead out the κῶμος-voice of a plurality of men. The voice of the ode thus issues from multiple performers, but it is at the same time the voice of Pindar himself—his composition—as the song soon makes plain. . . .

"I hope, while by the Peneus Ephyraean men pour out my sweet voice, to make Hippocleas yet more famous with my songs. . . ."

The future, θησέμεν, probably belongs to the class identified by Bundy and Slater as describing what will be done before this performance comes to its close. It occurs at the end of a sequence of metapoetical statements: I stop my mythic narration because praise demands that an ode touch on several subjects, and it is time now to celebrate the victor directly I will now make him yet more famous. However, even if this were a reference to a future measured in years—an example of the "hope for future victory" motif—the relation of ode to chorus would remain the same. Pindar says that his expectation of epinician success, now or later, depends upon men who "pour out" his voice, just as the Muses "poured out" the θρῆνος of Achilles that gave the victory ode its ideal form.

There is one more passage wherein the epinician purpose is clearly identified with a κῶμος that acts as its vehicle. At **"Pythian 8"** the ode, having finished its mythic account, is making its way back to the topic of the victor. There has been a brief prayer to Apollo, followed, as is often the case at this point, by a metapoetical discussion. Before closing, the ode must list the victor's past triumphs, fully but without ostentation, and this is the most dangerous part of the song. In the present case, indeed, this duty of boasting is peculiarly tricky because there is going to be a rare reference to defeated opponents, thrown by the boy wrestler. The song must validate its version of these events, and only if it strikes the right balance between the boy's achievement and the gods' aid can φθανος be avoided **"Pythian 8,"** however, proceeds with confidence because Dike has stood beside it in its making and its performance. Her presence inspires its continuation at this point. And how does Pindar make this all-important claim? He says: κώμωμὲν ἁδυμελεῖ / Δίκα πᾳρέστᾳκε. He cannot mean that Justice took part in some disorderly revel that has preceded the singing of his ode, for that would be both irrelevant and absurd. He can mean only that the justice-based validity of his epinician praise is located physically in a group of singing men—in a chorus, in other words.

In summary, then, we can say first that there is no trace of twittering or humming in the Pindaric odes. They frequently refer to a present group of young men, directly involved in their own performances, and the sound made by this group is described as the sound of song: a melodic enunciation of words, with instrumental guidance. Furthermore, Pindar specifies himself as the source from which this group takes its song, though the Muse stands behind all. It is thus plain that in many cases Pindar's odes were

meant to be sung and danced by choruses, just as the scholars of antiquity supposed. Nevertheless, someone might still ask whether there may not have been other cases in which Pindar expected a solo singer to perform, with or without a chorus of mutes. Since there is no evidence of any such practice, I shall attempt only the briefest and most speculative answer to this question.

An epinician ode was paid for, and the buyer got his money's worth only when the song was produced. Performance was everything, and consequently the modes of performance were determined by socio-economic factors as well as by poetic convention. Above all, each new example of praise had to be recognizable as being of its kind and worthy, for otherwise it would not serve its status-making purpose. And this means that, though the scale might change, we should expect the form of an epinician production to remain stable. Expenditure was a prime virtue in the patron of a victory ode, as Pindar often remarks, but a particular man could clearly surpass others only by doing again, more magnificently, just what they had already done. He would not want a different sort of performance; he would want the ὕμνου τεθμᾳς, with its traditional guarantee of fame. The music was expected to be properly identifiable as one of the ancient modes, and a "new fashion" meant only a more elegant manipulation of the dancers' voices. Victors wanted songs that seemed to "luxuriate" in their performances, as Pindar promised that his ode for Hagesidamus would do, but this did not mean innovation, it meant adding instruments, using pipe as well as lyre, or increasing length. Another sort of richness could be conveyed if a number of odes were presented in the course of a single celebration, as seems to have been the case with **"Isthmian 3 and 4."** And of course, the patron's open hand could be most spectacularly shown in choruses wherein the performers were unusually numerous or their dress was strikingly ornate.

Given this context of lavish conventionality, it is hard to see why a patron should ever have wanted his victory ode to be sung by just one stationary voice, if he had the option of a chorus. Nevertheless, let us suppose for the sake of argument that some victor did ask for just such a reduction in spectacle and sound. He surely would not have asked that his single performershould do, alone, what many voices did at other celebrations, for that could only seem thin by comparison with the ἐπικωμίᾳν ἀνδρῶν κλυτὰν ὄπᾳ. He would have insisted instead on a solo song of the showiest and most professional kind; one that made a musical display of a sort that only the trained citharode could provide. All of which means that, had it ever developed, the commissioned solo epinician would in all likelihood have sparkled with the endlessly varying melodies that were later the glory of the lyre-song. It would almost certainly not have retained the potentially tedious repetitions of the strophic system, whose function was to get a multiplicity of amateur performers through the difficulties of memorization. And since all of Pindar's epinicians show the strophes or triads that eased the work of a chorus but were alien to the citharodic art, there is no reason to think that any of them were meant for a solo voice. There is every reason, on the other hand, to assume that each was intended for a band of boys or men who represented the victor's class and his community, a group that Pindar could, with a kind of pun, term χώρᾱς ἄ γᾰλμᾰ.

FURTHER READING

Criticism

Bonnard, André. "Pindar, Prince of Poets and Poet of Princes." *Greek Civilization,* translated by A. Lytton Sells, pp. 104-24. New York: The Macmillan Company, 1959.
  Summarizes the content of several Pindaric odes.

Burton, R. W. B. *Pindar's Pythian Odes: Essays in Interpretation.* London: Oxford University Press, 1962, 202 p.
  Examines the structure and content of each ode as a finished work.

Cook, Albert. "Pindar: 'Great Deeds of Prowess Are Always Many-Mythed.'" *Myth and Language*, pp. 108-44. Bloomington: Indiana University Press, 1980.
  Examines Pindar's handling of myth as it relates to time in the language of his epinicions.

Finley, John H., Jr. "Pindar's Beginnings." *The Poetic Tradition,* edited by Don Cameron Allen and Henry T. Rowell, pp. 3-26. Baltimore: The Johns Hopkins Press, 1968.
  Traces the influence of Theognis and Simonides on Pindar's early odes.

Grant, Mary A. *Folktale and Hero-Tale Motifs in the Odes of Pindar.* Lawrence, KS: University of Kansas Press, 1967, 172 p.
  Presents many mythological motifs and the way Pindar used them in his odes.

Grube, G. M. A. À "The Beginnings of Criticism." *The Greek and Roman Critics,* pp. 1-21. Toronto: University of Toronto Press, 1965.
  Offers brief comments on reflexive literary criticism found in Pindar's odes, which contain "perhaps the first mention of the notion of appropriateness in literary criticism."

Hamilton, Richard. *Epinikion: General Form in the Odes of Pindar.* The Hague: Mouton, 1974, 126 p.
  Studies the form, or "the position of the elements of content," in forty-five Pindaric odes.

———. "The Pindaric Dithyramb." *Harvard Studies in Classical Philology,* Vol. 93, edited by Wendell V. Clausen, *et al.,* pp. 211-22. Cambridge, MA: Harvard University Press, 1990.
  Defines the Pindaric dithyramb and speculates on how they were performed.

Kirkwood, G. M. "*Nemean 7* and the Theme of Vicissitude in Pindar." *Poetry and Poetics from Ancient Greece to the Renaissance,* edited by G. M. Kirkwood, pp. 56-90. Ithaca,

NY: Cornell University Press, 1975.
  Applies Pindar's "brooding consciousness of fluctuation of vicissitude in human fortunes" to illuminate the meaning of "Nemean 7," the relevance of its parts, and some problematic passages.

Knust, Herbert. "What's the Matter with One-Eyed Riley?" *Comparative Literature* Vol. 17, No. 4 (Fall 1965): pp. 299-310.
  Discusses English poet Abraham Cowley's concept of Pindar's odic form and what Cowley's odes meant to his contemporary seventeenth-century audience.

Lefkowitz, Mary R. "Who Sang Pindar's Victory Odes?" *American Journal of Philology,* Vol. 109, No. 1 (Spring 1988): 1-11.
  Argues that Pindar's victory odes were sung as a solo, with or without choral dancing accompaniment.

———. *First-Person Fictions: Pindar's Poetic 'I.'* Oxford: Clarendon Press, 1991, 226 p.
  Addresses various aspects of Pindar's identity in his odes, centering on the question of why the odes seem more appropriate for a solo voice rather than a chorus, as traditionally has been suggested.

Pratt, Louise H. "Truth and Lies in Epinician." *Lying and Poetry from Homer to Pindar,* pp. 115-30. Ann Arbor. MI: The University of Michigan Press, 1993.
  Discusses the way truth claims are presented in epinician verse, distinguishing between the truth claims of victor praise and those of mythological narrative.

Race, William H. Climactic Elements in Pindar's Verse. *Harvard Studies in Classical Philology,* Vol. 92, edited by R. J. Tarrant, pp. 43-69. Cambridge, MA: Harvard University Press, 1989.
  Studies Pindar's poetic style in terms of the "climactic" interplay between style, rhetoric, and colometry, with particular reference to priamels, hymnal addresses, and catalogues in several odes.

Segal, Charles Paul. "God and Man in Pindar's First and Third *Olympian* Odes." Harvard Studies in Classical Philology, Vol. 68, pp. 211-67. Cambridge, MA: Harvard University Press, 1964.
  Elucidates the significance of the myths and structure of both odes in relation to the nature of heroic action and the link between the human and the divine.

Stoneman, Richard. "Pindar and the Mythological Tradition." *Philologus* 125 (1981): 44-63.
  Analyzes Pindar's treatment of episodes from legends of the Seven against Thebes andthe story of the marriage of Peleus and Thetis.

Young, David C. "Pindar." *Ancient Writers: Greece and Rome,* Vol. 1, edited by T. James Luce, pp. 157-78. New York: Charles Scribner's Sons, 1982.
  Reviews Pindar's life, works, and literary achievements. Also included selected annotated bibliography of Pindar's principal works and commentaries on Pindar's odes.

Additional coverage of Pindar's life and career is contained in the following source published by Gale Research: *Classical and Medieval Literature Criticism*, Vol. 12.

Poetry Criticism
INDEXES

Literary Criticism Series
Cumulative Author Index

Cumulative Nationality Index

Cumulative Title Index

How to Use This Index

The main references

Calvino, Italo
1923–1985 .... **CLC 5, 8, 11, 22, 33, 39,
73; SSC 3**

list all author entries in the following Gale Literary Criticism series:

BLC = *Black Literature Criticism*
CLC = *Contemporary Literary Criticism*
CLR = *Children's Literature Review*
CMLC = *Classical and Medieval Literature Criticism*
DA = *DISCovering Authors*
DAB = *DISCovering Authors: British*
DAC = *DISCovering Authors: Canadian*
DAM = *DISCovering Authors: Modules*
      DRAM: *Dramatists Module; **MST**: Most-Studied Authors Module;*
      MULT: *Multicultural Authors Module; **NOV**: Novelists Module;*
      POET: *Poets Module; **POP**: Popular Fiction and Genre Authors Module*
DC = *Drama Criticism*
HLC = *Hispanic Literature Criticism*
LC = *Literature Criticism from 1400 to 1800*
NCLC = *Nineteenth-Century Literature Criticism*
PC = *Poetry Criticism*
SSC = *Short Story Criticism*
TCLC = *Twentieth-Century Literary Criticism*
WLC = *World Literature Criticism, 1500 to the Present*

The cross-references

See also CANR 23; CA 85-88;
  obituary CA116

list all author entries in the following Gale biographical and literary sources:

AAYA = *Authors & Artists for Young Adults*
AITN = *Authors in the News*
BEST = *Bestsellers*
BW = *Black Writers*
CA = *Contemporary Authors*
CAAS = *Contemporary Authors Autobiography Series*
CABS = *Contemporary Authors Bibliographical Series*
CANR = *Contemporary Authors New Revision Series*
CAP = *Contemporary Authors Permanent Series*
CDALB = *Concise Dictionary of American Literary Biography*
CDBLB = *Concise Dictionary of British Literary Biography*
DLB = *Dictionary of Literary Biography*
DLBD = *Dictionary of Literary Biography Documentary Series*
DLBY = *Dictionary of Literary Biography Yearbook*
HW = *Hispanic Writers*
JRDA = *Junior DISCovering Authors*
MAICYA = *Major Authors and Illustrators for Children and Young Adults*
MTCW = *Major 20th-Century Writers*
NNAL = *Native North American Literature*
SAAS = *Something about the Author Autobiography Series*
SATA = *Something about the Author*
YABC = *Yesterday's Authors of Books for Children*

Literary Criticism Series
Cumulative Author Index

Arundel, Honor (Morfydd)
    1919-1973 .... **CLC 17**
    See also CA 21-22; 41-44R; CAP 2;
    CLR 35; SATA 4; SATA-Obit 24

Arzner, Dorothy   1897-1979 .... **CLC 98**

Asch, Sholem   1880-1957 .... **TCLC 3**
    See also CA 105

Ash, Shalom
    See Asch, Sholem

Ashbery, John (Lawrence)
    1927- ...... **CLC 2, 3, 4, 6, 9, 13, 15, 25,**
                    41, 77; DAM POET
    See also CA 5-8R; CANR 9, 37; DLB 5,
    165; DLBY 81; INT CANR-9; MTCW

Ashdown, Clifford
    See Freeman, R(ichard) Austin

Ashe, Gordon
    See Creasey, John

Ashton-Warner, Sylvia (Constance)
    1908-1984 .... **CLC 19**
    See also CA 69-72; 112; CANR 29; MTCW

Asimov, Isaac
    1920-1992 ...... **CLC 1, 3, 9, 19, 26, 76,**
                        92; DAM POP
    See also AAYA 13; BEST 90:2; CA 1-4R;
    137; CANR 2, 19, 36; CLR 12; DLB 8;
    DLBY 92; INT CANR-19; JRDA;
    MAICYA; MTCW; SATA 1, 26, 74

Assis, Joaquim Maria Machado de
    See Machado de Assis, Joaquim Maria

Astley, Thea (Beatrice May)
    1925- .... **CLC 41**
    See also CA 65-68; CANR 11, 43

Aston, James
    See White, T(erence) H(anbury)

Asturias, Miguel Angel
    1899-1974 .... **CLC 3, 8, 13;**
                    DAM MULT, NOV; HLC
    See also CA 25-28; 49-52; CANR 32;
    CAP 2; DLB 113; HW; MTCW

Atares, Carlos Saura
    See Saura (Atares), Carlos

Atheling, William
    See Pound, Ezra (Weston Loomis)

Atheling, William, Jr.
    See Blish, James (Benjamin)

Atherton, Gertrude (Franklin Horn)
    1857-1948 .... **TCLC 2**
    See also CA 104; 155; DLB 9, 78

Atherton, Lucius
    See Masters, Edgar Lee

Atkins, Jack
    See Harris, Mark

Atkinson, Kate .... **CLC 99**

Attaway, William (Alexander)
    1911-1986 .... **CLC 92; BLC;**
                            DAM MULT
    See also BW 2; CA 143; DLB 76

Atticus
    See Fleming, Ian (Lancaster)

Atwood, Margaret (Eleanor)
    1939- ..... **CLC 2, 3, 4, 8, 13, 15, 25, 44,**
        84; DA; DAB; DAC; DAM MST, NOV,
                POET; PC 8; SSC 2; WLC
    See also AAYA 12; BEST 89:2; CA 49-52;
    CANR 3, 24, 33; DLB 53;
    INT CANR-24; MTCW; SATA 50

Aubigny, Pierre d'
    See Mencken, H(enry) L(ouis)

Aubin, Penelope   1685-1731(?) .... **LC 9**
    See also DLB 39

Auchincloss, Louis (Stanton)
    1917- .... **CLC 4, 6, 9, 18, 45;**
                    DAM NOV; SSC 22
    See also CA 1-4R; CANR 6, 29, 55; DLB 2;
    DLBY 80; INT CANR-29; MTCW

Auden, W(ystan) H(ugh)
    1907-1973 ...... **CLC 1, 2, 3, 4, 6, 9, 11,**
            14, 43; DA; DAB; DAC; DAM DRAM,
                MST, POET; PC 1; WLC
    See also AAYA 18; CA 9-12R; 45-48;
    CANR 5; CDBLB 1914-1945; DLB 10,
    20; MTCW

Audiberti, Jacques
    1900-1965 ...... **CLC 38; DAM DRAM**
    See also CA 25-28R

Audubon, John James
    1785-1851 .... **NCLC 47**

Auel, Jean M(arie)
    1936- .... **CLC 31; DAM POP**
    See also AAYA 7; BEST 90:4; CA 103;
    CANR 21; INT CANR-21; SATA 91

Auerbach, Erich   1892-1957 ...... **TCLC 43**
    See also CA 118; 155

Augier, Emile   1820-1889 .... **NCLC 31**

August, John
    See De Voto, Bernard (Augustine)

Augustine, St.   354-430 ...... **CMLC 6; DAB**

Aurelius
    See Bourne, Randolph S(illiman)

Aurobindo, Sri   1872-1950 .... **TCLC 63**

Austen, Jane
    1775-1817 ..... **NCLC 1, 13, 19, 33, 51;**
            DA; DAB; DAC; DAM MST, NOV;
                        WLC
    See also AAYA 19; CDBLB 1789-1832;
    DLB 116

Auster, Paul   1947- .... **CLC 47**
    See also CA 69-72; CANR 23, 52

Austin, Frank
    See Faust, Frederick (Schiller)

Austin, Mary (Hunter)
    1868-1934 .... **TCLC 25**
    See also CA 109; DLB 9, 78

Autran Dourado, Waldomiro
    See Dourado, (Waldomiro Freitas) Autran

Averroes   1126-1198 .... **CMLC 7**
    See also DLB 115

Avicenna   980-1037 .... **CMLC 16**
    See also DLB 115

Avison, Margaret
    1918- .... **CLC 2, 4, 97; DAC;**
                        DAM POET
    See also CA 17-20R; DLB 53; MTCW

Axton, David
    See Koontz, Dean R(ay)

Ayckbourn, Alan
    1939- ...... **CLC 5, 8, 18, 33, 74; DAB;**
                        DAM DRAM
    See also CA 21-24R; CANR 31; DLB 13;
    MTCW

Aydy, Catherine
    See Tennant, Emma (Christina)

Ayme, Marcel (Andre)   1902-1967... **CLC 11**
    See also CA 89-92; CLR 25; DLB 72;
    SATA 91

Ayrton, Michael   1921-1975 .... **CLC 7**
    See also CA 5-8R; 61-64; CANR 9, 21

Azorin .... **CLC 11**
    See also Martinez Ruiz, Jose

Azuela, Mariano
    1873-1952 ..... **TCLC 3; DAM MULT;**
                        HLC
    See also CA 104; 131; HW; MTCW

Baastad, Babbis Friis
    See Friis-Baastad, Babbis Ellinor

Bab
    See Gilbert, W(illiam) S(chwenck)

Babbis, Eleanor
    See Friis-Baastad, Babbis Ellinor

Babel, Isaac
    See Babel, Isaak (Emmanuilovich)

Babel, Isaak (Emmanuilovich)
    1894-1941(?) ...... **TCLC 2, 13; SSC 16**
    See also CA 104; 155

Babits, Mihaly   1883-1941 .... **TCLC 14**
    See also CA 114

Babur   1483-1530 .... **LC 18**

Bacchelli, Riccardo   1891-1985 ..... **CLC 19**
    See also CA 29-32R; 117

Bach, Richard (David)
    1936- ...... **CLC 14; DAM NOV, POP**
    See also AITN 1; BEST 89:2; CA 9-12R;
    CANR 18; MTCW; SATA 13

Bachman, Richard
    See King, Stephen (Edwin)

Bachmann, Ingeborg   1926-1973 ..... **CLC 69**
    See also CA 93-96; 45-48; DLB 85

Bacon, Francis   1561-1626 .... **LC 18, 32**
    See also CDBLB Before 1660; DLB 151

Bacon, Roger   1214(?)-1292 ...... **CMLC 14**
    See also DLB 115

Bacovia, George .... **TCLC 24**
    See also Vasiliu, Gheorghe

Badanes, Jerome   1937- .... **CLC 59**

Bagehot, Walter   1826-1877 ...... **NCLC 10**
    See also DLB 55

Bagnold, Enid
    1889-1981 ...... **CLC 25; DAM DRAM**
    See also CA 5-8R; 103; CANR 5, 40;
    DLB 13, 160; MAICYA; SATA 1, 25

Bagritsky, Eduard   1895-1934 ..... **TCLC 60**

Bagrjana, Elisaveta
    See Belcheva, Elisaveta

Bagryana, Elisaveta .... **CLC 10**
    See also Belcheva, Elisaveta
    See also DLB 147

Barthelme, Donald
1931-1989 . . . . . . **CLC 1, 2, 3, 5, 6, 8, 13, 23, 46, 59; DAM NOV; SSC 2**
See also CA 21-24R; 129; CANR 20, 58; DLB 2; DLBY 80, 89; MTCW; SATA 7; SATA-Obit 62

Barthelme, Frederick 1943- . . . . **CLC 36**
See also CA 114; 122; DLBY 85; INT 122

Barthes, Roland (Gerard)
1915-1980 . . . . **CLC 24, 83**
See also CA 130; 97-100; MTCW

Barzun, Jacques (Martin) 1907- . . . . **CLC 51**
See also CA 61-64; CANR 22

Bashevis, Isaac
See Singer, Isaac Bashevis

Bashkirtseff, Marie 1859-1884 . . . **NCLC 27**

Basho
See Matsuo Basho

Bass, Kingsley B., Jr.
See Bullins, Ed

Bass, Rick 1958- . . . . **CLC 79**
See also CA 126; CANR 53

Bassani, Giorgio 1916- . . . . **CLC 9**
See also CA 65-68; CANR 33; DLB 128, 177; MTCW

Bastos, Augusto (Antonio) Roa
See Roa Bastos, Augusto (Antonio)

Bataille, Georges 1897-1962 . . . . **CLC 29**
See also CA 101; 89-92

Bates, H(erbert) E(rnest)
1905-1974 . . . . **CLC 46; DAB; DAM POP; SSC 10**
See also CA 93-96; 45-48; CANR 34; DLB 162; MTCW

Bauchart
See Camus, Albert

Baudelaire, Charles
1821-1867 . . . . **NCLC 6, 29, 55; DA; DAB; DAC; DAM MST, POET; PC 1; SSC 18; WLC**

Baudrillard, Jean 1929- . . . . **CLC 60**

Baum, L(yman) Frank 1856-1919 . . . **TCLC 7**
See also CA 108; 133; CLR 15; DLB 22; JRDA; MAICYA; MTCW; SATA 18

Baum, Louis F.
See Baum, L(yman) Frank

Baumbach, Jonathan 1933- . . . . . . **CLC 6, 23**
See also CA 13-16R; CAAS 5; CANR 12; DLBY 80; INT CANR-12; MTCW

Bausch, Richard (Carl) 1945- . . . . . . **CLC 51**
See also CA 101; CAAS 14; CANR 43; DLB 130

Baxter, Charles
1947- . . . . **CLC 45, 78; DAM POP**
See also CA 57-60; CANR 40; DLB 130

Baxter, George Owen
See Faust, Frederick (Schiller)

Baxter, James K(eir) 1926-1972 . . . . **CLC 14**
See also CA 77-80

Baxter, John
See Hunt, E(verette) Howard, (Jr.)

Bayer, Sylvia
See Glassco, John

Baynton, Barbara 1857-1929 . . . . . . **TCLC 57**

Beagle, Peter S(oyer) 1939- . . . . **CLC 7**
See also CA 9-12R; CANR 4, 51; DLBY 80; INT CANR-4; SATA 60

Bean, Normal
See Burroughs, Edgar Rice

Beard, Charles A(ustin)
1874-1948 . . . . **TCLC 15**
See also CA 115; DLB 17; SATA 18

Beardsley, Aubrey 1872-1898 . . . . . **NCLC 6**

Beattie, Ann
1947- . . . . **CLC 8, 13, 18, 40, 63; DAM NOV, POP; SSC 11**
See also BEST 90:2; CA 81-84; CANR 53; DLBY 82; MTCW

Beattie, James 1735-1803 . . . . **NCLC 25**
See also DLB 109

Beauchamp, Kathleen Mansfield 1888-1923
See Mansfield, Katherine
See also CA 104; 134; DA; DAC; DAM MST

Beaumarchais, Pierre-Augustin Caron de
1732-1799 . . . . **DC 4**
See also DAM DRAM

Beaumont, Francis
1584(?)-1616 . . . . **LC 33; DC 6**
See also CDBLB Before 1660; DLB 58, 121

Beauvoir, Simone (Lucie Ernestine Marie Bertrand) de
1908-1986 . . . . **CLC 1, 2, 4, 8, 14, 31, 44, 50, 71; DA; DAB; DAC; DAM MST, NOV; WLC**
See also CA 9-12R; 118; CANR 28; DLB 72; DLBY 86; MTCW

Becker, Carl (Lotus) 1873-1945 . . . . **TCLC 63**
See also CA 157; DLB 17

Becker, Jurek 1937-1997 . . . . **CLC 7, 19**
See also CA 85-88; 157; DLB 75

Becker, Walter 1950- . . . . **CLC 26**

Beckett, Samuel (Barclay)
1906-1989 . . . . . . **CLC 1, 2, 3, 4, 6, 9, 10, 11, 14, 18, 29, 57, 59, 83; DA; DAB; DAC; DAM DRAM, MST, NOV; SSC 16; WLC**
See also CA 5-8R; 130; CANR 33; CDBLB 1945-1960; DLB 13, 15; DLBY 90; MTCW

Beckford, William 1760-1844 . . . . **NCLC 16**
See also DLB 39

Beckman, Gunnel 1910- . . . . **CLC 26**
See also CA 33-36R; CANR 15; CLR 25; MAICYA; SAAS 9; SATA 6

Becque, Henri 1837-1899 . . . . **NCLC 3**

Beddoes, Thomas Lovell
1803-1849 . . . . **NCLC 3**
See also DLB 96

Bede c. 673-735 . . . . **CMLC 20**
See also DLB 146

Bedford, Donald F.
See Fearing, Kenneth (Flexner)

Beecher, Catharine Esther
1800-1878 . . . . **NCLC 30**
See also DLB 1

Beecher, John 1904-1980 . . . . **CLC 6**
See also AITN 1; CA 5-8R; 105; CANR 8

Beer, Johann 1655-1700 . . . . **LC 5**
See also DLB 168

Beer, Patricia 1924- . . . . **CLC 58**
See also CA 61-64; CANR 13, 46; DLB 40

Beerbohm, Max
See Beerbohm, (Henry) Max(imilian)

Beerbohm, (Henry) Max(imilian)
1872-1956 . . . . **TCLC 1, 24**
See also CA 104; 154; DLB 34, 100

Beer-Hofmann, Richard
1866-1945 . . . . **TCLC 60**
See also DLB 81

Begiebing, Robert J(ohn) 1946- . . . . . **CLC 70**
See also CA 122; CANR 40

Behan, Brendan
1923-1964 . . . . **CLC 1, 8, 11, 15, 79; DAM DRAM**
See also CA 73-76; CANR 33; CDBLB 1945-1960; DLB 13; MTCW

Behn, Aphra
1640(?)-1689 . . . . . . **LC 1, 30; DA; DAB; DAC; DAM DRAM, MST, NOV, POET; DC 4; PC 13; WLC**
See also DLB 39, 80, 131

Behrman, S(amuel) N(athaniel)
1893-1973 . . . . **CLC 40**
See also CA 13-16; 45-48; CAP 1; DLB 7, 44

Belasco, David 1853-1931 . . . . **TCLC 3**
See also CA 104; DLB 7

Belcheva, Elisaveta 1893- . . . . **CLC 10**
See also Bagryana, Elisaveta

Beldone, Phil "Cheech"
See Ellison, Harlan (Jay)

Beleno
See Azuela, Mariano

Belinski, Vissarion Grigoryevich
1811-1848 . . . . **NCLC 5**

Belitt, Ben 1911- . . . . **CLC 22**
See also CA 13-16R; CAAS 4; CANR 7; DLB 5

Bell, Gertrude 1868-1926 . . . . **TCLC 67**
See also DLB 174

Bell, James Madison
1826-1902 . . . . **TCLC 43; BLC; DAM MULT**
See also BW 1; CA 122; 124; DLB 50

Bell, Madison Smartt 1957- . . . . **CLC 41**
See also CA 111; CANR 28, 54

Bell, Marvin (Hartley)
1937- . . . . **CLC 8, 31; DAM POET**
See also CA 21-24R; CAAS 14; DLB 5; MTCW

Bell, W. L. D.
See Mencken, H(enry) L(ouis)

Bellamy, Atwood C.
See Mencken, H(enry) L(ouis)

Bellamy, Edward 1850-1898 . . . . . . **NCLC 4**
See also DLB 12

Bellin, Edward J.
See Kuttner, Henry

Bessie, Alvah 1904-1985. . . . . CLC 23
See also CA 5-8R; 116; CANR 2; DLB 26

Bethlen, T. D.
See Silverberg, Robert

Beti, Mongo. . . . CLC 27; BLC; DAM MULT
See also Biyidi, Alexandre

Betjeman, John
1906-1984 . . . . CLC 2, 6, 10, 34, 43;
DAB; DAM MST, POET
See also CA 9-12R; 112; CANR 33, 56;
CDBLB 1945-1960; DLB 20; DLBY 84;
MTCW

Bettelheim, Bruno 1903-1990 . . . . . . CLC 79
See also CA 81-84; 131; CANR 23; MTCW

Betti, Ugo 1892-1953 . . . . TCLC 5
See also CA 104; 155

Betts, Doris (Waugh) 1932- . . . . CLC 3, 6, 28
See also CA 13-16R; CANR 9; DLBY 82;
INT CANR-9

Bevan, Alistair
See Roberts, Keith (John Kingston)

Bialik, Chaim Nachman
1873-1934 . . . . TCLC 25

Bickerstaff, Isaac
See Swift, Jonathan

Bidart, Frank 1939- . . . . CLC 33
See also CA 140

Bienek, Horst 1930- . . . . CLC 7, 11
See also CA 73-76; DLB 75

Bierce, Ambrose (Gwinett)
1842-1914(?) . . . . TCLC 1, 7, 44; DA;
DAC; DAM MST; SSC 9; WLC
See also CA 104; 139; CDALB 1865-1917;
DLB 11, 12, 23, 71, 74

Biggers, Earl Derr 1884-1933 . . . . . TCLC 65
See also CA 108; 153

Billings, Josh
See Shaw, Henry Wheeler

Billington, (Lady) Rachel (Mary)
1942- . . . . CLC 43
See also AITN 2; CA 33-36R; CANR 44

Binyon, T(imothy) J(ohn) 1936- . . . . CLC 34
See also CA 111; CANR 28

Bioy Casares, Adolfo
1914- . . . . CLC 4, 8, 13, 88;
DAM MULT; HLC; SSC 17
See also CA 29-32R; CANR 19, 43;
DLB 113; HW; MTCW

Bird, Cordwainer
See Ellison, Harlan (Jay)

Bird, Robert Montgomery
1806-1854 . . . . NCLC 1

Birney, (Alfred) Earle
1904- . . . . CLC 1, 4, 6, 11; DAC;
DAM MST, POET
See also CA 1-4R; CANR 5, 20; DLB 88;
MTCW

Bishop, Elizabeth
1911-1979 . . . . . . CLC 1, 4, 9, 13, 15, 32;
DA; DAC; DAM MST, POET; PC 3
See also CA 5-8R; 89-92; CABS 2;
CANR 26; CDALB 1968-1988; DLB 5,
169; MTCW; SATA-Obit 24

Bishop, John 1935- . . . . CLC 10
See also CA 105

Bissett, Bill 1939- . . . . CLC 18; PC 14
See also CA 69-72; CAAS 19; CANR 15;
DLB 53; MTCW

Bitov, Andrei (Georgievich) 1937- . . . CLC 57
See also CA 142

Biyidi, Alexandre 1932-
See Beti, Mongo
See also BW 1; CA 114; 124; MTCW

Bjarme, Brynjolf
See Ibsen, Henrik (Johan)

Bjornson, Bjornstjerne (Martinius)
1832-1910 . . . . TCLC 7, 37
See also CA 104

Black, Robert
See Holdstock, Robert P.

Blackburn, Paul 1926-1971 . . . . . CLC 9, 43
See also CA 81-84; 33-36R; CANR 34;
DLB 16; DLBY 81

Black Elk
1863-1950 . . . . . TCLC 33; DAM MULT
See also CA 144; NNAL

Black Hobart
See Sanders, (James) Ed(ward)

Blacklin, Malcolm
See Chambers, Aidan

Blackmore, R(ichard) D(oddridge)
1825-1900 . . . . TCLC 27
See also CA 120; DLB 18

Blackmur, R(ichard) P(almer)
1904-1965 . . . . CLC 2, 24
See also CA 11-12; 25-28R; CAP 1; DLB 63

Black Tarantula
See Acker, Kathy

Blackwood, Algernon (Henry)
1869-1951 . . . . TCLC 5
See also CA 105; 150; DLB 153, 156, 178

Blackwood, Caroline
1931-1996 . . . . CLC 6, 9, 100
See also CA 85-88; 151; CANR 32;
DLB 14; MTCW

Blade, Alexander
See Hamilton, Edmond; Silverberg, Robert

Blaga, Lucian 1895-1961 . . . . CLC 75

Blair, Eric (Arthur) 1903-1950
See Orwell, George
See also CA 104; 132; DA; DAB; DAC;
DAM MST, NOV; MTCW; SATA 29

Blais, Marie-Claire
1939- . . . . CLC 2, 4, 6, 13, 22; DAC;
DAM MST
See also CA 21-24R; CAAS 4; CANR 38;
DLB 53; MTCW

Blaise, Clark 1940- . . . . CLC 29
See also AITN 2; CA 53-56; CAAS 3;
CANR 5; DLB 53

Blake, Nicholas
See Day Lewis, C(ecil)
See also DLB 77

Blake, William
1757-1827 . . . . NCLC 13, 37, 57; DA;
DAB; DAC; DAM MST, POET; PC 12;
WLC
See also CDBLB 1789-1832; DLB 93, 163;
MAICYA; SATA 30

Blake, William J(ames) 1894-1969 . . . PC 12
See also CA 5-8R; 25-28R

Blasco Ibanez, Vicente
1867-1928 . . . . TCLC 12; DAM NOV
See also CA 110; 131; HW; MTCW

Blatty, William Peter
1928- . . . . CLC 2; DAM POP
See also CA 5-8R; CANR 9

Bleeck, Oliver
See Thomas, Ross (Elmore)

Blessing, Lee 1949- . . . . CLC 54

Blish, James (Benjamin)
1921-1975 . . . . CLC 14
See also CA 1-4R; 57-60; CANR 3; DLB 8;
MTCW; SATA 66

Bliss, Reginald
See Wells, H(erbert) G(eorge)

Blixen, Karen (Christentze Dinesen)
1885-1962
See Dinesen, Isak
See also CA 25-28; CANR 22, 50; CAP 2;
MTCW; SATA 44

Bloch, Robert (Albert) 1917-1994 . . . CLC 33
See also CA 5-8R; 146; CAAS 20; CANR 5;
DLB 44; INT CANR-5; SATA 12;
SATA-Obit 82

Blok, Alexander (Alexandrovich)
1880-1921 . . . . TCLC 5
See also CA 104

Blom, Jan
See Breytenbach, Breyten

Bloom, Harold 1930- . . . . CLC 24
See also CA 13-16R; CANR 39; DLB 67

Bloomfield, Aurelius
See Bourne, Randolph S(illiman)

Blount, Roy (Alton), Jr. 1941- . . . . . CLC 38
See also CA 53-56; CANR 10, 28;
INT CANR-28; MTCW

Bloy, Leon 1846-1917. . . . . TCLC 22
See also CA 121; DLB 123

Blume, Judy (Sussman)
1938- . . . CLC 12, 30; DAM NOV, POP
See also AAYA 3; CA 29-32R; CANR 13,
37; CLR 2, 15; DLB 52; JRDA;
MAICYA; MTCW; SATA 2, 31, 79

Blunden, Edmund (Charles)
1896-1974 . . . . CLC 2, 56
See also CA 17-18; 45-48; CANR 54;
CAP 2; DLB 20, 100, 155; MTCW

Bly, Robert (Elwood)
1926- . . . . CLC 1, 2, 5, 10, 15, 38;
DAM POET
See also CA 5-8R; CANR 41; DLB 5;
MTCW

Boas, Franz 1858-1942. . . . . TCLC 56
See also CA 115

Bobette
See Simenon, Georges (Jacques Christian)

Boccaccio, Giovanni
1313-1375 . . . . CMLC 13; SSC 10

Bochco, Steven 1943- . . . . CLC 35
See also AAYA 11; CA 124; 138

Bodenheim, Maxwell 1892-1954 . . . TCLC 44
See also CA 110; DLB 9, 45

Bodker, Cecil 1927- . . . . **CLC 21**
See also CA 73-76; CANR 13, 44; CLR 23;
MAICYA; SATA 14

Boell, Heinrich (Theodor)
1917-1985 . . . . **CLC 2, 3, 6, 9, 11, 15, 27,
32, 72; DA; DAB; DAC; DAM MST,
NOV; SSC 23; WLC**
See also CA 21-24R; 116; CANR 24;
DLB 69; DLBY 85; MTCW

Boerne, Alfred
See Doeblin, Alfred

Boethius 480(?)-524(?) . . . . **CMLC 15**
See also DLB 115

Bogan, Louise
1897-1970 . . . . **CLC 4, 39, 46, 93;
DAM POET; PC 12**
See also CA 73-76; 25-28R; CANR 33;
DLB 45, 169; MTCW

Bogarde, Dirk . . . . **CLC 19**
See also Van Den Bogarde, Derek Jules
Gaspard Ulric Niven
See also DLB 14

Bogosian, Eric 1953- . . . . **CLC 45**
See also CA 138

Bograd, Larry 1953- . . . . **CLC 35**
See also CA 93-96; CANR 57; SAAS 21;
SATA 33, 89

Boiardo, Matteo Maria 1441-1494 . . . . **LC 6**

Boileau-Despreaux, Nicolas
1636-1711 . . . . **LC 3**

Bojer, Johan 1872-1959 . . . . **TCLC 64**

Boland, Eavan (Aisling)
1944- . . . . **CLC 40, 67; DAM POET**
See also CA 143; DLB 40

Bolt, Lee
See Faust, Frederick (Schiller)

Bolt, Robert (Oxton)
1924-1995 . . . . . . **CLC 14; DAM DRAM**
See also CA 17-20R; 147; CANR 35;
DLB 13; MTCW

Bombet, Louis-Alexandre-Cesar
See Stendhal

Bomkauf
See Kaufman, Bob (Garnell)

Bonaventura . . . . **NCLC 35**
See also DLB 90

Bond, Edward
1934- . . . **CLC 4, 6, 13, 23; DAM DRAM**
See also CA 25-28R; CANR 38; DLB 13;
MTCW

Bonham, Frank 1914-1989 . . . . **CLC 12**
See also AAYA 1; CA 9-12R; CANR 4, 36;
JRDA; MAICYA; SAAS 3; SATA 1, 49;
SATA-Obit 62

Bonnefoy, Yves
1923- . . . . . . **CLC 9, 15, 58; DAM MST,
POET**
See also CA 85-88; CANR 33; MTCW

Bontemps, Arna(ud Wendell)
1902-1973 . . . . **CLC 1, 18; BLC;
DAM MULT, NOV, POET**
See also BW 1; CA 1-4R; 41-44R; CANR 4,
35; CLR 6; DLB 48, 51; JRDA;
MAICYA; MTCW; SATA 2, 44;
SATA-Obit 24

Booth, Martin 1944- . . . . **CLC 13**
See also CA 93-96; CAAS 2

Booth, Philip 1925- . . . . **CLC 23**
See also CA 5-8R; CANR 5; DLBY 82

Booth, Wayne C(layson) 1921- . . . . . **CLC 24**
See also CA 1-4R; CAAS 5; CANR 3, 43;
DLB 67

Borchert, Wolfgang 1921-1947 . . . . . **TCLC 5**
See also CA 104; DLB 69, 124

Borel, Petrus 1809-1859 . . . . **NCLC 41**

Borges, Jorge Luis
1899-1986 . . . **CLC 1, 2, 3, 4, 6, 8, 9, 10,
13, 19, 44, 48, 83; DA; DAB; DAC;
DAM MST, MULT; HLC; SSC 4; WLC**
See also AAYA 19; CA 21-24R; CANR 19,
33; DLB 113; DLBY 86; HW; MTCW

Borowski, Tadeusz 1922-1951 . . . . . . **TCLC 9**
See also CA 106; 154

Borrow, George (Henry)
1803-1881 . . . . **NCLC 9**
See also DLB 21, 55, 166

Bosman, Herman Charles
1905-1951 . . . . **TCLC 49**

Bosschere, Jean de 1878(?)-1953 . . . **TCLC 19**
See also CA 115

Boswell, James
1740-1795 . . . . . . **LC 4; DA; DAB; DAC;
DAM MST; WLC**
See also CDBLB 1660-1789; DLB 104, 142

Bottoms, David 1949- . . . . **CLC 53**
See also CA 105; CANR 22; DLB 120;
DLBY 83

Boucicault, Dion 1820-1890 . . . . . . **NCLC 41**

Boucolon, Maryse 1937(?)-
See Conde, Maryse
See also CA 110; CANR 30, 53

Bourget, Paul (Charles Joseph)
1852-1935 . . . . **TCLC 12**
See also CA 107; DLB 123

Bourjaily, Vance (Nye) 1922- . . . . **CLC 8, 62**
See also CA 1-4R; CAAS 1; CANR 2;
DLB 2, 143

Bourne, Randolph S(illiman)
1886-1918 . . . . **TCLC 16**
See also CA 117; 155; DLB 63

Bova, Ben(jamin William) 1932- . . . . **CLC 45**
See also AAYA 16; CA 5-8R; CAAS 18;
CANR 11, 56; CLR 3; DLBY 81;
INT CANR-11; MAICYA; MTCW;
SATA 6, 68

Bowen, Elizabeth (Dorothea Cole)
1899-1973 . . . . . . **CLC 1, 3, 6, 11, 15, 22;
DAM NOV; SSC 3**
See also CA 17-18; 41-44R; CANR 35;
CAP 2; CDBLB 1945-1960; DLB 15, 162;
MTCW

Bowering, George 1935- . . . . **CLC 15, 47**
See also CA 21-24R; CAAS 16; CANR 10;
DLB 53

Bowering, Marilyn R(uthe) 1949- . . . **CLC 32**
See also CA 101; CANR 49

Bowers, Edgar 1924- . . . . **CLC 9**
See also CA 5-8R; CANR 24; DLB 5

Bowie, David . . . . **CLC 17**
See also Jones, David Robert

Bowles, Jane (Sydney)
1917-1973 . . . . **CLC 3, 68**
See also CA 19-20; 41-44R; CAP 2

Bowles, Paul (Frederick)
1910- . . . . **CLC 1, 2, 19, 53; SSC 3**
See also CA 1-4R; CAAS 1; CANR 1, 19,
50; DLB 5, 6; MTCW

Box, Edgar
See Vidal, Gore

Boyd, Nancy
See Millay, Edna St. Vincent

Boyd, William 1952- . . . . **CLC 28, 53, 70**
See also CA 114; 120; CANR 51

Boyle, Kay
1902-1992 . . . . . **CLC 1, 5, 19, 58; SSC 5**
See also CA 13-16R; 140; CAAS 1;
CANR 29; DLB 4, 9, 48, 86; DLBY 93;
MTCW

Boyle, Mark
See Kienzle, William X(avier)

Boyle, Patrick 1905-1982 . . . . **CLC 19**
See also CA 127

Boyle, T. C. 1948-
See Boyle, T(homas) Coraghessan

Boyle, T(homas) Coraghessan
1948- . . . . . . **CLC 36, 55, 90; DAM POP;
SSC 16**
See also BEST 90:4; CA 120; CANR 44;
DLBY 86

Boz
See Dickens, Charles (John Huffam)

Brackenridge, Hugh Henry
1748-1816 . . . . **NCLC 7**
See also DLB 11, 37

Bradbury, Edward P.
See Moorcock, Michael (John)

Bradbury, Malcolm (Stanley)
1932- . . . . **CLC 32, 61; DAM NOV**
See also CA 1-4R; CANR 1, 33; DLB 14;
MTCW

Bradbury, Ray (Douglas)
1920- . . . . . **CLC 1, 3, 10, 15, 42, 98; DA;
DAB; DAC; DAM MST, NOV, POP;
WLC**
See also AAYA 15; AITN 1, 2; CA 1-4R;
CANR 2, 30; CDALB 1968-1988; DLB 2,
8; INT CANR-30; MTCW; SATA 11, 64

Bradford, Gamaliel 1863-1932 . . . . . **TCLC 36**
See also DLB 17

Bradley, David (Henry, Jr.)
1950- . . . . . **CLC 23; BLC; DAM MULT**
See also BW 1; CA 104; CANR 26; DLB 33

Bradley, John Ed(mund, Jr.)
1958- . . . . **CLC 55**
See also CA 139

Bradley, Marion Zimmer
1930- . . . . **CLC 30; DAM POP**
See also AAYA 9; CA 57-60; CAAS 10;
CANR 7, 31, 51; DLB 8; MTCW;
SATA 90

Bradstreet, Anne
1612(?)-1672 . . . . . . **LC 4, 30; DA; DAC;
DAM MST, POET; PC 10**
See also CDALB 1640-1865; DLB 24

Brady, Joan 1939- . . . . **CLC 86**
See also CA 141

Bragg, Melvyn 1939- .... **CLC 10**
See also BEST 89:3; CA 57-60; CANR 10,
48; DLB 14

Braine, John (Gerard)
1922-1986 .... **CLC 1, 3, 41**
See also CA 1-4R; 120; CANR 1, 33;
CDBLB 1945-1960; DLB 15; DLBY 86;
MTCW

Bramah, Ernest 1868-1942....... **TCLC 72**
See also CA 156; DLB 70

Brammer, William 1930(?)-1978 .... **CLC 31**
See also CA 77-80

Brancati, Vitaliano 1907-1954..... **TCLC 12**
See also CA 109

Brancato, Robin F(idler) 1936- ..... **CLC 35**
See also AAYA 9; CA 69-72; CANR 11,
45; CLR 32; JRDA; SAAS 9; SATA 23

Brand, Max
See Faust, Frederick (Schiller)

Brand, Millen 1906-1980 .... **CLC 7**
See also CA 21-24R; 97-100

Branden, Barbara .... **CLC 44**
See also CA 148

Brandes, Georg (Morris Cohen)
1842-1927 .... **TCLC 10**
See also CA 105

Brandys, Kazimierz 1916- .... **CLC 62**

Branley, Franklyn M(ansfield)
1915- .... **CLC 21**
See also CA 33-36R; CANR 14, 39;
CLR 13; MAICYA; SAAS 16; SATA 4,
68

Brathwaite, Edward Kamau
1930- .... **CLC 11; DAM POET**
See also BW 2; CA 25-28R; CANR 11, 26,
47; DLB 125

Brautigan, Richard (Gary)
1935-1984 .... **CLC 1, 3, 5, 9, 12, 34, 42;**
DAM NOV
See also CA 53-56; 113; CANR 34; DLB 2,
5; DLBY 80, 84; MTCW; SATA 56

Brave Bird, Mary 1953-
See Crow Dog, Mary (Ellen)
See also NNAL

Braverman, Kate 1950- .... **CLC 67**
See also CA 89-92

Brecht, Bertolt
1898-1956 ...... **TCLC 1, 6, 13, 35; DA;**
DAB; DAC; DAM DRAM, MST; DC 3;
WLC
See also CA 104; 133; DLB 56, 124; MTCW

Brecht, Eugen Berthold Friedrich
See Brecht, Bertolt

Bremer, Fredrika 1801-1865 ..... **NCLC 11**

Brennan, Christopher John
1870-1932 .... **TCLC 17**
See also CA 117

Brennan, Maeve 1917- .... **CLC 5**
See also CA 81-84

Brentano, Clemens (Maria)
1778-1842 .... **NCLC 1**
See also DLB 90

Brent of Bin Bin
See Franklin, (Stella Maraia Sarah) Miles

Brenton, Howard 1942- .... **CLC 31**
See also CA 69-72; CANR 33; DLB 13;
MTCW

Breslin, James 1930-
See Breslin, Jimmy
See also CA 73-76; CANR 31; DAM NOV;
MTCW

Breslin, Jimmy .... **CLC 4, 43**
See also Breslin, James
See also AITN 1

Bresson, Robert 1901- .... **CLC 16**
See also CA 110; CANR 49

Breton, Andre
1896-1966 ..... **CLC 2, 9, 15, 54; PC 15**
See also CA 19-20; 25-28R; CANR 40;
CAP 2; DLB 65; MTCW

Breytenbach, Breyten
1939(?)- ...... **CLC 23, 37; DAM POET**
See also CA 113; 129

Bridgers, Sue Ellen 1942- .... **CLC 26**
See also AAYA 8; CA 65-68; CANR 11,
36; CLR 18; DLB 52; JRDA; MAICYA;
SAAS 1; SATA 22, 90

Bridges, Robert (Seymour)
1844-1930 .... **TCLC 1; DAM POET**
See also CA 104; 152; CDBLB 1890-1914;
DLB 19, 98

Bridie, James.................... TCLC 3
See also Mavor, Osborne Henry
See also DLB 10

Brin, David 1950- .... **CLC 34**
See also AAYA 21; CA 102; CANR 24;
INT CANR-24; SATA 65

Brink, Andre (Philippus)
1935- .... **CLC 18, 36**
See also CA 104; CANR 39; INT 103;
MTCW

Brinsmead, H(esba) F(ay) 1922- .... **CLC 21**
See also CA 21-24R; CANR 10; MAICYA;
SAAS 5; SATA 18, 78

Brittain, Vera (Mary)
1893(?)-1970 .... **CLC 23**
See also CA 13-16; 25-28R; CANR 58;
CAP 1; MTCW

Broch, Hermann 1886-1951....... **TCLC 20**
See also CA 117; DLB 85, 124

Brock, Rose
See Hansen, Joseph

Brodkey, Harold (Roy) 1930-1996 .. **CLC 56**
See also CA 111; 151; DLB 130

Brodsky, Iosif Alexandrovich 1940-1996
See Brodsky, Joseph
See also AITN 1; CA 41-44R; 151;
CANR 37; DAM POET; MTCW

Brodsky, Joseph
1940-1996 .. **CLC 4, 6, 13, 36, 100; PC 9**
See also Brodsky, Iosif Alexandrovich

Brodsky, Michael (Mark) 1948- .... **CLC 19**
See also CA 102; CANR 18, 41, 58

Bromell, Henry 1947-............. **CLC 5**
See also CA 53-56; CANR 9

Bromfield, Louis (Brucker)
1896-1956 .... **TCLC 11**
See also CA 107; 155; DLB 4, 9, 86

Broner, E(sther) M(asserman)
1930- .... **CLC 19**
See also CA 17-20R; CANR 8, 25; DLB 28

Bronk, William 1918-............. **CLC 10**
See also CA 89-92; CANR 23; DLB 165

Bronstein, Lev Davidovich
See Trotsky, Leon

Bronte, Anne 1820-1849......... **NCLC 4**
See also DLB 21

Bronte, Charlotte
1816-1855 ..... **NCLC 3, 8, 33, 58; DA;**
DAB; DAC; DAM MST, NOV; WLC
See also AAYA 17; CDBLB 1832-1890;
DLB 21, 159

Bronte, Emily (Jane)
1818-1848 .... **NCLC 16, 35; DA; DAB;**
DAC; DAM MST, NOV, POET; PC 8;
WLC
See also AAYA 17; CDBLB 1832-1890;
DLB 21, 32

Brooke, Frances 1724-1789 .... **LC 6**
See also DLB 39, 99

Brooke, Henry 1703(?)-1783 .... **LC 1**
See also DLB 39

Brooke, Rupert (Chawner)
1887-1915 .... **TCLC 2, 7; DA; DAB;**
DAC; DAM MST, POET; WLC
See also CA 104; 132; CDBLB 1914-1945;
DLB 19; MTCW

Brooke-Haven, P.
See Wodehouse, P(elham) G(renville)

Brooke-Rose, Christine 1926(?)- .... **CLC 40**
See also CA 13-16R; CANR 58; DLB 14

Brookner, Anita
1928- .... **CLC 32, 34, 51; DAB;**
DAM POP
See also CA 114; 120; CANR 37, 56;
DLBY 87; MTCW

Brooks, Cleanth 1906-1994 ..... **CLC 24, 86**
See also CA 17-20R; 145; CANR 33, 35;
DLB 63; DLBY 94; INT CANR-35;
MTCW

Brooks, George
See Baum, L(yman) Frank

Brooks, Gwendolyn
1917- ...... **CLC 1, 2, 4, 5, 15, 49; BLC;**
DA; DAC; DAM MST, MULT, POET;
PC 7; WLC
See also AAYA 20; AITN 1; BW 2;
CA 1-4R; CANR 1, 27, 52;
CDALB 1941-1968; CLR 27; DLB 5, 76,
165; MTCW; SATA 6

Brooks, Mel..................... CLC 12
See also Kaminsky, Melvin
See also AAYA 13; DLB 26

Brooks, Peter 1938-.............. **CLC 34**
See also CA 45-48; CANR 1

Brooks, Van Wyck 1886-1963...... **CLC 29**
See also CA 1-4R; CANR 6; DLB 45, 63,
103

Brophy, Brigid (Antonia)
1929-1995 .... **CLC 6, 11, 29**
See also CA 5-8R; 149; CAAS 4; CANR 25,
53; DLB 14; MTCW

Brosman, Catharine Savage 1934-.... **CLC 9**
See also CA 61-64; CANR 21, 46

Chernyshevsky, Nikolay Gavrilovich
1828-1889 . . . . **NCLC 1**

Cherry, Carolyn Janice 1942-
See Cherryh, C. J.
See also CA 65-68; CANR 10

Cherryh, C. J. . . . . **CLC 35**
See also Cherry, Carolyn Janice
See also DLBY 80; SATA 93

Chesnutt, Charles W(addell)
1858-1932 . . . . **TCLC 5, 39; BLC;**
DAM MULT; SSC 7
See also BW 1; CA 106; 125; DLB 12, 50,
78; MTCW

Chester, Alfred 1929(?)-1971 . . . . **CLC 49**
See also CA 33-36R; DLB 130

Chesterton, G(ilbert) K(eith)
1874-1936 . . . . **TCLC 1, 6, 64;**
DAM NOV, POET; SSC 1
See also CA 104; 132; CDBLB 1914-1945;
DLB 10, 19, 34, 70, 98, 149, 178; MTCW;
SATA 27

Chiang Pin-chin 1904-1986
See Ding Ling
See also CA 118

Ch'ien Chung-shu 1910- . . . . **CLC 22**
See also CA 130; MTCW

Child, L. Maria
See Child, Lydia Maria

Child, Lydia Maria 1802-1880 . . . . **NCLC 6**
See also DLB 1, 74; SATA 67

Child, Mrs.
See Child, Lydia Maria

Child, Philip 1898-1978 . . . . **CLC 19, 68**
See also CA 13-14; CAP 1; SATA 47

Childers, (Robert) Erskine
1870-1922 . . . . **TCLC 65**
See also CA 113; 153; DLB 70

Childress, Alice
1920-1994 . . . . **CLC 12, 15, 86, 96; BLC;**
DAM DRAM, MULT, NOV; DC 4
See also AAYA 8; BW 2; CA 45-48; 146;
CANR 3, 27, 50; CLR 14; DLB 7, 38;
JRDA; MAICYA; MTCW; SATA 7, 48,
81

Chin, Frank (Chew, Jr.) 1940- . . . . **DC 7**
See also CA 33-36R; DAM MULT

Chislett, (Margaret) Anne 1943- . . . . **CLC 34**
See also CA 151

Chitty, Thomas Willes 1926- . . . . **CLC 11**
See also Hinde, Thomas
See also CA 5-8R

Chivers, Thomas Holley
1809-1858 . . . . **NCLC 49**
See also DLB 3

Chomette, Rene Lucien 1898-1981
See Clair, Rene
See also CA 103

Chopin, Kate
. . . . **TCLC 5, 14; DA; DAB; SSC 8**
See also Chopin, Katherine
See also CDALB 1865-1917; DLB 12, 78;
YABC

Chopin, Katherine 1851-1904
See Chopin, Kate
See also CA 104; 122; DAC; DAM MST,
NOV

Chretien de Troyes
c. 12th cent. - . . . . **CMLC 10**

Christie
See Ichikawa, Kon

Christie, Agatha (Mary Clarissa)
1890-1976 . . . . . . **CLC 1, 6, 8, 12, 39, 48;**
DAB; DAC; DAM NOV
See also AAYA 9; AITN 1, 2; CA 17-20R;
61-64; CANR 10, 37; CDBLB 1914-1945;
DLB 13, 77; MTCW; SATA 36

Christie, (Ann) Philippa
See Pearce, Philippa
See also CA 5-8R; CANR 4

Christine de Pizan 1365(?)-1431(?) . . . . **LC 9**

Chubb, Elmer
See Masters, Edgar Lee

Chulkov, Mikhail Dmitrievich
1743-1792 . . . . **LC 2**
See also DLB 150

Churchill, Caryl 1938- . . . **CLC 31, 55; DC 5**
See also CA 102; CANR 22, 46; DLB 13;
MTCW

Churchill, Charles 1731-1764 . . . . **LC 3**
See also DLB 109

Chute, Carolyn 1947- . . . . **CLC 39**
See also CA 123

Ciardi, John (Anthony)
1916-1986 . . . . **CLC 10, 40, 44;**
DAM POET
See also CA 5-8R; 118; CAAS 2; CANR 5,
33; CLR 19; DLB 5; DLBY 86;
INT CANR-5; MAICYA; MTCW;
SATA 1, 65; SATA-Obit 46

Cicero, Marcus Tullius
106B.C.-43B.C. . . . . **CMLC 3**

Cimino, Michael 1943- . . . . **CLC 16**
See also CA 105

Cioran, E(mil) M. 1911-1995 . . . . **CLC 64**
See also CA 25-28R; 149

Cisneros, Sandra
1954- . . . . . **CLC 69; DAM MULT; HLC**
See also AAYA 9; CA 131; DLB 122, 152;
HW

Cixous, Helene 1937- . . . . **CLC 92**
See also CA 126; CANR 55; DLB 83;
MTCW

Clair, Rene . . . . **CLC 20**
See also Chomette, Rene Lucien

Clampitt, Amy 1920-1994 . . . **CLC 32; PC 19**
See also CA 110; 146; CANR 29; DLB 105

Clancy, Thomas L., Jr. 1947-
See Clancy, Tom
See also CA 125; 131; INT 131; MTCW

Clancy, Tom . . . . **CLC 45; DAM NOV, POP**
See also Clancy, Thomas L., Jr.
See also AAYA 9; BEST 89:1, 90:1

Clare, John
1793-1864 . . . . **NCLC 9; DAB;**
DAM POET
See also DLB 55, 96

Clarin
See Alas (y Urena), Leopoldo (Enrique
Garcia)

Clark, Al C.
See Goines, Donald

Clark, (Robert) Brian 1932- . . . . **CLC 29**
See also CA 41-44R

Clark, Curt
See Westlake, Donald E(dwin)

Clark, Eleanor 1913-1996 . . . . . . **CLC 5, 19**
See also CA 9-12R; 151; CANR 41; DLB 6

Clark, J. P.
See Clark, John Pepper
See also DLB 117

Clark, John Pepper
1935- . . . . **CLC 38; BLC; DAM DRAM,**
MULT; DC 5
See also Clark, J. P.
See also BW 1; CA 65-68; CANR 16

Clark, M. R.
See Clark, Mavis Thorpe

Clark, Mavis Thorpe 1909- . . . . **CLC 12**
See also CA 57-60; CANR 8, 37; CLR 30;
MAICYA; SAAS 5; SATA 8, 74

Clark, Walter Van Tilburg
1909-1971 . . . . **CLC 28**
See also CA 9-12R; 33-36R; DLB 9;
SATA 8

Clarke, Arthur C(harles)
1917- . . . . **CLC 1, 4, 13, 18, 35;**
DAM POP; SSC 3
See also AAYA 4; CA 1-4R; CANR 2, 28,
55; JRDA; MAICYA; MTCW; SATA 13,
70

Clarke, Austin
1896-1974 . . . . . . **CLC 6, 9; DAM POET**
See also CA 29-32; 49-52; CAP 2; DLB 10,
20

Clarke, Austin C(hesterfield)
1934- . . . . **CLC 8, 53; BLC; DAC;**
DAM MULT
See also BW 1; CA 25-28R; CAAS 16;
CANR 14, 32; DLB 53, 125

Clarke, Gillian 1937- . . . . **CLC 61**
See also CA 106; DLB 40

Clarke, Marcus (Andrew Hislop)
1846-1881 . . . . **NCLC 19**

Clarke, Shirley 1925- . . . . **CLC 16**

Clash, The
See Headon, (Nicky) Topper; Jones, Mick;
Simonon, Paul; Strummer, Joe

Claudel, Paul (Louis Charles Marie)
1868-1955 . . . . **TCLC 2, 10**
See also CA 104

Clavell, James (duMaresq)
1925-1994 . . . . **CLC 6, 25, 87;**
DAM NOV, POP
See also CA 25-28R; 146; CANR 26, 48;
MTCW

Cleaver, (Leroy) Eldridge
1935- . . . . . **CLC 30; BLC; DAM MULT**
See also BW 1; CA 21-24R; CANR 16

Cleese, John (Marwood) 1939- . . . . . **CLC 21**
See also Monty Python
See also CA 112; 116; CANR 35; MTCW

Cleishbotham, Jebediah
See Scott, Walter

Cleland, John 1710-1789 . . . . **LC 2**
See also DLB 39

Constant (de Rebecque), (Henri) Benjamin
1767-1830 . . . . NCLC 6
See also DLB 119

Conybeare, Charles Augustus
See Eliot, T(homas) S(tearns)

Cook, Michael 1933- . . . . CLC 58
See also CA 93-96; DLB 53

Cook, Robin 1940- . . . . CLC 14; DAM POP
See also BEST 90:2; CA 108; 111;
CANR 41; INT 111

Cook, Roy
See Silverberg, Robert

Cooke, Elizabeth 1948- . . . . CLC 55
See also CA 129

Cooke, John Esten 1830-1886 . . . . . NCLC 5
See also DLB 3

Cooke, John Estes
See Baum, L(yman) Frank

Cooke, M. E.
See Creasey, John

Cooke, Margaret
See Creasey, John

Cook-Lynn, Elizabeth
1930- . . . . CLC 93; DAM MULT
See also CA 133; DLB 175; NNAL

Cooney, Ray . . . . CLC 62

Cooper, Douglas 1960- . . . . CLC 86

Cooper, Henry St. John
See Creasey, John

Cooper, J(oan) California
. . . . CLC 56; DAM MULT
See also AAYA 12; BW 1; CA 125;
CANR 55

Cooper, James Fenimore
1789-1851 . . . . NCLC 1, 27, 54
See also CDALB 1640-1865; DLB 3;
SATA 19

Coover, Robert (Lowell)
1932- . . . . CLC 3, 7, 15, 32, 46, 87;
DAM NOV; SSC 15
See also CA 45-48; CANR 3, 37, 58;
DLB 2; DLBY 81; MTCW

Copeland, Stewart (Armstrong)
1952- . . . . CLC 26

Coppard, A(lfred) E(dgar)
1878-1957 . . . . TCLC 5; SSC 21
See also CA 114; DLB 162; 1

Coppee, Francois 1842-1908 . . . . . . TCLC 25

Coppola, Francis Ford 1939- . . . . CLC 16
See also CA 77-80; CANR 40; DLB 44

Corbiere, Tristan 1845-1875 . . . . . NCLC 43

Corcoran, Barbara 1911- . . . . CLC 17
See also AAYA 14; CA 21-24R; CAAS 2;
CANR 11, 28, 48; DLB 52; JRDA;
SAAS 20; SATA 3, 77

Cordelier, Maurice
See Giraudoux, (Hippolyte) Jean

Corelli, Marie 1855-1924 . . . . TCLC 51
See also Mackay, Mary
See also DLB 34, 156

Corman, Cid . . . . CLC 9
See also Corman, Sidney
See also CAAS 2; DLB 5

Corman, Sidney 1924-
See Corman, Cid
See also CA 85-88; CANR 44; DAM POET

Cormier, Robert (Edmund)
1925- . . . . CLC 12, 30; DA; DAB; DAC;
DAM MST, NOV
See also AAYA 3, 19; CA 1-4R; CANR 5,
23; CDALB 1968-1988; CLR 12; DLB 52;
INT CANR-23; JRDA; MAICYA;
MTCW; SATA 10, 45, 83

Corn, Alfred (DeWitt III) 1943- . . . . CLC 33
See also CA 104; CAAS 25; CANR 44;
DLB 120; DLBY 80

Corneille, Pierre
1606-1684 . . . . LC 28; DAB; DAM MST

Cornwell, David (John Moore)
1931- . . . . CLC 9, 15; DAM POP
See also le Carre, John
See also CA 5-8R; CANR 13, 33; MTCW

Corso, (Nunzio) Gregory 1930- . . . CLC 1, 11
See also CA 5-8R; CANR 41; DLB 5, 16;
MTCW

Cortazar, Julio
1914-1984 . . . . . . CLC 2, 3, 5, 10, 13, 15,
33, 34, 92; DAM MULT, NOV; HLC;
SSC 7
See also CA 21-24R; CANR 12, 32;
DLB 113; HW; MTCW

CORTES, HERNAN 1484-1547 . . . . . LC 31

Corwin, Cecil
See Kornbluth, C(yril) M.

Cosic, Dobrica 1921- . . . . CLC 14
See also CA 122; 138

Costain, Thomas B(ertram)
1885-1965 . . . . CLC 30
See also CA 5-8R; 25-28R; DLB 9

Costantini, Humberto
1924(?)-1987 . . . . CLC 49
See also CA 131; 122; HW

Costello, Elvis 1955- . . . . CLC 21

Cotes, Cecil V.
See Duncan, Sara Jeannette

Cotter, Joseph Seamon Sr.
1861-1949 . . . . TCLC 28; BLC;
DAM MULT
See also BW 1; CA 124; DLB 50

Couch, Arthur Thomas Quiller
See Quiller-Couch, Arthur Thomas

Coulton, James
See Hansen, Joseph

Couperus, Louis (Marie Anne)
1863-1923 . . . . TCLC 15
See also CA 115

Coupland, Douglas
1961- . . . . CLC 85; DAC; DAM POP
See also CA 142; CANR 57

Court, Wesli
See Turco, Lewis (Putnam)

Courtenay, Bryce 1933- . . . . CLC 59
See also CA 138

Courtney, Robert
See Ellison, Harlan (Jay)

Cousteau, Jacques-Yves 1910- . . . . . . CLC 30
See also CA 65-68; CANR 15; MTCW;
SATA 38

Coward, Noel (Peirce)
1899-1973 . . . . CLC 1, 9, 29, 51;
DAM DRAM
See also AITN 1; CA 17-18; 41-44R;
CANR 35; CAP 2; CDBLB 1914-1945;
DLB 10; MTCW

Cowley, Malcolm 1898-1989 . . . . CLC 39
See also CA 5-8R; 128; CANR 3, 55;
DLB 4, 48; DLBY 81, 89; MTCW

Cowper, William
1731-1800 . . . . . . NCLC 8; DAM POET
See also DLB 104, 109

Cox, William Trevor
1928- . . . . CLC 9, 14, 71; DAM NOV
See also Trevor, William
See also CA 9-12R; CANR 4, 37, 55;
DLB 14; INT CANR-37; MTCW

Coyne, P. J.
See Masters, Hilary

Cozzens, James Gould
1903-1978 . . . . CLC 1, 4, 11, 92
See also CA 9-12R; 81-84; CANR 19;
CDALB 1941-1968; DLB 9; DLBD 2;
DLBY 84; MTCW

Crabbe, George 1754-1832 . . . . NCLC 26
See also DLB 93

Craddock, Charles Egbert
See Murfree, Mary Noailles

Craig, A. A.
See Anderson, Poul (William)

Craik, Dinah Maria (Mulock)
1826-1887 . . . . NCLC 38
See also DLB 35, 163; MAICYA; SATA 34

Cram, Ralph Adams 1863-1942 . . . . TCLC 45

Crane, (Harold) Hart
1899-1932 . . . . . . TCLC 2, 5; DA; DAB;
DAC; DAM MST, POET; PC 3; WLC
See also CA 104; 127; CDALB 1917-1929;
DLB 4, 48; MTCW

Crane, R(onald) S(almon)
1886-1967 . . . . CLC 27
See also CA 85-88; DLB 63

Crane, Stephen (Townley)
1871-1900 . . . . TCLC 11, 17, 32; DA;
DAB; DAC; DAM MST, NOV, POET;
SSC 7; WLC
See also AAYA 21; CA 109; 140;
CDALB 1865-1917; DLB 12, 54, 78; 2

Crase, Douglas 1944- . . . . CLC 58
See also CA 106

Crashaw, Richard 1612(?)-1649 . . . . . LC 24
See also DLB 126

Craven, Margaret
1901-1980 . . . . CLC 17; DAC
See also CA 103

Crawford, F(rancis) Marion
1854-1909 . . . . TCLC 10
See also CA 107; DLB 71

Crawford, Isabella Valancy
1850-1887 . . . . NCLC 12
See also DLB 92

Crayon, Geoffrey
See Irving, Washington

Creasey, John 1908-1973 . . . . CLC 11
See also CA 5-8R; 41-44R; CANR 8;
DLB 77; MTCW

Darwin, Charles 1809-1882 ...... **NCLC 57**
See also DLB 57, 166

Daryush, Elizabeth 1887-1977.... **CLC 6, 19**
See also CA 49-52; CANR 3; DLB 20

Dashwood, Edmee Elizabeth Monica de la Pasture 1890-1943
See Delafield, E. M.
See also CA 119; 154

Daudet, (Louis Marie) Alphonse 1840-1897 .... **NCLC 1**
See also DLB 123

Daumal, Rene 1908-1944 .... **TCLC 14**
See also CA 114

Davenport, Guy (Mattison, Jr.) 1927- .... **CLC 6, 14, 38; SSC 16**
See also CA 33-36R; CANR 23; DLB 130

Davidson, Avram 1923-
See Queen, Ellery
See also CA 101; CANR 26; DLB 8

Davidson, Donald (Grady) 1893-1968 .... **CLC 2, 13, 19**
See also CA 5-8R; 25-28R; CANR 4; DLB 45

Davidson, Hugh
See Hamilton, Edmond

Davidson, John 1857-1909 .... **TCLC 24**
See also CA 118; DLB 19

Davidson, Sara 1943- .... **CLC 9**
See also CA 81-84; CANR 44

Davie, Donald (Alfred) 1922-1995 .... **CLC 5, 8, 10, 31**
See also CA 1-4R; 149; CAAS 3; CANR 1, 44; DLB 27; MTCW

Davies, Ray(mond Douglas) 1944- .. **CLC 21**
See also CA 116; 146

Davies, Rhys 1903-1978 .... **CLC 23**
See also CA 9-12R; 81-84; CANR 4; DLB 139

Davies, (William) Robertson 1913-1995 ..... **CLC 2, 7, 13, 25, 42, 75, 91; DA; DAB; DAC; DAM MST, NOV, POP; WLC**
See also BEST 89:2; CA 33-36R; 150; CANR 17, 42; DLB 68; INT CANR-17; MTCW

Davies, W(illiam) H(enry) 1871-1940 .... **TCLC 5**
See also CA 104; DLB 19, 174

Davies, Walter C.
See Kornbluth, C(yril) M.

Davis, Angela (Yvonne) 1944- .... **CLC 77; DAM MULT**
See also BW 2; CA 57-60; CANR 10

Davis, B. Lynch
See Bioy Casares, Adolfo; Borges, Jorge Luis

Davis, Gordon
See Hunt, E(verette) Howard, (Jr.)

Davis, Harold Lenoir 1896-1960.... **CLC 49**
See also CA 89-92; DLB 9

Davis, Rebecca (Blaine) Harding 1831-1910 .... **TCLC 6**
See also CA 104; DLB 74

Davis, Richard Harding 1864-1916 .... **TCLC 24**
See also CA 114; DLB 12, 23, 78, 79; DLBD 13

Davison, Frank Dalby 1893-1970 ... **CLC 15**
See also CA 116

Davison, Lawrence H.
See Lawrence, D(avid) H(erbert Richards)

Davison, Peter (Hubert) 1928- ..... **CLC 28**
See also CA 9-12R; CAAS 4; CANR 3, 43; DLB 5

Davys, Mary 1674-1732............. **LC 1**
See also DLB 39

Dawson, Fielding 1930- .... **CLC 6**
See also CA 85-88; DLB 130

Dawson, Peter
See Faust, Frederick (Schiller)

Day, Clarence (Shepard, Jr.) 1874-1935 .... **TCLC 25**
See also CA 108; DLB 11

Day, Thomas 1748-1789............. **LC 1**
See also DLB 39; 1

Day Lewis, C(ecil) 1904-1972 .... **CLC 1, 6, 10; DAM POET; PC 11**
See also Blake, Nicholas
See also CA 13-16; 33-36R; CANR 34; CAP 1; DLB 15, 20; MTCW

Dazai, Osamu .... **TCLC 11**
See also Tsushima, Shuji

de Andrade, Carlos Drummond
See Drummond de Andrade, Carlos

Deane, Norman
See Creasey, John

de Beauvoir, Simone (Lucie Ernestine Marie Bertrand)
See Beauvoir, Simone (Lucie Ernestine Marie Bertrand) de

de Brissac, Malcolm
See Dickinson, Peter (Malcolm)

de Chardin, Pierre Teilhard
See Teilhard de Chardin, (Marie Joseph) Pierre

Dee, John 1527-1608 .... **LC 20**

Deer, Sandra 1940-............... **CLC 45**

De Ferrari, Gabriella 1941-........ **CLC 65**
See also CA 146

Defoe, Daniel 1660(?)-1731 .... **LC 1; DA; DAB; DAC; DAM MST, NOV; WLC**
See also CDBLB 1660-1789; DLB 39, 95, 101; JRDA; MAICYA; SATA 22

de Gourmont, Remy(-Marie-Charles)
See Gourmont, Remy (-Marie-Charles) de

de Hartog, Jan 1914-............. **CLC 19**
See also CA 1-4R; CANR 1

de Hostos, E. M.
See Hostos (y Bonilla), Eugenio Maria de

de Hostos, Eugenio M.
See Hostos (y Bonilla), Eugenio Maria de

Deighton, Len .... **CLC 4, 7, 22, 46**
See also Deighton, Leonard Cyril
See also AAYA 6; BEST 89:2; CDBLB 1960 to Present; DLB 87

Deighton, Leonard Cyril 1929-
See Deighton, Len
See also CA 9-12R; CANR 19, 33; DAM NOV, POP; MTCW

Dekker, Thomas 1572(?)-1632 ..... **LC 22; DAM DRAM**
See also CDBLB Before 1660; DLB 62, 172

Delafield, E. M. 1890-1943 .... **TCLC 61**
See also Dashwood, Edmee Elizabeth Monica de la Pasture
See also DLB 34

de la Mare, Walter (John) 1873-1956 .... **TCLC 4, 53; DAB; DAC; DAM MST, POET; SSC 14; WLC**
See also CDBLB 1914-1945; CLR 23; DLB 162; SATA 16

Delaney, Franey
See O'Hara, John (Henry)

Delaney, Shelagh 1939- .... **CLC 29; DAM DRAM**
See also CA 17-20R; CANR 30; CDBLB 1960 to Present; DLB 13; MTCW

Delany, Mary (Granville Pendarves) 1700-1788 .... **LC 12**

Delany, Samuel R(ay, Jr.) 1942- .... **CLC 8, 14, 38; BLC; DAM MULT**
See also BW 2; CA 81-84; CANR 27, 43; DLB 8, 33; MTCW

De La Ramee, (Marie) Louise 1839-1908
See Ouida
See also SATA 20

de la Roche, Mazo 1879-1961 ...... **CLC 14**
See also CA 85-88; CANR 30; DLB 68; SATA 64

Delbanco, Nicholas (Franklin) 1942- .... **CLC 6, 13**
See also CA 17-20R; CAAS 2; CANR 29, 55; DLB 6

del Castillo, Michel 1933- .... **CLC 38**
See also CA 109

Deledda, Grazia (Cosima) 1875(?)-1936 .... **TCLC 23**
See also CA 123

Delibes, Miguel .... **CLC 8, 18**
See also Delibes Setien, Miguel

Delibes Setien, Miguel 1920-
See Delibes, Miguel
See also CA 45-48; CANR 1, 32; HW; MTCW

DeLillo, Don 1936- ..... **CLC 8, 10, 13, 27, 39, 54, 76; DAM NOV, POP**
See also BEST 89:1; CA 81-84; CANR 21; DLB 6, 173; MTCW

de Lisser, H. G.
See De Lisser, H(erbert) G(eorge)
See also DLB 117

De Lisser, H(erbert) G(eorge) 1878-1944 .... **TCLC 12**
See also de Lisser, H. G.
See also BW 2; CA 109; 152

Drummond, William Henry
1854-1907 .... **TCLC 25**
See also DLB 92

Drummond de Andrade, Carlos
1902-1987 .... **CLC 18**
See also Andrade, Carlos Drummond de
See also CA 132; 123

Drury, Allen (Stuart) 1918-........ **CLC 37**
See also CA 57-60; CANR 18, 52;
INT CANR-18

Dryden, John
1631-1700 .... **LC 3, 21; DA; DAB;**
DAC; DAM DRAM, MST, POET;
DC 3; WLC
See also CDBLB 1660-1789; DLB 80, 101,
131

Duberman, Martin 1930-.......... **CLC 8**
See also CA 1-4R; CANR 2

Dubie, Norman (Evans) 1945-...... **CLC 36**
See also CA 69-72; CANR 12; DLB 120

Du Bois, W(illiam) E(dward) B(urghardt)
1868-1963 .... **CLC 1, 2, 13, 64, 96;**
BLC; DA; DAC; DAM MST, MULT,
NOV; WLC
See also BW 1; CA 85-88; CANR 34;
CDALB 1865-1917; DLB 47, 50, 91;
MTCW; SATA 42

Dubus, Andre
1936-........ **CLC 13, 36, 97; SSC 15**
See also CA 21-24R; CANR 17; DLB 130;
INT CANR-17

Duca Minimo
See D'Annunzio, Gabriele

Ducharme, Rejean 1941-.......... **CLC 74**
See also DLB 60

Duclos, Charles Pinot 1704-1772 ..... **LC 1**

Dudek, Louis 1918-........... **CLC 11, 19**
See also CA 45-48; CAAS 14; CANR 1;
DLB 88

Duerrenmatt, Friedrich
1921-1990 ...... **CLC 1, 4, 8, 11, 15, 43;**
DAM DRAM
See also CA 17-20R; CANR 33; DLB 69,
124; MTCW

Duffy, Bruce (?)-................. **CLC 50**

Duffy, Maureen 1933-............ **CLC 37**
See also CA 25-28R; CANR 33; DLB 14;
MTCW

Dugan, Alan 1923-.............. **CLC 2, 6**
See also CA 81-84; DLB 5

du Gard, Roger Martin
See Martin du Gard, Roger

Duhamel, Georges 1884-1966 .... **CLC 8**
See also CA 81-84; 25-28R; CANR 35;
DLB 65; MTCW

Dujardin, Edouard (Emile Louis)
1861-1949 .... **TCLC 13**
See also CA 109; DLB 123

Dulles, John Foster 1888-1959 .... **TCLC 72**
See also CA 115; 149

Dumas, Alexandre (Davy de la Pailleterie)
1802-1870 .... **NCLC 11; DA; DAB;**
DAC; DAM MST, NOV; WLC
See also DLB 119; SATA 18

Dumas, Alexandre
1824-1895 .... **NCLC 9; DC 1**

Dumas, Claudine
See Malzberg, Barry N(athaniel)

Dumas, Henry L. 1934-1968 ..... **CLC 6, 62**
See also BW 1; CA 85-88; DLB 41

du Maurier, Daphne
1907-1989 .... **CLC 6, 11, 59; DAB;**
DAC; DAM MST, POP; SSC 18
See also CA 5-8R; 128; CANR 6, 55;
MTCW; SATA 27; SATA-Obit 60

Dunbar, Paul Laurence
1872-1906 ...... **TCLC 2, 12; BLC; DA;**
DAC; DAM MST, MULT, POET; PC 5;
SSC 8; WLC
See also BW 1; CA 104; 124;
CDALB 1865-1917; DLB 50, 54, 78;
SATA 34

Dunbar, William 1460(?)-1530(?) .... **LC 20**
See also DLB 132, 146

Duncan, Dora Angela
See Duncan, Isadora

Duncan, Isadora 1877(?)-1927..... **TCLC 68**
See also CA 118; 149

Duncan, Lois 1934-.............. **CLC 26**
See also AAYA 4; CA 1-4R; CANR 2, 23,
36; CLR 29; JRDA; MAICYA; SAAS 2;
SATA 1, 36, 75

Duncan, Robert (Edward)
1919-1988 .... **CLC 1, 2, 4, 7, 15, 41, 55;**
DAM POET; PC 2
See also CA 9-12R; 124; CANR 28; DLB 5,
16; MTCW

Duncan, Sara Jeannette
1861-1922 .... **TCLC 60**
See also CA 157; DLB 92

Dunlap, William 1766-1839 .... **NCLC 2**
See also DLB 30, 37, 59

Dunn, Douglas (Eaglesham)
1942-.................... **CLC 6, 40**
See also CA 45-48; CANR 2, 33; DLB 40;
MTCW

Dunn, Katherine (Karen) 1945-..... **CLC 71**
See also CA 33-36R

Dunn, Stephen 1939- .... **CLC 36**
See also CA 33-36R; CANR 12, 48, 53;
DLB 105

Dunne, Finley Peter 1867-1936.... **TCLC 28**
See also CA 108; DLB 11, 23

Dunne, John Gregory 1932-........ **CLC 28**
See also CA 25-28R; CANR 14, 50;
DLBY 80

Dunsany, Edward John Moreton Drax
Plunkett 1878-1957
See Dunsany, Lord
See also CA 104; 148; DLB 10

Dunsany, Lord............ **.... TCLC 2, 59**
See also Dunsany, Edward John Moreton
Drax Plunkett
See also DLB 77, 153, 156

du Perry, Jean
See Simenon, Georges (Jacques Christian)

Durang, Christopher (Ferdinand)
1949-.................... **CLC 27, 38**
See also CA 105; CANR 50

Duras, Marguerite
1914-1996 ..... **CLC 3, 6, 11, 20, 34, 40,**
68, 100
See also CA 25-28R; 151; CANR 50;
DLB 83; MTCW

Durban, (Rosa) Pam 1947-........ **CLC 39**
See also CA 123

Durcan, Paul
1944- .... **CLC 43, 70; DAM POET**
See also CA 134

Durkheim, Emile 1858-1917 ...... **TCLC 55**

Durrell, Lawrence (George)
1912-1990 .... **CLC 1, 4, 6, 8, 13, 27, 41;**
DAM NOV
See also CA 9-12R; 132; CANR 40;
CDBLB 1945-1960; DLB 15, 27;
DLBY 90; MTCW

Durrenmatt, Friedrich
See Duerrenmatt, Friedrich

Dutt, Toru 1856-1877.......... **NCLC 29**

Dwight, Timothy 1752-1817...... **NCLC 13**
See also DLB 37

Dworkin, Andrea 1946- .... **CLC 43**
See also CA 77-80; CAAS 21; CANR 16,
39; INT CANR-16; MTCW

Dwyer, Deanna
See Koontz, Dean R(ay)

Dwyer, K. R.
See Koontz, Dean R(ay)

Dylan, Bob 1941-...... **CLC 3, 4, 6, 12, 77**
See also CA 41-44R; DLB 16

Eagleton, Terence (Francis) 1943-
See Eagleton, Terry
See also CA 57-60; CANR 7, 23; MTCW

Eagleton, Terry .... **CLC 63**
See also Eagleton, Terence (Francis)

Early, Jack
See Scoppettone, Sandra

East, Michael
See West, Morris L(anglo)

Eastaway, Edward
See Thomas, (Philip) Edward

Eastlake, William (Derry)
1917-1997 .... **CLC 8**
See also CA 5-8R; 158; CAAS 1; CANR 5;
DLB 6; INT CANR-5

Eastman, Charles A(lexander)
1858-1939 ..... **TCLC 55; DAM MULT**
See also DLB 175; NNAL; 1

Eberhart, Richard (Ghormley)
1904- .. **CLC 3, 11, 19, 56; DAM POET**
See also CA 1-4R; CANR 2;
CDALB 1941-1968; DLB 48; MTCW

Eberstadt, Fernanda 1960-........ **CLC 39**
See also CA 136

Echegaray (y Eizaguirre), Jose (Maria Waldo)
1832-1916 .... **TCLC 4**
See also CA 104; CANR 32; HW; MTCW

Echeverria, (Jose) Esteban (Antonino)
1805-1851 .... **NCLC 18**

Echo
See Proust, (Valentin-Louis-George-Eugene-)
Marcel

Emecheta, (Florence Onye) Buchi
    1944- .. CLC 14, 48; BLC; DAM MULT
    See also BW 2; CA 81-84; CANR 27;
    DLB 117; MTCW; SATA 66

Emerson, Ralph Waldo
    1803-1882 ..... NCLC 1, 38; DA; DAB;
    DAC; DAM MST, POET; PC 18; WLC
    See also CDALB 1640-1865; DLB 1, 59, 73

Eminescu, Mihail 1850-1889 ..... NCLC 33

Empson, William
    1906-1984 .... CLC 3, 8, 19, 33, 34
    See also CA 17-20R; 112; CANR 31;
    DLB 20; MTCW

Enchi Fumiko (Ueda) 1905-1986.... CLC 31
    See also CA 129; 121

Ende, Michael (Andreas Helmuth)
    1929-1995 .... CLC 31
    See also CA 118; 124; 149; CANR 36;
    CLR 14; DLB 75; MAICYA; SATA 61;
    SATA-Brief 42; SATA-Obit 86

Endo, Shusaku
    1923-1996 .... CLC 7, 14, 19, 54, 99;
                                  DAM NOV
    See also CA 29-32R; 153; CANR 21, 54;
    MTCW

Engel, Marian 1933-1985.......... CLC 36
    See also CA 25-28R; CANR 12; DLB 53;
    INT CANR-12

Engelhardt, Frederick
    See Hubbard, L(afayette) Ron(ald)

Enright, D(ennis) J(oseph)
    1920- .... CLC 4, 8, 31
    See also CA 1-4R; CANR 1, 42; DLB 27;
    SATA 25

Enzensberger, Hans Magnus
    1929- .... CLC 43
    See also CA 116; 119

Ephron, Nora 1941- .... CLC 17, 31
    See also AITN 2; CA 65-68; CANR 12, 39

Epicurus 341B.C.-270B.C........ CMLC 21
    See also DLB 176

Epsilon
    See Betjeman, John

Epstein, Daniel Mark 1948- .... CLC 7
    See also CA 49-52; CANR 2, 53

Epstein, Jacob 1956- .... CLC 19
    See also CA 114

Epstein, Joseph 1937-............. CLC 39
    See also CA 112; 119; CANR 50

Epstein, Leslie 1938- .... CLC 27
    See also CA 73-76; CAAS 12; CANR 23

Equiano, Olaudah
    1745(?)-1797 .... LC 16; BLC;
                                  DAM MULT
    See also DLB 37, 50

Erasmus, Desiderius 1469(?)-1536.... LC 16

Erdman, Paul E(mil) 1932- .... CLC 25
    See also AITN 1; CA 61-64; CANR 13, 43

Erdrich, Louise
    1954- .... CLC 39, 54; DAM MULT,
                                  NOV, POP
    See also AAYA 10; BEST 89:1; CA 114;
    CANR 41; DLB 152, 175; MTCW;
    NNAL; SATA 94

Erenburg, Ilya (Grigoryevich)
    See Ehrenburg, Ilya (Grigoryevich)

Erickson, Stephen Michael 1950-
    See Erickson, Steve
    See also CA 129

Erickson, Steve .... CLC 64
    See also Erickson, Stephen Michael

Ericson, Walter
    See Fast, Howard (Melvin)

Eriksson, Buntel
    See Bergman, (Ernst) Ingmar

Ernaux, Annie 1940- .... CLC 88
    See also CA 147

Eschenbach, Wolfram von
    See Wolfram von Eschenbach

Eseki, Bruno
    See Mphahlele, Ezekiel

Esenin, Sergei (Alexandrovich)
    1895-1925 .... TCLC 4
    See also CA 104

Eshleman, Clayton 1935-........... CLC 7
    See also CA 33-36R; CAAS 6; DLB 5

Espriella, Don Manuel Alvarez
    See Southey, Robert

Espriu, Salvador 1913-1985........ CLC 9
    See also CA 154; 115; DLB 134

Espronceda, Jose de 1808-1842... NCLC 39

Esse, James
    See Stephens, James

Esterbrook, Tom
    See Hubbard, L(afayette) Ron(ald)

Estleman, Loren D.
    1952- ...... CLC 48; DAM NOV, POP
    See also CA 85-88; CANR 27;
    INT CANR-27; MTCW

Eugenides, Jeffrey 1960(?)- .... CLC 81
    See also CA 144

Euripides c. 485B.C.-406B.C. .... DC 4
    See also DA; DAB; DAC; DAM DRAM,
    MST; DLB 176; YABC

Evan, Evin
    See Faust, Frederick (Schiller)

Evans, Evan
    See Faust, Frederick (Schiller)

Evans, Marian
    See Eliot, George

Evans, Mary Ann
    See Eliot, George

Evarts, Esther
    See Benson, Sally

Everett, Percival L. 1956- .... CLC 57
    See also BW 2; CA 129

Everson, R(onald) G(ilmour)
    1903- .... CLC 27
    See also CA 17-20R; DLB 88

Everson, William (Oliver)
    1912-1994 .... CLC 1, 5, 14
    See also CA 9-12R; 145; CANR 20; DLB 5,
    16; MTCW

Evtushenko, Evgenii Aleksandrovich
    See Yevtushenko, Yevgeny (Alexandrovich)

Ewart, Gavin (Buchanan)
    1916-1995 .... CLC 13, 46
    See also CA 89-92; 150; CANR 17, 46;
    DLB 40; MTCW

Ewers, Hanns Heinz 1871-1943 ... TCLC 12
    See also CA 109; 149

Ewing, Frederick R.
    See Sturgeon, Theodore (Hamilton)

Exley, Frederick (Earl)
    1929-1992 .... CLC 6, 11
    See also AITN 2; CA 81-84; 138; DLB 143;
    DLBY 81

Eynhardt, Guillermo
    See Quiroga, Horacio (Sylvestre)

Ezekiel, Nissim 1924-............. CLC 61
    See also CA 61-64

Ezekiel, Tish O'Dowd 1943-....... CLC 34
    See also CA 129

Fadeyev, A.
    See Bulgya, Alexander Alexandrovich

Fadeyev, Alexander............... TCLC 53
    See also Bulgya, Alexander Alexandrovich

Fagen, Donald 1948-............. CLC 26

Fainzilberg, Ilya Arnoldovich 1897-1937
    See Ilf, Ilya
    See also CA 120

Fair, Ronald L. 1932-............. CLC 18
    See also BW 1; CA 69-72; CANR 25;
    DLB 33

Fairbairns, Zoe (Ann) 1948- .... CLC 32
    See also CA 103; CANR 21

Falco, Gian
    See Papini, Giovanni

Falconer, James
    See Kirkup, James

Falconer, Kenneth
    See Kornbluth, C(yril) M.

Falkland, Samuel
    See Heijermans, Herman

Fallaci, Oriana 1930-............. CLC 11
    See also CA 77-80; CANR 15, 58; MTCW

Faludy, George 1913-............. CLC 42
    See also CA 21-24R

Faludy, Gyoergy
    See Faludy, George

Fanon, Frantz
    1925-1961 .... CLC 74; BLC;
                                  DAM MULT
    See also BW 1; CA 116; 89-92

Fanshawe, Ann 1625-1680......... LC 11

Fante, John (Thomas) 1911-1983 ... CLC 60
    See also CA 69-72; 109; CANR 23;
    DLB 130; DLBY 83

Farah, Nuruddin
    1945- ..... CLC 53; BLC; DAM MULT
    See also BW 2; CA 106; DLB 125

Fargue, Leon-Paul 1876(?)-1947 ... TCLC 11
    See also CA 109

Farigoule, Louis
    See Romains, Jules

Farina, Richard 1936(?)-1966 .... CLC 9
    See also CA 81-84; 25-28R

Farley, Walter (Lorimer)
  1915-1989 . . . . **CLC 17**
  See also CA 17-20R; CANR 8, 29; DLB 22;
  JRDA; MAICYA; SATA 2, 43

Farmer, Philip Jose 1918- . . . . **CLC 1, 19**
  See also CA 1-4R; CANR 4, 35; DLB 8;
  MTCW; SATA 93

Farquhar, George
  1677-1707 . . . . **LC 21; DAM DRAM**
  See also DLB 84

Farrell, J(ames) G(ordon)
  1935-1979 . . . . **CLC 6**
  See also CA 73-76; 89-92; CANR 36;
  DLB 14; MTCW

Farrell, James T(homas)
  1904-1979 . . . . **CLC 1, 4, 8, 11, 66**
  See also CA 5-8R; 89-92; CANR 9; DLB 4,
  9, 86; DLBD 2; MTCW

Farren, Richard J.
  See Betjeman, John

Farren, Richard M.
  See Betjeman, John

Fassbinder, Rainer Werner
  1946-1982 . . . . **CLC 20**
  See also CA 93-96; 106; CANR 31

Fast, Howard (Melvin)
  1914- . . . . **CLC 23; DAM NOV**
  See also AAYA 16; CA 1-4R; CAAS 18;
  CANR 1, 33, 54; DLB 9; INT CANR-33;
  SATA 7

Faulcon, Robert
  See Holdstock, Robert P.

Faulkner, William (Cuthbert)
  1897-1962 . . . . . **CLC 1, 3, 6, 8, 9, 11, 14,
  18, 28, 52, 68; DA; DAB; DAC;
  DAM MST, NOV; SSC 1; WLC**
  See also AAYA 7; CA 81-84; CANR 33;
  CDALB 1929-1941; DLB 9, 11, 44, 102;
  DLBD 2; DLBY 86; MTCW

Fauset, Jessie Redmon
  1884(?)-1961 . . . . **CLC 19, 54; BLC;
  DAM MULT**
  See also BW 1; CA 109; DLB 51

Faust, Frederick (Schiller)
  1892-1944(?) . . . . . **TCLC 49; DAM POP**
  See also CA 108; 152

Faust, Irvin 1924- . . . . **CLC 8**
  See also CA 33-36R; CANR 28; DLB 2, 28;
  DLBY 80

Fawkes, Guy
  See Benchley, Robert (Charles)

Fearing, Kenneth (Flexner)
  1902-1961 . . . . **CLC 51**
  See also CA 93-96; DLB 9

Fecamps, Elise
  See Creasey, John

Federman, Raymond 1928- . . . . . . **CLC 6, 47**
  See also CA 17-20R; CAAS 8; CANR 10,
  43; DLBY 80

Federspiel, J(uerg) F. 1931- . . . . **CLC 42**
  See also CA 146

Feiffer, Jules (Ralph)
  1929- . . . . . . **CLC 2, 8, 64; DAM DRAM**
  See also AAYA 3; CA 17-20R; CANR 30;
  DLB 7, 44; INT CANR-30; MTCW;
  SATA 8, 61

Feige, Hermann Albert Otto Maximilian
  See Traven, B.

Feinberg, David B. 1956-1994 . . . . . . **CLC 59**
  See also CA 135; 147

Feinstein, Elaine 1930- . . . . **CLC 36**
  See also CA 69-72; CAAS 1; CANR 31;
  DLB 14, 40; MTCW

Feldman, Irving (Mordecai) 1928- . . . . **CLC 7**
  See also CA 1-4R; CANR 1; DLB 169

Felix-Tchicaya, Gerald
  See Tchicaya, Gerald Felix

Fellini, Federico 1920-1993 . . . . . **CLC 16, 85**
  See also CA 65-68; 143; CANR 33

Felsen, Henry Gregor 1916- . . . . **CLC 17**
  See also CA 1-4R; CANR 1; SAAS 2;
  SATA 1

Fenton, James Martin 1949- . . . . **CLC 32**
  See also CA 102; DLB 40

Ferber, Edna 1887-1968 . . . . **CLC 18, 93**
  See also AITN 1; CA 5-8R; 25-28R; DLB 9,
  28, 86; MTCW; SATA 7

Ferguson, Helen
  See Kavan, Anna

Ferguson, Samuel 1810-1886 . . . . . **NCLC 33**
  See also DLB 32

Fergusson, Robert 1750-1774 . . . . **LC 29**
  See also DLB 109

Ferling, Lawrence
  See Ferlinghetti, Lawrence (Monsanto)

Ferlinghetti, Lawrence (Monsanto)
  1919(?)- . . . . **CLC 2, 6, 10, 27;
  DAM POET; PC 1**
  See also CA 5-8R; CANR 3, 41;
  CDALB 1941-1968; DLB 5, 16; MTCW

Fernandez, Vicente Garcia Huidobro
  See Huidobro Fernandez, Vicente Garcia

Ferrer, Gabriel (Francisco Victor) Miro
  See Miro (Ferrer), Gabriel (Francisco
  Victor)

Ferrier, Susan (Edmonstone)
  1782-1854 . . . . **NCLC 8**
  See also DLB 116

Ferrigno, Robert 1948(?)- . . . . **CLC 65**
  See also CA 140

Ferron, Jacques 1921-1985 . . . **CLC 94; DAC**
  See also CA 117; 129; DLB 60

Feuchtwanger, Lion 1884-1958 . . . . . **TCLC 3**
  See also CA 104; DLB 66

Feuillet, Octave 1821-1890 . . . . . . **NCLC 45**

Feydeau, Georges (Leon Jules Marie)
  1862-1921 . . . . . **TCLC 22; DAM DRAM**
  See also CA 113; 152

Fichte, Johann Gottlieb
  1762-1814 . . . . **NCLC 62**
  See also DLB 90

Ficino, Marsilio 1433-1499 . . . . **LC 12**

Fiedeler, Hans
  See Doeblin, Alfred

Fiedler, Leslie A(aron)
  1917- . . . . **CLC 4, 13, 24**
  See also CA 9-12R; CANR 7; DLB 28, 67;
  MTCW

Field, Andrew 1938- . . . . **CLC 44**
  See also CA 97-100; CANR 25

Field, Eugene 1850-1895 . . . . **NCLC 3**
  See also DLB 23, 42, 140; DLBD 13;
  MAICYA; SATA 16

Field, Gans T.
  See Wellman, Manly Wade

Field, Michael . . . . **TCLC 43**

Field, Peter
  See Hobson, Laura Z(ametkin)

Fielding, Henry
  1707-1754 . . . . . . **LC 1; DA; DAB; DAC;
  DAM DRAM, MST, NOV; WLC**
  See also CDBLB 1660-1789; DLB 39, 84,
  101

Fielding, Sarah 1710-1768 . . . . **LC 1**
  See also DLB 39

Fierstein, Harvey (Forbes)
  1954- . . . . . **CLC 33; DAM DRAM, POP**
  See also CA 123; 129

Figes, Eva 1932- . . . . **CLC 31**
  See also CA 53-56; CANR 4, 44; DLB 14

Finch, Robert (Duer Claydon)
  1900- . . . . **CLC 18**
  See also CA 57-60; CANR 9, 24, 49;
  DLB 88

Findley, Timothy
  1930- . . . . . . **CLC 27; DAC; DAM MST**
  See also CA 25-28R; CANR 12, 42;
  DLB 53

Fink, William
  See Mencken, H(enry) L(ouis)

Firbank, Louis 1942-
  See Reed, Lou
  See also CA 117

Firbank, (Arthur Annesley) Ronald
  1886-1926 . . . . **TCLC 1**
  See also CA 104; DLB 36

Fisher, M(ary) F(rances) K(ennedy)
  1908-1992 . . . . **CLC 76, 87**
  See also CA 77-80; 138; CANR 44

Fisher, Roy 1930- . . . . **CLC 25**
  See also CA 81-84; CAAS 10; CANR 16;
  DLB 40

Fisher, Rudolph
  1897-1934 . . . . **TCLC 11; BLC;
  DAM MULT; SSC 25**
  See also BW 1; CA 107; 124; DLB 51, 102

Fisher, Vardis (Alvero) 1895-1968 . . . . **CLC 7**
  See also CA 5-8R; 25-28R; DLB 9

Fiske, Tarleton
  See Bloch, Robert (Albert)

Fitch, Clarke
  See Sinclair, Upton (Beall)

Fitch, John IV
  See Cormier, Robert (Edmund)

Fitzgerald, Captain Hugh
  See Baum, L(yman) Frank

FitzGerald, Edward 1809-1883 . . . . **NCLC 9**
  See also DLB 32

Fitzgerald, F(rancis) Scott (Key)
  1896-1940 . . . . . . **TCLC 1, 6, 14, 28, 55;
  DA; DAB; DAC; DAM MST, NOV;
  SSC 6; WLC**
  See also AITN 1; CA 110; 123;
  CDALB 1917-1929; DLB 4, 9, 86;
  DLBD 1; DLBY 81, 96; MTCW

Fitzgerald, Penelope   1916-... **CLC 19, 51, 61**
See also CA 85-88; CAAS 10; CANR 56;
DLB 14

Fitzgerald, Robert (Stuart)
1910-1985 .... **CLC 39**
See also CA 1-4R; 114; CANR 1; DLBY 80

FitzGerald, Robert D(avid)
1902-1987 .... **CLC 19**
See also CA 17-20R

Fitzgerald, Zelda (Sayre)
1900-1948 .... **TCLC 52**
See also CA 117; 126; DLBY 84

Flanagan, Thomas (James Bonner)
1923- .... **CLC 25, 52**
See also CA 108; CANR 55; DLBY 80;
INT 108; MTCW

Flaubert, Gustave
1821-1880 .... **NCLC 2, 10, 19, 62; DA;
DAB; DAC; DAM MST, NOV; SSC 11;
WLC**
See also DLB 119

Flecker, Herman Elroy
See Flecker, (Herman) James Elroy

Flecker, (Herman) James Elroy
1884-1915 .... **TCLC 43**
See also CA 109; 150; DLB 10, 19

Fleming, Ian (Lancaster)
1908-1964 ...... **CLC 3, 30; DAM POP**
See also CA 5-8R; CDBLB 1945-1960;
DLB 87; MTCW; SATA 9

Fleming, Thomas (James)   1927- .... **CLC 37**
See also CA 5-8R; CANR 10;
INT CANR-10; SATA 8

Fletcher, John   1579-1625 ...... **LC 33; DC 6**
See also CDBLB Before 1660; DLB 58

Fletcher, John Gould   1886-1950 ... **TCLC 35**
See also CA 107; DLB 4, 45

Fleur, Paul
See Pohl, Frederik

Flooglebuckle, Al
See Spiegelman, Art

Flying Officer X
See Bates, H(erbert) E(rnest)

Fo, Dario   1926-..... **CLC 32; DAM DRAM**
See also CA 116; 128; MTCW

Fogarty, Jonathan Titulescu Esq.
See Farrell, James T(homas)

Folke, Will
See Bloch, Robert (Albert)

Follett, Ken(neth Martin)
1949- ...... **CLC 18; DAM NOV, POP**
See also AAYA 6; BEST 89:4; CA 81-84;
CANR 13, 33, 54; DLB 87; DLBY 81;
INT CANR-33; MTCW

Fontane, Theodor   1819-1898 ..... **NCLC 26**
See also DLB 129

Foote, Horton
1916- .... **CLC 51, 91; DAM DRAM**
See also CA 73-76; CANR 34, 51; DLB 26;
INT CANR-34

Foote, Shelby
1916- ...... **CLC 75; DAM NOV, POP**
See also CA 5-8R; CANR 3, 45; DLB 2, 17

Forbes, Esther   1891-1967 .... **CLC 12**
See also AAYA 17; CA 13-14; 25-28R;
CAP 1; CLR 27; DLB 22; JRDA;
MAICYA; SATA 2

Forche, Carolyn (Louise)
1950- .... **CLC 25, 83, 86; DAM POET;
PC 10**
See also CA 109; 117; CANR 50; DLB 5;
INT 117

Ford, Elbur
See Hibbert, Eleanor Alice Burford

Ford, Ford Madox
1873-1939 .... **TCLC 1, 15, 39, 57;
DAM NOV**
See also CA 104; 132; CDBLB 1914-1945;
DLB 162; MTCW

Ford, John   1895-1973 .... **CLC 16**
See also CA 45-48

Ford, Richard .... **CLC 99**

Ford, Richard   1944- .... **CLC 46**
See also CA 69-72; CANR 11, 47

Ford, Webster
See Masters, Edgar Lee

Foreman, Richard   1937- .... **CLC 50**
See also CA 65-68; CANR 32

Forester, C(ecil) S(cott)
1899-1966 .... **CLC 35**
See also CA 73-76; 25-28R; SATA 13

Forez
See Mauriac, Francois (Charles)

Forman, James Douglas   1932- ...... **CLC 21**
See also AAYA 17; CA 9-12R; CANR 4,
19, 42; JRDA; MAICYA; SATA 8, 70

Fornes, Maria Irene   1930- ...... **CLC 39, 61**
See also CA 25-28R; CANR 28; DLB 7;
HW; INT CANR-28; MTCW

Forrest, Leon   1937- .... **CLC 4**
See also BW 2; CA 89-92; CAAS 7;
CANR 25, 52; DLB 33

Forster, E(dward) M(organ)
1879-1970 ..... **CLC 1, 2, 3, 4, 9, 10, 13,
15, 22, 45, 77; DA; DAB; DAC;
DAM MST, NOV; WLC**
See also AAYA 2; CA 13-14; 25-28R;
CANR 45; CAP 1; CDBLB 1914-1945;
DLB 34, 98, 162, 178; DLBD 10; MTCW;
SATA 57

Forster, John   1812-1876 .... **NCLC 11**
See also DLB 144

Forsyth, Frederick
1938- .. **CLC 2, 5, 36; DAM NOV, POP**
See also BEST 89:4; CA 85-88; CANR 38;
DLB 87; MTCW

Forten, Charlotte L. .... **TCLC 16; BLC**
See also Grimke, Charlotte L(ottie) Forten
See also DLB 50

Foscolo, Ugo   1778-1827 .... **NCLC 8**

Fosse, Bob .... **CLC 20**
See also Fosse, Robert Louis

Fosse, Robert Louis   1927-1987
See Fosse, Bob
See also CA 110; 123

Foster, Stephen Collins
1826-1864 .... **NCLC 26**

Foucault, Michel
1926-1984 .... **CLC 31, 34, 69**
See also CA 105; 113; CANR 34; MTCW

Fouque, Friedrich (Heinrich Karl) de la Motte
1777-1843 .... **NCLC 2**
See also DLB 90

Fourier, Charles   1772-1837 ...... **NCLC 51**

Fournier, Henri Alban   1886-1914
See Alain-Fournier
See also CA 104

Fournier, Pierre   1916- .... **CLC 11**
See also Gascar, Pierre
See also CA 89-92; CANR 16, 40

Fowles, John
1926- ...... **CLC 1, 2, 3, 4, 6, 9, 10, 15,
33, 87; DAB; DAC; DAM MST**
See also CA 5-8R; CANR 25; CDBLB 1960
to Present; DLB 14, 139; MTCW;
SATA 22

Fox, Paula   1923-................. **CLC 2, 8**
See also AAYA 3; CA 73-76; CANR 20,
36; CLR 1, 44; DLB 52; JRDA;
MAICYA; MTCW; SATA 17, 60

Fox, William Price (Jr.)   1926- ..... **CLC 22**
See also CA 17-20R; CAAS 19; CANR 11;
DLB 2; DLBY 81

Foxe, John   1516(?)-1587 .... **LC 14**

Frame, Janet
1924- .... **CLC 2, 3, 6, 22, 66, 96**
See also Clutha, Janet Paterson Frame

France, Anatole .... **TCLC 9**
See also Thibault, Jacques Anatole Francois
See also DLB 123

Francis, Claude   19(?)- .... **CLC 50**

Francis, Dick
1920- .... **CLC 2, 22, 42; DAM POP**
See also AAYA 5, 21; BEST 89:3; CA 5-8R;
CANR 9, 42; CDBLB 1960 to Present;
DLB 87; INT CANR-9; MTCW

Francis, Robert (Churchill)
1901-1987 .... **CLC 15**
See also CA 1-4R; 123; CANR 1

Frank, Anne(lies Marie)
1929-1945 .... **TCLC 17; DA; DAB;
DAC; DAM MST; WLC**
See also AAYA 12; CA 113; 133; MTCW;
SATA 87; SATA-Brief 42

Frank, Elizabeth   1945-............ **CLC 39**
See also CA 121; 126; INT 126

Frankl, Viktor E(mil)   1905-........ **CLC 93**
See also CA 65-68

Franklin, Benjamin
See Hasek, Jaroslav (Matej Frantisek)

Franklin, Benjamin
1706-1790 ..... **LC 25; DA; DAB; DAC;
DAM MST**
See also CDALB 1640-1865; DLB 24, 43,
73; YABC

Franklin, (Stella Maraia Sarah) Miles
1879-1954 .... **TCLC 7**
See also CA 104

Fraser, (Lady) Antonia (Pakenham)
1932- .... **CLC 32**
See also CA 85-88; CANR 44; MTCW;
SATA-Brief 32

Fraser, George MacDonald 1925-.... **CLC 7**
See also CA 45-48; CANR 2, 48

Fraser, Sylvia 1935-.............. **CLC 64**
See also CA 45-48; CANR 1, 16

Frayn, Michael
1933-.............. **CLC 3, 7, 31, 47;
DAM DRAM, NOV**
See also CA 5-8R; CANR 30; DLB 13, 14;
MTCW

Fraze, Candida (Merrill) 1945-..... **CLC 50**
See also CA 126

Frazer, J(ames) G(eorge)
1854-1941 .... **TCLC 32**
See also CA 118

Frazer, Robert Caine
See Creasey, John

Frazer, Sir James George
See Frazer, J(ames) G(eorge)

Frazier, Ian 1951-................ **CLC 46**
See also CA 130; CANR 54

Frederic, Harold 1856-1898...... **NCLC 10**
See also DLB 12, 23; DLBD 13

Frederick, John
See Faust, Frederick (Schiller)

Frederick the Great 1712-1786...... **LC 14**

Fredro, Aleksander 1793-1876..... **NCLC 8**

Freeling, Nicolas 1927-........... **CLC 38**
See also CA 49-52; CAAS 12; CANR 1, 17,
50; DLB 87

Freeman, Douglas Southall
1886-1953 .... **TCLC 11**
See also CA 109; DLB 17

Freeman, Judith 1946-........... **CLC 55**
See also CA 148

Freeman, Mary Eleanor Wilkins
1852-1930 .... **TCLC 9; SSC 1**
See also CA 106; DLB 12, 78

Freeman, R(ichard) Austin
1862-1943 .... **TCLC 21**
See also CA 113; DLB 70

French, Albert 1943- .... **CLC 86**

French, Marilyn
1929-................ **CLC 10, 18, 60;
DAM DRAM, NOV, POP**
See also CA 69-72; CANR 3, 31;
INT CANR-31; MTCW

French, Paul
See Asimov, Isaac

Freneau, Philip Morin 1752-1832.. **NCLC 1**
See also DLB 37, 43

Freud, Sigmund 1856-1939 ...... **TCLC 52**
See also CA 115; 133; MTCW

Friedan, Betty (Naomi) 1921-...... **CLC 74**
See also CA 65-68; CANR 18, 45; MTCW

Friedlander, Saul 1932-........... **CLC 90**
See also CA 117; 130

Friedman, B(ernard) H(arper)
1926-........................ **CLC 7**
See also CA 1-4R; CANR 3, 48

Friedman, Bruce Jay 1930-.... **CLC 3, 5, 56**
See also CA 9-12R; CANR 25, 52; DLB 2,
28; INT CANR-25

Friel, Brian 1929-........... **CLC 5, 42, 59**
See also CA 21-24R; CANR 33; DLB 13;
MTCW

Friis-Baastad, Babbis Ellinor
1921-1970 .... **CLC 12**
See also CA 17-20R; 134; SATA 7

Frisch, Max (Rudolf)
1911-1991 ..... **CLC 3, 9, 14, 18, 32, 44;
DAM DRAM, NOV**
See also CA 85-88; 134; CANR 32;
DLB 69, 124; MTCW

Fromentin, Eugene (Samuel Auguste)
1820-1876 .... **NCLC 10**
See also DLB 123

Frost, Frederick
See Faust, Frederick (Schiller)

Frost, Robert (Lee)
1874-1963 .... **CLC 1, 3, 4, 9, 10, 13, 15,
26, 34, 44; DA; DAB; DAC; DAM MST,
POET; PC 1; WLC**
See also AAYA 21; CA 89-92; CANR 33;
CDALB 1917-1929; DLB 54; DLBD 7;
MTCW; SATA 14

Froude, James Anthony
1818-1894 .... **NCLC 43**
See also DLB 18, 57, 144

Froy, Herald
See Waterhouse, Keith (Spencer)

Fry, Christopher
1907-..... **CLC 2, 10, 14; DAM DRAM**
See also CA 17-20R; CAAS 23; CANR 9,
30; DLB 13; MTCW; SATA 66

Frye, (Herman) Northrop
1912-1991 .... **CLC 24, 70**
See also CA 5-8R; 133; CANR 8, 37;
DLB 67, 68; MTCW

Fuchs, Daniel 1909-1993 .... **CLC 8, 22**
See also CA 81-84; 142; CAAS 5;
CANR 40; DLB 9, 26, 28; DLBY 93

Fuchs, Daniel 1934-.............. **CLC 34**
See also CA 37-40R; CANR 14, 48

Fuentes, Carlos
1928-...... **CLC 3, 8, 10, 13, 22, 41, 60;
DA; DAB; DAC; DAM MST, MULT,
NOV; HLC; SSC 24; WLC**
See also AAYA 4; AITN 2; CA 69-72;
CANR 10, 32; DLB 113; HW; MTCW

Fuentes, Gregorio Lopez y
See Lopez y Fuentes, Gregorio

Fugard, (Harold) Athol
1932-......... **CLC 5, 9, 14, 25, 40, 80;
DAM DRAM; DC 3**
See also AAYA 17; CA 85-88; CANR 32,
54; MTCW

Fugard, Sheila 1932- .... **CLC 48**
See also CA 125

Fuller, Charles (H., Jr.)
1939-.... **CLC 25; BLC; DAM DRAM,
MULT; DC 1**
See also BW 2; CA 108; 112; DLB 38;
INT 112; MTCW

Fuller, John (Leopold) 1937-...... **CLC 62**
See also CA 21-24R; CANR 9, 44; DLB 40

Fuller, Margaret .... **NCLC 5, 50**
See also Ossoli, Sarah Margaret (Fuller
marchesa d')

Fuller, Roy (Broadbent)
1912-1991 .... **CLC 4, 28**
See also CA 5-8R; 135; CAAS 10;
CANR 53; DLB 15, 20; SATA 87

Fulton, Alice 1952-.............. **CLC 52**
See also CA 116; CANR 57

Furphy, Joseph 1843-1912....... **TCLC 25**

Fussell, Paul 1924-................ **CLC 74**
See also BEST 90:1; CA 17-20R; CANR 8,
21, 35; INT CANR-21; MTCW

Futabatei, Shimei 1864-1909...... **TCLC 44**
See also DLB 180

Futrelle, Jacques 1875-1912 ...... **TCLC 19**
See also CA 113; 155

Gaboriau, Emile 1835-1873...... **NCLC 14**

Gadda, Carlo Emilio 1893-1973 .... **CLC 11**
See also CA 89-92; DLB 177

Gaddis, William
1922-..... **CLC 1, 3, 6, 8, 10, 19, 43, 86**
See also CA 17-20R; CANR 21, 48; DLB 2;
MTCW

Gage, Walter
See Inge, William (Motter)

Gaines, Ernest J(ames)
1933-......... **CLC 3, 11, 18, 86; BLC;
DAM MULT**
See also AAYA 18; AITN 1; BW 2;
CA 9-12R; CANR 6, 24, 42;
CDALB 1968-1988; DLB 2, 33, 152;
DLBY 80; MTCW; SATA 86

Gaitskill, Mary 1954-............. **CLC 69**
See also CA 128

Galdos, Benito Perez
See Perez Galdos, Benito

Gale, Zona
1874-1938 ...... **TCLC 7; DAM DRAM**
See also CA 105; 153; DLB 9, 78

Galeano, Eduardo (Hughes) 1940-... **CLC 72**
See also CA 29-32R; CANR 13, 32; HW

Galiano, Juan Valera y Alcala
See Valera y Alcala-Galiano, Juan

Gallagher, Tess
1943- .. **CLC 18, 63; DAM POET; PC 9**
See also CA 106; DLB 120

Gallant, Mavis
1922-............ **CLC 7, 18, 38; DAC;
DAM MST; SSC 5**
See also CA 69-72; CANR 29; DLB 53;
MTCW

Gallant, Roy A(rthur) 1924- .... **CLC 17**
See also CA 5-8R; CANR 4, 29, 54;
CLR 30; MAICYA; SATA 4, 68

Gallico, Paul (William) 1897-1976 ... **CLC 2**
See also AITN 1; CA 5-8R; 69-72;
CANR 23; DLB 9, 171; MAICYA;
SATA 13

Gallo, Max Louis 1932-........... **CLC 95**
See also CA 85-88

Gallois, Lucien
See Desnos, Robert

Gallup, Ralph
See Whitemore, Hugh (John)

Galsworthy, John
1867-1933 ...... **TCLC 1, 45; DA; DAB; DAC; DAM DRAM, MST, NOV; SSC 22; WLC 2**
See also CA 104; 141; CDBLB 1890-1914; DLB 10, 34, 98, 162

Galt, John 1779-1839 .... **NCLC 1**
See also DLB 99, 116, 159

Galvin, James 1951- .... **CLC 38**
See also CA 108; CANR 26

Gamboa, Federico 1864-1939 ..... **TCLC 36**

Gandhi, M. K.
See Gandhi, Mohandas Karamchand

Gandhi, Mahatma
See Gandhi, Mohandas Karamchand

Gandhi, Mohandas Karamchand
1869-1948 ..... **TCLC 59; DAM MULT**
See also CA 121; 132; MTCW

Gann, Ernest Kellogg 1910-1991 .... **CLC 23**
See also AITN 1; CA 1-4R; 136; CANR 1

Garcia, Cristina 1958- .... **CLC 76**
See also CA 141

Garcia Lorca, Federico
1898-1936 ... **TCLC 1, 7, 49; DA; DAB; DAC; DAM DRAM, MST, MULT, POET; DC 2; HLC; PC 3; WLC**
See also CA 104; 131; DLB 108; HW; MTCW

Garcia Marquez, Gabriel (Jose)
1928- .... **CLC 2, 3, 8, 10, 15, 27, 47, 55, 68; DA; DAB; DAC; DAM MST, MULT, NOV, POP; HLC; SSC 8; WLC**
See also AAYA 3; BEST 89:1, 90:4; CA 33-36R; CANR 10, 28, 50; DLB 113; HW; MTCW

Gard, Janice
See Latham, Jean Lee

Gard, Roger Martin du
See Martin du Gard, Roger

Gardam, Jane 1928- .... **CLC 43**
See also CA 49-52; CANR 2, 18, 33, 54; CLR 12; DLB 14, 161; MAICYA; MTCW; SAAS 9; SATA 39, 76; SATA-Brief 28

Gardner, Herb(ert) 1934- .... **CLC 44**
See also CA 149

Gardner, John (Champlin), Jr.
1933-1982 ..... **CLC 2, 3, 5, 7, 8, 10, 18, 28, 34; DAM NOV, POP; SSC 7**
See also AITN 1; CA 65-68; 107; CANR 33; DLB 2; DLBY 82; MTCW; SATA 40; SATA-Obit 31

Gardner, John (Edmund)
1926- .... **CLC 30; DAM POP**
See also CA 103; CANR 15; MTCW

Gardner, Miriam
See Bradley, Marion Zimmer

Gardner, Noel
See Kuttner, Henry

Gardons, S. S.
See Snodgrass, W(illiam) D(e Witt)

Garfield, Leon 1921-1996 .... **CLC 12**
See also AAYA 8; CA 17-20R; 152; CANR 38, 41; CLR 21; DLB 161; JRDA; MAICYA; SATA 1, 32, 76; SATA-Obit 90

Garland, (Hannibal) Hamlin
1860-1940 .... **TCLC 3; SSC 18**
See also CA 104; DLB 12, 71, 78

Garneau, (Hector de) Saint-Denys
1912-1943 .... **TCLC 13**
See also CA 111; DLB 88

Garner, Alan
1934- ...... **CLC 17; DAB; DAM POP**
See also AAYA 18; CA 73-76; CANR 15; CLR 20; DLB 161; MAICYA; MTCW; SATA 18, 69

Garner, Hugh 1913-1979 .... **CLC 13**
See also CA 69-72; CANR 31; DLB 68

Garnett, David 1892-1981 .... **CLC 3**
See also CA 5-8R; 103; CANR 17; DLB 34

Garos, Stephanie
See Katz, Steve

Garrett, George (Palmer)
1929- .... **CLC 3, 11, 51**
See also CA 1-4R; CAAS 5; CANR 1, 42; DLB 2, 5, 130, 152; DLBY 83

Garrick, David
1717-1779 .... **LC 15; DAM DRAM**
See also DLB 84

Garrigue, Jean 1914-1972 .... **CLC 2, 8**
See also CA 5-8R; 37-40R; CANR 20

Garrison, Frederick
See Sinclair, Upton (Beall)

Garth, Will
See Hamilton, Edmond; Kuttner, Henry

Garvey, Marcus (Moziah, Jr.)
1887-1940 .... **TCLC 41; BLC; DAM MULT**
See also BW 1; CA 120; 124

Gary, Romain .... **CLC 25**
See also Kacew, Romain
See also DLB 83

Gascar, Pierre .... **CLC 11**
See also Fournier, Pierre

Gascoyne, David (Emery) 1916- .... **CLC 45**
See also CA 65-68; CANR 10, 28, 54; DLB 20; MTCW

Gaskell, Elizabeth Cleghorn
1810-1865 .... **NCLC 5; DAB; DAM MST; SSC 25**
See also CDBLB 1832-1890; DLB 21, 144, 159

Gass, William H(oward)
1924- ... **CLC 1, 2, 8, 11, 15, 39; SSC 12**
See also CA 17-20R; CANR 30; DLB 2; MTCW

Gasset, Jose Ortega y
See Ortega y Gasset, Jose

Gates, Henry Louis, Jr.
1950- .... **CLC 65; DAM MULT**
See also BW 2; CA 109; CANR 25, 53; DLB 67

Gautier, Theophile
1811-1872 .... **NCLC 1, 59; DAM POET; PC 18; SSC 20**
See also DLB 119

Gawsworth, John
See Bates, H(erbert) E(rnest)

Gay, Oliver
See Gogarty, Oliver St. John

Gaye, Marvin (Penze) 1939-1984 ... **CLC 26**
See also CA 112

Gebler, Carlo (Ernest) 1954- .... **CLC 39**
See also CA 119; 133

Gee, Maggie (Mary) 1948- .... **CLC 57**
See also CA 130

Gee, Maurice (Gough) 1931- .... **CLC 29**
See also CA 97-100; SATA 46

Gelbart, Larry (Simon) 1923- ... **CLC 21, 61**
See also CA 73-76; CANR 45

Gelber, Jack 1932- .... **CLC 1, 6, 14, 79**
See also CA 1-4R; CANR 2; DLB 7

Gellhorn, Martha (Ellis) 1908- .. **CLC 14, 60**
See also CA 77-80; CANR 44; DLBY 82

Genet, Jean
1910-1986 ...... **CLC 1, 2, 5, 10, 14, 44, 46; DAM DRAM**
See also CA 13-16R; CANR 18; DLB 72; DLBY 86; MTCW

Gent, Peter 1942- .... **CLC 29**
See also AITN 1; CA 89-92; DLBY 82

Gentlewoman in New England, A
See Bradstreet, Anne

Gentlewoman in Those Parts, A
See Bradstreet, Anne

George, Jean Craighead 1919- ...... **CLC 35**
See also AAYA 8; CA 5-8R; CANR 25; CLR 1; DLB 52; JRDA; MAICYA; SATA 2, 68

George, Stefan (Anton)
1868-1933 .... **TCLC 2, 14**
See also CA 104

Georges, Georges Martin
See Simenon, Georges (Jacques Christian)

Gerhardi, William Alexander
See Gerhardie, William Alexander

Gerhardie, William Alexander
1895-1977 .... **CLC 5**
See also CA 25-28R; 73-76; CANR 18; DLB 36

Gerstler, Amy 1956- .... **CLC 70**
See also CA 146

Gertler, T. .... **CLC 34**
See also CA 116; 121; INT 121

gfgg .... **CLC XvXzc**

Ghalib .... **NCLC 39**
See also Ghalib, Hsadullah Khan

Ghalib, Hsadullah Khan 1797-1869
See Ghalib
See also DAM POET

Ghelderode, Michel de
1898-1962 .... **CLC 6, 11; DAM DRAM**
See also CA 85-88; CANR 40

Ghiselin, Brewster 1903- .... **CLC 23**
See also CA 13-16R; CAAS 10; CANR 13

Ghose, Zulfikar 1935- .... **CLC 42**
See also CA 65-68

Ghosh, Amitav 1956- .... **CLC 44**
See also CA 147

Giacosa, Giuseppe 1847-1906 ...... **TCLC 7**
See also CA 104

Gibb, Lee
See Waterhouse, Keith (Spencer)

Gibbon, Lewis Grassic .... TCLC 4
See also Mitchell, James Leslie

Gibbons, Kaye
1960- .... CLC 50, 88; DAM POP
See also CA 151

Gibran, Kahlil
1883-1931 .... TCLC 1, 9; DAM POET,
POP; PC 9
See also CA 104; 150

Gibran, Khalil
See Gibran, Kahlil

Gibson, William
1914- .... CLC 23; DA; DAB; DAC;
DAM DRAM, MST
See also CA 9-12R; CANR 9, 42; DLB 7;
SATA 66

Gibson, William (Ford)
1948- .... CLC 39, 63; DAM POP
See also AAYA 12; CA 126; 133; CANR 52

Gide, Andre (Paul Guillaume)
1869-1951 ...... TCLC 5, 12, 36; DA;
DAB; DAC; DAM MST, NOV; SSC 13;
WLC
See also CA 104; 124; DLB 65; MTCW

Gifford, Barry (Colby) 1946- .... CLC 34
See also CA 65-68; CANR 9, 30, 40

Gilbert, W(illiam) S(chwenck)
1836-1911 ..... TCLC 3; DAM DRAM,
POET
See also CA 104; SATA 36

Gilbreth, Frank B., Jr. 1911- .... CLC 17
See also CA 9-12R; SATA 2

Gilchrist, Ellen
1935- .... CLC 34, 48; DAM POP;
SSC 14
See also CA 113; 116; CANR 41; DLB 130;
MTCW

Giles, Molly 1942- .... CLC 39
See also CA 126

Gill, Patrick
See Creasey, John

Gilliam, Terry (Vance) 1940- .... CLC 21
See also Monty Python
See also AAYA 19; CA 108; 113;
CANR 35; INT 113

Gillian, Jerry
See Gilliam, Terry (Vance)

Gilliatt, Penelope (Ann Douglass)
1932-1993 .... CLC 2, 10, 13, 53
See also AITN 2; CA 13-16R; 141;
CANR 49; DLB 14

Gilman, Charlotte (Anna) Perkins (Stetson)
1860-1935 .... TCLC 9, 37; SSC 13
See also CA 106; 150

Gilmour, David 1949- .... CLC 35
See also CA 138, 147

Gilpin, William 1724-1804 ...... NCLC 30

Gilray, J. D.
See Mencken, H(enry) L(ouis)

Gilroy, Frank D(aniel) 1925- .... CLC 2
See also CA 81-84; CANR 32; DLB 7

Gilstrap, John 1957(?)- .... CLC 99

Ginsberg, Allen (Irwin)
1926-1997 ..... CLC 1, 2, 3, 4, 6, 13, 36,
69; DA; DAB; DAC; DAM MST, POET;
PC 4; WLC 3
See also AITN 1; CA 1-4R; 157; CANR 2,
41; CDALB 1941-1968; DLB 5, 16, 169;
MTCW

Ginzburg, Natalia
1916-1991 .... CLC 5, 11, 54, 70
See also CA 85-88; 135; CANR 33;
DLB 177; MTCW

Giono, Jean 1895-1970 .... CLC 4, 11
See also CA 45-48; 29-32R; CANR 2, 35;
DLB 72; MTCW

Giovanni, Nikki
1943- ...... CLC 2, 4, 19, 64; BLC; DA;
DAB; DAC; DAM MST, MULT, POET;
PC 19
See also AITN 1; BW 2; CA 29-32R;
CAAS 6; CANR 18, 41; CLR 6; DLB 5,
41; INT CANR-18; MAICYA; MTCW;
SATA 24; YABC

Giovene, Andrea 1904- .... CLC 7
See also CA 85-88

Gippius, Zinaida (Nikolayevna) 1869-1945
See Hippius, Zinaida
See also CA 106

Giraudoux, (Hippolyte) Jean
1882-1944 .... TCLC 2, 7; DAM DRAM
See also CA 104; DLB 65

Gironella, Jose Maria 1917- .... CLC 11
See also CA 101

Gissing, George (Robert)
1857-1903 .... TCLC 3, 24, 47
See also CA 105; DLB 18, 135

Giurlani, Aldo
See Palazzeschi, Aldo

Gladkov, Fyodor (Vasilyevich)
1883-1958 .... TCLC 27

Glanville, Brian (Lester) 1931- ...... CLC 6
See also CA 5-8R; CAAS 9; CANR 3;
DLB 15, 139; SATA 42

Glasgow, Ellen (Anderson Gholson)
1873(?)-1945 .... TCLC 2, 7
See also CA 104; DLB 9, 12

Glaspell, Susan 1882(?)-1948 ...... TCLC 55
See also CA 110; 154; DLB 7, 9, 78; 2

Glassco, John 1909-1981 .... CLC 9
See also CA 13-16R; 102; CANR 15;
DLB 68

Glasscock, Amnesia
See Steinbeck, John (Ernst)

Glasser, Ronald J. 1940(?)- .... CLC 37

Glassman, Joyce
See Johnson, Joyce

Glendinning, Victoria 1937- .... CLC 50
See also CA 120; 127; DLB 155

Glissant, Edouard
1928- .... CLC 10, 68; DAM MULT
See also CA 153

Gloag, Julian 1930- .... CLC 40
See also AITN 1; CA 65-68; CANR 10

Glowacki, Aleksander
See Prus, Boleslaw

Gluck, Louise (Elisabeth)
1943- .... CLC 7, 22, 44, 81;
DAM POET; PC 16
See also CA 33-36R; CANR 40; DLB 5

Glyn, Elinor 1864-1943 .... TCLC 72
See also DLB 153

Gobineau, Joseph Arthur (Comte) de
1816-1882 .... NCLC 17
See also DLB 123

Godard, Jean-Luc 1930- .... CLC 20
See also CA 93-96

Godden, (Margaret) Rumer 1907- ... CLC 53
See also AAYA 6; CA 5-8R; CANR 4, 27,
36, 55; CLR 20; DLB 161; MAICYA;
SAAS 12; SATA 3, 36

Godoy Alcayaga, Lucila 1889-1957
See Mistral, Gabriela
See also BW 2; CA 104; 131; DAM MULT;
HW; MTCW

Godwin, Gail (Kathleen)
1937- .... CLC 5, 8, 22, 31, 69;
DAM POP
See also CA 29-32R; CANR 15, 43; DLB 6;
INT CANR-15; MTCW

Godwin, William 1756-1836 ...... NCLC 14
See also CDBLB 1789-1832; DLB 39, 104,
142, 158, 163

Goebbels, Josef
See Goebbels, (Paul) Joseph

Goebbels, (Paul) Joseph
1897-1945 .... TCLC 68
See also CA 115; 148

Goebbels, Joseph Paul
See Goebbels, (Paul) Joseph

Goethe, Johann Wolfgang von
1749-1832 .... NCLC 4, 22, 34; DA;
DAB; DAC; DAM DRAM, MST,
POET; PC 5; WLC 3
See also DLB 94

Gogarty, Oliver St. John
1878-1957 .... TCLC 15
See also CA 109; 150; DLB 15, 19

Gogol, Nikolai (Vasilyevich)
1809-1852 .... NCLC 5, 15, 31; DA;
DAB; DAC; DAM DRAM, MST; DC 1;
SSC 4; WLC

Goines, Donald
1937(?)-1974 .... CLC 80; BLC;
DAM MULT, POP
See also AITN 1; BW 1; CA 124; 114;
DLB 33

Gold, Herbert 1924- .... CLC 4, 7, 14, 42
See also CA 9-12R; CANR 17, 45; DLB 2;
DLBY 81

Goldbarth, Albert 1948- .... CLC 5, 38
See also CA 53-56; CANR 6, 40; DLB 120

Goldberg, Anatol 1910-1982 .... CLC 34
See also CA 131; 117

Goldemberg, Isaac 1945- .... CLC 52
See also CA 69-72; CAAS 12; CANR 11,
32; HW

Golding, William (Gerald)
1911-1993 .... **CLC 1, 2, 3, 8, 10, 17, 27, 58, 81; DA; DAB; DAC; DAM MST, NOV; WLC**
See also AAYA 5; CA 5-8R; 141; CANR 13, 33, 54; CDBLB 1945-1960; DLB 15, 100; MTCW

Goldman, Emma 1869-1940 ...... **TCLC 13**
See also CA 110; 150

Goldman, Francisco 1955- .... **CLC 76**

Goldman, William (W.) 1931- .... **CLC 1, 48**
See also CA 9-12R; CANR 29; DLB 44

Goldmann, Lucien 1913-1970 ...... **CLC 24**
See also CA 25-28; CAP 2

Goldoni, Carlo
1707-1793 .... **LC 4; DAM DRAM**

Goldsberry, Steven 1949- .... **CLC 34**
See also CA 131

Goldsmith, Oliver
1728-1774 ...... **LC 2; DA; DAB; DAC; DAM DRAM, MST, NOV, POET; WLC**
See also CDBLB 1660-1789; DLB 39, 89, 104, 109, 142; SATA 26

Goldsmith, Peter
See Priestley, J(ohn) B(oynton)

Gombrowicz, Witold
1904-1969 .... **CLC 4, 7, 11, 49; DAM DRAM**
See also CA 19-20; 25-28R; CAP 2

Gomez de la Serna, Ramon
1888-1963 .... **CLC 9**
See also CA 153; 116; HW

Goncharov, Ivan Alexandrovich
1812-1891 .... **NCLC 1**

Goncourt, Edmond (Louis Antoine Huot) de
1822-1896 .... **NCLC 7**
See also DLB 123

Goncourt, Jules (Alfred Huot) de
1830-1870 .... **NCLC 7**
See also DLB 123

Gontier, Fernande 19(?)- .... **CLC 50**

Gonzalez Martinez, Enrique
1871-1952 .... **TCLC 72**
See also HW

Goodman, Paul 1911-1972 .... **CLC 1, 2, 4, 7**
See also CA 19-20; 37-40R; CANR 34; CAP 2; DLB 130; MTCW

Gordimer, Nadine
1923- .... **CLC 3, 5, 7, 10, 18, 33, 51, 70; DA; DAB; DAC; DAM MST, NOV; SSC 17**
See also CA 5-8R; CANR 3, 28, 56; INT CANR-28; MTCW; YABC

Gordon, Adam Lindsay
1833-1870 .... **NCLC 21**

Gordon, Caroline
1895-1981 ... **CLC 6, 13, 29, 83; SSC 15**
See also CA 11-12; 103; CANR 36; CAP 1; DLB 4, 9, 102; DLBY 81; MTCW

Gordon, Charles William 1860-1937
See Connor, Ralph
See also CA 109

Gordon, Mary (Catherine)
1949- .... **CLC 13, 22**
See also CA 102; CANR 44; DLB 6; DLBY 81; INT 102; MTCW

Gordon, Sol 1923- .... **CLC 26**
See also CA 53-56; CANR 4; SATA 11

Gordone, Charles
1925-1995 ..... **CLC 1, 4; DAM DRAM**
See also BW 1; CA 93-96; 150; CANR 55; DLB 7; INT 93-96; MTCW

Gorenko, Anna Andreevna
See Akhmatova, Anna

Gorky, Maxim .... **TCLC 8; DAB; WLC**
See also Peshkov, Alexei Maximovich

Goryan, Sirak
See Saroyan, William

Gosse, Edmund (William)
1849-1928 .... **TCLC 28**
See also CA 117; DLB 57, 144

Gotlieb, Phyllis Fay (Bloom)
1926- .... **CLC 18**
See also CA 13-16R; CANR 7; DLB 88

Gottesman, S. D.
See Kornbluth, C(yril) M.; Pohl, Frederik

Gottfried von Strassburg
fl. c. 1210- .... **CMLC 10**
See also DLB 138

Gould, Lois .... **CLC 4, 10**
See also CA 77-80; CANR 29; MTCW

Gourmont, Remy (-Marie-Charles) de
1858-1915 .... **TCLC 17**
See also CA 109; 150

Govier, Katherine 1948- .... **CLC 51**
See also CA 101; CANR 18, 40

Goyen, (Charles) William
1915-1983 .... **CLC 5, 8, 14, 40**
See also AITN 2; CA 5-8R; 110; CANR 6; DLB 2; DLBY 83; INT CANR-6

Goytisolo, Juan
1931- ..... **CLC 5, 10, 23; DAM MULT; HLC**
See also CA 85-88; CANR 32; HW; MTCW

Gozzano, Guido 1883-1916 .... **PC 10**
See also CA 154; DLB 114

Gozzi, (Conte) Carlo 1720-1806 .. **NCLC 23**

Grabbe, Christian Dietrich
1801-1836 .... **NCLC 2**
See also DLB 133

Grace, Patricia 1937- .... **CLC 56**

Gracian y Morales, Baltasar
1601-1658 .... **LC 15**

Gracq, Julien .... **CLC 11, 48**
See also Poirier, Louis
See also DLB 83

Grade, Chaim 1910-1982 .... **CLC 10**
See also CA 93-96; 107

Graduate of Oxford, A
See Ruskin, John

Grafton, Garth
See Duncan, Sara Jeannette

Graham, John
See Phillips, David Graham

Graham, Jorie 1951- .... **CLC 48**
See also CA 111; DLB 120

Graham, R(obert) B(ontine) Cunninghame
See Cunninghame Graham, R(obert) B(ontine)
See also DLB 98, 135, 174

Graham, Robert
See Haldeman, Joe (William)

Graham, Tom
See Lewis, (Harry) Sinclair

Graham, W(illiam) S(ydney)
1918-1986 .... **CLC 29**
See also CA 73-76; 118; DLB 20

Graham, Winston (Mawdsley)
1910- .... **CLC 23**
See also CA 49-52; CANR 2, 22, 45; DLB 77

Grahame, Kenneth
1859-1932 .... **TCLC 64; DAB**
See also CA 108; 136; CLR 5; DLB 34, 141, 178; MAICYA; 1

Grant, Skeeter
See Spiegelman, Art

Granville-Barker, Harley
1877-1946 .... **TCLC 2; DAM DRAM**
See also Barker, Harley Granville
See also CA 104

Grass, Guenter (Wilhelm)
1927- ..... **CLC 1, 2, 4, 6, 11, 15, 22, 32, 49, 88; DA; DAB; DAC; DAM MST, NOV; WLC**
See also CA 13-16R; CANR 20; DLB 75, 124; MTCW

Gratton, Thomas
See Hulme, T(homas) E(rnest)

Grau, Shirley Ann
1929- .... **CLC 4, 9; SSC 15**
See also CA 89-92; CANR 22; DLB 2; INT CANR-22; MTCW

Gravel, Fern
See Hall, James Norman

Graver, Elizabeth 1964- .... **CLC 70**
See also CA 135

Graves, Richard Perceval 1945- .... **CLC 44**
See also CA 65-68; CANR 9, 26, 51

Graves, Robert (von Ranke)
1895-1985 ...... **CLC 1, 2, 6, 11, 39, 44, 45; DAB; DAC; DAM MST, POET; PC 6**
See also CA 5-8R; 117; CANR 5, 36; CDBLB 1914-1945; DLB 20, 100; DLBY 85; MTCW; SATA 45

Graves, Valerie
See Bradley, Marion Zimmer

Gray, Alasdair (James) 1934- ...... **CLC 41**
See also CA 126; CANR 47; INT 126; MTCW

Gray, Amlin 1946- .... **CLC 29**
See also CA 138

Gray, Francine du Plessix
1930- .... **CLC 22; DAM NOV**
See also BEST 90:3; CA 61-64; CAAS 2; CANR 11, 33; INT CANR-11; MTCW

Gray, John (Henry) 1866-1934 .... **TCLC 19**
See also CA 119

Gray, Simon (James Holliday)
1936- .... **CLC 9, 14, 36**
See also AITN 1; CA 21-24R; CAAS 3;
CANR 32; DLB 13; MTCW

Gray, Spalding
1941- ...... **CLC 49; DAM POP; DC 7**
See also CA 128

Gray, Thomas
1716-1771 ...... **LC 4; DA; DAB; DAC;**
DAM MST; PC 2; WLC
See also CDBLB 1660-1789; DLB 109

Grayson, David
See Baker, Ray Stannard

Grayson, Richard (A.) 1951- .... **CLC 38**
See also CA 85-88; CANR 14, 31, 57

Greeley, Andrew M(oran)
1928- .... **CLC 28; DAM POP**
See also CA 5-8R; CAAS 7; CANR 7, 43;
MTCW

Green, Anna Katharine
1846-1935 .... **TCLC 63**
See also CA 112

Green, Brian
See Card, Orson Scott

Green, Hannah .... **CLC 3**
See also CA 73-76

Green, Hannah
See Greenberg, Joanne (Goldenberg)

Green, Henry 1905-1973 ..... **CLC 2, 13, 97**
See also Yorke, Henry Vincent
See also DLB 15

Green, Julian (Hartridge) 1900-
See Green, Julien
See also CA 21-24R; CANR 33; DLB 4, 72;
MTCW

Green, Julien .... **CLC 3, 11, 77**
See also Green, Julian (Hartridge)

Green, Paul (Eliot)
1894-1981 ...... **CLC 25; DAM DRAM**
See also AITN 1; CA 5-8R; 103; CANR 3;
DLB 7, 9; DLBY 81

Greenberg, Ivan 1908-1973
See Rahv, Philip
See also CA 85-88

Greenberg, Joanne (Goldenberg)
1932- .... **CLC 7, 30**
See also AAYA 12; CA 5-8R; CANR 14,
32; SATA 25

Greenberg, Richard 1959(?)- .... **CLC 57**
See also CA 138

Greene, Bette 1934- .... **CLC 30**
See also AAYA 7; CA 53-56; CANR 4;
CLR 2; JRDA; MAICYA; SAAS 16;
SATA 8

Greene, Gael .... **CLC 8**
See also CA 13-16R; CANR 10

Greene, Graham
1904-1991 .... **CLC 1, 3, 6, 9, 14, 18, 27,**
37, 70, 72; DA; DAB; DAC; DAM MST,
NOV; WLC
See also AITN 2; CA 13-16R; 133;
CANR 35; CDBLB 1945-1960; DLB 13,
15, 77, 100, 162; DLBY 91; MTCW;
SATA 20

Greer, Richard
See Silverberg, Robert

Gregor, Arthur 1923- .... **CLC 9**
See also CA 25-28R; CAAS 10; CANR 11;
SATA 36

Gregor, Lee
See Pohl, Frederik

Gregory, Isabella Augusta (Persse)
1852-1932 .... **TCLC 1**
See also CA 104; DLB 10

Gregory, J. Dennis
See Williams, John A(lfred)

Grendon, Stephen
See Derleth, August (William)

Grenville, Kate 1950- .... **CLC 61**
See also CA 118; CANR 53

Grenville, Pelham
See Wodehouse, P(elham) G(renville)

Greve, Felix Paul (Berthold Friedrich)
1879-1948
See Grove, Frederick Philip
See also CA 104; 141; DAC; DAM MST

Grey, Zane
1872-1939 .... **TCLC 6; DAM POP**
See also CA 104; 132; DLB 9; MTCW

Grieg, (Johan) Nordahl (Brun)
1902-1943 .... **TCLC 10**
See also CA 107

Grieve, C(hristopher) M(urray)
1892-1978 .... **CLC 11, 19; DAM POET**
See also MacDiarmid, Hugh; Pteleon
See also CA 5-8R; 85-88; CANR 33;
MTCW

Griffin, Gerald 1803-1840 .... **NCLC 7**
See also DLB 159

Griffin, John Howard 1920-1980.... **CLC 68**
See also AITN 1; CA 1-4R; 101; CANR 2

Griffin, Peter 1942- .... **CLC 39**
See also CA 136

Griffith, D(avid Lewelyn) W(ark)
1875(?)-1948 .... **TCLC 68**
See also CA 119; 150

Griffith, Lawrence
See Griffith, D(avid Lewelyn) W(ark)

Griffiths, Trevor 1935- .... **CLC 13, 52**
See also CA 97-100; CANR 45; DLB 13

Grigson, Geoffrey (Edward Harvey)
1905-1985 .... **CLC 7, 39**
See also CA 25-28R; 118; CANR 20, 33;
DLB 27; MTCW

Grillparzer, Franz 1791-1872...... **NCLC 1**
See also DLB 133

Grimble, Reverend Charles James
See Eliot, T(homas) S(tearns)

Grimke, Charlotte L(ottie) Forten
1837(?)-1914
See Forten, Charlotte L.
See also BW 1; CA 117; 124; DAM MULT,
POET

Grimm, Jacob Ludwig Karl
1785-1863 .... **NCLC 3**
See also DLB 90; MAICYA; SATA 22

Grimm, Wilhelm Karl 1786-1859 .. **NCLC 3**
See also DLB 90; MAICYA; SATA 22

Grimmelshausen, Johann Jakob Christoffel
von 1621-1676 .... **LC 6**
See also DLB 168

Grindel, Eugene 1895-1952
See Eluard, Paul
See also CA 104

Grisham, John 1955- .. **CLC 84; DAM POP**
See also AAYA 14; CA 138; CANR 47

Grossman, David 1954- .... **CLC 67**
See also CA 138

Grossman, Vasily (Semenovich)
1905-1964 .... **CLC 41**
See also CA 124; 130; MTCW

Grove, Frederick Philip .... **TCLC 4**
See also Greve, Felix Paul (Berthold
Friedrich)
See also DLB 92

Grubb
See Crumb, R(obert)

Grumbach, Doris (Isaac)
1918- .... **CLC 13, 22, 64**
See also CA 5-8R; CAAS 2; CANR 9, 42;
INT CANR-9

Grundtvig, Nicolai Frederik Severin
1783-1872 .... **NCLC 1**

Grunge
See Crumb, R(obert)

Grunwald, Lisa 1959- .... **CLC 44**
See also CA 120

Guare, John
1938- .... **CLC 8, 14, 29, 67;**
DAM DRAM
See also CA 73-76; CANR 21; DLB 7;
MTCW

Gudjonsson, Halldor Kiljan 1902-
See Laxness, Halldor
See also CA 103

Guenter, Erich
See Eich, Guenter

Guest, Barbara 1920- .... **CLC 34**
See also CA 25-28R; CANR 11, 44; DLB 5

Guest, Judith (Ann)
1936- .... **CLC 8, 30; DAM NOV, POP**
See also AAYA 7; CA 77-80; CANR 15;
INT CANR-15; MTCW

Guevara, Che .... **CLC 87; HLC**
See also Guevara (Serna), Ernesto

Guevara (Serna), Ernesto 1928-1967
See Guevara, Che
See also CA 127; 111; CANR 56;
DAM MULT; HW

Guild, Nicholas M. 1944-.......... **CLC 33**
See also CA 93-96

Guillemin, Jacques
See Sartre, Jean-Paul

Guillen, Jorge
1893-1984 ...... **CLC 11; DAM MULT,**
POET
See also CA 89-92; 112; DLB 108; HW

Guillen, Nicolas (Cristobal)
1902-1989 .... **CLC 48, 79; BLC;**
DAM MST, MULT, POET; HLC
See also BW 2; CA 116; 125; 129; HW

Guillevic, (Eugene) 1907-.......... **CLC 33**
See also CA 93-96

Guillois
See Desnos, Robert

Guillois, Valentin
See Desnos, Robert

Guiney, Louise Imogen
1861-1920 . . . . **TCLC 41**
See also DLB 54

Guiraldes, Ricardo (Guillermo)
1886-1927 . . . . **TCLC 39**
See also CA 131; HW; MTCW

Gumilev, Nikolai Stephanovich
1886-1921 . . . . **TCLC 60**

Gunesekera, Romesh . . . . **CLC 91**

Gunn, Bill . . . . **CLC 5**
See also Gunn, William Harrison
See also DLB 38

Gunn, Thom(son William)
1929- . . . . **CLC 3, 6, 18, 32, 81;**
DAM POET
See also CA 17-20R; CANR 9, 33;
CDBLB 1960 to Present; DLB 27;
INT CANR-33; MTCW

Gunn, William Harrison 1934(?)-1989
See Gunn, Bill
See also AITN 1; BW 1; CA 13-16R; 128;
CANR 12, 25

Gunnars, Kristjana 1948- . . . . **CLC 69**
See also CA 113; DLB 60

Gurdjieff, G(eorgei) I(vanovich)
1877(?)-1949 . . . . **TCLC 71**
See also CA 157

Gurganus, Allan
1947- . . . . **CLC 70; DAM POP**
See also BEST 90:1; CA 135

Gurney, A(lbert) R(amsdell), Jr.
1930- . . . . **CLC 32, 50, 54; DAM DRAM**
See also CA 77-80; CANR 32

Gurney, Ivor (Bertie) 1890-1937 . . . **TCLC 33**

Gurney, Peter
See Gurney, A(lbert) R(amsdell), Jr.

Guro, Elena 1877-1913 . . . . **TCLC 56**

Gustafson, James M(oody) 1925- . . **CLC 100**
See also CA 25-28R; CANR 37

Gustafson, Ralph (Barker) 1909- . . . . **CLC 36**
See also CA 21-24R; CANR 8, 45; DLB 88

Gut, Gom
See Simenon, Georges (Jacques Christian)

Guterson, David 1956- . . . . **CLC 91**
See also CA 132

Guthrie, A(lfred) B(ertram), Jr.
1901-1991 . . . . **CLC 23**
See also CA 57-60; 134; CANR 24; DLB 6;
SATA 62; SATA-Obit 67

Guthrie, Isobel
See Grieve, C(hristopher) M(urray)

Guthrie, Woodrow Wilson 1912-1967
See Guthrie, Woody
See also CA 113; 93-96

Guthrie, Woody . . . . **CLC 35**
See also Guthrie, Woodrow Wilson

Guy, Rosa (Cuthbert) 1928- . . . . **CLC 26**
See also AAYA 4; BW 2; CA 17-20R;
CANR 14, 34; CLR 13; DLB 33; JRDA;
MAICYA; SATA 14, 62

Gwendolyn
See Bennett, (Enoch) Arnold

H. D. . . . . **CLC 3, 8, 14, 31, 34, 73; PC 5**
See also Doolittle, Hilda

H. de V.
See Buchan, John

Haavikko, Paavo Juhani
1931- . . . . **CLC 18, 34**
See also CA 106

Habbema, Koos
See Heijermans, Herman

Hacker, Marilyn
1942- . . . . **CLC 5, 9, 23, 72, 91;**
DAM POET
See also CA 77-80; DLB 120

Haggard, H(enry) Rider
1856-1925 . . . . **TCLC 11**
See also CA 108; 148; DLB 70, 156, 174,
178; SATA 16

Hagiosy, L.
See Larbaud, Valery (Nicolas)

Hagiwara Sakutaro
1886-1942 . . . . **TCLC 60; PC 18**

Haig, Fenil
See Ford, Ford Madox

Haig-Brown, Roderick (Langmere)
1908-1976 . . . . **CLC 21**
See also CA 5-8R; 69-72; CANR 4, 38;
CLR 31; DLB 88; MAICYA; SATA 12

Hailey, Arthur
1920- . . . . **CLC 5; DAM NOV, POP**
See also AITN 2; BEST 90:3; CA 1-4R;
CANR 2, 36; DLB 88; DLBY 82; MTCW

Hailey, Elizabeth Forsythe 1938- . . . **CLC 40**
See also CA 93-96; CAAS 1; CANR 15, 48;
INT CANR-15

Haines, John (Meade) 1924- . . . . **CLC 58**
See also CA 17-20R; CANR 13, 34; DLB 5

Hakluyt, Richard 1552-1616 . . . . **LC 31**

Haldeman, Joe (William) 1943- . . . . . **CLC 61**
See also CA 53-56; CAAS 25; CANR 6;
DLB 8; INT CANR-6

Haley, Alex(ander Murray Palmer)
1921-1992 . . . . **CLC 8, 12, 76; BLC; DA;**
DAB; DAC; DAM MST, MULT, POP
See also BW 2; CA 77-80; 136; DLB 38;
MTCW

Haliburton, Thomas Chandler
1796-1865 . . . . **NCLC 15**
See also DLB 11, 99

Hall, Donald (Andrew, Jr.)
1928- . . **CLC 1, 13, 37, 59; DAM POET**
See also CA 5-8R; CAAS 7; CANR 2, 44;
DLB 5; SATA 23

Hall, Frederic Sauser
See Sauser-Hall, Frederic

Hall, James
See Kuttner, Henry

Hall, James Norman 1887-1951 . . . **TCLC 23**
See also CA 123; SATA 21

Hall, (Marguerite) Radclyffe
1886-1943 . . . . **TCLC 12**
See also CA 110; 150

Hall, Rodney 1935- . . . . **CLC 51**
See also CA 109

Halleck, Fitz-Greene 1790-1867 . . **NCLC 47**
See also DLB 3

Halliday, Michael
See Creasey, John

Halpern, Daniel 1945- . . . . **CLC 14**
See also CA 33-36R

Hamburger, Michael (Peter Leopold)
1924- . . . . **CLC 5, 14**
See also CA 5-8R; CAAS 4; CANR 2, 47;
DLB 27

Hamill, Pete 1935- . . . . **CLC 10**
See also CA 25-28R; CANR 18

Hamilton, Alexander
1755(?)-1804 . . . . **NCLC 49**
See also DLB 37

Hamilton, Clive
See Lewis, C(live) S(taples)

Hamilton, Edmond 1904-1977 . . . . . . **CLC 1**
See also CA 1-4R; CANR 3; DLB 8

Hamilton, Eugene (Jacob) Lee
See Lee-Hamilton, Eugene (Jacob)

Hamilton, Franklin
See Silverberg, Robert

Hamilton, Gail
See Corcoran, Barbara

Hamilton, Mollie
See Kaye, M(ary) M(argaret)

Hamilton, (Anthony Walter) Patrick
1904-1962 . . . . **CLC 51**
See also CA 113; DLB 10

Hamilton, Virginia
1936- . . . . **CLC 26; DAM MULT**
See also AAYA 2, 21; BW 2; CA 25-28R;
CANR 20, 37; CLR 1, 11, 40; DLB 33,
52; INT CANR-20; JRDA; MAICYA;
MTCW; SATA 4, 56, 79

Hammett, (Samuel) Dashiell
1894-1961 . . . . **CLC 3, 5, 10, 19, 47;**
SSC 17
See also AITN 1; CA 81-84; CANR 42;
CDALB 1929-1941; DLBD 6; DLBY 96;
MTCW

Hammon, Jupiter
1711(?)-1800(?) . . . . **NCLC 5; BLC;**
DAM MULT, POET; PC 16
See also DLB 31, 50

Hammond, Keith
See Kuttner, Henry

Hamner, Earl (Henry), Jr. 1923- . . . **CLC 12**
See also AITN 2; CA 73-76; DLB 6

Hampton, Christopher (James)
1946- . . . . **CLC 4**
See also CA 25-28R; DLB 13; MTCW

Hamsun, Knut . . . . **TCLC 2, 14, 49**
See also Pedersen, Knut

Handke, Peter
1942- . . . . **CLC 5, 8, 10, 15, 38;**
DAM DRAM, NOV
See also CA 77-80; CANR 33; DLB 85,
124; MTCW

Hanley, James 1901-1985 . . . **CLC 3, 5, 8, 13**
See also CA 73-76; 117; CANR 36; MTCW

Hannah, Barry 1942- . . . . **CLC 23, 38, 90**
See also CA 108; 110; CANR 43; DLB 6;
INT 110; MTCW

Hannon, Ezra
See Hunter, Evan

Hansberry, Lorraine (Vivian)
1930-1965 . . . . . . **CLC 17, 62; BLC; DA;
DAB; DAC; DAM DRAM, MST,
MULT; DC 2**
See also BW 1; CA 109; 25-28R; CABS 3;
CANR 58; CDALB 1941-1968; DLB 7,
38; MTCW

Hansen, Joseph 1923- . . . . **CLC 38**
See also CA 29-32R; CAAS 17; CANR 16,
44; INT CANR-16

Hansen, Martin A. 1909-1955 . . . . . **TCLC 32**

Hanson, Kenneth O(stlin) 1922- . . . . **CLC 13**
See also CA 53-56; CANR 7

Hardwick, Elizabeth
1916- . . . . **CLC 13; DAM NOV**
See also CA 5-8R; CANR 3, 32; DLB 6;
MTCW

Hardy, Thomas
1840-1928 . . . . . . **TCLC 4, 10, 18, 32, 48,
53, 72; DA; DAB; DAC; DAM MST,
NOV, POET; PC 8; SSC 2; WLC**
See also CA 104; 123; CDBLB 1890-1914;
DLB 18, 19, 135; MTCW

Hare, David 1947- . . . . **CLC 29, 58**
See also CA 97-100; CANR 39; DLB 13;
MTCW

Harford, Henry
See Hudson, W(illiam) H(enry)

Hargrave, Leonie
See Disch, Thomas M(ichael)

Harjo, Joy 1951- . . . **CLC 83; DAM MULT**
See also CA 114; CANR 35; DLB 120, 175;
NNAL

Harlan, Louis R(udolph) 1922- . . . . . **CLC 34**
See also CA 21-24R; CANR 25, 55

Harling, Robert 1951(?)- . . . . **CLC 53**
See also CA 147

Harmon, William (Ruth) 1938- . . . . . **CLC 38**
See also CA 33-36R; CANR 14, 32, 35;
SATA 65

Harper, F. E. W.
See Harper, Frances Ellen Watkins

Harper, Frances E. W.
See Harper, Frances Ellen Watkins

Harper, Frances E. Watkins
See Harper, Frances Ellen Watkins

Harper, Frances Ellen
See Harper, Frances Ellen Watkins

Harper, Frances Ellen Watkins
1825-1911 . . . . **TCLC 14; BLC;
DAM MULT, POET**
See also BW 1; CA 111; 125; DLB 50

Harper, Michael S(teven) 1938- . . **CLC 7, 22**
See also BW 1; CA 33-36R; CANR 24;
DLB 41

Harper, Mrs. F. E. W.
See Harper, Frances Ellen Watkins

Harris, Christie (Lucy) Irwin
1907- . . . . **CLC 12**
See also CA 5-8R; CANR 6; DLB 88;
JRDA; MAICYA; SAAS 10; SATA 6, 74

Harris, Frank 1856-1931 . . . . **TCLC 24**
See also CA 109; 150; DLB 156

Harris, George Washington
1814-1869 . . . . **NCLC 23**
See also DLB 3, 11

Harris, Joel Chandler
1848-1908 . . . . **TCLC 2; SSC 19**
See also CA 104; 137; DLB 11, 23, 42, 78,
91; MAICYA; 1

**Harris, John (Wyndham Parkes Lucas)
Beynon** 1903-1969
See Wyndham, John
See also CA 102; 89-92

Harris, MacDonald . . . . **CLC 9**
See also Heiney, Donald (William)

Harris, Mark 1922- . . . . **CLC 19**
See also CA 5-8R; CAAS 3; CANR 2, 55;
DLB 2; DLBY 80

Harris, (Theodore) Wilson 1921- . . . . **CLC 25**
See also BW 2; CA 65-68; CAAS 16;
CANR 11, 27; DLB 117; MTCW

Harrison, Elizabeth Cavanna 1909-
See Cavanna, Betty
See also CA 9-12R; CANR 6, 27

Harrison, Harry (Max) 1925- . . . . . . **CLC 42**
See also CA 1-4R; CANR 5, 21; DLB 8;
SATA 4

Harrison, James (Thomas)
1937- . . . . . . **CLC 6, 14, 33, 66; SSC 19**
See also CA 13-16R; CANR 8, 51;
DLBY 82; INT CANR-8

Harrison, Jim
See Harrison, James (Thomas)

Harrison, Kathryn 1961- . . . . **CLC 70**
See also CA 144

Harrison, Tony 1937- . . . . **CLC 43**
See also CA 65-68; CANR 44; DLB 40;
MTCW

Harriss, Will(ard Irvin) 1922- . . . . . . **CLC 34**
See also CA 111

Harson, Sley
See Ellison, Harlan (Jay)

Hart, Ellis
See Ellison, Harlan (Jay)

Hart, Josephine
1942(?)- . . . . **CLC 70; DAM POP**
See also CA 138

Hart, Moss
1904-1961 . . . . . . **CLC 66; DAM DRAM**
See also CA 109; 89-92; DLB 7

Harte, (Francis) Bret(t)
1836(?)-1902 . . . . **TCLC 1, 25; DA; DAC;
DAM MST; SSC 8; WLC**
See also CA 104; 140; CDALB 1865-1917;
DLB 12, 64, 74, 79; SATA 26

Hartley, L(eslie) P(oles)
1895-1972 . . . . **CLC 2, 22**
See also CA 45-48; 37-40R; CANR 33;
DLB 15, 139; MTCW

Hartman, Geoffrey H. 1929- . . . . **CLC 27**
See also CA 117; 125; DLB 67

Hartmann von Aue
c. 1160-c. 1205 . . . . **CMLC 15**
See also DLB 138

Hartmann von Aue 1170-1210 . . . . **CMLC 15**

Haruf, Kent 1943- . . . . **CLC 34**
See also CA 149

Harwood, Ronald
1934- . . . . **CLC 32; DAM DRAM, MST**
See also CA 1-4R; CANR 4, 55; DLB 13

Hasek, Jaroslav (Matej Frantisek)
1883-1923 . . . . **TCLC 4**
See also CA 104; 129; MTCW

Hass, Robert
1941- . . . . **CLC 18, 39, 99; PC 16**
See also CA 111; CANR 30, 50; DLB 105;
SATA 94

Hastings, Hudson
See Kuttner, Henry

Hastings, Selina . . . . **CLC 44**

Hathorne, John 1641-1717 . . . . **LC 38**

Hatteras, Amelia
See Mencken, H(enry) L(ouis)

Hatteras, Owen . . . . **TCLC 18**
See also Mencken, H(enry) L(ouis); Nathan,
George Jean

Hauptmann, Gerhart (Johann Robert)
1862-1946 . . . . . . **TCLC 4; DAM DRAM**
See also CA 104; 153; DLB 66, 118

Havel, Vaclav
1936- . . . . **CLC 25, 58, 65;
DAM DRAM; DC 6**
See also CA 104; CANR 36; MTCW

Haviaras, Stratis . . . . **CLC 33**
See also Chaviaras, Strates

Hawes, Stephen 1475(?)-1523(?) . . . . . **LC 17**

Hawkes, John (Clendennin Burne, Jr.)
1925- . . . . . . **CLC 1, 2, 3, 4, 7, 9, 14, 15,
27, 49**
See also CA 1-4R; CANR 2, 47; DLB 2, 7;
DLBY 80; MTCW

Hawking, S. W.
See Hawking, Stephen W(illiam)

Hawking, Stephen W(illiam)
1942- . . . . **CLC 63**
See also AAYA 13; BEST 89:1; CA 126;
129; CANR 48

Hawthorne, Julian 1846-1934 . . . . . **TCLC 25**

Hawthorne, Nathaniel
1804-1864 . . . . **NCLC 39; DA; DAB;
DAC; DAM MST, NOV; SSC 3; WLC**
See also AAYA 18; CDALB 1640-1865;
DLB 1, 74; 2

Haxton, Josephine Ayres 1921-
See Douglas, Ellen
See also CA 115; CANR 41

Hayaseca y Eizaguirre, Jorge
See Echegaray (y Eizaguirre), Jose (Maria
Waldo)

Hayashi Fumiko 1904-1951 . . . . **TCLC 27**
See also DLB 180

Haycraft, Anna
See Ellis, Alice Thomas
See also CA 122

Hayden, Robert E(arl)
1913-1980 . . . . . . **CLC 5, 9, 14, 37; BLC;
DA; DAC; DAM MST, MULT, POET;
PC 6**
See also BW 1; CA 69-72; 97-100; CABS 2;
CANR 24; CDALB 1941-1968; DLB 5,
76; MTCW; SATA 19; SATA-Obit 26

Hayford, J(oseph) E(phraim) Casely
See Casely-Hayford, J(oseph) E(phraim)

Hayman, Ronald 1932-............ **CLC 44**
See also CA 25-28R; CANR 18, 50;
DLB 155

Haywood, Eliza (Fowler)
1693(?)-1756 .... **LC 1**

Hazlitt, William 1778-1830 ...... **NCLC 29**
See also DLB 110, 158

Hazzard, Shirley 1931- .... **CLC 18**
See also CA 9-12R; CANR 4; DLBY 82;
MTCW

Head, Bessie
1937-1986 .... **CLC 25, 67; BLC;**
DAM MULT
See also BW 2; CA 29-32R; 119; CANR 25;
DLB 117; MTCW

Headon, (Nicky) Topper 1956(?)- ... **CLC 30**

Heaney, Seamus (Justin)
1939- ...... **CLC 5, 7, 14, 25, 37, 74, 91;**
DAB; DAM POET; PC 18
See also CA 85-88; CANR 25, 48;
CDBLB 1960 to Present; DLB 40;
DLBY 95; MTCW; YABC

Hearn, (Patricio) Lafcadio (Tessima Carlos)
1850-1904 .... **TCLC 9**
See also CA 105; DLB 12, 78

Hearne, Vicki 1946-............. **CLC 56**
See also CA 139

Hearon, Shelby 1931-............. **CLC 63**
See also AITN 2; CA 25-28R; CANR 18,
48

Heat-Moon, William Least......... **CLC 29**
See also Trogdon, William (Lewis)
See also AAYA 9

Hebbel, Friedrich
1813-1863 .... **NCLC 43; DAM DRAM**
See also DLB 129

Hebert, Anne
1916-............. **CLC 4, 13, 29; DAC;**
DAM MST, POET
See also CA 85-88; DLB 68; MTCW

Hecht, Anthony (Evan)
1923- ...... **CLC 8, 13, 19; DAM POET**
See also CA 9-12R; CANR 6; DLB 5, 169

Hecht, Ben 1894-1964 .... **CLC 8**
See also CA 85-88; DLB 7, 9, 25, 26, 28, 86

Hedayat, Sadeq 1903-1951........ **TCLC 21**
See also CA 120

Hegel, Georg Wilhelm Friedrich
1770-1831 .... **NCLC 46**
See also DLB 90

Heidegger, Martin 1889-1976 ...... **CLC 24**
See also CA 81-84; 65-68; CANR 34;
MTCW

Heidenstam, (Carl Gustaf) Verner von
1859-1940 .... **TCLC 5**
See also CA 104

Heifner, Jack 1946-............. **CLC 11**
See also CA 105; CANR 47

Heijermans, Herman 1864-1924 ... **TCLC 24**
See also CA 123

Heilbrun, Carolyn G(old) 1926-..... **CLC 25**
See also CA 45-48; CANR 1, 28, 58

Heine, Heinrich 1797-1856 .... **NCLC 4, 54**
See also DLB 90

Heinemann, Larry (Curtiss) 1944- .. **CLC 50**
See also CA 110; CAAS 21; CANR 31;
DLBD 9; INT CANR-31

Heiney, Donald (William) 1921-1993
See Harris, MacDonald
See also CA 1-4R; 142; CANR 3, 58

Heinlein, Robert A(nson)
1907-1988 ...... **CLC 1, 3, 8, 14, 26, 55;**
DAM POP
See also AAYA 17; CA 1-4R; 125;
CANR 1, 20, 53; DLB 8; JRDA;
MAICYA; MTCW; SATA 9, 69;
SATA-Obit 56

Helforth, John
See Doolittle, Hilda

Hellenhofferu, Vojtech Kapristian z
See Hasek, Jaroslav (Matej Frantisek)

Heller, Joseph
1923- .... **CLC 1, 3, 5, 8, 11, 36, 63; DA;**
DAB; DAC; DAM MST, NOV, POP;
WLC
See also AITN 1; CA 5-8R; CABS 1;
CANR 8, 42; DLB 2, 28; DLBY 80;
INT CANR-8; MTCW

Hellman, Lillian (Florence)
1906-1984 ...... **CLC 2, 4, 8, 14, 18, 34,**
44, 52; DAM DRAM; DC 1
See also AITN 1, 2; CA 13-16R; 112;
CANR 33; DLB 7; DLBY 84; MTCW

Helprin, Mark
1947- .... **CLC 7, 10, 22, 32;**
DAM NOV, POP
See also CA 81-84; CANR 47; DLBY 85;
MTCW

Helvetius, Claude-Adrien
1715-1771 .... **LC 26**

Helyar, Jane Penelope Josephine 1933-
See Poole, Josephine
See also CA 21-24R; CANR 10, 26;
SATA 82

Hemans, Felicia 1793-1835 ...... **NCLC 29**
See also DLB 96

Hemingway, Ernest (Miller)
1899-1961 .... **CLC 1, 3, 6, 8, 10, 13, 19,**
30, 34, 39, 41, 44, 50, 61, 80; DA; DAB;
DAC; DAM MST, NOV; SSC 25; WLC
See also AAYA 19; CA 77-80; CANR 34;
CDALB 1917-1929; DLB 4, 9, 102;
DLBD 1; DLBY 81, 87, 96; MTCW

Hempel, Amy 1951-.............. **CLC 39**
See also CA 118; 137

Henderson, F. C.
See Mencken, H(enry) L(ouis)

Henderson, Sylvia
See Ashton-Warner, Sylvia (Constance)

Henley, Beth .... **CLC 23; DC 6**
See also Henley, Elizabeth Becker
See also CABS 3; DLBY 86

Henley, Elizabeth Becker 1952-
See Henley, Beth
See also CA 107; CANR 32; DAM DRAM,
MST; MTCW

Henley, William Ernest
1849-1903 .... **TCLC 8**
See also CA 105; DLB 19

Hennissart, Martha
See Lathen, Emma
See also CA 85-88

Henry, O......... **TCLC 1, 19; SSC 5; WLC**
See also Porter, William Sydney

Henry, Patrick 1736-1799 .... **LC 25**

Henryson, Robert 1430(?)-1506(?).... **LC 20**
See also DLB 146

Henry VIII 1491-1547 .... **LC 10**

Henschke, Alfred
See Klabund

Hentoff, Nat(han Irving) 1925-..... **CLC 26**
See also AAYA 4; CA 1-4R; CAAS 6;
CANR 5, 25; CLR 1; INT CANR-25;
JRDA; MAICYA; SATA 42, 69;
SATA-Brief 27

Heppenstall, (John) Rayner
1911-1981 .... **CLC 10**
See also CA 1-4R; 103; CANR 29

Heraclitus
c. 540B.C.-c. 450B.C......... **CMLC 22**
See also DLB 176

Herbert, Frank (Patrick)
1920-1986 ...... **CLC 12, 23, 35, 44, 85;**
DAM POP
See also AAYA 21; CA 53-56; 118;
CANR 5, 43; DLB 8; INT CANR-5;
MTCW; SATA 9, 37; SATA-Obit 47

Herbert, George
1593-1633 .... **LC 24; DAB;**
DAM POET; PC 4
See also CDBLB Before 1660; DLB 126

Herbert, Zbigniew
1924- .... **CLC 9, 43; DAM POET**
See also CA 89-92; CANR 36; MTCW

Herbst, Josephine (Frey)
1897-1969 .... **CLC 34**
See also CA 5-8R; 25-28R; DLB 9

Hergesheimer, Joseph
1880-1954 .... **TCLC 11**
See also CA 109; DLB 102, 9

Herlihy, James Leo 1927-1993 ...... **CLC 6**
See also CA 1-4R; 143; CANR 2

Hermogenes fl. c. 175- .... **CMLC 6**

Hernandez, Jose 1834-1886 ...... **NCLC 17**

Herodotus c. 484B.C.-429B.C..... **CMLC 17**
See also DLB 176

Herrick, Robert
1591-1674 ..... **LC 13; DA; DAB; DAC;**
DAM MST, POP; PC 9
See also DLB 126

Herring, Guilles
See Somerville, Edith

Herriot, James
1916-1995 .... **CLC 12; DAM POP**
See also Wight, James Alfred
See also AAYA 1; CA 148; CANR 40;
SATA 86

Herrmann, Dorothy 1941-......... **CLC 44**
See also CA 107

Herrmann, Taffy
See Herrmann, Dorothy

Hersey, John (Richard)
1914-1993 .... **CLC 1, 2, 7, 9, 40, 81, 97;
DAM POP**
See also CA 17-20R; 140; CANR 33;
DLB 6; MTCW; SATA 25;
SATA-Obit 76

Herzen, Aleksandr Ivanovich
1812-1870 .... **NCLC 10, 61**

Herzl, Theodor 1860-1904 .... **TCLC 36**

Herzog, Werner 1942- .... **CLC 16**
See also CA 89-92

Hesiod c. 8th cent. B.C.- .... **CMLC 5**
See also DLB 176

Hesse, Hermann
1877-1962 .... **CLC 1, 2, 3, 6, 11, 17, 25,
69; DA; DAB; DAC; DAM MST, NOV;
SSC 9; WLC**
See also CA 17-18; CAP 2; DLB 66;
MTCW; SATA 50

Hewes, Cady
See De Voto, Bernard (Augustine)

Heyen, William 1940- .... **CLC 13, 18**
See also CA 33-36R; CAAS 9; DLB 5

Heyerdahl, Thor 1914- .... **CLC 26**
See also CA 5-8R; CANR 5, 22; MTCW;
SATA 2, 52

Heym, Georg (Theodor Franz Arthur)
1887-1912 .... **TCLC 9**
See also CA 106

Heym, Stefan 1913- .... **CLC 41**
See also CA 9-12R; CANR 4; DLB 69

Heyse, Paul (Johann Ludwig von)
1830-1914 .... **TCLC 8**
See also CA 104; DLB 129

Heyward, (Edwin) DuBose
1885-1940 .... **TCLC 59**
See also CA 108; 157; DLB 7, 9, 45;
SATA 21

Hibbert, Eleanor Alice Burford
1906-1993 .... **CLC 7; DAM POP**
See also BEST 90:4; CA 17-20R; 140;
CANR 9, 28; SATA 2; SATA-Obit 74

Hichens, Robert S. 1864-1950 ..... **TCLC 64**
See also DLB 153

Higgins, George V(incent)
1939- .... **CLC 4, 7, 10, 18**
See also CA 77-80; CAAS 5; CANR 17, 51;
DLB 2; DLBY 81; INT CANR-17;
MTCW

Higginson, Thomas Wentworth
1823-1911 .... **TCLC 36**
See also DLB 1, 64

Highet, Helen
See MacInnes, Helen (Clark)

Highsmith, (Mary) Patricia
1921-1995 .... **CLC 2, 4, 14, 42;
DAM NOV, POP**
See also CA 1-4R; 147; CANR 1, 20, 48;
MTCW

Highwater, Jamake (Mamake)
1942(?)- .... **CLC 12**
See also AAYA 7; CA 65-68; CAAS 7;
CANR 10, 34; CLR 17; DLB 52;
DLBY 85; JRDA; MAICYA; SATA 32,
69; SATA-Brief 30

Highway, Tomson
1951- ..... **CLC 92; DAC; DAM MULT**
See also CA 151; NNAL

Higuchi, Ichiyo 1872-1896 ...... **NCLC 49**

Hijuelos, Oscar
1951- .... **CLC 65; DAM MULT, POP;
HLC**
See also BEST 90:1; CA 123; CANR 50;
DLB 145; HW

Hikmet, Nazim 1902(?)-1963 ...... **CLC 40**
See also CA 141; 93-96

Hildegard von Bingen
1098-1179 .... **CMLC 20**
See also DLB 148

Hildesheimer, Wolfgang
1916-1991 .... **CLC 49**
See also CA 101; 135; DLB 69, 124

Hill, Geoffrey (William)
1932- ... **CLC 5, 8, 18, 45; DAM POET**
See also CA 81-84; CANR 21;
CDBLB 1960 to Present; DLB 40;
MTCW

Hill, George Roy 1921- .... **CLC 26**
See also CA 110; 122

Hill, John
See Koontz, Dean R(ay)

Hill, Susan (Elizabeth)
1942- .. **CLC 4; DAB; DAM MST, NOV**
See also CA 33-36R; CANR 29; DLB 14,
139; MTCW

Hillerman, Tony
1925- .... **CLC 62; DAM POP**
See also AAYA 6; BEST 89:1; CA 29-32R;
CANR 21, 42; SATA 6

Hillesum, Etty 1914-1943 .... **TCLC 49**
See also CA 137

Hilliard, Noel (Harvey) 1929- ...... **CLC 15**
See also CA 9-12R; CANR 7

Hillis, Rick 1956- .... **CLC 66**
See also CA 134

Hilton, James 1900-1954 .... **TCLC 21**
See also CA 108; DLB 34, 77; SATA 34

Himes, Chester (Bomar)
1909-1984 .... **CLC 2, 4, 7, 18, 58; BLC;
DAM MULT**
See also BW 2; CA 25-28R; 114; CANR 22;
DLB 2, 76, 143; MTCW

Hinde, Thomas .... **CLC 6, 11**
See also Chitty, Thomas Willes

Hindin, Nathan
See Bloch, Robert (Albert)

Hine, (William) Daryl 1936- .... **CLC 15**
See also CA 1-4R; CAAS 15; CANR 1, 20;
DLB 60

Hinkson, Katharine Tynan
See Tynan, Katharine

Hinton, S(usan) E(loise)
1950- .... **CLC 30; DA; DAB; DAC;
DAM MST, NOV**
See also AAYA 2; CA 81-84; CANR 32;
CLR 3, 23; JRDA; MAICYA; MTCW;
SATA 19, 58

Hippius, Zinaida .... **TCLC 9**
See also Gippius, Zinaida (Nikolayevna)

Hiraoka, Kimitake 1925-1970
See Mishima, Yukio
See also CA 97-100; 29-32R; DAM DRAM;
MTCW

Hirsch, E(ric) D(onald), Jr. 1928- ... **CLC 79**
See also CA 25-28R; CANR 27, 51;
DLB 67; INT CANR-27; MTCW

Hirsch, Edward 1950- .... **CLC 31, 50**
See also CA 104; CANR 20, 42; DLB 120

Hitchcock, Alfred (Joseph)
1899-1980 .... **CLC 16**
See also CA 97-100; SATA 27;
SATA-Obit 24

Hitler, Adolf 1889-1945 .... **TCLC 53**
See also CA 117; 147

Hoagland, Edward 1932- .... **CLC 28**
See also CA 1-4R; CANR 2, 31, 57; DLB 6;
SATA 51

Hoban, Russell (Conwell)
1925- .... **CLC 7, 25; DAM NOV**
See also CA 5-8R; CANR 23, 37; CLR 3;
DLB 52; MAICYA; MTCW; SATA 1,
40, 78

Hobbes, Thomas 1588-1679 .... **LC 36**
See also DLB 151

Hobbs, Perry
See Blackmur, R(ichard) P(almer)

Hobson, Laura Z(ametkin)
1900-1986 .... **CLC 7, 25**
See also CA 17-20R; 118; CANR 55;
DLB 28; SATA 52

Hochhuth, Rolf
1931- ..... **CLC 4, 11, 18; DAM DRAM**
See also CA 5-8R; CANR 33; DLB 124;
MTCW

Hochman, Sandra 1936- .... **CLC 3, 8**
See also CA 5-8R; DLB 5

Hochwaelder, Fritz
1911-1986 ...... **CLC 36; DAM DRAM**
See also CA 29-32R; 120; CANR 42;
MTCW

Hochwalder, Fritz
See Hochwaelder, Fritz

Hocking, Mary (Eunice) 1921- ..... **CLC 13**
See also CA 101; CANR 18, 40

Hodgins, Jack 1938- .... **CLC 23**
See also CA 93-96; DLB 60

Hodgson, William Hope
1877(?)-1918 .... **TCLC 13**
See also CA 111; DLB 70, 153, 156, 178

Hoeg, Peter 1957- .... **CLC 95**
See also CA 151

Hoffman, Alice
1952- .... **CLC 51; DAM NOV**
See also CA 77-80; CANR 34; MTCW

Hoffman, Daniel (Gerard)
1923- .... **CLC 6, 13, 23**
See also CA 1-4R; CANR 4; DLB 5

Hoffman, Stanley 1944- .... **CLC 5**
See also CA 77-80

Hoffman, William M(oses) 1939- ... **CLC 40**
See also CA 57-60; CANR 11

Hoffmann, E(rnst) T(heodor) A(madeus)
1776-1822 .... **NCLC 2; SSC 13**
See also DLB 90; SATA 27

Hofmann, Gert 1931-............ **CLC 54**
See also CA 128

Hofmannsthal, Hugo von
1874-1929 .... **TCLC 11; DAM DRAM;
DC 4**
See also CA 106; 153; DLB 81, 118

Hogan, Linda
1947- .... **CLC 73; DAM MULT**
See also CA 120; CANR 45; DLB 175;
NNAL

Hogarth, Charles
See Creasey, John

Hogarth, Emmett
See Polonsky, Abraham (Lincoln)

Hogg, James 1770-1835.......... **NCLC 4**
See also DLB 93, 116, 159

Holbach, Paul Henri Thiry Baron
1723-1789 .... **LC 14**

Holberg, Ludvig 1684-1754 .... **LC 6**

Holden, Ursula 1921-............. **CLC 18**
See also CA 101; CAAS 8; CANR 22

Holderlin, (Johann Christian) Friedrich
1770-1843 .... **NCLC 16; PC 4**

Holdstock, Robert
See Holdstock, Robert P.

Holdstock, Robert P. 1948-........ **CLC 39**
See also CA 131

Holland, Isabelle 1920- .... **CLC 21**
See also AAYA 11; CA 21-24R; CANR 10,
25, 47; JRDA; MAICYA; SATA 8, 70

Holland, Marcus
See Caldwell, (Janet Miriam) Taylor
(Holland)

Hollander, John 1929-...... **CLC 2, 5, 8, 14**
See also CA 1-4R; CANR 1, 52; DLB 5;
SATA 13

Hollander, Paul
See Silverberg, Robert

Holleran, Andrew 1943(?)-........ **CLC 38**
See also CA 144

Hollinghurst, Alan 1954-....... **CLC 55, 91**
See also CA 114

Hollis, Jim
See Summers, Hollis (Spurgeon, Jr.)

Holly, Buddy 1936-1959 .... **TCLC 65**

Holmes, John
See Souster, (Holmes) Raymond

Holmes, John Clellon 1926-1988.... **CLC 56**
See also CA 9-12R; 125; CANR 4; DLB 16

Holmes, Oliver Wendell
1809-1894 .... **NCLC 14**
See also CDALB 1640-1865; DLB 1;
SATA 34

Holmes, Raymond
See Souster, (Holmes) Raymond

Holt, Victoria
See Hibbert, Eleanor Alice Burford

Holub, Miroslav 1923-............. **CLC 4**
See also CA 21-24R; CANR 10

Homer
c. 8th cent. B.C.-..... **CMLC 1, 16; DA;
DAB; DAC; DAM MST, POET**
See also DLB 176; YABC

Honig, Edwin 1919-............. **CLC 33**
See also CA 5-8R; CAAS 8; CANR 4, 45;
DLB 5

Hood, Hugh (John Blagdon)
1928- .... **CLC 15, 28**
See also CA 49-52; CAAS 17; CANR 1, 33;
DLB 53

Hood, Thomas 1799-1845........ **NCLC 16**
See also DLB 96

Hooker, (Peter) Jeremy 1941-...... **CLC 43**
See also CA 77-80; CANR 22; DLB 40

hooks, bell .... **CLC 94**
See also Watkins, Gloria

Hope, A(lec) D(erwent) 1907-.... **CLC 3, 51**
See also CA 21-24R; CANR 33; MTCW

Hope, Brian
See Creasey, John

Hope, Christopher (David Tully)
1944- .... **CLC 52**
See also CA 106; CANR 47; SATA 62

Hopkins, Gerard Manley
1844-1889 .... **NCLC 17; DA; DAB;
DAC; DAM MST, POET; PC 15; WLC**
See also CDBLB 1890-1914; DLB 35, 57

Hopkins, John (Richard) 1931-...... **CLC 4**
See also CA 85-88

Hopkins, Pauline Elizabeth
1859-1930 .... **TCLC 28; BLC;
DAM MULT**
See also BW 2; CA 141; DLB 50

Hopkinson, Francis 1737-1791 ...... **LC 25**
See also DLB 31

Hopley-Woolrich, Cornell George 1903-1968
See Woolrich, Cornell
See also CA 13-14; CANR 58; CAP 1

Horatio
See Proust, (Valentin-Louis-George-Eugene-)
Marcel

Horgan, Paul (George Vincent O'Shaughnessy)
1903-1995 ...... **CLC 9, 53; DAM NOV**
See also CA 13-16R; 147; CANR 9, 35;
DLB 102; DLBY 85; INT CANR-9;
MTCW; SATA 13; SATA-Obit 84

Horn, Peter
See Kuttner, Henry

Hornem, Horace Esq.
See Byron, George Gordon (Noel)

**Horney, Karen (Clementine Theodore
Danielsen)** 1885-1952........ **TCLC 71**
See also CA 114

Hornung, E(rnest) W(illiam)
1866-1921 .... **TCLC 59**
See also CA 108; DLB 70

Horovitz, Israel (Arthur)
1939- .... **CLC 56; DAM DRAM**
See also CA 33-36R; CANR 46; DLB 7

Horvath, Odon von
See Horvath, Oedoen von
See also DLB 85, 124

Horvath, Oedoen von 1901-1938... **TCLC 45**
See also Horvath, Odon von
See also CA 118

Horwitz, Julius 1920-1986........ **CLC 14**
See also CA 9-12R; 119; CANR 12

Hospital, Janette Turner 1942-..... **CLC 42**
See also CA 108; CANR 48

Hostos, E. M. de
See Hostos (y Bonilla), Eugenio Maria de

Hostos, Eugenio M. de
See Hostos (y Bonilla), Eugenio Maria de

Hostos, Eugenio Maria
See Hostos (y Bonilla), Eugenio Maria de

Hostos (y Bonilla), Eugenio Maria de
1839-1903 .... **TCLC 24**
See also CA 123; 131; HW

Houdini
See Lovecraft, H(oward) P(hillips)

Hougan, Carolyn 1943- .... **CLC 34**
See also CA 139

Household, Geoffrey (Edward West)
1900-1988 .... **CLC 11**
See also CA 77-80; 126; CANR 58;
DLB 87; SATA 14; SATA-Obit 59

Housman, A(lfred) E(dward)
1859-1936 ...... **TCLC 1, 10; DA; DAB;
DAC; DAM MST, POET; PC 2**
See also CA 104; 125; DLB 19; MTCW;
YABC

Housman, Laurence 1865-1959..... **TCLC 7**
See also CA 106; 155; DLB 10; SATA 25

Howard, Elizabeth Jane 1923- ... **CLC 7, 29**
See also CA 5-8R; CANR 8

Howard, Maureen 1930- ..... **CLC 5, 14, 46**
See also CA 53-56; CANR 31; DLBY 83;
INT CANR-31; MTCW

Howard, Richard 1929- ...... **CLC 7, 10, 47**
See also AITN 1; CA 85-88; CANR 25;
DLB 5; INT CANR-25

Howard, Robert E(rvin)
1906-1936 .... **TCLC 8**
See also CA 105; 157

Howard, Warren F.
See Pohl, Frederik

Howe, Fanny 1940- .... **CLC 47**
See also CA 117; CAAS 27; SATA-Brief 52

Howe, Irving 1920-1993........... **CLC 85**
See also CA 9-12R; 141; CANR 21, 50;
DLB 67; MTCW

Howe, Julia Ward 1819-1910 ..... **TCLC 21**
See also CA 117; DLB 1

Howe, Susan 1937-................ **CLC 72**
See also DLB 120

Howe, Tina 1937-................. **CLC 48**
See also CA 109

Howell, James 1594(?)-1666 .... **LC 13**
See also DLB 151

Howells, W. D.
See Howells, William Dean

Howells, William D.
See Howells, William Dean

Howells, William Dean
1837-1920 .... **TCLC 7, 17, 41**
See also CA 104; 134; CDALB 1865-1917;
DLB 12, 64, 74, 79

Howes, Barbara 1914-1996 .... **CLC 15**
See also CA 9-12R; 151; CAAS 3;
CANR 53; SATA 5

Hrabal, Bohumil 1914-1997..... **CLC 13, 67**
　See also CA 106; 156; CAAS 12; CANR 57

Hsun, Lu
　See Lu Hsun

Hubbard, L(afayette) Ron(ald)
　　1911-1986 .... **CLC 43; DAM POP**
　See also CA 77-80; 118; CANR 52

Huch, Ricarda (Octavia)
　　1864-1947 .... **TCLC 13**
　See also CA 111; DLB 66

Huddle, David 1942- .... **CLC 49**
　See also CA 57-60; CAAS 20; DLB 130

Hudson, Jeffrey
　See Crichton, (John) Michael

Hudson, W(illiam) H(enry)
　　1841-1922 .... **TCLC 29**
　See also CA 115; DLB 98, 153, 174;
　　SATA 35

Hueffer, Ford Madox
　See Ford, Ford Madox

Hughart, Barry 1934-............. **CLC 39**
　See also CA 137

Hughes, Colin
　See Creasey, John

Hughes, David (John) 1930- .... **CLC 48**
　See also CA 116; 129; DLB 14

Hughes, Edward James
　See Hughes, Ted
　See also DAM MST, POET

Hughes, (James) Langston
　　1902-1967 ..... **CLC 1, 5, 10, 15, 35, 44;**
　　BLC; DA; DAB; DAC; DAM DRAM,
　　MST, MULT, POET; DC 3; PC 1;
　　SSC 6; WLC
　See also AAYA 12; BW 1; CA 1-4R;
　　25-28R; CANR 1, 34; CDALB 1929-1941;
　　CLR 17; DLB 4, 7, 48, 51, 86; JRDA;
　　MAICYA; MTCW; SATA 4, 33

Hughes, Richard (Arthur Warren)
　　1900-1976 ...... **CLC 1, 11; DAM NOV**
　See also CA 5-8R; 65-68; CANR 4;
　　DLB 15, 161; MTCW; SATA 8;
　　SATA-Obit 25

Hughes, Ted
　　1930- .... **CLC 2, 4, 9, 14, 37; DAB;**
　　DAC; PC 7
　See also Hughes, Edward James
　See also CA 1-4R; CANR 1, 33; CLR 3;
　　DLB 40, 161; MAICYA; MTCW;
　　SATA 49; SATA-Brief 27

Hugo, Richard F(ranklin)
　　1923-1982 .... **CLC 6, 18, 32;**
　　DAM POET
　See also CA 49-52; 108; CANR 3; DLB 5

Hugo, Victor (Marie)
　　1802-1885 .... **NCLC 3, 10, 21; DA;**
　　DAB; DAC; DAM DRAM, MST, NOV,
　　POET; PC 17; WLC
　See also DLB 119; SATA 47

Huidobro, Vicente
　See Huidobro Fernandez, Vicente Garcia

Huidobro Fernandez, Vicente Garcia
　　1893-1948 .... **TCLC 31**
　See also CA 131; HW

Hulme, Keri 1947- .... **CLC 39**
　See also CA 125; INT 125

Hulme, T(homas) E(rnest)
　　1883-1917 .... **TCLC 21**
　See also CA 117; DLB 19

Hume, David 1711-1776............. **LC 7**
　See also DLB 104

Humphrey, William 1924-......... **CLC 45**
　See also CA 77-80; DLB 6

Humphreys, Emyr Owen 1919-..... **CLC 47**
　See also CA 5-8R; CANR 3, 24; DLB 15

Humphreys, Josephine 1945-.... **CLC 34, 57**
　See also CA 121; 127; INT 127

Huneker, James Gibbons
　　1857-1921 .... **TCLC 65**
　See also DLB 71

Hungerford, Pixie
　See Brinsmead, H(esba) F(ay)

Hunt, E(verette) Howard, (Jr.)
　　1918- .... **CLC 3**
　See also AITN 1; CA 45-48; CANR 2, 47

Hunt, Kyle
　See Creasey, John

Hunt, (James Henry) Leigh
　　1784-1859 ...... **NCLC 1; DAM POET**

Hunt, Marsha 1946-................ **CLC 70**
　See also BW 2; CA 143

Hunt, Violet 1866-1942 .... **TCLC 53**
　See also DLB 162

Hunter, E. Waldo
　See Sturgeon, Theodore (Hamilton)

Hunter, Evan
　　1926- .... **CLC 11, 31; DAM POP**
　See also CA 5-8R; CANR 5, 38; DLBY 82;
　　INT CANR-5; MTCW; SATA 25

Hunter, Kristin (Eggleston) 1931-... **CLC 35**
　See also AITN 1; BW 1; CA 13-16R;
　　CANR 13; CLR 3; DLB 33;
　　INT CANR-13; MAICYA; SAAS 10;
　　SATA 12

Hunter, Mollie 1922-............. **CLC 21**
　See also McIlwraith, Maureen Mollie
　　Hunter
　See also AAYA 13; CANR 37; CLR 25;
　　DLB 161; JRDA; MAICYA; SAAS 7;
　　SATA 54

Hunter, Robert (?)-1734............. **LC 7**

Hurston, Zora Neale
　　1903-1960 .... **CLC 7, 30, 61; BLC; DA;**
　　DAC; DAM MST, MULT, NOV; SSC 4
　See also AAYA 15; BW 1; CA 85-88;
　　DLB 51, 86; MTCW; YABC

Huston, John (Marcellus)
　　1906-1987 .... **CLC 20**
　See also CA 73-76; 123; CANR 34; DLB 26

Hustvedt, Siri 1955-.............. **CLC 76**
　See also CA 137

Hutten, Ulrich von 1488-1523....... **LC 16**
　See also DLB 179

Huxley, Aldous (Leonard)
　　1894-1963 ..... **CLC 1, 3, 4, 5, 8, 11, 18,**
　　35, 79; DA; DAB; DAC; DAM MST,
　　NOV; WLC
　See also AAYA 11; CA 85-88; CANR 44;
　　CDBLB 1914-1945; DLB 36, 100, 162;
　　MTCW; SATA 63

Huysmans, Charles Marie Georges
　　1848-1907
　See Huysmans, Joris-Karl
　See also CA 104

Huysmans, Joris-Karl .... **TCLC 7, 69**
　See also Huysmans, Charles Marie Georges
　See also DLB 123

Hwang, David Henry
　　1957- .... **CLC 55; DAM DRAM; DC 4**
　See also CA 127; 132; INT 132

Hyde, Anthony 1946-............. **CLC 42**
　See also CA 136

Hyde, Margaret O(ldroyd) 1917- ... **CLC 21**
　See also CA 1-4R; CANR 1, 36; CLR 23;
　　JRDA; MAICYA; SAAS 8; SATA 1, 42,
　　76

Hynes, James 1956(?)-............. **CLC 65**

Ian, Janis 1951- .... **CLC 21**
　See also CA 105

Ibanez, Vicente Blasco
　See Blasco Ibanez, Vicente

Ibarguengoitia, Jorge 1928-1983.... **CLC 37**
　See also CA 124; 113; HW

Ibsen, Henrik (Johan)
　　1828-1906 .... **TCLC 2, 8, 16, 37, 52;**
　　DA; DAB; DAC; DAM DRAM, MST;
　　DC 2; WLC
　See also CA 104; 141

Ibuse Masuji 1898-1993.......... **CLC 22**
　See also CA 127; 141; DLB 180

Ichikawa, Kon 1915-............. **CLC 20**
　See also CA 121

Idle, Eric 1943-................. **CLC 21**
　See also Monty Python
　See also CA 116; CANR 35

Ignatow, David 1914-...... **CLC 4, 7, 14, 40**
　See also CA 9-12R; CAAS 3; CANR 31, 57;
　　DLB 5

Ihimaera, Witi 1944- .... **CLC 46**
　See also CA 77-80

Ilf, Ilya .... **TCLC 21**
　See also Fainzilberg, Ilya Arnoldovich

Illyes, Gyula 1902-1983............ **PC 16**
　See also CA 114; 109

Immermann, Karl (Lebrecht)
　　1796-1840 .... **NCLC 4, 49**
　See also DLB 133

Inchbald, Elizabeth 1753-1821 ... **NCLC 62**
　See also DLB 39, 89

Inclan, Ramon (Maria) del Valle
　See Valle-Inclan, Ramon (Maria) del

Infante, G(uillermo) Cabrera
　See Cabrera Infante, G(uillermo)

Ingalls, Rachel (Holmes) 1940-..... **CLC 42**
　See also CA 123; 127

Ingamells, Rex 1913-1955 .... **TCLC 35**

Inge, William (Motter)
　　1913-1973 .. **CLC 1, 8, 19; DAM DRAM**
　See also CA 9-12R; CDALB 1941-1968;
　　DLB 7; MTCW

Ingelow, Jean 1820-1897 .... **NCLC 39**
　See also DLB 35, 163; SATA 33

Ingram, Willis J.
　See Harris, Mark

Jensen, Johannes V. 1873-1950.... **TCLC 41**

Jensen, Laura (Linnea) 1948- ...... **CLC 37**
See also CA 103

Jerome, Jerome K(lapka)
1859-1927 .... **TCLC 23**
See also CA 119; DLB 10, 34, 135

Jerrold, Douglas William
1803-1857 .... **NCLC 2**
See also DLB 158, 159

Jewett, (Theodora) Sarah Orne
1849-1909 .... **TCLC 1, 22; SSC 6**
See also CA 108; 127; DLB 12, 74;
SATA 15

Jewsbury, Geraldine (Endsor)
1812-1880 .... **NCLC 22**
See also DLB 21

Jhabvala, Ruth Prawer
1927- .... **CLC 4, 8, 29, 94; DAB;**
DAM NOV
See also CA 1-4R; CANR 2, 29, 51;
DLB 139; INT CANR-29; MTCW

Jibran, Kahlil
See Gibran, Kahlil

Jibran, Khalil
See Gibran, Kahlil

Jiles, Paulette 1943-.......... **CLC 13, 58**
See also CA 101

Jimenez (Mantecon), Juan Ramon
1881-1958 ..... **TCLC 4; DAM MULT,**
POET; HLC; PC 7
See also CA 104; 131; DLB 134; HW;
MTCW

Jimenez, Ramon
See Jimenez (Mantecon), Juan Ramon

Jimenez Mantecon, Juan
See Jimenez (Mantecon), Juan Ramon

Joel, Billy .... **CLC 26**
See also Joel, William Martin

Joel, William Martin 1949-
See Joel, Billy
See also CA 108

John of the Cross, St. 1542-1591 .... **LC 18**

Johnson, B(ryan) S(tanley William)
1933-1973 .... **CLC 6, 9**
See also CA 9-12R; 53-56; CANR 9;
DLB 14, 40

Johnson, Benj. F. of Boo
See Riley, James Whitcomb

Johnson, Benjamin F. of Boo
See Riley, James Whitcomb

Johnson, Charles (Richard)
1948- .... **CLC 7, 51, 65; BLC;**
DAM MULT
See also BW 2; CA 116; CAAS 18;
CANR 42; DLB 33

Johnson, Denis 1949-............. **CLC 52**
See also CA 117; 121; DLB 120

Johnson, Diane 1934-........ **CLC 5, 13, 48**
See also CA 41-44R; CANR 17, 40;
DLBY 80; INT CANR-17; MTCW

Johnson, Eyvind (Olof Verner)
1900-1976 .... **CLC 14**
See also CA 73-76; 69-72; CANR 34

Johnson, J. R.
See James, C(yril) L(ionel) R(obert)

Johnson, James Weldon
1871-1938 .... **TCLC 3, 19; BLC;**
DAM MULT, POET
See also BW 1; CA 104; 125;
CDALB 1917-1929; CLR 32; DLB 51;
MTCW; SATA 31

Johnson, Joyce 1935-............ **CLC 58**
See also CA 125; 129

Johnson, Lionel (Pigot)
1867-1902 .... **TCLC 19**
See also CA 117; DLB 19

Johnson, Mel
See Malzberg, Barry N(athaniel)

Johnson, Pamela Hansford
1912-1981 .... **CLC 1, 7, 27**
See also CA 1-4R; 104; CANR 2, 28;
DLB 15; MTCW

Johnson, Robert 1911(?)-1938 ..... **TCLC 69**

Johnson, Samuel
1709-1784 ..... **LC 15; DA; DAB; DAC;**
DAM MST; WLC
See also CDBLB 1660-1789; DLB 39, 95,
104, 142

Johnson, Uwe
1934-1984 .... **CLC 5, 10, 15, 40**
See also CA 1-4R; 112; CANR 1, 39;
DLB 75; MTCW

Johnston, George (Benson) 1913-... **CLC 51**
See also CA 1-4R; CANR 5, 20; DLB 88

Johnston, Jennifer 1930-.......... **CLC 7**
See also CA 85-88; DLB 14

Jolley, (Monica) Elizabeth
1923- .... **CLC 46; SSC 19**
See also CA 127; CAAS 13

Jones, Arthur Llewellyn 1863-1947
See Machen, Arthur
See also CA 104

Jones, D(ouglas) G(ordon) 1929-.... **CLC 10**
See also CA 29-32R; CANR 13; DLB 53

Jones, David (Michael)
1895-1974 .... **CLC 2, 4, 7, 13, 42**
See also CA 9-12R; 53-56; CANR 28;
CDBLB 1945-1960; DLB 20, 100; MTCW

Jones, David Robert 1947-
See Bowie, David
See also CA 103

Jones, Diana Wynne 1934- .... **CLC 26**
See also AAYA 12; CA 49-52; CANR 4,
26, 56; CLR 23; DLB 161; JRDA;
MAICYA; SAAS 7; SATA 9, 70

Jones, Edward P. 1950-........... **CLC 76**
See also BW 2; CA 142

Jones, Gayl
1949- .... **CLC 6, 9; BLC; DAM MULT**
See also BW 2; CA 77-80; CANR 27;
DLB 33; MTCW

Jones, James 1921-1977.... **CLC 1, 3, 10, 39**
See also AITN 1, 2; CA 1-4R; 69-72;
CANR 6; DLB 2, 143; MTCW

Jones, John J.
See Lovecraft, H(oward) P(hillips)

Jones, LeRoi .... **CLC 1, 2, 3, 5, 10, 14**
See also Baraka, Amiri

Jones, Louis B. .... **CLC 65**
See also CA 141

Jones, Madison (Percy, Jr.) 1925- ... **CLC 4**
See also CA 13-16R; CAAS 11; CANR 7,
54; DLB 152

Jones, Mervyn 1922-.......... **CLC 10, 52**
See also CA 45-48; CAAS 5; CANR 1;
MTCW

Jones, Mick 1956(?)- .... **CLC 30**

Jones, Nettie (Pearl) 1941- .... **CLC 34**
See also BW 2; CA 137; CAAS 20

Jones, Preston 1936-1979 .... **CLC 10**
See also CA 73-76; 89-92; DLB 7

Jones, Robert F(rancis) 1934-....... **CLC 7**
See also CA 49-52; CANR 2

Jones, Rod 1953- .... **CLC 50**
See also CA 128

Jones, Terence Graham Parry
1942- .... **CLC 21**
See also Jones, Terry; Monty Python
See also CA 112; 116; CANR 35; INT 116

Jones, Terry
See Jones, Terence Graham Parry
See also SATA 67; SATA-Brief 51

Jones, Thom 1945(?)-............. **CLC 81**
See also CA 157

Jong, Erica
1942- .... **CLC 4, 6, 8, 18, 83;**
DAM NOV, POP
See also AITN 1; BEST 90:2; CA 73-76;
CANR 26, 52; DLB 2, 5, 28, 152;
INT CANR-26; MTCW

Jonson, Ben(jamin)
1572(?)-1637 ...... **LC 6, 33; DA; DAB;**
DAC; DAM DRAM, MST, POET;
DC 4; PC 17; WLC
See also CDBLB Before 1660; DLB 62, 121

Jordan, June
1936- ..... **CLC 5, 11, 23; DAM MULT,**
POET
See also AAYA 2; BW 2; CA 33-36R;
CANR 25; CLR 10; DLB 38; MAICYA;
MTCW; SATA 4

Jordan, Pat(rick M.) 1941- .... **CLC 37**
See also CA 33-36R

Jorgensen, Ivar
See Ellison, Harlan (Jay)

Jorgenson, Ivar
See Silverberg, Robert

Josephus, Flavius c. 37-100 ..... **CMLC 13**

Josipovici, Gabriel 1940-........ **CLC 6, 43**
See also CA 37-40R; CAAS 8; CANR 47;
DLB 14

Joubert, Joseph 1754-1824 .... **NCLC 9**

Jouve, Pierre Jean 1887-1976...... **CLC 47**
See also CA 65-68

Joyce, James (Augustine Aloysius)
1882-1941 .... **TCLC 3, 8, 16, 35, 52;**
DA; DAB; DAC; DAM MST, NOV,
POET; SSC 26; WLC
See also CA 104; 126; CDBLB 1914-1945;
DLB 10, 19, 36, 162; MTCW

Jozsef, Attila 1905-1937......... **TCLC 22**
See also CA 116

Juana Ines de la Cruz 1651(?)-1695 ... **LC 5**

Judd, Cyril
See Kornbluth, C(yril) M.; Pohl, Frederik

Julian of Norwich 1342(?)-1416(?) .... **LC 6**
See also DLB 146

Juniper, Alex
See Hospital, Janette Turner

Junius
See Luxemburg, Rosa

Just, Ward (Swift) 1935- .... **CLC 4, 27**
See also CA 25-28R; CANR 32;
INT CANR-32

Justice, Donald (Rodney)
1925- .... **CLC 6, 19; DAM POET**
See also CA 5-8R; CANR 26, 54;
DLBY 83; INT CANR-26

Juvenal c. 55-c. 127 .... **CMLC 8**

Juvenis
See Bourne, Randolph S(illiman)

Kacew, Romain 1914-1980
See Gary, Romain
See also CA 108; 102

Kadare, Ismail 1936- .... **CLC 52**

Kadohata, Cynthia................. **CLC 59**
See also CA 140

Kafka, Franz
1883-1924 .... **TCLC 2, 6, 13, 29, 47, 53;**
DA; DAB; DAC; DAM MST, NOV;
SSC 5; WLC
See also CA 105; 126; DLB 81; MTCW

Kahanovitsch, Pinkhes
See Der Nister

Kahn, Roger 1927- .... **CLC 30**
See also CA 25-28R; CANR 44; DLB 171;
SATA 37

Kain, Saul
See Sassoon, Siegfried (Lorraine)

Kaiser, Georg 1878-1945 .... **TCLC 9**
See also CA 106; DLB 124

Kaletski, Alexander 1946- .... **CLC 39**
See also CA 118; 143

Kalidasa fl. c. 400- .... **CMLC 9**

Kallman, Chester (Simon)
1921-1975 .... **CLC 2**
See also CA 45-48; 53-56; CANR 3

Kaminsky, Melvin 1926-
See Brooks, Mel
See also CA 65-68; CANR 16

Kaminsky, Stuart M(elvin) 1934- ... **CLC 59**
See also CA 73-76; CANR 29, 53

Kane, Francis
See Robbins, Harold

Kane, Paul
See Simon, Paul (Frederick)

Kane, Wilson
See Bloch, Robert (Albert)

Kanin, Garson 1912-.............. **CLC 22**
See also AITN 1; CA 5-8R; CANR 7;
DLB 7

Kaniuk, Yoram 1930-............. **CLC 19**
See also CA 134

Kant, Immanuel 1724-1804 ...... **NCLC 27**
See also DLB 94

Kantor, MacKinlay 1904-1977 ...... **CLC 7**
See also CA 61-64; 73-76; DLB 9, 102

Kaplan, David Michael 1946- ...... **CLC 50**

Kaplan, James 1951- .... **CLC 59**
See also CA 135

Karageorge, Michael
See Anderson, Poul (William)

Karamzin, Nikolai Mikhailovich
1766-1826 .... **NCLC 3**
See also DLB 150

Karapanou, Margarita 1946-....... **CLC 13**
See also CA 101

Karinthy, Frigyes 1887-1938 ...... **TCLC 47**

Karl, Frederick R(obert) 1927-..... **CLC 34**
See also CA 5-8R; CANR 3, 44

Kastel, Warren
See Silverberg, Robert

Kataev, Evgeny Petrovich 1903-1942
See Petrov, Evgeny
See also CA 120

Kataphusin
See Ruskin, John

Katz, Steve 1935-................ **CLC 47**
See also CA 25-28R; CAAS 14; CANR 12;
DLBY 83

Kauffman, Janet 1945-............ **CLC 42**
See also CA 117; CANR 43; DLBY 86

Kaufman, Bob (Garnell)
1925-1986 .... **CLC 49**
See also BW 1; CA 41-44R; 118; CANR 22;
DLB 16, 41

Kaufman, George S.
1889-1961 ...... **CLC 38; DAM DRAM**
See also CA 108; 93-96; DLB 7; INT 108

Kaufman, Sue .... **CLC 3, 8**
See also Barondess, Sue K(aufman)

Kavafis, Konstantinos Petrou 1863-1933
See Cavafy, C(onstantine) P(eter)
See also CA 104

Kavan, Anna 1901-1968...... **CLC 5, 13, 82**
See also CA 5-8R; CANR 6, 57; MTCW

Kavanagh, Dan
See Barnes, Julian (Patrick)

Kavanagh, Patrick (Joseph)
1904-1967 .... **CLC 22**
See also CA 123; 25-28R; DLB 15, 20;
MTCW

Kawabata, Yasunari
1899-1972 .... **CLC 2, 5, 9, 18;**
DAM MULT; SSC 17
See also CA 93-96; 33-36R; DLB 180

Kaye, M(ary) M(argaret) 1909-..... **CLC 28**
See also CA 89-92; CANR 24; MTCW;
SATA 62

Kaye, Mollie
See Kaye, M(ary) M(argaret)

Kaye-Smith, Sheila 1887-1956..... **TCLC 20**
See also CA 118; DLB 36

Kaymor, Patrice Maguilene
See Senghor, Leopold Sedar

Kazan, Elia 1909-........... **CLC 6, 16, 63**
See also CA 21-24R; CANR 32

Kazantzakis, Nikos
1883(?)-1957 .... **TCLC 2, 5, 33**
See also CA 105; 132; MTCW

Kazin, Alfred 1915- .... **CLC 34, 38**
See also CA 1-4R; CAAS 7; CANR 1, 45;
DLB 67

Keane, Mary Nesta (Skrine) 1904-1996
See Keane, Molly
See also CA 108; 114; 151

Keane, Molly..................... **CLC 31**
See also Keane, Mary Nesta (Skrine)
See also INT 114

Keates, Jonathan 19(?)-........... **CLC 34**

Keaton, Buster 1895-1966 .... **CLC 20**

Keats, John
1795-1821 .... **NCLC 8; DA; DAB;**
DAC; DAM MST, POET; PC 1; WLC
See also CDBLB 1789-1832; DLB 96, 110

Keene, Donald 1922- .... **CLC 34**
See also CA 1-4R; CANR 5

Keillor, Garrison .... **CLC 40**
See also Keillor, Gary (Edward)
See also AAYA 2; BEST 89:3; DLBY 87;
SATA 58

Keillor, Gary (Edward) 1942-
See Keillor, Garrison
See also CA 111; 117; CANR 36;
DAM POP; MTCW

Keith, Michael
See Hubbard, L(afayette) Ron(ald)

Keller, Gottfried
1819-1890 .... **NCLC 2; SSC 26**
See also DLB 129

Kellerman, Jonathan
1949- .... **CLC 44; DAM POP**
See also BEST 90:1; CA 106; CANR 29, 51;
INT CANR-29

Kelley, William Melvin 1937-...... **CLC 22**
See also BW 1; CA 77-80; CANR 27;
DLB 33

Kellogg, Marjorie 1922-............ **CLC 2**
See also CA 81-84

Kellow, Kathleen
See Hibbert, Eleanor Alice Burford

Kelly, M(ilton) T(erry) 1947-....... **CLC 55**
See also CA 97-100; CAAS 22; CANR 19,
43

Kelman, James 1946-......... **CLC 58, 86**
See also CA 148

Kemal, Yashar 1923- .... **CLC 14, 29**
See also CA 89-92; CANR 44

Kemble, Fanny 1809-1893 .... **NCLC 18**
See also DLB 32

Kemelman, Harry 1908-1996........ **CLC 2**
See also AITN 1; CA 9-12R; 155; CANR 6;
DLB 28

Kempe, Margery 1373(?)-1440(?) ..... **LC 6**
See also DLB 146

Kempis, Thomas a 1380-1471 .... **LC 11**

Kendall, Henry 1839-1882....... **NCLC 12**

Keneally, Thomas (Michael)
1935- ...... **CLC 5, 8, 10, 14, 19, 27, 43;**
DAM NOV
See also CA 85-88; CANR 10, 50; MTCW

Kubin, Alfred (Leopold Isidor)
1877-1959 .... **TCLC 23**
See also CA 112; 149; DLB 81

Kubrick, Stanley 1928-............ **CLC 16**
See also CA 81-84; CANR 33; DLB 26

Kumin, Maxine (Winokur)
1925- ..... **CLC 5, 13, 28; DAM POET;
PC 15**
See also AITN 2; CA 1-4R; CAAS 8;
CANR 1, 21; DLB 5; MTCW; SATA 12

Kundera, Milan
1929- .... **CLC 4, 9, 19, 32, 68;
DAM NOV; SSC 24**
See also AAYA 2; CA 85-88; CANR 19,
52; MTCW

Kunene, Mazisi (Raymond) 1930-... **CLC 85**
See also BW 1; CA 125; DLB 117

Kunitz, Stanley (Jasspon)
1905- .... **CLC 6, 11, 14; PC 19**
See also CA 41-44R; CANR 26, 57;
DLB 48; INT CANR-26; MTCW

Kunze, Reiner 1933-.............. **CLC 10**
See also CA 93-96; DLB 75

Kuprin, Aleksandr Ivanovich
1870-1938 .... **TCLC 5**
See also CA 104

Kureishi, Hanif 1954(?)-.......... **CLC 64**
See also CA 139

Kurosawa, Akira
1910- .... **CLC 16; DAM MULT**
See also AAYA 11; CA 101; CANR 46

Kushner, Tony
1957(?)- .... **CLC 81; DAM DRAM**
See also CA 144

Kuttner, Henry 1915-1958........ **TCLC 10**
See also Vance, Jack
See also CA 107; 157; DLB 8

Kuzma, Greg 1944-............... **CLC 7**
See also CA 33-36R

Kuzmin, Mikhail 1872(?)-1936 .... **TCLC 40**

Kyd, Thomas
1558-1594 .... **LC 22; DAM DRAM;
DC 3**
See also DLB 62

Kyprianos, Iossif
See Samarakis, Antonis

La Bruyere, Jean de 1645-1696...... **LC 17**

Lacan, Jacques (Marie Emile)
1901-1981 .... **CLC 75**
See also CA 121; 104

**Laclos, Pierre Ambroise Francois Choderlos
de** 1741-1803 .... **NCLC 4**

Lacolere, Francois
See Aragon, Louis

La Colere, Francois
See Aragon, Louis

La Deshabilleuse
See Simenon, Georges (Jacques Christian)

Lady Gregory
See Gregory, Isabella Augusta (Persse)

Lady of Quality, A
See Bagnold, Enid

**La Fayette, Marie (Madelaine Pioche de la
Vergne Comtes** 1634-1693....... **LC 2**

Lafayette, Rene
See Hubbard, L(afayette) Ron(ald)

Laforgue, Jules
1860-1887 .... **NCLC 5, 53; PC 14;
SSC 20**

Lagerkvist, Paer (Fabian)
1891-1974 .... **CLC 7, 10, 13, 54;
DAM DRAM, NOV**
See also Lagerkvist, Par
See also CA 85-88; 49-52; MTCW

Lagerkvist, Par .... **SSC 12**
See also Lagerkvist, Paer (Fabian)

Lagerloef, Selma (Ottiliana Lovisa)
1858-1940 .... **TCLC 4, 36**
See also Lagerlof, Selma (Ottiliana Lovisa)
See also CA 108; SATA 15

Lagerlof, Selma (Ottiliana Lovisa)
See Lagerloef, Selma (Ottiliana Lovisa)
See also CLR 7; SATA 15

La Guma, (Justin) Alex(ander)
1925-1985 .... **CLC 19; DAM NOV**
See also BW 1; CA 49-52; 118; CANR 25;
DLB 117; MTCW

Laidlaw, A. K.
See Grieve, C(hristopher) M(urray)

Lainez, Manuel Mujica
See Mujica Lainez, Manuel
See also HW

Laing, R(onald) D(avid)
1927-1989 .... **CLC 95**
See also CA 107; 129; CANR 34; MTCW

Lamartine, Alphonse (Marie Louis Prat) de
1790-1869 ..... **NCLC 11; DAM POET;
PC 16**

Lamb, Charles
1775-1834 .... **NCLC 10; DA; DAB;
DAC; DAM MST; WLC**
See also CDBLB 1789-1832; DLB 93, 107,
163; SATA 17

Lamb, Lady Caroline 1785-1828.. **NCLC 38**
See also DLB 116

Lamming, George (William)
1927- .... **CLC 2, 4, 66; BLC;
DAM MULT**
See also BW 2; CA 85-88; CANR 26;
DLB 125; MTCW

L'Amour, Louis (Dearborn)
1908-1988 .... **CLC 25, 55; DAM NOV,
POP**
See also AAYA 16; AITN 2; BEST 89:2;
CA 1-4R; 125; CANR 3, 25, 40;
DLBY 80; MTCW

Lampedusa, Giuseppe (Tomasi) di
1896-1957 .... **TCLC 13**
See also Tomasi di Lampedusa, Giuseppe
See also DLB 177

Lampman, Archibald 1861-1899 .. **NCLC 25**
See also DLB 92

Lancaster, Bruce 1896-1963........ **CLC 36**
See also CA 9-10; CAP 1; SATA 9

Lanchester, John .... **CLC 99**

Landau, Mark Alexandrovich
See Aldanov, Mark (Alexandrovich)

Landau-Aldanov, Mark Alexandrovich
See Aldanov, Mark (Alexandrovich)

Landis, Jerry
See Simon, Paul (Frederick)

Landis, John 1950-.............. **CLC 26**
See also CA 112; 122

Landolfi, Tommaso 1908-1979... **CLC 11, 49**
See also CA 127; 117; DLB 177

Landon, Letitia Elizabeth
1802-1838 .... **NCLC 15**
See also DLB 96

Landor, Walter Savage
1775-1864 .... **NCLC 14**
See also DLB 93, 107

Landwirth, Heinz 1927-
See Lind, Jakov
See also CA 9-12R; CANR 7

Lane, Patrick
1939- .... **CLC 25; DAM POET**
See also CA 97-100; CANR 54; DLB 53;
INT 97-100

Lang, Andrew 1844-1912........ **TCLC 16**
See also CA 114; 137; DLB 98, 141;
MAICYA; SATA 16

Lang, Fritz 1890-1976 .... **CLC 20**
See also CA 77-80; 69-72; CANR 30

Lange, John
See Crichton, (John) Michael

Langer, Elinor 1939- .... **CLC 34**
See also CA 121

Langland, William
1330(?)-1400(?) ...... **LC 19; DA; DAB;
DAC; DAM MST, POET**
See also DLB 146

Langstaff, Launcelot
See Irving, Washington

Lanier, Sidney
1842-1881 ...... **NCLC 6; DAM POET**
See also DLB 64; DLBD 13; MAICYA;
SATA 18

Lanyer, Aemilia 1569-1645 ...... **LC 10, 30**
See also DLB 121

Lao Tzu .... **CMLC 7**

Lapine, James (Elliot) 1949-....... **CLC 39**
See also CA 123; 130; CANR 54; INT 130

Larbaud, Valery (Nicolas)
1881-1957 .... **TCLC 9**
See also CA 106; 152

Lardner, Ring
See Lardner, Ring(gold) W(ilmer)

Lardner, Ring W., Jr.
See Lardner, Ring(gold) W(ilmer)

Lardner, Ring(gold) W(ilmer)
1885-1933 .... **TCLC 2, 14**
See also CA 104; 131; CDALB 1917-1929;
DLB 11, 25, 86; MTCW

Laredo, Betty
See Codrescu, Andrei

Larkin, Maia
See Wojciechowska, Maia (Teresa)

Larkin, Philip (Arthur)
1922-1985 .... **CLC 3, 5, 8, 9, 13, 18, 33,
39, 64; DAB; DAM MST, POET**
See also CA 5-8R; 117; CANR 24;
CDBLB 1960 to Present; DLB 27;
MTCW

Larra (y Sanchez de Castro), Mariano Jose de
        1809-1837 . . . . NCLC 17

Larsen, Eric   1941- . . . . CLC 55
        See also CA 132

Larsen, Nella
        1891-1964 . . . . CLC 37; BLC;
                                           DAM MULT
        See also BW 1; CA 125; DLB 51

Larson, Charles R(aymond)   1938- . . . CLC 31
        See also CA 53-56; CANR 4

Larson, Jonathan   1961(?)-1996 . . . . . CLC 99

Las Casas, Bartolome de   1474-1566 . . LC 31

Lasker-Schueler, Else   1869-1945 . . TCLC 57
        See also DLB 66, 124

Latham, Jean Lee   1902- . . . . CLC 12
        See also AITN 1; CA 5-8R; CANR 7;
        MAICYA; SATA 2, 68

Latham, Mavis
        See Clark, Mavis Thorpe

Lathen, Emma . . . . CLC 2
        See also Hennissart, Martha; Latsis, Mary
        J(ane)

Lathrop, Francis
        See Leiber, Fritz (Reuter, Jr.)

Latsis, Mary J(ane)
        See Lathen, Emma
        See also CA 85-88

Lattimore, Richmond (Alexander)
        1906-1984 . . . . CLC 3
        See also CA 1-4R; 112; CANR 1

Laughlin, James   1914- . . . . CLC 49
        See also CA 21-24R; CAAS 22; CANR 9,
        47; DLB 48; DLBY 96

Laurence, (Jean) Margaret (Wemyss)
        1926-1987 . . . . CLC 3, 6, 13, 50, 62;
                              DAC; DAM MST; SSC 7
        See also CA 5-8R; 121; CANR 33; DLB 53;
        MTCW; SATA-Obit 50

Laurent, Antoine   1952- . . . . CLC 50

Lauscher, Hermann
        See Hesse, Hermann

Lautreamont, Comte de
        1846-1870 . . . . NCLC 12; SSC 14

Laverty, Donald
        See Blish, James (Benjamin)

Lavin, Mary
        1912-1996 . . . . CLC 4, 18, 99; SSC 4
        See also CA 9-12R; 151; CANR 33;
        DLB 15; MTCW

Lavond, Paul Dennis
        See Kornbluth, C(yril) M.; Pohl, Frederik

Lawler, Raymond Evenor   1922- . . . . CLC 58
        See also CA 103

Lawrence, D(avid) H(erbert Richards)
        1885-1930 . . . . TCLC 2, 9, 16, 33, 48, 61;
                       DA; DAB; DAC; DAM MST, NOV,
                         POET; SSC 4, 19; WLC
        See also CA 104; 121; CDBLB 1914-1945;
        DLB 10, 19, 36, 98, 162; MTCW

Lawrence, T(homas) E(dward)
        1888-1935 . . . . TCLC 18
        See also Dale, Colin
        See also CA 115

Lawrence of Arabia
        See Lawrence, T(homas) E(dward)

Lawson, Henry (Archibald Hertzberg)
        1867-1922 . . . . TCLC 27; SSC 18
        See also CA 120

Lawton, Dennis
        See Faust, Frederick (Schiller)

Laxness, Halldor . . . . CLC 25
        See also Gudjonsson, Halldor Kiljan

Layamon   fl. c. 1200- . . . . CMLC 10
        See also DLB 146

Laye, Camara
        1928-1980 . . . . CLC 4, 38; BLC;
                                      DAM MULT
        See also BW 1; CA 85-88; 97-100;
        CANR 25; MTCW

Layton, Irving (Peter)
        1912- . . . . CLC 2, 15; DAC; DAM MST,
                                            POET
        See also CA 1-4R; CANR 2, 33, 43;
        DLB 88; MTCW

Lazarus, Emma   1849-1887 . . . . NCLC 8

Lazarus, Felix
        See Cable, George Washington

Lazarus, Henry
        See Slavitt, David R(ytman)

Lea, Joan
        See Neufeld, John (Arthur)

Leacock, Stephen (Butler)
        1869-1944 . . TCLC 2; DAC; DAM MST
        See also CA 104; 141; DLB 92

Lear, Edward   1812-1888 . . . . NCLC 3
        See also CLR 1; DLB 32, 163, 166;
        MAICYA; SATA 18

Lear, Norman (Milton)   1922- . . . . . . CLC 12
        See also CA 73-76

Leavis, F(rank) R(aymond)
        1895-1978 . . . . CLC 24
        See also CA 21-24R; 77-80; CANR 44;
        MTCW

Leavitt, David   1961- . . . CLC 34; DAM POP
        See also CA 116; 122; CANR 50; DLB 130;
        INT 122

Leblanc, Maurice (Marie Emile)
        1864-1941 . . . . TCLC 49
        See also CA 110

Lebowitz, Fran(ces Ann)
        1951(?)- . . . . CLC 11, 36
        See also CA 81-84; CANR 14;
        INT CANR-14; MTCW

Lebrecht, Peter
        See Tieck, (Johann) Ludwig

le Carre, John . . . . CLC 3, 5, 9, 15, 28
        See also Cornwell, David (John Moore)
        See also BEST 89:4; CDBLB 1960 to
        Present; DLB 87

Le Clezio, J(ean) M(arie) G(ustave)
        1940- . . . . CLC 31
        See also CA 116; 128; DLB 83

Leconte de Lisle, Charles-Marie-Rene
        1818-1894 . . . . NCLC 29

Le Coq, Monsieur
        See Simenon, Georges (Jacques Christian)

Leduc, Violette   1907-1972 . . . . CLC 22
        See also CA 13-14; 33-36R; CAP 1

Ledwidge, Francis   1887(?)-1917 . . . TCLC 23
        See also CA 123; DLB 20

Lee, Andrea
        1953- . . . . . CLC 36; BLC; DAM MULT
        See also BW 1; CA 125

Lee, Andrew
        See Auchincloss, Louis (Stanton)

Lee, Chang-rae   1965- . . . . CLC 91
        See also CA 148

Lee, Don L. . . . . CLC 2
        See also Madhubuti, Haki R.

Lee, George W(ashington)
        1894-1976 . . . . CLC 52; BLC;
                                           DAM MULT
        See also BW 1; CA 125; DLB 51

Lee, (Nelle) Harper
        1926- . . . . CLC 12, 60; DA; DAB; DAC;
                        DAM MST, NOV; WLC
        See also AAYA 13; CA 13-16R; CANR 51;
        CDALB 1941-1968; DLB 6; MTCW;
        SATA 11

Lee, Helen Elaine   1959(?)- . . . . CLC 86
        See also CA 148

Lee, Julian
        See Latham, Jean Lee

Lee, Larry
        See Lee, Lawrence

Lee, Laurie
        1914-1997 . . . CLC 90; DAB; DAM POP
        See also CA 77-80; 158; CANR 33;
        DLB 27; MTCW

Lee, Lawrence   1941-1990 . . . . CLC 34
        See also CA 131; CANR 43

Lee, Manfred B(ennington)
        1905-1971 . . . . CLC 11
        See also Queen, Ellery
        See also CA 1-4R; 29-32R; CANR 2;
        DLB 137

Lee, Stan   1922- . . . . CLC 17
        See also AAYA 5; CA 108; 111; INT 111

Lee, Tanith   1947- . . . . CLC 46
        See also AAYA 15; CA 37-40R; CANR 53;
        SATA 8, 88

Lee, Vernon . . . . TCLC 5
        See also Paget, Violet
        See also DLB 57, 153, 156, 174, 178

Lee, William
        See Burroughs, William S(eward)

Lee, Willy
        See Burroughs, William S(eward)

Lee-Hamilton, Eugene (Jacob)
        1845-1907 . . . . TCLC 22
        See also CA 117

Leet, Judith   1935- . . . . CLC 11

Le Fanu, Joseph Sheridan
        1814-1873 . . . . NCLC 9, 58; DAM POP;
                                            SSC 14
        See also DLB 21, 70, 159, 178

Leffland, Ella   1931- . . . . CLC 19
        See also CA 29-32R; CANR 35; DLBY 84;
        INT CANR-35; SATA 65

Leger, Alexis
        See Leger, (Marie-Rene Auguste) Alexis
        Saint-Leger

Leger, (Marie-Rene Auguste) Alexis
Saint-Leger
1887-1975 ...... **CLC 11; DAM POET**
See also Perse, St.-John
See also CA 13-16R; 61-64; CANR 43;
MTCW

Leger, Saintleger
See Leger, (Marie-Rene Auguste) Alexis
Saint-Leger

Le Guin, Ursula K(roeber)
1929- ...... **CLC 8, 13, 22, 45, 71; DAB;
DAC; DAM MST, POP; SSC 12**
See also AAYA 9; AITN 1; CA 21-24R;
CANR 9, 32, 52; CDALB 1968-1988;
CLR 3, 28; DLB 8, 52; INT CANR-32;
JRDA; MAICYA; MTCW; SATA 4, 52

Lehmann, Rosamond (Nina)
1901-1990 .... **CLC 5**
See also CA 77-80; 131; CANR 8; DLB 15

Leiber, Fritz (Reuter, Jr.)
1910-1992 .... **CLC 25**
See also CA 45-48; 139; CANR 2, 40;
DLB 8; MTCW; SATA 45;
SATA-Obit 73

Leibniz, Gottfried Wilhelm von
1646-1716 .... **LC 35**
See also DLB 168

Leimbach, Martha 1963-
See Leimbach, Marti
See also CA 130

Leimbach, Marti .... **CLC 65**
See also Leimbach, Martha

Leino, Eino .... **TCLC 24**
See also Loennbohm, Armas Eino Leopold

Leiris, Michel (Julien) 1901-1990 ... **CLC 61**
See also CA 119; 128; 132

Leithauser, Brad 1953-............. **CLC 27**
See also CA 107; CANR 27; DLB 120

Lelchuk, Alan 1938-............... **CLC 5**
See also CA 45-48; CAAS 20; CANR 1

Lem, Stanislaw 1921-........ **CLC 8, 15, 40**
See also CA 105; CAAS 1; CANR 32;
MTCW

Lemann, Nancy 1956-............. **CLC 39**
See also CA 118; 136

Lemonnier, (Antoine Louis) Camille
1844-1913 .... **TCLC 22**
See also CA 121

Lenau, Nikolaus 1802-1850 ...... **NCLC 16**

L'Engle, Madeleine (Camp Franklin)
1918- .... **CLC 12; DAM POP**
See also AAYA 1; AITN 2; CA 1-4R;
CANR 3, 21, 39; CLR 1, 14; DLB 52;
JRDA; MAICYA; MTCW; SAAS 15;
SATA 1, 27, 75

Lengyel, Jozsef 1896-1975......... **CLC 7**
See also CA 85-88; 57-60

Lenin 1870-1924
See Lenin, V. I.
See also CA 121

Lenin, V. I. .... **TCLC 67**
See also Lenin

Lennon, John (Ono)
1940-1980 .... **CLC 12, 35**
See also CA 102

Lennox, Charlotte Ramsay
1729(?)-1804 .... **NCLC 23**
See also DLB 39

Lentricchia, Frank (Jr.) 1940-..... **CLC 34**
See also CA 25-28R; CANR 19

Lenz, Siegfried 1926-............. **CLC 27**
See also CA 89-92; DLB 75

Leonard, Elmore (John, Jr.)
1925- ...... **CLC 28, 34, 71; DAM POP**
See also AITN 1; BEST 89:1, 90:4;
CA 81-84; CANR 12, 28, 53; DLB 173;
INT CANR-28; MTCW

Leonard, Hugh.................... **CLC 19**
See also Byrne, John Keyes
See also DLB 13

Leonov, Leonid (Maximovich)
1899-1994 .... **CLC 92; DAM NOV**
See also CA 129; MTCW

Leopardi, (Conte) Giacomo
1798-1837 .... **NCLC 22**

Le Reveler
See Artaud, Antonin (Marie Joseph)

Lerman, Eleanor 1952-............ **CLC 9**
See also CA 85-88

Lerman, Rhoda 1936-............. **CLC 56**
See also CA 49-52

Lermontov, Mikhail Yuryevich
1814-1841 .... **NCLC 47; PC 18**

Leroux, Gaston 1868-1927....... **TCLC 25**
See also CA 108; 136; SATA 65

Lesage, Alain-Rene 1668-1747....... **LC 28**

Leskov, Nikolai (Semyonovich)
1831-1895 .... **NCLC 25**

Lessing, Doris (May)
1919- ... **CLC 1, 2, 3, 6, 10, 15, 22, 40,
94; DA; DAB; DAC; DAM MST, NOV;
SSC 6**
See also CA 9-12R; CAAS 14; CANR 33,
54; CDBLB 1960 to Present; DLB 15,
139; DLBY 85; MTCW; YABC

Lessing, Gotthold Ephraim
1729-1781 .... **LC 8**
See also DLB 97

Lester, Richard 1932-............. **CLC 20**

Lever, Charles (James)
1806-1872 .... **NCLC 23**
See also DLB 21

Leverson, Ada 1865(?)-1936(?) .... **TCLC 18**
See also Elaine
See also CA 117; DLB 153

Levertov, Denise
1923- ...... **CLC 1, 2, 3, 5, 8, 15, 28, 66;
DAM POET; PC 11**
See also CA 1-4R; CAAS 19; CANR 3, 29,
50; DLB 5, 165; INT CANR-29; MTCW

Levi, Jonathan.................... **CLC 76**

Levi, Peter (Chad Tigar) 1931-..... **CLC 41**
See also CA 5-8R; CANR 34; DLB 40

Levi, Primo
1919-1987 .... **CLC 37, 50; SSC 12**
See also CA 13-16R; 122; CANR 12, 33;
DLB 177; MTCW

Levin, Ira 1929- ..... **CLC 3, 6; DAM POP**
See also CA 21-24R; CANR 17, 44;
MTCW; SATA 66

Levin, Meyer
1905-1981 .... **CLC 7; DAM POP**
See also AITN 1; CA 9-12R; 104;
CANR 15; DLB 9, 28; DLBY 81;
SATA 21; SATA-Obit 27

Levine, Norman 1924- .... **CLC 54**
See also CA 73-76; CAAS 23; CANR 14;
DLB 88

Levine, Philip
1928- .... **CLC 2, 4, 5, 9, 14, 33;
DAM POET**
See also CA 9-12R; CANR 9, 37, 52;
DLB 5

Levinson, Deirdre 1931-.......... **CLC 49**
See also CA 73-76

Levi-Strauss, Claude 1908- .... **CLC 38**
See also CA 1-4R; CANR 6, 32, 57; MTCW

Levitin, Sonia (Wolff) 1934- .... **CLC 17**
See also AAYA 13; CA 29-32R; CANR 14,
32; JRDA; MAICYA; SAAS 2; SATA 4,
68

Levon, O. U.
See Kesey, Ken (Elton)

Levy, Amy 1861-1889.......... **NCLC 59**
See also DLB 156

Lewes, George Henry
1817-1878 .... **NCLC 25**
See also DLB 55, 144

Lewis, Alun 1915-1944............ **TCLC 3**
See also CA 104; DLB 20, 162

Lewis, C. Day
See Day Lewis, C(ecil)

Lewis, C(live) S(taples)
1898-1963 ..... **CLC 1, 3, 6, 14, 27; DA;
DAB; DAC; DAM MST, NOV, POP;
WLC**
See also AAYA 3; CA 81-84; CANR 33;
CDBLB 1945-1960; CLR 3, 27; DLB 15,
100, 160; JRDA; MAICYA; MTCW;
SATA 13

Lewis, Janet 1899-.............. **CLC 41**
See also Winters, Janet Lewis
See also CA 9-12R; CANR 29; CAP 1;
DLBY 87

Lewis, Matthew Gregory
1775-1818 .... **NCLC 11, 62**
See also DLB 39, 158, 178

Lewis, (Harry) Sinclair
1885-1951 ..... **TCLC 4, 13, 23, 39; DA;
DAB; DAC; DAM MST, NOV; WLC**
See also CA 104; 133; CDALB 1917-1929;
DLB 9, 102; DLBD 1; MTCW

Lewis, (Percy) Wyndham
1882(?)-1957 .... **TCLC 2, 9**
See also CA 104; 157; DLB 15

Lewisohn, Ludwig 1883-1955...... **TCLC 19**
See also CA 107; DLB 4, 9, 28, 102

Leyner, Mark 1956-.............. **CLC 92**
See also CA 110; CANR 28, 53

Lezama Lima, Jose
1910-1976 .... **CLC 4, 10, 101;
DAM MULT**
See also CA 77-80; DLB 113; HW

L'Heureux, John (Clarke) 1934-.... **CLC 52**
See also CA 13-16R; CANR 23, 45

Liddell, C. H.
  See Kuttner, Henry

Lie, Jonas (Lauritz Idemil)
  1833-1908(?) .... **TCLC 5**
  See also CA 115

Lieber, Joel 1937-1971............ **CLC 6**
  See also CA 73-76; 29-32R

Lieber, Stanley Martin
  See Lee, Stan

Lieberman, Laurence (James)
  1935- .... **CLC 4, 36**
  See also CA 17-20R; CANR 8, 36

Lieksman, Anders
  See Haavikko, Paavo Juhani

Li Fei-kan 1904-
  See Pa Chin
  See also CA 105

Lifton, Robert Jay 1926-......... **CLC 67**
  See also CA 17-20R; CANR 27;
  INT CANR-27; SATA 66

Lightfoot, Gordon 1938-.......... **CLC 26**
  See also CA 109

Lightman, Alan P. 1948-......... **CLC 81**
  See also CA 141

Ligotti, Thomas (Robert)
  1953- .... **CLC 44; SSC 16**
  See also CA 123; CANR 49

Li Ho 791-817.................... **PC 13**

Liliencron, (Friedrich Adolf Axel) Detlev von
  1844-1909 .... **TCLC 18**
  See also CA 117

Lilly, William 1602-1681.......... **LC 27**

Lima, Jose Lezama
  See Lezama Lima, Jose

Lima Barreto, Afonso Henrique de
  1881-1922 .... **TCLC 23**
  See also CA 117

Limonov, Edward 1944-.......... **CLC 67**
  See also CA 137

Lin, Frank
  See Atherton, Gertrude (Franklin Horn)

Lincoln, Abraham 1809-1865..... **NCLC 18**

Lind, Jakov .... **CLC 1, 2, 4, 27, 82**
  See also Landwirth, Heinz
  See also CAAS 4

Lindbergh, Anne (Spencer) Morrow
  1906- .... **CLC 82; DAM NOV**
  See also CA 17-20R; CANR 16; MTCW;
  SATA 33

Lindsay, David 1878-1945....... **TCLC 15**
  See also CA 113

Lindsay, (Nicholas) Vachel
  1879-1931 .... **TCLC 17; DA; DAC;**
  DAM MST, POET; WLC
  See also CA 114; 135; CDALB 1865-1917;
  DLB 54; SATA 40

Linke-Poot
  See Doeblin, Alfred

Linney, Romulus 1930- .... **CLC 51**
  See also CA 1-4R; CANR 40, 44

Linton, Eliza Lynn 1822-1898.... **NCLC 41**
  See also DLB 18

Li Po 701-763................. **CMLC 2**

Lipsius, Justus 1547-1606 .... **LC 16**

Lipsyte, Robert (Michael)
  1938- .... **CLC 21; DA; DAC;**
  DAM MST, NOV
  See also AAYA 7; CA 17-20R; CANR 8,
  57; CLR 23; JRDA; MAICYA; SATA 5,
  68

Lish, Gordon (Jay) 1934-.. **CLC 45; SSC 18**
  See also CA 113; 117; DLB 130; INT 117

Lispector, Clarice 1925-1977...... **CLC 43**
  See also CA 139; 116; DLB 113

Littell, Robert 1935(?)- .... **CLC 42**
  See also CA 109; 112

Little, Malcolm 1925-1965
  See Malcolm X
  See also BW 1; CA 125; 111; DA; DAB;
  DAC; DAM MST, MULT; MTCW

Littlewit, Humphrey Gent.
  See Lovecraft, H(oward) P(hillips)

Litwos
  See Sienkiewicz, Henryk (Adam Alexander
  Pius)

Liu E 1857-1909................ **TCLC 15**
  See also CA 115

Lively, Penelope (Margaret)
  1933- .... **CLC 32, 50; DAM NOV**
  See also CA 41-44R; CANR 29; CLR 7;
  DLB 14, 161; JRDA; MAICYA; MTCW;
  SATA 7, 60

Livesay, Dorothy (Kathleen)
  1909- .... **CLC 4, 15, 79; DAC;**
  DAM MST, POET
  See also AITN 2; CA 25-28R; CAAS 8;
  CANR 36; DLB 68; MTCW

Livy c. 59B.C.-c. 17 .... **CMLC 11**

Lizardi, Jose Joaquin Fernandez de
  1776-1827 .... **NCLC 30**

Llewellyn, Richard
  See Llewellyn Lloyd, Richard Dafydd
  Vivian
  See also DLB 15

Llewellyn Lloyd, Richard Dafydd Vivian
  1906-1983 .... **CLC 7, 80**
  See also Llewellyn, Richard
  See also CA 53-56; 111; CANR 7;
  SATA 11; SATA-Obit 37

Llosa, (Jorge) Mario (Pedro) Vargas
  See Vargas Llosa, (Jorge) Mario (Pedro)

Lloyd Webber, Andrew 1948-
  See Webber, Andrew Lloyd
  See also AAYA 1; CA 116; 149;
  DAM DRAM; SATA 56

Llull, Ramon c. 1235-c. 1316..... **CMLC 12**

Locke, Alain (Le Roy)
  1886-1954 .... **TCLC 43**
  See also BW 1; CA 106; 124; DLB 51

Locke, John 1632-1704 .... **LC 7, 35**
  See also DLB 101

Locke-Elliott, Sumner
  See Elliott, Sumner Locke

Lockhart, John Gibson
  1794-1854 .... **NCLC 6**
  See also DLB 110, 116, 144

Lodge, David (John)
  1935- .... **CLC 36; DAM POP**
  See also BEST 90:1; CA 17-20R; CANR 19,
  53; DLB 14; INT CANR-19; MTCW

Loennbohm, Armas Eino Leopold 1878-1926
  See Leino, Eino
  See also CA 123

Loewinsohn, Ron(ald William)
  1937- .... **CLC 52**
  See also CA 25-28R

Logan, Jake
  See Smith, Martin Cruz

Logan, John (Burton) 1923-1987..... **CLC 5**
  See also CA 77-80; 124; CANR 45; DLB 5

Lo Kuan-chung 1330(?)-1400(?)...... **LC 12**

Lombard, Nap
  See Johnson, Pamela Hansford

London, Jack.. **TCLC 9, 15, 39; SSC 4; WLC**
  See also London, John Griffith
  See also AAYA 13; AITN 2;
  CDALB 1865-1917; DLB 8, 12, 78;
  SATA 18

London, John Griffith 1876-1916
  See London, Jack
  See also CA 110; 119; DA; DAB; DAC;
  DAM MST, NOV; JRDA; MAICYA;
  MTCW

Long, Emmett
  See Leonard, Elmore (John, Jr.)

Longbaugh, Harry
  See Goldman, William (W.)

Longfellow, Henry Wadsworth
  1807-1882 ..... **NCLC 2, 45; DA; DAB;**
  DAC; DAM MST, POET
  See also CDALB 1640-1865; DLB 1, 59;
  SATA 19; YABC

Longley, Michael 1939-.......... **CLC 29**
  See also CA 102; DLB 40

Longus fl. c. 2nd cent. - .... **CMLC 7**

Longway, A. Hugh
  See Lang, Andrew

Lonnrot, Elias 1802-1884....... **NCLC 53**

Lopate, Phillip 1943- .... **CLC 29**
  See also CA 97-100; DLBY 80; INT 97-100

Lopez Portillo (y Pacheco), Jose
  1920- .... **CLC 46**
  See also CA 129; HW

Lopez y Fuentes, Gregorio
  1897(?)-1966 .... **CLC 32**
  See also CA 131; HW

Lorca, Federico Garcia
  See Garcia Lorca, Federico

Lord, Bette Bao 1938-............ **CLC 23**
  See also BEST 90:3; CA 107; CANR 41;
  INT 107; SATA 58

Lord Auch
  See Bataille, Georges

Lord Byron
  See Byron, George Gordon (Noel)

Lorde, Audre (Geraldine)
  1934-1992 .... **CLC 18, 71; BLC;**
  DAM MULT, POET; PC 12
  See also BW 1; CA 25-28R; 142; CANR 16,
  26, 46; DLB 41; MTCW

Lord Houghton
See Milnes, Richard Monckton

Lord Jeffrey
See Jeffrey, Francis

Lorenzini, Carlo 1826-1890
See Collodi, Carlo
See also MAICYA; SATA 29

Lorenzo, Heberto Padilla
See Padilla (Lorenzo), Heberto

Loris
See Hofmannsthal, Hugo von

Loti, Pierre .... **TCLC 11**
See also Viaud, (Louis Marie) Julien
See also DLB 123

Louie, David Wong 1954- .... **CLC 70**
See also CA 139

Louis, Father M.
See Merton, Thomas

Lovecraft, H(oward) P(hillips)
1890-1937 .... **TCLC 4, 22; DAM POP;**
SSC 3
See also AAYA 14; CA 104; 133; MTCW

Lovelace, Earl 1935- .... **CLC 51**
See also BW 2; CA 77-80; CANR 41;
DLB 125; MTCW

Lovelace, Richard 1618-1657 .... **LC 24**
See also DLB 131

Lowell, Amy
1874-1925 .... **TCLC 1, 8; DAM POET;**
PC 13
See also CA 104; 151; DLB 54, 140

Lowell, James Russell 1819-1891 .. **NCLC 2**
See also CDALB 1640-1865; DLB 1, 11, 64,
79

Lowell, Robert (Traill Spence, Jr.)
1917-1977 ... **CLC 1, 2, 3, 4, 5, 8, 9, 11,**
15, 37; DA; DAB; DAC; DAM MST,
NOV; PC 3; WLC
See also CA 9-12R; 73-76; CABS 2;
CANR 26; DLB 5, 169; MTCW

Lowndes, Marie Adelaide (Belloc)
1868-1947 .... **TCLC 12**
See also CA 107; DLB 70

Lowry, (Clarence) Malcolm
1909-1957 .... **TCLC 6, 40**
See also CA 105; 131; CDBLB 1945-1960;
DLB 15; MTCW

Lowry, Mina Gertrude 1882-1966
See Loy, Mina
See also CA 113

Loxsmith, John
See Brunner, John (Kilian Houston)

Loy, Mina .... **CLC 28; DAM POET; PC 16**
See also Lowry, Mina Gertrude
See also DLB 4, 54

Loyson-Bridet
See Schwob, (Mayer Andre) Marcel

Lucas, Craig 1951- .... **CLC 64**
See also CA 137

Lucas, George 1944- .... **CLC 16**
See also AAYA 1; CA 77-80; CANR 30;
SATA 56

Lucas, Hans
See Godard, Jean-Luc

Lucas, Victoria
See Plath, Sylvia

Ludlam, Charles 1943-1987 ..... **CLC 46, 50**
See also CA 85-88; 122

Ludlum, Robert
1927- ... **CLC 22, 43; DAM NOV, POP**
See also AAYA 10; BEST 89:1, 90:3;
CA 33-36R; CANR 25, 41; DLBY 82;
MTCW

Ludwig, Ken .... **CLC 60**

Ludwig, Otto 1813-1865 .... **NCLC 4**
See also DLB 129

Lugones, Leopoldo 1874-1938 ..... **TCLC 15**
See also CA 116; 131; HW

Lu Hsun 1881-1936 ...... **TCLC 3; SSC 20**
See also Shu-Jen, Chou

Lukacs, George .... **CLC 24**
See also Lukacs, Gyorgy (Szegeny von)

Lukacs, Gyorgy (Szegeny von) 1885-1971
See Lukacs, George
See also CA 101; 29-32R

Luke, Peter (Ambrose Cyprian)
1919-1995 .... **CLC 38**
See also CA 81-84; 147; DLB 13

Lunar, Dennis
See Mungo, Raymond

Lurie, Alison 1926- .... **CLC 4, 5, 18, 39**
See also CA 1-4R; CANR 2, 17, 50; DLB 2;
MTCW; SATA 46

Lustig, Arnost 1926- .... **CLC 56**
See also AAYA 3; CA 69-72; CANR 47;
SATA 56

Luther, Martin 1483-1546 .... **LC 9, 37**
See also DLB 179

Luxemburg, Rosa 1870(?)-1919 .... **TCLC 63**
See also CA 118

Luzi, Mario 1914- .... **CLC 13**
See also CA 61-64; CANR 9; DLB 128

Lyly, John 1554(?)-1606 .... **DC 7**
See also DAM DRAM; DLB 62, 167

L'Ymagier
See Gourmont, Remy (-Marie-Charles) de

Lynch, B. Suarez
See Bioy Casares, Adolfo; Borges, Jorge
Luis

Lynch, David (K.) 1946- .... **CLC 66**
See also CA 124; 129

Lynch, James
See Andreyev, Leonid (Nikolaevich)

Lynch Davis, B.
See Bioy Casares, Adolfo; Borges, Jorge
Luis

Lyndsay, Sir David 1490-1555 ...... **LC 20**

Lynn, Kenneth S(chuyler) 1923- .... **CLC 50**
See also CA 1-4R; CANR 3, 27

Lynx
See West, Rebecca

Lyons, Marcus
See Blish, James (Benjamin)

Lyre, Pinchbeck
See Sassoon, Siegfried (Lorraine)

Lytle, Andrew (Nelson) 1902-1995 .. **CLC 22**
See also CA 9-12R; 150; DLB 6; DLBY 95

Lyttelton, George 1709-1773 .... **LC 10**

Maas, Peter 1929- .... **CLC 29**
See also CA 93-96; INT 93-96

Macaulay, Rose 1881-1958 ..... **TCLC 7, 44**
See also CA 104; DLB 36

Macaulay, Thomas Babington
1800-1859 .... **NCLC 42**
See also CDBLB 1832-1890; DLB 32, 55

MacBeth, George (Mann)
1932-1992 .... **CLC 2, 5, 9**
See also CA 25-28R; 136; DLB 40; MTCW;
SATA 4; SATA-Obit 70

MacCaig, Norman (Alexander)
1910- ..... **CLC 36; DAB; DAM POET**
See also CA 9-12R; CANR 3, 34; DLB 27

MacCarthy, (Sir Charles Otto) Desmond
1877-1952 .... **TCLC 36**

MacDiarmid, Hugh
.... **CLC 2, 4, 11, 19, 63; PC 9**
See also Grieve, C(hristopher) M(urray)
See also CDBLB 1945-1960; DLB 20

MacDonald, Anson
See Heinlein, Robert A(nson)

Macdonald, Cynthia 1928- ...... **CLC 13, 19**
See also CA 49-52; CANR 4, 44; DLB 105

MacDonald, George 1824-1905 ..... **TCLC 9**
See also CA 106; 137; DLB 18, 163, 178;
MAICYA; SATA 33

Macdonald, John
See Millar, Kenneth

MacDonald, John D(ann)
1916-1986 .... **CLC 3, 27, 44;**
DAM NOV, POP
See also CA 1-4R; 121; CANR 1, 19;
DLB 8; DLBY 86; MTCW

Macdonald, John Ross
See Millar, Kenneth

Macdonald, Ross ..... **CLC 1, 2, 3, 14, 34, 41**
See also Millar, Kenneth
See also DLBD 6

MacDougal, John
See Blish, James (Benjamin)

MacEwen, Gwendolyn (Margaret)
1941-1987 .... **CLC 13, 55**
See also CA 9-12R; 124; CANR 7, 22;
DLB 53; SATA 50; SATA-Obit 55

Macha, Karel Hynek 1810-1846 .. **NCLC 46**

Machado (y Ruiz), Antonio
1875-1939 .... **TCLC 3**
See also CA 104; DLB 108

Machado de Assis, Joaquim Maria
1839-1908 ..... **TCLC 10; BLC; SSC 24**
See also CA 107; 153

Machen, Arthur .... **TCLC 4; SSC 20**
See also Jones, Arthur Llewellyn
See also DLB 36, 156, 178

Machiavelli, Niccolo
1469-1527 .... **LC 8, 36; DA; DAB;**
DAC; DAM MST
See also YABC

MacInnes, Colin 1914-1976 ...... **CLC 4, 23**
See also CA 69-72; 65-68; CANR 21;
DLB 14; MTCW

Author Index

McDermott, Alice 1953- .... **CLC 90**
See also CA 109; CANR 40

McElroy, Joseph 1930- .... **CLC 5, 47**
See also CA 17-20R

McEwan, Ian (Russell)
1948- .... **CLC 13, 66; DAM NOV**
See also BEST 90:4; CA 61-64; CANR 14,
41; DLB 14; MTCW

McFadden, David 1940-.......... **CLC 48**
See also CA 104; DLB 60; INT 104

McFarland, Dennis 1950- .... **CLC 65**

McGahern, John
1934-.......... **CLC 5, 9, 48; SSC 17**
See also CA 17-20R; CANR 29; DLB 14;
MTCW

McGinley, Patrick (Anthony)
1937-...................... **CLC 41**
See also CA 120; 127; CANR 56; INT 127

McGinley, Phyllis 1905-1978 ...... **CLC 14**
See also CA 9-12R; 77-80; CANR 19;
DLB 11, 48; SATA 2, 44; SATA-Obit 24

McGinniss, Joe 1942-............ **CLC 32**
See also AITN 2; BEST 89:2; CA 25-28R;
CANR 26; INT CANR-26

McGivern, Maureen Daly
See Daly, Maureen

McGrath, Patrick 1950-.......... **CLC 55**
See also CA 136

McGrath, Thomas (Matthew)
1916-1990 .... **CLC 28, 59; DAM POET**
See also CA 9-12R; 132; CANR 6, 33;
MTCW; SATA 41; SATA-Obit 66

McGuane, Thomas (Francis III)
1939-................ **CLC 3, 7, 18, 45**
See also AITN 2; CA 49-52; CANR 5, 24,
49; DLB 2; DLBY 80; INT CANR-24;
MTCW

McGuckian, Medbh
1950- .... **CLC 48; DAM POET**
See also CA 143; DLB 40

McHale, Tom 1942(?)-1982...... **CLC 3, 5**
See also AITN 1; CA 77-80; 106

McIlvanney, William 1936-........ **CLC 42**
See also CA 25-28R; DLB 14

McIlwraith, Maureen Mollie Hunter
See Hunter, Mollie
See also SATA 2

McInerney, Jay
1955- .... **CLC 34; DAM POP**
See also AAYA 18; CA 116; 123;
CANR 45; INT 123

McIntyre, Vonda N(eel) 1948- ..... **CLC 18**
See also CA 81-84; CANR 17, 34; MTCW

McKay, Claude
.... **TCLC 7, 41; BLC; DAB; PC 2**
See also McKay, Festus Claudius
See also DLB 4, 45, 51, 117

McKay, Festus Claudius 1889-1948
See McKay, Claude
See also BW 1; CA 104; 124; DA; DAC;
DAM MST, MULT, NOV, POET;
MTCW; WLC

McKuen, Rod 1933-............ **CLC 1, 3**
See also AITN 1; CA 41-44R; CANR 40

McLoughlin, R. B.
See Mencken, H(enry) L(ouis)

McLuhan, (Herbert) Marshall
1911-1980 .... **CLC 37, 83**
See also CA 9-12R; 102; CANR 12, 34;
DLB 88; INT CANR-12; MTCW

McMillan, Terry (L.)
1951- ...... **CLC 50, 61; DAM MULT,
NOV, POP**
See also AAYA 21; BW 2; CA 140

McMurtry, Larry (Jeff)
1936- .... **CLC 2, 3, 7, 11, 27, 44;
DAM NOV, POP**
See also AAYA 15; AITN 2; BEST 89:2;
CA 5-8R; CANR 19, 43;
CDALB 1968-1988; DLB 2, 143;
DLBY 80, 87; MTCW

McNally, T. M. 1961- .... **CLC 82**

McNally, Terrence
1939- ... **CLC 4, 7, 41, 91; DAM DRAM**
See also CA 45-48; CANR 2, 56; DLB 7

McNamer, Deirdre 1950-......... **CLC 70**

McNeile, Herman Cyril 1888-1937
See Sapper
See also DLB 77

McNickle, (William) D'Arcy
1904-1977 ...... **CLC 89; DAM MULT**
See also CA 9-12R; 85-88; CANR 5, 45;
DLB 175; NNAL; SATA-Obit 22

McPhee, John (Angus) 1931- ...... **CLC 36**
See also BEST 90:1; CA 65-68; CANR 20,
46; MTCW

McPherson, James Alan
1943- .... **CLC 19, 77**
See also BW 1; CA 25-28R; CAAS 17;
CANR 24; DLB 38; MTCW

McPherson, William (Alexander)
1933-......................... **CLC 34**
See also CA 69-72; CANR 28;
INT CANR-28

Mead, Margaret 1901-1978........ **CLC 37**
See also AITN 1; CA 1-4R; 81-84;
CANR 4; MTCW; SATA-Obit 20

Meaker, Marijane (Agnes) 1927-
See Kerr, M. E.
See also CA 107; CANR 37; INT 107;
JRDA; MAICYA; MTCW; SATA 20, 61

Medoff, Mark (Howard)
1940- .... **CLC 6, 23; DAM DRAM**
See also AITN 1; CA 53-56; CANR 5;
DLB 7; INT CANR-5

Medvedev, P. N.
See Bakhtin, Mikhail Mikhailovich

Meged, Aharon
See Megged, Aharon

Meged, Aron
See Megged, Aharon

Megged, Aharon 1920-............. **CLC 9**
See also CA 49-52; CAAS 13; CANR 1

Mehta, Ved (Parkash) 1934-....... **CLC 37**
See also CA 1-4R; CANR 2, 23; MTCW

Melanter
See Blackmore, R(ichard) D(oddridge)

Melikow, Loris
See Hofmannsthal, Hugo von

Melmoth, Sebastian
See Wilde, Oscar (Fingal O'Flahertie Wills)

Meltzer, Milton 1915-............ **CLC 26**
See also AAYA 8; CA 13-16R; CANR 38;
CLR 13; DLB 61; JRDA; MAICYA;
SAAS 1; SATA 1, 50, 80

Melville, Herman
1819-1891 ..... **NCLC 3, 12, 29, 45, 49;
DA; DAB; DAC; DAM MST, NOV;
SSC 1, 17; WLC**
See also CDALB 1640-1865; DLB 3, 74;
SATA 59

Menander
c. 342B.C.-c. 292B.C........ **CMLC 9;
DAM DRAM; DC 3**
See also DLB 176

Mencken, H(enry) L(ouis)
1880-1956 .... **TCLC 13**
See also CA 105; 125; CDALB 1917-1929;
DLB 11, 29, 63, 137; MTCW

Mendelsohn, Jane 1965(?)- .... **CLC 99**
See also CA 154

Mercer, David
1928-1980 .... **CLC 5; DAM DRAM**
See also CA 9-12R; 102; CANR 23;
DLB 13; MTCW

Merchant, Paul
See Ellison, Harlan (Jay)

Meredith, George
1828-1909 .. **TCLC 17, 43; DAM POET**
See also CA 117; 153; CDBLB 1832-1890;
DLB 18, 35, 57, 159

Meredith, William (Morris)
1919- .. **CLC 4, 13, 22, 55; DAM POET**
See also CA 9-12R; CAAS 14; CANR 6, 40;
DLB 5

Merezhkovsky, Dmitry Sergeyevich
1865-1941 .... **TCLC 29**

Merimee, Prosper
1803-1870 .... **NCLC 6; SSC 7**
See also DLB 119

Merkin, Daphne 1954-............. **CLC 44**
See also CA 123

Merlin, Arthur
See Blish, James (Benjamin)

Merrill, James (Ingram)
1926-1995 .... **CLC 2, 3, 6, 8, 13, 18, 34,
91; DAM POET**
See also CA 13-16R; 147; CANR 10, 49;
DLB 5, 165; DLBY 85; INT CANR-10;
MTCW

Merriman, Alex
See Silverberg, Robert

Merritt, E. B.
See Waddington, Miriam

Merton, Thomas
1915-1968 .. **CLC 1, 3, 11, 34, 83; PC 10**
See also CA 5-8R; 25-28R; CANR 22, 53;
DLB 48; DLBY 81; MTCW

Merwin, W(illiam) S(tanley)
1927- ...... **CLC 1, 2, 3, 5, 8, 13, 18, 45,
88; DAM POET**
See also CA 13-16R; CANR 15, 51; DLB 5,
169; INT CANR-15; MTCW

Metcalf, John 1938-.............. **CLC 37**
See also CA 113; DLB 60

Metcalf, Suzanne
  See Baum, L(yman) Frank

Mew, Charlotte (Mary)
  1870-1928 .... **TCLC 8**
  See also CA 105; DLB 19, 135

Mewshaw, Michael 1943-.......... **CLC 9**
  See also CA 53-56; CANR 7, 47; DLBY 80

Meyer, June
  See Jordan, June

Meyer, Lynn
  See Slavitt, David R(ytman)

Meyer-Meyrink, Gustav 1868-1932
  See Meyrink, Gustav
  See also CA 117

Meyers, Jeffrey 1939- .... **CLC 39**
  See also CA 73-76; CANR 54; DLB 111

Meynell, Alice (Christina Gertrude Thompson)
  1847-1922 .... **TCLC 6**
  See also CA 104; DLB 19, 98

Meyrink, Gustav .... **TCLC 21**
  See also Meyer-Meyrink, Gustav
  See also DLB 81

Michaels, Leonard
  1933- .... **CLC 6, 25; SSC 16**
  See also CA 61-64; CANR 21; DLB 130;
  MTCW

Michaux, Henri 1899-1984 ...... **CLC 8, 19**
  See also CA 85-88; 114

Michelangelo 1475-1564........... **LC 12**

Michelet, Jules 1798-1874....... **NCLC 31**

Michener, James A(lbert)
  1907(?)- .... **CLC 1, 5, 11, 29, 60;
                           DAM NOV, POP**
  See also AITN 1; BEST 90:1; CA 5-8R;
  CANR 21, 45; DLB 6; MTCW

Mickiewicz, Adam 1798-1855 ..... **NCLC 3**

Middleton, Christopher 1926- ...... **CLC 13**
  See also CA 13-16R; CANR 29, 54;
  DLB 40

Middleton, Richard (Barham)
  1882-1911 .... **TCLC 56**
  See also DLB 156

Middleton, Stanley 1919-........ **CLC 7, 38**
  See also CA 25-28R; CAAS 23; CANR 21,
  46; DLB 14

Middleton, Thomas
  1580-1627 .... **LC 33; DAM DRAM,
                           MST; DC 5**
  See also DLB 58

Migueis, Jose Rodrigues 1901-..... **CLC 10**

Mikszath, Kalman 1847-1910 ..... **TCLC 31**

Miles, Jack .... **CLC 100**

Miles, Josephine (Louise)
  1911-1985 .... **CLC 1, 2, 14, 34, 39;
                           DAM POET**
  See also CA 1-4R; 116; CANR 2, 55;
  DLB 48

Militant
  See Sandburg, Carl (August)

Mill, John Stuart 1806-1873 .. **NCLC 11, 58**
  See also CDBLB 1832-1890; DLB 55

Millar, Kenneth
  1915-1983 .... **CLC 14; DAM POP**
  See also Macdonald, Ross
  See also CA 9-12R; 110; CANR 16; DLB 2;
  DLBD 6; DLBY 83; MTCW

Millay, E. Vincent
  See Millay, Edna St. Vincent

Millay, Edna St. Vincent
  1892-1950 ...... **TCLC 4, 49; DA; DAB;
                           DAC; DAM MST, POET; PC 6**
  See also CA 104; 130; CDALB 1917-1929;
  DLB 45; MTCW; YABC

Miller, Arthur
  1915- .... **CLC 1, 2, 6, 10, 15, 26, 47, 78;
                     DA; DAB; DAC; DAM DRAM, MST;
                     DC 1; WLC**
  See also AAYA 15; AITN 1; CA 1-4R;
  CABS 3; CANR 2, 30, 54;
  CDALB 1941-1968; DLB 7; MTCW

Miller, Henry (Valentine)
  1891-1980 .... **CLC 1, 2, 4, 9, 14, 43, 84;
                     DA; DAB; DAC; DAM MST, NOV;
                     WLC**
  See also CA 9-12R; 97-100; CANR 33;
  CDALB 1929-1941; DLB 4, 9; DLBY 80;
  MTCW

Miller, Jason 1939(?)- .... **CLC 2**
  See also AITN 1; CA 73-76; DLB 7

Miller, Sue 1943- ..... **CLC 44; DAM POP**
  See also BEST 90:3; CA 139; DLB 143

Miller, Walter M(ichael, Jr.)
  1923- .... **CLC 4, 30**
  See also CA 85-88; DLB 8

Millett, Kate 1934-................ **CLC 67**
  See also AITN 1; CA 73-76; CANR 32, 53;
  MTCW

Millhauser, Steven 1943-....... **CLC 21, 54**
  See also CA 110; 111; DLB 2; INT 111

Millin, Sarah Gertrude 1889-1968 .. **CLC 49**
  See also CA 102; 93-96

Milne, A(lan) A(lexander)
  1882-1956 .... **TCLC 6; DAB; DAC;
                           DAM MST**
  See also CA 104; 133; CLR 1, 26; DLB 10,
  77, 100, 160; MAICYA; MTCW; 1

Milner, Ron(ald)
  1938- .... **CLC 56; BLC; DAM MULT**
  See also AITN 1; BW 1; CA 73-76;
  CANR 24; DLB 38; MTCW

Milnes, Richard Monckton
  1809-1885 .... **NCLC 61**
  See also DLB 32

Milosz, Czeslaw
  1911- .... **CLC 5, 11, 22, 31, 56, 82;
                           DAM MST, POET; PC 8**
  See also CA 81-84; CANR 23, 51; MTCW;
  YABC

Milton, John
  1608-1674 ...... **LC 9; DA; DAB; DAC;
                           DAM MST, POET; PC 19; WLC**
  See also CDBLB 1660-1789; DLB 131, 151

Min, Anchee 1957-............... **CLC 86**
  See also CA 146

Minehaha, Cornelius
  See Wedekind, (Benjamin) Frank(lin)

Miner, Valerie 1947- .... **CLC 40**
  See also CA 97-100

Minimo, Duca
  See D'Annunzio, Gabriele

Minot, Susan 1956- .... **CLC 44**
  See also CA 134

Minus, Ed 1938-................. **CLC 39**

Miranda, Javier
  See Bioy Casares, Adolfo

Mirbeau, Octave 1848-1917...... **TCLC 55**
  See also DLB 123

Miro (Ferrer), Gabriel (Francisco Victor)
  1879-1930 .... **TCLC 5**
  See also CA 104

Mishima, Yukio
  .... **CLC 2, 4, 6, 9, 27; DC 1; SSC 4**
  See also Hiraoka, Kimitake

Mistral, Frederic 1830-1914 ...... **TCLC 51**
  See also CA 122

Mistral, Gabriela........... **TCLC 2; HLC**
  See also Godoy Alcayaga, Lucila

Mistry, Rohinton 1952-...... **CLC 71; DAC**
  See also CA 141

Mitchell, Clyde
  See Ellison, Harlan (Jay); Silverberg, Robert

Mitchell, James Leslie 1901-1935
  See Gibbon, Lewis Grassic
  See also CA 104; DLB 15

Mitchell, Joni 1943-.............. **CLC 12**
  See also CA 112

Mitchell, Joseph (Quincy)
  1908-1996 .... **CLC 98**
  See also CA 77-80; 152; DLBY 96

Mitchell, Margaret (Munnerlyn)
  1900-1949 ...... **TCLC 11; DAM NOV,
                           POP**
  See also CA 109; 125; CANR 55; DLB 9;
  MTCW

Mitchell, Peggy
  See Mitchell, Margaret (Munnerlyn)

Mitchell, S(ilas) Weir 1829-1914 .. **TCLC 36**

Mitchell, W(illiam) O(rmond)
  1914- ...... **CLC 25; DAC; DAM MST**
  See also CA 77-80; CANR 15, 43; DLB 88

Mitford, Mary Russell 1787-1855.. **NCLC 4**
  See also DLB 110, 116

Mitford, Nancy 1904-1973......... **CLC 44**
  See also CA 9-12R

Miyamoto, Yuriko 1899-1951 ..... **TCLC 37**
  See also DLB 180

Mizoguchi, Kenji 1898-1956 ...... **TCLC 72**

Mo, Timothy (Peter) 1950(?)-...... **CLC 46**
  See also CA 117; MTCW

Modarressi, Taghi (M.) 1931-...... **CLC 44**
  See also CA 121; 134; INT 134

Modiano, Patrick (Jean) 1945-..... **CLC 18**
  See also CA 85-88; CANR 17, 40; DLB 83

Moerck, Paal
  See Roelvaag, O(le) E(dvart)

Mofolo, Thomas (Mokopu)
  1875(?)-1948 .... **TCLC 22; BLC;
                           DAM MULT**
  See also CA 121; 153

Mohr, Nicholasa
     1935- . . . . . **CLC 12; DAM MULT; HLC**
     See also AAYA 8; CA 49-52; CANR 1, 32;
     CLR 22; DLB 145; HW; JRDA; SAAS 8;
     SATA 8

Mojtabai, A(nn) G(race)
     1938- . . . . **CLC 5, 9, 15, 29**
     See also CA 85-88

Moliere
     1622-1673 . . . . . **LC 28; DA; DAB; DAC;**
                     DAM DRAM, MST; WLC

Molin, Charles
     See Mayne, William (James Carter)

Molnar, Ferenc
     1878-1952 . . . . . **TCLC 20; DAM DRAM**
     See also CA 109; 153

Momaday, N(avarre) Scott
     1934- . . . . . **CLC 2, 19, 85, 95; DA; DAB;**
            DAC; DAM MST, MULT, NOV, POP
     See also AAYA 11; CA 25-28R; CANR 14,
     34; DLB 143, 175; INT CANR-14;
     MTCW; NNAL; SATA 48;
     SATA-Brief 30; YABC

Monette, Paul 1945-1995 . . . . **CLC 82**
     See also CA 139; 147

Monroe, Harriet 1860-1936 . . . . **TCLC 12**
     See also CA 109; DLB 54, 91

Monroe, Lyle
     See Heinlein, Robert A(nson)

Montagu, Elizabeth 1917- . . . . **NCLC 7**
     See also CA 9-12R

Montagu, Mary (Pierrepont) Wortley
     1689-1762 . . . . **LC 9; PC 16**
     See also DLB 95, 101

Montagu, W. H.
     See Coleridge, Samuel Taylor

Montague, John (Patrick)
     1929- . . . . **CLC 13, 46**
     See also CA 9-12R; CANR 9; DLB 40;
     MTCW

Montaigne, Michel (Eyquem) de
     1533-1592 . . . . . . **LC 8; DA; DAB; DAC;**
                        DAM MST; WLC

Montale, Eugenio
     1896-1981 . . . . **CLC 7, 9, 18; PC 13**
     See also CA 17-20R; 104; CANR 30;
     DLB 114; MTCW

Montesquieu, Charles-Louis de Secondat
     1689-1755 . . . . **LC 7**

Montgomery, (Robert) Bruce 1921-1978
     See Crispin, Edmund
     See also CA 104

Montgomery, L(ucy) M(aud)
     1874-1942 . . . . **TCLC 51; DAC;**
                          DAM MST
     See also AAYA 12; CA 108; 137; CLR 8;
     DLB 92; DLBD 14; JRDA; MAICYA; 1

Montgomery, Marion H., Jr. 1925- . . **CLC 7**
     See also AITN 1; CA 1-4R; CANR 3, 48;
     DLB 6

Montgomery, Max
     See Davenport, Guy (Mattison, Jr.)

Montherlant, Henry (Milon) de
     1896-1972 . . . . . **CLC 8, 19; DAM DRAM**
     See also CA 85-88; 37-40R; DLB 72;
     MTCW

Monty Python
     See Chapman, Graham; Cleese, John
     (Marwood); Gilliam, Terry (Vance); Idle,
     Eric; Jones, Terence Graham Parry; Palin,
     Michael (Edward)
     See also AAYA 7

Moodie, Susanna (Strickland)
     1803-1885 . . . . **NCLC 14**
     See also DLB 99

Mooney, Edward 1951-
     See Mooney, Ted
     See also CA 130

Mooney, Ted . . . . **CLC 25**
     See also Mooney, Edward

Moorcock, Michael (John)
     1939- . . . . **CLC 5, 27, 58**
     See also CA 45-48; CAAS 5; CANR 2, 17,
     38; DLB 14; MTCW; SATA 93

Moore, Brian
     1921- . . . . . . **CLC 1, 3, 5, 7, 8, 19, 32, 90;**
                   DAB; DAC; DAM MST
     See also CA 1-4R; CANR 1, 25, 42; MTCW

Moore, Edward
     See Muir, Edwin

Moore, George Augustus
     1852-1933 . . . . **TCLC 7; SSC 19**
     See also CA 104; DLB 10, 18, 57, 135

Moore, Lorrie . . . . **CLC 39, 45, 68**
     See also Moore, Marie Lorena

Moore, Marianne (Craig)
     1887-1972 . . . . **CLC 1, 2, 4, 8, 10, 13, 19,**
     47; DA; DAB; DAC; DAM MST, POET;
                            PC 4
     See also CA 1-4R; 33-36R; CANR 3;
     CDALB 1929-1941; DLB 45; DLBD 7;
     MTCW; SATA 20; YABC

Moore, Marie Lorena 1957-
     See Moore, Lorrie
     See also CA 116; CANR 39

Moore, Thomas 1779-1852 . . . . **NCLC 6**
     See also DLB 96, 144

Morand, Paul 1888-1976 . . **CLC 41; SSC 22**
     See also CA 69-72; DLB 65

Morante, Elsa 1918-1985 . . . . **CLC 8, 47**
     See also CA 85-88; 117; CANR 35;
     DLB 177; MTCW

Moravia, Alberto
     1907-1990 . . . . **CLC 2, 7, 11, 27, 46;**
                          SSC 26
     See also Pincherle, Alberto
     See also DLB 177

More, Hannah 1745-1833 . . . . **NCLC 27**
     See also DLB 107, 109, 116, 158

More, Henry 1614-1687 . . . . **LC 9**
     See also DLB 126

More, Sir Thomas 1478-1535 . . . . **LC 10, 32**

Moreas, Jean . . . . **TCLC 18**
     See also Papadiamantopoulos, Johannes

Morgan, Berry 1919- . . . . **CLC 6**
     See also CA 49-52; DLB 6

Morgan, Claire
     See Highsmith, (Mary) Patricia

Morgan, Edwin (George) 1920- . . . . . **CLC 31**
     See also CA 5-8R; CANR 3, 43; DLB 27

Morgan, (George) Frederick
     1922- . . . . **CLC 23**
     See also CA 17-20R; CANR 21

Morgan, Harriet
     See Mencken, H(enry) L(ouis)

Morgan, Jane
     See Cooper, James Fenimore

Morgan, Janet 1945- . . . . **CLC 39**
     See also CA 65-68

Morgan, Lady 1776(?)-1859 . . . . . . **NCLC 29**
     See also DLB 116, 158

Morgan, Robin 1941- . . . . **CLC 2**
     See also CA 69-72; CANR 29; MTCW;
     SATA 80

Morgan, Scott
     See Kuttner, Henry

Morgan, Seth 1949(?)-1990 . . . . **CLC 65**
     See also CA 132

Morgenstern, Christian
     1871-1914 . . . . **TCLC 8**
     See also CA 105

Morgenstern, S.
     See Goldman, William (W.)

Moricz, Zsigmond 1879-1942 . . . . . **TCLC 33**

Morike, Eduard (Friedrich)
     1804-1875 . . . . **NCLC 10**
     See also DLB 133

Mori Ogai . . . . **TCLC 14**
     See also Mori Rintaro

Mori Rintaro 1862-1922
     See Mori Ogai
     See also CA 110

Moritz, Karl Philipp 1756-1793 . . . . . . **LC 2**
     See also DLB 94

Morland, Peter Henry
     See Faust, Frederick (Schiller)

Morren, Theophil
     See Hofmannsthal, Hugo von

Morris, Bill 1952- . . . . **CLC 76**

Morris, Julian
     See West, Morris L(anglo)

Morris, Steveland Judkins 1950(?)-
     See Wonder, Stevie
     See also CA 111

Morris, William 1834-1896 . . . . **NCLC 4**
     See also CDBLB 1832-1890; DLB 18, 35,
     57, 156, 178

Morris, Wright 1910- . . . **CLC 1, 3, 7, 18, 37**
     See also CA 9-12R; CANR 21; DLB 2;
     DLBY 81; MTCW

Morrison, Arthur 1863-1945 . . . . . . **TCLC 72**
     See also CA 120; 157; DLB 70, 135

Morrison, Chloe Anthony Wofford
     See Morrison, Toni

Morrison, James Douglas 1943-1971
     See Morrison, Jim
     See also CA 73-76; CANR 40

Morrison, Jim . . . . **CLC 17**
     See also Morrison, James Douglas

Nakos, Lilika   1899(?)- . . . .   **CLC 29**

Narayan, R(asipuram) K(rishnaswami)
1906- . . . . . .   **CLC 7, 28, 47; DAM NOV;
SSC 25**
See also CA 81-84; CANR 33; MTCW;
SATA 62

Nash, (Frediric) Ogden
1902-1971 . . . . . .   **CLC 23; DAM POET**
See also CA 13-14; 29-32R; CANR 34;
CAP 1; DLB 11; MAICYA; MTCW;
SATA 2, 46

Nathan, Daniel
See Dannay, Frederic

Nathan, George Jean   1882-1958 . . .   **TCLC 18**
See also Hatteras, Owen
See also CA 114; DLB 137

Natsume, Kinnosuke   1867-1916
See Natsume, Soseki
See also CA 104

Natsume, Soseki   1867-1916 . . . . .   **TCLC 2, 10**
See also Natsume, Kinnosuke
See also DLB 180

Natti, (Mary) Lee   1919-
See Kingman, Lee
See also CA 5-8R; CANR 2

Naylor, Gloria
1950- . . . . .   **CLC 28, 52; BLC; DA; DAC;
DAM MST, MULT, NOV, POP**
See also AAYA 6; BW 2; CA 107;
CANR 27, 51; DLB 173; MTCW; YABC

Neihardt, John Gneisenau
1881-1973 . . . .   **CLC 32**
See also CA 13-14; CAP 1; DLB 9, 54

Nekrasov, Nikolai Alekseevich
1821-1878 . . . .   **NCLC 11**

Nelligan, Emile   1879-1941 . . . .   **TCLC 14**
See also CA 114; DLB 92

Nelson, Willie   1933- . . . .   **CLC 17**
See also CA 107

Nemerov, Howard (Stanley)
1920-1991 . . . .   **CLC 2, 6, 9, 36;
DAM POET**
See also CA 1-4R; 134; CABS 2; CANR 1,
27, 53; DLB 5, 6; DLBY 83;
INT CANR-27; MTCW

Neruda, Pablo
1904-1973 . . . . .   **CLC 1, 2, 5, 7, 9, 28, 62;
DA; DAB; DAC; DAM MST, MULT,
POET; HLC; PC 4; WLC**
See also CA 19-20; 45-48; CAP 2; HW;
MTCW

Nerval, Gerard de
1808-1855 . . . . .   **NCLC 1; PC 13; SSC 18**

Nervo, (Jose) Amado (Ruiz de)
1870-1919 . . . .   **TCLC 11**
See also CA 109; 131; HW

Nessi, Pio Baroja y
See Baroja (y Nessi), Pio

Nestroy, Johann   1801-1862 . . . . . .   **NCLC 42**
See also DLB 133

Netterville, Luke
See O'Grady, Standish (James)

Neufeld, John (Arthur)   1938- . . . . . .   **CLC 17**
See also AAYA 11; CA 25-28R; CANR 11,
37, 56; MAICYA; SAAS 3; SATA 6, 81

Neville, Emily Cheney   1919- . . . .   **CLC 12**
See also CA 5-8R; CANR 3, 37; JRDA;
MAICYA; SAAS 2; SATA 1

Newbound, Bernard Slade   1930-
See Slade, Bernard
See also CA 81-84; CANR 49;
DAM DRAM

Newby, P(ercy) H(oward)
1918- . . . .   **CLC 2, 13; DAM NOV**
See also CA 5-8R; CANR 32; DLB 15;
MTCW

Newlove, Donald   1928- . . . .   **CLC 6**
See also CA 29-32R; CANR 25

Newlove, John (Herbert)   1938- . . . . .   **CLC 14**
See also CA 21-24R; CANR 9, 25

Newman, Charles   1938- . . . .   **CLC 2, 8**
See also CA 21-24R

Newman, Edwin (Harold)   1919- . . . .   **CLC 14**
See also AITN 1; CA 69-72; CANR 5

Newman, John Henry
1801-1890 . . . .   **NCLC 38**
See also DLB 18, 32, 55

Newton, Suzanne   1936- . . . .   **CLC 35**
See also CA 41-44R; CANR 14; JRDA;
SATA 5, 77

Nexo, Martin Andersen
1869-1954 . . . .   **TCLC 43**

Nezval, Vitezslav   1900-1958 . . . . . .   **TCLC 44**
See also CA 123

Ng, Fae Myenne   1957(?)- . . . .   **CLC 81**
See also CA 146

Ngema, Mbongeni   1955- . . . .   **CLC 57**
See also BW 2; CA 143

Ngugi, James T(hiong'o) . . . .   **CLC 3, 7, 13**
See also Ngugi wa Thiong'o

Ngugi wa Thiong'o
1938- . . . . .   **CLC 36; BLC; DAM MULT,
NOV**
See also Ngugi, James T(hiong'o)
See also BW 2; CA 81-84; CANR 27, 58;
DLB 125; MTCW

Nichol, B(arrie) P(hillip)
1944-1988 . . . .   **CLC 18**
See also CA 53-56; DLB 53; SATA 66

Nichols, John (Treadwell)   1940- . . . .   **CLC 38**
See also CA 9-12R; CAAS 2; CANR 6;
DLBY 82

Nichols, Leigh
See Koontz, Dean R(ay)

Nichols, Peter (Richard)
1927- . . . .   **CLC 5, 36, 65**
See also CA 104; CANR 33; DLB 13;
MTCW

Nicolas, F. R. E.
See Freeling, Nicolas

Niedecker, Lorine
1903-1970 . . . .   **CLC 10, 42; DAM POET**
See also CA 25-28; CAP 2; DLB 48

Nietzsche, Friedrich (Wilhelm)
1844-1900 . . . .   **TCLC 10, 18, 55**
See also CA 107; 121; DLB 129

Nievo, Ippolito   1831-1861 . . . .   **NCLC 22**

Nightingale, Anne Redmon   1943-
See Redmon, Anne
See also CA 103

Nik. T. O.
See Annensky, Innokenty (Fyodorovich)

Nin, Anais
1903-1977 . . . . . .   **CLC 1, 4, 8, 11, 14, 60;
DAM NOV, POP; SSC 10**
See also AITN 2; CA 13-16R; 69-72;
CANR 22, 53; DLB 2, 4, 152; MTCW

Nishiwaki, Junzaburo   1894-1982 . . . .   **PC 15**
See also CA 107

Nissenson, Hugh   1933- . . . .   **CLC 4, 9**
See also CA 17-20R; CANR 27; DLB 28

Niven, Larry . . . .   **CLC 8**
See also Niven, Laurence Van Cott
See also DLB 8

Niven, Laurence Van Cott   1938-
See Niven, Larry
See also CA 21-24R; CAAS 12; CANR 14,
44; DAM POP; MTCW

Nixon, Agnes Eckhardt   1927- . . . . . .   **CLC 21**
See also CA 110

Nizan, Paul   1905-1940 . . . .   **TCLC 40**
See also DLB 72

Nkosi, Lewis
1936- . . . . .   **CLC 45; BLC; DAM MULT**
See also BW 1; CA 65-68; CANR 27;
DLB 157

Nodier, (Jean) Charles (Emmanuel)
1780-1844 . . . .   **NCLC 19**
See also DLB 119

Nolan, Christopher   1965- . . . .   **CLC 58**
See also CA 111

Noon, Jeff   1957- . . . .   **CLC 91**
See also CA 148

Norden, Charles
See Durrell, Lawrence (George)

Nordhoff, Charles (Bernard)
1887-1947 . . . .   **TCLC 23**
See also CA 108; DLB 9; SATA 23

Norfolk, Lawrence   1963- . . . .   **CLC 76**
See also CA 144

Norman, Marsha
1947- . . . .   **CLC 28; DAM DRAM**
See also CA 105; CABS 3; CANR 41;
DLBY 84

Norris, Benjamin Franklin, Jr.
1870-1902 . . . .   **TCLC 24**
See also Norris, Frank
See also CA 110

Norris, Frank
See Norris, Benjamin Franklin, Jr.
See also CDALB 1865-1917; DLB 12, 71

Norris, Leslie   1921- . . . .   **CLC 14**
See also CA 11-12; CANR 14; CAP 1;
DLB 27

North, Andrew
See Norton, Andre

North, Anthony
See Koontz, Dean R(ay)

North, Captain George
See Stevenson, Robert Louis (Balfour)

North, Milou
See Erdrich, Louise

Northrup, B. A.
See Hubbard, L(afayette) Ron(ald)

North Staffs
See Hulme, T(homas) E(rnest)

Norton, Alice Mary
See Norton, Andre
See also MAICYA; SATA 1, 43

Norton, Andre 1912- .... CLC 12
See also Norton, Alice Mary
See also AAYA 14; CA 1-4R; CANR 2, 31;
DLB 8, 52; JRDA; MTCW; SATA 91

Norton, Caroline 1808-1877...... NCLC 47
See also DLB 21, 159

Norway, Nevil Shute 1899-1960
See Shute, Nevil
See also CA 102; 93-96

Norwid, Cyprian Kamil
1821-1883 .... NCLC 17

Nosille, Nabrah
See Ellison, Harlan (Jay)

Nossack, Hans Erich 1901-1978..... CLC 6
See also CA 93-96; 85-88; DLB 69

Nostradamus 1503-1566............ LC 27

Nosu, Chuji
See Ozu, Yasujiro

Notenburg, Eleanora (Genrikhovna) von
See Guro, Elena

Nova, Craig 1945-.............. CLC 7, 31
See also CA 45-48; CANR 2, 53

Novak, Joseph
See Kosinski, Jerzy (Nikodem)

Novalis 1772-1801 .... NCLC 13
See also DLB 90

Nowlan, Alden (Albert)
1933-1983 .. CLC 15; DAC; DAM MST
See also CA 9-12R; CANR 5; DLB 53

Noyes, Alfred 1880-1958 .... TCLC 7
See also CA 104; DLB 20

Nunn, Kem 19(?)- .... CLC 34

Nye, Robert
1939- .... CLC 13, 42; DAM NOV
See also CA 33-36R; CANR 29; DLB 14;
MTCW; SATA 6

Nyro, Laura 1947- .... CLC 17

Oates, Joyce Carol
1938- ...... CLC 1, 2, 3, 6, 9, 11, 15, 19,
33, 52; DA; DAB; DAC; DAM MST,
NOV, POP; SSC 6; WLC
See also AAYA 15; AITN 1; BEST 89:2;
CA 5-8R; CANR 25, 45;
CDALB 1968-1988; DLB 2, 5, 130;
DLBY 81; INT CANR-25; MTCW

O'Brien, Darcy 1939-............. CLC 11
See also CA 21-24R; CANR 8

O'Brien, E. G.
See Clarke, Arthur C(harles)

O'Brien, Edna
1936- .... CLC 3, 5, 8, 13, 36, 65;
DAM NOV; SSC 10
See also CA 1-4R; CANR 6, 41;
CDBLB 1960 to Present; DLB 14;
MTCW

O'Brien, Fitz-James 1828-1862... NCLC 21
See also DLB 74

O'Brien, Flann....... CLC 1, 4, 5, 7, 10, 47
See also O Nuallain, Brian

O'Brien, Richard 1942- .... CLC 17
See also CA 124

O'Brien, (William) Tim(othy)
1946- ...... CLC 7, 19, 40; DAM POP
See also AAYA 16; CA 85-88; CANR 40,
58; DLB 152; DLBD 9; DLBY 80

Obstfelder, Sigbjoern 1866-1900... TCLC 23
See also CA 123

O'Casey, Sean
1880-1964 ...... CLC 1, 5, 9, 11, 15, 88;
DAB; DAC; DAM DRAM, MST
See also CA 89-92; CDBLB 1914-1945;
DLB 10; MTCW; YABC

O'Cathasaigh, Sean
See O'Casey, Sean

Ochs, Phil 1940-1976............. CLC 17
See also CA 65-68

O'Connor, Edwin (Greene)
1918-1968 .... CLC 14
See also CA 93-96; 25-28R

O'Connor, (Mary) Flannery
1925-1964 .... CLC 1, 2, 3, 6, 10, 13, 15,
21, 66; DA; DAB; DAC; DAM MST,
NOV; SSC 1, 23; WLC
See also AAYA 7; CA 1-4R; CANR 3, 41;
CDALB 1941-1968; DLB 2, 152;
DLBD 12; DLBY 80; MTCW

O'Connor, Frank........... CLC 23; SSC 5
See also O'Donovan, Michael John
See also DLB 162

O'Dell, Scott 1898-1989........... CLC 30
See also AAYA 3; CA 61-64; 129;
CANR 12, 30; CLR 1, 16; DLB 52;
JRDA; MAICYA; SATA 12, 60

Odets, Clifford
1906-1963 .... CLC 2, 28, 98;
DAM DRAM; DC 6
See also CA 85-88; DLB 7, 26; MTCW

O'Doherty, Brian 1934-........... CLC 76
See also CA 105

O'Donnell, K. M.
See Malzberg, Barry N(athaniel)

O'Donnell, Lawrence
See Kuttner, Henry

O'Donovan, Michael John
1903-1966 .... CLC 14
See also O'Connor, Frank
See also CA 93-96

Oe, Kenzaburo
1935- ..... CLC 10, 36, 86; DAM NOV;
SSC 20
See also CA 97-100; CANR 36, 50;
DLBY 94; MTCW

O'Faolain, Julia 1932-....... CLC 6, 19, 47
See also CA 81-84; CAAS 2; CANR 12;
DLB 14; MTCW

O'Faolain, Sean
1900-1991 .... CLC 1, 7, 14, 32, 70;
SSC 13
See also CA 61-64; 134; CANR 12;
DLB 15, 162; MTCW

O'Flaherty, Liam
1896-1984 .... CLC 5, 34; SSC 6
See also CA 101; 113; CANR 35; DLB 36,
162; DLBY 84; MTCW

Ogilvy, Gavin
See Barrie, J(ames) M(atthew)

O'Grady, Standish (James)
1846-1928 .... TCLC 5
See also CA 104; 157

O'Grady, Timothy 1951- .... CLC 59
See also CA 138

O'Hara, Frank
1926-1966 .... CLC 2, 5, 13, 78;
DAM POET
See also CA 9-12R; 25-28R; CANR 33;
DLB 5, 16; MTCW

O'Hara, John (Henry)
1905-1970 .... CLC 1, 2, 3, 6, 11, 42;
DAM NOV; SSC 15
See also CA 5-8R; 25-28R; CANR 31;
CDALB 1929-1941; DLB 9, 86; DLBD 2;
MTCW

O Hehir, Diana 1922- .... CLC 41
See also CA 93-96

Okigbo, Christopher (Ifenayichukwu)
1932-1967 .... CLC 25, 84; BLC;
DAM MULT, POET; PC 7
See also BW 1; CA 77-80; DLB 125;
MTCW

Okri, Ben 1959- .... CLC 87
See also BW 2; CA 130; 138; DLB 157;
INT 138

Olds, Sharon
1942- ..... CLC 32, 39, 85; DAM POET
See also CA 101; CANR 18, 41; DLB 120

Oldstyle, Jonathan
See Irving, Washington

Olesha, Yuri (Karlovich)
1899-1960 .... CLC 8
See also CA 85-88

Oliphant, Laurence
1829(?)-1888 .... NCLC 47
See also DLB 18, 166

Oliphant, Margaret (Oliphant Wilson)
1828-1897 .... NCLC 11, 61; SSC 25
See also DLB 18, 159

Oliver, Mary 1935-......... CLC 19, 34, 98
See also CA 21-24R; CANR 9, 43; DLB 5

Olivier, Laurence (Kerr)
1907-1989 .... CLC 20
See also CA 111; 150; 129

Olsen, Tillie
1913- ..... CLC 4, 13; DA; DAB; DAC;
DAM MST; SSC 11
See also CA 1-4R; CANR 1, 43; DLB 28;
DLBY 80; MTCW

Olson, Charles (John)
1910-1970 ..... CLC 1, 2, 5, 6, 9, 11, 29;
DAM POET; PC 19
See also CA 13-16; 25-28R; CABS 2;
CANR 35; CAP 1; DLB 5, 16; MTCW

Olson, Toby 1937- .... CLC 28
See also CA 65-68; CANR 9, 31

Olyesha, Yuri
See Olesha, Yuri (Karlovich)

Ondaatje, (Philip) Michael
1943- .... CLC 14, 29, 51, 76; DAB;
DAC; DAM MST
See also CA 77-80; CANR 42; DLB 60

Oneal, Elizabeth 1934-
See Oneal, Zibby
See also CA 106; CANR 28; MAICYA;
SATA 30, 82

Oneal, Zibby . . . . **CLC 30**
See also Oneal, Elizabeth
See also AAYA 5; CLR 13; JRDA

O'Neill, Eugene (Gladstone)
1888-1953 . . . . . . **TCLC 1, 6, 27, 49; DA;**
DAB; DAC; DAM DRAM, MST; WLC
See also AITN 1; CA 110; 132;
CDALB 1929-1941; DLB 7; MTCW

Onetti, Juan Carlos
1909-1994 . . . . **CLC 7, 10; DAM MULT,**
NOV; SSC 23
See also CA 85-88; 145; CANR 32;
DLB 113; HW; MTCW

O Nuallain, Brian 1911-1966
See O'Brien, Flann
See also CA 21-22; 25-28R; CAP 2

Oppen, George 1908-1984 . . . . **CLC 7, 13, 34**
See also CA 13-16R; 113; CANR 8; DLB 5,
165

Oppenheim, E(dward) Phillips
1866-1946 . . . . **TCLC 45**
See also CA 111; DLB 70

Origen c. 185-c. 254 . . . . **CMLC 19**

Orlovitz, Gil 1918-1973 . . . . **CLC 22**
See also CA 77-80; 45-48; DLB 2, 5

Orris
See Ingelow, Jean

Ortega y Gasset, Jose
1883-1955 . . . . . **TCLC 9; DAM MULT;**
HLC
See also CA 106; 130; HW; MTCW

Ortese, Anna Maria 1914- . . . . **CLC 89**
See also DLB 177

Ortiz, Simon J(oseph)
1941- . . . . **CLC 45; DAM MULT,**
POET; PC 17
See also CA 134; DLB 120, 175; NNAL

Orton, Joe . . . . **CLC 4, 13, 43; DC 3**
See also Orton, John Kingsley
See also CDBLB 1960 to Present; DLB 13

Orton, John Kingsley 1933-1967
See Orton, Joe
See also CA 85-88; CANR 35;
DAM DRAM; MTCW

Orwell, George
. . . . . **TCLC 2, 6, 15, 31, 51; DAB; WLC**
See also Blair, Eric (Arthur)
See also CDBLB 1945-1960; DLB 15, 98

Osborne, David
See Silverberg, Robert

Osborne, George
See Silverberg, Robert

Osborne, John (James)
1929-1994 . . . . . **CLC 1, 2, 5, 11, 45; DA;**
DAB; DAC; DAM DRAM, MST; WLC
See also CA 13-16R; 147; CANR 21, 56;
CDBLB 1945-1960; DLB 13; MTCW

Osborne, Lawrence 1958- . . . . **CLC 50**

Oshima, Nagisa 1932- . . . . **CLC 20**
See also CA 116; 121

Oskison, John Milton
1874-1947 . . . . . **TCLC 35; DAM MULT**
See also CA 144; DLB 175; NNAL

Ossoli, Sarah Margaret (Fuller marchesa d')
1810-1850
See Fuller, Margaret
See also SATA 25

Ostrovsky, Alexander
1823-1886 . . . . **NCLC 30, 57**

Otero, Blas de 1916-1979 . . . . **CLC 11**
See also CA 89-92; DLB 134

Otto, Whitney 1955- . . . . **CLC 70**
See also CA 140

Ouida . . . . **TCLC 43**
See also De La Ramee, (Marie) Louise
See also DLB 18, 156

Ousmane, Sembene 1923- . . . . **CLC 66; BLC**
See also BW 1; CA 117; 125; MTCW

Ovid
43B.C.-18(?) . . . **CMLC 7; DAM POET;**
PC 2

Owen, Hugh
See Faust, Frederick (Schiller)

Owen, Wilfred (Edward Salter)
1893-1918 . . . . . **TCLC 5, 27; DA; DAB;**
DAC; DAM MST, POET; PC 19; WLC
See also CA 104; 141; CDBLB 1914-1945;
DLB 20

Owens, Rochelle 1936- . . . . **CLC 8**
See also CA 17-20R; CAAS 2; CANR 39

Oz, Amos
1939- . . . . **CLC 5, 8, 11, 27, 33, 54;**
DAM NOV
See also CA 53-56; CANR 27, 47; MTCW

Ozick, Cynthia
1928- . . . . **CLC 3, 7, 28, 62; DAM NOV,**
POP; SSC 15
See also BEST 90:1; CA 17-20R; CANR 23,
58; DLB 28, 152; DLBY 82;
INT CANR-23; MTCW

Ozu, Yasujiro 1903-1963 . . . . **CLC 16**
See also CA 112

Pacheco, C.
See Pessoa, Fernando (Antonio Nogueira)

Pa Chin . . . . **CLC 18**
See also Li Fei-kan

Pack, Robert 1929- . . . . **CLC 13**
See also CA 1-4R; CANR 3, 44; DLB 5

Padgett, Lewis
See Kuttner, Henry

Padilla (Lorenzo), Heberto 1932- . . . **CLC 38**
See also AITN 1; CA 123; 131; HW

Page, Jimmy 1944- . . . . **CLC 12**

Page, Louise 1955- . . . . **CLC 40**
See also CA 140

Page, P(atricia) K(athleen)
1916- . . . . **CLC 7, 18; DAC; DAM MST;**
PC 12
See also CA 53-56; CANR 4, 22; DLB 68;
MTCW

Page, Thomas Nelson 1853-1922 . . . . **SSC 23**
See also CA 118; DLB 12, 78; DLBD 13

Paget, Violet 1856-1935
See Lee, Vernon
See also CA 104

Paget-Lowe, Henry
See Lovecraft, H(oward) P(hillips)

Paglia, Camille (Anna) 1947- . . . . . . **CLC 68**
See also CA 140

Paige, Richard
See Koontz, Dean R(ay)

Paine, Thomas 1737-1809 . . . . **NCLC 62**
See also CDALB 1640-1865; DLB 31, 43,
73, 158

Pakenham, Antonia
See Fraser, (Lady) Antonia (Pakenham)

Palamas, Kostes 1859-1943 . . . . **TCLC 5**
See also CA 105

Palazzeschi, Aldo 1885-1974 . . . . **CLC 11**
See also CA 89-92; 53-56; DLB 114

Paley, Grace
1922- . . . . **CLC 4, 6, 37; DAM POP;**
SSC 8
See also CA 25-28R; CANR 13, 46;
DLB 28; INT CANR-13; MTCW

Palin, Michael (Edward) 1943- . . . . . **CLC 21**
See also Monty Python
See also CA 107; CANR 35; SATA 67

Palliser, Charles 1947- . . . . **CLC 65**
See also CA 136

Palma, Ricardo 1833-1919 . . . . **TCLC 29**

Pancake, Breece Dexter 1952-1979
See Pancake, Breece D'J
See also CA 123; 109

Pancake, Breece D'J . . . . **CLC 29**
See also Pancake, Breece Dexter
See also DLB 130

Panko, Rudy
See Gogol, Nikolai (Vasilyevich)

Papadiamantis, Alexandros
1851-1911 . . . . **TCLC 29**

Papadiamantopoulos, Johannes 1856-1910
See Moreas, Jean
See also CA 117

Papini, Giovanni 1881-1956 . . . . **TCLC 22**
See also CA 121

Paracelsus 1493-1541 . . . . **LC 14**
See also DLB 179

Parasol, Peter
See Stevens, Wallace

Pareto, Vilfredo 1848-1923 . . . . **TCLC 69**

Parfenie, Maria
See Codrescu, Andrei

Parini, Jay (Lee) 1948- . . . . **CLC 54**
See also CA 97-100; CAAS 16; CANR 32

Park, Jordan
See Kornbluth, C(yril) M.; Pohl, Frederik

Parker, Bert
See Ellison, Harlan (Jay)

Parker, Dorothy (Rothschild)
1893-1967 . . . . **CLC 15, 68;**
DAM POET; SSC 2
See also CA 19-20; 25-28R; CAP 2;
DLB 11, 45, 86; MTCW

Parker, Robert B(rown)
1932- . . . . . . **CLC 27; DAM NOV, POP**
See also BEST 89:4; CA 49-52; CANR 1,
26, 52; INT CANR-26; MTCW

Peshkov, Alexei Maximovich 1868-1936
See Gorky, Maxim
See also CA 105; 141; DA; DAC;
DAM DRAM, MST, NOV

Pessoa, Fernando (Antonio Nogueira)
1888-1935 .... **TCLC 27; HLC**
See also CA 125

Peterkin, Julia Mood 1880-1961.... **CLC 31**
See also CA 102; DLB 9

Peters, Joan K(aren) 1945- .... **CLC 39**
See also CA 158

Peters, Robert L(ouis) 1924-........ **CLC 7**
See also CA 13-16R; CAAS 8; DLB 105

Petofi, Sandor 1823-1849....... **NCLC 21**

Petrakis, Harry Mark 1923-....... **CLC 3**
See also CA 9-12R; CANR 4, 30

Petrarch
1304-1374 .... **CMLC 20; DAM POET;
PC 8**

Petrov, Evgeny .... **TCLC 21**
See also Kataev, Evgeny Petrovich

Petry, Ann (Lane) 1908-1997... **CLC 1, 7, 18**
See also BW 1; CA 5-8R; 157; CAAS 6;
CANR 4, 46; CLR 12; DLB 76; JRDA;
MAICYA; MTCW; SATA 5;
SATA-Obit 94

Petursson, Halligrimur 1614-1674 .... **LC 8**

Philips, Katherine 1632-1664....... **LC 30**
See also DLB 131

Philipson, Morris H. 1926- .... **CLC 53**
See also CA 1-4R; CANR 4

Phillips, Caryl
1958- .... **CLC 96; DAM MULT**
See also BW 2; CA 141; DLB 157

Phillips, David Graham
1867-1911 .... **TCLC 44**
See also CA 108; DLB 9, 12

Phillips, Jack
See Sandburg, Carl (August)

Phillips, Jayne Anne
1952- .... **CLC 15, 33; SSC 16**
See also CA 101; CANR 24, 50; DLBY 80;
INT CANR-24; MTCW

Phillips, Richard
See Dick, Philip K(indred)

Phillips, Robert (Schaeffer) 1938-... **CLC 28**
See also CA 17-20R; CAAS 13; CANR 8;
DLB 105

Phillips, Ward
See Lovecraft, H(oward) P(hillips)

Piccolo, Lucio 1901-1969......... **CLC 13**
See also CA 97-100; DLB 114

Pickthall, Marjorie L(owry) C(hristie)
1883-1922 .... **TCLC 21**
See also CA 107; DLB 92

Pico della Mirandola, Giovanni
1463-1494 .... **LC 15**

Piercy, Marge
1936- .... **CLC 3, 6, 14, 18, 27, 62**
See also CA 21-24R; CAAS 1; CANR 13,
43; DLB 120; MTCW

Piers, Robert
See Anthony, Piers

Pieyre de Mandiargues, Andre 1909-1991
See Mandiargues, Andre Pieyre de
See also CA 103; 136; CANR 22

Pilnyak, Boris .... **TCLC 23**
See also Vogau, Boris Andreyevich

Pincherle, Alberto
1907-1990 ..... **CLC 11, 18; DAM NOV**
See also Moravia, Alberto
See also CA 25-28R; 132; CANR 33;
MTCW

Pinckney, Darryl 1953- .... **CLC 76**
See also BW 2; CA 143

Pindar 518B.C.-446B.C.... **CMLC 12; PC 19**
See also DLB 176

Pineda, Cecile 1942-.............. **CLC 39**
See also CA 118

Pinero, Arthur Wing
1855-1934 ..... **TCLC 32; DAM DRAM**
See also CA 110; 153; DLB 10

Pinero, Miguel (Antonio Gomez)
1946-1988 .... **CLC 4, 55**
See also CA 61-64; 125; CANR 29; HW

Pinget, Robert 1919- .... **CLC 7, 13, 37**
See also CA 85-88; DLB 83

Pink Floyd
See Barrett, (Roger) Syd; Gilmour, David;
Mason, Nick; Waters, Roger; Wright,
Rick

Pinkney, Edward 1802-1828 ..... **NCLC 31**

Pinkwater, Daniel Manus 1941-.... **CLC 35**
See also Pinkwater, Manus
See also AAYA 1; CA 29-32R; CANR 12,
38; CLR 4; JRDA; MAICYA; SAAS 3;
SATA 46, 76

Pinkwater, Manus
See Pinkwater, Daniel Manus
See also SATA 8

Pinsky, Robert
1940- .. **CLC 9, 19, 38, 94; DAM POET**
See also CA 29-32R; CAAS 4; CANR 58;
DLBY 82

Pinta, Harold
See Pinter, Harold

Pinter, Harold
1930- ..... **CLC 1, 3, 6, 9, 11, 15, 27, 58,
73; DA; DAB; DAC; DAM DRAM,
MST; WLC**
See also CA 5-8R; CANR 33; CDBLB 1960
to Present; DLB 13; MTCW

Piozzi, Hester Lynch (Thrale)
1741-1821 .... **NCLC 57**
See also DLB 104, 142

Pirandello, Luigi
1867-1936 ..... **TCLC 4, 29; DA; DAB;
DAC; DAM DRAM, MST; DC 5;
SSC 22; WLC**
See also CA 104; 153

Pirsig, Robert M(aynard)
1928- .... **CLC 4, 6, 73; DAM POP**
See also CA 53-56; CANR 42; MTCW;
SATA 39

Pisarev, Dmitry Ivanovich
1840-1868 .... **NCLC 25**

Pix, Mary (Griffith) 1666-1709....... **LC 8**
See also DLB 80

Pixerecourt, Guilbert de
1773-1844 .... **NCLC 39**

Plaatje, Sol(omon) T(shekisho)
1876-1932 .... **TCLC 71**
See also BW 2; CA 141

Plaidy, Jean
See Hibbert, Eleanor Alice Burford

Planche, James Robinson
1796-1880 .... **NCLC 42**

Plant, Robert 1948- .... **CLC 12**

Plante, David (Robert)
1940- .... **CLC 7, 23, 38; DAM NOV**
See also CA 37-40R; CANR 12, 36, 58;
DLBY 83; INT CANR-12; MTCW

Plath, Sylvia
1932-1963 ..... **CLC 1, 2, 3, 5, 9, 11, 14,
17, 50, 51, 62; DA; DAB; DAC;
DAM MST, POET; PC 1; WLC**
See also AAYA 13; CA 19-20; CANR 34;
CAP 2; CDALB 1941-1968; DLB 5, 6,
152; MTCW

Plato
428(?)B.C.-348(?)B.C..... **CMLC 8; DA;
DAB; DAC; DAM MST**
See also DLB 176; YABC

Platonov, Andrei .... **TCLC 14**
See also Klimentov, Andrei Platonovich

Platt, Kin 1911- .... **CLC 26**
See also AAYA 11; CA 17-20R; CANR 11;
JRDA; SAAS 17; SATA 21, 86

Plautus c. 251B.C.-184B.C.......... **DC 6**

Plick et Plock
See Simenon, Georges (Jacques Christian)

Plimpton, George (Ames) 1927-..... **CLC 36**
See also AITN 1; CA 21-24R; CANR 32;
MTCW; SATA 10

Plomer, William Charles Franklin
1903-1973 .... **CLC 4, 8**
See also CA 21-22; CANR 34; CAP 2;
DLB 20, 162; MTCW; SATA 24

Plowman, Piers
See Kavanagh, Patrick (Joseph)

Plum, J.
See Wodehouse, P(elham) G(renville)

Plumly, Stanley (Ross) 1939- ...... **CLC 33**
See also CA 108; 110; DLB 5; INT 110

Plumpe, Friedrich Wilhelm
1888-1931 .... **TCLC 53**
See also CA 112

Poe, Edgar Allan
1809-1849 .... **NCLC 1, 16, 55; DA;
DAB; DAC; DAM MST, POET; PC 1;
SSC 1, 22; WLC**
See also AAYA 14; CDALB 1640-1865;
DLB 3, 59, 73, 74; SATA 23

Poet of Titchfield Street, The
See Pound, Ezra (Weston Loomis)

Pohl, Frederik 1919- ..... **CLC 18; SSC 25**
See also CA 61-64; CAAS 1; CANR 11, 37;
DLB 8; INT CANR-11; MTCW;
SATA 24

Poirier, Louis 1910-
See Gracq, Julien
See also CA 122; 126

Pteleon
See Grieve, C(hristopher) M(urray)
See also DAM POET

Puckett, Lute
See Masters, Edgar Lee

Puig, Manuel
1932-1990 . . . . **CLC 3, 5, 10, 28, 65;**
DAM MULT; HLC
See also CA 45-48; CANR 2, 32; DLB 113;
HW; MTCW

Purdy, Al(fred Wellington)
1918- . . . . **CLC 3, 6, 14, 50; DAC;**
DAM MST, POET
See also CA 81-84; CAAS 17; CANR 42;
DLB 88

Purdy, James (Amos)
1923- . . . . **CLC 2, 4, 10, 28, 52**
See also CA 33-36R; CAAS 1; CANR 19,
51; DLB 2; INT CANR-19; MTCW

Pure, Simon
See Swinnerton, Frank Arthur

Pushkin, Alexander (Sergeyevich)
1799-1837 . . . . . **NCLC 3, 27; DA; DAB;**
DAC; DAM DRAM, MST, POET;
PC 10; WLC
See also SATA 61

P'u Sung-ling   1640-1715 . . . . **LC 3**

Putnam, Arthur Lee
See Alger, Horatio, Jr.

Puzo, Mario
1920- . . . . . **CLC 1, 2, 6, 36; DAM NOV,**
POP
See also CA 65-68; CANR 4, 42; DLB 6;
MTCW

Pygge, Edward
See Barnes, Julian (Patrick)

Pym, Barbara (Mary Crampton)
1913-1980 . . . . **CLC 13, 19, 37**
See also CA 13-14; 97-100; CANR 13, 34;
CAP 1; DLB 14; DLBY 87; MTCW

Pynchon, Thomas (Ruggles, Jr.)
1937- . . . . . **CLC 2, 3, 6, 9, 11, 18, 33, 62,**
72; DA; DAB; DAC; DAM MST, NOV,
POP; SSC 14; WLC
See also BEST 90:2; CA 17-20R; CANR 22,
46; DLB 2, 173; MTCW

Pythagoras
c. 570B.C.-c. 500B.C. . . . . **CMLC 22**
See also DLB 176

Qian Zhongshu
See Ch'ien Chung-shu

Qroll
See Dagerman, Stig (Halvard)

Quarrington, Paul (Lewis)   1953- . . . . **CLC 65**
See also CA 129

Quasimodo, Salvatore   1901-1968 . . . **CLC 10**
See also CA 13-16; 25-28R; CAP 1;
DLB 114; MTCW

Quay, Stephen   1947- . . . . **CLC 95**

Quay, The Brothers
See Quay, Stephen; Quay, Timothy

Quay, Timothy   1947- . . . . **CLC 95**

Queen, Ellery. . . . . **CLC 3, 11**
See also Dannay, Frederic; Davidson,
Avram; Lee, Manfred B(ennington);
Marlowe, Stephen; Sturgeon, Theodore
(Hamilton); Vance, John Holbrook

Queen, Ellery, Jr.
See Dannay, Frederic; Lee, Manfred
B(ennington)

Queneau, Raymond
1903-1976 . . . . **CLC 2, 5, 10, 42**
See also CA 77-80; 69-72; CANR 32;
DLB 72; MTCW

Quevedo, Francisco de   1580-1645. . . . **LC 23**

Quiller-Couch, Arthur Thomas
1863-1944 . . . . **TCLC 53**
See also CA 118; DLB 135, 153

Quin, Ann (Marie)   1936-1973 . . . . **CLC 6**
See also CA 9-12R; 45-48; DLB 14

Quinn, Martin
See Smith, Martin Cruz

Quinn, Peter   1947- . . . . **CLC 91**

Quinn, Simon
See Smith, Martin Cruz

Quiroga, Horacio (Sylvestre)
1878-1937 . . . . . **TCLC 20; DAM MULT;**
HLC
See also CA 117; 131; HW; MTCW

Quoirez, Francoise   1935- . . . . **CLC 9**
See also Sagan, Francoise
See also CA 49-52; CANR 6, 39; MTCW

Raabe, Wilhelm   1831-1910 . . . . **TCLC 45**
See also DLB 129

Rabe, David (William)
1940- . . . . . . **CLC 4, 8, 33; DAM DRAM**
See also CA 85-88; CABS 3; DLB 7

Rabelais, Francois
1483-1553 . . . . . . **LC 5; DA; DAB; DAC;**
DAM MST; WLC

Rabinovitch, Sholem   1859-1916
See Aleichem, Sholom
See also CA 104

Rachilde   1860-1953 . . . . **TCLC 67**
See also DLB 123

Racine, Jean
1639-1699 . . . . **LC 28; DAB; DAM MST**

Radcliffe, Ann (Ward)
1764-1823 . . . . **NCLC 6, 55**
See also DLB 39, 178

Radiguet, Raymond   1903-1923 . . . . **TCLC 29**
See also DLB 65

Radnoti, Miklos   1909-1944 . . . . **TCLC 16**
See also CA 118

Rado, James   1939- . . . . **CLC 17**
See also CA 105

Radvanyi, Netty   1900-1983
See Seghers, Anna
See also CA 85-88; 110

Rae, Ben
See Griffiths, Trevor

Raeburn, John (Hay)   1941- . . . . **CLC 34**
See also CA 57-60

Ragni, Gerome   1942-1991 . . . . **CLC 17**
See also CA 105; 134

Rahv, Philip   1908-1973 . . . . **CLC 24**
See also Greenberg, Ivan
See also DLB 137

Raine, Craig   1944- . . . . **CLC 32**
See also CA 108; CANR 29, 51; DLB 40

Raine, Kathleen (Jessie)   1908- . . . **CLC 7, 45**
See also CA 85-88; CANR 46; DLB 20;
MTCW

Rainis, Janis   1865-1929 . . . . **TCLC 29**

Rakosi, Carl. . . . . **CLC 47**
See also Rawley, Callman
See also CAAS 5

Raleigh, Richard
See Lovecraft, H(oward) P(hillips)

Raleigh, Sir Walter
1554(?)-1618 . . . . **LC 31, 39**
See also CDBLB Before 1660; DLB 172

Rallentando, H. P.
See Sayers, Dorothy L(eigh)

Ramal, Walter
See de la Mare, Walter (John)

Ramon, Juan
See Jimenez (Mantecon), Juan Ramon

Ramos, Graciliano   1892-1953 . . . . . **TCLC 32**

Rampersad, Arnold   1941- . . . . **CLC 44**
See also BW 2; CA 127; 133; DLB 111;
INT 133

Rampling, Anne
See Rice, Anne

Ramsay, Allan   1684(?)-1758 . . . . **LC 29**
See also DLB 95

Ramuz, Charles-Ferdinand
1878-1947 . . . . **TCLC 33**

Rand, Ayn
1905-1982 . . . . . . **CLC 3, 30, 44, 79; DA;**
DAC; DAM MST, NOV, POP; WLC
See also AAYA 10; CA 13-16R; 105;
CANR 27; MTCW

Randall, Dudley (Felker)
1914- . . . . **CLC 1; BLC; DAM MULT**
See also BW 1; CA 25-28R; CANR 23;
DLB 41

Randall, Robert
See Silverberg, Robert

Ranger, Ken
See Creasey, John

Ransom, John Crowe
1888-1974 . . . . **CLC 2, 4, 5, 11, 24;**
DAM POET
See also CA 5-8R; 49-52; CANR 6, 34;
DLB 45, 63; MTCW

Rao, Raja   1909- . . . **CLC 25, 56; DAM NOV**
See also CA 73-76; CANR 51; MTCW

Raphael, Frederic (Michael)
1931- . . . . **CLC 2, 14**
See also CA 1-4R; CANR 1; DLB 14

Ratcliffe, James P.
See Mencken, H(enry) L(ouis)

Rathbone, Julian   1935- . . . . **CLC 41**
See also CA 101; CANR 34

Rattigan, Terence (Mervyn)
1911-1977 . . . . **CLC 7; DAM DRAM**
See also CA 85-88; 73-76;
CDBLB 1945-1960; DLB 13; MTCW

Ratushinskaya, Irina 1954-........ **CLC 54**
See also CA 129

Raven, Simon (Arthur Noel)
1927-........................ **CLC 14**
See also CA 81-84

Rawley, Callman 1903-
See Rakosi, Carl
See also CA 21-24R; CANR 12, 32

Rawlings, Marjorie Kinnan
1896-1953 .... **TCLC 4**
See also AAYA 20; CA 104; 137; DLB 9,
22, 102; JRDA; MAICYA; 1

Ray, Satyajit
1921-1992 ... **CLC 16, 76; DAM MULT**
See also CA 114; 137

Read, Herbert Edward 1893-1968.... **CLC 4**
See also CA 85-88; 25-28R; DLB 20, 149

Read, Piers Paul 1941- ...... **CLC 4, 10, 25**
See also CA 21-24R; CANR 38; DLB 14;
SATA 21

Reade, Charles 1814-1884 .... **NCLC 2**
See also DLB 21

Reade, Hamish
See Gray, Simon (James Holliday)

Reading, Peter 1946- .... **CLC 47**
See also CA 103; CANR 46; DLB 40

Reaney, James
1926-...... **CLC 13; DAC; DAM MST**
See also CA 41-44R; CAAS 15; CANR 42;
DLB 68; SATA 43

Rebreanu, Liviu 1885-1944 .... **TCLC 28**

Rechy, John (Francisco)
1934-.............. **CLC 1, 7, 14, 18;**
DAM MULT; HLC
See also CA 5-8R; CAAS 4; CANR 6, 32;
DLB 122; DLBY 82; HW; INT CANR-6

Redcam, Tom 1870-1933 .... **TCLC 25**

Reddin, Keith..................... **CLC 67**

Redgrove, Peter (William)
1932-....................... **CLC 6, 41**
See also CA 1-4R; CANR 3, 39; DLB 40

Redmon, Anne.................... **CLC 22**
See also Nightingale, Anne Redmon
See also DLBY 86

Reed, Eliot
See Ambler, Eric

Reed, Ishmael
1938-........ **CLC 2, 3, 5, 6, 13, 32, 60;**
BLC; DAM MULT
See also BW 2; CA 21-24R; CANR 25, 48;
DLB 2, 5, 33, 169; DLBD 8; MTCW

Reed, John (Silas) 1887-1920 ...... **TCLC 9**
See also CA 106

Reed, Lou...................... **CLC 21**
See also Firbank, Louis

Reeve, Clara 1729-1807 .... **NCLC 19**
See also DLB 39

Reich, Wilhelm 1897-1957........ **TCLC 57**

Reid, Christopher (John) 1949-..... **CLC 33**
See also CA 140; DLB 40

Reid, Desmond
See Moorcock, Michael (John)

Reid Banks, Lynne 1929-
See Banks, Lynne Reid
See also CA 1-4R; CANR 6, 22, 38;
CLR 24; JRDA; MAICYA; SATA 22, 75

Reilly, William K.
See Creasey, John

Reiner, Max
See Caldwell, (Janet Miriam) Taylor
(Holland)

Reis, Ricardo
See Pessoa, Fernando (Antonio Nogueira)

Remarque, Erich Maria
1898-1970 .... **CLC 21; DA; DAB; DAC;**
DAM MST, NOV
See also CA 77-80; 29-32R; DLB 56;
MTCW

Remizov, A.
See Remizov, Aleksei (Mikhailovich)

Remizov, A. M.
See Remizov, Aleksei (Mikhailovich)

Remizov, Aleksei (Mikhailovich)
1877-1957 .... **TCLC 27**
See also CA 125; 133

Renan, Joseph Ernest
1823-1892 .... **NCLC 26**

Renard, Jules 1864-1910 .... **TCLC 17**
See also CA 117

Renault, Mary............... **CLC 3, 11, 17**
See also Challans, Mary
See also DLBY 83

Rendell, Ruth (Barbara)
1930-......... **CLC 28, 48; DAM POP**
See also Vine, Barbara
See also CA 109; CANR 32, 52; DLB 87;
INT CANR-32; MTCW

Renoir, Jean 1894-1979 .... **CLC 20**
See also CA 129; 85-88

Resnais, Alain 1922-.............. **CLC 16**

Reverdy, Pierre 1889-1960 .... **CLC 53**
See also CA 97-100; 89-92

Rexroth, Kenneth
1905-1982 ...... **CLC 1, 2, 6, 11, 22, 49;**
DAM POET
See also CA 5-8R; 107; CANR 14, 34;
CDALB 1941-1968; DLB 16, 48, 165;
DLBY 82; INT CANR-14; MTCW

Reyes, Alfonso 1889-1959 .... **TCLC 33**
See also CA 131; HW

Reyes y Basoalto, Ricardo Eliecer Neftali
See Neruda, Pablo

Reymont, Wladyslaw (Stanislaw)
1868(?)-1925 .... **TCLC 5**
See also CA 104

Reynolds, Jonathan 1942-....... **CLC 6, 38**
See also CA 65-68; CANR 28

Reynolds, Joshua 1723-1792 .... **LC 15**
See also DLB 104

Reynolds, Michael Shane 1937-.... **CLC 44**
See also CA 65-68; CANR 9

Reznikoff, Charles 1894-1976 .... **CLC 9**
See also CA 33-36; 61-64; CAP 2; DLB 28,
45

Rezzori (d'Arezzo), Gregor von
1914-..................... **CLC 25**
See also CA 122; 136

Rhine, Richard
See Silverstein, Alvin

Rhodes, Eugene Manlove
1869-1934 .... **TCLC 53**

R'hoone
See Balzac, Honore de

Rhys, Jean
1890(?)-1979 .... **CLC 2, 4, 6, 14, 19, 51;**
DAM NOV; SSC 21
See also CA 25-28R; 85-88; CANR 35;
CDBLB 1945-1960; DLB 36, 117, 162;
MTCW

Ribeiro, Darcy 1922-1997 .... **CLC 34**
See also CA 33-36R; 156

Ribeiro, Joao Ubaldo (Osorio Pimentel)
1941-..................... **CLC 10, 67**
See also CA 81-84

Ribman, Ronald (Burt) 1932- .... **CLC 7**
See also CA 21-24R; CANR 46

Ricci, Nino 1959-................ **CLC 70**
See also CA 137

Rice, Anne 1941- ..... **CLC 41; DAM POP**
See also AAYA 9; BEST 89:2; CA 65-68;
CANR 12, 36, 53

Rice, Elmer (Leopold)
1892-1967 .... **CLC 7, 49; DAM DRAM**
See also CA 21-22; 25-28R; CAP 2; DLB 4,
7; MTCW

Rice, Tim(othy Miles Bindon)
1944-..................... **CLC 21**
See also CA 103; CANR 46

Rich, Adrienne (Cecile)
1929-.... **CLC 3, 6, 7, 11, 18, 36, 73, 76;**
DAM POET; PC 5
See also CA 9-12R; CANR 20, 53; DLB 5,
67; MTCW

Rich, Barbara
See Graves, Robert (von Ranke)

Rich, Robert
See Trumbo, Dalton

Richard, Keith.................... **CLC 17**
See also Richards, Keith

Richards, David Adams
1950-................. **CLC 59; DAC**
See also CA 93-96; DLB 53

Richards, I(vor) A(rmstrong)
1893-1979 .... **CLC 14, 24**
See also CA 41-44R; 89-92; CANR 34;
DLB 27

Richards, Keith 1943-
See Richard, Keith
See also CA 107

Richardson, Anne
See Roiphe, Anne (Richardson)

Richardson, Dorothy Miller
1873-1957 .... **TCLC 3**
See also CA 104; DLB 36

Richardson, Ethel Florence (Lindesay)
1870-1946
See Richardson, Henry Handel
See also CA 105

Richardson, Henry Handel......... **TCLC 4**
See also Richardson, Ethel Florence
(Lindesay)

Author Index

Richardson, John
1796-1852 . . . . **NCLC 55; DAC**
See also DLB 99

Richardson, Samuel
1689-1761 . . . . . . **LC 1; DA; DAB; DAC;**
DAM MST, NOV; WLC
See also CDBLB 1660-1789; DLB 39

Richler, Mordecai
1931- . . . . **CLC 3, 5, 9, 13, 18, 46, 70;**
DAC; DAM MST, NOV
See also AITN 1; CA 65-68; CANR 31;
CLR 17; DLB 53; MAICYA; MTCW;
SATA 44; SATA-Brief 27

Richter, Conrad (Michael)
1890-1968 . . . . **CLC 30**
See also AAYA 21; CA 5-8R; 25-28R;
CANR 23; DLB 9; MTCW; SATA 3

Ricostranza, Tom
See Ellis, Trey

Riddell, J. H. 1832-1906 . . . . **TCLC 40**

Riding, Laura . . . . **CLC 3, 7**
See also Jackson, Laura (Riding)

Riefenstahl, Berta Helene Amalia 1902-
See Riefenstahl, Leni
See also CA 108

Riefenstahl, Leni . . . . **CLC 16**
See also Riefenstahl, Berta Helene Amalia

Riffe, Ernest
See Bergman, (Ernst) Ingmar

Riggs, (Rolla) Lynn
1899-1954 . . . . . **TCLC 56; DAM MULT**
See also CA 144; DLB 175; NNAL

Riley, James Whitcomb
1849-1916 . . . . . . **TCLC 51; DAM POET**
See also CA 118; 137; MAICYA; SATA 17

Riley, Tex
See Creasey, John

Rilke, Rainer Maria
1875-1926 . . . . **TCLC 1, 6, 19;**
DAM POET; PC 2
See also CA 104; 132; DLB 81; MTCW

Rimbaud, (Jean Nicolas) Arthur
1854-1891 . . . . . **NCLC 4, 35; DA; DAB;**
DAC; DAM MST, POET; PC 3; WLC

Rinehart, Mary Roberts
1876-1958 . . . . **TCLC 52**
See also CA 108

Ringmaster, The
See Mencken, H(enry) L(ouis)

Ringwood, Gwen(dolyn Margaret) Pharis
1910-1984 . . . . **CLC 48**
See also CA 148; 112; DLB 88

Rio, Michel 19(?)- . . . . **CLC 43**

Ritsos, Giannes
See Ritsos, Yannis

Ritsos, Yannis 1909-1990 . . . . . **CLC 6, 13, 31**
See also CA 77-80; 133; CANR 39; MTCW

Ritter, Erika 1948(?)- . . . . **CLC 52**

Rivera, Jose Eustasio 1889-1928 . . . **TCLC 35**
See also HW

Rivers, Conrad Kent 1933-1968 . . . . . . **CLC 1**
See also BW 1; CA 85-88; DLB 41

Rivers, Elfrida
See Bradley, Marion Zimmer

Riverside, John
See Heinlein, Robert A(nson)

Rizal, Jose 1861-1896 . . . . **NCLC 27**

Roa Bastos, Augusto (Antonio)
1917- . . . . . **CLC 45; DAM MULT; HLC**
See also CA 131; DLB 113; HW

Robbe-Grillet, Alain
1922- . . . . . . **CLC 1, 2, 4, 6, 8, 10, 14, 43**
See also CA 9-12R; CANR 33; DLB 83;
MTCW

Robbins, Harold
1916- . . . . **CLC 5; DAM NOV**
See also CA 73-76; CANR 26, 54; MTCW

Robbins, Thomas Eugene 1936-
See Robbins, Tom
See also CA 81-84; CANR 29; DAM NOV,
POP; MTCW

Robbins, Tom . . . . **CLC 9, 32, 64**
See also Robbins, Thomas Eugene
See also BEST 90:3; DLBY 80

Robbins, Trina 1938- . . . . **CLC 21**
See also CA 128

Roberts, Charles G(eorge) D(ouglas)
1860-1943 . . . . **TCLC 8**
See also CA 105; CLR 33; DLB 92;
SATA 88; SATA-Brief 29

Roberts, Elizabeth Madox
1886-1941 . . . . **TCLC 68**
See also CA 111; DLB 9, 54, 102;
SATA 33; SATA-Brief 27

Roberts, Kate 1891-1985 . . . . **CLC 15**
See also CA 107; 116

Roberts, Keith (John Kingston)
1935- . . . . **CLC 14**
See also CA 25-28R; CANR 46

Roberts, Kenneth (Lewis)
1885-1957 . . . . **TCLC 23**
See also CA 109; DLB 9

Roberts, Michele (B.) 1949- . . . . **CLC 48**
See also CA 115; CANR 58

Robertson, Ellis
See Ellison, Harlan (Jay); Silverberg, Robert

Robertson, Thomas William
1829-1871 . . . . **NCLC 35; DAM DRAM**

Robeson, Kenneth
See Dent, Lester

Robinson, Edwin Arlington
1869-1935 . . . . **TCLC 5; DA; DAC;**
DAM MST, POET; PC 1
See also CA 104; 133; CDALB 1865-1917;
DLB 54; MTCW

Robinson, Henry Crabb
1775-1867 . . . . **NCLC 15**
See also DLB 107

Robinson, Jill 1936- . . . . **CLC 10**
See also CA 102; INT 102

Robinson, Kim Stanley 1952- . . . . . . **CLC 34**
See also CA 126

Robinson, Lloyd
See Silverberg, Robert

Robinson, Marilynne 1944- . . . . **CLC 25**
See also CA 116

Robinson, Smokey . . . . **CLC 21**
See also Robinson, William, Jr.

Robinson, William, Jr. 1940-
See Robinson, Smokey
See also CA 116

Robison, Mary 1949- . . . . **CLC 42, 98**
See also CA 113; 116; DLB 130; INT 116

Rod, Edouard 1857-1910 . . . . **TCLC 52**

Roddenberry, Eugene Wesley 1921-1991
See Roddenberry, Gene
See also CA 110; 135; CANR 37; SATA 45;
SATA-Obit 69

Roddenberry, Gene . . . . **CLC 17**
See also Roddenberry, Eugene Wesley
See also AAYA 5; SATA-Obit 69

Rodgers, Mary 1931- . . . . **CLC 12**
See also CA 49-52; CANR 8, 55; CLR 20;
INT CANR-8; JRDA; MAICYA;
SATA 8

Rodgers, W(illiam) R(obert)
1909-1969 . . . . **CLC 7**
See also CA 85-88; DLB 20

Rodman, Eric
See Silverberg, Robert

Rodman, Howard 1920(?)-1985 . . . . . **CLC 65**
See also CA 118

Rodman, Maia
See Wojciechowska, Maia (Teresa)

Rodriguez, Claudio 1934- . . . . **CLC 10**
See also DLB 134

Roelvaag, O(le) E(dvart)
1876-1931 . . . . **TCLC 17**
See also CA 117; DLB 9

Roethke, Theodore (Huebner)
1908-1963 . . . . . . **CLC 1, 3, 8, 11, 19, 46,**
101; DAM POET; PC 15
See also CA 81-84; CABS 2;
CDALB 1941-1968; DLB 5; MTCW

Rogers, Thomas Hunton 1927- . . . . . **CLC 57**
See also CA 89-92; INT 89-92

Rogers, Will(iam Penn Adair)
1879-1935 . . . **TCLC 8, 71; DAM MULT**
See also CA 105; 144; DLB 11; NNAL

Rogin, Gilbert 1929- . . . . **CLC 18**
See also CA 65-68; CANR 15

Rohan, Koda . . . . **TCLC 22**
See also Koda Shigeyuki

Rohmer, Eric . . . . **CLC 16**
See also Scherer, Jean-Marie Maurice

Rohmer, Sax . . . . **TCLC 28**
See also Ward, Arthur Henry Sarsfield
See also DLB 70

Roiphe, Anne (Richardson)
1935- . . . . **CLC 3, 9**
See also CA 89-92; CANR 45; DLBY 80;
INT 89-92

Rojas, Fernando de 1465-1541 . . . . . . **LC 23**

Rolfe, Frederick (William Serafino Austin
Lewis Mary) 1860-1913 . . . . . . **TCLC 12**
See also CA 107; DLB 34, 156

Rolland, Romain 1866-1944 . . . . **TCLC 23**
See also CA 118; DLB 65

Rolle, Richard c. 1300-c. 1349 . . . **CMLC 21**
See also DLB 146

Rolvaag, O(le) E(dvart)
See Roelvaag, O(le) E(dvart)

Romain Arnaud, Saint
See Aragon, Louis

Romains, Jules 1885-1972 . . . . **CLC 7**
See also CA 85-88; CANR 34; DLB 65;
MTCW

Romero, Jose Ruben 1890-1952 . . . **TCLC 14**
See also CA 114; 131; HW

Ronsard, Pierre de
1524-1585 . . . . **LC 6; PC 11**

Rooke, Leon
1934- . . . . **CLC 25, 34; DAM POP**
See also CA 25-28R; CANR 23, 53

Roosevelt, Theodore 1858-1919 . . . . **TCLC 69**
See also CA 115; DLB 47

Roper, William 1498-1578 . . . . **LC 10**

Roquelaure, A. N.
See Rice, Anne

Rosa, Joao Guimaraes 1908-1967 . . . **CLC 23**
See also CA 89-92; DLB 113

Rose, Wendy
1948- . . . . **CLC 85; DAM MULT; PC 13**
See also CA 53-56; CANR 5, 51; DLB 175;
NNAL; SATA 12

Rosen, Richard (Dean) 1949- . . . . **CLC 39**
See also CA 77-80; INT CANR-30

Rosenberg, Isaac 1890-1918 . . . . **TCLC 12**
See also CA 107; DLB 20

Rosenblatt, Joe . . . . **CLC 15**
See also Rosenblatt, Joseph

Rosenblatt, Joseph 1933-
See Rosenblatt, Joe
See also CA 89-92; INT 89-92

Rosenfeld, Samuel 1896-1963
See Tzara, Tristan
See also CA 89-92

Rosenstock, Sami
See Tzara, Tristan

Rosenstock, Samuel
See Tzara, Tristan

Rosenthal, M(acha) L(ouis)
1917-1996 . . . . **CLC 28**
See also CA 1-4R; 152; CAAS 6; CANR 4,
51; DLB 5; SATA 59

Ross, Barnaby
See Dannay, Frederic

Ross, Bernard L.
See Follett, Ken(neth Martin)

Ross, J. H.
See Lawrence, T(homas) E(dward)

Ross, Martin
See Martin, Violet Florence
See also DLB 135

Ross, (James) Sinclair
1908- . . . . . . **CLC 13; DAC; DAM MST;
SSC 24**
See also CA 73-76; DLB 88

Rossetti, Christina (Georgina)
1830-1894 . . . . . **NCLC 2, 50; DA; DAB;
DAC; DAM MST, POET; PC 7; WLC**
See also DLB 35, 163; MAICYA; SATA 20

Rossetti, Dante Gabriel
1828-1882 . . . . **NCLC 4; DA; DAB;
DAC; DAM MST, POET; WLC**
See also CDBLB 1832-1890; DLB 35

Rossner, Judith (Perelman)
1935- . . . . **CLC 6, 9, 29**
See also AITN 2; BEST 90:3; CA 17-20R;
CANR 18, 51; DLB 6; INT CANR-18;
MTCW

Rostand, Edmond (Eugene Alexis)
1868-1918 . . . . . . **TCLC 6, 37; DA; DAB;
DAC; DAM DRAM, MST**
See also CA 104; 126; MTCW

Roth, Henry 1906-1995 . . . . **CLC 2, 6, 11**
See also CA 11-12; 149; CANR 38; CAP 1;
DLB 28; MTCW

Roth, Joseph 1894-1939 . . . . **TCLC 33**
See also DLB 85

Roth, Philip (Milton)
1933- . . . . **CLC 1, 2, 3, 4, 6, 9, 15, 22,
31, 47, 66, 86; DA; DAB; DAC;
DAM MST, NOV, POP; SSC 26; WLC**
See also BEST 90:3; CA 1-4R; CANR 1, 22,
36, 55; CDALB 1968-1988; DLB 2, 28,
173; DLBY 82; MTCW

Rothenberg, Jerome 1931- . . . . **CLC 6, 57**
See also CA 45-48; CANR 1; DLB 5

Roumain, Jacques (Jean Baptiste)
1907-1944 . . . . **TCLC 19; BLC;
DAM MULT**
See also BW 1; CA 117; 125

Rourke, Constance (Mayfield)
1885-1941 . . . . **TCLC 12**
See also CA 107; 1

Rousseau, Jean-Baptiste 1671-1741 . . . **LC 9**

Rousseau, Jean-Jacques
1712-1778 . . . . **LC 14, 36; DA; DAB;
DAC; DAM MST; WLC**

Roussel, Raymond 1877-1933 . . . . . **TCLC 20**
See also CA 117

Rovit, Earl (Herbert) 1927- . . . . **CLC 7**
See also CA 5-8R; CANR 12

Rowe, Nicholas 1674-1718 . . . . **LC 8**
See also DLB 84

Rowley, Ames Dorrance
See Lovecraft, H(oward) P(hillips)

Rowson, Susanna Haswell
1762(?)-1824 . . . . **NCLC 5**
See also DLB 37

Roy, Gabrielle
1909-1983 . . . . **CLC 10, 14; DAB; DAC;
DAM MST**
See also CA 53-56; 110; CANR 5; DLB 68;
MTCW

Rozewicz, Tadeusz
1921- . . . . **CLC 9, 23; DAM POET**
See also CA 108; CANR 36; MTCW

Ruark, Gibbons 1941- . . . . **CLC 3**
See also CA 33-36R; CAAS 23; CANR 14,
31, 57; DLB 120

Rubens, Bernice (Ruth) 1923- . . . **CLC 19, 31**
See also CA 25-28R; CANR 33; DLB 14;
MTCW

Rubin, Harold
See Robbins, Harold

Rudkin, (James) David 1936- . . . . . . **CLC 14**
See also CA 89-92; DLB 13

Rudnik, Raphael 1933- . . . . **CLC 7**
See also CA 29-32R

Ruffian, M.
See Hasek, Jaroslav (Matej Frantisek)

Ruiz, Jose Martinez . . . . **CLC 11**
See also Martinez Ruiz, Jose

Rukeyser, Muriel
1913-1980 . . . . **CLC 6, 10, 15, 27;
DAM POET; PC 12**
See also CA 5-8R; 93-96; CANR 26;
DLB 48; MTCW; SATA-Obit 22

Rule, Jane (Vance) 1931- . . . . **CLC 27**
See also CA 25-28R; CAAS 18; CANR 12;
DLB 60

Rulfo, Juan
1918-1986 . . . . **CLC 8, 80; DAM MULT;
HLC; SSC 25**
See also CA 85-88; 118; CANR 26;
DLB 113; HW; MTCW

Rumi, Jalal al-Din 1297-1373 . . . . **CMLC 20**

Runeberg, Johan 1804-1877 . . . . . . **NCLC 41**

Runyon, (Alfred) Damon
1884(?)-1946 . . . . **TCLC 10**
See also CA 107; DLB 11, 86, 171

Rush, Norman 1933- . . . . **CLC 44**
See also CA 121; 126; INT 126

Rushdie, (Ahmed) Salman
1947- . . . . **CLC 23, 31, 55, 100; DAB;
DAC; DAM MST, NOV, POP**
See also BEST 89:3; CA 108; 111;
CANR 33, 56; INT 111; MTCW; YABC

Rushforth, Peter (Scott) 1945- . . . . . **CLC 19**
See also CA 101

Ruskin, John 1819-1900 . . . . **TCLC 63**
See also CA 114; 129; CDBLB 1832-1890;
DLB 55, 163; SATA 24

Russ, Joanna 1937- . . . . **CLC 15**
See also CA 25-28R; CANR 11, 31; DLB 8;
MTCW

Russell, George William 1867-1935
See Baker, Jean H.
See also CA 104; 153; CDBLB 1890-1914;
DAM POET

Russell, (Henry) Ken(neth Alfred)
1927- . . . . **CLC 16**
See also CA 105

Russell, Willy 1947- . . . . **CLC 60**

Rutherford, Mark . . . . **TCLC 25**
See also White, William Hale
See also DLB 18

Ruyslinck, Ward 1929- . . . . **CLC 14**
See also Belser, Reimond Karel Maria de

Ryan, Cornelius (John) 1920-1974 . . . **CLC 7**
See also CA 69-72; 53-56; CANR 38

Ryan, Michael 1946- . . . . **CLC 65**
See also CA 49-52; DLBY 82

Ryan, Tim
See Dent, Lester

Rybakov, Anatoli (Naumovich)
1911- . . . . **CLC 23, 53**
See also CA 126; 135; SATA 79

Ryder, Jonathan
See Ludlum, Robert

Ryga, George
1932-1987 . . **CLC 14; DAC; DAM MST**
See also CA 101; 124; CANR 43; DLB 60

S. S.
  See Sassoon, Siegfried (Lorraine)

Saba, Umberto 1883-1957 .... **TCLC 33**
  See also CA 144; DLB 114

Sabatini, Rafael 1875-1950 ...... **TCLC 47**

Sabato, Ernesto (R.)
  1911- .... **CLC 10, 23; DAM MULT;**
                                    HLC
  See also CA 97-100; CANR 32; DLB 145;
    HW; MTCW

Sacastru, Martin
  See Bioy Casares, Adolfo

Sacher-Masoch, Leopold von
  1836(?)-1895 .... **NCLC 31**

Sachs, Marilyn (Stickle) 1927- ..... **CLC 35**
  See also AAYA 2; CA 17-20R; CANR 13,
    47; CLR 2; JRDA; MAICYA; SAAS 2;
    SATA 3, 68

Sachs, Nelly 1891-1970 .... **CLC 14, 98**
  See also CA 17-18; 25-28R; CAP 2

Sackler, Howard (Oliver)
  1929-1982 .... **CLC 14**
  See also CA 61-64; 108; CANR 30; DLB 7

Sacks, Oliver (Wolf) 1933- .... **CLC 67**
  See also CA 53-56; CANR 28, 50;
    INT CANR-28; MTCW

Sade, Donatien Alphonse Francois Comte
  1740-1814 .... **NCLC 47**

Sadoff, Ira 1945-................... **CLC 9**
  See also CA 53-56; CANR 5, 21; DLB 120

Saetone
  See Camus, Albert

Safire, William 1929-............. **CLC 10**
  See also CA 17-20R; CANR 31, 54

Sagan, Carl (Edward) 1934-1996.... **CLC 30**
  See also AAYA 2; CA 25-28R; 155;
    CANR 11, 36; MTCW; SATA 58;
    SATA-Obit 94

Sagan, Francoise .... **CLC 3, 6, 9, 17, 36**
  See also Quoirez, Francoise
  See also DLB 83

Sahgal, Nayantara (Pandit) 1927-... **CLC 41**
  See also CA 9-12R; CANR 11

Saint, H(arry) F. 1941- .... **CLC 50**
  See also CA 127

St. Aubin de Teran, Lisa 1953-
  See Teran, Lisa St. Aubin de
  See also CA 118; 126; INT 126

Sainte-Beuve, Charles Augustin
  1804-1869 .... **NCLC 5**

**Saint-Exupery, Antoine (Jean Baptiste Marie
  Roger) de**
  1900-1944 .... **TCLC 2, 56; DAM NOV;**
                                    WLC
  See also CA 108; 132; CLR 10; DLB 72;
    MAICYA; MTCW; SATA 20

St. John, David
  See Hunt, E(verette) Howard, (Jr.)

Saint-John Perse
  See Leger, (Marie-Rene Auguste) Alexis
    Saint-Leger

Saintsbury, George (Edward Bateman)
  1845-1933 .... **TCLC 31**
  See also DLB 57, 149

Sait Faik .... **TCLC 23**
  See also Abasiyanik, Sait Faik

Saki .... **TCLC 3; SSC 12**
  See also Munro, H(ector) H(ugh)

Sala, George Augustus .... **NCLC 46**

Salama, Hannu 1936-............. **CLC 18**

Salamanca, J(ack) R(ichard)
  1922- .... **CLC 4, 15**
  See also CA 25-28R

Sale, J. Kirkpatrick
  See Sale, Kirkpatrick

Sale, Kirkpatrick 1937- .... **CLC 68**
  See also CA 13-16R; CANR 10

Salinas, Luis Omar
  1937- ...... **CLC 90; DAM MULT; HLC**
  See also CA 131; DLB 82; HW

Salinas (y Serrano), Pedro
  1891(?)-1951 .... **TCLC 17**
  See also CA 117; DLB 134

Salinger, J(erome) D(avid)
  1919- ...... **CLC 1, 3, 8, 12, 55, 56; DA;**
    DAB; DAC; DAM MST, NOV, POP;
                                 SSC 2; WLC
  See also AAYA 2; CA 5-8R; CANR 39;
    CDALB 1941-1968; CLR 18; DLB 2, 102,
    173; MAICYA; MTCW; SATA 67

Salisbury, John
  See Caute, David

Salter, James 1925- .... **CLC 7, 52, 59**
  See also CA 73-76; DLB 130

Saltus, Edgar (Everton)
  1855-1921 .... **TCLC 8**
  See also CA 105

Saltykov, Mikhail Evgrafovich
  1826-1889 .... **NCLC 16**

Samarakis, Antonis 1919- .... **CLC 5**
  See also CA 25-28R; CAAS 16; CANR 36

Sanchez, Florencio 1875-1910..... **TCLC 37**
  See also CA 153; HW

Sanchez, Luis Rafael 1936-........ **CLC 23**
  See also CA 128; DLB 145; HW

Sanchez, Sonia
  1934- ...... **CLC 5; BLC; DAM MULT;**
                                    PC 9
  See also BW 2; CA 33-36R; CANR 24, 49;
    CLR 18; DLB 41; DLBD 8; MAICYA;
    MTCW; SATA 22

Sand, George
  1804-1876 .... **NCLC 2, 42, 57; DA;**
    DAB; DAC; DAM MST, NOV; WLC
  See also DLB 119

Sandburg, Carl (August)
  1878-1967 .... **CLC 1, 4, 10, 15, 35; DA;**
    DAB; DAC; DAM MST, POET; PC 2;
                                    WLC
  See also CA 5-8R; 25-28R; CANR 35;
    CDALB 1865-1917; DLB 17, 54;
    MAICYA; MTCW; SATA 8

Sandburg, Charles
  See Sandburg, Carl (August)

Sandburg, Charles A.
  See Sandburg, Carl (August)

Sanders, (James) Ed(ward) 1939- ... **CLC 53**
  See also CA 13-16R; CAAS 21; CANR 13,
    44; DLB 16

Sanders, Lawrence
  1920- .... **CLC 41; DAM POP**
  See also BEST 89:4; CA 81-84; CANR 33;
    MTCW

Sanders, Noah
  See Blount, Roy (Alton), Jr.

Sanders, Winston P.
  See Anderson, Poul (William)

Sandoz, Mari(e Susette)
  1896-1966 .... **CLC 28**
  See also CA 1-4R; 25-28R; CANR 17;
    DLB 9; MTCW; SATA 5

Saner, Reg(inald Anthony) 1931- .... **CLC 9**
  See also CA 65-68

Sannazaro, Jacopo 1456(?)-1530...... **LC 8**

Sansom, William
  1912-1976 ...... **CLC 2, 6; DAM NOV;**
                                    SSC 21
  See also CA 5-8R; 65-68; CANR 42;
    DLB 139; MTCW

Santayana, George 1863-1952..... **TCLC 40**
  See also CA 115; DLB 54, 71; DLBD 13

Santiago, Danny .... **CLC 33**
  See also James, Daniel (Lewis)
  See also DLB 122

Santmyer, Helen Hoover
  1895-1986 .... **CLC 33**
  See also CA 1-4R; 118; CANR 15, 33;
    DLBY 84; MTCW

Santoka, Taneda 1882-1940....... **TCLC 72**

Santos, Bienvenido N(uqui)
  1911-1996 ...... **CLC 22; DAM MULT**
  See also CA 101; 151; CANR 19, 46

Sapper .... **TCLC 44**
  See also McNeile, Herman Cyril

Sapphire 1950- .... **CLC 99**

Sappho
  fl. 6th cent. B.C.- .... **CMLC 3;**
                            DAM POET; PC 5
  See also DLB 176

Sarduy, Severo 1937-1993 .... **CLC 6, 97**
  See also CA 89-92; 142; CANR 58;
    DLB 113; HW

Sargeson, Frank 1903-1982 .... **CLC 31**
  See also CA 25-28R; 106; CANR 38

Sarmiento, Felix Ruben Garcia
  See Dario, Ruben

Saroyan, William
  1908-1981 ..... **CLC 1, 8, 10, 29, 34, 56;**
    DA; DAB; DAC; DAM DRAM, MST,
                        NOV; SSC 21; WLC
  See also CA 5-8R; 103; CANR 30; DLB 7,
    9, 86; DLBY 81; MTCW; SATA 23;
    SATA-Obit 24

Sarraute, Nathalie
  1900- .... **CLC 1, 2, 4, 8, 10, 31, 80**
  See also CA 9-12R; CANR 23; DLB 83;
    MTCW

Sarton, (Eleanor) May
  1912-1995 .... **CLC 4, 14, 49, 91;**
                                 DAM POET
  See also CA 1-4R; 149; CANR 1, 34, 55;
    DLB 48; DLBY 81; INT CANR-34;
    MTCW; SATA 36; SATA-Obit 86

Search, Alexander
　　See Pessoa, Fernando (Antonio Nogueira)

Sebastian, Lee
　　See Silverberg, Robert

Sebastian Owl
　　See Thompson, Hunter S(tockton)

Sebestyen, Ouida 1924- . . . . **CLC 30**
　　See also AAYA 8; CA 107; CANR 40;
　　CLR 17; JRDA; MAICYA; SAAS 10;
　　SATA 39

Secundus, H. Scriblerus
　　See Fielding, Henry

Sedges, John
　　See Buck, Pearl S(ydenstricker)

Sedgwick, Catharine Maria
　　　　1789-1867 . . . . **NCLC 19**
　　See also DLB 1, 74

Seelye, John 1931- . . . . **CLC 7**

Seferiades, Giorgos Stylianou 1900-1971
　　See Seferis, George
　　See also CA 5-8R; 33-36R; CANR 5, 36;
　　MTCW

Seferis, George . . . . **CLC 5, 11**
　　See also Seferiades, Giorgos Stylianou

Segal, Erich (Wolf)
　　　　1937- . . . . **CLC 3, 10; DAM POP**
　　See also BEST 89:1; CA 25-28R; CANR 20,
　　36; DLBY 86; INT CANR-20; MTCW

Seger, Bob 1945- . . . . **CLC 35**

Seghers, Anna . . . . **CLC 7**
　　See also Radvanyi, Netty
　　See also DLB 69

Seidel, Frederick (Lewis) 1936- . . . . . **CLC 18**
　　See also CA 13-16R; CANR 8; DLBY 84

Seifert, Jaroslav
　　　　1901-1986 . . . . **CLC 34, 44, 93**
　　See also CA 127; MTCW

Sei Shonagon c. 966-1017(?) . . . . . . **CMLC 6**

Selby, Hubert, Jr.
　　　　1928- . . . . **CLC 1, 2, 4, 8; SSC 20**
　　See also CA 13-16R; CANR 33; DLB 2

Selzer, Richard 1928- . . . . **CLC 74**
　　See also CA 65-68; CANR 14

Sembene, Ousmane
　　See Ousmane, Sembene

Senancour, Etienne Pivert de
　　　　1770-1846 . . . . **NCLC 16**
　　See also DLB 119

Sender, Ramon (Jose)
　　　　1902-1982 . . **CLC 8; DAM MULT; HLC**
　　See also CA 5-8R; 105; CANR 8; HW;
　　MTCW

Seneca, Lucius Annaeus
　　　　4B.C.-65 . . . . . . **CMLC 6; DAM DRAM;
　　　　　　　　　　　　　　　　　　　DC 5**

Senghor, Leopold Sedar
　　　　1906- . . . . . **CLC 54; BLC; DAM MULT,
　　　　　　　　　　　　　　　　　　　POET**
　　See also BW 2; CA 116; 125; CANR 47;
　　MTCW

Serling, (Edward) Rod(man)
　　　　1924-1975 . . . . **CLC 30**
　　See also AAYA 14; AITN 1; CA 65-68;
　　57-60; DLB 26

Serna, Ramon Gomez de la
　　See Gomez de la Serna, Ramon

Serpieres
　　See Guillevic, (Eugene)

Service, Robert
　　See Service, Robert W(illiam)
　　See also DAB; DLB 92

Service, Robert W(illiam)
　　　　1874(?)-1958 . . . . . . **TCLC 15; DA; DAC;
　　　　　　　　　　　　　　DAM MST, POET; WLC**
　　See also Service, Robert
　　See also CA 115; 140; SATA 20

Seth, Vikram
　　　　1952- . . . . **CLC 43, 90; DAM MULT**
　　See also CA 121; 127; CANR 50; DLB 120;
　　INT 127

Seton, Cynthia Propper
　　　　1926-1982 . . . . **CLC 27**
　　See also CA 5-8R; 108; CANR 7

Seton, Ernest (Evan) Thompson
　　　　1860-1946 . . . . **TCLC 31**
　　See also CA 109; DLB 92; DLBD 13;
　　JRDA; SATA 18

Seton-Thompson, Ernest
　　See Seton, Ernest (Evan) Thompson

Settle, Mary Lee 1918- . . . . **CLC 19, 61**
　　See also CA 89-92; CAAS 1; CANR 44;
　　DLB 6; INT 89-92

Seuphor, Michel
　　See Arp, Jean

**Sevigne, Marie (de Rabutin-Chantal) Marquise
　　de** 1626-1696 . . . . **LC 11**

Sewall, Samuel 1652-1730 . . . . **LC 38**
　　See also DLB 24

Sexton, Anne (Harvey)
　　　　1928-1974 . . . . **CLC 2, 4, 6, 8, 10, 15, 53;
　　　　　　　DA; DAB; DAC; DAM MST, POET;
　　　　　　　　　　　　　　　　　　　PC 2; WLC**
　　See also CA 1-4R; 53-56; CABS 2;
　　CANR 3, 36; CDALB 1941-1968; DLB 5,
　　169; MTCW; SATA 10

Shaara, Michael (Joseph, Jr.)
　　　　1929-1988 . . . . **CLC 15; DAM POP**
　　See also AITN 1; CA 102; 125; CANR 52;
　　DLBY 83

Shackleton, C. C.
　　See Aldiss, Brian W(ilson)

Shacochis, Bob . . . . **CLC 39**
　　See also Shacochis, Robert G.

Shacochis, Robert G. 1951-
　　See Shacochis, Bob
　　See also CA 119; 124; INT 124

Shaffer, Anthony (Joshua)
　　　　1926- . . . . **CLC 19; DAM DRAM**
　　See also CA 110; 116; DLB 13

Shaffer, Peter (Levin)
　　　　1926- . . . . . . **CLC 5, 14, 18, 37, 60; DAB;
　　　　　　　　　　　　DAM DRAM, MST; DC 7**
　　See also CA 25-28R; CANR 25, 47;
　　CDBLB 1960 to Present; DLB 13;
　　MTCW

Shakey, Bernard
　　See Young, Neil

Shalamov, Varlam (Tikhonovich)
　　　　1907(?)-1982 . . . . **CLC 18**
　　See also CA 129; 105

Shamlu, Ahmad 1925- . . . . **CLC 10**

Shammas, Anton 1951- . . . . **CLC 55**

Shange, Ntozake
　　　　1948- . . . . **CLC 8, 25, 38, 74; BLC;
　　　　　　　　　　　　DAM DRAM, MULT; DC 3**
　　See also AAYA 9; BW 2; CA 85-88;
　　CABS 3; CANR 27, 48; DLB 38; MTCW

Shanley, John Patrick 1950- . . . . **CLC 75**
　　See also CA 128; 133

Shapcott, Thomas W(illiam) 1935- . . **CLC 38**
　　See also CA 69-72; CANR 49

Shapiro, Jane . . . . **CLC 76**

Shapiro, Karl (Jay) 1913- . . **CLC 4, 8, 15, 53**
　　See also CA 1-4R; CAAS 6; CANR 1, 36;
　　DLB 48; MTCW

Sharp, William 1855-1905 . . . . **TCLC 39**
　　See also DLB 156

Sharpe, Thomas Ridley 1928-
　　See Sharpe, Tom
　　See also CA 114; 122; INT 122

Sharpe, Tom . . . . **CLC 36**
　　See also Sharpe, Thomas Ridley
　　See also DLB 14

Shaw, Bernard . . . . **TCLC 45**
　　See also Shaw, George Bernard
　　See also BW 1

Shaw, G. Bernard
　　See Shaw, George Bernard

Shaw, George Bernard
　　　　1856-1950 . . . **TCLC 3, 9, 21; DA; DAB;
　　　　　　　　　　DAC; DAM DRAM, MST; WLC**
　　See also Shaw, Bernard
　　See also CA 104; 128; CDBLB 1914-1945;
　　DLB 10, 57; MTCW

Shaw, Henry Wheeler
　　　　1818-1885 . . . . **NCLC 15**
　　See also DLB 11

Shaw, Irwin
　　　　1913-1984 . . . . **CLC 7, 23, 34;
　　　　　　　　　　　　　　　DAM DRAM, POP**
　　See also AITN 1; CA 13-16R; 112;
　　CANR 21; CDALB 1941-1968; DLB 6,
　　102; DLBY 84; MTCW

Shaw, Robert 1927-1978 . . . . **CLC 5**
　　See also AITN 1; CA 1-4R; 81-84;
　　CANR 4; DLB 13, 14

Shaw, T. E.
　　See Lawrence, T(homas) E(dward)

Shawn, Wallace 1943- . . . . **CLC 41**
　　See also CA 112

Shea, Lisa 1953- . . . . **CLC 86**
　　See also CA 147

Sheed, Wilfrid (John Joseph)
　　　　1930- . . . . **CLC 2, 4, 10, 53**
　　See also CA 65-68; CANR 30; DLB 6;
　　MTCW

Sheldon, Alice Hastings Bradley
　　　　1915(?)-1987
　　See Tiptree, James, Jr.
　　See also CA 108; 122; CANR 34; INT 108;
　　MTCW

Sheldon, John
　　See Bloch, Robert (Albert)

Shelley, Mary Wollstonecraft (Godwin)
      1797-1851 .... **NCLC 14, 59; DA; DAB;**
            DAC; DAM MST, NOV; WLC
      See also AAYA 20; CDBLB 1789-1832;
      DLB 110, 116, 159, 178; SATA 29

Shelley, Percy Bysshe
      1792-1822 ...... **NCLC 18; DA; DAB;**
            DAC; DAM MST, POET; PC 14; WLC
      See also CDBLB 1789-1832; DLB 96, 110,
      158

Shepard, Jim   1956-............... **CLC 36**
      See also CA 137; SATA 90

Shepard, Lucius   1947-............ **CLC 34**
      See also CA 128; 141

Shepard, Sam
      1943- .... **CLC 4, 6, 17, 34, 41, 44;**
            DAM DRAM; DC 5
      See also AAYA 1; CA 69-72; CABS 3;
      CANR 22; DLB 7; MTCW

Shepherd, Michael
      See Ludlum, Robert

Sherburne, Zoa (Morin)   1912-...... **CLC 30**
      See also AAYA 13; CA 1-4R; CANR 3, 37;
      MAICYA; SAAS 18; SATA 3

Sheridan, Frances   1724-1766........ **LC 7**
      See also DLB 39, 84

Sheridan, Richard Brinsley
      1751-1816 .... **NCLC 5; DA; DAB;**
            DAC; DAM DRAM, MST; DC 1; WLC
      See also CDBLB 1660-1789; DLB 89

Sherman, Jonathan Marc........... **CLC 55**

Sherman, Martin   1941(?)-......... **CLC 19**
      See also CA 116; 123

Sherwin, Judith Johnson   1936-... **CLC 7, 15**
      See also CA 25-28R; CANR 34

Sherwood, Frances   1940-......... **CLC 81**
      See also CA 146

Sherwood, Robert E(mmet)
      1896-1955 ...... **TCLC 3; DAM DRAM**
      See also CA 104; 153; DLB 7, 26

Shestov, Lev   1866-1938.......... **TCLC 56**

Shevchenko, Taras   1814-1861 .... **NCLC 54**

Shiel, M(atthew) P(hipps)
      1865-1947 .... **TCLC 8**
      See also CA 106; DLB 153

Shields, Carol   1935-......... **CLC 91; DAC**
      See also CA 81-84; CANR 51

Shields, David   1956-............. **CLC 97**
      See also CA 124; CANR 48

Shiga, Naoya   1883-1971... **CLC 33; SSC 23**
      See also CA 101; 33-36R; DLB 180

Shilts, Randy   1951-1994 .... **CLC 85**
      See also AAYA 19; CA 115; 127; 144;
      CANR 45; INT 127

Shimazaki, Haruki   1872-1943
      See Shimazaki Toson
      See also CA 105; 134

Shimazaki Toson   1872-1943 .... **TCLC 5**
      See also Shimazaki, Haruki
      See also DLB 180

Sholokhov, Mikhail (Aleksandrovich)
      1905-1984 .... **CLC 7, 15**
      See also CA 101; 112; MTCW;
      SATA-Obit 36

Shone, Patric
      See Hanley, James

Shreve, Susan Richards   1939-...... **CLC 23**
      See also CA 49-52; CAAS 5; CANR 5, 38;
      MAICYA; SATA 46; SATA-Brief 41

Shue, Larry
      1946-1985 ...... **CLC 52; DAM DRAM**
      See also CA 145; 117

Shu-Jen, Chou   1881-1936
      See Lu Hsun
      See also CA 104

Shulman, Alix Kates   1932- ...... **CLC 2, 10**
      See also CA 29-32R; CANR 43; SATA 7

Shuster, Joe   1914- .... **CLC 21**

Shute, Nevil...................... **CLC 30**
      See also Norway, Nevil Shute

Shuttle, Penelope (Diane)   1947- ..... **CLC 7**
      See also CA 93-96; CANR 39; DLB 14, 40

Sidney, Mary   1561-1621 .... **LC 19, 39**

Sidney, Sir Philip
      1554-1586 ...... **LC 19, 39; DA; DAB;**
            DAC; DAM MST, POET
      See also CDBLB Before 1660; DLB 167

Siegel, Jerome   1914-1996 .... **CLC 21**
      See also CA 116; 151

Siegel, Jerry
      See Siegel, Jerome

Sienkiewicz, Henryk (Adam Alexander Pius)
      1846-1916 .... **TCLC 3**
      See also CA 104; 134

Sierra, Gregorio Martinez
      See Martinez Sierra, Gregorio

Sierra, Maria (de la O'LeJarraga) Martinez
      See Martinez Sierra, Maria (de la
      O'LeJarraga)

Sigal, Clancy   1926-............... **CLC 7**
      See also CA 1-4R

Sigourney, Lydia Howard (Huntley)
      1791-1865 .... **NCLC 21**
      See also DLB 1, 42, 73

Siguenza y Gongora, Carlos de
      1645-1700 .... **LC 8**

Sigurjonsson, Johann   1880-1919... **TCLC 27**

Sikelianos, Angelos   1884-1951 .... **TCLC 39**

Silkin, Jon   1930- .... **CLC 2, 6, 43**
      See also CA 5-8R; CAAS 5; DLB 27

Silko, Leslie (Marmon)
      1948- .... **CLC 23, 74; DA; DAC;**
            DAM MST, MULT, POP
      See also AAYA 14; CA 115; 122;
      CANR 45; DLB 143, 175; NNAL; YABC

Sillanpaa, Frans Eemil   1888-1964... **CLC 19**
      See also CA 129; 93-96; MTCW

Sillitoe, Alan
      1928- .... **CLC 1, 3, 6, 10, 19, 57**
      See also AITN 1; CA 9-12R; CAAS 2;
      CANR 8, 26, 55; CDBLB 1960 to
      Present; DLB 14, 139; MTCW; SATA 61

Silone, Ignazio   1900-1978 .... **CLC 4**
      See also CA 25-28; 81-84; CANR 34;
      CAP 2; MTCW

Silver, Joan Micklin   1935-........ **CLC 20**
      See also CA 114; 121; INT 121

Silver, Nicholas
      See Faust, Frederick (Schiller)

Silverberg, Robert
      1935- .... **CLC 7; DAM POP**
      See also CA 1-4R; CAAS 3; CANR 1, 20,
      36; DLB 8; INT CANR-20; MAICYA;
      MTCW; SATA 13, 91

Silverstein, Alvin   1933-........... **CLC 17**
      See also CA 49-52; CANR 2; CLR 25;
      JRDA; MAICYA; SATA 8, 69

Silverstein, Virginia B(arbara Opshelor)
      1937-......................... **CLC 17**
      See also CA 49-52; CANR 2; CLR 25;
      JRDA; MAICYA; SATA 8, 69

Sim, Georges
      See Simenon, Georges (Jacques Christian)

Simak, Clifford D(onald)
      1904-1988 .... **CLC 1, 55**
      See also CA 1-4R; 125; CANR 1, 35;
      DLB 8; MTCW; SATA-Obit 56

Simenon, Georges (Jacques Christian)
      1903-1989 .... **CLC 1, 2, 3, 8, 18, 47;**
            DAM POP
      See also CA 85-88; 129; CANR 35;
      DLB 72; DLBY 89; MTCW

Simic, Charles
      1938- .... **CLC 6, 9, 22, 49, 68;**
            DAM POET
      See also CA 29-32R; CAAS 4; CANR 12,
      33, 52; DLB 105

Simmel, Georg   1858-1918 .... **TCLC 64**
      See also CA 157

Simmons, Charles (Paul)   1924-..... **CLC 57**
      See also CA 89-92; INT 89-92

Simmons, Dan   1948-... **CLC 44; DAM POP**
      See also AAYA 16; CA 138; CANR 53

Simmons, James (Stewart Alexander)
      1933-....................... **CLC 43**
      See also CA 105; CAAS 21; DLB 40

Simms, William Gilmore
      1806-1870 .... **NCLC 3**
      See also DLB 3, 30, 59, 73

Simon, Carly   1945-............... **CLC 26**
      See also CA 105

Simon, Claude
      1913- .... **CLC 4, 9, 15, 39; DAM NOV**
      See also CA 89-92; CANR 33; DLB 83;
      MTCW

Simon, (Marvin) Neil
      1927- .... **CLC 6, 11, 31, 39, 70;**
            DAM DRAM
      See also AITN 1; CA 21-24R; CANR 26,
      54; DLB 7; MTCW

Simon, Paul (Frederick)   1941(?)- ... **CLC 17**
      See also CA 116; 153

Simonon, Paul   1956(?)- .... **CLC 30**

Simpson, Harriette
      See Arnow, Harriette (Louisa) Simpson

Simpson, Louis (Aston Marantz)
      1923- .... **CLC 4, 7, 9, 32; DAM POET**
      See also CA 1-4R; CAAS 4; CANR 1;
      DLB 5; MTCW

Simpson, Mona (Elizabeth)   1957-... **CLC 44**
      See also CA 122; 135

Simpson, N(orman) F(rederick)
 1919- .... **CLC 29**
 See also CA 13-16R; DLB 13

Sinclair, Andrew (Annandale)
 1935- .... **CLC 2, 14**
 See also CA 9-12R; CAAS 5; CANR 14, 38;
 DLB 14; MTCW

Sinclair, Emil
 See Hesse, Hermann

Sinclair, Iain 1943- .... **CLC 76**
 See also CA 132

Sinclair, Iain MacGregor
 See Sinclair, Iain

Sinclair, Irene
 See Griffith, D(avid Lewelyn) W(ark)

Sinclair, Mary Amelia St. Clair 1865(?)-1946
 See Sinclair, May
 See also CA 104

Sinclair, May.................. **TCLC 3, 11**
 See also Sinclair, Mary Amelia St. Clair
 See also DLB 36, 135

Sinclair, Roy
 See Griffith, D(avid Lewelyn) W(ark)

Sinclair, Upton (Beall)
 1878-1968 ...... **CLC 1, 11, 15, 63; DA;**
  DAB; DAC; DAM MST, NOV; WLC
 See also CA 5-8R; 25-28R; CANR 7;
  CDALB 1929-1941; DLB 9;
  INT CANR-7; MTCW; SATA 9

Singer, Isaac
 See Singer, Isaac Bashevis

Singer, Isaac Bashevis
 1904-1991 .... **CLC 1, 3, 6, 9, 11, 15, 23,**
  38, 69; DA; DAB; DAC; DAM MST,
  NOV; SSC 3; WLC
 See also AITN 1, 2; CA 1-4R; 134;
  CANR 1, 39; CDALB 1941-1968; CLR 1;
  DLB 6, 28, 52; DLBY 91; JRDA;
  MAICYA; MTCW; SATA 3, 27;
  SATA-Obit 68

Singer, Israel Joshua 1893-1944 ... **TCLC 33**

Singh, Khushwant 1915-.......... **CLC 11**
 See also CA 9-12R; CAAS 9; CANR 6

Sinjohn, John
 See Galsworthy, John

Sinyavsky, Andrei (Donatevich)
 1925- .... **CLC 8**
 See also CA 85-88

Sirin, V.
 See Nabokov, Vladimir (Vladimirovich)

Sissman, L(ouis) E(dward)
 1928-1976 .... **CLC 9, 18**
 See also CA 21-24R; 65-68; CANR 13;
  DLB 5

Sisson, C(harles) H(ubert) 1914-..... **CLC 8**
 See also CA 1-4R; CAAS 3; CANR 3, 48;
  DLB 27

Sitwell, Dame Edith
 1887-1964 .... **CLC 2, 9, 67;**
  DAM POET; PC 3
 See also CA 9-12R; CANR 35;
  CDBLB 1945-1960; DLB 20; MTCW

Sjoewall, Maj 1935-.............. **CLC 7**
 See also CA 65-68

Sjowall, Maj
 See Sjoewall, Maj

Skelton, Robin 1925- .... **CLC 13**
 See also AITN 2; CA 5-8R; CAAS 5;
  CANR 28; DLB 27, 53

Skolimowski, Jerzy 1938- .... **CLC 20**
 See also CA 128

Skram, Amalie (Bertha)
 1847-1905 .... **TCLC 25**

Skvorecky, Josef (Vaclav)
 1924- .... **CLC 15, 39, 69; DAC;**
  DAM NOV
 See also CA 61-64; CAAS 1; CANR 10, 34;
  MTCW

Slade, Bernard................. **CLC 11, 46**
 See also Newbound, Bernard Slade
 See also CAAS 9; DLB 53

Slaughter, Carolyn 1946-......... **CLC 56**
 See also CA 85-88

Slaughter, Frank G(ill) 1908- ...... **CLC 29**
 See also AITN 2; CA 5-8R; CANR 5;
  INT CANR-5

Slavitt, David R(ytman) 1935-.... **CLC 5, 14**
 See also CA 21-24R; CAAS 3; CANR 41;
  DLB 5, 6

Slesinger, Tess 1905-1945 .... **TCLC 10**
 See also CA 107; DLB 102

Slessor, Kenneth 1901-1971....... **CLC 14**
 See also CA 102; 89-92

Slowacki, Juliusz 1809-1849 ..... **NCLC 15**

Smart, Christopher
 1722-1771 ... **LC 3; DAM POET; PC 13**
 See also DLB 109

Smart, Elizabeth 1913-1986........ **CLC 54**
 See also CA 81-84; 118; DLB 88

Smiley, Jane (Graves)
 1949- .... **CLC 53, 76; DAM POP**
 See also CA 104; CANR 30, 50;
  INT CANR-30

Smith, A(rthur) J(ames) M(arshall)
 1902-1980 .... **CLC 15; DAC**
 See also CA 1-4R; 102; CANR 4; DLB 88

Smith, Adam 1723-1790............ **LC 36**
 See also DLB 104

Smith, Alexander 1829-1867 ..... **NCLC 59**
 See also DLB 32, 55

Smith, Anna Deavere 1950-........ **CLC 86**
 See also CA 133

Smith, Betty (Wehner) 1896-1972... **CLC 19**
 See also CA 5-8R; 33-36R; DLBY 82;
  SATA 6

Smith, Charlotte (Turner)
 1749-1806 .... **NCLC 23**
 See also DLB 39, 109

Smith, Clark Ashton 1893-1961 .... **CLC 43**
 See also CA 143

Smith, Dave................... **CLC 22, 42**
 See also Smith, David (Jeddie)
 See also CAAS 7; DLB 5

Smith, David (Jeddie) 1942-
 See Smith, Dave
 See also CA 49-52; CANR 1; DAM POET

Smith, Florence Margaret 1902-1971
 See Smith, Stevie
 See also CA 17-18; 29-32R; CANR 35;
  CAP 2; DAM POET; MTCW

Smith, Iain Crichton 1928- .... **CLC 64**
 See also CA 21-24R; DLB 40, 139

Smith, John 1580(?)-1631 .... **LC 9**

Smith, Johnston
 See Crane, Stephen (Townley)

Smith, Joseph, Jr. 1805-1844 .... **NCLC 53**

Smith, Lee 1944-.............. **CLC 25, 73**
 See also CA 114; 119; CANR 46; DLB 143;
  DLBY 83; INT 119

Smith, Martin
 See Smith, Martin Cruz

Smith, Martin Cruz
 1942- ..... **CLC 25; DAM MULT, POP**
 See also BEST 89:4; CA 85-88; CANR 6,
  23, 43; INT CANR-23; NNAL

Smith, Mary-Ann Tirone 1944-..... **CLC 39**
 See also CA 118; 136

Smith, Patti 1946- .... **CLC 12**
 See also CA 93-96

Smith, Pauline (Urmson)
 1882-1959 .... **TCLC 25**

Smith, Rosamond
 See Oates, Joyce Carol

Smith, Sheila Kaye
 See Kaye-Smith, Sheila

Smith, Stevie .... **CLC 3, 8, 25, 44; PC 12**
 See also Smith, Florence Margaret
 See also DLB 20

Smith, Wilbur (Addison) 1933-..... **CLC 33**
 See also CA 13-16R; CANR 7, 46; MTCW

Smith, William Jay 1918- .... **CLC 6**
 See also CA 5-8R; CANR 44; DLB 5;
  MAICYA; SAAS 22; SATA 2, 68

Smith, Woodrow Wilson
 See Kuttner, Henry

Smolenskin, Peretz 1842-1885.... **NCLC 30**

Smollett, Tobias (George) 1721-1771 .. **LC 2**
 See also CDBLB 1660-1789; DLB 39, 104

Snodgrass, W(illiam) D(e Witt)
 1926-............ **CLC 2, 6, 10, 18, 68;**
  DAM POET
 See also CA 1-4R; CANR 6, 36; DLB 5;
  MTCW

Snow, C(harles) P(ercy)
 1905-1980 .... **CLC 1, 4, 6, 9, 13, 19;**
  DAM NOV
 See also CA 5-8R; 101; CANR 28;
  CDBLB 1945-1960; DLB 15, 77; MTCW

Snow, Frances Compton
 See Adams, Henry (Brooks)

Snyder, Gary (Sherman)
 1930- .. **CLC 1, 2, 5, 9, 32; DAM POET**
 See also CA 17-20R; CANR 30; DLB 5, 16,
  165

Snyder, Zilpha Keatley 1927-...... **CLC 17**
 See also AAYA 15; CA 9-12R; CANR 38;
  CLR 31; JRDA; MAICYA; SAAS 2;
  SATA 1, 28, 75

Soares, Bernardo
 See Pessoa, Fernando (Antonio Nogueira)

Sobh, A.
See Shamlu, Ahmad

Sobol, Joshua. . . . . CLC 60

Soderberg, Hjalmar 1869-1941 . . . . TCLC 39

Sodergran, Edith (Irene)
See Soedergran, Edith (Irene)

Soedergran, Edith (Irene)
1892-1923 . . . . TCLC 31

Softly, Edgar
See Lovecraft, H(oward) P(hillips)

Softly, Edward
See Lovecraft, H(oward) P(hillips)

Sokolov, Raymond 1941- . . . . CLC 7
See also CA 85-88

Solo, Jay
See Ellison, Harlan (Jay)

Sologub, Fyodor . . . . TCLC 9
See also Teternikov, Fyodor Kuzmich

Solomons, Ikey Esquir
See Thackeray, William Makepeace

Solomos, Dionysios 1798-1857 . . . NCLC 15

Solwoska, Mara
See French, Marilyn

Solzhenitsyn, Aleksandr I(sayevich)
1918- . . . . . . CLC 1, 2, 4, 7, 9, 10, 18, 26,
34, 78; DA; DAB; DAC; DAM MST,
NOV; WLC
See also AITN 1; CA 69-72; CANR 40;
MTCW

Somers, Jane
See Lessing, Doris (May)

Somerville, Edith 1858-1949 . . . . . . TCLC 51
See also DLB 135

Somerville & Ross
See Martin, Violet Florence; Somerville,
Edith

Sommer, Scott 1951- . . . . CLC 25
See also CA 106

Sondheim, Stephen (Joshua)
1930- . . . . CLC 30, 39; DAM DRAM
See also AAYA 11; CA 103; CANR 47

Sontag, Susan
1933- . . . . CLC 1, 2, 10, 13, 31;
DAM POP
See also CA 17-20R; CANR 25, 51; DLB 2,
67; MTCW

Sophocles
496(?)B.C.-406(?)B.C. . . . . CMLC 2; DA;
DAB; DAC; DAM DRAM, MST; DC 1
See also DLB 176; YABC

Sordello 1189-1269 . . . . CMLC 15

Sorel, Julia
See Drexler, Rosalyn

Sorrentino, Gilbert
1929- . . . . CLC 3, 7, 14, 22, 40
See also CA 77-80; CANR 14, 33; DLB 5,
173; DLBY 80; INT CANR-14

Soto, Gary
1952- . . . . CLC 32, 80; DAM MULT;
HLC
See also AAYA 10; CA 119; 125;
CANR 50; CLR 38; DLB 82; HW;
INT 125; JRDA; SATA 80

Soupault, Philippe 1897-1990 . . . . . . CLC 68
See also CA 116; 147; 131

Souster, (Holmes) Raymond
1921- . . . CLC 5, 14; DAC; DAM POET
See also CA 13-16R; CAAS 14; CANR 13,
29, 53; DLB 88; SATA 63

Southern, Terry 1924(?)-1995 . . . . CLC 7
See also CA 1-4R; 150; CANR 1, 55;
DLB 2

Southey, Robert 1774-1843 . . . . NCLC 8
See also DLB 93, 107, 142; SATA 54

Southworth, Emma Dorothy Eliza Nevitte
1819-1899 . . . . NCLC 26

Souza, Ernest
See Scott, Evelyn

Soyinka, Wole
1934- . . . . CLC 3, 5, 14, 36, 44; BLC;
DA; DAB; DAC; DAM DRAM, MST,
MULT; DC 2; WLC
See also BW 2; CA 13-16R; CANR 27, 39;
DLB 125; MTCW

Spackman, W(illiam) M(ode)
1905-1990 . . . . CLC 46
See also CA 81-84; 132

Spacks, Barry (Bernard) 1931- . . . . . CLC 14
See also CA 154; CANR 33; DLB 105

Spanidou, Irini 1946- . . . . CLC 44

Spark, Muriel (Sarah)
1918- . . . . . CLC 2, 3, 5, 8, 13, 18, 40, 94;
DAB; DAC; DAM MST, NOV; SSC 10
See also CA 5-8R; CANR 12, 36;
CDBLB 1945-1960; DLB 15, 139;
INT CANR-12; MTCW

Spaulding, Douglas
See Bradbury, Ray (Douglas)

Spaulding, Leonard
See Bradbury, Ray (Douglas)

Spence, J. A. D.
See Eliot, T(homas) S(tearns)

Spencer, Elizabeth 1921- . . . . CLC 22
See also CA 13-16R; CANR 32; DLB 6;
MTCW; SATA 14

Spencer, Leonard G.
See Silverberg, Robert

Spencer, Scott 1945- . . . . CLC 30
See also CA 113; CANR 51; DLBY 86

Spender, Stephen (Harold)
1909-1995 . . . . . . CLC 1, 2, 5, 10, 41, 91;
DAM POET
See also CA 9-12R; 149; CANR 31, 54;
CDBLB 1945-1960; DLB 20; MTCW

Spengler, Oswald (Arnold Gottfried)
1880-1936 . . . . TCLC 25
See also CA 118

Spenser, Edmund
1552(?)-1599 . . . . . . LC 5, 39; DA; DAB;
DAC; DAM MST, POET; PC 8; WLC
See also CDBLB Before 1660; DLB 167

Spicer, Jack
1925-1965 . . . . CLC 8, 18, 72;
DAM POET
See also CA 85-88; DLB 5, 16

Spiegelman, Art 1948- . . . . CLC 76
See also AAYA 10; CA 125; CANR 41, 55

Spielberg, Peter 1929- . . . . CLC 6
See also CA 5-8R; CANR 4, 48; DLBY 81

Spielberg, Steven 1947- . . . . CLC 20
See also AAYA 8; CA 77-80; CANR 32;
SATA 32

Spillane, Frank Morrison 1918-
See Spillane, Mickey
See also CA 25-28R; CANR 28; MTCW;
SATA 66

Spillane, Mickey . . . . CLC 3, 13
See also Spillane, Frank Morrison

Spinoza, Benedictus de 1632-1677 . . . . LC 9

Spinrad, Norman (Richard) 1940- . . . CLC 46
See also CA 37-40R; CAAS 19; CANR 20;
DLB 8; INT CANR-20

Spitteler, Carl (Friedrich Georg)
1845-1924 . . . . TCLC 12
See also CA 109; DLB 129

Spivack, Kathleen (Romola Drucker)
1938- . . . . CLC 6
See also CA 49-52

Spoto, Donald 1941- . . . . CLC 39
See also CA 65-68; CANR 11, 57

Springsteen, Bruce (F.) 1949- . . . . . . CLC 17
See also CA 111

Spurling, Hilary 1940- . . . . CLC 34
See also CA 104; CANR 25, 52

Spyker, John Howland
See Elman, Richard

Squires, (James) Radcliffe
1917-1993 . . . . CLC 51
See also CA 1-4R; 140; CANR 6, 21

Srivastava, Dhanpat Rai 1880(?)-1936
See Premchand
See also CA 118

Stacy, Donald
See Pohl, Frederik

Stael, Germaine de
See Stael-Holstein, Anne Louise Germaine
Necker Baronn
See also DLB 119

Stael-Holstein, Anne Louise Germaine Necker
Baronn 1766-1817 . . . . NCLC 3
See also Stael, Germaine de

Stafford, Jean
1915-1979 . . . . CLC 4, 7, 19, 68; SSC 26
See also CA 1-4R; 85-88; CANR 3; DLB 2,
173; MTCW; SATA-Obit 22

Stafford, William (Edgar)
1914-1993 . . . CLC 4, 7, 29; DAM POET
See also CA 5-8R; 142; CAAS 3; CANR 5,
22; DLB 5; INT CANR-22

Stagnelius, Eric Johan
1793-1823 . . . . NCLC 61

Staines, Trevor
See Brunner, John (Kilian Houston)

Stairs, Gordon
See Austin, Mary (Hunter)

Stannard, Martin 1947- . . . . CLC 44
See also CA 142; DLB 155

Stanton, Maura 1946- . . . . CLC 9
See also CA 89-92; CANR 15; DLB 120

Stanton, Schuyler
See Baum, L(yman) Frank

Stapledon, (William) Olaf
1886-1950 . . . . **TCLC 22**
See also CA 111; DLB 15

Starbuck, George (Edwin)
1931-1996 . . . . **CLC 53; DAM POET**
See also CA 21-24R; 153; CANR 23

Stark, Richard
See Westlake, Donald E(dwin)

Staunton, Schuyler
See Baum, L(yman) Frank

Stead, Christina (Ellen)
1902-1983 . . . . **CLC 2, 5, 8, 32, 80**
See also CA 13-16R; 109; CANR 33, 40;
MTCW

Stead, William Thomas
1849-1912 . . . . **TCLC 48**

Steele, Richard 1672-1729 . . . . **LC 18**
See also CDBLB 1660-1789; DLB 84, 101

Steele, Timothy (Reid) 1948- . . . . **CLC 45**
See also CA 93-96; CANR 16, 50; DLB 120

Steffens, (Joseph) Lincoln
1866-1936 . . . . **TCLC 20**
See also CA 117

Stegner, Wallace (Earle)
1909-1993 . . . **CLC 9, 49, 81; DAM NOV**
See also AITN 1; BEST 90:3; CA 1-4R;
141; CAAS 9; CANR 1, 21, 46; DLB 9;
DLBY 93; MTCW

Stein, Gertrude
1874-1946 . . . . . . **TCLC 1, 6, 28, 48; DA;**
DAB; DAC; DAM MST, NOV, POET;
PC 18; WLC
See also CA 104; 132; CDALB 1917-1929;
DLB 4, 54, 86; MTCW

Steinbeck, John (Ernst)
1902-1968 . . . . . . **CLC 1, 5, 9, 13, 21, 34,**
45, 75; DA; DAB; DAC; DAM DRAM,
MST, NOV; SSC 11; WLC
See also AAYA 12; CA 1-4R; 25-28R;
CANR 1, 35; CDALB 1929-1941; DLB 7,
9; DLBD 2; MTCW; SATA 9

Steinem, Gloria 1934- . . . . **CLC 63**
See also CA 53-56; CANR 28, 51; MTCW

Steiner, George
1929- . . . . **CLC 24; DAM NOV**
See also CA 73-76; CANR 31; DLB 67;
MTCW; SATA 62

Steiner, K. Leslie
See Delany, Samuel R(ay, Jr.)

Steiner, Rudolf 1861-1925 . . . . **TCLC 13**
See also CA 107

Stendhal
1783-1842 . . . . **NCLC 23, 46; DA; DAB;**
DAC; DAM MST, NOV; WLC
See also DLB 119

Stephen, Leslie 1832-1904 . . . . **TCLC 23**
See also CA 123; DLB 57, 144

Stephen, Sir Leslie
See Stephen, Leslie

Stephen, Virginia
See Woolf, (Adeline) Virginia

Stephens, James 1882(?)-1950 . . . . . . **TCLC 4**
See also CA 104; DLB 19, 153, 162

Stephens, Reed
See Donaldson, Stephen R.

Steptoe, Lydia
See Barnes, Djuna

Sterchi, Beat 1949- . . . . **CLC 65**

Sterling, Brett
See Bradbury, Ray (Douglas); Hamilton,
Edmond

Sterling, Bruce 1954- . . . . **CLC 72**
See also CA 119; CANR 44

Sterling, George 1869-1926 . . . . **TCLC 20**
See also CA 117; DLB 54

Stern, Gerald 1925- . . . . **CLC 40, 100**
See also CA 81-84; CANR 28; DLB 105

Stern, Richard (Gustave) 1928- . . . **CLC 4, 39**
See also CA 1-4R; CANR 1, 25, 52;
DLBY 87; INT CANR-25

Sternberg, Josef von 1894-1969 . . . . . **CLC 20**
See also CA 81-84

Sterne, Laurence
1713-1768 . . . . . . **LC 2; DA; DAB; DAC;**
DAM MST, NOV; WLC
See also CDBLB 1660-1789; DLB 39

Sternheim, (William Adolf) Carl
1878-1942 . . . . **TCLC 8**
See also CA 105; DLB 56, 118

Stevens, Mark 1951- . . . . **CLC 34**
See also CA 122

Stevens, Wallace
1879-1955 . . . . **TCLC 3, 12, 45; DA;**
DAB; DAC; DAM MST, POET; PC 6;
WLC
See also CA 104; 124; CDALB 1929-1941;
DLB 54; MTCW

Stevenson, Anne (Katharine)
1933- . . . . **CLC 7, 33**
See also CA 17-20R; CAAS 9; CANR 9, 33;
DLB 40; MTCW

Stevenson, Robert Louis (Balfour)
1850-1894 . . . . . **NCLC 5, 14; DA; DAB;**
DAC; DAM MST, NOV; SSC 11; WLC
See also CDBLB 1890-1914; CLR 10, 11;
DLB 18, 57, 141, 156, 174; DLBD 13;
JRDA; MAICYA; 2

Stewart, J(ohn) I(nnes) M(ackintosh)
1906-1994 . . . . **CLC 7, 14, 32**
See also CA 85-88; 147; CAAS 3;
CANR 47; MTCW

Stewart, Mary (Florence Elinor)
1916- . . . . **CLC 7, 35; DAB**
See also CA 1-4R; CANR 1; SATA 12

Stewart, Mary Rainbow
See Stewart, Mary (Florence Elinor)

Stifle, June
See Campbell, Maria

Stifter, Adalbert 1805-1868 . . . . . . **NCLC 41**
See also DLB 133

Still, James 1906- . . . . **CLC 49**
See also CA 65-68; CAAS 17; CANR 10,
26; DLB 9; SATA 29

Sting
See Sumner, Gordon Matthew

Stirling, Arthur
See Sinclair, Upton (Beall)

Stitt, Milan 1941- . . . . **CLC 29**
See also CA 69-72

Stockton, Francis Richard 1834-1902
See Stockton, Frank R.
See also CA 108; 137; MAICYA; SATA 44

Stockton, Frank R. . . . . **TCLC 47**
See also Stockton, Francis Richard
See also DLB 42, 74; DLBD 13;
SATA-Brief 32

Stoddard, Charles
See Kuttner, Henry

Stoker, Abraham 1847-1912
See Stoker, Bram
See also CA 105; DA; DAC; DAM MST,
NOV; SATA 29

Stoker, Bram
1847-1912 . . . . **TCLC 8; DAB; WLC**
See also Stoker, Abraham
See also CA 150; CDBLB 1890-1914;
DLB 36, 70, 178

Stolz, Mary (Slattery) 1920- . . . . **CLC 12**
See also AAYA 8; AITN 1; CA 5-8R;
CANR 13, 41; JRDA; MAICYA;
SAAS 3; SATA 10, 71

Stone, Irving
1903-1989 . . . . **CLC 7; DAM POP**
See also AITN 1; CA 1-4R; 129; CAAS 3;
CANR 1, 23; INT CANR-23; MTCW;
SATA 3; SATA-Obit 64

Stone, Oliver (William) 1946- . . . . . . **CLC 73**
See also AAYA 15; CA 110; CANR 55

Stone, Robert (Anthony)
1937- . . . . **CLC 5, 23, 42**
See also CA 85-88; CANR 23; DLB 152;
INT CANR-23; MTCW

Stone, Zachary
See Follett, Ken(neth Martin)

Stoppard, Tom
1937- . . . . . . **CLC 1, 3, 4, 5, 8, 15, 29, 34,**
63, 91; DA; DAB; DAC; DAM DRAM,
MST; DC 6; WLC
See also CA 81-84; CANR 39;
CDBLB 1960 to Present; DLB 13;
DLBY 85; MTCW

Storey, David (Malcolm)
1933- . . . . . . **CLC 2, 4, 5, 8; DAM DRAM**
See also CA 81-84; CANR 36; DLB 13, 14;
MTCW

Storm, Hyemeyohsts
1935- . . . . **CLC 3; DAM MULT**
See also CA 81-84; CANR 45; NNAL

Storm, (Hans) Theodor (Woldsen)
1817-1888 . . . . **NCLC 1**

Storni, Alfonsina
1892-1938 . . . . . **TCLC 5; DAM MULT;**
HLC
See also CA 104; 131; HW

Stoughton, William 1631-1701 . . . . **LC 38**
See also DLB 24

Stout, Rex (Todhunter) 1886-1975 . . . **CLC 3**
See also AITN 2; CA 61-64

Stow, (Julian) Randolph 1935- . . **CLC 23, 48**
See also CA 13-16R; CANR 33; MTCW

Stowe, Harriet (Elizabeth) Beecher
1811-1896 . . . . . **NCLC 3, 50; DA; DAB;**
DAC; DAM MST, NOV; WLC
See also CDALB 1865-1917; DLB 1, 12, 42,
74; JRDA; MAICYA; 1

Strachey, (Giles) Lytton
1880-1932 . . . . **TCLC 12**
See also CA 110; DLB 149; DLBD 10

Strand, Mark
1934- . . **CLC 6, 18, 41, 71; DAM POET**
See also CA 21-24R; CANR 40; DLB 5;
SATA 41

Straub, Peter (Francis)
1943- . . . . **CLC 28; DAM POP**
See also BEST 89:1; CA 85-88; CANR 28;
DLBY 84; MTCW

Strauss, Botho 1944- . . . . **CLC 22**
See also CA 157; DLB 124

Streatfeild, (Mary) Noel
1895(?)-1986 . . . . **CLC 21**
See also CA 81-84; 120; CANR 31;
CLR 17; DLB 160; MAICYA; SATA 20;
SATA-Obit 48

Stribling, T(homas) S(igismund)
1881-1965 . . . . **CLC 23**
See also CA 107; DLB 9

Strindberg, (Johan) August
1849-1912 . . . . . . **TCLC 1, 8, 21, 47; DA;**
DAB; DAC; DAM DRAM, MST; WLC
See also CA 104; 135

Stringer, Arthur 1874-1950 . . . . . . **TCLC 37**
See also DLB 92

Stringer, David
See Roberts, Keith (John Kingston)

Stroheim, Erich von 1885-1957 . . . . **TCLC 71**

Strugatskii, Arkadii (Natanovich)
1925-1991 . . . . **CLC 27**
See also CA 106; 135

Strugatskii, Boris (Natanovich)
1933- . . . . **CLC 27**
See also CA 106

Strummer, Joe 1953(?)- . . . . **CLC 30**

Stuart, Don A.
See Campbell, John W(ood, Jr.)

Stuart, Ian
See MacLean, Alistair (Stuart)

Stuart, Jesse (Hilton)
1906-1984 . . . . **CLC 1, 8, 11, 14, 34**
See also CA 5-8R; 112; CANR 31; DLB 9,
48, 102; DLBY 84; SATA 2;
SATA-Obit 36

Sturgeon, Theodore (Hamilton)
1918-1985 . . . . **CLC 22, 39**
See also Queen, Ellery
See also CA 81-84; 116; CANR 32; DLB 8;
DLBY 85; MTCW

Sturges, Preston 1898-1959 . . . . . . **TCLC 48**
See also CA 114; 149; DLB 26

Styron, William
1925- . . . . **CLC 1, 3, 5, 11, 15, 60;**
DAM NOV, POP; SSC 25
See also BEST 90:4; CA 5-8R; CANR 6, 33;
CDALB 1968-1988; DLB 2, 143;
DLBY 80; INT CANR-6; MTCW

Suarez Lynch, B.
See Bioy Casares, Adolfo; Borges, Jorge
Luis

Su Chien 1884-1918
See Su Man-shu
See also CA 123

Suckow, Ruth 1892-1960 . . . . **SSC 18**
See also CA 113; DLB 9, 102

Sudermann, Hermann 1857-1928 . . **TCLC 15**
See also CA 107; DLB 118

Sue, Eugene 1804-1857 . . . . **NCLC 1**
See also DLB 119

Sueskind, Patrick 1949- . . . . **CLC 44**
See also Suskind, Patrick

Sukenick, Ronald 1932- . . . . . **CLC 3, 4, 6, 48**
See also CA 25-28R; CAAS 8; CANR 32;
DLB 173; DLBY 81

Suknaski, Andrew 1942- . . . . **CLC 19**
See also CA 101; DLB 53

Sullivan, Vernon
See Vian, Boris

Sully Prudhomme 1839-1907 . . . . . **TCLC 31**

Su Man-shu . . . . **TCLC 24**
See also Su Chien

Summerforest, Ivy B.
See Kirkup, James

Summers, Andrew James 1942- . . . . . **CLC 26**

Summers, Andy
See Summers, Andrew James

Summers, Hollis (Spurgeon, Jr.)
1916- . . . . **CLC 10**
See also CA 5-8R; CANR 3; DLB 6

Summers, (Alphonsus Joseph-Mary Augustus)
Montague 1880-1948 . . . . **TCLC 16**
See also CA 118

Sumner, Gordon Matthew 1951- . . . . **CLC 26**

Surtees, Robert Smith
1803-1864 . . . . **NCLC 14**
See also DLB 21

Susann, Jacqueline 1921-1974 . . . . . . **CLC 3**
See also AITN 1; CA 65-68; 53-56; MTCW

Su Shih 1036-1101 . . . . **CMLC 15**

Suskind, Patrick
See Sueskind, Patrick
See also CA 145

Sutcliff, Rosemary
1920-1992 . . . . **CLC 26; DAB; DAC;**
DAM MST, POP
See also AAYA 10; CA 5-8R; 139;
CANR 37; CLR 1, 37; JRDA; MAICYA;
SATA 6, 44, 78; SATA-Obit 73

Sutro, Alfred 1863-1933 . . . . **TCLC 6**
See also CA 105; DLB 10

Sutton, Henry
See Slavitt, David R(ytman)

Svevo, Italo
1861-1928 . . . . **TCLC 2, 35; SSC 25**
See also Schmitz, Aron Hector

Swados, Elizabeth (A.) 1951- . . . . **CLC 12**
See also CA 97-100; CANR 49; INT 97-100

Swados, Harvey 1920-1972 . . . . **CLC 5**
See also CA 5-8R; 37-40R; CANR 6;
DLB 2

Swan, Gladys 1934- . . . . **CLC 69**
See also CA 101; CANR 17, 39

Swarthout, Glendon (Fred)
1918-1992 . . . . **CLC 35**
See also CA 1-4R; 139; CANR 1, 47;
SATA 26

Sweet, Sarah C.
See Jewett, (Theodora) Sarah Orne

Swenson, May
1919-1989 . . . . **CLC 4, 14, 61; DA; DAB;**
DAC; DAM MST, POET; PC 14
See also CA 5-8R; 130; CANR 36; DLB 5;
MTCW; SATA 15

Swift, Augustus
See Lovecraft, H(oward) P(hillips)

Swift, Graham (Colin) 1949- . . . . **CLC 41, 88**
See also CA 117; 122; CANR 46

Swift, Jonathan
1667-1745 . . . . . . **LC 1; DA; DAB; DAC;**
DAM MST, NOV, POET; PC 9; WLC
See also CDBLB 1660-1789; DLB 39, 95,
101; SATA 19

Swinburne, Algernon Charles
1837-1909 . . . . **TCLC 8, 36; DA; DAB;**
DAC; DAM MST, POET; WLC
See also CA 105; 140; CDBLB 1832-1890;
DLB 35, 57

Swinfen, Ann . . . . **CLC 34**

Swinnerton, Frank Arthur
1884-1982 . . . . **CLC 31**
See also CA 108; DLB 34

Swithen, John
See King, Stephen (Edwin)

Sylvia
See Ashton-Warner, Sylvia (Constance)

Symmes, Robert Edward
See Duncan, Robert (Edward)

Symonds, John Addington
1840-1893 . . . . **NCLC 34**
See also DLB 57, 144

Symons, Arthur 1865-1945 . . . . **TCLC 11**
See also CA 107; DLB 19, 57, 149

Symons, Julian (Gustave)
1912-1994 . . . . **CLC 2, 14, 32**
See also CA 49-52; 147; CAAS 3; CANR 3,
33; DLB 87, 155; DLBY 92; MTCW

Synge, (Edmund) J(ohn) M(illington)
1871-1909 . . . . **TCLC 6, 37;**
DAM DRAM; DC 2
See also CA 104; 141; CDBLB 1890-1914;
DLB 10, 19

Syruc, J.
See Milosz, Czeslaw

Szirtes, George 1948- . . . . **CLC 46**
See also CA 109; CANR 27

Szymborska, Wislawa 1923- . . . . **CLC 99**
See also CA 154; DLBY 96

T. O., Nik
See Annensky, Innokenty (Fyodorovich)

Tabori, George 1914- . . . . **CLC 19**
See also CA 49-52; CANR 4

Tagore, Rabindranath
1861-1941 . . . . **TCLC 3, 53;**
DAM DRAM, POET; PC 8
See also CA 104; 120; MTCW

Taine, Hippolyte Adolphe
1828-1893 . . . . **NCLC 15**

Talese, Gay 1932- . . . . **CLC 37**
See also AITN 1; CA 1-4R; CANR 9, 58;
INT CANR-9; MTCW

Tallent, Elizabeth (Ann) 1954- ..... **CLC 45**
See also CA 117; DLB 130

Tally, Ted 1952- .... **CLC 42**
See also CA 120; 124; INT 124

Tamayo y Baus, Manuel
1829-1898 .... **NCLC 1**

Tammsaare, A(nton) H(ansen)
1878-1940 .... **TCLC 27**

Tam'si, Tchicaya U
See Tchicaya, Gerald Felix

Tan, Amy (Ruth)
1952- .... **CLC 59; DAM MULT, NOV,
POP**
See also AAYA 9; BEST 89:3; CA 136;
CANR 54; DLB 173; SATA 75

Tandem, Felix
See Spitteler, Carl (Friedrich Georg)

Tanizaki, Jun'ichiro
1886-1965 ...... **CLC 8, 14, 28; SSC 21**
See also CA 93-96; 25-28R; DLB 180

Tanner, William
See Amis, Kingsley (William)

Tao Lao
See Storni, Alfonsina

Tarassoff, Lev
See Troyat, Henri

Tarbell, Ida M(inerva)
1857-1944 .... **TCLC 40**
See also CA 122; DLB 47

Tarkington, (Newton) Booth
1869-1946 .... **TCLC 9**
See also CA 110; 143; DLB 9, 102;
SATA 17

Tarkovsky, Andrei (Arsenyevich)
1932-1986 .... **CLC 75**
See also CA 127

Tartt, Donna 1964(?)- .... **CLC 76**
See also CA 142

Tasso, Torquato 1544-1595 .... **LC 5**

Tate, (John Orley) Allen
1899-1979 .... **CLC 2, 4, 6, 9, 11, 14, 24**
See also CA 5-8R; 85-88; CANR 32;
DLB 4, 45, 63; MTCW

Tate, Ellalice
See Hibbert, Eleanor Alice Burford

Tate, James (Vincent) 1943- ... **CLC 2, 6, 25**
See also CA 21-24R; CANR 29, 57; DLB 5,
169

Tavel, Ronald 1940- .... **CLC 6**
See also CA 21-24R; CANR 33

Taylor, C(ecil) P(hilip) 1929-1981... **CLC 27**
See also CA 25-28R; 105; CANR 47

Taylor, Edward
1642(?)-1729 .... **LC 11; DA; DAB;
DAC; DAM MST, POET**
See also DLB 24

Taylor, Eleanor Ross 1920- .... **CLC 5**
See also CA 81-84

Taylor, Elizabeth 1912-1975 ... **CLC 2, 4, 29**
See also CA 13-16R; CANR 9; DLB 139;
MTCW; SATA 13

Taylor, Henry (Splawn) 1942- ..... **CLC 44**
See also CA 33-36R; CAAS 7; CANR 31;
DLB 5

Taylor, Kamala (Purnaiya) 1924-
See Markandaya, Kamala
See also CA 77-80

Taylor, Mildred D. .... **CLC 21**
See also AAYA 10; BW 1; CA 85-88;
CANR 25; CLR 9; DLB 52; JRDA;
MAICYA; SAAS 5; SATA 15, 70

Taylor, Peter (Hillsman)
1917-1994 ..... **CLC 1, 4, 18, 37, 44, 50,
71; SSC 10**
See also CA 13-16R; 147; CANR 9, 50;
DLBY 81, 94; INT CANR-9; MTCW

Taylor, Robert Lewis 1912- .... **CLC 14**
See also CA 1-4R; CANR 3; SATA 10

Tchekhov, Anton
See Chekhov, Anton (Pavlovich)

Tchicaya, Gerald Felix
1931-1988 .... **CLC 101**
See also CA 129; 125

Tchicaya U Tam'si
See Tchicaya, Gerald Felix

Teasdale, Sara 1884-1933 .... **TCLC 4**
See also CA 104; DLB 45; SATA 32

Tegner, Esaias 1782-1846 .... **NCLC 2**

Teilhard de Chardin, (Marie Joseph) Pierre
1881-1955 .... **TCLC 9**
See also CA 105

Temple, Ann
See Mortimer, Penelope (Ruth)

Tennant, Emma (Christina)
1937- .... **CLC 13, 52**
See also CA 65-68; CAAS 9; CANR 10, 38;
DLB 14

Tenneshaw, S. M.
See Silverberg, Robert

Tennyson, Alfred
1809-1892 .... **NCLC 30; DA; DAB;
DAC; DAM MST, POET; PC 6; WLC**
See also CDBLB 1832-1890; DLB 32

Teran, Lisa St. Aubin de .... **CLC 36**
See also St. Aubin de Teran, Lisa

Terence
195(?)B.C.-159B.C..... **CMLC 14; DC 7**

Teresa de Jesus, St. 1515-1582 ...... **LC 18**

Terkel, Louis 1912-
See Terkel, Studs
See also CA 57-60; CANR 18, 45; MTCW

Terkel, Studs .... **CLC 38**
See also Terkel, Louis
See also AITN 1

Terry, C. V.
See Slaughter, Frank G(ill)

Terry, Megan 1932- .... **CLC 19**
See also CA 77-80; CABS 3; CANR 43;
DLB 7

Tertz, Abram
See Sinyavsky, Andrei (Donatevich)

Tesich, Steve 1943(?)-1996...... **CLC 40, 69**
See also CA 105; 152; DLBY 83

Teternikov, Fyodor Kuzmich 1863-1927
See Sologub, Fyodor
See also CA 104

Tevis, Walter 1928-1984 .... **CLC 42**
See also CA 113

Tey, Josephine .... **TCLC 14**
See also Mackintosh, Elizabeth
See also DLB 77

Thackeray, William Makepeace
1811-1863 .... **NCLC 5, 14, 22, 43; DA;
DAB; DAC; DAM MST, NOV; WLC**
See also CDBLB 1832-1890; DLB 21, 55,
159, 163; SATA 23

Thakura, Ravindranatha
See Tagore, Rabindranath

Tharoor, Shashi 1956- .... **CLC 70**
See also CA 141

Thelwell, Michael Miles 1939- ..... **CLC 22**
See also BW 2; CA 101

Theobald, Lewis, Jr.
See Lovecraft, H(oward) P(hillips)

Theodorescu, Ion N. 1880-1967
See Arghezi, Tudor
See also CA 116

Theriault, Yves
1915-1983 .. **CLC 79; DAC; DAM MST**
See also CA 102; DLB 88

Theroux, Alexander (Louis)
1939- .... **CLC 2, 25**
See also CA 85-88; CANR 20

Theroux, Paul (Edward)
1941- .... **CLC 5, 8, 11, 15, 28, 46;
DAM POP**
See also BEST 89:4; CA 33-36R; CANR 20,
45; DLB 2; MTCW; SATA 44

Thesen, Sharon 1946- .... **CLC 56**

Thevenin, Denis
See Duhamel, Georges

Thibault, Jacques Anatole Francois
1844-1924
See France, Anatole
See also CA 106; 127; DAM NOV; MTCW

Thiele, Colin (Milton) 1920- .... **CLC 17**
See also CA 29-32R; CANR 12, 28, 53;
CLR 27; MAICYA; SAAS 2; SATA 14,
72

Thomas, Audrey (Callahan)
1935- .... **CLC 7, 13, 37; SSC 20**
See also AITN 2; CA 21-24R; CAAS 19;
CANR 36, 58; DLB 60; MTCW

Thomas, D(onald) M(ichael)
1935- .... **CLC 13, 22, 31**
See also CA 61-64; CAAS 11; CANR 17,
45; CDBLB 1960 to Present; DLB 40;
INT CANR-17; MTCW

Thomas, Dylan (Marlais)
1914-1953 ... **TCLC 1, 8, 45; DA; DAB;
DAC; DAM DRAM, MST, POET;
PC 2; SSC 3; WLC**
See also CA 104; 120; CDBLB 1945-1960;
DLB 13, 20, 139; MTCW; SATA 60

Thomas, (Philip) Edward
1878-1917 ...... **TCLC 10; DAM POET**
See also CA 106; 153; DLB 19

Thomas, Joyce Carol 1938- .... **CLC 35**
See also AAYA 12; BW 2; CA 113; 116;
CANR 48; CLR 19; DLB 33; INT 116;
JRDA; MAICYA; MTCW; SAAS 7;
SATA 40, 78

Thomas, Lewis 1913-1993 .... **CLC 35**
See also CA 85-88; 143; CANR 38; MTCW

Thomas, Paul
　See Mann, (Paul) Thomas

Thomas, Piri 1928- . . . . CLC 17
　See also CA 73-76; HW

Thomas, R(onald) S(tuart)
　1913- . . . . CLC 6, 13, 48; DAB;
　　　　　　　　　　　　　　DAM POET
　See also CA 89-92; CAAS 4; CANR 30;
　　CDBLB 1960 to Present; DLB 27;
　　MTCW

Thomas, Ross (Elmore) 1926-1995 . . CLC 39
　See also CA 33-36R; 150; CANR 22

Thompson, Francis Clegg
　See Mencken, H(enry) L(ouis)

Thompson, Francis Joseph
　1859-1907 . . . . TCLC 4
　See also CA 104; CDBLB 1890-1914;
　　DLB 19

Thompson, Hunter S(tockton)
　1939- . . . . CLC 9, 17, 40; DAM POP
　See also BEST 89:1; CA 17-20R; CANR 23,
　　46; MTCW

Thompson, James Myers
　See Thompson, Jim (Myers)

Thompson, Jim (Myers)
　1906-1977(?) . . . . CLC 69
　See also CA 140

Thompson, Judith . . . . CLC 39

Thomson, James
　1700-1748 . . . . . LC 16, 29; DAM POET
　See also DLB 95

Thomson, James
　1834-1882 . . . . . NCLC 18; DAM POET
　See also DLB 35

Thoreau, Henry David
　1817-1862 . . . . NCLC 7, 21, 61; DA;
　　　　　　　DAB; DAC; DAM MST; WLC
　See also CDALB 1640-1865; DLB 1

Thornton, Hall
　See Silverberg, Robert

Thucydides c. 455B.C.-399B.C. . . . . CMLC 17
　See also DLB 176

Thurber, James (Grover)
　1894-1961 . . . . CLC 5, 11, 25; DA; DAB;
　　　　DAC; DAM DRAM, MST, NOV; SSC 1
　See also CA 73-76; CANR 17, 39;
　　CDALB 1929-1941; DLB 4, 11, 22, 102;
　　MAICYA; MTCW; SATA 13

Thurman, Wallace (Henry)
　1902-1934 . . . . TCLC 6; BLC;
　　　　　　　　　　　　　　DAM MULT
　See also BW 1; CA 104; 124; DLB 51

Ticheburn, Cheviot
　See Ainsworth, William Harrison

Tieck, (Johann) Ludwig
　1773-1853 . . . . NCLC 5, 46
　See also DLB 90

Tiger, Derry
　See Ellison, Harlan (Jay)

Tilghman, Christopher 1948(?)- . . . . . CLC 65

Tillinghast, Richard (Williford)
　1940- . . . . CLC 29
　See also CA 29-32R; CAAS 23; CANR 26,
　　51

Timrod, Henry 1828-1867 . . . . NCLC 25
　See also DLB 3

Tindall, Gillian 1938- . . . . CLC 7
　See also CA 21-24R; CANR 11

Tiptree, James, Jr. . . . . CLC 48, 50
　See also Sheldon, Alice Hastings Bradley
　See also DLB 8

Titmarsh, Michael Angelo
　See Thackeray, William Makepeace

Tocqueville, Alexis (Charles Henri Maurice
　Clerel Comte) 1805-1859 . . . . . NCLC 7

Tolkien, J(ohn) R(onald) R(euel)
　1892-1973 . . . . CLC 1, 2, 3, 8, 12, 38;
　　　　DA; DAB; DAC; DAM MST, NOV,
　　　　　　　　　　　　　　POP; WLC
　See also AAYA 10; AITN 1; CA 17-18;
　　45-48; CANR 36; CAP 2;
　　CDBLB 1914-1945; DLB 15, 160; JRDA;
　　MAICYA; MTCW; SATA 2, 32;
　　SATA-Obit 24

Toller, Ernst 1893-1939 . . . . TCLC 10
　See also CA 107; DLB 124

Tolson, M. B.
　See Tolson, Melvin B(eaunorus)

Tolson, Melvin B(eaunorus)
　1898(?)-1966 . . . . CLC 36; BLC;
　　　　　　　　　　　　DAM MULT, POET
　See also BW 1; CA 124; 89-92; DLB 48, 76

Tolstoi, Aleksei Nikolaevich
　See Tolstoy, Alexey Nikolaevich

Tolstoy, Alexey Nikolaevich
　1882-1945 . . . . TCLC 18
　See also CA 107; 158

Tolstoy, Count Leo
　See Tolstoy, Leo (Nikolaevich)

Tolstoy, Leo (Nikolaevich)
　1828-1910 . . . . . . TCLC 4, 11, 17, 28, 44;
　　　　DA; DAB; DAC; DAM MST, NOV;
　　　　　　　　　　　　　　SSC 9; WLC
　See also CA 104; 123; SATA 26

Tomasi di Lampedusa, Giuseppe 1896-1957
　See Lampedusa, Giuseppe (Tomasi) di
　See also CA 111

Tomlin, Lily . . . . CLC 17
　See also Tomlin, Mary Jean

Tomlin, Mary Jean 1939(?)-
　See Tomlin, Lily
　See also CA 117

Tomlinson, (Alfred) Charles
　1927- . . . . CLC 2, 4, 6, 13, 45;
　　　　　　　　　　　　　DAM POET; PC 17
　See also CA 5-8R; CANR 33; DLB 40

Tomlinson, H(enry) M(ajor)
　1873-1958 . . . . TCLC 71
　See also CA 118; DLB 36, 100

Tonson, Jacob
　See Bennett, (Enoch) Arnold

Toole, John Kennedy
　1937-1969 . . . . CLC 19, 64
　See also CA 104; DLBY 81

Toomer, Jean
　1894-1967 . . . . . . CLC 1, 4, 13, 22; BLC;
　　　　　　　　　DAM MULT; PC 7; SSC 1
　See also BW 1; CA 85-88;
　　CDALB 1917-1929; DLB 45, 51; MTCW;
　　YABC

Torley, Luke
　See Blish, James (Benjamin)

Tornimparte, Alessandra
　See Ginzburg, Natalia

Torre, Raoul della
　See Mencken, H(enry) L(ouis)

Torrey, E(dwin) Fuller 1937- . . . . . . CLC 34
　See also CA 119

Torsvan, Ben Traven
　See Traven, B.

Torsvan, Benno Traven
　See Traven, B.

Torsvan, Berick Traven
　See Traven, B.

Torsvan, Berwick Traven
　See Traven, B.

Torsvan, Bruno Traven
　See Traven, B.

Torsvan, Traven
　See Traven, B.

Tournier, Michel (Edouard)
　1924- . . . . CLC 6, 23, 36, 95
　See also CA 49-52; CANR 3, 36; DLB 83;
　　MTCW; SATA 23

Tournimparte, Alessandra
　See Ginzburg, Natalia

Towers, Ivar
　See Kornbluth, C(yril) M.

Towne, Robert (Burton) 1936(?)- . . . . CLC 87
　See also CA 108; DLB 44

Townsend, Sue 1946- . . CLC 61; DAB; DAC
　See also CA 119; 127; INT 127; MTCW;
　　SATA 55, 93; SATA-Brief 48

Townshend, Peter (Dennis Blandford)
　1945- . . . . CLC 17, 42
　See also CA 107

Tozzi, Federigo 1883-1920 . . . . TCLC 31

Traill, Catharine Parr
　1802-1899 . . . . NCLC 31
　See also DLB 99

Trakl, Georg 1887-1914 . . . . TCLC 5
　See also CA 104

Transtroemer, Tomas (Goesta)
　1931- . . . . CLC 52, 65; DAM POET
　See also CA 117; 129; CAAS 17

Transtromer, Tomas Gosta
　See Transtroemer, Tomas (Goesta)

Traven, B. (?)-1969 . . . . CLC 8, 11
　See also CA 19-20; 25-28R; CAP 2; DLB 9,
　　56; MTCW

Treitel, Jonathan 1959- . . . . CLC 70

Tremain, Rose 1943- . . . . CLC 42
　See also CA 97-100; CANR 44; DLB 14

Tremblay, Michel
　1942- . . . . . . CLC 29; DAC; DAM MST
　See also CA 116; 128; DLB 60; MTCW

Trevanian . . . . CLC 29
　See also Whitaker, Rod(ney)

Trevor, Glen
　See Hilton, James

Trevor, William
1928- . . . . . **CLC 7, 9, 14, 25, 71; SSC 21**
See also Cox, William Trevor
See also DLB 14, 139

Trifonov, Yuri (Valentinovich)
1925-1981 . . . . **CLC 45**
See also CA 126; 103; MTCW

Trilling, Lionel 1905-1975 . . . . **CLC 9, 11, 24**
See also CA 9-12R; 61-64; CANR 10;
DLB 28, 63; INT CANR-10; MTCW

Trimball, W. H.
See Mencken, H(enry) L(ouis)

Tristan
See Gomez de la Serna, Ramon

Tristram
See Housman, A(lfred) E(dward)

Trogdon, William (Lewis) 1939-
See Heat-Moon, William Least
See also CA 115; 119; CANR 47; INT 119

Trollope, Anthony
1815-1882 . . . . . **NCLC 6, 33; DA; DAB;
DAC; DAM MST, NOV; WLC**
See also CDBLB 1832-1890; DLB 21, 57,
159; SATA 22

Trollope, Frances 1779-1863 . . . . . **NCLC 30**
See also DLB 21, 166

Trotsky, Leon 1879-1940 . . . . **TCLC 22**
See also CA 118

Trotter (Cockburn), Catharine
1679-1749 . . . . **LC 8**
See also DLB 84

Trout, Kilgore
See Farmer, Philip Jose

Trow, George W. S. 1943- . . . . **CLC 52**
See also CA 126

Troyat, Henri 1911- . . . . **CLC 23**
See also CA 45-48; CANR 2, 33; MTCW

Trudeau, G(arretson) B(eekman) 1948-
See Trudeau, Garry B.
See also CA 81-84; CANR 31; SATA 35

Trudeau, Garry B. . . . . **CLC 12**
See also Trudeau, G(arretson) B(eekman)
See also AAYA 10; AITN 2

Truffaut, Francois 1932-1984 . . . **CLC 20, 101**
See also CA 81-84; 113; CANR 34

Trumbo, Dalton 1905-1976 . . . . **CLC 19**
See also CA 21-24R; 69-72; CANR 10;
DLB 26

Trumbull, John 1750-1831 . . . . **NCLC 30**
See also DLB 31

Trundlett, Helen B.
See Eliot, T(homas) S(tearns)

Tryon, Thomas
1926-1991 . . . . . . **CLC 3, 11; DAM POP**
See also AITN 1; CA 29-32R; 135;
CANR 32; MTCW

Tryon, Tom
See Tryon, Thomas

Ts'ao Hsueh-ch'in 1715(?)-1763 . . . . . . **LC 1**

Tsushima, Shuji 1909-1948
See Dazai, Osamu
See also CA 107

Tsvetaeva (Efron), Marina (Ivanovna)
1892-1941 . . . . **TCLC 7, 35; PC 14**
See also CA 104; 128; MTCW

Tuck, Lily 1938- . . . . **CLC 70**
See also CA 139

Tu Fu 712-770 . . . . **PC 9**
See also DAM MULT

Tunis, John R(oberts) 1889-1975 . . . **CLC 12**
See also CA 61-64; DLB 22, 171; JRDA;
MAICYA; SATA 37; SATA-Brief 30

Tuohy, Frank . . . . **CLC 37**
See also Tuohy, John Francis
See also DLB 14, 139

Tuohy, John Francis 1925-
See Tuohy, Frank
See also CA 5-8R; CANR 3, 47

Turco, Lewis (Putnam) 1934- . . . **CLC 11, 63**
See also CA 13-16R; CAAS 22; CANR 24,
51; DLBY 84

Turgenev, Ivan
1818-1883 . . . . **NCLC 21; DA; DAB;
DAC; DAM MST, NOV; DC 7; SSC 7;
WLC**

Turgot, Anne-Robert-Jacques
1727-1781 . . . . **LC 26**

Turner, Frederick 1943- . . . . **CLC 48**
See also CA 73-76; CAAS 10; CANR 12,
30, 56; DLB 40

Tutu, Desmond M(pilo)
1931- . . . . . **CLC 80; BLC; DAM MULT**
See also BW 1; CA 125

Tutuola, Amos
1920- . . . . **CLC 5, 14, 29; BLC;
DAM MULT**
See also BW 2; CA 9-12R; CANR 27;
DLB 125; MTCW

Twain, Mark
. . . . **TCLC 6, 12, 19, 36, 48, 59; SSC 26;
WLC**
See also Clemens, Samuel Langhorne
See also AAYA 20; DLB 11, 12, 23, 64, 74

Tyler, Anne
1941- . . . . **CLC 7, 11, 18, 28, 44, 59;
DAM NOV, POP**
See also AAYA 18; BEST 89:1; CA 9-12R;
CANR 11, 33, 53; DLB 6, 143; DLBY 82;
MTCW; SATA 7, 90

Tyler, Royall 1757-1826 . . . . **NCLC 3**
See also DLB 37

Tynan, Katharine 1861-1931 . . . . . . **TCLC 3**
See also CA 104; DLB 153

Tyutchev, Fyodor 1803-1873 . . . . . **NCLC 34**

Tzara, Tristan
1896-1963 . . . . . . **CLC 47; DAM POET**
See also Rosenfeld, Samuel; Rosenstock,
Sami; Rosenstock, Samuel
See also CA 153

Uhry, Alfred
1936- . . . . . **CLC 55; DAM DRAM, POP**
See also CA 127; 133; INT 133

Ulf, Haerved
See Strindberg, (Johan) August

Ulf, Harved
See Strindberg, (Johan) August

Ulibarri, Sabine R(eyes)
1919- . . . . **CLC 83; DAM MULT**
See also CA 131; DLB 82; HW

Unamuno (y Jugo), Miguel de
1864-1936 . . . **TCLC 2, 9; DAM MULT,
NOV; HLC; SSC 11**
See also CA 104; 131; DLB 108; HW;
MTCW

Undercliffe, Errol
See Campbell, (John) Ramsey

Underwood, Miles
See Glassco, John

Undset, Sigrid
1882-1949 . . . . **TCLC 3; DA; DAB;
DAC; DAM MST, NOV; WLC**
See also CA 104; 129; MTCW

Ungaretti, Giuseppe
1888-1970 . . . . **CLC 7, 11, 15**
See also CA 19-20; 25-28R; CAP 2;
DLB 114

Unger, Douglas 1952- . . . . **CLC 34**
See also CA 130

Unsworth, Barry (Forster) 1930- . . . . **CLC 76**
See also CA 25-28R; CANR 30, 54

Updike, John (Hoyer)
1932- . . . . . . **CLC 1, 2, 3, 5, 7, 9, 13, 15,
23, 34, 43, 70; DA; DAB; DAC;
DAM MST, NOV, POET, POP;
SSC 13; WLC**
See also CA 1-4R; CABS 1; CANR 4, 33,
51; CDALB 1968-1988; DLB 2, 5, 143;
DLBD 3; DLBY 80, 82; MTCW

Upshaw, Margaret Mitchell
See Mitchell, Margaret (Munnerlyn)

Upton, Mark
See Sanders, Lawrence

Urdang, Constance (Henriette)
1922- . . . . **CLC 47**
See also CA 21-24R; CANR 9, 24

Uriel, Henry
See Faust, Frederick (Schiller)

Uris, Leon (Marcus)
1924- . . . . . **CLC 7, 32; DAM NOV, POP**
See also AITN 1, 2; BEST 89:2; CA 1-4R;
CANR 1, 40; MTCW; SATA 49

Urmuz
See Codrescu, Andrei

Urquhart, Jane 1949- . . . . **CLC 90; DAC**
See also CA 113; CANR 32

Ustinov, Peter (Alexander) 1921- . . . . **CLC 1**
See also AITN 1; CA 13-16R; CANR 25,
51; DLB 13

U Tam'si, Gerald Felix Tchicaya
See Tchicaya, Gerald Felix

U Tam'si, Tchicaya
See Tchicaya, Gerald Felix

Vaculik, Ludvik 1926- . . . . **CLC 7**
See also CA 53-56

Vaihinger, Hans 1852-1933 . . . . **TCLC 71**
See also CA 116

Valdez, Luis (Miguel)
1940- . . . . . **CLC 84; DAM MULT; HLC**
See also CA 101; CANR 32; DLB 122; HW

Valenzuela, Luisa
1938- . . . **CLC 31; DAM MULT; SSC 14**
See also CA 101; CANR 32; DLB 113; HW

Valera y Alcala-Galiano, Juan
1824-1905 . . . . **TCLC 10**
See also CA 106

Valery, (Ambroise) Paul (Toussaint Jules)
1871-1945 . . . . **TCLC 4, 15;**
DAM POET; PC 9
See also CA 104; 122; MTCW

Valle-Inclan, Ramon (Maria) del
1866-1936 . . . . . **TCLC 5; DAM MULT;**
HLC
See also CA 106; 153; DLB 134

Vallejo, Antonio Buero
See Buero Vallejo, Antonio

Vallejo, Cesar (Abraham)
1892-1938 . . . . **TCLC 3, 56;**
DAM MULT; HLC
See also CA 105; 153; HW

Vallette, Marguerite Eymery
See Rachilde

Valle Y Pena, Ramon del
See Valle-Inclan, Ramon (Maria) del

Van Ash, Cay 1918- . . . . **CLC 34**

Vanbrugh, Sir John
1664-1726 . . . . **LC 21; DAM DRAM**
See also DLB 80

Van Campen, Karl
See Campbell, John W(ood, Jr.)

Vance, Gerald
See Silverberg, Robert

Vance, Jack . . . . **CLC 35**
See also Kuttner, Henry; Vance, John
Holbrook
See also DLB 8

Vance, John Holbrook 1916-
See Queen, Ellery; Vance, Jack
See also CA 29-32R; CANR 17; MTCW

Van Den Bogarde, Derek Jules Gaspard Ulric
Niven 1921-
See Bogarde, Dirk
See also CA 77-80

Vandenburgh, Jane . . . . **CLC 59**

Vanderhaeghe, Guy 1951- . . . . **CLC 41**
See also CA 113

van der Post, Laurens (Jan)
1906-1996 . . . . **CLC 5**
See also CA 5-8R; 155; CANR 35

van de Wetering, Janwillem 1931- . . **CLC 47**
See also CA 49-52; CANR 4

Van Dine, S. S. . . . . **TCLC 23**
See also Wright, Willard Huntington

Van Doren, Carl (Clinton)
1885-1950 . . . . **TCLC 18**
See also CA 111

Van Doren, Mark 1894-1972 . . . . . **CLC 6, 10**
See also CA 1-4R; 37-40R; CANR 3;
DLB 45; MTCW

Van Druten, John (William)
1901-1957 . . . . **TCLC 2**
See also CA 104; DLB 10

Van Duyn, Mona (Jane)
1921- . . . . **CLC 3, 7, 63; DAM POET**
See also CA 9-12R; CANR 7, 38; DLB 5

Van Dyne, Edith
See Baum, L(yman) Frank

van Itallie, Jean-Claude 1936- . . . . **CLC 3**
See also CA 45-48; CAAS 2; CANR 1, 48;
DLB 7

van Ostaijen, Paul 1896-1928 . . . . . **TCLC 33**

Van Peebles, Melvin
1932- . . . . **CLC 2, 20; DAM MULT**
See also BW 2; CA 85-88; CANR 27

Vansittart, Peter 1920- . . . . **CLC 42**
See also CA 1-4R; CANR 3, 49

Van Vechten, Carl 1880-1964 . . . . . . **CLC 33**
See also CA 89-92; DLB 4, 9, 51

Van Vogt, A(lfred) E(lton) 1912- . . . . . **CLC 1**
See also CA 21-24R; CANR 28; DLB 8;
SATA 14

Varda, Agnes 1928- . . . . **CLC 16**
See also CA 116; 122

Vargas Llosa, (Jorge) Mario (Pedro)
1936- . . . . **CLC 3, 6, 9, 10, 15, 31, 42, 85;**
DA; DAB; DAC; DAM MST, MULT,
NOV; HLC
See also CA 73-76; CANR 18, 32, 42;
DLB 145; HW; MTCW

Vasiliu, Gheorghe 1881-1957
See Bacovia, George
See also CA 123

Vassa, Gustavus
See Equiano, Olaudah

Vassilikos, Vassilis 1933- . . . . **CLC 4, 8**
See also CA 81-84

Vaughan, Henry 1621-1695 . . . . **LC 27**
See also DLB 131

Vaughn, Stephanie . . . . **CLC 62**

Vazov, Ivan (Minchov)
1850-1921 . . . . **TCLC 25**
See also CA 121; DLB 147

Veblen, Thorstein (Bunde)
1857-1929 . . . . **TCLC 31**
See also CA 115

Vega, Lope de 1562-1635 . . . . **LC 23**

Venison, Alfred
See Pound, Ezra (Weston Loomis)

Verdi, Marie de
See Mencken, H(enry) L(ouis)

Verdu, Matilde
See Cela, Camilo Jose

Verga, Giovanni (Carmelo)
1840-1922 . . . . **TCLC 3; SSC 21**
See also CA 104; 123

Vergil
70B.C.-19B.C. . . . . . **CMLC 9; DA; DAB;**
DAC; DAM MST, POET; PC 12
See also YABC

Verhaeren, Emile (Adolphe Gustave)
1855-1916 . . . . **TCLC 12**
See also CA 109

Verlaine, Paul (Marie)
1844-1896 . . . . **NCLC 2, 51;**
DAM POET; PC 2

Verne, Jules (Gabriel)
1828-1905 . . . . **TCLC 6, 52**
See also AAYA 16; CA 110; 131; DLB 123;
JRDA; MAICYA; SATA 21

Very, Jones 1813-1880 . . . . **NCLC 9**
See also DLB 1

Vesaas, Tarjei 1897-1970 . . . . **CLC 48**
See also CA 29-32R

Vialis, Gaston
See Simenon, Georges (Jacques Christian)

Vian, Boris 1920-1959 . . . . **TCLC 9**
See also CA 106; DLB 72

Viaud, (Louis Marie) Julien 1850-1923
See Loti, Pierre
See also CA 107

Vicar, Henry
See Felsen, Henry Gregor

Vicker, Angus
See Felsen, Henry Gregor

Vidal, Gore
1925- . . . . . **CLC 2, 4, 6, 8, 10, 22, 33, 72;**
DAM NOV, POP
See also AITN 1; BEST 90:2; CA 5-8R;
CANR 13, 45; DLB 6, 152;
INT CANR-13; MTCW

Viereck, Peter (Robert Edwin)
1916- . . . . **CLC 4**
See also CA 1-4R; CANR 1, 47; DLB 5

Vigny, Alfred (Victor) de
1797-1863 . . . . . . **NCLC 7; DAM POET**
See also DLB 119

Vilakazi, Benedict Wallet
1906-1947 . . . . **TCLC 37**

Villiers de l'Isle Adam, Jean Marie Mathias
Philippe Auguste Comte
1838-1889 . . . . **NCLC 3; SSC 14**
See also DLB 123

Villon, Francois 1431-1463(?) . . . . **PC 13**

Vinci, Leonardo da 1452-1519 . . . . . . **LC 12**

Vine, Barbara . . . . **CLC 50**
See also Rendell, Ruth (Barbara)
See also BEST 90:4

Vinge, Joan D(ennison)
1948- . . . . **CLC 30; SSC 24**
See also CA 93-96; SATA 36

Violis, G.
See Simenon, Georges (Jacques Christian)

Visconti, Luchino 1906-1976 . . . . **CLC 16**
See also CA 81-84; 65-68; CANR 39

Vittorini, Elio 1908-1966 . . . . . . **CLC 6, 9, 14**
See also CA 133; 25-28R

Vizinczey, Stephen 1933- . . . . **CLC 40**
See also CA 128; INT 128

Vliet, R(ussell) G(ordon)
1929-1984 . . . . **CLC 22**
See also CA 37-40R; 112; CANR 18

Vogau, Boris Andreyevich 1894-1937(?)
See Pilnyak, Boris
See also CA 123

Vogel, Paula A(nne) 1951- . . . . **CLC 76**
See also CA 108

Voight, Ellen Bryant 1943- . . . . **CLC 54**
See also CA 69-72; CANR 11, 29, 55;
DLB 120

Voigt, Cynthia 1942- . . . . **CLC 30**
See also AAYA 3; CA 106; CANR 18, 37,
40; CLR 13; INT CANR-18; JRDA;
MAICYA; SATA 48, 79; SATA-Brief 33

Voinovich, Vladimir (Nikolaevich)
1932- . . . . **CLC 10, 49**
See also CA 81-84; CAAS 12; CANR 33;
MTCW

Vollmann, William T.
1959- . . . . . . **CLC 89; DAM NOV, POP**
See also CA 134

Voloshinov, V. N.
See Bakhtin, Mikhail Mikhailovich

Voltaire
1694-1778 . . . . . **LC 14; DA; DAB; DAC;
DAM DRAM, MST; SSC 12; WLC**

von Daeniken, Erich 1935- . . . . **CLC 30**
See also AITN 1; CA 37-40R; CANR 17,
44

von Daniken, Erich
See von Daeniken, Erich

von Heidenstam, (Carl Gustaf) Verner
See Heidenstam, (Carl Gustaf) Verner von

von Heyse, Paul (Johann Ludwig)
See Heyse, Paul (Johann Ludwig von)

von Hofmannsthal, Hugo
See Hofmannsthal, Hugo von

von Horvath, Odon
See Horvath, Oedoen von

von Horvath, Oedoen
See Horvath, Oedoen von

von Liliencron, (Friedrich Adolf Axel) Detlev
See Liliencron, (Friedrich Adolf Axel)
Detlev von

Vonnegut, Kurt, Jr.
1922- . . . . . . **CLC 1, 2, 3, 4, 5, 8, 12, 22,
40, 60; DA; DAB; DAC; DAM MST,
NOV, POP; SSC 8; WLC**
See also AAYA 6; AITN 1; BEST 90:4;
CA 1-4R; CANR 1, 25, 49;
CDALB 1968-1988; DLB 2, 8, 152;
DLBD 3; DLBY 80; MTCW

Von Rachen, Kurt
See Hubbard, L(afayette) Ron(ald)

von Rezzori (d'Arezzo), Gregor
See Rezzori (d'Arezzo), Gregor von

von Sternberg, Josef
See Sternberg, Josef von

Vorster, Gordon 1924- . . . . **CLC 34**
See also CA 133

Vosce, Trudie
See Ozick, Cynthia

Voznesensky, Andrei (Andreievich)
1933- . . . . . . **CLC 1, 15, 57; DAM POET**
See also CA 89-92; CANR 37; MTCW

Waddington, Miriam 1917- . . . . **CLC 28**
See also CA 21-24R; CANR 12, 30;
DLB 68

Wagman, Fredrica 1937- . . . . **CLC 7**
See also CA 97-100; INT 97-100

Wagner, Richard 1813-1883. . . . . . . **NCLC 9**
See also DLB 129

Wagner-Martin, Linda 1936- . . . . . . **CLC 50**

Wagoner, David (Russell)
1926- . . . . **CLC 3, 5, 15**
See also CA 1-4R; CAAS 3; CANR 2;
DLB 5; SATA 14

Wah, Fred(erick James) 1939-. . . . . . **CLC 44**
See also CA 107; 141; DLB 60

Wahloo, Per 1926-1975 . . . . **CLC 7**
See also CA 61-64

Wahloo, Peter
See Wahloo, Per

Wain, John (Barrington)
1925-1994 . . . . **CLC 2, 11, 15, 46**
See also CA 5-8R; 145; CAAS 4; CANR 23,
54; CDBLB 1960 to Present; DLB 15, 27,
139, 155; MTCW

Wajda, Andrzej 1926-. . . . . **CLC 16**
See also CA 102

Wakefield, Dan 1932-. . . . . **CLC 7**
See also CA 21-24R; CAAS 7

Wakoski, Diane
1937- . . . . **CLC 2, 4, 7, 9, 11, 40;
DAM POET; PC 15**
See also CA 13-16R; CAAS 1; CANR 9;
DLB 5; INT CANR-9

Wakoski-Sherbell, Diane
See Wakoski, Diane

Walcott, Derek (Alton)
1930- . . . . **CLC 2, 4, 9, 14, 25, 42, 67, 76;
BLC; DAB; DAC; DAM MST, MULT,
POET; DC 7**
See also BW 2; CA 89-92; CANR 26, 47;
DLB 117; DLBY 81; MTCW

Waldman, Anne 1945- . . . . **CLC 7**
See also CA 37-40R; CAAS 17; CANR 34;
DLB 16

Waldo, E. Hunter
See Sturgeon, Theodore (Hamilton)

Waldo, Edward Hamilton
See Sturgeon, Theodore (Hamilton)

Walker, Alice (Malsenior)
1944- . . . . **CLC 5, 6, 9, 19, 27, 46, 58;
BLC; DA; DAB; DAC; DAM MST,
MULT, NOV, POET, POP; SSC 5**
See also AAYA 3; BEST 89:4; BW 2;
CA 37-40R; CANR 9, 27, 49;
CDALB 1968-1988; DLB 6, 33, 143;
INT CANR-27; MTCW; SATA 31;
YABC

Walker, David Harry 1911-1992. . . . **CLC 14**
See also CA 1-4R; 137; CANR 1; SATA 8;
SATA-Obit 71

Walker, Edward Joseph 1934-
See Walker, Ted
See also CA 21-24R; CANR 12, 28, 53

Walker, George F.
1947- . . . . **CLC 44, 61; DAB; DAC;
DAM MST**
See also CA 103; CANR 21, 43; DLB 60

Walker, Joseph A.
1935- . . . . **CLC 19; DAM DRAM, MST**
See also BW 1; CA 89-92; CANR 26;
DLB 38

Walker, Margaret (Abigail)
1915- . . . . **CLC 1, 6; BLC; DAM MULT**
See also BW 2; CA 73-76; CANR 26, 54;
DLB 76, 152; MTCW

Walker, Ted. . . . . **CLC 13**
See also Walker, Edward Joseph
See also DLB 40

Wallace, David Foster 1962-. . . . . . . **CLC 50**
See also CA 132

Wallace, Dexter
See Masters, Edgar Lee

Wallace, (Richard Horatio) Edgar
1875-1932. . . . . **TCLC 57**
See also CA 115; DLB 70

Wallace, Irving
1916-1990 . . . . . **CLC 7, 13; DAM NOV,
POP**
See also AITN 1; CA 1-4R; 132; CAAS 1;
CANR 1, 27; INT CANR-27; MTCW

Wallant, Edward Lewis
1926-1962 . . . . **CLC 5, 10**
See also CA 1-4R; CANR 22; DLB 2, 28,
143; MTCW

Walley, Byron
See Card, Orson Scott

Walpole, Horace 1717-1797. . . . . **LC 2**
See also DLB 39, 104

Walpole, Hugh (Seymour)
1884-1941 . . . . **TCLC 5**
See also CA 104; DLB 34

Walser, Martin 1927-. . . . . **CLC 27**
See also CA 57-60; CANR 8, 46; DLB 75,
124

Walser, Robert
1878-1956 . . . . **TCLC 18; SSC 20**
See also CA 118; DLB 66

Walsh, Jill Paton. . . . . **CLC 35**
See also Paton Walsh, Gillian
See also AAYA 11; CLR 2; DLB 161;
SAAS 3

Walter, Villiam Christian
See Andersen, Hans Christian

Wambaugh, Joseph (Aloysius, Jr.)
1937- . . . . **CLC 3, 18; DAM NOV, POP**
See also AITN 1; BEST 89:3; CA 33-36R;
CANR 42; DLB 6; DLBY 83; MTCW

Wang Wei 699(?)-761(?). . . . . **PC 18**

Ward, Arthur Henry Sarsfield 1883-1959
See Rohmer, Sax
See also CA 108

Ward, Douglas Turner 1930-. . . . . . . **CLC 19**
See also BW 1; CA 81-84; CANR 27;
DLB 7, 38

Ward, Mary Augusta
See Ward, Mrs. Humphry

Ward, Mrs. Humphry
1851-1920 . . . . **TCLC 55**
See also DLB 18

Ward, Peter
See Faust, Frederick (Schiller)

Warhol, Andy 1928(?)-1987. . . . . **CLC 20**
See also AAYA 12; BEST 89:4; CA 89-92;
121; CANR 34

Warner, Francis (Robert le Plastrier)
1937- . . . . **CLC 14**
See also CA 53-56; CANR 11

Warner, Marina 1946-. . . . . **CLC 59**
See also CA 65-68; CANR 21, 55

Warner, Rex (Ernest) 1905-1986. . . . **CLC 45**
See also CA 89-92; 119; DLB 15

Warner, Susan (Bogert)
    1819-1885 .... **NCLC 31**
    See also DLB 3, 42

Warner, Sylvia (Constance) Ashton
    See Ashton-Warner, Sylvia (Constance)

Warner, Sylvia Townsend
    1893-1978 .... **CLC 7, 19; SSC 23**
    See also CA 61-64; 77-80; CANR 16;
    DLB 34, 139; MTCW

Warren, Mercy Otis 1728-1814... **NCLC 13**
    See also DLB 31

Warren, Robert Penn
    1905-1989 .... **CLC 1, 4, 6, 8, 10, 13, 18,**
        39, 53, 59; DA; DAB; DAC; DAM MST,
            NOV, POET; SSC 4; WLC
    See also AITN 1; CA 13-16R; 129;
    CANR 10, 47; CDALB 1968-1988;
    DLB 2, 48, 152; DLBY 80, 89;
    INT CANR-10; MTCW; SATA 46;
    SATA-Obit 63

Warshofsky, Isaac
    See Singer, Isaac Bashevis

Warton, Thomas
    1728-1790 .... **LC 15; DAM POET**
    See also DLB 104, 109

Waruk, Kona
    See Harris, (Theodore) Wilson

Warung, Price 1855-1911........ **TCLC 45**

Warwick, Jarvis
    See Garner, Hugh

Washington, Alex
    See Harris, Mark

Washington, Booker T(aliaferro)
    1856-1915 .... **TCLC 10; BLC;**
                                    DAM MULT
    See also BW 1; CA 114; 125; SATA 28

Washington, George 1732-1799...... **LC 25**
    See also DLB 31

Wassermann, (Karl) Jakob
    1873-1934 .... **TCLC 6**
    See also CA 104; DLB 66

Wasserstein, Wendy
    1950- .... **CLC 32, 59, 90;**
                                DAM DRAM; DC 4
    See also CA 121; 129; CABS 3; CANR 53;
    INT 129; SATA 94

Waterhouse, Keith (Spencer)
    1929- .... **CLC 47**
    See also CA 5-8R; CANR 38; DLB 13, 15;
    MTCW

Waters, Frank (Joseph)
    1902-1995 .... **CLC 88**
    See also CA 5-8R; 149; CAAS 13; CANR 3,
    18; DLBY 86

Waters, Roger 1944-.............. **CLC 35**

Watkins, Frances Ellen
    See Harper, Frances Ellen Watkins

Watkins, Gerrold
    See Malzberg, Barry N(athaniel)

Watkins, Gloria 1955(?)-
    See hooks, bell
    See also BW 2; CA 143

Watkins, Paul 1964-.............. **CLC 55**
    See also CA 132

Watkins, Vernon Phillips
    1906-1967 .... **CLC 43**
    See also CA 9-10; 25-28R; CAP 1; DLB 20

Watson, Irving S.
    See Mencken, H(enry) L(ouis)

Watson, John H.
    See Farmer, Philip Jose

Watson, Richard F.
    See Silverberg, Robert

Waugh, Auberon (Alexander) 1939-.. **CLC 7**
    See also CA 45-48; CANR 6, 22; DLB 14

Waugh, Evelyn (Arthur St. John)
    1903-1966 ...... **CLC 1, 3, 8, 13, 19, 27,**
        44; DA; DAB; DAC; DAM MST, NOV,
                    POP; WLC
    See also CA 85-88; 25-28R; CANR 22;
    CDBLB 1914-1945; DLB 15, 162; MTCW

Waugh, Harriet 1944- .... **CLC 6**
    See also CA 85-88; CANR 22

Ways, C. R.
    See Blount, Roy (Alton), Jr.

Waystaff, Simon
    See Swift, Jonathan

Webb, (Martha) Beatrice (Potter)
    1858-1943 .... **TCLC 22**
    See also Potter, Beatrice
    See also CA 117

Webb, Charles (Richard) 1939-...... **CLC 7**
    See also CA 25-28R

Webb, James H(enry), Jr. 1946-.... **CLC 22**
    See also CA 81-84

Webb, Mary (Gladys Meredith)
    1881-1927 .... **TCLC 24**
    See also CA 123; DLB 34

Webb, Mrs. Sidney
    See Webb, (Martha) Beatrice (Potter)

Webb, Phyllis 1927-.............. **CLC 18**
    See also CA 104; CANR 23; DLB 53

Webb, Sidney (James)
    1859-1947 .... **TCLC 22**
    See also CA 117

Webber, Andrew Lloyd............. **CLC 21**
    See also Lloyd Webber, Andrew

Weber, Lenora Mattingly
    1895-1971 .... **CLC 12**
    See also CA 19-20; 29-32R; CAP 1;
    SATA 2; SATA-Obit 26

Weber, Max 1864-1920 .... **TCLC 69**
    See also CA 109

Webster, John
    1579(?)-1634(?) ...... **LC 33; DA; DAB;**
        DAC; DAM DRAM, MST; DC 2; WLC
    See also CDBLB Before 1660; DLB 58

Webster, Noah 1758-1843 .... **NCLC 30**

Wedekind, (Benjamin) Frank(lin)
    1864-1918 ...... **TCLC 7; DAM DRAM**
    See also CA 104; 153; DLB 118

Weidman, Jerome 1913-............. **CLC 7**
    See also AITN 2; CA 1-4R; CANR 1;
    DLB 28

Weil, Simone (Adolphine)
    1909-1943 .... **TCLC 23**
    See also CA 117

Weinstein, Nathan
    See West, Nathanael

Weinstein, Nathan von Wallenstein
    See West, Nathanael

Weir, Peter (Lindsay) 1944- .... **CLC 20**
    See also CA 113; 123

Weiss, Peter (Ulrich)
    1916-1982 .... **CLC 3, 15, 51;**
                                    DAM DRAM
    See also CA 45-48; 106; CANR 3; DLB 69,
    124

Weiss, Theodore (Russell)
    1916- .... **CLC 3, 8, 14**
    See also CA 9-12R; CAAS 2; CANR 46;
    DLB 5

Welch, (Maurice) Denton
    1915-1948 .... **TCLC 22**
    See also CA 121; 148

Welch, James
    1940- ..... **CLC 6, 14, 52; DAM MULT,**
                                            POP
    See also CA 85-88; CANR 42; DLB 175;
    NNAL

Weldon, Fay
    1933- .... **CLC 6, 9, 11, 19, 36, 59;**
                                    DAM POP
    See also CA 21-24R; CANR 16, 46;
    CDBLB 1960 to Present; DLB 14;
    INT CANR-16; MTCW

Wellek, Rene 1903-1995........... **CLC 28**
    See also CA 5-8R; 150; CAAS 7; CANR 8;
    DLB 63; INT CANR-8

Weller, Michael 1942-......... **CLC 10, 53**
    See also CA 85-88

Weller, Paul 1958-............... **CLC 26**

Wellershoff, Dieter 1925-.......... **CLC 46**
    See also CA 89-92; CANR 16, 37

Welles, (George) Orson
    1915-1985 .... **CLC 20, 80**
    See also CA 93-96; 117

Wellman, Mac 1945- .... **CLC 65**

Wellman, Manly Wade 1903-1986 .. **CLC 49**
    See also CA 1-4R; 118; CANR 6, 16, 44;
    SATA 6; SATA-Obit 47

Wells, Carolyn 1869(?)-1942 ...... **TCLC 35**
    See also CA 113; DLB 11

Wells, H(erbert) G(eorge)
    1866-1946 .... **TCLC 6, 12, 19; DA;**
        DAB; DAC; DAM MST, NOV; SSC 6;
                                    WLC
    See also AAYA 18; CA 110; 121;
    CDBLB 1914-1945; DLB 34, 70, 156, 178;
    MTCW; SATA 20

Wells, Rosemary 1943-............. **CLC 12**
    See also AAYA 13; CA 85-88; CANR 48;
    CLR 16; MAICYA; SAAS 1; SATA 18,
    69

Welty, Eudora
    1909- ...... **CLC 1, 2, 5, 14, 22, 33; DA;**
        DAB; DAC; DAM MST, NOV; SSC 1;
                                    WLC
    See also CA 9-12R; CABS 1; CANR 32;
    CDALB 1941-1968; DLB 2, 102, 143;
    DLBD 12; DLBY 87; MTCW

Wen I-to 1899-1946 .... **TCLC 28**

Wentworth, Robert
See Hamilton, Edmond

Werfel, Franz (V.) 1890-1945 . . . . . . **TCLC 8**
See also CA 104; DLB 81, 124

Wergeland, Henrik Arnold
1808-1845 . . . . **NCLC 5**

Wersba, Barbara 1932-. . . . . **CLC 30**
See also AAYA 2; CA 29-32R; CANR 16,
38; CLR 3; DLB 52; JRDA; MAICYA;
SAAS 2; SATA 1, 58

Wertmueller, Lina 1928- . . . . **CLC 16**
See also CA 97-100; CANR 39

Wescott, Glenway 1901-1987. . . . . . . **CLC 13**
See also CA 13-16R; 121; CANR 23;
DLB 4, 9, 102

Wesker, Arnold
1932- . . . . **CLC 3, 5, 42; DAB;
DAM DRAM**
See also CA 1-4R; CAAS 7; CANR 1, 33;
CDBLB 1960 to Present; DLB 13;
MTCW

Wesley, Richard (Errol) 1945-. . . . . . . **CLC 7**
See also BW 1; CA 57-60; CANR 27;
DLB 38

Wessel, Johan Herman 1742-1785 . . . . **LC 7**

West, Anthony (Panther)
1914-1987 . . . . **CLC 50**
See also CA 45-48; 124; CANR 3, 19;
DLB 15

West, C. P.
See Wodehouse, P(elham) G(renville)

West, (Mary) Jessamyn
1902-1984 . . . . **CLC 7, 17**
See also CA 9-12R; 112; CANR 27; DLB 6;
DLBY 84; MTCW; SATA-Obit 37

West, Morris L(anglo) 1916-. . . . . **CLC 6, 33**
See also CA 5-8R; CANR 24, 49; MTCW

West, Nathanael
1903-1940 . . . . . **TCLC 1, 14, 44; SSC 16**
See also CA 104; 125; CDALB 1929-1941;
DLB 4, 9, 28; MTCW

West, Owen
See Koontz, Dean R(ay)

West, Paul 1930- . . . . **CLC 7, 14, 96**
See also CA 13-16R; CAAS 7; CANR 22,
53; DLB 14; INT CANR-22

West, Rebecca 1892-1983 . . **CLC 7, 9, 31, 50**
See also CA 5-8R; 109; CANR 19; DLB 36;
DLBY 83; MTCW

Westall, Robert (Atkinson)
1929-1993 . . . . **CLC 17**
See also AAYA 12; CA 69-72; 141;
CANR 18; CLR 13; JRDA; MAICYA;
SAAS 2; SATA 23, 69; SATA-Obit 75

Westlake, Donald E(dwin)
1933- . . . . **CLC 7, 33; DAM POP**
See also CA 17-20R; CAAS 13; CANR 16,
44; INT CANR-16

Westmacott, Mary
See Christie, Agatha (Mary Clarissa)

Weston, Allen
See Norton, Andre

Wetcheek, J. L.
See Feuchtwanger, Lion

Wetering, Janwillem van de
See van de Wetering, Janwillem

Wetherell, Elizabeth
See Warner, Susan (Bogert)

Whale, James 1889-1957 . . . . **TCLC 63**

Whalen, Philip 1923- . . . . **CLC 6, 29**
See also CA 9-12R; CANR 5, 39; DLB 16

Wharton, Edith (Newbold Jones)
1862-1937 . . . . . . **TCLC 3, 9, 27, 53; DA;
DAB; DAC; DAM MST, NOV; SSC 6;
WLC**
See also CA 104; 132; CDALB 1865-1917;
DLB 4, 9, 12, 78; DLBD 13; MTCW

Wharton, James
See Mencken, H(enry) L(ouis)

Wharton, William (a pseudonym)
. . . . **CLC 18, 37**
See also CA 93-96; DLBY 80; INT 93-96

Wheatley (Peters), Phillis
1754(?)-1784 . . . . **LC 3; BLC; DA; DAC;
DAM MST, MULT, POET; PC 3; WLC**
See also CDALB 1640-1865; DLB 31, 50

Wheelock, John Hall 1886-1978 . . . . **CLC 14**
See also CA 13-16R; 77-80; CANR 14;
DLB 45

White, E(lwyn) B(rooks)
1899-1985 . . **CLC 10, 34, 39; DAM POP**
See also AITN 2; CA 13-16R; 116;
CANR 16, 37; CLR 1, 21; DLB 11, 22;
MAICYA; MTCW; SATA 2, 29;
SATA-Obit 44

White, Edmund (Valentine III)
1940- . . . . **CLC 27; DAM POP**
See also AAYA 7; CA 45-48; CANR 3, 19,
36; MTCW

White, Phyllis Dorothy James 1920-
See James, P. D.
See also CA 21-24R; CANR 17, 43;
DAM POP; MTCW

White, T(erence) H(anbury)
1906-1964 . . . . **CLC 30**
See also CA 73-76; CANR 37; DLB 160;
JRDA; MAICYA; SATA 12

White, Terence de Vere
1912-1994 . . . . **CLC 49**
See also CA 49-52; 145; CANR 3

White, Walter F(rancis)
1893-1955 . . . . **TCLC 15**
See also White, Walter
See also BW 1; CA 115; 124; DLB 51

White, William Hale 1831-1913
See Rutherford, Mark
See also CA 121

Whitehead, E(dward) A(nthony)
1933- . . . . **CLC 5**
See also CA 65-68; CANR 58

Whitemore, Hugh (John) 1936-. . . . . **CLC 37**
See also CA 132; INT 132

Whitman, Sarah Helen (Power)
1803-1878 . . . . **NCLC 19**
See also DLB 1

Whitman, Walt(er)
1819-1892 . . . . . **NCLC 4, 31; DA; DAB;
DAC; DAM MST, POET; PC 3; WLC**
See also CDALB 1640-1865; DLB 3, 64;
SATA 20

Whitney, Phyllis A(yame)
1903- . . . . **CLC 42; DAM POP**
See also AITN 2; BEST 90:3; CA 1-4R;
CANR 3, 25, 38; JRDA; MAICYA;
SATA 1, 30

Whittemore, (Edward) Reed (Jr.)
1919- . . . . **CLC 4**
See also CA 9-12R; CAAS 8; CANR 4;
DLB 5

Whittier, John Greenleaf
1807-1892 . . . . **NCLC 8, 59**
See also DLB 1

Whittlebot, Hernia
See Coward, Noel (Peirce)

Wicker, Thomas Grey 1926-
See Wicker, Tom
See also CA 65-68; CANR 21, 46

Wicker, Tom . . . . **CLC 7**
See also Wicker, Thomas Grey

Wideman, John Edgar
1941- . . . . **CLC 5, 34, 36, 67; BLC;
DAM MULT**
See also BW 2; CA 85-88; CANR 14, 42;
DLB 33, 143

Wiebe, Rudy (Henry)
1934- . . . . **CLC 6, 11, 14; DAC;
DAM MST**
See also CA 37-40R; CANR 42; DLB 60

Wieland, Christoph Martin
1733-1813 . . . . **NCLC 17**
See also DLB 97

Wiene, Robert 1881-1938. . . . . **TCLC 56**

Wieners, John 1934-. . . . . **CLC 7**
See also CA 13-16R; DLB 16

Wiesel, Elie(zer)
1928- . . . . . . **CLC 3, 5, 11, 37; DA; DAB;
DAC; DAM MST, NOV**
See also AAYA 7; AITN 1; CA 5-8R;
CAAS 4; CANR 8, 40; DLB 83;
DLBY 87; INT CANR-8; MTCW;
SATA 56; YABC

Wiggins, Marianne 1947-. . . . . **CLC 57**
See also BEST 89:3; CA 130

Wight, James Alfred 1916-
See Herriot, James
See also CA 77-80; SATA 55;
SATA-Brief 44

Wilbur, Richard (Purdy)
1921- . . . **CLC 3, 6, 9, 14, 53; DA; DAB;
DAC; DAM MST, POET**
See also CA 1-4R; CABS 2; CANR 2, 29;
DLB 5, 169; INT CANR-29; MTCW;
SATA 9

Wild, Peter 1940-. . . . . **CLC 14**
See also CA 37-40R; DLB 5

Wilde, Oscar (Fingal O'Flahertie Wills)
1854(?)-1900 . . . . **TCLC 1, 8, 23, 41; DA;
DAB; DAC; DAM DRAM, MST, NOV;
SSC 11; WLC**
See also CA 104; 119; CDBLB 1890-1914;
DLB 10, 19, 34, 57, 141, 156; SATA 24

Cumulative Nationality Index

AMERICAN

Ammons, A(rchie) R(andolph) **16**
Auden, W(ystan) H(ugh) **1**
Baraka, Amiri **4**
Bishop, Elizabeth **3**
Blake, William J(ames) **12**
Bogan, Louise **12**
Bradstreet, Anne **10**
Brodsky, Joseph **9**
Brooks, Gwendolyn **7**
Bukowski, Charles **18**
Carruth, Hayden **10**
Clampitt, Amy **19**
Clifton, (Thelma) Lucille **17**
Crane, (Harold) Hart **3**
Cummings, E(dward) E(stlin) **5**
Dickinson, Emily (Elizabeth) **1**
Doolittle, Hilda **5**
Dove, Rita (Frances) **6**
Dunbar, Paul Laurence **5**
Duncan, Robert (Edward) **2**
Eliot, T(homas) S(tearns) **5**
Emerson, Ralph Waldo **18**
Ferlinghetti, Lawrence (Monsanto) **1**
Forche, Carolyn (Louise) **10**
Frost, Robert (Lee) **1**
Gallagher, Tess **9**
Ginsberg, Allen (Irwin) **4**
Giovanni, Nikki **19**
Gluck, Louise (Elisabeth) **16**
Hammon, Jupiter **16**
Hass, Robert **16**
Hayden, Robert E(arl) **6**
H. D. **5**
Hughes, (James) Langston **1**
Jeffers, (John) Robinson **17**
Knight, Etheridge **14**
Kumin, Maxine (Winokur) **15**
Kunitz, Stanley (Jasspon) **19**

Levertov, Denise **11**
Lorde, Audre (Geraldine) **12**
Lowell, Amy **13**
Lowell, Robert (Traill Spence Jr.) **3**
Loy, Mina **16**
Madhubuti, Haki R. **5**
Masters, Edgar Lee **1**
McKay, Claude **2**
Merton, Thomas **10**
Millay, Edna St. Vincent **6**
Moore, Marianne (Craig) **4**
Olson, Charles (John) **19**
Ortiz, Simon J(oseph) **17**
Plath, Sylvia **1**
Poe, Edgar Allan **1**
Pound, Ezra (Weston Loomis) **4**
Rich, Adrienne (Cecile) **5**
Robinson, Edwin Arlington **1**
Roethke, Theodore (Huebner) **15**
Rose, Wendy **13**
Rukeyser, Muriel **12**
Sanchez, Sonia **9**
Sandburg, Carl (August) **2**
Schwartz, Delmore (David) **8**
Sexton, Anne (Harvey) **2**
Stein, Gertrude **18**
Stevens, Wallace **6**
Swenson, May **14**
Toomer, Jean **7**
Wakoski, Diane **15**
Wheatley (Peters), Phillis **3**
Whitman, Walt(er) **3**
Williams, William Carlos **7**
Zukofsky, Louis **11**

AUSTRALIAN

Wright, Judith (Arandell) **14**

CANADIAN

Atwood, Margaret (Eleanor) **8**
Bissett, Bill **14**
Page, P(atricia) K(athleen) **12**

CHILEAN

Neruda, Pablo **4**

CHINESE

Li Ho **13**
Tu Fu **9**
Wang Wei **18**

ENGLISH

Arnold, Matthew **5**
Auden, W(ystan) H(ugh) **1**
Behn, Aphra **13**
Blake, William **12**
Bradstreet, Anne **10**
Bronte, Emily (Jane) **8**
Browning, Elizabeth Barrett **6**
Browning, Robert **2**
Byron, George Gordon (Noel) **16**
Carroll, Lewis **18**
Chaucer, Geoffrey **19**
Coleridge, Samuel Taylor **11**
Day Lewis, C(ecil) **11**
Donne, John **1**
Eliot, T(homas) S(tearns) **5**
Graves, Robert (von Ranke) **6**
Gray, Thomas **2**
Hardy, Thomas **8**
Herbert, George **4**
Herrick, Robert **9**
Hopkins, Gerard Manley **15**
Housman, A(lfred) E(dward) **2**
Hughes, Ted **7**
Jonson, Ben(jamin) **17**
Keats, John **1**

PC Cumulative Title Index

515

Title Index

Title Index

Title Index

Title Index

ISBN 0-7876-1546-3